Encyclopedia of Fairies
in World Folklore
and Mythology

Encyclopedia of Fairies in World Folklore and Mythology

THERESA BANE

McFarland & Company, Inc., Publishers
Jefferson, North Carolina, and London

Library of Congress Cataloguing-in-Publication Data

Bane, Theresa, 1969–
Encyclopedia of fairies in world folklore and mythology /
Theresa Bane.
p.   cm.
Includes bibliographical references and index.

ISBN 978-0-7864-7111-9
softcover : acid free paper ∞

1. Fairies—Encyclopedias.
I. Title.
BF1552.B27 2013
398.21—dc23   2013028639

British Library cataloguing data are available

On the cover: *Fairies on Tree Limbs* (© 2013 PicturesNow)

Manufactured in the United States of America

*McFarland & Company, Inc., Publishers
Box 611, Jefferson, North Carolina 28640
www.mcfarlandpub.com*

For Barbara Bane.
Thank you for everything.

Table of Contents

Preface   1

Introduction   5

THE ENCYCLOPEDIA   9

Bibliography   351

Index   379

Preface

After encyclopedias on the historical and mythological demons and vampires of world cultures and religions it seemed only logical my next book would be about fairies. Like demons and vampires, fairies have not been proven to exist, yet many people from all over the world, from all walks of life, rich and poor, young and old, believe they are real.

For example, I imagine one would be hard-pressed to find someone who has not at least heard the expression "kiss the Blarney Stone," even if the person did not know what it meant or where it originated. Nevertheless, one of Ireland's most popular tourist attractions has its roots in fairy lore. CLIDNA was a FAIRY QUEEN of southwest Ireland whose seat of power is within a fairy hill in County Cork called *Carrig Cliodna*. She was a BANSHEE to the MacCarthy clan but she also gifted it with the *Cloch na Blarnan*, more commonly known as the Blarney Stone. According to the stone's legend, the clan's chieftain was involved in a lawsuit during the construction of the family castle and appealed to CLIDNA for assistance. CLIDNA bade MacCarthy to kiss the first stone he happened across that morning; in return, he would be gifted with the ability to speak eloquently. Doing as he was told, MacCarthy saw and kissed a wedge of bluestone and won his case. To honor his FAIRY QUEEN he placed the stone in the parapet of his castle around the year 1446. Statesmen,

nobility, celebrities and untold numbers of tourists have risked their safety to lean backwards over the parapet to kiss the stone and hopefully gain the blessing of CLIDNA.

As a professional vampirologist—a mythologist who specializes in cross-cultural vampire studies—I collected data as I did research for my previous books. I found several hundred different ancestral and NATURE SPIRITS that are, for all intents and purposes, essentially fairies. According to the folklore and regional beliefs of various cultures from throughout history, these beings, be they wispy ghost-like spirits or alleged flesh and blood beings capable of interbreeding with humans, are, generally speaking, all described very similarly as being otherworldly and here upon the earth to interact intentionally with mankind, be it for good or ill.

It was my initial assessment there were but a handful of different species of fay, maybe no more than a dozen or so whose only true difference was a regional name. However, as often is the case, a bit of hard work doing research proved me wrong. What I first believed was going to be a humble book of a couple hundred entries quickly grew much larger than I ever anticipated.

I don't feel the term *fairyologist* will ever be applicable to the study of the fay, because in my professional opinion to properly appreciate and comprehend these beings one must understand not only the people who believe in them but also have a complete understanding of the geographic terrain where they are said to originate. The word *fairyologist*, although growing in popularity as a descriptor, is simply just too small a title. There are so many legends and tales of the fay connected to land, to a particular glen, a specific standing stone or a copse of trees. So powerful is the belief of the fay and the power these creatures hold that the trees alleged to be dedicated or occupied by those beings have been left untouched for their entire life cycle.

Although Celtic and European fairies such as BANSHEES, BROWNIES, and LEPRECHAUNS are the sort of fairy-folk that most immediately come to mind, the NYMPHS and OCEANIDS of ancient Greece and the NATURE SPIRITS of Africa are also deeply tied to their respective lands. Many times the legend of one area is tied directly to the lore of another, such as the character Arcas appearing in the story of CALLISTO as well as in the story of CHRYSOPELIA.

To explain, HAMADRYADS are NYMPHS of the forest but the DRYADS are NYMPHS specifically associated with oak groves. In one legend the beautiful NYMPH and sworn virgin CALLISTO was seduced by the god Zeus. It is unclear if the intercourse was consensual but nevertheless a child was born of the union, a son named Arcas. At this point, Hera, Zeus' rightfully jealous wife, discovers the tryst. Unable to punish her husband, she transforms CALLISTO into a bear. Arcas was left in the care to the ATLANTID NYMPH MENA to raise.

Many years later, the DRYAD CHRYSOPELIA's sacred oak tree, located on the side of a mountain in Arcadia, was in danger of being washed away by seasonal floodwaters—and CHRYSOPELIA herself was in danger. Arcas, the now-heroic adult, rushes to her aid. He saves her by quickly constructing a dyke. After the flood passes and the water recedes, the grateful NYMPH agrees to become his wife. More years pass, and one day Arcas is hunting when he comes upon a bear. Unknown to him, the bear is his mother, CALLISTO. She flees to Zeus' sanctuary on Mount Lykaion, and he takes pity on her, but he cannot undo his wife's curse. To save CALLISTO from being accidentally slain by her own son, Zeus transforms the NYMPH into the constellation Ursa Major and her son Arcas into the constellation Arcturus.

Meanwhile, in AFRICAN FAIRY LORE, NATURE SPIRITS are believed to be the cause of FAIRY RINGS, the exact same sort appearing throughout the European countryside. Although most of these NATURE SPIRITS come in one of two varieties, earth or sky spirits, they have individual personalities, are considered intelligent, and are identified with specific natural locations or seasonal forces of nature.

As with my previous books, *Encyclopedia of Vampire Mythology* (2010) and *Encyclopedia of Demons in World Religions and Cultures* (2012), I put my research skills to the test in collecting as many of the historically-named fairies from all the folklores and mythologies I could find. I utilized not only architectural, artistic, geographic, historical, medical, and religious texts, but also books on mythologies from around the world.

Additionally, I made use of older books claiming to be the written transcriptions of the original oral tales traditionally told. Whenever possible I reference the oldest edition of each book I could find, as I personally feel the earlier editions are more accurate even if the language and spelling are often antiquated. There are more than a few books I relied heavily upon whose date of publication is listed in the middle to late 1700 and the 1800s.

Publishers such as Forgotten Books and Kessinger tend to republish old and out of print books that are in the public domain. They use the text exactly as it originally appeared in print, typos and all.

Once all my facts were compiled, sorted, and sourced, I condensed the information to its barest but most essential points, making sure all the sources cited for each entry were in agreement. If the specifics were not consistent in my sources, the fairy did not make it into this book. My goal, now as ever, is to present to the reader a concise description in each entry based on the collected raw data. It was intentional on my part to keep entries brief and precise without personal commentary, be it speculation or editorial comment, as there were more than 2,000 fairies total to be cataloged.

The *Encyclopedia of Fairies in World Folklore and Mythology* is the first of its kind. There are many books on the market purporting to be spell books containing methods for summoning the fay and utilizing them in magical crafts. Many of these occult and paranormal books also explain how to open channels of communication with the fay so practitioners of what is called the Fairy Faith (variously spelled) can freely interact with these beings. Whether or not I believe in the fay or any of their incarnations is and was irrelevant in the writing of this book, as I sought to collect only the mythological and historically consistent facts regarding fairy-kind. I was extremely mindful which of these New Age-style books I choose to use, for although I found many of them unhelpful because they weren't of a level appropriate for the academic work I wanted to write, there were a few that contained relevant information verified by other sources and therefore useful. In no circumstance did I use a book or a source in which the author focused on his or her personal, one-on-one encounters with the fay, as these events could not, by the author's own admission in many cases, be confirmed by an outside source.

I would like to take a moment to recommend books I consider highly relevant and important in the field. Katharine Mary Briggs has written several books on fairy and fairy folk belief, including *Abbey Lubbers, Banshees, and Boggarts: An Illustrated Encyclopedia of Fairies*; *An Encyclopedia of Fairies: Hobgoblins, Brownies, Bogies, and Other Supernatural Creatures*; *The Fairies in Tradition and Literature*; *The Vanishing People: Fairy Lore and Legends*; and *A Dictionary of British Folk-Tales in the English Language: Folk Narratives*. All of these books are excellent for providing new bits of minutiae to add to well-known lore of the established fay. These books are also a valuable resource for comparative studies of European fairies, noting the ways in which species and stories are similar to one another. This is especially apparent in Jacob Ludwig C. Grimm's work and more so in W. Y. Evans-Wentz's *The Fairy-Faith in Celtic Countries*. The only fault I have with Briggs' books is that they tend to concentrate primarily on traditional Celtic and European fairies common to familiar lore. Readers of these books will find little in the way of new, rare, or unique knowledge.

Thomas Keightley's *The Fairy Mythology: Illustrative of the Romance and Superstition of Various Countries*, originally published more than two hundred years ago, is still in print. It is full of wonderful tales of the fay and gives as much insight into their motivations as can clearly be explained by anyone. Keightley's book also gives the reader an excellent idea of how tied the fay are to the regions there they live.

Louis Herbert Gray was the editor of an epic work entitled *Mythology of All Races*; if ever a book could live up to its impressive title, this one has. Entries range from a few sentences to several pages and cover a vast array of beliefs. *Mythology of All Races* can only be challenged by the works of mythologist and researcher Lewis Spence.

A modern author I find I am especially partial to is Patricia Monaghan and her books *The Encyclopedia of Celtic Mythology and Folklore* and *Encyclopedia of Goddesses and Heroines* in particular. Each entry is rich in information and arranged so names and locations can easily be cross-referenced, a must for any truly useful modern research book. I only wish her indexes were more inclusive.

Besides Briggs, Evans-Wentz, Keightley, Monaghan, and Spence I would like to acknowledge other folklorists and mythologists who have contributed much to the field, including Apollodorus of Athens, John Bell, Thomas Bulfinch, John Francis Campbell, Cassandra Eason, Lady Augusta Greg-ory, Rosemary Ellen Guiley, James Hastings, Hesiod, Homer, Donald Alexander MacKenzie, Harry Mountain, John Rhys, Carol Rose, William Shakespeare, Sir William Smith, Lewis Spence, and William Butler Yeats.

I would also like to express my deep appreciation to those who assisted me with this undertaking: my beta-readers, Barbara Bane, Gina Farago, Holley B. Drye, Angela McGill, Tracey McGill, Pam Parisi, and Joy Poger; my French translator, Richard Shecky; and especially my husband, T. Glenn Bane. Without this dedicated cadre of individuals, this book would not have been possible.

Introduction

Fairies are curious beings, complicated and fickle, acting without thought even when their intent only moments ago was crystal clear. Nothing in fairy mythology is fixed or permanent; even the most malicious and foul of their kind has been known to assist a person in need while the kindest and most benign will put a generational curse upon a poor soul for a slight offense.

Most cultures have a version of a fairy, whether they call it an ancestral spirit or a NATURE SPIRIT or consider it an actual being dwelling underground or living on a mysterious, invisible, floating island. The fay, as a species, are of a mind we as mere mortals cannot understand. When interaction between our kind and their kind occurs one side always seems to come out on top, forever changing the other, scarring them in some way, be it emotionally if not physically.

In a world with fairies, Man does not sit nicely atop the food chain.

When I set out to write this book, from the very beginning I intended to create what I hope will become an established single-volume encyclopedia of fairies. My research revealed to me that numerous books on the subject have been written on the fay over the years but they are neatly divided by cultural mythology and geographic region, with fairy tales and folklore being found in tomes separate and apart. I wanted my work to be a definitive stand-alone, all-encompassing book. I worked especially hard to make sure even the most obscure and infrequently mentioned fairy would find its way into these pages. I knew this would be a huge undertaking as I had decided to include the fairy-like beings from not only classical sources but from cultural mythologies from around the world.

The words *fairy* and *fay* are used interchangeably throughout this book; this was a conscious choice on my part. In the *Merriam-Webster's Collegiate Dictionary*, the word *fay* appears as a noun and is likened in its secondary definition to *fairy*. It should be pointed out some authors and self-proclaimed experts opt to use the word *fey* when referencing fairy kind; this is incorrect. *Fey*, according to the same dictionary, refers to a soothsayer or an individual who is fated to die. Although the source does claim the word may have come from the Middle English word *feye*, which may have originated from the Old German word *feigi*, or even the Old English word *fāh*, it still refers back to an outlaw or hostile force.

The reader of this book need not believe fairies are or were actual beings. Did the TUATHA DE DANANN immigrate to Ireland from Falias, Finias, Gorias, and Murias as the *Book of Invasions* describes? Are FAUTHS actually living in the fresh- and saltwater lochs of Scotland? Did they ever? In my professional opinion as a mythologist, it does not matter; it is important to know and understand, however, the message of the mythology and story of the fay. I leave it to the reader to decide if the fay are or were real.

The fairies of Europe, particularly those from the United Kingdom, are perhaps the best known and the very ones whose image is imagined when fairy-kind is spoken of, especially here in the West. However, it is fascinating to see that other cultures in lands far from Europe—and whose histories tell us have had no contact with one another—have in their mythology very similar beings, albeit with different names. It is uncertain if this is due to stories being somehow transmitted from one culture to another by means that we are unaware of, or if it happened naturally as cultures develop and produce similar mythologies—even without contact with one another.

Interestingly, fairies, unlike vampires or demons, are never considered to be wholly good or evil but rather have the propensity for either, depending on their mood and inclination. Perhaps this is because many of the fay were at one time considered to be gods and worshiped as such. As divine beings they would have had followers and an established set of rules regarding their worship. When a follower obeyed the established rules he could, at the very least, expect no sort of malicious interference from the god if not given an outright blessing; however, when the rules were broken, the practitioner could anticipate his god to punish him by some means, hopefully in direct proportion to the seriousness of the sin. Even after the introduction of Christianity, which did much to quell the worship of fairies and diminish them in power to nothing more than NATURE SPIRITS, people continued, if not to worship them, to go out of their way to show respect and deference to their sacred places. This still occurs today, even in our most modern cities around the world.

The Church was never able to wholly end the tradition of fairy folklore. People were reluctant to fell a grove of fairy-protected oaks. There are reports of construction workers walking off the job rather than plow up a sacred oak. Today, many of those forests remain untouched.

Regarding traditional and regional fairy tales, I chose to include many of their fairies. Even though in some instances these fairies may have been fictional creations used to tell stories, others are not just an integral part of our early childhood but have their origins in mythos. In fact, many of our favorite and beloved children's fairy tales, such as *Cinderella* and *The Little Mermaid*, originate from Christian authors in predominantly Christian countries. Fictional fairies that will not be found herein, because of their lack of regional folkloric origins, include Tinker Bell from J.M. Barrie's 1911 novel *Peter Pan; or The Boy Who Wouldn't Grow Up*. Although Tinker Bell is well known thanks to Walt Disney's *Peter Pan*, she was not based on a mythological character from a tale told in a small but quaint town; rather she was created by Barrie himself.

When the fay interfered in the lives of men, for good or ill, more often than not they visited the humble farmer or the lone traveler rather than a member of the powerful ruling class. Unlike mortal nobility, it was hardly uncommon for a FAIRY KING or FAIRY QUEEN to openly address such a person without introduction or to freely and physically interact with him or her, offering hospitality and entertainment. This is not to say the fay paid nobility the same respect they were given by their subjects; often a fairy would single out a prince or princess for the sole purpose of testing his or her morality to determine if he or she was worthy of his or her position and the right to rule. When the nobility passed these secret tests they were always richly rewarded with prosperous lands, beautiful or handsome and devoted spouses, and the security of fairy friendship. When the ruler did not perform to the fairy's exacting expectations, he or she was harshly and swiftly punished. Rarely were offenders given the opportunity to amend their behavior, see the error of their ways, and change for the better.

Perhaps a contributing factor to the endurance of the fay is their amazing fickleness. If they are imaginary beings, they were apparently created for no real or particular reason. Already existing in the countless cultures I researched were numerous other beings already held responsible for mysterious deaths and the subjects of cautionary tales and seen as natural phenomena. Fairies were not necessarily needed to explain why it rained or didn't rain, so why were they created? The answer to this question is as elusive as the fairy itself.

The purpose of this encyclopedia is to identify and describe each fairy being and race from folklore and mythology the world over and provide, when appropriate, a brief summary of the fairy's story. I intentionally did not include my interpretation of a moral lesson, if there was one to be had. I feel I would have tainted the material, projecting my modern interpretation and way of thinking upon a lesson whose origins dated back hundreds, if not thousands, of years.

For example, I personally find violence perpetrated against women particularly criminal, sexual violence even worse. However, the literature of ancient Greece and Rome is filled with stories of the rape of both men and women. The gods were often the worst of the perpetrators, unable or unwilling to restrain themselves in the presence of an attractive NYMPH or NAIAD. The only defense I can offer for the gods, as thin as it may be, is there is no word in ancient Greek or Latin that is comparable to our English word *rape*; rather, it was

looked upon as an act of violence, worse than a mugging but not as bad as murder.

Sometimes the moral of the story is clear, such as with JENNY GREENTEETH, a fairy who is renowned in Lancashire and Yorkshire, England. This NURSERY BOGIE snatches up children who wander too close to the water's edge and violently takes them to her watery domain where they drown. River banks have soft edges and children tend not to heed the warnings of their parents; however, with visions of a monstrous, duckweed-covered HAG, the child of his own volition may decide not to risk an encounter.

Other times the message may be murkier or outright unclear as is the case with the OVINNIK from Slavic lore. This fairy will live in one's barn in the form of a black cat. Should it ever become displeased—and the mythology does not say how this unhappy event can happen—the fairy will simply make sure one's children are inside the barn when it sets the structure on fire and burns it to the ground. One would suppose the OVINNIK would be a cautionary tale about leaving children by themselves in the barn; however, this fairy is not interested in unattended children. When this is the case, the mythology clearly says so, the OVINNIK is enacting an extreme punishment upon a mortal who inadvertently committed some misdeed worthy of extreme tragedy. And yet, even knowing how harsh and violent this particular fairy can be, it is customary for people to enter their barns on New Year's Eve for the fairy's assistance in divining their personal future for the next year. Is it likely that somewhere, somehow, two very separate bits of regional folklore were combined and attached to a singular being? That may or may not be; there is no other fairy who could have been a likely progenitor.

As with all my books, this one has cross-references that enable readers and researchers alike to track down additional information as they choose without having to go to an outside source for more details. All words in SMALL CAPS are entries to be found in the book.

Fairies may be known by different names or have different ways of spelling their names. In these instances, I chose the most commonly used among the listed references and the most familiar. Variants immediately follow under the heading "Variations."

I'll warn readers here and now that if they picked up this book hoping to discover spells or means by which to call up, summon, or otherwise make contact with the fay, they will find themselves sorely disappointed. I do know, however, that academics, researchers, and scholars alike will be pleased with what they discover here—a collection of fairies from world folklore and mythology, alphabetically arranged, fully described, and hand-chosen.

The Encyclopedia

A-senee-ki-wakw

In the Abenaki mythology of the Algonquian speaking Native American tribes of northeastern North America, the A-senee-ki-wakw were a race of stone GIANTS as well as the first race created by the mythical and cultural hero, Gluskab. Sadly, because the A-senee-ki-wakw were so large they crushed many animals and did damage to the earth when they moved; for this, Gluskab had them destroyed.

Source: Books, *Native American Legendary Creatures*, 127

Aba

Aba was a NYMPH from of the town of Ergiske in Kikonia, in northern Greece according to the mythology of ancient Greece. By the god of the sea, Poseidon (Neptune), she was the mother of the town's founder, Ergiskos.

Source: McInerney, *Folds of Parnassos*, 130

Abarbarea

Variations: The Barbarian NYMPH

Abarbarea was a NYMPH from the mythology of ancient Greece and Rome. One of the NAIADS, she was named in Homer's *Iliad* as having been the mother of Æsepus and Padasus and the consort of Bucolion by which she bore two sons, Aesepus and Pedasus.

Sources: Day, *God's Conflict with the Dragon and the Sea*, 394; Munn, *Mother of the Gods, Athens, and the tyranny of Asia*, 140; Rose, *Spirits, Fairies, Leprechauns, and Goblins*, 1, 351; Smith, *Dictionary of Greek and Roman Biography and Mythology*, 516

Abarbaree

Abarbaree ("unmuddy") was a spring–NYMPH from the mythology of classical Greece and Rome. One of the NAIADS, she once joined the NYMPH KALYBE in a sexual encounter with the fresh corpse of a mortal ox-herder named Hymnos. Later, Abarbaree bore the Trojan prince Boukolion two sons in an illicit affair.

Sources: Kirk, *The Iliad: Volume 2*, 158; Larson, *Greek Nymphs*, 22, 196

Abatwa

According to South African lore, the Abatwa are a tiny race of fay living peacefully alongside ants; at night they sleep in their colonies. The abatwa do not have villages of their own but rather live wherever they kill game, moving only when the carcass is consumed. When it is time to move, they mount up upon a horse sitting one behind another from the length of its neck and all the way down its back to the top of its tail. If they cannot find game in a reasonable amount of time the abatwa will slay and consume the horse. These fay ambush game from hidden positions in the tall grass.

On occasion the abatwa reveal themselves but only to children, pregnant women, and wizards. It is believed if a pregnant woman sees an Abatwa during her seventh month it will ensure the birth of a male child.

As bothersome as fleas, the abatwa will harass and torment a man, keeping him awake at night by giving him chest palpitations.

Sources: Callaway, *Nursery Tales, Traditions, and Histories of the Zulus*, 352–5; Gray, *Mythology of all races, Volume 7*, 262, 268; Illes, *Encyclopedia of Spirits*, 6

Abbey Lubbers

Variations: Buttery Spirits, BUTTERY SPRITES

An abbey lubber is a type of injurious fay from the folklore of England; they live in abbeys and other religious houses that have allowed themselves to become over indulgent and wanton. These fay are described as wearing a red cap, leather apron, and long, light-blue stockings. Since the fifteenth century, the abbey lubbers have tried to tempt the brothers and monks to stray from their life of piety and give into drunkenness, gluttony, and an array of other excesses in order to damn their souls. In some circles these fay are considered to be a type of lesser demon. BUTTERY SPIRITS are the lay version of the Abbey Lubber.

In more modern times the phrase "abbey lubber" has come to be a term of reproach for an idle person.

Sources: Briggs, *Encyclopedia of Fairies*, 1, 109; Monaghan, *Encyclopedia of Celtic Mythology and Folklore*, 1; Rose, *Spirits, Fairies, Leprechauns, and Goblins*, 1, 351; Wright, *Dictionary of Obsolete and Provincial English*, 5

Abcán

Variations: Abcán mac Bicelmois

A DWARF and a poet of the TUATHA DÉ DANANN, Abcán ("little DWARF") possessed a bronze boat with a sail made of tin; it is in this vessel, according to lore, he ferries the goddess Ruad from the Otherworld to ours so she can seduce the human, Aed Srónmár. In another story, Abcán was once captured by the hero Cúchulainn, but was able to free himself by playing lullabies so enthralling the warrior fell asleep.

Sources: Meyer, *Contributions to Irish Lexicography*, 7; Monaghan, *Encyclopedia of Celtic Mythology and Folklore*, 1–2

Abdullah al-Kazwini

First named in the tale, *Thousand and One Tales of the Arabian Nights* the MERMAN Abdullah al-Kazwini befriended and assisted a poor fisherman.

Source: Rose, *Spirits, Fairies, Leprechauns, and Goblins*, 1, 351

Abhartach

Variations: Murbhheo

The oldest known recorded vampire story in Western Europe comes from ancient Celtic lore and is said to have taken place in the rural parish of Glenullin, Londonderry, in the town of Slaughtaverty, Ireland. It's the tale of the merciless tyrant and powerful sorcerer, Abhartach ("DWARF"). Traditionally, he is described as being a short man, a DWARF in many tellings, and having a physical deformity. Abhartach, although possessing magical abilities and being described as a DWARF, is likely not a fay nor a member of fairy-kind, but rather a man of uncommonly short stature.

Nevertheless, the story says one night Abhartach, a jealous and suspicious man, convinced himself his wife was being unfaithful to him. Unwilling to confront her directly and wanting to catch her in the act of adultery, he climbed out of a window and crept along the ledge toward his wife's bedroom. Before he could clear the distance and have a peek into his wife's room, he slipped and fell to his death. Abhartach's body was discovered in the morning and the people of the town buried him as if he were a king, standing upright in his grave.

The day after his funeral, Abhartach returned to Slaughtaverty demanding each person cut their wrist and bleed into his bowl daily in order to sustain his life. His people complied—they were too terrified of Abhartach to oppose his will while he was alive, they certainly did not want to do anything to further upset him now that he was dead. However, it did not take them long to decide they were unwilling to live under the tyranny of such an obvious revenant, so the citizenry hired an assassin to kill him. Although the attempt was initially successful, Abhartach returned, demanding his daily allotment of blood. Undeterred, another assassin was hired, but with the same results. After several more failed assassination attempts, a druid came forward and promised he could free them from the creature, Abhartach, once and for all. The druid explained because of the nature of the magic used to return the tyrant combined with the type of creature he became, a *murbhheo* (ancient Gaelic for vampire), their evil ruler could not be permanently destroyed, only trapped. The druid, using a sword made of yew wood, ran Abhartach through and while he was in a weakened state, was buried upside down in a grave and then covered it with ash branches, thorns, and a large boulder.

It is said in the town of Slaughtaverty (the name means "Abhartach's grave") even to this day Abhartach will attack anyone who comes too near his gravesite, as he is unable to fully escape it. Next to the boulder that helps imprison him, a large thorn tree now grows out of the burial site, pinning him to the earth.

Sources: Recorded by Dr. Geoffrey Keating in *The History of Ireland* (Seathrun Ceitinn, *Foras Feasa na Eireann*) circa 1634; Joyce, *Origin and History of Irish Names of Places*, 59

Abonde

Variations: ABUNDIA, HABONDE, Dame Ab, DAME ABONDE, Wandering Dame Abonde

In French mythology Abonde was a FAIRY QUEEN; living in the forest of Lorraine, France; she was described as being tall, star-crowned, and the consort of the Worcestershire HOB, Hobany. In some folklore she was also described as being one of the *dames blanches* ("WHITE LADIES") of French lore, a peer of LA DAME D'APRIGNY.

Abonde was the equivalent of the French Father Christmas or SANTA CLAUS, delivering toys to children on New Year's Day night.

Sources: Bayley, *Archaic England*, 165; Brewer, *Dictionary of Phrase and Fable*, 4

Abundia

Variations: Abundantina, Abunde, Dame Abunde, Dame Habonde, Domina Abundia, HABONDE

A Fairy Queen, Abundia ("abundant") and her band of fairies haunt stables. At night they enter into barns and twist the manes of horses into tangled knots, causing them to sweat; however these fay can be placated with offerings of food and wine.

Sources: Dorson, *Peasant Customs and Savage Myths*, 582; Keightly, *World Guide to Gnomes, Fairies, Elves, and Other Little People*, 476; White, *Notes and queries, Volume 96*, 314

Acalica

The acalica are a species of weather fay (see Nature Spirits) from Bolivian lore; they have a particular influence over frost, hail, and rain. Rarely seen as they live underground in caves these fairies are described as looking like tiny wizened men.

Sources: Illes, *Encyclopedia of Spirits*, 6; Matthews, *Element Encyclopedia of Magical Creatures*, 6

Acamantis

In Greek mythology Acamantis was a water–Nymph and one of the named Danaids, the collective name for the daughters of Danaus; her name appears in a list of the Danaids generated by Gaius Julius Hyginus (ca. 64 B.C.–A.D. 17), a Latin author. Acamantis was wedded to Ecnomius and killed him on their wedding night.

Sources: Hyginus, *Myths of Hyginus*, 133; Parada, *Genealogical Guide to Greek Mythology*, 59

Acaste

Born one of the 3,000 daughters of the Titians, Oceanus and Tethys, Acaste was one of the named Oceanids in classical Greek mythology; Acaste was also the name of one of the Nereids, the daughters of Nerues and Doris.

Sources: Boswell, *What Men or Gods Are These*, 58; Hesiod, *Works of Hesiod, Callimachus, and Theognis*, 20; Westmoreland, *Ancient Greek Beliefs*, 24

Achachilas

Variations: Acacila, Apus

The achachilas are a group of Nature Spirits from the folklore of the Aymara people of Bolivia whose ancestral home is located in the Andes Mountains. These fairies keep a watchful eye on the Aymara, assisting them as needed and oftentimes sending dreams to warn of upcoming dangerous or unfortunate situations. Described as looking like old people and said to live underground, the achachilas control the weather and send frost, hail, or rain to a region depending on

how benevolent they are feeling (see Nature Spirits).

In the high mountain passes stone alters dedicated to the achachilas have been erected; to this day travelers leave offerings of alcohol and coca.

Sources: Illes, *Encyclopedia of Spirits*, 119; Read, *Rough Guide to Bolivia*, 151; Rose, *Spirits, Fairies, Leprechauns, and Goblins*, 2; Senior, *Illustrated Who's Who in Mythology*, 15

Achelous

Born one of the 6,000 children of the Titians, Oceanus and Tethys, Achelous is one of the few male named Oceanid; he was the King of the river spirits in classical Greek mythology. In addition to ensuring the proper maturing of young men as well as being a spirit of prosperity he also begot bodies of water such as rivers, springs, and streams. Like all river spirits Achelous is fertile; he fathered the Nymphs, Sirens, and many of the sea spirits.

In one story, Achelous and Hercules did combat against one another competing for the same woman. During the battle, Hercules ripped off one of Achelous' horns; as the blood landed upon the earth, the Sirens were born. Being a prosperity spirit, this spontaneous birth is a prime example of his fertility; this has led some to theorize Achelous' loosed horn is the true Horn of Plenty.

Sources: Boswell, *What Men or Gods Are These*, 58; Day, *God's Conflict with the Dragon and the Sea*, 64; Hesiod, *Works of Hesiod, Callimachus, and Theognis*, 20; Illes, *Encyclopedia of Spirits*, 119–20

Acheron

Born one of the 3,000 daughters of the Titians, Oceanus and Tethys, Acheron ("woe") was one of the named Oceanids; she was a Nymph and the guardian of a small river in ancient Greece.

Sources: Boswell, *What Men or Gods Are These*, 58; Day, *God's Conflict with the Dragon and the Sea*, 64; Hesiod, *Works of Hesiod, Callimachus, and Theognis*, 20

Actaea

A sea–Nymph, Actaea was the Nereid of the rocky shore line in classical Greek mythology; she was born of Nereus and Doris. Additionally in Greek mythology Actaea was a water–Nymph and one of the named Danaids, the collective name for the daughters of Danaus. In a list compiled by Apollodorus, a Greek scholar and grammarian, she was one of the daughters of Pieria and was wedded to Periphas, one of the sons of Gorgo.

Sources: Apollodorus, *Apollodorus' Library and Hyginus' Fabulae*, 95; Gould, *Historic Magazine and Notes and Queries*, Volume 14, 212; Hesiod, *Theogony*, 103

Actaia

A sea–NYMPH, Actaia, was one of the named NEREIDS in classical Greek mythology; she was born the daughter of Nerues and DORIS.

Sources: Homer, *The Iliad*, 503; Trzaskoma, *Anthology of Classical Myth*, 18; Westmoreland, *Ancient Greek Beliefs* 25

Actea

A sea–NYMPH from Greek mythology, Actea, was the NYMPH of the shore and the NEREIDS of despair; she was born the daughter of Nerues and DORIS.

Sources: Betham, *Transactions of the Royal Irish Academy*, Volume 17, 88; Parada, *Genealogical guide to Greek mythology*, 125

Ad-Hene

In the Manx Gaelic language *ad-hene* ("themselves") is the euphemistic word used when referring to the fairies of the Isle of Man, as it is believed the fay can be directly summoned by saying their name aloud.

Sources: Killip, *Folklore of the Isle of Man*, 32; Monaghan, *Encyclopedia of Celtic Mythology and Folklore*, 2–3; Rose, *Spirits, Fairies, Leprechauns, and Goblins*, 3

Adhunall

In Irish mythology Adhunall was a FAIRY ANIMAL, one of the many hunting dogs of the cultural hero, Finn Mac Cumhaill; his other dogs were Bran, Luath Luchar, SCEOLAN, and Sear Dugh.

Sources: Gregory, *Gods and Fighting Men*, 238, 398; Monaghan, *Encyclopedia of Celtic Mythology and Folklore*, 3

Adiante

In Greek mythology Adiante was a water–NYMPH and one of the named DANAIDS, the collective name for the daughters of Danaus. In a list compiled by Apollodorus, a Greek scholar and grammarian, she was one of the daughters of Herse and was wedded to Daiphron, one of the sons of Hephaestine.

Sources: Apollodorus, *Apollodorus' Library and Hyginus' Fabulae* 2; Grimal, *Dictionary of Classical Mythology*, 127; Parada, *Genealogical Guide to Greek Mythology*, 7

Adite

In Greek mythology Adite was a water–NYMPH and one of the named DANAIDS, the collective name for the daughters of Danaus. In a list compiled by Apollodorus, a Greek scholar and grammarian, she was one of the daughters of Pieria and was wedded to Menalces, one of the sons of Gorgo.

Sources: Apollodorus, *Apollodorus' Library and Hyginus' Fabulae* 20; Parada, *Genealogical Guide to Greek Mythology*, 7

Admete

Variations: Admeta, Admeto

Born one of the 3,000 daughters of the Titians, Oceanus and Tethys, Admete was one of the OCEANID, and a companion of Persephone (Proserpina) in classical Greek mythology. She was also one of the named NEREIDS, and as such said to be one of the daughters of Nerues and DORIS.

Sources: Boswell, *What Men or Gods Are These*, 58; Hesiod, *Theogony*, 103; Hesiod, *Works of Hesiod, Callimachus, and Theognis*, 20; Westmoreland, *Ancient Greek Beliefs*, 24

Adraste

One of the HYAD, Adraste was a NYMPH of Mount Ida on the island of Crete in the Greek Aegean Sea; she was one of the nurses to the infant god, Zeus (Jupiter). Adraste was commonly grouped with fellow NYMPHS, ALTHAEA and IDOTHEA.

Source: Smith, *Dictionary of Greek and Roman Biography and Mythology: Earinus-Nyx*, 533

Adrastea

Variations: NEMESIS

In ancient Roman mythology, Adrastea and IDA were the mountain NYMPHS who lived in Dictaea; they were wet-nurses to the infant god Zeus (Jupiter). In Greek mythology, Adrastea was born the daughter of the god, Zeus, and his lover, Anank.

Sources: Lanier, *Book of Giants*, 4–5; Lethbridge, *Gogmagog*, 163

Adrasteia

Adrasteia ("inescapable") was a NYMPH of Mount Ida on the island of Crete in the Greek Aegean Sea according to the mythology of classical Greece and Rome; she was one of the many nurses of the infant god, Zeus (Jupiter).

Sources: Cook, *Zeus*, Volume 3, 931; Day, *God's Conflict with the Dragon and the Sea*, 325; Hard, *Routledge Handbook of Greek Mythology*, 75

Áed Abrat

Variations: Aed Abrat

Áed Abrat was a FAIRY KING in Irish mythology; he was also the father of the FAIRY QUEEN, FAND and LIBAN.

Sources: Gray, *Mythology of All Races*, Volume 3, 87; Layzer, *Signs of Weakness*, 136, 142; Monaghan, *Celtic Encyclopedia of Mythology and Folklore*, 3

Aegeirus

In ancient Greek mythology Aegeirus was a HAMADRYAD of the black poplar tree; she was born from the incestuous relationship between Oxylus and his sister.

Sources: Athenaeus of Naucratis, *Deipnosophists*, Volume 1, 131; Smith, *Dictionary of Greek and Roman Geography*, 35

Ægina

Variations: Aegina, Aigina

The river NYMPH Ægina was born of the river goddess, ASOPUS and the male NYMPH, METOPE according to classical Greek mythology; this NAIAD was the guardian of the island in the Saronic Gulf that bears her name.

Although there are a few tales claiming Ægina and the god Zeus (Jupiter) shared a mutual romantic interlude the stories of her abduction and rape by the god far outnumber them. Her father attempted to rescue her but was driven off by Zeus' thunderbolts. Ultimately Ægina ended up have two children with the god, a godling named Aeacus and a mortal son named Menoetius.

Sources: Gardner, *Journal of Hellenic Studies, Volume 9*, 55; Illes, *Encyclopedia of Spirits*, 126; Pindar, *Pindar's Odes*, 318; Tripp, *Meridian Handbook of Classical Mythology*, 19

Aegle

Variations: Ægle

In Greek lore, Aegle ("dazzling light") was a daughter of Zeus (Jupiter) and considered to be the most beautiful of the NAIADS. There is also a DRYAD by this name, who is one of the daughters of Atlas and PLEIONE, making her one of the PLEIADES as well. Aegle is also one of the four HESPERIDES, a group of four NAIAD sisters who were charged with the protection of a golden apple tree that grew the golden apples the goddess Gaia gave the goddess Hera (Juno) and were stolen by the godling, Herakles (Hercules) (see also ARETHUSA, ERYTHEIA, and HESPERIA). Another NYMPH named Aegle was the one who stole the love of Theseus from Ariadne ("very

holy"). A final NYMPH named Aegel was one of the seven Daughters of Helios (Sol); AEGLE, AETHERIE, DIOXIPPE, Helie (see HELIADES, THE), LAMPETIE, MEROPE, and PHOEBE.

Sources: Bell, *Bell's New Pantheon or Historical Dictionary of the Gods*, 112; Daly, *Greek and Roman Mythology A to Z*, 53; Day, *God's Conflict with the Dragon and the Sea*, 394; Littleton, *Gods, Goddesses, and Mythology, Volume 11*, 998, 1454, 1000; Rose, *Spirits, Fairies, Leprechauns, and Goblins*, 5

Aelfdane

In Denmark, the word *aelfdane* means "coming from the ELF valley" or "Danish ELF."

Source: Newcomb, *Faerie Treasury*, 66

Aengus

Variations: Aonghus, Aengus MacOg, Oenghus

Aengus, son of DAGDA and BOANN, was the handsome and witty harpist of the TUATHA DÉ DANANN in Irish mythology; he was also a fairy and counted among the SÍDHE as an invisible being with power or mortals. Aengus had the ability to reanimate corpses and let them speak to his followers. Sometimes he was regarded as the Irish god of fatal love.

Sources: McCoy, *Celtic Myth and Magick*, 254; Rose, *Spirits, Fairies, Leprechauns, and Goblins*, 3, 351; Wentz, *Fairy-Faith in Celtic Countries*, 414–5

Aetherie

Aetherie ("upper-air") was a NYMPH in the mythology of classical Greece and Rome. According to the Greek oral poet, Hesiod, when her brother, Phaethon, died, she and her seven sisters were transformed into amber-weeping poplar tree. The sisters were collectively known as The Daughters of Helios (Sol); their names are AEGLE, AETHERIE, DIOXIPPE, Helie (see HELIADES, THE), LAMPETIE, MEROPE, and PHOEBE.

Sources: Hyginus, *Myths of Hyginus*, 26, 125; Trzaskoma, *Anthology of Classical Myth*, 264–65

Aethra

Born one of the 3,000 daughters of the Titians, Oceanus and Tethys, Aethra ("bright sky") was one of the named OCEANIDS. Sometimes she is referred to as the wife of Atlas, making her the mother of the PLEIADES and the half sisters of the Hyades.

Sources: Dibbley, *From Achilles' Heel to Zeus's Shield*, 58; Littleton, *Gods, Goddesses, and Mythology, Volume 11*, 1130

Aeval

Variations: Aebhel, Aebill, Aibell, Aibhinn, Aobiheall, Aoibheal, Aoibhell, Aoibhil, Eevell, Eevil, Eevinn

The Fairy Queen of Munster, Aeval ("burning with fire") held her Midnight Court to determine whether husbands were meeting their wives sexual needs. Predisposed to say the men were lazy and prudish she would hear both sides of the case before ruling the husband must bow to the wife's needs. The ancestral mother of the O'Brian clan, Aeval served as their Banshee and overseen a dozen more additional families. Her personal adversary was the sea–Nymph Clídna who once turned her into a white cat.

At Killaloe in east Clare County there is a mound or Fairy Fort said to belong to her; a nearby well called Tobereevul ("well of Aeval") comes up from a crag known as Craganeevul ("rock of Aeval"). In recent years the residents of Inchiquin Lake in the south west region of Munster claim to have seen her; unfortunately, her appearance foretells of an impending disaster.

Sources: Evan-Wentz, *Fairy Faith in Celtic Countries*, 300; Monaghan, *Encyclopedia of Goddesses and Heroines*, 304; Monaghan, *Encyclopedia of Celtic Mythology and Folklore*, 5

Affric

Variations: Affrica, Afric, Oirig

Affric was a water Nymph of Scottish lore. Her name may have originated from the name Aithbrecc, a name from ancient Brittany. It is possibly, originally Aithbrecc was the name of a Scottish river goddess who was demoted to Nymph with the introduction of Christianity, and thereby renamed Affric.

Sources: Campbell, *Celtic Dragon Myth*, xxviii; Henderson, *Norse Influence on Celtic Scotland*, 5; Rose, *Spirits, Fairies, Leprechauns, and Goblins*, 4

Afreda

Variations: Aafreeda, Aelfraed, Afredah, Afreeda, Afreedah, Afrida, Afridah, Afryda, Afrydah

The Arabic word *afreda* means "Elf councilor" or "Elf power."

Sources: Newcomb, *Faerie Treasury*, 66; Wells, *Treasury of Names*, 34

African Fairy Lore

The fay of Africa consists of ancestral spirits, elves, Dwarf-like men, Goblins, Nature Spirits, and Seasonal Fairies (see Elf). Fairy Rings are found quite frequently in the grasslands of the western regions of southern Africa, an interesting event as these rings are usually only found in northern Europe. Like their European counterparts, scientists are uncertain what causes these rings but the oral tradition of the Himba people in the Kunene region claim the rings are created by the local Nature Spirits.

Also similar to the European fairy traditions is the habit of African elves appearing to children and playing with them. Just like their cousins to the far north, as soon as an adult nears, they vanish.

Nature Spirits in African lore consist of two varieties, sky- and the numerous earth-spirits. In general, these spirits tend to have the ability to take various animal forms. Identified with natural locations and forces of nature, these fairy spirits have personalities and are considered to be intelligent, invisible beings. Although some Nature Spirits were said to have been created by God, others are the spirits of those people who lived a very long time ago, too far in the past to be considered ancestral spirits. Nature Spirits commonly have the ability to propagate and reproduce more of their own kind. Powerful spirits have authority and dominion over less powerful spirits. Generally, Nature Spirits are not offered sacrifices or prayers but rather left to reside in legends, myths, and stories.

Some examples of African fay include Asamanukpai, Tokoloshes, and Yumboes.

Sources: Koch, *Occult ABC*, 82; Mbiti, *Introduction to African Religion*, 70–2; McCoy, *Witch's Guide to Faery Folk*, 33

Aganippe

Aganippe ("the mare who destroys mercifully") was a Crinaeae, a sub-species of the Naiad. The Nymph of Mount Helikon in Boiotia, central Greece according to the mythology of classical Greece and Rome, her name described both the fountain she occupied and the Naiad who lived in it. The fountain was created by the hooves of Pegasus and was associated with the Muses; the fountain itself was said to be in the ancient Greek city of Boetia near the Thespiae River, located at the base of Mount Helicon. These waters were considered sacred to the Canonical Muses. Aganippe, a daughter of the river-god Termessus, gave the gift of poetic inspiration to any who drank from her well.

Sources: Falkner, *Mythology of the Night Sky*, 178;

Larson, *Greek Nymphs*, 138; Lemprière, *Classical Dictionary*, 570; Smith, *Dictionary of Greek and Roman Biography and Mythology*, 59

Agave

Variations: Agaue

A sea–NYMPH, Agave ("illustrious") was one of the named NEREID and the NYMPH of the boistorous waves in classical Greek mythology; she was born of Nereus and DORIS. Hesiod refers to her as the "fair cheeked"; she was the mother of Pentheus, a king of Thebes as well as one of the named NEREID who accompanied THETIS in mourning the loss of her son, Achilles.

As Agaue, she, along with AUTONOE and Ino, nursed the infant god, Dionysus (Bacchus), who was born from the thigh of Jupiter.

Agave was also the name of one of the named DANAIDS, the collective name for the daughters of Danaus. In a list compiled by Apollodorus, a Greek scholar and grammarian, she was one of the daughters of Europe and was wedded to Lycus, one of the sons of Argyphia.

Sources: Apollodorus, *Apollodorus' Library and Hyginus' Fabulae*, 95; Collignon, *Manual of Mythology*, 18; Hesiod, *Theogony*, 12; Hesiod, *Works of Hesiod, Callimachus, and Theognis*, 15, 48; Trzaskoma, *Anthology of Classical Myth*, 18

Aglaopheme

Variations: Aglaope, AGLAOPHONOS

In classical Greek mythology, Aglaopheme ("illustrious of voice") was one of the named SIRENS, a type of injurious NYMPH born the offspring of the ancient sea god, Phorcys. Half bird and half woman, she and her sisters would perch on the rocky Sicilian coastline and lure sailors in with their melodious song; once caught, their prey were eaten alive. Although they hunted along the coastline Aglaopheme and her sisters lived inland in a meadow.

Sources: Rose, *Spirits, Fairies, Leprechauns, and Goblins*, 6; Smith, *Dictionary of Greek and Roman Biography and Mythology*, 817

Aglaophonos

In classical Greek mythology, Aglaophonos ("lovely voice") was one of the named SIRENS, a type of malicious NYMPH born the offspring of the ancient sea god, Phorcys. Half bird and half woman, she and her sisters would perch on the rocky Sicilian coastline and lure in sailor with their melodious song; once caught, their prey were eaten alive. Although they hunted the coast-

line, Aglaophonos and her kind lived inland in a meadow.

Sources: Austern, *Music of the Sirens*, 40; Graves, *The Greek Myths*, N.p.; Lemprière, *Classical Dictionary*, 162

Aglaurides

Variations: Agraulos, Cercropids, Kekropides

Aglaurides ("children of Aglauros") was the collective name for the three daughters of Aglauros, a NYMPH, and Cecrops, a snake spirit, who was also the first King of Athens. The eldest daughter was named after her mother, Aglauros ("dweller on tilled land"); Herse ("dewfall") was the middle daughter and Pandrosos ("all bedewed") the youngest. Since the oldest daughter was named after her mother this tell researchers she was born before the ancient Greek city of Athens was dedicated to the goddess Athena (Minerva); subsequent to that time children were named after their father.

According to legend, Cecrops was devoted to Athena and had his daughters attend her shrine. The goddess entrusted into their care a large chest, asking them to protect it but forbid them to ever open it or look within. For a while the half–NYMPH sisters did as they were told but eventually curiosity got the better of them. Aglauros and Herse opened the chest and looked within. Sources vary as to what they saw, some claim it was a very large snake, some say it was an infant child guarded by a snake, while others say it was a snake-child hybrid similar to a hydra. No matter what it was they saw, the two sisters were instantly driven insane by the sight and jumped from the rock to their death. Later, the location they lept from would become the location of the Acropolis.

Sources: Hard, *Routledge Handbook of Greek Mythology*, 365; Illes, *Encyclopedia of Spirits*, 133; Petiscus, *Gods of Olympos*, 196

Agloolik

A NATURE SPIRIT from Inuit mythology, Agloolik lived under the ice; when properly prayed to, he would give his assistance to fishermen and lead hunters to seal holes.

Sources: Andrews, *Dictionary of Nature Myths*, 14; Bilby, *Among Unknown Eskimo*, 72; Drew, *Wiccan Bible*, 278; Rose, *Spirits, Fairies, Gnomes, and Goblins*, 5

Aguane

The aguane were a type of female fairy or NATURE SPIRIT found in the Austrian Alps in northern Italy near the Slovenia boarder; they live in the hills and in the rivers and streams that cross them. These fay are said to be very beautiful with long, luxurious hair and large breasts, but some sources say they also have either the feet of a goat or those of a horse. Expert shape-shifters, the aguane act as protectors of mountain streams and rivers, much like the subspecies of NYMPH known as a NAPAEAE. Before entering into a body of water it is advised to ask for their permission, as the aguane have been known to eat trespassers. In spite of their harsh treatment of intruders, the aguane are said to be fond of children and will carry them safely across water.

Aguane were said to be able to successfully mate with the SILVANI thereby producing offspring known as *SALVANELLI*.

Sources: Arrowsmith, *Field Guide to the Little People*, 103–4; Euvino, *Complete Idiot's Guide to Italian History and Culture*, 274; Grimassi, *Hereditary Witchcraft: Secrets of the Old Religion*, 83; Illes, *Encyclopedia of Spirits*, 11

Agun Kuguza

Usually invisible, Agun Kuguza ("drying house old man") was a fairy spirit from the folk lore of the Mari people in what was once Eastern Russia. Living in buildings used for drying and storing grain this fairy, if not offered the sacrifice of a small animal each autumn, would ruin the harvest. The remains of the sacrifice were buried under the building.

Sources: Rose, *Spirits, Fairies, Leprechauns, and Goblins*, 5; Sebeok, *Studies in Cheremis: the Supernatural*, 78

Ahermanabâd

Variations: Ahermanabad, City of Principal Evil

In Persian lore, the fairy metropolis of Ahermanabâd was peopled by the DEV; this was the location of King ARZSHENK's enchanted castle.

Sources: Keightly, *World Guide to Gnomes, Fairies, Elves, and Other Little People*, 16; Richardson, *Dissertation on the Languages*, 144; Yardley, *Supernatural in Romantic Fiction*, 53

Ahi At-Trab

A type of mischievous fairy spirit from Muslim-Tureg lore, the ahi at-trab lived just below the surface of the Sahara desert. Seldom seen in their true form they would manifest as a small whirling column of sand; the ahi at-trab caused many problems for the nomadic people of the desert including drinking an oases dry and causing camels to trip.

Source: Rose, *Spirits, Fairies, Leprechauns, and Goblins*, 5–6

Ai

Ai ("from a river" and "great grandfather") was one of the many DWARFS named in the *Voluspa*, the first and best known poem of the *Poetic Edda*, a collection of Old Norse poems dating back to about A.D. 985.

Sources: Crossley-Holland, Norse Myths, 183; Daly, *Norse Mythology A to Z*, 22; Sykes, *Who's Who in Non-Classical Mythology*, 53; Wilkinson, *Book of Edda called Völuspá*, 12

Aia

In classical Greek mythology, Aia was a NYMPH of the town of Aia or Kollhos, which was located near the Kaukasos Mountains; she was loved by the river god, Phasis.

Source: Cook, *Zeus*, Volume 2, 904

The Aiaiai

Variations: Aiaia

According to Homer, the greatest ancient Greek poet and the author of the *Iliad*, the Aiaiai were a collection of NYMPHS who lived on the goddess CIRCE's Isle of Wails.

Sources: Brann, *Homeric Moments*, 192; Hansen, *Handbook of Classical Mythology*, 170

Aibell

Variations: Aebill, AEVAL, Aibell, Aibhinn, AOIBHEALL, Aoibhell ("fire" or "radiance"), Aoibhil, Aoibinn ("beautiful" or "happy")

Originally an Irish earth goddess, the FAIRY QUEEN of North Munster, Aibell ("most beautiful"), was the BANSHEE to the O'Briens and the Dalcassians families. Aibell may also have been a guardian of the Irish sovereignty, as it was said before the battle of Clontarf on 1014 C.E. she appeared to the high King, Brian Boru. Not only did she warn him of his death but also advised as to which of his children should rule after him.

Aibell owned a golden harp and was such a skilful harpest if a human should ever happen to hear her playing upon it, they would soon die. In addition to her harp, she also owned the Cloak of Darkness; it rendered the wearer invisible.

Aibell's palace, Crageevil ("grey rock"), was located two miles north of Killaloe in a deep and wooded valley. All the trees of this valley have long since been felled and without them she would not reside there, however, the well named for her, Tobereevil ("Aibell's well"), still springs from the mountain side.

Aibell was rivals with the Fairy Queen, Cliodna.

Sources: Illes, *Encyclopedia of Spirits*, 140; Mahon, *Ireland's Fairy Lore*, 138: McCoy, *Celtic Myth and Magick*, 173; Monaghan, *Encyclopedia of Celtic Mythology and Folklore*, 5

Aíbell

Variations: Aoibhell ("fire" or "radiance")

In Irish mythology Aíbell is the Fairy Queen of Connacht. The lusty and powerful Fairy King, Mongan, shape-shifted himself into the likeness of her husband, Áed, in order to spend a night of passion with her. Aíbell possessed a magical harp, to hear its music was a death omen. Aíbell's personal rival was Fairy Queen, Clidna, who transformed her into a white cat by use of a magical spell.

Sources: Matson, *Celtic Mythology A to Z*, 2; Monaghan, *Encyclopedia of Celtic Mythology and Folklore*, 4

Aibheaeg

In Irish mythology Aibheaeg was originally an ancient goddess of fire later demoted to the status and position of Fairy Queen of Donegal after the introduction of Christianity; she was worshiped at the Well of Fire whose water was said to cure toothaches if the petitioner left a white stone at the location.

Sources: Logan, *Holy Wells of Ireland*, 67; Monaghan, *Encyclopedia of Celtic Mythology and Folklore*, 6

Aicha Kandida

Aicha Kandida was a female water Djinn from the folklore of Morocco; she lived along the banks of the river Sebu and could also be found in the sultan's palace grounds. Married to the afrit, Hamou Ukaiou, Aicha Kandida took appearance of a dazzlingly beautiful woman who approached men who traveled alone. Aicha Kandida would call to him by name and give chase if he should run. She hated mankind and if she caught her victim she would drag him to a watery grave and consume him there. There have been a few stories of men able to sexually gratify her and in doing so were released, laden down with gifts.

Sources: Legey, *Folklore of Morocco*, 73; Rose, *Spirits, Fairies, Leprechauns, and Goblins*, 6; Yolen, *Fish Prince and Other Stories*, 107

Aigeiros

In Greek mythology Aigeiros ("poplar") was one of the eight Hamadryad born of Hamadryas; she was the Hamadryad of the black poplar tree.

Sources: Buxton, *Forms of Astonishment*, 211; Larson, *Greek Nymphs*, 283; Room, *Who's Who in Classical Mythology*, 121

Aigel

In classical Greek mythology the Nymph Aigle ("radiant") was the mother of the Kharites by the sun god, Helios (Sol).

Sources: Brown, *Eridanus*, 32; Trzaskoma, *Anthology of Classical Myth*, 39

Aiken Drum

Variations: The Brownie of Blednoch

Aiken Drum was an individual Brownie from Scottish lore who lived in Blednoch in Galloway. Described as only wearing a kilt made of green rushes, during the night Aiken Drum would complete household tasks left undone by the time the sun set. On occasions when people tried to exorcise him by use of prayers from the Bible, he proved resistant. Like all Brownies, if ever he were to be given clothes, he would leave his current location forever.

A popular Scottish balled commonly titled *The Brownie of Blednoch* written by William Nicholson explains how this fay came to Blednoch, the work he did while he was there, the newlywed wife who was shocked by his lack of clothing, and why he left the region; it was first published in *Dumfries Magazine* in 1825.

Sources: *Notes on Superstition and Folk Lore*, 44–6; Rose, *Spirits, Fairies, Leprechauns, and Goblins*, 6

Ailill

Variations: Ailbill, Ailill of Leinster, the Honey Tongued, Oilill

Ailill ("Elf" or "Sprite") was a Milesian Fairy King of Leinster, Ireland although he had a right to lay claim to Connacht through his mother's bloodline. He married Medbh, the sovereign of Ireland for the bride price of a wedding band of red gold as wide as his face, twenty-one slaves, the weight of silver equal to his shield arm, and the clothing for twelve men. Ailill was also the father of Etain (see Edain). He agreed to the marriage of his daughter to the Fairy King, Midir on the provision the would-be groom cleared twelve vast agricultural fields, twelve rivers to be created in order to irrigate those fields, and a cash settlement of her weight in both gold and silver. Ailill was described as being a tall individual with reddish skin and a golden diadem rested on his head.

Sources: Evan-Wentz, *Fairy Faith in Celtic Countries*, 301; Monaghan, *Encyclopedia of Celtic Mythology and Folklore*, 8; Mountain, *Celtic Encyclopedia*, Volume 2, 296–7

Aillen Mac Midhna

Variations: Aillen Mac Midna, Aillen Mac-Modha, the Wondrous Elfin Man

In the folklore and legends of Ireland, Aillen Mac Midhna was the fairy musician of the TUATHA DE DANANN; he was described as being particularly dark, having fiery breath, and carrying an evil and poisonous spear. Mac Midhna played a magical *tuinpan* (an Irish harp or tambourine); he was so proficient with this instrument anyone who heard him play would soon drift off to sleep.

For twenty-three consecutive years Aillen Mac Midhna left his home in Finnachaidh and traveled south to play at the festival of Samhain held at Tara. Each year as he played his audience would drift off to sleep and each year, greatly annoyed at their having done so, he would blast three plumes of fire from his nostrils, setting Tara ablaze. Finn Mac Cumhaill of the Fianna, also a SÍDHE, tired of this annual burning and took Mac Midhna's spear from him and forced the musician to inhale its poisonous fumes. The noxious gas killed the harpist.

Sources: Mountain, *Celtic Encyclopedia*, Volume 2, 300; Rose, *Spirits, Fairies, Leprechauns, and Goblins*, 6, 351; Wentz, *Fairy-Faith in Celtic Countries*, 298–9

Aine

Variations: Aíne, Aine Cliach, Aine Marina, Aine Marine, Aine of Knockaine, Aine of the Sight, Aine of the Whip, Ainé, Fennel, Finnen

Originally an Irish goddess of fertility and love who was demoted to the rank of fay after the introduction of Christianity, the beautiful FAIRY QUEEN Aine ("bright") of Knockaine in Limerick County in West Munster, along with FAIRY QUEEN AOIBHINN of North Munster, owed their allegiances to the FAIRY QUEEN, CLIODNA. Her FAIRY FORT, Cnoc Aine ("Aine's hill"), was a hill located three miles south-west of Lough Gur; it was known as Knock Aine. Atop this hill's summit sacrifices and ancient sacred rites were performed.

Born the daughter of King Egobagal, one of the TUATHA DE DANANN, Aine was already one of the SÍDHE when she was taken and enchanted by the fay. While she was still part human, she possessed a magical ring that could reveal fairies. Before her marriage to Gerald, the Earl of Desmond, she had many mortal men as her lovers and bore several fairy-blooded children. After giving birth to their son, GEROID Iarla, Earl Fitzgerald, she left her husband in a fit of disgust when he broke his *gess*; she retreated to her mound or FAIRY FORT, Cnoc Aine.

Sources: Evan-Wentz, *Fairy Faith in Celtic Countries*, 79; McCoy, *Celtic Myth and Magick*, 175; Mountain, *Celtic Encyclopedia*, Volume 2, 301; Rose, *Spirits, Fairies, Leprechauns, and Goblins*, 7, 351; Squire, *Celtic Myth and Legend*, 162

Ainsel

Variations: Brollachan ("a shapeless thing")

In the folklore of Rothly, Northumberland, England Ainsel ("own self"), an individual fairy, appeared as a playful, female child. According to legend, one winter night a mother tried to send her son to bed but he was not sleepy and refused to go. The mother warned should he stay up the fairies would take him away but laughing at his mother, the son ignored the warning. Not long after she left the room, a beautiful, doll-size fairy came down the chimney and introduced itself to the child as Ainsel. The two played nicely together until the fire began to die; when the child poked at the logs a single hot ember struck the fay causing it to scream out in magnificent pain. The mother came dashing into the room asking her son "Who hurt you?" to which he replied "It was my Ainsel!" The mother, assuming her son had confessed to hurting himself, spanked and chided him for making so much noise when there was no one to blame but himself.

Sources: Hartland, *English Fairy and Folk Tales*, 149–50; Keightley, *Fairy Mythology*, 313; Rose, *Spirits, Fairies, Leprechauns, and Goblins*, 7, 351

Airmed

Variations: Airmed, Airmid

An Irish fairy-goddess of herbal lore and witchcraft, Airmed was born the daughter of the renowned physician, Dian Cecht, one of the TUATHA DE DANANN; she assisted her father in protecting his sacred, healing spring. When her brother Miach died she mourned so profoundly at his gravesite all the herbs of the world grew from its location and revealed their secrets to her.

Sources: Matson, *Celtic Mythology A to Z*, 3; Monaghan, *New Book of Goddesses and Heroines*, 37; Reidling, *Faery Initiations*, 278

Aithousa

In classical Greek mythology the NYMPH Aithousa was born the daughter of the god of the sea, Poseidon (Neptune) and the OREADS, ALCYONE. Aithousa was the mother of Eleuther by the god, Apollo.

Sources: Apollodorus of Athens, *Apollodorus' Library and Hyginus' Fabulae*, 58; Hard, *Routledge Handbook of Greek Mythology*, 521

Aitvaras

A HOUSE-SPIRIT of Lithuanian folklore, Aitvaras could assume shapes in accordance to its environment, for example inside of a house it looked like a black cat or a roosters but when outdoors it looked like a dragon or a serpent with a fiery tail. Traditionally, aitvaras were powerful beings who lived in the forest but could be persuaded to serve as a family guardian; they brought abundance, good fortune, happiness, and wealth to those they favor. The aitvaras did not get along well with Perkunas, the god of thunder.

Sources: Illes, *Encyclopedia of Spirits*, 147; Rose, *Spirits, Fairies, Leprechauns, and Goblins*, 7

Aiwel

Variations: Aiwel Longar

Aiwel was a NATURE SPIRIT and cultural hero from the folklore of the Dinka people of the Sudan. Born the son of a river spirit and an elderly widow woman, Aiwel was responsible for helping people and their herds with his magical powers. His attitude, disposition, and values were considered Dinka ideals. Embracing both his humanity and spirituality he overcame great adversity and rose to become the leader of his mother's people. He founded a priesthood known as the Spear Masters; the symbol of his power was the spear.

Sources: Asante, *Encyclopedia of African religion*, Volume 1, 22; Lynch, *African Mythology A to Z*, 5–6; Rose, *Spirits, Fairies, Leprechauns, and Goblins*, 8

Aix

Variations: Amaltheia

In classical Greek mythology the NYMPH of Mount Ida on the island of Crete in the Greek Aegean Sea was called Aix ("goat"); typically described as looking like a goat she was also one of the many nurses to the god, Zeus (Jupiter). The appearance of Aix was so shocking, especially to the Titians, Zeus used her hide to create the aegis he carried into battle.

Sources: Cook, *Zeus*, 933, Fontenrose, *Python*, 353–54

Akaia

Variations: Acraia

Akaia was a NYMPH born the daughter of the river god, Asterion; along with her sisters EUBOIA and PROSYMNA, she was a nurse to the infant goddess, Hera (Juno).

Sources: Lemprière, *Classical Dictionary*, 642; Pausânias, *Guide to Greece, Central*, 169; Trzaskoma, *Anthology of Classical Myth*, 346

Akakasoh

Similar to the HAMADRYADS of classical Greek mythology, the akakasoh were tree spirits or NATS from Burmese folklore. They lived in the highest branches of the trees; there presence could be detected by the shivering of the leaves.

Sources: Porteous, *Forest in Folklore and Mythology*, 125; Rose, *Spirits, Fairies, Leprechauns, and Goblins*, 8; Scott, *Burman: His Life and Notions*, Volume 1, 286

Akaste

Akaste was one of the NAIADES, according to the Greek oral poet, Homer.

Source: Homer, *Homeric Hymns*, 13

Akeste

Born one of the 3,000 daughters of the Titians, Oceanus and Tethys, Akeste was one of the named OCEANIDS in ancient Greek mythology; she was one of the playmates of Persephone (Proserpina) and present when the goddess was kidnapped.

Source: Fowler, *Archaic Greek Poetry*, 14, 322

The Akheloides

Variations: Acheloides, SIRENS

The akheloides was the collective name for the NAIADS of the river Akheloios in Anatolia, central Greece; they were born the daughters of the river god, Acheloos. The akheloides were very similar to the SIRENS, in that they would use their sweet, melodious voice to lure sailors and fishermen to drive their ship in towards shore to hear their song where they would be dashed against the rocky shoreline.

Sources: Avant, *Mythological Reference*, 207; Smith, *New Classical Dictionary of Greek and Roman Biography, Mythology and Geography*, Volume 1, 561

Akraia

One of the three NYMPHS of the river Asterion in Argos, southern Greece, Akraia ("she dominates the hills"), along with EUBOIA and PROSYMNA, was one of the nurses to the infant goddess, Hera (Juno).

Sources: Larson, *Greek Nymphs*, 150; Pausânias, *Guide to Greece: Central Greece*, 169

Aktaie

Aktaie ("anointed") was the NEREID of the sound of the lapping of the waves upon the shore; she was one of the named NEREID who accompanied THETIS in mourning the loss of her son, Achilles.

Sources: Collignon, *Manual of Mythology*, 187; Sammons, *Art and Rhetoric of the Homeric Catalogue*, 10

Al-A'war

According to the Koran, Al-A'war ("the one-eyed") was a DJINN and one of the five sons of IBLIS. He was considered to be the demon of debauchery.

Sources: Cramer, *Devil Within*, 292; Singer, *Jewish Encyclopedia*, 521; Tabarī, *Sāsānids, the Byzantines, the Lakhmids, and Yemen*, 75

al Naddaha

Variations: Ginneyya

In the Arabic folklore in Egypt al naddaha ("the caller") haunts the Nile River; similar to the BANSHEE, only this fairy's call is considered to be a death omen, it is more closely related to the LORELEI, MERMAID, or SIREN. Although no one who has ever seen an al naddaha has survived to tell the tale, it is described as looking like a slender, tall, beautiful woman with flowing long hair. Standing at the river bank in transparent clothing, her hands by her side, she would call out in her calm, loud, yet soft voice. In some tales al naddaha is described as having a translucent or simi-solid body, causing some folklorists to liken it to the DJINN. Anyone who hears the voice of al naddaha is either devoured by it or pulled into the river and drowned, but either way, the victim is never seen alive again.

Source: Illes, *Encyclopedia of Spirits*, 735–36

Alan

The alan were a species of NATURE SPIRITS from the folklore of the Tinguian people of the Philippines. Alans lived in the forests and appeared to be half bird and half human; the size of humans, their fingers bent back towards their wrists and their toes sprug from their heels. Although they were said to have homes made of gold, alans could be found at rest hanging batlike from tree branches. They had a wide and varied array of magical abilities, such as taking afterbirth and creating a child from it, healing the sick, and traveling the world. Generally the alan were considered to be mischievous yet benevolent, acting as the guardians or foster parent of mythological cultural heroes.

Sources: Cole, *Traditions of the Tinguian*, 14–5. 64; Gale, *Tinguian*, 301; Rose, *Spirits, Fairies, Leprechauns, and Goblins*, 8–9

Albastor

Variations: Labasta

A species of fairy from the Mari people of Russia, the Albastor lived in the bathhouse disguised as an old man or woman; however, they could also take on the appearance of a GIANT with long flowing hair. Created when an illegitimate child died unbaptized these fairies could shape-shift into any animal so long as it remained upon the ground. As it traveled through the sky it looked like a shooting star.

Like the demonic succubus, the albastor engaged in sexual intercourse with humans; it punished those who overindulge themselves with excessive sex, slowing killing them with exhaustion. Victims of this sort of assault would have a sore on their lips, left there by the fairy's kiss. Any human lover the victim took on would also become sick and may die as well. An albastor could be defeated by catching it and breaking the fingers of its left hand or by hanging a cross over each doorway of the house to prevent its entry.

Sources: Rose, *Spirits, Fairies, Leprechauns, and Goblins*, 9; Sebeok, *Studies in Cheremis*, 51

Alberich

Variations: Aelfric, Albrich, Alferich, Alpris, ANDVARI, ELBERICH

In Scandinavian and Teutonic mythology Alberich was the King of the DWARFS (also known as the DARK ELVES, see also DWARF) and was the brother to King Goldmar. Described as looking like a hideous GNOME he lived in an underground castle decorated with precious gems. Alberich was the keeper of a belt of strength; a magical ring; cloak of invisibility; and the invincible sword, Balmung; he was also the individual who forged many of the god's magical items, such as Freya's necklace.

It has been speculated Alberich, whose name means "ELF ruler" or "ELF king" had dominion over elves in the same fashion King Solomon had dominion over demons.

Sources: Illes, *Encyclopedia of Spirits*, 17, 156; Keightly, *World Guide to Gnomes, Fairies, Elves, and Other Little People*, 206; Rose, *Spirits, Fairies, Leprechauns, and Goblins*, 9, 13; Wägner, *Epics and Romances of the Middle Ages*, 59, 236

Alcheringa

From the Arunta tribes of Central Australia the alcheringa were a race of fairy spirits who live in an invisible realm, also call Alcheringa; it was similar to FAIRYLAND. Only medicine men had the ability to see these ancestral or NATURE SPIRITS; they were described as being shadowy, thin, and young in appearance. The alcheringa lived in stones and trees and were propitiated in order to secure their favor and protection.

Sources: Chisholm, *Encyclopædia Britannica*, Volume 19, 135; Evan-Wentz, *Fairy Faith in Celtic Countries*, 227; Narváez, *Good People*, 488

Alcina

A FATE, luxury-driven Alcine was said to have used her magic to create a splendid palace surrounded by a wall of gold on Alcina Island but was displeased with the island's location. She conspired with her lascivious sister Morgana against their virtuous half-sister and rightful heir to their father's throne, LOGISTILLA. The unfortunate sister's castle was on the same island as Alcina's but was in a far less accessible and ideal location.

Alcina was known to lure great numbers of men onto the island, take them on as lovers, and when she tired of them, transform them into plants and stones. Although old and rather ugly, she appeared to be dazzlingly beautiful by means of her glamour magic. Commanding an army of ape-men, cat-men, centaurs, and dog-men she went to war against her sister LOGISTILLA, but lost when all the men she had transformed were restored and rallied against her.

Sources: Brewer, *Character Sketches of Romance, Fiction and the Drama*, 5; Hankins, *Source and Meaning in Spenser's Allegory*, 59; Keightly, *World Guide to Gnomes, Fairies, Elves, and Other Little People*, 452–3; Manguel, *Dictionary of Imaginary Places*, 14

Alcinda

Alcinda ("light") was a NYMPH from Greek mythology; she was charged with the care and feeding of the infant god, Zeus (Jupiter).

Source: Pausanias, *Pausanias's Description of Greece*, Volume 1, 434

Alcinoe

Alcinoe was a NYMPH from the mythology of classical Greece and Rome. One of the NAIADS, she was one of the many nurses of the infant god, Zeus (Jupiter).

Sources: Bell, *Women of Classical Mythology*, 19, 462; Parada, *Genealogical Guide to Greek Mythology*, 13

Alcyone

Variations: Alkyone

One of the OREADS, Alcyone was a NYMPH from classical Greek mythology. Born one of the daughters of the Titian Atlas and the ocean NYMPH, PLEIONE, she was the eldest of the PLEIADES, the seven sisters and daughters of PLEIONE; these sisters were also known as the ATLANTIDES. Alcyone had a long standing love affair with the god of the sea, Poseidon (Neptune), by which she bore many children.

Sources: Ardinger, *Pagan Every Day*, 190; Illes, *Encyclopedia of Spirits*, 158

Alecto

Variations: Alekto

One of the three FURIES from classical Greek mythology, Alecto ("envy") was the sister who specialized in maintaining justice. She, like her sisters, were described as looking like an old HAG with bat wings, bloodshot eyes, and snakes in her hair; sometime they were confused as being a gorgon. The ancient Greek tragedian, Aeschylus (525 B.C.–456 B.C.), claimed the sisters were the daughters of Night while the tragedian Sophocles (497 B.C.–406 B.C.) said they were the daughter of Skotos, the personification of darkness, and the earth.

Sources: Chopra, *Academic Dictionary of Mythology*, 112, 284; Drury, *Dictionary of the Esoteric*, 93; Hard, *Routledge Handbook of Greek Mythology*, 39

Alexirhoe

Variations: Alyxothoe

Alexirhoe was a NYMPH of the springs of the River Grenikos on Mount Ida from the mythology of classical Greece and Rome. One of the NAIADS, she was born one of the daughters of the twin-horned river god, Granicus. By King Priam of Troy she bore a son named Aesacus (Aisakos) who grieved deeply the loss of his lover, or wife, the NYMPH, CEBREN.

Sources: Larson, *Greek Nymphs*, 195, 198; Lempière, *Classical Dictionary*, 44, 198

Alf

Variations: ELF, Elv

An alf is a lesser known type of benevolent German fairy. The origin of the word is unknown but there is speculation among scholars it may mean "spirit."

Source: Keightly, *World Guide to Gnomes, Fairies, Elves, and Other Little People*, 66, 206, 601

Alf (2)

Alf was one of the many DWARFS named in the *Voluspa*, the first and best known poem of the *Poetic Edda*, a collection of Old Norse poems dating back to about A.D. 985.

Sources: Daly, *Norse Mythology A to Z*, 22; Crossley-Holland, *Norse Myths*, 183; Gray, *Mythology of All Races*, Volume 2, 220

Alfa

Variations: Alfa-folk, ALFAR

In Scandinavian and Teutonic mythology the alfa (also known as elves) are divided up into two clans, the LIOSALFAR and the SVARTALFAR. Both species of elves are said to have been created from the maggots that ate the decomposing flesh of YMIR, the GIANT (see ELF). Powerful beings, the alfas are seldom truly malicious toward mankind.

Clan LIOSALFAR ("LIGHT ELVES") are light bringers; they are described as being tall, exceedingly beautiful, and having skin more white and pale than the sun. They live in Alfhime, a place located between Earth and the Heavens.

Clan SVARTALFAR ("DARK ELVES") have very dark skin, and are described as being darker than a night sky without stars. Dwelling beneath the earth they are reputed as being magnificent smiths, creating magical armor and weapons. Although they have a reputation for being evil the SVARTALFAR are associated with fertility, giving them a substantial following among the ancient Norse people.

The creation origins of the Alfa are varied; some claim they were created after Adam but before Eve while others say they were spontaneously created by God. There is a belief they may have an immortal soul making them HALF-KIN.

Alfa are well organized for fay; they live under the same political form of government Icelanders do. There are two viceroys ruling over the alfa and every other year they travel to Norway where they present themselves to the ruling FAIRY KING of their kind. There, they give a full and honest detailed report concerning his subjects' fidelity, good conduct, and obedience.

Sources: Illes, *Encyclopedia of Spirits*, 17; Keightly, *World Guide to Gnomes, Fairies, Elves, and Other Little People*, 150

Alfar, DWARF

Variations: Alb, Alberich, Alfa-blot, Álfr

Alfar came from Scandinavian folklore and was named in the *Nibelungen Saga*; he is a singular entity who was originally seen as being half god and half DWARF. After the introduction of Christianity, he was demoted into the demon of diseases and nightmares.

Sources: Du Chaillu, *Viking Age*, 409–10; Keightley, *Fairy Mythology*, 108–9, 135; Sykes, *Who's Who in Non-Classical Mythology*, 53; Turner, *Dictionary of Ancient Deities*, 166

Alfar

Variations: Ælf, Alf, Elben, Elfvor, Ellen, Elven

In Teutonic mythology the alfar is the Old Norse word for ELF and is commonly used, even now, to refer to the elves of northern Europe. The Icelandic historian and scholar, Snorri Sturluson, wrote the *Prose Edda* around the year 1220; in it he described two different types of elves: the DÖCKALFAR and the LIOSALFAR.

Sources: Keightly, *World Guide to Gnomes, Fairies, Elves, and Other Little People*, 78; McCoy, *A Witch's Guide to Faery Folk*, 30

Alfheim

Variations: Alf-heim

In Scandinavian mythology Alfheim was the city inhabited by the LIGHT ELVES, the LIOSALFAR; it was also the location of the home of the god of rain, sunshine, and vegetation, Freyr.

Sources: Dunham, *History of Denmark, Sweden, and Norway*, Volume 2, 57, 133; Keightly, *World Guide to Gnomes, Fairies, Elves, and Other Little People*, 64

Alfreikr

Alfreikr was one of the many DWARFS named in the *Voluspa*, the first and best known poem of the *Poetic Edda*, a collection of Old Norse poems dating back to about A.D. 985.

Sources: Daly, *Norse Mythology A to Z*, 22; Sykes, *Who's Who in Non-Classical Mythology*, 53

Alfrigg

Variations: Alfrik

In Norse mythology Alfrigg ("whole beloved") was one of the four BRISINGAMEN DWARFS who created the prized necklace for the goddess Freyr (see also BERLING, DVALIN, and GERR). He once spent a night with the goddess discussing and debating the many aspects of the world.

Alfrigg and BERLING are uncommon names for DWARFS and only appear in *Sorla Thattr* in the *Flateyjarbok* manuscript.

Sources: Daly, *Norse Mythology A to Z*, 2, 11, 32–3; Grimes, *Norse Myths*, 131–2, 254; Pentikäinen, *Shamanism and Northern Ecology*, 87, 94

Alfs

Variations: ELF

The alfs are one of the three races of NORNIR, a type of FATE, in Norse mythology; the DWARFS and the Æser are the other two. Described as looking like tiny children wearing caps they dance in circles in the woods where fire is said to spew up from the earth. In the morning the ground where these fay have danced is scorched but quickly grows back, thicker and greener than before. On occasion they become possessive of a particular tree and will see to its protection going so far as to physically assault anyone who would chop it down.

Uncommon to fairy-kind the alfs have an ability known as an *alf-gust* ("ELF-blast"). When one of these fay breathe upon a person they will fall sick and oftentimes die.

Typically only children who are born on a Sunday have the ability to see the alfs but they are known to occasionally grant this ability to those who happen to come across them as they dance in the woods.

Sources: Burke, *Saint James's Magazine, and Heraldic and Historical Register*, Volume 1, 419; Keightly, *World Guide to Gnomes, Fairies, Elves, and Other Little People*, 64

Alkinoe

In classical Greek mythology Alkinoe was a NYMPH of Mount Lykaios in Arcadia, the Peloponnesos, central Greece; she was one of the nurses of the infant god, Zeus (Jupiter).

Sources: Cook, *Zeus*, 112; Larson, *Greek Nymphs*, 153

Alkippe

In classical Greek mythology Alkippe was a fountain NYMPH; one of the AGLAURIDES, she was born the daughter of the god of war, Ares (Mars) by the NYMPH, Aglauros. Alkippe was in love with the godling Halirrhotios, a son of the god of the sea, Poseidon (Neptune); her beloved was slain by her father, Ares.

Sources: Avant, *Mythological Reference*, 222; Hard, *Routledge Handbook of Greek Mythology*, 365

The Alkyonides

In classical Greek mythology the Alkyonides were the seven daughters of the GIANT, Alkyoneus (Alcyineus). When the godling Herakles (Hercules) slew their father the sisters threw themselves into the sea but AMPHITRITE transformed them all into kingfishers.

Sources: Avant, *Mythological Reference*, 215–16; Falkner, *Mythology of the Night Sky*, 195

Alom-bag-winno-sis

Variations: Alom-begwi-no-sis

In the mythology of the Abenaki Indians of New England, Alom-bag-winno-sis were a race of injurious aquatic DWARFS who lived in deep pool, rivers and lakes. In areas where the water was particularly turbulent they came up underneath canoes and capsized them in the hopes of drowning its occupants. Powerful fay, they had the ability to increase their size at will becoming either extremely large or incredibly small. Generally the Alom-bag-winno-sis lived in underwater communities but there were stories of an isolated individual living on its own. They possessed a magical pot; when a few grains of maize were added to it, the pot inflated to a huge size making more than enough food for the community, they were described as being about three feet tall and having incredibly black and straight hair growing down past their waist; they did not wear clothing of any sort. Normally these fay prefered to remain hidden and avoided contact with mankind, but to see one of the Alom-bag-winnosis was considered a death omen, a prediction one's death by drowning.

Source: Maberry, *They Bite*, 192

Alp-Luachra

Normally the alp-luachra ("joint eater") of Irish lore was harmless to humans except in one particular circumstance: should a person fall asleep beside a stream and accidently swallows a newt. If this singular event should occur then the alp-luachra would cause its victim to be consumed with eating but prevented him from gaining any nourishment from the food consumed.

When not in its newt form, this fairy was completely invisible and unable to be detected until it was too late to help the victim.

In Douglas Hyde's *Beside the Fire*, one victim was able to rid himself of the fey by eating great quantizes of salted beef without drinking any water. Then he went back to the stream he acquired the fey from and fell back asleep. The alpluachra, desperate and thirsty, returned of its own accord to the water.

Sources: Hyde, *Beside the Fire*, 51–60; Monaghan, *Encyclopedia of Celtic Mythology and Folklore*, 15; Rose, *Spirits, Fairies, Leprechauns, and Goblins*, 10, 351

Alpheus

Born the son of the Titians Oceanus and Tethys, Alpheus was a river god and one of the named OCEANIDS. He fell in love first with the goddess Artemis (Diana) and when thoroughly rejected by her, he fell in love with ARETHUSA, one of the goddesses NYMPH attendants. She too refused to return his love and fled to the island of ORTYGIA where she was transformed into a spring by her goddess to keep her safe from Alpheus.

Sources: Boswell, *What Men or Gods Are These*, 58; Day, *God's Conflict with the Dragon and the Sea*, 64; Grimal, *Dictionary of Classical Mythology*, 35; Hesiod, *Works of Hesiod, Callimachus, and Theognis*, 20

Alseid

Variations: Alsea, Alseides

The alseids ("groves") of classical Greek mythology were a sub-species of the LIMONIAD, they were the NYMPHS of sacred groves but they also appeared in glens, lightly forested areas, and meadows. These fairies had a reputation as being pranksters and enjoyed playing tricks on travelers.

Sources: Custer, *Treasury of New Testament Synonyms*, 76; Hesiod, *Hesiod, the Homeric Hymns, and Homerica*, 413; Homer, *Iliad of Homer, Books 1–6*, 9; Illes, *Encyclopedia of Spirits*, 161; Littleton, *Gods, Goddesses, and Mythology*, Volume 4, 440

Alston

Alston is British surname whose origins come from Old English; it translats to mean "from the ELF's abode."

Sources: Ames, *What Shall We Name the Baby*, 129; Newcomb, *Faerie Treasury*, 66

Althaea

One of the HYAD, Althaea was a NYMPH of Mount Ida on the island of Crete in the Greek Aegean Sea; she was one of the nurses to the infant god, Zeus (Jupiter). Althaea was commonly grouped with fellow NYMPHS, Adraste and IDOTHEA.

Source: Smith, *Dictionary of Greek and Roman Biography and Mythology: Earinus-Nyx*, 533

Althaia

Variations: Amaltheia

Althaia was a NYMPH of Mount Ida on the island of Crete in the Greek Aegean; she was one of the nurses to the infant god, Zeus (Jupiter).

Source: Larson, *Greek Nymphs*, 137

Althiof

Althiof was one of the many DWARFS named in the *Voluspa*, the first and best known poem of the *Poetic Edda*, a collection of Old Norse poems dating back to about A.D. 985.

Sources: Wägner, *Asgard and the Gods*, 311; Wilkinson, *Book of Edda called Völuspá*, 12

Althiolf

Variations: Althjof

Althiolf ("mighty thief") was one of the many DWARFS named in the *Voluspa*, the first and best known poem of the *Poetic Edda*, a collection of Old Norse poems dating back to about A.D. 985.

Sources: Daly, *Norse Mythology A to Z*, 22; Sturluson, *Edda*, 16

Althjófr

Variations: Althjof

Althjófr ("all thief") was one of the many DWARFS named in the *Voluspa*, the first and best known poem of the *Poetic Edda*, a collection of Old Norse poems dating back to about A.D. 985.

Sources: Crossley-Holland, Norse Myths, 183; Daly, *Norse Mythology A to Z*, 22; Sykes, *Who's Who in Non-Classical Mythology*, 53

Alux (plural: aluxob)

Variations: A'lus, Ahlu't, Aigypans, Aluche, Barux, Curinqueans, Curupiras, DUENDE, Goazis, Guayazis, Ixtabay, Kax, Matuyus, Vasitris

The Mayan people of the Yucatán Peninsula and Guatemala had in their fairy mythology a being known as an alux. Standing only about knee high and dressed in traditional Mayan clothing the aluxob remained invisible except to frighten humans or when congregating together. A type of NATURE SPIRIT, these fay were associated with a natural features such as a cave, forest, or large stone but it was believed with proper offerings an alux could be enticed to move to a different location.

Small one- and two-story shrines called *kahtal alux* ("houses of the alux") dot the countryside; farmers would sometimes build such a structure in their maize field for the aluxob to move into. It was said for seven years the fairy would dwell in the shrine and care for the crops even causing proper amounts of rain to fall. At the end of seven years the doors and windows of the shrine must be closed, trapping the aluxob inside; if this was not done the fairies would become injurious tricksters.

Sources: Bond-Freeman, *Maya Preclassic Ceramic Sequence at the Site of Ek Balam, Yucatan, Mexico*, 126–37; Eberhart, *Mysterious Creatures*, 16; Montemayor, *Words of the True Peoples*, 265

Alvar

Variations: Allvar, Allvaro, Allvarso, Alva, Alvara, Alvare, Alvaria, Alvarie, Alvarr, Alvarso, Alvie

In German, the word *alvar* means "army or elves."

Sources: Larson, *Best Baby Names Treasury*, 115, 380; Newcomb, *Faerie Treasury*, 66

Alven

Variations: Ottermaaner

In the fairy lore from the Netherlands, the alven ("elves") were a species of LIGHT ELVES and were described as having transparent and translucent bodies. These very powerful fay were said to have control over the lakes, ponds, and rivers in which they lived; interestingly they were also said to have a strong dislike of fish. Mainly associated with the River Elbe the wingless alven flew through the air by riding upon or within bubbles or eggshells. Especially fond of night blooming plants, such as nightwort, they would cause illness or even death to any cattle or human who harms these plants.

Sources: Newcomb, *Faerie Treasury*, 47; McCoy, *Witch's Guide to Faery Folk*, 147, 174

Alvin

In old English, the word *alvin* means "ELF wine" and "noble friend."

Source: Newcomb, *Faerie Treasury*, 66

Alvina

Variations: Aelfwen, Aelfwenn, Aelfwenne, Aelfwin, Aelfwine, Aelfwinn, Aelfwyne, Aelfwynn, Aelfwynne, Aethelwine, Aethelwyne, Arthelwine

In Old English, the word *alvina* means "friend of the elves."

Sources: Larson, *Best Baby Names Treasury*, 108, 377; Lorenz, *Pacific Islander's Book of Names*, 14

Alvis

Variations: Alvíss, Alviss, Alwis

Alvis ("all wise") was one of the kings of the DWARF in Nordic mythology; his story is told in the *Alvis-Mal-Edda*. Alvis had fallen in love with THRUD ("power"), a VALKYRIE and a daughter of the god, Thor. When he asked for her hand in marriage it was granted if Alvis would stand before Thor that evening and correctly answer thirteen questions about the naming of beer, clouds, fire, forest, moon, night, sea, sky, stillness, sun, wheat wind, and the world in the languages of the Æsir, the Elves, the GIANTs, the Gods, and the Vanir. The questions were simple enough but took a great deal of time to answer fully. Just as Alvis had correctly answered the last one and took a step to take the hand of the woman he had rightfully won, the first rays of the sun fell upon him turning the DWARF king into stone.

Sources: Bennett, *Gods and Religions of Ancient and Modern Times*, Volume 1, 382; Daly, *Norse Mythology A to Z*, 22; Rose, *Spirits, Fairies, Leprechauns, and Goblins*, 11; Terry, *Poems of the Elder Edda*, 90–6

Amadán

Variations: Amadáin Mhóir, Amadáin, Amadán Mór, Amadán na Briona, Amadán na Bruidne, Stroke Lad

Amadán was the Fool of the Irish SÍDHE, choosing people at random to curse or punish with his incurable crippling touch. This injurious fey disfigured an individual in such a way it would cause them to be ridiculed for the rest of their lives; fortunately his presence alone was not enough to do damage. Even the famed fairy doctor, BIDDY EARLY, was unable to cure Amadán's touch. In more severe cases Amadán would strike a person dead on the spot. Although active all year long, he was particularly active during the month of June.

According to Lady Isabella Augusta Gregory, an Irish dramatist and folklorist, if Amadán was seen, a difficult prospect as he was not only a shape-shifter but could also become invisible, his assault could be prevented by repeating the prayer "The Lord between us and harm" until he left the area or you have moved far enough away from him. Because this fairy was insane, even by fairy standards, there was no reasoning with him and no way to appeal to him to reverse the harm he has caused.

Sources: Illes, *Encyclopedia of Spirits*, 162; Monaghan, *Encyclopedia of Celtic Mythology and Folklore*, 15; Rose, *Spirits, Fairies, Leprechauns, and Goblins*, 11, 351

Amalthea

Variations: Amalthéa, Amaltheia, Amáltheia

Amalthea ("tender goddess") was a NYMPH from classical Greek mythology who nursed the god, Zeus (Jupiter), while he was an infant with goat's milk. In some telling, she was described having horns or being a goat. She was rewarded for her services to the god by being placed among the stars of heaven, making her the constellation known as the "celestial goat."

Amalthea was said to be a goat first by Hellenistic authors, a reference which continued onward; however, the Greek author and philosopher Phereceydes of Syros (sixth century B.C.) and Pindar, the Greek lyric poet (ca. 522–443 B.C.) each previously established she was a NYMPH. No matter what sort of being she was, there are several tales in which Zeus (Jupiter) removed one of Amalthea's horns, gave it to the daughters of King Melisseus, and endowed the horn with the magical ability to be filled with whatever the owner wished.

Sources: Day, *God's Conflict with the Dragon and the Sea*, 64; Rose, *Spirits, Fairies, Leprechauns, and Goblins*, 11; Smith, *New Classical Dictionary of Biography, Mythology, and Geography*, 41

Amathea

Variations: Amathëa, Amatheia ("she is sparkling water")

A sea–NYMPH, Amathea ("queen of voice") was one of the NEREIS named in Homer's *The Iliad*; she was described as having "azure locks luxuriant" or as some translations put it "long, heavy hair."

Sources: Gould, *Historic Magazine and Notes and Queries*, Volume 14, 212; Homer, *Iliad of Homer*, 209; Meredith, *Works of George Meredith*, Volume 23, 80

Amathia

Born one of the 3,000 daughters of the Titians,

Oceanus and Tethys, ALPHEUS was one of the named OCEANIDS. She was described by Homer, the greatest ancient Greek epic poet and author of the *Iliad* and the *Odyssey* as having "beauteous hair."

There was also a sea–NYMPH, by the name of Amathia who was listed as one of the named NEREID. In this instance, she was said to have been born of Nereus and DORIS.

Sources: Apollodorus, *Apollodorus' Library and Hyginus' Fabulae*, 95; Bell, *Bell's New Pantheon*, 112; Boswell, *What Men or Gods Are These*, 58; Hesiod, *Works of Hesiod, Callimachus, and Theognis*, 20; Homer, *Iliad of Homer*, Volume 2, 161

Amatongo (plural: umzimu)

Variations: Abapansi, Azimo, Bazimo

In AFRICAN FAIRY LORE the amatongo ("ancestors") were a type of ancestral spirit similar to the fairies of Scottish lore. The very first amatongo was created by the death of the first man, Umvelinqangi. Since that time more of these fay were created when an existing amatongo "takes" the life of a person; those "so taken" were now amatongo and worshiped as such. Each family worshiped the previous head of the house but seldom further back, as the names of the long dead were quickly forgotten. When proper sacrifices and prayer requests were made, the amatongo appeared either in a dream, as a lizard, or as a snake.

Uncommon for the fay, these fairies had the ability to possess a person causing convulsions and hysteria; when they took up residence in a human body they anchored themselves between the person's shoulders. In addition to causing illness in animals and humans, the amatongo could also cure illness if proper supplications were made. Doctors would often pray to them as part of their healing process.

Sources: Callaway, *Religious System of the Amazulu*, 130–1, 141, 144; Evan-Wentz, *Fairy Faith in Celtic Countries*, 228; Peek, *African Divination Systems*, 30, 34, 35

Amberabad

Variations: Amberabâd

Amberabad ("Amber City") was one of the cities or provinces in Jinnistan, the Persian mythological equivalent of FAIRYLAND.

Sources: Keightly, *World Guide to Gnomes, Fairies, Elves, and Other Little People*, 16; Smedley, *Occult Sciences*, 19, 775; Spence, *Encyclopædia of Occultism*, 177; Yardley, *Supernatural in Romantic Fiction*, 53

Ambrosia

According to classical Greek mythology Ambrosia was one of the DODONIDES, the seven NYMPHS who cared for the infant god, Zeus (Jupiter).

Sources: Larson, *Greek Nymphs*, 161; Rigoglioso, *Cult of Divine Birth in Ancient Greece*, 144

The Amnisiades

Variations: Amnisides

In classical Greek mythology the amnisiades were the NYMPHS of the river Amnisos on the island of Crete in the Aegean Sea; they were the attendants of the goddess, Artemis (Diana).

Sources: Bell, *Bell's New Pantheon*, 56; Smith, *New Classical Dictionary of Greek and Roman Biography, Mythology and Geography*, Volume 1, 561

Amoret

In Greek mythology, Amoret was the epitome of grace and charm. She and her twin sister, BELPHOEBE, were born the daughters of the NYMPH, Chrysogonee; their father was the warm sunlight that fell on the sleeping Chrysogonee after she bathed one afternoon. Born in the woods, the infants were found by the goddesses Diana and Venus as they were searching for the lost god, Cupid. BELPHOEBE was taken and raised by Diana while Amoret was raised by Venus who took her to the gardens of Adonis. Amoret fell in love with a knight named Scudamour; he courted her and won her love over twenty suitors.

Sources: Cavanagh, *Wanton Eyes and Chaste Desires*, 133; Keightly, *World Guide to Gnomes, Fairies, Elves, and Other Little People*, 58; Morley, *English Writers*, Volume 11, 354–5

Ampelos

Variations: Ampelus

In ancient Greek mythology Ampelos was one of the HAMADRYAD born of from the incestuous relationship between Oxylus and his sister, HAMADRYAS. Ampelos was the HAMADRYAD of vines, especially vitis.

Sources: Athenaeus of Naucratis, *Deipnosophists*, Volume 1, 131; Buxton, *Forms of Astonishment*, 211; Larson, *Greek Nymphs*, 283

Amphicomone

In Greek mythology Amphicomone was a water–NYMPH and one of the named DANAIDS, the collective name for the daughters of Danaus; her name appears in a list of the DANAIDS generated by Gaius Julius Hyginus (ca. 64 B.C.–A.D.

17), a Latin author. Amphicomone was wedded to Plexippus and killed him on their wedding night.

Sources: Apollodorus, *Apollodorus' Library and Hyginus' Fabulae*, 170; Parada, *Genealogical Guide to Greek Mythology*, 59

Amphinome

A sea–NYMPH born of Nereus and DORIS, Amphinome ("the surrounder") was the NEREIS who "feeds Neptune's' flock" according to *The Iliad*, the epic poem written by the ancient Greek poet, Homer. She was also one of the named NEREID who accompanied THETIS in mourning the loss of her son, Achilles.

Sources: Apollodorus, *Apollodorus' Library and Hyginus' Fabulae*, 95; Bell, *Bell's New Pantheon or Historical Dictionary of the Gods*, 112; Collignon, *Manual of Mythology*, 18; Gould, *Historic Magazine and Notes and Queries*, Vol 14, 212; Homer, *The Iliad of Homer*, Volume 2, 239

Amphirho

Born one of the 3,000 daughters of the Titians, Oceanus and Tethys, Amphirho was one of the named OCEANIDS.

Sources: Bell, *Women of Classical Mythology*, 33; Grimal, *Dictionary of Classical Mythology*, 315; Westmoreland, *Ancient Greek Beliefs*, 24

Amphiro

Born one of the 3,000 daughters of the Titians, Oceanus and Tethys, Amphiro ("she is flowing water" or "surrounding stream") was one of the named OCEANIDS.

Sources: Boswell, *What Men or Gods Are These*, 58; Hesiod, *Works of Hesiod, Callimachus, and Theognis*, 20; Phylactopoulos, *History of the Hellenic World*, 184

Amphithoe

Variations: Amphithoë

A sea–NYMPH born of Nereus and DORIS, Amphithoe ("the shouter") was the NEREID of sea currents in classical Greek mythology. She was one of the named NEREID who accompanied THETIS in mourning the loss of her son, Achilles.

Sources: Apollodorus, *Apollodorus' Library and Hyginus' Fabulae*, 95; Collignon, *Manual of Mythology*, 18; Gould, *Historic Magazine and Notes and Queries*, Vol 14, 212; Rose, *Spirits, Fairies, Leprechauns, and Goblins*, 12

Amphitrite

Variations: Amphytrite

Born one of the 3,000 daughters of the Titians,

Oceanus and Tethys, ALPHEUS was one of the named OCEANIDS. Amphitrite was also the NEREID of hollow sea caves as well as a NYMPH who, in classical Greek mythology, reluctantly married the god of the sea, Poseidon (Neptune). She tired of her husband's affair with SCYLLA and changed her into a sea monster. As a NEREID, she was born the daughter of Nerues and DORIS.

According to the writings of both Apollodorus of Athens, a Greek grammarian and scholar, and the Greek oral poet, Hesiod, "neat-ankled" Amphitrite, along with her sisters CYMATOLEGE and CYMOTHOE had the power to calm the sea and still the winds.

Sources: Boswell, *What Men or Gods Are These*, 58; Day, *God's Conflict with the Dragon and the Sea*, 64; Hesiod, *Theogony*, 104; Hesiod, *Works of Hesiod, Callimachus, and Theognis*, 14, 15, 20; Rose, *Spirits, Fairies, Leprechauns, and Goblins*, 12

Amymone

Variations: HYPERMNESTRA

In classical Greek mythology, there are two different versions of Amymone's story.

In the pre–Olympian myth Amymone was a beautiful NYMPH who caught the eye of the god of the ocean, Poseidon (Neptune). A SATYER attempted to rape her but the god intervened. Rather than continuing the assault himself he chose to court her and promised her many springs, one of which was the hidden spring, Lerna; it also housed one of the entryways into Hades. Amymone accepted Poseidon's promises and is said to live in Lerna to this day.

Amymone may also be one of Danaus' fifty daughters, collectively known as the DANAIDS, the name for the daughters of Danaus; her name appears on a list of the DANAIDS generated by Gaius Julius Hyginus (ca. 64 B.C.–A.D. 17), a Latin author. Amymone was wedded to Midanus and killed him on their wedding night. However, on a list compiled by Apollodorus, a Greek scholar and grammarian, she was one of the daughters of Europe and was wedded to the son of Argyphia, Enceladus. As a reward for not committing murder she was gifted the spring, Lerna, from the god Poseidon.

Sources: Bonnefoy, *Greek and Egyptian Mythologies*, 100; Illes, *Encyclopedia of Spirits*, 171; Trzaskoma, *Anthology of Classical Myth*, 266

An

An was one of the many DWARFS named in the *Voluspa*, the first and best known poem of the *Poetic Edda*, a collection of Old Norse poems dating back to about A.D. 985.

Sources: Daly, *Norse Mythology A to Z*, 22; Sykes, *Who's Who in Non-Classical Mythology*, 53

Ana

From the folklore of the Romanian gypsies, Ana was the Queen of the Fay (see FAIRY QUEEN). Tall and lithe, Ana was staggeringly beautiful, generous and kind; she lived in a magnificent mountain-top castle.

According to legend, Ana lived an charmed life in her enchanted castle located in the Transylvanian mountains. Her life was idealic until she captured the eye of the King of Demons. Ana refused his advances and proposals of marriage until his demonic hoard attacked her castle and began to eat her fairy entourage. In order to save her remaining people she agreed to marry him.

Ana, being a goddess of fertility, conceived a child with her very first sexual encounter with the King of Demons, forever thereafter condemning her offspring to be born as demonic beings. After a lengthy and horrific pregnancy she gave birth to a demon of disease. After ten such ordeals she was able to convince the King of Demons to set her free on the promise whenever one of her fey reached the age of 999 years of age it would marry one of his *locolico*, a type of malevolent spirit. Filled with remorse and shame FAIRY QUEEN Ana almost never left her castle in the Carpathian Mountains; however when she does, she travels in the form of a golden toad. If she is approached with great veneration she will fulfill *any* wish asked of her.

In the Celtic language *ana* translates to mean "abundant," while in Romanian it means "nourishment" or "sustenance."

Sources: de Vere, *Dragon Legacy*, 204; Illes, *Encyclopedia of Spirits*, 171–2; Rose, *Spirits, Fairies, Leprechauns, and Goblins*, 12, 351

Ananta-Shesha

Variations: Ananta ("endless"), Ananta Sesha

The king of the NAGA and the cosmic serpent in Hindu mythology, Ananta-Shesha was described as being immense and having either seven or one-thousand heads; he was a protector and supporter of the god, Vishnu. Ananta-Shesha's bit was not only poisonous but it could also spit fire; this was the same fire it would use to destry the earth at the end of each cycle.

Sources: Chopra, *Academic Dictionary of Mythology*, 159, Rose, *Giants, Monsters, and Dragons*, 16, 261

Anarr

Variations: Ánaar, Anar, Ánarr, ANNAR, Annarr, Annaver, Fjorgyn, Onar, Ónar, Onarr, ÓNARR

Anarr ("sword part") was one of the many DWARFS named in the *Voluspa*, the first and best known poem of the *Poetic Edda*, a collection of Old Norse poems dating back to about A.D. 985.

Sources: Daly, *Norse Mythology A to Z*, 22; Gray, *Mythology of All Races*, Volume 2, 200; Wägner, *Asgard and the Gods*, 311

Anaxibia

In Greek mythology Anaxibia was a water–NYMPH and one of the named DANAIDS, the collective name for the daughters of Danaus. In a list compiled by Apollodorus, a Greek scholar and grammarian, she was one of the daughters of an unnamed Ethiopian woman and was wedded to Archelaus, one of the sons of an unnamed Phoenician woman.

Sources: Bell, *Women of Classical Mythology*, 36, 37; Grimal, *Dictionary of Classical Mythology*, 127; Lemprière, *Classical Dictionary*, 236; Smith, *Dictionary of Greek and Roman Biography and Mythology*, 1169

Anaxithea

In Greek mythology Anaxithea, was a NYMPH and one of the named DANAIDS; she was said to be the mother of Olenus by the god, Zeus (Jupiter).

Sources: Bell, *Women of Classical Mythology*, 37, 151; Lemprière, *Classical Dictionary*, 31

Anchirhoe

Anchirhoe was a NYMPH from the mythology of classical Greece and Rome. One of the NAIADS and born a daughter of the river god, Erasinus, she was one of the many nurses to the infant god, Zeus (Jupiter). Anchirhoe, along with BYZE, MAERA, and MELITE, was also one of the attendants to the goddess, BRITOMARTIS.

Sources: Bell, *Women of Classical Mythology*, 38; Larson, *Greek Nymphs*, 153; Parada, *Genealogical Guide to Greek Mythology*, 19

Anchiroe

Born one of the 3,000 daughters of the Titians, Oceanus and Tethys, Anchiroe was one of the named OCEANIDS.

Sources: Bell, *Women of Classical Mythology*, 38; Larson, *Greek Nymphs*, 96; Smith, *Dictionary of Greek and Roman Biography and Mythology*, 12

Andvari

Andvari was a DWARF from Norse mythology. He once spied a great hoard of gold belonging to a school of river NYMPHS. As he stole their gold, the NYMPHS begged him to return it, promising a array of sensuous delights if he did. Andvari knew he was so deformed, hideous, and ugly the only way he would ever have the love and affection of a woman would be to buy it. In his realization and rage he swore an oath to the gods claming from that moment on he would love nothing but gold. Using his innate magical abilities, he turned his stolen treasure into a magical, golden ring he named Andvaranaut ("Andvari's Gift"); it had the ability to both locate and generate gold. By use of the ring, Andvari had an amazing hoard of magical armor, weapons, and items of incredible value. In one fell swoop, the entire collection was stolen by the god, Loki when he needed to pay a ransom. Initially the DWARF was not devastated by his loss as he intended to remake his beloved hoard but Loki forced him to surrender the ring Andvaranaut as well. Andvari knew he had no choice to comply with the god's demands; before doing so he used his innate magical abilities to place a curse upon the ring, dooming anyone who possessed it.

Sources: Greene, *Mythic Journey*, 205–10; Illes, *Encyclopedia of Spirits*, 182; Sparling, *Völsunga Saga*, 46–48; Sykes, *Who's Who in Non-Classical Mythology*, 53

Anglesey

Anglesey is one of the FAIRY ISLANDS; an actual island, it is located off the coast the western coast of England in the Irish Sea, south of the Isle of Mann. In addition to being populated by humans, it is said to be the home of a race of fay known as TYLWYTH TEGS. It is not uncommon for locals of Anglesey to claim to be descended from the fay.

Sources: Hopkins, *Shakespeare on the Edge*, 89; McCoy, *Witch's Guide to Faery Folk*, 43; Wentz, *Fairy-Faith in Celtic Countries*, 138, 141

Angus

Angus was a fairy from Irish folklore whose sweet little kisses would turn into birds.

Source: Wallace, *Folk-lore of Ireland*, 79

Angus Og

Variations: AENGUS, Aengus Mac Óg, Angus Oc, Angus of the Birds, Aonghus, Engus Mac Og, Oengus, Young Son

Born the son of the TUATHA DE DANANN, DAGDA and a FAIRY QUEEN of the SÍDHE, Angus Og, the Lord of Love, resided in his castle, Bruigh na Bóinne in Ireland. It was said he owned a cloak of invisibility and had the magical ability to not only shape-shift into a swan but also control time. He fell in love with the SWAN MAIDEN, Ibormeith but she was only able to take human form every other year. As swans they lived on Lough Bel Dracon where it was said anyone who heard them singing their love song together would fall into a magical sleep. When in human form they resided in Bruigh na Bóinne.

Sources: Yeats, *Gods and Fighting Men*, 81–3; Illes, *Encyclopedia of Spirits*, 185; MacKillop, *Myths and Legends of the Celts*, 17; Rose, *Spirits, Fairies, Leprechauns, and Goblins*, 16, 351

Anhanga

Anhanga was an ancient forest or vegetation fairy from the folklore of the Tupi people of Brazil; he guarded animals, field-game, and the forest; any who would hunt an animal with young ran the risk of being struck with fever or madness. Anhanga was described as taking the form of a white deer with red eyes; in more modern times this fairy spirit has been demonized and made out to be an evil entity.

Sources: Pinkerton, *General Collection of the Best and Most Interesting Voyages and Travels in all Parts of the World*, 875; Rose, *Spirits, Fairies, Leprechauns, and Goblins*, 16; Smith, *Brazil, the Amazons and the Coast*, 570

The Anigrides

Variations: Anigriades

In classical Greek mythology the Anigrides were the NAIADS of the river Anigros in Elis, in the Peloponessos, southern Greece. It was believed their springs could cure skin diseases.

Sources: Bell, *Bell's New Pantheon*, 66; Larson, *Greek Nymphs*, 159

Anippe

Anippe was a NYMPH from the mythology of classical Greece and Rome. One of the NAIADS, she was born of the Nile River as one of the daughters of the god Poseidon (Neptune) and was the mother of Busiris, king of Egypt.

Sources: Bell, *Women of Classical Mythology*, 42; Graves, *Larousse Encyclopedia of Mythology*, 135

Las Anjanas

In Hispanic lore the anjanas were small, female fairies who appeared to mankind as old women in order to test their charity and compassion for animals. If the person passes the test, the anjanass would reveal itself in its true form, a young and beautiful maiden with long golden hair and blue eyes, carrying a golden staff, and wearing green stockings and clothes made of flowers and star-silver. Anything the staff touched turned into an item of value.

Sources: Andrews, *Enchantment of the Faerie Realm*, 200; Cirlot, *Dictionary of Symbols*, 13

Ankou

Variations: Death, the Grim Reaper, Father Time

In the fairy lore of Brittany Ankou ("death") was similar to the Grim Reaper; he also appeared in the fairy lore in Cornwall and Wales in Britain as well as in the fairy lore of Ireland. This singular individual was described as looking like a man dressed in dark robes; sometimes he was said to drive a black cart pulled by four black horses, other reports say he was headless. Rare reports say he has two skeleton assistants who hurl bodies upon his cart. He travels the countryside along a particular path (see FAIRY TRAIL). Typically he appeared at dusk; active all year long he was especially powerful on November Eve (October 31). This benevolent and comforting fay collected the souls of those who died and took them to the Summerlands.

Ankou was a personification of death and to see him was a sure sign of your eminent death; an old Irish proverb claims "When Ankou comes, he will not go away empty."

In Brittany, each parish had its own King of the Dead, an ankou, the last man to die each calendar year. Never holding the office for more than a year, the ankou was said to be seen entering into a house when a tenant's death was near, making a BANSHEE's mournful cry as he crosses the threshold.

Sources: Curran, 257–8; McCoy, *Witch's Guide to Faery Folk*, 174–5; Wentz, *Fairy-Faith in Celtic Countries*, 218, 220

Anna Perenna

A NYMPH from ancient Italian lore, Anna Perenna was once worshiped by the ancient Romans; sacrifices both public and private were offered to her. She was associated with the River Numicus and her feast day celebrated on March 15. Her grove and spring were identified at the piazza Euclide in Rome.

Sources: Adams, *Cyclopaedia of Female Biography*,

45; Harvey, *Religion in Republican Italy*, 168; Keightly, *World Guide to Gnomes, Fairies, Elves, and Other Little People*, 448; Larson, *Greek Nymphs*, 222

Annaed

Annaed was a NAIAD from the mythology of classical Greece and Rome.

Source: Day, *God's Conflict with the Dragon and the Sea*, 394

Annar

Annar was one of the many DWARFS named in the *Voluspa*, the first and best known poem of the *Poetic Edda*, a collection of Old Norse poems dating back to about A.D. 985.

Sources: Daly, *Norse Mythology A to Z*, 22; Sykes, *Who's Who in Non-Classical Mythology*, 53

Anthedon

Anthedon was a NYMPH of the town of Anthedon in Boiotia, in the mythology of classical Greece and Rome.

Sources: Larson, *Greek Nymphs*, 143; Parada, *Genealogical Guide to Greek Mythology*, 128

Anthelia

In Greek mythology Anthelia was a water–NYMPH and one of the named DANAIDS, the collective name for the daughters of Danaus. In a list compiled by Apollodorus, a Greek scholar and grammarian, she was one of the daughters of the NAIAD, POLYXO and was wedded to Cisseus, one of the sons of the NAIAD, CALIADNE.

Sources: Apollodorus, *Gods and Heroes of the Greeks*, 69; Parada, *Genealogical Guide to Greek Mythology*, 7, 59

Anthoussai

Variations: Anthousai

In ancient Greek mythology the anthoussai were the NYMPHS of flowers.

Source: Rigoglioso, *Cult of Divine Birth in Ancient Greece*, 87

Anthracia

Anthracia was a NYMPH and one of the OCEANID; she was charged with the care and feeding of the infant god, Zeus (Jupiter). In art, Anthracia was depicted holding a torch.

Sources: Bell, *Women of Classical Mythology*, 44, 209; Pausanias, *Pausanias's Description of Greece*, Volume 1, 414, 434

Anthrakia

A NYMPH who lived on Mount Lykaios in Arcadia, southern Greece, Anthrakia was one of the nurses to the infant god, Zeus (Jupiter).

Sources: Larson, *Greek Nymphs*, 153; Pausânias, *Guide to Greece: Southern Greece*, 487

Anthropophagi

Variations: Anthropohagi

A flesh-eating fairy from British lore, the anthropophagi preyed upon humans when hungry. Headless, their eyes are located in their shoulders and their mouths in the middle of their chest. Having no nose benefited them, allowing them to consume human flesh without gagging. The anthropophagi appeared in William Shakespeare's plays *The Merry Wives of Windsor* and *Othello*.

Sources: McCoy, *Witch's Guide to Faery Folk*, 176; Shakespeare, *Merry Wives of Windsor*, 186; Shakespeare, *Othello*, 38

Antiope

Antiope was a NYMPH from classical Greek mythology; she was born the daughter of the river god, ASOPUS. Antiope was driven insane by the god Dionysus (Bacchus) which caused her to wander Greece aimlessly. Ultimately she was cured by Phoeus who married her.

Sources: Roman, *Encyclopedia of Greek and Roman Mythology*, 71; Rose, *Spirits, Fairies, Leprechauns, and Goblins*, 16; Smith, *New Classical Dictionary of Biography, Mythology, and Geography*, 67–8

Antonoe

A sea–NYMPH from Greek mythology, Antonoe was the NEREID of the spark of the wave.

Sources: Bell, *Bell's New Pantheon*, 102; Betham, *Transactions of the Royal Irish Academy*, Volume 17, 89

Aoibheall

A BANSHEE of the royal house of Munster, Ireland, Aoibheall appeared to the Dunlang O'Hartigan before the historic battle of Clontarf fought near Dublin on April 23, 1014. Aoibheall begged O'Hartigan to delay the fighting for one day and if he did so she would gift him with a life of happiness for 200 years. However if he fought without delay the fairy predicted he, his son, his friends, and all the nobles of Erin would fall in battle. O'Hartigan did not follow Aoibheall's advice and choose to fight; her prediction came to pass.

Sources: Curran, *Field Guide to Irish Fairies*, 53; Evan-Wentz, *Fairy Faith in Celtic Countries*, 305; Ó hÓgáin, *Myth, Legend and Romance,* 311

Aoibhinn

Aoibhinn ("beautiful") was the Queen of the Fairies of Northern Munster, according to Irish folklore (see FAIRY QUEEN). One of the SÍDHE, she oweed her allegiance to FINVARRA and ONAGH the King and Queen of the Connaught Fairies as well as their provincial Queen, CLIODNA (see FAIRY QUEEN).

Sources: D'Amato-Neff, *Book of Clouds*, 6; Rose, *Spirits, Fairies, Leprechauns, and Goblins*, 16, 248, 351; Squire, *Celtic Myth and Legend*, 162

Aoide

Variations: Aoede
One of the original three muses according to Pausanias, a second century Greek geographer and traveler, Aoide ("song" or "voice") was the MUSE of singing and associated with Mount Helicon.

Sources: Littleton, *Gods, Goddesses, and Mythology*, Volume 11, 924; Peterson, *Mythology in Our Midst*, 121

Aos Sí

Variations: Aes SÍDHE, Daoine Sìdh, Daoine SÍDHE, Daoine Sìth ("People of Peace")
In ancient Irish mythology the aos sí ("the people of the mounds") were said to have been a race of powerful, supernatural fairy beings; it was believed they lived in an invisible world and coexisted with the world of humans, someplace across the western sea, or underground in FAIRY FORTS. These fay were variously believed to be ancestor spirits, gods, or NATURE SPIRITS. Some believed the aos sí were the last remaining survivors of the TUATHA DÉ DANANN; as such the aos sí were described as being both incredibly beautiful or terribly hideous.

In folk belief offerings were left for the aos sí and great care was taken to avoid angering or insulting these fairy spirits; they are usually referenced by euphemisms such as "the good neighbors" and "the little people." The aos sí were fierce guardians of their home or sacred location, be it a hill, FAIRY RING, notable boulder, or tree.

Sources: Ellis, *Celtic Myths and Legends*, 34; Maberry, *They Bite*, 82; MacRitchie, *Fians, Fairies, and Picts*, 71

Apci'lnic

The apci'lnic were a type of fairy or DWARF from the folklore of the Montagnais of Labrador, Canada. Living in the mountainous wilderness these LITTLE PEOPLE stood only a foot or two tall but their presence was associated with danger. The apci'lnic had the ability to appear anyplace at will and were known to steal human children.

Sources: Blackman, *Field Guide to North American Monsters*, 123; Rose, *Spirits, Fairies, Leprechauns, and Goblins*, 17

Apoiaueue

A benevolent NATURE SPIRIT from the folklore of the Tupi Guarani people of Amazonian, Brazil, Apoiaueue maked sure the earth received the amount of rain water necessary for sustaining life. He also carried news of earthly events to the Supreme Deity. Some sources claim Apoiaueue was not a singular entity but rather a species of fay.

Sources: Bingham, *South and Meso-American Mythology A to Z*, 7; Graves, *Larousse Encyclopedia of Mythology*, 447; Rose, *Spirits, Fairies, Leprechauns, and Goblins*, 17

Apopa

In the folklore from the Inuit and Ihalmiut people of North America the apopa were DWARF-like creatures, deformed and hideously ugly. These fairies behaved much like the KOBOLD of Europe and PUCK from classical mythology, they were mischievous, never benevolent, but relatively harmless. Some sources claim Apopa was a singular entity and not a species of fay.

Sources: Mowat, *People of the Deer*, 254; Rose, *Spirits, Fairies, Leprechauns, and Goblins*, 17

Apotamkin

Variations: Ponca
The Maliseet-Passamaquoddy people of the northeastern coast of the Unites States of America have in their mythology a FAIRY ANIMAL called an apotamkin. Described as looking like an extremely hairy humanoid with enormous teeth, it predates on children who wander out on thin ice, venture onto the beach alone, or otherwise misbehaive; this essentially makes it a NURSERY BOGIE.

Sources: Malinowski, *Gale Encyclopedia of Native American Tribes*, 108, 225; Rose, *Giants, Monsters, and Dragons*, 7

Appias

Appias was a CRINAEAE, a sub-species of the NAIAD from Greek mythology; she was the NYMPH who lived in the Appian well located near the temple of Venus Genetrix. The well itself was said to be surrounded by statues of nymphs called *appiades*.

Sources: Peck, *Harper's Dictionary of Classical Literature and Antiquities*, Volume 1, 103; Smith, *New Classical Dictionary of Biography, Mythology, and Geography*, 79

Appletree Man

In the folklore from Cornwall, Devon, and Somerset, England the fairy spirit resided in the oldest tree in the orchard was given the title of Appletree Man. To ensure a good crop each year on the Eve of the Epiphany the (January 5) the farmer and his hands took a pail of good cider and roasted apples to the Appletree Man's tree; toasting him they said "Health to tee, old apple tree; well to bear pocketfuls, hatsful, pecksful, bushelful." Any remaining cider was poured over the tree's roots to a cheering crowd.

Sources: Briggs, *Dictionary of British Folk-Tales in the English Language*, 107; Rose, *Spirits, Fairies, Leprechauns, and Goblins*, 18

Apseudes

A sea–NYMPH born of Nereus and DORIS in Greek mythology, Apseudes ("the shiner") was one of the named NEREID who accompanied THETIS in mourning the loss of her son, Achilles.

Sources: Apollodorus, *Apollodorus' Library and Hyginus' Fabulae*, 95; Collignon, *Manual of Mythology*, 18; Gould, *Historic Magazine and Notes and Queries*, Vol 14, 212, Smith, *New Classical Dictionary of Biography, Mythology, and Geography*, 79

Apu

The apu ("lord") were mountain spirits of the Andes Mountains (see NATURE SPIRIT); they were a part of the mountain itself but were able to move about freely. Apu played a part in the religion practiced by the Quechua people of Peru. Each mountain peak in the Andes had its own apu; they appeared as helpful, playful, but mischievous children. Typically an apu was male but there were some females of the species; they were referred to as "mama."

Sources: Illes, *Encyclopedia of Spirits*, 198; Rose, *Spirits, Fairies, Leprechauns, and Goblins*, 18; Steele, *Handbook of Inca Mythology*, 213

Apuku

Fairy spirits from the Afro-South American folklore of Surinam, the apuku lived in clearings found naturally in the bush and jungle. Described as looking like Dwarfs from European mythologies, the apuku had a frightening appearance and were powerfully built (see DWARF).

Sources: Jones, *Encyclopedia of Religion*, Volume 1, 126; Rose, *Spirits, Fairies, Leprechauns, and Goblins*, 18

Arallu

Variations: PAZUZU, UTUKKU

Arallu were a type of DJINN in Assryo-Babylonian demonology born from the bile of Ea (Enki) and the stagnant water under the KUR. They were described as "the storm, which breaks loose with fury in the skies" or "the rising wind, which casts darkness over the bright day" and were depicted as having a human male body, the head and paws of a lion, large wings, and small goat horns upon their head. Arallu were extremely powerful and immortal beings and had the power to cause disease, corrupt the unity of a family, inspire criminal acts, and kill livestock. When they possessed a person a very powerful exorcist was required to exorcize and cast them out. Arallu hated mankind and there was no way to appease them.

They were the adversaries of the gods, especially the moon god, Sin (Nanna). According to mythology, an eclipse was caused when they attacked him. They tied him up in a sack, causing him to have to fight his way out. Fortunately, there was a finite number of arallu, as they were all male and could not reproduce.

Sources: Jastrow, *Religion of Babylonia and Assyria*, 260; Langdon, *Semitic Mythology*, 161; Rogers, *Religion of Babylonia and Assyria*, 147

Arapteš

The arapteš were female forest fey from the folklore of the Mari people of Russia. Only appearing after nightfall and in bathhouses, they were described as looking like a pretty young girl.

Source: Rose, *Spirits, Fairies, Leprechauns, and Goblins*, 18

Arcadia

In Greek mythology Arcadia was a water–NYMPH and one of the named DANAIDS, the collective name for the daughters of Danaus; her name appears in a list of the DANAIDS generated by Gaius Julius Hyginus (ca. 64 B.C.–A.D. 17), a Latin author. Arcadia was wedded to Xanthus and killed him on their wedding night.

Sources: Apollodorus, *Gods and Heroes of the Greeks*, 35, 37; Bell, *Women of Classical Mythology*, 59

Arche

One of the Mousai Titanides ("Titian MUSES"), Arche ("Beginning") was born the daughter of the Titian, Uranus, according to Greek mythology.

Sources: Day, *God's Conflict with the Dragon and the Sea*, 293; Falkner, *Mythology of the Night Sky*, 178; Smith, *Classical Dictionary of Biography, Mythology, and Geography*, 460

Archiroe

Archiroe was a NYMPH and one of the OCEANID from Greek mythology; she was charged with the care and feeding of the infant god, Zeus (Jupiter). In art, she and the NYMPH MYRTOESSA were depicted holding a water pot from which water flowed.

Sources: Bell, *Women of Classical Mythology*, 214; Pausanias, *Pausanias's Description of Greece*, Volume 1, 414, 434; Smith, *New Classical Dictionary of Biography, Mythology, and Geography*, 1132

Arethusa

Variations: Arethousa, Aretusa

In classical Greek and Roman mythology Arethusa was one of the named NEREID, a NYMPH of the Mediterranean Sea in general. According to Greek mythology, as Arethusa was bating she was seen by Alpheios, a river spirit, who emerged from the water to embrace her. Rejecting his attention Arethusa fled appealing the goddess Artemis (Diana) for help. Her prayers were answered and the NEREID found she had been moved to ORTYGIA, Sicily and transformed into a stream. Alpheios searched until he found her and when he did he sent his waters to merge with hers. In Greek myth this is how the Alpheios River came to emerge in the Springs of Arethusa.

Arethusa was also the name of one of the four HESPERIDES, a group of four NAIAD sisters who were charged with the protection of a golden apple tree that grew the golden apples the goddess Gaia gave the goddess Hera (Juno) and were stolen by the godling, Herakles (Hercules) (see also AEGLE, ERYTHEIA, and HESPERIA).

Sources: Apollodorus, *Apollodorus' Library and Hyginus' Fabulae*, 95; Bell, *Bell's New Pantheon or*

Historical Dictionary of the Gods, 112; Littleton, *Gods, Goddesses, and Mythology*, Volume 11, 1000, 1454; Illes, *Encyclopedia of Spirits*, 204; Rose, *Spirits, Fairies, Leprechauns, and Goblins*, 19

Argante

Variations: Morgain

Argante, the Silver Queen, was a FAIRY QUEEN and the Queen of the Island of AVALON; she appeared only once in Arthurian lore, in the first English translation of the story written near the end of the twelfth century by a parish priest named Layamon.

In the story, Arthur was mortally wounded; with his dying breath asks to be taken to see the fairest of the fay, Argante, who could heal him, enabling him to return home to Britain. Because of this, some scholars believe Argante was a title that could be given, and one granted to MORGAN LE FEY; others feel Argante was a queen in her own right and a separate individual from the King's half-sister.

Sources: Illes, *Encyclopedia of Spirits*, 205; Paton, *Studies in the Fairy Mythology of Arthurian Romance*, 16, 26; Schofield, *English Literature*, 232, 353

Argia

Variations: MELIA

Born one of the 3,000 daughters of the Titians, Oceanus and Tethys, the NYMPH Argia was one of the named OCEANIDS from Greek mythology. The wife of the river-god Inakhos, Argia was the NYMPH of the town Argos in southern Greece.

Sources: Apollodorus of Athens, *Apollodorus' Library and Hyginus' Fabulae*, 95; Grant, *Who's Who in Classical Mythology*, 531; Lemprière, *Classical Dictionary*, 85

Argiope

In classical Greek mythology, Argiope was a NYMPH of Mount Parnassos in Phokis, central Greece. By the bard Philammon, she gave birth to an even greater musician, her son Thamyris.

Sources: Apollodorus of Athens, *Library of Greek Mythology* 30; Hard, *Routledge Handbook of Greek Mythology*, 435

Argyra

In classical Greek and Roman mythology Argyra was one of the NEREID; she was a sea–NYMPH of the town of Argyra in Akhaia, southern Greece and was loved by Solemnos (Selemnos), a shepherd, until his youthful beauty faded.

Sources: Keightley, *Mythology of Ancient Greece and Italy*, 453; Pausanias, *Pausanias's Description of*

Greece, Volume 1, 363; Rose, *Spirits, Fairies, Leprechauns, and Goblins*, 19

Ariā

Variations: Aira

The ariā was the fairy form or the physical manifestation of the ATUA spirit in the beliefs of the Maori people of New Zealand; it could take the shape of a dog, an insect, a star, or other forms as needed. It was commonly believed the ariā caused misfortune and spread diseases; to see one was considered terrible luck and the most fearsome of them took the form of a green gecko.

Sources: Best, *Māori Religion and Mythology*, 33–4; Polynesian Society (N.Z.), *Journal of the Polynesian Society*, Volume 6, 43; Rose, *Spirits, Fairies, Leprechauns, and Goblins*, 19–20

Ariel

Ariel was the name of the "airy spirit" in William Shakespeare's "*The Tempest*"; he flew through the air on the back of a bat (Act 5). Ariel was invisible but took form when he acted; like air and fire there was no place on the earth he could not go. His voice was like music, his ideas were associated with liberty, to "be as free as the wind"; although moody, he reflected human emotions but being of the fay, could not feel them. He was immune to human illness, capricious, rebellious and motivated by mere promises.

The name of the FAIRY QUEEN of the SEASONAL FAIRIES known as PILLYWIGGINS was ARIEL.

Sources: Ashliman, *Fairy Lore*, 52; Shakespeare, *Complete Works of William Shakespeare*, 20–1; Shakespeare, *The Tempest*, 83

Arkan Sonney

Variations: Fairy Pig of Man, Lucky Piggies, Lucky Piggy, Tucky Piggy

Arkan Sonney was a fairy pig from the lore of the Isle of Man. Like the Hounds of Annwn from Welsh mythology, Arkan Sonney was described as being white with red ears; it had the ability to change its size at will (see ANNWN, HOUNDS OF). Although it was a difficult undertaking, it was considered to be very lucky to catch one. According to the lore, if did caught it, you would find a piece of silver in your pocket.

Sources: Briggs, *Encyclopedia of Fairies*, 10; Monaghan, *Encyclopedia of Celtic Mythology and Folklore*, 51; Smith, *W.B. Yeats and the Tribes of Danu*, 126

L'Armée Furieuse

In Swiss folklore a L' Armée Furieuse ("Furious Host" or "Raging Host") was the name given

to the WILD HUNT; it was said during this event unbaptized babies were abducted.

Sources: Macdowall, *Asgard and the Gods*, 78; Rose, *Spirits, Fairies, Leprechauns, and Goblins*, 20

Arsalte

In Greek mythology Arsalte was a water–NYMPH and one of the named DANAIDS, the collective name for the daughters of Danaus; her name appeared in a list of the DANAIDS generated by Gaius Julius Hyginus (ca. 64 B.C.–A.D. 17), a Latin author. Arsalte was wedded to Ephialtes and killed him on their wedding night.

Sources: Bell, *Women of Classical Mythology*, 68, 149; Hyginus, *Myths of Hyginus*, 133

Arshenk

Variations: ARZSHENK

Arshenk was a DJINN or DEEV who was the King of Jinnestân; he was said to have a "splendid palace."

Sources: Keightly, *World Guide to Gnomes, Fairies, Elves, and Other Little People*, 16; Tennant, *Thane of Fife*, 74

Arzshenk

In Persian lore, Arzshenk was a DEV and the king of the fairy metropolis AHERMANABÂD; he lived there in an enchanted castle filled with plundered treasure. He was described as having a humanoid body and the head of a bull. His army was commanded by DEEV SEFEED.

Sources: Keightly, *World Guide to Gnomes, Fairies, Elves, and Other Little People*, 18; Richardson, *Dictionary, Persian, Arabic and English*, Volume 1, Liv, Lv; Richardson, *Dissertation on the Languages*, 144; Yardley, *Supernatural in Romantic Fiction*, 53

As-Iga

As-Iga ("old man of the Ob") was a benevolent WATER SPIRIT from the fairy folklore of the Ostyaks people of Siberia. This fay acted as a guardian to the creatures of the river; he protected the people who depend upon the river for a living.

Sources: Dixon-Kennedy, *Encyclopedia of Russian and Slavic Myth and Legend*, 18; Graves, *Larousse Encyclopedia of Mythology*, 307; Rose, *Spirits, Fairies, Leprechauns, and Goblins*, 22

Asamanukpai

Around the size of a monkey, the asamanukpai of Ghana, West Africa were DWARF-like men described as having backward turned feet and black, red, or white beards. When sighted, they were said to be dancing on outcropping of quartz which they polish with their feet as they dance; continued use of the same spot would cause a hole to be worn straight through. Offerings of dolls, rum, sweet fruits, water, and yarn were left for them; if the gifts were accepted and the fairy decide they especially like you, they would squeeze magical fairy-fruit juice into your eyes gifting you with the ability to read people's mind and see the future. However, if the asamanukpai were disturbed or angered, they would trick the offender into following them into the jungle where they will lose them.

Sources: Bord, *Fairies*, 60; Harpur, *Philosophers' Secret Fire*, 21; McCann, *Finding Fairies*, n.p.

Asdeev

A DEV from Persian lore who could take the form of a white dragon, Asdeev was slain by the cultural hero, Roostem (Rustam).

Sources: Dekirk, *Dragonlore*, 33; Keightly, *World Guide to Gnomes, Fairies, Elves, and Other Little People*, 81; Rose, *Giant, Monsters and Dragons*, 27

Asteria

In ancient Greek mythology Asteria was a water–NYMPH and one of the named DANAIDS, the collective name for the daughters of Danaus. In a list compiled by Apollodorus, a Greek scholar and grammarian, she was one of the daughters of HAMADRYAD, ATLANTEIA or (PHOEBE, sources vary) and was wedded to Chaetus, one of the sons of an unnamed Arabic woman.

Sources: Bell, *Women of Classical Mythology*, 75, 149; Grimal, *Dictionary of Classical Mythology*, 127; Lemprière, *Classical Dictionary*, 5, 236

Ash Boys

Variations: ASHES MAN, Fire Boys, Flint Boys, Poker Boys

Ash boys were a type of fairy spirit of fire in the folklore of the Zuñi tribe of America.

Sources: Parsons, *Pueblo Indian religion*, Volume 2, 963; Rose, *Spirits, Fairies, Leprechauns, and Goblins*, 22, 130

Ashes Man

Ashes Man was a fairy spirit of fire in the folklore of the Zuñi tribe of America.

Sources: Rose, *Spirits, Fairies, Leprechauns, and Goblins*, 22, 130; Parsons, *Pueblo Indian religion*, Volume 2, 196

Ashinaga and Tenaga

First appearing the Chinese classic, *Sankaikyo*, an eighteen volume work depicting creatures and ghosts of land and sea, the bearded Ashinaga ("long legs") and Tenaga ("long arms") were a pair of symbiotic GOBLINS who worked together to achieve goals, such as food gathering and catching fish. Ashinaga had only one overly long leg and Tenaga had one overly long arm; it was believed they lived on an island off the North China coast near Hung Sheung Tree. Ashinaga would wade into the water with Tenaga on his shoulders and snatch up the fish. Tales of their cooperative nature were popular in both Chinese and Japanese art and tales.

Sources: Barbanson, *Fables in Ivory*, 106; Joly, *Legend in Japanese Art*, 13; Tomita, *Japanese Treasure Tales*, 12, 25

Ashray

Variations: Asrai, Water Lover

In Scottish fairy lore, ashrays were translucent fairies occasionally mistaken for ghosts; they could appear to be either female or male and looked like a human in their late teens or early twenties. Unable to live on land, the ashrays were completely nocturnal; should one ever be captured and exposed to the rays of the sun it would melt into a puddle of water.

Sources: Begley, *Faith of Legacy*, 420; Briggs, *Encyclopedia of Fairies*, 10–11, 111; McCoy, *Witch's Guide to Faery Folk*, 147, 176–7; Tongue, *Forgotten Folk-Tales*, 24–6

Asia

Variations: CLYMENE

Born one of the 3,000 daughters of the Titians, Oceanus and Tethys, Aisa was a NYMPH and one of the named OCEANIDS. She was the sister to the NYMPH, EUROPA. In classical Greek and Roman mythology Asia was named as the mother of Prometheus; however in English literature she was said to be his wife.

Sources: Apollodorus, *Apollodorus' Library and Hyginus' Fabulae*, 95; Bell, *Bell's New Pantheon or Historical Dictionary of the Gods*, 112; Boswell, *What Men or Gods Are These*, 58; Day, *God's Conflict with the Dragon and the Sea*, 64; Hesiod, *Works of Hesiod, Callimachus, and Theognis*, 20

Asie

In classical Greek mythology Asie was one of the OCEANID NYMPHS of the Anatolian peninsula; she was possibly the wife of the Titian, Iapetos, and by him gave birth to four sons, Atlas, Epimetheus, Menoitios, and Prometheus.

Sources: Day, *God's Conflict with the Dragon and*

the Sea, 59; Hard, *Routledge Handbook of Greek Mythology*, 49

Askre

In Greek mythology, Askre ("sterile oak") was a NYMPH of the town Askra in Boiotia in classical Greece; she was loved by the god of the sea, Poseidon (Neptune) and gave birth to a son named Oioklos who founded the town of Askra.

Sources: Luce, *Ancient Writers*, 64; Nagy, *Greek Mythology and Poetics*, 74

The Asopides

Variations: Daughters of the Sea

In classical Greek mythology the Asopides were the NAIADS daughters of ASOPUS; they were the NYMPHS of the river Asopos in Sikyonia and Boiotia, central and southern Greece. These twelve NAIADS were all abducted and raped by Zeus (Jupiter) and many of the other Olympian gods; their names were Aegina (ÆGINA), Asopis, CHALCIS, CLEONE, CORCYRA, OINIA, PIRENE, SALAMIS, SINOPE, TANAGRA, THEBE, and THESPIAN.

Sources: Larson, *Greek Nymphs*, 11; Quiggin, *Essays and Studies Presented to William Ridgeway*, 224

Asopis

In classical Greek mythology Asopis was one of the twelve ASOPIDES, the NAIADS daughters of ASOPUS; they were the NYMPHS of the river Asopos in Sikyonia and Boiotia, central and southern Greece. She and each of her sisters were abducted and raped by Zeus (Jupiter) and many of the other Olympian gods.

Sources: Classical Association, *Classical Review*, Volume 12, 125; Larson, Greek Nymphs, 141; Quiggin, *Essays and Studies Presented to William Ridgeway*, 224

Asopus

Born one of the 3,000 daughters of the Titians, Oceanus and Tethys, Asopus was one of the named OCEANIDS.

Sources: Boswell, *What Men or Gods Are These*, 58; Day, *God's Conflict with the Dragon and the Sea*, 64; Hesiod, *Works of Hesiod, Callimachus, and Theognis*, 20

Astakides

The astakides was the collective name for the NYMPHS who originated from Lake Astakos in Bithynia, a Roman province in northwest Asia Minor, now located in modern Turkey.

Sources: Chaniótis, *From Minoan Farmers to Roman Traders*, 204; Larson, *Greek Nymphs*, 196

Asteriai

In ancient Greek mythology the asteriai were the NYMPHS of stars.

Source: Rigoglioso, *Cult of Divine Birth in Ancient Greece*, 87

Asterodeia

A NYMPH of a stream in the Kaukasos Mountains, east of Black Sea, Asterodeia from Greek mythology was born the daughter of the Aiolid, Deion and married Phokos.

Sources: Barthell, *Gods and Goddesses of Ancient Greece*, 55; Hard, *Routledge Handbook of Greek Mythology*, 435

Asterodia

Born one of the 3,000 daughters of the Titians, Oceanus and Tethys, Asterodia was one of the named OCEANIDS; she was the wife of Endymion.

Sources: Lemprière, *Classical Dictionary*, 87; Smith, *Dictionary of Greek and Roman Biography and Mythology*, 389

Asterope

Variations: Merope

One of the OREADS, Asterope was a mountain NYMPH from classical Greek mythology; she was born one of the daughters of the Titian, Atlas and the ocean NYMPH, PLEIONE. As the seven daughters of Atlas, she and her sisters are sometime referred to as the ATLANTIDES.

Asterope was also the name of one of the PLEIADES. Born in Arcadia, she and her sisters, ALCYONE, CELAENO, DRYOPE (Aero or MEROPE), ELECTRA, MAIA, and TAYGETE, are sometimes referred to as the Seven Sisters.

Sources: Ardinger, *Pagan Every Day*, 190; Smith, *Dictionary of Greek and Roman Biography and Mythology*, 389

Astris

Astris was a NYMPH born the daughter of the sun god, Helios (Sol) and CETO the NAIAD; she was the wife of the Indian river-god, Hydaspes according to classical Greek mythology.

Source: *Asiatic Journal and Monthly Miscellany*, Volume 6, 170–71

Astyokhe

Variations: Astyoche

Astyokhe was a NYMPH of the town of Troy in the Troad, Anatolia; she was the wife of the Trojan King Erikhthonios in classical Greek mythology.

Sources: Hard, *Routledge Handbook of Greek Mythology*, 522; Lemprière, *Classical Dictionary*, 400

Ataman

Ataman was the name or title belonging to the chief of the NATURE SPIRITS in particularly large forests according to Russian folklore.

Sources: Ivanits, *Russian Folk Belief*, 67; Rose, *Spirits, Fairies, Leprechauns, and Goblins*, 25

Athach

Athach ("GIANT" or "monster") was a gigantic FAIRY ANIMAL living in isolated glens and lochs in the Irish highlands. Examples of such a creature would be the BOCAN, the DIREACH, and the LUIDEAG.

Sources: Campbell, *Popular Tales of the West Highlands*, Volume 3, 365; Ellis, *Chronicles of the Celts*, 223–4; Rose, *Giants, Monsters, and Dragons*, 30

Atlanteia

A HAMADRYAD of Libya in North Africa, Atlanteia was one of the many wives of King Danaus in Greek mythology.

Sources: Apollodorus of Athens, *Library of Greek Mythology*, 61; Springborg, *Western Republicanism and the Oriental Prince*, 129

Atlantid

The Atlantid were one of twelve species of NYMPHS, they were any of the offspring of the primordial Titian, Atlas (see PLEIADES).

Sources: Littleton, *Gods, Goddesses, and Mythology*, Volume 11, 999; Serviss, *Astronomy with the Naked Eye*, 28

The Atlantides

In classical Greek mythology the Atlantides were the seven NYMPH daughters of the Titian, Atlas; their names were ALCYONE, ASTEROPE, CELOENO, ELECTRA, MAIA, MEROPE (Aero or DRYOPE) and TAYGETE. Each of the ATLANTIDES married one of the gods or an earthly heroic prince; they were well known for their wisdom and being just.

Sources: Bell, *Bell's New Pantheon*, 105; Blacket, *Researches into the Lost Histories of America*, 215

Atropos

Atropos ("inevitable") was one of the three FATES (MOERAE) from classical Greek mythology; representative of the Past, she was depicted in art as holding a pair of cutting shears, cutting the thread of human life.

Sources: Anthon, *Classical Dictionary*, 976; Rose, *Spirits, Fairies, Leprechauns, and Goblins*, 25

Attorcroppe

Variations: Attercroppe ("spider")

The attorcroppe ("little poison head") were a species of injurious fay from Saxon lore; as curious as they were ill-natured, they were described as looking like a small snake with human arms and legs. Walking upright through the forests of England, the attorcroppe were best avoided.

Sources: Cunliffe, *Glossary of Rochdale*, 15; Illes, *Encyclopedia of Spirits*, 43; Newcomb, *Faerie Treasury*, 47

Atua

Atua (generally translated to mean either "god" or "good") can be a confusing word and concept as it was used by the Maori people of New Zealand for both the extremely poisonous elemental spirits inhabiting the bodies of animals and monstrous creatures as well as referring to beloved ancestral spirits.

An atua was created when a person dies. These spirits could be summoned through ceremonial magic and have questions put to them; in these instances it was said the atua of a still born child was the most powerful. Atua of friends and family could be summoned if they were dearly missed through similar ceremonies, even being invited to possess a person. Injurious atua could be captured and have their power negated by use of fishing nets.

There were many different atua in the mythology, such as KOROKIORWEK, MAKAWE, MOKOTITI, TARAKIKA, and TITIHAL. The atua were similar to the NUKIR MAI TORE of Polynesian mythology.

Sources: Illes, *Encyclopedia of Spirits*, 44; Mageo, *Spirits in Culture, History, and Mind*, 123, 124, 125; White, *Ancient History of the Maori*, 2, 4

Au Co

In Vietnamese lore, Au Co was a beautiful mountain fairy who deeply loved and was loved by Lac Long Quan, the Dragon Prince of the Sea. She bore him an egg sack hatching one hundred children. Although the two were passionate for one another they could not remain together for she longed to be in the mountains and he need to be in the sea. Eventually the couple separated, each taking half the children with them; the fifty who went with Au Co developed into the Vietnamese people, one of which was Dinh Tien Hoang, the first Vietnamese emperor.

Sources: Chapuis, *History of Vietnam*, 11–12; Fujii, *Neuropsychology of Asian-Americans*, 181; Illes, *Encyclopedia of Spirits*, 230

Aughisky

In Ireland the aughisky was a water-horse very similar to the EACH UISCE of Scottish Highlands lore, the Welsh CEFFYL DWFR, and the SHOOPILTEE from the Shetlands except it was never seen galloping along the shores of the inland lakes where it lived. It was also different from the Scottish KELPIE which inhabited running water.

Unlike the beautiful lake-dwelling horse known as Cúchulainn, the aughisky could not be permanently tamed. If a halter was placed on one, the aughisky would be a faithful mount so long as it never laid eyes on its lake. Should this happen, the fairy horse would make a dash for its old home, taking its rider with it; there, it would tear its former master into bloody pieces. Once wild again, it would return to its normal diet of eating cattle.

Most sightings of this of fairy horse were made in the month of November when they left their lake to come on land to graze. Generally regarded as being a benign fay, stories say most people will not to go a lake reported to be the home of an aughissky after dark.

Sources: Briggs, *Encyclopedia of Fairies*, 13; Conway, *Magickal, Mystical Creatures*, 45; Froud, *Faeries*, 108; Kölbing, *Englische Studien*, Volume 5, 396

Auki

Variations: El Auki

The auki were a type of mountain fey from the folklore of the Quechua people of Peru. Living high up in the Andes Mountains, these fey lived in haciendas and looked like the ones lived in by the local populace. The vicuñas (a species of wild camelids) were the auki's spirit servants, condors were kept as their poultry, and CCOAS as their cats. Auki were called upon by the *brujos* (shamans) to assist them in curing the sick.

Sources: Edwards, *Visual Sense*, 159; Lambright, *Creating the Hybrid Intellectual*, 79, 95–6; Rose, *Spirits, Fairies, Leprechauns, and Goblins*, 25

Aulanerk

Aulanerk was a sea- and NATURE SPIRIT and spirit of joyfulness from the folklore of the Inuit people of North America. Described as looking like a naked man, Aulanerk lived in the sea much like a MERMAN; it was said his movement in the oceans causes the waves. It was said he was always cold and when he shook, his movement created the waves.

Sources: Andrews, *Dictionary of Nature Myths*, 15, 223; Rose, *Spirits, Fairies, Leprechauns, and Goblins*, 25–6

Auloniad

Variations: Napææ

The Auloniad ("ravine" or "valley") were a sub-species of the NAPAEA, they were the NYMPHS of mountain pastures and vales; oftentimes they were seen in the company of Pan (Faunus), the god of nature. EURYDICE, for whom Orpheus traveled into Hades, was a lovely and beloved auloniad.

Sources: Bechtel, *Dictionary of Mythology*, 152; Maberry, *Cryptopedia*, 112; Murray, *Manual of Mythology*, 183

Aumanil

Aumanil was a beneficent fairy from Inuit mythology although he lived on land, he controled the movement of whales and guides them to hunting grounds.

Sources: Eason, *Mammoth Book of Ancient Wisdom*, 426; Graves, *Larousse Encyclopedia of Mythology*, 436; Rose, *Spirits, Fairies, Gnomes and Goblins*, 26

Aurai

The aurai of ancient Greek mythology were the NYMPHS of the moist, cool breeze; they were born the daughters of the wind-god Boreas.

Sources: Lerner, *Lotus Transcendent*, 62; Rigoglioso, *Cult of Divine Birth in Ancient Greece*, 87

Aurvang

Aurvang ("muddy wolf") was one of the many DWARFS named in the *Voluspa*, the first and best known poem of the *Poetic Edda*, a collection of Old Norse poems dating back to about A.D. 985.

Sources: Daly, *Norse Mythology A to Z*, 22; Crossley-Holland, *Norse Myths*, 183; Sturluson, *Prose Edda*, 123

Aurvangr

Aurvangr ("sandy") was one of the many DWARFS named in the *Voluspa*, the first and best known poem of the *Poetic Edda*, a collection of Old Norse poems dating back to about A.D. 985.

Source: Wilkinson, *Book of Edda called Völuspá*, 12

Ausangate

Ausangate was an APU who liveed on a mountain peak in the Andes Mountains; he was described as looking like a blond headed, fair-skinned child wearing white clothing and riding upon a white horse. Of all the APU, Ausangate was said to be the most powerful; he bestowed health and prosperity while increasing the fertility of animals and the yield of crops. He was the owner of wild animals, all of which were subject to his commands; he was especially associated with alpacas and llamas.

Sources: Heckman, *Woven Stories*, 15; Illes, *Encyclopedia of Spirits*, 198; Reinhard, *Ice Maiden*, 128

Austri

Austri ("east") was one of the many DWARFS named in the *Voluspa*, the first and best known poem of the *Poetic Edda*, a collection of Old Norse poems dating back to about A.D. 985. One of the four DWARFS of the four main compass points, Austri, along with NORDI (north), and SUDRI (south) and WESTRI ("west") each held up one corner of the earth which is described as a flat, plate-like piece of land.

Sources: Crossley-Holland, Norse Myths, 183; Daly, *Norse Mythology A to Z*, 22; Sykes, *Who's Who in Non-Classical Mythology*, 53; Wägner, *Asgard and the Gods*, 311

Autodice

In Greek mythology Autodice was a water–NYMPH and one of the named DANAIDS, the collective name for the daughters of Danaus; her name appears in a list of the DANAIDS generated by Gaius Julius Hyginus (ca. 64 B.C.–A.D. 17), a Latin author. Autodice was wedded to Clytus and killed him on their wedding night.

Sources: Bell, *Women of Classical Mythology*, 90, 149; Hyginus, *Myths of Hyginus*, 133

Automate

In Greek mythology Automate was a water–NYMPH and one of the named DANAIDS, the collective name for the daughters of Danaus. In a list compiled by Apollodorus, a Greek scholar and grammarian, she was one of the daughters of Europe and was wedded to Busiris, one of the sons of Argyphia.

Sources: Apollodorus, *Gods and Heroes of the Greeks,* 69; Lemprière, *Classical Dictionary*, 236; Smith, *Dictionary of Greek and Roman Biography and Mythology*, 518

Autonoe

A sea–NYMPH, Autonoe ("sensible" or "with her own mind") was one of the named NEREID in ancient Greek mythology. Along with AGAVE and Ino she nursed the infant god, Dionysus (Bacchus), who was born from the thigh of Jupiter (see AGAVE).

Autonoe was also named as one of the named DANAIDS, the collective name for the daughters of Danaus. In a list compiled by Apollodorus, a Greek scholar and grammarian, she was one of the daughters of the NAIAD, POLYXO and was wedded to Eurylochus, one of the sons of the NAIAD, CALIADNE.

Sources: Dalby, *Bacchus*, 24, 30; Falkner, *Mythology of the Night Sky*, 178; Hesiod, *Works of Hesiod, Callimachus, and Theognis*, 15; Lemprière, *Classical Dictionary*, 236; Trzaskoma, *Anthology of Classical Myth*, 18

Avalon

Variations: Apple Island, Insuls Avallonis ("Isle of Apples")

In the Welsh Arthurian tradition the Island of Avalon was the land of the dead, a place where no one ever grew old and their needs were fulfilled by thought. According to Geoffrey of Monmouth, one of the major figures in the development of British historiography it was ruled by MORGAN LE FEY who lead a sisterhood of nine. Avalon was associated with Glastonbury Tor a hill near Sumerset England was once nearly encircled by water. Since 1191 the hill has been considered a FAIRY ISLAND.

Sources: Ashliman, *Fairy Lore*, 16; Keightly, *World Guide to Gnomes, Fairies, Elves, and Other Little People*, 45

Aveline

In the French fairy-tale *The Princess Minion-Minette* the fairy Aveline lived in a country near the lands of young King Souci. In the hopes of teaching Souci the lessons of how to please others, the fairy Aveline disguised herself as an old woman carrying a bundle of faggots as the young king had never been taught proper manners by his FAIRY GODMOTHER, INCONSTANCY, who raised him.

Source: Lang, *Pink Fairy Book*, 274–88

Awd Goggie

In east Yorkshire, England, there lived an individual fairy known as Awd Goggie. Similar to a type of fairy known as a BOGIE, Awd Goggie hunted for unsupervised children in forest and orchards; children were warned to "be good or Awd Gogie will git thee." He was especially watchful over unripe apples.

Sources: Briggs, *Abbey Lubbers, Banshees, and Boggarts*, 21; Nicholson, *Folk Lore of East Yorkshire*, 79; Peach, *Curious Tales of old East Yorkshire*, 77; Wright, *Rustic Speech and Folk-Lore*, 198

Awki

Awki was an earth or NATURE SPIRIT from the folklore of the Quechua people of southern Peru; he lived in *moqo* (knolls or rounded hills) in the region.

Sources: Bolin, *Growing up in a Culture of Respect*, 179; Rose, *Spirits, Fairies, Leprechauns, and Goblins*, 27

Awl

Awl was one of the many DWARFS named in the *Voluspa*, the first and best known poem of the *Poetic Edda*, a collection of Old Norse poems dating back to about A.D. 985, Awl was the brother to BROC and SINDRI.

Source: Wilkinson, *Book of Edda called Völuspá*, 12

Aynia

Variations: ÁINE

In Irish folklore Aynia was one of the SÍDHE and the FAIRY QUEEN of Ulster and Tyrone in Northern Ireland. One of her sacred places was a large stone located near Dunany called Aynia's Chair. This place attracted both rabid dogs and people who were mentally unstable. It was believed anyone who sat on the stone ran the risk of becoming insane.

It was possible Aynia, a lunar spirit, was at one time also Aine, a solar spirit, and a goddess of Irish mythology. Likely a diminished goddess, Aynia was most powerful on Fridays, Saturdays, and Sundays. Out of respect to this fay, locals did not bath or fish on those days.

There was an immense stone in Dunany, Ireland called the "chair of Aynia" by some and the "chair of lunatics" by others. The stone was believed to attract rabid dogs and people with mental illness. They were said to gather there and linger about until a great compulsion overtook them to walk out into the ocean and to the underwater lands of Aynia.

Sources: Illes, *Encyclopedia of Spirits*, 237–8; Rose, *Spirits, Fairies, Leprechauns, and Goblins*, 27, 351; Squire, *Celtic Myth and Legend*, 245; Wood-Martin, *Traces of the Elder Faiths of Ireland*, 356

'Azâzeel

Variations: El-HÂRITH

According to Arabian lore 'Azâzeel was the name of a young DJINN; he was eaid to have been raised by the Angels.

Source: Keightly, *World Guide to Gnomes, Fairies, Elves, and Other Little People*, 25

Aziza

Variations: Azizan

The aziza were a race of fairy from the folklore of the Dahomey people of Africa. These generally benign fay lived deep in the forest and had been known to share some of their supernatural knowledge with the hunters who lived there. Considered to bring luck with them, the aziza were often called upon by the native people for assistants in hunting and luck in general.

Sources: Argyle, *Fon of Dahomey*, 164; Illes, *Encyclopedia of Spirits*, 47; Peek, *African Folklore*, 179; Rose, *Spirits, Fairies, Leprechauns, and Goblins*, 27

Azrail

Azrail was a GIANT in Armenian lore who lived on Mount Djandjavaz. According to legend, the GIANT captured and took into slavery the brother of three fairies (see HOURI). Although many tired no one was able to rescue him. A young man known only as "the apprentice" told the king for the price of eleven goblets he would slay Azrail. In addition to the goblets the king gave "the apprentice" a mace, a suit of armor, and a war house. The slayer first killed the two serpents guarding Azrail's castle before confronting the GIANT himself. A terrific battle ensued and "the apprentice" managed to land two blows. Azrail begged to be finished off but the youth previously learned a third strike would magically restore the GIANT to full health and vigor. Rather than striking his opponent, he left Azrail to bleed to death.

Sources: Dixon-Kennedy, *Encyclopedia of Russian and Slavic Myth and Legend*, 22; Rose, *Giants, Monsters, and Dragons*, 33

Bà-Dúc-Chúa

In the Annamese belief of Vietnam, there was three NATURE SPIRITS known collectively as the Three Mothers; their names were DÚC-BÀ, Bà-Dúc-Chúa, and DÚC-THÀNH BÀ. These NATURE SPIRITS were worshiped in small rooms in pagodas dedicated to the Buddha.

Bà-Dúc-Chúa was the Spirit of the Air and was created by the Jade Emperor.

Sources: Leach, *Funk and Wagnalls Standard Dictionary of Folklore, Mythology, and Legend*, 778; Rose, *Spirits, Fairies, Leprechauns, and Goblins*, 92

Baba

The fairy name, Baba, dates back to the early folk belief of Hungary; however, the fay gradually evolved over time into an evil spirit resembling a HAG or witch.

Sources: Lurker, *Routledge Dictionary of Gods and Goddesses*, 29; Rose, *Spirits, Fairies, Leprechauns, and Goblins*, 29, 351

Baba Yaga

Variations: Бáба-Ягá ("Baba Yaga"), Баба Яга ("Baba Yaga"), Баба Яга ("Baba Yaga"), Baba Yaga Kostianaya Noga ("bone-legs"), Grandmother Bony-shanks, Grandmother in the Forest, Iron Nosed Witch, Iron Nosed Woman, Jaga Baba, JEŽIBABA, Jezi-Baba

Originally from Hungarian lore Baba Yaga ("old woman Yaga" or ("old woman Jadwiga") was a kind and benevolent fairy; over time her stories changed and she became a cannibalistic old crone or witch, small and ugly; in some stories Baba Yaga was a race of evil fay and not an individual. The name and character of Baba Yaga appeared in a number of eastern European and Slavic myths.

As an evil individual, Baba Yaga is described as being old, short, skinny, and ugly with particularly distorted and large nose and long, crooked teeth. Her behavior has earned her the reputation of being the Devil's own grandmother.

In instances where Baba Yaga was a fairy race rather than a singular individual, such as in the fairy tale of "*The Feather of Finist the Falcon*," the hero was met by not one but three baba yagas. In these instances, the baba yagas were commonly benevolent, gifting the hero with both advice and magical presents he would later need to succeed in his quest.

Baba Yaga, as a character, was hardly set in her way; she was used seemingly to fulfill a storyteller's need. There were numerous stories of her kidnapping children and threatening to eat them; in fact, many versions of cruel and evil witches living in houses of cake and candy were named Baba Yaga. In some stories heroes would make the brave and dangerous decision to seek out Baba Yaga for advice or assistance in completing a quest; in these stories there was always an emphasis placed on the hero's level of politeness, his need for proper preparation, and purity

of his spirit. Sometimes she played the role of an antagonist while other times she was a necessary source of guidance. No matter what role she was fulfilling, she drove a hard bargain, and was the one who sets the conditions and terms of the agreement; it mattered not to her if the hero accepted or refused the deal. All of her verbal contracts allowed her the right to eat anyone who was later unable or unwilling to fulfill their end of the deal (see BABA YAGA'S HUT).

By use of a gigantic mortar BABA YAGA could fly amazingly fast through the forest steering by use of the accompanying pestle in her right hand while with her left she uses her magical broom made out of silver birch to sweep away any sign of her having passed through the area. As she traveled it was believed a host of spirits trail behind her.

Sources: Dixion, *Encyclopedia of Russian and Slavic Myth and Legend*, 23–8; Evan-Wentz, *Fairy Faith in Celtic Countries*, 247; Lurker, *Routledge Dictionary of Gods and Goddesses*, 29; Rose, *Spirits, Fairies, Leprechauns, and Goblins*, 29; Rosen, *Mythical Creatures Bible*, 234

Baba Yaga's Hut

Baba Yaga lived in a hut surrounded by a picket fence, the tops of which were decorated with the skulls of her victims. The hut itself, windowless and with a false door, had proportionally large chicken legs which it rested upon. When wanting to enter into her home, BABA YAGA must enchant a magical spell which would compel the hut to lower itself to ground level. Anyone who tried to pick the lock to her home would be surprised to discover the keyhole was nothing more than a mouth full of sharp teeth. The hut was filled with scores of invisible servants who protected and served BABA YAGA.

It has been theorized the concept of BABA YAGA's Hut was not so farfetched. The nomadic tribal hunter of Serbia would build log cabins upon the tall stumps of two or three trees. The way the tree stump roots grow and spread looked just like chicken feet. These huts would have a trap-door built into the floor that could only be reached by ladder, as a bear was not only strong enough to break in a sturdy door but also stubborn enough to keep at it until it broke it open. Bears, no matter their size or strength, cannot climb a ladder. Small shrines containing clay figurines have also been found with this same sort of construction. Russian archaeologists, Yefimenko and Tretyakov, discovered in 1948 some small huts fitting the description of BABA YAGA's Hut; as circular fences surrounded the hut and inside they found traces of corpse cremation as well.

There are many versions of BABA YAGA's hut; in some tales it was connected with three mysterious riders. The first dressed in black and rode upon a black horse decked out in black barding and tack, he was the personification of the night; likewise there was a second rider dressed in red upon a red horse who personification of the sun, and the third rider dressed all in white upon a white horse was the personification of the day. If a visitor asked about the riders she would explain what they are but if she was ever asked about her invisible house servants, she will try to kill the person.

Sources: Johns, *Baba Yaga*, 141–2, 146; Rose, *Spirits, Fairies, Leprechauns, and Goblins*, 29; Rosen, *Mythical Creatures Bible*, 234; Wikimedia, *Slavic Mythology*, 117

Babau

A famous OGRE and a NURSERY BOGIE from French lore, Babau was used by nurses in hospitals to frighten their charges into behaving. The nursing staff would tell the children the OGRE sprinkled naughty children on his evening salad.

Sources: Drury, *Dictionary of the Esoteric*, 25; Spence, *Encyclopædia of Occultism: A Compendium of Information*, 57

Babban Ny Mheillea

On the Isle of Man, England, Babban Ny Mheillea ("harvest baby") was a fertility spirit; it lived in the last sheaf of corn at the time of harvest. This sheaf, cut by a young maiden, was to be made into an effigy of the corn spirit, decorated, paraded, and then held in honor at a feast. The effigy of Babban Ny Mheillea was kept until sowing season when the spirit was then released back into the field.

Other traditions involving corn dolls require some form of sacrifices, be it a simulation or an actual spilling of blood.

Sources: Killip, *Folklore of the Isle of Man*, 174; Rose, *Spirits, Fairies, Leprechauns, and Goblins*, 29

Bacche

Variations: Bakkhe

A NYMPH from the mythical Mount Nysa, Bacche was a nurse to the infant god, Dionysus (Bacchus) in classical Greek mythology. Collectively these NYMPHS were known as the BACCHANTS; their names were Bacche, BROMIE, ERATO, KISSEIS, KELLIA, KORONIS, MACRIS, and NYSA.

Sources: Daly, *Greek and Roman Mythology A to Z*, 22; Hyginus, *Myths of Hyginus*, 140

Bachna Rachna

Variations: Bakhna Rakhna, Good People, YUMBOES

In the folklore from the Republic of Senegal in western Africa in the Pap Mountain region comes the dark eyed, fair skinned, silver hair fairies known as the bachna rachna ("the Good People"). Standing two to three-foot tall these good-natured fay were known to dance and feast on moon-lit nights, inviting humans to freely join them. According to the Jaloff people of Goree Island if the bachna rachna were low on the supplies they needed to make their feast they would steal what they needed.

Sources: Allardice, *Myths, Gods and Fantasy*, 227; Keightley, *Fairy Mythology*, Volume 2, 327, 495; Maberry, *Crypopedia*, 119

Bäckahästen

Variations: Nykur

The bäckahästen ("brook horse") was a beautiful white fairy horse from in Scandinavian folklore. Very similar to the KELPIE from Scottish lore and the NÄCKEN and NIXEN of Polish lore, it rose up from the river and lurked along the banks looking too magnificent to not to be ridden. Anyone who climbed upon its back would find they would not be able to climb off again as the bäckahästen charged headlong into the water, drowning its rider. In the Middle Ages there was the belief in saying *"Bäckahästen go back to your watery place and set me free in the name of our Lady and the Holy Trinity"* three times the rider would be allowed to dismount from the FAIRY ANIMAL before being murdered.

There are stories of it being harnessed and made to plow but sometimes this is because it was all part of the bäckahästen's plan while other times it's domestication came about because it was tricked by the hero of the story.

Sources: Craigie, *Scandinavian Folk-Lore*, 233; Eason, *Fabulous Creatures, Mythical Monsters, and Animal Power Symbols*, 142; Scales, *Poseidon's Steed*, n.p.

Bad

In Persian demonology Bad was a DJINN and the demon of tempests; he could control the wind. Bad is most powerful on the twenty-second day of every month.

Source: Drury, *Dictionary of the Esoteric*, 26

Bademagu

Variations: MELWAS

A kindly FAIRY KING of the fairy underworld kingdom, Gorre, Bademagu was the father of the FAIRY KING MELEAGANT who once kidnapped Queen Guinevere, according to Arthurian lore. Ultimately, he forced his son to return the stolen queen. Bademagu was re-crowned king annual on the feast day of Mary Magdalene.

Sources: Berg, *Red Tree, White Tree*, 93, 105; Karr, *Arthurian Companion*, 54–5; Monaghan, *Goddesses in World Culture*, 32

Baetata

From the folklore of the Tupi-Guarani speaking people who lived in the Brazilian Amazon Basin comes the baetata ("marsh-fire"). An injurious water-spirit with the ability to make it rain, it was similar to the WILL O' THE WISP in that this fairy would lure humans off into the woods until they were hopelessly lost.

Sources: Graves, *Larousse Encyclopedia of Mythology*, 447; Hemming, *Red Gold*, 59; Rose, *Spirits, Fairies, Leprechauns, and Goblins*, 31

Báfurr

Variations: Bafur, Bofur

Báfurr, one of the great DWARF lords, was one of the many DWARFs named in the *Voluspa*, the first and best known poem of the *Poetic Edda*, a collection of Old Norse poems dating back to about A.D. 985.

Sources: Crossley-Holland, Norse Myths, 183; Sturluson, *Prose Edda*, 123

Baghlet el Qebour

Variations: Mule of the Graves

The Baghlet el Qebour was a specific and singular DJINN from Arabic lore; it was created when a Marrakesh widow by the name of Baghlet el Qebour broke Islamic law and remarried before the proper mourning period has passed. Having broken this law, it would have been impossible to determine paternity should the question arise; consequently, when the woman died eternal peace and rest was denied. With the exception of Wednesday nights, Baghlet el Qebour returned to earth between midnight and dawn in the form of a saddled mule and roams the marketplace looking for cavorting men. Whenever she found

one, she would allow them to mount upon her back and take them on a wild ride into the desert where she would bury them alive.

Sources: Evan-Wentz, *Fairy Faith in Celtic Countries*, 251–52; Illes, *Encyclopedia of Spirits*, 252; Legey, *Folklore of Morocco*, 34

Bahaman

A DJINN from Persian demonology, Bahaman was the demonic fay of appeasing anger. He had power over oxen, sheep, and all animals of a peaceful nature.

Sources: De Claremont, *Ancients' Book of Magic*, 119; Spence, *Encyclopedia of Occultism*, 62; Susej, *Demonic Bible*, 70

Bahlindjo

Variations: Balandjo, Balendjo

Similar to the river-NYMPHS of Greek mythology, the bahlindjo of Nigeria was the spirit of the Ogun River; he was associated with fertility and healing.

Sources: Evan-Wentz, *Fairy Faith in Celtic Countries*, 252; Illes, *Encyclopedia of Spirits*, 252

Bakemono

The word *bakemono* ("changing things") was a general term for injurious, little spirits from Japanese folklore; they were described as looking similar to a GOBLIN but could also be evil spirits or witches. Buddhists believe some bakemono can cause illnesses and plagues.

Sources: Figal, *Civilization and Monsters*, 4–5; Roberts, *Japanese Mythology A to Z*, 11, 94; Rose, *Spirits, Fairies, Leprechauns, and Goblins*, 31

The Bakkhai

Variations: BACCHANTS, Bacchantes, Maenades, THYIADES

According to Greek mythology the bakkhai, were the female NYMPH companions to the god of wine, Dionysus (Bacchus); their male equivalents were called the *bakkhoi*.

Sources: Dixon-Kennedy, *Encyclopedia of Greco-Roman Mythology*, 197; Ogden, *Companion to Greek Religion*, 327, 338

Bakru

A race of evil fairies or DWARFS living in the Paramaribo and coastal region of Surinam, the bakru were described as being half flesh and half wood, black skin and hair, and having very large black eyes set in their very large heads on their child-like bodies. Some sources claim they were the constructs of evil magicians. Always appearing in two's, one male and one female, the bakru were similar to the APUKU of West African lore.

If one wishes to have a bakru as a servant the person must agree to a pact with the being, signing away their soul for whatever riches the bakru will bring them, much like the AITVARAS of European lore. Other sources claim they can be created and purchased from evil magicians and kept as servants. If someone were to strike their master, the bakru dashes in the way, taking the shot with the wooden side of their body; later they will kill the assailant. When the owner of bakru dies the fairy is then free and will wander the roads looking for children to tease; if a child should ever accept a drink from a bakru, it will die.

Sources: Begley, *Faith of Legacy*, 420; Herskovits, *Myth of the Negro Past*, 254–5; Rose, *Spirits, Fairies, Leprechauns, and Goblins*, 31

Bakš Ia

Variations: Bakš Kuba ("Mill Old Woman"), Bakš Kuguza, Bakš Oza ("Mill Master"), Haks Oza

The Mari people of Russia have in their folk beefs a being known as Bakš Ia ("Mill Devil"). Similar to the KILLMOULIS, Bakš Ia protected the mill and its workings so long as a bowl of porridge with butter was left for him; should the offering be forgotten the fey would become angry and take its revenge by causing mechanical problems and spoiling the grain. He lived in the crawl space under the floorboards or behind the water wheel.

As Bakš Kuba, this fay appears as an old woman wearing traditional peasant garb decorated with silver coins.

Sources: Rose, *Spirits, Fairies, Leprechauns, and Goblins*, 31; Sebeok, *Studies in Cheremis*, 61

Baku

Variations: Youkai

Originating in Chinese folklore the baku ("dream eaters") made their way into traditional Japanese fairy lore as early as the Muromachi period (14th-15th century). These generally benign fairies literally devour a person's dreams and nightmares. Normally they do this of their own free will, grazing through the night; however there are some stories of a baku being called to a person for assistance in fighting off a nightmare. It is believed when a baku eats a person's dream it gives them good luck in return.

Physical descriptions of the baku are chimera-

like at best and vary widely; they are said to have the head of an elephant and the body of a lion while other sources claim they have the head of a lion but the body of horse with a cow tail and legs and feet of a tiger. In some regions they are described as being more piglike and its color anywhere between black and pink.

Sources: Davis, *Myths and Legends of Japan*, 358–9; Jōya, *Japanese Customs and Manners*, 151–3

Balanos

Variations: Balanus

In ancient Greek mythology Balanos was a HAMADRYAD of the acorn bearing oak tree or walnut, sources conflict; she was born from the incestuous relationship between the NATURE SPIRIT Oxylus and his sister, HAMADRYAS.

Sources: Athenaeus of Naucratis, *Deipnosophists*, Volume 1, 131; Buxton, *Forms of Astonishment*, 211; Gerber, *Greek Iambic Poetry*, 391; Larson, *Greek Nymphs*, 283

Balderich

Variations: Baldarich

In traditional German fairy lore, Balderich ("prince ruler") was a GIANT living on the Isle of Rugen in the Baltic Sea. According to the story Balderich did not like wading through the ocean each time he wanted to visit Pomerania or the mainland; donning an apron and filling it with earth he intended to connect Rugen to to them by making a huge dam. As he walked, a hole tore in his apron and as clay and dirt fell from it in clumps it formed what was later named the Nine-hills. Balderich repaired the hole and traveled on but another seam became loose and thirteen more hills were created. By the time the GIANT reached the shoreline and began to use the earth he had left, it was only enough to form the hook of Prosnitz and the peninsula of Drigge. Enrage his plan did not work, Balderich threw a fit and died where he fell, his dam uncompleted.

Sources: Arndt, *Fairy Tales from the Isle of Rügen*, 1; Bunce, *Fairy Tales, Their Origin and Meaning*, 150; Keightly, *World Guide to Gnomes, Fairies, Elves, and Other Little People*, 177

Balkin

Variations: Balkin, Lord of the Northern Mountains

In northern Scotland comes the fairy lore of Balkin, a SATYER-like fairy said to feed upon the air. He had a wife and over 12,000 children, all of which makes up fairy population of Catenes, Sutherland, and the adjacent islands. He and his massive brood speak ancient Irish and lived in caves. Balkin had a servant named LURIDAN; he was sent on errands to Finland, Lapland and the northern parts of Russia. Balkin and his fairies of the air were at constant war with the fairies of fire who lived on Mount Hekla, Iceland.

Sources: Henderson, *Scottish Fairy Belief*, 22–3; Keightly, *World Guide to Gnomes, Fairies, Elves, and Other Little People* 173; Shah, *Occultism,* 206

Ballybog

Variations: Bog-a-boo, Boggan, BOGGIE, BOGLE, Mudbog, Peat Faeries

Living in peat bogs and mud holes throughout England, Ireland, and Wales, the ill-tempered ballybogs were described as mud-covered, round-bodied fay; they hed no necks but long and spindly arms and legs. Believed by some to be the guardian of the peat bogs, the ballybogs communicated by use of grunts and slobbering sounds. Agile and quick-tempered, the ballybogs were said to fixate on people who were guilty of crimes or lazy and would lead them astray while crossing the bogs.

Sources: Begley, *Faith of Legacy*, 420; Maberry, *Cryptopedia*, 101; McCoy, *Witch's Guide to Faery Folk,* 178

Balor

Variations: Balar, Balior, Balor mac Doit, Balor of the Evil Eye, Balrog, Balroth, Balur, Bolar, Ri Balor

A king of the FORMORIAN, Balor was described as having only one huge leg and a supernatural eye. When he was young, Balor leaned over a cauldron his father's druids were concocting a potion in; the fumes rose up and settled in his eye inadvertently giving him the power to kill hundreds at a glance. He and his wife, Cethlenn, lived on Tory Island in a castle on Tor Mor, located nine miles northwest of Ireland.

According to legend, a prophecy declared his grandson would one day kill him, so Balor locked is daughter Etheline up in a crystal tower. In spite of this precaution the hero Cain dressed as an old crone made his way into the tower and fathered a child they named Lugh. When Balor discovered this he threw the infant into the sea, but it survived and grew to slay his grandfather by use of a sling.

Sources: Curtin, *Hero-Tales of Ireland*, 283–95; Matson, *Celtic Mythology A to Z*, 8; Mountain, *Celtic Encyclopedia*, Volume 2, 343–4

Balte

In Greek mythology, Balte was the NYMPH of Crete, Greece.

Sources: Grote, *History of Greece*, Volume 2, 114; Larson, *Greek Nymphs*, 283

Bamapama

Variations: Crazyman

In the folklore of the Murgin people from Arnhem, Australia, Bamapama, a trickster, was well known for his ability for causing bitterness, conflicts, hostility, and otherwise stirring up trouble between humans by violating tribal taboos, such as incest. In one popular story, he raped and killed his own sister; when his crime was discovered he was stoned and became mad, spearing dogs and vegetables.

Sources: Morphy, *Ancestral Connections*, 209; Rose, *Spirits, Fairies, Leprechauns, and Goblins*, 32

Ban Naomha

Variations: Ban-na-Naomha

The elusive Ban Naomha ("woman of the well") was an oracular fairy spirit associated with a sacred well known as Tober Kil-na-Greina ("Well of the Font of the Sun") located in Cork County, Ireland. Typically, this fairy chose to remain invisible but when she manifested did so in the form of a trout.

Sources: Evan-Wentz, *Fairy Faith in Celtic Countries*, 256; Illes, *Encyclopedia of Spirits*, 256; McCoy, *Celtic Myth and Magick*, 72, 372–73

Ban Nighechain

Variations: Bean-nigh, Bean-nighidh ("washer woman"), Nigheag ("little washer"), Nigheag bheag a bhroin ("little washer or the sorrow"), Nigheag na H-ath ("little washer of the fords")

In Celtic Scottish folklore Ban Nighechain ("little washer") was a female fairy spirit that forewarned of doom. Described as looking like an old woman with one nostril, protruding teeth, and webbed feet she was seen at the fords washing the blood-soaked clothed of those slain in battle. Death or some sort of disaster was imminent for anyone who saw her unless they could catch her before she fled. If caught she would give up the name of the fated person and grant her captor three wishes.

Sources: Jones, *Power of Raven*, 186; Rose, *Spirits, Fairies, Leprechauns, and Goblins*, 32; Watson, *Carmina Gadelica*, Volume 2, 226

Bannaia

Variations: Bainikha

In northern Russian folklore Bannaia was the wife of the evil spirit of the bathhouse, BANNIK.

Sources: Ivanits, *Russian Folk Belief*, 59; Rose, *Spirits, Fairies, Leprechauns, and Goblins*, 32; Ryan, *Bathhouse at Midnight*, 51, 65

Bannik

Variations: Bainik, Baennik, Bainushko

In northern Russian folklore Bannik was the evil spirit of the bathhouse; he was said to have the ability to predict the future. He looked like a wizened old man with wild white hair and beard but would sometimes shape-shift to look like a family member. His wife was named BANNAIA.

The bathhouse traditionally was set some distance away from the main house; essentially a sauna with an outer changing room and an inner steaming room, this outbuilding was seen as an unclean place where evil spirits gathered; however, they were also places where women gave birth and the art of divination was practiced. Bannik was seldom alone in the bathhouse, as he would invite other fairies to join him to partake in the sauna. To ensure he and his company were not disturbed all religious jewelry and belts were removed before entering, Christian imagery was not hung inside, boisterous activity, loud talking and singing were also forbidden. To guarantee Bannik was appeased, the third or fourth turn of steam was his alone to enjoy; during this time other fairies, demons, and spirits may be invited to join him. And as a final precaution, slam offerings of fir branches, soap, and water would be left for Bannik as a "thank you."

In some regions it was believed Bannik welcomed guests into the bathhouse and only after there was a birth in family did he truly settle down and move into the bathhouse permanently. If a bather wanted a divination, he could expose his naked back to the outside of the bathhouse; if the reading was positive Bannik would gently touch their spine, if it was negative, he would scratch them.

Sources: Dixon-Kennedy, *Encyclopedia of Russian and Slavic Myth and Legend*, 32; Ivanits, *Russian Folk Belief*, 58–60; Rose, *Spirits, Fairies, Leprechauns, and Goblins*, 33; Rhyne, *Supplement to the Modern Encyclopedia of Russian, Soviet and Eurasian History*, Volume 3, 197–8

Banshee

Variations: Bean Chaointe (keening woman), Bean Chaointe, Bean Si, Bean-Nighe, Bean-SÍDHE ("woman of the fairy" or "woman of the mounds"), Beansidhe, Benshi, CAOINEAG, Coin-teach, Cyhiraeth, Cyoerraeth, Eur-Cunnere Noe, GWRACH Y RHIBYN, Kannerez-Noz, Lady of Death, Little Washer by the Ford, Spirit of the Air, Washer at the Banks, Washer at the Ford, Washer of the Shrouds, White Lady of Sorrow, Woman of Peace

In Irish folklore the banshee was originally a singularity entity, an ancestral spirit wailing to announce an upcoming death for one of the five major families: the Kavanaghs, the O'Briens, the O'Connors, the O'Gradys, and the O'Neills. In modern times, it is still believed the mournful cry of the banshee can still be heard; it is considered to be a death omen, those who hear it will know someone who will die the following night. When a chorus of banshee gathers and wails together it is said someone holy or great is going to die.

Seldom seen, the banshee appeared naked when washing shrouds at the riverbank, her long, pendulous breasts getting in the way. When not at the river, it was hunting in the hills near lakes and running water for young men, wearing a gray cloak over a green gown; its long white hair worn loose, let to blow in the wind. If it could, a banshee lured its victim to a secluded place and drained him of his blood.

If you caught a glimpse of a banshee as it was washing shrouds, it was advised not to run from it. Rather, wait quietly until it slings its breast over its shoulder and carefully sneak up behind it. Then, place one of its nipples in your mouth and pretend you are nursing from it. As soon as you are caught, declare to the banshee it is your foster mother; should it accept you as its foster child, it will answer any question you have. A far less intimate way of gaining information from a banshee is to capture it and threaten it at sword point.

Should you happen upon a banshee while it is washing a shirt at the river and it sees you before you can act, it may speak, saying it is washing the shirt of an enemy. Name an enemy of yours aloud and then do not try to stop it from finishing its task or else the person you named will most certainly die. If you do not name an enemy for it, the banshee will attack and drain you of your blood.

Sources: Maberry, *Cryptopedia*, 101–2; Rose, *Spirits, Fairies, Leprechauns, and Goblins*, 33, 351; Yeats, *Fairy and Folk Tales of the Irish Peasantry*, 108–12

Baobhan Sith

In Scottish fairy-lore the baobhan sith ("woman of the fairies") was a vampire-like fay; it took the form of a beautiful woman and wandered the woods and roads looking for hunters or men walking alone at night. Once one was discovered, it danced with him until he was completely exhausted, then it drained him dry of his blood. Like most fay, the baobhan sith have a susceptibility to iron and can be slain by it.

The baobhan sith was similar to the BANSHEE of Irish lore, the HULI JING of Chinese lore, and the LHIANNAN SHEE of Manx lore, but they are all different beings.

Sources: Briggs, *Encyclopedia of Fairies*, 16; Guiley, *Encyclopedia of Vampires, Werewolves and other Monsters*, 19–20; Rose, *Spirits, Fairies, Leprechauns, and Goblins*, 34

Bar

A beautiful WATER SPIRIT from Scandinavian lore, Bar became the wife of Ögir the Dane who went on to become the King of the Sea because of her love for him. Bar was said to actively seek humans to pull beneath the water's surface to drown after which she buried them on the bottom of the ocean's floor.

Sources: Rose, *Spirits, Fairies, Leprechauns, and Goblins*, 34; Wägner, *Asgard and the Gods*, 242

Barbegazi

The barbegazi were a small GNOME-like race of fairy living in the Alps between France and Switzerland; their name was likely a corruption of the French words *barbe glacées* translated to mean "frozen beards." They had overly large feet allowing them to ski over snow easily. They also had the ability to completely cover themselves up with snow and disappear within moments. They were described as having long and thick frozen hair resembling icicles. The barbegazi communicated to one another over long distances by use of an eerie hooting oftentimes mistaken as the wind whistling through the mountain peaks. Living in a network of caves they dug out by use of their oversized feet, the barbegazi were only seen in the winter months and never below the tree line.

Sources: Begley, *Faith of Legacy*, 420; Conway, *Magickal, Mystical Creatures*, 198–9; Page, *Encyclopedia of Things that Never Were*, 52–3

Bardha

The bardha ("white ones") were NATURE SPIRITS in the folklore of Albania; they were described as formless white beings living in the ground. Housewives would leave sugar and sweet cakes on the ground for them to ensure their kindness.

Sources: Lurker, *Routledge Dictionary of Gods and Goddesses*, 30; Rose, *Spirits, Fairies, Leprechauns, and Goblins*, 35

Barguest

Variations: Bargeist, Bargest, Bargheist, Bargtjest, Barguist, Bo-guest

Originating from the fairy lore of Yorkshire England, the barguests were a species of shapeshifting fairy. Although they could take any form they pleased combing such features as claws, fiery eyes, horns, and vicious teeth, they usually took on the appearance of a mastiff dog or some other domestic animal. Its name likely originated from the words *barn ghaist* meaning "barn spirit." In Manchester, England, the barguest was said to be headless.

Haunting the wastelands between Headingley Hill near Leeds and Wreghorn in west Yorkshire, the barguest, like the BANSHEE, was most active at the death of a notable person or prominent figure. It gathered together all the dogs of the community and lead them on a howling procession through the streets. To see a barguest was a death omen and those who saw it died within a few days; to catch a fleeting glimpse would allow the viewer to live on, but only for a few months.

Barguests seem to become a staple fixture in an area or community and several have been named, such as the Barghest of Burnley, the BLACK DOG of Winchester, BLACK SHUCK, the Demon of Tidworth, the Dogs of Hell, Gwyllgi the Dog of Darkness, Hounds of Annwn (see ANNWN, HOUNDS OF), MODDEY DHOO, the PADFOOT of Wakefield, PICKTREE BRAG, SHOCK, SKRIKER, STRIKER, and TRASH.

Sources: Chisholm, *Encyclopædia Britannica*, Volume 3, 399; Keightly, *World Guide to Gnomes, Fairies, Elves, and Other Little People*, 317, 442; Rose, *Spirits, Fairies, Leprechauns, and Goblins*, 35

Bari

Bari ("feisty") was one of the many DWARFS named in the *Voluspa*, the first and best known poem of the *Poetic Edda*, a collection of Old Norse poems dating back to about 985, A.D; he was instrumental in building Lyr, Mengloth's hall.

Bari was also named as being one of the Ijosalfar, the SONS OF IVALDI. These DWARFS were the ones who created many of the magical items of the gods, including the golden wig of Sif; the ship, Skidbladnir; and the spear of Odin.

Sources: Crossley-Holland, *Norse Myths*, 183; Grimes, *Norse Myths*, 9, 285; Hollander, *Poetic Edda*, Volume 1, 150; Sturluson, *Prose Edda*, 123

Bariaua

From the folklore of the Tubetube and Wagawaga people of Melanesia comes the bariaua, a race of benign and shy NATURE SPIRITS. Keeping far from humans they live deep in the forest in the trunks of ancient trees. It was said they were incapable of making any sort of water-going vessel and on occasion they would borrow a person's canoe. Bariaua abhor the very thought of being seen by human eyes and if they were ever spotted they disappeared instantly.

Sources: Renner, *Primitive Religion in the Tropical Forests*, 84; Rose, *Spirits, Fairies, Leprechauns, and Goblins*, 35; Seligman, *Melanesians of British New Guinea*, 647

Basa-Andre

Variations: Basaandre

In the fairy lore of Basque, Basa-Andre ("wild woman") was best known as being the wife of BASA-JUAN. A sorceress, she was not necessarily evil but her actions and motivations were always supportive of her husband and their continued comfort and existence. When a story took place in a remote mountain area Basa-Andre was typically described as a beautiful woman sitting upon a rock just inside of a cave, combing out her long hair with a golden comb, much like a MERMAID. Although in none of the stories she or her husband portrayed as a danger to the Church or Christianity, the couple both hate the sound of church bells and will flee from their peeling.

Sources: Cobham, *Character Sketches of Romance,* Volume 1, 182; Evan-Wentz, *Fairy Faith in Celtic Countries*, 263; Webster, *Basque Legends*, 47–8

Basa-Juan

Variations: Basajuan

From the Basque folklore of northwest Spain comes the NATURE SPIRIT known as Basa-Juan. Taking the appearance of a FAUN or wood SPRITE, this fairy was said to have taught humans agriculture and iron-working. Similar to the French fairy known as HOMME DE BOUC ("he-goat man"), Basa-Juan was mischievous and enjoyed playing tricks. Living high up in the Pyrenean Mountains with his wife BASA-ANDRE, a SIREN-like fairy often seen sitting and combing her hair,

Basa-Juan protected the wandering flocks of goats and sheep from predators and thunderstorms.

In one isolated Basque story of Basa-Juan, he was not portrayed as his typical SATYER or wood spirit self but rather as a vampiric being; his wife, BASA-ANDRE, remained a sorceress. Although in none of their stories are he or his wife portrayed as a danger to the Church or Christianity, the couple both hate the sound of church bells and will flee from their peeling.

Sources: Cobham, *Character Sketches of Romance,* Volume 1, 182; Evan-Wentz, *Fairy Faith in Celtic Countries*, 263–64; Rose, *Spirits, Fairies, Leprechauns, and Goblins*, 35; Webster, *Basque Legends*, 47–8

Basadone

In northern Italy there was a species of FOLLETTI known as the basadone ("woman kisser"); they glided along on the wind and stole kisses from women as they drifted by.

Sources: Arrowsmith, *Field Guide to the Little People*, 22; Euvino, *Complete Idiot's Guide to Italian History and Culture*, 274; Wilborn, *Witches' Craft*, 85

Basilisk

Variations: Regulus

A basilisk was a highly poisonous FAIRY ANIMAL from Greek mythology; it was so lethal it could kill not just by looking at its prey, but also by breathing on or touching them. Described as having the body of a large golden colored snake with two arms protruding from the top of its head, this species of injurious fairy hates mankind.

Although the basilisk originated in Greek mythology, it did not figure much into it. Pliny the Elder, a Roman author, army and naval commander, natural philosopher, and naturalist wrote of the basilisk in his book, *Naturalis Historia*; in it he inscribed it was a small creature native to the province of Cyrenaica, walked upright on a set of rear legs, had a white diamond shape mark on its head, and was only about twelve inches long. Pliny goes on to say the basilisk was so poisonous it could kill bushes, scorch grass, and cause rocks to burst.

It was very difficult to kill a basilisk. If a person saw the creature before they themselves were seen, then the creature would die. If a person was gazed upon by a basilisk and they were quick enough to hold up an empty glass vial to catch the poison as it mysteriously travels through the air to catch it, the bottle could be thrown against the creature, breaking the glass, and its own poison would kill it.

Sources: Eason, *Fabulous Creatures, Mythical Monsters, and Animal Power Symbols*, 30; Magnanini, *Fairy-Tale Science*, 126; Pliny, *Natural History of Pliny*, Volume 2, 282

Bassai

In Greek mythology, Bassai was the Nymph of Arcadia, Greece.

Source: Larson, *Greek Nymphs*, 156–7

Bateia

Bateia was a Nymph from the mythology of ancient Greece and Rome. One of the Naiads, she bore King Oebalus of Sparta three sons Hippocoon, Icarios, and Tyndareus.

Sources: Apollodorus, *Library of Greek Mythology*, 120; Bell, *Women of Classical Mythology*, 93; Day, *God's Conflict with the Dragon and the Sea*, 394; Larson, *Greek Nymphs*, 195

Bathing Fairies

Dating back as far as the sixteenth century, tales of small, wingless, green-clad fairies or Nymphs with bird-like voices frolicking in the water were found not only in European fairy lore but from India as well. Both cultures told the tale of beautiful maidens bating in the water and were spied upon by a man who falls madly in love with one of them. Stealing her clothes the fairy seems to have no choice but to succumb to his desires and become his wife. Usually these tales end in tragedy as some years later the dutiful and faithful fairy-wife and mother discovers her long lost garment; upon reclaiming her fairy heritage by donning the garment she only leaves her mortal husband but flees with their children, returning to the water, never to be seen again. It was not uncommon in these tales for the fairy to murder her children just prior to or as she returns to the water.

Sources: Briggs, *Encyclopedia of Fairies*, 17–18; Clouston, *Popular Tales and Fictions*, 187; Parker, *Village Folktales of Ceylon*, Part 2, 347–8

Bauchan

Variations: Bòcan, Bogan, Buckawn

The bauchan was a type of extremely hairy Hobgoblin from the folklore of England; it had been known to be both benevolent and injurious. These fairies could become attached to a person or family and stay with them for great periods of times, sometimes giving assistance when there was a need and othertimes being overly mischevious for no apparent cause.

Sources: Campbell, *Popular tales of the West Highlands*, 101; Briggs, *Encyclopedia of Fairies*, 19; Rose, *Spirits, Fairies, Leprechauns, and Goblins*, 36; Spence, *Fairy Tradition in Britain*, 58

Baumbur

Baumbur was one of the many Dwarfs named in the *Voluspa*, the first and best known poem of the *Poetic Edda*, a collection of Old Norse poems dating back to about A.D. 985.

Sources: Daly, *Norse Mythology A to Z*, 22; Sykes, *Who's Who in Non-Classical Mythology*, 53

Baumesel

The baumesel ("ass of the trees") was a type of Goblin from the folklore of Germany; he lived in the trees of the forest.

Sources: Folkard, *Plant Lore, Legends, and Lyrics*, 83–4; Porteous, *Forest Folklore*, 42; Rose, *Spirits, Fairies, Leprechauns, and Goblins*, 36

Bavorr

Variations: Bavor

Bavorr ("grumbler") was one of the many Dwarfs named in the *Voluspa*, the first and best known poem of the *Poetic Edda*, a collection of Old Norse poems dating back to about A.D. 985.

Sources: Daly, *Norse Mythology A to Z*, 22; Sykes, *Who's Who in Non-Classical Mythology*, 53

Bayard

Bayard was the enchanted, fairy horse (see Fairy Animal) to the French hero, Maugis Renadu who quested and won him. The horse was said to understand the human language and possess edsupernatural intelligence, loyalty, power, and speed. Bayard, a beautiful white charger, was able to bear the weight of three riders and still perform perfectly in combat as a war-horse. When fighting, Charlemagne's army and faced with starvation, Bayard knelt before his master and offered up his life so the men of the army could eat his flesh. When Charlemagne tried to drown the animal in the River Meuse, the horse broke the millstone was tied to him, swam to the opposite side of the river, escaped pursuit through the woods, and joined his handler.

Sources: Akehurst, *Stranger in Medieval Society*, 112–3; Hausman, *Mythology of Horses*, 216–8; Keightly, *World Guide to Gnomes, Fairies, Elves, and Other Little People*, 33

Bažaloshtsh

Variations: Boialoshtsh

A BANSHEE from the Wend folklore of the eastern Germany, the bažaloshtsh ("God's plaint") was described as looking like a tiny, long-haired woman. This fairy only appeared beneath the window of someone who was about to die; there it sat and wept.

Sources: Hastings, *Encyclopedia of Religion and Ethics,* Part 8, 627; Rose, *Spirits, Fairies, Leprechauns, and Goblins*, 36, 351

Bean Fionn

Variations: Ban-Shoan, Greentoothed Woman, Jenny Greentooth, JENNY GREENTEETH, PEG POWLER, Water Woman, Weiss Frau

The bean fionn ("white woman") was the general name given to any type of fairy involved with drowning in England, Germany, and Ireland. Usually these fairies were described as dressing in white and live in lakes and streams. They waited for a child to come near the edge of their domain and then grabbed them up and pulled them down beneath the water's surface.

Sources: Eason, *Complete Guide to Faeries and Magical Beings*, 196; McCoy, *Witch's Guide to Faery Folk*, 180–1; Newcomb, *Faerie Treasury*, 47

Bean Nighe

Variations: an Nighechain ("little washerwoman"); Nigheag Na H-Ath ("little washer at the ford"), Washer at the Ford

The bean nighe ("washer wife") of Irish and Scottish fairy lore was similar to the BANSHEE, as it too could be found at isolated streams washing the blood-stained garments of those who were about to die. According to lore, a bean nighe was created when a woman died in childbirth; they became this sort of fairy ghost and remained in such a state until the day they normally would have died. They were described as being small in stature, dressing all in green, and having red webbed feet.

If a person could find a bean nighe and get between it and the river before it sees her, the bean nighe would grant three wishes. She would also answer and three questions put to her on the provision she can ask and expect to have answered honestly, three questions back.

Sources: Eason, *Complete Guide to Faeries and Magical Beings*, 196; Campbell, *Superstitions of the Highlands and Islands of Scotland*, 42–3; Froud, *Faeries*, 105; Spence, *Minor Traditions of British Mythology*, 22

Bean Sidhe

Variations: BANSHEE, Bean Si ("fairy woman"), Bean Sídhe, Beansidhe, Beansidhe, Cointeach ("one who keens"), Cyoerraeth, Cyrhiraeth, Eur-Cunnere Noe, GWRACH Y RHIBYN, Little Washer of Sorrow, Washer at the Banks, Washer at the Fords, Washer of the Shrouds

The bean sidhe ("woman of the hills") were a type of fairy spirit from Irish lore very similar to the BANSHEE. They are most often seen lingering near a house, either alone or in a group, where a person was likely to die; once one starts their *keening* ("mourning wail"), the person's fate was set. If one can be capture it could be compelled to say the name of the person who will die.

The bean sidhe were described as dressed in a green dress and grey cloak and having long, wild hair and bloodshot eyes from their constant crying. There were also regional variations to the descriptions of the bean sidhe, sometimes having one large bucked tooth, other times having overly large and pendulous breasts. In a few stories she was said to have slimly and wet skin, similar to pond scum.

Bean sidhe were also seen at river banks washing a blood stained shirt, a burial shroud, an article of clothing, or a shirt, the item varies from region.

Aiobhill was the name of the bean sidhe who presided over the Dalcassians of North Munster; CLIODNA was the bean sidhe of the MacCarthys as well as other families of South Munster.

Sources: Eason, *Complete Guide to Faeries and Magical Beings*, 90, 196–7; Evans-Wentz, *Fairy-Faith in Celtic Countries*, 305; McCoy, *Witch's Guide to Faery Folk*, 181–3; Mountain, *Celtic Encyclopedia*, 1322

Bean Tighe

Variations: Bean a'Tighe, Bean-Tighe, Our Housekeeper

In Irish fairy lore the bean tighe was a species of kindly house fay which were described as looking like a kindly little old peasant woman with a round, dimpled face. These benevolent little fairies lived near the hearth and helped with household chores, such as looking after the children and keeping the home clean.

Bean Tighe was also the name of the fairy housekeeper to the Earl of Desmond and his wife, FAIRY QUEEN, AINE. Bean Tighe was said to appear sitting atop an ancient earth-mound which was shaped like a GIANT chair known as Suidheachan ("Housekeeper's little seat").

Sources: Eason, *Complete Guide to Faeries and Magical Beings*, 197; Evans-Wentz, *Fairy-Faith in Celtic Countries*, 81–2; McCoy, *Witch's Guide to Faery Folk*, 147, 183–5

Becfhola

Variations: Beafhola, Becfola

In Irish mythology, Becfhola ("small fortune") was the FAIRY QUEEN of Tara, the wife of King Diarmaite, and the mortal lover of FLANN UA FEDACH, a FAIRY KING. The queen was desirous of her foster son, Crimthann, but this would-be tryst cost the king his throne making the people question who was the rightful ruler. While attempting to assassinate Crimthann, the lovely Becfhola met Flann and spent an evening with him on his enchanted island, Lough Erne enjoying a blissful affair. As time passes differently in FAIRYLAND than it does elsewhere, she was able to enjoy herself. When she returned, no one suspected the affair with her new lover let alone for how long it had been going on. However, soon after her return, FLANN UA FEDACH returned to Tara and whisking her away; they went off forever to FAIRYLAND.

Sources: Monaghan, *Encyclopedia of Celtic Mythology and Folklore*, 38, Monaghan, *Encyclopedia of Goddesses*, 308; Tolstoy, *Oldest British Prose Literature*, 85–6

Becuma

Variations: Becuma Cneisgel ("of the fair skin")

Possibly one of the TUATHA DE DANANN, Becuma cheated on her husband with one of the sons of Manannan mac Lir, god of the sea. When the liaison was discovered Manannan declared she be burned at the stake or set adrift in the sea; choosing the latter, Becuma was cast out in a small boat never again to return to her magical realm and forever denied access to the spirits.

When the recently widowed king of Ireland, Conn, first laid eyes upon Becuma he fell deeply in love. The pair quickly wed but soon after Ireland began to fail; the fertility of the land dwindled. This was seen by everyone, save the king, as the goddess Sovereignty not supporting the union. One day when Becuma defeated Art, Conn's son, in a game of chess she sent him to retrieve a spirit for her by the name of DELUCAEM. After a great adventure, Art was able to do so, and in the process fell in love with the powerful spirit and sorceress. When the pair returned home, DELUCAEM was able to force Becuma to leave court. In some versions of the story she re-turned to her small ship and drifted off to parts unknown while in other versions she landed in England and there created and fostered the hatred between England and Ireland.

Sources: Evan-Wentz, *Fairy Faith in Celtic Countries*, 269; Illes, *Encyclopedia of Spirits*, 267; Mountain, *Celtic Encyclopedia*, 353

Bediadari

Variations: Bidadari

The word *bediadari* ("good people") was a euphemism used when referring to the LITTLE PEOPLE or fairies in the folklore of the Malay people of West Malaysia.

Sources: Clifford, *Dictionary of the Malay Language*, 182; Rose, *Spirits, Fairies, Leprechauns, and Goblins*, 36; Skeat, *Malay Magic*, 106

Befana

Variations: Befana, La Befana, La Strega (the Witch) La Vecchia (the Old), Saint Befana

A good house-fairy from the folklore of Italy, Befana was usually described as looking like an old HAG, however, on Twelfth Night, the Feast of the Epiphany (January 6) she took on the appearance of a kindly old grandmother. Her name was a mispronunciation of the word *epiphania* (Epiphany).

There were various Christian Christmas legends about Befana. In one she was too busy with her housework to be hospitable when the Magi stopped by her house on the way to see the newborn Christ child, but she promised to offer it on their return trip. In another, she was invited to travel with them but wanted to finish her housework and promised to follow behind; however, when she did, she got lost and missed delivering her offering. Because of her shortcomings, every Twelfth Night she sets out a feast just in case the Magi return. She also fills children's shoes with sweets and small presents.

Sources: Corsaro, *Sociology of Childhood*. 122; Illes, *Encyclopedia of Spirits*, 269; Rose, *Spirits, Fairies, Leprechauns, and Goblins*, 37, 351

Béfind

Variations: Be Bind, Be Find, Befind, Befionn

The béfind were a species of fairy from Celtic lore. In Irish lore Béfind was singular entity, one of the SÍDHE, and one of three guardian fay who attend the birth of each child in order to give it the gift of an ability or character as well as to make predictions of its life. It was likely she was once an Irish goddess of birth. Béfind was likely the progenitor of the FAIRY GODMOTHER. Typically she would only make three appearances in a person's life, once at their birth, again on their wedding day, and finally on the day of their death, to bestow blessings and reveal their fate.

Up until the end of last century it was the custom in Brittany, France to set a festival table and invite the three fairies to attend a celebratory meal. In Breton she was considered to be a FAIRY QUEEN.

Sources: Evan-Wentz, *Fairy Faith in Celtic Countries*, 269; Illes, *Encyclopedia of Spirits*, 269; Monaghan, *Encyclopedia of Celtic Mythology and Folklore*, 38; Rose, *Spirits, Fairies, Leprechauns, and Goblins*, 37, 351

Behir

Variations: Beithir ("bear")

In the Highlands of Scotland's the behir were said to be one of a group of fearsome spirits. Associated with lightening and snakes the behir lived in caves and corries and kept away from humans as much as possible. Behirs were rarely seen but when sighted it was during the summer nights when lightning strikes. The word *behir* was used to mean both "lightening" and "serpent." The behir were also one of the FUATH, a collective name for the malicious and monstrous water fay in Scottish folklore.

Sources: Briggs, *Encyclopedia of Fairies*, 20; O'Reilly, *Irish-English Dictionary*, 60; Rose, *Spirits, Fairies, Leprechauns, and Goblins*, 37

Belphoebe

Belphoebe was a fairy known for her great talent of healing; she was seen as the epitome of the beauty of womanhood, chastity, and purity. She and her twin sister, AMORET, were born the daughters of the NYMPH Chrysogonee; their father was the warm sunlight that fell on the sleeping Chrysogonee after she bathed one afternoon. Born in the woods, the infants were found by the goddesses Diana and Venus as they were searching the woods for the lost god, Cupid. Belphoebe was taken and raised by Diana while her sister was raised by Venus.

Sources: Cavanagh, *Wanton Eyes and Chaste Desires*, 129; Keightly, *World Guide to Gnomes, Fairies, Elves, and Other Little People*, 58; Morley, *English Writers*, Volume 11, 354–5

Ben Baynac

Ben Baynac and his quarrelsome wife, CLASHNICHD AULNIAC, were GOBLINS who lived in the area of Craig Aulniac, Scotland. Like all SPRITES,

Ben Baynac was nearly immortal except for the vulnerable mole on his chest. It was said he beats his wife so badly her wailing and screams kept the neighbors awake all night. James Gray, a Highlander, heard the sad cries one night and put an end to Ben Baynac forever by shooting him with an arrow right in the center of his mole. CLASHNICHD AULNIAC, was so thankful for being rescued she attached herself to the local families. Unfortunately, GOBLIN greed knows no bounds; one day an enrage housewife doused CLASHNICHD AULNIAC with boiling water causing her to flee, screaming, never to return.

Sources: Anonymous. *Folk-Lore and Legends: Scotland*, 21–2; Rose, *Spirits, Fairies, Leprechauns, and Goblins*, 37; Stewart, *Popular Superstitions and Festive Amusements of the Highlanders of Scotland*, 10–13

Ben Socia

Variations: Bensocia, Frau HILDE, Pharaildis, Vrouelden

In French folklore ben socia ("good neighbor") was a euphemism for the word fairy. The name originated with the Norse goddess, Frigg, who, with the introduction of Christianity, lost her divine status.

Sources: Rose, *Spirits, Fairies, Leprechauns, and Goblins*, 38, 351; Wägner, *Asgard and the Gods*, 104

Ben Varrey

Variations: Ben-Varrey

On the Isle of Man, England, *ben varrey* was the Manx word for MERMAID, a beautiful sea creature with long golden hair enchanting fishermen to lure them to their deaths. The ben varrey had the same general description and disposition as other mermaids but in Manx tales they tend to be genrally kinder. There are more than a few folktales where the ben varrey was benevolent, such as in Dora Broome's *Fairy Tales from the Isle of Man* where a grateful MERMAID told a fisherman where to find a treasure hoard. In another tale a ben varrey rose up from the water and called out "shiaull er thalloo" ("sail to land") just as a violent storm was about to roll up; those who heed its warning lived, the rest were lost to the sea forever.

Sources: Briggs, *Encyclopedia of Fairies*, 22–3; Conway, *Magical, Mystical Creatures*, 156; Rose, *Spirits, Fairies, Leprechauns, and Goblins*, 38

Bendith Y Mamau

Variations: Bendith Mamau, TYLWYTH TEG

Traditionally members of the UNSEELIE COURT,

the bendith y mamau ("mother's blessing") were a species of BROWNIE but it was also the general name given to the fairies of Carmarthenshire and Glamorganshire counties, Wales. Mothers who lived in this county had to be especially careful with their infants because the bendith y mamau were know to steal children and replace them with their own CHANGELING offspring known as CRIMBILS. Sometimes the child would be returned to the parents after the bendith blessed it with the gift of music and song but usually the parents would have to hire a witch to rescue their child. No matter how the babe was returned, the child never remembered anything of its time with the fay except for a vague memory of having heard some beautiful and sweet music.

Other than stealing children the bendith y mamau—also ELF—rode horses, leaving them sweat covered and with tangled manes. Bowls of milk were left out to keep these deformed and ugly fairies appeased.

Over time, the words bendith y mamau became a saying spoken like a short prayer in order to ward fairies off.

Sources: Begley, *Faith of Legacy*, 420; Evans-Wentz, *Fairy Faith in Celtic Countries*, 153; Rose, *Spirits, Fairies, Leprechauns, and Goblins*, 38; Rhys, *Celtic Folklore*, 257

Benthesikyme

A sea–NYMPH of classical Greek mythology, Benthesikyme ("wave of the deep") was born the daughter of the god of the sea, Poseidon (Neptune); she was the wife to the Aithiopian King, Enalos.

Sources: Avant, *Mythological Reference*, 253; Hard, *Routledge Handbook of Greek Mythology*, 105

Berberoka

Living in the swamps of the Philippines, the berberoka are a species of cannibalistic water fairy; they are renowned for their predation on the Apayao people who live along the Apayao River. The fairies would move to a small pond or section of swamp and drink up so much water fish could easily been seen swimming near the surface. Fishermen are then lured to the area by the prospect of a fast and plentiful catch; then, berberoka release the water, drowning or knocking out their prey. Once the trap is sprung, they drag their food down to the watery depths where it is consumed.

Sources: Ramos, *Creatures of Philippine Lower Mythology*, 104

Berchta

Variations: Berkta, BERTHA, Brechta, Butzenbercht, Eisenberta, Frau Berchta, Frau Berta, Percht Perchta, Precht, Spinnstubenfrau, Stomach-slasher

In Alsatian, Austrian, German, and Swiss folklore comes the spirit of winter or WEISSE FRAU, Berchta. Once worshiped as an earth goddess by both northern and southern Germans, she was said to be a prophet.

Depending on the role she was playing in the lore determines her physical description but Berchta could always be identified by her one overly long and flat foot which was deformed by all the hours she spent at the spinning wheel. She has been described as a HAG with bright eyes, a hooked nose, long straggly grey hair wearing worn out clothes and carrying a staff. In many stories she appeared as an enchantress or trapped enchanted-maiden who gifted the hero who rescued her with many fine treasures. With the rise of Christianity, her appearance and disposition both turned dark and ugly.

As a NURSERY BOGIE she was used most often around Christmas time to threaten naughty children into changing their behavior. As Butzenbercht she delivered presents to good children on the Epiphany.

As Stomach-Slasher she made good on her name if not given offerings of dumplings and herrings or pancakes on feast days. If she caught anyone who has not eaten dumplings and fish on her holy day, she will slash open their stomach, remove the offending contents, fill it with straw, and stitch the person sloppily back together with a plowshare for a needle and lengths of chain for thread.

Appearing as Brechta she is described as a tall and lovely youthful looking woman wearing her long flaxen hair in a braid down her back; her pale face was hidden behind a white veil extending out and down into her gown. In one hand she carried the keys of happiness, in the other a sprig of mayflower.

In her guise of Perchta ("shining") she was the guardian of the barns, cornfield, and those who practiced the art of spinning. If the areas she watched over were left unattended she would cause a plague to befall the livestock.

Sources: *Teutonic Mythology*, Volume 1, 273; Rose, *Spirits, Fairies, Leprechauns, and Goblins*, 38; Wägner, *Asgard and the Gods*, 116, 117

Beregini

Variations: Bóginki ("little goddesses")

Beregini ("river bank") were the benevolent WATER SPIRIT in Russian folklore associated with rivers and streams; little is known of them beyond their name and that they lived in the banks over the river where the RUSALKA are found. Sacrificial offerings were believed to be thrown into the river for them.

In Polish fairy lore, the Bóginki ("little goddesses") were the forerunners of the RUSALKA; they were said to steal human infants and leave behind a type of CHANGELING called *ODMIENCE* (or *oborotni* in Russian).

Sources: Evan-Wentz, *Fairy Faith in Celtic Countries*, 276; Ivanits, *Russian Folk-Beliefs*, 78; Rose, *Spirits, Fairies, Leprechauns, and Goblins*, 38; Warner, *Russian Myths*, 11

Bereginya

Variations: Berehynias

The bereginya were a very obscure and little known and understood fairy, first mentioned in the fifteenth century Novgorod manuscript *The Lay of Saint Gregory the Theologian of the Idols*. The source, heavily edited and re-translated since the twelfth century makes the claim "vampires and bereginyas" were the first creatures worshiped by ancient Slavs, a form of dualistic animism practiced in their most ancient times. Although the text does not offer any details on the bereginya it has been speculated since their name is the Slavic word for *riverbank* they must be a sort of benevolent MERMAID.

Sources: Kravchenko, *World of the Russian Fairy Tale*, 201; Warner, *Russian Myths*, 11

Berg People

Variations: Bergfolk, Bjerg-Trolds, Hill-Men, SKOVTROLDE ("wood TROLL")

Said to resemble DWARFS, the berg people of Dutch lore were a species of fairly benign TROLL often appearing to humans as a toad. The god Thor was particularly hostile to them.

Sources: Briggs, *Vanishing People*, 195; Gray, *Mythology of All Races*, Volume 2, 224; Keightley, *Fairy Mythology*, 106; Rose, *Spirits, Fairies, Leprechauns, and Goblins*, 39

Berggeist

In Swiss lore the berggeist ("mountain spirit") was a type of fairy who lived in mines, particulary iron mines. The berggeist was described as looking like an elderly white man sporting a long white beard and wearing a red coat and a wide brimmed hat. Originally offerings were made to the local berggeist as a means of seeking permission before digging; however, after the introduction of Christianity, these fairies were blamed for mining disasters and were accused of being in league with the Devil.

Sources: Folklore Society (Great Britain). *The Folk-Lore Journal*, Volume 6, 218; Grimm, *German Legends of the Brothers Grimm*, Volume 1, 317; Illes, *Encyclopedia of Spirits*, 277

Berkhyas

Born the son of Akvan, the DEV Berkhyas of Persian fairy lore was described as being a large as a mountain with a body covered in bristling, needle-like hair; his black face hosted eyes as red as blood, and two large boar-like tusks protruded from his mouth, and pigeons nested in his beard. He had command of his father's army.

Sources: Bunce, *Fairy Tales, Their Origin and Meaning*, 110–11; Keightly, *World Guide to Gnomes, Fairies, Elves, and Other Little People*, 19

Berling

Variations: Berlingr

In Norse mythology, Berling ("handspike ") was one of the four BRISINGAMEN DWARFS who created the prized necklace for the goddess Freyr (see also ALFRIGG, DVALIN, and GERR).

The names ALFRIGG and Berling were uncommon names for DWARF; they only appeared in the *Sorla Thattr* in the *Flateyjarbok* manuscript.

Sources: Daly, *Norse Mythology A to Z*, 2, 11, 32–3; Grimes, *Norse Myths*, 131–2, 254; Pentikäinen, *Shamanism and Northern Ecology*, 87, 94

Bero

A sea–NYMPH, Bero was one of the named NEREID in classical Greek mythology; she was born of Nereus and DORIS.

Sources: Apollodorus, *Apollodorus' Library and Hyginus' Fabulae*, 95; Bell, *Bell's New Pantheon or Historical Dictionary of the Gods,* 112

Beroe

A sea–NYMPH, Beroe was one of the named NEREID; she was born of the goddess Aphrodite (Venus) and Adonis. According to the ancient Greek legend, Beroe was beloved by both the god of the sea, Poseidon (Neptune) and the god of the grape harvest, Dionysus (Bacchus); in the end the latter won her hand.

Sources: Hill, *Church Quarterly Review*, Volume 66, 137; Lemprière, *Classical Dictionary*, 468

Bertha

Variations: Bertha of Rosenberg, Brechta, Lady Bertha, Lady Perchta, White Lady

A fairy from German folklore, Bertha, appeared in the castles of nobility, quietly sliped into nurseries, and gently rocked infants to sleep; however, she was a nightmare and terrorizeed naughty children. She was described as being dressed in snowy-white clothes with a massive set of keys hanging from her belt and down her side. It was likely she was once the nature goddess, Berhta ("brilliant shining white") who in the advent of Christianity was reduced in power and status to a fairy. Several noble German families claim to be her ancestral descendants. She was first sighted in the early sixteenth century and reports of her appearance continued until 1850. In Thuringia, Germany Bertha was said to live in a hollow mountain where she kept watch over the souls of unborn children and those who died before they were baptized.

Sources: Chambers, *Chambers's Encyclopaedia*, Volume 10, 179; Guerber, *Hammer of Thor*, 39

The Bethen

Variations: Beden

A triad of female fertility spirits the Bethen of German lore were associated with birth, fertility and good fortune. After the introduction of Christianity, the bethen were absorbed into local traditions.

Source: Illes, *Encyclopedia of Spirits*, 278

Betikhân

A NATURE SPIRIT or FAUN from the folklore of southern India, the Betikhân was said to hunt the animals of the Neilgherry Hills.

Sources: Porteous, *Lore of the Forest*, 123; Reclus, *Les Primitifs*, 276; Rose, *Spirits, Fairies, Leprechauns, and Goblins*, 39

Bia

Bia was a river spirit from the folklore of the Akan people of Ghana.

Sources: Parrinder, *Religion in Africa*, 57; Rose, *Spirits, Fairies, Leprechauns, and Goblins*, 39

Bianca

Variations: Le Fate Bianca, Fata Bianca

Bianca was one of the FATES appearing in Matteo Maria Boiardo's epic poem *Orlando Innamorato* ("Orlando in Love," 1495) from the Italian Renaissance period. In the poem, Bianca and fellow FATE, NERA, were the protectors of Aquilante, son of Ricciardetto, and Guidone, son of Boveto d'Antona, but the poem was vague and misleading as to his parentage.

Sources: Boiardo, *Orlando Innamorato Di Bojardo*, 421; Brewer, *Character Sketches of Romance, Fiction and the Drama*, 5; Keightly, *World Guide to Gnomes, Fairies, Elves, and Other Little People*, 452

Biasd Bheulach

Variations: The Beast of Odail Pass

The biasd bheulach was a strict nocturnal FAIRY ANIMAL living in the Odail Pass on the Isle of Skye in the Scottish Highlands. Sometimes it appeared as a greyhound or man while other times it appeared as a man with only one leg. It was said to make a horrific wail; some stories claimed the biasd bheulach was a spirit of a vengeful ghost of murdered man, on the hunt and hungry for revenge. Victims of this FAIRY ANIMAL were found dead on the roadside with two piercing wounds on their side and one on their leg; a hand was said to be pressed to each wound.

Sources: Avant, *Mythological Reference*, 79; Briggs, *Encyclopedia of Fairies*, 23, Campbell, *Witchcraft and Second Sight in the Highlands and Islands of Scotland*, 207–8

Bibung

Bibung was the DWARF who acted as the protector of the ice FAIRY QUEEN, VIRGINIAL, in the ancient German work compiled in the fifteenth century by Kaspar von der Rhon, *Book of Heroes*. He was the ruler of all the DWARFS and GIANTS in the mountains. By reputation he was unconquerable, however it was under his watch the lovely VIRGINIAL fell into the hands of the magician Ortgis. She was kept imprisoned in a castle and each new moon was required to deliver up one of her attendants, known as the Snow Maidens, to be fattened up and then consumed by the cannibal magician. Ortgis was slain by the cultural hero, Hildebrand.

Sources: Guerber, *Legends of the Middle Ages*, 113–14; Rose, *Spirits, Fairies, Leprechauns, and Goblins*, 40; Wägner, *Epics and Romances of the Middle Ages*, 114

Biča Ia

Biča Ia ("pen devil") was a domestic fairy from the lore of the Mari people, Russia. A guardian of livestock, he shared this responsibility with fellow fay, BIČA OZA ("pen master"). Biča Ia had his favorite animal and at night, just like the Pixies of England, would take it out for a ride returning it back to its stall or pen, covered in sweat.

Sources: Ingemann, *Studies in Cheremis*, 53; Rose, *Spirits, Fairies, Leprechauns, and Goblins*, 40

Biča Kuba

Biča Kuba ("old woman of the animal pen") and her husband Biča Kuguza ("old man of the animal pen") were from the folklore of the Mari people of Russia; as her name implies, she was a guardian of livestock who shared her responsibility with Biča Ia ("pen devil") and Biča Oza ("pen master").

Described as looking like a little old woman dress in white, Biča Kuba could be seen inspecting animals in the early evening hours. Just as she may have a favorite animal she lavishes attention on, she may also have one she dislikes and singles out to torment.

Sources: Ingemann, *Studies in Cheremis*, 53; Rose, *Spirits, Fairies, Leprechauns, and Goblins*, 40

Biča Kuguza

Biča Kuguza ("old man of the animal pen") and his wife Biča Kuba ("old woman of the animal pen") were from the folklore of the Mari people of Russia; as his name implies, he was a guardian of livestock who shared his responsibility with Biča Ia ("pen devil") and Biča Oza ("pen master").

Sources: Ingemann, *Studies in Cheremis*, 53; Rose, *Spirits, Fairies, Leprechauns, and Goblins*, 40

Biča Oza

Biča Oza ("pen master") was a domestic fairy from the lore of the Mari people, Russia. A guardian of livestock, he shared this responsibility with fellow fay, Biča Ia ("pen devil").

Sources: Ingemann, *Studies in Cheremis*, 53;Rose, *Spirits, Fairies, Leprechauns, and Goblins*, 40

Biddy Early

Variations: Wise Woman Early

Biddy Early (1798–April 1874) was one of Ireland's most popular fairy doctor and herbalist; by the number of documented cases she was accredited of having worked on, she seems to have been an actual person who bore the title of Fairy. All who knew of her said she lived in a cottage located between Feakle and Tulla. Reputed to have been charitable and kind, it was said she could cure any ailment except for the debilitating touch caused by the Sídhe, Amadán. She could interpret dreams and visions and foretell events

by gazing into a glass bottle, as she could not afford a proper crystal ball.

Sources: Illes, *Encyclopedia of Spirits*, 162; MacManus, *Middle Kingdom*, 153–8; Yeats, *Visions and Beliefs in the West of Ireland*, Volume 1, 35–40, 276

Biersal

A Goblin or Kobold from the Saxony region of Germany, a biersal was a household fey who made his home in the *bierkeller* (cellar) of inns. In exchange for his own stein of beer he would gladly clean all other bottles, jugs, and steins in the establishment.

Source: Rose, *Spirits, Fairies, Leprechauns, and Goblins*, 40

Bifurr

Variations: Bivaurr, Bivorr

Bifurr ("trembler"), one of the great Dwarf lords, was one of the many Dwarfs named in the *Voluspa*, the first and best known poem of the *Poetic Edda*, a collection of Old Norse poems dating back to about A.D. 985.

Sources: Crossley-Holland, Norse Myths, 183; Hollander, *Poetic Edda*, Volume 1, 322; Wägner, *Asgard and the Gods*, 311

Big Ears

Big Ears was monstrous, catlike creature originating from the fairy lore of the Scottish Highlands. It was summoned through use of the Taghairm, an ancient magical rite, for the purpose of granting wishes. For four consecutive days cats were roasted alive over an open fire until it appeared. Stones with deep ruts in them were said to be places where Big Ears appeared, his claw marks left behind as evidence of his presence. Described as having evil-looking yellow eyes and gigantic ears it was believed it is the King of the Underworld cats. Big Ears was sometimes associated to the Cait Sith, a witch transformed into a cat.

Sources: Avant, *Mythological Reference*, 86, 89; Briggs, *Encyclopedia of Fairies*, 23; Conway, *Mysterious, Magickal Cat*, 88

Bild

Bild was one of the many Dwarfs named in the *Voluspa*, the first and best known poem of the *Poetic Edda*, a collection of Old Norse poems dating back to about A.D. 985.

Sources: Daily, *Norse Mythology A to Z*, 22; Wilkinson, *Book of Edda called Völuspá*, 12

Billingr

Billingr ("twin") was one of the many DWARFS named in the *Voluspa*, the first and best known poem of the *Poetic Edda*, a collection of Old Norse poems dating back to about A.D. 985.

Sources: McKinnell, *Meeting the Other in Norse Myth and Legend*, 168; Wilkinson, *Book of Edda called Völuspá*, 12

Billy Blind

Variations: Belly Blin, Billie Blin, Billy Blin, Billy Blynde, Blind Barlow

Billy Blind was household fairy akin to the HOBGOBLIN or BROWNIE; he was primarily found in the border region between England and Scotland but seemed to exist only in ballads and songs. Described as wearing a blindfold, this fay was concerned with family matters and maintaining marital happiness. In many ballads, songs, and stories he gave good advice or told how to undo a spell or evil enchantment.

In Arthurian lore, Billy Blind was a seven-headed fiend who hid in a barrel and spied on the court of King Arthur. Beaten in combat by the Green Knight, Sir Bredbedal, he was turned over to the King and made a servant of the other knights.

Sources: Briggs, *Fairies in Tradition and Literature*, 32–3; Henderson, *Scottish Fairy Belief*, 49; Rose, *Spirits, Fairies, Leprechauns, and Goblins*, 40

Billy Winker

Variation: The Dustman, Old Luk Oie, Wee Willie Winkie

Billy Winker was a NURSERY BOGIE who was called upon by mothers and nursemaids to induce sleep in children; he was from the folklore of Lancashire but elsewhere in England and in Scotland he was known as Wee Willie Winkie. As Old Luk Oie he walked through the home very quietly in his stocking feet and was otherwise said to be very well dressed, carrying an umbrella under each arm. His silk coat was blue, green, or red, depending on which direction he was facing. He sprinkled a small amount of sand into children's eyes so they couldnot awake and see him, then he breaths gently on their necks. For good children he opens up his highly decorated umbrella and holds it over them all night long to ensure they have pleasant dreams but for naughty children he hold his plain umbrella over them preventing them from having any dreams at all.

Sources: Andersen, *Tales and Fairy Stories*, 82–3; Briggs, *Encyclopedia of Fairies*, 24; Rose, *Spirits, Fairies, Leprechauns, and Goblins*, 40–1, 333

Biloko

Variations: Elokos

Biloko was a species of injurious DWARF from the folklore of Zaire; they were described as having a very large mouth and hair resembling grass. These fairy or NATURE SPIRITS have enormous claws and wears clothes made of leaves; they live in hollow trees and wait for someone to pass by to attack.

Although the word *biloko* translates to literally mean "object" or "thing," the fairy race of biloko have become sunomous with the word "bogyman," especially among the Nkundo people of central Zaire.

Sources: Knappert, *Aquarian Guide to African Mythology*, 83; Knappert, *Bantu Myths and Other Tales*, Volume 7, 142; Rose, *Spirits, Fairies, Leprechauns, and Goblins*, 41

Bilwis

Variation: Bimesschneider, Pilwiz

During the Middle Ages, Bilwis was a spirit from the fairy lore of Austria and Germany. Living in trees, this fay was invoked to assist in curing illnesses. Originally a kindly wood fairy or NATURE SPIRIT, Bilwis was demonized during the Middle Ages and described as having large sickles sticking out of the tops of his toes. Said to plague humans by making crop circles called Bilwis Reaping's, tying their hair into knots, and spoiling the harvest Bilwis was left small offerings to keep him away from children and the fields. In more modern times he looked upon as a type of BOGIE. Believed to live in trees offerings of children's clothing were left for it in the hopes of deterring him from spreading childhood diseases and illnesses.

Sources: Hastings, *Encyclopedia of Religion and Ethics*, Part 8, 632; Lindahl, *Medieval Folklore*, 393–4; Rose, *Spirits, Fairies, Leprechauns, and Goblins*, 41

Birds of Rhiannon

The birds of Rhiannon were FAIRY ANIMALS of British folk lore; typically their number was given as three. These birds were wonderful musicians with the ability to sing the dead back to life. According to the *"Mabinogi of Branwen, Daughter of Llyr"* a warrior came upon the birds and was so enchanted by their song he stopped and listened to them sing for 80 consecutive years; there are many versions of this story.

Sources: Evan-Wentz, *Fairy Faith in Celtic Countries*, 334; Parker, *Mythology*, 214; Sikes, *British Goblins*, 89

Bisan

A species of female NATURE SPIRITS from the folklore of the Malay people of West Malaysia, the bisan are the guardians of, specifically, the camphor-bearing trees (*Cinnamonium camphora*); at night is makes a shrill cry identical to the call of the cicadas. Appearing to humans in the form of the cicada these fairies must be approached using the correct method, such as only speaking *bahasa kapor* (camphor language), sacrificing a white rooster, and leaving a small offering of food. While hunting for camphor-bearing trees one must eat his trail rations without any form of condiment or the bisan will be offended.

Sources: Rose, *Spirits, Fairies, Leprechauns, and Goblins*, 41; Skeat, *Malay Magic*, 213; Watts, *Dictionary of Plant Lore*, 55

Bistonis

Bistonis was a NYMPH from the mythology of classical Greece and Rome. One of the NAIADS, she was the mother of the cruel and wicked king of Thrace, Tereus, by the god, Mars.

Sources: Bell, *Bell's New Pantheon*, 272; Day, *God's Conflict with the Dragon and the Sea*, 394

Bivor

Bivor ("the tremulous") was one of the many DWARFS named in the *Voluspa*, the first and best known poem of the *Poetic Edda*, a collection of Old Norse poems dating back to about A.D. 985.

Sources: Daly, *Norse Mythology A to Z*, 22; Sykes, *Who's Who in Non-Classical Mythology*, 53

Bjerg-trolde

Variations: Bjergtrolde
In Scandinavian fairy lore the bjerg-trolde ("hill TROLL") lives in the hills, underground. Standing only about twelve feet tall and being stout of body, the bjerg-trolde hunt GIANT salmon in the lakes.

Sources: Dunham, *History of Denmark, Sweden, and Norway*, Volume 2, 65; Keightly, *World Guide to Gnomes, Fairies, Elves, and Other Little People*, 63; Pritchett, *Gamle Norg*, 56

Black Angus

Variations: BARGUEST, CuSith ("fairy dog"), Cwn Annw, Gurt Dog
A Black Angus is a fairy hound from the folklore of England and Scotland; it is uncertain if this is a species of FAIRY ANIMAL or an individual being. Appearing as a large black dog with yel-

low glowing eyes and a maw full of sharp teeth, it roams the countryside as a sort of death omen, as anyone who sees it will die within a fortnight. Reports of Black Angus sightings date back as far as the seventeenth century.

Sources: Conway, *Magickal, Mystical Creatures*, 139; Jones, *Modern Science and the Paranormal*, 61; McCoy, *Witch's Guide to Faery Folk*, 147, 185

Black Annis

Variations: Black Agnes
Black Annis is a blue-faced HAG well known in the Dane Hills region near Leicester, England. Described as having long claws and yellow fangs, this powerful fairy lives in a cave called by locals Black Annis' Bower. Legend has it she made the cave herself by hewing out the stone with her own talon-tipped fingers. Her antipathist is a being named GENTLE ANNIS. Black Annis catches children and lambs who linger in the Dane Hills near twilight, removing the skin from their bodies, devouring their flesh and scattering their bones over the land.

As late as the eighteenth century, on Easter Monday, a dead cat soaked in aniseed was dragged past the opening of Black Annis' Bower with a pack of hunting hounds in pursuit. It was hoped she would follow suit and be exposed to purifying sunlight. In modern times she is consider to be little more than a NURSERY BOGIE although she is associated with sightings of monstrous cats and Alien Big Cats.

Sources: Briggs, Encyclopedia of Fairies, 24; Monaghan, *Encyclopedia of Goddesses and Heroines*, 335; Rose, *Spirits, Fairies, Leprechauns, and Goblins*, 41

Black Dog

Variations: Bakgest, Barghest, BARGUEST, CAPELTHWAITE, Choin Dubh ("Muckle Black Tyke"), Devil Dog, BLACK ANGUS, BLACK SHUCK, Black Shug, Gurt Dog, Gytrash, Hell Hound, Hounds of Annwn (see ANNWN, HOUNDS OF), Mauthe Dhoog, Morphing Shuck, PADFOOT, Pooka, SKRIKER, Shuck, Suicide Shuck, Tchian du Bouolay, TRASH

There are many different species of black dogs in fairy mythology, especially in the British Isles; generally these injurious fairy creatures are described as being a large and fierce dog, typically with a black coat. Its eyes are said to glow red or yellow, its mouth filled with vicious teeth. To see one, or hears its howl is a death omen, only a few rare stories exist of the black dog playing the role of a guardian and protector. Black dogs patrol deserted roads usually invisible right up until the moment it attacks; prior to that, only the clicking of its claws can be heard; crossroads and midnight are also common additions to black dog lore.

In the British Isles the black dog is shaggy and the size of a calf while in German lore it is every bit as large but its coat is more akin to that of a poodle's. Appearance and size differs only slightly from region to region; black dogs are reported in some fashion or another throughout the world.

Although traveling alone is never a good idea at night if fairy-country, having a companion offers no protection from the black dog, as one person may see and hear it while the other does not. According to legend, the best protection from one of these creatures is to travel with a descendant of Ean MacEndroe of Loch Ewe, as he once reportedly saved the life of a fairy who in return gave him and his family line perpetual and eternal immunity from black dogs.

Sources: Bois, *Jersey Folklore and Superstitions*, 103; Budd, *Weiser Field Guide to Cryptozoology*, 98–9; Choron, *Planet Dog*, 28; Godfrey, *Mythical Creatures*, 92–3

Black Dwarf (plural: dwarfs)

Living under the coastal hills of the Isle of Rügen, Germany's largest island, the black dwarfs were said to plunder the jetsam and flotsam of the ships wrecked along the coastline. They kept to the hills and seldom ventured out in the daylight; when they did, they never traveled too far from their home. In the summer months they were known to sit under elder trees. The black dwarfs did not dance or have any music to call their own.

Injurious, malicious, and of a foul disposition, the black dwarfs could hardly stand each other others company, seldom gathering in groups of more than three in number. They took pleasure in causing great mischief among mankind.

Dressed in black capes and jackets and described as being exceedingly ugly, they were expert craftsmen when it came to steel; their wares were always in high demand. It is said the swords of the black dwarfs were of unparallel craftsmanship, bending like a willow yet as hard as a diamond, no corset or shield could withstand a blow from one. The chainmail shirts knitted by them were as fine and delicate as the web of a spider; no bullet or sword could stand up against it.

Sources: Briggs, *Encyclopedia of Fairies*, 115; Keightly, *World Guide to Gnomes, Fairies, Elves, and Other Little People*, 176, 178; Ruoff, *Standard Dictionary of Facts*, 354

Black Elf (plural: elves)

Variations: Dark Elf, Swart Elves

The injurious black elves (Svartdlfar) from Scandinavian fairy lore live in Svartalfaheim, their underground domain. Described in the Old Norse *Edda* (thirtheenth century) as having skin "blacker than pitch," these elves would frequently cause harm and illness to mankind. Those who were victimized by them had to seek out the healing remedies of a specific kind of doctor known as a *kloka*.

It should be noted scholars are of a divided opinion as to whether or not black elves and DARK ELVES are in fact the same beings; some see them as being the same species of fairy as the DWARF.

Sources: Gardner, *Faiths of the World*, Part 2, 813; Keightly, *World Guide to Gnomes, Fairies, Elves, and Other Little People*, 78; Lindow, *Norse Mythology*, 110; Littleton, *Gods, Goddesses, and Mythology*, Volume 11, 59

Black Shanglan

Black Shanglan, was a warhorse, a FAIRY ANIMAL from Irish folklore; along with WOMAN RULER, they lived invisibly inside their FAIRY FORT. These two fairies come out only when it involves the freeing of Ireland in order to aid and comfort the people during a national uprising.

Source: Wallace, *Folk-lore of Ireland*, 81

Black Shuck

Variations: Doom Dog, Galleytrot, MODDEY DHOO of Norfolk, Old SHOCK, Old Shuck, Shucky Dog

Black Shuck is the name given to the BLACK DOG (see BARGUEST) that roams the lonely roads in East Anglia, Essex, Norfolk, and the Suffolk coastline. Sightings of this HELL HOUND are still made periodically; legends of him date back thousands of years to the time of Viking invasions. It has been speculated Black Shuck was named after Shukir, the war dog of Odin and Thor although it is equally as possible it was derived from the local dialect word *shucky*, which means "hairy" or "shaggy."

Black Shuck has been described in appearance in a number of ways; he is said to have two large saucer-like glowing green or red eyes, sometimes it is said he had only a single eye. Reports vary to his size, in one report he is as large as a horse while in another he is just as big as any large-sized dog, but headless. What apparently sets this particular BLACK DOG apart from others is its haunting of a specific region and that he has very seldom been accredited with doing anything more than frightening people nearly to their death. Nevertheless, sightings of him are still considered to be a death-omen; those who encounter him will die within a year.

Appearing just before bad weather and most active on stormy nights when the sea is dark and roiling, Black Shuck will sound out, its cry being carried out over the roar of the waves.

Sources: Dutt, *Highways and Byways in East Anglia*, 216; Eberhart, *Mysterious Creatures: A Guide to Cryptozoology*, Volume 1, 63; Guiley, *Encyclopedia of Witches, Witchcraft and Wicca*, 24; Mitchell, *Slow Norfolk and Suffolk*, 47

Blainn

Blainn ("corpse blue") was possibly the first of the DWARFS; his funeral which was held at the beginning of time was mentioned in the *Voluspa*, the first and best known poem of the *Poetic Edda*, a collection of Old Norse poems dating back to about A.D. 985.

Sources: Bellows, *Poetic Edda*, 6; Sturluson, *Proe Edda*, 28

Blathnat

Variations: Blanid, Blathnad, Blathnait, Blathnet

In Irish lore the Blathnat ("little flower") was a SÍDHE woman and the foster daughter of ANGUS OG. Legends vary, but generally it was said Blathnat either eloped with the cultural hero, Cu Chulain or was abducted by him. She may have played a part in the looting of her father's burial mound, but if she did, it was not clear if she was a willing participant or not. The only consistent part of her story occurs when she betrayed Cu Roi to Cu Chulain by revealing to him the only way his rival could be slain was with his own sword. Once the information was givem Cu Roi was then either killed while he slept or bathing. In the end, Blathnat either rode off happily with Cu Chulair or was slain by Cu Roi's bard.

Sources: Illes, *Encyclopedia of Spirits*, 288; Monaghan, *Encyclopedia of Celtic Mythology and Folklore*, 48; Mountain, *Celtic Encyclopedia*, 365–66

Bloody-Bones

Variations: Old Bloody Bones

Bloody-Bones is a NURSERY BOGIE from the folklore of England and the Unites States of America primarily. Ugly beyond description with his bloody and raw flesh exposed, Bloody-Bones and his companion, RAWHEAD, were often used as NURSERY BOGIES by parents to trick children into good behavior or for avoiding a certain activity or area, which ever was appropriate.

Sources: Brewer, *Reader's Handbook of Famous Names in Fiction*, 129, 743; Monaghan, *Encyclopedia of Celtic Mythology and Folklore*, 450; Wright, *Rustic Speech and Folk-Lore*, 198

Blud

Variations: Dickenpoten, Irrlicht, Will the Smith

In Slavic fairy lore Blud ("wanderer") is an injurious fairy causing disorientation; much like the WILL O' THE WISP, it leads people aimlessly around. Blud was also the ancient Slavic word for "illicit fornication."

Sources: Hastings, *Encyclopedia of Religion and ethics*, Volumes 3–4, 629; Levin, *Sex and Society in the World of the Orthodox Slavs*, 164; Rose, *Spirits, Fairies, Leprechauns and Goblins*, 336

Blue Burches

Variations: Blue Britches

Blue Burches is a HOBGOBLIN from Somerset, England; although known to take the shape of a small black pig his true form is said to be an old man wearing baggy blue britches. Considered to be harmless he plays mild pranks such as making the sound of heavy boots stomping down steps or causing wisps of smoke to appear in a room. In one story he took the form of an old white horse who allowed itself to be bridled and ridden; unfortunately the rider was a parson and took offence to the fairy and condemned it on the spot. Blue Bruchers ran off into a duck pond with the parson; although the parson was not harmed, the HOBGOBLIN was said never to be seen again.

Sources: Alexander, *British Folklore*, 129; Briggs, *Encyclopedia of Fairies*, 27

Blue-Cap

Variations: Blue-Bonnet

Similar to a KNOCKER, Blue-Cap of northern England is a fairy who lives in mines and assisted miners in pushing full coal carts all by himself; he would land on the handle of the cart as a ball of blue flame and push the load where it needed to go. Unlike the helpful BROWNIE, Blue-cap demanded fair wages for his services; every two week his pay would be left for him in a lonely corner of the mine. If ever his wager were short or more than he had earned he'd become indignant and not accept any of it.

Sources: Briggs, *Encyclopedia of Fairies*, 27–8; Fish, *Folklore of the Coal Miners of the Northeast of England*, 125; Ginswick, *Labour and the Poor in England and Wales 1849–1851*, 65; Mack, *Field Guide to Demons, Fairies, Fallen Angels, and Other Subversive Spirits*, 68

Blue Men of the Minch

Variations: Fir Ghorma, Fir Gorm, Storm KELPIES

In Scottish fairy lore the Blue Men of the Minch cause ships to wreck by creating sudden and violent thunderstorms; they are most active in the winter months, but during the summer they are said to be seen swimming just below the water's surface. These blue-skinned fairies, possibly descended from seals, live in underwater caves between Long Island and the Shiant Islands, an area know to sailors as the Blue Man's Stream and the Current of Destruction. Some sources add to their description claiming them to wear blue hats and have long grey arms and faces. These man-sized water fairies may be thwarted from their violence; as a ship passes by they call out a rhyme and a if a clever couplet is shouted back, they let the vessel pass in peace.

In one a local belief, the Blue Men are not fairies but rather fallen angels.

Sources: Eberhart, *Mysterious Creatures*, 64–5; Mackenzie, *Scottish Wonder Tales from Myth and Legend*, 76–8; Monaghan, *Encyclopedia of Celtic Mythology and Folklore*, 50

Boann

Variations: Boand, Boanna, Boind, Bouvindea

One of the TUATHA DÉ DANANN Boann ("white cow") was the river spirit of the Boyne river in Ireland; she was born the daughter of Danu. According to a twelfth century document entitled "*History of Places*" Boann was married to Nechtan, the guardian and owner of a Well of Wisdom. Forbidden to ever visit the well, Boann defiantly walked around it counter-clockwise; this action caused the water in the well to react violently. The water churned up and engulfed her, transforming Boann into the river which to this day bears her name.

Sources: Illes, *Encyclopedia of Spirits*, 291; Mountain, *Celtic Encyclopedia*, 367–68

Bocan

Variations: BAUCHAN, Bauken, Bawken, Boccan, Bocian, Bogan, Bugan

Found in both Ireland and the highlands of Scotland, the bocan are similar to the HOBGOBLIN; they have a reputation for being both helpful and injurious. There are numerous tales of a bocan being used as a sort of NURSERY BOGIE, attacking a child who has ventured into a place they were told not to enter.

Sources: Brigs, *Encyclopedia of Fairies*, 28; McCoy, *Witch's Guide to Faery Folk*, 186; Spence, *Fairy Tradition in Britain*, 58; Pratt, *Dictionary of Prince Edward Island English*, 20

Bodach (plural: Bodaich)

Variations: Bodach a Chipein, Bodach Glas ("Dark Grey Man"), Bug-A-Boo, BUGBEAR

In Celtic lore the bodach was a type of NURSERY BOGIE or GOBLIN said to creep down chimneys and kidnap children. In Scottish the word *bodach* means "old man," however in Irish it refers to a "churlish person, clown; peasant, or serf." As the Bodach Glas ("Dark Grey Man") it was very similar to the BANSHEE, except it appeared in a male form; to see one was a certain sign of one's impending death. As Bodach a Chipein ("Old Man with a Peg") it was a friendly and helpful fairy who watcheed over people as they performed their everyday chores and weep as funerals passed by.

Sources: McKay, *More West Highland Tales*, Volume 2, 489; Monaghan, *Encyclopedia of Celtic Mythology and Folklore*, 51; Pratt, *Dictionary of Prince Edward Island English*, 21

Bodachan Sabhaill

According to Scottish folk-ballads, Bodachan Sabhail ("Little old Man of the Barn") was a BROWNIE who took piety on old men by threshing corn and making straw bundles for them during the night. Never anything but helpful, has each village had its own Bodachan Sabhail, a small little fairy looking like a wise old man.

Sources: Avant, *A Mythological Reference*, 82; Briggs, Encyclopedia of Fairies, 29; Campbell, *Superstitions of the Highlands and Islands of Scotland*, 190

Bogart

Variations: BAUCHANS, Blobs, Bogans, Boggans, Boggart, Boggle, BOGLE, Boogey Man, Boogies, Gobelins, Gobs, Hobbers, HOBGOBLIN, PADFOOT

Originating in Celtic lore a bogart is an injurious species of fairy, it adopts a family and causes havoc in their life, acting exactly like a poltergeist, eating the wool, tossing about the items in the kitchen and ruining the butter. Some fairy lore says a bogart is created when a BROWNIE or HOBGOBLIN becomes insulted, transforming into an ugly, haired cover being with sharp and nasty teeth.

In modern times the word boggart is a verb and is used when meaning *"to steal," "to take more than one's fair share,"* or *"to refuse to share."*

Sources: Briggs, *Encyclopedia of Fairies*, 29; Keightly, *World Guide to Gnomes, Fairies, Elves, and Other Little People*, 317; Moorey, *Fairy Bible*, 290–1

Bogeyman (plural: bogeymen)

Variations: Bogey-beast, BOGIE, BOGLE, Bogy, Boogeyman, Bug, Bug-a-Boo, BUGBEAR

A bogeyman is any type of injurious fairy; while some are just slightly more than a minor nuisance others can be deadly. Shape-shifters who cause disruptions and move objects about, a bogeyman usually attaches itself to and then consequently plagues a specific family.

Their appearance is often vague and usually they are described as looking like nothing more than a puff of dust. The only known way to see a bogeyman is to look through a keyhole of a wooden door; if one is on the other side, you may be able to catch the gleam off of its dull eyes.

There are many regional stories of the local bogeyman carrying off naughty children. Usually this being will not have a name, however, once this NURSERY BOGIE gains one, the fairy is then typically, said to be a GOBLIN.

A bogel is a particular classification of the bogeymen; particularly evil and malicious, they specifically target liars and murders.

Sources: Ashliman, *Folk and Fairy Tales*, 181; Briggs, *Encyclopedia of Fairies*, 30–1; Drury, 35, *Dictionary of the Esoteric*; World Book, *World Book Encyclopedia*, Volume 7, 10

Bogie

Variations: BOGEYMAN, BOGLE, Bug, Bug-a-Boo, Bugger, GOBLIN

Bogie is the generic name for various types of GOBLIN whose temperament ranges from mild annoyance to deadly.

Sources: Briggs, *Fairies in Tradition and Literature*, 37–8; Froud, *Faeries*, 92; McCoy, *Witch's Guide to Faery Folk*, 28

Bogle

Variations: Bugell, Bugil

In Scottish fairy lore the bogle is similar to the BOGART and BOGEYMAN, having a foul disposi-

tion and taking extreme delight in frightening its victims it is also said to be virtirous. Folklore says when dealing with this type of fairy, you must have the last word with it.

Sources: Briggs, *Encyclopedia of Fairies*, 32–3; Douglas, *Scottish Fairy Tales, Folklore, and Legends*, 184; Jacobs, *English Fairy Tales Collected by Joseph Jacobs*, 203–4

Bokwus

Bokwus ("Wild Man of the Woods") is a NATURE SPIRIT found in the folklore of the Kwakiutl tribe of Native Americans of northwest America. Described as a skeletal being and wearing fearsome war paint it uses the sound of rushing water to mask its movement through the spruce wood forest, then, sneaking up on an unsuspecting fisherman it pushes him in the water and tries to drown him. If he succeeds, Bokwus captures his soul. If ever Bokwus offers a person a piece of dried salmon they should not accept it, as in truth it is actually a piece of dried tree bark; if it is eaten, it will transform the person into a ghost under his control.

Sources: Avant, *Mythological Reference*, 497; Eason, *Complete Guide to Faeries and Magical Being*, 197; Ingpen, *Ghouls and Monsters*, 43

Bolbe

Born one of the 3,000 daughters of the Titians, Oceanus and Tethys, Bolbe was one of the named OCEANIDS. According to Greek mythology she lived in the Thessalian lake Bolbe; in modern times it is known as Lake Volvi. Her offspring were LIMNADES, fresh-water lake NYMPHS; she was also the mother of Olynthus by Herakles (Hercules) according to Athenaeus, the second century Greek rhetorician and grammarian.

Sources: Boswell, *What Men or Gods Are These*, 58; Hesiod, *Works of Hesiod, Callimachus, and Theognis*, 20; Osborn, *Romancing the Goddess*, 190–1

Bolina

A NYMPH of the town of Bolina in Akhaia, southern Greece Bolina was pursued by the god, Apollo in classical Greek mythology; she leapt into the sea to escape his pursuits and remain a virgin. Impressed with her virtue the god bestowed the mantle of immortality upon her.

Sources: Bell, *Bell's New Pantheon*, 135; Endsjø, *Greek Resurrection Beliefs and the Success of Christianity*, 67; King, *Historical Account of the Heathen Gods and Heroes*, 79

Bolotnyi

Bolotnyi "(swamp") is a female marsh fairy or NATURE SPIRIT in Russian folklore, she is considered to be an injurious spirit.

Sources: Ivanits, *Russian Folk Belief*, 64; Rose, *Spirits, Fairies, Gnomes, and Goblins*, 47

Bombor

Variations: Bömburr ("swollen")

Bombor, one of the great DWARF lords, was one of the many DWARFs named in the *Voluspa*, the first and best known poem of the *Poetic Edda*, a collection of Old Norse poems dating back to about A.D. 985.

Source: Crossley-Holland, Norse Myths, 183

Bon Garçon

Variations: Bon Garcon, LUTIN

The LUTIN, a GOBLIN from the fairy lore of Normandy, was known by various names depending on the region and the shape it assumes; it was known as Bon Garcon ("handsome young man") when he takes on a human form. As it plays the role of man-about-town it flatters everyone it meets.

Sources: Keightly, *World Guide to Gnomes, Fairies, Elves, and Other Little People*, 477; Sherman, *Trickster Tales*, 149

Bonga Maidens

Variations: Bonga

The bonga maidens from the folklore of the Santal people of India are said to be both beautiful and dangerous NATURE SPIRITS. These fairies entice and marry men only to ultimately leave them alone, haggard, and "palely loitering." When a bonga is not involved in a relationship it plays injurious tricks on people however, on occasions, it can reward a person with a gift, such as "second sight" to those who have assisted it.

Sources: Leach, *Dictionary of Folklore*, n.p.; Rose, *Spirits, Fairies, Gnomes, and Goblins*, 48

Boobrie

The boobrie is a fairy-bird from the Scottish Highlands haunting lakes and salt-water wells; it is said to fly through the water. Its favorite food is cattle and sheep and will attack any ship carrying them. The boobrie mimics the sound of a calf or lamb in the hopes of luring an adult animal to the side of the ship; if successful, it will use it long talons to grab the animal and drag it underwater and drown it. When cows and sheep are not available, it eats otters.

The boobrie has the ability to shape-shift into a horse; in this form it can run across the surface of the water and when it does so, its hoof beats sound as if it were running over solid ground. It also shape-shifts into the form of a large insect with tentacles and feeds off horse blood. The foot-print of the boobrie looks like the imprint of an antler.

Sources: Briggs, *Encyclopedia of Fairies*, 34; Campbell, *Popular Tales of the West Highland*, 307–8; Howey, *Horse in Magic and Myth*, 146; Mccoy, *Witch's Guide to Faery Folk*, 88–9; Monaghan, *Encyclopedia of Celtic Myth and Folklore*, 53

Booman

The booman is a BROWNIE-like HOBGOBLIN from the Orkney and Shetland islands; his name is sung in the funeral game called "Shoot, Booman, shoot," and "Booman is Dead and Gone." In these songs the singer mimes digging grave, lowering a body into it, presumably Booman's, and throwing flowers after it.

Sources: Briggs, *Fairies in Tradition and Literature*, 269; Gomme, *Dictionary of British Folklore*, 497

Boomasoh

Similar to the HAMADRYADS of classical Greek mythology, the Boomasoh are tree spirits or NATS from Burmese folklore. They live in the roots of the trees.

Sources: Porteous, *Forest in Folklore and Mythology*, 125; Scott, *Burman: His Life and Notions*, Volume 1, 286

Boruta

In Polish folklore Bourta is a female NATURE SPIRIT, similar to a DRYAD; she is said to inhabit and protect the fir trees.

Sources: Arrowsmith, *Field Guide to the Little People*, 182; Porteous, *Forest in Folklore and Mythology*, 108; Rose, *Spirits, Fairies, Leprechauns, and Goblins*, 48

Bostonis

Bostonis was one of the NAIADS from classical Greek mythology.

Source: Day, *God's Conflict with the Dragon and the Sea*, 394

Brag

A brag is a species of mischievous, ugly, shape-shifting GOBLIN from the northern counties of England; it oftentimes shape-shifts into the form of a horse. In its horse form it is similar to the KELPIE and SHELLYCOAT and the PHOOKA of

Ireland. Sir Cuthbert Sharp in his book *The Bishoprick Garland* (1834) describes the fairy PICK-TREE BRAG, as a fantastic shape-shifter taking numerous forms such as a calf with a bushy tail wearing a white kerchief, four men holding a white sheet, headless naked man, and the "shape of a galloway." Some reports say when the brag cannot be seen it can be heard; on these instances it sounds like a coach being drawn by six horses.

Sources: Briggs, *Fairies in Tradition and Literature*, 70, 269; Moorey, *Fairy Bible*, 388; Sharp, *Bishoprick Garland*, 41–3

Breena

In Celtic lore, the word *breena* in Gaelic means "fairy land."

Sources: Newcomb, *Faerie Treasury*, 66; Samuelson, *Baby Names for the New Generation*, 35

Brenin Llwyd

Variations: The Monarch of the Mists

In Welsh fairy lore Brenin Llwyd ("Grey King") lives in the misty mountain tops of Snowdonia in northern Wales, although he has been placed in various mountain passes throughout the northern part of the country. Brooding, mighty, and powerful, he waits for a lone traveler to cross his path and when they do, are never seen again; he is especially quick to snatch up a child. Brenin Llwyd is an independent individual and is not associated with any particular group of Welsh fairies; he is said to wear a grey robe.

Sources: Budd, *Weiser Field Guide to Cryptozoology*, 48; Eberhart, *Mysterious Creatures*, 68; Trevelyan, *Folk-lore and Folk-Stories of Wales*, 69

Brísingamen Dwarfs

Variations: Brisinga Men ("Brising's Necklace"), Brosingamene

In Norse mythology the Brísingamen DWARFS are ALFRIGG, BERLING, DVALIN, and GERR, the four grotesque DWARFS who forged *Brísingamen* ("flaming ornament"), the necklace of the goddess, Freyja; it is thought to be made of amber or quartz. The only time these DWARFS were ever moved by anything but gold and silver was the moment they saw the look of Freyja's face when the necklace was presented to her and she recognized it craftsmanship and beauty as the most wonderful necklace she had ever seen.

Sources: Daly, *Norse Mythology A to Z*, 14; Knight, *Little Giant Encyclopedia: Runes*, 256; Pentikäinen, *Shamanism and Northern Ecology*, 87, 94

Britomartis

Variations: Dictynna ("daughter of the net")

Born a daughter of Zeus (Jupiter) and Carme and a virgin NYMPH of the mountains, Britomartis ("gentle virgin") was a companion to the goddess Artemis (Diana) and one of the OREADS; she was a guardian of fishermen. She had attracted the unwanted attention of Minos and fled from him for nine months, escaping his clutches only by throwing herself into the sea, leaping from the heights of Diktynnaion. Rescued from the water by fishermen and their nets, she traveled to Aigina and changed her name to Aphaia. She was depicted as being surrounded by hunting dogs and is dressed as a hunter.

Sources: Cox, *Mythology of the Aryan Nations*, 379; Daly, *Greek and Roman Mythology A to Z*, 107; Grimal, *Dictionary of Classical Mythology*, 78

Britomatis

Originally a Cretan mother-goddess, Britomatis became a NYMPH of the island of Crete in Greek mythology.

Sources: Guthrie, *Greeks and Their Gods*, 105; Larson, *Greek Nymphs*, 187

Broc

Variations: Brock, Brokk ("trotter"), Brokkr

The DWARF, Broc, is the brother to EITRI, a smith. Loki had wagered Broc his brother could not smith three items as wonderful as the golden hair of Fryja, the ship Skidblad, and the spear Gugner as made by the DWARFs known as the Sons of Ivallda. The brothers took up the bet; Broc blew on the fire and worked the bellows to keep it hot as his brother, EITRI, went to work making the golden boar, Gullinbursti; the golden arm-ring, DRAUPNIR, and the hammer, Mjolner.

Sources: Evans, *Greek and Norse Legends*, 105; Keightly, *World Guide to Gnomes, Fairies, Elves, and Other Little People*, 68; Tibbits, *Folk-Lore and Legends, Scandinavian*153–4

Bromie

A NYMPH from the mythical Mount Nysa, Bromie was a nurse to the infant god, Dionysus (Bacchus) in classical Greek mythology. Collectively these NYMPHS were known as the BACCHANTS; their names were BACCHE, BROMIE, ERATO, KISSEIS, KELLIA, KORONIS, MACRIS, and NYSA.

Sources: Daly, *Greek and Roman Mythology A to Z*, 22; Hyginus, *Myths of Hyginus*, 140

Brother Mike

Brother Mike is a local fairy from the folklore if Suffolk, England; his name was called out in a desperate cry of help by a fairy who had been captured by a local farmer.

Sources: Briggs, *Encyclopedia of Fairies*, 44; Rose, *Spirits, Fairies, Leprechauns, and Goblins*, 51, 351

Brown Dwarfs

In German fairy lore the Brown DWARFS are said to live on the Isle of Rügen, Germany's largest island, under the nine hills near Rambin; these mounds are said by some to be hünengräber, or "*giant's graves*." Described as standing more than eighteen inches tall they are decked out in brown outfits topped off with shiny black shoes and a cap upon their heard with a silver bell. The cap they wear renders them invisible; only those who wear a similar cap can see them. Generally a cheerful race they have handsome faces and beautifully delicate hands and feet. Said to be fantastic gold- and silver-smiths, the Brown DWARFS leave their underground homes and come out at night to dance under the stars. At their dances, their black shoes are fashioned with red laces.

Brown DWARFS are known to slip invisible and silently into a person's home and take a child away with them; they have an unlimited ability to shape-shift into any form and can reduce their size to crawl through any key hole. Any such taken child must serve the brown DWARFS for fifty years. Sometimes they will leave golden ducats in the home of a poor widow or play invisibly with a child, keeping an eye on it and making sure it does not fall into danger.

Lazy man-servants and slovenly maids will find they are made the target of a great many pranks played on them by the brown DWARFS. Plagues of nightmare, unrelenting flea-bites and mysterious scratches will suddenly and painfully appear on their body.

Sources: Keightly, *World Guide to Gnomes, Fairies, Elves, and Other Little People*, 175–8; Maclaren, *Fairy Family*, 127–8; Whittier, *Writings*, Volume 1, 421–7

Brown Man of the Muirs

Variations: Brown Man of the Moors, Brown Man of the Moors and Mountains

The Brown Man of the Muirs is a square and stout DWARF with red hair wearing clothes made of bracken; he is a NATURE SPIRIT and a guardian of the animals living in the border country of Scotland. A strict vegetarian surviving solely on apples, nuts, and whortleberries, this fairy is particularly injurious to those who hunt for sport and not for food. There are many stories of this SOLITARY FAIRY enacting his own brand of justice on greedy sportsmen; however according to Skamble's *Fairy Tales*, an angered Brown Man may be appeased and calmed by chanting the phrase "Munko tiggle snobart tolwol dixy crambo," having done so, the red-eyed DWARF will not only be civil but courteous and helpful.

Sources: Briggs, *Encyclopedia of Fairies*, 44–5; Moorey, *Fairy Bible*, 388; Rose, *Spirits, Fairies, Gnomes, and Goblins*, 51; Skamble, *Fairy Tales*, 152–3

Brown Men

Variations: Moor Men

Not to be confused with the SOLITARY FAIRY, BROWN MAN OF THE MUIRS, the Brown Men are a species of Scottish BROWNIE who live on Bodmin Moor, a granite moorland in northeastern Cornwall, England. Described as being short, thin, and always male, these coppery-redheaded fairies are the protectors of the wildlife living on the moor. Brown men are shy by nature and if at all possible will not show themselves to humans.

Sources: Conway, *Magickal, Mystical Creatures*, 56; McCoy, *Witch's Guide to Faery Folk*, 191; Tregarthen, *North Cornwall Fairies and Legends*, 182

Browney

Browney is the guardian of bees in Cornish fairy lore; when the insects swarm, call "Browney! Browney" aloud and the fairy will come invisibly, rounding them up and calming them down. There is some speculation "browney" is the name of the bees themselves, called such after their coloring.

Sources: Briggs, *Encyclopedia of Fairies*, 45; Hitchins, *History of Cornwall*, 712; Rose, *Encyclopedia of Spirits, Fairies, Leprechauns, and Goblins*, 51; Spence, *Fairy Tradition in Britain*, 22

Brownie

Variations: BENDITH Y MAMAU ("the Mother's Blessing"), Bockle, BODACH, Boggart, Brounie (Lowland Scotland), Bookha, Broonie, Brouny, Browny, Budagh, Bwbachod, Bwca, CHIN-CHIN KOBAKAMA, Choa Phum Phi, Dobbie, Domonvoi, Fenodoree, GOBLIN, Good Folk, Heinzelmännchen, HOBGOBLIN, HOB, House Brownie, KILLMOULIS, KOBOLD, Little Man, NIÄGRUISAR, Nis, PIXIE, Psgie, SHELLYCOAT, TIGHE, Tomtgubbe ("old man of the house," Sweden), Tomtra, URISK, YUMBOES

A species of domestic fairy or HOUSE-SPIRIT

from Scottish fairy lore, the brownie is short of stature, only standing about three feet tall. If clothed at all, these brown faced and shaggy headed fairies wears ragged brown clothing. Brownies tend to become attached to one member of a family; generally nocturnal, they finish the housework left undone by the servants. They will also help out on the farm, herding sheep, running errands, and reaping the fields. Care should be taken not to criticize their work or they may become offended; at least they could turn mischievous and at worst they could become an injurious BOGGART. When offended or mistreated, a brownie turns into a BOGGART. The brownie hates cats, cheats, misers, ministers, and teetotalers.

In Scotland the brownies are said to live in the hollow of trees or abandoned houses so long as they are near the family they adopt. According to Highland lore the way to banish a troublesome brownie is to leave a small green hooded-cloak for it by the kitchen fire. The brownie will find the clothing and wear it with great delight but will leave the household, never to been again. Although brownies were active in a household they were seldom if ever actually seen by those who lived there. However, brownies are very social fairies and they frequently hold conferences among themselves. These meeting were typically held along remote rocky shorelines. In one such known meeting place in Scotland is called *Peallaidh an Spùit* (PEALLAIDH of the Spout), another is called *Stochdail a' Chùirt*, and *Brùnaidh an Easain* (Brownie of the little waterfall). Brownies in the Scottish Highlands are said to not have any fingers or toes and Lowland brownies are said not to have a nose.

In England brownies will become very affronted if they are offered anything like a bribe or *doucer* however it will allow itself to succumb and accept a nice bowl of cream or a bit of fresh honeycomb if it was left in private and snug corner. A DOBBIE is a species of brownie, not very intelligent, but basically harmless and means well.

Sources: Bord, *Fairies*, 110; Briggs, *Encyclopedia of Fairies*, 45–9; Froud, *Faeries*, 122; Keightly, *World Guide to Gnomes, Fairies, Elves, and Other Little People*, 402, 418, 443; Moorey, *Fairy Bible*, 55, 57, 284–5; Rose, *Encyclopedia of Spirits, Fairies, Leprechauns, and Goblins*, 51–2

Brownie-Clod

One of the more famous Scottish Highland BROWNIES, Brownie-Clod, so named for his habit of throwing clumps of turf at passer-bys, is the companion and possible husband or son of MEG MOULACH. A humorous individual attached to the Tullochgorm family, Brownie-Clod was simplistic in nature, even for a BROWNIE. It is commonly believed he was scaled to death at the mill of Fincastle.

Sources: Briggs, *Encyclopedia of Fairies*, 49; Dégh, *Folklore on Two Continents*, 81–2; McPherson, *Primitive Beliefs in the Northeast of Scotland*, 107

The Brownie of the Lake

In the fairy-tale *The Brownie of the Lake* by Emile Souvestres the BROWNIE had the ability to take any form he choose and with some difficulty could become invisible. Most often the BROWNIE took the form of a little DWARF all dressed in green. The BROWNIE of the Lake and his people were at war with the KORRIGAN who lived in the White Corn country.

Source: Lang, *Lilac Fairy Book*, 341–348

Brownie Stone

In the Orkney Islands a brownie stone is any stone with a little hole in it; locals will pour milk and wort in it for the fairies to drink.

In the Scottish Highlands there is a town on the outskirts of Inverness called Drumashie; it has a remarkably large brownie stone in it. According to the modern local story, there once were two BROWNIES each standing one side of Loch Bunachton throwing these large stones at one another. The reason for the stone-toss is lost but the fairy on the west side of the river missed his mark. The fairy on the east side of the loch struck his partner and killed him instantly; to this day the boulder is known as Clach-an-duine-mbairbh ("stone of the dead man"). The brownie stone is measured at 25' × 18' × 10' and is estimated to weigh 300 tons.

Sources: Edinburgh Geological Society, *Transactions of the Edinburgh Geological Society*, Volume 4, 65–6; Keightly, *World Guide to Gnomes, Fairies, Elves, and Other Little People*, 172; Kohl, *Travels in Scotland*, 200

Brucie

Brucie is a French word; translated it means "forest SPRITE."

Sources: Kenyon, *Writer's Digest Character Naming Sourcebook*, 124; Newcomb, *Faerie Treasury*, 66

Brugh

Variations: Bru, Bruighean, Bruighin Sithein

In Irish fairy lore a brugh ("fairy place") is a

hill, natural or man-made, where a collection of fairies live. Many burial mounds are also considered to be a brugh, especially if it is where one of the TUATHA DE DANANN are said to be buried.

Sources: Briggs, *Encyclopedia of Fairies*, 50; Evans-Wentz, *Fairy Faith in Celtic Countries*, 327; Mahon, *Ireland's Fairy Lore*, 85–6

Brunhilde

Variations: Brynhilde

In Nordic and Teutonic mythology Brunhilde was one of the named VALKYRIES; she was one of a handful of her kind who not only named but had adventures apart from her cohorts. In the *Poetic Edda*, Brunhilde was strong-minded and strong willed with super-human abilities; she goes against Odin will and is punished for it by being place in a magical sleep and surrounded by a wall of fire. In the story, Brunhilde and the great hero Sigurd exchange oaths of fidelity as well as promise rings. Sigurd is later tricked into drinking a potion which makes him forget Brunhilde and instead he marries Gudrun. Sigurd shape-shifts into his bride's brother, King Gunnar, and completes difficult quests in order to win the love of Brunhilde in the hope she will want to marry the real Gunnar. Although the shape-shifted Sigurd never had intercourse with Brunhilde she tells Gunnar they did as her anger against Sigurd has overshadowed her love for him. By the time the story ends, Brunhilde is an embittered shrew of a woman but nevertheless, lays atop Sigurd's funeral pyre in an attempt to unite with in the grave.

Sources: Doty, *Mythosphere: Issue 4*, 529–30; Rose, *Spirits, Fairies, Leprechauns, and Goblins*, 325

Bruni

Bruni ("brown") was one of the many DWARFS named in the *Voluspa*, the first and best known poem of the *Poetic Edda*, a collection of Old Norse poems dating back to about A.D. 985.

Sources: Daly, *Norse Mythology A to Z*, 22; Wilkinson, *Book of Edda called Völuspá*, 12

Brunissen

In French mythology Brunissen ("the brown one") was a FAIRY QUEEN of Provence. An orphan who raised herself in the magical forest of Broceliande, she grieved after the loss of her parents by crying for seven continuous years. Only the sound of magical songbirds could ease her suffering until Giflet, a knight of the Round Table

who had fallen into a magical sleep, drew her attention and fell in love with him.

Sources: Larrington, *King Arthur's Enchantresses*, 93; Markale, *Women of the Celts*, 74–5; Monaghan, *Encyclopedia of Goddesses*, 63

Bryce

In Greek mythology Bryce was a water–NYMPH and one of the named DANAIDS, the collective name for the daughters of Danaus. In a list compiled by Apollodorus, a Greek scholar and grammarian, she was one of the daughters of the NAIAD, POLYXO and was wedded to Chthonius, one of the sons of the NAIAD, CALIADNE.

Sources: Apollodorus, *Gods and Heroes of the Greeks,* 69; Grimal, *Dictionary of Classical Mythology*, 127; Lemprière, *Classical Dictionary*, 189

Buachailleen

In the fairy lore of Ireland and Scotland the buachailleen ("little boys" or "little herd boys") were well known shape-shifters. Described as wearing pointed red hats and looking like small young men these fairies enjoyed spending their time playing pranks of herds of sheep, such as smearing their coats with mud the night before their shearing. Shepherds would collar their sheep with iron bells to protect them from these little pranksters. The DWARF of Loch Gur, FER FI, assumed the form of a buachailleen very often.

Sources: Evans-Wentz, *Fairy Faith in Celtic Countries*, 82, 409; McCoy, *Witch's Guide to Faery Folk*, 192; Newcomb, *Faerie Treasury*, 48

Bucca

Variations: Bucca-Boo ("fool" or "bogey"), Bug, Bug-a-Boo, Bwca, Bwci, BWBACH, Bwciod, COBLYN, Pwca

In Cornish fairy lore the bucca is a type of GOBLIN living off of the Cornish coast; it is an omen of an upcoming shipwreck. Fishermen, in an attempt to appease it, would leave three fishes on the sandy beach in the hopes of having a good catch; at lunch time some beer and bread were tossed overboard for it as well. In addition to a species of bucca said to live in tin mines the bucca was also used to frighten children to bed and sleep, promising if they did not it would sneak into the home and kidnap them.

It has been supposed by some scholars the bucca was originally a god of the sea reduced to the status of fairy. There is also the Slavic *Bucca-Du* (Black Bucca) and the much rarer *Bucca-*

Widn (White Bucca). Black Bucca may be associated with the Black God, Czernobog and Bucca-Widn may be the corresponding white god, Bielobog.

Sources: Bottrell, *Stories and Folk-Lore of West Cornwall*, 156; Briggs, *Encyclopedia of Fairies*, 50; Evans-Wentz, *Fairy Faith in Celtic Countries*, 147, 164, 175; Monaghan, *Encyclopedia of Celtic Mythology and Folklore*, 64

Bucca Dhu

Variations: Bucca Boo, the God of Darkness

In Cornish folklore bucca dhu ("black bucca" or "evil bucca") is the name given to a bucca that has proven itself to be injurious. Originally the bucca dhu was regarded as an evil divinity; sacrifices of fish were made to its honor order to ward off its wrath. Later, the name evolved into bucca boo and the malicious divinity was described more like a sea-serpent, occasionally it would rear up from the ocean, destroy nets, frighten fishermen, and on occasion attack their vessels. After the introduction and acceptance of Christianity, bucca dhu lost its god status and was reduced to a fairy, a mere NURSERY BOGIE to threaten children who misbehave into being good.

Sources: Koch, *Celtic Culture*, 731; Rose, *Encyclopedia of Spirits, Fairies, Leprechauns, and Goblins*, 51–2; Wright, *Records of the Past*, Volume 10, 144

Bucca Gwidden

Variations: Bucca Guidder, the God of Light

In Cornish folklore bucca Gwidden ("good bucca" or "white bucca") is the name given to a BUCCA proven to be benevolent. Originally the bucca gwidden was regarded as a benign divinity. Sacrifices to it were humble, a bit of bread tossed over the left shoulder and some beer poured on the ground; this was done by fishermen in order to gain its support and have it protect their fishing nets.

After the introduction and acceptance of Christianity, bucca gwidden lost its god status and was reduced to a fairy.

Sources: Monaghan, *Encyclopedia of Celtic Mythology and Folklore*, 64; Rose, *Encyclopedia of Spirits, Fairies, Leprechauns, and Goblins*, 51–2; Wright, *Records of the Past*, Volume 10, 144, 149

Buecubu

Variations: Algue, Guecubu, Huecuvu ("the wanderer without")

In the fairy lore from Chili the buecubu is a type of NATURE SPIRIT. Among its many malicious activities, these injurious fairies said to ride horse to a state of exhaustion; the day after the animal appear sick, its mane and tail tangled and coated in sweat. They are also said to cause earthquakes and anyone who dies in their sleep was suffocated to death by one of them.

Sources: Falkner, *Description of Patagonia*, 115; Hastings, *Encyclopedia of Religion and Ethics*, Part 6, 547; Spence, *Encyclopædia of Occultism*, 98

Bugarik

The tribal people known as the Garos of Assam, a northeastern state of India, have in their fairy lore the seductive SIREN, Bugarik. She is said to live in still pools and is described as having the upper body and arms of a woman but no legs; sometimes her head with its long beautiful hair is said to be seen floating down the river with the current. She will attempt to kill anyone who she can catch, adding their hair to her own.

Sources: Crooke, *Religion and Folklore of Northern India*, 60; Hastings, *Encyclopedia of Religion and Ethics*, Part 24, 718; Playfair, *The Garos*, 99, 116

Bugbear

Variations: Bogey, Boggle-Boo, BOGLE Boo, Bucca Boo, Bug Boy, Bug, Bug-A-Boo, Bugaboo, Bugbeare, Buggy Bow

The bugbear of European folklore is a type of HOBGOBLIN described as looking like a monsterous bear or horrific beast. Fond of eating naughty children it is used as a NURSERY BOGIE to frighten children into good behavior. The word *bugbear* is also a synonym for a scarecrow.

Sources: Briggs, *Encyclopedia of Fairies*, 52; Daniels, *Encyclopaedia of Superstitions, Folklore, and the Occult Sciences of the World*, 1415; Edwards, *Hobgoblin and Sweet Puck*, 91, 97

Buggane

An injurious and malicious fairy from the Isle of Man, the buggane is a variant of the BOGGART. Bugganes are described as OGRE-like beings, covered in black hair and sporting claws, a maw of sharp teeth, and jagged tusks. It also popularly takes the shape of a BLACK DOG with a white collar; a GIANT, with or without a head; and a hideous black cow without a head or tail. These fairies are a favorite companion to evil magicians.

Other sources describe the bugganes as being a type of water fairy living in streams and waterfalls. These bugganes are shape-shifters most often take the form or a cow or horse; when they assume a human form they are easily known for what they are, as they cannot hide their long hair, nails, and teeth.

There are many stories of the evils of the buggane, but the most popular of them all is called *The Buggane of Saint Trinion*. To summarize, as the local church was being constructed an offended buggane would come each night and undo, or worse, the work which was done each day. Although the church was named Saint Trinian's Church it is called to this day Keeill Vrisht ("Broken Church") as its roof was never completed.

Sources: Briggs, *Encyclopedia of Fairies*, 51; Moore, *Folk-Lore of the Isle of Man*, 60–1; Rose, *Giants, Monsters, and Dragons*, 59–60

Buggar

A buggar is a type of shape-shifting fairy in British folklore similar to the BROWNIE and GOBLIN of Scotland.

Sources: Edwards, *Hobgoblin and Sweet Puck*, 91; McCoy, *Witch's Guide to Faery Folk*, 28

Buggare

Variations: Boggane

At the foot of Greeba Mountain on the Isle of Man lies Saint Trinian's church; it has walls and a tower but no roof, as it is said the injurious and malicious fairy Buggare tore it off in a fit of rage. Some say it lives within a rock in nearby Laxey. *Boggane* is a general Manx word applied to any frightful visiage.

Sources: Moore, *Manx Note Book*, Volume 1, 42; Sutton, *Drama of Storytelling in T.E. Brown's Manx Yarns*, 141; Thomas, *World of Islands*, 91

Bugul-Noz

In Breton fairy mythology Bugul-Noz ("Night Shepherd") is a tall and alarming NATURE SPIRIT living in the rural forests of Brittany. The last of his kind, this fairy is desperately lonely; he is so hideous and ugly the animals of the woods avoid him and will flee when he approaches. Aware of his frightful visage the gentle and kind Bugul-Noz is considerate enough to call out as he wanders the woodlands during twilight, least he surprise a person and frighten them to death. Bugul-Noz is a sort of NURSERY BOGIE for adults, as he is said to appear at dusk, a time when adults should quit their work for the day and head back to their homes; once indoors, they can lock themselves in and safely rest and sleep.

Sources: Evans-Wentz, *Fairy-Faith in Celtic Countries*, 192; McCoy, *Witch's Guide to Faery Folk*, 193–4

Bukura e dheut

Variations: E Bukura e Dynjas, E Bukura e dheut

In Albanian fairy lore Bukura e dheut ("the beauty of the earth ") is a beautiful, crafty, and magic weilding FAIRY QUEEN, the very epitome of happiness; the fairies of her court of capricious and unpredictable, sometimes beneficial and other times injurious. Although she may have an underwater realm at her disposal, Bukura e dheut is believed to live in a magnificent castle high in the mountains of the underworld; it is guarded day and night by a three-headed dog or *kulshedra*, similar to Cerberus of Greek lore. The magical powers Bukura e dheut weild with great art and ease originates from her dress; her favorite spell is transforming men into pigs, similar to the Greek sorceress, CIRCE. In many tales a hero sets forth to steal a single strand of her golden hair; if he is able to succeed in the perilous task she will reward him but should he fail she will steal his possessions and further punish him in any number of ways.

At one time in ancient Albanian mythology Bukura e dheut was considered to be a goddess, the lover of Tomor, the supreme god of the Illyrians; her sister was named as Bukura e detit ("the beauty of the sea").

Sources: Illes, *Encyclopedia of Spirits*, 378; Robert, *Dictionary of Albanian Religion, Mythology, and Folk Culture*, 79–80; Rose, *Spirits, Fairies, Leprechauns, and Goblins*, 351

Bukwas

Variations: Bakwas, Boks, Bowis, Bukwis, Pi'kis, Pokwas, Pukmis, Puks, Pukwubis

A NATURE SPIRIT of the Kwakiutl people of Vancouver Island Bukwas ("ape" or "man of the woods") lived deep within the Pacific Northwest forests; he was most often sighted early in the morning along the seashore to gather cockles and shellfish. Described as having a hair covered body with long arms and a broad chest, it walks with a looping gate; often times it whistles. If ever Bukwas presented food to a traveler they should never eat it, as doing so will cause them to enter into the land of the dead. Bukwas was seen also as a spirit of death; seeing him was considered to be a death omen.

Sources: Eberhart, *Mysterious Creatures*, 73–74; Illes, *Encyclopedia of Spirits*, 307

Bullbeggar

Variations: Boe Bulbagger, Bull-Beggar, Bullebeggar, Scare Bug

In Surrey England, a bullbeggar is said to b a non-descript HOBGOBLIN or fairy spirit of a generally frightening appearance. Assuming the form of an injured person the bullbeggar will lie on the road and wait for a good Samaritan to come along and help. When the person leans down to offer assistance the bullbeggar will spring up to its full height and assume its enormous and shadowy form. Wailing out, the fairy will chase the person, never catching them but frightening them all the same, until they reach safety. Less dramatic but just as frightening the bullbeggar will stalk behind a traveler, become a vague black shadow, and make the sound of foot falls.

Sources: Briggs, *Encyclopedia of Fairies*, 52; Monaghan, *Encyclopedia of Celtic Mythology and Folklore*, 64; Nares, *Glossary of Words, Phrases, Names,* 118; Rose, *Spirits, Fairies, Leprechauns, and Goblins*, 54–5

Bumburr

Bumburr was one of the many DWARFS named in the *Voluspa*, the first and best known poem of the *Poetic Edda*, a collection of Old Norse poems dating back to about A.D. 985.

Sources: Pfeiffer, *Visit to Iceland and the Scandinavian North*, 325; Wägner, *Asgard and the Gods*, 311

Bunyip

Variations: Buneep

An Australian fairy-creature standing only about four-foot tall, the shy and seldom seen bunyip ("devil" or "spirit") looks like a small, plump human with backward facing feet. Living in lakes, rivers, and swamplands, these mud-covered fairies will bark out a warning if danger is near although there are some stories in which it will attack anyone who enters into its territory.

The first sighting of the bunyip came in the New South Wales area in 1800 and continued on into the twentieth century. It is believed by the Abonorigials lakes Bathurst and George are sacred to the bunyip however after a dam was built across the Murray River in the 1920s and 30s, sightings of the bunyip all but stopped. Although most native bunyip drawings depict this FAIRY ANIMAL in a wide array of shapes and sizes most often it is shown as having flippers, walrus-like tusks, and a horse-like tail; it has been speculated the bunyip are nothing more than a fur-seals.

Sources: Coleman, *Cryptozoology A to Z*, 49–50; Ho, *Mysteries Unwrapped*, 26–7; McCoy, *Witch's Guide to Faery Folk*, 194–5

Buri

Variations: Burinn

Buri ("son") was one of the many DWARFS named in the *Voluspa*, the first and best known poem of the *Poetic Edda*, a collection of Old Norse poems dating back to about A.D. 985.

Sources: Daly, *Norse Mythology A to Z*, 22; Wilkinson, *Book of Edda called Völuspá*, 12

Buschfrauen

Variations: Buschweiber ("wild maidens"), Dziwozony, Moosfraulein (Moss-damsels)

The German NYMPH-like NATURE SPIRITS known as the buschfrauen ("bush women") live communally in the hollows of trees but they only appear alone. Standing a little taller than a DWARF they have golden hair and are most likely to be seen when bread is baking. The white-haired and mossy-footed FAIRY QUEEN of the buschfrauen is named Buschgrossmutter ("Grandmother of the Bushes"); she is both respected and feared.

Sources: Elliott, *Modern Language Notes*, Volume 16, 65; Monaghan, *New Book of Goddesses and Heroines*, 76

Buttery Sprites

Variations: Buttery Spirits, Cellar Demon

Buttery Sprites are the laymen's equivalent of the ABBEY LUBBER. British folklore says these fairies can eat any human food not marked with a cross; the buttery sprites feed off of any food abused as a gift, belittled, dishonestly prepared, ill-gotten, or ungratefully received.

Sources: Briggs, *Encyclopedia of Fairies*, 54–5; McCoy, *Witch's Guide to Faery Folk*, 195; Rose, *Spirits, Fairies, Gnomes, and Goblins*, 56

Bwaganod

Variations: Boobach, BWBACH ("BUGBEAR")

In Welsh fairy lore the bwaganod is very similar to the Scottish BROWNIE, especially in its domestic helpfulness and ability to turn injurious when angered or insulted. With a strong dislike for dissenting ministers and teetotalers the bwaganod will use their shape-shifting ability to assume an animal or human form to cause all manner of mischief, however, these fairies have not perfected this ability and if one looks carefully at it, the flaws of its altered form will be apparent. These fairies enjoy a full pipe, a good ale, and a seat close to the fire.

Sources: Briggs, *Encyclopedia of Fairies*, 55–6; Sikes, *British Goblins*, 27

Bwbach (plural: bwbachod)

Variations: Boobach, Bucca, Bwbachod, Bwca, Bwci, Coblyn

The bwbach ("Goblin") was a good-natured Welsh household fairy similar to the Brownie which enjoyed playing pranks; among its favorites were lifting up the skirts of old women, making dogs bark, pinching faces, and scaring babies. The bwbach were said to dress like a farmer, have dark skin, and a long nose. They disdained abstinence in any form and so long as the maid remembered to leave out a small offering of cream for it every night the bwbach would assist her in chores; it was especially partial to cwrw da (ale). However, if the cream was forgotten or the little fairy wasdispleased in any way it would become an injurious poltergeist-like spirit. If its name was ever asked the bwbach would leave the house in a fit of anger.

Sources: Arrowsmith, *Field Guide to the Little People*, 63; Eason, *Complete Guide to Faeries and Magical Beings* 37; Monaghan, *Encyclopedia of Celtic Mythology and Folklore*, 64; Sikes, *British Goblins*, 27, 33–35

Bwcca (plural: bwci)

Variations: Bucca, Bwca, Gwarwyn-a-Throt

Bwcca is the Welsh version of the Cornish Bucca and the Scottish Brownie and Puck. While the family it has adopted is asleep the bwcca will perform menial household tasks in exchange for a bowl of flummery with wheat bread or some sweet milk. Bwcca are benign and loyal but if provoked can turn injurious and malicious becoming a Boggart. When a bwcca has been turned a *dyn cynnil* ("wise man") must be call to "lay it low" or exorcize the fairy. This process involves discovering where the Boggart is hiding and reading scriptures at it, banishing it typically to the Red Sea for several generations.

Sources: Briggs, *Encyclopedia of Fairies*, 56–7; Froud, *Faeries*, 123; Narváez, *Good People*, 244; Rose, *Spirits, Fairies, Gnomes, and Goblins*, 58

Bwgan (plural: bwganod)

Appearing at dusk in an array of various animal forms the bwganod ("ghost," "Hobgoblin," "specter," or "Sprite") of Welsh lore was believed to live in the roots of trees near a well in Llanllughan-Adfa-Cefn Coch in Montgomeryshire.

Sources: Hooke, *Trees in Anglo-Saxon England*, 105; Illes, *Encyclopedia of Spirits*, 145

Bwyd ellyllon

Bwyd ellyllon ("elves food" or "goblins meat") was a poisonous mushroom in Welsh fairy lore was considered to be Fairy Food.

Sources: Brayley, *Graphic and Historical Illustrator*, 294; Keightly, *World Guide to Gnomes, Fairies, Elves, and Other Little People*, 412; Sikes, *British Goblins*, 12

Byblis

Byblis was a Nymph of Ionia. She was in love with her twin brother, Caunos (Kaunos), but when her feelings were not reciprocated she threw herself off a cliff in an attempt to commit suicide. She was saved from death when the local Nymph transmuted the falling Byblis into a Nymph. Still grieving, her constant flow of tears transformed her into a fountain.

Sources: Buxton. *Forms of Astonishment*, 199; Larson, *Greek Nymphs*, 204

Byze

A Naiad of the river Erasinos in Argos in classical Greek mythology, Byze, along with Anchirhoe, Maera, and Melite, was one of the attendants to the goddess, Britomartis.

Source: Antoninus Liberalis, *Metamorphoses of Antoninus Liberalis*, 100

Byzia

Byzia was one of the Naiads; she was said to have raised Byzas, the founder of Byzantine.

Source: Day, *God's Conflict with the Dragon and the Sea*, 394

Cabyll-Ushtey

Variations: Glashtinhe

In Manx fairy lore the pale grey cabyll-ushtey ("water horse") is a species of water horse similar to the Scottish Each Uisce, although not as injurious. Occasionally this Fairy Animal will prey upon cattle and humans alike, ripping them to pieces; stampede horse herds, and steal children. The cabyll-ushtey also has the ability to shapeshift into a handsome young man.

Sources: Briggs, *Encyclopedia of Fairies*, 57; Conway, *Magickal, Mystical Creatures*, 45; Monaghan, *Encyclopedia of Celtic Mythology and Folklore*, 67

Caccavecchia

Variations: Buffardello, Linchetto, Mazapegolo

Possibly originating in Etruscan lore, the caccavecchia of Italian folklore are a species of small house elves, they cannot stand disorder of any type. These fairies are said to cause nightmares and make strange noises in the house during the night.

Sources: Arrowsmith, *Field Guide to the Little People*, 188; Euvino, *Complete Idiot's Guide to Italian History and Culture*, 274

Cacy Taperere

Variations: SACI, Sasy Perere

In southern Brazilian fairy lore Cacy Taperere is a DWARF-like spirit; he is described as having fiery eyes, one leg, smoking a pipe, and wearing a red cap. A household fairy similar to the BROWNIE, when not being helpful the cacy taperere enjoys playing little pranks, such as hiding objects or moving belongings.

Sources: Leach, *Funk and Wagnalls Standard Dictionary of Folklore, Mythology, and Legend*, n.p.; Rose, *Spirits, Fairies, Gnomes, and Goblins*, 58

Caelia

A FAIRY QUEEN of British legend and literature, Caelia ("heavenly"), she was the mother of the Fairy Knight, Tom a' Lincoln, an illegitimate son of King Arthur. Despite the fact he was married, she took her son as a lover and they had a son who grew to become the Red Rose Fairy Knight. Caelia bore three daughters, Charissa (charity), Fidelia (faith), and Speranza (hope). She committed suicide, drowning herself when her son and lover quit her for Anglitora, the daughter of Prester John. Her body is said to be interred in King Arthur's realm.

Sources: Bruce, *Arthurian Name Dictionary*, 94; Hughes, *British Chronicles*, Volume 1, 199; Spence, *Dictionary of Medieval Romance and Romance Writers*, 357, Spencer, *Faerie Queen*, Book 1, 209

Caer

Variations: Caer Ibormeith

In the lore of Connacht, Ireland, Caer ("yew berry") is a beautiful fairy maiden living in the shape-shifted form of a swan; it was adorned with necklaces of golden chains and bells.

When the handsome God of Love, Angus, saw the beautiful Caer in a dream, he fell so deeply in love with her he immediately fell ill upon waking because he was not with her.

In one version of the myth Angus sought out Caer's father, Ethal, one of the TUATHA DE DANANN, and asked permission to marry her; it was given on the provision the young suitor could pick out his beloved from a flock of swans.

Angus agreed and on the selected day went to the lake where he immediately knew his beloved Caer from all other swans. As he called out her name he transformed into a swan himself; together, the couple flew away.

In an alternative version of the myth Angus had to have his father, the DAGDA, imprison Ethal to persuade him to give Caer marriage. In a final version, it was Caer who lured Angus to the lake in order to transform him into a swan so they could be together, forever.

Sources: Aldhouse-Green, *Celtic Myths*, 38–9; Evan-Wentz, *Fairy Faith in Celtic Countries*, 310–11; Illes, *Encyclopedia of Spirits*, 310; Mountain, *Celtic Encyclopedia*, Volume 2, 401

Caillagh ny Groamagh

Variations: Cailliagh ny Gueshag

In Manx lore, Caillagh ny Groamagh ("HAG of the sulks") was an Irish witch who was thrown into the sea and floated over and landed on the Isle of Man. She is associated with the weather. It is believed at the beginning of spring she intends to leave her house to collect twigs for her woodpile. If the weather is unpleasant and keeps her indoors she burns through her stores and winter ends early. If the weather in pleasant and she is able to collect what she needs winter will linger on.

Sources: Briggs, *Encyclopedia of Fairies*, 57–8; Killip, *Folklore of the Isle of Man*, 171; Monaghan, *Encyclopedia of Celtic Mythology and Folklore*, 68–9

Cailleac Bhuer

Variations: BLACK ANNIS, Blue HAG, Cally Berry, Daughter of Grianan, Stone Woman

Cailleac Bhuer is a personification of winter and likely a diminished goddess who was reduced to fairy status. A nocturnal, SOLITARY FAIRY she described as looking like an old woman wearing black or blue and white tattered clothes. Some descriptions of her have a crow sitting on her left shoulder. The holly staff she carries has the ability to kill a person with a single touch. As she flies over the Scottish Highlands, she drops stones on people as she passes overhead.

On May Eve Cailleac Bhuer will throw her staff under a holly bush and shape-shifted into a grey stone, then on each All Hallows Eve she would be reborn and set out blighting the earth, calling down the snow.

Sources: Briggs, *Encyclopedia of Fairies*, 58–9; Eason, *Complete Guide to Faeries and Magical Being*, 162; McCoy, *Witch's Guide to Faery Folk*, 139

Cailleach Bera

Variations: Beara, Cailleach Beara, Cailleach Bhearra, Cailleach Bheirre, Cailleach Bearra, Cailleach Beare, Cailleach Bherri, Calliagh Birra

Cailleach Bera ("HAG of Bera") of Irish fairy lore is a gigantic HAG of supernatural cunning and strength who is credited as being a great mountain builder. She is very similar to CAILLEAC BHUER, but not as closely associated to winter. Local legend says one day while carrying stones in her apron the strong broke, spilling the load and thereby creating the Beare Peninsula near Cork and the Hebrides Islands, Scotland.

Sources: Briggs, *Encyclopedia of Fairies*, 58; Rose, *Giants, Monsters, and Dragons*, 64

Caipora

Variations: Caapora

Caipora ("forest-dweller") is an individual fairy from the folklore of the tupi-guarani speaking people of Brazil. Described as looking like a small, dark-skinned native it wears no clothing but its body is covered by its mane of long black hair; sighting include it smoking a cigar or riding upon a large pecari, a species of small wild hog. Occasionally the caipora is described as being more anthropomorphic and having the head of a fox or only having one leg; more rarely, it is said to be female.

With its backward turned feet this forest dwelling fairy or NATURE SPIRIT lures people off into the woods. It is believed the Caipora see itself as the King of the animals and will punish any hunter who does not track and stalk game fairly, becoming vengeful if unacceptable methods of hunting are employed. Offerings of cachaça (a Brazilian drink), carvings of pigs, and tobacco are left for him.

Sources: Cau, *Brazil*, 81–2; Freyre, *Masters and the Slaves*, 99–100

Cait Sith

Variations: Cat SÍDHE, Cat Sith, Elfin Cats

The cait sith ("fairy cat") is spoken of in the fairy lore of both Ireland and the Scottish Highlands. Described as looking like a black cat with white mark on the center of its chest, this FAIRY ANIMAL is said to somewhere between the size of a large dog or a small calf. Large and ferocious, especially if surprised, the caith sith are said to have a king among their kind called BIG EARS.

In the Scottish Highlands it is a popular belief the cait sith is not a FAIRY ANIMAL at all but a transformed witch. It has been proposed by some the cat sith is a hybrid animal between the European Wildcats and the domestic cats only found in Scotland; these large black hybrids are typically called Kellas Cats. These animals cannot be domesticated.

Sources: Avant, *Mythological Reference*, 86; Briggs, *Encyclopedia of Fairies*, 60; Campbell, *Superstitions of the Highlands and Islands of Scotland*, 5, 32

Caliadne

Variations: Caliadna, Kaliadne

Caliadne ("beautiful holy") was a NYMPH from the mythology of classical Greece and Rome. One of the Naiads of the Nile River, she was the wife of the Egyptian king, Aigyptos. Their twelve sons marry the twelve daughters of her sister, POLYXO.

Sources: Bell, *Women of Classical Mythology*, 436; Lemprière, *Classical Dictionary*, 118; Parada, *Genealogical Guide to Greek Mythology*, 48, 128

Callianassa

Born one of the 3,000 daughters of the Titians, Oceanus and Tethys, Callianassa ("beautiful queen") was one of the named OCEANIDS.

Sources: Apollodorus, *Apollodorus' Library and Hyginus' Fabulae*, 5; Day, *God's Conflict with the Dragon and the Sea*, 64

Callianira

Callianira was one of the named NEREID who accompanied THETIS in mourning the loss of her son, Achilles.

Sources: Chapman, *Chapman's Homer*, 373; Homer, *Iliads of Homer*, 137

Callicantzaroi

In the fairy lore from Albania, Greece, and Italy the callicantzaroi are a species of nude, skinny, and small, TROOPING FAIRIES; they suffer from some degree of blindness. Some sources describe these fairies as being violently dangerous, terrorizing the countryside during the twelve days after Christmas, raping women whenever the opportunity presents itself. They are believed to be terrified of fire and driven off by brandishing fire-brands. In Greek lore they are associated more as a creature and kin to the centaurs, living in caves during the day, eating frogs and snakes. Offerings of pig bones or pork sausages were made to them. Less explicit lore says these fairies are merely malicious a mischievous NATURE SPIRITS riding around of chickens and wearing elaborate headdresses during their Yule-time rides.

Sources: Euvino, *Complete Idiot's Guide to Italian History and Culture*, 274; Kingsley, *Heroes*, 171; Livo, *Storytelling Folklore Sourcebook*, 171; McCoy, *Witch's Guide to Faery Folk*, 139

Callidice

In classical Greek mythology Callidice was a water–NYMPH and one of the named DANAIDS, the collective name for the daughters of Danaus. In a list compiled by Apollodorus, a Greek scholar and grammarian, she was one of the daughters of Crino and was wedded to Pandion, one of the sons of Hephaestine.

Sources: Bell, *Women in Classical Mythology*, 150, 455; Grimal, *Dictionary of Classical Mythology*, 127

Calliope

One of the nine CANONICAL MUSES Calliope ("beautiful voice"), born one of the many daughter of the god, Zeus (Jupiter), was the chief of the CANONICAL MUSES and the MUSE of the epic poetry and song; she is depicted in art as carrying a writing tablet. By Oeager, king of Thrace, she became the mother of Orpheus, the legendary musician, poet, and prophet of Greek mythology.

Sources: Hesiod, *Homeric Hymns and Homerica*, 85, 571; Littleton, *Gods, Goddesses, and Mythology*, Volume 11, 921; Peterson, *Mythology in Our Midst*, 121

Calliphaea

Variations: Kalliphaeia

A NAIAD from classical Greek mythology Calliphaea ("lovely shining") was one of the four NYMPHS of the healing springs of the river Kytheros in Elis, located in southern Greece. Collectively they were known as the IODINES and they names were CALLIPHAEA, IASIS, PEGAEA, and SYNALLAXIS and it was believed to bathe in one of their springs was a cure-all for an array of illnesses and pains.

Sources: Larson, *Greek Nymphs*, 158; Pausanias, *Commentary on Book I: Attica*, 319

Callirrhoe

Variations: Callirrhoë

Born one of the 3,000 daughters of the Titians, Oceanus and Tethys, Callirrhoe ("beautiful stream") was one of the named OCEANIDS. Fathered by Chrysaor, she gave birth to Geryon, a GIANT with the bodies of three men joined together at the waist. This NAIAD had three husbands, Chrysaor, who fathered Geryon and Echidna; Neilus who fathered Chione; and Poseidon (Neptune) who fathered Minyas. With her lover Tros, she gave birth to Ganymede.

Sources: Boswell, *What Men or Gods Are These*, 58; Day, *God's Conflict with the Dragon and the Sea*, 64; Hesiod, *Works of Hesiod, Callimachus, and Theognis*, 20; Westmoreland, *Ancient Greek Beliefs*, 24

Callisto

Variations: Kallisto, THEMISTO

In ancient Greek mythology Callisto was a sworn virginal NYMPH seduced by the god, Zeus (Jupiter); through this union she bore a son named Arcas. According to legend, Hera (Juno), the wife of Zeus (Jupiter) transformed Callisto into a bear as punishment for her tryst but some versions of the myth say Zeus did this to Callisto himself to save her from the wrath of his jealous wife. As an adult, Arcas unaware of his mother's form, came across the bear and hunted her. As Callisto fled to Zeus' sanctuary on Mount Lykaion the god took pity on the developing situation and transformed them both into constellations, Arcturus and Ursa Major.

Sources: Anderson, *King Arthur in Antiquity*, 25, 34; Evan-Wentz, *Fairy Faith in Celtic Countries*, 311–12; Littleton, *Gods, Goddesses, and Mythology*, Volume 4. 441; Roman, *Encyclopedia of Greek and Roman Mythology*, 78–9

Calypso

Variations: Atlantis, KALYPSO

A NYMPH from Greek mythology, Calypso ("to conceal," "to cover," "concealing the knowledge," or "to hide") was born one of the 3,000 daughters of the Titians, Oceanus and Tethys, Calypso was one of the named OCEANIDS; she was said to have lived on the island of Ogygia where she detained the hero Odysseus for five or seven years, sources conflict. Both a NYMPH and a goddess, in very ancient Greek lore Calypso may have originally been a death goddess.

Homer, the greatest ancient Greek epic poet and author of the *Iliad* and the *Odyssey*, dose not mention Calypso as having children. Some accounts say after the *Odyssey* takes place she bore Odysseus a son, Latinus, although the NYMPH CIRCE is commonly named as his mother. Other accounts claim Calypso and Odysseus had two children together, Nausithous and Nausinous.

Sources: Bell, *Bell's New Pantheon or Historical Dictionary of the Gods*, 112; Boswell, *What Men or Gods Are These*, 58; Day, *God's Conflict with the Dragon and the Sea*, 64; Grimal, *Dictionary of Classical Mythology*, 86; Hesiod, *Works of Hesiod, Calli-*

machus, and Theognis, 20; Keightly, *World Guide to Gnomes, Fairies, Elves, and Other Little People,* 444; Westmoreland, *Ancient Greek Beliefs,* 24

Camenae

In ancient Roman lore the camenae were a species of water NYMPH, their fountains were considered sacred in Roman groves. Over time the rustic camenaes were absorbed into the collection of MUSES; they oversaw the celebrations of national exploits, a unique blending of Greek and Roman mythology.

Sources: Barchiesi, *Rituals in Ink,* 46, 54; Myers, *Ovid's Causes,* 110

Cancaline

In the fairy-tale *The Good Little Mouse* by Madame d'Aulnoy, Cancaline was a cruel fairy and the enemy of the kind and good but unnamed fairy of the story; this fairy is refered to as the MOUSE FAIRY. Older and therefore more powerful than her unnamed adversary, Cancaline stole the infant Princess Delicia out from under the protective care of her unnamed FAIRY GODMOTHER.

Sources: Lang, *Red Fairy Book,* 146–57

Candelas

In Italian folklore the candelas ("candles") are a species of tiny fairies; small in size, they appear in groups and look like the twinkling lights of fireflies.

Sources: Euvino, *Complete Idiot's Guide to Italian History and Culture,* 274; Mccoy, *Witch's Guide to Faery Folk,* 338

Cannered-Noz

In the northwestern region of Brittany, France, the cannered-noz ("washerwomen of the night") live along river banks, these fairies are normally invisible but when they materialize they appear as small peasant women. Similar to the Bean-Sidhe, the cannere-noz are seen at night washing the death shrouds or clothing of those individuals who died without first having gained absolution from the Church.

Sources: Evans-Wentz, *Fairy-Faith in Celtic Countries,* 185; Rose, *Spirits, Fairies, Leprechauns, and Goblins,* 61, 351

Canonical Muses

Variations: Mousai, the Pierides

In Greek mythology the canonical muses were a collection of nine MUSES; they were the protectors of the arts, music, poetry, song and the sciences related to civilization and culture. The muses were born the daughters of the god Zeus (Jupiter) and Mnemosyne ("Memory"); because they were born at the springs of Pieria on Mount Olympus these nine sisters are sometimes referred to as the Pierides.

The names of the canonical muses are CALLIOPE, CLIO, ERATO, EUTERPE, MELPOMENE, POLYHYMIA, TERPSICHORE, TRALIA, and URANIA.

Sources: Hunt, *Masonic Symbolism,* 468; Thomassen, *Canon and Canonicity,* 118

Caoineag

Variations: CAOINTEACH

A fairy spirit or NAIAD similar to the BANSHEE, the caoineag ("weeper") of the Scottish Highlands was often heard wailing out in the night near waterfalls, but was never seen and could not be approached to grant wishes. The caoineag was active just before a death in the clan it adopted; the person who first hears the cry will either face death or a great sorrow.

Sources: Avant, *Mythological Reference,* 88; Briggs, *Encyclopedia of Fairies,* 61; Rose, *Giants, Monsters and Dragons,* 61; Thompson, *Supernatural Highlands,* 127

Caointeach

A female fairy spirit, the caointeach ("wailer") was a localized version of the CAOINEAG, a species of Scottish Highland BANSHEE; it was specific to Argyllshire and Skye islands and was associated to the Currie, Kelly, Mackay, Macmillan, Mathison, Mcfarlane, and Shaw families. Sometimes it was described as beating cloths against a river stone as if washing wearing a green gown and white night cap.

Sources: Avant, *Mythological Reference,* 88; Briggs, *Encyclopedia of Fairies,* 61; Illes, *Encyclopedia of Spirits,* 318

Capelthwaite

Capelthwaite is a fairy creature, a BLACK DOG said to be the size of a calf; it roams Westmorland, an area in North West England and the adjacent Yorkshire. With the ability to assume any quadropedal form it likes, Capelthwaite prefers its canine visage. When one of these fairies takes up residence on a farm it will help round-up and herd sheep and will pleasantly regard the residing family; however, it will be injurious and malicious to strangers.

Sources: Briggs, *Encyclopedia of Fairies,* 62; Henderson, *Notes on the Folk-Lore of the Northern Coun-*

ties of England and the Borders, 275–6; Monaghan, *Encyclopedia of Celtic Mythology and Folklore*, 47

Capheira

Born one of the 3,000 daughters of the Titians, Oceanus and Tethys, Capheira ("her Breath is Thunderstorms") was one of the named OCEANIDS in classical Greek mythology; she was also said to be of one of the NEREIDS, the daughters of Nerues and DORIS.

Sources: Daly, *Greek and Roman Mythology A to Z*, 120; Grimal, *Dictionary of Classical Mythology*, 88; Smith, *New Classical Dictionary of Greek and Roman Biography, Mythology and Geography*, Volume 2, 860

Carabosse

In the French fairy-tale, "*The Princess Mayblossom*" ("*Le Princesse Printaniere*") by Par Mme. d' Aulnoy, the fairy Carabosse appeared in the royal court as a dark-skinned and ugly nurse seeking to enact vengeance on the king. As a child the monarch placed some sulfur in her porridge as a prank. By use of her magic wand Carabosse can summon her chariot of fire which is drawn by winged DRAGONS. In order to protect his infant daughter he and his counselors decided to invite every fairy for a thousand miles to the child's christening ceremony without inviting Carabosse for fear she would ruin it. On the thousand fairies invited only five could attend but each one bestowed the child with a blessing. the first promised the child would be beautiful; the second said the infant would have perfect understanding of anything explained to her the very first time; the third fairy blessed the child with the ability to sing like a nightingale; and the fourth foretold the child would succeed in every task she undertook. Before the fifth fairy could give her gift to the child, the fairy Carabosse appeared and doomed the infant to be the unluckiest of all the unlucky until she was twenty years old. After her parting the first fairy then blessed the child, promising her a long and happy life once her twentieth birthday had passed.

Source: Lang, *Red Fairy Book*, 13–29

Carlin

Variations: Carline

In Scotland Carlin ("old woman") is the spirit of Samhain (Halloween) eve. At the end of the harvest, the last sheaf of barley or corn is cut and dressed up to look like her, an old woman, and hung inside the home to ward off evil spirits.

Sources: Avant, *Mythological Reference*, 185; Mon-aghan, *Encyclopedia of Celtic Mythology and Folklore*, 69, 75; Morton, *Halloween Encyclopedia*, 54

Carya

In ancient Greek mythology Carya was a HAMADRYAD of the nut tree; she was born from the incestuous relationship between Oxylus and his sister.

Sources: Athenaeus of Naucratis, *Deipnosophists*, Volume 1, 131; Gerber, *Greek Iambic Poetry*, 391

Caryatid

Variations: Catyatids, Karyatis

The Caryatids were a species of NYMPHS living in and protect nut trees.

Sources: Larson, *Greek Nymphs*, 152; Littleton, *Gods, Goddesses, and Mythology*, Volume 4, 440; Newcomb, *Faerie Treasury*, 17

Castalia

Castalia was one of the NAIADS, a NYMPH, and a daughter of Achelous, was loved by the god, Apollo. Rejecting his affections, she fled from him and threw herself into the spring at the base of Mount Parnassos at Delphi; the spring was then named after her. Water from this sacred spring was used to clean the Delphian temples and to inspire poets.

Sources: Adkins, *Handbook to Life in Ancient Rome*; 283; Day, *God's Conflict with the Dragon and the Sea*, 394; Illes, *Encyclopedia of Spirits*, 320

The Cauld Lad

Variations: Cauld Lad of Hilton, Cauld Lad of Hylton

The Cauld Lad was a BROWNIE living in Hilton Hall, in the vale of the Wear, England. Servants claimed they could hear him knocking around in the kitchen at night and singing a sad song. The servants were not appreciative of how Cauld Lad would rearrange the utensils and cookware every night so they conspired to rid themselves of him in the usual way. A small green cloak and hat were left out for him to discover neatly folded next to the kitchen hearth. They spied on him, saw him try the clothes on and then dance about the room in great delight. At the first crow of the cock he disappeared, calling out he never would be seen there again.

There are many version of the story, one claims Cauld Lad was not a BROWNIE but rather a ghost dating back to the 16th or 17th century. Another rendition tells the tale of a stable boy who was murdered by Baron Hylton because the servant was caught courting the nobleman's daughter. Yet another version says the nobleman ordered his horse to be tacked and ready early in the morning but the stable boy, Robert Skelton, overslept; in a sudden fit of anger, the Barron beat him to death in a number of way including beating him with a riding crop decapitating him, and stabbing him with a nearby pitchfork. No matter how he died, the body was thrown into a pond or well and was discovered some months later. The Baron was tried for the boys murder but had a proven alibi, the arrest and trial of Robert Hylton, 13th Baron Hylton is a matter of historical record; he was pardoned in 1609. Shortly after, strange occurrences began to happen in the castle, off noises were heard and mysterious lights were seen. A cook once said he saw the spirit of a naked boy shivering and saying "I'm cauld" ("I'm cold").

Sources: Briggs, *Encyclopedia of Fairies* 68; Jacobs, *English Fairy Tales*, 203–5; Keightly, *World Guide to Gnomes, Fairies, Elves, and Other Little People*, 296

Ccoa

Ccoa is an injurious spirit from the folklore of the Quechua tribes in the highlands of Peru. Described as looking like a flying catlike being, this NATURE SPIRIT brings hail and lightning, destroys crops, urinates rain, and kills with its lightning. Larger than a domestic cat, it is said to be grey with black stripes; it arches it back and spits hail when threatened. Ccoa sponsors sorcerers and gives them their powers; it will not harm farmers who make daily offerings to it.

Sources: Bingham, *South and Meso-American Mythology A to Z*, 23; Rose, *Giants, Monsters, and Dragons*, 70; Steward, *Handbook of South American Indians*, Volume 2, 463

Cearb

A Scottish fairy Cearb ("the killing one") is a murderous fairy of the Highlands; it has a reputation for killing both cattle and men. Cearb was recorded by Donald A. Mackenzie in his book *Scottish Folk-Lore and Folk Life* (1935).

Sources: Briggs, *Encyclopedia of Fairies*, 69; MacKenzie, *Scottish Folk-Lore and Folk Life*, 244; Rose, *Spirits, Fairies, Gnomes and Goblins*; 63

Ceasg

Variations: Maighdean Mhara ("maid of the sea"), Maighdean na Tuinne ("maid of the wave")

In the Scottish Highland the ceasg ("tuft") is a MERMAID, having the upper body of a woman and the lower body of a salmon. Injurious by nature, the only way to kill this creature is to discover where it has hidden it soul, usually in an egg or shell, and then destroy it. To see one while out on the sea is considered to be an ill omen. Fishermen would take the chance of confronting this FAIRY ANIMAL for if they were successful in capturing one it was compelled to grant its captor three wishes. If the fisherman is kind hearted and good looking and can convince the ceasg to live with him, his luck would be perpetual; the ceasg will shape-shift into a beautiful woman and be his wife. There are some Scottish families who claim to be descendants of a male fisherman and a ceasg mother.

Sources: Conway, *Magickal Mermaids and Water Creatures*, 60; Evan-Wentz, *Fairy Faith in Celtic Countries*, 25; Monaghan, *Encyclopedia of Celtic Mythology and Folklore, 80*; Snow, *Incredible Mysteries and Legends of the Sea*, 112

Cebren

Born one of the 3,000 daughters of the Titians, Oceanus and Tethys, Cebren was one of the named OCEANIDS. She was the lover or wife to Aisakos, the son of the NYMPH, ALEXIRHOE.

Sources: Boswell, *What Men or Gods Are These*, 58; Day, *God's Conflict with the Dragon and the Sea*, 64; Hesiod, *Works of Hesiod, Callimachus, and Theognis*, 20

Ceffyl-Dwr

In Welsh fairy lore the ceffyl-dwr ("water horse") is a water-horse, similar to the Scottish EACH UISGUE and KELPIE. Described as looking like a small but beautiful animal grazing alongside the riverbank, it will tempt the unwary to climb up on its back; as soon as it is mounted the ceffyl-dwr will jump into the air, fly about and buck its rider off from a fatal height. There are a few stories of one of these creatures being put successfully under the bridle and used as a cart horse, but eventually it breaks free and plunges back to its watery domain.

In South Wales the ceffyl-dwr appeared as a small horse; it allowed weary travelers to ride upon its back and after a wild ride, unceremoniously dump him in a river; it was described as being a luminous and sometimes winged steed. However in North Wales this FAIRY ANIMAL was a shape-shifter with a murderous addendum; there it was described as being dark and having fiery eyes. Most often the ceffyl-dwr was seen along the coastal shore appearing as having a dappled grey or sand colored coat. Its hoofs were pointed backward and if it could entice someone to ride it would plunge its rider into the ocean foam.

In various locations all throughout Wales the ceffyl-dwr is said to be a large, hulking chestnut or piebald horse trotting along the coast after a storm. Prior to a storm this water horse is said to be seen as a dapple, grey, or white horse clumsily stomping about in the oceans waves, possibly brewing up the very storm its sightings precedes. In storm seasons, the ceffyl-dwr always appears with a sea-foam white coat.

Sources: Evans, *History of Llangynwyd Parish*, 170; Palmer, *Dragons, Unicorns, and Other Magical Beasts*, 14; Radford, *Tales of South Wales*, 148–9; Trevelyan, *Folk-Lore and Folk-Stories of Wales*, 64–5

Celaeno

One of the OREADS, Celaeno was a NYMPH from classical Greek mythology; she was born one of the daughters of the Titian, Atlas and the ocean NYMPH, PLEIONE. She and her sisters, ALCYONE, ASTEROPE, DRYOPE (Aero or MEROPE), ELECTRA, MAIA, and TAYGETE, are sometimes referred to as the Seven Sisters (see PLEIADES).

Additionally in Greek mythology Celaeno was a water–NYMPH and one of the named DANAIDS, the collective name for the daughters of Danaus; her name appears in a list of the DANAIDS generated by Gaius Julius Hyginus (ca. 64 B.C.–A.D. 17), a Latin author. Celaeno was wedded to Aristonoos and killed him on their wedding night. In a list compiled by Apollodorus, a Greek scholar and grammarian, she was one of the daughters of Crino and was wedded to the son of Hephaestine, Hyperbius.

Sources: Ardinger, *Pagan Every Day*, 190; Grant, *Gods and Mortals in Classical Mythology*, 292; Grimal, *Dictionary of Classical Mythology*, 313

Celoeno

Variations: Celaeno

As one of the seven daughters of Atlas, Celoeno and her sisters are sometime referred to as the ATLANTIDES in classical Greek mythology. As Celaeno, she was one of the three harpies born to ELECTRA, one of the OCEANID.

Sources: Blacket, *Researches into the Lost Histories of America*, 215

Cephissus

Born one of the 3,000 daughters of the Titians, Oceanus and Tethys, Cephissus was one of the named OCEANIDS.

Sources: Boswell, *What Men or Gods Are These*, 58; Day, *God's Conflict with the Dragon and the Sea*, 64; Hesiod, *Works of Hesiod, Callimachus, and Theognis*, 20

Cerceis

Variations: Cercestis

Born one of the 3,000 daughters of the Titians, Oceanus and Tethys, Cerceis ("gorgeous in form") was one of the named OCEANIDS.

Sources: Avant, *Mythological Reference*, 296; Bell, *Bell's New Pantheon or Historical Dictionary of the Gods*, 112; Lemprière, *Classical Dictionary*, 236; Westmoreland, *Ancient Greek Beliefs*, 24

Cethlion

Variations: Caitlín, Ceithlenn, Cethleann, Cethlenn, Céthlionn, Kethlenda of the Crooked Teeth

In Irish mythology Cethlion is the queen of the FORMORIANS; said to be buck-tooth, she was the wife of the FORMORIAN king, BALOR. A prophet she saw the downfall of her people and their defeat to the TUATHAN DE DANANN. Although the FORMORIANS did not win at the battle of Mag Tuired, Cethlion armed with foreknowledge and a poisoned casting spear was able to kill the TUATHAN DE DANANN chief, Dadga.

Sources: Gregory, *Gods and Fighting Men*, 58; McCoy, *Celtic Myth and Magic*, 192; Monaghan, *Encyclopedia of Celtic Mythology and Folklore*, 86

Ceto

Born one of the 3,000 daughters of the Titians, Oceanus and Tethys, Ceto ("whale") was one of the named OCEANIDS in classical Greek mythology. She was also considered to be one of the NAIAD and one of the NEREIDS, the daughter of Nerues and DORIS. As a consort of Helios (Sol), Ceto bore the god a daughter named ASTRIS; by her brother a god of the sea, Phorcys, she begot the Gorgons, GRAEAE, the Hesperian dragon and the Heaprides.

Sources: Day, *God's Conflict with the Dragon and the Sea*, 388; Daly, *Greek and Roman Mythology A to Z*; 34; Smith, *New Classical Dictionary of Biography, Mythology, and Geography*, 571; Trzaskoma, *Anthology of Classical Myth*, 18

Chalcis

In classical Greek mythology Chalcis was one of the twelve ASOPIDES, the NAIADS daughters of ASOPUS; they were the NYMPHS of the river Asopos in Sikyonia and Boiotia, central and southern Greece. She and each of her sisters were abducted and raped by Zeus (Jupiter) and many of the other Olympian gods.

Sources: Classical Association, *Classical Review, Volume 12, 125*; Quiggin, *Essays and Studies Presented to William Ridgeway*, 224

Chalcomede

A NYMPH in classical Greek mythology, Chalcomede was one of the MAENADS, the collective name of the daughter born of the CANONICAL MUSE, Mnemosyne, the personification of memory, and the god Zeus (Jupiter), after nine days of continuous intercourse. Chalcomede was protected by the god Dionysus (Bacchus) when a warrior tried to rape her.

Sources: Monaghan, *Encyclopedia of Goddesses and Heroines*, 419

Changeling

Variations: Callicanzaris, Changeling Child ("Plentyn Newid"), Crimbil, Gremlins, Hosentefel, Kontsodaimonas, Leurre, Sibhreach

A changeling is, in brief, the fairy being left behind by a fairy when it steals a human child; this being looks at best like a sickly version of the stolen child; but only a child who had not been christened could be taken. In some traditions, a log rather than a being is left behind to punish the mother. The changeling is believed to be the deformed child of a DWARF or ELF or a senile or old and withered fairy. This lore may have originated to explain why a child is born with a physical or mental defect. This belief exists in the mythology and folklore of China, France, Germany, Great Britain, Greece, Ireland, the Native Americans, Scotland, and the Scandinavian countries.

The reason for stealing human babies and replacing them with a fairy changeling are numerous; some sources claim this was done because the fairies, also known as the TUATHA DE DANANN, are a real race of hidden people who need to replenish their bloodlines due to years of their own inbreeding. Other possible explanations include taking a human child to deliver to the Tithe, a seven year tribute paid to the Devil; fairies see human babies as wonderfully beautiful and desire to have one, be it as a lover, plaything, or slave.

Common to the changeling fairy lore is a means by which the being can be exposed for what it is and a method for the return of the human child. To expose a changeling for what it is may be as simple as making it laugh or doing something so amazing it shocks the fairy into

leaving of its own accord, but usually the process involves some sort of torture on the being. Common methods employed to expose a changeling in folklore include abandoning it on a hillside, bathing it in scalding water, chasing after it with a red-hot poker, dropping it into a racing river, dumping it in a dung heap, dunking it into a well, force foxglove tea down its throat and wait for it to immolate, placing it in a pot over a roaring fire, stabbing the suspected babe with a knife, threatening it with a sword, or tossing it into a chimney fire. There are many reports of women killing infants by trying to drive out the changeling and have their own child returned to them. For example, in 1826 a woman was acquitted of the murder of her son by drowning because she was trying to compel the changeling to leave.

In Great Britain, changelings are described as looking like a baby having some sort of physical deformity, noticeable intellectual disabilities, an overly large head, and pale skin. They are known to play little tricks, such as breaking sentimental or valuable object, playing music that forces people to dance against their will, and stealing items when no one is looking.

In some parts of Germany it was believed when a child did not thrive it was a changeling. The fairy being was then taken to Cyriac's Mead, a place near Neuhausen, and was forced to drink from Cyriacc's well. Then, the child was left there unattended for nine days where it would either die from exposure or recover. Jacob and Wilhelm Grimm, noted German academics, authors, cultural researchers, and linguists who collected folklore, recorded a story how a woman suspected her child to have been swapped out with a changeling. She had been advised to brew beer in an acorn where the child could watch. The changeling was so amazed at the spectacle it exclaimed *"I am as old as any oak in the wood but never have I seen beer brewed in an accord"* and then disappeared.

In Ireland, it is sometimes thought left handed people are changelings. Although the belief in the lore of fairy changelings is older than recorded history, as recently as 1894 woman named Bridget Cleary of Clommel, Ireland, had been accused of being a changeling by her husband and family when she recovered from a case of phenomena. Nine members of her family had been charged with her murder, they burned her to death trying to drive the changeling away. Although arrested on murder charges the most sever charge pressed was manslaughter; most other charges of "wounding" were dropped.

In Welsh lore it is not immediately apparent when a changeling has been placed, only after a period of time does its natural behavior reveal it for what it is by gradually becoming deformed, ill-tempered, ugly, and having fits of uncontrollable biting and crying. In addition to its difficult behavior, the child will also show cunning and wisdom more appropriate to an adult. As a sort of payment for caring for the changeling, the fay will leave some money to be found, every day in the same place. so long as the family cares for the changeling and does not reveal the source of the money, they will continued to be paid but if the secret is revealed, the money will cease to appear. To discover if a child has been replaced for a changeling Welsh lore says to bathe it in foxglove, hold it over an open fire, or place it in a hot oven. Similar to the German idea of brewing beer in an acorn, in Wales it is advised to cook the family's evening meal in an eggshell; this will so confound the fairy it will leave, returning the human child to its family.

In Scandinavian fairy mythology fairies are said to have an extreme aversion to steel, so parents would place a steel item, such as a knife or a pair of scissors in the bed of an unbaptized child. If the steel deterrent did not work it was believed if the changeling was treated badly the fay would return the human baby; methods employed included inserting the changeling into a heated over and whippings.

Sources: Briggs, *Encyclopedia of Fairies*, 69–74; Evan-Wentz, *Fairy Faith in Celtic Countries*, 58; Keightly *World Guide to Gnomes, Fairies, Elves, and Other Little People*, 227, 418; Mccoy, *Witch's Guide to Faery Folk,* 7, 71; Sikes, *British Goblins*, 50–56

Chao Phum Phi

The chao phum phi ("gods of the earth") of Thai lore are similar to the BROWNIES, CORRIGANS, and Pixies; they correspond to the PENATES from the mythology of the ancient Romans.

Sources: Allardice, *Myths, Gods and Fantasy*, 170; Evan-Wentz, *Fairy Faith in Celtic Countries*, 229; Spence, *British Fairy Origins*, 108

Chariolo

Variations: Chariclo, Chariklo

In the mythology of ancient Greece, Chariolo was a NYMPH born one of the daughters of Apollo; she was the wife of the centaur Chiron and the mother of their two children, a son named Carystus and a NYMPH daughter, OCYROE. Char-

iolo and Chiron raised and tutored many of the heroes of the ancient world. Chariolo was best friend and lover to the goddess Athena.

Sources: Chambers *Chambers's Encyclopaedia*, Volume 3, 198; Evan-Wentz, *Fairy Faith in Celtic Countries*, 327; Smith, *New Classical Dictionary of Greek and Roman Biography*, 195

The Charities

Variations: The Graces, Gratiae

In ancient Greece the Charities (known as the Graces in ancient Roman mythology) were the three sisters, according to the Greek oral poet Hesiod, Aglaia ("the wonderful"), Euphrosyne ("Joy"), and THALIA ("Plenty") who were born of the OCEANID EURYNOME and the god Zeus (Jupiter). The travel writer, Pausanias, however claimed the Graces were born the daughters of the sun god, Helios and the HESPERIDES NYMPH, AEGLE. Homer, the greatest ancient Greek poet and the author of the *Iliad*, made a differentiation between Elder Graces and Younger Graces, adding five more names, Antheia, Eudaimonia, Paidia, Pandaisia, and Pannykhis.

The Charities were the attendants of the goddess Aphrodite and the god Hermes but were also venerated independently as MUSES of botanical abundance, creative inspiration, human fertility, and moisture. They were the personification of beauty, charm, and grace and sometimes associated with love. The Graces were the ones who wove and created the robe of Immortality for the goddess, Aphrodite.

Sources: Evan-Wentz, *Fairy Faith in Celtic Countries*, 326–27; Hard, *Routledge Handbook of Greek Mythology*, 208; Littleton, *Gods, Goddesses, and Mythology*, Volume 11, 582

Charopeia

A NYMPH in classical reek mythology, Charopeia was one of the MAENADS, the collective name of the daughter born of the CANONICAL MUSE, Mnemosyne, the personification of memory, and the god Zeus (Jupiter), after nine days of continuous intercourse. Charopeia along with her sister PHASYLEIA, would oftentimes lead her sisters and religious followers in dance.

Source: Monaghan, *Encyclopedia of Goddesses and Heroines*, 418

Charybdis

Charybdis was an ugly NYMPH from the mythology of classical Greece and Rome. One of the NAIADS, she was born of the gods Zeus and Gaia and is the personification of the whirlpools of the oceans. She and her sister SCYLLA lived in a narrow strait off the coast of Sicily. Born greedy and monstrous in appearance Zeus (Jupiter) cast his tempestuous and violent daughter down into the ocean where she continuously gulps down water and then spits it back out. If any ship sails too near her, she would try to sink it.

Sources: Andrews, *Dictionary of Nature Myths*, 171; Brewer, *Dictionary of Phrase and Fable*, 1116; Parada, *Genealogical Guide to Greek Mythology*, 46; Rosen, 335

Chelone

A mountain NYMPH from Greek mythology, Chelone ("tortoise") spoke out against the marriage of the god Zeus to the goddess Hera. As a warning to others who may also want to voice an objection, Zeus transformed Chelone into a turtle.

Sources: Day, *God's Conflict with the Dragon and the Sea*, 120; Evan-Wentz, *Fairy Faith in Celtic Countries*, 330; Illes, *Encyclopedia of Spirits*, 330

Cheney's Hounds

Variations: Dandy-Dogs, WISH HOUNDS

From the local folklore of Cornwall, England, in the Parish of Saint Teath comes the story of Cheney, the old squire. It is said after his death, Cheney and his pack of spectral fairy-hounds would hunt an area now called Cheney's Downs. The baying hounds can be seen and heard most often during bad weather.

WISH HOUNDS, a breed of fairy-dog popular in the folklore of Dartmoor, England is likely the same story of Cheney but retold in a different area. The WILD HUNT, said to be led by the Devil himself, was sometimes called Cheney's Hounds, Dando's and his Dogs, and Herla's Rade.

Sources: Briggs, *Encyclopedia of Fairies*, 72; Conway, *Magickal, Mystical Creatures*, 148; Howey, *Cults of the Dog*, 170; Hunt, *Popular Romances of the West of England*, 146

Chesiad

Chesiad was the NYMPH of Mount Keretes in classical Greek mythology.

Source: Larson, *Greek Nymphs*, 299

Chesme

Variations: Cesme, Chesma

The chesme ("fountain") is a vampiric fairy cat-NYMPH from Turkish mythology; it lives in the water and lures young men to their death by singing hypnotically, much like a SIREN.

Sources: De Claremont, *Ancient's Book of Magic*, 123; Leland, *Gypsy Sorcery and Fortune Telling*, 133; Spence, *Encyclopædia of Occultism*, 100

Le Cheval Bayard

Variations: LUTIN

In the folklore of Normandy, France when a LUTIN appears in the guise of a horse bridled and saddled it is called a le cheval bayard. This malicious fairy will then attempt to entice a rider to mount up on its back. Should this happen, it will begin to kick and rear and eventually, after a long and wild ride, dump it rider into some body of water.

The le cheval bayard may also appear in the guise of a handsome young man and court married women. In one such story a jealous husband discovered this and placed an iron rod to heat in the fire. When the rod was glowing red he then donned his wife's clothing and pretended to spin at her spinning wheel. Not too long later the le cheval bayard appeared and began to romance the husband. When the fairy asked for a name the husband yelled "myself" and stabbed the le cheval bayard in his eye. When the other fairies asked the le cheval bayard what happened he claimed "Myself did it" causing them all to laugh at him. This is similar to the story of AINSEL.

Sources: Bois, *Jersey Folklore and Superstitions*, 404, 426, 437; Keightly, *World Guide to Gnomes, Fairies, Elves, and Other Little People*, 477; Rose, *Giants, Monsters, and Dragons*, 78

Chi Spirits

In Chinese fairy lore chi spirits are helpful, invisible household spirits known to attach themselves to families, similar to BROWNIES; these spirits are best known to rearrange furniture to ensure a better flow of energy. Chi spirits are made of pure energy and have no physical form.

Source: McCoy, *Witch's Guide to Faery Folk*, 200–01

Chih Nü

Variations: the Spinning Damsel, Vega, Weaving Sister

In Chinese folklore Chih Nü is the celestial NYMPH who is tasked with the responsibility of weaving the beautiful cloth was used to tailor into clothes for the gods. The Chinese holiday, Ch'i His (similar to Saint Valentine's Day), originated from folktale telling the story of the love between Niu Lang, a simple cow herder and the very beautiful Chih Nü. There are several versions of the tale told throughout China, Japan, and Korea all dwelling on the strength of their enduring love.

Sources: Beeler *(More) Parents, Family, 44;* Monaghan, *Encyclopedia of Goddesses and Heroines*, 113; Rose, *Spirits, Fairies, Leprechauns, and Goblins*, 67, 351

Chin-Chin Kobakama

Although attributed to Japanese lore, the chin-chin kobakama ("lovely little spirit wearing a skirt") likely originated in Chinese mythology. These elflike beings are described as looking like small but spry elderly men and women. They are most active during the Hour of the Ox, or 2 A.M. Although considered benevolent, the chin-chin kobakama can be something of a nuisance as they are extremely fastidious in keeping a clean house; they are particularly concerned with the thick mats covering the wooden floors in the home. So long as the home is clean, neat, and orderly, these fairies will be content but they are known to gently tease those who are careless and messy, causing an array of little annoyances to occur.

Sources: Conway, *Magickal, Mystical Creatures*, 208; Hearn, *Japanese Fairy Tales*, 15; McCoy, *Witch's Guide to Faery Folk*, 201

Chlidanope

Chlidanope ("delicate face") was a NYMPH from the mythology of classical Greece and Rome. One of the NAIADS, she was married to the king of Lapiths, Hypseus and bore him a daughter named Cyrene.

Sources: Bell, *Women of Classical Mythology*, 146; Room, *Who's Who in Classical Mythology*, 93

Chrysa

Chrysa was the NYMPH of Lemnos; she was born the daughter of Halmus and Phelegyas; she was the sister of CHRYSE in Greek mythology.

Sources: Bell, *Bell's New Pantheon*, 179; Larson, *Greek Nymphs*, 179; Parada, *Genealogical Guide to Greek Mythology*, 47

Chryse

Chryse was the NYMPH of Lemnos; she was born the daughter of Halmus and Phelegyas; she was the sister of CHRYSA in Greek mythology.

Sources: Bell, *Bell's New Pantheon*, 179; Larson, *Greek Nymphs*, 179; Parada, *Genealogical Guide to Greek Mythology*, 47

Chryseis

Born one of the 3,000 daughters of the Titians, Oceanus and Tethys, Chryseis ("gold") was one of the named OCEANIDS; she bore Herakles (Hercules) a son named Onesippus. Her name in the *Iliad* (1194–1184 B.C.) the epic poem commonly attributed to the ancient Greek author Homer, there meant "Chryses' daughter"; however, later writers give her real name as being Astynome. In medieval literature, Chryseis was developed into the character Cressida in the retellings of the Trojan War.

Sources: Avant, *Mythological Reference*, 236; Dixon-Kennedy, *Encyclopedia of Greco-Roman Mythology*, 86; Westmoreland, *Ancient Greek Beliefs*, 24, 702

Chrysis

A sea–NYMPH, Chrysis was a NEREIS; she was the mistress of Demetrius in classical Greek mythology.

Sources: Hesiod, *Theogony*, 103; Lemprière, *Classical Dictionary*, 346

Chrysopelia

Variations: Chrysopeleia, ERATO ("lovely"), Khrysopeleia

In Greek mythology, Chrysopelia ("golden dove") was a DRYAD and a NYMPH of Arcadia in southern Greece; her oak tree grew in the mountainous of Arcadia. According to legend, after a particularly fierce season of storms a great wall of floodwater was rushing down the mountain destined to destroy her tree and consequently end her life. As she cried out for help, Arcas (also known as Arkas), the son of the NYMPH CALLISTO happened to be hunting the area and heard her cries of desperation. Moved by her situation he quickly built a dyke strong enough to divert the floodwaters. The grateful Chrysopelia married her hero and bore him two sons; they would go on to be the progenitors of the music loving people known as the Arcadians, Amphidamas, and Elatus.

Sources: Grimmel, *Dictionary of Classical Mythology*, 102; Larson, *Greek Nymphs*, 155; Littleton, *Gods, Goddesses, and Mythology*, Volume 4. 441

Chrysothemis

In Greek mythology Chrysothemis ("golden light") was a water–NYMPH and one of the named DANAIDS, the collective name for the daughters of Danaus; her name appears in a list of the DANAIDS generated by Gaius Julius Hyginus (ca. 64 B.C.–A.D. 17), a Latin author. Chrysothemis was wedded to Asterides and killed him on their wedding night.

Sources: Bell, *Women of Classical Mythology*, 123, 149; Parada, *Genealogical Guide to Greek Mythology*, 30, 47

Chu Pa-Chiai

Variations: Chu Pa-chieh

Originally a celestial official, Chu Pa-Chiai ("eating watermelon") is known as the pig fairy in Chinese lore. He was stripped of his rank for drunkenness, banished to earth, and reincarnated as a piglet. Enraged over his situation, he consumed his sow and littermates and ran off to the Fu-Lung Mountains where he continued his rampage against anyone he ventured across. The goddess of mercy, Kwan Yin eventually converted Chu Pa-Chiai over to Buddhism; he was then admitted into the western Paradise where he was given the rank of Chief Alter Washer, the highest office for which he was eligible to achieve due to his greed.

Chu Pa-Chiai represents mankind's more coarse passions and his desire to cast off all self-restraint.

Sources: Heath, *Echoing Green*, 29; Rose, *Spirits, Fairies, Leprechauns, and Goblins*, 131, 351; Werner, *Myths and Legends of China*, 221, 249

Churn Milk Peg

Variations: Acorn Lady, Churnmilk Peg

In the folklore of West Yorkshire, England the arthritic, lazy, and pipe-smoking Churn Milk Peg guards over unripe nut thickets; she is used by mothers as a NURSERY BOGIE to keep children from picking and eating unripe food by pinching them. If they persist and eat the nut, Churn Milk Peg will cause them to suffer with bloating and stomach cramps. Her male counterpart is MELSH DICK.

Sources: Arrowsmith, *Field Guide to the Little People*, 182; Briggs, *Encyclopedia of Fairies*, 75; McCoy, *Witch's Guide to Faery Folk*, 202; Wright, *Rustic Speech and Folk-Lore*, 198

Circe

Variations: Kirke

Born one of the 3,000 daughters of the Titians, Oceanus and Tethys, Circe was one of the named OCEANIDS. A divine shape-shifting enchantress who appears in many Greek myths she is best known from her appearance in Homer's *Odyssey*. When Odysseus and his crew land on the island of Aiaia, her home, she transforms them in baboons and lions but mostly pigs. Circe and Odysseus have a son together named Telegonus.

Sources: Boswell, *What Men or Gods Are These*, 58; Day, *God's Conflict with the Dragon and the Sea*, 64; Hesiod, *Works of Hesiod, Callimachus, and Theognis*, 20

Circeis

Born one of the 3,000 daughters of the Titians, Oceanus and Tethys, Circeis ("gorgeous in form") was one of the named OCEANIDS; she is said by Hesiod to have an amiable nature.

Sources: Boswell, *What Men or Gods Are These*, 58; Hesiod, *Works of Hesiod, Callimachus, and Theognis*, 20; Westmoreland, *Ancient Greek Beliefs*, 85

Ciuthach

Variations: Ceathach, Citheach, Kewach, URISK

In Scottish lore Ciuthach ("mist") was originally a noble cave-dwelling GIANT and possibly even a hero. Eventually he disintegrated into a monster. In more modern times, in Gaelic folktales the ciuthach are said to be a race of naked wild-men who live in caves; one of these fairy-creatures plays a dominant role in the story of Diarmaid and Grainne.

Sources: Avant, *Mythological Reference*, 90; Briggs, *Encyclopedia of Fairies*, 75–6; MacRitchie, *Fians, Fairies, and Picts*, 36

Clap-Cans

Variations: Clapcans

A NURSERY BOGIE from the folklore of Lancaster, England, Clap-Cans is an invisible fairy-spirit or HOBGOBLIN. Considered to be one of the least offensives of its kind, Clap-Cans is known to make scary noises, sounding like the beating of empty cans.

Sources: Briggs, *Encyclopedia of Fairies*, 76; Buckton, *Notes and Queries*, 156; Rose, *Spirits, Fairies, Gnomes, and Goblins*, 69; Wright, *Rustic Speech and Folk-Lore*, 194

Clashnichd Aulniac

The GOBLIN Clashnichd Aulniac is the quarrelsome wife of BEN BAYNAC; they live in the area of Craig Aulniac, Scotland. Like all fairy-kind she is nearly immortal, which is fortunate as her husband frequently beats her so badly her screams and wails can be heard across the countryside all night long. When James Gray, a Highlander who lived near the couple killed BEN BAYNAC, Clashnichd Aulniac was so grateful she attached herself to his family. She stayed with them until one day when a housewife splashed her with boiling water, causing her to flee and never return.

Source: Rose, *Spirits, Fairies, Leprechauns, and Goblins*, 37

Cleio

A sea–NYMPH from Greek mythology, Cleio was one of the named NEREID in classical Greek mythology; she was born of Nereus and DORIS.

Sources: Apollodorus, *Apollodorus' Library and Hyginus' Fabulae*, 95; Bell, *Bell's New Pantheon or Historical Dictionary of the Gods,* 112; Lemprière, *Classical Dictionary*, 468

Cleo

In Greek mythology Cleo was a water–NYMPH and one of the named DANAIDS, the collective name for the daughters of Danaus; her name appears in a list of the DANAIDS generated by Gaius Julius Hyginus (ca. 64 B.C.–A.D. 17), a Latin author. Cleo was wedded to Asterius and killed him on their wedding night.

Sources: Bell, *Women of Classical Mythology*, 127; Hyginus, *Myths of Hyginus*, 132

Cleochareia

From the mythology of classical Greece and Rome Cleochareia was one of the NAIADS. This river NYMPH was the wife of King Lelex, the first inhabitant and king of Lamnia; together they had three sons, Eurotas, Myles, and Polycaon and a daughter named Therapne.

Sources: Apollodorus, *Gods and Heroes of the Greeks,* 189; Bell, *Bell's New Pantheon*, 184; Lemprière, *Classical Dictionary*, 189; Parada, *Genealogical Guide to Greek Mythology*, 48, 49

Cleodora

Variations: KLEODORA

Born one of the 3,000 daughters of the Titians, Oceanus and Tethys, Cleodora was one of the named OCEANIDS. She was beloved by the god of the sea, Poseidon (Neptune), however, with her mortal husband, Thueyd, she had a son, Parnassus; Mount Parnassus was named for him. It is supposed by scholars she had two husbands simultaneously, one divine and one mortal. When Cleodora was included among the DANAID it was as the wife of Lyxus. If Cleodora was the NYMPH, KLEODORA, she was able to divine the future by use of birds.

Sources: Bell, *Bell's New Pantheon*, 184; Halliday, *Greek Divination*, 80; Lemprière, *Classical Dictionary,* 189, 191

Cleodore

In classical Greek mythology Cleodore was a water–NYMPH and one of the named DANAIDS, the collective name for the daughters of Danaus.

In a list compiled by Apollodorus, a Greek scholar and grammarian, she was one of the daughters of the NAIAD, POLYXO and was wedded to Lixus, one of the sons of the NAIAD, CALIADNE.

Sources: Apollodorus, *Gods and Heroes of the Greeks,* 69; Bell, *Women of Classical Mythology*, 159

Cleone

Variation: Kleone

In classical Greek mythology Cleone was one of the twelve ASOPIDES, the NAIADS daughters of ASOPUS; they were the NYMPHS of the river Asopos in Sikyonia and Boiotia, central and southern Greece. She and each of her sisters were abducted and raped by Zeus (Jupiter) and many of the other Olympian gods.

Sources: Classical Association, *Classical Review,* Volume 12, 125; Quiggin, *Essays and Studies Presented to William Ridgeway*, 224

Cleopatra

In classical Greek mythology Cleopatra was a water–NYMPH and one of the named DANAIDS, the collective name for the daughters of Danaus; her name appears in a list of the DANAIDS generated by Gaius Julius Hyginus (ca. 64 B.C.–A.D. 17), a Latin author. Cleopatra was wedded to Hermus (or Metalces, sources vary) and killed him on their wedding night. In a list compiled by Apollodorus, a Greek scholar and grammarian, she was one of the daughters of the HAMADRYAD, ATLANTEIA (or PHOEBE, sources conflict) and was wedded to Agenor, the son of an unnamed Arabic woman.

Sources: Apollodorus, *Gods and Heroes of the Greeks,* 69; Grimal, *Dictionary of Classical Mythology*, 127

Clethrad

The alder tree was said to be watched over by the alder-fairy, Clethrad, a water- SPRITE.

Source: Newcomb, *Faerie Treasury*, 16

Clidna

Variations: Centfind, Cleena, Clídna, Clídna of the Fair Hair, Cliodna, Clíodna, Clíona

Originally an Irish goddess of birds and the afterlife, Clidna was reduced to being a member of the TUATHA DE DANANN and the FAIRY QUEEN of southwest Ireland after the introduction of Christianity; her seat of power was in Munster but FAIRY QUEEN AEVAL claimed this region as her own. Clidna's home was within a fairy hill in Cork called Carrig Cliodna. She was associated with off-shore rocks, called *carrigcleena*. According to legend, every ninth wave coming to shore was called Clidna's wave and was said to be the largest.

Reported to be the world's most beautiful woman in her time, there were many romantic tales involving Clidna. She was connected to many important Irish families and was even said to have had an affair with Earl Gerald Fitzgerald of the Desmond Geraldines; she was also the BANSHEE to the MacCarthy family to whom she told the secret of the Blarney stone to, kissing it would make the person eloquent.

Sources: Evans-Wentz, *Fairy-Faith in Celtic Countries*, 288; Gray, *Mythology of all races*, Volume 7, 116; Monaghan, *Encyclopedia of Celtic Mythology and Folklore*, 90–1

Clio

Not to be confused with the MUSE of the same name, Clio ("fame-giver") the OCEANID was born one of the 3,000 daughters of the Titians, Oceanus and Tethys.

Sources: Bell, *Bell's New Pantheon or Historical Dictionary of the Gods*, 112; Farrell, *Vergil's Georgics and the Traditions of Ancient Epic*, 105; Hesiod, *Works of Hesiod, Callimachus, and Theognis*, 20

Clio 2

One of the nine CANONICAL MUSES Clio ("fame-giver") was the MUSE of lyrical songs; she was depicted in art as carrying a books and scrolls. In some accounts it was Clio who introduced the Phoenician alphabet to the Greeks.

Sources: Hunt, *Masonic Symbolism*, 469; Littleton, *Gods, Goddesses, and Mythology*, Volume 11, 921; Peterson, *Mythology in Our Midst*, 121

Cliodna

Variations: Cleeona, Cleena, Clidna, Cliodhna
Cliodna is the FAIRY QUEEN of South Munster, and owes her alliance to King FINVARRA and Queen ONAGH. One of the TUATHA DE DANANN and a woman of the SÍDHE, Cliodna resdies in a *sidh* in Cork County, Ireland. The fairy Queens AOIBHINN of North Munster and AINE of South Munster owe their allegiances to her.

A foreigner from FAIRYLAND, it is said she accidentally drowned in Glandore Harbor in South Cork. At the base of the ocean-side cliffs where Cliodna fell to her death are caverns; it is believed the occasional loud and melancholy roars hear are the sea expressing its grief for her death. It has been noted this wail coincides with the death of the Kings of Munster associating

Cliodna with the BANSHEE; she is said to live on as a fairy claiming a cairn some five miles away in Mallow as her home.

Sources: Evan-Wentz, *Fairy Faith in Celtic Countries*, 300; Mahon, *Ireland's Fairy Lore*, 137–8; Rose, *Spirits, Fairies, Leprechauns, and Goblins*, 69, 351; Squire, *Celtic Myth and Legend*, 162

Clite

In Greek mythology Clite was a water–NYMPH and one of the named DANAIDS, the collective name for the daughters of Danaus. In a list compiled by Apollodorus, a Greek scholar and grammarian, she was one of the daughters of MEMPHIS and was wedded to Clitus, one of the sons of Tyria; since these children were namesakes of one another, they were matched up without drawing lots.

Sources: Grimal, *Dictionary of Classical Mythology*, 127; Lemprière, *Classical Dictionary*, 236

Clitemneste

Born one of the 3,000 daughters of the Titians, Oceanus and Tethys, the NYMPH Clitemneste was one of the named OCEANIDS in classical Greek mythology.

Source: Apollodorus of Athens, *Apollodorus' Library and Hyginus' Fabulae*, 95

Clitunno

Born one of the 3,000 daughters of the Titians, Oceanus and Tethys, Clitunno was one of the named OCEANIDS in classical Greek mythology.

Sources: Boswell, *What Men or Gods Are These*, 58; Day, *God's Conflict with the Dragon and the Sea*, 64; Hesiod, *Works of Hesiod, Callimachus, and Theognis*, 20

Cluracaun

Variations: Clooracaun, FINVARRA
A SPRITE from Munster, Ireland, cluracaun is similar to the LEPRECHAUN but has a mischievous streak; it was often blamed for breaking eggs, curdling milk, stealing butter and tipping over milk buckets.

Sources: Evan-Wentz, *Fairy Faith in Celtic Countries*, 30; Muirithe, *Words We Use*, 149

Cluricaun

Variations: Cluricaune, Cluricauns, Cluri-chauns, His Nibs, Monciello
In Cork County, Ireland Cluricaunes are a species of BOGGART or Nis are similar to the LEP-RECHAUN. Described as wearing a tall, green cap with a feather sticking out of it, long blue stock-

ings, and a red jacket, and silver-buckled shoes these fairies look like wizened old men. Cluricaunes like to be indoors and avoid work of any kind. Fond of alcoholic beverages these fairies are found in wine cellars. Typically drunk the cluricaun manages to chase away anyone who would slip into the cellar and steal a quick drink, prevent casks from leaking, and keeps wine from turning bad.

The solitary cluricaun enjoys riding on the back of sheep and sheep dogs at night; evidence of its nocturnal activities is these animals found covered in mud and panting in the morning. It is unsure if the cluricaun is BOGGART-like in his mischief, breaking dishes, hiding things, knocking over fences, and raiding the larder or if this activity is all just its brand of drunken revelry.

Sources: Briggs, *Encyclopedia of Fairies*, 77; Curran, *Field Guide to Irish Fairies*, 59; Keightly, *World Guide to Gnomes, Fairies, Elves, and Other Little People*, 369; Spence, *Fairy Tradition in Britain*, 107–8

Clymene

Born one of the 3,000 daughters of the Titians, Oceanus and Tethys, Clymene ("mountain rusher"), the wife of the Titian, Iapetus and mother of their children Atlas, Epimetheus, Menoetius, and Prometheus, was one of the named OCEANIDS in classical Greek mythology. Clymene was also the name of one of the NEREIDS, the daughters of Nerues and DORIS and by the god of the sun, Helios (Sol), was the mother of their seven daughters known colectivly as the HELIADES.

Sources: Apollodorus, *Apollodorus' Library and Hyginus' Fabulae*, 95; Bell, *Bell's New Pantheon or Historical Dictionary of the Gods*, 112; Boswell, *What Men or Gods Are These*, 58; Hesiod, *Works of Hesiod, Callimachus, and Theognis*, 20; Westmoreland, *Ancient Greek Beliefs*, 24

Clytia

Variations: Clytie, Klytie
Born one of the 3,000 daughters of the Titians, Oceanus and Tethys, Clytia was one of the named OCEANIDS in classical Greek mythology. A water NYMPH, she pinned for the the love of the god Apollo and eventually was changed into a heliotrope flower.

Sources: Bell, *Bell's New Pantheon or Historical Dictionary of the Gods*, 112; Boswell, *What Men or Gods Are These*, 58; Day, *God's Conflict with the Dragon and the Sea*, 64; Hesiod, *Works of Hesiod, Callimachus, and Theognis*, 20

Clytic

Variations: CHRYSEIS
Born one of the 3,000 daughters of the Titians, Oceanus and Tethys, Clytic was one of the named OCEANIDS in classical Greek mythology. According to *The Iliad*, the epic poem written by the ancient Greek poet, Homer she was described as being "fair" and "light."

Sources: Benjamin, *Troy*, 20–30; Homerus, *The Iliad*, Volume 1, 34, 57; Westmoreland, *Ancient Greek Beliefs*, 24

Co-Walker

Variations: Companion, Copy, Doubleman, ECHO, Living Picture, Man, Reflex-Man, Resemblance, Twin-Brother, Waff

Irish and Scottish men who claimed to have the ability to see fairies would say many times at a funeral banquet they would see a fairy-sprit known as a co-walker. When this fay was present they would not eat any of the meat offered for fear it had been poisoned by the spirit. These seers said co-walkers were present to assist the pole bearers in carrying the coffin to the grave and describe the beings as looking exactly as a human being, perfect in every way, except for the fact it had taken on the guise of the deceased and was not acting properly, considering the somber occasion. The term, co-walker, was believed to have coined by the 17th century fairy scholar, Reverend Rovert Kirk.

Sources: Briggs, *Encyclopedia of Fairies*, 80; Kirk, *Secret Commonwealth of Elves, Fauns, and Fairies*, 69; Stepanich, *Faery Wicca*, Book One, 88

Coblyn

Variations: BUCCA
Described as looking like British soldiers wearing red handkerchief with yellow spots, the coblyn of Welsh lore were most often seen in mining communities. These fairies were described as being almost as tall as an average sized person.

Sources: Monaghan, *Encyclopedia of Celtic Mythology and Folklore*, 64; Sikes, *British Goblins*, 32

Coblynau

Variations: Cobylynau, Koblernigh
In Welsh fairy lore the perpetually dirty coblynau ("knocker, thumper" and "fiend, SPRITE") was a GOBLIN living in mines and dressed itself to look like a miner with a red handkerchief with yellow spots worn upon its head. Standing only about a foot and a half tall (45.6 cm) with cop-

per-colored skin, this ugly but good-natured fairy always looked to be busy carrying pails and using tools but it never accomplished anything. Similar to the KNOCKERS of Cornish lore, the coblynau were helpful in finding ore deposits; hearing their hammers and picks at work was a sign a rich load was near. Should one of these fairies overhear a miner dismissing their existence, it would throw a stone at him, but the rock would not do any harm. Apart from being seen working in mines the coblynau enjoyed daning and there a few reports of them doing so in large numbers. Their homes were invisible to mortal eyes.

Sources: Allardice, *Myths, Gods and Fantasy*, 56; Briggs, *Encyclopedia of Fairies*, 77; Froud, *Faeries*, 82; Guiney, *Brownies and Bogles*, 42; Sikes, *British Goblins*, 28, 31

Cobweb

Cobweb is a FLOWER FAIRY and an attendant of TITANIA, the FAIRY QUEEN. Along with fellow fairies MOTH, MUSTARDSEED, and PEASE BLOSSOM, it attends a human peasant named Bottom whose head was changed into an ass' by OBERON, the FAIRY KING.

Sources: Lamb, *Works of Charles and Mary Lamb*, 18; Rose, *Spirits, Fairies, Leprechauns, and Goblins*, 255, 351; Shakespeare, *Shakespeare's a Midsummer Night's Dream*, 26

Colbronde

Variations: Colbrand, Colbrond

Colbronde was a GIANT slain by Guy of Warwick in Winchester, freeing the England from Dutch tribute. According to the folklore, invading Kings Conelock of Noweay and Havelock of Denmark had burned and pillaged every town they came upon until reaching Winchester where the British King, Athelstan was besieged. The invading nobility promised to abandon their conquest if a champion would meet and defeat their GIANT, Colbronde. King Athelstan prayed for an answer and was granted a vision; in it he learned if he went to the gates of the city the following day he would find a pilgrim who could answer the challenge. There Guy of Warwick was found and agreed to meet the GIANT. It was a difficult battle but in the end, he defeated Colbronde decapitating him with one of his own axes.

Sources: Ashton, *Romances of Chivalry Told and Illustrated in Facsimile*, 295–6; Brewer, *Dictionary of Phrase and Fable*, 565; Rose, *Giants, Monsters, and Dragons*, 85

Coleman Gray

Coleman Gray was the name of a little pixy boy adopted by a Cornish couple. The story goes one day a farmer came across a miserable and pathetic looking child which had been abandoned in his field. Suspecting it was left there by fairies he decided to take it home for fear it would anger the fay if he didn't. Adopted into the family the CHANGELING child quickly began to thrive, an uncommon event, becoming active, good humored, strong, and showing signs of being very intelligent. The family prospered and loved the child very much. One day as it lingered near the door a male voice called out "Coleman Gray, Coleman Gray!" The CHANGELING child clapped its hands and became wonderfully excited; calling back to the family it said "My daddy has come to take me home!" and before their eyes, disappeared.

Sources: Briggs, *Encyclopedia of Fairies*, 77; Hunt, *Popular Romances of the West of England*, 96; Rose, *Spirits, Fairies, Gnomes, and Goblins*, 71

Colt-Pixy

In the fairy-lore from Hampshire, England the colt-pixy is species of mischievous fairies similar to the BRAG; they are said to look like a young colt and leads horses into bogs. In Somerset, England they are said to guard apple orchards from thieves.

The phrase "to colt-pixy" is to take something which belongs to the pixies; it is used most often when picking an apple from a tree after the crop has been taken in, as it was the custom of whatever fruit left behind then belonged to the fairies.

Sources: Brand, *Brand's Popular Antiquities of Great Britain*, 141; Brewer, *Dictionary of Phrase and Fable*, 277; Keightly, *World Guide to Gnomes, Fairies, Elves, and Other Little People*, 305

Coluinn gun Chean

Variations: Colann Gun Cheann, Coluinn Gan Ceann

The Coluinn gun Chean ("headless trunk") was a BAUCHAN that once acted as the guardian of the Macdonalds of Morar and is extremely hostile to anyone else. By day it was said to be hovering over Morar House, located on the Isle of Skye, but by night it patrolled the "smooth mile," the road running from the river to the house. Any solitary man it found walking along the road at night would have his mutilated remains discovered in the morning. It never harmed children or women or those who walked in a group but when it killed a friend and distant cousin of the Macleods of Raasay, "Big" John Macleod sought it destruction. A man of remarkable size, strength and fighting prowess he found Coluinn gun Chean one evening just after sunset and fought it all night, eventually defeating it. As the sun rose "Big" John Macleod held tightly onto his prize hoping the break of day will reveal to him what the BAUCHAN looked like. It begged for its release and Macleod took pity on it, making it swear by "book, candle, and black stockings ('on its knees')" to leave and never return. It did as was asked and fled, lamenting its plight in song.

Sources: Briggs, *Encyclopedia of Fairies*, 79; Gordon, *Highways and Byways in the West Highlands*, 74–6; Rose, *Giants, Monsters, and Dragons*, 86

Corcyra

In classical Greek mythology Corcyra was one of the twelve ASOPIDES, the NAIADS daughters of ASOPUS; they were the NYMPHS of the river Asopos in Sikyonia and Boiotia, central and southern Greece. She and each of her sisters were abducted and raped by Zeus (Jupiter) and many of the other Olympian gods.

Sources: Classical Association, *Classical Review*, Volume 12, 125; Quiggin, *Essays and Studies Presented to William Ridgeway*, 224

Coronis

A NYMPH in classical reek mythology, Coronis was one of the MAENADS, the collective name of the daughter born of Mnemosyne, the personification of memory, and the god Zeus (Jupiter), after nine days of continuous intercourse. When the god Dionysus (Bacchus) was unable to save her from being raped he cursed her assailant with madness and eventually committed suicide.

Source: Monaghan, *Encyclopedia of Goddesses and Heroines*, 419

Corrigan

Variations: Fées, KORRIGAN, Ozeganned

An injurious female NATURE-SPIRIT in the folklore of Brittany, the Corrigan ("fairy" or "little DWARF") was associated with ghosts and spirits of the dead. Fond of beautiful human children, they were said take them from their homes and leave a CHANGELING in their place. In lower Brittany Corrigan tribes were collectively known as *corriket*. There, when a farmer slaughtered his fattened cow or ox the Corrigan was always invited. If the fairy partook in the feast, displayed

perfect manners and was of a good humor than the animal would be found whole and alive in the morning. If the fairy refused the invitation the animal remained slaughtered.

In some lore the Corrigan was a singular individual, the fairy spirit of an ancient druid aggressive toward Christian priests. In other Breton lore she was described as looking like a beautiful blond haired woman by night and a hideous HAG by day. If a human man fell in love with her one night and was open-minded enough to love her throughout the day, she will transform into a human and be a permanent vision of loveliness.

Sources: Bord, *Fairies*, 59; Evans-Wentz, *Fairy-Faith in Celtic Countries*, 159, 181, 419; McCoy, *Witch's Guide to Faery Folk*, 203–4; Monaghan, *Encyclopedia of Celtic Mythology and Folklore*, 275

Corycia

Variations: Corycae

A NYMPH from Greek mythology, Corycia was said to be one of the "triple muses of divination at Delphi" along with DAPHNUS, KLEODORA, MELAINA, and THIUA. She was one of the NAIADS and one of a trio of NYMPHS known collectively as the Thriae or the Thriai. By the god, Apollo, she gave birth to a son named Lycorus (Lycoreus or Lycorua). The corycian cave located above Delphi and figures heavily in Delphian myth is named for her; it is where the priestess attempted conception rituals.

Sources: Brewer, *Dictionary of Phrase and Fable*, 296; Lemprière, *Classical Dictionary*, 75; Monaghan, *Goddesses in World Culture*, 147; Rigoglioso, *Cult of Divine Birth in Ancient Greece*, 198

Couril

In the folklore of northwest Brittany, France, the couril are a type of DWARF or fairy; they are said to live in the stone circles that are plentiful throughout the region, such as in Tresmalaouen. They are said to look like tiny humans with but have webbed feet and a malignant disposition. The couril have a great love of dancing and at night, should a man approach too close during their festivities the will be compelled to join in until the dawn; sadly, sometimes he may die of exhaustion before sunrise. On the other hand, if a woman is forced to dance with the couril, nine months late she will give birth to a child the wicked mined fairies have made to look like someone in the village.

Sources: Croker, *Fairy Legends and Traditions of the South of Ireland*, Volumes 1–3, 150; Keightly, *World Guide to Gnomes, Fairies, Elves, and Other Little Peo-*

ple, 441; Rose, *Spirits, Fairies, Leprechauns, and Goblins*, 73, 351

Cowlug Sprites

Fairy spirits seen on in the border villages of Bowden and Gateside in Roxburghshire, the cowlug sprites are described only as having broad ears like a cow. These fairy spirits only appear on certain undisclosed nights of the year called Cowlug E'en.

Sources: Briggs, *Encyclopedia of Fairies*, 80–1; Henderson, *Folk-Lore of the Northern Countries*, 262; Spence, *Fairy Tradition in Britain*, 141

Craneus

Variations: Craneia

In ancient Greek mythology Craneus was a HAMADRYAD of the cornel tree; she was born from the incestuous relationship between Oxylus and his sister.

Sources: Athenaeus of Naucratis, *Deipnosophists*, Volume 1, 131; Gerber, *Greek Iambic Poetry*, 391

Cranto

Variations: Kranto

A sea–NYMPH, Cranto was one of the NEREIDS, the daughters of Nerues and DORIS in classical Greek mythology.

Sources: Apollodorus, *Library of Greek Mythology*, 308; Bell, *Women of Classical Mythology*, 140; Day, *God's Conflict with the Dragon and the Sea*, 388; Grimal, *Dictionary of Classical Mythology*, 308

Cred

Variations: Créd, Creide ingen Guaire

Cred is an Irish FAIRY QUEEN and a poet; her home is located the mountains known as the Paps of Danu in Kerry County. The beautiful and young Cred is married to an old king named Marcan, whom she hates; Cano is her lover. The universal love triangle of an aged husband, a young wife and her youthful lover makes Cano, Cred and Marcan the prototypes of Iseult, Marc'h and Tristan.

Sources: Monaghan, *Red-Haired Girl from the Bog*, 255, 256; Williams, *Irish Literary Tradition*, 136

Crenaeis

Born one of the 3,000 daughters of the Titians, Oceanus and Tethys, Crenaeis was one of the named OCEANIDS; she was described only as wearing a saffron colored robe.

Sources: Boswell, *What Men or Gods Are These*, 58; Hesiod, *Works of Hesiod, Callimachus, and Theognis*, 20

Crendé

According to Irish lore, Crendé was the fairy bronze-worker of the TUATHA DÉ DANANN.

Sources: Rose, *Spirits, Fairies, Leprechauns, and Goblins*, 74, 351

Creneis

Born one of the 3,000 daughters of the Titians, Oceanus and Tethys, Creneis was one of the named OCEANIDS.

Sources: Apollodorus, *Apollodorus' Library and Hyginus' Fabulae*, 95; Boswell, *What Men or Gods Are These*, 58; Hesiod, *Works of Hesiod, Callimachus, and Theognis*, 20

Crenis

A sea–NYMPH, Crenis was one of the named NEREID; she was born of Nereus and DORIS in classical Greek mythology.

Source: Lemprière, *Classical Dictionary*, 494

Creusa

Creusa was a NYMPH from the mythology of ancient Greece and Rome; she was born of Eaia, the personification of mother earth, and Oceanus. A Thessalonian NAIAD, she was loved by the river PENEUS and with him bore two sons, Hypseus and STILBE. Sometimes she was said to be the mother of a third son, Andreus.

Sources: Day, *God's Conflict with the Dragon and the Sea*, 13; Grimal, *Dictionary of Classical Mythology*, 114; Smith, *Dictionary of Greek and Roman Biography and Mythology*, 196

Crimbils

Variations: Cryfaglach, Cyrfaglach

In Welsh fairly lore, crimbils are the offspring born of the fairies known as BENDITH Y MAMAU; these are very often the babes left behind when a human baby has been stolen and a CHANGELING has been left in its place. Crimbils are ugly but have a calm temperament. Because of their appearance they tend to have lonely childhoods. Born with a natural gift for music and song the crimbil will use it to gain attention and parise.

Sources: Briggs, *Encyclopedia of Fairies*, 81; Page, *Encyclopedia of Things that Never Were*, 54; Rhys, *Celtic folklore: Welsh and Manx*, Volume 1, 496

Crinaeae

In Greek mythology the crinaeae are a subspecies of the NAIAD, they are the NYMPHS of fountains.

Sources: Chopra, *Academic Dictionary of Mythol-*

ogy, 198; Day, *God's Conflict with the Dragon and the Sea*, 391, 394; Maberry, *Cryptopedia*, 112

Crinisus

Born one of the 3,000 daughters of the Titians, Oceanus and Tethys, Crinisus was one of the named OCEANIDS in classical Greek mythology.

Sources: Boswell, *What Men or Gods Are These*, 58; Day, *God's Conflict with the Dragon and the Sea*, 64; Hesiod, *Works of Hesiod, Callimachus, and Theognis*, 20

Crions

Variations: COURILS, Gorics, Kouril, Koril

These GOBLINS from the lore of French Brittany stand only between two and three feet tall but are said to possess the strength of GIANTS; they are accredited as being the ones who created Ti Goriquet ("House of the Gorics"), 4,000 large stones standing in an open field. At night crions would dance among the stone and anyone who happened across them was compelled to join them, dancing and whirling about until they fell from exhaustion. Like Nains, they frequent abandoned Druidical monuments, such as Carnac and Tresmalouen, as well as the remnants of castle foundations, like Morlaix.

Legend tell us the crions are the guardians of the golden treasures hidden beneath Carnac and they themselves have a treasure hoard as great as any of the GNOMES in Germany or Norway. On occasion they will let a mortal take a handful of treasure, but if they attempt to take more, what they already have will vanish and their ears will be soundly boxed by invisible hands.

Sources: Keightly, *World Guide to Gnomes, Fairies, Elves, and Other Little People*, 440; Summers, *Geography of Witchcraft*, 389; Thoms, *Lays and Legends of Various Nations*, 38

Critomedia

In Greek mythology Critomedia was a water–NYMPH and one of the named DANAIDS, the collective name for the daughters of Danaus; her name appears in a list of the DANAIDS generated by Gaius Julius Hyginus (ca. 64 B.C.–A.D. 17), a Latin author. Critomedia was wedded to Antipaphus and killed him on their wedding night.

Sources: Hyginus, *Myths of Hyginus*, 133; Parada, *Genealogical Guide to Greek Mythology*, 22, 59

Crocale

Variations: Krokalê

Born one of the 3,000 daughters of the Titians, Oceanus and Tethys, Crocale ("sea-shore") was one of the named OCEANIDS in classical Greek mythology; she was one of the OCEANID NYMPHS to the goddess, Artemis (Diana) as her hairdresser. Crocale was with HYALE and NEPHELE the day Artemis was bathing and spied upon by Actaeon.

Sources: Bulfinch, *Illustrated Age of Fable*, 32; Monaghan, *New Book of Goddesses and Heroines*, 340; Salmonson, *Encyclopedia of Amazons*, 65

Crodh Mara

Variations: Crodh Sidhe

Less dangerous than the EACH UISCE, the crodh mara ("cattle of the sea") from the Scottish Highlands are a breed of fairy-cattle described as being dun colored and hummel ("hornless"), although those in Skye are said to be black or red. On occasion one of the fair bulls will mate with a mortal cow and greatly improve the bloodline. If a crodh mara cow joins a mortal herd they will instinctually follow her, should the fairy-cow return to her *knowe* the herd will follow her in, never to return.

As the crodh sidhe ("fairy cow") this breed of friendly fairy-cow is typically described as being hummel, round eared, and white bodied with red speckles (see FAIRY ANIMAL), similar to the GWARTHEG Y LLYN. Dwelling in the sea and living on seaweed the crodh sidhe would sometimes join up with a mortal herd to improve the stocks quality but eventually, they would always make their way back home to the sea.

Sources: Briggs, *Encyclopedia of Fairies*, 81; Eberhart, *Mysterious Creatures*, 580; Monaghan, *Encyclopedia of Celtic Mythology and Folklore*, 105

Croquemitaine

Variations: Carabibounet, Croque-Mitaine, Miare-Couette, Micaraouda, Papotchantel, Ratepenate

In France the croquemitaine ("to crunch") is an ugly BOGEYMAN used to frighten children into good behavior. He is described as having a bulbous nose, empty eyes, huge teeth, pointy ears, spiky white hair, thick mouth, and Newcastle styled white beard. Popularized in the eighteenth and nineteenth century through cartoons and wooden cut outs, he was often depicted with his equally ugly wife, Dame Croquemitaine (or Vipérine) and their servant, Bras-de-Fer (or Mordillard, Brique-à-Brac).

Sources: Gilman, *New International Encyclopædia*, Volume 5, 605; Rose, *Giants, Monsters, and Dragons*, 89

Cu Sith

Variations: Cusith, Cu Sìth

Cu Sith is a fairy-dog from the Scottish Highlands. Described as having huge feet, long and shaggy dark green hair, and a long but coiled up tail resting on its back. It is different from other fairy-dogs which are typically described as being white with red ears, such as the Hounds of Annwn (see ANNWN, HOUNDS OF). Cu sith is as large as a two-year old bull but this monstrous canine whose feet was as broad as a man's chest glided along the earth in near silence, traveling in straight lines. When it hunts unlike other dogs the cu sith does not cry out continuously but rather gives three sharp barks which could be heard by ships out to sea.

Sources: Briggs, *Encyclopedia of Fairies*, 83; Campbell, *Superstitions of the Highlands and Islands of Scotland*, 141–3; Rosen, *Mythical Creatures Bible*, 114

Cuachag

The cuachag ("cuckoo" or "little cup") is an injurious species of water fairy living in the Scottish Highlands; it is most often associated with Glen Cuaich in Inverness-shire. The cuachag is one of the FUATH, a collective name for the malicious and monstrous water fay in Scottish folklore.

Sources: Briggs, *Encyclopedia of Fairies*, 84; Macleod, *Dictionary of the Gaelic Language,* 209; Mackenzie, *Scottish Folk-Lore and Folk Life*, 233

Cuarahu-Yara

Variations: El Dueno del Sol ("the Owner of the Sun")

A nocturnal fairy from Brazilian lore, a cuarahu-yara appears only when its name is spoken, making a nuisance of itself by opening farm gates, impregnating women with its hand, and spooking horses. It is described as being hairy, tall, and wearing a large hat. If one can be persuaded, ca urahu-yara will adopt a family, live in their house, and perform small household tasks, much like the BROWNIE. It will help find lost items with offerings of cigarettes, items he likely hid. Cuarahu-yara also watches over birds preventing children from shooting them. It will alert others of danger by making a loud hissing sound.

Sources: Ambrosetti, *Supersticiones y Leyendas*, 50; Morel, *Diccionario Mitológico Americano*, 42

Cuco

Variations: Abuelo ("grandfather"), Calaca ("skeleton"), Chamucho, Chumcho, Coca, Coco, Coco Man, Cuca, Cucui, Cucuy

The cuco is a BOGEYMAN or NURSERY BOGIE found in many Hispanic and Lusophone speaking countries. Parents will tell their children if they do not go to sleep the cuco will take them away. There is no consistent description of this FAIRY ANIMAL but traditionally it is represented by a Jack-o'-Lantern, a carved vegetable lantern made from a pumpkin. The coca, the female version of this creature, is represented as a dragon in Galician and Portuguese folklore.

Sources: Herrera-Sobek, *Chicano Folklore*, 223, 226; Landy, *Tropical Childhood*, 34, 129; Maberry, *They Bite*, 337

Cuilenn

Variations: Culann, Cullen

In Irish mythology Cuilenn ("holly") was the FAIRY KING ruling from his seat of power, a mountain known as Slieve Gullion; it was located within the Ring of Gullion, a huge circular mountain created by an ancient volcano. The lake located near the mountain's summit is said to turn anyone who swims in it grey.

Sources: Lincoln, *Death, War, and Sacrifice*, 56; Monaghan, *Encyclopedia of Celtic Mythology and Folklore*, 109

Curupira

Variations: Caapora ("inhabitant of the woods"), Caipira, CAIPORA, Curupura

A NATURE SPIRIT from the Tupi people of Brazil, the curupira ("boy body") is a guardian of the forest, protecting it from the devastation of man; this fairy will allow anyone who hunts for food to do so with event but will cause no end of trouble for those who hunt for pleasure. It has the ability to summon a hunter by calling out his name. Once the greedy hunter is confused and lost in the jungle the curupira will lure him into the pitfalls and traps it has set throughout the jungle. Its high-pitched shrill whistle is enough to stun an adult, knocking him to his knees.

The curupira is described as looking like a boy with backward facing feet, green teeth, large pointy ears, and hair made of living flames. Occasionally it will assume the form of a brocket, a frog, an old man, a very tall man, or a paca. It rides of the back of a wild boar and has a special fondness for the white-lipped peccaries and brocket deer. Although it wanders the wilderness freely and calls not particular location home, it routinely sleeps at the base of the kapok tree. The mythology is confusing as to whether this is a singular entity or a race of fairies.

Sources: de Almeida, *Brazilian Folktales*, 41; Mac-Donald, *Earth Care*, 75; Smith, *Enchanted Amazon Rain Forest*, 43

Cururipur

In South American folklore the cururipur is a powerful NATURE SPIRIT, similar to the CUCUPIRA, except it is especially protective of tortoises; it will attack anyone who would try to harm or hunt one.

Sources: Eason, *Complete Guide to Faeries and Magical Beings*, 148; Eason, *Scrying the Secrets of the Future*, 100

Cutty Soams

In Cornish mining lore Cutty Soams is a coal-pit BOGLE, similar to a BROWNIE. Typically this fairy is mischievous, cutting rope to bits is his specialty, but on occasion he will do a good deed, such as cutting the rope-traces (or *soams*) the assistant putters use to yoke the wooden trams.

Sources: Briggs, *Encyclopedia of Fairies*, 85; Denham, *Denham Tracts*, 362; Ginswick, *Labour and the Poor in England and Wales 1849–1851*, 65

Cwn Annwfn

Variations: Cwn Annwn ("Hounds of Annwn," see ANNWN, HOUNDS OF), Cwn Cyrff, Cwn Mamau, Cwn Wyber, GABRIEL HOUNDS

The Cwn Annwfn ("the dogs of the In-World") are the red-eared and white bodied fairy-hounds of the underworld in Welsh fairy mythology. These hounds specialize in revenge, hunting down those who have overhunted the area or ran an animal to death; they will find the guilty and chance him until he can run no more, only then will they move in for the kill.

Most often seen on the mountains of Cadair Idris it is said their bays carry off the mountain at night. The growling of the cwn annwfn is very misleading, as it is at its loudest when they are far off; as they near, the sound decreases as their attack becomes more and more imminent. When not hunting, the cwn annwfn fly through the sky and hover over house where a death will soon occur, acting like a death omen.

Ownership of the cwn annwfn has fallen to both Bran the Blessed and GWYN AP NUDD (the Devil); no matter who they answer to, the pack goes out with their master to partake on the WILD HUNT on the eves of All Saints' Day, Christmas, Good Friday, New Year, Saint Agnes' Day, Saint David's Day, Saint John's Day, Saint Martin's Day, and Saint Michael the Archangel's Day.

Sources: Hastings, *Encyclopedia of Religion and Ethics*, Part 8, 575; Lindahl, *Medieval Folklore*, 190; Matthews, *Encyclopaedia of Celtic Myth and Legend*, 484; Monaghan, *Encyclopedia of Celtic Mythology and Folklore*, 112

Cycais

Cycais was a NYMPH of Telos in classical Greek mythology.

Source: Müller, *Ancient Art and Its Remains*, 540

Cydippe

A sea–NYMPH, Cydippe was one of the named NEREID; she was born of Nereus and DORIS in classical Greek mythology.

Sources: Apollodorus, *Apollodorus' Library and Hyginus' Fabulae*, 95; Bell, *Bell's New Pantheon or Historical Dictionary of the Gods*, 112; Lemprière, *Classical Dictionary*, 468

Cyhyraeth

Variations: CAOINEAG

A BANSHEE-like spirit from the folklore of Glamorganshire, Wales Cyhyraeth was infrequently seen but often heard crying and wailing. Associated with specific families, this fairy frequents crossroads and walks along the Glamorganshire coastline prior to shipwrecks. When Cyhyraeth walks through village streets she was said to be crying and wailing as she opened doors at random and rattled window shutters. She was most often seen near populated areas right before an epidemic broke out.

Sources: Briggs, *Fairies in Tradition and Literature*, 279; Illes, *Encyclopedia of Spirits*, 339; Sikes, British Goblins, 221

Cymadoce

A sea–NYMPH from Greek mythology, Cymadoce was the NYMPH of the foamy white waves in classical Greek mythology.

Source: Betham, *Transactions of the Royal Irish Academy*, Volume 17, 89

Cymatolege

Variations: KYMATOLEGE

A sea–NYMPH from Greek mythology, Cymatolege was the NEREIS of the breakers. Along with her sisters AMPHITRITE and CYMOTHOE, they have control over the waves when the sea is misty and there are blasts of violent wind; they were born the daughters of Nerues and DORIS.

Sources: Betham, *Transactions of the Royal Irish Academy*, Volume 17, 88; Hesiod, *Works of Hesiod, Callimachus, and Theognis*, 15

Cymodoce

Variations: Cymodocè

A sea–NYMPH, Cymodoce ("wave receiver") was one of the named NEREIS in classical Greek mythology.

Sources: Apollodorus, *Apollodorus' Library and Hyginus' Fabulae*, 95; Gould, *Historic Magazine and Notes and Queries*, Vol 14, 212

Cymothoe

A sea–NYMPH, Cymothoe, was the NEREIDS of gentle and quiet waves in classical Greek mythology; she was born the daughter of Nerues and DORIS (see AMPHITRITE and CYMATOLEGE) in classical Greek mythology.

Sources: Betham, *Transactions of the Royal Irish Academy*, Volume 17, 88; Homer, *The Iliad*, 503; Trzaskoma, *Anthology of Classical Myth*, 18; Westmoreland, *Ancient Greek Beliefs* 25

Cynosura

Variations: KYNOSOURA

In ancient Greek mythology Cynosura ("dog's tail") was an OREAD, a NYMPH of Mount Ida, Crete. She, along with HELIKE, nursed the infant god, Zeus (Jupiter), while he was in hiding from his father, Cronus.

Sources: Grimal, *Dictionary of Classical Mythology*, 121; Smith, *New Classical Dictionary of Biography, Mythology, and Geography*, 235

Cyoeraeth

Variations: Cy-oer-aeth, GWRACH Y RHIBYN

In Welsh mythology the cyoeraeth is a fairy spirit similar to the GWRACH Y RHIBYN. It has a cold and chilling voice, disheveled hair, cadaverous body, long black teeth, and long withered arms; most often it is said to be female. Seldom seen but often heard the cyoeraeth's roar was enough to cause a man to freeze up, his body locked with fear. It is sometimes heard making gentle splashing sounds near water while weeping, "my husband, my, husband" or "my child, my child" in a woman's voice or "my wife, my wife" if in a man's. In some regions hearing the cyoeraeth is considered to be a death omen.

Sources: Allardice, *Myths, Gods, and Fantasy*, 60; Barber, *Monsters Who's Who*, 22; Howels, *Cambrian Quarterly Magazine and Celtic Repertory*, Volume 3, 73–4

Dactyl

In ancient Greek mythology the dactyls ("fingers") were a species of NATURE SPIRIT who lived on Mount Ida in Phrygia who discovered iron and perfected the art of ironworking. Although the original number of dactyls was three, Acmon ("anvil"), Celmis ("smelter"), and Damnameneus (" hammer") there numbers have also been said to be five or ten (five females representing the left hand and five males to represent the right), fifty-two, and one hundred. Other dactly named by various ancient authors were Acesidas, Cyllenus, Delas, Epimedes, Heracles, Idas, Jasius, Paconius, Scythes, and Titias; typically their names were said to be a well-guarded secret.

In addition to having invented ironworking, the dactyls were also accredited with the discovery of the dactylic rhythm and music.

Sources: Graves, *Greek Myths*, 53; Guiley, *Encyclopedia of Angels*, 84; Smith, *Dictionary of Greek and Roman Biography and Mythology*, 926

Dagda

Variations: Dagda the Good God, Eoachaid Ollathif ("Father of All"), Great Dagda, Ruad Rofessa ("Red One of Great Knowledge"), The Dagda

Dagda is the High King of the TUATHA DE DANANN in Irish mythology; originally he was a god but has since been reduced to FAIRY KING. A powerful leader known for his knowledge, prowess with a war club, magical ability, and wisdom, after he and his people were defeated by the invading Milesians they retreated underground but were still able to exert some control over the land. Dagda, cruel, greedy, and uncouth, used his influence and prohibited crops from growing or cows from giving milk until the Milesians agreed upon a peace treaty with them.

He had four sons, Angus Mac Og, Aedh, Lug, and Ogme; each of them like their father is an immortal who can only be killed in combat. He also possessed four magnificent underground palaces; his magical harp could fly through the air at his command and make its listeners, cry or laugh depending the music being played. Associated with abundance, Dagda also possessed a magical cauldron capable of feeding any number of people and oftentimes was taxed by his own enormous appetite.

Sources: Briggs, *Encyclopedia of Fairies*, 86–7; Matthews, *Encyclopaedia of Celtic Myth and Legend*, 17, 24, 487; Monaghan, *Encyclopedia of Celtic Mythology and Folklore*, 114

Dagfinnr

Variations: Dagfinn

Dagfinnr ("day finder") was one of the many

DWARFS named in the *Voluspa*, the first and best known poem of the *Poetic Edda*, a collection of Old Norse poems dating back to about 985, A.D.

Sources: Anderson, *A Certain Text,* 175; Di Lauro, *Through a Glass Darkly,* 70

Dagwanoenyent

Variations: Dagwano'ĕñ'iĕn, Flying Heads, Hatdedases

Dagwanoenyent ("what habitually hits or knocks our heads") are flying NATURE SPIRITS from the mythology of the Seneca People of North America, one of the five Iroquoi tribes; they are the personification of the cyclone or whirlwind. These fairy creatures have veracious appetites and will eat anything when they are hungry, even rocks; when they do, the crunching sound of it can be heard for miles. Sometimes Dagwanoenyent is portrayed in stories as a singular individual, an elderly female witch.

Sources: Avant, *Mythological Reference,* 36; Hewitt, *Seneca Fiction, Legends, and Myths,* 85, 800; Maberry, *Cryptopedia,* 56

Daimones

Variations: Daemones

Wild and rustic NATURE SPIRITS from the mythology of ancient Greece, the daimones ("divine beings") lived in the forests, mountains, and uncultivated fields. Apart from dancing, drinking, playing the flute and having sex, these raucous fairies were a part of the entourage of the gods Artemis (Diana), Dionysus (Bacchus), Hermes (Mercury), Cybele, and Pan (Faunus). Daimones were less powerful than the gods but more powerful than mankind and were often seen as a protective spirit, similar to a guardian angel of modern Christian beliefs. Diamones could be of either gender and act as a force of evil or good; those who were generally benign were called eudaimones while those who were chaotic or malicious were known as kakodiamones. Entities who were considered to be of the daimones were Corybantes (Korybantes), Curetes, DACTYLS, Genii (DJINN), NATURE SPIRITS, SATYERS, and the Sileni.

Sources: Belanger, *Dictionary of Demons,* 107; Guiley, *Encyclopedia of Angels,* 84; Illes, *Encyclopedia of Fairies,* 343

Dain

Variations: Dáinn

Dain ("dead") was a DWARF or ELF named in the *Poetic Edda,* a collection of ancient Norse poems preserved in the mediaeval manuscript

Codex Regius. He was one of the four DWARFS in Nordic mythology whose name was those of the hart's that ate the buds off of Yggdrasil, the World Tree (see DAVALIN, DUNEYR, and DURATHROR). The four DWARFS were likely the guardians of it.

Sources: Bellows, *Poetic Edda,* 62, 220; Lindow, *Norse Mythology,* vii; Rose, *Spirits, Fairies, Leprechauns, and Goblins,* 79; Sykes, *Who's Who in Non-Classical Mythology,* 53

Daira

Variations: Daeira

Born one of the 3,000 daughters of the Titians, Oceanus and Tethys, Daira was one of the named OCEANIDS in ancient Greek mythology; she was a NYMPH of the town of Eleusis in Attika, southern Greece. By the god Hermes (Mercury) she was the mother of Eleusis.

Sources: Conti, *Natale Conti's Mythologiae: Books VI–X,* 701; Wright, *Eleusinian Mysteries and Rites,* 18

Dâl Peri

In Persian fairy lore, Dâl Peri and his brother, MILÂN SHÂH PERI, tried to save their sister the beautiful PERI MERJÂN ("Fairy Pearl"), from the fierce DEEV, DEMRUSH, but failed.

Sources: Hunt, *Leigh Hunt's London Journal,* Volumes 1–2, 235; Keightly, *World Guide to Gnomes, Fairies, Elves, and Other Little People,* 18

Dama Dagenda

In the mythology of the Huli people of Papua New Guinea, the dama dagenda are a species of NATURE SPIRIT that create nose bleeds and painful open sores on the bodies of anyone who invade their territory. The only known way to protect yourself from their attack is to have a shaman teach you a language the dama dagenda do not know and then using it, speak to yourself as you transverse their terrain.

Sources: Chopra, *Academic Dictionary,* 79; Page, *Encyclopedia of Things That Never Were,* 58; Parratt, *Papuan Belief and Ritual,* 7

Dame Abonde

Variations: Dame Abundia, Dame Habonde, the Giver of Abundance, HABONDE, HABUNDIA

In French fairy lore, Dame Abonde was a FAIRY QUEEN; her lands were located in the forests of Lorraine. This star crowned queen was associated with the full moon and Saint John's Day. Dame Abonde is said to bring good luck and treasure wherever she goes; her companion is called Hobany.

Sources: Bayley, *Archaic England*, 165; Keightly, *World Guide to Gnomes, Fairies, Elves, and Other Little People*, 474; Maclaren, *Fairy Family*, 43

La Dame d'Aprigny

One of the *dames blanches* ("WHITE LADIES") of French lore, La Dame d'Aprigny is said to appear in a narrow ravine of Rue Saint Quentin at Bayeux. There, upon seeing a traveler, she will extend her hand inviting him to join her in a dance. If the traveler accepts after a round or two, she curtsies, thanks, and dismisses him; however if the traveler refuses or shows signs of fear la dame d'Aprigny will leap upon him and throw him into a ditch full of briars and thorns. La Dame d'Aprigny is a peer of ABONDE.

Sources: Brewer, *Dictionary of Phrase and Fable*, 1269; Keightly, *World Guide to Gnomes, Fairies, Elves, and Other Little People*, 427

Dame du Lac

Variations: Du Lac, LADY OF THE LAKE, Niniane, Vivienne

Born near Paradise and skilled in the magical arts, Dame du Lac is oftentimes compared to MORGAN LA FAY, as both fairy women were said to be loved by Merlin the Magician of Arthurian lore. Beautiful and possessing many natural gifts, Dame du Lac seeks to do good and help the knights of Arthur's court, whereas MORGAN LA FAY is evil and tries to thwart them at every turn. In a few stories it was said she was taught her magic by Merlin but most often her knowledge was natural and innate due to her fairy nature. She was Lancelot's adoptive mother, nurse and protector while he recovered from his wounds and madness; she gifted him with a fairy-forged sword and a ring capable of breaking any enchantment. She was a friend of IBLIS, the wife of Lancelot but also encouraged the love between Queen Guinevere and Lancelot. Dame du Lac wears white at all times and insists her entourage does as well.

Sources: Keightly, *World Guide to Gnomes, Fairies, Elves, and Other Little People*, 31; Littleton, *From Scythia to Camelot*, 154–7; Paton, *Studies in the Fairy Mythology of Arthurian Romance*, 195–6, 200

Dame Hirip

Variations: Tünder

In Hungarian lore Dame Hirip is a fairy-woman who was known for abducting young women. She would stand upon her tower located in Varoldal near Gyergyo-Szens-Miklos, holding a wreath in her hands as she waited for her two sons to return home, as they were the one who did actual abduction. Her sons were eventually slain by a pair of heroes who were dressed in mourning clothing.

Sources: Jones, *Notes and Queries*, 501; Monaghan, *Encyclopedia of Goddesses and Heroines*, 361; Rose, *Spirits, Fairies, Leprechauns, and Goblins*, 351

Dame Tryamoug

Variations: Dame Tryamour

In French Arthurian lore, Dame Tryamoug was a sexually aggressive fairy maiden, the daughter of a FAIRY KING. She loved Sir Launfal and solicited a promise from him to never speak of her or their romance. When Queen Guinevere, who did not initially like the knight, shuns him and does him a disservice, Launfal is forced to live at some level of poverty. Tryamoug, wanting her lover to be happy and well liked, gifted to him with a never-failing purse as well as many lavish gifts. Upon his return to court, the Queen tries to discover the source of his wealth but the knight will not tell. Angered she accuses him of being a homosexual for there is not obvious sign of his having a lover. Shamed, he confessed the source and instantly all his fairy-given wealth melt away.

Sources: Keightly, *World Guide to Gnomes, Fairies, Elves, and Other Little People*, 37; Neal, *Masculine Self in Late Medieval England*, 211; Wells, *Manual of the Writings in Middle English, 1050–1500*, Volume 1, 138–9

Dames Blanches

In Normandy the dames blanches ("WHITE LADIES") are a species of fairy or NATURE SPIRIT living in bogs, under bridges, on fords, and in pools and ravines. Described as being beautiful and dressed in revealing fashion theses injurious fairies draw attention to themselves, and then force people to dance with them, usually until they pass out or die from exhaustion.

Sources: Bois, *Jersey Folklore and Superstitions*, 516; Keightly, *World Guide to Gnomes, Fairies, Elves, and Other Little People*, 474

Damone

In Greek mythology Damone was a water–NYMPH and one of the named DANAIDS, the collective name for the daughters of Danaus; her name appears in a list of the DANAIDS generated by Gaius Julius Hyginus (ca. 64 B.C.–A.D. 17), a Latin author. Damone was wedded to Amyntor and killed him on their wedding night.

Sources: Bell, *Women of Classical Mythology*, 147,

149; Lemprière, *Classical Dictionary*, 46; Parada, *Genealogical Guide to Greek Mythology*, 18, 59

Dana O'Shee

Variations: DAOINE SIDHE ("People of the Mounds"), Daoine O'Sidhe

Originally a divine race in Irish folklore known as the TUATHA DE DANANN, they later came to be known as the Dana O'Shee. Described as being aristocratic and beautiful, they live in Tir-nan-Og ("Land of the Ever-Young") where there they are exempt from death under the rulership of their own kings and queens. These TROOPING FAIRIES are fond of dancing, feasting, horseback riding, hunting game, and parading; they are renown for healing the sick and warding off diseases. Resembling humans the Dana O'Shee can shape-shift and become invisible.

Sources: Jestice, *Encyclopedia of Irish Spirituality*, 102; Monaghan, *Encyclopedia of Celtic Mythology and Folklore*, 117; Rose, *Spirits, Fairies, Gnomes, and Goblins*, 79

Danaid (plural: Danaids)

Variations: Danaides, Danaïdes, Daughters of Danaus

In Greek mythology a Danaid is a water–NYMPH; collectively they are the fifty daughters of Danaus who are jointly known as the Danaids. In the most popular version of the mythology the sisters are each set to marry one of the fifty sons of Aegyptus, a mythical king of Egypt. Their father, King Danaus, not pleased with the arrangement he agreed to, ordered his daughters to murder their spouses. On their wedding night the Danaids killed their husbands save for one daughter named AMYMONE; she chose not to join her sisters in the murderous plot because her husband, Lynceus (Enceladus) respected her desire to remain a virgin. For their crime the Danaids are condemned to spend eternity carrying water in a sieve in an attempt to fill a leaky tub in order to wash away their sin of their crime; they come to represent the futility of repeating a task that can never be completed.

Apollodorus, a Greek scholar and grammarian, listed not only the daughters and who they married but also the names of the mothers:

ACTAEA, one of the six daughters of Pieria was given to Periphas, one of the six sons of Gorgo; ADIANTE, one of the two daughters of Herse was given to Daiphron (different one), one of the two sons of Hephaestine; ADITE, one of the six daughters of Pieria was given to Menalces, one of the six sons of Gorgo; AGAVE, one of the four daughters of Europe was given to Lycus, one of the four sons of Argyphia; AMYMONE, one of the four daughters of Europe was given to Enceladus, one of the four sons of Argyphia; ANAXIBIA, one of the seven daughters of an unnamed Ethiopian woman to Archelaus, one of the seven sons of an unnamed Phoenician woman; Antheli, one of the twelve daughters of POLYXO and a NAIAD was given to Cisseus, one of the twelve sons of CALIADNE who was also a NAIAD; ASTERIA, one of the ten daughters of either ATLANTEIA or of PHOEBE, the HAMADRYADS was given to Chaetus, one of the ten sons of an unnamed Arabic woman; AUTOMATE, one of the four daughters of Europe was given to Busiris, one of the four sons of Argyphia; AUTONOE, one of the twelve daughters of POLYXO and a NAIAD was given to Eurylochus, one of the twelve sons of CALIADNE who was also a NAIAD; BRYCE, one of the twelve daughters of POLYXO and a NAIAD was given to Chthonius, one of the twelve sons of CALIADNE who was also a NAIAD; Callidice, one of the four daughters of Crino was given to Pandion, one of the four sons of Hephaestine; CELAENO, one of the four daughters of Crino was given to Hyperbius, one of the four sons of Hephaestine; CHRYSIPPE, one of the three daughters of MEMPHIS was given to Chrysippus, one of the three sons of Tyria without the casting of lots since they were namesakes; CLEODORE, one of the twelve daughters of POLYXO and a NAIAD was given to Lixus, one of the twelve sons of CALIADNE who was also a NAIAD; CLEOPATRA (not the Egyptian queen), one of the twelve daughters of POLYXO and a NAIAD was given to Hermus, one of the twelve sons of CALIADNE who was also a NAIAD; CLEOPATRA, one of the ten daughters of either ATLANTEIA or of PHOEBE, the HAMADRYADS was given to Agenor, one of the ten sons of an unnamed Arabic woman; CLITE, one of the three daughters of MEMPHIS was given to Clitus, one of the three sons of Tyria without the casting of lots since they were namesakes; DIOXIPPE, one of the six daughters of Pieria was given to Aegyptus, one of the six sons of Gorgo; Dorion, one of the seven daughters of an unnamed Ethiopian woman to Cercetes, one of the seven sons of an unnamed Phoenician woman; ELECTRA, one of the twelve daughters of POLYXO and a NAIAD was given to Peristhenes, one of the twelve sons of CALIADNE who was also a NAIAD; ERATO, one of the twelve daughters of POLYXO and a NAIAD was given to Bromius, one of the twelve sons of CALIADNE who was also a NAIAD; EURYDICE, one of the twelve daughters of POLYXO and a NAIAD was given to Dryas, one of the twelve sons of CALIADNE who was also a NAIAD; EVIPPE (different one), one of the twelve daughters of POLYXO and a NAIAD was given to Imbrus, one of the twelve sons of CALIADNE who was also a NAIAD; EVIPPE, one of the seven daughters of an unnamed Ethiopian woman to Argius, one of the seven sons of an unnamed Phoenician woman; GLAUCE, one of the ten daughters of either ATLANTEIA or of PHOEBE, the HAMADRYADS was given to Alces, one of the ten sons of an unnamed Arabic woman; GLAUCIPPE, one of the twelve daughters of POLYXO and a NAIAD was given to Potamon, one of the twelve sons of CALIADNE who was also a NAIAD; GORGE, one of the ten daughters of either ATLANTEIA or of PHOEBE, the HAMADRYADS was given to Hippothous, one of the ten sons of an unnamed Arabic woman; GORGOPHONE, one of the two daughters of Elephantis was given to Proteus, one of the two sons of Queen Argyphia; HIPPODAMIA (different one), one of the ten daughters of either ATLANTEIA or of PHOEBE, the HAMADRYADS was given to Diocorystes, one of the ten sons of an unnamed Arabic woman; HIPPODAMIA, one of the ten daughters of either ATLANTEIA or of PHOEBE, the HAMADRYADS was given to Istrus, one of the ten sons of an unnamed Arabic woman; HIPPODICE, one of the two daughters of Herse was given to Idas, one of the two sons of Hephaestine; HIPPOMEDUSA, one of the ten daughters of either ATLANTEIA or of PHOEBE, the HAMADRYADS was given to Alcmenor, one of the ten sons of an unnamed Arabic woman; HYPERIPPE, one of the four daughters of Crino was given to Hippocorystes, one of the four sons of Hephaestine; HYPERMNESTRA, one of the two daughters of Elephantis was given to Lyncaeus, one of the two sons of Queen Argyphia; IPHIMEDUSA, one of the ten daughters of either ATLANTEIA or of PHOEBE, the HAMADRYADS was given to Euchenor, t one of the ten sons of an unnamed Arabic woman; MNESTRA, one of the seven daughters of an unnamed Ethiopian woman to Aegius, one of the seven sons of an unnamed Phoenician woman; NELO, one of the seven daughters of an unnamed Ethiopian woman to Menemachus, one of the seven sons of an unnamed Phoenician woman; OCYPETE, one of the six daughters of Pieria was given to Lampus, one of the six sons of Gorgo; OEME, one of the four daughters of Crino was given to Arbelus, one of the four sons of Hephaestine; PHARTIS, one of the

seven daughters of an unnamed Ethiopian woman to Eurydamas, one of the seven sons of an unnamed Phoenician woman; PIRENE, one of the seven daughters of an unnamed Ethiopian woman to Agaptolemus, one of the seven sons of an unnamed Phoenician woman; PODARCE, one of the six daughters of Pieria was given to Oeneus, one of the six sons of Gorgo; PYLARGE, one of the six daughters of Pieria was given to Idmon, one of the six sons of Gorgo; RHODE, one of the ten daughters of either ATLANTEIA or of PHOEBE, the HAMADRYADS was given to Hippolytus, one of the ten sons of an unnamed Arabic woman; RHODIA, one of the ten daughters of either ATLANTEIA or of PHOEBE, the HAMADRYADS was given to Chalcodon, one of the ten sons of an unnamed Arabic woman; SCAEA, one of the four daughters of Europe was given to Daiphron, one of the four sons of Argyphia; STHENELE, one of the three daughters of MEMPHIS was given to Sthenelus, one of the three sons of Tyria without the casting of lots since they were namesakes; STYGNE, one of the twelve daughters of POLYXO and a NAIAD was given to Polyctor, one of the twelve sons of CALIADNE who was also a NAIAD; and THEANO, one of the twelve daughters of POLYXO and a NAIAD was given to Phantes, one of the twelve sons of CALIADNE who was also a NAIAD.

Gaius Julius Hyginus (ca. 64 B.C.–A.D. 17), a Latin author and a freedman of Caesar Augustus has also compiled a list of the Danaid and their husbands. It should be noted his list has little in common with Apollodorus,' he makes only forty-nine pairs, and does not name all the Danaid:

An unnamed Danaid was married to Armoasbus; ACAMANTIS to Ecnomius; AMPHICOMONE to Plexippus; AMYMONE to Midanus; ARCADIA to Xanthus; ARSALTE to Ephialtes; AUTODICE to Clytus; CELAENO to Aristonoos; CHRYSOTHEMIS to Asterides;CLEO to Asterius;CLEOPATRA to Hermus; CLEOPATRA (a second daughter with the same name) to Metalces; CRITOMEDIA to Antipaphus; DAMONE to Amyntor; DANAÏS to Pelops; DAPLIDICE to Pugno; DEMODITAS to Chrysippus; DEMOPHILE to Pamphilus; ELECTRA to Hyperantus; ERATO to Eudaemon; EUBULE to Demarchus; EUPHEME to Hyperbius; EUROPOME to Athletes; EURYDICE to Canthus; EVIPPE, to Agenor; GLAUCIPPE to Niauius; HECABE to Dryas; HELICE to Evidea; HELICTA to Cassus; HERO to Andromachus; Hipparete to Protheon; HIPPOTHOE to Obrimus; HYALE to Perius; ITEA to Antiochus; MIDEA to Antimachus; MONUSTE to Eurysthenes; MYRMI-

DONE to Mineus; OEME to Polydector; PHILA to Philinus; PHILOMELA to Panthius; PIRENE to Dolichus; POLYBE to Itonomus; POLYXENA to Aegyptus; PYRANTE to Athamas; PYRANTIS to Plexippus; SCYLLA to Proteus; THEMISTAGORA to Podasimus; and TRITE to Enceladus. HYPERMNESTRA saved her husband, Lynceus.

Throughout Greek mythology there are a few other women who are mentioned in passing as being one of the Danaid: Amphimedusa, the mother of Erythras by the god, Poseidon (Neptune); ANAXITHEA, the mother of Olenus by the god, Zeus (Jupiter); EURYTHOE, was one of the possible mothers of Oenomaus by the god Ares (Mars) (she may also be the mother of HIPPODAMIA by Oenomaus); HIPPODAMIA and Isione, wives of Olenus and Orchomenus or Chryses respectively, who were both seduced by the god Zeus (Jupiter); ISONOE, mother of Orchomenus by the god Zeus (Jupiter); PHAETHUSA, one of the possible mothers of Myrtilus by the god Hermes (Mercury); PHYLODAMEIA, mother of Pharis by the god Hermes (Mercury); PHYSADEIA, who, like her sister AMYMONE, gave her name to a freshwater source; POLYDORA, mother of Dryops (Oeta) by the river god Spercheus; and Side, a mythical eponym of a town in Laconia.

Sources: Antoninus Liberalis, *Metamorphoses of Antoninus Liberalis*, 32; Bowlby, *Freudian Mythologies*, 392–3; Callimachus, *Hymn 5 to Athena*, 47–48; Hastings, *Encyclopedia of Religion and Ethics*, Part 7, 392–3; Parada, *Genealogical Guide to Greek Mythology*, 59

Danais

A NYMPH from the town of Pisa in Elis, southern Greece, Danais ("she lives forever") was loved by the Elean King Pelops and their son, Chrysippus was said to have incomprehensible beauty in classical Greek mythology.

Sources: Bell, *Bell's New Pantheon*, 179; Smith, *New Classical Dictionary of Greek and Roman Biography*, 621

Danaïs

In Greek mythology Danaïs was a water–NYMPH and one of the named DANAIDS, the collective name for the daughters of Danaus; her name appears in a list of the DANAIDS generated by Gaius Julius Hyginus (ca. 64 B.C.–A.D. 17), a Latin author. Danaïs was wedded to Pelops and killed him on their wedding night.

Sources: Bell, *Bell's New Pantheon*, 179; Smith, *New Classical Dictionary of Greek And Roman Biography*, 621

Daoine Maithe

In Celtic lore the daoine maithe ("good people") are believed to be the fairies present at the Fall of the angels from Heaven. These fairies, similar to the GENTRY, are expecting salvation. Daoine maithe is a euphemism for the GENTRY, the SÍDHE, to ward off their trickery.

Sources: Briggs, *Fairies in Tradition and Literature*, 172; Monaghan, *Encyclopedia of Celtic Mythology and Folklore* 117; Rose, *Spirits, Fairies, Leprechauns, and Goblins*, 78

Daoine Shi'

Variations: Daoine Matha ("Good Men")

Daoine shi' is a Scottish word for fairies used mostly in the Highlands; the word translates to mean variously fairy people, men of peace, perhaps the still-folk, and the still people, all euphuism used out of respect for the fay, lest they become upset and vengeful. These fairies dress in green and are said to live in *shians* or *tomhans*, masses of rocks or hillocks are the entryway to their underground homes. Similar to the fairies of England the daoine shi' are not overtly injurious or malicious but rather joyous and overall content.

Sources: Froud, *Faeries*, 39, 41; Keightly, *World Guide to Gnomes, Fairies, Elves, and Other Little People*, 384; Keltie, *History of the Scottish Highlands*, 302–5

Daoine Sidhe

Variations: Aso Sidhe ("people of the mounds"), Daoine Beaga ("little folk"), Daoi-Sith, SIDHE, the People of Peace

In Ireland the daoine sidhe ("DARK ELVES") were a race of human-sized fairies, some scholars would suggest they were the last remnants of the TUATHA DE DANANN who were driven to live underground by the Milesians (Gaels). Other lore suggests they were the fallen angels who were too good to be banished to Hell.

As a race, they enjoy doing battle, hurling, playing chess, and riding their milk white horses. Described as being more or less human in size, and wearing green clothing and red hats, the daoine sidhe were generally benign or indifferent to mankind. There are some stories of them using their magic to prevent milk from being churned into butter in the churn and stealing children. Typically they lived underground or underwater in lakes or the sea.

The king of the daoine sidhe was FINVARRA and he held court within his fairy-hill Cnoc Meadha (Knockma) in Galway.

Sources: Briggs, *Encyclopedia of Fairies*, 90–1; Jestice, *Encyclopedia of Irish Spirituality*, 102; Knight, *Celtic Traditions*, 114, 116; Stepanich, *Faery Wicca*, Book One, 24

Daphne

Daphne was a wood-NYMPH from the mythology of ancient Greece and Rome; she was born the daughter of Peneios, the river god. She refused the love of the god, Apollo, and fled from him, as she desired to remain a virgin. Upon reaching a riverbank she implored her father to save her and was answered by being rooted to the spot, bark covering her body and being transformed into a laurel tree.

Sources: Littleton, *Gods, Goddesses, and Mythology*, Volume 11, 367; Evan-Wentz, *Fairy Faith in Celtic Countries*, 348; Salisbury, *Women in the Ancient World*, 78

Daphnus

Daphnus was one of the names given as being one of the NYMPHS of the cave at Corycian. She was said to be one of the "triple muses of divination at Delphi" along with CORYCIA, KLEODORA, MELAINA, and THIUA. She was one of the NAIADS and one of a trio of NYMPHS known collectively as the Thriae or the Thriai.

Source: Monaghan, *Goddesses in World Culture*, 147

Daplidice

In Greek mythology Daplidice was a water–NYMPH and one of the named DANAIDS, the collective name for the daughters of Danaus; her name appears in a list of the DANAIDS generated by Gaius Julius Hyginus (ca. 64 B.C.–A.D. 17), a Latin author. Daplidice was wedded to Pugno and killed him on their wedding night.

Sources: Hyginus, *Myths of Hyginus*, 133; Parada, *Genealogical Guide to Greek Mythology*, 60

Dark Elves

Variations: Daoi-Sith, Dökkálfar ("Darkelves"), Drow, Obscure Elves, Swartelves ("black elves"), Swarthy-Elves

In Norse mythology the dark elves live in the subterranean world Svartálfheim. Neither innately benevolent nor injurious they worked the forges under the deepest root of the world-tree, near the northern gate to the lower world (*iormungrundar i iodyr, nyrdra*). Constantly near the flames and soot covered thereby earning their name. Dark elves are considered by some to be synonymous with the *DUERGAR* ("DWARFS").

In Germanic traditions the Dökkálfar ("Darkelves") are ancestral spirits, always male, protecting their family line. Although not strictly subterranean, they avoid light and can be quite intimidating when provoked.

In fairy mythology from the Orkney Islands the cave and mine dwelling TROW are similar to the DWARFS and TROLLS of Scandinavian lore. Typically injurious, the TROW can be benevolent or indifferent to mankind.

In the Shetland Islands the drow are essentially the same beings as the TROW except they are exclusively injurious. Like DWARFS, the diminutive drow work their mines and are expert metalworkers. However, in Irish mythology, the drow is more like the TROLL of Scandinavian folklore and is considered to be a creature of stone aligned to the Fomori.

Sources: Daly, *Norse Mythology A to Z*, 26; Guerber, *Hammer of Thor*, 174, 237; Lindow, *Norse Mythology*, 54, 110; Maberry, *Cryptopedia*, 104–5; Rydberg, *Teutonic Mythology*, 553

Dark Man

Variations: DULLAHAN, Durahan, Durrachan ("Malicious Anger"), Gan Ceann

In Irish lore the Dark Man ("Far Dorocha") is the physical and solid embodiment of death. Exclusively serving the FAIRY QUEENS, the Dark Man of the UNSEELIE court is sent out on his black horse to abduct a human and take them to FAIRYLAND. Some sources claim he is headless. Never speaking to his victims they always understand his intent; unable to resist, they mount up behind him, a willing passenger. Although many have been take to FAIRYLAND very few have return; those who do are warned never to betray fairy secrets they learned, traitors will be visited by the Dark Man a second time; he will remove an eye or wither a limb. Some lore says if a person sees him as he rides down the road he will use his spinal-cord whip to lash out an eye or toss a basin of blood in their face.

Sources: Croker, *Fairy Legends and Traditions of the South of Ireland*, 311–12; Haughton, *Famous Ghost Stories*, 54–5; White, *History of Irish Fairies*, 101–2

Darrant

In the Derwent River in Derbyshire, England lives the water-fairy Darrant. Similar to JENNY GREENTEETH, Darrant lurks along the river banks and grabs out anyone who gets too close, pulling them into the water and drowning them.

Sources: Rose, *Spirits, Fairies, Leprechauns, and*

Goblins, 79; Spence, *Minor Traditions of British Mythology*, 14

Dasyus

Dasyus ("dark folk") are the DWARFS in the folklore in of India; they are described as dark, over-powerful beings adorning their bodies with ornaments of gold; they are the likely precursor of demons. Dasyus are the natural enemies of the Aryas and the god, INDRA, and are susceptible to fire.

Sources: Rose, *Spirits, Fairies, Leprechauns, and Goblins*, 79; Shendge, *Civilized Demons*, 36, 317

Datan

Originally an ancient Polish god of tilling the soil, Datan has since been reduced to a NATURE SPIRIT.

Sources: Aldington, *Larousse Encyclopedia of Mythology*, 291; Rose, *Spirits, Fairies, Leprechauns, and Goblins*, 79

Dathkin

Variations: The Strong Limbed

Dathkin was a fairy with magical legs from Irish folklore; he had the ability to make himself short or tall.

Sources: O'Sheridan, *Gaelic Folk Tales*, 221, 239; Wallace, *Folk-lore of Ireland*, 85

Daulis

In classical Greek mythology Daulis was born the daughter of CEPHISSUS and was the NYMPH of the town of Daulis in Boiotia located in central Greece.

Sources: Pausanias, *Pausanias' Description of Greece*, Volume 2, 225; Smith, *Dictionary of Greek and Roman Geography: Abacaenum-Hytanis*, 756

Davalin

Devalin was one of the four DWARFS in Nordic mythology whose name was those of the hart's that ate the buds off of Yggdrasil, the World Tree (see DAIN, DUNEYR, and DURATHROR). The four DWARFS were likely the guardians of it.

Sources: Rose, *Spirits, Fairies, Leprechauns, and Goblins*, 79; Sykes, *Who's Who in Non-Classical Mythology*, 53, 217

Death Candle

Appearing as a spot of bright light the death candle of Swiss lore was not a flame rather but a luminous mass, light blue in color. Dancing with a life of its own, no matter how dark the room may be this little fairy would light up the room as bright as day. Sometimes this fairy light acts like a WILL O' THE WISP, other times it simply would hover over a grave; in Scottish lore the death candle was considered to be a death omen.

Sources: Daniels, *Encyclopedia of Superstitions, Folklore, and the Occult Sciences of the World*, 139; Evan-Wentz, *Fairy Faith in Celtic Countries*, 155; Jamieson, *Scottish Dictionary and Supplement*, Volume 3, 302

Death Coach

Variations: Headless Coach ("Coiste-gan-Cheann"), Cóiste Bodhar

In Celtic lore there is a vampiric fairy-spirit known as a death coach; it appears after the wail and subsequent attack of a BANSHEE. The death coach descends from the sky, looking like a funeral coach drawn by a team black horses, although in some regions it is said the horses are white. The death coach collects the soul of the BANSHEE's victim, traveling through the air and over the ground without making a sound. The death coach may be the transmuted concept of Charon, the Ferryman from Greek mythology; it is similar to the DULLAHAN.

Sources: Keegan, *Legends and Poems*, 131; Leach, *Funk and Wagnalls Standard Dictionary of Folklore*, 300; Radford, *Encyclopedia of Superstitions*, 70–71, 101–2; Wentz, *Fairy Faith in Celtic Countries*, 71

Deev

Variations: Daeva, DEV, Deva, Deve, Devi, Deeve, Div, Dive

In Persian lore the deev live in the mountains of Kâf with the JINN and the PERIES. This mountain range composed of green chrysolite reflects a greenish tint to the sky. Kâf was believed to surround the circular and flat earth like a gigantic fence some 2,000 miles high, outside of which flows the ocean.

The malignant deev and the PERIES wage constant war against one another. When PERIES are taken prisoner they are locked up in an iron cage hung from the top of the tallest trees. Not only are the PERIES in pain from constantly touching the iron bars of the cage but also they are exposed to the persistent chilling wind. The deev deny the PERIES the only food they can comsume, the fragrance of perfume, as the deev find it to be a natural repellant.

Just as in European fairly lore where a person can claim ancestral descent from fairy-kind, so could the ancient Persians. Being born with white hair is said to be proof of being from deev descent. In modern lore both the deev and the PERIES are subject to the will of the JINN.

Famous deevs are ARSHENK, ARZSHENK, AS-DEEV DEEV AKVAN, DEEV SEFEED, DEMRUSH, HOUNDKONZ, and Tahmuras.

Sources: Benjamin, *Story of Persia*, 38; Keightly, *World Guide to Gnomes, Fairies, Elves, and Other Little People*, 15–7; Ouseley, *Oriental Collections*, 52; Porteous, *Lore of the Forest*, 121; Rose, *Spirits, Fairies, Leprechauns, and Goblins*, 80; Yar-Shater, *Encyclopædia Iranica*, 308

Deev Akvan

Variations: Deeve Akvan, DEV Akvan, Div Akvan

Deev Akvan, from Persian lore, was huge and had the power of flight, to turn invisible, and disappear and reappear at will. It was described as looking like a wild ass; his skin shone like the sun and a black strip ran down his back. Known for slaying the horses of the royal house and haunting springs, this DEEV was ultimately defeated by the cultural hero, Roostem. Deev Akvan's son, Deev BERKHYAS and his army confronted Roostem but the hero not only slew the son seeking avenge but also two-thirds of his army.

Sources: Keightly, *World Guide to Gnomes, Fairies, Elves, and Other Little People*, 19; Rose, *Spirits, Fairies, Gnomes, and Goblins*, 8; Yar-Shater, *Encyclopædia Iranica*, 308

Deev Sefeed

Variations: Deeve Sefeed

Deev Sefeed ("white GIANT") of Persian lore lived in a gloomy cleft in the mountains; his DEEV army was commanded by ARZSHENK. Having unspecified magical powers he had the ability to cause vast numbers of people to suddenly become blind. Deev Sefeed sought to destroy the Persians but was slain by the cultural hero, Roostem.

Sources: Benjamin, *Story of Persia*, 38; Keightly, *World Guide to Gnomes, Fairies, Elves, and Other Little People*, 18; Ouseley, *Oriental Collections*, 52

Deiopea

A sea–NYMPH, Deiopea was one of the named NEREID in classical Greek mythology; she was born of Nereus and DORIS and was the loveliest attendant of the goddess, Hera ("Juno").

Sources: Apollodorus, *Apollodorus' Library and Hyginus' Fabulae*, 95; Bell, *Women of Classical Mythology*, 155; Sievers, *Master Drawings from the Smith College Museum of Art*, 94

Deive

Variations: Dieva

Originally a goddess in Lithuanian mythology Deive was reduced to the status of NATURE SPIRIT with the introduction of Christianity; later she was debased even further and said to be a species of fairy. These fay are described as having beautiful, long blond hair, blue eyes and voluptuous breasts. Making for excellent mothers and wives the deive were highly sought after, captured and married, however, if a taboo was broken, such as doing laundry at night, they would return to the wild. They insisted men show them respect and resented greed and insincerity.

Sources: Lurker, *Routledge Dictionary of Gods and Goddesses*, 48; Rose, *Spirits, Fairies, Gnomes, and Goblins*, 80

Deliades

Deliades was the collective name for the NYMPHS of Greek mythology of the springs of the River Inopos on the island of Delos in the Greek Aegean Sea.

Source: Larson, *Greek Nymphs*, 182

Dellingr

Dellingr ("glowing") was a DWARF from ancient Norse mythology; he is the personification of twilight and is said to have existed before Vallhalla was walled. The saying, "to stand before the doors of Dellingr" may mean the equivalent of "facing the day." Dellingr was also named in the *Voluspa*, the first and best known poem of the *Poetic Edda*, a collection of Old Norse poems dating back to about A.D. 985. The third husband of Nott, Dellingr is the father of the hero, Dagr.

Sources: Adnerson, *A Certain Text*, 179; Grimm, *Teutonic Mythology*, Volume 4, 1511

Delphin

Variations: Delphinus

In ancient Greek mythology Delphin ("dolphin") was a water-based NATURE SPIRIT in the employ of the god, Poseidon (Neptune). When Dephin's sister, AMPHITRITE spurned Poseidon's advances, he was able to convince his sister to marry the god.

Sources: Evan-Wentz, *Fairy Faith in Celtic Countries*, 352; Falkner, *Mythology of the Night Sky*, 141–42; Graves, *Greek Myths*, 16

Delucaem

Variations: Delbchaem, Delvcaem

In Irish mythology Delucaem ("fair shape")

was a powerful fairy spirit and sorceress; she lived on an island ruled by her parents, King Morgan and Queen Coinchend ("Doghead"). An oracle had once predicted to the royal couple that when their daughters were courted the queen would die. Art, son of Conn of the Hundred Battles and the King of Ireland, had been quested to return home with Delucaem; eventually he was able to convince the king to allow Delucaem to return to Ireland with him. Art had not only fallen in love with the fairy but also knew by returning home with her he would save his father's kingdom, driving off the current queen, BECUMA. Once the queen was gone, Art and Delucaem were married.

Sources: Illes, *Encyclopedia of Spirits*, 352–53; McCoy, *Celtic Myth and Magick*, 193; Mountain, *Celtic Encyclopedia*, 330

Demoditas

In Greek mythology Demoditas was a water–NYMPH and one of the named DANAIDS, the collective name for the daughters of Danaus in classical Greek mythology; her name appears in a list of the DANAIDS generated by Gaius Julius Hyginus (ca. 64 B.C.–A.D. 17), a Latin author. Demoditas was wedded to Chrysippus and killed him on their wedding night.

Sources: Bell, *Women of Classical Mythology*, 160, 442; Hyginus, *Myths of Hyginus*, 132; Parada, *Genealogical Guide to Greek Mythology*, 47, 59

Demogorgon

Variations: Gorgon

First referenced by Lucius Caecilius Firmianus Lactantius (ca. 240–ca. 320) a rhetorician and early Christian author, the demogorgon is a creature said to have power over fairies and witches. He is also mentioned in John Milton's epic poem, *Paradise Lost* (1667). According to Voltaire, the French, historian, philosopher, and writer, Demogorgon was the Lieutenant of the Great Architect, he was entrusted to building the world, but being dim-witted he is blamed for all the evils of life.

Sources: Keightly, *World Guide to Gnomes, Fairies, Elves, and Other Little People*, 451; Rose, *Spirits, Fairies, Gnomes, and Goblins*, 80; Yardley, *Supernatural in Romantic Fiction*, 45

Demophile

In Greek mythology Demophile was a water–NYMPH and one of the named DANAIDS, the collective name for the daughters of Danaus; her name appears in a list of the DANAIDS generated by Gaius Julius Hyginus (ca. 64 B.C.–A.D. 17), a Latin author. Demophile was wedded to Pamphilus and killed him on their wedding night.

Sources: Bell, *Women of Classical Mythology*, 149, 161; Hyginus, *Myths of Hyginus*, 133; Parada, *Genealogical Guide to Greek Mythology*, 59, 136

Demrush

In Persian lore Demrush was a DEEV fiercer than ARSHENK; he lived in a dark cave filled with all of the treasure he had plundered from India and Persia. Demrush had kidnapped and held captive PERI MERJÂN, chaining her to the center of his mountain dwelling. Her two brothers, DÂL PERI and MILÂN SHÂH PERI, tried to save her but failed, ultimately she was rescued when the mortal hero, Tahmuras, slew Demrush.

Sources: Blavatsky, *Anthropogenesis*, 398; Hunt, *Leigh Hunt's London Journal*, Volumes 1–2, 235; Keightly, *World Guide to Gnomes, Fairies, Elves, and Other Little People*, 18

Deohako

The deohako ("life supporters") from the mythology of the Iroquois and Seneca people of North America are NATURE-SPIRITS, three sisters who are the personification of beans, corn, and squash. The oldest sister, Onatha, was tall, wore a long green shawl and had yellow hair that blew in the breeze. The middle sister wore a yellow dress and loved to run in the sunshine. The youngest sister wore green clothing and crawled after her sisters. The three sisters were never separated from one another until a young man appeared and carried off the two youngest sisters. The eldest sister cried until the man return and feeling sorry for her took her to where her two sisters were living happily.

Sources: Avant, *Mythological Reference*, 38; Monaghan, *Encyclopedia of Goddesses and Heroines*, 538; Savill, P*ears Encyclopaedia of Myths and Legends: Oceania and Australia, the Americas*, Book 4, 195

Deopea

A sea–NYMPH, Deopea was one of the named NEREID; she was born of Nereus and DORIS in classical Greek mythology.

Source: Lemprière, *Classical Dictionary*, 494

Dero

A sea–NYMPH, Dero, was one of the named NEREIDS; she was born the daughter of Nerues and DORIS in classical Greek mythology.

Sources: Apollodorus, *Apollodorus' Library and Hyginus' Fabulae*, 3; Parada, *Genealogical Guide to*

Greek Mythology, 125; Trzaskoma, *Anthology of Classical Myth*, 18

Derrick

A derrick is specific type of uncommon fairy in Devonshire, England. The name of this being is supposed to come from the old English word, *dweorg*, which translates to mean "DWARF." Derricks are considered to maligned and enjoy leading travlers astray.

Sources: Bord, *Fairies*, 2; Briggs, *Encyclopedia of Fairies*, 97; King, *Fraser's Magazine*, Volume 88, 781; Wright, *Dictionary of Obsolete and Provincial English*, 382

Dev (plural: devs)

Variations: Divs (DIV), Drauga, DRUJ, Durugh

In Persian mythology a dev is a demon (DJINN) of war. They were created by ANGRA MAINYU, are immoral and ruthless, and intended to be the counterparts to the Amesha Spentas.

Sources: Blavatsky, *Isis Unveiled*, 482; Ford, *Luciferian Witchcraft*, 288; Turner, *Dictionary of Ancient Deties*, 147–8

Devas

In Persian lore devas ("shining ones") were a type of NATURE SPIRIT and considered to be the soul of the plant they inhabited. These fairies appeared as glowing balls of light they flew through the air and tended to plants; they were well versed in herbal medicines.

Sources: Beliefnet, *Big Book of Angels*, 109–110; Hodson, *Fairy Kingdom*, 12; McCoy, *Witch's Guide to Faery Folk,* 204–6; Stepanich, *Faery Wicca*, Book One, 23

Dewas

In the Buddhist folk beliefs the dewas ("gods") are NATURE SPIRIT; they are the guardians of trees. They can inhabit mountains, rice stalks, and streams as well as trees. The word dewas is used interchangeably with *bakat*, a kind of Jinn, *nyiwa* ("soul") and epens ("twin shadow"). According to the lore, each person is born with a dewas and each one is different, some are strong while others are weak; people who are energetic, talented, verile, wealthy, and wise are believed to have a powerful dewas where people who lack these abilities are said to have a weak dewas.

Sources: Hay, *Remembering to Live*, 75; Rose, *Spirits, Fairies, Gnomes, and Goblins*, 85

Dexamene

A sea–NYMPH in classical Greek mythology, Dexamene ("powerful one") was one of the named NEREID who accompanied THETIS in mourning the loss of her son, Achilles.

Sources: Collignon, *Manual of Mythology*, 18; Gould, *Historic Magazine and Notes and Queries*, Vol 14, 212

Diancecht

Variations: Cainte, Canta, Dian Cécht Diancécht

In Irish mythology, Diancecht was the great healer of the TUATHA DE DANANN; he had the ability to restore the dead to life so long as the person's head is intact. He could also replace lost limbs with ones made of silver. He was the progenitor of a clan of extremely powerful and highly skilled healers. He and his three children had the ability to restore the dead through the use of herbs, incantations, and metallurgy. Diancecht was jealous of his son, Miach, who was so skilled healer he could replace lost limbs with ones of flesh, that he killed him. Diancecht died of plague; he likely contracted it when struck with a bladed weapon covered in plague carrying poison.

Sources: Evan-Wentz, *Fairy Faith in Celtic Countries*, 359; Jayne, *Healing Gods of Ancient Civilizations*, 510, 516–7; Mountain, *Celtic Encyclopedia*, Volume 3, 546

Dievini

In Latvian folklore Dievini was once a minor god but has since been reduced to the status of household-fairy; as a species, they are protective of the families and household they live look after.

Sources: Lurker, *Routledge Dictionary of Gods and Goddesses*, 51; Rose, *Spirits, Fairies, Gnomes, and Goblins*, 86

Dike

In Greek mythology, Dike ("Justice") and her two sisters, EIRENE ("Peace") and EUNOMIA ("Lawful Order"), were collectively known as the HORAE ("the correct moment"), the guardians of natural law; they were born the daughters of the Titian goddess of Law, Themis, and the god, Zeus (Jupiter). The NATURE SPIRIT-like sisters were entrusted with guarding the gate to Olympus. Dike, like her sisters, was described as being a beautiful young maiden with beautiful hair, light footsteps, and wearing golden diadems. Representing the seasons, each one held a blooming flower, and ear of corn, and a vine stock. Dike executed the laws of justice and sentencing; she was the mother of Hesychia ("Tranquility" or "Quiet").

Sources: Gall, *Lincoln Library of Greek and Roman Mythology*, 20; McLean, *Triple Goddess*, 49; Roman, *Encyclopedia of Greek and Roman Mythology*, 172

Diktynna

Originally a Cretan mother-goddess, Diktynna ("net") became a NYMPH of the island of Delos and was associated with Mount Dikte.

Sources: Guthrie, *Greeks and Their Gods*, 105; Larson, *Greek Nymphs*, 182

The Diminutive Fairy

Variations: Forgetful People, the Gentry, Good Neighbors, Hill Folk, Honest Folk, the Literary Fairy, Little Fairy, Little Folk, People of Peace

This species of fairy was created near the end of the fifteenth century when the ideas of the ME-DIEVAL FAIRY merged with the Heroic Fairy. The alert and invisible diminutive fairy became the standard image of what a fairy looked like.

Also known as the literary fairy, this species of fairy was introduced by John Lyly in the dramatic play he wrote for the court of Queen Elizabeth, *Endimion*, in the 16th century. In the play the fairies brought justice to the villain by severely pinching him; he was being punished for the wrong he did to Endimion but also for the crime of infringing upon fairy privacy.

During this time fairies were not necessarily welcomed into the home; speaking their name aloud was believed to be enough to summon one to appear so a list of euphemistic names was invented to reference them. To know the true name of a fairy would ensure the fairy would depart from your presence never to return because knowing the name would give you the power to control it.

During this time there was a belief that the human soul was a tiny creature living within the body. At night the soul had the ability to leave the body and act of its own accord; its wild adventures were the sleeper's dreams.

Sources: Haase, *Greenwood Encyclopedia of Folktales and Fairy Tales*, 625; Lyly, *Endymion*, 54, 154–55; Stepanich, *Faery Wicca*, Book One, 21, 26, 269

Dindonette

In the fairy-tale *A Fairy's Blunder*, the fairy Dindonette was said to have the kindest heart but not much in the way of common sense; she claimed Fountain Island, located in the middle of the sea, as being under her special protection. Whenever she would try to help someone Dindonette would inevitably cause distress and pain.

Among her attempts to help, she enchanted a spring so when children drank from it they would become adults and when grown men and women drank from it they would become children. Embarrassed by the damage she did, Dindonette left the island swearing never to return. it was decided by the assembly of fairies since Dindonette's actions were done with no maliciousness she would be given the power to restore half of the afflicted people.

Sources: Lang, *Grey Fairy Book*, 353–65; Romanowski, *Homage to Paul Bénichou*, 284

Dinnshenchas

In Irish lore the dinnshenchas are female DWARFS serving the goddess of cattle and protector of women, AINE. The dinnshenchas use their ability to shape-shift into various forms in order to avenge women who have been harmed or otherwise wronged by men. They are also guardians of cattle. There is also a book of Irish mythology named "*Dinnshenchas.*"

Sources: McCoy, *Witch's Guide to Faery Folk*, 206–7; Monaghan, *Encyclopedia of Celtic Mythology and Folklore*, 129

Dinny-Mara

Variations: Doinney Marrey ("man of the sea"), Dooinney Marrey, Duny Mara

Dinny-Mara was the amiable MERMAN from the Isle of Man; they were said to be far less fierce than the mermen of England and more easygoing, like the MERROW of Ireland. As benign as these MERMAN may have been there was the belief if one whistles onboard a sail ship the dinny-mara would send more wind than is needed to the ship. This aquatic FAIRY ANIMAL was described as having large, piglike eyes, and a bright red nose from drinking too much brandy salvaged from sunken ships. Their break smelled like the raw fish they ate.

Sources: Briggs, *Encyclopedia of Fairies*, 102; Monaghan, *Encyclopedia of Celtic Mythology and Folklore*, 327; Rose, *Spirits, Fairies, Gnomes, and Goblins*, 86–7

Diogeneia

Diogeneia was a NYMPH from the mythology of classical Greece and Rome. One of the NAIADS, she was born the daughter of CEPHISSUS, the god of the Cephissus River in Attica. She was the wife of the Athenian lord Phrasimos; her brother, by the same father is the famed character, Narcissus.

Sources: Bell, *Women of Classical Mythology*, 380; Smith, *Dictionary of Greek and Roman Biography and Mythology*, Volume 1, 671

Dione

Born one of the 3,000 daughters of the Titians, Oceanus and Tethys, Dione was one of the named OCEANIDS in classical Greek mythology. As a sea–NYMPH, Dione was also listed as one of the named NEREIDS, born the daughter of Nerues and DORIS. Some sources claim she and the god Zeus (Jupiter) are the parents of the goddess, Aphrodite (Venus).

Sources: Bell, *Bell's New Pantheon or Historical Dictionary of the Gods*, 112; Boswell, *What Men or Gods Are These*, 58; Day, *God's Conflict with the Dragon and the Sea*, 64; Hesiod, *Works of Hesiod, Callimachus, and Theognis*, 20; Trzaskoma, *Anthology of Classical Myth*, 18; Westmoreland, *Ancient Greek Beliefs*, 24

Dioxippe

In Greek mythology Dioxippe ("steed of light") was a water–NYMPH and one of the named DANAIDS, the collective name for the daughters of Danaus. In a list compiled by Apollodorus, a Greek scholar and grammarian, she was one of the daughters of Pieria and was wedded to Aegyptus, one of the sons of Gorgo. According to the Greek oral poet Hesiod, Dioxippe was one of the seven sisters collectively known as The Daughters of Helios (Sol); their names are AEGLE, AETHERIE, DIOXIPPE, Helie (see HELIADES, THE), LAMPETIE, MEROPE, and PHOEBE.

Sources: Bell, *Women of Classical Mythology*, 168–9; Grimal, *Dictionary of Classical Mythology*, 127

Dip

In Catalan mythology, Dip is a hell hound, a hairy, injurious, blood-drinking doglike creature similar to the BLACK DOGS of the British Isles. Like many evil beings in Catalan lore he is lame in one leg.

Source: Maberry, *They Bite*, 145

Direach

Variations: Direach Ghlinn Eitidh, Dithreach, FACHAN

The direach was an ATHACH, a type of fairy-creature living in the Highlands of Scotland in Glen of Eiti near Ballachulish. This fairy-creature was described as having one eye, one leg, one hand, and an arm coming directly out of its chest; its head had random tuffs of wirily hair. Examples of similar creatures are the BOCAN and the LUIDEAG.

Sources: Briggs, *Encyclopedia of Fairies*, 102–3; Monaghan, *Encyclopedia of Celtic Mythology and Folklore*, 166; Rose, *Giants, Monsters and Dragon*, 99

Dirke

A NYMPH of the spring Dirke on Mount Kithairon, in Boiotia located in central Greece, Dirke was born the daughter of Acheloos by Euripides. Dirke was killed by Amphion and Zethos who bound her to a wild bull as a means of punishment for her cruelty to their mother. The god Dionysus (Bacchus) transformed her into a fountain after her death.

Sources: Hard, *Routledge Handbook of Greek Mythology*, 304; Larson, *Greek Nymphs*, 6–7

Dirne Weibl

A NATURE SPIRIT in German folklore Dirne Weibl was a type of WOOD-WIFE who dressed all in white and wandered the forest asking travelers to accompany her; if they refused, she wept and then suddenly vanished. In Bavaria she was said to wear all red and carry a basket of apples that turned into money for some lucky recipients.

Sources: Grimm, *Teutonic Mythology*, Volume 4, 1370; Porteous, *Lore of the Forest*, 91–2; Rose, *Spirits, Fairies, Leprechauns, and Goblins*, 87

Disir

In Norse lore the disir are female ancestral spirits who watch over their descendants; they usually attach themselves to a man-made structure, like a house, and can be either helpful or injurious. They are said to be nocturnal and when seen are described as looking like ghostly women. On occasion a disir would appear to its descendant in animal form, something that would suit the character of the individual and be recognized for what it was; for example a powerful leader may see a bear or a bull whereas a crafty individual may see a fox.

Even long after the introduction of Christianity the disir were worshiped. An assembly of or for the disir was called a *disathing*; it was usually celebrated on the full moon in October; sacrifices for the disir were left in their temples called *disir salen*.

Sources: Grimm, *Teutonic Mythology*, Volume 1, 4012; Lindow, *Handbook of Norse Mythology*, 95; Yonge, *History of Christian Names*, Volume 2, 218

Diuturna

Variations: JUTURNA

In ancient Roman mythology Diuturna was a NYMPH transformed into a fountain by the god,

Jupiter; she was rewarded with immortality and was given dominion over water. The fountain was said to stand in Latium, Italy and its water had incredible healing powers. A guardian of healing springs and well Diuturna was also a protector against fire.

Sources: Rose, *Spirits, Fairies, Leprechauns, and Goblins*, 87; Smith, *Smaller Classical Dictionary*, 295

Divozenky

Variations: Dziwozony

In Slavic lore the Divozenky ("WILD WOMEN") were fairies who looked like beautiful women with large, square heads, long thick black or ruddy hair, long fingers and hairy bodies; they lived in caves in the woods and kept a household very closely resembled a humans. Knowing the secrets of nature these fairy-being can become invisible by use of their herbology. Fond of dancing and singing, they can cause storms when enjoying this activity. Friendly toward humans they will do housework in exchange for food or borrowing household items, some will even take a man for a husband.

Divozenky will steal a human baby and leave one of their own in its place; these fairy-babe are called Divous ("wild brats") or Premien ("CHANGE-LINGS") and are noticeably ugly.

Source: Gray, *Mythology of All Races*, Volume 3, 263

Diwata

Variations: Encantada, Lambana

In Philippine mythology, the diwata were original seen and worshiped as gods but in modern times they are comparable to fairies, NATURE SPIRITS, or NYMPHS. Description of their appearance varies, but generally they are said to look human, ageless and beautiful with a singular distinct characteristic; this can be anything from having perfectly smooth, wrinkle-free skin even in places like the knees and elbows to not having a philtrum. Diwata live in large trees, such as acacia and balete; they will bless those who benefit and protect the forest and mountains and will curse those who attempt to exploit or harm them.

A male diwata is called an *enkanto* (also spelt *encanto*, ENCANTADO, *encantada*, and *ingkanto*) and lives in the sea. Filipino fishermen will make offerings of meat to them after a successful day.

Sources: Demetrio, *Myths and Symbols, Philippines*, 346; Olupọna, *Beyond Primitivism*, 257–8

Djinn

Variations: Ajnan (male), Ande, Cin, Cinler, the "concealed ones," the "dark ones," Div, Djin, Djinnee, Djinni, Djinny, Dschin, Duh, Džin, Dzsinn, Genii, GENIE, Génie, Gênio, Ghaddar, Ginn, HALTIJA, Hengetär, JANN, Jin, Jinn, Jinnee (plural Jineeyeh), Jinni, Jinniyah (female), Jinnie, Jinniy, Ka-Jinn ("fire demon"), Kijini, MARID, Mareed, Maride, Nar, Nara, QUTRUB, Se'irim, Skyddsande, Szellem, Xhind

In Islamic mythology the djinn ("angry, possessed") are a race of demons; they are divided into two species. The first has five classes: Afreet, GHILAN, JANN, MARID, and the Sheitan. The other has only three: Ghul, IFRIT, and SILA. They were created by Allah out of smokeless fire and were given permission to attempt to seduce and tempt men away from God's teachings. They are immortal and unless slain they will live indefinitely. When a djinn has been mortally wounded it bleeds fire; eventually the flames will consume the demon. They will also avoid direct sunlight, salt, and steel. These demons fear the "falling stars" God can throw at them and the sound of singing. In general they are known to be quick-tempered and vain.

All djinn were ruled by a succession of seventy-two kings or "Suleyman." Their homeland is called Jinnistan; its capital city is called the City of Jewels and its main district is called the Country of Delight. Outside of their homeland they live in abandoned buildings, caves, graveyards, places of darkness, and underground. If a djinn is near, cattle will refuse to drink if driven to water.

Nocturnal demons of fire, the djinn have the ability to shape-change into a variety of animals, insects, inanimate objects, and reptiles, frogs, heavily muscled youths, lizards, scorpions, snakes, and wrinkled old men. They will even take the form of a hybrid animal, such as a hyena-wolf crossbreed. Additionally, djinn can become invisible, cause insanity, foretell the future, possess inanimate objects, and spread diseases.

Djinn are capable of procreation with their own species as well as with humans. They have Incubus-like tendencies and the offspring of a djinn and human coupling take the best attributes of each parent. These children are very cunning and are considered dangerous, but fortunately, like all djinn, are immortal, unless slain.

Unlike other demons, djinn have free will, and with it they have the ability to choose to be good or evil. Evil djinn can be redeemed if they are converted to Islam. King Solomon is said to have gained control over the djinn by use of magical spells given to him by an archangel.

Sources: Hughes, *Dictionary of Islam*, 135; Hyatt, *Book of Demons*, 54–5; Knowles, *Nineteenth century,* Volume 31, 449

Do-gakw-ho-wad

Variations: The Spreader

In the folklore of the Abenaki people, a tribe of Native American Indians who live in the northeast United States, there is a race of NATURE SPIRITS called the Do-gakw-ho-wad ("one who props open"). These small fairy beings are quick enough to use a stick and prop open the maw of an attacking animal. The Do-gakw-ho-wad make their homes near the side of cliffs or on steep river banks and do like when people make camp near them.

Source: Sturtevant, *Handbook of North American Indians,* Volume 17, 193

Dobby

Variations: Dobbs, Dobie, Master Dobbs

Dobbies are a type of house-fairy, similar to BROWNIES, in the folklore from England. Playful and prone to pranks they are very kind to children and servants. They are described as looking shaggy and thin. Although they watched over the family and their valuables, especially in times of trouble, the dobby usually stayed in the stable where it could keep better watch over the animals. Unnatched dobbies are said to be particularly injurious and malicious living in or near isolated and derelict ruins or water sources. It has been suggested the word *dobby* is a nickname for the name Robin, and the supernatural dobby may be a reference to ROBIN GOOD FELLOW.

Regional beliefs of the dobby vary greatly; in Northumberland they were said to be gullible, lazy, and unintelligent; in Lancashire any sort of outside ghost is called a dobby, and in Morecambe Bay they live along the shoreline. In some regions dobbies are a type of NATURE SPIRIT known to attack travelers and has control over deer. In Durham County the Shonton dobby appears at the birth and death of prominent people in the form of a cow, dog, donkey, goose, or horse.

Sources: Briggs, *Encyclopedia of Fairies*, 103; Rose, *Spirits, Fairies, Gnomes, and Goblins*, 88; Simpson, *Dictionary of English Folklore*, n.p.

Döckalfar

Variations: Black Alfs, Döcalfar, Svartalfar, Swartalfar

In Norse mythology the döckalfar ("DARK ELVES") are the ALFAR born from the decaying remains of the GIANT, YMIR. They lived in underground dwellings in the mountains or in burial mounds; they were associated with the dead. Originally the döckalfar were "dark" in the sense they were the same color as the ore and stones they lived near; they had no interest in human affairs at all. It was not until later these fay were said to be malicious and misshapen, kidnapping human children and replacing them with CHANGELINGS. Their association and connection to the dead further tarnish their reputation and eventually they were paired with the SVARTALFAR, the black elves.

Sources: Littleton, *Gods, Goddesses, and Mythology*, Volume 11, 58; Rose, *Spirits, Fairies, Leprechauns, and Goblins*, 10

Dodone

Born one of the 3,000 daughters of the Titans, Oceanus and Tethys, Dodone was one of the named OCEANIDS in classical Greek mythology; she married Deukalion who, after consulting an oracle, founded a city where a dove perched upon an oak tree and named it after her.

Sources: Bell, *Women of Classical Mythology*, 328; Day, *God's Conflict with the Dragon and the Sea*, 47

Dodonides

The Dodonides were the seven NYMPHS of the oracles of Zeus (Jupiter) at Dodone, the god's birthplace in classical Greek mythology; their names were AMBROSIA, DIONE, Eudore, KORONIS (CORONIS), Phaio (PHAENO), PHAISYLE, and POLYXO.

Sources: Larson, *Greek Nymphs*, 161; Rigoglioso, *Cult of Divine Birth in Ancient Greece*, 87, 144

Dodore

Variations: KAKAMORA, Kakangora, Katu, Mumu, Mumulou, Pwaronga, Toku, Tutu-Langi, Waitarohia

According to the Malaita people of the Solomon Islands the dodore are the local species of fairy. Described as being large, having only one arm, eye, and leg and very long red hair reminiscent of a horse's tail, these injurious fay have been said to kill men by scratching them to death with their long fingernails or spitting into their eyes. Dodore always walk in the woods in pairs and if they catch the scent of a man will track him down, hunting him. Fortunately, the dodore are dim-witted and can usually be outwitted.

Sources: *History of Civilization*, 139; Rose, *Spirits, Fairies, Gnomes, and Goblins*, 88–9

Dola

In Polish lore the dola are protective spirits attached to a person at birth and remaining with them for the entirety of their life guiding them; they are the personifications of FATE. Although they usually appear as a woman or a young maiden working at a spinning wheel with a golden thread they can also take the form of a cat, God, man, or mouse. The dola will help its person by caring for his fields, looking after their flocks, and seeing after their welfare in general.

Sources: Grimal, *Larousse World Mythology*, 414; Kmietowicz, *Slavic Mythical Beliefs*, 212

Dolgthrasir

Variations: Dani

Dolgthrasir ("strife keen") was one of the many DWARFS named in the *Voluspa*, the first and best known poem of the *Poetic Edda*, a collection of Old Norse poems dating back to about A.D. 985. He is known to be a contentious, obstinate, persisting warrior.

Sources: Daly, *Norse Mythology A to Z*, 22; Sykes, *Who's Who in Non-Classical Mythology*, 53; Wilkinson, *Book of Edda called Völuspá*, 12

Dolgthvari

Variations: Dólgthvari

Dolgthvari ("eager to fight") was one of the many DWARFS named in the *Voluspa*, the first and best known poem of the *Poetic Edda*, a collection of Old Norse poems dating back to about A.D. 985.

Sources: Crossley-Holland, Norse Myths, 183; Haugen, *Language and Its Ecology*, 446

Dolya

In Ukrainian folklore Dolya is a house fairy liveing behind the stove; when it is in a good mood, this little fay described as looking like an old woman, brings good fortune and luck to the family. However, if Dolya is annoyed or offended he is then known as Nedolya; its appearance changes to look like a shabbily dressed HAG and will bring misfortune to the household. Originally, Dolya may have once been a goddess who was reduced to the status of fairy.

Sources: Eason, *Complete Guide to Faeries and*

Magical Beings, 16; Gray, *Mythology of All Races*, Volume 3, 252; Monaghan, *New Book of Goddesses and Heroines*, 105

Domovik (plural: domovye)

Variations: Dedek, Dedushka Dobrokhot ("Grandfather Well-Wisher"), Djadek, Domaći, Domoviyr, Domovoi, Domovoi Djedoe, Domovoj, Domovoy, Domowije, Domowoj, Grandfather, Stopan

In Russian folklore, especially in the Bulgarian, Croatian, Czech, Polish, Serbian, Slovene, and Ukrainian lore, the domovik is a male household spirit similar to the BROWNIE; it appears as an old grey-haired man. Loving fire, it lives behind the stove. Sometimes the domovik will assist the family by feeding the livestock if the chore is otherwise forgotten to be completed or by lending a hand with field work. It would also punish the women of the house who broke social taboos, such as spinning on a Friday or leaving the house without their head properly covered.

At night, food is left out for him so it will bring luck and prosperity to the household; it preferred bread, incense, juniper, porridge, salt, and tobacco. If the domovik is abused or neglected he will burn down the house. Domovik is said to have a wife named DOMOVIKHA.

The domovik was also consulted as an oracle. If a question was asked of it and his invisible touch was soft and gentle than it was a sign of coming happiness; a cold or prickly touch foretold of death or misfortune. When this fairy took a liking to a particular horse or cow it was said never to fall ill but if it did not an animal, or even an animal's color, it would scatter its food, tie its hair in knots, and keep the animal constantly bothered so it was never at rest.

Sources: Bord, *Fairies*, 59; Dixon-Kennedy, *Encyclopedia of Russian and Slavic Myth and Legend*, 73; Evan-Wentz, *Fairy Faith in Celtic Countries*, 368; Ivanits, *Russian Folk Belief*, 55–7; McCoy, *Witch's Guide to Faery Folk*, 34, 207–8

Domovikha

Variations: Dedeks, Domania, Domavichka, Domavikha, Domawiczka, Domikha, KIKIMORA, Setek, Shishimora, Stopan

In Russian folklore the domovikha is a female household spirit similar to the BROWNIE; it appears as woman with the beak and legs of a chicken. Living in either the hen-house or in the basement of the family home, this little fairy will help a good-natured wife with her household chores, but if the woman of the home is ill-natured the domovikha will kick her children awake and cause them to cry all night long.

As the wife of DOMOVOI she lives under the floorboards of the family home, emerging only at night to do her spinning. As Domawiczka she is a HOUSE-SPIRIT similar to a BROWNIE that appears in the form of a snake.

Sources: Borrero, *Russia*, 131; Dixon-Kennedy, *Encyclopedia of Russian and Slavic Myth and Legend*, 73; Eason, *Complete Guide to Faeries and Magical Beings*, 16, 199; Rose, *Spirits, Fairies, Gnomes, and Goblins*, 89–90

Donagh

Variations: ONAGH, Onaugh, Oona, Oonagy, Una

In Western Ireland, Donagh was a FAIRY QUEEN, she ruled over the DAOINE SIDHE; her fairy hill, Knockshegouna ("Hill of the Fairy-calf"), was located in Tipperary County. Described as being more compellingly beautiful than any living mortal woman Donagh had long blond hair and dressed in robes made of silver gossamer glimmering with drops of dew, shining like diamonds. As often was the case, her husband FINVARRA, a FAIRY KING was a cad who incessantly pursued and took human women.

Sources: Maberry, *Cryptopedia*, 116; Squire, *Mythology of the British Islands*, 243–4; Wilde, *Ancient Legends, Mystic Charms, and Superstitions of Ireland*, 132

Donn Fírinne

Donn Fírinne ("brown truth") was a FAIRY KING in Irish fairy lore; he ruled from his seat of power on Knockfierna Mountain in Limerick County. Well known to kidnap mortal women from the back of his magical white horse and force them to join him at his dances, Donn Fírinne was associated with the Underworld, as his victims were never seen again. He was also associated with storms and the weather in general.

Sources: MacLeod, *Celtic Myth and Religion*, 56; Monaghan, *Encyclopedia of Celtic Mythology and Folklore*, 136

Dooinney-Oie

Variations: The Nightman

In Manx lore the dooinney-oie is a NATURE SPIRIT, a fairy taking a misty humanoid shape and giving warning of incoming storms by sounding off with a great lamenting howl. When this BANSHEE-like cry, sounding like "*HOWLAA*" or "*howaa*" is heard in the winter it is a warning of a great and violent storm approaching.

Sources: Brand, *Observations on the Popular Antiquities of Great Britain*, 414; Briggs, *Encyclopedia of Fairies*, 105–6; Rose, *Spirits, Fairies, Gnomes, and Goblins*, 90

Doonie

In Scottish lore the doonie appears as either an old man, old woman, or as a pony. Unlike the DUNNIE and other fay that assume these guises, the doonie will guide lost travelers and help these in need.

Sources: Monaghan, *Encyclopedia of Celtic Mythology and Folklore*, 142; Rose, *Spirits, Fairies, Gnomes, and Goblins*, 90

Dóri

Variations: Dori ("boarer")

Dóri ("spearman") was one of the many DWARFS named in the *Voluspa*, the first and best known poem of the *Poetic Edda*, a collection of Old Norse poems dating back to about A.D. 985.

Sources: Daly, *Norse Mythology A to Z*, 22; Sykes, *Who's Who in Non-Classical Mythology*, 53

Dorion

In Greek mythology Dorion was a water–NYMPH and one of the named DANAIDS, the collective name for the daughters of Danaus. In a list compiled by Apollodorus, a Greek scholar and grammarian, she was one of the daughters of an unnamed Ethiopian woman and was wedded to Cercetes, one of the sons of an unnamed Phoenician woman.

Sources: Apollodorus, *Apollodorus' Library and Hyginus' Fabulae*, 22; Grimal, *Dictionary of Classical Mythology*, 127

Doris

Born one of the 3,000 daughters of the Titians, Oceanus and Tethys, Doris ("all voice" or "invisible") was the OCEANID of pure water; she and her husband Nerues, god of the sea, were the parents of the NEREID. She was the NEREID of the bountiful catch and she was one of the named NEREID who accompanied THETIS in mourning the loss of her son, Achilles. Doris' sister, CLYMENE, was the mother of the Titan, Atlas.

Sources: Apollodorus, *Apollodorus' Library and Hyginus' Fabulae*, 95; Bell, *Bell's New Pantheon or Historical Dictionary of the Gods*, 112; Collignon, *Manual of Mythology*, 18; Hesiod, *Works of Hesiod, Callimachus, and Theognis*, 20; Westmoreland, *Ancient Greek Beliefs*, 98

La Dormette

Variations: La Dormette de Poitou

Similar to the SANDMAN of British lore and OLE LUK ØJ of Denmark, the la dormette ensures pleasant dreams and sleep for infants in the neighborhood of Poitou, located in western France. She is described as a kindly woman who sprinkles sand and sleep in sleeping children's eyes.

Sources: Martinengo-Cesaresco, *Essays in the Study of Folk-Songs*, 337; Rose, *Spirits, Fairies, Leprechauns, and Goblins*, 91, 351

Doto

A sea–NYMPH, Doto ("the milk-white") was the NEREID of the safe voyage or safe fishing expedition in classical Greek mythology; she was born the daughter of Nerues and DORIS. Doto was one of the named NEREID who accompanied THETIS in mourning the loss of her son, Achilles.

Sources: Apollodorus, *Apollodorus' Library and Hyginus' Fabulae*, 95; Collignon, *Manual of Mythology*, 18; Gould, *Historic Magazine and Notes and Queries*, Volume 14, 212; Homer, *Iliads of Homer*, 137

Drac

Variations: d'Oc, Nix Dracae

Very similar to the DRACAE of Scotland, the dracs of southern France shape change in gold cups or rings and float down streams where they will be seen by lactating women or boys who are bathing. When the person touches the item the drac then drags their victim down to their underwater abode; women are forced to spend up to seven years breast-feeding the drac's children.

These fairies are also said to be able to assume human form and go shopping in the market. Their true form is said to be large purple blobs floating along the surface of the water. The dracs were most populous in the English Channel, but their previous home and sacred kingdom was the Seine River.

Sources: Keightly, *World Guide to Gnomes, Fairies, Elves, and Other Little People*, 465; McCoy, *Witch's Guide to Faery Folk*, 208–9; Moorey, *Fairy Bible*, 129

Dracae

In the Scottish Lowlands the dracae are water fairies living in the lochs and rivers. Leaving golden cups floating on the surface or bits of jewelry just below it, these fay lure women and children to water's edge, snatch them up, and drag them into their watery domain uses their victims as slaves. After the introduction of Christianity,

it was said a quick blessing, or *saining*, over the items were then safe to take.

Sources: Cox, *Mythology of the Aryan Nations*, Volume 2, 116; Douglas, *Scottish Fairy Tales*, 117–8; Monaghan, *Encyclopedia of Celtic Mythology and Folklore*, 136

Dragons

Variations: Drachen, Drake, Firedrake, Worm, Wurm, Wyrm

Existing in some form in virtually every culture the dragon, basically resembling a huge serpent, is also tied to fairy lore. Powerful beings like the fay, dragons abduct beautiful women, can be male or female, represent good or evil, are aquatic and terrestrial, and are associated with the elements: air, earth, fire, and water.

In most British tales and in Scandinavian lore, dragons are described as wingless creatures, having long scaly bodied, living in pools or wells, and having poisonous breath. These dragons hoard treasure, have a preference for eating young maidens, and are notoriously difficult and dangerous to kill. To slay a dragon is almost a guarantee to win the hand of the local princess and become the new king. Fairies with densely hairy bodies will commonly have a dragon as a pet in German folklore.

Sources: Briggs, *Encyclopedia of Fairies*, 106–8; Haase, *Greenwood Encyclopedia of Folktales and Fairy Tales*, 278–9; McCoy, *Witch's Guide to Faery Folk*, 30; Rose, *Giants, Monsters, and Dragons*, 104–5

Dragontina

Dragontina and FALERINA are FATES, neutrally aligned; they are the owners and caretakers of a beautiful garden. Dragontina is an erotic enchantress and seductress. She stands near at river, the Stream of Love, and offers to unsuspecting knights a cup filled with the elixir of blissful oblivion. By drinking it the victim forgets who they were, obliterating their identity, and completely destroying the person they were. At her father's request, she created a garden, pleasure palace, and temple to enchant a young prince, Orlando and keep him there. He travels in a flying wagon.

Sources: Cavallo, *Boiardo's Orlando Innamorato*, 42; Keightly, *World Guide to Gnomes, Fairies, Elves, and Other Little People*, 454

Drake

In British folklore a drake ("dragon") is a benevolent, invisible HOUSE-SPIRIT similar to a

BROWNIE; it keeps the firewood dry and hearth burning in exchange for being able to live in the family home. As kind as these fairies are, they smell like rotten eggs. If a Drake discovers it is not welcome it leave the house without holding a grudge; there has never been a story told of a drake acting out or reacting negatively to an insult, slight, or ill treatment they may have received.

Source: McCoy, *Witch's Guide to Faery Folk*, 209–10

Draupnir

Draupnir was one of the many DWARFS named in the *Voluspa*, the first and best known poem of the *Poetic Edda*, a collection of Old Norse poems dating back to about A.D. 985.

Sources: Crossley-Holland, *Norse Myths*, 183; Daly, *Norse Mythology A to Z*, 22; Sykes, *Who's Who in Non-Classical Mythology*, 53

Drosera

Drosera was a NYMPH from the mythology of ancient Greece and Rome. One of the NAIADS, she was known as "the dewy."

Sources: Bowersock, *Hellenism in Late Antiquity*, 48; Parada, *Genealogical Guide to Greek Mythology*, 128

Druggen Hill Boggle

In Cumberland, England the singular entity known as the Druggen Hill Boggle was first sighted in the nineteenth century; its appearance coincided with the disappearance of a local peddler and the appearance of a BLACK DOG that began to terrorize the area. When the community made the connection they went and searched the area, eventually finding the body of the peddler. As soon as the recovered body was interred in the churchyard the Druggen Hill Boggle disappeared forever. The wounds it had inflicted on its victims began to heal.

Source: Rose, *Spirits, Fairies, Leprechauns, and Goblins*, 91

Dryad

Variations: HAMADRYAD

Although originating in the lore of ancient Greece the dryads are well known all throughout the Celtic countries. The Dryads are one of twelve species of NYMPHS; they are the NYMPHS of the forests and trees, particularly oak trees. They have to power to both punish those who abridge the life of the trees under their protection or reward those who actively extend and protect their trees. The life of the dryad is tied to its tree; it is only as long lived as its tree. Ash, oak, and thorn trees are especially important in the Celtic traditions; when these three species of trees are found together they form what is call a FAIRY TRIAD. The trees in these groves are considered sacred to fairies, more so to the dryads.

Described as looking like the perfection of female beauty and youth a dryad woman will take a human male as her lover; when it does, it is not uncommon for the dryad to solicit a vow from the man asking him to avoid sexual intercourse will all other women. If the lover breaks the vow, he will be struck blind.

DAPHNE, the dryad associated with the laurel tree, was loved and pursued by the god, Apollo. Another famous dryad was AEGLE.

Sources: Evan-Wentz, *Fairy Faith in Celtic Countries*, 372; Hansen, *Classical Mythology*, 240–1; Keightly, *World Guide to Gnomes, Fairies, Elves, and Other Little People*, 447; Littleton, *Gods, Goddesses, and Mythology*, Volume 4, 440–42

Drymo

A sea–NYMPH, Drymo was one of the named NEREID; she was born of Nereus and DORIS and described by Virgil as having bright, waving locks of hair and a slender pale neck.

Sources: Apollodorus, *Apollodorus' Library and Hyginus' Fabulae*, 95; Bell, *Bell's New Pantheon or Historical Dictionary of the Gods*, 112; Virgil, *The Fourth Georgic of Virgil*,, 49

Dryope

Variations: Aero, MEROPE

One of the OREADS, Dryope was a NYMPH from classical Greek mythology. She was born one of the daughters of the god Atlas and the ocean NYMPH, PLEIONE. She and her sisters, ALCYONE, ASTEROPE, CELAENO, ELECTRA, MAIA, and TAYGETE, are sometimes referred to as the the ATLANTIDES or the Seven Sisters (see PLEIADES). In the guise of a serpent, the god Apollo fathered a son named Amphissos with her.

Sources: Antoninus, *Metamorphoses of Antoninus Liberalis* 91; Ardinger, *Pagan Every Day*, 190; Larson, *Greek Nymphs*, 165, 168; Rose, *Spirits, Fairies, Leprechauns, and Goblins*, 91–2

Dualin

In Scandinavian lore, Dualin was one of the two most ingenious and expert DWARF smiths, DYREN was the other; he forged the magical sword Trifing for the godling hero, Suaforlami, the second in descent from the god Odin and King over Gardarike (Russia). Dualin warned the magical sword "shall be the bane of man every time it is drawn. Done three of the greatest atrocities, it shall also be thy bane." Not long after, Dualin was slain by the weapon.

Sources: Keightly, *World Guide to Gnomes, Fairies, Elves, and Other Little People*, 72; Tibbits, *Folk-Lore and Legends, Scandinavian*, 190

Duallach

Duallach was a fairy piper from Irish folklore; he was the piper who played fairy music for the fay to dance to.

Source: Wallace, *Folk-lore of Ireland*, 85

Dúc-Bà

In the Annamese belief of Vietnam, there are three NATURE SPIRITS known collectively as the Three Mothers; their names are Dúc-Bà, Bà-Dúc-Chúa, and Dúc-Thành Bà. These NATURE SPIRITS are worshiped in small room in pagodas dedicated to the Buddha.

Dúc-Bà is the Spirit of the Forest and was created by the Jade Emperor.

Sources: Leach, *Funk and Wagnalls Standard Dictionary of Folklore, Mythology, and Legend*, 778; Rose, *Spirits, Fairies, Leprechauns, and Goblins*, 92

Dúc-Thành Bà

In the Annamese belief of Vietnam, there are three NATURE SPIRITS known collectively as the Three Mothers; their names are Dúc-Bà, Bà-Dúc-Chúa, and Dúc-Thành Bà. These NATURE SPIRITS are worshiped in small room in pagodas dedicated to the Buddha.

Dúc-Thành Bà is the Spirit of the Waters and was created by the Jade Emperor.

Sources: Leach, *Funk and Wagnalls Standard Dictionary of Folklore, Mythology, and Legend*, 778; Rose, *Spirits, Fairies, Leprechauns, and Goblins*, 92

Duende

Variations: Dueño de casa, Trasgo

In the fairy lore of Latin America, the Philippines, Portugal, and Spain, the duende is a SOLITARY FAIRY more often heard than seen as it whistles while walking through the woods. It is a HOUSE-SPIRIT but unlike the helpful BROWNIE, the duende hates humans and shows its dislike by throwing bits of clay and stones at people. Fortunately there are very few of them are left.

Most often this diminutive fairy is described as looking like either a small middle-age or elderly woman, having long fingers looking like icicles, and wearing a green-robe and a large hat. In the Hispanic folklore from the American Southwest, the duendes are considered to be malicious and described as having green skin and red eyes. They live inside the walls of the children's room and tempt them into misbehaving, attempting to steal their soul. In Central American folklore, particularly in Belize, the duendes are considered to be more of a NATURE SPIRIT and has no thumbs. They call it "Tata Duende."

Sources: Evan-Wentz, *Fairy Faith in Celtic Countries*, 373; Garza, *Creepy Creatures and other Cucuys*, 4, 6–7; Keightly, *World Guide to Gnomes, Fairies, Elves, and Other Little People*, 464; McCoy, *Witch's Guide to Faery Folk*, 212–13

Duergar

Variations: Dvergr ("DWARF")

According to Scandinavian lore, the duergar were the maggots who consumed the flesh of the dead GIANT, YMIR; as they ate they were gifted with human knowledge and took on the general appearance of mankind but were short, having stubby lega but long arms that almost touched the ground. The name of the very first duergar was MODSOGNER, and the name of the second was Dyrin. Silled gold-, iron-, metal-, and silversmiths they forged many magical items for both the Æsar and mortal heroes. They are said to reside in the underground realm of Nidavellir, one of the nine worlds fixed to the world-tree Yggdrasil according to Norse cosmology.

Sources: Briggs, *Encyclopedia of Fairies*, 111–12; Keightly, *World Guide to Gnomes, Fairies, Elves, and Other Little People*, 66–7; McCoy, *Witch's Guide to Faery Folk*, 213

Duergarrs

Variations: DUERGAR

In the folklore of France and northern England the duergarrs is a malicious species of DWARF; it gains no greater pleasure than in tricking people into dying, usually by pretending to be the flickering of a light and leading them through the dark off a cliff ledge. It will also turn around the signs on signposts causing travelers to become lost. A SOLITARY FAIRY and skilled metallurgists, the duergar can be either male or female and are described as standing only about two foot tall and wearing green hats, lambskin coats, and moleskin shoes; it is most often the male that leads travelers to their death as they believe the hills and the rocks they live in are theirs alone and do tolerate the presence of others.

Sources: McCoy, *Witch's Guide to Faery Folk*, 213; Tibbits, *Folk Lore and Legends, English*, 181–4

Dúfr

Variations: Dufr, Duf, Duri ("sleepy"), Durinn

Dúfr ("snoozy") was one of the many DWARFS named in the *Voluspa*, the first and best known poem of the *Poetic Edda*, a collection of Old Norse poems dating back to about A.D. 985.

Sources: Daly, *Norse Mythology A to Z*, 22; Sykes, *Who's Who in Non-Classical Mythology*, 53

Dugani

In Slavic lore Dugani was a singular entity, a household fairy spirit that looked after bread dough and prevented it from turning sour.

Sources: Guirand, *New Larousse Encyclopedia of Mythology*, 290; Rose, *Spirits, Fairies, Leprechauns, and Goblins*, 92

Dullahan

Variations: Dulachan, Dullaghan, Durahan, Far Dorocha, Gan Ceann, Headless Horseman

Before the Irish potato famine began in 1845 no such fairy being as the dullahan existed, but once the famine had begun people started to claim a BANSHEE was being accompanied by a headless man riding upon a horse at midnight; sightings were most numerous on Feast Days. The being traveling with the BANSHEE was described as carrying his head, a smile on its face from ear to ear. The head was said to be the color and texture of moldy cheese. Sometimes the hose was headless as well. Other times the dullahan was described more like the DEATH COACH, made of human thigh bones and was pulled by six black horses with skull heads, their eyes lit by candles in their sockets. No matter its appearance, the dullahan races down roads spreading disease and causing households to fall ill. The fairy-being uses a bullwhip to lash out the eyes of anyone on the roadside who sees him; he is cursed with poor eyesight himself. Lucky victims only get covered with a bucket of blood he throws at them as he charges by. The dullahan is a member of the UNSEELIE COURT; it is exceedingly greedy and any momentary offering thrown to it will be accepted.

Sources: Curran, *Field Guide to Irish Fairies*, 62–5; Haughton, *Famous Ghost Stories: Legends and Lore*, 54–5; Monaghan, *Encyclopedia of Celtic Mythology and Folklore*, 140

Duln Glichd

A duln glichd ("wise woman") was a woman who had a great deal of knowledge about fairies, herbs, and sometimes magical abilities she was either born with or were gifted to her by the fay. Usually duln glichd can see the fairies out of one of their eyes; sometimes this ability was given to them as payment for acting as a midwife to a fairy or by accidentally having some fairy oil rubbed into an eye.

Sources: J. T. C. J. T. *Folk-Lore and Legends: England and Scotland*, 111; Keightly, *World Guide to Gnomes, Fairies, Elves, and Other Little People*, 386

Dund

Variations: Dhundh

In the folklore from India, the dund was a terrifying fairy spirit described as looking like a rider with no hands, head, or feet riding upon a horse; it is similar to the DULLAHAN of Celtic lore. The limbs are sometime said to be tied to the saddle. As it travels, the dund calls out the names of the occupants of the nearby houses. The people must not answer his call or they will go insane or die.

Sources: Crooke, *North Indian Notes and Queries*, Volumes 1–2, 32; Rose, *Spirits, Fairies, Leprechauns, and Goblins*, 92

Duneyr

Duneyr was one of the four DWARFS in Nordic mythology whose name was those of the hart's that ate the buds off of Yggdrasil, the World Tree (see DAIN, DAVALIN, and DURATHROR). The four DWARFS were likely the guardians of it.

Sources: Rose, *Spirits, Fairies, Leprechauns, and Goblins*, 79; Sykes, *Who's Who in Non-Classical Mythology*, 53

Dunnie

Variations: DOONIE

In the fairy-lore of Northumbria, England, a dunnie is a shape-shifting practical joker. Its favorite trick is to look like a midwife's horse and as soon as it is needs, disappear, leaving her stranded. It would also play a similar prank on plowmen. Some sources say the dunnie is an individual entity rather than a species of fairy. In Scotland, the dunnie is known as a DOONIE, but has a much kinder disposition.

Sources: Briggs, *Encyclopedia of Fairies*, 114; Monaghan, *Encyclopedia of Celtic Mythology and Folklore*, 142; Rose, *Spirits, Fairies, Gnomes, and Goblins*, 90

Dunter

Variations: Powries, RED CAP

Dunters are a type of fairy spirit living in old peel-towers and keeps along the border lands between England and Scotland. These spirits make a constant noise like the grinding of flax seed against stone; it is believed if the sound increases in volume it is an omen of an impending death. It has been speculated the foundations of the old keeps were made from ancient Picts who, according to their tradition, made a blood sacrifice over the stones making the dunters the spirits of those sacrifices, be they animal or human.

Sources: Briggs, *Encyclopedia of Fairies*, 115; Monaghan, *Encyclopedia of Celtic Mythology and Folklore*, 385; Rose, *Spirits, Fairies, Gnomes, and Goblins*, 92–3

Durathror

Durathror was one of the four DWARFS in Nordic mythology whose name was those of the hart's that ate the buds off of Yggdrasil, the World Tree (see DAIN, DAVALIN, and DUNEYR). The four DWARFS were likely the guardians of it.

Sources: Rose, *Spirits, Fairies, Leprechauns, and Goblins*, 79; Sykes, *Who's Who in Non-Classical Mythology*, 53, 217

Durin

Variations: Durinn ("dripper"), Dyrin

In old German lore Durin ("slumberer") was the name of a DWARF who resided within a stone. One of three powerful DWARF leaders, Durin, along with DVALIN and MODSOGNIR, forged many fantastic and magical weapons. Any weapon demanded from them would ultimately kill its owner.

As Durinn ("dripper") he was one of the many DWARFS named in the *Voluspa*, the first and best known poem of the *Poetic Edda*, a collection of Old Norse poems dating back to about A.D. 985. With the DWARF DVALIN he forged the magic sword, Tyrfing. As the first of Mimir's sons, he is the eldest of the DWARFS and knows the destiny of the elders of his kind. He and his father built the World Mill to create fertile soil so there could be life on Midgard.

Sources: Bunsen, *God in History*, 506; Daly, *Norse Mythology A to Z*, 22; Rose, *Spirits, Fairies, Leprechauns, and Goblins*, 93; Sturluson, *Younger Edda*, 70; Sykes, *Who's Who in Non-Classical Mythology*, 53

Dush

Variations: Dusii, Pilosi ("hairy ones")

In the mythology from the ancient Gauls of France the dush were a hairy species of fairy similar to the HOBGOBLIN of Celtic lore. The dush are essentially a furred version of the BROWNIE.

Sources: Roscher, *Pan and the Nightmare*, 57; Rose, *Spirits, Fairies, Leprechauns, and Goblins*, 93

Dvalin

Variations: Dvalin Brisings, Dvalinn, Dwalin

Dvalinn ("dawdler") was one of the many DWARFS named in the *Voluspa*, the first and best known poem of the *Poetic Edda*, a collection of Old Norse poems dating back to about A.D. 985.

In Norse mythology the Dvalin is one of the four BRISINGAMEN DWARFS who created the prized necklace for the goddess Freyr (see also ALFRIGG, BERLING, and GERR). He once spent a night with the goddess discussing and debating the many aspects of the world. He also invented runes, created a golden wig for the goddess Sif, constructed the spear Gungnir, and the ship Skidbladnir.

Sources: Bellows, *Poetic Edda*, 6, 7, 62; Daly, *Norse Mythology A to Z*, 22; Pentikäinen, *Shamanism and Northern Ecology*, 87, 94; Wilkinson, *Book of Edda called Völuspá*, 12

Dvorovoi

Variations: Dvoroi

In Russia, a dvorovoi is a fairy spirit of the house's yard; typically it resembles the male head of the household and demonstrates a distinct preference as to the color of pets and livestock are kept. Although the dvorovoi is injurious it is not deadly. Offerings of sheep's wool, shiny objects, or a slice of bread left in the barn are left in the barn for it while saying "*Master Dvorovik, I offer you this gift in gratitude. Please look after the cattle and feed them well*"; doing this can appease it. If the dvorovoi becomes too malicious and needs to be banished or at least brought back into line a three-tailed whip must be made from a used burial shroud. Then, it must be dipped in wax, set on fire and then used, whipping each corner of the barn, hoping to hit the fairy and bring it back into submission.

Sources: Dixon-Kennedy, *Encyclopedia of Russian and Slavic Myth and Legend*, 78; Graves, *Larousse Encyclopedia of Mythology*, 287; Ivanits, *Russian Folk Belief*, 58

Dwarf (plural: dwarfs)

Variations: Berg-Mänlein ("Hill-Mannikins"), Berg-Mänlein ("Hill-Mannikins"), Dorch, Drerge, Dverg, Dweeorg, Dwerger, Dwergugh, DUERGAR, Dworh, Erd-Mänlein ("Ground-Mannikins"), HÄRDMANDLE, Hel-kaplein, Hill TROLLS, Kleine Volk ("Little People"), MOSS PEOPLE, OENNERBANSKE, Oennereeske, Stele Volk ("Still People"), Tarnkapppe, Tele Volk ("Still People"), Timber, Trold, TROLL, Unnerorske ("Underground folks"), Wichtelweib, Wichtlein ("Little Wights"), Wild, Zwerge, Zzwerg

The dwarf is a popular and staple figure in fairy lore. Generally these short but powerfully built beings are beneficent and will assist those who treat them with respect; however if injured or offended they will quickly vent their rage on cattle. They appear to be old, reach maturity at three years of age, and the male of the species will have long, grey beards. dwarfs who live underground do not involve themselves with humans if they can help it, as they would rather mine for their gold and precious gems. If they venture above ground, the dwarf will do so at night. They have the ability to become invisible and can walk through rocks and walls. The lore varies as to why they do not venture out into the light, sometimes it is said they will turn to stone but other times it is said they spend their daylight hours in the guise of a frog. Because they are such isolationists they are said to be members of the UNSEELIE COURT.

The Fairies of England are the dwarfs of Germany and the lands to its north.

In Iceland dwarfs are said to wear red clothing. The fullest account of Icelandic dwarfs comes from the learned Bishop of Skalholt, Finnus Johannaeus in his book *"The Ecclesiastical History of Iceland,"* but it is make almost distinction between elves and dwarfs.

In Brenton dwarfs are called KORRIGAN.

In Finland and Lapland it is believed dwarfs live in a magnificent underground land and sometimes mortals are allowed to enter. While a guest, they are spectacularly entertained and given copious amounts of brandy and tobacco.

In the Friesland, Netherlands, dwarfs are called oennereeske and tend to fall in love with mortal women and steal them away, keeping them for long periods of time. They also steal children and leave CHANGELINGS in their place. Oennereeske will also borrow and lend plates and pots as well as money, sometimes even charging interest. They will assist in the construction of churches and homes, helping when a cart is stuck in the mud, and bring field workers pancakes and water.

In Switzerland dwarfs are called dverg ("spider") and are described as being generous, kind and having a joyous nature. Fond of strolling throughout the land they will randomly take part in random act of kindness, such as driving sheep and leaving berries where poor children can find them. In Scandinavian lore, the more common word used for the dwarf if TROLL or trold.

The fifteenth century German manuscript entitled *The Heldenbuch* (*"Book of Heroes"*) claims "God created the GIANTS that they might kill the wild beasts, and the great DRAGONS, that the dwarfs might be more secure."

Dwarfs in southern Germany live in large communal groups but tend to appear to man alone. They are described as being small, grey and old looking, hairy and covered in moss, standing as tall as a three year old child. Female dwarfs in southern Germany have a nicer disposition than their male counterparts; they were green clothing trimmed in red and cocked hats upon their head. They live deep back in the woods and will give woodcutters good advice, assist in cooking and washing clothes. They most often appear where people are baking so they can use the fire. A bit of dough is left for them as an offering. The male dwarfs in southern Germany live in mines and dress like miners, carrying a hammer, lantern, and mallet. They enjoy throwing stones at miners but unless they have been offended, the assault is harmless.

In Lusatia, Germany, it is believed dwarfs are actually fallen angels.

In some German tales when a dwarf's hat is knocked off of their head it becomes visible. They can also bestow physical strength, curse a family to poverty, foresee future events, gift prosperity upon a family, and shape-shift into any form.

Interestingly, there are no dwarfs in Italian lore.

Sources: Bord, Fairies, 60; Briggs, *Encyclopedia of Fairies*, 115; Evan-Wentz, *Fairy Faith in Celtic Countries*, 374–75; Keightly, *World Guide to Gnomes, Fairies, Elves, and Other Little People*, 216–17, 229–30, 264, 281, 448; Lindow, *Norse Mythology*, 99–101

Dwende

Variations: Duwende

Filipino fairy lore says the dwende are a type of NATURE SPIRIT living in caves, old trees, rocks, and in the unused, dark areas of the home. They are partial to acacia, balete, caimito, and mango trees. Living in hills, the white dwende are considered to be beneficent while the black dwende are malicious. They enjoy playing with children. Descriptions are varies, they are said to be between two and three feet tall, have red skin, hairy bodies, long beards, pointed ears, smell of either damp earth or dried feces and wear pointed hats and shoes.

Able to shape-shift into the form of a human

man these fairies will sometimes fall in love with a married woman and try to take her on as its lover. The only way the woman can rid herself of this fairy is to be sure she is always in the company of two men.

Sources: Henry, *Filipino Spirit World*, 30, 32; Licauco, J. *Dwarfs and Other Nature Spirits*, 169; Llamzon, *Handbook of Philippine Language Groups*, 78

Dynamene

Variations: Dynamenè

A sea–NYMPH, Dynamene ("the bringer") was the NEREID of the power of the sea in classical Greek mythology; she had the ability to appear and disappear rapidly. Born the daughter of Nerues and DORIS, she was one of the named NEREID who accompanied THETIS in mourning the loss of her son, Achilles.

Sources: Collignon, *Manual of Mythology*, 18; Gould, *Historic Magazine and Notes and Queries*, Volume 14, 212; Hesiod, *Works of Hesiod, Callimachus, and Theognis*, 15; Trzaskoma, *Anthology of Classical Myth*, 18

Dyombie

Variations: Yorba

From the folklore of Surinam in South Africa Dyombie is the NATURE SPIRIT of the Kankantree (cotton tree). Born the son of the gods Gereonsu and Tinne he will punish anyone who harms the tree or fails to properly respect it with liquid libations. In more modern times, Dyombie is considered to be a species of NATURE SPIRIT and not a singular entity.

Sources: Rose, *Spirits, Fairies, Leprechauns, and Goblins*, 96; Thompson, *Face of the Gods*, 123

Dyren

In Scandinavian lore, Dyren was one of the two most ingenious and expert DWARF smiths, DUALIN was the other; he forged the magical sword Trifing for the godling hero, Suaforlami, the second in descent from the god Odin and King over Gardarike (Russia).

Sources: Keightly, *World Guide to Gnomes, Fairies, Elves, and Other Little People*, 72

Dziwitza

In Polish folklore Dziwitza is a NATURE SPIRIT and a *knenye* ("princess"); it appears as a beautiful young woman. Armed with a zylba ("javelin") and a pack of hunting hounds Dziwitza will appear suddenly in front of people who are in the woods at the noon and midnight hours and terrify

them. Although startling, she has never been said to harm anyone.

Sources: Grimm, *Teutonic Mythology*, Volume 3, 933; Porteous, *Forest in Folklore and Mythology*, 108; Rose, *Spirits, Fairies, Leprechauns, and Goblins*, 96

Dzunukwa

Variations: Sasquatch, Tsonoqua, Tsonokwa

A type of NATURE SPIRIT who lived in the mountains and deep forests of the Pacific Northwest, Dzunukwa was a cannibal who was especially fond of eating children. Described as having large, round sleepy eyes large breasts, and thick red lips, she adorns herself with the skulls of the children she has eaten. Acting as a NURSERY BOGIE to keep children from wandering out into the woods alone, Dzunukwa was also physically strong and had a wide array of supernatural powers. An extremely literal thinker, she was easy to trick and outwit but this should not be confused with being dimwitted. Dzunukwa possessed tremendous esoteric knowledge on animals, death, life, nature, and the woods. Becoming easily disoriented when outside of her forest, Dzunukwa was a generally hostile being but could be calmed down by men; she may bestow good fortune or wealth on someone who sooths her as in addition to having great knowledge she was also the guardian of the Water of Life.

Sources: Illes, *Encyclopedia of Spirits*, 377; Shearar, *Understanding Northwest Coast Art*, 42

E Bukura e Dheut

The FAIRY QUEEN of the Albanian fairies, E Bukura e Dheut ("the earthly beauty"), rules over a host of beautiful, capricious, and completely unpredictable court of subject. E Bukura e Dheut was considered to be the epitome of beauty and happiness and may be asked to intervene if her subjects became too volatile.

Originally a goddess of beauty and love, E Bukura e Dheut had taken Tomor, the supreme god of the Illyrians, as her lover. In addition to living in an underworld real she also had a castle atop a mountain surrounded by fabulous beasts and magical creatures.

Sources: Elsie, *Dictionary of Albanian Religion, Mythology, and Folk Culture*, 48; Illes, *Encyclopedia of Spirits*, 378

Each Uisce

Variations: AUGHISKY, Eač Uisge, Each Uisge

One of the many species of water horse, the each uisce ("water monster") of Scottish fairy lore is a fearsome creature, beautiful and sleek; it offers itself to be ridden. So long as the fairy-horse never catches a glimpse of a body of salt water it will be a fine riding horse; however as soon as it does it will bound into the water, taking its rider with it. Once submerged the each uisce then turns and attacks it rider, devouring him if it is able, leaving only the liver behind. Untamed, unbridled each uisce will roam the countryside and consume cattle.

Similar to the AUGHISKY of Irish lore, CEFFYL DWFR from Wales, and the SHOOPILTEE from the Shetlands, the each uisce differs from the KELPIE in that it lives in running water. Typically, it is sighted during the month of November, running down the sandy beaches.

Sources: Briggs, *Encyclopedia of Fairies*, 115–16; Eberhart, *Mysterious Creatures*, 580; Illes, *Encyclopedia of Spirits*, 378; Rose, *Spirits, Fairies, Leprechauns, and Goblins*, 97

Eager

In Nottingham, England Eager is the name of a NATURE SPIRIT, the personification of the Trent River Tidal Bore. This malicious WATER SPIRIT was responsible for causing floods in the region; it has been speculated its name is diverived from the Scandinavian god of the sea, Ægir, a deity familiar to the Danish who settled the area after the Roman occupation.

Sources: Rose, *Spirits, Fairies, Leprechauns, and Goblins*, 97; Spence, *Minor Traditions of British Mythology*, 14

The Earthmen

Variations: Earth-Men, Earth People

The earthmen are the general name applies to the fairy and GNOME mines. A solitary race, they enjoy dancing and laughing. In Scandinavia earthmen are known as TROLLS while in other mythologies they were called DWARFS. They are sometimes described as being NATURE SPIRITS and are said to live in mounds and throughout the night the sounds of their laboring can be heard on the surface.

Sources: Brewer, *Dictionary of Phrase and Fable*, 401; Hunter-Duvar, *Stone, Bronze and Iron Ages*, 259

Echenais

Variations: HEDINA, Lyce, LYKA, NOMIA, THALEIA, Xenon

Echenais was a NYMPH from the mythology of ancient Greece and Rome. One of the NAIADS, she had been given different names by various authors. Echenais fell in love with a handsome Sicilian poet and shepherd named Daphnis, son of the god, Hermes (Mercury); before she would fully give her herself to him she solicited a promise from him—he would resist the temptations of all other women. Eventually, he forgot his vow and Echenais struck him blind, or turned him to stone, sources vary.

Sources: Bell, *Women of Classical Mythology*, 172; Platthy, *Mythical Poets of Greece*, 68; Smith, *Dictionary of Greek and Roman Biography and Mythology*, 939

Echo

Variations: Ekho

Echo was a NYMPH from the mythology of ancient Greece. One of the OREADS, she deeply offended the goddess, Hera (Juno) with her artful loquacity; Echo was cursed and deprived of the ability to speak except to say the last thing said by another. Echo fell in love with Narcissus but he only loved his reflection. The NYMPH eventually pined away, only her voice remaining in the mountains where she lived. Her story is told by the Roman poet Ovid in his masterpiece work of the Golden age of Latin literature, *Metamorphoses* (A.D. 8).

Sources: Daly, *Greek and Roman Mythology A to Z*, 44; Keightly, *World Guide to Gnomes, Fairies, Elves, and Other Little People*, 3; Pavlock, *Image of the Poet in Ovid's Metamorphoses*, 29

Edain

Variations: Achtan, Aideen, Édain, Etain, Étain, Etain Echraide, Etaine

Edain ("swift one") is the mortal, human wife of the FAIRY KING, MIDIR in Irish mythology; his first wife, FUAMNACH, a powerful sorceress, transformed her rival into a fly. As an insect, Edain flew about for years until she landed in a cup and was consumed by a princess of Ulster, making her pregnant. The princess gave birth to a baby girl and named her Etain who grew up to be the most beautiful woman in all of Ireland. Having forgotten her past life, she married King EOCHAID but MIDIR had not forgotten about her. The FAIRY KING concocted a plan to win his wife back; he traveled to earth and challenged EOCHAID to a game of fidchell. The mortal king played well but was determined to win, putting his wife, Etain up as a prize. The kings played and MIDIR won, claiming his prize he kissed Etain and all her memories were restored. Together they fled. EOCHAID perused the couple and fell victim to a clever ploy where he fell in love with his own daughter, Esa. He did not realize the tragedy until after he and his new wife had a child together.

Sources: Briggs, *Encyclopedia of Fairies*, 123–4; Knapp, *Women, Myth, and the Feminine Principle*, 188; Monaghan, *Encyclopedia of Celtic Mythology and Folklore*, 162–3; Russell, *Irish Monthly*, Volume 20, 219–22

Eddy winds

Variations: Oiteag Sluaigh ("the People's Puff of Wind"), Furl of Fairy Wind

In Scottish lore it is said whenever straw is lifted up on the wind the fairy court is on the move and traveling. These whirlwinds, or eddy winds, are reputed to pick up people, especially those who are traveling at night, and fly them over the land, depositing them in an unfamiliar area. To protect this from happening it is advised to toss one's left shoe at the eddy; this will cause the fairy to momentarily lose it power. Another method is to toss the dirt from beneath your feet at the wind; this too will cause the fairy to temporarily lose it power.

Sources: Campbell, *Superstitions of the Highlands and Islands of Scotland*, 22–25; MacKenzie, *Migration of Symbols*, 75

Eeyeekalduk

Eeyeekalduk is a benevolent NATURE SPIRIT in the mythology of the Inuit people; it lived in stones. Described as a tiny man with a jet-black face he is called upon to assist in healing the sick. Eeyeekalduk would look at a sick person and draw the sickness out of them along his line of sight; however it was considered dangerous to look directly into his eyes.

Sources: Avant, *Mythological Reference*, 36; Chopra, *Academic Dictionary of Mythology*, 95; Rose, *Spirits, Fairies, Leprechauns, and Goblins*, 97

Egeria

Egeria was a NYMPH from the mythology of ancient Rome. Worshiped by pregnant women because she, like the goddess, Diana, could grant an easy delivery, Egeria also had the power to assist in conception. The water in her grotto was considered sacred and votive offerings were left. Egeria was one of the oak-NYMPHS, a DRYAD specifically associated with the grove in Nemi; her fountain was said to have sprung from the trunk of an oak tree and whoever drank it water was blessed with fertility, prophetic visions, and wisdom. Her lover (or husband sources vary) was the OAK KING, Numa. Egeria was described as looking like a beautiful woman as well as a MERMAID.

Sources: Bell, *Bell's New Pantheon*, 278–9; Frazer, *Golden Bough*, 150; Keightly, *World Guide to Gnomes, Fairies, Elves, and Other Little People*, 448

Eggmoinn

Eggmoinn ("slain by the sword," literally "sword mown") was one of the many DWARFS named in the *Voluspa*, the first and best known poem of the *Poetic Edda*, a collection of Old Norse poems dating back to about A.D. 985.

Sources: Anderson, *A Certain Text*, 175; Di Lauro, *Through a Glass Darkly*, 67

Eido

Variations: Eidothea, Theonoe

A sea–NYMPH, Eido ("she is wisdom") was a daughter of the early sea god, Proteus, according to ancient Greek mythology. As Eidothea she advised Menelaus how to approach and question her father, a talented shape-shifter who had visions.

Sources: Larson, *Greek Nymphs*, 167; Westmoreland, *Ancient Greek Beliefs*, 719

Eidyia

Variations: IDYIA

Born one of the 3,000 daughters of the Titians, Oceanus and Tethys, Eidyia ("the fair faced"), one of the named OCEANIDS was the wife of King Aeetes and the mother of the sorceress Medea.

Sources: Bell, *Bell's New Pantheon or Historical Dictionary of the Gods*, 112; Boswell, *What Men or Gods Are These*, 58; Hesiod, *Works of Hesiod, Callimachus, and Theognis*, 20

The Eight Fairies of the Kingdom of Matakin

In the fairy-tale *The Sleeping Beauty in the Woods* there were mentioned but never named seven good fairies and one very old fairy. Upon the birth of a princess all the fairies of the kingdom were invited to her christening but since no one had seen or heard from the eldest fairy for some fifty years she was not invited. The first fairy blessed the child so she would be the most beautiful woman in the world; the second fairy blessed her so she would have the wit of an angel; the third fairy blessed with child with a wonderful grace which would be apparent in all she did; the fourth fairy blessed the child so she would always dance perfectly; the fifth fairy bless the child with the ability to sing like a nightingale; and the sixth fairy blessed the princess so she would be able to play all kinds of musical instruments with the utmost perfection. Before the seventh fairy could deliver her blessing the old fairy appeared, insulted she was not invited, and laid a curse upon the infant—if ever her finger should be pierced by a spindle, she would die. The seventh fairy could not undo the magical spell but was able to alter the magic so the princess would not die but rather fall into a profound sleep which would last one hundred years; when the time had passed, a prince will awaken her.

Eventually, in spite of the royal decrees and care taken to protect the princess, she did one day prick her finger on a spindle. When this happened the seventh fairy left her home located 12,000 leagues away, and flew by means of fiery chariot pulled by DRAGONS. Upon her arrival, she placed everyone in the kingdom in a deep sleep so when the enchantment was lifted everyone would awake and be ready to serve her. While the princess slept, the seventh fairy sent her a plethora of pleasant dreams.

Source: Lang, *Blue Fairy Book*, 54–60

Eikinskjaldi

Eikinskjaldi ("Oak Shield") was one of the many DWARFS named in the *Voluspa*, the first and best known poem of the *Poetic Edda*, a collection of Old Norse poems dating back to about A.D. 985. He was known to be a skilful artist.

Sources: Crossley-Holland, Norse Myths, 183; Daly, *Norse Mythology A to Z*, 22; Wilkinson, *Book of Edda called Völuspá*, 12

Eilian of Garth Dorwen

Eilian of Garth Dorwen is the golden haired maidservant who would spin with the TYLWYTH TEG on moonlit nights. Eilian was especially loved by the fairies because of her beautiful hair and one spring was invited to live with them. According to folklore, she is one of the few humans who became a willing bride to a fairy husband; when she became pregnant and needed a midwife one was called to the mound or FAIRY FORT to assist in the birth.

Sources: Brigs, *Encyclopedia of Fairies*, 117; Rhys, *Celtic Folklore Welsh and Manx*, Volume 1, 212–13; Westwood, *Albion*, 281

Eingsaung

Variations: Enig Saung, Min-magayi

The eingsaung is a species of NAT from the mythology of the Burman and Talaing people of Burma. Considered benevolent guardians of the home, the eingsaung live in a post decorated with leaves in the southern corner of the house. All other posts in the home are covered in white cloth. Votive coconuts are hung in a rectangular bamboo frame draped with a red cloth in the house to honor the enigsaung.

Sources: Gray, *Mythology of All Races*, Volume 12, 344–5; Hardiman, *Gazetteer of Upper Burma and the Shan States, Part 1*, Volume 2, 20; Rose, *Spirits, Fairies, Leprechauns, and Goblins*, 98

Eione

Variations: Heione

A sea–NYMPH, Eione was the NEREID of beach sand; she was born the daughter of Nerues and DORIS and was said by the ancient writer, Philodemus, the Epicurean philosopher and poet, to be "sweet."

Sources: Gigante, *Books from Herculaneum*, 51; Hesiod, *Works of Hesiod, Callimachus, and Theognis*, 15; Trzaskoma, *Anthology of Classical Myth*, 18

Eirene

In Greek mythology, Eirene (Peace) and her two sisters, DIKE ("Justice") and EUNOMIA ("Lawful Order"), were collectively known as the HORAE ("the correct moment"), the guardians of natural law; they were born the daughters of the Titian goddess of Law, Themis, and the god, Zeus (Jupiter). The NATURE SPIRIT-like sisters were entrusted with guarding the gate to Olympus. Eirene, like her sisters, was described as being a beautiful young maiden with beautiful hair, light footsteps, and wearing golden diadems. Representing the seasons, each one held a blooming flower, and ear of corn, and a vine stock. She was worshiped in Athens and sacrifices were made upon an alter dedicated to her.

Sources: Gall, *Lincoln Library of Greek and Roman Mythology*, 20; McLean, *Triple Goddess*, 49; Roman, *Encyclopedia of Greek and Roman Mythology*, 172

Eithne

Variations: ETHNE

A beautiful, charming, and modest woman of the TUATHA DE DANANN; after having been deeply insulted by a visiting Chieftan of the TUATHA DE DANANN Eithne was no longer able to eat or drink anything except for the milk from two special cows imported from India; they were milked daily into a golden cup.

In a Christianized version of the tale the insult said to Eithne so damaged her pure soul and so offended her, the demon with her fled and was quickly replaced by a guardian angel. She chose to not eat the flesh of the magical pork or drink the enchanted ale of her people; rather she was sustained miraculously by the true God. Eventually her father came across two divine cows that gave perpetual milk while traveling in India. He returned home with them and gave them to his daughter who milked them herself.

Sources: de Jubainville, *Irish Mythological Cycle and Celtic Mythology*, 157; van Doorn-Harder, *Coping with Evil in Religion and Culture*, 44

Eitri

Eitri ("poisonous"), a DWARF was the smith who made Gullinbursti ("golden bristles"), the boar with the bristles of bold. This creature-item was able to run through the air both day and night and was said to be better than any horse. He also made the magical gold ring Drupner, and the hammer of Thor, Miolner which would never fail to hit a TROLL. Eitri was the brother of BROC.

Sources: Conway, *Norse Magic*, 143–4; Keightly, *World Guide to Gnomes, Fairies, Elves, and Other Little People*, 68–9; Tibbits, *Folk-Lore and Legends, Scandinavian*, 153–4

Ekimmu

A malicious spirit from the mythology of the ancient Assyrians the ekimmu, much like the BANSHEE of Irish folklore, appeared outside a home and released an long, frightful, wailing cry just before the death of one of its occupants.

Sources: Avant, *Mythological Reference*, 469; Eason, *Complete Guide to Faeries and Magical Beings*, 200; Haining, *Ghosts*, 18

Ekke Nekkepem

Ekke Nekkepem is the name of a DWARF from Friesian lore that had fallen in love with a beautiful, young girl, Inge of Rantum. He became engaged to her against her will but Ekke Nekkepem promised her if she could correctly guess his name before their wedding day he would release her. Just as in the popular tale, RUMPELSTILTSKIN, the girl overhears the DWARF gloating and singing a song with his own name in it.

Sources: Guiney, *Brownies and Bogles*, 142; Keightly, *World Guide to Gnomes, Fairies, Elves, and Other Little People*, 233

Ekkekko

Variations: Ekako, Ekeko, Eq'eq'o

In the folklore of the Aymara people of Peru and the Mestizos people of Brazil the ekkekko is revered as a benevolent HOUSE-SPIRIT. Described as looking like a small, plump man carrying household utensils he brings fertility and good luck with him. Little statues made of clay, gold, rock, silver, and tin were made of ekkekko and kept in the home; a feast day was dedicated to him and celebrated in midsummer but Spanish invaders put an end to the celebration and the spirits worship. In 1871 the feast day to ekkekko was reinstated but it is now celebrated on January 24.

Sources: Meisch, *Traveler's Guide to El Dorado and the Inca Empire*, 389–90; Chopra, Academic Dictionary of Mythology, 97; Rose, *Spirits, Fairies, Leprechauns, and Goblins*, 98

Elaby Gathan

In the seventeenth century in England, Elaby Gathan was the name if a fairy who was invoked in magical spells. It has been suggested the word, *lullaby*, was taken from this fay; nurses would call upon it to watch over sleeping babies so other, malicious fairies would not swap out their baby for a CHANGELING.

Sources: Briggs, *Encyclopedia of Fairies*, 117; Hupfeld, *Encyclopedia of Wit and Wisdom*, 697; Rose, *Spirits, Fairies, Leprechauns, and Goblins*, 98, 351

Elayne

Variations: Elain, Elaine, Elane

According to legend, Elayne of Astolat, the Lady of Shalott, was imprisoned in a tower; in order to see the outside world she would weave magical tapestries giving her images of events and people. One day she saw the face of Sir Lancelot and fell in love with. Even knowing it would mean her death she set out in a small boat to Camelot meet him, dying as she traveled.

The original Elayne was likely a SIREN of the Scotland's Clyde River where she lived in a stone castle on the rock, Dumbarton. She owned a magic mirror and on its surface she could see events happening all over the world.

Another Elayne from Arthurian mythology was said to be the fairy-lover of the Arthurian knight, Sir Lancelot. This Elayne was said to live on the Joyous Isle where she and Lancelot were the parents of Sir Galahad.

Sources: Evan-Wentz, *Fairy Faith in Celtic Countries*, 316–17; Monaghan, *Encyclopedia of Celtic Mythology and Folklore*, 149; Spence, *Minor Traditions of British Mythology*, 18

Elberich

Variations: Albrich, Auberich, Auberon, OBERON

A DWARF king named in the Middle High German epic poem *The Nibelungenlied* (*The Song of the Nibelungs*), Elberich defends his hoard of treasure against the cultural hero, Siegfried. Cunning Elberich is described as being "very ancient," and since his appearance in the book as a character in a very old story, it lends credence to this claim. He also has the ability to become invisible. It has been suggested Elberich is none other than the graceful and petulant OBERON.

Sources: Carlyle, *Essays on the Greater German Poets and Writers*, 152; Keightly, *World Guide to Gnomes, Fairies, Elves, and Other Little People*, 38; Yonge, *History of Christian Names*, Volume 2, 346–7

Elbgast

In Teutonic mythology Elbgast, a DWARF, is the brother of King Goldmar and ALBERICH.

Sources: Rose, *Spirits, Fairies, Leprechauns, and Goblins*, 98, 351

Eldrich

Variations: Alriche, Eldriche, Eldritch, Elphrish, Elrage, Elraige, Elrisch, Elrish, Eltrich

In Scottish folklore Eldrich is a house ELF so hideously ugly it causes fear in anyone who sees it.

Sources: Jamieson, *Scottish Dictionary and Supplement: In Four Volumes. A-Kut*, Volume 1, 357; Rose, *Spirits, Fairies, Leprechauns, and Goblins*, 98

Electra

Variations: Elektra, Ozomene

Born one of the 3,000 daughters of the Titians, Oceanus and Tethys, Electra, was one of the named OCEANIDS; she was one of the playmates of Persephone (Proserpina) and present when the goddess was kidnapped. The wife of Thaumas she was the mother of Arke, Iris the rainbow goddess, and the Harpies, Aello, CELAENO, and OCYPETE. Electra and her sisters, ALCYONE, ASTEROPE, CELAENO, DRYOPE (Aero or MEROPE), MAIA, and TAYGETE, are sometimes referred to as the ATLANTIDES or the Seven Sisters (see PLEIADES).

Additionally, in Greek mythology Electra was a water–NYMPH and one of the named DANAIDS, the collective name for the daughters of Danaus; her name appears in a list of the DANAIDS generated by Gaius Julius Hyginus (ca. 64 B.C.–A.D. 17), a Latin author. Electra was wedded to Hyperantus and killed him on their wedding night. In a list compiled by Apollodorus, a Greek scholar and grammarian, she was one of the daughters of the NAIAD, POLYXO and was wedded to the son of the NAIAD CALIADNE, Peristhenes.

Sources: Apollodorus, *Gods and Heroes of the Greeks,* 69; Bell, *Bell's New Pantheon or Historical Dictionary of the Gods,* 112; Boswell, *What Men or Gods Are These*, 58; Day, *God's Conflict with the Dragon and the Sea,* 64; Hesiod, *Works of Hesiod, Callimachus, and Theognis,* 20; Westmoreland, *Ancient Greek Beliefs,* 24

Eleionomae

The Eleionomae are a sub-species of the LIMNIAD or NAIADS in Greek mythology, they are the NYMPHS of fresh water marshes.

Sources: Bell, *Women of Classical Mythology,* 179; Day, *God's Conflict with the Dragon and the Sea,* 394; Littleton, *Gods, Goddesses, and Mythology,* Volume 11, 999; Maberry, *Cryptopedia,* 112

The Elemental Fairy

In the 20th century fairies became a primal power linked to the elemental forces of nature. There were four primary classifications of the fay, Air, Earth, Fire, and Water; each was considered to be their own species. Elemental fairies that dwell within the air are known as SYLPH, within the earth are GNOMES; within fire are called SALAMANDERS, and within the water are the NEREIDS (see UNDINE).

Sources: Little, *Spirits, Angels, Demons, and Gods,* 267; Stepanich, *Faery Wicca,* Book One, 23, 31, 33

Elf (plural: elves)

Variations: Elb, Elfin, Ellyll (plural ELLYLLON), ELLYLLON, Erl, Fary, Fay, Fée, HULDRAFOLK, Mannikin, Ouph, Wight

The word elf is a generic word used worldwide to describe a wide array of fairy-folk, including DWARFS, GNOMES and TROLLS; it is used interchangeably with the word *fairy*. They answer to their own royalty having their own kings and queens and greatly enjoy celebrating and feasting banquets and weddings. Descriptions of these creatures, from their appearance to their dress, vary widely, as does their disposition and personalities.

In England the elves are divided into two distinct classes: domestic and rural. Domestic elves are a type of household spirit and live symbiotically with mankind on their farms and in their homes, such as the BROWNIES and HOBGOBLINS do. Rural elves live in the caverns, fields, mountains and wilderness. TROOPING FAIRIES are small, benevolent, and kind, freely helping humans whereas SOLITARY FAIRIES have a tendency to be injurious and if they choose to assist a person will set a price on their services. Generally speaking, each are skilled at spinning cloth and thread as well as making shoes.

Like British lore, elves are divided into two classes in Scandinavian, the LIGHT ELVES of the SEELIE COURT and the DARK ELVES of the UNSEELIE COURT. The voice of the elves in this part of the world is said to be soft and sweet, like the air. Children who are born on a Sunday have the natural ability to see elves and similar such beings.

In Scotland fairies are human size and are often called elves; their FAIRYLAND was known as Elfame.

Common folklore in Wales claims the ELLYLLON should be respected, as they are the souls of the ancient druids who are too good to be condemned to Hell but not good enough to be allowed to enter Heaven. The ELLYLLON are assigned the punishment of wandering upon the earth among mankind until Judgment day when they will be allowed to rise into a higher state of being.

In Africa elves are SEASONAL FAIRIES and more akin to NATURE SPIRITS.

Teutonic and Norse folklore claims fairies (HULDRAFOLK) were once the spirits of the dead bringing fertility to the land. Later, they evolved into small, humanoid beings; the beautiful one were considered to be elves of light while ugly one were call black or DARK ELVES. Dutch elves (ellefolk) are beautiful creatures with hollow backs.

Sources: Ashliman, *Fairy Lore*, 199; Bord, *Fairies*, 2; Illes, *Encyclopedia of Spirits*, 383; Keightly, *World Guide to Gnomes, Fairies, Elves, and Other Little People*, 57, 81; McCoy, *Witch's Guide to Faery*, 171; Stepanich, *Faery Wicca*, Book One, 270

Elf Arrows

Variations: Aithadh, Elf-Bolt, Elf-Dart, ELF-SHOT, Elfin Arrow, Fairy Arrows, Lamiarum Sagittas

Small triangular bits of flint about an inch long and half an inch wide which are found in many countries but especially Scotland; it was supposed these little artifacts were the arrow heads to the arrows of the elves and fairies. It is believed in Aberdeen, Scotland, these objects fall out of the sky.

When a cow suddenly falls it is said to have been shot with one of these arrows; the only way to save it is to rub it with an elf-arrow and give

it water to drink the arrow has been dipped in. The TROW of Shedland Island mythology use elf arrows when they want beef or mutton to bring down game.

Sources: Brand, *Brand's Popular Antiquities of Great Britain*, 208; Evans, *Ancient Stone Implements, Weapons and Ornaments of Great Britain*, 365–6, Keightly, *World Guide to Gnomes, Fairies, Elves, and Other Little People*, 352; Spence, *Encyclopædia of Occultism*, 139

Elf-Fire

Variations: Ignis-Fatuus ("foolish fire"), Jack o' Lanthorn, Kit o' the Canstick ("candlestick"), Peg-a-Lantern, WILL O' THE WISP

Elf-fire is the name given to fire obtained by rubbing two pieces of wood together and used in magical and superstitious practices.

Sources: Brand, *Faiths and Folklore*, 208–9; Brewer, *Dictionary of Phrase and Fable*, 413; Spence, *Encyclopædia of Occultism*, 139

Elf-King's Tune

Variations: Huldreslaut

Norwegian fiddlers claim there is a tune they all know but never play called the Elf-King's Tune; they say they learned it by carefully listening to the elves play and memorizing the cords. This piece of music will compel both the young and ill to dance, even objects begin to join in. Once the fiddler has begun playing the tune he cannot stop unless he can play the air backwards or someone manages to come up from behind him and cut his fiddle's strings.

Sources: Bunce, *Fairy Tales, Their Origin and Meaning*, 130; Keightly, *World Guide to Gnomes, Fairies, Elves, and Other Little People*, 79; Ripley, *American Cyclopaedia*, Volume 7, 64

Elf-Mills

Variations: Alfavakir, Alfquarnar, Elfinmills, Elf-Quarnor

It is believed in Scandinavian lore any cup-shaped divit in a stone was created by elves sitting in it. These stones were once considered to be sacred, treated with respect; offerings were left near them. This beliefe is also held in Scottish lore. In Iceland, these stones are called *alfavakir*.

Sources: Croker, *Fairy Legends and Traditions of the South of Ireland*, Volumes 1–3, 81; Dunham, *History of Denmark, Sweden, and Norway*, Volume 2, 68; Keightly, *World Guide to Gnomes, Fairies, Elves, and Other Little People*, 81

Elf-Shot

A person or domestic animal afflicted with some mysterious disease or stroke is said to have been elf-shot and struck with an ELF-ARROW.

Sources: Bord, *Fairies* 20; Brand, Faiths and Folklore, 208; Brewer, *Dictionary of Phrase and Fable*, 413; Evans, *Ancient Stone Implements, Weapons and Ornaments of Great Britain*, 365

Elfland

Variations: ALFHEIM, Alfheimr ("ELF home"), FAIRYLAND

Elfland is one of the many names given to the mythical homeland of the elves and fairies; it is very often associated with the land of the dead. According to folklore descriptions, there is no sun or moon, no day or night, only perpetual twilight. All cultures have elves and fairies in their mythology also have an equivalent of Elfland.

On very rare occasions the fay will invite a human there and treat them well, as an honored guest. Of those who make the trip to Elfland, few do it of their own free will. Typically mortals who enter into Elfland are kidnapped and taken there or have been tricked in going. Humans who are taken are only released if they are able to perform some task or valuable service for the fairies. Few make the trip back home. Sightings of people who have died and ghosts are said to be from Elfland.

Those who visit are subject to a distorted sense of time, what seemed to be the passing of a few minutes or an evening is later revealed to have been hours, weeks, or even years. Most unfortunate is once a human leaves Elfland, the lost time catches up to them, ageing them appropriately, even if they are to turn instantly to dust.

There are many and varied stories describing the entrance to Elfland as being both celestial and terrestrial; the entry is speculated to be located in an "other-space," in-between dimensions, or in a parallel dimension. The actual doorway to Elfland has been in numerous places, in the forest, the hills, upon stone, up in the mountains, off on an island, over the sea, beneath the earth, and under the water.

Elfland itself has been described as a land of unequaled beauty. The nobility's court is a splendid place, filled with music and dancing.

Sources: Brewer, *Dictionary of Phrase and Fable*, 413; Guiley, *Encyclopedia of Magic and Alchemy*, 99; Henderson, *Scottish Fairy Belief*, 44–7; Vallee, *Other Worlds, Other Universes*, 84–6

Elle-King

The concept of an elle-king ("elder king") comes from Danish fairy lore. These mythical rulers are under the denomination of Promontory-Kings (*klintekonger*) and keep watch over the country. If any misfortune, such as war, should threaten the country an elle-king is said to be seen with his armies ready to defend the land. The elle-king of Bornnholm was often both heard and seen with his fife and drum when war was at hand.

One such elle-king is said to live at Möen on Kongsbjerg in Zealand. His unnamed queen is alleged to be the most beautiful of all beings and resides at a location known as the Queen's Chair (Dronningstolen). Another elle-king has his bed chamber in the wall of the church of the Danish town of Store Hedding; the oaks in the churchyard are his royal guard by day but at night transform into his valiant soldiers. It was once believed no mortal king could come to Stevns, Zealand as the elle-king would not permit other nobility to corss the rivers surrounding the land; and if one did the ell-king would not tolerate his presence for more than three consecutive nights. However the king of Denmark Norway, Christian IV (1588–1648) not only crossed over onto the little island but remained well past the three days. Since then, several other kings have also visited.

Sources: Keightly, *World Guide to Gnomes, Fairies, Elves, and Other Little People*, 91–3; Killikelly, *Curious Questions in History, Literature, Art, and Social Life*, 261

Elle-maid

Variations: Elve-Woman, Wood-Woman

The elle-maids of German and Scandinavian lore are a nocturnal species of fairy. Similar to the cruel and lovely KORRIGAN of Brittany, France, they dance in the grass with such grace that when they offer themselves to a young man resistance is seldom meet. These elves are known to also sit by the roadside with food and wine, offering a cup to men as they pass; should any accept and drink the wine, they will go insane. Hauntingly beautiful when seen from the front, the elle-maid is revealed to be hollow when seen from behind. To drive an elle-maid away, make the sign of the Cross in her presence and she will disappear.

Sources: Chambers, *Chambers's Journal*, Volumes 19–20, 256; Colburn, *New Monthly Magazine*, 78; Keightly, *World Guide to Gnomes, Fairies, Elves, and Other Little People*, 81, 323

Elle-people

Variations: Ellefolk ("Elve-People"), Ellen, Elle Folk, Elle-Folk

In Danish lore the elle-people live in the elle-moors; the male of the species is described as looking like an old man wearing a low-crowned hat on his head and are often seen sun-bathing on the moors. If approached they will exhale their breath, a toxic stench producing pestilence and sickness. The elle-woman is by day and is described as being young and vibrant. When seen from the front she is a vision of lovlyness but when seen from behind is revealed to be hollow (see ELLE-MAID). In spite of her physical deformity she is still difficult to resist when applying her charms, more so when she plays her harp.

Elle-people raise their own cattle, large and blue; they can be seen in the fields licking up the dew in the mornings, as it is the only substance that nourishes them. Mortal cattle will not go where elle-people and their cattle have been. If an animal happens upon the place where an elle-person has spit, or worse, the creature will suddenly fall ill with an sickness that can only be cured by forcing it to eat a handful of Saint John's wort harvested at midnight on Saint John's Day (June 24).

Sources: Arrowsmith, *Field Guide to the Little People*, 7; Biggs, *Vanishing People*, 75; Keightly, *World Guide to Gnomes, Fairies, Elves, and Other Little People*, 81

Ellerkonge

Variations: Alder King, Elerkonge, Elver-konge, Erl King, Erlking, Erlkönig ("ELF King"), ERLKONIG, Harlequin, Hellekin, Herleekin, Herleking, Herlequin, OAK KING

Ellerkonge is the ELF King of Denmark; he has a malicious disposition toward mankind, especially toward children, leading them off to their death in the Black Forest of Germany. Ellerkonge was first introduced into German lore by Johann Gottfried von Herder's translation of a Danish ballad entitled *The Erlking's Daughter* (1778) and popularized by Johann Wolfgang von Goethe's poem *Erlkonig* (1782).

As the consort of the goddess, Hel, he was the god and protector of the elder tree and the land of the dead. A mistranslation of the Danish Ellerkonge made him the king of the elves in a Germanic saga.

Sources: Chisholm, *Encyclopedia Americana*, Volume 10, 479; Lima, *Stages of Evil*, 51, 75; Spence, *Dictionary of Non-Classical Mythology*, 204

Ellydan

Variation: Ellylldan, Jacky Lantern, Pooka, Pwca, Spunkie

Similar to the WILL O' THE WISP, the ellydan ("luring ELF-fire") of Welsh fairy lore leads travelers astray at night. It will lure unsuspecting travelers to dangerous precipices or into bogs. It is described as looking like a GOBLIN, having wide ears, wings, and wearing a tall cap and carrying two torches.

Sources: Ashliman, *Fairy Lore,* 126; Guiney, *Brownies and Bogles,* 116; Parry-Jones, *Welsh Legends and Fairy Lore,* 5; Sikes, British Goblins, 18–24

Ellyllon

In Wales, elves are called ellyllon; they are benevolent and described as being tiny, almost transparent beings under the rulership of their FAIRY QUEEN, MAB. The ellyllon consume FAIRY BUTTER, a fungus found in the roots of old trees and in limestone crevices, and toadstools. Similar to the BROWNIE, the ellyllon will help with household chores but leave forever if offended or if their privacy is intruded upon, however they are fonder of living in the wild and rocky northlands. They are blamed if the corn crop is blighted or if cows start giving up little milk.

In Cornwall, these elves are said to be lake dwelling fairies riding in eggshells floating along the wind for transportation and are the guardians of the LADY OF THE LAKE of Arthurian lore.

The ellyllon possessed a magical item known as the cap of oblivion. When this hat worn by a mortal, it would make the person follow him and join in on his fairy dance. The cap also prevented the person from correctly remembering the events which took place.

Sources: Brayley, *Graphic and Historical Illustrator,* 348–50; Briggs, *Enyclopedia of Fairies,* 121; McCoy, *Witch's Guide to Faery Folk,* 215; Rose, *Spirits, Fairies, Leprechauns, and Goblins,* 100; Sikes, *British Goblins,* 69

Elves of Light

Variations: LIOSALFAR

In Algonquin lore the elves of light are a race of tiny, forest dwelling elves; they greatly en-joy dancing. The Queen of the Elves of Light is Summer, a diminutive yet very beautiful being; she was once captured by the god, Glooskap, and was kept in a moose hide. When she was carried into the wigwam of the GIANT, Winter, her presence caused him to melt away allowing Spring to arrive and awaken the hibernating elves.

Sources: McNeese, *Myths of Native America*, 19; Rose, *Spirits, Fairies, Leprechauns, and Goblins*, 100; Spence, *Myths and Legends of the North American Indians*, 148–9

Emandwa

Variations: Emandwa Zabakazi

In the folklore of the Ankore people of Uganda the emandwa ("of the women") are a species of protective household guardians made up of the spirits of ancient kings. Benevolent, the emandwa is called upon to assist the women of the family to conceive. Ceremonies and offerings were made to them; shrines dedicated to them are typical in the home. When a person who had a guardian spirit dies, it was said to move onto another member of the family; if the deceased was male the emandwa went to his heir, if the deceased was a woman it went to the senior wife of her eldest son.

Sources: Edel, *Chiga of Uganda*, 146–7; Nzita, *Peoples and Cultures of Uganda*, 35; Rose, *Spirits, Fairies, Leprechauns, and Goblins*, 100

Empedo

Variations: Klepsydra

Empedo was the Nymphs of a spring in Athens in Greek mythology.

Sources: Larson, *Greek Nymphs,* 97, 126; Ogden, *Companion to Greek Religion, 62*

Encantado

Variations: Boto, Buefo Colorado ("reddish dolphin")

In South America, there is said to exist a fairy spirit called an encantado ("enchanted"). Living in an underwater utopia called Encante, full of wealth and where death and pain do not exist, the encantado shape-shift into dolphins, humans, and snakes. Known for attending parties, their musical talent, and their sexual desire these fairies are said to have fathered a great number of illegitimate children. In addition to these abilities the encantado also have the ability to use magic and with it they can control storms, dominate mortals into doing their bidding, inflict illness, insanity, or death and can even transform a person into an encantado. Kidnapping is a common activity for these fairies to take part in, stealing both mortals they fall in love with as well as their own illegitimate children, and returning to Encante with them.

According to lore the encantado is typically in its dolphin form. On the rare occasion when it takes human form, it will do so only at night and then only to attend a party when it will seek to fulfill its sexual desires. While in its pale-skinned human guise the graceful and beautifully dressed fay wears a hat to hide its blow hole. These fairies are curious about human society and crave to experience both the hardships and the pleasures of the mortal world.

Sources: Arnold, *Monsters, Tricksters, and Sacred Cows*, 158–9; Budd, *Weiser Field Guide to Cryptozoology*, 105–7; Montgomery, 2, 78, 90

Endeis

A Nymph of Mount Pelion in Thessalia from classical Greek mythology, Endeis ("she loves her nation") was born the daughter of Charicol by the centaur, Chiron. Endeis was also the wife of King Aiakos, ruler of the island Aigina.

Sources: Grant, *Who's Who in Classical Mythology*, 12; Lempriere, *Classical Dictionary*, 48, 340

Engkanto

Variations: Engkantada

In the Philippines it is believed the engkanto ("enchanters") are a species of fairy spirit associated with ancestral spirits; although they can shape-shift in virtually any animal or plant they also have the ability to take on a human guise. In its natural form it is taller than a human, has a fair complexion, light colored hair, a high-bridge nose, and lacks a philtrum. The Engkanto are fairly unique among fairy-kind as both the males and the females of their species are susceptible to age and may also suffer from illnesses and die. These fairies live in large balete trees or in rocks. When these fairy spirits like a person they will bring them power and wealth, but normally the presence of the engkanto is harmful to humans causing boils, depression, fevers, madness, and skin diseases.

Belief in the engkanto exists to this day, even in the urban area of the Philippines. Modern additions to the lore say these fairies have "Caucasian" features and being wealthy, send their children to private schools, sometimes as far away as America. Young women claim to be courted romantically by an invisible engkanto.

Sources: Aguilar, *Clash of Spirits*, 34, 42; Demetrio, *Myths and Symbols, Philippines*, 124–7; Tan, *Revisiting Usog, Pasma, Kulam*, 63–5

Enipeus

Born one of the 3,000 daughters of the Titians, Oceanus and Tethys, Enipeus was one of the named Oceanids in Greek mythology.

Sources: Boswell, *What Men or Gods Are These*, 58; Day, *God's Conflict with the Dragon and the Sea*, 64; Hesiod, *Works of Hesiod, Callimachus, and Theognis*, 20

Ennesiades

Ennesiades ("NYMPHS of the islands") was the collective name for the NYMPHS of Lesbos in Greek mythology.

Source: Larson, *Greek Nymphs*, 197

Entella

Entella was the NYMPHS of Sicily; she was the wife of the godling, Egestus (Aigestes, AKESTES) in Greek mythology.

Sources: Bell, *Women of Classical Mythology*, 181; Larson, *Greek Nymphs*, 221

Eochaid

Variations: ECHO ("horse"), Echu, Eochaid Mac Eirc, Eochaide, Eochaidhe, Eochaidu, Eoched, Eocho, Eochu, Eochy

When the TUATHAN DE DANANN invaded Ireland, Eochaid was the ninth king of the FIRBOLGS and ruled them with great wisdom for the years; he passed laws against deception and lies during his rule. He was the first person to die of wounds inflicted by spears in Ireland. At his death darkness fell across the land and it rained fire and blood for three days.

Sources: Briggs, *Encyclopedia of Fairies*, 123; Chisholm, *Encyclopedia Britannica*, Volume 14, 758; Mountain, *Celtic Encyclopedia*, Volume 3, 590–1

Ephesus

In ancient Greek mythology Ephesus was one of the HAMADRYAD who was born of the incestuous relationship between Oxylus and his sister, Hamadryas.

Sources: Kloppenborg, *Tenants in the Vineyard*, 227

Ephyra

Variations: Ephira, Ephyre

A sea–NYMPH of the town Korinthos in Korinthia, southern Greece, Ephyra, wife of the Titan Epimetheus, was one of the named NEREID. Ephyra was born the daughter of Nereus and DORIS.

Sources: Apollodorus, *Apollodorus' Library and Hyginus' Fabulae*, 95; Conti, *Natale Conti's Mythologiae: Books VI–X*, 701; Lemprière, *Classical Dictionary*, 494

Epimeliad

The Epimeliad were a sub-species of the HAMADRYAD, they were the NYMPHS of apple trees in Greek mythology.

Sources: Parada, *Genealogical Guide to Greek Mythology*, 70, 128; Pausanias, *Pausanias's Description of Greece*, Volume 3, 359

Epimeliades

Variations: Boukolai, EPIMELIDES

In the mythology of the ancient Greeks the epimeliades ("those who care for flocks") were the NYMPHS dedicated to tending sheep.

Sources: Antoninus Liberalis, *Metamorphoses of Antoninus Liberalis*, 197; Avant, *Mythological Reference*, 251; Rigoglioso, *Cult of Divine Birth in Ancient Greece*, 87

Epimelides

Variations: Meliades, Melias, Melides

The epimelides were, in ancient Greek mythology, the NYMPHS of pastures; they were born the daughters of the god Apollo and MELIA.

Sources: Clark, *Classical Manual,* 587; Rigoglioso, *Cult of Divine Birth in Ancient Greece*, 87

Eranno

Eranno was a NYMPH of Telos is classical Greek mythology.

Sources: Larson, *Greek Nymphs*, 322; Müller, *Ancient Art and Its Remains*, 540; Murray, *Manual of Mythology*, 207

The Erasinides

The erasinides were the four NAIADS of the river Erasinos in Argos located in central Greece. According to Greek mythology they, ANCHIRHOE, BYZE, MAERA, and MELITE, were the attendants of the goddess, BRITOMARTIS.

Sources: Antoninus Liberalis, *Metamorphoses of Antoninus Liberalis*, 100; Cox, *Mythology of the Aryan Nations*, 379; Gould, *Historic Magazine and Notes and Queries*, Volume 14, 212

Erato

Variations: Erata

A sea–NYMPH, Erato ("loveliness") was one of the named NEREID; referred to as "the lovely" she was born the daughter of Nerues and DORIS. Erato was one of the named DANAIDS, the collective name for the daughters of Danaus; her name appears in a list of the DANAIDS generated by Gaius Julius Hyginus (ca. 64 B.C.–A.D. 17), a Latin author. Erato was wedded to Eudaemon and killed him on their wedding night. In a list compiled by Apollodorus, a Greek scholar and grammarian, she was one of the daughters of the NAIAD, POLYXO and was wedded to the son of the NAIAD CALIADNE, Bromius.

A second NYMPH named Erato ("lyre") was a DRYAD and a NYMPH of Arcadia; she gave prophecies to the god, Pan (Faunus). This Erato married Arkas son of CALLISTO. There is yet another NYMPH named Erato, during a musical competition, she judged in favor of the god, Apollo.

One of the nine CANONICAL MUSES Erato ("awakener of desire") was the MUSE of erotic poetry; she is depicted in art as carrying a crown of roses and a lyre.

Erato was also a NYMPH from the mythical Mount Nysa who was a nurse to the infant god, Dionysus (Bacchus). Collectively these NYMPHS were known as the BACCHANTS; their names were BACCHE, BROMIE, ERATO, KISSEIS, KELLIA, KORONIS, MACRIS, and NYSA.

Sources: Grimal, *Dictionary of Classical Mythology*, 127; Hesiod, *Works of Hesiod, Callimachus, and Theognis*, 15; Lemprière, *Classical Dictionary*, 236; Littleton, *Gods, Goddesses, and Mythology*, Volume 11, 921; Pausânias, *Guide to Greece*, 466; Peterson, *Mythology in Our Midst*, 121; Trzaskoma, *Anthology of Classical Myth*, 18

Erchia

Erchia was a NYMPH of Attica in Greek mythology; sacrifices of all black goats and sheep were made to her.

Sources: Larson, *Greek Nymphs*, 135; Parker, *Polytheism and Society at Athens*, 416

Erdleute

Erdleute is a DWARF from the folklore of Germany. Along with the words bergsmiedlein, bjergfolk, erdmannlein, stillevolk, unterirdische, and unterjordiske, in the German language erdleute ("earth people") is also used to describe a DWARF.

Sources: MacCulloch, *Eddic*, 270; Rose, *Spirits, Fairies, Leprechauns, and Goblins*, 102

Erdluitle

Variations: Females: Erdbibberli, Erdweibchen ("earth wives"), Heidenweibchen, Herdweibchen; Males: Bergmanli, Gotwergi, GURIUZ, Härdmandlene, Heidenmanndli

The DWARF-like erdluitle ("earth folk") can be found in the folklore of Switzerland, northern Italy, and western Austria. The lore of this species is varied, but they all agree the erluitle do not like to show their feet. Generally, the erdluitle stand between one and three feet tall and have earthtone skin; when they are young their hair is dark but turns white as they age. They were hooded robes and cloaks, long enough to cover their feet. Their favorite foods are berries, peas, pork, and roots and live in dark caves or underground. Erdluitle can control the weather, causing avalanches, floods, and storms and can transform dry leaves into diamonds.

Long ago there were tales of these fairies being helpful towards humans, acting much like the BROWNIE, however in more modern times they seem to have turned against mankind and are becoming more injurious and malicious.

Sources: Arrowsmith, *Field Guide to the Little People*, 26–8; Livo, *Storytelling Folklore Sourcebook*, 33; McCoy, *Witch's Guide to Faery Folk*, 218

Eri

Variations: Eri of the Golden Hair

Eri is a fairy goddess in Irish mythology; she is one of the TUATHA DE DANAAN. In spite of the fact her people were enemies of the FORMORIAN she and Elatha, the handsome son of a FORMORIAN king, fell in love with one another as soon as they met. In some telling, Eri was a virgin but in others she was already married to another member of the TUATHA DE DANAAN; no matter the case, she and Elatha were married and had a son named Bres who went on to become the consort of Brigid.

Sources: O'Conor, *Battles and Enchantments*, 16–21; Monaghan, *New Book of Goddesses and Heroines*, 115; Monaghan, *Women in Myth and Legend*, 97

Eriphia

One of the HYAD, Eriphia was one of the NYMPHS who nursed the infant god Dionysus (Bacchus) on Mount Nysa in classical Greek mythology; she was one of the many daughters born of the Titians, Atlas and AETHRA.

Sources: Howe, *Handbook of Classical Mythology*, 181; Smith, *Smaller Classical Dictionary of Biography, Mythology, and Geography*, 274

ErlKonig

Variations: ELLERKONGE, Elver-Konge ("king of the elle-folk")

In Dutch and German lore the ErlKonig is the King of the Elves; he is described as wearing a large golden crown and expensive, tailored clothing. Appearing outside the home of someone about to die, he otherwise lives in the forest and lures mortals to their doom, especially children. He is also said to lead the WILD HUNT.

Sources: Chisholm, *Encyclopedia Americana*, Volume 10, 479; Lima, *Stages of Evil*, 51, 75; McCoy, *Witch's Guide to Faery Folk*, 217–8

Erytheia

Variations: Erytheir, Erytheis

Erytheia was a DRYAD, one of the twelve species of NYMPH in Greek mythology; she is also one of the daughters of Atlas and PLEIONE, making her one of the PLEIADES as well. Erytheia was also one of the four HESPERIDES, a group of four NAIAD sisters charged with the protection of a golden apple tree that grew the golden apples the goddess Gaia gave the goddess Hera (Juno); they were stolen by the godling, Herakles (Hercules) (see also AEGLE, ARETHUSA, and HESPERIA).

Sources: Daly, *Greek and Roman Mythology A to Z*, 53; Littleton, *Gods, Goddesses, and Mythology*, Volume 11, 1454; Westmoreland, Ancient Greek Beliefs, 150

Espiet

In the epic poem, *Orlando Innamorato* (*Orlando in Love*) written by the Italian Renaissance author Matteo Maria Boiardo, Espiet is a roguish DWARF. He described as having hair as fine and yellow as gold standing no more than three feet tall and looking to be no more than seven years old despite the fact he was over one hundred. Espiet, himself a learned magician, a necromancer, and the close friend and assistant of the character Maugis.

Sources: Boiardo, *Orlando Innamorato di Bojardo*, Volume 1, 71; Briggs, Vanishing People, 145; Keightly, *World Guide to Gnomes, Fairies, Elves, and Other Little People*, 33

Esprit Follet

Variations: Friar's Lantern, Ignis Fatuus

A HOUSE-SPIRIT in France, the esprit follet is a type of BOGLE that enjoys in misleading and tormenting mortals. Esprit follets are essentially the French version of the WILL O' THE WISP.

Sources: Douglas, *Scottish Fairy Tales, Folklore, and Legends*, 184; Keightly, *World Guide to Gnomes, Fairies, Elves, and Other Little People*, 491

Esterelle

Variations: Esterel, Esterello

In Provence, France there is a legend dating back to 1300 of a fairy name Esterelle; it was said she would give barren women an elixir to drink making them fertile. Sacrifices and offerings were left for her on a stone called *la Lauza de la Fado*.

Sources: Hastings, *Encyclopedia of Religion and Ethics*, Part 10, 681; Keightly, *World Guide to Gnomes, Fairies, Elves, and Other Little People*, 468

Ethne

Variations: EITHNE, Ethniu

A woman of the TUATHA DE DANANN and the daughter of BALOR she married Cian the son of Dianceht of the FORMORIANS; their son was the much famed and *samildannach*, Lug. She was also said to have been one of the wives of Conchobar after Medba left him. There was also an Ethne who was part of the pagan conversion to Christianity tale, but the tale was more popularly told with her being given as EITHNE.

Sources: de Jubainville, *Irish Mythological Cycle and Celtic Mythology*, 157; Gray, *Mythology of All Races*, Volume 3, 25, 29, 207–8; MacCulloch, *Celtic Mythology*, 29; van Doorn-Harder, *Coping with Evil in Religion and Culture*, 44

Euadne

Euadne ("very holy") was the NYMPH of the town of Argos in Argolis located in southern Greece in ancient Greek mythology; she was born of the rape of the Laconian NYMPH, PITANE by the god of the sea, Poseidon (Neptune). Euadne herself was raped by the god Apollo and bore him a son she left to die of exposure. The infant was saved by the gods and returned to Euadne to raise; she named the child Iamos. Euadne eventually became the wife of King Argos.

Sources: Hard, *Routledge Handbook of Greek Mythology*, 548; Rose, *Handbook of Greek Mythology*, 289

Euagore

Variations: Euagoreis

A sea–NYMPH, Euagore ("good speech"), was the NEREID of "good assembling," which may refer to a fishing vessel or a naval ship. She was born the daughter of Nerues and DORIS in ancient Greek mythology.

Sources: Apollodorus, *Apollodorus' Library and Hyginus' Fabulae*, 95; Hesiod, *Homeric Hymns and Homerica*, 99; Trzaskoma, *Anthology of Classical Myth*, 18

Euarne

A sea–NYMPH from Greek mythology, Euarne ("unblemished"), was one of the named NEREIDS; she was born the daughter of Nerues and DORIS and described as being "lovely of shape and without blemish of form."

Sources: Bell, *Women of Classical Mythology*, 192; Boswell, *What Men or Gods Are These?*, 24; Westmoreland, *Ancient Greek Beliefs*, 25

Euboia

Variations: Khalkis, Markis

Euboia was a NYMPH in ancient Greek lore; along with AKAIA and PROSYMNA, she was a nurse to the infant goddess, Hera (Juno). By the god of the sea, Poseidon (Neptune), Euboia bore the hero, Tychios.

Sources: Larson, *Greek Nymphs*, 144; Lemprière, *Classical Dictionary*, 642

Eubule

In Greek mythology Eubule was a water–NYMPH and one of the named DANAIDS, the collective name for the daughters of Danaus; her name appeared in a list of the DANAIDS generated by Gaius Julius Hyginus (ca. 64 B.C.–A.D. 17), a Latin author. Eubule was wedded to Demarchus and killed him on their wedding night.

Sources: Bell, *Women of Classical Mythology*, 150, 192; Parada, *Genealogical Guide to Greek Mythology*, 59, 73

Eucrante

A sea–NYMPH from Greek mythology, Eucrante was one of the named NEREID; she was born the daughter of Nerues and DORIS.

Sources: Hesiod, *Works of Hesiod, Callimachus, and Theognis*, 14; Trzaskoma, *Anthology of Classical Myth*, 18

Eucrate

A sea–NYMPH from Greek mythology, Eucrate ("swan"), was one of the named NEREID; she was born the daughter of Nerues and DORIS.

Sources: Betham, *Transactions of the Royal Irish Academy*, Volume 17, 88; Hesiod, *Works of Hesiod*, 154; Lemprière, *Classical Dictionary*, 392

Eudora

Variations: Eudore

Born one of the 3,000 daughters of the Titians, Oceanus and Tethys, Eudora ("early" or "leading") was one of the named OCEANIDS. Eudora is also the NEREID of sailing and a good fish-catch; she was born the daughter of Nerues and DORIS.

Sources: Bell, *Bell's New Pantheon or Historical Dictionary of the Gods*, 112; Boswell, *What Men or Gods Are These*, 58; Hesiod, *Works of Hesiod, Callimachus, and Theognis*, 14, 20; Trzaskoma, *Anthology of Classical Myth*, 18; Westmoreland, *Ancient Greek Beliefs*, 24

Eugel

Variations: Engel, Engelein

In the Norse poem *Hurnen Sifrift* ("Horny Siegfred"), the DWARF Eugel is the heroic companion to the hero of the poem, Sifrift.

Sources: Croker, *Fairy Legends and Traditions of the South of Ireland*, Volumes 1–3, 75–6; Keightly, *World Guide to Gnomes, Fairies, Elves, and Other Little People*, 207–8

Euis

Euis was a NYMPH of Attica from Greek mythology; goats were sacrificed to her.

Source: Larson, *Greek Nymphs*, 137

Eukrante

A sea–NYMPH, Eukrante ("bringer of fulfillment" or "good ruler") was the NEREIS of the successful voyage or fishing-catch from Greek mythology. She was born one of the daughters of Nereus and DORIS in ancient Greek mythology.

Sources: Caldwell, *Origin of the Gods*, 99, 122; Hesiod. *Hesiod, the Poems and Fragments*, 40; Kerényi, *Gods of the Greeks*, 64; Sluiter, *Free Speech in Classical Antiquity*, 33

Eulimene

A sea–NYMPH from Greek mythology, Eulimene ("good harbor") was the NEREID of good harborage and the lapping of water upon the shoreline in ancient Greek mythology; she was born the daughter of Nerues and DORIS.

Sources: Collignon, *Manual of Mythology*, 187; Hesiod, *Works of Hesiod, Callimachus, and Theognis*, 15; Sluiter, *Free Speech in Classical Antiquity*, 33; Trzaskoma, *Anthology of Classical Myth*, 18

Eulimine

A sea–NYMPH from Greek mythology, Eulimine ("good harbor woman"), was the NEREIDS who danced on the waves; she was born the daughter of Nerues and DORIS.

Sources: Betham, *Transactions of the Royal Irish Academy*, Volume 17, 88; Rose, *Handbook of Greek Mythology*, 19

Eumendies

Variations: Dirae, Erinyes ("avenging ones"), FURIES, Semnai Theai ("revered goddesses")

In Greek mythology, the eumendies ("benevolent ones") were originally the avenging spirits of the dead, specifically the ghosts of murdered men crying out for vengeance and were known as the Erinyes. Over time they were said to have been the daughters of the earth goddess, Gaia, and took on a more benevolent aspect, were associated with earth spirits, and were akin to NATURE SPIRITS.

Sources: Harrison, *Mythology*, 72; Keightly, *World Guide to Gnomes, Fairies, Elves, and Other Little People*, 495; Rose, *Spirits, Fairies, Leprechauns, and Goblins*, 288

Eumolpe

A sea–NYMPH, Eumolpe, was one of the named NEREIDS from Greek mythology; she was born the daughter of Nerues and DORIS.

Sources: Bell, *Bell's New Pantheon*, 297; Grimal, *Dictionary of Classical Mythology*, 308; Trzaskoma, *Anthology of Classical Myth*, 18

Eunica

Eunica ("night lady") was a NYMPH of a fountain on the island of Propontis. Along with the NYMPHS MALIS and NYCHEIA, as they were preparing to dance, saw a young boy name Hylas who traveled with the Argonauts; instantly enamored with him, they took him by the hand and pulled him into the fountain.

Sources: *Encyclopaedia Britannica*, Volume 16, Issue 1, 313; Lang, *Tales of Troy and Greece*, 196

Eunice

A sea–NYMPH, Eunice was one of the named NEREID; she was born the daughter of Nerues and DORIS from Greek mythology. According to Hesiod she is "rosy-armed" and is described as leaping and dancing from wave to wave.

Sources: Hesiod, *Works of Hesiod, Callimachus, and Theognis*, 15; Rose, *Spirits, Fairies, Leprechauns, and Goblins*, 104; Trzaskoma, *Anthology of Classical Myth*, 18

Eunika

Eunika was a NYMPH of Kios from Greek mythology; she was described as having "spring time in her eyes."

Sources: Larson, *Greek Nymphs*, 67; Pache, *Moment's Ornament*, 161

Eunike

A sea–NYMPH, Eunike ("good victory") was one the NEREID of good maritime victory from Greek mythology; she was born the daughter of Nerues and DORIS. According to Hesiod she was "rosy-armed."

Sources: Caldwell, *Origin of the Gods*, 122; Hesiod, *Works of Hesiod, Callimachus, and Theognis*, 15; Kerényi, *Gods of the Greeks*, 64

Eunoe

Eunoe was a NYMPH of Troad; she was the mother of the NAIAD NYMPH, Euagora from Greek mythology.

Source: Larson, *Greek Nymphs*, 195

Eunomia

In Greek mythology, Eunomia ("Lawful Order") and her two sisters, DIKE ("Justice") and EIRENE (Peace), were collectively known as the Horae ("the correct moment"), the guardians of natural law; they were born the daughters of the Titian goddess of Law, Themis, and the god, Zeus (Jupiter). The NATURE SPIRIT-like sisters were entrusted with guarding the gate to Olympus. Eunomia, like her sisters, was described as being a beautiful young maiden with beautiful hair, light footsteps, and wearing golden diadems. Her services were primarily involved in political life and her worship was never neglected by the state. Representing the seasons, each one held a blooming flower, and ear of corn, and a vine stock. She was e mother of Hesychia ("quiet" or "tranquility").

Sources: Gall, *Lincoln Library of Greek and Roman Mythology*, 20; McLean, *Triple Goddess*, 49; Roman, *Encyclopedia of Greek and Roman Mythology*, 172

Eunoste

Eunoste was a NYMPH of Tanagra from Greek mythology; she raised Eunostos ("happy return") the tutelary god of corn mills.

Sources: Larson, *Greek Nymphs: Myth, Cult, Lore*, 304; Smith, *Dictionary of Greek and Roman Biography and Mythology*, 95

Eupheme

In Greek mythology Eupheme was a water–NYMPH and one of the named DANAIDS, the collective name for the daughters of Danaus; her name appears in a list of the DANAIDS generated by Gaius Julius Hyginus (ca. 64 B.C.–A.D. 17), a Latin author. Eupheme was wedded to Hyperbius and killed him on their wedding night.

Sources: Bell, *Women of Classical Mythology*, 150, 195; Crabb, *Mythology of All Nations Adapted to the Biblical, Classical and General Reader*, 66; Grimal, *Dictionary of Classical Mythology*, 116

Eupome

A sea–NYMPH, Eupome ("good journey"), was one of the named NEREIDS in ancient Greek mythology; she was born the daughter of Nerues and DORIS.

Sources: Sluiter, *Free Speech in Classical Antiquity*, 33

Eupompe

A sea–NYMPH, Eupompe was the NEREIS of a good festive or a processional voyage from Greek mythology; she was known as the NYMPH of the conc.

Sources: Betham, *Transactions of the Royal Irish Academy*, Volume 17, 88; Hesiod, *Theogony*, 107; Hesiod, *Works of Hesiod, Callimachus, and Theognis*, 15; Westmoreland, *Ancient Greek Beliefs*, 25

Europa

Born one of the 3,000 daughters of the Titians, Oceanus and Tethys, Europa was one of the named OCEANIDS from Greek mythology. She should not to be confused with the woman of the same name who was kidnapped by the god Zeus (Jupiter) in the form of a white or multicolored bull, taken to the isle of Crete, and raped.

Sources: Bell, *Bell's New Pantheon or Historical Dictionary of the Gods,* 112; Boswell, *What Men or Gods Are These*, 58; Hesiod, *Theogony*, 107; Hesiod, *Works of Hesiod, Callimachus, and Theognis*, 20; Westmoreland, *Ancient Greek Beliefs*, 24

Europe

An Egyptian NYMPH, Europe was born the daughter of the river god Neilos (Nile); she was the mother of four of the DANAID, by King Danaos, AGAVE, AMYMONE, AUTOMATE, and SCAEA.

Sources: Apollodorus, *Apollodorus' Library and Hyginus' Fabulae*, 22, 95; Apollodorus of Athens, *Gods and Heroes of the Greeks*, 69

Europome

In Greek mythology Europome was a water–NYMPH and one of the named DANAIDS, the collective name for the daughters of Danaus; her name appears in a list of the DANAIDS generated by Gaius Julius Hyginus (ca. 64 B.C.–A.D. 17), a Latin author. Europome was wedded to Athletes and killed him on their wedding night.

Sources: Apollodorus, *Apollodorus' Library and Hyginus' Fabulae*, 213; Hyginus, *Myths of Hyginus*, 133; Parada, *Genealogical Guide to Greek Mythology*, 59, 75

Eurydice

A sea–NYMPH, Eurydice was one of the named NEREID; she was born of Nereus and DORIS. Additionally in Greek mythology Eurydice was one of the named DANAIDS, the collective name for the daughters of Danaus; her name appears in a list of the DANAIDS generated by Gaius Julius Hyginus (ca. 64 B.C.–A.D. 17), a Latin author. Eurydice was wedded to Canthus and killed him on their wedding night. In a list compiled by Apollodorus, a Greek scholar and grammarian, she

was one of the daughters of the NAIAD, POLYXO and was wedded to the son of the NAIAD CALIADNE, Dryas.

Sources: Apollodorus, *Apollodorus' Library and Hyginus' Fabulae*, 95; Apollodorus, *Gods and Heroes of the Greeks,* 69; Grimal, *Dictionary of Classical Mythology*, 127; Lemprière, *Classical Dictionary*, 236

Eurynome

Born one of the 3,000 daughters of the Titians, Oceanus and Tethys, Eurynome was one of the named OCEANIDS from Greek mythology. She and the god Zeus (Jupiter) were the parents of the CHARITIES. Eurynome was worshiped near the convergence of the Lymax and NEDA rivers and was represented by a statue portraying her as a MERMAID.

Sources: Boswell, *What Men or Gods Are These*, 58; Day, *God's Conflict with the Dragon and the Sea*, 64; Hesiod, *Works of Hesiod, Callimachus, and Theognis*, 20; Westmoreland, *Ancient Greek Beliefs*, 24

Eurythoe

In Greek mythology Eurythoe, was a NYMPH and one of the named DANAIDS; she was said to be one of the possible mothers of Oenomaus by the god, Ares (Mars). Alternatively, it was said Eurythoe was the mother of HIPPODAMIA by Oenomaus.

Sources: Bell, *Women of Classical Mythology*, 204; Sergent, *Homosexuality in Greek Myth*, 76; Grimal, *Dictionary of Classical Mythology*, 214

Euterpe

Variations: Uterpe

One of the nine CANONICAL MUSES from Greek mythology Euterpe ("joy-giver") was the MUSE of lyrical songs; she is depicted in art as carrying a flute.

Sources: Hunt, *Masonic Symbolism*, 470; Littleton, *Gods, Goddesses, and Mythology*, Volume 11, 921; Peterson, *Mythology in Our Midst*, 121

Evagora

A sea–NYMPH from Greek mythology, Evagora was known to be kind and smiling.

Sources: Barthell, *Gods and Goddesses of Ancient Greece*, 12, 48; Betham, *Transactions of the Royal Irish Academy*, Volume 17, 89

Evagore

A sea–NYMPH, Evagore was one of the named NEREID from Greek mythology.

Sources: Bell, *Bell's New Pantheon*, 102; Grimal, *Dictionary of Classical Mythology*, 308; Hesiod, *Works of Hesiod, Callimachus, and Theognis*, 15

Evarne

A sea–NYMPH from the mythology of classical Greece, Evarne was the named NEREID of marble rocks. According to the Greek oral poet, Hesiod, she is "both lovely in shape and in beauty flawless."

Sources: Betham, *Transactions of the Royal Irish Academy*, Volume 17, 89; Bell, *Bell's New Pantheon*, 102; Grimal, *Dictionary of Classical Mythology*, 308; Hesiod, *Works of Hesiod, Callimachus, and Theognis*, 15

Evippe

Variations: Evidea

In Greek mythology Evippe was a water–NYMPH and one of the named DANAIDS, the collective name for the daughters of Danaus; her name appears in a list of the DANAIDS generated by Gaius Julius Hyginus (ca. 64 B.C.–A.D. 17), a Latin author. According to Greek mythology, Evippe was wedded to Agenor and killed him on their wedding night. There was a second daughter with the name Evippe who was one of the daughters of an unnamed Ethiopian woman to Argius, one of the sons of an unnamed Phoenician woman. In a list compiled by Apollodorus, a Greek scholar and grammarian, she was one of the daughters of an unnamed Ethiopian woman and was wedded to Argius, one of the sons of an unnamed Phoenician woman.

Sources: Apollodorus, *Gods and Heroes of the Greeks,* 69; Grimal, *Dictionary of Classical Mythology*, 127; Hyginus, *Myths of Hyginus*, 133; Lemprière, *Classical Dictionary*, 236

Fachan

Variations: Fachen, Fachin, Peg Leg Jack

A breed of fairy from the West Highlands of Scotland, the fachan are described as being ugly; a hand protrudes from the chest, thick fur covers their body, and they have only one leg and eye. They dress in a girdle of deer skins donned in a mantle of blue feathers as they are jealous of fairies capable of flight. Some lore claims the fachan are so physically repulsive seeing one may induce a heart attack. An expert leaper, the fachan are not nearly as agile as a person. Known for their malevolent disposition and hating all living things, they carry a spiked club they use liberally when chasing people out of their territory. It will also use its club or wickedly spiked chain to destroy an entire orchard in a single night. A Fachan from a popular Highland tale is told of NESNAS MHICCALLAIN.

Sources: Avant, *Mythological Reference*, 187; Briggs, *Encyclopedia of Fairies*, 129; Campbell, *Popular Tales of the West Highlands*, 298; Maberry, *Vampire Universe*, 116

Fada

Variations: Hada, Hadada

Fada is the provincial word in both the Italian and Spanish languages for fairies.

In the south of France the fada were considered to be a species of fairy well known to take a human lover. If a man who had a fada for a lover ever married a mortal woman, his bride would die before the marriage could be consummated.

Sources: Grimm, *Grimm's Goblins, Grimm's Household Stories*, xv; Keightly, *World Guide to Gnomes, Fairies, Elves, and Other Little People*, 4, 468; McCoy, *Witch's Guide to Faery Folk*, 30

Fafnir

Variations: Fafner, Fáfnir, Frænir

Fafnir was a son of the magician DWARF king, HREIDMAR and the brother of ÓTR and REGIN in Norse mythology. The most aggressive and the strongest of the brothers, Fafnir was blessed with a fearless soul and a powerful arm. Wearing the Aegis helmet he guarded his father's house of gems and gold. Driven by greed, Fafnir killed his father in front of his two sisters, Lofnheid and Lyngheid, for possession of the hoard and transformed into a dragon to better guard it; ultimately he was slain by the cultural hero, Sigurd. This tragic story is told in the legendary thirteenth century saga, *Volsunga Saga* ("Saga of the Völsungs").

Sources: Daly, *Norse Mythology*, 78–9; Dekirk, *Dragonlore*, 72–3; Gentry, *Nibelungen Tradition*, 69

Fair Family

Variations: Fair Folk, TYLWYTH TEG, y Tylwyth Tegyny Coed ("the fair family in the wood")

The term, fair family, is a euphemistic phrase used by the Welsh when referring to the fairies.

Sources: Croker, *Fairy Legends and Traditions of the South of Ireland*, 134; Keightley, *Fairy Mythology*, 408; Sikes, *British Goblins*, 11

Fair Lady

A very powerful species of fairy from Hungarian folklore a Fair Lady will often shape-shift into a beautiful horse, naked women, or a long-haired woman dressed in white looking like a typical housewife. These fairies will walk through a town looking for a home to stay in;

when invited into one it would cast a spell and strike the home owner deaf, mute, or worse. Each Fair Lady also has a magical "platter," some item enchanted, such as a spoon, an actual platter, or even a puddle of water on the ground. Anyone who touches one of these "platters" will fall under its injurious and malicious spells. To see a Fairy Lady is an omen of hard times approaching; when one is seen, it is often said she is dancing in the rain or flying enemas through the sky. Known to steal children, the Fair Ladies have an irresistible singing voice they will use to lure a man into its arm and then systematically dance to death. Like many of the fay, the Fair Ladies are repelled by church bells, the use of the Lord's name, and human laughter.

Sources: Dömötör, *Hungarian Folk Beliefs*, Volume 1981, 93; Mack, *Field Guide to Demons*, n.p.

Fairy

Variations: BENDITH Y MAMAU ("Their Mother's Blessing"); Blessed Folk, the; Blessed Ones, the; DAOINE MAITH ("Good People"); Daoine Shi; DAOINE SIDHE ("fairy people"); Elfins; Elfs; FADA; Fae Eire ("green friend"); Faërie; Faerie; Faery Folk; Faery; Faes; Fai; Faierie; Faiery; Faine, FAIR FAMILY; Fair Folk; Fair; Fairies; Fairye; Farie; Farisees; Fary; Farys; Fas; FATA; Fay; Faye; Fayerie; Fayery; Fayry; Fays; FEE; Fée; Feen; Fees; Fées; Feinen Feiri; FENODEREE, Fenodrerr; Ferier; Ferisher; Ferrie; Ferrishyn; Fery; Fey; Feyrie; Feyrye; the Folk; the Forgetful People; Frairiesv; the GENTRY; the Good Folk; the Good Neighbors; Good People, GREENCOATIES, Greenies, Green Goons, the Green Men; the Grey Neighbours; Guillyn Veggey ("little boys"), Hada; Hadada; Hadas; Hill Crowd; the Hill Folk; Honest Folks; Kleine Volk ("little folk"); KLIPPE; Little Fellas; the Little Folks; the Little People; the Lordly Ones; the Men of Peace; Middle World Ones; Mooinjer-Veggey ("little people"); Muintir Bheaga, the Natives; the Neighbors; the Neighbours; the Night Walkers; the Old People; Pebel Vean ("small people"); the People of Peace; the People of the Hills; the People; Phairie; Pharie; Phenodyree; Pherie; Pixies; Prowlies; Púcaí; the Restless People; SEELIE; Shee; Sheeè; Sheeidh; Shia; Shicáre; Shifa; Shifra; SÍDHE ("hill folk"); the SILENT MOVING FOLK; Sisth; Sleeth Ma; Sleagh Maith ("good people"); Sleight Beggey; Small People of Cornwall; Smallfolk; Still Folk; Still Peoople; the Strangers; Them; Them That's in It; Them Who Be; Them Who Prowl; Themselves; They; TUATHA DE DANANN; TYLWYTH TEG; the Wee Folk; the Wee Ones; Wights; Y Tylwyth Teg ("fairy family")

The word *fairy* is used to represent the species of folkloric, legendary, and mythological creatures falling into the category of DWARF, elemental spirit, ELF, NATURE SPIRIT, SÍDHE, TUATHA DE DANANN, as well as similarly described animals, beings, monsters, and spirits. The word *fay*, a noun, albeit somewhat archaic, is beginning to regain popularity as an interchangeable descriptor for the word *fairy*.

Although the fay of Anglo-Saxon, Germanic, Norse, and Scandinavian lore are most popular, most cultures have an array of similar beings, such as in the Middle East, the Orient, and ancient Greece.

Where the fay live and what they wear vary, generally speaking, fairies are benign or indifferent to mankind and appear as beautiful but small humanoids. When one of the fay are said to be ugly, they are truly hideous in appearance; when warned a fairy is injurious or malicious this should not be taken lightly as that fairy is beyond a doubt a dangerous and spiteful being.

Albanian fairies are stunningly beautiful and live capricious lives, interacting with humans and other spirits freely; they are deeply involved in the folklore of these people. Most Albanian fay are beautiful and live in a castle high up in the mountains.

Before the introduction and acceptance of Christianity, the people worshiped nature in cults. In England, there are two types of fairies, the elves living in the caves, fields, mountains, and woods; and the domestic fay, such as the HOB-GOBLINS.

The fairies of British lore are interwoven into the arts, culture and literature of the people from the very beginning. For instance the gentle TROOPING FAIRIES of the SEELIE COURT are small in stature, resemble perfectly proportioned humans with wings, and are always dressed in exquisite clothing of blue, gold, and green. They have supernatural speed and the ability to become invisible and shape-shift; they live in kingdoms underground ruled over by FAIRY KINGS and queens. They love dancing, feasting, and music, sometimes inviting humans to join in the merry-making. The fairies of the UNSEELIE COURT however are perpetually injurious and malicious toward mankind. Hideous and completely evil without a means of reproducing themselves, they kidnap and transform mortals into one of their own. In Yorkshire, England has more fairy mythology concerning GIANTS and OGERS than any other part of the world. Yorkshire fairies are well known for their cravings for fresh milk.

Canadian fairies tend to be more like NATURE SPIRITS or are otherwise modified from European lore to suite the regions needs. CHANGELINGS are common here.

The CHU PA-CHIAI in Chinese mythology is similar to the role fairies play in Western cultures. They are far less powerful than the gods but take a much more active hand in the control of human affairs and destiny.

In Cornwall, England fairies are called the old people.

The fée of French fairy lore are almost always female dressed in either the finest fashion or in common peasant clothing but are fearfully unpredictable. Many of the French kings will claim to have been descended from one of the fée. These fairies have the ability to shape-shift into any form, from the most beautiful to something utterly horrifying; they can even become invisible.

Gaelic fairies are always described as being very handsome and wearing green clothes. Dancers and singers who both borrow and lend freely with humans these fay are also expert cloth and shoe makers. Gaelic fay raid low country settlements and take mortal women and children back to their *shians* or *tomhans*, a mass of hillocks or rocks. Those humans fortunate enough to leave the next morning will sadly discover upwards to one-hundred years will have passed.

The fairies of German lore include the countries of Austria, Hungary, Lusatia, and parts of Switzerland. The mythology is deeply tied to the heroic literature of these ancient people. Fairies here tend to be likened to the dead and live underground. Typically in popular German belief fairies are divided into four classes: DWARF, KOBOLD, NIXES, and WILD WOMEN. Taken babies and CHANGELINGS are also found in German fairy lore.

In the Hindu mythology fairies are described as pointy-eared, small, and quick moving winged beings; they are most often seen on or near the holy days.

Hungarian fay are predominantly female, generally benevolent, are human in appearance and size but have a magical nature about them.

In the countries that make up Iberia, Andorra, Gibraltar, Portugal, and Spain, fairy lore is extremely scant.

The bishop of Skalholt, Iceland Finnus Johannaeus, wrote a book entitled *The Ecclesiastical History of Iceland* (1754); it contains the fullest account of the ELVES and DWARFS in Icelandic lore.

The fairies of Ireland are very similar to the fay if England and Scotlans; they are commonly referred to as the DAOINE SIDHE and are believed to be fallen angels or the ancient gods of the earth however more often than not they are one of the TUATHAN DE DANANN. When they are visible, these small fairies are said to be beautiful and very slender, although they are expert shape-shifters. Their clothing is either of the most resplendent silk or of the corset rags, but always green. Living in ancient barrows, mounds, and stone circles throughout the land, these fairies live in organized communities and are under the rulership of kings and queens. They are overly fond of dancing, feasting, hunting, and making music. Like many species of fay, the fairies of Ireland will steal not only a human baby and leave a CHANGELING in its place, but they will also make off with a human bride. The SOLITARY FAIRIES of Ireland can be benevolent but are very quick to anger and will take revenge out on any mortal who is disrespectful to them or tries to harm one. In Irish fairy lore, there are no water fairies similar to the KELPIE or the NIXEN.

Italian fairies are called FATA and tend to be deeply driven by evil and malicious intent or are genuinely compassionate, kind, and good natured.

Lithuanian fairies are blond haired, blue-eyed beauties, former gods reduced in power and regulated to giving mortal women protection.

There are two species of fay in Malaysian fairy lore, the BEDIADARI, similar to the TROOPING FAIRIES of Europe, and the Orang Bunyian, fickle, mischievous, and unsophisticated.

On the Isle of Man the fairies are similar to those of the suroundnd regions, and are called the Li'l Fellas, the *cloan ny moyrn* ("children of pride"), and Mooinjer-Veggey ("little People"). It is believed they are fallen angels were cast out of Heaven but were too good for eternal damnation in Hell. Although they can be kind toward humans they are more likely to be merely mischievous; however it is said they have no power whatsoever over any person who is on a mission of mercy. Manx fairies, when visible are seen fishing in the sea or watching their cattle as they graze on land; they stand only a few feet tall and are especially fond of the company of goats.

These fay are said to enjoy churning butter and have a particular talent for herbalism. Knowing the name of fairy is to have power over it in Manx lore.

Native American fairy lore is a rich tradition encompassing FAIRY ANIMALS, creatures, beings and NATURE SPIRITS alike.

Native American NATURE SPIRITS very often take the form of an animal. The fairies in this mythology tend to be driven off by excess smoke; this belief holds true among the Irish, Polynesians, and Welsh.

Nigerian fairies are small and live in the forest; they have more in common with NATURE SPIRITS.

Similar to the fairy lore of Germany, the feés Normandy are also like those of northern France.

There is very little information on the Orcadian fairies of the Orkney Islands other than they are frequently seen dancing. Similar to the fay of Scotland and the Shetland Islands the Orcadian fairies are described as wearing armor.

Called peries in Persian folklore, these gossamer winged, lightweight, tiny beings are completely benevolent; they live off the scent of flowers and perfume. The peries are enemy of the thoroughly evil DEEVS.

Treasures hoarding Polynesian fairies are believed to live in *heiaus*, nature temples constructed with lava stones. Although these fairies are fond of fire they do not like excess smoke; Polynesian islanders, just like the Irish, Native Americans, and the Welsh people will smoke clay pipes as a means of protection, creating clouds of smoke in the area.

The fairies in the folklore of the Romanian gypsies are ruled over by a FAIRY QUEEN named ANA; she was forced to marry a demon and through this unfortunate union all human disease and ill came into being.

Russian word for fairy is *domovoi*, and SEASONAL FAIRIES are very popular in their folklore. These Slavic fairies are spiteful, enjoying ruining butter, spilling milk, and stealing cheese and yogurt. To protect oneself from fairies invading the home and causing trouble it was customary to hang a scythe over the home's door; the scythe prevented the fay from entering.

Scandinavia has their fair lore tied to their ancient heroic literature, similar to the German tradition. Mostly consisting of DWARFS, ELLEMAIDS and TROLLS play a role while other typed of fairy spirits are far less common. Generally the fay are mischievous but love a clean home, gladly rewarding servants who keep their homes

neat; they are described as having a voice as soft as the air. The fay of Scandinavia are also exceedingly fond of dancing and wherever they do so a patch of deep green grass called regionally *elfdans* ("ELF-dance") will grow. In this country's fairy lore there are four classes of the fay: elves, DWARFS (or TROLLS), the NECKS, Mermen (see MERMAN) and MERMAIDS, and the NISSES. The white elves of Scandinavia live in the air, dance on the grass and sit in the trees; they are considered to be benign; the black elves on the other hand lived underground and would cause illness and injury to humans. People who fall ill to fairy illness must seek out a specific sort of doctor who specializes fairy- illness known as a *kloka män*.

Scottish fairies, or *sith* as they are there called, are very similar to those found in England except they are more likely to be mischievous and less likelt to be offended by some real or imagined human slight; they are also similar to Irish fairies ones in both manner and appearance. Scottish fairies are divided into two classes, domestic and rural and live in burghs called *bowers, bruthain*, and *sithean*. Described most commonly as wearing green, generally these fay tend to be small in stature but are also expert shape-shifters and can take any form or size they choose. The female fairies of Scottish lore are dazzlingly beautiful but especially malicious with an unpredictable nature. Having both a SEELIE and UNSEELIE COURT they are both generally aloof and tend to avoid human contact; they prefer to live in isolated areas where there are brochs, dolmens, hill forts, and peel towers. Ash tree wands give the weilder power over fairies and can tell them to leave, a sometime necessary item to have, as Scottish fairies lend and borrow freely, although it is uncommon to refuse them.

In South America there are two different classes of fairy; one set of mythology originates with the native Americans of the region and the other comes from the folklore or Portugal and Spain.

Spanish fairies are called FADA and as the name implies, they have some control over human fate. Sometimes these fairies will live indoors in human habitations but more often than not they dwell in the mountains. Similar to the SOLITARY FAIRIES, the FADA have a natural ability for deception and are deeply vindictive in their cruelty, even against their own kind. Partial to olive trees Spanish fay cannot stand to hear the word Sunday spoke aloud as it is a holy day and one on which they have no power.

The oldest written account of Welsh fairies appears in *Hinerary of Giraldus Cambrensis* (1188) written by Gerallt Gymro ("Gerald of Wales") the archdeacon of Brecon as he accompanied Archbishop Baldwin on his tour throughout Wales. Although known by many different names, such as BENDITH Y MAMAU ("their mother's blessing"), Ellyll, Fair Folk, Korid-gwen ("korid-women"), Night Walkers, Them Who Be, Y Dynon Bach Têg ("little fair people"), and Y Tylwyth Teg ("fairy family") Welsh fay are most commonly known as the TYLWYTH TEG, although regional names abound, such as in Gower Wales where the benign *verry volk* dressed in scarlet and green dance beneath the moon. Described as beautiful, golden haired humans half of these fairies are diminutive while the other half reaches only up to the height of a man's knee; however both sizes are shape-shifters and may appear any height they choose. The smaller of the species are physically more attractive than their larger counterparts. Larger Welsh fay are more prone to steal babies, butter, cows, goats, and milk. CHANGELINGS are left behind whenever a child is taken; they also lure humans into their world. Welsh fairies of both sizes are usually said to have a courtly appearance and dress in red and white. White dogs are strictly considered to be FAIRY ANIMALS. The harp was the musical instrument of choice among Welsh fairies; on especially grand occasions they would play the bag pipes or a bugle. On occasion there would be fiddle playing but in almost every occasion where this happens it is later revealed the fiddler was not a fairy but rather a mortal who had been captured by the fairies. To protect hoes from unwanted fairies entering gorse hedes are planted all around the outside of the home. Like the fay of Native American and Polynesian lore, Welsh fairies do not like excessive smoke, although they do appreciate fire.

The fairies of Wales live off of milk and saffron and enjoy dancing, music, and making FAIRY RINGS. They wear green clothing, although the nobility will don silk clothing of blue and red. The females are known to take a mortal husband and stay with him so long as he never breaks the taboo placed upon him. Welsh fay live in lakes or the woods, on lonely islands, and under hills.

Sources: Bord, *Fairies*, 66, 110; Keightly, *World Guide to Gnomes, Fairies, Elves, and Other Little People*, 12, 216–17, 230–31; McCoy, *Witch's Guide to Faery Folk*, 4, 22, 28–30; Rose, *Spirits, Fairies, Leprechauns, and Goblins*, 107–112

Fairy Animal

Variations: Fairy Creature

Throughout the fairy lores of the various cultures, there are those animals that have many of the magical or otherworldly qualities of the fay but lack the level of empathy, intelligence, and understanding associated with sentient beings. Oftentimes theses fairy animals are kept by the fay for domestic use, such as with their cattle the CRODH MARA or their hunting hounds, as in the Hounds of Annwn (see ANNWN, HOUNDS OF), the ARKAN SONNEY and the CU SITH.

When one of these other worldly animals is not domesticated but rather runs wild throughout the countryside causing fear and wreaking havoc in the lives of mortals, it is considered to be a fairy creature, such as in the case of the BOOBRIE.

There are those fairy who are described as having animal physical characteristics but due to their behavior and obvious displays of intelligence, such as the ability to communicate by use of language, these being would not be considered to be a strictly a fairy animal but a species of fay. A few examples of this would be any of the GIANTS, the BAKU, and the BARGUESTS.

Sources: Briggs, *Encyclopedia of Fairies*, 1034; Campbell, *Superstitions of the Highlands and Islands of Scotland*, 141–3; Davis, *Myths and Legends of Japan*, 358–9; Howey, *Horse in Magic and Myth*, 146; Monaghan, *Encyclopedia of Celtic Mythology and Folklore*, 105

Fairy Artifacts

Fairy artifacts are tiny household items found buried in the Scottish Highlands typically attributed to fairies, such as flint arrowheads (also known as ELF ARROWS) and small clay pipes whose bowl in not even big enough to place the tip of one's little finger tip in. The Fairy Flag of Dunvegan Castle and the Fairy Cup of Edenhal are more popularly know artifacts and have established folklore attached to these items. In southwest Ireland on the Beara Peninsula a laborer found what he called a fairy shoe in 1835. This minuscule shoe fashioned like one belonging to an eighteenth century gentleman measured $2\frac{7}{8}$ inches long but only $\frac{7}{8}$ inches wide. Made of mouse skin and having a worn down heal this fairy artifact was examined under a microscope at Harvard University revealing handmade stitches and eyelets. One such item, a mirror with a brass plate on a molded handle, is currently in the Scottish Highland Folk Museum located in Inverness-Shire.

Sources: Ashliman, *Fairy Lore*, 155, 157; Bord, *Fairies*, 19; Hamilton, *Am Bratach Sith of Dunvegan*, 237

Fairy Bush

In British fairy lore, any bush growing in the direct path of a FAIRY RADE or FAIRY TRAIL was called a fairy bush and considered untouchable; some of those plants remained intact for ages. Common species of fairy bushes were elderberry, holly, maybush, rowan, and whitethorn. If ever the wood of one of these bushes was burned for fuel it would spit sparks and send forth a noxious fume which would cause anyone who inhaled it to linger in sickness before they finally died.

Sources: Bayley, *Archaic England*, 602; Evan-Wentz, *Fairy Faith in Celtic Countries*, 33; Narváez, *Good People*, 199

Fairy Butter

Variations: Menyn Tylna Teg ("fairies' butter"), Pixy-Puffs, Tremella, TROLL's Butter, Witch's Butter

According to popular fairy lore, fairy butter is a species of fungus and one of the staple foods of the fay; it is described as being gelatinous and yellow. Growing on the exposed roots on old trees; after it rains and some time has passed the fungus putrefies to a state of looking like and having the consistency of butter. Another possible substance that could be the source of fairy butter may be limestone in a semi-indurated state.

Sources: Bord, *Fairies*, 20; Friend, *Flowers and Flower-Lore*, 19; Keightly, *World Guide to Gnomes, Fairies, Elves, and Other Little People*, 309; Rolfe, *Romance of the Fungus World*, 12–13

Fairy Food

Variations: BWYD ELLYLLON ("elves food")

The food the fairies serve at their festivals has been described by those few who have been fortunate enough to have eaten it and returned to tell the tale, as having the most delicious flavor. Fairy food is said to taste like wheaten-bread, mixed with wine and honey. Humans who consume fairy food are said to never become full, and oftentimes will remain hungry. When a blessing or a prayer is said over fairy food it transforms into horse-dung. Mortals who consume fairy food are not allowed to leave FAIRYLAND, but are forever physically transformed, no longer wholly mortal or human.

When fairies eat human food they are not actually consuming the physical object but rather the *toradh*, the spiritual essence and sustenance of the food. When the fay actually eat a physical object they eat barley meal, poisonous mushrooms, the milk of goats and red deer hine, the roots of silver weed (*brisgein*), the stalks of heather (*cuiseagan an fhraoich*), toadstools, and the weeds gathered in the fields. Oatmeal is a food that will not necessarily repel the fay but will do nothing to lure them in.

Sources: Campbell, *Superstitions of the Highlands and Islands of Scotland*, 21–2; Keightly, *World Guide to Gnomes, Fairies, Elves, and Other Little People*, 354; Moorey, *Fairy Bible*, 54

Fairy Fort

Variations: Barrow Mound, Burghs, Cashel, Fairy Mound, Forth, Lios, Place of the Fairies, RATH, Ring Fort, Rusheen, Stone Fort, Taigh Shidhe ("fairy house")

Found all over Ireland a fairy fort was the remains of a hill fort or some other circular dwelling; most of these locations date back to the Iron Age. At one time there was said to be as many as sixty-thousand such locations over the country; fairies were said to frequent these locations, thereby giving the name. It was believed damage to these ancient sites would anger the fairies who dwelt within and would cause some disaster to befall the perpetrator. Fairy forts were also believed to the entryway to FAIRYLAND.

Sources: Bord, *Fairies*, 49; Eason, *Complete Guide to Faeries and Magical Beings*, 123–4; Illes, *Encyclopedia of Spirits*, 909; Narváez, *Good People*, 314

Fairy Godmother

Variations: Faery Godmother, sa Maraine qui estoit FÉE

A fairy godmother was a good natured fairy first popularized in the French fairy tale, *Cinderella*, from the latter half of the seventeenth century. The story's origin is ancient and unknown but the fairy godmother was a concept well familiar to the peasants who believed fairies could be invited into a person's live and become an active participant in it.

The fairy godmother as a character in folklore and fairy tales acts as a personal mentor or surrogate mother delivering a loving and nurturing relationship, typically the person being helped is a young maiden whose own mother is deceased. In the 18th century she became a relentless moralist. The fairy godmother will help the maiden achieve her goal and fulfill her needs so she will be able to win her prize, typically the love and protection of a husband who will stand up for her against her enemies, and help her claim her birthright. In very old fairy-tales the fairy god-mother is actually the returned spirit of the maiden's mother.

Sources: Elsie, *Dictionary of Albanian Religion, Mythology, and Folk Culture*, 59; Hartland, *Mythology and Folktales*, 18; Indick, *Movies and the Mind*, 49, 96; Stepanich, *Faery Wicca*, Book One, 29

Fairy Island

A fairy island is an island only visible or able to be seen part of the time. In areas where these islands are said to appear sailors make a point to be cautious; landing on one of these islands is never considered to be a good idea, although in conflicting reports it is also believed anyone who goes to one of these islands will enjoy a lifetime of joy and pleasure. Examples of a fairy island would be AVALON and Anglesey of England; Gresholm of Wales; and Isle of the Blest, Hy Brasil of Ireland.

Sources: Degidon, *New Catholic World*, Volume 85, 98; Froud, *Faeries*, 24–25; McCoy, *Witch's Guide to Faery Folk*, 43; Olcott, *Book of Elves and Fairies*, 91

Fairy King

Especially popular in British and Scottish fairy lore, fairy kings are those individual fairy beings who rule over a fairy court of subjects, in as much as the fay can be ruled. Some of them are literary, some are folkloric, while others are remained gods or historical figures. In Scotland, the royal Fairy King and Queen are even recognized as such by ancient law.

Some of the named fairy kings are: ÁED ABRAT, a King in Ireland; AILILL, a Milesian King of Leinster; Connla; Cóle, an Irish King; CUILENN, King of the mountain, Slieve Gullion; DONN FÍRINNE, an Irish Fairy King of Knock-fierna mountain; FIACHRA, King of Western Sea Fairies; FINVARRA, King of Connacht; FLANN UA FEDACH, an Irish King; Gwynn ap Nudd, a King in Celtic lore; IUBDAN, a King of Ulster; Manannan mac Lir, the half human King; MELEAGANT, King of Somerset; Midhir, last King of the TUATHA DE DANANN; Midir, a Milesian King of Leinster; and OBERON, a British Fairy King.

Sources: McCoy, *Witch's Guide to Faery Folk*, 21; Monaghan, *Encyclopedia of Celtic Mythology and Folklore*, 3, 8, 97, 127, 136, 217

Fairy Loaf

Variations: Pharisee Loaf

A fairy loaf is, according to lore, a loaf of bread a fairy gives to a mortal out of charity; the loaf will always remain fresh and never reduce in size so long as some condition is meet, such as never revealing the source of the loaf or en-suring your children always eat a slice.

Fossilized sea-urchins are called fairy loafs and there is a saying in Norfolk, "If you keep a fairy-loaf you will never want bread." Interest-ingly, fairies are also euphemism referred to as urchins.

Sources: McNamara, *Star-Crossed Stone*, 119, 128; Spence, *Legends and Romances of Brittany*, 53; Wright, *Rustic Speech and Folk-Lore*, 208

Fairy Money

In all of the folklore, legends, and stories in-volving fairies and money it is imprrtant to note the money they offer is perfectly good and by all measures actual currency so long as the source of the income was kept a secret. Should ever the recipitant of the gift tell anyone of how he came into in, the money and all purchased with it, would instantly vanish.

Sources: Ashliman, *Fairy Lore*, 200; Croker, *Fairy Legends and Traditions of the South of Ireland*, Vol-umes 1–3, 227–28; Sikes, *British Goblins*, 117, 119

Fairy of the Beech-Woods

In the fairy-tale *Prince Featherhead and the Princess Celandine* by Le Prinze Muguet the Fairy of the Beech-woods lived in a lovely valley where a kind but displaced king and queen took refuge with their infant son; the fairy put the royal family under her protection. The Fairy of the Beech-Woods lived in Leafy Palace, an enchanted place filled with treasures. She had the ability to send dreams and mask visibly a person's appear-ance causing them to appear unattractive. He chariot is dressed with honeysuckle and jasmine.

Source: Lang, *Green Fairy Book*, 86–99

The Fairy of the Dawn

In the fairy tale, *Fairy of the Dawn* by Ruman-ian author Rümänische Märchen, the NYMPH-like Fairy of the Dawn was the guardian of a fountain whose water contained magical properties. To reach the fountain one must pass a three-headed fire breathing dragon, defeat the evil Welwa (GOBLIN) of the Copper Woods, the Welwa of the Silver Woods, the Welwa of the Gold Woods, safely pass through the frozen and icy kingdom of the goddess Mittwoch (feminine form of the Roman god, Mercury), pass safely through the kingdom of the goddess of thunder, Donnerstag (feminine form of the Roman god, Jupiter) and finally through the kingdom of Vineri (feminine form of the Roman god, Venus).

Sources: Haughton, *Tales from Eternity*, 57, 146; Lang, *Violet Fairy Book*, 167–87

The Fairy of the Desert

In the fairy-tale *The Yellow Dwarf* by Madame d'Aulnoy, the Fairy of the Desert, one of a dozen sisters, was guarded by a pride of fierce lions. Known to be exceptionally wise, this fairy is described as wearing a ruff of black taffeta, a red velvet hood, and a farthingale of rags. The Fairy of the Desert leans heavily upon a cane as she stands and walks; aside from being very tall, she is also very old and has eagle-like feet. The entourage of this fairy contains two great BASILISKS, a winged griffin and an array of snakes she keeps worn about her neck. Her chariot is pulled by bats. Although she may assume any form she chooses, there is no amount of magic or enchantment strong enough to hide the ugliness of her feet. She has the ability to call up storms.

The moment she laid eyes upon the King of the Gold Mine, she fell in love with him; because he did not return her affection she captured him and intended to bend his will to her liking by use of her magic. The best friend and closest allie of the Fairy of the Desart was the YELLOW DWARF.

Sources: Aulnoy, *Fairy Tales of Madame d'Aulnoy*, 239–42; Lang, *Blue Fairy Book*, 30–50

The Fairy of the Fields

In the fairy-tale *The Punishment of the Fairy Gangans* from the collection *Le Cabinet de Fees* the Fairy of the Fields was the fairy who had appeared to Queen Gillette on her wedding night. In a dream the fairy bade the queen to bake a barley cake and a small platter of cream cheese then place these items under a rose-tree in the garden. The fairy would, in the form of a beautiful blue mouse, take the food each day. When captured, she transformed the queen and her six children into various animals ad disappeared with them. The fairy left a note for the queen promising "everything comes to him who knows how to wait." In the end, the queen's patience paid off and she was reunited with her children.

Source: Lang, *Olive Fairy Book*, 320–25

The Fairy of the Forest

In the fairy-tale *Jackal or Tiger* there was a fairy called the Fairy of the Forest who was obliged to assist Prince Ameer Ali as he was kind enough to assist her when he believed she was was an old woman whose water vessel had broken. In her true form this fairy appears as a young and beautiful woman; she assisted the prince in acquiring lovely anklets and necklaces. In the end, when the prince gained his throne, he married the Fairy of the Forest.

Source: Lang, *Olive Fairy Book*, 71

Fairy of the Meadows

In the fairy-tale *Sylvain and Jocosa* by Comte de Caylus, the Fairy of the Meadows was attracted to two beautiful and intelligent children, Sylvain and Jocosa, and decided to become their FAIRY GODMOTHER and protector. When the children were grown she appeared to them as a slender and tall woman dressed all in green and wearing a crown of flowers upon her head. From time to time she would appear to teach them many things and show them the marcels of her fairy kingdom. In exchange she asked the two keep her favorite fountain clear of leafs and twigs before the morning sun shown down on it. The two friends did as they were asked, as they were promised never to be parted from one another as they loved one another deeply. For many years they were diligent in their daily chore but one morning they each ran late and were unable to clean the fountain in time. As they arrived, the fountain caused a great churning river to pour fourth and roiling up, parted the friends, one on each side of the bank. For three years they each walked down the river looking for a way to cross over to one another; eventually the river fed out into the ocean. The friends were overcome with sorrow and were about to drown themselves when the Fairy of the Meadow removed the spell of the river allowing the friends to reunite. Sylvain and Jocosa became lovers married, and lived all the days of their life together.

Sources: Aldrich, *Young Folks' Library*, 124–127; Lang, *Green Fairy Book*, 56–59

The Fairy of the Well

The Fairy of the Well is described as being hideous in appearance with bewitching owl-like eyes, a foxlike face, and catlike claws upon her fingertips. As ugly as this fairy is her entourage is strikingly beautiful. The palace of the Fairy of the Well is located a two day ride through a flowery meadow; he land is in perpetual twilight and the temperature is comfortable and otherwise moderate. There is a river of milk which runs around her castle and the river bottom is covered with pearls and precious gems.

Source: Lang, *Violet Fairy Book*, 192

Fairy Path

Variations: Doodweg ("death-way" or "death-road"), Fairy Avenue, Fairy Pass, Fairy Passage, Geisterweg ("ghost-way" or "ghost-road"), Helweg ("hell-way" or "hell-road"), Spirit Paths

In Brittany, Germany, Ireland, and Scotland, a fairy path is a sacred fairy space, a rout said to be walked by the fay between traditional significant sites, such as a FAIRY FORT and a Stone Age monument. These paths are almost always a straight line directly from one place to another. Sometimes these paths are invisible but locals always seem to be able to know where they are and how they run. Typically the grass is greener along the fairy path. Many fairy paths run on top of established ley lines. Builders would determine if a fairy path was present by placing a pile of stones in an area; if in the morning the stones were untouched the area was declared safe but if they were moved work would not begin.

Buildings constructed along a fairy path fail to prosper. People who are chronically ill or have perpetual bad luck are believed to live in a house built atop a fairy path; these houses are said to be in a "contrary place."

Underwater fairy path run through marshes; some connect one island to another and are made of coral. Water fairy paths are only used by the fay and sometimes fishermen say as they pass overhead they can see fairies along it.

Sources: Bord, *Fairies*, 7; McCoy, *Witch's Guide to Faery Folk*, 23

Fairy Queen

Especially popular in British and Scottish fairy lore, fairy queens were those individual fairy beings who ruled over a fairy court of subjects, in as much as the fay could be ruled. Some of them were literary; some were folkloric, while others were remained goddesses or historical figures; all of them were sexually assertive. In Scotland, the royal FAIRY KING and Queen were even recognized as such by ancient law. More often than not, FAIRYLAND was said to be ruled by a queen.

Some of the named fairy queens are: AEVAL, Queen of southwest Munster; Aíbell, Queen of Connacht; Aibheag, Queen of Donegal; Aibheall; AINE, Queen of Munster; ARGANTE, Queen of the Island of AVALON; AYNIA; BECFHOLA, Queen of Tara; Befind; BRUNISSEN, French Fairy Queen;

CETHLION, Queen of the FORMORIANS; CLIDNA, and Irish Queen; CRED, Irish queen of Paps of Danu; Crunniuc, an Irish Queen; FAND, Queen of Scotland; FINDCHÓEM, Queen of Ulster; Maeve; NIAMH, a golden-haired queen of Ireland; Titania.

Sources: Illes, *Encyclopedia of Spirits*, 407; Keightley, *Fairy Mythology*, 628; Monaghan, *Encyclopedia of Celtic Mythology and Folklore*, 177

Fairy Rade

Variations: Fairy Raed, RADE, WILD HUNT

A fairy rade is a grand procession of the fay and such an event occurring is considered to be of great importance. Although a rade can occur any time of the year they are especially significant when they occur on the onset of summer. Typically these rades consist of fairies wearing their finest clothes and riding upon their favorite mounts that are equally adorned with resplendent trappings; sometimes ghosts and witches are said to accompany the fay. In ancient times it was believed GWYN AP NUDD, a FAIRY KING, led many a fairy rade out of FAIRYLAND through a portal on Glastonbury Tor.

To see a rade occurring is dangerous; by placing a rowan branch over the door to the family home one is them able to watch is pass from inside the house. In Scotland the SLUAG of the SEELIE COURT will use the opportunity of a rade to fly through the sky and kidnap travelers who are on the road at midnight. They would always fly towards the West in order to catch the souls of dying men before the souls dissipate.

Sources: Eason, *Complete Guide to Faeries and Magical Beings*, 21; Froud, *Faeries*, 22–23; Jamieson, *Scottish Dictionary and Supplement*, 383; Keightly, *World Guide to Gnomes, Fairies, Elves, and Other Little People*, 354–5

Fairy Riding

Variations: A' Mharcachd-Shìth, Marcachd Shìth, Marcachd-Shìth, Na Marcachd-Shìth

Fairy riding is a sort of paralysis said to occur in the livestock of Scotland whenever a fairy mouse would take them out and ride them or sleep on their back. In doing so, the fairy would damage the animal's spine. In Wales fairy riding is common. In both locations to counter the ill affects a shrew mouse, either alive or deceased, is rubbed along the back of the afflicted animal.

Sources: Evans-Wentz, *Fairy-Faith in Celtic Countries*, 85; Hurd, *Sleep Paralysis*, 41; Spence, *Fairy Tradition in Britain*, 164

Fairy Ring

Variations: ELF Circle, Fairy Circle, PIXIE Circle

A fairy ring is a dark ring of grass, mushrooms, or withered grass perfectly, or nearly perfectly round; the discolored grass is distinctly darker than the grass which surrounds it. It is a common folklore belief the ring was made by dancing fairies and the location is where they would use their magic and it is a portal into FAIRYLAND. In modern times it is suspected a type of fungus in the soil is the actual cause. It is interesting to note Welsh sheep are the only animals which will eat grass that grows inside a fairy ring.

Fairies seen by mortals dancing in a fairy ring are sometimes lured into the ring to dance with them; when this happens the person can become trapped within. Fortunately, a glove thrown into the ring first is said to make it safe for them to enter and leave. If someone is trapped inside the fairy ring and is dancing uncontrollably he can be pulled out and save if he is removed by three friends.

Fairy rings are not common in Ireland. In Northern France the FEÉ are said to create fairy rings as they dance about in a circle. If anyone should see them, they will be mystically compelled to join in but as the speed of the dance increases, the person cannot keep up and will ultimately fall of exhaustion or be killed when the FEÉ toss him about in the air. In Germany fairy rings are called *hexenringe* ("witch ring") because it is believed dancing witches created the ring. In Central Europe it iss said a fairy ring of mushrooms had been created by a dragon and for the next seven years only toadstools will grow there. Entering into a fair ring is a bad idea even if one does not see dancing fay, as lore warns it will cause an array of problems for the violator ranging from becoming prone to seeing illusions, becoming insane, developing skin problems, or even losing an eye.

Sources: Bord, *Fairies*, 15; Keightly, *World Guide to Gnomes, Fairies, Elves, and Other Little People*, 363; McCoy, *Witch's Guide to Faery Folk*, 42; Sikes, *British Goblins*, 99, 105

Fairy Trail

Similar to a FAIRY RING, a fairy trail is a long trail of dark colored grass believed to be used as a regular walkway by the TROOPING FAIRIES when they parade on their FAIRY RADE.

Source: McCoy, *Witch's Guide to Faery Folk*, 43, 68

Fairy Triad

In the Celtic fairy tradition a fairy triad is a place where ash, oak, and thorn trees are all growing together; where this occur it is considered to be a sacred grove and a place inhabited by the DRYADS. Carrying a small bundle of oak, and thorn twigs bound together with black, red, and white thread will offer protection against the fay.

Sources: Cunningham, *Cunningham's Encyclopedia of Magical Herbs*, 132; McCoy, *Witch's Guide to Faery Folk*, 52, 61; Moorey, *Fairy Bible*, 79

The Fairy Truth

In the fairy tale *Prince Darling* the fairy, Truth, tested a king to see if he was indeed as good and merciful as everyone in his kingdom claimed him to be. After having passed her test Truth swore to be his friend forever and promised to give him anything he asked for; the king asked Truth to make his son, Prince Darling, into a good man. Truth gave the prince a gold ring to wear telling him each time he did a bad deed the ring would prick his finger. If he continued with his act of evil she would become his personal enemy. The prince one day let himself be seduced by evil influenced and Truth, keeping her promise, transformed the young man into the monstrous animal his behavior mimicked—a bull for his churlishness, a lion by his anger, a snake for his ungratefulness and turning on a friend, and a wolf by his greediness. This new appearance gave him the head of a lion, bull horns, wolf feet, and a snake's body. As the prince modified his behavior he transformed into a little dog, a dove, and finally having become a good, his original form.

Source: Lang, *Blue Fairy Book*, 278–89

Fairyland

Variations: ELFLAND, Faërieland, Faeryland, Fairy Kingdom, Fairy-Land, Faylinn ("fairy kingdom"), Feerieland, Tir Nan Og ("land of the young"), Tír na nÓg ("land of perpetual youth")

The homeland of the fairies, Fairyland is described as being an enchanting place where happiness abounds; there is no illness or death, time stands still. It is not uncommon for a mortal who travels to Fairyland never to return, as in many mythologies the homeland of the fay is not merely located underground but is actually some sort of afterlife destination, perhaps even and alternative or parallel universe.

Although the entryways into the realm of the fay are located here on earth Fairyland said sometimes said to be underground or underwater while other times it is described as being in some other nearby dimension or in-between place. These entry ways are usually located in a cave, in the side of a hill, or under the water. On the occasion Fairyland is said to be actually located on our world, it is described as being on top of a hill, but invisible to the human eye.

Unlike other designated lands, Fairyland is almost always described as being ruled over by a FAIRY QUEEN, rather than a king, although there are many named FAIRY KINGS, few have been the King of Fairyland.

Sources: Board, *Fairies*, 5–6, 122; Keightly, *World Guide to Gnomes, Fairies, Elves, and Other Little People*, 8, 56, 289; Stepanich, *Faery Wicca*, Book One, 23, 87

Falerina

DRAGONTINA and Falerina are FATES, neutrally aligned; they are the owners and caretakers of a beautiful garden it has taken them seven months to create. A powerful haughty enchantress who spends time in introspection (a sign of divinity) she cast a magical spell on the sword of Orlando so no magic could stand up to it. In the story of Orlando, Falerina goes through a transformation and become good.

Sources: Bulfinch, *Bulfinch's Mythology*, 424; Cavallo, *Boiardo's Orlando Innamorato*, 92, 95; Kisacky, *Magic in Boiardo and Ariosto* 44–5

Falr

Variations: Fal

Falr ("socket") was one of the many DWARFS named in the *Voluspa*, the first and best known poem of the *Poetic Edda*, a collection of Old Norse poems dating back to about A.D. 985.

Sources: Crossley-Holland, Norse Myths, 183; Thorpe, *Northern Mythology*, Volume 1, 183

Falsirena

Variations: Felisinda

Falsirena is the fairy of fortune or gold in the Adone of Marini; later she becomes identified as the fairy of romance. Falsirena falls in love with the beautiful mortal, Adonis and keeps him as a prisoner in her garden of pleasure. In spite of her natural beauty and use of magical elixirs and spells, Adonis does not return her affections; enraged the lascivious Falsirena transforms the youth into a parrot and forces him to watch love scenes between Mars and Venues.

Sources: Beachem, *Critical Survey of Poetry*, 976;

Keightly, *World Guide to Gnomes, Fairies, Elves, and Other Little People*, 453; Quint, *Epic and Empire*, 310

Fand

A Manx deity absorbed into Irish mythology, Fand, the greatest of the Irish FAIRY QUEENS, the "pearl of beauty," and a minor goddess of earthly pleasures, health, and the sea, was once married to Manannan the god of the sea. When her husband abandoned her, Fand was challenged by three FORMORIAN warriors in a battle for control of the Irish Sea. Unable to win, she beseeched the cultural hero, Cuchulainn, to fight for her but he would not agree to do so unless she agreed to marry him. Reluctantly the SÍDHE consented; as soon as the two met they fell deeply in love with one another. Manannan knew if a relationship between a fairy and a mortal continued it would ultimately destroy the fay. Using his magical mantle he erased the memory of the lovers from each other's mind.

In a different telling of the story Manannan decides to reconcile with his wife and asks her to choose between her husband and her lover. Fand prefers Cuchulainn but knows he will not leave his wife, Emer, who had been plotting to kill her. Fand returns to Manannan but Cuchulainn is inconsolable, retreating into the wilderness refusing to eat or drink. Eventually the druids found and saved him; they gave him and Emer a magic potion to drink; it lett them move beyond the affair. Manannan used his magical mantle to ensure his wife and her lover would never see each other again.

Sources: Evans-Wentz, *Fairy-Faith in Celtic Countries*, 345–6; Hathaway, *Friendly Guide to Mythology*, 331; McCoy, *Witch's Guide to Faery Folk*, 5

Fantine

In Swiss fairy lore, in the spring time the fantines of the Vaudois valley, would watch over and water the flowers as the bloomed. A type of NATURE SPIRIT, the fantines were also concerned with the welfare of the herds that grazed in the Alpine pastures.

Sources: Bonnerjea, *Allborough New Age Guide*, 95; Robinson, *Margaret of Angoulême*, 262; Rose, *Spirits, Fairies, Leprechauns, and Goblins*, 113

Far Darric

Far Darric was a fairy practical joker from Irish folklore; he presides over evil dreams and nightmares.

Source: Wallace, *Folk-lore of Ireland*, 86

Farfadet

Variations: Fadas, Fades, Fadet, Fadhas, Follets

In the folklore of Brittany the farfadet ("SPRITE") is a species GOBLIN or LUTIN. These small, furry, kindly fairies not only guards treasures but also help out around the house; sometimes they are a little mischievous.

Sources: Keightly, *World Guide to Gnomes, Fairies, Elves, and Other Little People*, 476; Livia, *Queerly Phrased*, 138

Farvann

Farvann was a green fairy dog from the folklore of Scotland (see FAIRY ANIMAL). According to legend, he was as large as a two year old heifer and was once set lose on Hugh MacLeod who had stolen a fairy chalice. The dog will bay three time when on the hunt, pausing between each sonorous howl; the sound of it could strike fear in a man's heart. The tail of Farvann was said to sometimes curl up over its back while other times it was braided in a long plait. The fairy dog was said to act as a guardian to the entryway of FAIRYLAND and would accompany fairy women as they went out to fetch milk. Moving in perfect silence, Farvann's paw prints were as large as a man's hand.

Sources: Briggs, *Encyclopedia of Fairies*, 165; Simpson, *Folk Lore in Lowland Scotland*, 108–9

Fata

Variations: INCANTATRICE, Maga

In Italian poetry there are two classifications of the FATES. The first is benign and protective of mankind while the other is malicious and seductive. The words *fata*, *incantatrice*, and *maga* are used freely and interchangeably to describe each group.

Sources: Keightly, *World Guide to Gnomes, Fairies, Elves, and Other Little People*, 453

Fata della Fonte

Variations: Fata della Fonti

Fata della Fonte is one of the FATES appearing in Matteo Maria Boiardo's epic poem *Orlando Innamorato* ("*Orlando in Love*," 1495) from the Italian Renaissance period. In the poem, Fata della Fonte assists Mandricardo in obtaining the love of Hector.

Sources: Brewer, *Character Sketches of Romance, Fiction and the Drama*, 5; Keightly, *World Guide to Gnomes, Fairies, Elves, and Other Little People*, 452

Fata Morgana

Variations: Fata Morga'na, Lady Fortune

Said to be the sister of King Arthur and taught magic by the sorcerer Merlin, Fata Morgana was introduced as a FATE in Matteo Maria Boiardo's epic poem *Orlando Innamorato* ("*Orlando in Love*," 1495) initially as Lady Fortune. She is portrayed as an enchantress in the poem. In Tasso her three daughters are introduced, Carvilia, Nivetta, and Morganetta.

Fata Morgana is also said to be the fairy presumed to have caused the mirages in the Straits of Messina.

Sources: Brewer, *Character Sketches of Romance, Fiction and the Drama*, 5; Keightly, *World Guide to Gnomes, Fairies, Elves, and Other Little People*, 451; Rose, *Spirits, Fairies, Leprechauns, and Goblins*, 113, 351

Fata Silvanella

Silvanella is a FATE appearing in Matteo Maria Boiardo's epic poem *Orlando Innamorato* ("*Orlando in Love*," 1495) from the Italian Renaissance period. In the poem, Silvanella is presented as an enchantress.

Sources: Brewer, *Character Sketches of Romance, Fiction and the Drama*, 5; Rose, *Spirits, Fairies, Leprechauns, and Goblins*, 113, 351

The Fates

Variations: Destines, FATA, Fatal Sisters, Moirai ("allotter" or "cutter-off"), Parcae ("those who bring forth the child")

Depicted as three sisters who guide over the fate of man rather than control or determine it, many of the classical Greek authors saw them as beings more powerful than the gods. In mythology, the do not play an active part.

In Late Greek tradition, Clotho's name with its reference to spinning lent to the the Fates being depicted as three elderly women spinning out the thread of a man's life, measuring it, and then cutting it at a specific length.

Homer, the greatest ancient Greek epic poet and author of the *Iliad* and the *Odyssey*, says there was only one god who presided over fate, Moipa, and even the gods were subject to her plans. However, according to Hesiod, the Greek oral poet (750 and 650 B.C.), and all poets after him, said there were three such beings born the daughters of Nyx ("night"); their names were ATROPOS ("inevitable"), Clotho ("the spinner"), and Lachesis ("drawer of lots").

In Upper Brittany, the Fates are referred to as the fetes.

Sources: Dixon-Kennedy, *Encyclopedia of Greco-Roman Mythology*, 133; Grant, *Who's Who in Classical Mythology*, 136–7; Huffington, *Gods of Greece*, 22; Roman, *Encyclopedia of Greek and Roman Mythology*, 171; Society for the Diffusion of Useful Knowledge. *The Penny Cyclopædia of the Society for the Diffusion of Useful Knowledge,* Volume 17, 242

Fati (plural: fatit)

Variations: Miren

A fati is a type of birth fairy from southern Albanian lore; beautiful and extremely powerful, these female fairies are small enough to ride on the back of a butterfly. It was believed three fatit appear to a child three days after its birth to determine its destiny.

Sources: Illes, *Encyclopedia of Spirits*, 409; Lurker, *Routledge Dictionary of Gods and Goddesses, Devils and Demons*, 61

Faun

Variations: Faunus, Phaunos

A FAIRY ANIMAL from Roman mythology the faun is often associated with Greek SATYERS and the Greek god Pan (Faunus). Described as a horned human from the waist up and a goat from the waist down, this NATURE SPIRIT would guide those who were lost in the woods or terrorize those who traveled through the woods; it depends of the fairy's whimsy. Fauns, the fairy creatures, should not be confused with the Roman god, Faunus nor the goddess Fauna.

Sources: Dixon-Kennedy, *Encyclopedia of Greco-Roman Mythology*, 133; Euvino, *Complete Idiot's Guide to Italian History and Culture*, 274; McCoy, *Witch's Guide to Faery Folk*, 31; Roman, *Encyclopedia of Greek and Roman Mythology*, 171

Fay

Variations: ELF, FADA, Fae, Fairy, Fas, FATA, FEE, Fey

The word fay is another word meaning fairy when used as a noun; albeit somewhat archaic in use, it is beginning to regain some of its lost popularity. The word fay has also been used to refer to the FATES. In Albania fay are said to be a species of fairy, small winged NATURE SPIRITS loving to play harmless jokes.

Originally the word *fairy* was *fayerie*, an enchantment or magical application of the fay; by the Middle Ages, women who were said to be able to create charms, knew gemology, herbalism, and used enchantments were called fay. It

was suspected by use of their secret knowledge these fay were able to acquire riches and retain their youthful appearance.

Sources: Allied. *Chembers 21 Century Dictionary*, 469; Briggs, *Encyclopedia of Fairies*, 169; Keightly, *World Guide to Gnomes, Fairies, Elves, and Other Little People*, 31; McCoy, *Witch's Guide to Faery Folk*, 219–20; Narváez, *Good People*, 464

Fear Darrig (plural: Fir Darrig)

Variations: Far Darrig, Fear Dearc of Donegal, Fear Dearc, Fear-Dearg, Fir Dhearga

Fear Darrig ("RED MAN") is a fairy from Irish folklore; his appearance varies across the country. In Munster Fear Darrig is said to look like a wizened GNOME standing only two and a half feet tall. He has long grey hair and wears a scarlet coat and sugarloaf hat. He goes from home to home and begs to warm himself by the fire; good luck falls on those who let him in. When Fear Darrig has red hair it is said he is a practical joker. However, when this fay wears an all red outfit and calls himself Fear Dearc of Donegal, he is especially ill-behaved. Not only is he a practical joker but will use cruel and evil hallucinations. In some lore, Fear Darrig is a species of fairy and not an individual being.

Sources: Rose, *Spirits, Fairies, Leprechauns, and Goblins*, 115, 351; Monaghan, *Encyclopedia of Celtic Mythology and Folklore*, 180; O'Hanlon, *Legend Lays of Ireland*, 150

Fear Gorta (plural: fir gorta)

Variations: Far Gorta, Gorta Man

In Irish folklore the fear gorta ("hungry man") is a fairy spirit, possibly the ghost of someone who has died of hunger. Standing the by the roadside he begs for food; anyone who gives him an offering is blessed with good fortune. However, it is believed in Kiltubrid a fear gorta is a sudden onset of hunger occuring to a person while they travel through the mountains; if this hunger is not quickly satisfied the situation would be fatal. In Slieve-an-irain there is a fear gorta stone that if trod upon causes an overwhelming fit of hunger to overtake the person.

Sources: Jacobs, *Folklore*, Volume 4, 183; Monaghan, *Encyclopedia of Celtic Mythology and Folklore*, 180; Yeats, *Fairy and Folk Tales of the Irish Peasantry*, 81

Fear Liath More

Variations: Am Fear Liath Mor ("big grey man"), Fear Liath Mór, Fer-Las Mhór, Ferla Mór, Ferlie More, Fomor

Living on the summit cairn of Ben MacDhui, one of the great peaks of the Scottish Cairngorm Mountains Fear Liath More ("the grey man") has been physically and psychically attacking people for generations. Of the few times it has been seen this FAIRY ANIMAL has been described as standing over ten-feet tall, having olive toned skin, long arms, and broad shoulders. More commonly the fear liath more is said to be experienced as an icy feeling in the air or a cold brushing against the skin. It also will make unusually crunching noises and mimic the sound of echoing footsteps.

Sources: Eberhart, *Mysterious Creatures*, 51; Townsend, *Scotland*, 283; Wilson, *Mammoth Encyclopedia of the Unsolved*, 168

Fee

Variations: CORRIGANS, Fée, Fetes, Fions

In upper Brittany fairies are called fees; however in Brenton fairies are divided into two classes, the fee (fairies) and the nains (DWARFS). In Normandy, fee will steal children and leave a CHANGELING in its place.

In North France the fee are described as being both physically attractive and very small. Particularly fond of dancing, they create a FAIRY RING as they do so; anyone who overhears their music will be compelled to join in, but as the speed of the dance increases the mortal will find himself unable to keep up, he will fall from exhaustion or be found battered and bruised. The fee are also said to be seen at isolated springs washing their linen and letting them dry on druid stones. Such areas are sometimes called *grottes des fees.* At night the fee will visit its favorite farm and borrow a horse to go joy riding or to complete some personal chores. Farms they frequent are said to prosper and thrive.

Sources: Bord, *Fairies*, 59; Keightly, *World Guide to Gnomes, Fairies, Elves, and Other Little People*, 431, 473

Feeorin

The feeorin are a type of very small fairy found in the folklore of England. They are described as wearing green coats and red hats; the feeorin love to dance inside FAIRY RINGS.

Sources: Briggs, *Encyclopedia of Fairies*, 169; Rose, *Spirits, Fairies, Leprechauns, and Goblins*, 115, 351; Stepanich, *Faery Wicca*, Book One, 270

Fees des Houles

The fees des houles ("faeries of the billows") in Upper Brittany live in grottos or natural caves

along the sea cliffs, particularly near Saint-Cast. They are said to be storm fairies and dress themselves in all the colors of the rainbow. Before a storm their FAIRY QUEEN will leave their FAIRYLAND and head up a FAIRY RADE upon a boat made from the nautilus of the southern seas. Her boat is drawn by twin crabs.

Source: Evans-Wentz, *Fairy-Faith in Celtic Countries*, 175

Fenoderee

Variations: Fenodyree, Finnoderee, Fynnoderee, PHYNNODDEREE, Yn Foldyr Gastey

A species of BROWNIE from the Isle of Man, the brown furred fenoderee ("nimble mower") was an expert in farming; they were extremely strong and were said to take great enjoyment form ploughing fields, reaping crops, and sowing seeds. At night during snowy weather, they would gather in the sheep.

According to one legend, Fenoderee was not a species of BROWNIE but rather an individual fairy, a member of the Ferrishyn fairies. One day while out courting a mortal girl in Glen Rushen, Fenoderee missed attending his people's sacred autumn festival, Harvest Moon. As punishment, his handsome looks were taken from him and became a SOLITARY and ugly fay.

Sources: Allardice, *Myths, Gods and Fantasy*, 82; Briggs, *Vanishing People*, 57, 163; Evan-Wentz, *Fairy Faith in Celtic Countries*, 120; Froud, *Faeries*, 124; Randles, *Super Natural Isle of Man*, 90

Fer Fi

In Ireland, the locals who reside around Lough Gur believe the red-haired DWARF, Fer Fi, was the ruler of the lough and not GEROID. Fer Fi, a highly skilled shape-shifter who often took the form of a BEAN NIGHE or a BROWNIE, was born the son of Eogabal, the brother to the FAIRY QUEEN, AINE. Fer Fi was an expert three-string harpist; when he played *suantraighe* ("sleep music") everyone who heard it fell into a deep sleep; when he played *gentraighe* ("laughter music") listeners burst into delighted laughter.

Sources: Evan-Wentz, *Fairy Faith in Celtic Countries*, 82; Monaghan, *Encyclopedia of Celtic Mythology and Folklore*, 184; Spence, *History and Origins of Druidism*, 65

Ferrish (plural: ferrishyn)

Variations: Ferrishin, Sleih Beggey

TROOPING FAIRIES on the Isle of Man, the ferrishyn are a tribe of fay, as they have no king or queen to rule over them. Described as standing between one and three feet tall they have incredible hearing, as anything said about them outdoors, they can hear. Ferrishyn were also known to steal human babies and leave a CHANGELING in its place. These fairies were also fond of hunting; they rode beautiful horses following their red-eared hounds; the ferrishyn wore hunting outfits of green with red hats. The Ferrishyn are less aristocratic than the fairies of Ireland and Wales; they have no named King or Queen. The name of this fairy tribe is thought to be a combination of the English word *fairy* and the Irish word, *SÍDHE*; if true ferrish would translate as "fairy fairy."

Sources: Briggs, *Encyclopedia of Fairies*, 173; Moore, *Folk-Lore of the Isle of Man*, 13, 34; Stepanich, *Faery Wicca*, Book One, 270

Ferusa

A sea–NYMPH from Greek mythology, Ferusa, was the NEREIDS who sports in the devious contortions; she was born the daughter of Nerues and DORIS.

Sources: Betham, *Transactions of the Royal Irish Academy*, Volume 17, 88; Perry, *Study of Poetry*, 62

Feux follets

Variations: Fi-Follet, WILL O' THE WISP
In the fairy lore of Quebec, the feux follets are a species of injurious and vicious NATURE SPIRIT that enjoys playing tricks on mortals. Described as looking like blue flame, these fairy spirits lure travelers into ponds intending to drown them.

Sources: Fowke, *Canadian Folklore*, 34; Narváez, *Good People*, 18–19

Fiachra

Variations: Fiaghra
In Scottish lore, Fiachra ("eagle") was the FAIRY KING of the Western Sea fairies.

In Irish lore, Fiachra and her three sisters were turned into swans by their jealous step mother; the curse would remain until a man from the north married a woman from southern Ireland. It took 900 years for the condition to be met, freeing them. Unfortunately, within a moment, age and time caught up to them; they crumbled into dust and blew away in the wind.

Sources: Matson, *Celtic Mythology A to Z*, 56; McCoy, *Witch's Guide to Faery Folk*, 21, 244; Yonge, *History of Christian names*, Volume 2, 96

Fialarr

Fialarr was one of the many DWARFS named in the *Voluspa*, the first and best known poem of the

Poetic Edda, a collection of Old Norse poems dating back to about A.D. 985.

Sources: Grimm, *Teutonic Mythology*, Volume 2, 453; Wilkinson, *Book of Edda called Völuspá*, 12

Fideal

The fideal is one of the FUATH, a collective name for the malicious and monstrous water fay in Scottish folklore; she is personification of the entangling marsh grass and reeds. Singing a compelling and lovely song as it walks through the reedy edges of lakes, the voluptuous fideal will lure in her prey, with a cold kiss and chilling embrace. It is said her victims die happily embraced in her arms.

Near Loch Maree Hotel is the isolated Loch na Fideil in Gairloch, Scotland where a fideal was once said to haunt. The last encounter of this fairy was said to be in a fatal confrontation between it and a strong young man named Eoghainn. In their conflict, they killed one another.

Sources: Briggs, *Encyclopedia of Fairies*, 175; Mackenzie, *Scottish Folk-Lore and Folk Life*, 234; Rose, *Spirits, Fairies, Leprechauns, and Goblins*, 121; Watson, *Place-Names of Ross and Cromarty*, 81, 281

Fidr

Variations: Fid
Fidr was one of the many DWARFS named in the *Voluspa*, the first and best known poem of the *Poetic Edda*, a collection of Old Norse poems dating back to about A.D. 985.

Sources: Crossley-Holland, *Norse Myths*, 183; Sturluson, *Prose Edda*, 27

Fíli

Variations: Fili
Fíli ("file") was one of the many DWARFS named in the *Voluspa*, the first and best known poem of the *Poetic Edda*, a collection of Old Norse poems dating back to about A.D. 985.

Sources: Crossley-Holland, Norse Myths, 183; Daly, *Norse Mythology A to Z*, 22; Sykes, *Who's Who in Non-Classical Mythology*, 53; Wägner, *Asgard and the Gods*, 311

Fin Folk

Variations: Fin Finn, Fin wizards, Finn-Men, Fion, the Lady's Own, Muckle Men, Sea Gardeners
In Cornwall, Scotland, and Wales, the fin folk are small humanoid fay tending to gardens under water in the lochs of Scotland. These anthropomorphic faeries tend to avoid human contact.

Sources: Beck, *Folklore and the Sea*, 220; Kynes, *Sea Magic*, 131; McCoy, *Witch's Guide to Faery Folk*, 220–1

Findchóem

Variations: Finncháem, Fionnchaomh

Originally a goddess in Irish mythology Findchóem was reduced in power and designated to the position of the FAIRY QUEEN of Ulster after the introduction of Christianity. According to lore when she drew a cup of water up from a holy well, it contained a worm in it. Hoping to conceive a hero, she drank the contents, worm and all, and bore a son she named Conall who albeit not as powerful or memorable as his step-brother Cu Chulainn, he was indeed a hero.

Source: Monaghan, *Encyclopedia of Celtic Mythology and Folklore*, 187

Finn

Variations: Fdnn, FINNR

Finn ("magician") was one of the many DWARFS named in the *Voluspa*, the first and best known poem of the *Poetic Edda*, a collection of Old Norse poems dating back to about A.D. 985.

Sources: Smart, *Norroena,* 524; Wilkinson, *Book of Edda called Völuspá*, 12

Finncaev

Variations: Sighe Finncaev

Finncaev ("fair love") is a benevolent and powerful FAIRY QUEEN in Irish lore. She was the tutelary protector of the family the hero Fearghal came from; Finncaev promised her assistance at his utmost need.

Source: Kennedy, *Legendary Fictions of the Irish Celts*, 236

Finnine

Variations: Fennel, Finnen, Fininne, White Lady of Lough Gur

Finnine was the sister of the beautiful FAIRY QUEEN, AINE. As the White Lady of Lough Gur, Finnine was a BANSHEE. Her FAIRY FORT, Cnoc Finnine ("Finnine's Hill") was in Munster, Ireland. The highest hill on the lake shore of Lough Gur was called Knock Fennel ("Hill of Fennel") and was one of her FAIRY FORTS.

Sources: Cork Historical, *Journal of the Cork Historical and Archaeological Society*, 244; Evans-Wentz, *Fairy-Faith in Celtic Countries*, 81; Monaghan, *Encyclopedia of Celtic Mythology and Folklore*, 190

Finnr

Variations: Ivalde

Finnr in Norse mythology is named as being one of the Ijosalfar, the SONS OF IVALDI. These DWARFS were the ones who created many of the magical items of the gods, including the golden wig of Sif; the ship, Skidbladnir; and the spear of Odin. Finnr has a son named Slagfiu who is allied to VIRFIR.

Sources: Grimes, *Norse Myths*, 9, 285; Rydberg, *Teutonic Mythology*, 119

Finvarra

Variations: Fin Bheara, Finbheara, Findabair, Fionnbharr, Finn Bheara, Finvara, Finvarr, Fionnbharr

A FAIRY KING, Finvarra rules over the Connaught Fairies of Ireland and the land of the dead; his fairy wife and queen is named ONAGH (or NUALA, sources conflict) and together they are the supreme king and queen of the SÍDHE (see FAIRY QUEEN). The FAIRY QUEENS AINE, AOIBHINN, and CLIODNA owe their allegiance to him and his queen.

King Finvara rules from his mound or FAIRY FORT in Cnoc Meadha (Knockma) in Galway; he is well known for his benevolence towards humans, providing fine breeding stock, good harvests, and wealth for those not afraid to work with him. Like all of his kind he enjoys plays chess, and no human has ever beaten him at the game. In spite of his good reputation, Finvarra, a known womanizer, is prone to run off with any new bride he desires, especially beautiful mortal women. In one story he even ran off with Etain, the wife of the Lord Kirwan. After her safe return, Finvarra became the guardian spirit and patron of the family and all their possessions.

Sources: Briggs, *Encyclopedia of Fairies*, 125–6; Evan-Wentz, *Fairy Faith in Celtic Countries*, 28, 300; Rose, *Spirits, Fairies, Leprechauns, and Goblins*, 118, 351; Squire, *Celtic Myth and Legend*, 162

Fir Chlis

Variations: Merry Dancers, Nimble Men, Perry Dancers

The fir chlis of the Scottish Highlands are the two clans of fairies who are at war; their fairy chiefs are fighting for the love of a FAIR LADY. When the Aurora Borealis or Northern Lights is bright red it is a pool of blood from the warring chiefs. Heliotrope, also known as bloodstone, is said to be splashed with the blood of the wounded fairies. There is also the belief the fir chlis are fallen angels who were arrested before they arrived on earth.

Sources: Briggs, *Encyclopedia of Fairies*, 177; Campbell, *Superstitions of the Highlands*, 200; Mark, *Gaelic-English Dictionary*, 305

Fir Darrig

Variations: Fear Durgs, Fir Dhearga, Rat Boys

A species of FORMORIAN, the fir darrig ("RED MAN") are malevolent and malicious practical jokers. Possibly originating in Scotland, these Irish fairies are described as looking rather ratlike, having dark hair and skin, fat-bodied, long snouts, and skinny tails. The clothing they wear is extremely shabby and worn, looking as if it were pulled from a sewer. They are carrion eaters, preferring fish. Typically these fairies can be found along polluted coastlines, at coastal ruins, in damp raths, or in marshes near the sea. When they can, they deeply enjoy the warmth of a fireplace.

Some lore claims the fir darrig were once humans, unfortunate individuals who had wandered into FAIRYLAND and are now trying to warn others not to do the same. Unfortunately, their way of thinking has changed and in attempting to warn they end up using deadly tricks in an attempt to convey their message.

Sources: Briggs, *Encyclopedia of Fairies*, 177–8; Guiney, *Brownies and Bogles*, 87; McCoy, *Witch's Guide to Faery Folk*, 221

Firbolgs

Variations: Aithech Tuatha ("rent-paying people"), Fir Bholg, Fir Bolg, Firbourage, Gamanraide

Tradition says there were five different colorizations of Ireland, all of which are said to have originated in Mediterranean. The first two people were the Parthalons and the Nemedians. After a point about half of the nemedians returned to their homeland as slaves. There, they were forced to carry soil from the plains of Thrace up to the mountain side to enrich the quality of soil in the vineyards earning them the name of *firbolgs* ("men of the leather sack"). Eventually, these uncultured people returned to Ireland, ugly, dark eyed and skinned. Forty years later the TUATHA DE DANANN arrived. EOCHAID, the Firbolg king had a premonition of the coming of the TUATHA DE DANANN. Fearful, he decided these newcomers to the land were destined to be his enemy and prepared for war. The TUATHA DE DANANN demanded half of the island be given to them,

and when EOCHAID refused, they went to war. After five days of battle, the Firbolgs who had the advantage of heavy spears and overwhelming numbers lost to the more skilled and highly trained invaders. EOCHAID was slain in the conflict. Conquered and subdued, they were not wholly driven off.

Sources: Bynum, *African Unconscious*, 53; Evan-Wentz, *Fairy Faith in Celtic Countries*, 32; Gwynn, *Fair Hills of Ireland*, 64–9; MacManus, *Story of the Irish Race*, 2–3, 28, 36; Yeats, *Gods and Fighting Men*, 1–3

Fireesin

Variations: Farm Faeries, Farin Faeries, the Harvesters

On the Isle of Man the fireesin are SOLITARY FAIRIES known to assist farmers but are not always successful, as they are not very intelligent. Described as nude and having patches of coarse, brown hair. Hibernating throughout the winter, these fay are seen in fields about to be worked are or being newly worked.

Sources: McCoy, *Witch's Guide to Faery Folk*, 222; Newcomb, *Faerie Treasury*, 50

Fith

Fith was one of the many DWARFS named in the *Voluspa*, the first and best known poem of the *Poetic Edda*, a collection of Old Norse poems dating back to about A.D. 985.

Sources: Daly, *Norse Mythology A to Z*, 22; Sykes, *Who's Who in Non-Classical Mythology*, 53

Fiura

In the fairy lore of Chile, Fiura is a GOBLIN, the only daughter of the Condená and the woman of the virile TRAUCO, a TROLL so ugly woman cannot resist his sexual advance. Fiura is described as ample breasts and long hair but a hideous face. Her breath is so foul it can cause back-aches, lameness or even scar an individual. An irresistible seductress, coquettishly she bathes in waterfall cascades, combing out her dark hair with a crystal comb. Afterwards, she lounges nude on a bed of moss, sunbathing. Those she peruses, be they animals or men are driven insane after her sexual desire is sated. Those who manage to rebuff her have a spell cast upon them

Sources: Eberhart, *Mysterious Creatures*, 555; Roth, *American Elves*, 59

Fjalar

Variations: Fjalarr

Fjalar ("hider, deceiver") was one of the many

DWARFS named in the *Voluspa*, the first and best known poem of the *Poetic Edda*, a collection of Old Norse poems dating back to about A.D. 985. Along with his brother, GALAR, they killed KVASIR and made the Mead of Poetry from his blood.

Sources: Daly, *Norse Mythology A to Z*, 22; Sykes, *Who's Who in Non-Classical Mythology*, 53

Fjolsvidr

Variations: Fjolsvior, Fjolsvinnr

Fjolsvidr ("much wise") was one of the many DWARFS named in the *Voluspa*, the first and best known poem of the *Poetic Edda*, a collection of Old Norse poems dating back to about A.D. 985.

Sources: Acker, *Poetic Edda*, 218; Hastings, *Encyclopedia of Religion and Ethics*, Volume 9, 161; Sturluson, Prose Edda, 34

Flann ua Fedach

Flann ua Fedach was an Irish FAIRY KING. He eloped with the queen of Tara, BECFHOLA after spending only one night with her on the island of Lough Erne.

Sources: Monaghan, *Encyclopedia of Celtic Mythology and Folklore*, 127, 197; Tolstoy, *Oldest British Prose Literature*, 85–6

Flora

Variations: Chloris, Khloris

A NYMPH of springtime and of the mythical Islands of the Blessed in the River Okeanos, Flora is associated with vegetation, especially grains. According to Ovid's six-book epic poem, *Fasti*, Flora was literally swept off of her feet by Zephyrus, a wind of one of the cardinal points. After their marriage Flora carried spring with her; Zephyrus gave her dominion over flowers.

Sources: Fox, *Greek and Roman, 294;* Grimal, *Dictionary of Classical Mythology*, 165; Roman, *Encyclopedia of Greek and Roman Mythology*, 172

The Flower Fairy

In the fairy-tale *Fairy Gifts* by Comte de Caylus the Flower Fairy is said to live in a lovely palace surrounded by a beautiful garden. Said to be charming and kind this fairy is well loved by all who encounter her. Many Princes and Princesses are set by their royal parents to live with her in her beautiful world until they reach adulthood; when the time of their departure is upon them they are each allowed to ask of her for one gift or fairy blessing. The Flower Fairy travels the world in a chariot pulled by butterflies.

Source: Lang, *Green Fairy Book,* 64

The Flower Fairy

During the eighteenth century fairies were associated with flowers and were seen as beautiful, capricious, gentle, willful fertility NATURE SPIRITS. Flower fairies love beauty and luxury and hold in absolute contempt the very idea of economy and thrift. These fairies deeply enjoy bathing in fresh water, flattery, and offerings of food and wine left out for them; no matter how much they drink they cannot become drunk.

Sources: Illes, *Encyclopedia of Spirits*, 404; Stepanich, *Faery Wicca*, Book One, 22, 29

Foawr

The foawr ("GIANT") are hideous, humorless, stone throwing GIANTS on the Isle of Man; they are similar to the FORMORIANS. Foawr hunt and devour cattle. Like many of the fay, they are unable to cross running water.

Sources: Briggs, *Encyclopedia of Fairies*, 178, Briggs, *Fairies in Tradition and Literature*, 77; Rhys, *Celtic Folklore*, 347

The Folk-Tale Fairy

In the eighteenth century fairies were reimagined; described as airy beings, tenuous beings made of nothing more than froth and whimsy. For the first time, books were being written expressly for children and it with the creation of this market in which the concept of the FAIRY GODMOTHER was popularized.

Sources: Haase, *Greenwood Encyclopedia of Folktales and Fairy Tales*, xvi–xviii; Stepanich, *Faery Wicca*, Book One, 22, 29

Follet

Follets live in the homes of those who dwell out in the country of northern France. Although invisible, the pelt people with domestic utensils, sticks, and stones. The voices of the fairies can also be heard. The follet, once they attach to a location cannot be driven off, not even by an exorcism.

Sources: Keightly, *World Guide to Gnomes, Fairies, Elves, and Other Little People*, 468

Folletti

Variations: GRANDINILLI, SALVANELLI, SUMASCAZZO, Wind Knots

On the island of Sicily the folletti are weather fairies so light and small they are almost invisible. Riding upon grasshoppers and playing a game similar to polo, the folletti have backward facing toes and love to call up hail storms; their laughing can be heard over the downpour. Completely oblivious to mortals it appears the folletti call up storms for their own amusement.

Sources: Arrowsmith, *Field Guide to the Little People* 22; McCoy, *Witch's Guide to Faery Folk*, 222–3

Formorian (plural: formori or formorians)

Variations: Fomhoraiah, Fomhoraigh, Formor

At one point in it time the Formorians were the fairy race ruling over the country of Ireland long before the Great Flood and were skilled in the magical arts; they were a warlike people and ruled the land with brutality. The Formorian were literally driven off the land and into the sea by the invading TUATHA DE DANANN. Over time these fairies began to de-evolve, and their physical appearance changed into misshapen bodies with an animal-like appearance; no two were alike, some having one leg while another had three, some had the head of a man while another had the head of a goat. These monstrous Formorians became foul tempered, uncultured, and unintelligent.

Historically, the Formorians, tall and strong, were likely an African sea-going people who had joined with some of the Nemedians, now called FIRBOLGS, as they escaped slavery in Thrace seeking to return to Ireland. The Formorians reach extended far up into the Atlantic, including Ireland, with their strongest beachhead established on Torrey Island. Most authorities place their arrival in Ireland around 1448 B.C.E. (though 1000 B.C.E. is an early date cited); these Formorians may be the origin of the pejorative phrase, "the black Irish." From their launching point on Torrey Island the Formorians both traded and raided with the FIRBOLGS until they encountered the TUATHA DE DANANN in 710 B.C.E.

Sources: Bynum, *African Unconscious*, 53; Bonwick, *Our Nationalities*, 23–4; McCoy, *Witch's Guide to Faery Folk*, 223–4; O'Hanlon, *Irish Folk Lore*, 172

Fornbogi

Fornbogi ("ancient bow") was one of the many DWARFS named in the *Voluspa*, the first and best known poem of the *Poetic Edda*, a collection of Old Norse poems dating back to about A.D. 985.

Sources: Grimes, *Norse Myths*, 7; Wägner, *Asgard and the Gods*, 311

Fossegrin

Variations: Fosse-Grim ("waterfall grim"), STRÖMKARL

The fossegrin are a species of Norwegian fairy guarding waterfalls as the play the harp and sing. Described as looking like small but perfectly formed and physically attractive humans, their feet taper off into misty nothingness. Unpredictable by nature they can change both their mood and gender at a moment's notice.

There was the belief in Norway the fossegrin would teach the art of playing the violin to anyone who sacrificed a white goat to it by throwing the animal into a waterfall that flowed northward on the night of Holy Thursday. The fossegrin would then appear and take the right hand of its new pupil and pull it over the strings of the instrument until all the blood ran from their fingers. Once this was accomplished the person would be able to play with the skill of a master, his music making the trees dance and the rivers stay in their course.

Sources: Heron-Allen, *Violin-Making, as it Was and Is*, 16–17; Keightly, *World Guide to Gnomes, Fairies, Elves, and Other Little People*, 152; McCoy, *Witch's Guide to Faery Folk*, 224

Fountain Fairies

Variations: NAIAD

Fountain fairies, as Homer the greatest ancient Greek epic poet and author of the *Iliad* and the *Odyssey* calls them, preside after perennial springs. Some examples of fountain fairies are: AGANIPPE, ALKIPPE, BYBLIS, DIUTURNA, EUNICA, GARGAPHIA, GLAUKE, and JUTURNA; a few examples of the species of fountain are the CAMENAE, the CHESME, and the CRINAEAE.

Sources: Chopra, *Academic Dictionary of Mythology*, 198; Lambe, *Exact and Circumstantial History of the Battle of Floddon*, 89; Smith, *Dictionary of Greek and Roman Biography and Mythology*, 59

Fraegr

Fraegr ("famous") was one of the many DWARFS named in the *Voluspa*, the first and best known poem of the *Poetic Edda*, a collection of Old Norse poems dating back to about A.D. 985.

Sources: Daly, *Norse Mythology A to Z*, 22; Wilkinson, *Book of Edda called Völuspa*, 12

Frag

Frag was one of the many DWARFS named in the *Voluspa*, the first and best known poem of the *Poetic Edda*, a collection of Old Norse poems dating back to about A.D. 985.

Sources: Crossley-Holland, *Norse Myths*, 183; Smart, *Norroena*, 541

Frar

Variations: Frarr

Frar ("swift") was one of the many DWARFS named in the *Voluspa*, the first and best known poem of the *Poetic Edda*, a collection of Old Norse poems dating back to about A.D. 985.

Sources: Crossley-Holland, *Norse Myths*, 183; Daly, *Norse Mythology A to Z*, 22; Wilkinson, *Book of Edda called Völuspá*, 12

Frau Holle

Variations: Fray Holle, Holle, HYLDEMOER ("elder mother"), Mother Holle

In Germany Frau Holle ("mother spirit") was likely at one time a goddess reduced to the status of fairy. She has the ability to confer fertility on women who wish to conceive a child. Frau Holle is believed to live on the bottom of a pond where she tends to her beautiful garden of flowers and fruits; oftentimes this fay will gift visitors to her pond with cakes or pastries. Babies are also said to be delivered up from her pond. Frau Holle will take advantage of children who walk to near to the edge of her territory and pull them down into the water with her. Good children are said to live a life of fortune and well-being beneath the waves while she will transform naughty children into CHANGELINGS for later use.

An extremely tidy individual, it is said when it snows Frau Holle is shaking out her feather bed. She will reward diligent spinners with new needles and doing some of their work for them while punishing lazy spinners with dirtying and tangling their flax. Housewives who do their work well will sometimes find a silver coin on the bottom of their pail, placed there by Frau Holle as a reward for their hard work.

Each year she takes a walk through the fields and meadows making them bountiful, however she will also lead her hounds on a WILD HUNT through the forest; her pack will tear apart any unfortunate human or benign fairy they come across.

Sources: Altmann, *Seven Swabians*, 211–12; Ashliman, *Fairy Lore*, 131; Keightly, *World Guide to Gnomes, Fairies, Elves, and Other Little People*, 93; Rose, *Spirits, Fairies, Leprechauns, and Goblins*, 154, 351

Frau Wachholder

A GOBLIN and HAMADRYAD of the Juniper tree, Frau Wachholder of German fairy lore is called upon to make thieves give up their ill-gotten gains. It is believed if the person who was robbed goes to a juniper tree and bends down one of its branches to the ground and pins it there with a stone the thief will present himself and return the item he stole.

Sources: Elworthy, *Evil Eye*, 103; Porteous, *Forest Folklore*, 93–4; Rose, *Spirits, Fairies, Leprechauns, and Goblins*, 120–1, 351

Frau Welt

Frau Welt is a fairy paramour from the ecclesiastical and secular folklore of medieval Germany. She was said to visit brothers, clerics, and monks in their monastic houses. From a distance she appears to be a beautiful woman but when someone approaches too close she turns her body to reveal her other side, a façade of rotten flesh covered in maggots, snakes, and worms. In some German and Bohemian manuscripts dating from the fifteenth century Frau Welt is depicted as an amalgamated female, having human arms, head, and torso but each animal appendage representing one of the cardinal sins. The tiara on her head has peacock feathers; a charm worn on her neck reads *Luxuria*. Inscribed on her arms is the word *Accadia*; she has bat wings and stands upon one leg ending in an avian claw marked *Vita* while her other leg, that of the long neck and head of dragon labeled *Mors* chews upon it.

Sources: Cohen, *Animals as Disguised Symbols in Renaissance Art*, 224–5; Rose, *Spirits, Fairies, Leprechauns, and Goblins*, 121, 351; Žižek, *Plague of Fantasies*, 66

Frid (plural: fridean)

Variations: Frideag, Fridich

In the Highlands of Scotland the fridean are said to be fairy creatures dwelling inside rocks and living off of breadcrumbs and milk split on the ground. Glen Liadail in South Uist is believed to have a colony of frid live there; although these fay are friendly to the locals who live there they are resentful of strangers. Anyone who wished to travel through their glen was advised to sing a propitiatory song before entering.

Sources: Briggs, *Encyclopedia of Fairies*, 182; Rose, *Spirits, Fairies, Leprechauns, and Goblins*, 121; Thompson, *Supernatural Highlands*, 145–6

Fridur

Fridur ("beautiful" or "fine") was the beautiful daughter of the GIANT, THIASSE and the human woman, Dofri. Her father was slain by the hero, Suaforlami with his magical sword, Tirfing. With her father slain, Fridur was taken by Suaforlami.

Sources: Brown, *Early English and Norse Studies*, 143; Keightly, *World Guide to Gnomes, Fairies, Elves, and Other Little People*, 72; Tibbits, *Folk-Lore and Legends, Scandinavian*, 190

Frosti

Frosti ("frosty") was one of the many DWARFS named in the *Voluspa*, the first and best known poem of the *Poetic Edda*, a collection of Old Norse poems dating back to about A.D. 985.

Sources: Crossley-Holland, *Norse Myths*, 183; Daly, *Norse Mythology A to Z*, 22; Sykes, *Who's Who in Non-Classical Mythology*, 53

Fuamnach

Variations: Fuaieach, Fuaimnech

Fuamnach ("the Resonant") was a powerful FAIRY QUEEN; she was married to the FAIRY KING, MIDIR the Proud, son of the DAGDA, one of the TUATHA DE DANANN. Many years into their marriage MIDIR took a second, younger wife named EDAIN. Enraged Fuamnach used her magical talents to turn her rival first into a pool of water and then a purple butterfly kept aloft in a perpetual wind, but still MIDIR was in love with his young bride. EDAIN eventually landed in the palace of Angus, the god of love; he was able to transform her back into a beautiful young woman each day from dusk to dawn. The two fell in love and became lovers. When Fuamnach heard this she was more anger than ever and transformed EDAIN into a fly and used a tempest to blow her out to sea. Blind with fury at the loss of his love, Angus killed Fuamnach and took her head as a trophy.

Sources: Evan-Wentz, *Fairy Faith in Celtic Countries*, 375; Monaghan, *Encyclopedia of Celtic Mythology and Folklore*, 201; Mountain, *Celtic Encyclopedia*, 698; Rolleston, *Celtic Myths and Legends*, 156

Fuath (plural: fuathan or fauths)

In Scottish lore the fuath ("hate") is a generic term applied to any type of WATER SPIRIT liveing in water, be it fresh or salt water, a loch, river or sea. On occasion this title is given to a Highland or NATURE SPIRIT, but when this happens, the being is always malaligned. Descriptions of fuaths vary widely, but generally speaking, they look like terribly deformed humans covered with long yellow fur or just have a mane running down their back. Typically dressed in green, spikes, tails, and webbed feet are also common features however they are rarely seen because of the remote regions they live in. Susceptible to sunlight, the fuath are far more mindful of cold steel, as it will kill them instantly. Interestingly, they be-come restless when crossing a stream. Although the fuath are similar to the KELPIE or UISGES in Northern Ireland, they will intermarry with humans; their offspring will have the telltale sign of sporting a mane, tail, or webbed toes. Fairies who would fall into this category are the BEHIR, CAOINEAG, FACHAN, FIDEAL, GLAISTIG, PEALLAIDH, SHELLYCOAT, URISK, and the VOUGH, to name but a few.

Sources: Briggs, *Fairies and Traditions in Literature*, 52; Illes, *Encyclopedia of Spirits*, 420; Macleod, *Dictionary of the Gaelic Language*, 208; Rose, *Spirits, Fairies, Leprechauns, and Goblins*, 121

Fullangr

Fullangr ("fully long" or "tall enough") was one of the many DWARFS named in the *Voluspa*, the first and best known poem of the *Poetic Edda*, a collection of Old Norse poems dating back to about A.D. 985.

Source: Anderson, *A Certain Text*, 175

Fundin

Variations: Fundinn

Fundin ("found") was one of the many DWARFS named in the *Voluspa*, the first and best known poem of the *Poetic Edda*, a collection of Old Norse poems dating back to about A.D. 985.

Sources: Crossley-Holland, Norse Myths, 183; Daly, *Norse Mythology A to Z*, 22; Sykes, *Who's Who in Non-Classical Mythology*, 53

Furies

Variations: Angry Ones, Dirae, Erinyes ("disturbers of the mind"), Errinys, Eumenides, Furies, Kindly Ones, Night Born Sisters, Strong Ones

The Furies of Greek mythology, three sisters named ALECTO ("envy" or "never ending"), MEGAERA ("envious anger" or " slaughter"), and TISIPHONE ("face of retaliation" or "rage") are the opposite of the MUSES who were associated with upholding cosmic order and proper behavior; the Furies primary concern was with the retribution for the killing of family members. Linked with darkness, death, night and the Underworld, the furies drink human blood rather than wine. Born the daughters of Gia ("earth") and Uranus ("heaven") they find the practice of human sacrifice reprehensible and will lash out their anger on those who practice it. Described as having a ghastly physical appearance is comparable to the Gorgons, the Furies wear black robes, their eyes ooze and their breath reeks. In art the Furies are depicted as sucking the life-blood out of their victims, gnawing on flesh. Self-imposed outcast of Olympia the Furies are associated with death, pain, torture, and violence. Although the opposite of the clean and beautiful Olympians the Furies play an important role in Greek mythology, as without these unclean spirits mortals would have no fear of punishment and live in total anarchy. When the Furies punished someone with obvious compassion they were called the Eumenides ("mild").

Sources: Illes, *Encyclopedia of Spirits*, 390; Keightly, *World Guide to Gnomes, Fairies, Elves, and Other Little People*, 495; Robbins, *Elements of Mythology*, 106–7; Roman, *Encyclopedia of Greek and Roman Mythology*, 173

Füttermarinchen

A subspecies of the WICHTLN from the folklore of southern Germany the Füttermarinchen are a type of house-fairy, similar to the BROWNIE of Scottish lore, who specialize in feeding farm animals.

Source: Arrowsmith, *Field Guide to the Little People*, 51–3

Fuwch Gyfeiliorn

Variations: The Cow, Stray Cow, LLYN BARFOG, Y Fuwch Frech, Y Fuwch Gyfeiliorn

In Welsh folklore Fuwch Gyfeiliorn was a FAIRY ANIMAL, one of the LLYN BARFOG; One day a farmer was fortunate enough to have one of the FAIRY ANIMALS fall in love with a bull from his herd; he named this fairy cow Fuwch Gyfeiliorn. The cow birthed the most amazing calves and gave the most delicious milk which was churned into the tastiest butter and cheese. The farmer grew rich off of the proceeds his fairy cow but the time came when he left it was too old to be of any further profit and began fattening it up for market. When the time of Fuwch Gyfeiliorn killing came people from all over the region came to witness the event. The butcher's bludgeon hit the correct place on the cows head but magically passed harmlessly through the cow but knocked over nine men who stood close watching. From a crag which overlooked the lake the crowd saw a woman dressed in green and heard her call out "Come yellow anvil, stray horns, speckled one of the lake, and of the hornless Dodlin, arise and come home." Not only did Fuwch Gyfeiliorn begin to make her way into the lake in response to the call but all of her progeny going back four generations; only one cow remained behind and

it turned raven black. The farmer, now financially ruined, drowned himself in the lake but the black cow became the progenitor of the Welsh black cattle.

Sources: Narváez, *Good People*, 163; Rhys, *Celtic Folklore Welsh and Manx*, Volume 1, 244–5; Thomas, *Welsh Fairy Book*, 79–80; Sikes, *British Goblins*, 39–40

Gabriel Hounds

Variations: Cron Annwn, Cwn Annwn, Dogs of Hell, Gabble Retchets, Gabriel Ratchets, Gabriel Ratchet's Hounds, Gobble-ratches, Gytrash, Heath Hounds, Hell Hounds, Sky Yelpers, WISH HOUNDS, Wisk, Yell Hounds, Yesk, Yell Hounds, Yeth Hounds

Similar to CWN ANNWFN (see ANNWN, HOUNDS OF) in Welsh fairy lore, the Gabriel hounds are a pack of spectral hounds prowling Durham, Lancashire, North Devon, Staffordshire and Yorkshire, England led by the archangel Gabriel when the WILD HUNT is under way. Described as being overly large and having red ears and eyes, their bodies glow eerily green or white, they fly through the air; sometimes the hounds are said to have a human head. A Gabriel hound is believed to be created when an unbaptized baby dies. If seen hovering over a house, it is reputed these spectral hounds foretell death for one of its occupants.

Sometimes the cries and the wing beats of geese Bean Goose (*Anser segetum*) flying at night are mistakenly misinterpreted as the sounding of the hounds.

Sources: Allardice, *Myths, Gods and Fantasy*, 88; Briggs, *Encyclopedia of Fairies*, 183; Chambers, *Book of Days*, 430; Wright, *English Dialect Dictionary*, 530

Gahonga

The gahonga ("stone throwers") are one of three types of mountain dwelling NYMPH or *JOGAH* ("DWARF people") from the folklore of the Iroquois people of North America; the GANDAYAH and the OHDOWS are the other two. Gahonga live in rivers in rocky terrain. Remarkably strong they are called stone throwers because they are fond of playing with boulders as a child would plays balls.

Sources: Beauchamp, *Iroquois Folk Lore*, 46; Chopra, *Academic Dictionary of Mythology*, 113; Gray, *Mythology of All Races*, Volume 10, 28

Galar

Variations: Galarr

Galar ("chanter") was one of the many

DWARFS named in the *Voluspa*, the first and best known poem of the *Poetic Edda*, a collection of Old Norse poems dating back to about A.D. 985. Along with his brother, FJALAR, killed KVASIR and made the Mead of Poetry from his blood.

Sources: Daly, *Norse Mythology A to Z*, 22; Sykes, *Who's Who in Non-Classical Mythology*, 53

Galatea

Variations: Galataea, Galateia

A sea–NYMPH, Galatea ("milk white") was one of the named NEREID, the daughters of Nerues and DORIS, one of the OCEANID; she lived off the coast of Sicily. According to Hesiod Galatea is "beauteous." The object of the attention of Polyphemus, a crude and monstrous Cyclops, Galatea spurned his affection, as she was in love with the young and hansom Acis. Polyphemus would have crushed the youth to death but Galatea saved his live by turning him into a river; unfortunately, she was not able to turn him back into a human. In a different version of the mythology, Polyphemus eventually won the love of Galatea and together they had a son named Galas (or Galates, sources conflict); their son went on to become the founder of the Gaul people.

Sources: Apollodorus, *Apollodorus' Library and Hyginus' Fabulae*, 95; Bell, *Bell's New Pantheon or Historical Dictionary of the Gods*, 112; Gould, *Historic Magazine and Notes and Queries*, Volume 14, 212; Hesiod, *Works of Hesiod, Callimachus, and Theognis*, 15

Galaxaura

Born one of the 3,000 daughters of the Titians, Oceanus and Tethys, Galaxaura was one of the named OCEANIDS from Greek mythology.

Sources: Avant, *Mythological Reference*, 296; Hesiod, *Homeric Hymns and Homerica*, 105

Galaxaure

Born one of the 3,000 daughters of the Titians, Oceanus and Tethys, Galaxaure ("the charmer" or "like the refreshing coolness of a shady stream") was one of the named OCEANIDS from Greek mythology.

Sources: Boswell, *What Men or Gods Are These*, 58; Hesiod, *Works of Hesiod, Callimachus, and Theognis*, 20; Westmoreland, *Ancient Greek Beliefs*, 24

Galene

A sea–NYMPH, Galene ("calm" or "tranquility") was the NEREID of calm seas from Greek mythology. According to Hesiod she was also associated as a *maenad*, one of the female nurses

dressed in special attire who served in the circle of Dionysus (Bacchus).

Sources: Birch, *History of Ancient Pottery*, Volume 1, 135; Collignon, *Manual of Mythology*, 187; Hesiod, *Works of Hesiod, Callimachus, and Theognis*, 15; Stafford, *Personification in the Greek World*, 215, 223

Gallena

A sea–NYMPH from Greek mythology, Gallena, was the NEREID of the rock from Greek mythology; she was born the daughter of Nerues and DORIS.

Source: Betham, *Transactions of the Royal Irish Academy*, Volume 17, 88

Galley-Beggar

A ferocious skeleton apparition from Somerset and Suffolk in the North of England the Galley-Beggar carries its own severed head while walking about terrifying anyone who sees it. Like the scream like a BANSHEE of Scotland, the galley-begger has a scream capable of freezing a man where he stands. Like the BULLBEGGER of Surrey, England the galley-begger seems to exist for the sole purpose of frightening people. Most often this fairy is sighted tobogganing from Over Stowey to Nether Stowey, its head tucked under its arm.

Sources: Allardice, *Myths, Gods and Fantasy*, 88–9; Briggs, *Encyclopedia of Fairies*, 183; Maberry, *They Bite*, 255; Rose, *Spirits, Fairies, Gnomes, and Goblins*, 183

Gally-Trot

Variations: Churchyard Dog, Galleytrot, Hell Beast, Swooning Shadow

The gally-trot is a FAIRY ANIMAL from British lore, typically said to roam in Bath-Slough and Woodbridge; it is very similar to the BARGUEST and the BLACK SHUCK but is described as looking like a shaggy, shadowy white dog (rather than black) about the size of a bullock. Fearsome to behold its soulful and terrible howl is heard before it is ever seen, typically in graveyards or along the side of lonesome roads. Apparently harmless, the gally-trot is unable to actually catch anyone who it chases.

Sources: Buckland, *Weiser Field Guide to Ghosts*, 25; Hartland, *Gloucestershire*, 85; Wright, *Rustic Speech and Folk-Lore*, 194

Gan Ceanach

Variations: GEANCANACH, Gean-Canach, Gean-Cannah, Gancanagh, Ganconer

In the folklore of Ireland and Scotland the solitary Gan Ceanach ("love talker") appears in secluded glens as a debonair little man smoking on a *dudeen* (clay pipe). He casts no shadow and a mist lingers near him. Birds stop singing when Gan Ceanach is near. It is unlucky for a young man to run into this fairy, as they will then be compelled to spend all of their money of trinkets and presents for their ladies. Women find themselves seduced by his conversation, gentle voice, and twinkling black eyes. If a maiden should ever kiss Gan Ceanach he will instantly disappear leaving his victim to pine to death in his absence.

Sources: Briggs, *Encyclopedia of Fairies*, 183–4; Evan-Wentz, *Fairy Faith in Celtic Countries*, 30; McCoy, *Witch's Guide to Faery Folk*, 226; Rose, *Spirits, Fairies, Leprechauns, and Goblins*, 124, 351; Squire, *Celtic Myth and Legend*, 163

Gandalf

Variations: Gandalfr, Gandálfr ("wand ELF")

Gandalf ("magic ELF") was one of the many DWARFS named in the *Voluspa*, the first and best known poem of the *Poetic Edda*, a collection of Old Norse poems dating back to about A.D. 985.

Sources: Crossley-Holland, Norse Myths, 183; Daly, *Norse Mythology A to Z*, 22; Sykes, *Who's Who in Non-Classical Mythology*, 53; Wägner, *Asgard and the Gods*, 311

Gandayah

The Gandayah are one of three types of mountain dwelling NYMPH or *JOGAH* ("DWARF people") from the folklore of the Iroquois people of North America; the GAHONGA and the OHDOWS are the other two. Gandayah are the NATURE SPIRITS of the earth's fertility. The gandayah create *dewcup charms* that attract fruits and grains and causes them to bloom and sprout. These NYMPHS will also release fish caught in fishermen's traps.

Sources: Alexander, *North American [mythology]*, 28; Chopra, *Academic Dictionary of Mythology*, 114; Converse, *Myths and Legends of the New York State Iroquois*, 101; Gray, *Mythology of All Races*, Volume 10, 28

Gandharvas

Variations: Gandhabba, Gandharbas

In India the gandharvas are a species of shy, small fairies living underground in caves; they are renown for their amazing musical talent. Similar to the NYMPHS of Grecian mythology the gandharvas are male NATURE SPIRITS of the wilderness, husbands of the Apsaras; they were created by Brahma from the stray droplets of water that created the gods and men. Associated with flowers and trees they live within the scent of bark, blossoms, and sap. The gandharvas are always described as being part animal, typically a bird or a horse, but they are always beautiful and artful dancers. The chieftain of the gandharvas is named Timbaru.

According to Hindu law, a Gandharva marriage is one contracted by mutual consent and without formal rituals. One of the lowest-ranking DEVAS in Buddhist theology the gandharva are capable of flight and when the opportunity presents itself will disturb a meditation monk.

Sources: Keightly, *World Guide to Gnomes, Fairies, Elves, and Other Little People*, 510; McCoy, *Witch's Guide to Faery Folk*; 226–7; MacDonnell, *Vedic Mythology*, 134–7

Gangana

In the fairy-tale *The Punishment of the Fairy Gangans* from the collection *Le Cabinet de Fees* the fairy Gangana made an arrangement with the king and queen wherein their son, Petaldo, would marry her niece, if ever she were to have one.

Source: Lang, *Olive Fairy Book*, 305–27

Gans

The gans are a species of mountain OREAN NATURE SPIRIT from the folklore of the Apache people of North America; neither good nor evil but sent to teach the Apache the art of civilization, the gan are described as being vaporous in form. Shaman would offer prayers to the gans asking them to bring good fortune, improve agriculture, protect wildlife, and drive away evil spirits. In religious ceremonies four dancers will each wear a colored headdress to represent one of four different types of gan: black for eagle feather, blue for turquoise, white for pollen, and yellow for deerskin.

Sources: Chopra, *Academic Dictionary of Mythology*, 116; McCoy, *Witch's Guide to Faery Folk*, 227–8; Waldman, *Encyclopedia of Native American Tribes*, 16

Gargaphia

Variations: Gargaphie, Oeroe, Plataia

Gargaphia was a NYMPH of the Gargaphian spring in ancient Greece near Plataia; this was the fountain where the goddess Artemis (Diana) was disturbed while bathing by the hero, Aktaion.

Sources: Cox, *Mythology of the Aryan Nations*, Volume 2, 288; Larson, *Greek Nymphs: Myth, Cult, Lore*, 142

Geancanach

In Ireland and Scotland the geancanach is a PIXY-like fay said to be the guardian of the hearth and home. Described as standing only a few inches tall, it had large blue slanted eyes and long, pointed ears. The geancanach are also winged but would rather dematerialize in one place and rematerialized in another. These milk-drinking fay, albeit helpful do enjoy playing pranks from time to time. Like the BROWNIE, they are most active at night.

Sources: Evans-Wentz, *Fairy-Faith in Celtic Countries*, 40; McCoy, *Witch's Guide to Faery Folk*; 228; Woodfield, *Celtic Lore and Spellcraft of the Dark Goddess*, 166

Geirolul

In Nordic and Teutonic mythology Geirolul ("Spear-alimentrix") was one of the named VAL-KYRIES, a NYMPH of battle. Always depicted as beautiful women who are sometimes immortal, they are the attendants of the god, Odin.

Sources: Grimm *Teutonic Mythology*, Volume 1, 421; Sigfusson, *Elder Eddas of Saemund Sigfusson Younger Eddas of Snorre Sturleson*, 23, 338

Genderuwa

Variations: Gandaruwo, Genderuwo, Gendruwo, Setan

Originally from Persian mythology the genderuwa was believed to be a type of haunting spirit created when a person died in a violent way. When the genderuwa came over into Javanese lore it is seen as a benevolent FAIRY ANIMAL that usually remains invisible. When the genderuwa appears it is sometimes described as looking like a large red and black furred ape although on a few rare occasions it is described as taking the form of a dignified old man dressed all in white; in this form it has been known to seduce women. In either form, the genderuwa can change its size, shrinking down to as small as just a few centimeters tall. During the day it may take the form of a predatory beast, such as a bird of prey, crocodile, snake, or tiger. Living in areas around large trees, old damp buildings, and water; male genderuwa are called *memedis* and females are call *wéwé*.

Sources: Bruun, *Asian Perceptions of Nature*, 51–2; Geertz, *Religion of Java*, 16, 18

Genesta

In the fairy-tale *Heart of Ice* written by Comte de Caylus, the fairy Genesta took under her protection and became the FAIRY GODMOTHER of a prince. On the day of the child's christening he was about to have placed on him a dozen or more undesirable traits by a unknown fairy from a distant land who claimed to have been slighted by the child's parents. Genesta had the ability to fly through the air as if skating on ice, send dreams, feed people food while they slept, teaches knowledge of magical herbs, enchant people so they will see what she wants them to see, and place adventures in the paths of her favored people so they would develop into brave, courageous individuals with a good character.

Source: Lang, *Green Fairy Book*, 108–09, 127

Genie (plural: genies)

Variations: DJINN, Dyinyinga, Genii

From the demonology of the Mende people of Sierra Leone comes the genie. Originally Mende ancestral spirits, genies evolved into generic good or evil spirits, then NATURE SPIRITS, and in some places, demonic spirits. They are described as looking like a person of Portuguese descent and being white skinned. Genies live deep in the forest or on isolated mountain sides or wherever Islam is practiced.

Genies have well-defined human emotions and passions. They are highly receptive to flattery and are notoriously fickle, a quality they especially share with the fairies of Europe. Genies have the ability to shape-shift into animals and people and are also capable of causing good fortune to enter into a person's life by use of their innate magical abilities. Occasionally they will have sexual relations with humans or visit one while they sleep, but a genie will only attack when it is displeased with the personality of the Mende it encounters. There is no formulated approach on how to deal with a genie who has been angered except to act boldly. If dominance is not quickly established, it will claim dominance and have power over you. If this should happen, to escape out from under a genie's power, a sacrifice of something dearly loved or treasured must be offered, such as the life of your firstborn son. If a person becomes possessed by a genie, a magical Mende ceremony must be performed.

Sources: Forde, *African Worlds*, 115, 124, 137; Hughes, *Dictionary of Islam*, 135; Rose, *Spirits, Fairies, Gnomes, and Goblins*, 96

Genius Cucullatus (plural: genii cucullati)

Genii cucullati ("hooded spirits") are a species of NATURE SPIRITS which may have originally been a now forgotten fertility goddess from ancient Celtic beliefs but evolved into a masculine figure that appeared all throughout the Romano-Celtic region from Britain to Pannonia, particularly in Gaul and Germany. Described as DWARFS wearing Gaulish hooded cloaks they are depicted in art and sculpture usually in sets of threes. The hood the fairy wears is sometimes depicted in sculptures as being overtly phallic, further evidence these spirits were associated with fertility. Traditionally an exposed phallus is a ward against the evil eye, promotes personal fertility, and prevents unnatural deaths from occurring. The male genii cucullati are associated with the supernatural world and believed to be invisible to the eyes of mortal men.

It is possible the Genii cucullati are the progenitor of the BROWNIE, a domestic fay bringing fertility and prosperity to a family.

Sources: Aldhouse-Green, *Gods of Roman Britain*, 55–6; Bord, *Fairies*, 110; Henig, 46; Illes, *Encyclopedia of Spirits*, 438–9

Gentle Annis

Variations: Gentle Annie

On the FIRTH of Cromarty in the Highlands of Scotland Gentle Annis the weather spirit and a HAG who controls the southwesterly gales and winds in the region. The terrain of the Firth is guarded against wind on the north and east by tall hill but a gap allows sporadic and violent wind bursts to rush through earning the fay a reputation for treachery. It has been speculated by some folklorists Gentle Annis is an aspect of CAILLEAC BHUER, as her name implies an association to the Celtic goddess Anu whose own origins lay in BLACK ANNIS of the Dane Hills.

Sources: Briggs, *Encyclopedia of Fairies*, 185; Monaghan, *Encyclopedia of Celtic Mythology and Folklore*, 210; Rose, *Spirits, Fairies, Gnomes, and Goblins*, 126

The Gentry

Variations: The Shining Ones, SÍDHE

In Ireland the Gentry (*daoine uaisle*) was a euphemistic term applied to the most noble of the fairy tribes; they lived in the hills and mountains. Described as being large, near seven foot tall, and glowing with a white aura, these fay were worshiped and shown a great deal of respect for fear of their wrathful retribution. They both sang and spoke in a beautifuly silvery voice. Some people hold the belief the Gentry were the spirits or soul of their departed loved ones while others felt these fay originated on another planet or realm.

The Gentry, as a race, have always taken a great interest in human affairs and were moved to action when matters of justice and right came into question. It was believed whichever side they favored in battle, won. Military-aristocratic, the Gentry had the ability to cause paralysis in humans but seldom did so, as they craved Salvation; they also had eye-sight so keen they could see what lay buried beneath the earth.

When one of the Gentry happens upon a person they find to be particularly interesting they would kidnap the person and transform their body into one like their own; this transformation was permanent so long as the individual never returned home. The Gentry stay eternally young and never die.

Sources: Ashliman, *Fairy Lore*, 144, 146; Evans-Wentz, *Fairy-Faith in Celtic Countries*, 46–47, 62; Monaghan, *Encyclopedia of Celtic Mythology and Folklore*, 168

Geroid

Variations: Geroid Iarla, Earl Fitzgerald, the Red Earl

Born the son of the Earl of Desmond and the FAIRY QUEEN, AINE, Geroid was believed to live in the underwater kingdom located beneath Lough Gur. Once every seven years on a full moon, Geroid would emerge from the lake as a fairy spirit mounted upon a great, white horse, leading a fairy cavalcade (see FAIRY RADE).

Sources: Avant, *Mythological Reference*, 69; Evan-Wentz, *Fairy Faith in Celtic Countries*, 79; Monaghan, *Encyclopedia of Celtic Mythology and Folklore*, 211

Gerr

Variations: Geer, Geri, Grer

In Norse mythology the Gerr ("covetous" or "greedy") is one of the four BRISINGAMEN DWARFS who created the prized necklace for the goddess Freyr (see also ALFRIGG, BERLING, and DVALIN). He once spent a night with the goddess discussing and debating the many aspects of the world.

Sources: Pentikäinen, *Shamanism and Northern Ecology*, 87, 94; Sigfusson, 197; Thornton, *Kings, Chronologies, and Genealogies*, 43

Ghilan

Variations: Algul, Ghillan, Ghoul, Ghul

From Islamic mythology and mentioned in the Koran are two genuses of DJINN. The first is divided into five classes: the Afreet (IFRIT), Ghilan, JANN, MARID, and the SHAITAN. In their genus, they are the fourth strongest of the DJINN.

The ghilan are born the children of IBLIS. They

have innate magical abilities and are expert shape-shifters; no matter the form they choose to appear in, they will always have hooves rather than feet. They use their shape-shifting to take on the appearance of a beautiful woman to lure a traveler away from his companions, at which point the ghilan will kill and consume him. Grave robbers, ghilan live in cemeteries. They are capable of being destroyed, but they must be hit hard enough to be killed with a single blow; a second assault will restore a ghilan to full health.

Sources: Houtsma, *E.J. Brill's First Encyclopaedia of Islam*, Volume 3, 165; Oesterley, *Immortality and the Unseen World*, 33

Ghillie Dhu

Variations: Gille Dubh ("dark haired lad"), Gillee Doo, Gillee Yoo, Ghillie Yu

In Scottish folklore Ghillie Dhu ("dark shoe") is a nocturnal SOLITARY FAIRY acting as a guardian of the trees, much like a DRYAD or NATURE SPIRIT, in the area of Gairloch and Loch a Druing; it is especially protective of birch trees. Described as having dark hair and clothed in leaves and moss, much like the GREEN MAN, this fairy is not fond of humans and will capture anyone who endangers his trees. Offenders are either crushed to death in his strong, green arms, becoming compost or, by use of fairy magic, enslaved for all eternity.

Sources: Briggs, *Encyclopedia of Fairies*, 186; Froud, *Faeries*, 64; Maberry, *Cryptopedia*, 108; McCoy, *Witch's Guide to Faery Folk,* 229

Gianes

In the fairy lore of northern Italy, more specifically Sardinia, the gaines are a female species of SOLITARY FAIRY; they are master weavers. They are found in living in the cliffs, forests, and hills. By use of their spinning wheel they are able to tell the future by scrying into the wheel as it turns; they also can divine the location of buried treasures. Shy and fearful of man-made machines, these woodland fay have been known to assist humans.

In the original mythology of the gianes it was said these beautiful fairies stood around five foot tall, had breasts long enough to place over their shoulders, and fingernails made of steel. Although otherwise beautiful, they had a difficult time finding a proper mate for themselves as the DWARFS are too small for them and GIANTS are too brute-like. Driven into a sexual frenzy when a mortal man happened across one of them, he was quickly pounced upon and raped while the

giane drained him dry of his blood. Three days later she would give birth to a fairy half-breed having a taste for raw meat. During its infancy the baby was carried in a wicker basket its mother carried on her back.

In modern lore there are male and female gianes and they are both described as being small, around ten inches high, and overly shy. Gianes of both genders wear brightly colored peasant clothing and lavish gold, hand crafted jewelry; male gianes wear and thick furs and females wear handkerchief on their head. In well furnished caves these magnificent weavers live off of a diet of herbs.

Sources: Source: Arrowsmith, *Field Guide to the Little People*, 103-4; Euvino, *Complete Idiot's Guide to Italian History and Culture*, 274; McCoy, *Witch's Guide to Faery Folk*, 229-30

Giant

Variations: Iöunn, OGRES

Giants are a species of FAIRY ANIMAL common to most of the world's mythologies. Universally described as being larger and taller than a humans, be it by a few or several hundred feet, there the similarity ends. Depending on the culture, religion, and reason for having a giant in a tale, these beings come in a wide variety of characteristics, descriptions, and personalities. Giants have been wizened war chiefs capable of leading armies while others of their species are barely intelligent enough to talk and walk at the same time, easily out witted by the Simple Jacks of folklore. Some have said to be gods and the creators of the universe and pother are the proginators of the great noble families, while others yet are more animal-like, living in caves, barely clothed in furs, wielding a misshapen club, and robbing the countryside of its goats and sheep.

Having great strength is common among giants as well, but this is typically in proportion to their size and not otherwise remarkable. Traditionally, they represent an obstacle a Hero must overcome and defeat on his quest. Many tales have characters in them who are described as being a half-giant, where one of its parents was a human.

Giants, like the rest of the fay, are good or evil depending on their motivation; for instance, Paul Bunyan from American folklore is a giant who is helpful to humans, assisting in taming the west and bringing civilization to mankind. Also, like the fay, many natural landmarks are named after them, for giants are often accredited with having created islands, mountains, rivers, and standing stones.

It appears whenever a giant is particularly

bloodthirsty, cruel and preys on humans to consume for their flesh it is called an OGRE; this would be incorrect, for although an OGRE can be gigantic in size, not all are, most are in fact human size but monstrous in appearance due to their physical deformities.

Giants play a particularly important role in reek and Norse mythology, representing the force of nature and violent natural phenomena.

Sources: Briggs, Encyclopedia of Fairies, 186–90; Daniels, *Encyclopedia of Superstitions, Folklore, and the Occult Sciences of the World*, 1375–8; Keightly, *World Guide to Gnomes, Fairies, Elves, and Other Little People*, 321; Leeming, *Oxford Companion to World Mythology*, 149; Rose, *Giants, Monsters, and Dragons*, 136–9

Ginnarr

Variations: Ginar, Ginnar

Ginnarr ("deceiver") was one of the many DWARFS named in the *Voluspa*, the first and best known poem of the *Poetic Edda*, a collection of Old Norse poems dating back to about A.D. 985.

Sources: Crossley-Holland, Norse Myths, 183; Daly, *Norse Mythology A to Z*, 22; Sykes, *Who's Who in Non-Classical Mythology*, 53

Girle Guairle

In Irish folklore Girle Guairle ("stormy storm") is a fairy in a story very similar to those of PEERIFOOL, RUMPELSTILTSKIN, and TIT TOT. According to the story a very busy wife worked late into the night as she was very anxious over her spinning and weaving of flax. A fairy overheard the wife's distress and offered to do the work for her on the condition his name, Girle Guairle, be remembered. The wife agreed but the fairy disappeared with the spinning; furthermore, as soon as the fairy was gone from sight his name was forgotten as well. The wife was afraid of what her family would think but more fearful of the vengeance of the fairy whose name she had forgotten. Nervous she went walking in the field and happened upon a FAIRY RING where she heard the fairy she had bargained with signing "If yon woman knew my name to be Girle Guairle, I would have neither frieze nor canvas." The wife happily returned home and waited for the fey to return with the spinning completed, and as soon as he appeared the wife greeted him by name. Girle Guairle handed over the spinning as promised and disappeared in a fit of rage.

Sources: Rose, *Spirits, Fairies, Leprechauns, and Goblins*, 127, 351; Súilleabháin, *Handbook of Irish Folklore*, 473

Girouette

In the French fairy-tale *The Princess Minion-Minette* the fairy Girouette was said to have a kind heart but was difficult to live with as she was never able to make up her mind or stick to a decision. Girouette, in a position similar to a FAIRY GODMOTHER, was given the task of ruling the court of young King Souci's until he was of age to assume his royal duties and responsibilities. Before she left the court, Girouette was determined to see the king married and selected Princess Diaphana was a perfect choice.

Source: Lang, *Pink Fairy Book*, 274–88

Girp

In the Swedish fairy-tale *The Bird Girp* it was said the FAIRY ANIMAL, a bird by the name of Girp, had the ability to restore sight to the blind with its song. This bird was kept in a cage by a king and was guarded as his greatest treasure.

Source: Lang, *Pink Fairy Book*, 132–42

Glaistig

Variations: Glaestig, GLASHTIN, Glastig, GRUAGACH ("long-haired one"), Gruagach Sheombair, Green Glaistig ("a ghlaistig uaine") Maighdean Sheombair ("chamber-maid"), MAIGHDEAN UAINE ("green maiden")

The glaistig ("grey crouching object") is one of the FUATH, a collective name for the malicious and monstrous water fay in Scottish folklore. There are two sets of descriptions for this fairy. The first has it as being a monstrous creature, part human and part goat; the ratio of human to animal varies depending on the story. Sometimes it is able to hide its animal characteristics under a long, green dress. This form of the glaistig says it will lure a man to dance with it and then like a vampire, will drain him dry of his blood. In true fairy fashion, it can also be benign and assist children and the elderly in herding cattle.

The glaistig is also described as looking like a woman with a wan, grey face, dusky skin, and long blond hair. In this guise it is more like a tutelary guardian attached to a particular location. In most stories involving the glaistig it is typically invisible, seeing it is very rare.

Disliking dogs and protecting people of weak intellect the glaistig is said to be physically stronger than most other fairies. It has a particular interest in dairy cows and will go out of its way to protect them. A portion of milk is set out to the glaistig each evening to ensure its ongoing protection.

There are many legends associated with the glaistig, and almost none of them match up to one another painting it as benign and injurious, helpful and harmful to mortals. One legend tells us the glaistig was once a mortal noblewoman who was either cursed with the legs of a goat and immortality or had been given a fairy nature and eventually became a fay. Some tales say it is fulfilling the role of a BANSHEE, wailing out at the death of prominent individuals, such as with the MacQuarries and the Mac Ian families. Many stories tell how it will drain the blood from a man but there also stories of how it will only throw stones at those who travel at night.

Sources: Campbell, *Superstitions of the Highlands and Islands of Scotland,* 155–64; Froud, *Faeries,* 115; Mackenzie, *Scottish Folk-Lore and Folk Life,* 179–81; McCoy, *Witch's Guide to Faery Folk,* 233; Rose, *Spirits, Fairies, Leprechauns, and Goblins,* 121

Glas Ghailbhleann

In Welsh lore Glas Ghailbhleann was a fairy cow renowned for giving copious amounts of milk. The FAIRY ANIMAL would, each day, make its rounds from farm to farm to be milked until one day a greedy woman tried to take more than her fair share. Once the woman was finished milking Glas Ghailbhleann, like the GLASGAVLEN of Irish lore, walked off and was never seen again.

Source: Monaghan, *Encyclopedia of Celtic Mythology and Folklore,* 233

Glasgavlen

Variations: Dun Cow, Dun Cow of Kirkham, Dun Cow of Mac Brandy's Thicket, Glas Gaivlen

A fairy cow from Irish lore the glasgavlen would present itself to every household in the anticipation of being milked. Described as being milk-white and studded with bright green spots it was said this FAIRY ANIMAL regularly made the rounds until one day a greedy woman was determined to obtain more than her daily pail and milked the glasgavlen into a sieve, running it dry and causing the cow to leave Ireland forever. There are various versions of this lore told all over Wales and Ireland, but the basic premise of a generous cow being used up by an avaricious or evil person, such as a witch, remains consistent. It is said wherever the glasgaven walks the grass grows greener, the hay is reaped in greater abundance, and the potatoes grow larger.

Sources: Briggs, *Encyclopedia of Fairies,* 113, 191; Wood-Martin, *Traces of the Elder Faiths of Ireland,* 127–8

Glashtin

Variations: Hawlaa, Howlies, Howlers

On the Isle of Man the glashtin was a species of GOBLIN described as being half cow and half horse. If the head of the glashtin was a cow, than the fairy was unintelligent but if the was a horse than it was cunning and shrewd. Sighted during storms, it howled loudly, taking delight in the chaos and havoc it caused.

Source: McCoy, *Witch's Guide to Faery Folk,* 232

Glashtyn

Variations: GLASHTIN, Glaistyn, Glashan, Glastyn

A FAIRY ANIMAL from the Isle of Man, the glashtyn is a water horse similar to the Irish AUGHISKY and the Scottish EACH UISCE. In its human guise this fairy is described as looking like a handsome, curly, dark haired youth; his horse ears are hidden well beneath his hair. Typically, the glashtyn keeps his equine shape and lingers along the banks of lochs and rivers enticing people to mount up on its back. As soon as it has a rider this water horse takes its prey into the water and devours it.

Sources: Briggs, *Encyclopedia of Fairies,* 191–2; Rose, *Giants, Monsters and Dragons,* 144; Spence, *Fairy Tradition in Britain,* 84; Varner, *Creatures in the Mist,* 23

Glauce

Variations: Glaucè

A sea–NYMPH, Glauce ("bright green" or "sea-green") was one of the named NEREIS in Greek mythology; she was associated with the care and feeding of the infant god, Zeus (Jupiter). She was also named as one of the DANAIDS, the collective name for the daughters of Danaus. In a list compiled by Apollodorus, a Greek scholar and grammarian, Glauce was one of the daughters of HAMADRYAD, ATLANTEIA or (PHOEBE, sources vary) and was wedded to Alces, one of the sons of an unnamed Arabic woman.

Sources: Apollodorus, *Apollodorus' Library and Hyginus' Fabulae,* 95; Gould, *Historic Magazine and Notes and Queries,* Vol 14, 212; Grimal, *Dictionary of Classical Mythology,* 127; Hesiod, *Works of Hesiod, Callimachus, and Theognis,* 15; Pausanias, *Pausanias's Description of Greece,* Volume 1, 434

Glaucippe

Variations: Glaueippe

In Greek mythology Glaucippe was a water–NYMPH and one of the named DANAIDS, the collective name for the daughters of Danaus; her name appears in a list of the DANAIDS generated by Gaius Julius Hyginus (ca. 64 B.C.–A.D. 17), a Latin author. Glaucippe was wedded to Potamon and killed him on their wedding night. In a list compiled by Apollodorus, a Greek scholar and grammarian, she was one of the daughters of the NAIAD, POLYXO and was wedded to the son of the NAIAD CALIADNE, Dryas.

Sources: Apollodorus, *Gods and Heroes of the Greeks,* 69; Bell, *Women of Classical Mythology,* 150; Lemprière, *Classical Dictionary,* 236

Glauconome

A sea–NYMPH, Glauconome was one of the named NEREID in Greek mythology; she was born the daughter of Nerues and DORIS. According to the Greek oral poet Hesiod, she was "blithe" and described as having long flowing hair.

Sources: Bell, *Women of Classical Mythology,* 210, 321; Betham, *Transactions of the Royal Irish Academy,* Volume 17, 89; Hesiod, *Works of Hesiod, Callimachus, and Theognis,* 15; Trzaskoma, *Anthology of Classical Myth,* 18

Glauke

Glauke was the NEREID of grey waters and made the shimmering lights on the sea; she was one of the named NEREID who accompanied THETIS in mourning the loss of her son, Achilles in Greek mythology. Glauke was also a NYMPH of fountains in Corinth.

Sources: Collignon, *Manual of Mythology,* 187; Conway, *Maiden, Mother, Crone,* 122; Homer, *Illiad,* 9; Larson, *Greek Nymphs: Myth, Cult, Lore,* 148; Perry, *Women of Homer,* 146

Glaukia

Variations: Glaucia

A NYMPH of the river Skamandros in the Troad, Anatolia, Glaukia of Greek mythology, was loved by Deimakhos (Drimachos), a companion of the godling, Herakles (Hercules) during his Trojan expedition. The couple had a child together, a son named Skamander.

Sources: Bell, *Place-Names in Classical Mythology,* 138; Larson, *Greek Heroine Cults in their Social and Literary Contexts,* Volume 2, 203; Smith, *Dictionary of Greek and Roman Biography and Mythology: Earinus-Nyx,* 272

Glaukonome

Glaukonome is the NEREID of the green-sea in Greek mythology; she was described by Hesiod as being "laughter-loving."

Sources: Hesiod, *Theogony; and, Works and Days,* 31; Kerényi, *Gods of the Greeks,* 65; Thury, *Introduction to Mythology,* 696

Gloi

Variations: Gloinn

Gloi ("glowing") was one of the many DWARFS named in the *Voluspa,* the first and best known poem of the *Poetic Edda,* a collection of Old Norse poems dating back to about A.D. 985.

Sources: Daly, *Norse Mythology A to Z,* 22; Wilkinson, *Book of Edda called Völuspá,* 12

Glóinn

Glóinn was one of the many DWARFS named in the *Voluspa,* the first and best known poem of the *Poetic Edda,* a collection of Old Norse poems dating back to about A.D. 985.

Sources: Daly, *Norse Mythology A to Z,* 22; Sykes, *Who's Who in Non-Classical Mythology,* 53

Gnome

Variations: Álfur, Djendoes, Djude, Domovoi Djedoe ("earth fairy"), Domovoi, Dudje, DUENDE, Dvergur, Erdmanlein, Erd-Mänlein, Erdmanleins, Foddenskkmaend, FOLLET, Gartenzwerg ("garden gnome"),Gnom, Gommes, Gnomiko, Gnomo, Gnomos, GOBLIN, Ground Manikins, Hammerlinge, Heinzemannchens, Hill manikins, HOB, Hustomte, Kabauter, KABOUTER, Kaukis, Kepec, Klabauter, Kleinmanneken, Krasnoludek, Maahinen, Mano, Manó, Menninkäinen, Nains, Nanu, NISSE, Nissen, Patuljak, Polutan, Škriatok, SKRITEK, Skřítek, Skrzat, Småtomte, TOMTE, Tomtenisse, Tontti, VÆTTIR, Wichtel, Гном (gnom), Патуљак (patuljak), Полушан (polušan)

The hermetic and neo-Platonic doctrine from which all medieval medicine and science was founded describes four Elemental classes, Air, Earth, Fire, and Water; accordingly the Gnomes belong to the Earth class, NEREIDS to water, SALAMANDERS to Fire, and SLYPHS to Air (see EARTH FAIRY, THE).

In the earliest mythology, gnomes lived underground and moved through it as easily as a fish moves through water, they acted as the protectors of the treasures of the earth. Paracelsus describes them as standing two spans high (a *span* is the distance from the tip of an adults thumb to the tip of his pinky finger, fingers spread), and inclined to silence.

Gnomes are traditionally a part of fairy lore but in truth have no folkloric stories or legends of their own; they have little in common with the

DWARFS and KNOCKERS they are likened to except by physical appearance. In the late middle age German folklore said the gnomes had a king named Number-nip or RUBEZAHL, but it was not until very modern times the gnome was fleshed out and fully described, re-imagined into a kindly, forest dwelling being with a highly developed culture.

Sources: Briggs, *Encyclopedia of Fairies*, 192–3; McCoy, *Witch's Guide to Faery Folk*, 219; Monaghan, *Encyclopedia of Celtic Mythology and Folklore*, 218; Patrick, *Chambers's Encyclopædia*, Volume 4, 174

Gob

In German folklore, Gob is a king of the GNOMES; this is very rare as individual gnomes are seldom the feature or a character in a story. Gob has a magical sword and is has the ability to manipulate the melancholy temperament of humans; this associates him with the humor black bile of alchemic medicine.

Sources: Merriam-Webster, Inc. *Merriam-Webster's Encyclopedia of Literature*, 468–9; Rosen, *Mythical Creatures Bible*, 253; Webster, *Flower and Tree Magic*, 166

Goblin

Variations: Blobins, Boggarts, BOGIES, BOGLES, Brags, FARFADET, FOLLET, Gobbies, Gobelin, Goblin, Gouvelin, Grim, Hobgobs, Hob-thrush, KOBOLD, LUTIN, Nis, Robin Goblin

The word goblin has many meanings in fairy lore.

Originally the word goblin was simply a general term for any of the grotesque, small but friendly BROWNIE-like creatures among the fay. It later evolved to cover the sub-terrain species as well. Again the word changed and goblin now encompassed any fairy with an injurious and malicious intent, such as the KNOCKER KOBOLD, PHOOKAS, SPRIGGAN, TROLL and TROW. Goblin, in this context are seldom welcomed by its own kind and disliked by humans. Any of the fay described as being ugly is said to be a goblin or is described as being goblin-like.

However a goblin is also a specific species of fairy being in the same way the BROWNIES, CUCO, DUSH, ESPRIT FOLLET, and FIREESIN are. In British and German lore, as a species they are described as being malicious, small, swarthy thieves; they have the ability to shape-shift and when doing so will typically take the form of whatever an animal best reflects its beastlike nature. Standing about a foot in height (30 centimeters), with bod-

ies covered in a thick coat of black or grey fur, the goblin's actions can range from the mild prank to outright murderous. There were three nights of the year when goblins were most active, and those evenings were called *teir-nos yspry-dion*.

A house goblin will work against the family living there, making their life more difficult by banging pots and pans, digging up graves and scattering the bones, knocking on doors and walls rearranging items in the house, and tangling horses manes and tails.

Goblins dwelling in mines are on occasionally taken as a good omen, believing they linger only near the richest loads. In the mine, the goblin will make noise to annoy the miners or cause little accidents attempting to frighten and intimidate them.

Sources: Bord, *Fairies*, 2; Briggs, *Encyclopedia of Fairies*, 194, 205; Froud, *Faeries*, 76–77; Keightly, *World Guide to Gnomes, Fairies, Elves, and Other Little People*, 357, 468, 476; McCoy, *Witch's Guide to Faery Folk*, 173, Sikes, *British Goblins*, 68

The Goblin Pony

In the French fairy-tale *The Goblin Pony* a grandmother by the name of old Peggy warns her grandchildren not to go out on Hallow-e'n night as witches and goblins are about. The children do not listen to their elder and go outdoors; immediately they see a little black pony. The six of them mount up upon its back and rode it all across the countryside until they came upon the ocean. As soon as the pony saw the water it neighed lustily and charged into the wave drowning its riders.

Source: Lang, *Grey Fairy Book*, 17–18

Godda

Variations: Goda, GONDUL

In the folklore from Shropshire, England, the fairy Godda married and became the wife of Wild Eric. She and her husband along with his faithful band of followers were said to ride out and take the field when ever England is threatened. As GONDUL, she was one of the VALKYRIE.

Sources: Buckland, *Weiser Field Guide to Ghosts,* 78–9; Rose, *Spirits, Fairies, Leprechauns, and Goblins*, 128, 351; Sheard, *Llewellyn's Complete Book of Names*, 254

Godmother

Variations: FAIRY GODMOTHER

In the fairy-tale *Cinderella, or the Little Glass Slipper* written by Charles Perrault, Godmother was the FAIRY GODMOTHER to the cinderwretch, Cinderella. To enable her godchild to attend a ball being hosted by the king's son, she turned a rat into a fat and jolly coachman, hollowed out pumpkin into a fine coach gilded in gold, six lizards into footman dressed in gold and silver, and six mice into beautiful dapple-grey horses. The normally ragged dress worn by her godchild was transformed into cloth of gold and silver which was beset with jewels; upon her feet she placed the world's prettiest pair of glass slippers. The enchantments, although beautiful, would only last until midnight.

Source: Lang, *Blue Fairy Book*, 64–71

Goibniu

Variations: Gaibnenn, Gobnenn, Gofannon, Goibhniu, Goibne

One of the TUATHA DE DANANN Goibniu was not only the weaponsmith who created his people's magical weapons but he was also a brew master. In his Otherworld roadhouse, Goibniu brewed ale made from the fruit of the Otherworld trees. Anyone who drank his ale would remain eternally vital and youthful.

Sources: Illes, *Encyclopedia of Spirits*, 446; Monaghan, *Encyclopedia of Celtic Mythology and Folklore*, 221–22

Goll

In Nordic and Teutonic mythology Goll ("grim" or "herald") was one of the named VALKYRIES, a NYMPH of battle. Always depicted as beautiful women who are sometimes immortal, they are the attendants of the god, Odin.

Sources: Grimm *Teutonic Mythology*, Volume 1, 421; Sigfusson, *Elder Eddas of Saemund Sigfusson Younger Eddas of Snorre Sturleson*, 57, 306

Gonconer

Variations: Gancanagh, Ganconagh, Gean-Canach ("love-talker")

In Irish lore the gonconer is a species of hopelessly idle fairy living in remote valleys; they enjoy pipe smoking and making love to milkmaids and shepherdesses (see GAN CEANACH).

Sources: Booss, *Treasury of Irish Myth, Legend, and Folklore*, 323; Wallace, *Folk-lore of Ireland*, 87; Wright, *English Dialect Dictionary*: D-G, 553

Gondul

In Nordic and Teutonic mythology Gondul ("she wolf") was one of the named VALKYRIES, a NYMPH of battle. Always depicted as beautiful

women who are sometimes immortal, they are the attendants of the god, Odin.

Sources: Grimm *Teutonic Mythology*, Volume 1, 421, 435; Sigfusson, *Elder Eddas of Saemund Sigfusson Younger Eddas of Snorre Sturleson*, 8, 306

Good Lubber

In the fairy lore of Mansfield, Germany, the Good Lubber was a fay to whom the bones of animals were offered up in sacrifice to.

Sources: Dyer, *Folklore of Shakespeare*, 8; Grimm, *Deutsche Mythologie*, 492; Thompson, *Landmarks in Ancient Dover*, 133

Gooseberry Wife

Variations: Awd Goggin

In the folklore of England, on the Isle of Wight, the Gooseberry Wife is a fairy appearing as a large and wooly caterpillar; it guards over gooseberries growing in gardens.

Sources: Baker, *Discovering the Folklore of Plants*, 62; Watts, *Dictionary of Plant Lore*, 169; Wright, *Rustic Speech and Folk-Lore*, 198

Gorge

In Greek mythology Gorge was a water–NYMPH and one of the named DANAIDS, the collective name for the daughters of Danaus. In a list compiled by Apollodorus, a Greek scholar and grammarian, she was one of the daughters of HAMADRYAD, ATLANTEIA or (PHOEBE, sources vary) and was wedded to Hippothous, one of the sons of an unnamed Arabic woman.

Sources: Grimal, *Dictionary of Classical Mythology*, 127; Lemprière, *Classical Dictionary*, 236

Gorgonzola

In the fairy-tale *Heart of Ice* by Comte de Caylus, the fairy Gorgonzola appeared as an old HAG who had the ability to grow gigantic in size and magically transform her staff into a dragon, her cloak into a golden mantle, and her shoes into rockets. Malicious and vengeful by nature Gorgonzola was known to transform herself into a black cat, sneak into a home, and steal the heart of a person thereby rendering them loveless and unable to love.

Source: Lang, *Green Fairy Book*, 121–22

Gorgophone

In Greek mythology Gorgophone was a water–NYMPH and one of the named DANAIDS, the collective name for the daughters of Danaus. In a list compiled by Apollodorus, a Greek scholar and grammarian, she was one of the daughters of Elephantis and was wedded to Proteus, one of the sons of Queen Argyphia.

Sources: Grimal, *Dictionary of Classical Mythology*, 127; Lemprière, *Classical Dictionary*, 236

Görzoni

The Vends of Lüneburg, Germany have in their fairylore a species of subterranean fay they call the görzoni. Known to borrow bread from humans, portions would be left outside the family's door each night for them. When the görzoni came by to retrieve their meal they would show their appreciation by knocking at the window and leaving an extra loaf of bread to show their appreciation.

Sources: Grimm, *Deutsche Mythologie*, 376; Keightly, *World Guide to Gnomes, Fairies, Elves, and Other Little People*, 227

Graeae (singular: graia)

Variations: Crones, Graiai, Graiae

The graeae were the grey-haired sea–NYMPHS from the mythology of ancient Greece; they were born the daughters of KETO (CETO) and Phorkys, making them the sisters of the Gorgons. In some descriptions, the graeae were said to have wings. Originally there were only two graeae, Enyo ("saffron-robed") and Pemphredo ("well-clad"); Enyo is not the same being as the Enyo who is named as being a member of the entourage of the god Ares. A third graia, Deino ("the terrible") was later added. The graeae were said to live in Kisthene, the land of the rock rose, in a sea cave where they guard the road leading to the Gorgons. A personification of the terror of the sea, these three sisters were said to only have one eye and one tooth between them which they would pass back and forth, sharing.

Sources: Bulfinch, *Golden Age of Myth and Legend*, 103–04; Illes, *Encyclopedia of Spirits*, 450; Roman, *Encyclopedia of Greek and Roman Mythology*, 181

Grain

Variations: Grain of the Bright Cheeks, Grainne ("hateful goddess"), Grania, Greine, Grian, Grian of the Bright Cheeks, Grian

A FAIRY QUEEN from Leinster, Ireland, Grain ("sun") holds court in Tipperary on top of Pallas Green Hill also known as Cnoc Greine. There are numerous stories of Grain, such as the one of her turning her father's enemies into badgers, but most of her stories are about her romance, elopement and life with Diarmuid of the Love Spot.

Although these tales vary, essentially Grain was promised by her father, King Cormac Mac Art to be married to the head of his bodyguards, Finn MacCool. At the wedding fest she met and fell hopelessly in love with Diarmuid and by use of her magical abilities, they were able to escape. For sixteen years they fled MacCool living outdoors in makeshift camps with their four sons. Eventually the god of love intervened, Finn forgave Grain and the happy couple was finally able to settle down. Sadly, Diarmuid was soon thereafter killed by a boar while hunting. At first Grain blamed Finn for his death but eventually he managed to convince her otherwise; soon thereafter they were finally wed.

Sources: Mahon, *Ireland's Fairy Lore*, 138; McCoy, *Celtic Myth and Magick*, 214; Monaghan, *Encyclopedia of Celtic Mythology and Folklore*, 229

Le Grand Colin

A famous household fairy from France, le Grand Colin and his constant companion, PETIT COLIN, lived in or on the hearth. Normally invisible this fairy would show its appreciation from time-to-time by assisting in household chores, similar to the BROWNIE. le Grand Colin and his companion enjoy playing ball on the fields of les Paysans; one of the large standing stones there is said to be his bat planted firmly into the ground during a moment's annoyance with PETIT COLIN.

Sources: Bois, *Jersey Folklore and Superstitions* Volume Two, 113, 396; MacCulloch, *Guernsey Folk Lore*, 214–15

Grandinilli

Variations: SUMASCAZZO

In Sardinia, Italy the fairy Grandinilli causes whirlwinds; to see him is an omen of misfortune.

Sources: Arrowsmith, *Field Guide to the Little People*, 22; McCoy, *Witch's Guide to Faery Folk*, 222

Grant

Variations: Gervase of Tilbury

In British fairy lore the grant is a species of fay described as looking like an oddly misshapen little horse walking on its hind legs. Although a fearful sight to behold, it is actually quite friendly and warns humans of impending dangers. Each grant will attach itself to a particular place, be it a meadow or village. When a grant is sighted it will be either during the heat of the day or near sunset. If there will be a fire within a day's time the grant will run up and down through the streets of the town getting dogs to chase after it.

Sources: Briggs, *Encyclopedia of Fairies*, 196; Keightly, *World Guide to Gnomes, Fairies, Elves, and Other Little People*, 286

Green Children of Woolpit

Variations: Green Children, Green Children of Wolf Pit

According to folklore in Woolpit, England during the middle of the 12th century, sometime between A.D. 1135 to 1154 two children, a boy and a girl, were discover trapped in the deep wolf pits near the Thefford Forest. The skin of the children was green, their clothing was made of a material unfamiliar to the locals, and they spoke a language no one understood. Taken to the local landowner, the children cried and would not eat any of the food given to them save for freshly picked beans. It took many months for them to become acclimated to local cuisine. As time passed the boy, who was the youngest of the pair, fell into a state of depression and eventually died. The girl managed to adapt to her new surroundings, took the name took the name Agnes Barre, learned to speak English, was baptized a Christian, and soon thereafter her skin color began to take on a more traditional hue.

When questioned about herself she was able to relate she and the boy were brother and sister and were from a land of perpetual twilight called the Land of Saint Martin where everyone was green skinned; she mentioned another land could be seen off in the distance, across a river of considerable size. She was able to recall one day while herding their father's cattle she and her brother saw a cave and from it hear the distant sound of bells; intrigued, they followed the sound and found themselves trapped in the pit, bedazzled by the blinding light of the sun and terrified from the sound of the farmers reapers. Agnes, even with a reputation for being "loose and wanton in conduct" married a senior ambassador of Henry II.

There are two historical texts retell the story of the Green Children; the first entitled *Historia rerum Anglicarum* ("*History of English Affairs*") which covers the events of England from 1066 to 1198 was written by a historian and monk named William of Newburgh. The second book, *Chronicon Anglicanum* ("English Chronicle") was written by an abbot of Coggeshall Abby by the name of Ralph Coggeshall. Both books were written about 100 years after the events were said to have taken place.

Sources: Briggs, *Encyclopedia of Fairies*, 200–01; Clark, *Unexplained!*, 390–2; Cohen, *Cultural Diversity in the British Middle Ages*, 75, 82–91; Haughton, *Hidden History*, 234–6

The Green Lady of Caerphilly

Similar to the Irish BANSHEE, the Green Lady of Caerphilly releases a mournful moan which could be hear all throughout the ruined Welsh fortress of Caerphilly and in the surrounding countryside, although who or what she was grieving after remains unknown. Described as being airy and light in her movements, walking from one turrent to the next, wearing a long green robe it was said she has the ability to shape-shift into ivy. Cardif folklore says she was in life a French princess who married the Norman Lord of Caerphilly but was in love with a handsome Welsh prince. When the husband learned of this he exiled his wife but her spirit returned to the castle after her eventual death.

Sources: Evan-Wentz, *Fairy Faith in Celtic Countries*, 10; Hall, *Book of South Wales, the Wye, and the Coast*, 237, 327; Porter, *Frommer's England 2011*, 700; Sikes, *British Goblins*, 116

Greencoaties

Variations: Greenies, the Strangers, the Tiddy Mun, Tiddy People, YARTHKINS

In Lincolnshire Fen country, England, greencoaties were the local euphemistic name given to the YARTHKINS fairies for fear of offending them. They were described as wearing green coats and red caps. The greencoaties were sometimes said to be benevolent like the BROWNIE while at other times they were more akin to the YALLERY BROWN.

Sources: Avant, *Mythological Reference*, 471; Briggs, *Encyclopedia of Fairies*, 204; Varner, *Creatures in the Mist*, 56

Gremlin

Variations: Spandule

In England and Germany the gremlin was originally believed to be a fairy being described as being covered with brownish fur, bearing a malicious grin and sporting stubby terrier-like ears; they range in size from being very small to as tall as a human. Lore says once these fairies were able to fly but have since lost the ability. Strong enough to tear through metal, gremlins are said to have little or need to eat or drink and live in high altitudes. Because they can no longer fly they despise the fact humans have achieved it, albeit through the use of machines. Nevertheless the gremlin so resents this they will sneak aboard airplanes and cause havoc, destroying the plane as it flies. This idea of gremlins sabotaging planes was first recorded by British Air Force pilots during World War Two, reports were especially persistent from the Photographic Reconnaissance Units (PRU) of RAF Benson, Wick and St. Eval.

Sources: Ashliman, *Fairy Lore*, 183, 203; Edwards, *Hobgoblin and Sweet Puck*, 216, 220; McCoy, *Witch's Guide to Faery Folk*, 237–8

Grerr

Grerr was one of the many DWARFS named in the *Voluspa*, the first and best known poem of the *Poetic Edda*, a collection of Old Norse poems dating back to about A.D. 985.

Source: Daly, *Norse Mythology A to Z*, 21

Grey Man

Variations: Far Liath, Fir Liath

The Grey Man is an individual fairy and is greatly feared, so much so there is a special road at Fair Head in Antrim reserved just for him to walk upon. Although he lacks the ability to speak he takes great delight in causing the loss of human life. Using his ability to create fog and known as "the Grey Man's Breath," this malicious and murderous fay will obscure the rocks along the Irish and Scottish coasts in the hope ships will crash into the jetties. The Grey Man will also cause darkness on the road so those who travel along it will step off a cliff and fall to their death. Although the Grey Man can be warded off by use of holy items, metal, or the sprinkling of holy water, it is only a temporary fix; he will return with a vengeance.

Sources: Curran, *Field Guide to Irish Fairies*, 21–3; White, *History of Irish Fairies*, 102

Grig

The griggs are a species of small merry fairy dressed in green and wear red hats and stockings. "Grigging apples," the small apples left on the trees after harvest time in Somerset, are said to remain there for the fairies. The Oxford Dictionary defines *grig* as a baby eel, a cricket, a DWARF, or something small.

Sources: Briggs, *Encyclopedia of Fairies*, 205; Siefring, *Oxford Dictionary of Idioms*, 130; Tongue, *Forgotten Folk-tales of the English Counties*, 76

Grim

Grim was one of the fairies mentioned being in the company of ROBIN GOOD FELLOW in a sev-enteenth century pamphlet. He and his fellow fairies, GULL, PATCH, and PINCH are all said to have shape-shifting abilities. According to William Shakespeare's play, *A Midsummer Night's Dream*, Grim would bother those who traveled at night appearing to them as a fire, headless bear, horse, or hound, and making frightening sounds chase after them. In *The Tempest*, he was said to ride upon the back of bats to fly through the night sky, to roost with the owl, and drink nectar from cowslip blossoms.

Sources: Briggs, *Encyclopedia of Fairies*, 327; Wilson, *Life in Shakespeare's England*, 42, 44–45

Grindylow

In the folklore of Yorkshire, England Grindy-low was a NYMPH or water-fairy who lived at the bottom of pits, ponds, and wells; when children came to close to her domain, she reached out, grabbed, and held them under the water until they were drowned. She was used by parents as a NURSERY BOGIE.

Sources: Briggs, Encyclopedia of Fairies, 206; Maberry, *Vampire Universe*, 144; Wright, *English Dialect Dictionary*, 730; Wright, *Rustic Speech and Folk-Lore*, 198–9

Groac'h

In the British fairy-tale *The Groac'h of the Isle of Lok* by Emile Souvestres the groac'h was a fairy living on an island in the middle of the lake; it was said this fairy was richer than all the kings of the world combined. To reach his island palace one must find a small ship, painted blue, and shaped like a swan with its head tucked under its wing. Upon boarding the skiff it will animate and take its passenger to the underwater palace which is made of blue, green, pink, lilac, and white shells. The staircases of the palace are made of crystals, the gardens are full of plants and diamonds grow there as if they were flowers. Men who seek the groac'h for the treasures are tricked into falling in love with her. When they try to marry her she transforms them into fish and tosses them into her pond.

The groac'h is described as having a pink and white face, long black hair intertwined with strings of coral, and a dress of green silk. Her husband, Korandon, was bound to sit upon six stone eggs until they hatched; he is described as looking like a ting black man who is greatly wrinkled.

Source: Lang, *Lilac Fairy Book*, 312–321

Grogan

Variations: Grogach, Groagach, GRUAGACH

A BROWNIE-like fairy from the lore of the Scottish Highlands the grogan, a SOLITARY FAIRY, was described as being broad of shoulders, hairy, richly dressed, short, and strong. Specifically in the highlands, the grogan had golden hair and watched over cattle while in Ulster these fairies were said to be hairy, naked men standing about four feet tall. Sometimes they are said to have large heads, a soft body, and no bones.

Sources: Briggs. *Encyclopedia of Fairies*, 206; Narváez, *Good People*, 243; Rose, *Giants, Monsters, and Dragons*, 156

Grogoch

Variations: PHYNNODDEREE

According to Irish lore the grogoch were originally a species of half human and half fairy natives who left Kintyre, Scotland and settled in Ireland; there are no females. Described as looking like a small elderly man covered with coarse reddish hair these fairies do not wear clothing but rather cover themselves in dirt and twigs; they are well known for their lack of hygiene. Impervious to the cold and heat of the elements, the grogoch live in caves or in clefts in the landscape; large stones dotting the countryside are known as grogochs' houses. BROWNIE-like in their desire to be helpful the grogoch will assist farmers in daily tasks; although they will gladly accept any milk left out for them these fay will become insulted if ever they are offered anything in payment for the services they freely give. Apart from being a very strong and a tireless worker the grogoch have the ability to become invisible.

Sources: Avant, *Mythological Reference*, 96; Briggs. *Encyclopedia of Fairies*, 206; Curran, *Field Guide to Fairies*, 17

Gruagach

The Scottish equivalent of a BROWNIE, the gruagach ("long-haired one") was a female, SOLITARY FAIRY who was utterly grotesque in appearance but extremely kind hearted. Female gruagach were associated with water and described as having long blond or golden hair and wearing a green dress; sometimes it was said to be attractive but more often it was described as a HAG but always it was dripping wet. Male gruagach were typically naked except for a thick fur covering their body; on occasion it would be described as looking like a handsome youth dressed in green and red clothing. Both genders enjoy assisting mortals in household tasks; the females herd and protect cattle while the males will work alongside the farm hands in field shredding and thrashing grain. Although they work because they want to the gruagach become very annoyed if a bowl of milk is not left out for them each evening.

In the highlands of Scotland, Gruagach was a FAIRY QUEEN who watched over cows; she was often seen pouring libations of milk over BROWNIE STONES, natural huen stones with a hole or deep impression in it.

In the fairy-tale *The King of the Waterfalls*, as it appeared in *West Highland Tales*, the gruagach was said to be a malicious and injurious species of fairy. Described as having long, curly brown hair, they were fond of playing games.

Sources: Briggs, *Encyclopedia of Fairies*, 206–7; Evan-Wentz, *Fairy Faith in Celtic Countries*, 93; Frazer, *Folk-Lore in the Old Testament*, 72; Lang, *Lilac Fairy Book*, 61; McCoy, *Witch's Guide to Faery Folk*, 230–40

Guild-folk

Variations: Guild Neighbors

The guild-folk are a species of TROLL living in the interior of green hill; the interior walls of their subterranean homes are lines with gold and silver. Usually these fairies are described dressed in grey or green clothing. When traveling across the land they ride upon bulrushes through the air. If ever one of the guild-folk is seen and you are not carrying a bible in your person quickly draw a circle on the ground around you and in the Lord's name forbid it to approach.

Sources: Keightly, *World Guide to Gnomes, Fairies, Elves, and Other Little People*, 164

Gull

Gull was one of the fairies mentioned being in the company of ROBIN GOOD FELLOW in a seventeenth century pamphlet. He and his fellow fairies, GRIM, PATCH, and PINCH are all said to have shape-shifting abilities. According to William Shakespeare's play, *Romeo and Juliet* Gull was a midwife to the fay; in *A Midsummer Night's Dream*, Gull confesses at nigh to using a disguised voice to deceive men. She admits to lying atop the stomachs of both men and women causing them great pain and in those instances she is referred to as a HAG or night mare. Gull also steals human infants leaving CHANGELINGS in their place as well as stealing cream and milk which she shares with her brothers, GRIM, PATCH, and PINCH as well as her sisters, LICKE, LULL, SIB, and TIB.

Sources: Briggs, *Encyclopedia of Fairies*, 327; Wilson, *Life in Shakespeare's England*, 42, 44

Gumnut Babies

Created by Cecelia May Gibbs (1877–1969), Gumnut Babies made their literary début in January 1914. Like the flower fairies of England, of which Gibbs was a native of, theses fictional fairies became a part of many Australian's childhoods.

Described as being small and chubby with blond or red hair, each fairy dressed according to the flower it represented. Gumnut Babies populate Gumnut Town said to be located out in the wild Australian bush. These fairies successfully live in any environment and enjoy visiting their friends who live in the air and under water. The most popular of the Gumnut Babies were Bib and Bub, Chucklebud, Cuddlepie, Narnywo, Nittersing, Ragged Blossom, and Snugglepot.

Sources: Holden, *Bunyips*, 79; Rose, *Spirits, Fairies, Leprechauns, and Goblins*, 40, 351

Gunlod

Variations: Gunnold

A lonely TROLL queen from Norse mythology, Gunlod was the guardian of the three containers of the Mead of Poetry which was made from the blood of Kvasir; the drink bestows poetic skills upon any who consumed it. The god Odin traveled to Hnitbjorg Mountain in order to steal the mead from her but instead spent three days enjoying her company. Gunlod bore Odin a daughter named Bragi.

Sources: Daly, *Norse Mythology A to Z*, 43, 77; Illes, *Encyclopedia of Spirits*, 458

Gunn

Gunn is a male fairy known to steal children and leave a CHANGELING in their place.

Sources: Keightly, *World Guide to Gnomes, Fairies, Elves, and Other Little People*, 289

Gunna

Variations: Goona

In Ireland, on the Isle of Tyree there is a SOLITARY FAIRY-spirit called a gunna; much like the BROWNIE the gunna will assist families in household chores, especially herding cattle, keeping them from falling off cliff and from wandering into crop fields. According to the lore the gunna has been banished from FAIRYLAND by the FAIRY QUEEN and is to forever wander the world of man. Rarely seen as only those who have the gift of second-sight can see it, the gunna is described as having long blond hair that falls over its shoulders and down its back. In winter months he wears layers of fox furs trying to keep warm, as part of its punishment is it is forbidden to enter into a human's home and warm itself by the fire. Surviving on the scraps of food left for it by people the gunna remains very thin.

Sources: Briggs, *Encyclopedia of Fairies*, 209; MacKenzie, *Wonder Tales from Scottish Myth and Legend*, 136–7; Monaghan, *Encyclopedia of Celtic Mythology and Folklore*, 233

Guriuz

In Italian fairy-lore the guriuz are fairies with some control over the weather; these fay have not been seen in many years and it is unknown if they are in hiding or have died out.

Sources: Arrowsmith, *Field Guide to Little People*, 26; McCoy, *Witch's Guide to Faery Folk*, 240

Gustr

Gustr ("wind") was one of the many DWARFS named in the *Voluspa*, the first and best known poem of the *Poetic Edda*, a collection of Old Norse poems dating back to about A.D. 985.

Sources: Grimm, *Teutonic Mythology*, Volume 2, 461; Rydberg, *Teutonic Mythology: Gods and Goddesses of the Northland*, Volume 3, 977

Guytrash

Variations: Guytrash PADFOOT, Gytrash, Shagfoal, TRASH

Guytrash was a large black and white fairyhound in Horton, England, it had the ability to take the shape of a cow, horse, or mule; it took its name from the sound its feet makes, similar to of heavy boot on a mired road. It has also been seen in Lincolnshire and Yorkshire. Sometimes Guytrash is said to roam the roads with chains dragging behind it and other times not. This fairyhound was said to be malevolent, chasing travelers or leading them astray but there are no stories of it actually hurting anyone. Its presence was said to foretell disaster.

Sources: Briggs, *Encyclopedia of Fairies*, 209; Campbell, *Strange World of the Brontës*, 115, 116; Peacock, *Folklore Journal*, Volume 18, 266–7; Wright, *English Dialect Dictionary*, 226

Gwartheg Y Llyn

In Welsh lore the gwartheg y llyn ("kine of the lake") are the fairy cows (see FAIRY ANIMAL) belonging to the GWRAGEDD ANNWN; they are similar to the CRODH MARA of the Scottish Highlands. Described as being milk-white with the occasional one having red ears these fairy bovines were capable of interbreeding with mortal cattle producing a hybrid cow that would yield a prodigious amount of milk. Interestingly, in Ireland and Scotland the gwartheg y llyn are said to be red bodied and have white ears. FUWCH GYFEILIORN and GLAS GHAILBHLEANN are each specific famous gwartheg y llyn.

Sources: Briggs, *Encyclopedia of Fairies*, 209–10; Monaghan, *Encyclopedia of Celtic Mythology and Folklore*, 233

Gwenhidw

Variations: GWYDION AB DON, Gwenhudwy, Gwenhidwy

Gwenhidw was the FAIRY QUEEN and wife to the FAIRY KING of the TYLWYTH TEG, GWYDION AB DON, according to Welsh fairy lore. Together they resided in Caer Gwydion, located among the stars. Gwenhidw was said to resemble a ghost-like being, similar to the WEISSE FRAU of German lore.

Sources: Briggs, *Fairies in Tradition and Literature*, 176; Evan-Wentz, *Fairy Faith in Celtic Countries*, 151–52

Gwrach Y Rhibyn

Variations: Cunnere Noe, Gwrach-y'r-oerboen, Gwrachyribin, Gwrarch Er Hreebin, HAG of Warning, Witch Rhibyn

A vampiric fairy from Wales, Gwrach Y Rhibyn is described as having two different forms. The first guise is that of a hunchbacked being beneath a green cloak. Under the hood only darkness can be seen. The other description says under the hood of the green cloak is a being so hideous and ugly it causes madness to anyone who looks at it. A constant string of drool, either saliva or blood, hangs from the corners of its mouth. It has one tusklike tooth, a hooked nose with one nostril, webbed (or clawed) feet and hands, ridiculously long thin breasts, a long barbed tongue, long thin gray hair, and skin with a greenish or bluish tint to it. It also has a pair of large, leathery bat wings that hang at its side.

Gwrach Y Rhibyn attacks sleeping people, especially the bedridden, children, and the old. It drains blood from them, but not so much the victim dies. Rather, it returns to the person several times, only taking a little more than they can fully recover from, until the person eventually becomes too weak and dies.

Living in secluded forest glades or along waterways, Gwrach Y Rhibyn can tell when someone of pure Welsh descent is about to die. It will turn invisible, find the person, and travel alongside them waiting until they reach a crossroads. There, Gwrach Y Rhibyn cries out a warning to the person: "My husband!" if a man, "My wife!" if a woman, or "My child!" if a child. Usually, upon being so suddenly surprised, the person who Gwrach Y Rhibyn was trying to warn of imminent death drops over dead or goes insane with the shock of the experience.

Sources: Jacobs, *Celtic Fairy Tales*, 259–64; Motley, *Tales of the Cymry*, 88; Rhy, *Celtic Folklore*, 453; Trevelyan, *Folk-Lore*, 65–68

Gwragedd Annwn

Variations: Gragedd Annwn

The gwragedd annwn ("wives of the lower world") were affable, beautiful, courteous, female Welsh water-fairies who lived in isolated mountain lakes. There underwater homeland were said to be a submerged human settlement. These fairies, accompanied by their fairy hounds, would drive their milk-white cows, the GWARTHEG Y LLYN ("kine of the lake") out of the water to graze in the meadow (See FAIRY ANIMAL). The gwragedd annwn have been known to take a mortal man as a spouse and children born of this union would have webbed fingers and toes. There are some families who claim to be their descendants, such as the Morgan's, whose name loosely translates to mean "of the sea." There was a strict taboo of striking a fairy bride, for even the slightest slap would cause her to leave taking all of her fairy wealth with her.

Sources: Briggs, *Encyclopedia of Fairies*, 211; Froud, *Faeries*, 33; Monaghan, *Encyclopedia of Celtic Mythology and Folklore*, 234; Penwyche, *World of Fairies*, 84; Sikes, *British Goblins*, 30–2, 37, 48

Gwydion ab Don

Gwydion ab Don ("like a god") was said to be the FAIRY KING of the TYLWYTH TEG, according to Welsh fairy lore; his residence, known as Caer Gwydion, was located among the stars. Gwydion ab Don's wife was the FAIRY QUEEN, GWENHIDW.

Sources: Evan-Wentz, *Fairy Faith in Celtic Countries*, 151–52; Rhys, *Celtic folklore: Welsh and Manx*, Volume 1, 504

Gwyllion

In Wales, the gwyllion are malicious, nocturnal, female mountain fairies known to mislead leads travelers. Especially susceptible to iron these fairies can be warded off by drawing a knife on them. The gwyllion have the ability to shape-shift into the form of a goat and are especially friendly to these animals. One well known gwyllion was called the OLD WOMAN OF THE MOUNTAIN; it lived on Lanhyddel Mountain in Monmouthshire. In the town of Aberystruth the gwyllion were said to enter into people's homes during storms. On these nights clean water was left out for the fairies and special attention was taken to make sure no cutting implements were left out as the gwyllion would be sure to ues it in some fashion.

Sources: Briggs, *Encyclopedia of Fairies*, 212; McCoy, *Witch's Guide to Faery Folk*, 242; Sikes, *British Goblins*, 51, 54; Spence, *The Minor Traditions of British Mythology*, 98

Gwyn ap Nudd

Variations: Fionn macCumhil, Gwyneb y Nyth, Gwynn ap Nudd

Born the son of Nudd, the Celtic god of War, Gwyn ap Nudd ("white leather" or "white blessed") was a FAIRY KING, ruler of the GOBLINS, leader of the WILD HUNT, pack master of the Cwn Annwn, and ruler of the Otherworld (see ANNWN, HOUNDS OF and GABRIEL HOUNDS); each Beltane he battled Gwythyr ap Greidal for the hand of Creiddylad, who may be his sister.

Sources: Chopra, *Academic Dictionary of Mythology*, 125; Croker, *Fairy Legends and Traditions of the South of Ireland*, 197–8; Schreiber, *Mabinogion*, Volume 2, 305; Sikes, *British Goblins*, 12

Gyl Burnt-tayl

In Warwickshire England, the gyl burnt-tayl was a female version of the WILL O' THE WISP.

Sources: Briggs, *Encyclopedia of Fairies*, 213; Edwards, *Hobgoblin and Sweet Puck*, 175; Rose, *Spirits, Fairies, Gnomes and Goblins*, 139

Gyre-Carlin

Variations: Gy-Carling, Gyre-Carling

Gyre-Carlin was the FAIRY QUEEN of the Fyfe area of Scotland. It was believed if any flax was left unspun by the end of the year Gyre Carlin would carry it away. Like the GLAISTIG she was said to always carry a child and bathe it each night before going to bed for the evening; for this reason a basin of fresh spring water was left out for her each evening.

Sources: Briggs, *Encyclopedia of Fairies*, 213; Jamieson, *Scottish Dictionary and Supplement*, Volume 1, 476; Rose, *Spirits, Fairies, Gnomes and Goblins*, 139; Spence, *Fairy Tradition in Britain*, 69

Habetrot

Variations: Gy-Carlin, GYRE-CARLING, Habetrot the Spinstress, Habitrot, Habtrot

In Scottish fairy lore Habetrot and her fellow spinners live under the root of a tree and can only be seen by a mortal when looking through a stone with a hole through it. As kindly as she is, Habetrot is ugly, as all her spinning has deformed her lip, flattened her thumb and given her a flipper for a foot. Habetrot is befriended by a lazy but beautiful girl whose mother has bragged to the local laird her daughter was the best and fastest spinner even known. The laird is taken by the beauty of the girl but before he will marry her demands she spin an enormous pile of flax in a single night. Assisted by Habetrot and her friends the task is easily done, the laird is impressed and set a wedding date; however all is not well, as the soon-to-be-bride learns her husband intends for her to continue spinning. Habetrot intervenes on the wedding day, showing herself to the laird and all present, warning her own hideous form came as a result of spinning. The laird declares his wife is forever forbidden to even touch a spinning wheel. Now happily married, the girl is thankful for the friendship and assistant of her fairy friend.

Sources: Briggs, *Encyclopedia of Fairies*, 214–15; Davidson, Davidson, 106; Monaghan, *Encyclopedia of Celtic Mythology and Folklore*, 237; Rose, *Spirits, Fairies, Leprechauns, and Goblins*, 141, 351

Habonde

Variations: ABUNDIA, DAME ABONDE, HABUNDIA, Wandering Dame Abonde

Habonde is a beautiful fairy from English and French folklore described as having dark plaited hair and wearing a golden circlet with a star on it upon her head. The circlet could possibly signify she is a FAIRY QUEEN.

Sources: Bayley, *Archaic England*, 557; Henderson, *Scottish Fairy Belief*, 136; Rose, *Spirits, Fairies, Leprechauns, and Goblins*, 141, 351

Habundia

Variations: Dame Ab, Dame Hab, Dame Habundia, Dame MAB

Habundia is a nocturnal FAIRY QUEEN, benevolent of nature; she is most pleased when a family retires for the evening and their house is left in a neat and orderly fashion. In the early medieval period Habundia was a night-flying, fairy goddess with witch-like abilities associated with fertility rites. In Normandy Habundia is said to be the Queen of the WHITE LADIES, a species of fay whose presence is believed to be a death omen. Many folklorists have associated Habundia as one of the many names and guises of Queen MAB.

Sources: Dowe, *Sharpe's London Magazine*, 14; Gerwig, *Crowell's Handbook for Readers and Writers*, 711; Spence, *Fairy Tradition in Britain*, 24

Hag

The idea of a hag, an elderly, immortal, ugly, witch-like woman dates back to ancient Egypt and Greece, as Hecate, as well as in ancient Celtic lore. The term is used in both fairy lore and in reference to witches, although the later is considered to be a derogatory term.

In the fairy lore of the British Isles hags are fairy beings; likely at one time they were ancient goddess. In the winter months the hag is depicted as being old and ugly but as the season changes it becomes younger and more attractive as spring nears. Sometimes the hag is said to be cannibalistic. There are many individual beings considered to be a hag throughout Celtic mythology.

Norse hags may have originally been sacrificial priestesses to the death-goddess, Hel.

In Irish and Scottish lore the hag is also an ugly being, blind or one-eyed, hairy chinned, hunchbacked, and decrepitly old but if it is kissed then the hag transforms into a beautiful young woman, a common theme. A good hag will oftentimes assist with spinning while malevolent hags are aligned with dark fay and spirits of the dead seeking to do harm to mankind and livestock.

Sources: Guiley, *Encyclopedia of Witches*, 152; Monaghan, *Encyclopedia of Celtic Mythology and Folklore*, 237–8

Hagno

Hagno was a NYMPH and one of the OCEANID; she was associated with the care and feeding of the infant god, Zeus (Jupiter), along with NEDA and THEISOA. In art, she was depicted holding a goblet in one hand and a water pot in the other. Hango has the ability to lessen the intensity of a drough if beseeched for assistance through Zeus.

Sources: Larson, *Greek Nymphs*, 153; Pausanias, *Pausanias's Description of Greece*, Volume 1, 414, 434

Hairy Jack

In Lincolnshire, England, Hairy Jack was a well known BARGUEST. This large, black, shaggy fairy dog attacked those who traveled alone, especially near the area of Willoughton. Usually

invisible this FAIRY ANIMAL could only be felt as a presence. When it wanted not to be noticed it was believed it took the guise of a lame, small man.

Sources: Eberhart, *Mysterious Creatures*, 299; Monaghan, *Encyclopedia of Celtic Mythology and Folklore*, 238; Steiger, *Real Monsters, Gruesome Critters, and Beasts from the Darkside*, 46

Half-Kin

Variations: Half-Kyn

A half-kin is a fairy, like the ALFA, having an immortal soul or was created by God.

Sources: Keightly, *World Guide to Gnomes, Fairies, Elves, and Other Little People*, 159–60; Wylie, *Pattern of Love*, 75

Halia

Variations: Leukothea

A sea–NYMPH, Halia ("sea woman") was the NEREID of the sea's brine. Hesiod refers to her as being "charming." Halia, along with the NYMPH, KAPHEIRA, was a nurse of the god of the sea, Poseidon (Neptune).

Sources: Bell, *Bell's New Pantheon or Historical Dictionary of the Gods,* 112; Fontenrose, *Didyma*, 154; Hesiod, *Works of Hesiod, Callimachus, and Theognis*, 15

Haliai

In ancient Greek mythology the haliai ("salt" and "sea") were the NYMPHS of the sea, specifically the rocky and sandy shores.

Sources: Larson, *Ancient Greek Cults*, 139; Nardo, *Gods and Goddesses of Greek Mythology*, 45; Rigoglioso, *Cult of Divine Birth in Ancient Greece*, 87

Halie

Variations: Haliè

A sea–NYMPH in Greek mythology, Halie ("the briney") was one of the named NEREID who accompanied THETIS in mourning the loss of her son, Achilles; she was born the daughter of Nerues and DORIS.

Sources: Collignon, *Manual of Mythology*, 18; Gould, *Historic Magazine and Notes and Queries*, Vol 14, 212; Trzaskoma, *Anthology of Classical Myth*, 18

Halimede

A sea–NYMPH in Greek mythology, Halimede was one of the named NEREID and was called the walking NYMPH of the rocks; she was born the daughter of Nerues and DORIS. According to the Greek oral poet, Hesiod, she had "beauteous wreath."

Sources: Hesiod, *Works of Hesiod, Callimachus, and Theognis*, 15; Trzaskoma, *Anthology of Classical Myth*, 18

Haltija

In Finland the haltija are GNOME-like creatures, similar to BROWNIES, guard or protect items or people. Each person has their own haltija, similar to the guardian angel of Christian mythology.

The haltija are divided into races called *väki*, and there are many different species, such as metsän väki ("forest folk") and veden väki ("water folk").

Sources: Cavendish, *Man, Myth and Magic: An Illustrated Encyclopedia of the Supernatural*, Volume 3, 958; Hastings, *Encyclopedia of Religion and Ethics*, Part 6, 24; Hultkrantz, *Supernatural Owners of Nature*, 13; Talve, *Finnish Folk Culture*, 223–4

Halykos

Halykos was a NYMPH in Greek mythology from a spring in Attica. A sacred law in Attica decreeded anyone who drank from Halykos' spring should pay and annual fee of one *obol* for the rites. An *obol* is one sixth of a *drachma*, the standard monetary unit.

Sources: Larson, *Greek Nymphs*, 136; Parker, *On Greek Religion*, 76

Hamadryad

Variations: DRYADS, Hamadryádes, HAMA-DRYAS, Wood-Women

The hamadryad of Greek mythology were one of twelve species of NYMPHS, they were the NYMPHS of oak trees. It was believed each tree has its own NYMPH and if either one dies, than so did the other. Because their life was tied to their tree these NATURE SPIRITS would punish or reward those who abridged or lengthened their existence. *The Deipnosophistae*, written by Athenaeus, an ancient Greek grammarian and rhetorician, named eight different species of hamadryad born of their mother, HAMADRYAS: AIGEIROS (black poplar), AMPELOS (vines, especially vitis), BALANOS (oak), KARYA (walnut or hazelnut), KRANEIA (dogwood), MOREA (mulberry), PTELEA (elm), and SYKE (fig).

Sources: Littleton, *Gods, Goddesses, and Mythology, Volume 11*, 999; Keightly, *World Guide to Gnomes, Fairies, Elves, and Other Little People*, 446

Hamadryadnik

Variations: HAMADRYAD

In the folklore of Czechoslovakia, Greece, and Yugoslavia, the hamadryadniks, a species of DRYAD, are NATURE SPIRITS which appear to be living foliage.

Sources: Eason, *Scrying the Secrets of the Future*, 101; McCoy, *Witch's Guide to Faery Folk*, 243

Hamadryas

Hamadryas was the mother of eight different tree-specific species of HAMADRYAD by her brother, the NATURE SPIRIT, Oxylos, according to ancient Greek mythology. The daughters of Hamadryas were AIGEIROS (popular), AMPELOS (vine), BALANOS (acorn), KARYA (nut), KRANEIA (cornel), MORIA (oleaster), PTELEA (elm), and SKYE (fig).

Sources: Kerenyi, *Eleusis*, 135; Larson, *Greek Nymphs*, 283

Hamou Ukaiou

Variations: Hamu Ukaiou

Hamou Ukaiou is the husband to the DJINN, AICHA KANDIDA in Moroccan folklore. A nocturnal demon, he preys upon women who travel alone at night, stalking up and then devouring them. Sharpening a knife on the ground in his presence will prevent him from attacking.

Sources: Illes, *Encyclopedia of Spirits*, 145; Rose, *Giants, Monsters, and Dragons*, 20; Yolen, *Fish Prince and Other Stories*, 107

Hannarr

Variations: Hanarr, Hannar

Hannarr ("skilful") was one of the many DWARFS named in the *Voluspa*, the first and best known poem of the *Poetic Edda*, a collection of Old Norse poems dating back to about A.D. 985.

Sources: Daly, *Norse Mythology A to Z*, 22; Wägner, *Asgard and the Gods*, 311; Wilkinson, *Book of Edda called Völuspá*, 12

Hans

In the Danish fairy-tale *Hans, the Mermaid's Son*, a smith named Basmus went out fishing for three days and came back with a boatful of fish. Six years later he confessed he spent the time as a guest of a MERMAID on the bottom of the sea. A year later Basmus was greeted by a handsome young man who looked to be eighteen years of age; this individual claimed his name was Hans and the son born of the union between the MERMAID whose company Basmus had kept.

Hans had a vivacious appetite and was immensely strong, able to break an iron rod as thick as a wagon pole easily over his knee. Hans was able to do the work of any twelve farmhands but also was a sound sleeper who never missed an opportunity to nap.

Source: Lang, *Pink Fairy Book*, 112–25

Härdmandle (plural: härdmändlen)

In Switzerland the härdmändlen a joyous species of DWARF; they enjoy walking through valleys and enjoying taking part in agriculture labor, such as finding stray lambs and farming. Their primary chore is keeping cattle and making the most excellent and well formed cheese.

Source: Keightly, *World Guide to Gnomes, Fairies, Elves, and Other Little People*, 264

El-Hârith

Variations: ʿAZÂZEEL, Iblees

According to Arabian lore El-Hârith was a young DJINN taken prisoner by the angels and raised by them; he went on to become one of their chiefs. After the creation of Adam, God commanded his angels to worship him but El-Hârith refused and became a sheytân or devil, and he became the father of the sheytâns.

Source: Keightly, *World Guide to Gnomes, Fairies, Elves, and Other Little People*, 25

Harpina

In Greek mythology Harpina was a NAIAD of the town of Pisa in Elis located in southern Greece and one of the NYMPH daughters of the river god, ASOPUS. She and the god of war, Ares (Mars), were the parents of the brutal and violent Oinomaos.

Sources: Hard, *Routledge Handbook of Greek Mythology*, 504; Howe, *Handbook of Classical Mythology*, 191; Larson, *Greek Nymphs*, 139

Hárr

Variations: Har

Hárr ("high" or "lofty one") was one of the many DWARFS named in the *Voluspa*, the first and best known poem of the *Poetic Edda*, a collection of Old Norse poems dating back to about A.D. 985. Hárr is a king; all who come to Hárr Hall may drink and eat without cost.

Sources: Clarke, *Ten Great Religions,* 370; Daly, *Norse Mythology A to Z*, 22; Sykes, *Who's Who in Non-Classical Mythology*, 53; Wilkinson, *Book of Edda called Völuspá*, 12

Hathors

In contemporary fairy lore the ancient Egyptian goddess, Hathor has been associated with fairies. There is an aspect of Hathor named Neith, the goddess of trees. She is associated with the seven Hathors, the beings, like FAIRY-GODMOTHERS, preside over births and make prophecies.

Sources: Benson, *Temple of Mut in Asher*, 94; McCoy, *Witch's Guide to Faery Folk,* 32

Haugspori

Haugspori was one of the many DWARFS named in the *Voluspa*, the first and best known poem of the *Poetic Edda*, a collection of Old Norse poems dating back to about A.D. 985.

Sources: Daly, *Norse Mythology A to Z*, 22; Wilkinson, *Book of Edda called Völuspá*, 12

Haumia

Variations: Haumia-tiketike

In the fairy lore of the Naori people of New Zealand Haumai ("fern root") was a type of aquatic TANIWHA, or tutelary water-fay intentionally trapped and consequently kill the TANIWHA whale, Ureia. Born one of the many offspring of Rangi (Heaven) and Papa (Earth) Haumia was personified by the fern root and lived in the Manukau.

Sources: Best, *Transactions and Proceedings of the New Zealand Institute*, Volume 40, 221; Tregear, *Maori-Polynesian Comparative Dictionary*, 54

Haur

Haur was one of the many DWARFS named in the *Voluspa*, the first and best known poem of the *Poetic Edda*, a collection of Old Norse poems dating back to about A.D. 985.

Source: Crossley-Holland, Norse Myths, 183

Haus-Schmiedlein

In Bohemia there was a species of KNOCKER known as the haus-schmiedlein ("little house-smiths"); these underground fairies lived in mines and usually made the sound of a smith hard at work at his anvil. However, whenever a miner' death is eminent, they would knock three times upon the wall; when an accident was about to occur they will imitate the sounds of miners at work.

Sources: Fish, *Folklore of the Coal Miners of the Northeast of England*, 82; Keightly, *World Guide to Gnomes, Fairies, Elves, and Other Little People*, 230; Sikes, British Goblins, 26

Hausmanner

A domestic house ELF from German folklore, the hausmanner was typically helpful but had occasional bouts of being mischievous especially when it was not fairly compensated for the work did.

Sources: Franklin, *Working with Fairies*, 133, 230; Sikes, *British Goblins*, 23

Havfrue

The havfrue ("half-woman") of Denmark is a species of MERMAID; to see one of these fairy-creatures is an omen of both poor fishing and an upcoming storm. It is believed the havfrue have the ability to predict the future, a common gift among sea-people. Fishermen say the best time to see a havfrue is during the summer months when a mist is over the sea. During this time it will be at the surface of the water combing out its long, golden hair with a comb or driving its snowy-white cattle onto shore to graze.

Sources: Blankner, *History of the Scandinavian Literatures*, 165; Keightly, *World Guide to Gnomes, Fairies, Elves, and Other Little People,* 153; Rose, *Giants, Monsters, and Dragons,* 169

Havmand

Variations: Havman

The havmand ("half-man") of Denmark is a species of MERMAN, the male counterpart to the MERMAID; they live at the bottom of the sea or in the cliffs near the shoreline. Considered benign, the havmand are described as being handsome and although bald as having either a green or black beard.

Sources: Keightly, *World Guide to Gnomes, Fairies, Elves, and Other Little People*, 152; Lysaght, *Islanders and Water-Dwellers*, 94; Rose, *Giants, Monsters, and Dragons,* 169

Heather Pixies

Found on the Scottish moors and in Yorkshire, England, heather pixies are winged fay that enjoy playing pranks.

Source: McCoy, *Witch's Guide to Faery Folk*, 243–4

Hecabe

In Greek mythology Hecabe was a water–NYMPH and one of the named DANAIDS, the collective name for the daughters of Danaus; her name appears in a list of the DANAIDS generated by Gaius Julius Hyginus (ca. 64 B.C.–A.D. 17), a Latin author. Hecabe was wedded to Dryas and killed him on their wedding night.

Sources: Bell, *Women of Classical Mythology*, 149; Grant, *Who's Who in Classical Mythology*, 445

Hedina

Hedina was a NYMPH from the mythology of ancient Greece and Rome. One of the NAIADS, she fell in love with a handsome Sicilian goatherder and hunter named Daphnis, son of the god, Hermes (Mercury) (see ECHENAIS); before she would fully give her herself to him she either solicited a promise he would resist the temptations of all other women or foretold is should he fall into the arms of another would become blind (or be turned to stone, sources conflict). The daughter of the king fell in love with Daphnis and seduced him by giving him too much wine to drink; in his drunken stupor, he forgot his vow to Hedina and consequently became blind.

Source: Fontenrose, *Orion*, 189–92

Hedley Kow

Variations: Boneless, It

A shape-changing, harmless SOLITARY FAIRY trickster of British fairy lore Hedley Kow of Hedley, England near Ebchester was well known for its neighing-like laughter; it was an individual fairy-being. One of its favorite pranks is to shape-shift into a bundle of straw; once picked up and carried for a while, it would become so heavy it would ultimately have to be placed back down. Once released, it would bounce off with its trademark laughter. Other tricks it enjoys are feeding cream to cats, mimicking the voice of a lover, and spilling bowls of soup.

Sources: Ashliman, *Fairy Lore*, 122–3; Hartland, *English Fairy and Other Folk Tales*, 141–2; Sherman, *Trickster Tales*, 33–4

Hegetoria

Hegetoria was a NYMPH of Rhodes in Greek mythology; she was married to the Rhodian King Ochimus, the son of the god Helios (Sol) and the NYMPH, RHODOS.

Sources: Bell, *Women of Classical Mythology*, 145, 223; Larson, *Greek Nymphs*, 207; Lemprière, *Classical Dictionary*, 329

Heinzelmanchen

In Cologne, Germany the heinzelmanchen are a species of naked, nocturnal, TROOPING FAIRIES working nightly for humans they have taken a liking to or for those whom they feel indebted to. The sort of labor these fairies invisibly perform would be baking bread, household chores, and washing, similar to BROWNIE and KOBOLD. According to legend, at one point the city of Cologne was replete with heinzelmanchen; they did all the work for all the citizenry of the city each night enabling the inhabitants to be as lazy as they pleased. This continued on for many years until one day a curious tailor's wife sprinkled peas over the floor of her husband's workshop in the hopes one of the little fairies would slip and fall and she would b able to see what they looked like. This plan so infuriated the heinzelmanchen they left the city, never to return. To commemorate the folklore there is a fountain, Heinzelmännchenbrunnen, erected in the city.

Sources: Briggs, *Vanishing People*, 60; Guiney, *Brownies and Bogles*, 67–8; Keightly, *World Guide to Gnomes, Fairies, Elves, and Other Little People*, 257

Hekaerge

Variations: Arge

In classical Greek mythology Hekaerge was one of the three NYMPH attendants of the goddess Artemis (Diana) who came from the mythical land to the north, Hyperborea (see LOXO and UPIS).

Sources: Hard, *Routledge Handbook of Greek Mythology*, 190; Keightley, *Mythology of Ancient Greece and Italy*, 119

The Hekaterides (singular: Hekateride)

The Hekaterides were the five NYMPH daughters of Hekateros, the ancient Greek god of a rustic dance. The Hekaterides were the mothers of the Curetes, OREADS, and the SATYERS.

Sources: Avant, *Mythological Reference*, 262; Sheard, *Llewellyn's Complete Book of Names*, 323

The Heliades

Variations: The Helie, the Phaethonides

The heliades ("children of the sun") were the seven daughters born of the sun god Helios (Sol) and the OCEANID, CLYMENE; their names have been given by various sources as AEGIALE, AEGLE, AETHERIA, AETHERIE, AETHERIA, DIOXIPPE, HELIA, Helie (see THE HELIADES), LAMPETIA, LAMPETIE, MEROPE, PHAETHOUSA, and PHOEBE. According to the Greek oral poet, Hesiod, when their brother Phaethon ("gleaming") died, his sisters, the heliades wept for months until they transformed into poplar trees. It is believed the amber colored sap bleeding from these trees are the continuing tears of the mourning sisters.

Sources: Brown, *Eridanus*, 32; Hyginus, *Myths of Hyginus*, 26, 125; Keightley, *Mythology of Ancient Greece and Italy*, 57; Littleton, *Gods, Goddesses, and Mythology*, Volume 11, 1117

Helice

In Greek mythology Helice was a water–NYMPH and one of the named DANAIDS, the collective name for the daughters of Danaus; her name appears in a list of the DANAIDS generated by Gaius Julius Hyginus (ca. 64 B.C.–A.D. 17), a Latin author. Helice was wedded to Evidea and killed him on their wedding night.

Sources: Bell, *Place-Names in Classical Mythology: Greece*, 141; Hyginus, *Myths of Hyginus*, 133; Parada, *Genealogical Guide to Greek Mythology*, 59

Heliconian

The heliconian were a species of NYMPH in Greek mythology living in and protecting willow trees.

Sources: Littleton, *Gods, Goddesses, and Mythology*, Volume 4, 440; Newcomb, *Faerie Treasury*, 18

Helicta

In Greek mythology Helicta was a water–NYMPH and one of the named DANAIDS, the collective name for the daughters of Danaus; her name appears in a list of the DANAIDS generated by Gaius Julius Hyginus (ca. 64 B.C.–A.D. 17), a Latin author. Helicta was wedded to Cassus and killed him on their wedding night.

Sources: Bell, *Women of Classical Mythology*, 150; Hyginus, *Myths of Hyginus*, 133; Parada, *Genealogical Guide to Greek Mythology*, 59

Helike

In ancient Greek mythology Helike was an OREAD, a NYMPH of Mount Ida, Crete. She, along with CYNOSURA, nursed the infant god, Zeus (Jupiter), while he was in hiding from his father, Cronus. Helike was also a NYMPH of Arcadia; she was transformed into the constellation Ursa Major.

Sources: Grimal, *Dictionary of Classical Mythology*, 121; Larson, *Greek Nymphs*, 185; Smith, *New Classical Dictionary of Biography, Mythology, and Geography*, 235

Hen Wen

Variations: Henwen, Hen-Wen, the sow of Dallweir Dallpenn

In Welsh lore Coll ap Collfrewy was one of the three powerful swine herders on the Isle of Britain; he kept the fairy-swine of Dallwyr Dallben in the valley of Dallwyr in Cornwall (see FAIRY ANIMAL). One of the swine under Coll ap Collfrewy's protection was named Hen Wen. It had been prophesied when this pig gave birth it would bring evil to the land. King Arthur assembles a troop of men to seek out the animal and destroy. Hen Wen, about to give birth, became frightened and ran but her herder caught her by the bristles; unfortunately he was not strong enough to stop her charge. The man held on as Hen Wen ran across the country and swam through the sea, delivering its offspring as it went: in Arvon she delivered a grain of rye, in Dyved she delivered a grain of barley and a piglet, in Gwent she delivered three grains of wheat and three bees, in Maen Du she delivered a kitten, and in Rhiwgyverthwch she delivered an eagle and wolf cub. It is believed by scholars the story is a device used to explain how food and animals not native to the island arrived there.

Sources: Morgan, *Notes on Wentwood, Castle Troggy, and Llanvair Castle*, 13; Schreiber, *The Mabinogion*, 330–2

Henkies

On the Orkney and Shetland Islands the henkies are a species of TROLL or TROW that *henks* ("limps") as they dance. *Henkie knows* are the knolls these fairies would gambol and play around at night.

Sources: Briggs, *Abbey Lubbers, Banshees, and Boggarts*, 99; Rose, *Giants, Monsters, and Dragons*, 170; Wright, *Rustic Speech and Folk-Lore*, 170

Hepti

Hepti ("grip") was one of the many DWARFS named in the *Voluspa*, the first and best known poem of the *Poetic Edda*, a collection of Old Norse poems dating back to about A.D. 985.

Sources: Daly, *Norse Mythology A to Z*, 22; Sykes, *Who's Who in Non-Classical Mythology*, 53; Wilkinson, *Book of Edda called Völuspá*, 12

Heptifíli

Heptifíli ("file with handle") was one of the many DWARFS named in the *Voluspa*, the first and best known poem of the *Poetic Edda*, a collection of Old Norse poems dating back to about A.D. 985.

Sources: Daly, *Norse Mythology A to Z*, 22; Sturluson, *Prose Edda*, 25; Sykes, *Who's Who in Non-Classical Mythology*, 53

Herbaline

In the German fairy-tale *The History of Dwarf Long-Nose*, the fairy Herbaline was described as looking rather ragged; small of stature and having a small and sharp wrinkled face with red eyes and a thin hooked nose which almost touched her chest. Her hands were a hideous shade of brown sporting skinny fingers and her neck was as thin as a cabbage stalk. Once every fifty-five years Herbaline went into town to purchase produce.

A vengeful fairy by nature, Herbaline kidnapped a twelve-year old boy by the name of Jem who had mocked her appearance. Once captured, Herbaline transformed him by use of her magic and tremendous herbal lore into a squirrel and forced him to do household chore sand prepare her meals. This spell lasted for seven years.

Once this initial spell was broken, Jem was not free of Herbaline's vengeance,, for rather than returning to his true form he was transformed into a misshapen DWARF with small piglike eyes, a long hooked nose that almost touched his chin, and his throat removed so his head had to sit squarely upon his shoulders. In addition, Jem was given two humps upon his back small spindly legs and long over-developed arms. Eventually, with the assistance of an enchanted goose, the evil enchantment was broken.

Source: Lang, *Violet Fairy Book*, 226–48

Heri

Heri ("fighter" or "hare") was one of the many DWARFS named in the *Voluspa*, the first and best known poem of the *Poetic Edda*, a collection of Old Norse poems dating back to about A.D. 985.

Sources: Daly, *Norse Mythology A to Z*, 22; Wilkinson, *Book of Edda called Völuspá*, 12

Herkyna

A NYMPH of the river Herkyna near Lebadeia in central Greece, Herkyna was a companion to the goddess, Persephone (Proserpina) as well as the male healing hero, Trophonios. In art Herkyna is depicted holding a goose.

Sources: Larson, *Greek Heroine Cults*, 85; Larson, *Greek Nymphs*, 143

Hero

In Greek mythology Hero was a water–NYMPH and one of the named DANAIDS, the collective name for the daughters of Danaus; her name appears in a list of the DANAIDS generated by Gaius Julius Hyginus (ca. 64 B.C.–A.D. 17), a Latin author. Hero was wedded to Andromachus and killed him on their wedding night.

Sources: Bell, *Women of Classical Mythology*, 150; Hyginus, *Myths of Hyginus*, 133

The Heroic Fairy

The Irish knights and ladies of Celtic legends and medieval romances were described as possessing "shining beauty" and being human sized, or slightly larger, in stature. Unless placed under a magical spell, Heroic fay were nearly always beautiful; on the rare occasion they were disgustingly ugly. These beings enjoyed spending their time is aristocratic pursuits, such as dancing, fighting, hunting, music, and riding. Heroic fairies oftentimes took a human lover.

Sources: Stepanich, *Faery Wicca*, Book One, 25–26

Herophilos

A male NYMPH in classical Greek mythology, Herophilos was born of the god of the sea, Poseidon (Neptune) and the goddess of love, Aphrodite (Venus); his sister was the NYMPH, RHODOS.

Sources: Budin, *Origin of Aphrodite* 18; Dalby, *Story of Venus*, 43, 131

Hesiod, Types of Nymph

Hesiod, the ancient Greek oral poet and contemporary of Homer, describes two classes of NYMPH in his poem *Theogony* ("Birth of the Gods" 8–7th century B.C.). The first of the two classes are the MELIAI, tree NYMPHS of the hills and mountains were born when the heavens meet with the earth; the second are the OCEANID, the 3,000 divine daughter NYMPHS of fresh water springs, streams, and water meadows. In Hesiod's mythological compendium, the *Catalogues of Women*, he introduces the NAIAD, daughters of the River-gods and the OREIADES of the mountains; they are similar to the MELIAI.

Accord to a fragment of one of Hesiod's poems, a NAIAD declares "a crow lives for nine human generations, a stag lives four times as long as a crow, a raven three times as long as a stag, a phoenix nine times as long as a raven, and a NYMPH 10 times as long as a phoenix." Assuming a human generation is 20 years, a NYMPH can reasonably expect to live 194,000 years.

Sources: Gray, *Mythology of all Races*, Volume 1, 256; Hansen, *Classical Mythology: A Guide to the Mythical World of the Greeks and Romans*, 41; Penglase, *Greek Myths and Mesopotamia*, 206

Hesione

Variations: Asyn, PRONOIA

Born one of the 3,000 daughters of the Titians, Oceanus and Tethys, Hesione was one of the named OCEANIDS and the wife of the Titan Prometheus in Greek mythology.

Sources: Bell, *Women of Classical Mythology*, 238–9; Schmidt, *Larousse Greek and Roman Mythology*, 133; Thorburn, *Facts on File Companion to Classical Drama*, 262

Hesperia

Variations: ASTEROPE, Hespera, Hespere, Hespereia, Hesperidian Nymphs, Hesperethoosa, Hesperusa

Hesperia ("evening") was a DRYAD, one of the twelve species of NYMPH in Greek mythology; she was also one of the daughters of Atlas and PLEIONE, making her one of the PLEIADES as well.

Additionally, Hesperia was one of the four HESPERIDES, a group of four NAIAD sisters who were charged with the protection of a golden apple tree (see also AEGLE, ARETHUSA, and ERYTHEIA). They lived in a celestial garden with Ladon, a reptilian creature, the guardian of the golden apples.

Sources: Daly, *Greek and Roman Mythology A to Z.*, 72; Littleton, *Gods, Goddesses, and Mythology, Volume 11*, 1000

Hesperides

The Hesperides were a group of four NAIAD sisters from Greek mythology who guarded the golden apple tree the goddess Gaia gave to the goddess Hera (Juno) as a wedding present. It was from this tree Herakles (Hercules) stole a golden apple to complete his eleventh labor. The names of these four sisters, the daughters of Atlas, are AEGLE, ARETHUSA, ERYTHEIR, and HESPERIA. The Hesperides lived in a garden located in the Underworld; this garden was protected by a dragonlike creature called Landon.

Sources: Day, *God's Conflict with the Dragon and the Sea*, 402; Littleton, *Gods, Goddesses, and Mythology*, Volume 11, 1000

Hestyaea

Born one of the 3,000 daughters of the Titians, Oceanus and Tethys, the NYMPH Hestyaea was one of the named OCEANIDS in Greek mythology.

Sources: Apollodorus of Athens, *Apollodorus' Library and Hyginus' Fabulae*, 95

Hieromneme

A NYMPH from classical Greek mythology Hieromneme was a NAIAD of Mount Ida in the Troad, Anatolia; she was the wife of the Dardanian prince Assarakos (Assaracus).

Sources: Laeson, *Greek Nymphs*, 320; Littleton, *Gods, Goddesses, and Mythology*, Volume 11, 1453; Parada, *Genealogical Guide to Greek Mythology*, 19, 128

Hilde

In Nordic and Teutonic mythology Hilde ("war") was one of the named VALKYRIES, a NYMPH of battle. Always depicted as beautiful women who are sometimes immortal, they are the attendants of the god, Odin. When Hilde's father declared war on her lover she fought on her lover's side; each night she would perform a magical ceremony to rais up the dead so they may return to the battle.

Sources: Monaghan, *Encyclopedia of Goddesses and Heroines*, 485; Welch, *Goddess of the North*, 67

Hildur

In Nordic and Teutonic mythology Hildur ("warrior") was one of the named VALKYRIES, a NYMPH of battle. Always depicted as beautiful women who are sometimes immortal, they are the attendants of the god, Odin.

Sources: Salmonson, *Encyclopedia of Amazons*, 117; Sykes, *Who's Who in Non-Classical Mythology*, 86

Hill People

Variations: Bjergfolk, Hill-People, Högfolk

Hill people are a species of Elves living in cave in small hills. Described as looking like handsome humans they seem to radiate a feeling of melancholy; it has been put forth during the introduction of Christianity these fairy beings were the spirits of the people's forefathers who had died without the benefit of having known Christ and were bewailing the lost opportunity for their personal redemption. Hill people are also said to be most magnificent singers; to speak against their hope of salvation will turn their song into great lamentation. It was also believed if a person wanted to learn to play the fiddle in an instant it could be done if they promised the Hill people religious salvation.

TROLL, who also live in caves in hills both alone or with their families, are called hill people (bjergfolk).

Sources: Keightly, *World Guide to Gnomes, Fairies, Elves, and Other Little People*, 79, 147–8

Hille Bingels

Hille Bingels was the wife of HINZELMANN, a fairy spirit; they lived in Lüneburg, Germany, during the sixteenth century.

Sources: Arrowsmith, *Field Guide to the Little People*, 113; Briggs, *Vanishing People*, 53; Keightly, *World Guide to Gnomes, Fairies, Elves, and Other Little People*, 240

Himalia

Himalia was a NYMPH of Arcadia or Rhodes, sources conflict; she was transformed into the constellation Ursa Major according to Greek mythology. After Zeus (Jupiter) defeated the Titans he became enchanted with Himalia and seduced her by means of a rain shower. She bore the god Zeus three sons, Cronios, Cytos, Spartacos.

Sources: Avant, *Mythological Reference*, 265; Larson, *Greek Nymphs*, 206, 322; Torr, *Rhodes in Ancient Times*, 148

Himera

In Greek mythology, Himera was a NYMPH of Sicily; her symbol was the rooster, representing the dawn.

Sources: Larson, *Greek Nymphs*, 37; Leake, *Numismata Hellenica*, 58, 69

Hine-Korako

Variations: Hinekorako

In the Maori mythology the Hine-Korako ("pale woman") was a female water-fairy, similar to a NATURE SPIRIT, it lived in the Wairoa River; she was married to Tane-Kino, a human chief, and bore him a son named Tuarenga. The woman of the tribe began to taunt her maternal abilities but Hine-Korako could not tolerate their taunts and left her family, returning to her home under Regina Falls. It is believed she also resides in lunar rainbows.

Sources: Gudgeon, *Journal of the Polynesian Society*, Volume 14, 187; Tregear, *Maori-Polynesian Comparative Dictionary*, 71

Hine-Pukohurangi

Variations: Hine-pukohu-rangi

In the Maori mythology Hine-Pukohurangi ("woman of the mist") is a female NATURE SPIRIT; she is the personification of the mist covering the mountain tops; she is married to Te Maunga, the personification of the mountains.

Sources: Cowan, *New Zealand*, 180; Gudgeon, *Journal of the Polynesian Society*, Volume 14, 209

Hine-Ruru

Hine-Ruru is an owl-woman in the belief of the native people of New Zealand; a nocturnal tutelary NATURE SPIRIT, she gives advice and protects people from harm. A death omen seen by those who are about to die, Hine-Ruru will woot out an alarm to warn of approaching strangers.

Sources: Orbell, *Illustrated Encyclopedia of Māori Myth and Legend*, 63

Hine-Wai

In the Maori mythology Hine-Wai ("water woman") was born the daughter of HINE-PUKO-HURANGI. A female mountain-fairy, similar to a NATURE SPIRIT, Hine-Wai is personified by the light rain of the mountain tops.

Sources: Orbell, *Concise Encyclopedia of Māori Myth and Legend*, 39–40; Parker, *Mythology*, 406

Hinzelmann

Variations: Luring

Hinzelmann was a house fairy living in an old castle in Hüdemuhlen Lüneburg, Germany, during the sixteenth century with his wife, HILLE BINGELS. At first Hinzelmann was feared when his spectral voice was heard but over time he grew to become friendly, laughing and singing; he was very similar to the German KOBOLD and the Scottish BROWNIE. Hinzelmann who normally remained invisible claimed he had the ability to shape-shift into a white feather; in this form he would fly through the air and follow the master of the house whenever he would travel. Although he was said to be fond of playing tricks, Hinzelmann never hurt anyone; he would work in the kitchen cleaning, drying, and putting away dishes; if anything was misplaced, he knew exactly where it was; he tended to the horses and curried them daily; and he encouraged maids who did their work well but would switch those who slacked off.

Sources: Briggs, *Vanishing People*, 58; Grimm, *German Legends of the Brothers Grimm*, Volume 1, 76; Keightly, *World Guide to Gnomes, Fairies, Elves, and Other Little People*, 240–5

Hipparete

In Greek mythology Hipparete was a water–NYMPH and one of the named DANAIDS, the collective name for the daughters of Danaus; her name appears in a list of the DANAIDS generated by Gaius Julius Hyginus (ca. 64 B.C.–A.D. 17), a Latin author. Hipparete was wedded to Protheon and killed him on their wedding night.

Sources: Bell, *Women of Classical Mythology*, 241; Hyginus, *Myths of Hyginus*, 132; Parada, *Genealogical Guide to Greek Mythology*, 59

Hippo

Born one of the 3,000 daughters of the Titians, Oceanus and Tethys, Hippo ("like a swift current") was one of the named OCEANIDS in Greek mythology.

Sources: Bell, *Bell's New Pantheon or Historical Dictionary of the Gods*, 112; Boswell, *What Men or Gods Are These*, 58; Hesiod, *Theogony*, 108; Hesiod, *Works of Hesiod, Callimachus, and Theognis*, 20; Westmoreland, *Ancient Greek Beliefs*, 24

Hippodamia

In a list compiled by Apollodorus, a Greek scholar and grammarian, Hippodamia was one of the daughters of the HAMADRYAD, ATLANTEIA (or PHOEBE, sources vary) and was wedded to Diocorystes (or Istrus, sources vary) one of the sons of an unnamed Arabic woman. She is also a NYMPH in Greek mythology and was seduced by the god, Zeus (Jupiter).

Sources: Lemprière, *Classical Dictionary*, 236; Parada, *Genealogical Guide to Greek Mythology*, 59

Hippodice

In Greek mythology Hippodice was a water–NYMPH and one of the named DANAIDS, the collective name for the daughters of Danaus. In a list compiled by Apollodorus, a Greek scholar and grammarian, she was one of the daughters of Herse and was wedded to Idas, one of the sons of Hephaestine.

Sources: Grimal, *Dictionary of Classical Mythology*, 127; Lemprière, *Classical Dictionary*, 236

Hippomedusa

In Greek mythology Hippomedusa was a water–NYMPH and one of the named DANAIDS, the collective name for the daughters of Danaus. In a list compiled by Apollodorus, a Greek scholar and grammarian, she was one of the daughters of HAMADRYAD, ATLANTEIA or (PHOEBE, sources vary) and was wedded to Alcmenor, one of the sons of an unnamed Arabic woman.

Sources: Grimal, *Dictionary of Classical Mythology*, 127; Lemprière, *Classical Dictionary*, 236

Hipponay

In ancient Greek mythology Hipponay was one of the HAMADRYAD who was born of the incestuous relationship between Oxylus and his sister, HAMADRYAS.

Source: Kloppenborg, *Tenants in the Vineyard*, 227

Hipponoe

A sea–NYMPH, Hipponoe was the named NEREID of "the temper of horses" (ie: the waves); she was born the daughter of Nerues and DORIS. According to Hesiod she was "rosy-armed."

Sources: Hesiod, *Works of Hesiod, Callimachus, and Theognis*, 15; Trzaskoma, *Anthology of Classical Myth*, 18

Hippothe

A sea–NYMPH from Greek mythology, Hippothe was a happy and silent NYMPH.

Source: Betham, *Transactions of the Royal Irish Academy*, Volume 17, 89

Hippothoe

A sea–NYMPH in Greek mythology, Hippothoe was the named NEREID of "running horses" (i.e: the waves); she was born the daughter of Nerues and DORIS. According to Hesiod she was "lovely." Hippothoe was also, according to Gaius Julius Hyginus (ca. 64 B.C.–A.D. 17), a Latin author, one of the named DANAIDS, the collective name for the daughters of Danaus; she kill her husband Obrimus on their wedding night.

Sources: Hesiod, *Works of Hesiod, Callimachus, and Theognis*, 15; Trzaskoma, *Anthology of Classical Myth*, 18

Hlaevang

Varaiations: Hlaevangr

Hlaevang was one of the many DWARFS named in the *Voluspa*, the first and best known poem of the *Poetic Edda*, a collection of Old Norse poems dating back to about A.D. 985.

Sources: Daly, *Norse Mythology A to Z*, 22; Wägner, *Asgard and the Gods*, 311; Wilkinson, *Book of Edda called Völuspá*, 12

Hledjólfr

Hledjólfr ("protecting wolf") was one of the many DWARFS named in the *Voluspa*, the first and best known poem of the *Poetic Edda*, a collection of Old Norse poems dating back to about A.D. 985.

Sources: Sturluson, *Younger Edda,* 25; Universität Münster, *Frühmittelalterliche Studien*, 106

Hliodolf

Hliodolf was one of the many DWARFS named in the *Voluspa*, the first and best known poem of the *Poetic Edda*, a collection of Old Norse poems dating back to about A.D. 985.

Source: Daly, *Norse Mythology A to Z*, 22

Hljodjolfr

Hljodjolfr ("howling wolf") was one of the many DWARFS named in the *Voluspa*, the first and best known poem of the *Poetic Edda*, a collection of Old Norse poems dating back to about A.D. 985.

Sources: Daly, *Norse Mythology A to Z*, 22; Sykes, *Who's Who in Non-Classical Mythology*, 53; Wilkinson, *Book of Edda called Völuspá*, 12

Hlokk

In Nordic and Teutonic mythology Hlokk was one of the named VALKYRIES, a NYMPH of battle. Always depicted as beautiful women who are sometimes immortal, they are the attendants of the god, Odin.

Sources: Grimm *Teutonic Mythology*, Volume 1, 422; Sigfusson, *Elder Eddas of Saemund Sigfusson Younger Eddas of Snorre Sturleson*, 57, 310

Hmin

Similar to the HAMADRYADS of classical Greek mythology, the Hmin are tree spirits or NATS from Burmese folklore. This NATURE SPIRIT wanders throughout the forest violently shaking anyone it happens across; they are sometimes said to be demons of ague and fevers.

Sources: Porteous, *Forest in Folklore and Mythology*, 125; Scott, *The Burman: His Life and Notions*, Volume 1, 286

Hnikur

Variations: Nickur, Nikar, Ninner, Nok

In the fairy lore of the Faroe Islands and Iceland the hnikur is a water-fairy similar to the KELPIE and NECK. Appearing as a fine apple-grey horse with reversed hooves, it stands on the seashore awaiting someone foolish enough to limb up on its back. Should ever this FAIRY ANIMAL get a rider it would charge off into the sea.

Sources: Keightly, *World Guide to Gnomes, Fairies, Elves, and Other Little People*, 162; Thorpe, *Northern Mythology*, Volume 1, 22

Hob

Variations: HOBGOBLIN, HOBTHRUST, Hob of T'hurst, Hob Thrush, Hob Thrust, LOB, ROBIN GOOD FELLOW, Thurse

In northern England a hob is a species of friendly but mischievous fairy although it is oftentimes used to reference the fay in general. According to the lore the hob would help the farmer in the field, the shopkeeper in his store, or the wife with her household chores until one day he is given a coat or thanked for his services; deeply insulted and infuriated, the hob leaves.

Sources: Addy, *Folk Tales and Superstitions*, 39–40; Ashliman, *Fairy Lore*, 203; Bord, *Fairies*, 2; Briggs, *Encyclopedia of Fairies*, 222

Hobgoblin

Variations: HOB, Hob-Goblin, Hobgoblinet, Hobtrust, LOB, Rob Goblin, Rob-Goblin, ROBIN GOOD FELLOW

Originally the hobgoblin of England was a good natured house fairy, quick to help with chores, similar to the Danish Nis, the German KOBOLD, and the Scottish BROWNIE; however, it was fond of playing practical jokes. Eventually, under Puritan influence, the word came to take on a negative tone and referred to any form of a malicious being. As the word became more connected to injurious beings the appearance of the hobgoblin changed as well, they were described as having a horrifying appearance easily frightening anyone. Eventually, to see one became a death omen.

Sources: Keightly, *World Guide to Gnomes, Fairies, Elves, and Other Little People*, 281; Monaghan, *Encyclopedia of Celtic Mythology and Folklore*, 247; Rose, *Spirits, Fairies, Leprechauns, and Goblins*, 351

Hobmen

Hobmen is the generic name for the category in which the various species of HOB belong. Fairies fall into the hobmen category include BOGARTS, FENODEREE, GRUAGACH, KILLMOULIS, LUBBARD FIEND, PHOOKA, Pixies, PUCK, ROBIN GOOD FELLOW, SILKIES, and the WILL O' THE WISP.

Sources: Briggs, Encyclopedia of Fairies, 223; Burns, *Witch Hunts in Europe and America*, 85; Wilby, *Cunning Folk and Familiar Spirits*, 107

Hobthrust

Variations: Hob-Thrust

A BROWNIE-like fairy said to live in the north of England, Hobthrust was different from other fairies in that he was reported to carry an iron pot, stirring the thumb-bones of children he kept in it as he walked about.

Sources: Spense, *Minor Traditions of British Mythology*, 90–91; Peacock, *Folklore*, Volume 12, 170; Westwood, *Lore of the Land*, 445

Hobyahs

Cannibalistic GOBLINS in English fairy lore the hobyahs are malicious and murderous; they will kidnap children and tear down crops. These nocturnal fairies are fearful of dogs.

Sources: Briggs, *Encyclopedia of Fairies*, 223–4; Jacobs, *English Fairy Tales*, 270–3; Proudfit, *Journal of American Folk-Lore*, Volume 4, 173–4

Hödeken

Variations: Hütchen, Hatekin ("little hat")

Hödeken was a KOBOLD once living in the palace of the bishop of Hildesheim, Lower Saxony, Germany. Said to be kind and having an obliging disposition, even making announcements of events about to happen, Hödeken wore a little felt hat low on its head, so much so its face was covered. Unfortunately Hödeken had extreme reactions to being affronted; his good nature was replaced with a murderous and violent one. Eventually the bishop had to banish and exorcise him.

Sources: Keightly, *World Guide to Gnomes, Fairies, Elves, and Other Little People*, 255; Roscoe, *German Novelists*, 250–4

Hodge-Poker

The GOBLIN Hodge-Poker was a NURSERY-BOGY from the folklore of England. His two brothers were MUM-POKER and TOM-POKER.

Sources: American Philological Association, *Transactions of the American Philological Association*, Volume 26, 110; Halliwell, *Dictionary of Archaic and Provincial Words*, 453; Narváez, *Good People*, 469

Hoggstari

Hoggstari was one of the many DWARFS named in the *Voluspa*, the first and best known poem of the *Poetic Edda*, a collection of Old Norse poems dating back to about A.D. 985.

Sources: Daly, *Norse Mythology A to Z*, 22; Sykes, *Who's Who in Non-Classical Mythology*, 53; Wilkinson, *Book of Edda called Völuspá*, 12

Hogmen

Variations: Hillmen

Hogmen are the most feared of fairy people on the Isle of Man. November 11 is known as *Hollantide*, it is believed to be the night the hogmen move their home; using FAIRY PATHS they travel along those straight lines to suitable fairy hills. Offerings of fruit and small gifts are left for them.

Sources: Briggs, Encyclopedia of Fairies, 225; Dewdney, *Acquainted with the Night*, 195; Spence, *Fairy Tradition in Britain*, 83

Hollenmadchen

In the fairy-tale *The Dragon of the North* the hollenmadchen ("witch-maiden") was a fairy who had possession of King Solomon's lost ring. The hollenmadchen had no permanent dwelling but rather moved about as the wind took her. Once a month the fairy needed to go to a particular spring and wash her face in the light of the full moon; if she did not do so the hollenmadchen would lose her bloom of youth and instantly grow old and wrinkled.

Source: Lang, *Yellow Fairy Book*, 9–20

The Holly King

A protector of holly trees, Holly King is a HAMADRYAD and the king of winter. Prior to the introduction of Christianity, the Holly king was the personification of the tenacity of life and was in power from midsummer to midwinter; after which the OAK KING came into power. Depicted as an old man wearing winter clothing he wears a wreath of holly and carries a holly branch as a staff. He was once the Celtic god of the dying year.

Sources: Hooke, *Trees in Anglo-Saxon England*, 213; Monaghan, *Encyclopedia of Celtic Mythology and Folklore*, 248

Homeric Nymphs

Homer, the greatest ancient Greek epic poet and author of the *Iliad* and the *Odyssey* classifies NYMPHS, the daughters of Zeus (Jupiter), by their habitat: NYMPHS of the grassy meadows are known as the *pisea poiêenta*; NYMPHS of the groves are known as the *alsea*; NYMPHS of the mountain-tops are known as the *OREA*; NYMPHS of the rivers are known as the *potamoi*, NYMPHS of the river-springs are known as the *pegai potamon*; NYMPHS of the sacred rivers flowing seawards are known as the *potamoi*; NYMPHS of the springs are known as the *krênai*; NYMPHS of the springs of rivers are known as the *pegai potamon*; NYMPHS of the tree groves are known as the *alsea*. Later authors would call these beings Dryades, LEIMONIDES, OREIADES, and the Naiades.

Homer's NYMPHS frequently took on heroes as their lover or spouse; many warriors who fought before the battle of Troy made the claim they were descendents of a NAIAD or NERERD, as it was believed their offspring were of "surpassing excellence in quality."

Sources: Keightly, *World Guide to Gnomes, Fairies, Elves, and Other Little People*, 445; Larson, *Greek Nymphs*, 29

Homme de Bouc

Variations: Ancho. BASA-JUAN

In French fairy lore Homme de Bouc ("he-goat man") was once a god but had been reduced to the status of fairy, living in the forests between France and Spain. In some stories he is described as being similar to the Scottish BROWNIE; in this role Homme de Bouc is on occasion referred to as Ancho. He lives in shepherd's huts in the mountains, drinks their milk, eats their cheese, and by the fire side will converse with them. Al-though these encounters seem innocent enough there is always a feeling of dread associated with them.

Sources: Illes, *Encyclopedia of Spirits*, 263–4; Rose, *Giants, Monsters, and Dragons*, 30; Webster, *Basque Legends*, 76

Hooper of Sennen Cove

In Sennen Cove, West Cornwall, England there is believed to live a NATURE SPIRIT called Hooper who warns the locals of approaching storms. Described as looking like a large sheet of cloud mist stretched across the bay with a dull light in the middle of it, Hooper will appear before a storm and make distinctive yet strange hooping sounds. The fog this fairy created was thick enough even if his calls were ignored a fisherman would have to intentionally make a very poor decision to sail out into it; those who did were inevitably lost at sea.

Sources: Briggs, Encyclopedia of Fairies, 225; Morvan, *Legends of the Sea*, 134; Westwood, *Lore of the Land*, 113

Horae

In the mythology of the ancient Greeks the horae ("the correct moment") were the three NYMPHS born of the union between Zeus (Jupiter) and the Titian goddess of Law, Themis; their names were DIKE ("just retribution"), EIRENE ("Peace"), and EUNOMIA ("lawful order"). Collectively these NATURE SPIRIT-like sisters controlled the changing of the seasons, were the guardians of natural law, and were entrusted with guarding the gate to Olympus.

Sources: Gall, *Lincoln Library of Greek and Roman Mythology*, 20; McLean, *Triple Goddess*, 49; Roman, *Encyclopedia of Greek and Roman Mythology*, 172

Hornbori

Hornbori ("horn carrier") was one of the many DWARFS named in the *Voluspa*, the first and best known poem of the *Poetic Edda*, a collection of Old Norse poems dating back to about A.D. 985.

Sources: Crossley-Holland, *Norse Myths*, 183; Daly, *Norse Mythology A to Z*, 22; Wilkinson, *Book of Edda called Völuspá*, 12

Horr

Variations: Hor, Hörr

Horr was one of the many DWARFS named in the *Voluspa*, the first and best known poem of the *Poetic Edda*, a collection of Old Norse poems dating back to about A.D. 985.

Sources: Anderson, *Norse Mythology*, 108; Sturluson, *Prose Edda*, 26

Houndkonz

Houndkonz was a powerful DEEV; according to ancient Persian lore he slew Tamnuras, the King of Persia, also known as the DEEV-Binder.

Sources: Brewer, *Dictionary of Phrase and Fable*, 340; Keightly, *World Guide to Gnomes, Fairies, Elves, and Other Little People*, 18

Hounds of Annwn

Variations: Cwn Annwn, Herla's Hounds, Hounds of the Hills

The Hounds of Annwn were the spectral fairy hounds associated with Annwn, the underworld in Welsh mythology. Owned by Arawn, Lord of Annwn, the pack was usually sent out on their own to retrieve souls for Annwn or to reveal and occasionally consume a corpse. In the *First Branch of the Mabinogi* (*Pedair Cainc y Mabinogi*), the hounds were described as being shining white with red ears but other sources say they were small, grey hounds with red speckles. To see them was an omen of death.

After the introduction of Christianity the Hounds of Annwn were reclassified as hell hounds; however Annwn itself was more accurately defined as a paradise.

Sources: Conway, *Magickal, Mystical Creatures*, 147; Green, *Animals in Celtic Life and Myth*, 168, 190; Illes, *Encyclopedia of Spirits*, 188–9

House-Spirit

Variations: Domestic Fairy, Domestic Fay, Domestic spirit, Domovoj House Fairy, TOMTE-GUBBE

In British fairy lore a house-spirit is a domestic fay, one of two classes of fairy; typically these fairies are called BROWNIES, HOBGOBLINS or ROBIN GOOD FELLOW. The other class of fairy would be the Elves, those fairies living in the caves, fields, mountains, and woods. Well know house-spirits include CAULD LAD, HINZELMAN, ISKRZYCKI, ORTHONE, and TONTTY.

Sources: Ashiman, *Fairy Lore*, 144; Hastings, *Encyclopedia of Religion and Ethics*, Part 10, 683; Keightly, *World Guide to Gnomes, Fairies, Elves, and Other Little People*, 281

Howlaa

Variations: Dooiney-oie, Howa-a, Howaa, the Night Man

On the Isle of Man the howlaa is a fairy known to call out from the mountains just prior to a storm; this NATURE SPIRIT received its name from the distinct sound of it dismal call, "*howlaa, howlaa!*"

Sources: Briggs, Encyclopedia of Fairies, 226; Cumming, *Guide to the Isle of Man*, 23; Jenkinson, *Jenkinson's Practical Guide to the Isle of Man*, 40

Hreidmar

Variations: Reidmar

Hreidmar was a magician DWARF king, and the father of three sons, FAFNIR, ÓTR, and REGIN and two daughters, Lofnheid and Lyngheid, in Norse mythology. When his son ÓTR was killed in a hunting accident by the god Loki, Hreidmar was gifted with a treasure hoard of gold. To ensure the safety of bounty, Hreidmar placed his strongest son, FAFNIR in charge of its protection but his son was driven by greed and killed his father for possession of it. This tragic story is told in the legendary thirteenth century saga, *Volsunga Saga* ("*Saga of the Völsungs*").

Sources: Daly, *Norse Mythology*, 51; Dekirk, *Dragonlore*, 72–3; Gentry, *Nibelungen Tradition*, 92

Hrist

In Nordic and Teutonic mythology Hrist ("storm") was one of the named VALKYRIES, a NYMPH of battle. Always depicted as beautiful women who are sometimes immortal, they are the attendants of the god, Odin.

Sources: Grimm *Teutonic Mythology*, Volume 1, 422; Sigfusson, *Elder Eddas of Saemund Sigfusson Younger Eddas of Snorre Sturleson*, 57, 310

Hu hsien

In China the hu hsien ("a fox fairy") is a malicious fox-fairy; they are powerful shape-shifters. Hu hsien are believed to be the guardian spirit of the seal of some of the high officials.

Sources: Moorey, *Fairy Bible*, 388; Rose, *Spirits, Fairies, Gnomes, and Goblins*, 155; Sullivan, *Introduction to Chinese Art*, 202

Huacas

In Incan mythology the huacas are a type of NATURE SPIRIT, the stone forms or sacred object or place of divine beings or spirits; a carved stone huacas is called an *inti huatana*. Specific huacas had definite powers and responsibilities; each one protected a particular area, be it a bridge, cave, field, hill, river, spring, temple, tomb, or a well. Hierarchically ranked the larger the huacas was the more raw power it had, therefore the most powerful huacas were the snow-covered mountain peaks.

Sources: Andrews, *Dictionary of Nature Myths,* 94; McEwan, *The Incas,* 158; Roza, *Incan Mythology and Other Myths of the Andes,* 18

Hugstari

Hugstari was one of the many DWARFS named in the *Voluspa,* the first and best known poem of the *Poetic Edda,* a collection of Old Norse poems dating back to about A.D. 985.

Sources: Crossley-Holland, *Norse Myths,* 183; Grimes, *Norse Myths,* 7; Sturluson, *Prose Edda,* 23

Huldafolk

Variations: Hulda-Folk

Huldafolk ("hidden people") are species of reclusive fairies in Scandinavian folklore. Although their interaction with humans is very rare when it occurs they will deal fairly and reward good and honest behavior. To ask a hulfafolk for a knife is considered very unlucky and ensures having a curse being laid.

Sources: Avant, *Mythological Reference,* 472; Jeaffreson, *Farӧe Islands,*96–7

Huldra

Variations: Hulla, Skogsrå, SKOGSFRU ("lady (ruler) of the forest"), Skogsnerte, TALLEMAJA ("pine tree Mary")

In Norwegian folklore it is believed an individual fairy-woman or NYMPH named Huldra ("covered" or "secret") lives in the forest and mountains. Descriptions of Huldra vary across the country, sometimes she is said to be beautiful but when seen from behind reveled to be hollow; other times she is said to be blue-skinned. In areas where she is known as Skogsnerte ("blue") she is said to be blue colored and wearing a green petticoat. As Huldra, as she is most commonly known, she is said to be beautiful, wearing a blue petticoat and a white snood that nearly hides her long, cowlike tail; a physical trait she is most embarrassed of. Particularly fond of brindled colored cattle, she keeps a handsome and thriving heard of hornless cows. In the mountains her song can be hear over a great distance, a low and mournful tune.

Sources: Conway, *Magickal Mystical Creatures,* 233–4; Rosen, *Mythical Creatures Bible,* 245; Thorpe, *Scandinavian Popular Traditions and Superstitions,* Volume 2, 2–3

Huldrafolk (plural: Huldre)

Variations: Uldra

In regions sporadic throughout the country HULDRA is not thought of as an individual being but rather a race of fairy. The Huldre, or Huldre-folk as they are also known, are said to live in the mountains, wearing nothing but green colored clothing and raise herds of blue cattle known to yield copious amounts of milk. Huldre-men tend to their herds in pasture lands mortals have abandoned. The music of the huldrafolk is called *huldraslaat*; is in a minor key and known for its dull and mournful sound.

In Lapland the huldrafolk are considered to be beneficent NATURE SPIRITS living underground coming to the surface quite regularly to work with the animals of the woods. In the winter the Huldre are said to feed the hibernating, especially the bears, so gently as not to wake them.

Sources: Conway, *Magickal Mystical Creatures,* 233–4; Keightly, *World Guide to Gnomes, Fairies, Elves, and Other Little People,* 79; Rosen, *Mythical Creatures Bible,* 245; Thorpe, *Scandinavian Popular Traditions and Superstitions,* Volume 2, 2–3

Huldufólk

In Iceland the huldufólk ("hidden people") are a race of people with many characteristics similar to the fay. Living a life cycle similar to humans—they mature, marry, and have children—the huldufólk live in communities called *huldubyggd,* and are usually associated with sacred boulders or hillocks.

Sources: Bord, *Fairies,* 59; Swatos, *Icelandic Spiritualism,* 46–7

Humuhumu

A tutelary NATURE SPIRIT from the Maori mythology, Hummuhumu escorted the cultural hero Mahuhu on his journey. Hummuhumu had the ability to shape-shift into animals and could take on the form of natural phenomena.

Sources: Orbell, *Concise Encyclopedia of Māori Myth and Legend,* 47

Huorco

Variations: Huerco, Huergo, Orco, Uerco

Huorco was a famous GIANT or OGRE from the seventeenth-century fairy tale collection, *The Pentamerone,* by the Italian poet Giambattista Basile; he was portrayed as being a cruel, maneating, and ugly being. The word *huorco* is sometimes used as a synonym for a BOGEYMAN.

Sources: Grimm, *Teutonic Mythology,* Volume 4, 1428; Keightley, *Fairy Mythology,* 640

Hyad

Variations: The Hyades, Thyades

The Hyad ("rainer") were one of twelve species of NYMPHS, they were any of the daughters born of Atlas and AETHRA. As a reward for having nursed the infant god Dionysus (Bacchus) on Mount Nysa, they were transformed into a cluster of stars.

In a different version of the myth it was said when their brother Hyas was killed while on a hunting expedition they wept so much they were transformed into a constellation. The names of the sisters vary wildly among the ancient writers but common groupings of the sister are Adraste, ALTHAEA, and IDOTHEA; AESYLE, AMBROSIA, AND EUDORA; AGAVE, Autone, Ino, and Semele; AMBROSIA, CORONIS, EUDORA, PEDILE, PHAENO, Phaesyla, POLYXO, and Thyone (DIONE); Bromia, Cisseis, ERATO, ERIPHIA, NYSA, and POLYHYMNO; Cleeia (KLEEIA), CORONIS, EUDORA, Phaeote, and Phaesyle; Cleis, Coronia, and PHILIA; and Phileto, Plexaris, PRODICE, Python, Suculae, and TYCHE.

Sources: Clark, *Classical Manual*, 246; Grant, *Who's Who in Classical Mythology*, 79; Littleton, *Gods, Goddesses, and Mythology*, Volume 11, 999; Smith, *Dictionary of Greek and Roman Biography and Mythology: Earinus-Nyx*, 533

Hyale

Variations: Hyalê

In Greek mythology Hyale ("crystal") was a water–NYMPH and one of the named DANAIDS, the collective name for the daughters of Danaus; her name appears in a list of the DANAIDS generated by Gaius Julius Hyginus (ca. 64 B.C.–A.D. 17), a Latin author. Hyale was wedded to Perius and killed him on their wedding night. According to the ancient Greek oral poet, Hesiod, Hyale was one of the OCEANID NYMPHS which formed the retinue of the goddess, Artemis (Diana).

Sources: Bell, *Bell's New Pantheon or Historical Dictionary of the Gods,* 112; Hyginus, *Myths of Hyginus*, 132; Parada, *Genealogical Guide to Greek Mythology*, 59

Hyde

In classical Greek mythology Hyde was a NYMPH and a NAIAD of the town of Hyde in Lydia; she was the wife of a local lord named Otrynteus.

Sources: Homer, *Iliads of Homer*, 136; Larson, *Greek Nymphs*, 22

Hyele

Variations: Elea ("glassy stream"), Velia

In ancient Greek mythology Hyele ("moist girl") was a NYMPH of springs in Southern Italy.

Sources: Larson, *Greek Nymphs*, 224; Seltman, *Masterpieces of Greek Coinage*, 70

Hyldemoer

Variations: Hylde-moer (Elder-mother), Hyldermoder, Hyldeqvinde (Elder-wife)

In Copenhagen, Denmark Hyldemoer are a species of fairy being similar to the NYMPHS of ancient Greece; as they live in elder trees and avenge any injury done to them. If a moveable object is made from elder wood, such as a child's cradle, the infant will never know a moment's peace as the hyldemoer will poke at it and pull its legs. It is believed before an elder tree is cut one needs to ask permission by saying aloud *"hyldemoer, hyldemoer, allow me to cut thy branches."*

Sources: Folkard, *Plant Lore, Legends, and Lyrics*, 318; Keightly, *World Guide to Gnomes, Fairies, Elves, and Other Little People*, 93; Thorpe, *Northern Mythology*, Volume 1, 167–8

Hylleis

In ancient Greek mythology, Hylleis was a NYMPH of Thera.

Sources: Dixon-Kennedy, *Encyclopedia of Greco-Roman Mythology*, 167; Larson, *Greek Nymphs*, 188

Hypate

One of the MUSES, Hypate ("highest") was the MUSE of the highest cord of the lyre; she represented one of the three strings on the popular Greek musical instrument, they lyre (see also MESE and NETE). Hypate was associated with Delphi, Greece.

Sources: Hastings, *Encyclopædia of Religion and Ethics*, Volume 9, 4; Peterson, *Mythology in Our Midst*, 121; Smith, *Dictionary of Greek and Roman Biography and Mythology*, 1125

Hypereia

In classical Greek mythology, Hypereia was a NYMPH of a spring in the town of Argos, in the Peloponnesos located in southern Greece. This NAIAD was a daughter of Peneios.

Sources: Cook, *Zeus*, 1228; Larson, *Greek Nymphs*, 166

Hyperippe

In Greek mythology Hyperippe was a water–NYMPH and one of the named DANAIDS, the collective name for the daughters of Danaus. In a list compiled by Apollodorus, a Greek scholar and grammarian, she was one of the daughters of Crino and was wedded to Hippocorystes, one of the sons of Hephaestine.

Sources: Bell, *Women of Classical Mythology*, 250; Grimal, *Dictionary of Classical Mythology*, 127; Parada, *Genealogical Guide to Greek Mythology*, 89

Hypermnestra

In Greek mythology Hypermnestra ("excessive wooing" or "special intent") was a water–NYMPH and one of the named DANAIDS, the collective name for the daughters of Danaus; her name appears in a list of the DANAIDS generated by Gaius Julius Hyginus (ca. 64 B.C.–A.D. 17), a Latin author. Hypermnestra was wedded to Lynceus and was the only one of her sisters not to kill her husband on their wedding night because he respected her desire to remain a virgin. In a list compiled by Apollodorus, a Greek scholar and grammarian, she was one of the daughters of Elephantis and was wedded to one of the sons of Queen Argyphia, Lyncaeus.

Sources: Bell, *Women of Classical Mythology*, 250–1; Grimal, *Dictionary of Classical Mythology*, 127; Parada, *Genealogical Guide to Greek Mythology*, 190

Hyter Sprite

Variations: Hyster

In East Anglia and Lincolnshire, England hyster sprites are a type of fairy which shape-shift into sand martins, a species of regional bird. Naturally sandy-brown in color with bright green eyes hyster sprites are known together in groups and fly dangerously close to humans.

Sources: Briggs, *Encyclopedia of Fairies*, 230; McCoy, *Witch's Guide to Faery Folk*, 247; Rye, *Glossary of Words used in East Anglia*, Volume 31, 109

Iache

Born one of the 3,000 daughters of the Titians, Oceanus and Tethys, Iache (shriek" or "wail") was one of the named OCEANIDS in ancient Greek mythology; she was one of the playmates of Persephone (Proserpina) and present when the goddess was kidnapped.

Sources: Allen, *Homeric Hymns*, 51; Fowler, *Archaic Greek Poetry*, 14; Morford, *Classical Mythology*, 613

Iaera

A mountain NYMPH, Iaera ("the honeyed") was the NEREIS associated with Mount Ida, located in Phrygia. She was the mother of Pandarus and Bitias in Greek mythology.

Sources: Apollodorus, *Apollodorus' Library and Hyginus' Fabulae*, 95; Gould, *Historic Magazine and*

Notes and Queries, Vol 14, 212; Virgi, *Aeneid of Vergill*, 69

Iaira

Iaira was one of the named NEREID of Greek mythology who accompanied THETIS in mourning the loss of her son, Achilles.

Sources: Collignon, *Manual of Mythology*, 18; Homer, *The Iliad*, 503; Perry, *Women of Homer*, 146

Iakhe

Born one of the 3,000 daughters of the Titians, Oceanus and Tethys, Iakhe was one of the named OCEANIDS in ancient Greek mythology.

Source: Crudden, *Homeric Hymns*, 19

Ianassa

Variations: Ianesse

A NYMPH from Greek mythology, Ianassa ("wedded to voice") was one of the NEREIS who accompanied THETIS in mourning the loss of her son, Achilles.

Sources: Apollodorus, *Apollodorus' Library and Hyginus' Fabulae*, 95; Gould, *Historic Magazine and Notes and Queries*, Vol 14, 212; Homer, *Iliads of Homer*, 137; Perry, *Women of Homer*, 146

Ianeria

Variations: Iæneria

A sea–NYMPH from Greek mythology, Ianeria ("the famous"), was one of the named NEREIDS who accompanied THETIS in mourning the loss of her son, Achilles. Born the daughter of Nerues and DORIS, she was one of the NYMPHS gathering flowers with Persephone (Proserpina).

There is another Ianeira ("lady of the Ionians") who was said to have been born one of the 3,000 daughters of the Titians, Oceanus and Tethys, and was one of the named OCEANIDS. Ianeira was one of the playmates of Persephone and present when the goddess was kidnapped.

Sources: Crudden, *Homeric Hymns*, 19; Gould, *Historic Magazine and Notes and Queries*, Vol 14, 212; Perry, *Women of Homer*, 146; Trzaskoma, *Anthology of Classical Myth*, 18

Ianira

Born one of the 3,000 daughters of the Titians, Oceanus and Tethys, Ianira was one of the named OCEANIDS from Greek mythology. She was also a sea–NYMPH, one of the named NEREID; some sources say she was born of Nereus and DORIS.

Sources: Apollodorus, *Apollodorus' Library and Hyginus' Fabulae*, 95; Avant, *Mythological Reference*, 296; Boswell, *What Men or Gods Are These*, 58;

Fowler, *Archaic Greek Poetry*, 14; Hesiod, *Works of Hesiod, Callimachus, and Theognis*, 20

Ianthe

Born one of the 3,000 daughters of the Titians, Oceanus and Tethys, Ianthe was one of the named OCEANIDS from Greek mythology. She was also known to be the NYMPH of violet flowers or violet rainclouds. Ianthe was one of the playmates of Persephone (Proserpina) and present when the goddess was kidnapped.

Sources: Bell, *Bell's New Pantheon or Historical Dictionary of the Gods,* 112; Boswell, *What Men or Gods Are These,* 58; Conti, *Natale Conti's Mythologiae: Books VI–X,* 701; Hesiod, *Works of Hesiod, Callimachus, and Theognis,* 20

Iara

Variations: Mae d'Agua, Vira, Yara

Iara are Brazilian NATURE SPIRITS who live in the Amazon River. Described as looking like beautiful women, the iara are often found sitting on a rock near the river, seductively singing and combing out their long, silky blond hair. Similar to the SIREN of ancient Greece, the green-eyed iara has an irresistible singing voice, luring only bachelors and young men who wish to marry begging them abandon everything and come into the water, almost always with lethal results.

Sources: Illes, *Encyclopedia of Spirits*, 502; Smith, *Enchanted Amazon Rain Forest*, 84–5

Iasis

A NAIAD from classical Greek mythology Iasis ("healer") was one of the four NYMPHS of the healing springs of the river Kytheros in Elis, located in southern Greece. Iasis was most directly associated with warm sulphur springs. Collectively they were known as the IODINES and they names were CALLIPHAEA, IASIS, PEGAEA, and SYNALLAXIS and it was believed to bathe in one of their springs was a cure-all for an array of illnesses and pains.

Sources: Larson, *Greek Nymphs*, 158; Pausanias, *Commentary on Book I: Attica*, 319; Selbie, *Encyclopædia of Religion and Ethics*, 548

Iblis

Variations: "The Bruised One," El-Harith, Enais, "Father of the Sheitans," Haris, SHAITAN, Shaytan, Sheitan

Originating in Hasidic and Muslim lore and adopted into Christian demonology, Iblis ("despair") has been mentioned in the Book of Rev-

elation, the *Book of the Yezidi*, and the Koran. He has been called the Chief of the spirits of evil and the Ruler of Hell, as well as a fallen angel and a DJINN. He is often depicted as having the head of a donkey and wearing a peacock-feathered headdress, or as a hermaphrodite.

Created by God out of the element of fire, Iblis is the father of five evil DJINN sons. Sworn to tempt mankind until Judgment Day, he has the ability to lay eggs from which demons are born, can shape-shift into any form, self-impregnate to give birth to evildoers, and knows the three sacred words that grant immortality. Proud Iblis loves the idea of divinity, but he is powerless against Allah and his followers.

Sources: Guiley, *Encyclopedia of Demons and Demonology*, 67, 117–8; Houtsma, *E.J. Brill's First Encyclopaedia of Islam*, 187, 296, 351; Hyatt, *Book of Demons*, 53; McHugh, *Hantu Hantu*, 121

Ida

Variations: NEMESIS

In ancient Greek and Roman mythology, ADRASTEA and Ida were the mountain NYMPHS living in Dictaea; they were wet-nurses to the infant god Zeus (Jupiter).

Sources: Lanier, *Book of Giants*, 4–5; Lethbridge, *Gogmagog*, 163; Pausanias, *Pausanias's Description of Greece*, Volume 1, 434

Idaia

Variations: Idaean Mother, Kybele

Idaia was a NYMPH of Mount Ida in the Troad, Anatolia from the classical mythology of ancient Greece; she was the wife of the river god, Skamandros (SCAMANDER).

Sources: Apollodorus of Athens, *Library of Greek Mythology* 123; Fontenrose, *Python*, 416, 481

Ide

Ide was one of the NYMPHS of Ida on the island of Crete in the Greek Aegean Sea who was a nurse to the infant god, Zeus (Jupiter), according to classical Greek mythology.

Sources: Cook, *Zeus*, 982; Larson, *Greek Nymphs*, 185

Idothea

One of the HYAD, Idothea was a NYMPH of Mount Ida on the island of Crete in the Greek Aegean Sea; she was one of the nurses to the infant god, Zeus (Jupiter). She was commonly grouped with fellow NYMPHS, ADRASTE and ALTHAEA.

Sources: Cook, *Zeus*, 112; Smith, *Dictionary of Greek and Roman Biography and Mythology: Earinus-Nyx*, 533

Idya

Born one of the 3,000 daughters of the Titians, Oceanus and Tethys, Idya was one of the named OCEANIDS from Greek mythology.

Sources: Boswell, *What Men or Gods Are These*, 58; Hesiod, *Works of Hesiod, Callimachus, and Theognis*, 20

Idyia

Variations: EIDYIA

Born one of the 3,000 daughters of the Titians, Oceanus and Tethys, Idyia ("the knowing") was one of the named OCEANIDS from Greek mythology; she was married to King Aectes and bore him two children a son named Apsyrtus and a daughter named Medea.

Sources: Grant, *Who's Who in Classical Mythology*, 12; Monaghan, *Encyclopedia of Goddesses and Heroines*, 414; Westmoreland, *Ancient Greek Beliefs*, 24

Ieles

In eastern European fairy lore, ieles were a species of malevolent, vampiric fairies described as looking like large bipedal cats. At crossroads and villiage fountains, they attacked humans and drank their blood. The ieles had the ability to cast an array of maladies on humans but would also on occasion fall in love with one. These fairies are very fond of music. eles are likely a type of NEREID or NYMPH who were changed into malicious being after the introduction of Christianity.

Sources: Evan-Wentz, *Fairy Faith in Celtic Countries*, 230–31; McCoy, *Witch's Guide to Faery Folk*, 247–8; Newcomb, *Faerie Treasury*, 52

Ielle

Variations: Iele, Rusalii

The ielle ("they") of Romanian lore were the extremely beautiful but injurious fairies. Said to dan in the forests and dressed in white, the ielle caused general mischief, illness, and storms. Like the WILL O' THE WISP, they also lead people deep into the forest where they became fatally lost. They are led by their FAIRY QUEEN, IRODEASA.

Source: Illes, *Encyclopedia of Spirits*, 504

Ifrit

Variations: Afreet, Afrit, Afrite, Efreet, Ifreet

The ifrit is a species of DJINN from Arabic mythology. A subterranean spirit, it looks like an enormous, winged demon made of smoke. Cunning, immortal, and strong, their veins flow with fire, not blood. When an ifrit is mortally wounded it combusts into flames. Ifrit live underground and in ruins in a structured tribal society under the command of their tribal leader. The female of the species is known as an 'ifritah. These demons fear lightning bolts.

Sources: Hyatt, *Book of Demons*, 55; Merriam-Webster, Inc., *Merriam-Webster's Encyclopedia of World Religions*, 498; Rose, *Giants, Monsters, and Dragons*, 6

Ifrita

In Arabic mythology an ifrita is a type of DJINN looking like a woman with huge breasts and large buttocks. Natural seductresses, these fairies can shape-shift into a beautiful woman.

Sources: Gibb, *Shorter Encyclopaedia of Islam*, 159; Knappert, *Encyclopaedia of Middle Eastern Mythology and Religion*, 154

Igosha

In Slavic folklore the igosha is a species of Household spirite, the spirit of an infant who died without being baptized; they are usually buried just outside the house they were born in. The igosha are described as being headless, legless and fond of playing pranks. To keep an igosha appeased, acknowledge its presence loudly and leave it an offering of a loaf of bread, a spoon, and in the winter months, a hat and mittens.

Sources: Gorky, *Childhood*, 209; Franklin, *Working with Fairies*, 133

Illes

Illes are a species of nocturnal TROLL living underground in Icelandic and Scandinavian folklore. Described as being dark skinned and very hairy these fairies try to lure mortals into their lairs by shape-shifting into a sexually attractive member of the opposite sex.

Sources: Conway, *Magickal Mystical Creatures*, 222

Ina Pic Winna

In Worlebury Hill, North Somerset, England it was the custom of local fishermen to leave a small white stone at the nearby fairy mound and say "Ina Pic Winna, send me a good dinner." According to lore, those fishermen who practice this belief will return with a load of fish.

Sources: Briggs, *Encyclopedia of Fairies*, 232; Hole, *English Folklore*, 39

Inachus

Born one of very few sons of the Titians Oceanus and Tethys, Inachus was one of the named OCEANIDS from Greek mythology. He was married to the OCEANID, MELIA; together they had a son named Phoroneos.

Sources: Boswell, *What Men or Gods Are These*, 58; Day, *God's Conflict with the Dragon and the Sea*, 64; Hesiod, *Works of Hesiod, Callimachus, and Theognis*, 20

Incantatrice

Variations: FATA, Incantatori, Maga, Maliarda, Streghe

In the fairy lore based on Italian poetry there are two classes of FATE, there known as FATA. The first is beneficent and protective of mortals while the other in malicious and seductive. The terms FATA, *incantatrice*, and *maga* are used interchangeably between the classes.

Sources: Keightly, *World Guide to Gnomes, Fairies, Elves, and Other Little People*, 453; Levack, *Demonology, Religion, and Witchcraft*, 158

Inconstancy

In the French fairy-tale *The Princess Minion-Minette* the fairy Inconstancy was the FAIRY GODMOTHER to the young king, Souci; she raised him to adulthood from his infancy.

Source: Lang, *Pink Fairy Book*, 274–88

Incubo

In Italian folk lore Incubo is a small, individual fairy said to watch over hidden treasure. If his cap is ever stolen he will give up the location of treasure to get it back.

Sources: Keightly, *World Guide to Gnomes, Fairies, Elves, and Other Little People*, 449; Ripley, *American Cyclopaedia*, Volume 7, 163

Indra

In the fairy-tale *Dorani*, Indra was the FAIRY KING of FAIRYLAND; he held the beautiful maiden, Dorani and her friend, the fairy Indra, in high regard because not only could they sing beautifully but also because no one in the kingdom of Hindustan could match their beauty and grace.

Source: Lang, *Olive Fairy Book*, 190–97

Ingi

Variations: Ing

Ingi ("lordly") was one of the many DWARFS named in the *Voluspa*, the first and best known poem of the *Poetic Edda*, a collection of Old Norse poems dating back to about A.D. 985.

Sources: Crossley-Holland, *Norse Myths*, 183; Sturluson, *Edda*, 17

Io

Variations: Kallithyia

A NAIAD of the river Inakhos in Argos located in southern Greece, Io was a beautiful NYMPH born the daughter of the river god Inachus; she who was seduced by the god, Zeus (Jupiter). In order to hide the affair from this jealous wife, Hera (Juno), Zeus transformed Io into a pure white heifer so he may take the form of a bull when he visited her. Unfortunately Hera discovered the liaison thanks to her 1,000 eyed servant, Argus, and plagued Io with a gladfly. Once bitten by the insect, Io was compelled to run aimlessly and continuously. One day she came upon the chained and suffering Prometheus who prophesied she would stop her endless running at the Nile river where Zeus would touch her and she would conceive a son. The prophecy came to pass and Io went on to marry the king of Egypt.

In the oldest versions of this story Io was a mortal priest of Hera and was raped by Zeus.

Sources: Illes, *Encyclopedia of Spirits*, 511; Littleton, *Gods, Goddesses, and Mythology*, Volume 11, 1435; Rigoglioso, *Cult of Divine Birth in Ancient Greece*, 131

Ione

A sea–NYMPH, Ione, was one of the named NEREIDS in classical Greek mythology; she was born the daughter of Nerues and DORIS; she was described as being "sweet."

Sources: Apollodorus, *Apollodorus' Library and Hyginus' Fabulae*, 2; Landor, *Hellenics and Gebir of Walter Savage Landor*, 51; Trzaskoma, *Anthology of Classical Myth*, 18

The Ionides

Variations: Ioniades

NAIADS from classical Greek mythology the Ionides were four NYMPHS of the healing springs of the river Kytheros in Elis, located in southern Greece; their names were CALLIPHAEA, IASIS, PEGAEA, and SYNALLAXIS. It was believed to bathe in one of their springs was a cure-all for an array of illnesses and pains. The ionides were named after Ion, the son of Gargettus.

Sources: Jayne, *Healing Gods of Ancient Civilizations*, 339; Larson, *Greek Nymphs*, 158; Pausanias, *Commentary on Book I: Attica*, 319

Iphianassa

A sea–NYMPH, Iphianassa ("rule strongly"), was one of the named NEREIDS in classical Greek mythology; she was born the daughter of Nerues and DORIS; according to Homer she was one of the daughters of Agamenmon along with CHRYSOTHEMIS ("golden light") and Laodice ("justice for the people").

Sources: Edwards, *Homer,* 151; Grimal, *Larousse World Mythology,* 159

Iphimedusa

In Greek mythology Iphimedusa was a water–NYMPH and one of the named DANAIDS, the collective name for the daughters of Danaus. In a list compiled by Apollodorus, a Greek scholar and grammarian, she was one of the daughters of HAMADRYAD, ATLANTEIA or (PHOEBE, sources vary) and was wedded to Euchenor, one of the sons of an unnamed Arabic woman.

Sources: Bell, Women of Classical Mythology, 149; Grimal, *Dictionary of Classical Mythology,* 127; Lemprière, *Classical Dictionary,* 236

Ircenrraq (plural: ircenrraat)

Among the Inuit people in Yup'ik, central Alaska, United States of America, the ircenrraat are a species of fairy living under the low hills on Nelson Island. Described as being small and standing only two or three feet tall, the ircenrraat appear as a normal person or even as a fox or wolf; it is not until days later the person realizes they had an encounter with a fairy being. There are many stories of people walking up on one of these hills, seeing a window dug into it and stealing a peek inside; after what seems to be only a moment it is later discovered a great deal of time has passed. To spend a night in the company of one of the ircenrraq one will later discover a year has passed.

Sources: Fienup-Riordan, *Boundaries and Passages,* 63–4; Meade, *Ciuliamta Akluit,* 81, 291

Iri

Variations: UNI

Iri was one of the many DWARFS named in the *Voluspa,* the first and best known poem of the *Poetic Edda,* a collection of Old Norse poems dating back to about A.D. 985; in the poem it was said the Iri existed "before Valhalla was walled."

Iri was also named as being one of the Ijosalfar, the SONS OF IVALDI. These DWARFS were the ones who created many of the magical items of the gods, including the golden wig of Sif; the ship, Skidbladnir; and the spear of Odin.

Sources: Grimes, *Norse Myths,* 9, 285; Rydberg, *Our Fathers' Godsaga,* 186; Smart, *Norroena,* 356

Irodeasa

Variations: Arada, Aradia, Doamna Zinelor, Herodiada, Herodias, Irodiada

A beautiful and dangerous FAIRY QUEEN of the IELLE fairies from Romanian lore, Irodeasa was worshiped as goddess, the Romanian equivalent of Diana.

Sources: Grimassi, *Hereditary Witchcraft,* 224; Illes, *Encyclopedia of Spirits,* 513

Isione

In Greek mythology Isione was a water–NYMPH; she was one of the DANAID, the fifty daughters of Danaus. The wife of Chryses, she was seduced by the god, Zeus (Jupiter), by which she bore a son named Orchomenos.

Sources: Myres, *Who Were the Greek,* 328; Roberts, *Writings of Tatian and Theophilus,* 440

Iskrzycki

Iskrzycki ("firestone" or "spark") was a specific and singular fairy being described as having horse hooves for feet. According to Polish folklore, Iskrzycki offered his services to a noble family which was accepted and a contract was drawn up and signed. After the nobleman saw Iskrzycki's feet and tried to dismiss him but the fairy would not leave, rather he took up residence, invisibly, by the fireplace doing the tasks assigned to him. The Lady of the house was unsettled by Iskrzycki and convinced her husband to move the family. As they traveled to their new residence, the wagon came upon a rough patch of road and nearly toppled over. The lady cried out in panic but Iskrzycki came to her rescue exclaiming for everyone to hear "Fear not my masters, Iskrzycki is here." With that, the family returned to their old home and learned to live with their fairy servant. He was good and reliable and quietly left when his contract expired.

Sources: Grimm, *Teutonic Mythology,* Volume 2, 513; Keightly, *World Guide to Gnomes, Fairies, Elves, and Other Little People,* 491

Ismene

Ismene was a NYMPH of Telos in classical Greek mythology.

Sources: Larson, *Greek Nymphs,* 304; Müller, *Ancient Art and Its Remains,* 540, Murray, *Manual of Mythology,* 207

Ismenis

Ismenis was a NYMPH from the mythology of classical Greece and Rome. One of the NAIADS, she was born the daughter of the river god, Ismenus. She and the god Fanus had a son together named Crenaeus.

Sources: Duncan, *Influence of Art on Description in the Poetry of P. Papinius Statius*, 59, 61; Smith, *Smaller Classical Mythology*, 143

Isonoe

In Greek mythology Isonoe, was a NYMPH and one of the named DANAIDS; she is said to be the mother of Orchomenus by the god, Zeus (Jupiter) and with the assistance of Minerva she was able to escape Egypt and flee to Argos.

Sources: Blunck, *Solar System Moons*, 40; Falkner, *Mythology of the Night Sky*, 183

Issa

In Greek mythology, Issa was a NYMPH of Lesbos; she was married to Cadmus.

Sources: Larson, *Greek Nymphs: Myth, Cult, Lore*, 197; Shields, *Cults of Lesbos*, 37

Itea

In Greek mythology Itea was a water–NYMPH and one of the named DANAIDS, the collective name for the daughters of Danaus; her name appears in a list of the DANAIDS generated by Gaius Julius Hyginus (ca. 64 B.C.–A.D. 17), a Latin author. Itea was wedded to Antiochus and killed him on their wedding night.

Sources: Bell, *Women of Classical Mythology*, 438; Hyginus, *Myths of Hyginus*, 133

Ithome

In ancient Greek mythology Ithome and NEDA were the two NYMPHS of Mount Ithome who nursed the infant god, Zeus (Jupiter) while he was in hiding from his father, Cronus; she was also one of the named OCEANID.

Sources: Hesiod, *Works of Hesiod*, 122; Smith, *Springs and Wells in Greek and Roman Literature*, 96

Iubdan

A FAIRY KING of Ulster, Iubdan was described as being both boastful and small; he ruled over a diminutive race of people known as the Faylinn; they stood only a few inches tall. Iubdan's equally small FAIRY QUEEN was named Bebo. The Faylinn, being so small, believed Ireland was populated by GIANTS.

Sources: Monaghan, *Encyclopedia of Celtic Mythol-ogy and Folklore*, 265; Mountain, *Celtic Encyclopedia*, 767; Rolleston, *Celtic Myths and Legends*, 246

Ívaldi

Variations: Ivald, Ivallda

Ívaldi was one of the many DWARFS named in the *Voluspa*, the first and best known poem of the *Poetic Edda*, a collection of Old Norse poems dating back to about 985, A.D; he was the father of BROKKR and SINDRI.

Sources: Daly, *Norse Mythology A to Z*, 22; Sykes, *Who's Who in Non-Classical Mythology*, 53

Iynx

An OREAD from classical Greek mythology Iynx was a NYMPH of Boiotia, in central Greece; she was the daughter the god, Pan (Faunus) and the NYMPH, ECHO. Iynx seduced the god Zeus (Jupiter) by the means of a love potion. Hera (Juno), the god jealous wife transformed Iynx into a wryneck bird. Other ancient writers say Iynx was one of the nine daughters of PEITHO and created the magical potion was used by Io to cause Zeus to fall in love with her; in this version her punishment was to be turned into stone.

Sources: Arnott, *Birds in the Ancient World from A to Z*, 119; Grant, *Who's Who in Classical Mythology*, 297

Jack Frost

Variations: Father Frost, OLD MAN WINTER

In British fairy lore Jack Frost was a singular individual SEASONAL FAIRY-being, a NATURE-SPIRIT of the cold and frost and the personification of winter. He was said to be ELF-like in appearance and displaying a childlike innocence. It has been speculated by some scholars Jack Frost originated in Norse folklore as either the DWARF Jokul ("icicle") or FROSTI ("frost").

In Russia there is a very strong connection to Jack Frost; on Christmas Eve a spoonful of *kissel*, a type of pudding, is offered to him in exchange for his not spoiling their oat stores and for his driving the flax and hemp roots deep into the ground. It is also believed knocking icicles off of the house will anger Jack Frost to the point where he will freeze the offender to death. In many Russian tales of Jack Frost he is portrayed as a hero who lives in a hut of ice and snow; he bestows gift to the good and deserving people while delivering misfortune to the evil ones. Jack Frost is especially fond of children who are singled out and harassed; he has a particular and singular hatred for hypocrisy, pride, and selfishness.

Sources: Brewer, *Dictionary of Phrase and Fable*, 320; Chamberlain, *Child and Childhood in Folk Thought*, 66–7; Hall, *Pedagogical Seminary*, Volume 10, 62; Rose, *Spirits, Fairies, Gnomes, and Goblins*, 165

Jack-in-Irons

Jack-in-Irons was a nocturnal GIANT from the folklore of Yorkshire, England. Covered in chains and the heads of his past victims, Jack-in-Irons patroled the more isolated and lonely roads with his large spiked club.

Sources: Avant, *Mythological Reference*, 473; Froud, *Faeries*, 102; Monaghan, *Encyclopedia of Celtic Mythology and Folklore*, 266; Wright, *Rustic Speech and Folk-Lore*, 194

Jack-Muh-Lantern

Variations: Joac-O-Lantern

Along the southern coast of the United States of America comes the story of Jack-Muh-Lantern, a hideous creature with a fur-cover body, goggling eyes, and a huge mouth. Standing around five-foot tall, this fairy being leaps through the air like a GIANT grasshopper; stronger than a man and moving faster than a horse it has the supernatural ability to compel its victims to follow it deep into the swamp. Once its prey has been isolated, its abandons them there to die.

Sources: Newell, *Journal of American Folklore*, Volumes 17–18, 41; Sikes, *British Goblins*, 23

Jack o' the Bowl

In Switzerland, Jack o' the Bowl is a household fairy similar to a BROWNIE; each night a bowl of fresh cream is placed for his consumption in the cow house. By morning, the contents of the bowl are always gone.

Sources: Brewer, *Dictionary of Phrase and Fable*, 451; Fisher, *National Geographic Traveler Switzerland*, 52

The Jacobean Fairy

Variations: Greenies

Described as being very small and having gossamer wings this species of fairy was introduced after the ELIZABETHAN FAIRY, in the seventeenth century. The fashion of the fay was extended during this time but the emphasis of fairies here was placed on their small size. Under Puritan influence the fay were regarded as devils.

Source: Stepanich, *Faery Wicca*, Book One, 22, 27, 271

Jafnhar

Jafnhar ("equal to the high") was one of the many DWARFS named in the *Voluspa*, the first and best known poem of the *Poetic Edda*, a collection of Old Norse poems dating back to about A.D. 985. Jafnhar is a king.

Sources: Clarke, *Ten Great Religions*, 370; Keightly, *World Guide to Gnomes, Fairies, Elves, and Other Little People*, 61

Jan

Variations: Jan the Sun

According to Burmese folklore, the jan are one of four different species of the NATS of the Air; generally the jan are considered to be beneficial towards mankind. Once a year they are worshiped by the village chief; sacrifices are not required.

Sources: Hastings, *Encyclopedia of Religion and Ethics*, Part 5, 22; Porteous, *Forest in Folklore and Mythology*, 125; Scott, *Burman: His Life and Notions*, Volume 1, 286

Jan-Ibn-Jan

Variations: Jan bin Jan, Jann al-Jann

The last of the seventy-two Suleymans (kings) of the DJINN, Jan-Ibn-Jan is the ruler of Jinnestan with command over all of his kind, according to Arabic mythology. His name means "Jan son of Jan." Builder of the great pyramids of Egypt, his shield was a powerful magical item that came into the hands of King Solomon, allowing him to bind demons. This demon's personal adversary is the angel IBLIS, not to be confused with the demonic King of the SHAITANS, IBLIS.

Sources: Hyatt, *Book of Demons*, 54; Keightley, *Fairy Mythology*, 18, 25; Lieber, *Encyclopædia Americana*, Volume 5, 412

Janaina

Variations: Aiuka, Dona Janaina ("Lady Janaina"), Dona Maria, Lemanja ("Queen of the Fish"), Princess of the Sea

A beautiful MERMAID from Brazilian lore, Janaina was a benign being who protects fishermen and those who travel by sea. In Afro-Brazilian mythology she was said to have created fish, the oceans, and starfishes; after being raped by own son, Janaina gave birth to the divinities of the Afro-Brazilian, the Orixas.

Sources: Herrera-Sobek, *Celebrating Latino Folklore*, 160; Illes, *Encyclopedia of Spirits*, 522

Jann

Variations: JAN

There are two classes of DJINN in Islamic

mythology. The first and higher class is divided into five genera: the Afreet (IFRIT), GHILAN, Jann, MARID, and the SHAITAN. Born the children of IBLIS, the jann ("spirit") are the weakest of their genus. A type of FAMILIAR spirit, these demons steal animals from farmers.

The author of *One Thousand and One Arabian Nights*, Sir Richard F. Burton, considered the word *jann* to be the plural form of the word GENIE.

Sources: Borges, *Book of Imaginary Beings*, 133–4; Eberhart, *Mysterious Creatures*, 136; Mercatante, *Good and Evil*, 69

Jari

Jari ("fighter") was one of the many DWARFS named in the *Voluspa*, the first and best known poem of the *Poetic Edda*, a collection of Old Norse poems dating back to about A.D. 985.

Sources: Crossley-Holland, *Norse Myths*, 183; Daly, *Norse Mythology A to Z*, 22; Wilkinson, *Book of Edda called Völuspá*, 12

Jengu (plural: miengu)

Among the Duala people of the Cameroonian coast a jengu are a species of water-spirit still widely and openly worship in modern times. The miengu are said to live in rivers and in the sea and described as looking rather like MERMAIDS, having long wooly hair and a gap-tooth smile. Having the ability to control the quality of fishing the miengu are worship and allowed to take part in possession rituals.

Sources: Austen, *Middlemen of the Cameroons Rivers*, 21; Rosen, *Mythical Creatures Bible*, 143

Jenny Greenteeth

Variations: LORELEI with Green Tresses, PEG POWLER

In the folklore of Lancashire and Yorkshire, England Jenny Greenteeth was a NYMPH or water-fairy who lived in the Yorkshire River; when children came too close to her domain, she reached out, grabbed, and held them under the water until they drowned. She was described as looking like a HAG with long green hair and sharp teeth. Similar to PEG POWLER, she was used by parents as a NURSERY BOGIE. Associated with duckweed, a plant that covers the surface of stagnant water, this water fairy would lure children to step out onto the plants, then when the child was away from the bank, the plants would part, the child would fall into the water, and the plants would come back together, hiding any evidence of the child's disappearance.

Jenny Greenteeth was the feminine version of an injurious NATURE SPIRIT known as BLOODY-BONES, RAWHEAD, and Tommy Rawhead.

Sources: Froud, *Faeries*, 117; Watts, *Dictionary of Plant Lore*, 123, 214; Wright, *English Dialect Dictionary*, 730; Wright, *Rustic Speech and Folk-Lore*, 198–9

Jezibaba

Similar to BABA YAGA, Jezibaba ("granny witch") of western Slavic lore lives in a little hut on the shore of a lake. Although not as frightening or vicious as BABA YAGA, Jezibaba is nevertheless the fierce but a helpful fairy witch.

Sources: Folklore Society (Great Britain), *The Folk-Lore Journal*, Volume 6, 200–05; Illes, *Encyclopedia of Spirits*, 528; Johns, *Baba Yaga*, 61, 63

Jimaninos

In Mexican folklore and throughout Central America the jimaninos ("little children") are SEASONAL FAIRIES only appearing on the Day of the Dead festival (November 2), as they are exceedingly shy by nature. Described as looking like chubby, winged children these fairies are unaware they are the souls of deceased children. Male fairy-spirits are called *jimaninos*, and female fairy-spirits are known as *jimaninas*.

Sources: Dunwich, *Witch's Halloween*, 27–8; McCoy, *Witch's Guide to Faery Folk*, 251

Jimmy Squarefoot

Likely originating from the story of Squarefoot, a colossal pig carried about by a stone-throwing GIANT, Jimmy Squarefoot survives on in British and Manx fairy-lore as having a frightening appearance but being otherwise harmless. As the story of Jimmy Squarefoot goes, he was described as having the body of a man but the head of a pig, complete with boarlike tusks, this transformation happened when his wife left him because he used to throw stones at her.

Sources: Allardice, *Myths, Gods and Fantasy*, 125; Avant, *Mythological Reference*, 473; Briggs, *Encyclopedia of Fairy Lore*, 242; Froud, *Faeries*, 103

Joan the Wad

Variations: The Consort of Jack o' Lantern, the Queen of the Piskies

Joan the wad ("Joan of the torch") was a WILL O' THE WISP from the folklore of Polperro, a fishing village in south-east Cornwall; she is also considered to be a FAIRY QUEEN of Cornwall. Based on an old rhyme it is considered lucky to carry a small carving of her to ensure safety when traveling. The carvings depict this PIXIE fairy as being small and squat.

Sources: Briggs, *Encyclopedia of Fairy Lore*, 242; Illes, *Encyclopedia of Spirits*, 531; Simpson, *Dictionary of English Folklore*, N.p.

Jogah

The jogah ("DWARF people") are small NATURE-SPIRITS similar to NYMPHS, in the folklore of the Iroquois people of North America. Each jogah represent different aspects of nature; for instance the GAHONGA are the jogah of rocky terrains and are associated with stones.

Sources: Chopra, *Academic Dictionary of Mythology*, 155; Savill, *Pears Encyclopaedia of Myths and Legends*, 202

Juturna

Variations: DIUTURNA

Juturna was a fountain NYMPH from ancient Roman mythology; her sacred well was located in Latium and was well known for its healing qualities. Water from her source was believed to have healing properties and was used by the Vestal Virgins. Juturna, as a mythological character, was older than Rome, she was said to be the sister to the hero, Turnus and the siblings had fought to keep the Romans from occupying their land.

Juturna was not born a NYMPH but rather transformed into one; it was a means of compensation for Jupiter having raped her. Wed to the god Janus, she was the mother of a son named Fontus, a NYMPH of fountains, springs, and wells.

Sources: Keightly, *World Guide to Gnomes, Fairies, Elves, and Other Little People*, 448; Smith, *Smaller Classical Dictionary*, 295

The Kabeirides

According to classical Greek mythology the NYMPH, KABEIRO and her husband the god, Hephaistos had a son named Kadmilos (Kamillos) who in turned fathered three children collectively known as the Kabeiroi; these children fathered three daughters, the Kabeirides, NEREIDS NYMPHS who lived on or near Samothrake island in the Greek Aegean Sea.

Sources: Brown, *Great Dionysiak Myth*, Volume 2, 217; Larson, *Green Nymphs*, 177

Kabeiro

Variations: Cabeiro, Kabira

Kabeiro ("she is beyond human comprehension") was a NEREID, NYMPH, and an OCEANID from of the island of Lemnos in the north Aegean Sea in classical Greek mythology; she was born one of the daughter of Proteus, the Old Man of the Sea. Kabeiro was married to the god, Hephaistos.

Sources: Evan-Wentz, *Fairy Faith in Celtic Countries*, 308; Hard, *Routledge Handbook of Greek Mythology*, 220; Larson, *Green Nymphs*, 177

Kabouter

Variations: Kaboutermannikin

The kabouter are a friendly Dutch species of Irish LEPRECHAUN or German KOBOLD; they lend a hand by cleaning and cooking, feeding the cattle, fetching water, lighting household fires, threshing grain, and other daily household and farm chores.

Sources: Allardice, *Myths, Gods, and Fantasy*, 130; Arrowsmith, *Field guide to the Little People*, 120

Kaboutermannekin

In the lowlands of Holland the kaboutermannekin is a species of domestic fairy, similar to the BROWNIE but are easily identified by their green face and hands and bright red hats. Kaboutermannekin enjoy doing household chores such as maintain the hearth's fire. If ever offered a set of clothing the kaboutermannekin will become offended and leave the home.

Sources: Briggs, *Encyclopedia of Fairies*, 247; Currie, *Goblins*, 59; Rose, *Spirits, Fairies, Gnomes, and Goblins*, 173

Kachina

Variations: Cachina, Kacina, Katchina, Katcina

In the mythology of the Hopi, Kerese, Pueblo, Tewa, and Zuni Indians of North America the kachina are a species of powerful NATURE-SPIRITS having power over grain fertility and rain. Kachina can appear as animals, birds, or plants and can be either female or male. There are several hundred different named kachina and each one is represented by a special mask and ceremonial costume worn during religious ceremonies.

The Hopi believe the kachinas to be the souls of virtuous deceased people but the general belief is the kachina came to earth and lived among the southwestern tribes as honored guardians and teachers. After a period of time the kachinas began to feel as if they were being taken for granted. Before returning to their home in the start they taught the tribes how to fashion mask and costumes to invoke their power and influence nature.

Sources: Illes, *Encyclopedia of Spirits*, 540; Lynch, *Native American Mythology A to Z*, 55–6; Parker, *Mythology*, 434; Parsons, *Pueblo Indian Religion*, Volume 2, 554, 736

Kafizin

From Greek mythology, Kafizin was a NYMPH of Cyprus.

Source: Larson, *Greek Nymphs: Myth, Cult, Lore*, 257

Kakamora

In the Solomon Islands the kakamora are NATURE-SPIRITS living in limestone caves and trees subsisting on fruit, nuts, and possums. Although generally benign toward humans they will attack with their long, sharp nails and tiny teeth if provoked. Described as having a dark complexion, although some have be said to be fair skinned; their long straight hair comes down to their knees and they wear no clothes. The kakamora are exceedingly strong, stand about three feet tall, and stoop over as they run.

Sources: Forth, *Images of the Wildman in Southeast Asia*, 243; Stanley, *South Pacific Handbook*, 920

Kaliya

The colossal, four headed NAGA king of the river Yamuna, Kaliya was said to be four leagues long and so poisonous nothing near him could survive. He lives within a whirlpool and was made gentle by the Krishna, according to Hindu mythology.

Sources: Chopra, *Academic Dictionary of Mythology*, 159; Seth, *Gods and Goddesses of India*, 63

Kallianassa

A NYMPH from Greek mythology, Kallianassa ("the infallible") was one of the named NEREID who accompanied THETIS in mourning the loss of her son, Achilles.

Sources: Collignon, *Manual of Mythology*, 18; Gould, *Historic Magazine and Notes and Queries*, Vol 14, 212; Perry, *Women of Homer*, 146

Kallianeira

A NYMPH from Greek mythology, Kallianeira ("the truthful") was one of the NEREID who accompanied THETIS in mourning the loss of her son, Achilles.

Sources: Collignon, *Manual of Mythology*, 18; Gould, *Historic Magazine and Notes and Queries*, Volume 14, 212

Kalligeneia

A NYMPH of Eleusis in Attika, southern Greece, Kalligeneia ("beautiful birth") was a nurse to both the goddess Demeter (Ceres) as well as her daughter, Persephone (Proserpina).

Sources: Larson, *Green Nymphs*, 45; Ogden, *Companion to Greek Religion*, 212

Kallirhoe

Born one of the 3,000 daughters of the Titians, Oceanus and Tethys, Kallirhoe ("lovely flowing") was one of the named OCEANIDS in ancient Greek mythology; she was one of the playmates of Persephone (Proserpina) and present when the goddess was kidnapped. A spring NYMPH of the city of Athens, she supplied the water for the nuptial baths Athenian brides.

Sources: Crudden, *Homeric Hymns*, 19; Fowler, *Archaic Greek Poetry*, 14; Larson, *Greek Nymphs: Myth, Cult, Lore*, 127

Kalliste

Given as a gift to the hero, Euphemos by her father, Triton, Kalliste ("most beautiful") was a NEREID NYMPH of the island Kalliste located in the Greek Aegean; she was the personification of the island. According to classical Greek lore, Kalliste's mother was named LIBYA.

Sources: Foxhall, *When Men Were Men*, 102; Grant, *Who's Who in Classical Mythology*, 73

Kallraden

Variations: Spring-nixen

The kallraden were a type of water-fairy in Swedish fairy lore; they were similar to the NEREID of ancient Greece.

Sources: Arrowsmith, *Field Guide to Little People*, 99; Froud, *Fairies*, N.p.

Kalybe

Variations: Calybe

Kalybe ("hut") was a NYMPH of Troad; she was the daughter of Laomedon, a legendary king of Troy, and the mother of Boukolion (Bucolion). One of the NAIADS, she devoted herself to chastity and hunting. She was deeply loved by a mortal ox-hearder named Hymnos but continuously rejected his advances. One day she shot him through the throat with an arrow and joined the NYMPH ABARBAREE, engaged in a sexual encounter with the herder's fresh corpse.

Sources: Larson, *Greek Nymphs*, 22, 195–6; Ramsay, *Ovid*, 278

Kalypso

Variations: CALYPSO

Born one of the 3,000 daughters of the Titians, Oceanus and Tethys, Kalypso ("like the hidden tide") was one of the named OCEANIDS in ancient Greek mythology; she was one of the playmates of Persephone (Proserpina) and present when the goddess was kidnapped. One of the NEREIS Kalypso is perhaps best known for her role in the *Odyssey*. After a seven year stay on her island Kalypso offered Odysseus immortality if he choose to remain on her island and be her lover; Odysseus rejected her as he wished to return to his home, wife, and son. It was only at the bidding of the god, Hermes (Mercury), she finally assisted Odysseus in constructing a raft allowing him to leave the island of Ogygia.

Sources: Cox, *Mythology of the Aryan Nations*, Volume 2, 179; Crudden, *Homeric Hymns*, 19; Fowler, *Archaic Greek Poetry*, 14; Hard, *Routledge Handbook of Greek Mythology*, 497

Kamapua'a

A sensual hog spirit from Hawaiian mythology, Kamapua'a was described as looking like a human-pig hybrid. Living in the swamp, this NATURE SPIRIT was also associated with abundance, fertility, precipitation, sex, and well-being. Born the son of the goddess Hina and her illicit lover, a handsome chief named Kahiki-ula, Kamapua'a had many affairs himself, including Pele the volcano goddess and Poliahu the snow goddess. A skilled shape-shifter Kamapua'a was immensely strong in his pig form and could use his supernatural strength to destroy crops and farms.

Sources: Andrews, *Dictionary of Nature Myths*, 109; Avant, *Mythological Reference*, 147; Illes, *Encyclopedia of Spirits*, 548

Kami

Kami ("deity") are NATURE-SPIRITS in Shinto, the national religion of Japan; they were born of the union between the god Izanagi and Izanami. Sometimes the kami are seen as representations of the Buddhas.

Sources: Leeming, *Oxford Companion to World Mythology*, 225; McCoy, *Witch's Guide to Faery Folk*, 34; Roberts, *Japanese Mythology A to Z*, 74

Kamarina

A NYMPH of the town Kamarina in Sicily, southern Italy, Kamarina was an OCEANIAD in classical Greek mythology. In art, she was depicted riding upon a swan.

Sources: Charlesworth, *Good and Evil Serpent*, 133; Freeman, *History of Sicily from the Earliest Times*, Volume 2, 29–30

Kapheira

An OCEANID and a NEREID NYMPH from the island of Rhodes in the Greek Aegean Sea, Kapheira, along with the NYMPH, HALIA, was a nurse of the god of the sea, Poseidon (Neptune).

Sources: Fontenrose, *Didyma*, 154–55; Illes, *Encyclopedia of Spirits*, 308

Kappa

Variations: Kawako

In Japan there is a vampiric creature living in ponds called a *kappa* ("river child"). It looks like a green child with a long nose, round eyes, tortoise shell on its back, webbed fingers and toes, and smells like fish. However, its most interesting physical feature is a dent in the top of its head deep enough to hold water. The water sitting in the dent is representative of its power. Should a kappa attempt to attack you, quickly bow to it. As it is a stickler for courteousness and ritual, the kappa will take pause to return the bow. When it does so, the water in the dent will spill out, rendering the creature powerless.

The kappa hunts from its home in the water. It waits until a cow or horse comes to drink and then it pulls the animal down into the water. As the animal drowns, the kappa bites into the animal's anus to drain it of its blood. The only time a kappa will leave its watery home is to steal cucumbers and melons, rape women, and to rip the liver out of people.

The kappa is incredibly strong and a highly skilled sumo wrestler. It is also a skilled teacher in the art of bone setting and medical skills.

It may well be the kappa is the only vampire with a cucumber fetish. No matter what may be happening all around it, a kappa will stop whatever it is doing to steal away with one should the opportunity arise. By writing one's family name on a cucumber and giving it to a kappa, the entire family will be temporarily protected from its attacks.

Kappas can be surprisingly courteous, honorable, and trustworthy beings. They are highly respectful of ritual and tradition, even going so far as to challenge one of its would-be victims to a wrestling match. A kappa can even be bargained with, willing to enter into contractual agreements not to attack certain people.

Sources: Davis, *Myths and Legends of Japan*, 350–

52; Mack, *Field guide to Demons*, 17–18; Rowthorn, *Japan*, 511

Karakoncolos

Variations: Black Bogey, Black Werewolf, Karakondjol, Karakondjul

The karakoncolos is a species of nocturnal fairies from the folklore of Northeast Anatolian Turkey and Bulgaria. Described as having an ugly face and brown or red fur covering their body the karakoncolos are most active during the first ten days of winter.

Source: Curran, *Dark Fairies*, 108

Karya

In Greek mythology Karya was one of the eight HAMADRYAD who was born of HAMADRYAS; she was the HAMADRYAD of chestnut, hazle, and walnut trees.

Sources: Buxton, *Forms of Astonishment*, 211; Larson, *Greek Nymphs: Myth, Cult, Lore*, 152

Karzelek

Variations: Karzeł

The karzelek were DWARFS or GNOMES living underground in mines in Polish folklore. Known to lead workers to veins of ore they would throw dirt and small stones at anyone who insults them.

Sources: Maberry, *Cryptopedia*, 232

Kassotis

In Greek mythology, Kassotis was a NYMPH of Mount Parnassos, Greece; her spring, which gave women the gift of prophetic inspiration, was located in the sanctuary of Apollo.

Sources: Larson, *Greek Nymphs: Myth, Cult, Lore*, 147; Pausânias, *Guide to Greece*, 469

Kastalia

Kastalia was a NYMPH of the Kastalian spring at the shrine of Delphi, located in central Greece; she was said to have the ability to make women prophetic inside "the god's holy place." According to Greek mythology, she was born the daughter of the river god, Acheloos; some sources say Kastalian threw herself in a river to avoid being raped by the god, Apollo while other sources say she was the wife of Delphos and the mother of Kastalios and Phemonoe.

Sources: Fontenrose, *Orion*, 298; Larson, *Greek Nymphs*, 147–48, 306

Kataw

In the Visayan islands of the Philippines, the kataw is believed to be a species water fairy sim-
ilar to the MERMAID or SIREN. Described as looking like a beautiful, light skinned woman from the waist up, the lower body of the kataw is a fish, covered in shiny scales; they are said to have a notable fishy smell. In addition to having control over fish the kataw had the ability to haunt a person's dreams.

Sources: Dumont, *Visayan Vignettes*, 200; Ramos, *Creatures of Midnight*, 67

Kaukas (plural: kaukai)

Variations: Barstukai, Bezdukai

The kaukai are a species of fairy in Lithuanian lore associated with prosperity and wealth. It is said if a single piece of straw is found atop a few kernels of grain it is a sign the kaukas has blessed you with never-ending fortune. This blessing is not necessarily a financial gain that can be measured but rather the kaukas embeds objects with the idea of an infinite supply.

Housewives will make a garment from a single piece of thread and bury it in the corner of the home in hopes of luring a kaukas into living there. If one of these fairies takes up residence it will stay in the dark places, such as in the cellar or in dark storehouses. The kaukai represents *skalsd*, the consistency of the earth.

Sources: Gimbutas, *Living Goddesses*, 211–12; Trinkauske, *Seeing the Swarming Dead*, 69–70

Kelaino

According to classical Greek mythology, the NYMPH Kelaino ("she is a black as night") was the daughter of Hyamos. By the god Apollo Kelaino was the mother of Delphos and by the god Poseidon (Neptune) she was the mother of a son named Lykos.

Sources: Hard, *Routledge Handbook of Greek Mythology*, 520; Pausânias, *Guide to Greece: Central Greece*, 419

Kelouse

Variations: Celusa ("abnormal delivery")

A fresh-water NYMPH of Sikyonia in southern Greece, Kelouse was a NAIAD and the mother of the river god, Asopos, by the god of the sea, Poseidon (Neptune).

Source: Pausânias, *Guide to Greece: Central Greece*, 159

The Kelpie

Variations: Afanc, ANTHROPOPHAGI, AUGHISKY, BÄCKAHÄSTEN ("brook horse"), Each Uisge, Eisges, Endrop, FUATH, Goborchinu, HNIKUR, NECK,

Nicker, Nickur, Nix, Nuggies, SHOOPILTEE, Shoney, Sjofn, Uisges, Water-Spirit

Originating in Scottish lore and spreading into Cornish, Icelandic, Irish, German, Orkney, and Shetland fairy lore, the kelpie is a cannibalistic, foul-tempered, and malicious water-fay. Rarely seen, when fairy or humans are not available to consume the kelpie will kill deer that wander too near its watery home.

In Ireland the kelpie is known as the AUGHISKY or the EACH UISGE and are described as looking like web-footed women with the mane and tail of a horses; however, in Scotland the kelpie is said to look like a hose wandering along the seashore; it first allows humans to ride upon it before taking them off into the ocean and drowning them. Socttish kelpies also have the ability to shape-shift and can appear as a hairy man.

There are several names the kelpie is known by in Iceland, such as the HNIKUR, NECK, Nickur, Ninner, and Water-Spirit to name a few. There, this FAIRY ANIMAL appears as an apple-grey horse with reversed hooves hunting along the seashore.

Interestingly, there are no kelpies in the Avon, the Thames, or any other English streams.

There is also the belief it is possible to capture and tame a kelpie by managing to get a bridle over its head, however, this is a difficult and dangerous task as the kelpie is physically powerful and strong and has a singularly willful nature. If a kelpie is bridled it will serve its new master well and make for a wonderful and versatile horse.

Sources: Briggs, *Encyclopedia of Fairies*, 246; Froud, *Faeries*, 109; Keightly, *World Guide to Gnomes, Fairies, Elves, and Other Little People*, 162, 360, 370, 385; McCoy, *Witch's Guide to Faery Folk*, 253–4

Kepler's Fairy

Johannes Kepler (1571–1630) was a German astrologer, astronomer, and mathematician who made the claim each of the planets was guided along its elliptical orbit by a fairy.

Source: Brewer, *Dictionary of Phrase and Fable*, 699

Kerkeis

The OCEANID and NYMPH from Greek mythology, Kerkeis was described as being lovely with a beautiful form by the ancient Greek oral poet Hesiod.

Source: Hesiod, *Hesiod, the Poems and Fragments*, 44

Keshalyi

In the Romani gypsy lore the keshalyi ("spindles") was a type of fairy similar to the FATES of Greek lore. Living in solicitude in remote forests and mountains, these beautiful, benevolent, generous, and gentle fairies are both long lived and fertile; they are invoked to cure infertility.

According to legend the keshalyi once lived atop a mountain as the entourage to the FAIRY QUEEN, ANA. The king of the evil spirits, Locolico, fell in love with ANA; when she spurned his advances the demon sent his minion hoard to devour the keshalyi. In order to save her people, ANA married Locolico. After years of degradation, she was able to persuade her husband to divorice her; however, the price was steep—in exchanged for her freedom, whenever any of the keshalyi reached the age of 999 years, they must marry one of the minions of Locolico.

Sources: Clébert, *The Gypsies*, 188, 192; Illes, *Encyclopedia of Spirits*, 563

Keto

Variations: CETO, Cetus

A sea–NYMPH born of Nereus and DORIS, Keto was the NEREIS of sea-monsters in ancient Greek mythology; she married her brother, Phorkys; together they begot Deino, Echidna, Enyo, the Graiai, Pemphredo, as well as the three Gorgons, Euryale, Medusa, and Stenni; collectively their children are known as the Phorcids.

Sources: Graves, *Greek Myths*, 33; Illes, *Encyclopedia of Spirits*, 564; Rose, *Handbook of Greek Mythology*, 22, 24

Khariklo

Greek mythology Khariklo was the NYMPH of Mount Pelion in Thessalia, northern Greece. Although she was a companion to the goddess Athena (Minerva), Khariklo's son, Teiresias, was struck blind by the goddess because he almost saw her bathing in the river.

Source: Callimachus, *Callimachus*, 75

Khione

In classical Greek mythology Khione was a NYMPH of snow in the region of Thrake, north of Greece; she was born the daughter of Boreas, the god of wind, and the Amazon, Oreithyia.

Source: Avant, *Mythological Reference*, 299

Khryseis

Variations: CHRYSEIS

Born one of the 3,000 daughters of the Titians,

Oceanus and Tethys, Khryseis was one of the named OCEANIDS in ancient Greek mythology; she was one of the playmates of Persephone (Proserpina) and present when the goddess was kidnapped.

Sources: Avant, *Mythological Reference*, 296; Crudden, *Homeric Hymns*, 19; Fowler, *Archaic Greek Poetry*, 14; Westmoreland, *Ancient Greek Beliefs*, 24, 702

Kijimuna

Variations: Akakanaza, Bungaya, Ki No Mono ("monster of trees"), Kijimun, Kiji-mun, Kijimunaa

Specific to the island of Okinawa, Japan, the kijimuna are a type of DRYAD or NYMPH living in the trees and guiding and protecting humans. Described as being hairy these NATURE SPIRITS will try to assist fishermen in their task; it is believed any fish caught with one eye was through the assistance of the kijimuna, as it is prone to take a bite of the catch. The temperament of the kijimuna ranges from delightfully playful to slightly annoying and it is described as having red fur or hair. Walking in the shallow water at night, they carry a lantern; the kijimuna are afraid of octopuses.

Sources: Hendry, *Interpreting Japanese Society*, 172; Sered, *Women of the Sacred Groves*, 52; Sakihara, *Okinawan-English Wordbook*, 93

Kikimora

Variations: Kikimera, Domania, DOMOVIKHA, Shishimora

A species of household fairy in Eastern Europe the kikimora are described as looking like a tiny or invisible woman with a small head and a skinny body; they live territorial and with only one to a house, this little fairy being lives behind the stove or in the cellar. Like the DIVOZENKY of Slavic lore, the kikimora enjoys cleaning the house, feeding the chickens and doing needlework. A kikimora if married, it will have a DOMOVIK as its husband. To see a kikimora at working spinning is a death omen.

Sources: Dixon-Kennedy, *Encyclopedia of Russian and Slavic Myth and Legend*, 150; Illes, *Encyclopedia of Spirits*, 571; Ivanits, *Russian Folk Belief*, 57

Kíli

Variations: Kili

Kíli ("wedge") was one of the many DWARFS named in the *Voluspa*, the first and best known poem of the *Poetic Edda*, a collection of Old Norse poems dating back to about A.D. 985.

Sources: Crossley-Holland, Norse Myths, 183; Daly, *Norse Mythology A to Z*, 22; Sykes, *Who's Who in Non-Classical Mythology*, 53

The Killmoulis

Throughout Belgium, Germany, and Holland the killoulis ("miller's servant") was known as being a particularly ugly species of BROWNIE living in mills. Described as having a gigantic nose but no mouth; it ate by shoving its food up its nostrils. Although a hard worker it would grievously bemoan any misfortune which fell upon the mill it lived in, the killmoulis enjoyed playing pranks and could be a hindrance. Its favorite food was pork.

Sources: Avant, *Mythological Reference*, 473; Briggs, *Encyclopedia of Fairies*, 246–7; Froud, *Faeries*, 125; Henderson, *Notes on the Folk-Lore of the Northern Counties of England and the Borders*, 252–3

King Goldemar

Variations: King Goldmar, King Vollmar, King Volmar

King Goldemar was the KOBOLD living with an individual named Neveling von Hardenberg at Hardenstein Castle along the Ruhr River, Germany. According to legend, King Goldemar called von Hardenberg his brother-in-law and played the harp beautifully for him with his cold, soft, froglike hands. He was never actually seen but very often people claimed to feel his physical form. King Goldear enjoyed playing dice and making the clergy blush by revealing their secrets. The fairy insisted a place always be set for him at the table and stall always be left for his horse; it was said the food and the grain would always disappear. For three years King Goldemar lived at Hardenstein Castle until one day a visitor desirous to see the fay sprinkled ashes along the floor to get at least a look at his foot-prints. King Goldemar took great offence to this breach of trust, killed the man, cut the body into pieces, roasted the body and boiled the head and legs, afterwhich he consumed the remains. A note was said to have been found the next day saying all the luck once enjoyed by the Castle was leaving; it was signed by King Goldemar.

Sources: Croker, *Fairy Legends and Traditions of the South of Ireland*, 112; Grimm, *Teutonic Mythology*, Volume 2, 609; Keightly, *World Guide to Gnomes, Fairies, Elves, and Other Little People*, 256

King Loc

Variations: Little King Loc

From the French fairy-tale *Abeille* by M. Anatole France which was adapted into the tale *The Story of Little King Loc* there was said to be a lake both beautiful and dangerous as UNDINES lived in it; these water fairies were well known to lure passerby's to their death. The lake was described as being blue and silvery with gold and purple irises growing all along the banks; white water lilies floated along its bottom. A light mist fell on the lake during the night but when the moonlight hit its surface it looked like FAIRY-LAND. When these events occurred beautiful women with long green hair wold appear with outstretched hands toward anyone they saw.

In addition to the UNDINES in the story were also Bog, Nur, Pau, Pig, Rug, Tad, all GNOMES with long white beards. The FAIRY KING, Loc, ruled over them all; he held Princess Abeille in his underground kingdom for many years in the hopes she would one day want to marry him. Loc and his court, all immortal beings though kind and good had never felt either great joy or great sorrow. These GNOMES were said to walk slowly. King Loc was described as having a long beard and kind eyes.

Source: Lang, *Olive Fairy Book*, 43–63

King Under-Wave

King Under-Wave sits upon a golden throne in his palace where there is continual feasting; a few passing days in his palace was actually the passing of a year and a day. King Under-Wave appears out of his lake and then suddenly disappears again.

Sources: Evan-Wentz, *Fairy Faith in Celtic Countries*, 354; Gregory, *Gods and Fighting Men*, 285–91; Hyde, *Giolla an Fhiugha Lad of the Ferrule*, 63–64

Kirkegrim

Variations: Church Grim, Church Lamb

A BROWNIE that specifically looks after a church is known as a kirkegrim in Scandinavia; it will typically live in the tower but any area in the building where it can hide itself is acceptable. Kirkegrim are said to keep order in the church during ceremonies and deliver punishments whenever a scandal occurs.

Sources: Guiney, *Brownies and Bogles,* 76; Keightly, *World Guide to Gnomes, Fairies, Elves, and Other Little People*, 140; Thorpe, *Northern Mythology*, Volume 1, 166

Kirkonwaki

Similar to the KIRKEGRIM of Scandinavia, in the fairy lore of Finland the kirkonwaki ("church folk") are a race of little misshapen fairy beings living under the alter in a church. Whenever one of the kirkonwaki women are having a difficult labor they will have their suffering eased if a Christian woman lays her hands upon it; such a charitable act is often rewarded with the gift of a gold coin.

Sources: Arrowsmith, *Field Guide to the Little People*, 25; Grimm, *Teutonic Mythology*, Volume 3, 457; Tyson, *Philological Essay Concerning the Pygmies of the Ancients*, lxxxiv

Kisseis

Variations: Cisseis

A NYMPH of the mythical Mount Nysa in classical Greek mythology, Kisseis was one of the BACCHANTS; a nurse of the infant god, Dionysus (Bacchus); her name also appears as one of the nurses to the infant god, Zeus (Jupiter).

Source: Cook, *Zeus*, 111

Klabautermann

Variations: Klaboutermannikins, Kalfater ("caulker"), Kluterman ("joiner")

The klabautermann ("knocking fairy") is a fairy of the Baltic Sea assisting fishermen and sailors with their duties; it is essentially a seafaring version of the BROWNIE. Having a diligent and merry nature the klabautermann is an expert of watercraft and a musician of unsurpassed talent. His likeness varies, typically it is given as a small man in a yellow coat, woolen sailor's cap and tobacco pipe, but this little fairy, standing only about two foot tall has also been said to wear a red jacket, wide sailor pants, and a round hat. On rare occasions, the klabautermann is described as being nude. However it is described, its image is carved and attached to the ship's masthead for good luck.

The birth of a klabautermann occurs in a very precise manner; when an unbaptized child dies and is buried outside of the churchyard if a tree should grow over the child grave it is believed its soul becomes part of the tree. Then, should the tree be harvested and its wood used to construct a boat, then a DRAYAD of a ship, the klabautermann, is created.

In the original lore the klabautermann was helpful and only seen by those who sailed on a doomed ship, however, in modern times the klabautermann has been demonized into a cruel creature known to plays malicious and harmful pranks on the crew, damaging the ship.

Sources: Altmann, *Seven Swabians*, 232–3; McCoy,

Witch's Guide to Faery Folk, 147, 254–5; Thorpe, *Northern Mythology*, Volume 3, 49–50

Klaia

A sea–NYMPH, Klaia was one of the named NEREID; she was born of Nereus and DORIS in classical Greek mythology. She had been given by the god, Dionysus (Bacchus), the ability to transform anything she wished into corn, oil, or wine. The sacred cave of Klaia was located on Mount Kalathion, Greece.

Source: Pausânias, *Guide to Greece*, 100, 137

Kleeia

Variations: Cleeia

A NYMPH of the mythical Mount Nysa in classical Greek mythology, Kleeia was one of the BACCHANTS; a nurse of the infant god, Dionysus (Bacchus).

Sources: Howe, *Handbook of Classical Mythology*, 181; Lemprière, *Lempriere's Classical Dictionary for Schools and Academies*, 121

Kleide

A NYMPH of Mount Drios on the island of Naxos in the Greek Aegean Sea, Kleide, along with KORONIS and PHILIA, was entrusted by the god Zeus (Jupiter) to care for the infant god, Dionysus (Bacchus).

Sources: Dalby, *Bacchus*, 105; Larson, *Greek Nymphs*, 181

Kleocharia

In Greek mythology, Kleocharia was a NAIAD of Lakonia; she was married to Lelex.

Source: Larson, *Greek Nymphs: Myth, Cult, Lore*, 152

Kleodora

Variations: CLEODORA

Kleodora was a NYMPH of Parnassos; she was the mother of the hero Parnassos by the god, Poseidon (Neptune). Kleodora had the ability to divine the future by cleromancy, the art of throwing pebbles to cast lots.

Kleodora was also one of the names given as one of the NYMPHS of the cave at Corycian. She was said to be one of the "triple muses of divination at Delphi" along with CORYCIA, DAPHNUS, MELAINA, and THIUA. She was one of the NAIADS and one of a trio of NYMPHS known collectively as the Thriae or the Thriai.

Sources: Day, *God's Conflict with the Dragon and the Sea*, 395; Larson, *Greek Nymphs: Myth, Cult, Lore*, 147; Monaghan, *Goddesses in World Culture*, 147

Kleokhareia

Variations: Cleocharia

A NYMPH of the river Eurotas in Lakedaimonia located in southern Greece, Kleokhareia was the wife of King Lelex and the mother of Eurotas in Greek mythology.

Sources: Apollodorus of Athens, *Gods and Heroes of the Greeks*, 170; Lemprière, *Classical Dictionary* (1875), 169

Klippe

Klippe ("cliff" or "crag") is the name used for the fairy in Forfarshire, Scotland. They are described as being small and brown-faced and wander along the roads.

Sources: Briggs, *Encyclopedia of Fairies*, 254; Monaghan, *Encyclopedia of Celtic Mythology and Folklore,* 272; Simpson, *Folk lore in Lowland Scotland,* 93

Klonia

Variations: Klonie

The NYMPH of the town Hyria in Boiotia located in central Greece, the NAIAD Klonia was the wife of King Hyrieus in classical Greek mythology who bares him two sons, Lykos and Nykteus ("of the night").

Sources: Dowden, *Death and the Maiden*, 182; Gantz, *Early Greek Myth*, 215; Hard, *Routledge Handbook of Greek Mythology*, 520; Larson, *Greek Nymphs: Myth, Cult, Lore*, 142

Kludde

Variations: Kleure

Kludde is a malicious shape-shifting fairy found in Brabant and Flanders, Belgium. Typical pranks it will play on unsuspecting travelers will be to take on the guise of a large black dog and on its hind legs, chase its prey or it will transform into a wonderful shade tree and as its victim lays for a rest, suddenly grow in size, taking the mortal into the dizzying heights of the clouds. The favorite trick of the kludde is to take on the appearance of an old and starving horse; when a stable-boy or groom approaches it lures them up onto its back and then runs off at a furious speed throwing itself into a lake or river. As the person makes their way out of the water and back onto the bank, the kludde lays flat on its stomach, laughing.

No matter the form the kludde assumes, bat, cat, crow, frog, stone, or what have you, there will always be the presence of two small blue flames before the animal; these lights are believed to be the creature's eyes.

Sources: Henderson, *Notes on the Folk-Lore of the Northern Counties of England and the Borders*, 273; Maberry, *Vampire Universe*, 178; Thorpe, *Northern Mythology*, Volume 3, 193–5

Klymene

Klymene ("flame") was one of the named NEREID who accompanied THETIS in mourning the loss of her son, Achilles. Klymene married Kephalos, Deion's son, and bore him a child named Iphiklos.

Sources: Hard, *Routledge Handbook of Greek Mythology*, 355; Pausânias, *Guide to Greece*, 481; Perry, *Women of Homer*, 146

Knock Ma Fairies

Variations: Cnoc Ma Fairies, Cnoc Meadhe ("Hill of the Plain")

Knock Ma was the place where the fairies were believed to live, a hill with many passages and an entrance into an underground world. In Knock Ma were all the people the fairies had taken over the years; those of note were people who were said to have died of consumption but within Knock Ma were enjoying good health. The sick person was taken, body and soul, into FAIRYLAND where their health was restored. It was believed the palace of FINVARA, FAIRY KING of Connaught, resided there.

Sources: Briggs, *Encyclopedia of Fairies*, 125–26; Evan-Wentz, *Fairy Faith in Celtic Countries*, 37, 42; Mahon, *Ireland's Fairy Lore*, 117

Knockers

Variations: Black DWARFS, BUCCAS, Bwca, COBLYN, Cobylnaus, Gommes, Koblernigh, Knackers, SPRIGGANS, Tommyknockers, Wichlein Paras

In Cornwall, England knockers were DWARFS or a species of KOBOLD who lived in caves and mines; they earned their name by the knocking noises they made to direct miners where to dig. When danger was near they would knock in rapid successions. Knockers did not like the sound of whistling and would throw handfuls of gravel, harmlessly, at the offender. To keep on their good side, miners would leave a portion of their food for them.

Generally the knocker were described as standing about two foot tall and dressed as if it were a miner carrying a lunch pail and pick. There was also the belief knockers were the souls of the Jewish individuals who were responsible for the crucifixion and death of Jesus Christ; as punishment they had been condemned to work in tin-mines until the Resurrection.

Sources: Courtney, *Cornish Feasts and Folk-Lore*, 61, 128; Evan-Wentz, *Fairy Faith in Celtic Countries*, 165; Illes, *Encyclopedia of Spirits*, 576; McCoy, *Witch's Guide to Faery Folk*, 147, 255–6

Knocky-Boh

Variations: Boh-Thing

Knocky-Boh is a BOGGART from British folklore that does seemingly nothing else but make knocking sounds from behind the *wainscoting*, the decorative boards or paneling that extend part way up a wall, of a home. The noise it makes is said to be frightening and keep people awake.

Sources: Briggs, *Encyclopedia of Fairies*, 333; Harland, *Glossary of Words Used in Swaledale, Yorkshire*, Volume 4, 22; Wright, *Rustic Speech and Folk-Lore*, 198

Knossia

Variations: Cnossia

A NYMPH of the town of Knossos of the island of Crete in the Greek Aegean Sea, the NAIAD Knossia was the wife of King Menelaos (Menelaus) of Sparta; she bore a son named Xenodamus.

Sources: Apollodorus of Athens, *Apollodorus' Library and Hyginus' Fabulae*, 61; Bell, *Bell's New Pantheon*, 187; Parada, *Genealogical Guide to Greek Mythology*, 51

Kobold

Variations: Bullerkate, Bullermann, Bullihann, Bullerkater, Butzemann, Chimmeken, Claus, Cobald, Heinsel-mannchen, Hutchens, Heinzel-mannchens, KABOUTER, Kobauld, Kobolde, Kolbalds, Kaboutermannikin, Nis, Niagruisar, PARA, Poltergeist, Popanz, PUK, Rumpelgeist, Tatermann, Wichtelmannchen, Wolterken

The kobold ("good house" or "rogue") of German fairy lore are a species of fay very similar to the KNOCKERS of England living in mine and take great pleasure in playing tricks on people.

Throughout the sixteenth and seventeenth century the kobold were depicted as wearing conical hats and pointy shoes; they were shown to have bald feet and hairy tails.

Kobolds have also been compared to the BROWNIE, but they are very particular about the temperament of the family they adopt. It is said the kobold will carry sawdust and wood chips into the home and throw dirt into the fresh milk. If the head of the household leaves the mess, the kobold will move in and stay in the home for as long as the family lives.

According to Jacob Ludwig Carl Grimm, a German jurist, mythologist, and philologist, claimed the kobold was not mentioned by any writer prior to the thirteenth century.

Sources: Bord, *Fairies*, 66; Froud, *Faeries*, 80; Herrmann, *Deutsche Mythologie*, 1436–53; Keightly, *World Guide to Gnomes, Fairies, Elves, and Other Little People*, 239, 316; Sikes, *British Goblins*, 32–33

Kodin-Haltia

In Finnish folklore the kodin-haltia is a household spirit.

Source: Franklin, *Working with Fairies*, 133

Koko

Variations: Ka-Ka, Kokko

The koko ("rain people") are a species of NA-TURE SPIRITS from the Zuni mythology known as the kachinas. When properly venerated by dance, the koko make not only the rains come but also bring blessings and prosperity.

Sources: Illes, *Encyclopedia of Spirits*, 578; Lyon, *Encyclopedia of Native American Healing*, 137

Kollimalaikanniyarka

Variations: Seven Maidens

A type of NYMPH from the mythology of India the Kollimalaikanniyarka ("Seven Maidens from the Kolli Mountains") were charged with the task of educating Kattavarayan, the son of Parvati and Siva. They assisted him in learning magic. There were at least two sets of the Kollimalaikanni-yarka, some names include: Annamuttu, Cavutayi, Karuppalaki, Karuppayi, Nallatankaj, Nallatankal, Nalli, Ontayi, Puvayi, Ukantalaki, and Valli.

Sources: Hiltebeitel, *Criminal Gods and Demon Devotees*, 86, 440; Rose, *Spirits, Fairies, Leprechauns, and Goblins*, 183

Korkyra

Variations: CORCYRA

The NYMPH of a town on the island of Korkyra in central western Greece, the NAIAD Korkyra was born the daughter of Asopos, a river god of Boiotia, and the river NYMPH, METOPE. Korkyra was abducted by the god of the sea, Poseidon (Neptune), and taken to an unnamed island, thereby naming it after her; there, Korkyra bore the god a son named Phaiak.

Sources: Dow, *Ancient Coins Through the Bible*, 249; Grant, *Who's Who in Classical Mythology*, 142

Kornbocke

Variations: PHOOKA

The kornbocke of Germany fairy lore guards the grain and causes it to ripen.

Sources: Conway, *Magickal, Mythical, Mystical Beasts*, 55; Franklin, *Working with Fairies*, 98, 231

Kornmutter

Variations: Roggenmutter ("rye mother")

A German NATURE SPIRIT, the kornmutter ("corn mother") was an agriculture fairy of the growing grain. It was believed swaying shafts of wheat and rye was caused by the kornmutter flying invisibly over the crop. As the kornmutter hovered over the field, if her gown touched a kernel of corn, the grain turned black, was considered sacred, and thereafter known as kornmutter-korn.

Sources: Bové, *Story of Ergot*, 5; Hastings, *Encyclopedia of Religion and Ethics*, Part 8, 634

Korokiorwek

One of the ATUA from the mythology of the Maori people of New Zealand, korokiorwek was blamed for causing birth defects.

Source: Illes, *Encyclopedia of Spirits*, 44

The Koronides

In classical Greek mythology the Koronides were two NYMPHS of Thebes in Boiotia located in central Greece. These sisters were named MENIPPE and METIOCHE and were born the daughters of the hunter, Orion. The goddess Aphrodite (Venus) taught them beautiful manners and the goddess Athena (Minerva) taught them how to weave. When a plague came to Boiotia the oracles declared everyone would die unless there was a sacrifice of two maidens. The sisters sacrificed themselves, using their shuttles to take their life; as they died the gods Hades (Pluto) and Persephone (Proserpina) took pity on the sisters and transformed them into comets.

Sources: Fontenrose, *Orion*, 16–17; Monaghan, *Encyclopedia of Goddesses and Heroines*, 415

Koronis

A NYMPH of Mount Drios on the island of Naxos in the Greek Aegean Sea, KORONIS, along with KLEIDE and PHILIA, were entrusted by the god Zeus (Jupiter) to care for the infant god, Dionysus (Bacchus).

Sources: Dalby, *Bacchus*, 105; Larson, *Greek Nymphs*, 181

Korred

Variations: COURIL, Crion, Goric, Kores, Korrig, KORRIGAN, Korrs, Pyrenee

The korred of Brittany are very similar to the TROLLS of Scandinavian lore, described as being short and stocky with clawed hands, dark wrinkled faces, deep-set eyes as bright as carbuncles, goatlike feet, and shaggy hair; they speak with a voice cracked and hollow sounding. All sightings of korred describe them as being male. Expert coiners and smiths the korred keep large stockpiles of treasure in the dolems in which they live and dance around during the night.

Korred enjoy dancing and will oftentimes invite mortals to join them, however, this is dangerous, as those who accept the invitation are often found dead with a broken back or from exhaustion. To prevent being lured into one of the korred's dances, a *fourche* ("short stick"), a type of plough paddle, may be employed.

Sources: Keightly, *World Guide to Gnomes, Fairies, Elves, and Other Little People*, 432, 439; McCoy, *Witch's Guide to Faery Folk*, 153, 257–8

Korrigan

Variations: Cornik, CORRIGAN, Koril, Kornikaned, Ozeganned, Poulpikan, Teuz

Believed to have originated in ancient Gaul on the Isles des Saints in the British sea the korrigaan stand no more than two feet tall but have perfectly proportioned bodies and a head full of flowing, long hair that they take great care of. Sometimes they are said to have wasp-like wings. The only clothing they wear is a long white veil they wrap and wind around their body. Typically the korrigan are seen at night when they are at their most beautiful; by day their eyes are red, their hair white, and their faces deeply wrinkled. Fond of music and with a voice suitable for singing, the korrigan are one of the few species of fairy not fond of dancing.

Although the korrigan will steal children they do not leave a CHANGELING in its place; rather they take children they consider need to be protected. Only those children who wear a scapular or rosary about their neck are safe from abduction as they have a great abhorrence to the holy Virgin Mary. The sound of peeling church bells will drive them away.

There is the general belief the korrigan were created when the princesses of Armorica refused to convert to Christianity; they were cursed by God, transformed into fairy-beings. Although their breath is said to be deadly, the all-female race of the korrigan must take mortal men as their lovers in order to perpetuate their race. These fairies have the ability to shape-shift into any form they desire, can predict the future, can travel from one location to another with the speed of thought, cure most illnesses by means of charms they create.

Sources: Keightly, *World Guide to Gnomes, Fairies, Elves, and Other Little People*, 420, 431–2; Monaghan, *Encyclopedia of Celtic Mythology and Folklore*, 275; Spence, *Legends and Romances of Brittany*, 35–8

Korykia

Korykia was a NYMPH of Parnasso from Greek mythology; she and the god Apollo were the parents of the hero Lykoros.

Sources: Fontenrose, *Python*, 416; Larson, *Greek Nymphs*, 147; Pausânias, *Guide to Greece*, 489

Koumyoumin

A NAT from Burmese lore, Koumyoumin ("Lord of the Nine Towns") is a regional NATURE SPIRIT; it oversees the land around Kyankse, Burma. Koumyoumin greatly dislikes and will cause great harm to anything appearing in groups of nines; for instance, when traveling through his region, people are mindful to move in groups of less than or more than nine individuals. If a person cannot be found to increase the number a large stone will be used to symbolically represent a person; if this tradition is not followed it is believed a tragedy will occur.

Sources: Illes, *Encyclopedia of Spirits*, 583; Spiro, *Burmese Supernaturalism*, 97

Kraneia

In Greek mythology Kraneia was one of the eight HAMADRYAD who was born of HAMADRYAS; she was the HAMADRYAD of cornel-cherry.

Sources: Buxton, *Forms of Astonishment*, 211; Larson, *Greek Nymphs: Myth, Cult, Lore*, 283

Kremara

A NATURE SPIRIT in Polish folklore Kremara was the guardian spirit of adult pigs after they left the care and watchful eye of fellow NATURE SPIRIT PRIPARCHIS. Kremara would look after his adult, domestic pigs to ensure their good health. To show their appreciation, farmers would pour libations of beer into roaring fires creating a horrible stench Kremara was said to find pleasing. It was believed his brother was the NATURE SPIRIT, KURWAICHIN, the guardian of domestic sheep.

Sources: Dixon-Kennedy, *Encyclopedia of Russian and Slavic Myth and Legend*, 157–58; Graves, *Larousse Encyclopedia of Mythology*, 291; Rose, *Spirits, Fairies, Leprechauns, and Goblins, an Encyclopedia*, 266–67

Kreousa

In classical Greek mythology, the OCEANID Kreousa was a NYMPH of Thessalia in northern Greece; she was the wife of the river god, Peneios. Kreousa is frequently depicted in art as holding a serpent.

Sources: Charlesworth, *Good and Evil Serpent*, 136; Larson, *Greek Nymphs*, 41

Kretheis

According to Greek mythology the NYMPH of the town of Smyrna in Lydia, the NAIAD Kretheis, was, by the river god Meles, the mother of Homer, the greatest ancient Greek epic poet and the author of *The Iliad* and *The Odyssey*.

Sources: Kirk, *Iliad: A Commentary:* Volume 1, 2; Nagy, *Homer the Preclassic*, 258

Kruzimugeli

Kruzimugeli is the name of a DWARF from Austrian lore that fell in love with a black eyed and haired charcoal-burner's daughter. Kruzimugeli promised she would marry the king and be queen but if at the end of three years she did know his name, she would be forever his. The girl agreed married the king and lived happily for three years until she suddenly remembered the promise she made the DWARF. Just as in the popular tale, RUMPELSTILTSKIN, the girl overheard the DWARF gloating and singing a song with his own name in it.

Sources: Guiney, *Brownies and Bogles,* 142; Harrison, *Bric-A-Brac Stories*, 83–91; Vernaleken, *In the Land of Marvels*, 26–8

Kunal-Trow

Variations: King-Trows
The kunal-trow is a particular species of TROW found in the Shetland Islands. There are only male kunal-trow and to perpetuate their kind they must take a mortal woman as a wife. These fairy-beings are monogamous and mate for life but unfortunately their wives always die during childbirth; perhaps this is why, as a species, they are all morose in nature.

Sources: Briggs, *Encyclopedia of Fairies*, Henderson, *Scottish Fairy Belief: A History*, 15; Saxby, *Shetland Traditional Lore*, 128

Kupara

In Greek mythology, Kupara was a NYMPH of a spring in Sicily.

Source: Larson, *Greek Nymphs*, 220

Kuperan

Variations: Kuppiron, Kuprian
Kuperan was a GIANT and an ally of the dragon in the middle High German epic poem, *Nibelungenlied* ("*The Song of the Nibelungs*"). Living high up in the mountains with the dragon, Kuperan is the guardian of the only sword by which the dragon can be slain and commands a legion of GIANTS as well. Bearing a shield a foot thick and "hardened with dragon's blood," Kuperan does battle against the hero Seyfrid (Siegfried). He wore gilded armor, a helm that increased his strength, and wielded a four cornered club razor sharp at every angel.

It has be speculated Kuperan and the dragon of the poem are in fact the same character as they never appear in the same place at the same time; although the hero of the poem, Seyfrid, does battle and kill each in turn.

Sources: Keightly, *World Guide to Gnomes, Fairies, Elves, and Other Little People*, 208; McConnell, *Companion to the Nibelungenlied*, 56–8; Thoms, *Lays and Legends of Germany*, 67–8

Kura

Variations: Cyrene, Kurana, Kurene, KYRENE, Qrennah
A NYMPH from the mythology of the North African Berber, Kura was the guardian of a spring in Cyrene, the location of which is where the plant silphium came from; a herbal aphrodisiac and contraceptive. In art she is often depicted as slaying large beasts.

Sources: Illes, *Encyclopedia of Spirits*, 593; Oden, *Early Libyan Christianity*, 57

Kurupira

Variations: CURUPIRA, Curupiri, Kuru-Pira
In the mythology of the Guaraní people of Argentina, Bolivia, Brazil, and Paraguay the NATURE SPIRIT known as Kurupira was born one of the seven monstrous children of Tau and Kerana. Described as being hairy, short and ugly with backward facing feet, Kurupira lives in the jungle and acts as its protector. He is known to attack and oftentimes kill greedy hunters who take more than they need or do not show the woods proper respect. At one time, in addition to being considered the lord of the wilderness, Kurupira was also

revered as a fertility spirit as he has an enormous, prehensile penis he wraps around his waist like a belt.

Sources: Helms, *Creations of the Rainbow Serpent*, 64; Mack, *Field Guide to Demons*, 100–01; Stookey, *Thematic Guide to World Mythology*, 138

Kurwaichin

A NATURE SPIRIT in Polish folklore Kurwaichin was the guardian spirit of adult domestic sheep. To show their appreciation, farmers would pour libations of beer into their fireplace, creating a horrible stench Kurwaichin was said to find pleasing. It was believed his brother was the NATURE SPIRIT, KREMARA, the guardian of adult, domestic pigs.

Sources: Dixon-Kennedy, *Encyclopedia of Russian and Slavic Myth and Legend*, 160; Graves, *Larousse Encyclopedia of Mythology*, 291; Rose, *Spirits, Fairies, Leprechauns, and Goblins, an Encyclopedia*, 266–67

Kyane

Variations: Cyane

Kyane ("blue") was a blue-haired NYMPH of a spring in Syracuse; she was the wife of the river, Anapos. Kyane was the dear friend of Persephone (Proserpina) who tried to come to her aid when she was being abducted by the god, Hades (Pluto). As the only witness of the kidnapping, Kyane protested loudly as Hades (Pluto) opened a portal to his realm right over her freshwater spring. From here, different versions of the myth exist; some say Kyane latterly wept herself into tears and mingled into the water of her spring; in another version Hades struck her mute so she could not call for assistance or tell anyone what she witnessed.

Sources: Cameron, *Greek Mythography in the Roman World*, 12–3; Illes, *Encyclopedia of Spirits*, 599; Larson, *Greek Nymphs: Myth, Cult, Lore*, 213

Kyanee

Variations: Cyanee, Cyanea

Born the daughter of Maeander, Kyanee was the river NYMPH of the town of Miletos in Karia, Anatolia. This NAIAD was the wife of the eponymous king, Miletus, one of the godling sons of Apollo; they were the parents of BYBLIS and Caunus. Some sources give their mother as being the NYMPH, TRAGASIA.

Sources: Larson, *Greek Nymphs*, 203; Lemprière, *Classical Dictionary* (1839), 86

Kykais

In Greek mythology, Kykais was a NYMPH of a spring in Telos in classical Greek mythology.

Sources: Collignon, *Manual of Mythology*, 207; Larson, *Greek Nymphs*, 322; Murray, *Manual of Mythology*, 207

Kyllene

Variations: Cyllene

In Greek mythology, Kyllene was a mountain NYMPH of Kyllene, a region in Arcadia; she was born the daughter of NAIS. Kyllene was the nurse of the infant god, Hermes (Mercury). It is possible Kyllene was the wife of the first man of Arcadia, Pelasgos, and the mother of his son, Lykaon; other potential wives were the OCEANIAD, MELIBOIA and Deianeira.

Sources: Fox, *Greek and Roman*, 20; Larson, *Greek Nymphs*, 154

Kymatolege

A sea–NYMPH, Kymatolege ("wave-stiller") was the NEREIS of the waves (or the end of the waves). Along with her sisters AMPHITRITE and KYMODOKE, they had the power to still the winds and calm the sea.

Sources: Hard, *Routledge Handbook of Greek Mythology*, 52; Hesiod, *Poems of Hesiod*, 41

Kymo

A sea–NYMPH, Kymo was one of the named NEREID in classical Greek mythology; she was born the daughter of Nerues and DORIS.

Source: Hesiod, *Poems of Hesiod*, 41

Kymodoke

Kymodoke was the NEREIS of steadying waves who, with her sisters, AMPHITRITE and KYMATOLEGE, possessed the power to still the winds and calm the sea. She was one of the named NEREID who accompanied THETIS in mourning the loss of her son, Achilles.

Sources: Collignon, *Manual of Mythology*, 187; Perry, *Women of Homer*, 146

Kymopoleia

A sea–NYMPH in classical Greek mythology, Kymopoleia ("wave walker") was born a daughter of the god of the sea, Poseidon (Neptune). She was given as a wife by her father to Briareos (Briareus) the hundred-handed GIANT.

Sources: Hard, *Routledge Handbook of Greek Mythology*, 67; Rose, *Handbook of Greek Mythology*, 75

Kymothoe

The NEREIS of the running waves, Kymothoe was also one of the named NEREID who accompanied THETIS in mourning the loss of her son, Achilles.

Sources: Collignon, *Manual of Mythology*, 18; Hesiod, *Poems of Hesiod*, 41

Kynosoura

Variations: CYNOSURA

Kynosoura ("a dog's tail") was a NYMPH of Crete; she was transformed into the constellation Ursa Minor. According to some stories she and HELIKE were the two Creatan NYMPHS who nursed the infant god, Zeus (Jupiter).

Sources: Cook, *Zeus*, 112; Larson, *Greek Nymphs*, 185; Gorrell, *What's in a Word*, 95

Kyrene

A NYMPH of the Greek colony of Kyrene in Libya, North Africa, Kyrene was a NAIAD who successfully wrestled a deadly lion who had been plaguing her father's lands; she was depicted in art as holding the head of a lion. The god Apollo fell in love with her upon seeing her defeat the animal and took her away to Thessalia where she became queen. Kyrene bore the god two sons, Aristaios and Autychos.

Sources: Foxhall, *When Men Were Men*, 100; Larson, *Greek Nymphs*, 188–89

Kyrtones

In Greek mythology, Kyrtones was a NYMPH of a cold water spring in Boiotia.

Sources: Larson, *Greek Nymphs*, 143; Pausânias, *Guide to Greece*, 359

Lolotte

In the fairy-tale *Prince Vivien and the Princess Placida* by Nonchalante et Papillon, the good fairy Lolotte was the FAIRY GODMOTHER of Prince Vivien and Princess Placida; she cultivated their characters in order to make them not only love oneanother but also to become beloved rulers of their subjects.

Source: Lang, *Green Fairy Book*, 238–61

Lady Banana Ghost

Variations: Phit Nang Tani

A NATURE SPIRIT from Thailand, Lady Banana Ghost is a spirit of NAIAD who lives within small banana trees. Rarely leaving its tree without great provocation, these spirits are extremely displeased if forcibly displaced. Lady Banana Ghost are believed to be at the peak of their power when the tree they possess is flowering; they will use their magic to play pranks intended to frighten but never harm; they will also use this power to make gifts of alms to itinerant monks.

Sources: Guelden, *Thailand into the Spirit World*, 75; Illes, *Encyclopedia of Spirits*, 604–05

The Lady of Gollerus

The Lady of Gollerus of Smerwick, Ireland was similar to a MERROW but rather than a special hat she had a magical dress called a *cohuleen driuth*, if ever it was taken from her she could not return to her watery abode. She was beautiful with a head of long green hair; there was a very thin, clear or pale white webbing between her fingers. She was said to have been a wonderful wife, keeping house and rearing the children until the day she discovered where her husband had her *cohuleen driuth*. Upon its discovery she donned her dress, went down to the sea and never looking back at her life ashore, dove headfirst into the water.

Sources: Croker, *Fairy Legends and Traditions of the South of Ireland*, 239–47; Keightly, *World Guide to Gnomes, Fairies, Elves, and Other Little People*, 370

The Lady of the Lake

Variations: Nimue, VIVIAN

According to Arthurian mythology the Lady of the Lake resides in Dosemary Pool, a lake in Cornwall, England. Most often she is depicted only with her arm extended up out of the water holding tightly onto the legendary sword, Excalibur.

It seems in the earliest texts, the Lady of the Lake was a FAIRY QUEEN who ruled over an underwater or otherworld land called Tir na Mban ("Land of Women"). There was an island in the middle of the lake where she resided with her servants. The Lady took Lancelot when he was a child and raised him to be her protector and eventual lover, earning him the title of Lancelot of the Lake. In some versions of the old texts they had a child together, Galahad, the most pure of Arthur's knights.

In later version of the story, the Lady of the Lake was said to be a mortal sorceress; her name became a title and was held by at least two different women in Welsh Arthurian lore, Morgause and Nimue and her lake became a magical illusion created to secure her privacy.

No matter the age or the version of the myth

the Lady of Lake was always King Arthur's greatest ally, protecting him in life and seeing to him and his funerary needs in death.

Sources: Evan-Wentz, *Fairy Faith in Celtic Countries*, 315, 327; McCoy, *Witch's Guide to Faery Folk*, 259; Monaghan, *Encyclopedia of Celtic Mythology and Folklore*, 279; Rose, *Spirits, Fairies, Leprechauns, and Goblins*, 191, 351

Laimos

Similar to the FATES of the lore of ancient Greece, the Laimos of Baltic mythology are the seven fairies who spin and weave the fate of a person shortly after their birth. Appearing only in groups of three, these fairies decide if the child will live, if so, when it will die, and the quality of life it will experience while alive.

Sources: Illes, *Encyclopedia of Spirits*, 610; Lurker, *Routledge Dictionary of Gods and Goddesses, Devils and Demons*, 108

Lalla Malika

A beautiful DJINN from Moroccan lore, Lalla Malika was coquettish, elegant, and flirtatious; she has a reputation for taking married men as lovers and only speaks in French.

Sources: Illes, *Encyclopedia of Spirits*, 613–14; Rose, *Spirits, Fairies, Leprechauns, and Goblins, an Encyclopedia*, 220

Lalla Mira

Variations: Lalla Mira al-Mtiriyya, Lalla Mira Bent Hartya, Lalla Mirra

A DJINN from Moroccan lore, Lalla Mira was both beloved and feared for her power. Possibly originating amongst the Berber tribes, Lalla Mira had a reputation for seducing unmarried men.

Sources: Illes, *Encyclopedia of Spirits*, 614; Rose, *Spirits, Fairies, Leprechauns, and Goblins, an Encyclopedia*, 220

Lalla Mkouna Bent Mkoun

Variations: The Lady

A benevolent DJINN from Moroccan lore, Lalla Mkouna Bent Mkoun, watches over the family home. As a species, Djinn are attracted to newly constructed houses, so it was believed vital to appease this domestic spirit with offerings of incense with the intent she will intervene and protect the family from malicious DJINN who would try to move into the home.

Sources: Illes, *Encyclopedia of Spirits*, 616; Rose, *Spirits, Fairies, Leprechauns, and Goblins, an Encyclopedia*, 191

Lalla Rekya Bint el Khamar

Variations: Lalla Raqya, Lalla Reqya, Lalla Rkia

The sister of LALLA MKOUNA BENT MKOUN, Lalla Rekya Bint el Khamar ("Lady Rekya Daughter of the Red One") is a Queen among the DJINN. A guardian of *hummam* (bathhouses) and freshwater springs, this benevolent and diplomatic fairy is traditionally introduced to a child on or near their first birthday in the *hummam*; this celebration is accompanied with feasting and the lighting of oil lamps with twelve floating wicks.

Sources: Illes, *Encyclopedia of Spirits*, 616; Rose, *Spirits, Fairies, Leprechauns, and Goblins, an Encyclopedia*, 191

Lamas

The lamas ("GIANT") of ancient Chaldea was a propitious and protecting female, winged DJINN; later they were associated with the lamassu of ancient Assyria. Nirgallu, the winged lions sometimes acted as palace guardians were considered to be a species of lamas.

Sources: Lenormant, *Chaldean Magic*, 24; Rose, *Spirits, Fairies, Gnomes, and Goblins*, 192

Lamia of the Sea

Variations: Lamia of the Shore, Queen of the Sea-NYMPHS

In ancient Greek lore, Lamia of the Sea was a MERMAID or a NYMPH who would seductively dance and sing from the water. As she would dance, Lamia would attract the attention of men who when they approached her, she would then drown. On occasion, Lamia is said to emerge from the water and ask a passer-by if Alexander the Great still lives. If the person tells the fairy the king of Macedon is deceased she will fly into a rage and attempt to kill the person, by drowning if she can. She is said to be the cause of waterspouts.

Sources: Illes, *Encyclopedia of Spirits*, 618; Lawson, *Modern Greek Folklore and Ancient Greek Religion*, 52, 172–73

Lamiae

According to the *Malleus Maleficarum* ("*Hammer of the Witches*"), a treatise on witches written by Inquisitors Heinrich Kramer and Jacob Sprenger in 1486, the lamiae ("render") were a species of evil fairy or a FAIRY ANIMAL described as having a human face but a beastial body. Sent by a witch, the lamiae would sneak into a home, tear an infant to pieces, and then restore it to life.

Sources: Briggs, *Encyclopedia of Fairies*, 260–61; Broedel, *Malleus Maleficarum and the Construction of Witchcraft*, 104–5; Latham, *Elizabethan Fairies*, 52–3

Laminak

Variations: Lamin'ak

In Basque fairy lore the laminak are said to be a species of fay living underground. Although their presence is believed to bring good luck, these tiny fays are also dreaded; they enter into peoples home by coming down the chimney and once inside they steal unbaptized infants and various household items. Laminak, when they speak, always say exactly the opposite of what they mean; they are described as having the feet of a chicken, duck, goat, or goose. Excessively fond of neat homes the laminak, like BASA-ANDRE and BASA-JUAN, are easily driven off by the sound of peeling church bells. All laminak are named Guillen (William).

Sources: Cobham, *Character Sketches of Romance, Fiction and the Drama*, Volume 4, 193; Gimbutas, *Living Goddesses*, 174; Webster, *Basque Legends*, 48–9

Lampades

The Lampades were torch-bearing infernal NYMPHS of the Underworld, inhabiting the rivers there. Although Greek in origin, their parentage is uncertain; it is possible they were the daughters of the goddess Nyx and any number of river gods of Hades. The lampades were described by Alkman, an ancient Greek lyrical poet from Sparta who worked in the 7th century B.C.; he described them as being the lamp-bearing entourage of Hekate as well as prophets.

Sources: Illes, *Encyclopedia of Spirits*, 619; Rigoglioso, *Cult of Divine Birth in Ancient Greece*, 87

Lampetie

Variation: Lampetia ("to shine")

In Greek mythology Lampetie ("gleaming and shining"), was a NYMPH of the sun and one of the named DANAIDS. Other sources say she and her sister, PHAETHUSA ("radiance"), were born the daughters of the Titan, Hyperion (Heilos) and tended after his sacred herds on the mythical island of Thrinakie. Each sister was described by Homer, the greatest ancient Greek epic poet, in *The Odyssey* as having "redundant locks" of hair. According to the Greek oral poet, Hesiod, when her brother, Phaethon, died, she and her seven sisters were transformed into amber-weeping poplar tree. The sisters were collectively known as The Daughters of Helios (Sol); their names are AEGLE, AETHERIE, DIOXIPPE, Helie (see THE HELIADES), MEROPE, and PHOEBE.

Sources: Homer, *The Odyssey*, Volume 1, 307; Keightley, *Mythology of Ancient Greece and Italy*, 56

Landvaettir

Variations: Landvættir

In ancient Icelandic literature and stories the landvaettir are chthonic guardians inhabiting animals, rivers, tones, specific land, trees, and the like. These NATURE SPIRITS have, in addition to natural magical ability, the ability to shape-shift into TROLL-like animals with greatly increased strength. In addition to be tutelary guardians, the landvaettir have been known to take special interest in individual humans, protecting them as well. In the ancient Icelandic language the word *landvaettir* is grammatically a feminine noun, however, in the stories they are described as being either animals or men.

One of the laws written in the medieval Icelandic text entitled *Landnámabók* ("Book of Settlements") demands when coming ashore, seafarers first remove the carved figureheads from their longships least they frighten or offend the landvaettir, causing them to attack.

Sources: Hastings, *Encyclopedia of Religion and Ethics*, Part 23, 252; Jolly, *Witchcraft and Magic in Europe*, 95, 125

Laneria

Born one of the 3,000 daughters of the Titians, Oceanus and Tethys, Laneria was one of the named OCEANIDS in Greek mythology.

Source: Westmoreland, *Ancient Greek Beliefs*, 24

Langia

Langia was a NYMPH from the mythology of classical Greece and Rome. One of the NAIADS, it is believed among the ancient Greeks the Nemean games were established to honor her as a show of appreciation for her kindness of not allowing her spring to dry up. She also gave the questing godling, Perseus, water from her spring.

Sources: Ballentine, *Nymphs as Water-deities Among the Greeks and Roman*, 6, 7

Lanthe

Born one of the 3,000 daughters of the Titians, Oceanus and Tethys, Lanthe was one of the named OCEANIDS in Greek mythology.

Sources: Bell, *Women of Classical Mythology*, 358; Westmoreland, *Ancient Greek Beliefs*, 24

Lantukh

A domestic fairy from Jewish lore, the lantukh lives in the corners of the family home. Typically there is only one of these little fairies in a home, as they tend to become emotionally attached to their people. Similar to the HOBGOBLIN, the lantukh likes to play pranks by frightening people; there are no stories of this species of fairy ever harming anyone.

Sources: Illes, *Encyclopedia of Spirits*, 620–21; Singer, *Stories for Children*, 231–36; Weinreich, *Lantukh*, 243–51

Laomedeia

Variations: Laomedia

A sea–NYMPH, Laomedeia ("counsel the people," "mid-day" or "noon") was one of the NEREIS named by Hesiod; she was born the daughter of Nerus and DORIS in ancient Greek mythology.

Sources: Bell, *Women of Classical Mythology*, 273; Hesiod, *Works of Hesiod, Callimachus, and Theognis*, 15; Hesiod, *Poems of Hesiod*, 41; Westmoreland, *Ancient Greek Beliefs*, 755

Lara

Variations: Larunda, Mana, Muta

In ancient Greek mythology, Lara was a NAIAD; she was believed to been born the daughter of the river god, Almo. When Lara reported to the goddess Hera (Juno) her husband, Zeus (Jupiter) had an affair with a fountain NYMPH named JUTURNA the angry goddess had Lara's tongue ripped out before banishing her to Hades. Lara, by the god Mercury (Hermes) was the mother of the LARES, twin brothers who guarded cities and crossroads.

Sources: Bell, *Bell's New Pantheon or Historical Dictionary of the Gods*, 112; Littleton, *Gods, Goddesses, and Mythology*, Volume 11, 1454, Parada, *Genealogical Guide to Greek Mythology*, 87

Lares

Variations: Genii loci, Lases

According to ancient Roman mythology the Lares were born the twin sons of the NAIAD, LARA and the god Hermes (Mercury); she was raped by him as he escorted her to her Hades. The Lares were the tutelary guardians of at first cities and crossroads and then later fertility to the fields, blessings to the households, and the good fortune pertaining to the sea. Depicted as dancing youth holding a bowl in hone and horn cup in the other, the lares were also accompanied by phallic looking serpents.

There were many different species of lares, most important were the domestic household spirits known as the lares familiars ("guardians of the family"). Other lares were the lares compitales ("guardians of crossroads"), lares domestici ("guardians of the house"), lares patria, lares permarini ("guardians of the sea"), lares praestitis ("guardians of the state"), lares privati, lares rurales ("guardians of the land"), and the lares viales ("guardians of travelers").

Sources: Adkins, *Handbook to Life in Ancient Rome*, 274; Allen, *Encyclopedia Britannica*, Volume 14, 313; Jones, *Encyclopedia of Religion*, 3937, Littleton, *Gods, Goddesses, and Mythology*, Volume 11, 861

Larissa

In Greek mythology, Larissa was a NYMPH of a fountain or a spring in Argos, Greece.

Sources: Chisholm, *Encyclopædia Britannica*, Volume 19, 882; Larson, *Greek Nymphs*, 165

Laudine

Variations: Alundyne, Analida, the Lady of the Fountain

In Arthurian lore Laudine was the one of the SÍDHE, the fairy woman to whom Sir Iwain (Sir Ywain) married; she lived in a sacred well which her husband knight guarded. This character from Arthurian mythology appeared in the poem *Yvain, the Knight with the Lion* (1170) by the French poet and troubadour, Chrétien de Troyes. The poem tells the tale of how Laudine marries Sir Iwain after he kills her husband, Sir Esclandos; their marriage is based on her need for a protector of her fountain and his sexual desires. Laudine rejects her new husband when the knight deserts her for a year to persue his adventures. By the end of the story, Laudine and the Knight are reunited. In some versions of the story, she later fails a purity test in Arthur's court.

Sources: Bruce, *Arthurian Name Dictionary*, 312; Evan-Wentz, *Fairy Faith in Celtic Countries*, 325; Fenster, *Arthurian Women*, xxxvi

Lauma

Variations: Laume

Originally a goddess in Baltic and Latvian mythology Lauma became a NATURE SPIRIT or a woodland fairy after the introduction of Christianity. Described as being very beautiful with long blond hair, she appears naked near her home by water or notable, feminine shaped stones. On some occasions she is said to have the feet of a bird or pendulous breasts. If a man should see her and laugh because of her appearance, the Lauma will change him into an animal.

Lauma, in addition to being an individual has also been considered to be a species of fay. As such, the lauma are said to be sexually aggressive in their pursuit and dominance of men. Manifesting as a either a trio or a large number of their kind, the set out at night to commit acts of mischief, such as riding horses to exhaustion, milking cows dry, and shearing too much wool from sheep. On Thursday evening they will go out with their spinning wheel and will spin into thread anything they can get their hands no, such as moss, human hair, and even intestines.

The laumès, no doubt named for Lauma, were fairies of Baltic lore who were believed to have the ability to bestow or remove abundance, fertility, and wealth. Sometimes the laumès were known to steal infants but there are no tales of them ever harming anyone, although they tend to be as volatile as they can be compassopnate. The male version of the lauma is known as the *laumiukas*.

Sources: Dexter, *Whence the Goddesses*, 56–7; Gimbutas, *Living Goddesses*, 207–8; Illes, *Encyclopedia of Spirits*, 622; Monaghan, *Encyclopedia of Goddesses and Heroines*, 287

Laurin

A DWARF king, Laurin was said to own a magical ring, a magical girdle purported to give him the strength of ten men, a magical sword capable of cutting through iron and stone, and a *hel keplein*, a magical cap that could make him invisible at will.

Laurin once carried off a mortal woman named Kunhild to his kingdom in the Tyroleso mountains; he eventually married her and made her his queen. They lived in a subterranean palace covered with carbuncle, diamonds, and other precious stones. The hero Dietrich came to the rescue of Kunhild and bested Laurin in combat. Spearing the DWARF's life the two warriors then became friends.

Sources: Keightly, *World Guide to Gnomes, Fairies, Elves, and Other Little People*, 207; Pope, *German Composition*, 71–3; Wägner, *Great Norse, Celtic and Teutonic Legends*, 69–77

Lausks

Variations: Granfather Lausks, Lauskis, OLD MAN WINTER

In Latvian mythology Lausks ("frost") is a NATURE SPIRIT, the personification of the cold.

Lausks carries a large golden axe with him; it is believed when the frost is particularly strong he cracks the earth with his axe. When a tree branch snaps suddenly in the cold it said Lauks is cracking his axe.

Sources: Bunkśe, *Geography and the Art of Life*, 96; Olcott, *Baltic Wizards*, 86

Lazy Lawrence

Variations: Lazy Larrence, Lazy Laurence, Sir Lazy Lawrence, Lazy Lawrence of Lubberland

Lazy Lawrence was a Scottish fairy whose presence induces lethargy in people according to Durrant Cooper in his 1853 book entitled *Sussex Vocabulary*; this individual fairy was considered to be a NURSERY BOGIE in the folklore of Hampshire and Somerset, England.

Sources: Brewer, *Dictionary of Phrase and Fable*, 736; Green, *Cassell's Dictionary of Slang*, 866; Hazlitt, *Faiths and Folklore*, 361

Leagore

Variations: Leiagore ("addressing the people")

A sea–NYMPH from Greek mythology, Leagore was the NEREIS of assembling (fish or navies) according to the ancient reek oral poet, Hesiod; she was born the daughter of Nerues and DORIS.

Sources: Eco, *Infinity of Lists*, 21; Hesiod, *Theogony, Works and Days,* 20; Sluiter, *Free Speech in Classical Antiquity*, 33

Leanhaum-Shee

Variations: Leanan-Sidhe, Leanhaun-Shee, Leanhaun-Sidhe, Lhiannan Shee

On the Isle of Man, located in the middle of the northern Irish Sea, there is a type of vampiric fay appearing to its victims as a beautiful young woman but to everyone else is invisible; it is called a leanhaum-shee. It will try to seduce a man, and if it is successful, its magic will cause him to fall in love with it. If he does, the leanhaum-shee will take him as a lover; if he does not, it will strangle him to death and then drain his corpse of blood. Little by little it will drain off its lover's life-energy during intercourse. The leanhaum-shee also collects his blood and stores it in a red cauldron, which adds to its magical properties. (It is believed the cauldron is the source of its power, what gives the leanhaum-shee its ability to shape-shift into a white deer and keeps it looking young and beautiful.) The vampire also feeds small amounts of the blood to her lover so he will be inspired to write love poems. Eventually, the man will become nothing more than a used-up husk and die.

Sources: Jones, *On the Nightmare;* Moorey, *Fairy Bible*, 162–5; O'Connor, *Book of Ireland*, 50–2; Wilde, *Ancient Legends*, 169, 257–9

Leimakid

The Leimakids were a sub-species of the LIMONIAD from Greek mythology; they were the NYMPHS of meadows.

Source: Conner, *Everything Classical Mythology Book*, 275

Leimonides

The Leimonides were in ancient Greek mythology the NYMPHS of flowery meadows.

Source: Rigoglioso, *Cult of Divine Birth in Ancient Greece*, 87

Leiriope

Variations: Liriope

Leiriope was the NYMPH of the lily plant. Raped by the river god, Cephisus (Kephisos), the blue NYMPH, Leiriope gave birth to Narcissus and the NYMPH, DIOGENEIA.

Sources: Graves, *Greek Myths*, 85; Larson, *Greek Nymphs*, 11, 147

Lelegian

In Greek mythology, Lelegian was a NYMPH in ancient Carian.

Sources: Larson, *Greek Nymphs*, 204; Rigoglioso, *Cult of Divine Birth in Ancient Greece*, 127

Lemures

Variations: Larvae

In ancient Rome a MANE is the spirit of a departed person; there are two types of manes, LARES, beneficial household spirits, and Lemures, a type of BOGEYMAN. Created when a family member died theses malicious spirits lived in the family home and would frighten the inhabitants by taking on a frightening aspect and making mysterious noises. The festival of Lemuralia was held each year on May 9, 11, and 13 was held to placate the lemures. The counterpart to the lemurs was the LARES.

Sources: Adkins, *Handbook to Life in Ancient Rome*, 274; Bell, *Bell's New Pantheon*, 43; Berens, *Myths and Legends of Ancient Greece and Rome*, 185–6

Len

Variations: Len of Killarney, Len of the Many Hammers

Len was a fairy goldsmith from Irish folklore; it was from his furnace the rainbow and fiery dew came from. Len's forge was near Locha Lein ("Lakes of Len").

Sources: Rolleston, *Celtic Myths and Legends*, 123; Wallace, *Folk-lore of Ireland*, 90

Leprechaun

Variations: FIR DARRIG, Lepracaun, Lobaircin, Logheryman, Lubberkin, Lubrican, Luchorpain ("small bones"), Luchuiro ("little bodies"), Luporipan

According to Irish mythology leprechauns are a species of antisocial fairy spending its time cobbling shoes. Although they preferred to avoid human contact these fairies would live in a person's cellar and assist them in small household task or by gifting them with a lucky charm. At the end of a work day, these fairies enjoy celebrating by dancing, drinking and feasting heavily. Typically the leprechaun, a SOLITARY FAIRY, was depicted wearing a green suit, waistcoat, hat, and stockings. Their shoes are always perfect and sport large buckles. They are also said to be clever troublemakers who love to play practical jokes on humans. Carrying an iron horseshoe will protect a person from the pranks of the leprechauns, as not only iron a natural repellant to their kind but they are said to love horses to the point of distraction.

Associated with the leprechaun is its pot of gold, or other such treasure. By use of their innate magical abilities they protect their hoard from any who would want to have it. Depending on the version of the story a person will capture the fay and coheres it into giving up the location of its treasure, but nearly always by the end of the story the leprechaun will somehow have managed to turn the tables and escape with its treasure. Legends are divided as to the source of the leprechaun's wealth; some sources say it is their savings from all the hard work they do creating and selling shoes while other stories say they are the protectors of the remaining wealth of the TUATHA DE DANANN.

Although the leprechaun is a fairy from Irish folklore there are similar fairies in other countries to it. In Holland there is the myth of the KABOUTER, on the Isle of Man there is the PHYNNODDEREE, and in Polynesian lore there are the MENEHUNA. In the United Kingdom and the United States of America the leprechaun is seen as a symbol of the Irish and of luck.

Sources: Evan-Wentz, *Fairy Faith in Celtic Coun-*

tries, 52–53; Keightly, *World Guide to Gnomes, Fairies, Elves, and Other Little People*, 371; Ó hÓgáin, *Myth, Legend and Romance*, 196–7; McCoy, *Witch's Guide to Faery Folk*, 32; Peterson, *Mythology in Our Midst*, 93–4; Venable, *Gold*, 196–7

Leshy (plural: lechies)

Variations: Lešak, Leshii, Lesiy, Lesní mužík, Lesnik, Lesný mužík ("forest man"), Lesny mužik/ded, Lesovij, Lesovik, Lesovy, Lesun, Lešy, Leszi, Leszy

Originally a god or NATURE SPIRIT of the forest in Slavonic mythology, a leshy ("forest") was named as a type of terrestrial devil in Colin de Plancy's *Dictionaire Infernale* (1818, 1863); the male of the species was known as leshouikha. SATYER-like humans from the waist up with notable beards, ears, and the horns of a she-goat, these NATURE SPIRITS used their ability to imitate voices as a way to lure people back to their caves. Once the victim was inside, they would be tickled to death. Lechies, as they are called in numbers, have a BANSHEE-like cry and the ability to shrink down to the height of grass when marching through fields. They can also grow as tall as a tree when running through the forest where it lives.

Sources: Johnson, *Slavic Sorcery*, 8, 88; Mack, *Field Guide to Demons, Fairies, Fallen Angels, and Other Subversive Spirits*, 111–13; Varner, *Mythic Forest*, 30–1

Lesidhe

Variations: Leshes, Leshiye, Vodyaniye, Zuibotshniks

In Irish lore the lesidhe are tutelary guardian spirits of the forests; although they have been known to appear in the form of an owl or wolf they typically disguise themselves as foliage. These SOLITARY FAIRIES are androgynous and will mimic the call of mockingbirds in order to confuse hikers and travelers. The lesidhe do not like humans, presumably because of their mistreatment of the land; although these fairies have never been accredited with hurting anyone they are said to play cruel pranks, foremost of which is luring people deep into the woods until they are lost.

Sources: McCoy, *Witch's Guide to Faery Folk*, 263–4; Newcomb, *Faerie Treasury*, 53

Lesovikha

In Russian folklore the lesovikha is the female version or the wife of the LESHY. Described as a naked young girl, a woman in a white *sarafan*, and as an ugly old woman with large breasts the lesovikha played a prominent role in forest lore. If a lesovikha is encountered while walking in the woods it was likely to ask if the person wished for money or a good life. If money was the answer it was granted but as soon as you left the woods the coins would turn to coal. However if the person asked for nothing they would be blessed with good luck. Additionally, it was said if ever one was to encounter the lesovikha in the woods as she was giving birth they were to throw something over the child and without making the sign of the cross, walk away.

Sources: Gilchrist, *Russian Magic*, 135; Ivanits, *Russian Folk Belief*, 67

Lethe

Lethe ("forgetfulness") was a NYMPH from the mythology of ancient Greece and Rome. One of the NAIADS, Lethe was born the daughter of Eris (Discordia), the goddess of discord and strife. It was believed anyone who came to her river, located in the Underworld, and drank from it would forget their earthy concerns and troubles. Lethe was the mother of the god of wine, Dionysus (Bacchus).

Sources: Avant, *Mythological Reference*, 280; Monaghan, *Encyclopedia of Goddesses and Heroines*, 416

Leuce

Variations: Leuka, Leukas

The Leuce ("white") were a sub-species of the HAMADRYAD, they were the NYMPHS of white poplar trees in Greek mythology.

Leuce was also the name of the individual HAMADRYAD who was raped by the god of the Underworld, Hades (Pluto). According to the legend his wife, Persephone (Proserpina), was so angry she turned the NYMPH into a white poplar tree.

Sources: Day, *God's Conflict with the Dragon and the Sea*, 410; Larson, *Greek Nymphs*, 160–1; Littleton, *Gods, Goddesses, and Mythology*, Volume 11, 603

Leucippe

Born one of the 3,000 daughters of the Titians, Oceanus and Tethys, Leucippe ("white horse") was the OCEANIDS present when Persephone (Proserpina) was kidnapped by Hades (Pluto).

Sources: Allen, *Homeric Hymns*, 51; Bell, *Bell's New Pantheon*, 44; Conti, *Natale Conti's Mythologiae: Books VI–X*, 701; Monaghan, *Encyclopedia of Goddesses and Heroines*, 27

Leucosia

Variations: LIGEIA, Legia

In classical Greek mythology, Leucosia ("white goddess") was one of the named SIRENS, a type of malicious sea NYMPH born the offspring of the ancient sea god, Phorcys. Half bird and half woman, she and her sisters would perch on the rocky Sicilian coastline and lure in sailor with their melodious song; once caught their prey were eaten alive. Although they hunted the coastline they lived inland in a meadow.

Sources: Monaghan, *Encyclopedia of Goddesses and Heroines,* 282; Smith, *Dictionary of Greek and Roman Biography and Mythology,* 817; Smith, *Smaller Classical Mythology,* 34

Leucothoe

A sea–NYMPH, Leucothoe was one of the named NEREID; she was born of Nereus and DORIS in classical Greek mythology. Leucothoe was beloved by the god, Apollo; sadly she met with an untimely death when her father ordered her to be buried alive. In his grief Apollo sprinkled her grave with AMBROSIA and nectar and from it sprang the first frankincense tree.

Sources: Apollodorus, *Apollodorus' Library and Hyginus' Fabulae,* 95; Francillon, *Gods and Heroes* 50–2; Ovid, *Mythological Fables,* 42; Lemprière, *Classical Dictionary,* 468

Leuke

Born one of the 3,000 daughters of the Titians, Oceanus and Tethys, Leuke ("white") was one of the named OCEANIDS. In Greek lore, Leuke was abducted by the god Hades (Pluto) and taken to the Elysium Fields to be his mistress; the NYMPH was so distressed with the idea she died. Hades transformed her body into a white poplar tree.

Sources: Hard, *Routledge Handbook of Greek Mythology,* 125; Keightley, *Mythology of Ancient Greece and Italy,* 80

Leukippe

Born one of the 3,000 daughters of the Titians, Oceanus and Tethys, Leukippe was one of the named OCEANIDS in ancient Greek mythology; she was one of the playmates of Persephone (Proserpina) and present when the goddess was kidnapped.

Sources: Barthell, *Gods and Goddesses of Ancient Greece,* 136; Fowler, *Archaic Greek Poetry,* 14

Lhiannah-Shee

Variations: Lhiannan-Shee, Lianhan Shee, Lliannan-She

The Lhiannah-Shee of the Isle of Man is very different than the fairy of the same name from Irish folklore. The British version of this fey is described as a very beautiful woman wearing a yellow silk robe and is known for enticing young men. To the victim, Lhiannah-Shee appears stunning and completely irresistible but to his companions she is invisible. Once the young man is under her spell, he is doomed; eventually he will pine away for want of her touch.

The Lhiannah-Shee ("peaceful spirit") of Ballafletcher is slightly different, as she is said to be a guardian of the Fletcher family of Kirk Braddan; it was to him she gave the Fairy Cup, a miraculous crystal cup ensuring the family line so long as the cup remained in the family's possession. Each year the head of the family was to toast the fey in thanks for their prosperity. The Fairy Cup of Ballafletcher is now in the possession of the Bacon family of Seafeild, as the Fletchers have died out and their house is in ruins.

Sources: Briggs, *Encyclopedia of Fairies,* 266; Moore, *Folk-Lore of the Isle of Man,* 49–50; Rose, *Spirits, Fairies, Leprechauns, and Goblins,* 197–8, 351

Liagora

A sea–NYMPH from Greek mythology, Liagora was the NEREID of the beautiful countenance.

Sources: Betham, *Transactions of the Royal Irish Academy,* Volume 17, 89; Lemprière, *Classical Dictionary,* 494

Liagore

A sea–NYMPH from Greek mythology, Liagore is named as one of the NEREID in Hesiod's poem, *Theogony* (7–8th B.C.E).

Sources: Bell, *Bell's New Pantheon* 102; Hesiod, *Works of Hesiod, Callimachus, and Theognis,* 15; Randall, *Sources of Spenser's Classical Mythology,* 21

Liban

Variations: Li Ban

In Irish mythology, Liban was born the daughter of the FAIRY KING ÁED ABRAT. She and her sister, the FAIRY QUEEN FAND, were the cause of the wasting sickness suffered by the hero, Cu Chulsinn. Liban was one of the SÍDHE, born the daughter of EOCHAID, son of the god, Etain.

Sources: Briggs, *Encyclopedia of Fairies,* 266; Gray, *Mythology of All Races,* Volume 3, 87; Layzer, *Signs of Weakness,* 136–7

Libya

A NYMPH in classical Greek mythology, Libya was born the daughter of the Egyptian god,

Epaphos and Memphis; by Triton, she was the mother of the Nymph, Kalliste.

Sources: Foxhall, *When Men Were Men*, 102; Grant, *Who's Who in Classical Mythology*, 73

Licke

Variations: Lick

Licke was one of the fairies who appear in *The Life of Robin Goodfellow* (London, 1628). It was likely this British fairy's name was taken from its duties of being a cook in the Otherworld. Licke had three brothers, Grim, Patch, and Pinch and four sisters, Gull, Lull, Sib, and Tib.

Sources: Briggs, *Encyclopedia of Fairies*, 5, 267; Monaghan, *Encyclopedia of Celtic Mythology and Folklore*, 289; Wilson, *Life in Shakespeare's England*, 42, 44

Lidskjalfr

Variations: Lidscialfr

Lidskjalfr ("limb shaker") in Norse mythology is named as being one of the Ijosalfar, the Sons of Ivaldi. These Dwarfs were the ones who created many of the magical items of the gods, including the golden wig of Sif; the ship, Skidbladnir; and the spear of Odin.

Sources: Grimes, *Norse Myths*, 9, 285; Rydberg, *Teutonic Mythology*, 356

Liega

A sea–Nymph, Liega was one of the named Nereid in classical Greek mythology; she was born of Nereus and Doris.

Sources: Apollodorus, *Apollodorus' Library and Hyginus' Fabulae*, 95; Bell, *Bell's New Pantheon or Historical Dictionary of the Gods*, 112

Ligea

A sea–Nymph from Greek mythology, Ligea was one of the named Nereid in classical Greek mythology; she was born of Nereus and Doris and described by Virgil as having bright, waving locks of hair and a slender pale neck.

Sources: Lemprière, *Classical Dictionary*, 468; Virgil, *Fourth Georgic of Virgil*, 49

Ligeia

In classical Greek mythology, Ligeia ("soprano") was one of the named Sirens, a type of malicious Nymph born the offspring of the ancient sea god, Phorcys. Half bird and half woman, she and her sisters would perch on the rocky Sicilian coastline and lure in sailor with their melodious song; once caught, their prey

were eaten alive. Although they hunted the coastline, Ligeia and her kind lived inland in a meadow.

Sources: Austern, *Music of the Sirens*, 40; Lemprière, *Classical Dictionary*, 721

Light Elves

Variations: Alfs, High Elves, White Elves

In the original Scandinavian lore, light elves were the benign elves most often seen dancing on the grass or sitting upon a tree branch. These fairies were similar to Nature Spirits in that they were concerned with the well-being of flowers, plants, and trees. Light elves were typically described as being pale bodied and winged. The land these fairies lived in was called Alfheim. Over the centuries the appearance and temperament of the light eves changed. When they were being kind they were described as being beautiful but when they were acting in a malicious manner they were said to be ugly.

Sources: Guiney, *Brownies and Bogles*, 46, 62; Keightly, *World Guide to Gnomes, Fairies, Elves, and Other Little People*, 78; McCoy, *Witch's Guide to Faery Folk*, 30

Ligia

In classical Greek mythology, Ligia was one of the named Sirens, a type of malicious sea Nymph born the offspring of the ancient sea god, Phorcys. Half bird and half woman, she and her sisters would perch on the rocky Sicilian coastline and lure in sailor with their melodious song; once caught their prey were eaten alive.

Sources: Rose, *Spirits, Fairies, Leprechauns, and Goblins*, 335; Smith, *Smaller Classical Mythology*, 34

Lilaea

Lilaea was a Nymph from the mythology of ancient Greece and Rome. Born the daughter of Cephissus, it is believed the town Lilaea was named for her.

Sources: Bell, *Place-Names in Classical Mythology*, 165; Smith, *Dictionary of Greek and Roman Biography and Mythology*, 786

Lilaia

In Greek mythology, the Nymph Lilaia was a Naiad in the town of Lilaia in Phokis, central Greece, according to classical Greek mythology. Lilaia was a daughter of the river god of Attika, Kephisos (Cephisus).

Sources: Larson, *Greek Nymphs*, 147; Pausânias, *Guide to Greece: Central Greece*, 495

Lilyi

In the Romani gypsy lore from the region of Transylvania, Lilyi was born the daughter of the FAIRY QUEEN of the KESHALYI, ANA, and her demon husband the king of the Locolico. Melalo, the first born child of the royal couple, was desirous of a wife but there was no other half-fairy and half-demon being for him to wed. Melalo had his father cook a fish in donkey milk and pour the juice over the vulva of his mother while she slept. Next, the king had sex with his wife and nine days later, Lilyi was born. Described as having a human head but a fish's body, this grotesque being was considered to be the spirit of Catarrhal illness.

Sources: Clébert, *The Gypsies*, 187; Illes, *Encyclopedia of Spirits*, 641

Limnades

Variations: Leimenides, Limnatides

The Limnades were a sub-species of the NAIADS. NYMPHS of fresh water lakes, they were born the children of BOLBE, one of the named OCEANIDS, according to classical Greek lore.

Sources: Avant, *Mythological Reference*, 291; Bell, *Bell's New Pantheon*, 47; Chopra, *Academic Dictionary*, 198; Maberry, *Cryptopedia*, 112

Limnaee

Variation: Limniace

In Greek mythology, the NYMPH Limnaee was the daughter of Ganges, a river god in India; she was the mothers of Attis, a Phrygian vegetation god.

Sources: Bell, *Bell's New Pantheon*, 46; Ovid, *Metamorphoses*, Volume 2, 467

Limniad

The limniades are one of twelve species of NYMPHS; they are the NYMPHS of lakes, marshes, and swamps and are known to be dangerous to travelers.

Sources: Bell, *Bell's New Pantheon*, 47; Littleton, *Gods, Goddesses, and Mythology*, Volume 11, 999

Limnoria

A NYMPH, Limnoria was the NEREIS of the salt marshes in classical Greek mythology; she was born the daughter of Nerues and DORIS. She was one of the named NEREID who accompanied THETIS in mourning the loss of her son, Achilles.

Sources: Apollodorus, *Apollodorus' Library and Hyginus' Fabulae*, 2; Collignon, *Manual of Mythology*, 18; Gould, *Historic Magazine and Notes and Queries*, Volume 14, 212; Perry, *Women of Homer*, 146; Trzaskoma, *Anthology of Classical Myth*, 18

Limoniad

Variations: LIMNIAD

The Limoniad were one of twelve species of NYMPHS in Greek mythology; they were the NYMPHS of flowers and meadows.

Sources: Bell, *Bell's New Pantheon*, 47; Chopra, *Academic Dictionary of Mythology*, 176; Littleton, *Gods, Goddesses, and Mythology, Volume 11*, 999

Linchetto

In Italian folklore from Tuscany the linchetto are ELF-like beings; they dwell in dark places and are only active at night. The linchetto cause nightmares and literally make things go bump in the night.

Sources: Arrowsmith, *Field Guide to the Little People*, 187–8; Grimassi, *Hereditary Witchcraft: Secrets of the Old Religion*, 83–4

Liosalfar

Variations: Liosálfar

In Scandinavian and Teutonic mythology the liosalfar ("LIGHT ELVES") are light bringers; they are described as being tall, exceedingly beautiful, and having skin paler than the sun. They live in Alfhime, a place located between Earth and the Heavens.

Sources: Grimm, *Teutonic mythology*, Volume 2, 446; Illes, *Encyclopedia of Spirits*, 17; Keightley, *World Guide to Gnomes, Fairies, Elves, and Other Little People*, 64

Lit

Variations: Litr ("hue")

Lit was one of the many DWARFS named in the *Voluspa*, the first and best known poem of the *Poetic Edda*, a collection of Old Norse poems dating back to about A.D. 985. According to legend, as Balder's funeral boat was being pushed out to sea, Lit was running around. Thor, brother of Balder, was enraged and the moment Lit was in his way, kicked the little DWARF into the funeral fire.

Sources: Crossley-Holland, *Norse Myths*, 183; Daly, *Norse Mythology A to Z*, 22; Wägner, *Asgard and the Gods*, 311; Wilkinson, *Book of Edda called Völuspá*, 12

Little Men of Morlaix

Living in holes under castle Morlaix, France, these fairies stand less than a foot tall. Said to possess great treasure the Little Men sometimes allow people who are walking by to take a handful of it. If anyone should take more than their share the money will vanish and the fairies will invisibly box their ears.

Sources: Keightly, *World Guide to Gnomes, Fairies, Elves, and Other Little People*, 441

The Little People of the Passamaquoddy Indians

In the mythology of the Passamaquoddy Indians there are two species of fairies the Nagumwasuck and the Mekumwasuck. Each of these little people are said to stand between two and three feet tall and are grotesquely ugly as well. Said to be made of stone the Little People are described as wearing a wild array of fantastic clothing, each one unique. These fays can only be seen by the Passamaquoddy Indians.

The Nagumwasuck fairies involve themselves with human affairs, merrily dancing at weddings and sadly singing at funerals. Because they are so self-conscious of their terrible appearance it is dangerous to laugh at them, as unfortunate accidents soon befall the offender.

The Mekumwasuck little people live in the wilderness. Said to dress in outlandish outfits, these hairy-faced fairies are considered to be the guardians of the Catholic Church. Should a Mekumwasuck ever look directly at a person they will either acquire a contagious disease or die.

Sources: Avant, *Mythological Reference*, 474; Briggs, *Encyclopedia of Fairies*, 268–69; Stepanich, *Faery Wicca*, Book One, 272

Litur

Litur was one of the many DWARFS named in the *Voluspa*, the first and best known poem of the *Poetic Edda*, a collection of Old Norse poems dating back to about A.D. 985.

Sources: Daly, *Norse Mythology A to Z*, 22; Sykes, *Who's Who in Non-Classical Mythology*, 53

Llamhigyn Y Dwr

In Welsh folklore a FAIRY ANIMAL called the llamhigyn y dwr ("the WATER LEAPER") was described as looking like a toad but having a tail and a set of wings. Living in various lakes it was said to break fishing lines and come ashore to eat sheep.

Sources: Eberhart, *Mysterious Creatures*, 299; Monaghan, *Encyclopedia of Celtic Mythology and Folklore*, 469; Rhys, *Celtic folklore: Welsh and Manx*, Volume I, 95–6

Llyn Barfog

Variations: Elfin cow

The llyn barfog were the Welsh black cattle born from the droves owned by the PLANT ANNWN and tended to by their women, the GWRAGEDD ANNWN. According to legend, a band of green clad GWRAGEDD ANNWN would emerge from a lake located near Aberdover near dusk, driving their cows, the GWARTHEG Y LLYN.

Sources: Avant, *Mythological Reference*, 68; Eberhart, *Mysterious Creatures*, 5; Sikes, *British Goblins*, 39–40

Loathly Lady

There are two versions of the tale of the Loathly Lady, who is in truth a FAIRY QUEEN, and of the young knight she marries.

Generally the story opens with the introduction of a young knight, handsome, pure, and true. The knight is then threatened with death; usually his own but on occasion that of someone close to him. In order to save his life, or that of the other, it is discovered the knight's salvation is through an old and ugly HAG. Sometimes she only asks for a kiss from the knight but more often she demands they marry. Either way, the knight will agree and be true to his word. Soon after because of his nobility not only is he allowed to live but the old HAG transforms into a beautiful young woman.

In the old, Irish versions of the story of the Loathly Lady the old woman is the personification of the sovereignty of Ireland and the knight who submits to her becomes the high king. Also in this older version there is a ceremonial drink involved; it is offered to the king and his acceptance of it seals his kingship and the marriage.

The newer versions of the Loathly Lady are usually British. In these tales are basically the same but with the addition of the young knight having to answer the question "What do women most desire?" The answer is learned from the HAG, "sovereignty over herself." Even knowing the correct answer the knight still must marry the HAG. At the end of the story the HAG ask the young knight which he would prefer, for his wife to be beautiful and unfaithful or ugly but devoted to him (or to be beautiful by day but ugly by night). The knight wisely answers he would have her make the decision, demonstrating sovereignty. The knight is rewarded with a beautiful and faithful wife.

Sources: Archibald, *Arthurian Literature XXVII*, 62, 64–6; Matson, *Celtic Mythology A to Z*, 74–5; Osborn, *Nine Medieval Romances of Magic*, 8

Lob

Variations: Loby, Looby, Lubbard, Lubber, Lubberkin

In German and Welsh fairy lore the lob is described as looking like a small, dark raincloud with arms. Attracted to arguments, fights, and raw emotions the lob enjoys causing trouble. It has been speculated the lob was not the name of a species of fairy but rather the name of an individual fay. Lob is also a word used to describe any fairy-like spirit throughout British folklore.

Sources: Keightly, *World Guide to Gnomes, Fairies, Elves, and Other Little People*, 335–6; McCoy, *Witch's Guide to Faery Folk*, 265–6; Monaghan, *Encyclopedia of Celtic Mythology and Folklore*, 292

Lob Lie-by-the-fire

Lob Lie-by-the-fire was the name of a GIANT who was born the son of a witch. Very much like a BROWNIE, Lob Lie-by-the-fire was described as being hairy, strong, ugly, and enjoyed helping humans. He was a good farmhand and a hard worker in spite of his lazy sounding name.

Sources: Briggs, *Encyclopedia of Fairies*, 270; Keightly, *World Guide to Gnomes, Fairies, Elves, and Other Little People*, 318; Monaghan, *Encyclopedia of Celtic Mythology and Folklore*, 292

Lofar

Variations: Lofarr

Lofar ("praiser" or "stopper") is one of the earliest known DWARFS if not their progenitor. It is possible Lofar is an alias of the fire god, Loki, as all DWARFS needed his assistance in their labors.

Sources: Macdowall, *Asgard and the Gods*, 38; Thorpe, *Northern Mythology*, Volume 1, 9–10

Logistilla

Logistilla was the virtuous heir to her father's throne but was also the half-sister to the, luxury-driven ALCINE and the lascivious MORGANA. Logistilla's personal castle was located on her sister's land, Alcina Island. ALCINE had an army of ape-men, cat-men, centaurs, and dog-men she marched against her sister's much smaller forces. Fortunately Logistilla knew her sister had lured vast numbers of men, seduced them, and then transformed them into plants and stones. Using her own magic, Logistilla reversed her sister's evil spell and was able to win the day.

Sources: Hankins, *Source and Meaning in Spenser's Allegory*, 59; Keightly, *World Guide to Gnomes, Fairies, Elves, and Other Little People*, 452–3; Manguel, *Dictionary of Imaginary Places*, 14

Loireag

Variations: Lorryack

In the Hebrides Islands, Scotland the Loireag, similar to HABETROT, was said to be an individual water fairy heavily involved in the traditional lore of spinning and weaving, specifically presiding over the warping, weaving, waulking, and washing of the web. If during the process one of the traditional or ceremonial routines was omitted Loireag would become enraged and cause some sort of major problem to arise.

Loireag, described as being cunning, plaintive, stubborn, and very small, had a beautiful voice, singing songs with heavy rhythms, suitable for women who worked the heavy looms. Because of her talent the fairy was very critical of others who sang as they worked. If a song was sung twice in a row Loireag would cause the web to be too thin and the women would have to redo all their work. Loireag was especially harsh on women who sang out of tune, more so if the offender had a metallic tone to her voice.

Libations of milk were always left to Loireag, as she loved milk and dairy products. If the offering was not left the fay would go directly to nearest field of cows or sheep and suck them dry of their milk. She had the magical ability to cast a spell over the animals to prevent them from running off from her while she drank.

Sources: Briggs, *Encyclopedia of Fairies*, 271; Monaghan, *Encyclopedia of Celtic Mythology and Folklore*, 293; Watson, *Carmina Gadelica*, 300–01

Lokria

In Greek mythology, Lokria was a NYMPH of a spring in a town that later bore her name. The Greek city of Lokria was known for its laws.

Sources: Barnstone, *Ancient Greek Lyrics*, 144; Larson, *Greek Nymphs,* 252

Lolmischo

According to the lore of the Romany Gypsy, Lolmischo ("red mouse") was the name of the seventh son born of ANA, Queen of the KESHALYI (see FAIRY QUEEN). Ana was suffering from a severe skin ailment; her son, Melalo was a magician and advised his mother to allow mice to lick her sore. ANA did as her son suggested and the treatment worked, however, one of the mice penetrated into her body and caused her to conceive a child. Lolmischo, the child born of this bizarre conception is half fairy, however he is considered to be the demon of eczema.

Sources: Clébert, *The Gypsies*, 147; Illes, *Encyclopedia of Spirits*, 648

Loni

Loni ("dawdler") was one of the many Dwarfs named in the *Voluspa*, the first and best known poem of the *Poetic Edda*, a collection of Old Norse poems dating back to about A.D. 985.

Sources: Crossley-Holland, *Norse Myths*, 183; Daly, *Norse Mythology A to Z*, 22; Wilkinson, *Book of Edda called Völuspá*, 12

Lorelei

There are two versions on the origins of the water maiden Lorelei ("lurking girl" or "murmuring rock"); in one version she was born an immortal Nymph as the daughter of the Father Rhine. However, she is better known by the more popular German folklore version. According to the lore, between the towns of Colbentz and Mayence there is a large black rock named Lorelei that jets up from the Rhine River; it was named for a young woman who threw herself into the river when she was spurned by her lover. According to the story, at twilight when there is a cool breeze blowing across the water a Siren in the guise of a young maiden sits there combing her golden hair while singing to herself. Her song is so soft and compelling, fishermen will try to steer their vessel near to hear her more clearly, but rather, they wreck on the rocks.

Sources: Cartwright, *English Illustrated Magazine*, Volume 4, 303–04; Evan-Wentz, *Fairy Faith in Celtic Countries*, 28; Guerber, *Hammer of Thor*, 136–8; Mccoy, *Witch's Guide to Faery Folk*, 266

Lotis

Born the daughter of the god Neptune, Lotis was a Nymph of mount Othrys in Malis located in northern Greece. This beautiful Naiad of Greek mythology attracted desire of the deformed god, Priapus who attempted to rape her. While fleeing from her assailant she prayed to the gods for assistance; her prayers were answered and she was transformed into a lotos-tree.

Sources: Folkard, *Plant Lore*, 417; Littleton, *Gods, Goddesses, and Mythology*, Volume 11, 1170; Monaghan, *Encyclopedia of Goddesses and Heroines*, 426

Loxo

In classical Greek mythology Loxo was one of the three Nymph attendants of the goddess Artemis (Diana) who came from the mythical land to the north, Hyperborea (see Hekaerge and Upis).

Sources: Hard, *Routledge Handbook of Greek Mythology*, 190; Keightley, *Mythology of Ancient Greece and Italy*, 119

Lubbard Fiend

Variations: Lob Lie-By-The-Fire, Lob, Lubberkin, Lurdane

In English folklore the lubbard fiend is a Hobgoblin; like the Brownie of Scotland, it assists in household chores and threshing.

Sources: Briggs, *Encyclopedia of Fairies*, 271–2; Kennedy, *Legendary Fictions of the Irish Celts*, 107

Lubin

In Normandy, lubins are a species of fay with the ability to shape-shift into wolves. Under the guidance of their leader, a lubin much larger than the rest and black skinned, they gather in churchyards to dig up the dead. Lubins are very timid and any strange noise will cause them to cry out *"Robert est mort!"* Lubins may be a variant of the Lutins, the fairies have the ability to shape-shift into the form of a horse called a Le Cheval Bayard.

Sources: Keightly, *World Guide to Gnomes, Fairies, Elves, and Other Little People*, 478; Venedey, *Excursions in Normandy*, 90

Ludki

Variations: Kransnoludi, Krasnoludki, Lutky

In Serbia the ludki ("little people") are a species of fairy people inhabiting Lusatia (Lausitz) under the leadership of their own Fairy King. Before mankind settled the area, the ludki, described as being small in size with oversized heads and bulging eyes, abandoned the area. It was believed these fays wore fancy clothes and large hats or red caps. The ludki not only had language but also a particular way of speaking; whenever they said some positive assertion it was always followed by a negative expression or statement.

The homes of the ludki were described as looking like a baker's oven and were found up the mountains or deep in the woods; they were furnished within much like ant home would have been. Living in large family groups the ludki celebrated everything, especially weddings, with much singing and dancing as they played the cymbals. They grew corn and thrashed and grounded it into a brown, course, doughy, and sandy bread. Ludki would also borrow vegetables from humans and taught them the art of smithing.

Although the ludki were family oriented they

did not get along well with one another. Many violent wars were waged between the families and clans. When one of the ludki died, its body was cremated and the ashes were placed in a clay urn that was then buried.

Similar to most Celtic fay, the ludki do not like the sound of bells tolling.

Sources: Gray, *Mythology of All Races*, Volume 3, 246–8; MacCulloch, *Celtic Mythology*, 247–8; Perkowski, *Vampire Lore*, 85–6

Lugovik

Variations: Lugovnik

In Russian folklore Lugovik is a male NYMPH of the meadow.

Sources: Grimassi, *Encyclopedia of Wicca and Witchcraft*, 382; Ivanits, *Russian Folk Belief*, 64; Rose, *Spirits, Fairies, Gnomes, and Goblins*, 204

Luideag

The luideag ("little shaggy woman" or "the rag") was a type of ATHACH, a FAIRY ANIMAL haunting Loch nam Breacan Dubha ("Loch of the Black Trout") in Skye, Scotland. Said to be evil and injurious by nature it was described as looking squalid with a mop of shaggy hair atop her head.

Sources: Briggs, *Encyclopedia of Fairies*, 272–3; Monaghan, *Encyclopedia of Celtic Mythology and Folklore*, 299; Thompson, *Supernatural Highlands*, 152

Lull

In *The Life of Robin Goodfellow*, the female fairy Lull was a nurse who cared for baby fairies; she had three brothers, GRIM, PATCH, and PINCH and four sisters, GULL, LICKE, SIB, and TIB.

Sources: Collier, *Mad Pranks and Merry Jests of Robin Goodfellow*, 39; Rose, *Spirits, Fairies, Leprechauns, and Goblins*, 204, 351

Lunantishee

Variations: Lunantishess, Lunantisidhe

The Lunantishee were a clan of Irish fairies who guard black thorn tree, one of the favored trees of the fay. These fairies would not allow the cutting of these plants on May 11th, the original day for May Day nor on November 11th, the original date for All Hallows Eve; other sources claim the days are August 1st (the Summer feast of Lughnasa) and November 1st (the Winter feast of Samhain). Described as looking like small, bald men, great misfortune would befall anyone who harmed the black thorn on either one of those two days.

Sources: Allardice, *Myths, Gods and Fantasy*, 140; Evan-Wentz, *Fairy Faith in Celtic Countries*, 53; McCoy, *Witch's Guide to Faery Folk*, 267; Monaghan, *Encyclopedia of Celtic Mythology and Folklore*, 299

Luridan

Variations: Belelah, Elgin, Wadd, Wrthin

In the Orkney Islands of Scotland Luridan was a well-known BROWNIE, he was especially popular on Pomonia, the largest of the islands. Luridan was said to sweep rooms, wash dishes, and start the daily fire. Luridan himself claimed when he lived in Jerusalem during the rule of King Solomon and David he was called Belelah (Belial). From there he traveled to Wales where he was called Elgin, Wadd, and Wrthin; there he taught the Druidic bards prose and prophecy. Luridan, a spirit of the air, claimed he always took part in the wars between his kind and the fire spirits of Hecla; during those battles he said many of each of their kind was slain as they fought in the air over the sea. When the fighting happens over the mountains, as the fairy spirits of each side die, Luridan claimed their cries and wails could be heard in Iceland, Norway, and Russia for many days afterwards.

Luridan, whose story originated in 1665, has since retired and handed over his responsibilities to a fairy named BALKIN, the lord of the Northern Mountains. When summoned, Luridan is said to look like a DWARF with a crooked nose.

Sources: Keightly, *World Guide to Gnomes, Fairies, Elves, and Other Little People*, 172–3; Monaghan, *Encyclopedia of Celtic Mythology and Folklore*, 299–300; Schofield, *Mythical Bards and the Life of William Wallace*, 35–6

Lutin

Variations: LE CHEVAL BAYARD, LUITION, Netun

In Normandy lutin was a type of GOBLIN similar to many of the HOUSE-SPIRITS of Germany, the female is known as a lutinos; like ROBIN GOOD FELLOW these fairies had many names and forms they assumed. When this fairy species appeared in the form of a horse tacked up and ready to ride it was called LE CHEVAL BAYARD. When this fairy took a human form and played the part of a man-about-town, flattering everyone it meets, it was called a BON GARÇON. The LOB and the LUBIN may also be other forms the lutin can assume.

The lutin will choose a farm to live on and make use of its horses, sitting on the animals' neck as it rides them during the night; when it is finished the fairy will *lutines* their manes plaits and tangle up their hair into horrid knots. Having one of these kind and obliging fay living on a farm is considered to be lucky, as they seem to make the cattle thrive. The lutins are said to be fond of children, giving them nice things to eat, however, it will pinch and whip them just as quickly if the child misbehaves.

NAIN ROUGE is the name of a specific, individual lutin who is said to haunt the Normandy coast. Although he is, in his own way, kind to fishermen he will punish those who do not give him the proper respect.

Sources: Brewer, *Dictionary of Phrase and Fable*, 783–4; Illes, *Encyclopedia of Spirits*, 656; Keightly, *World Guide to Gnomes, Fairies, Elves, and Other Little People*, 473, 476; Spence, *Encyclopædia of Occultism*, 254–5

Ly Erg

In Scottish lore, particularly in the Glenmore area, the Ly Erg is a singular, individual fairy longing to be a solider. Dressing as such, it cannot be distinguished from actual soldiers except for the fact he has a blood stained right hand. While walking down the road Ly Erg will stop on the road near water and by raising his red, right hand will challenge you to combat. Win or lose anyone who engages Ly Erg dies within a fortnight.

Sources: McCoy, *Witch's Guide to Faery Folk*, 268–9; Scott, *Minstrelsy of the Scottish Border*, cvii; Spence, *Magic Arts in Celtic Britain*, 91

Lycorias

A sea–NYMPH, Lycorias was one of the named NEREID in classical Greek mythology; she was born of Nereus and DORIS in classical Greek mythology.

Sources: Apollodorus, *Apollodorus' Library and Hyginus' Fabulae*, 95; Bell, *Bell's New Pantheon or Historical Dictionary of the Gods,* 112; Lemprière, *Classical Dictionary*, 468

Lyka

Lyka was a NYMPH from the mythology of ancient Greece and Rome. One of the NAIADS, she fell in love with a handsome Sicilian goat-herder and hunter named Daphnis, son of the god, Hermes (Mercury) (see ECHENAIS); before she would fully give her herself to him she either solicited a promise he would resist the temptations of all other women or foretold if he should fall into the arms of another would become blind (or be turned to stone, sources conflict). The daughter

of the king fell in love with Daphnis and seduced him by giving him too much wine to drink; in his drunken stupor, he forgot his vow to Lyka and consequently became blind.

Sources: Fontenrose, *Orion*, 189–92

Lyris

Born one of the 3,000 daughters of the Titians, Oceanus and Tethys, the NYMPH Lyris was one of the named OCEANIDS in Greek mythology.

Sources: Apollodorus of Athens, *Apollodorus' Library and Hyginus' Fabulae*, 95; Hyginus, *Myths of Hyginus,* 25

Lysianassa

A sea–NYMPH, Lysianassa ("lady deliverance") was one the NEREID of royal delivery and the NYMPH of the royal promontory in ancient Greek mythology; she was born the daughter of Nerues and DORIS.

Sources: Betham, *Transactions of the Royal Irish Academy*, Volume 17, 89; Hesiod, *Works of Hesiod, Callimachus, and Theognis*, 15; Trzaskoma, *Anthology of Classical Myth*, 18

Lysithea

Born one of the 3,000 daughters of the Titians, Oceanus and Tethys, Lysithea was one of the named OCEANIDS from Greek mythology.

Sources: Boswell, *What Men or Gods Are These*, 58; Day, *God's Conflict with the Dragon and the Sea*, 64; Hesiod, *Works of Hesiod, Callimachus, and Theognis*, 20

Lytgubhe

Variations: Lyktgubhe

Similar to the ELLYDAN of Wales and the SAND YAN Y TAD of Brenton, the lytgubhe from the fairy lore of Scandinavian leads travelers astray at night exactly as the WILL O' THE WISP does.

Sources: Guiney, *Brownies and Bogles*, 116; Sikes, *British Goblins*, 23

Maahiset

Variations: Maanalaiset ("subterranean ones")

Maahiset ("earth dwellers") are Finnish DWARF-like NATURE SPIRITS typically usually helpful to humans but have been known to turn malicious. It is believed their subterranean world is the place where skin diseases originated from. When the maahiset are displeased they will cause pimples, ringworm and other such ailments to befall the offenders; they tend to single out those who disrespect the subterranean homes of the masshiset; those who enter into new home for the first time and do no bow to the four corners; and those who neglect their baking, brewing and entertainment duties.

Described as being very small and usually invisible, the maahiset look exactly like a human and live in a very similar society.

Sources: da Cherda, *Eclectic Magazine of Foreign Literature,* Volume 42, 361–2; Lurker, *Routledge Dictionary of Gods and Goddesses, Devils and Demons,* 115; Merriam-Webster, Inc., *Merriam-Webster's Encyclopedia of World Religions, 674*

Mab

In the English fairy tradition, Mab is considered to be the high Queen of the Fairies (see FAIRY QUEEN); although her exact origins are unknown, it is commonly believed she likely originated in Celtic lore either from the goddess Mab ("youth") of Welsh mythology or from Maeve (Maebhe) of the Cuchullain tales. There is also the possibility she could be a version of the Norse goddess Mara from Scandinavian folklore; this is suspected as both Mara and Mab are said to have the ability to infiltrate and manipulate a person's dreams. As with many divinities, Mab was reduced in power and status, descending from goddess to NATURE SPIRIT or fairy after the introduction of Christianity.

As a mere midwife to the fay and said to be no bigger than an agate stone, Mab was mentioned in William Shakespeare tragedy *Romeo and Juliet* as having her coach pulled by a pair of tiny insects over the nose of people as they slept. Mab as a FAIRY QUEEN first appeared in sixteenth century English literature; first in the Jacobean work, *The Entertainment at Althorp,* by Ben Jonson and then later by Michael Drayton gave a list of Mab's Maids of Honor in *Nymphidia* (1627) Dryp, Fib, Hop, Jil, Jin, Mop, Nit, Pin, PINCH, Pip, Quick, Skip, TIB, Tick, Tit, Trip, Wap, and Win. It was in the work of Joshua Poole, *Parnassus* (1657), where Mab was first said to be not only the Queen of the Fay but also the consort of OBERON, Emperor of the FAIRIES.

Sources: Briggs, *Encyclopedia of Fairies,* 5; Cooper, *Brewer's Book of Myth and Legend,* 170; Keightly, *World Guide to Gnomes, Fairies, Elves, and Other Little People,* 331; Rose, *Spirits, Fairies, Leprechauns, and Goblins,* 207, 351

Macha

One of the TUATHA DÉ DANANN, Macha was a malevolent fairy-being of conflict and death. She was known to take the form of a hooded crow and gloats over humans who have fallen in battle.

It is likely Macha, in this guise was one of the three aspects of the triple goddess, Mórrígan.

Sources: Evan-Wentz, *Fairy Faith in Celtic Countries,* 302; Matson, *Celtic Mythology A to Z,* 79; Monaghan, *Encyclopedia of Celtic Mythology and Folklore,* 304

Macieh

Appearing in the form of a laughing, young boy with a cap on his head Macieh, an individual fairy from the folklore of Dalmatia, would appear before a person and instantly be placed under their control. If he was told to brim them money this fairy would go and steal it from their neighbors. If repeatedly asked for more money, eventually he would come back with treasures retrieved from the sea.

Source: Keightly, *World Guide to Gnomes, Fairies, Elves, and Other Little People,* 494

Macris

Variations: Makris

A NYMPH from the mythical Mount Nysa, Macris was a nurse to the infant god, Dionysus (Bacchus) in classical Greek mythology. Collectively these NYMPHS were known as the BACCHANTS; their names were BACCHE, BROMIE, ERATO, MACRIS, and NYSA.

Sources: Daly, *Greek and Roman Mythology A to Z,* 22; Hyginus, *Myths of Hyginus,* 140

Maenad

The maenads ("mad-women") were the daughters born of the CANONICAL MUSE Mnemosyne and the god Zeus (Jupiter) after nine days of continuous intercourse. The maenads were devoted to the god of wine, Dionysus (Bacchus) and were also known as the BAKKHAI. According to classical Greek mythology the daughters were named CHALCOMEDE, CHAROPEIA, CORONIS, METHE, PHASYLEIA, TERPSICHORE, and THYIA. These female devotees of Dionysus dressed in fawn- and panther-skins, worshiped their god through dance and song, and while in an inebriated state hunt animals and kill them by ripping them limb from limb.

Sources: Dixon-Kennedy, *Encyclopedia of Greco-Roman Mythology,* 197; Monaghan, *Encyclopedia of Goddesses and Heroines,* 418–19; Sacks, *Encyclopedia of the Ancient Greek World,* 198

Maera

Variations: Mæra

A sea–NYMPH, Maera ("the giver") was one of the named NEREID in classical Greek mythology;

she was born of Nereus and Doris. Maera, along with Anchirhoe, Byze, and Melite, was one of the attendants to the goddess, Britomartis.

Sources: Apollodorus, *Apollodorus' Library and Hyginus' Fabulae*, 95; Gould, *Historic Magazine and Notes and Queries*, Volume 14, 212

Maia

One of the Oreads, Maia was a mountain Nymph from classical Greek mythology; she was born one of the daughters of the Titian Atlas and the ocean Nymph, Pleione. She and her sisters, Alcyone, Asterope, Celaeno, Dryope (Aero or Merope), Electra, and Taygete, are sometimes referred to as the Atlantides or the Seven Sisters (see Pleiades). Maia was the mother of the god, Hermes (Mercury) and was described as being a "lovely-haired Nymph, modest, for she avoids the company of the blessed gods, living in a deep, shady cave."

Sources: Ardinger, *Pagan Every Day*, 190; Larson, *Greek Nymphs*, 154; Perry, *Women of Homer*, 146

Maighdean Uaine

One of the Fuath of Scottish mythology, maighdean uaine ("green maiden") was always described as being beautiful, even when taking on the form of a goat, a half goat and half woman, or as a woman. Sitting by the side of a brook, river, or stream, she waited for someone to come along so she may ask for assistance in crossing. Those who agreed were found with their throats cut.

There was also the belief the maighdean uaine was a species of fairy similar to the Brownie. Attached to a family it would do chores around the house while the family slept and would wail out like a Banshee when one of her chosen family died.

Sources: Rose, *Giants, Monsters, and Dragons*, 234; Swire, *Skye*, 197

Mainades

In ancient Greek mythology the mainades ("mad women") were the orgiastic Nymphs of Dionysus (Bacchus); they were known to nurse panther cubs.

Sources: Devereux, *Dreams in Greek Tragedy*, 193; Rigoglioso, *Cult of Divine Birth in Ancient Greece*, 87

Maira

A Naiad of the river Erasinos in Argos, southern Greece, Maira was one of the attendants of the goddess, Britomartis; she was also one of the named Nereids from Greek mythology. By the god Zeus (Jupiter), Maira gave birth to a son named Lokros but was soon thereafter slain by the goddess Artemis (Diana) for ceasing to attend her hunts.

Sources: Cook, *Zeus*, 709; Hard, *Routledge Handbook of Greek Mythology*, 191

Makawe

Variations: Te Makawe

One of the Atua from the mythology of the Maori people of New Zealand, Makawe ("hair") was a war god and a trickster; his favorite ruse is to drive people into hot pools where they are scalded.

Sources: Illes, *Encyclopedia of Spirits*, 44; Rose, *Spirits, Fairies, Gnomes, and Leprechauns*, 25

Mal-de-Mer

Said to have lived in the sea near Brittany and Cornwall the nocturnal mal-de-mer ("evil of the sea" or "seasickness") preyed upon ships. There is no description of these fairies as they have never been seen by a human but when false lights are seen luring ships into the rocky coatline these fairies are often blamed.

Source: McCoy, *Witch's Guide to Faery Folk*, 269

Malekin

Variations: Malkin, Mawkin

Malekin, the fairy said to haunt Dagworthy Castle in Suffolk, England, was first described by the thirteenth century chronicler, Ralph of Coggeshall. Typically this fairy was said to be invisible but it spoke with the voice of a one-year old child. Malekin made the claim she had been abduct by the fay while her mother worked the field. Taken in by a knight and his wife, they were initially frightened by her but eventually came to enjoy her little pranks. She was very conversational with the staff of the castle and spoke Latin with the priests. Food was left for her was always taken. Malekin appeared only once to a chamber-maid who later described the fairy as looking like a tiny child wearing a white tunic.

Sources: Briggs, *Encyclopedia of Fairies*, 290; Monaghan, *Encyclopedia of Celtic Mythology and Folklore*, 310; Rose, *Spirits, Fairies, Leprechauns, and Goblins*, 209, 351

Malis

Malis was a Nymph of Kios in Greek mythology; she is described as having "spring time in her eyes." Along with the Nymphs Eunica and

NYCHEIA, as they were preparing to dance saw a young boy name Hylas who traveled with the Argonauts; instantly enamored with him, they took him by the hand and pulled him into the fountain.

Sources: *Encyclopaedia Britannica*, Volume 16, Issue 1, 313; Larson, *Greek Nymphs*, 67; Pache, *Moment's Ornament*, 161

Mallebron

Mallebron is the fairy servant of OBERON, King of the Fay according to the thirteenth century ballad *Huon de Bordeaux*. Mallebron was sent to assist knights on their journey to the holy lands, rescuing them when they got into trouble, and delivering them from harm whenever necessary.

Sources: Lang, *Red Romance Book*, 229–30; Lee, *Boke of Duke Huon of Burdeaux*, 168–9; Rose, *Spirits, Fairies, Leprechauns, and Goblins*, 351

Mama Dlo

Variations: Mama Dglo, Mama Glow, Maman de l' eau

In the mythology of the people from the Republic of Trinidad and Tobago comes the NATURE SPIRIT, Mama Dlo ("Mother of the Water"). She has the head and shoulders of a beautiful woman with long hair and the body of a snake. This aquatic devil uses her beauty to lure men off to their deaths by crushing their bodies during her lovemaking; restoring them back to life and killing them anew, for all time her sex slaves. Although she will prey upon any man she can get, Mama Dlo particularly hunts out those who destroy the natural swamp habitat where she lives.

Telltale signs of Mama Dlo's presence in an area are reports of men on work crews disappearing. Survivors also say they heard a loud cracking sound, which is said to be the noise she makes with her tail as she slaps it on the surface of a mountain pool or a still lagoon. Should this demon ever be encountered, remove your left shoe and place it upside-down on the path before you, then walking backwards, quickly return to your home.

Sources: Jones, *Evil in Our Midst,* 126–9; Lewis, *Guinea's Other Suns*, 179; Philpott, *Trinidad and Tobago*, 53, 89

Mama Putukusi

Variations: Apu Putukusi, Mamita Putukusi

Mama Putukusi ("flowering beauty") was the only female APU living on Machu Pichu in the Andes Mountains.

Sources: Illes, *Encyclopedia of Spirits*, 198; Toor, *Three Worlds of Peru*, 132

Mama Simona

Mama Simona is a female tutelary APU living on the Cuzo peak in the Andes Mountains.

Sources: Illes, *Encyclopedia of Spirits*, 198; Toor, *Three Worlds of Peru*, 132

Mama Veronica

Variations: Wakay Willca

Mama Veronica is a female APU living on a mountain peak in the Andes Mountains near Cuzco.

Sources: Daniel, *Incas*, 122; Illes, *Encyclopedia of Spirits*, 198

Mamagwasewug

In Canada the mamagwasewug ("the hidden beings") were the fairies of the poplar forest; although they can be friendly these fay have a tendency to quickly turn violent. Preferring to live along the riverbanks or in wetlands the mamagwasewug usually remained invisible but of the people who claim to have seen them describe these fairies as standing about two feet tall and look exactly like humans except their face is covered with hair. The mamagwasewug loved brightly colored bits of cloth and shooting off guns and to anyone who helpd them come into possession of both of these items was blessed with long life and prosperous hunting.

Sources: Plain, *Ways of Our Grandfathers*, 45; Porteous, *Forest Folklore*, 145; Rose, *Spirits, Fairies, Gnomes, and Goblins*, 210

Mane

Variations: Di Manes

In the mythology of the ancient Romans the manes are the tutelary fairy spirits of a family's deified deceased. Manes were revered as the gods were, holding an important place in daily, domestic life. The practice of worshiping the manes began in the earliest periods of the Roman Republic and was continued largely throughout the empire's rule, however, in spite of an abundance of documented evidence of their respect and worship most scholars characterize manes as nothing more than ghosts, supernatural-beings people would wish to avoid. Historical documents show manes were invoked routinely for intervention into the major events of the family's life.

There were two distinct classes of manes, LARES and LEMURES. Initially, lare were the guardians of cities and crossroads before becoming more domestic fertility NATURE SPIRITS and domestic household spirits. LEMURES were a type of BOGEYMAN created when a family member died, returning to the home as a malicious poltergeist-like spirit.

Sources: Adkins, *Handbook to Life in Ancient Rome*, 274; Berens, *Myths and Legends of Ancient Greece and Rome*, 185–6; Pu, *Rethinking Ghosts in World Religions*, 95–7

Manesto

Born one of the 3,000 daughters of the Titians, Oceanus and Tethys, Manesto was one of the named OCEANIDS in Greek mythology.

Sources: Boswell, *What Men or Gods Are These*, 58; Hesiod, *Works of Hesiod, Callimachus, and Theognis*, 20

Manitou

Variations: Manidoo, Manito, Manittoes, Manitu, Mannittos

A NATURE SPIRIT in the mythology of the Algonquin Indians of eastern, North America in the Great Lakes region, the manitou ("being") are oftentimes employed as the assistances of shamans; when this spirit manifests it takes on a human guise. The Manitou is not a singular being but rather a species of natural forces, qualities, and spirits combined.

Sources: Lyon, *Encyclopedia of Native American Healing*, 164; Mauss, *General Theory of Magic*, 141; *New International Encyclopedia*, Volume 15, 11

Manuel Pinta

Manuel Pinta is an APU living on a mountain peak in the Andes Mountains.

Sources: Illes, *Encyclopedia of Spirits*, 198; Museo Nacional de Historia, *Historia y Cultura*, Volume 16, 157

Mara

Variations: Mera

In Scandinavian and Teutonic folklore the mara was a GOBLIN known to seize men as they slept, stealing away their ability to move and speak. It was known to disrupt sleep and induce nightmares.

Mara was the Old English word for *demon* and during medieval times in Europe this being was better known as an incubus.

Sources: Briggs, *Encyclopedia of Fairies*, 280–1; Rose, *Spirits, Fairies, Gnomes, and Goblins*, 212

Marid

Islamic mythology tells us the marid ("rebellious") were the favored troops of IBLIS, as they were the most powerful of all the species of DJINN even though they were the least numerous. Unique for a demon, they were said to have free will. Marid were arrogant and proud, and as such could be compelled to perform chores. They were knowledgeable, physically powerful, and very evil. They could grant wishes to mortals but it involved battle, imprisonment, rituals, or copious amounts of flattery.

Sources: Hughes, *Dictionary of Islam*, 134; Mack, *Field Guide to Demons, Fairies, Fallen Angels, and Other Subversive Spirits*, 146; Waardenburg, *Islam: Historical, Social, and Political Perspectives*, 39

Marool

The marool is an extremely malevolent FAIRY ANIMAL from the fairy lore of Scotland. This creature was described as looking like a large fish with a crest of flame running down its back and many sets of eyes covering its head. Appearing when the sea-foam was phosphorescent, the marool was especially active during storms, calling out with a wild triumphant song.

Sources: Briggs, *Encyclopedia of Fairies*, 281; Saxby, *Shetland Traditional Lore*, 140

Marsontine

In the fairy-tale *Heart of Ice* by Comte de Caylus, the fairy Marsontine restored King Bayard and all the people of his kingdom from spaniels back to their human form.

Source: Lang, *Green Fairy Book*, 136

Mary Player

Variations: LORELEI, Meerweibers, Merewipers

In British, German and Greek fairy lore Mary Player was a SIREN. Described as looking like a beautiful young woman sitting upon the cliff edge, Mary Player would sing a song so alluring sailors would steer their ships to closer to her to get a better listen. Unfortunately, this waterfairy's location was always in a place where it would cause ships to wreck in rocky shoals. It was also believed if this fairy being swum around a ship three times, the vessel would sink.

Sources: Conway, *Magickal Mystical Creatures*, 164; McCoy, *Witch's Guide to Faery Folks*, 266

Masseriol

Dressing all in red clothing the masseriol ("little farmer") of the fairy mythology of the Iberian peninsula and northern Italy, has a booming laugh said to sound something like the cross between the neigh of a horse and the bleat of a goat. Highly opinionated, these fairies have been known to assist in daily farm and kitchen chores but only so long as they do not get dirty.

Sources: McCoy, *Witch's Guide to Faery Folk*, 270; Newcomb, *Faerie Treasury*, 15–16, 53

Mazikeen

Variations: Shedeem, Shehireem

In Hebrew lore the mazikeen are a species of being corresponding almost to the DJINN of Arabic lore; however, they have three qualities strikingly similar to angels—they have wings allowing them the ability of flight, they have foreknowledge of the future, and they can see the events of the world while remaining invisible to it. Additionally the mazikeen that already physically resemble humans, have three aspects akin to mankind, they must eat and drink to survive, can marry and have children, and are subject to death. Said to have been created when Adam and Eve were excommunicated from the Garden of Eden, these fairy beings have a great deal of magical talent and have the natural ability to shapeshift.

Sources: Avant, *Mythological Reference*, 474; Keightly, *World Guide to Gnomes, Fairies, Elves, and Other Little People*, 497–8; McCoy, *Witch's Guide to Faery Folk*, 270

Mazilla

The devoted FAIRY GODMOTHER to Turritella, the ill-tempered and ugly daughter of the sorrowful daughter in the fairy-tale *The Blue Bird* by L'Olseau Bleu and Par Mme d'Aulnoy, the fairy Mazilla lives in a brilliantly laminated castle. Mazilla turned King Charming into a blue bird for seven years as punishment when he realized he was being tricked into marrying Turritella and not his beloved Princess Fiordelisa. Fairy Mazilla has a sister, also a fairy and an enchantress, but he name is not given in the story.

Source: Lang, *Green Fairy Book*, 2–3, 7, 19

Mazzamarelle

In Abruzzo, Calabria, and Lazio, Italy the species of wind-fairy known as the mazzamarelle; in different location their descriptions varies. In Abruzzo specifically these fairies are said to appear as little boys wearing silk hats and ride upon whirlwinds, banging and crashing around inside of homes. They are described as

standing only about two foot tall and having the ability to shape-shit into a grasshopper.

Source: Arrowsmith, *Field Guide to the Little People*, 22

Mbōn

The mbōn are NATURE SPIRITS or NATS from Burmese folklore, specifically of the wind. Worshiped only during the national harvest the mbōn are accredited for bringing the fertilizing rains.

Sources: Hastings, *Encyclopedia of Religion and Ethics*, Part 5, 22; Porteous, *Forest in Folklore and Mythology*, 125; Scott, *The Burman: His Life and Notions*, Volume 1, 286

Medb

Variations: Maeve, Meadhbh ("she who is mead" or "she who intoxicates"), Meave, Medbh, Medhbh

According to Irish legend, Medb was a FAIRY QUEEN of the TUATHA DÉ DANANN and a woman of the SÍDHE of Connaugh, Ireland. Said to have had numerous husbands, Medb would not allow a man to rule Tara unless he took her for a wife.

Sources: Evan-Wentz, *Fairy Faith in Celtic Countries*, x301; Ó Hógáin, *Sacred Isle*, 133; Monaghan, *Encyclopedia of Celtic Mythology and Folklore*, 319

The Medieval Fairy

Variations: The Green Children

During the medieval era, the fifth to the fifteenth centuries, fairies were integrated into tales of magic, sorcery, witches, and wizards. These being had no set appearance or size; although they were often described as being beautiful maidens with long flowing red hair and startling white skin they could as easily be hideous with a monstrous appearance or tiny and rustic looking.

For a brief period of time the HEROIC FAIRY reappears and then merged with the medieval ideal creating the DIMINUTIVE FAIRY which goes on to be the tradition image of fairies thereafter.

Source: Stepanich, *Faery Wicca*, Book One, 25, 271

Medma

Variations: Mesma

In Greek mythology, Medma was a NYMPH of a spring in Sicily.

Source: Larson, *Greek Nymphs*, 222

Meg Mullach

Variations: Hairy Meg, Maggie Moloch, Maug Moulack, Maug Moulach, Maug Vuluchd

In Scottish folklore Meg Mullach was one of two BROWNIES living in Tullochgorm Castle assisting the family who live there, the Grants of Strathspey, in their daily household tasks; the other was called BROWNIE-CLOD. Described as looking like a small child with an impressive head of hair she is also described in some lore as having hairy hands as well. In other stories Meg Mullach reached down chimneys and snatched up children.

Sources: Briggs, Encyclopedia of Fairies, 28405; Monaghan, *Encyclopedia of Celtic Mythology and Folklore*, 322; Shaw, *Scottish Myths and Customs*, 166

Megaera

Variations: Megaira

One of the three FURIES from classical Greek mythology, Megaera ("envious anger" or "slaughter") was the sister who specialized in jealously. She like her sisters, were described as looking like an old HAG with bat wings, bloodshot eyes, and snakes in her hair; sometime they were confused as being a gorgon. The ancient Greek tragedian, Aeschylus (525 B.C.–456 B.C.), claimed the sisters were the daughters of Night while the tragedian Sophocles (497 B.C.–406 B.C.) said they were the daughter of Skotos, the personification of darkness, and the earth.

Sources: Drury, *Dictionary of the Esoteric*, 93; Hard, *Routledge Handbook of Greek Mythology*, 39

Melaina

Melaina was a NYMPH from the mythology of ancient Greece and Rome. One of the NAIADS, she was one of a trio of NYMPHs known collectively as the Thriae or the Thriai. Their spring was located inside of a Corycian cave and the only name it was consistently given as being one of the "triple muses of divination at Delphi" was CORYCIA; other names apart from Melaina included DAPHNUS, KLEODORA, and THIUA.

Sources: Fontenrose, *Python*, 368, 416; Monaghan, *Goddesses in World Culture*, 147

Melanippe

Variations: Arne

Melanippe was the NYMPH of Boiotia; she was born the daughter of Aiolos and a daughter of the god, Cheiron. Melanippe bore the god of the sea, Poseidon (Neptune), twin sons named Aiolos and Boiotos. This NYMPH of Artemis (Diana) married to Itonus, was also the mother of Melampus, the woman who cured the daughter of Proetus of their madness.

Sources: Bell, *Bell's New Pantheon*, 66; Larson, *Greek Nymphs*, 166; Salmonson, *Encyclopedia of Amazons*, 180

Meleagant

Variations: Malewas, Meleagraunce, Meles, Mellyagraunce, MELWAS

A FAIRY KING of Somerset, Meleagant once kidnapped Queen Guinevere, taking her back to his Underworld palace, Summer Land where he tried to force her to be his consort, according to Arthurian lore. There are many versions of the story, but ultimately, Meleagant was forced to return the stolen queen by order of his father, the kindly FAIRY KING, BADEMAGU.

Sources: Anderson, *King Arthur in Antiquity*, 89; Chisholm, *Encyclopedia Britannica*, Volume 16, 151; Monaghan, *Goddesses in World Culture*, 322–3

Melete

Variations: NETE

One of the original three MUSES according to Pausanias, a second century Greek geographer and traveler, Melete ("occasion" or "practice") was a MUSE associated with Mount Helicon.

Sources: Monaghan, *Encyclopedia of Goddesses and Heroines*, 422; Peterson, *Mythology in Our Midst*, 121; Smith, *Dictionary of Greek and Roman Biography and Mythology*, 1125

Melia

There are many Nymphs in classical Greek mythology who have the name Melia; she was said to have been from Argos in southern Greece, the Ismenian spring of Thebes in central Greece, the Malean peninsula in Lakedaimonia in southern Greece, the town of Kios in Bithynia, the town of the Bebrykes in eastern Bithynia, and the town on the island of Keos in the Greek Aegean Sea. Melia was also said to have been the lover of the god, Apollo; the god, Poseidon (Neptune); the god, Seilenos; and the river-god Inakhos.

Sources: Fontenrose, *Python*, 317–19; Larson, *Greek Nymphs*, 40–41, 142, 149

Meliads

Variations: Meliade, MELIAE, MELIAI

In the mythology of the ancient Greeks the Meliads were a sub-species of the HAMADRYAD, a NYMPH living in and protecting ash and fruit trees, specifically apple trees. These NYMPHS were born the children of the goddess Gaea from the spilt blood of the god, Uranus; they were the guardians to the golden apples that belonged to the goddess, Hera (Juno).

Sources: Antoninus Liberalis, *Metamorphoses of Antoninus Liberalis*, 197; Littleton, *Gods, Goddesses, and Mythology*, Volume 4, 440; Parada, *Genealogical Guide to Greek Mythology*, 128; Westmoreland, *Ancient Greek Beliefs*, 117, 775

Meliae

Born one of the 3,000 daughters of the Titians, Oceanus and Tethys, Meliae, an ash tree NYMPH, was one of the named OCEANIDS; she was the mother of Amykos.

Sources: Boswell, *What Men or Gods Are These*, 58; Day, *God's Conflict with the Dragon and the Sea*, 64; Hesiod, *Works of Hesiod, Callimachus, and Theognis*, 20; Larson, *Greek Nymphs: Myth, Cult, Lore*, 187

Meliai

Meliai was a specific named NYMPH of the island of Crete, Greece. Meliai was also one of the alternate names for a species of NYMPHS that were the guardians of bees, honey, and the mountain ash tree.

Sources: Larson, *Greek Nymphs*, 168; Rigoglioso, *Cult of Divine Birth in Ancient Greece*, 87

Melian

The Melian was the name of the race of people who inhabited the earth before the creation of Pandora. These men whom the god Zeus (Jupiter) withheld fire from, were born of the Melian NYMPHS who themselves were born of the Earth and Heavens.

Melian was also the name of a NYMPH of Thessaly.

Sources: Larson, *Greek Nymphs*, 164; Penglase, *Greek Myths and Mesopotamia*, 199, 206

Meliboea

Born one of the 3,000 daughters of the Titians, Oceanus and Tethys, Meliboea was one of the named OCEANIDS in classical Greek mythology. Possibly the mother of Lycaon, she was said to have been loved by Orontes, a river god, who stopped his water from flowing out of love for her, flooding the land.

Sources: Boswell, *What Men or Gods Are These*, 58; Hesiod, *Works of Hesiod, Callimachus, and Theognis*, 20

Meliboia

An OCEANIAD from classical Greek mythology, Meliboia was a NYMPH of Arcadia, southern Greece as well as in Syria in western Asia. Meliboia was the wife of King Pelasgos and the lover of the river god, Orontes.

Sources: Hard, *Routledge Handbook of Greek Mythology*, 538; Larson, *Greek Nymphs*, 154

Melinette

In the fairy-tale *Prince Narcissus and the Princess Potentilla* by La Princess Pimrenella et Le Prince Romarin, the fairy Melinette was given the youngest son, Prince Narcissus, of a late king and queen to raise. Melinette was very kind and powerful and taught her charge everything he would ever need to know about the world, including some fairy lore. He castle floats in the air. Melinette was the enemy of the evil enchanter, Grumedan.

Sources: Lang, *Green Fairy Book*, 69–84; Larkin, *Snow White and Other Stories*, 196–220

Melior

Melior was a beautiful fairy from the fifteenth century French romance, *Parthenopex of Blois*. In the story Melior insisted her love, PARTHENOPE, not look at her until after they were married. She was one of three triplets born between the fountain NYMPH, PRESSYNE and Elynas, the King of Albany.

Sources: Keightly, *World Guide to Gnomes, Fairies, Elves, and Other Little People*, 34; Vives, *Instruction of a Christen Woman*, 215

Melissa

Melissa was a bee NYMPH of Peloponnese, Greece. Melissa was also a common name for NYMPHS to have and have long been associated with bees, possibly because both live in the hollow of caves and trees. In one myth, the NYMPH Melissa discovered the creation of mead by mixing the honeycomb with water.

Sources: Larson, *Greek Nymphs*, 86, 88; Ransome, *Sacred Bee in Ancient Times and Folklore*, 96

Melissai

The melissai ("bees") were in ancient Greek mythology the NYMPHS of honeybees. These nymphs were nourishing, prophetic, pure beings, the symbol of rebirth. The title of *melissai* was given to the priestess of Artemis (Diana), Demeter (Ceres), and Ephesos.

Sources: Bernal, *Black Athena*, 289; Rigoglioso, *Cult of Divine Birth in Ancient Greece*, 87

Melita

A sea–NYMPH from Greek mythology, Melita ("she is honey sweet"), was the NEREIDS who sports on the waves; she was born the daughter of Nerues and DORIS.

Sources: Betham, *Transactions of the Royal Irish Academy*, Volume 17, 88; Ransome, *Sacred Bee in Ancient Times and Folklore*, 96

Melite

Variations: MELITA, Melité

A sea–NYMPH from Greek mythology, Melite ("glorious" or "splendid") was the NEREIS of the calm seas; she was born the daughter of Nerues and DORIS in classical Greek mythology. Hesiod refers to her as being "graceful." She was one of the named NEREID who accompanied THETIS in mourning the loss of her son, Achilles. Melite was also one of the playmates of Persephone (Proserpina) and present when the goddess was kidnapped. Melite, along with ANCHIRHOE, BYZE, and MAERA, was one of the attendants to the goddess, BRITOMARTIS.

Sources: Apollodorus, *Apollodorus' Library and Hyginus' Fabulae*, 95; Bell, *Bell's New Pantheon or Historical Dictionary of the Gods*, 112; Collignon, *Manual of Mythology*, 18; Gould, *Historic Magazine and Notes and Queries*, Volume 14, 212; Hesiod, *Works of Hesiod, Callimachus, and Theognis*, 15; Homer, *Iliads of Homer*, 137

Melobosis

Born one of the 3,000 daughters of the Titians, Oceanus and Tethys, Melobosis was one of the named OCEANIDS in Greek mythology; she was one of the playmates of Persephone (Proserpina) and present when the goddess was kidnapped.

Sources: Boswell, *What Men or Gods Are These*, 58; Crudden, *Homeric Hymns*, 19; Hesiod, *Theogony*, 111; Conti, *Natale Conti's Mythologiae: Books VI–X*, 701; Hesiod, *Works of Hesiod, Callimachus, and Theognis*, 20

Melolosis

Born one of the 3,000 daughters of the Titians, Oceanus and Tethys, Melolosis ("like a river that waters the meadows") was one of the named OCEANIDS in ancient Greek mythology; she was one of the playmates of Persephone (Proserpina) and present when the goddess was kidnapped.

Sources: Larned, *Old Tales Retold from Grecian Mythology*, 445; Murray, *Manual of Mythology*, 154

Melpomene

One of the nine CANONICAL MUSES Melpomene was the MUSE of tragedy in Greek mythology; she was depicted in art as carrying a tragic mask and on occasion a club or sword. In some accounts, she was the mother of the SIRENS.

Sources: Littleton, *Gods, Goddesses, and Mythology*, Volume 11, 921; Peterson, *Mythology in Our Midst*, 121; Stafford, *Personification in the Greek World*, 154

Melsh Dick

Variations: Melch Dick

In the West Riding of Yorkshire, England the NURSERY BOGIE known as Melsh Dick protects unripe nuts from being picked by children, although elsewhere in the north this duty is held by the pipe-smoking CHURN MILK PEG.

Sources: Briggs, *Encyclopedia of Fairies*, 285; Rose, *Spirits, Fairies, Gnomes, and Goblins*, 356

Melusina

Variations: Melusine

In French mythology Melusina was a beautiful NYMPH or fresh-water MERMAID. As is the case with many of half-fish, half woman stories a mortal man falls in love with her; she promises to marry him but sets aside one condition which must never be broken; when the condition is broken he loses her and may or may not be able to restore their love.

In one version of the myth Melusina, with her golden hair and inexpressible beauty instantly won the heart of a nobleman named Raymond. She confessed to him she was a water-fay of great power and wealth and constructed for their use a great palace on the spot where they met, Castle Lusinia. He asked the fairy to be his wife but before Melusina would agree she elicited from him a promise, if they were to wed she must be able to spend Saturdays in complete seclusion. They lived many years together in great happiness and had many children together, all of which grew up to be great heroes. One day however Raymond accidently saw his wife in her seclusion and was horror struck by her half-fish appearance. Soon thereafter in a fit of grief over one of his sons, Geoffrey with the Tooth, having burned an abbey to the ground rejected Melusina when she came to comfort him; he said to her "Away you odious serpent, contaminator of the human race." The NYMPH was heart-broken and bade her husband to look after their two youngest children, as they would now be forced to grow up without a mother. With a long, BANSHEE-like cry, she transformed as she leapt from the window into the water below.

Sources: Baring-Gould, *Curious Myths of the Middle Ages*, Volume 2, 220, 228; Keightly, *World Guide to Gnomes, Fairies, Elves, and Other Little People*, 479; Rose, *Spirits, Fairies, Leprechauns, and Goblins*, 217, 351

Melwas

Variations: BADEMAGU, Maelwas

Melwas ("princely youth") was the abductor of Arthur's wife, Guinevere (Gwenhwyvar, "white phantom") in Celtic lore; he was described as wearing a green cloak.

The realm of Melwas was a place from which no man had ever returned; access to it was by one of two narrow bridges. The less perilous bridge was called Li Ponz Evages ("water bridge"); it was a foot and a half wide and tall with water above, below and on both sides. The second bridge was called Li Ponz de L' Espee ("sword bridge") and it was made of the edge of a sword two lances long.

Sources: Evan-Wentz, *Fairy Faith in Celtic Countries*, 310–12; Matthews, *Encyclopaedia of Celtic Myth and Legend*, 340–42

Memphis

Memphis was a NYMPH from the mythology of classical Greece and Rome. One of the NAIADS, she was born one of the daughters the god of the Nile River, and married the son of Zeus (Jupiter) and IO, Epaphos; they had a daughter named LIBYA.

Sources: Larson, *Greek Nymphs*, 191; Lemprière, *Classical Dictionary*, 455; Parker, *Mythology*, 95

Men Made of Bark

In Eastern European fairy lore the Men Made of Bark were NATURE SPIRITS known to seduce young women; while some were said to be dangerous others were accredited as being generous and tender lovers.

Source: Datlow, *Green Man,* 10

Mena

In ancient Greek lore Mena was one of the ATLANTID NYMPHS in Greek mythology; she was charged by the god Zeus (Jupiter) to rais his illegitimate son Arcas he father by the NYMPH, CALLISTO.

Sources: Lemprière, *Classical Dictionary,* 303; Russell, *History and Heroes of the Art of Medicine,* 5

Menaka

In Hindu mythology Menaka was considered to be one of the most beautiful of the Apsaras ("born of the waters"), second only to URVASI. Described as having slender waist, Menaka was the first of the Apsaras to be born and the mother of Parvati. In all there are twelve apsaras but only four of them stand out in Sanskirt literature, Menaka, RAMBHA, TILOTTAMA and URVASI.

Sources: Hudson, *Body of God*, 593; Rajan, *Complete Works of Kālidāsa*, 168, 373

Menehunes

Variations: Menehuna, Menihuni

The menehunes are a class of GNOME in Polynesian lore which is not associated to ancestral gods. In Hawaii, United States of America, these fay are considered to be fairy servants of the lowest class. Working all night long performing prodigious task after sunrise the menehunes were never allowed to touch them again. Not all scholars agree on this however; some will say the menehunes are ancestral spirits and are well known for their stone work, accrediting them with the construction two fish ponds and nine of the ten temples on the island of Honolulu as well as twenty-four additional temples and various standing stones on the other islands.

Sources: Adelson, *Lives of Dwarfs*, 106–7; Westervelt, *Legends of Gods and Ghosts*, 255

Menestho

Born one of the 3,000 daughters of the Titians, Oceanus and Tethys, Menestho was one of the named OCEANIDS from Greek mythology; she had the ability to remember everything she heard.

Sources: Hesiod, *Works of Hesiod, Callimachus, and Theognis*, 299; Lemprière, *Classical Dictionary,* 450; Westmoreland, *Ancient Greek Beliefs*, 24

Menippe

A sea–NYMPH, Menippe ("sipper") was one of the named NEREID from Greek mythology. According to the Greek oral poet, Hesiod, she was "divine"; Menippe was born the daughter of the river god, Peneios she married Pelasgos. Menippe was also the name of one of the NYMPH sisters who were collectively known as the KORONIDES.

Sources: Betham, *Transactions of the Royal Irish Academy*, Volume 17, 89; Hesiod, *Works of Hesiod, Callimachus, and Theognis*, 15; Larson, *Greek Nymphs*, 122, 165

Mentis

Born one of the 3,000 daughters of the Titians, Oceanus and Tethys, the NYMPH Mentis was one of the named OCEANIDS from Greek mythology.

Source: Apollodorus of Athens, *Apollodorus' Library and Hyginus' Fabulae*, 95

Mermaid

Variations: Ben-Varrey, Gorgone, Maighdean-Mara, Mary Morgan, MORGENS, Morrough, Moruach ("sea maid"), Muir-Gheilt, Murdhuch'a, Moruadh, NEREIS, Samhghubh'a, SIREN, Sirena, Suire

Mermaids ("sea maidens"), beings half fish and half women, have permeated the lore of the ocean since ancient times. Described as beautiful enchantresses, destructive and seductive as the ocean itself, the mermaid also personifies the dangers of rocky coastlines and treacherous waters.

The physical appearance of the mermaid likely dates back to the ancient Babylonians god of the sea, OANNES, and his companions, the Atargatis (Derketo). These companions were in their earliest times depicted as wearing cloaks but over time the cloaks evolved into fish tails. OANNES, an early adaptation of the Sumerian fish-god, Ea, was worshiped as the beneficial aspects of the ocean and a sun god; conversely the Atargatis came to be worshiped as moon-goddesses and represented the ocean's more destructive aspects.

The physical description of the mermaid has not changed much since its early inception. Typically described as having flowing and long hair either sea-green or sun-ray yellow they hold mirrors in their hands, symbolic of the moon, as they sit upon the rocks grooming. There are some folklores where the mermaid is not attractive, said to have green teeth, a pig-like nose, and red eyes, The domain of the mermaid is said to be on the bottom of the sea, made of priceless pearls and coral.

These FAIRY CREATURES possess a natural fear of man and will quickly flee as soon as they realize they have been seen by mortal eyes. Both mermaids and mermen (see MERMAN) alike long to have a mortal's soul and according to the legend any one of the merfolk can acquire one if a human falls in love with it. In tales involving the romance of a MERMAID and a mortal, the creature will uses its singing to lure the sailor in. In the tragic versions of the tales the ship is dashed along the rocky coast or the mermaid takes her would-be loved down to the depth where it inadvertently drowns him. In the less romanticized tales, mermaids are vicious and cause the ships to wreck, drowning the survivors at will.

The mermaid of ancient Greece did not have any *Piscean* attributes but rather looked exactly like a human. Greek mermaids can however, change their form at will. Usually benevolent, merfolk in Greek lore can become malevolent and unpredictable.

In European lore the mermaids wore a sap upon their heads called a *cohuleen druith*; this magical garment granted them some degree of protection. Should a mermaid be taken as a wife this cap needed to be stolen and kept by the husband, as it would prevent her from return to the ocean; this is similar to the lore of the SEAL WOMEN's coat and SWAN MAIDEN's cloak.

Sources: Andrews, *Dictionary of Nature Myths*, 118–19; Briggs, *Encyclopedia of Fairies*, 287–89; Dixon-Kennedy, *Encyclopedia of Greco-Roman Mythology*, 205; Matson, *Celtic Mythology A to Z*, 82–3; Monaghan, *Encyclopedia of Celtic Mythology and Folklore*, 325–7

Merman (plural: mermen)

Variations: Blue Men, DINNY-MARA, Dooinney Marrey, Dunya Mara, HAVMAND

Mermen are the male counterpart of the MERMAID. In the lore of ancient Greece, mermen were traditionally offspring of a sea god, such as Poseidon (Neptune), but could also be identified with the conch shell dwelling TRITONS.

In Irish and Scottish lore the merman is rarely attractive, described as having piggy eyes, breath stinking of rotting fish, and a nose blushed red from having consumed too much brandy from the ships it wrecked.

As the Scandinavian HAVMAND, the merman is rather handsome and has a black or green beard and hair. Living on the bottom of the sea or in the caves in the cliffs along the shore this version of the merman is considered to be a benign creature.

Sources: Briggs, *Encyclopedia of Fairies*, 290; Dixon-Kennedy, *Encyclopedia of Greco-Roman Mythology*, 205; Knightly, *Fairy Mythology*, 152; Monaghan, *Encyclopedia of Celtic Mythology and Folklore*, 327

Merope

Born one of the 3,000 daughters of the Titians, Oceanus and Tethys, Merope was one of the named OCEANIDS as well as one of the OREAD and the PLEIADES. According to the Greek oral poet, Hesiod, when her brother, Phaethon, died, she and her seven sisters were transformed into amber-weeping poplar tree. The sisters were collectively known as The Daughters of Helios (Sol); their names are AEGLE, AETHERIE, DIOXIPPE, Helie (see THE HELIADES), LAMPETIE, MEROPE, and PHOEBE. As one of the seven daugh-

ters of the Titian Atlas she was one of the AT-
LANTIDES.

Sources: Boswell, *What Men or Gods Are These*,
58; Day, *God's Conflict with the Dragon and the Sea*,
64; Hesiod, *Works of Hesiod, Callimachus, and Theognis*, 20

Merrow

Variations: Moruach, Moruadh, Murdhuacha

The merrow is a species of merfolk from
British folklore. The females, very similar to
many of the MERMAID myths, are known to wear
a magical cap called a *cohuleen druith*, it pro-
vides protection as they swim in the ocean.
Should this cap ever be lost or stolen this water
fairy cannot return to its subterranean home. Merrows have clear or white webbing between their
fingers and although have been known to form
unions with mortal men would rather lure one to
the ocean's depths. If ever a female merrow is
takne as a wife its *cohuleen druith*, must be kept
from it. So long as it never gains possession of
its cap the merrow will be able to resist the call
of the sea, but the instant it is return it will abandon its family and return to the ocean as quickly
as possible.

The male merrow are as hideously ugly as they
are aggressive; they have been described as having green hair, long green teeth, a pig-like nose
and red eyes. On the bottom of the ocean they
are said to keep the souls of all the sailors they
have drowned locked up in cages. Male merrows
also wear a *cohuleen druith* and although there
are tales of them loaning an extra cap to a mortal
there are virtually no stories of them taking a
human bride.

Sources: Eason, *Fabulous Creatures, Mythical Monsters, and Animal Power Symbols*, 151; Froud, *Faeries*,
121; Knightly, *Fairy Mythology*, 152; Spence, *Minor
Traditions of British Mythology*, 50–2; Wallace, *Folklore of Ireland*, 90

Mese

One of the muses, Mese was the MUSE of the
middle cord of the lyre; she represented one of
the three strings on the popular Greek musical
instrument, the lyre (see also HYPATE and NETE).
Mese was associated with Delphi, Greece.

Sources: McLean, *Triple Goddess*, 54; Peterson,
Mythology in Our Midst, 121

Messana

In Greek mythology, Messana was a NYMPH
of Sicily; she was depicted on coins as a charia-
teer diving mules.

Sources: Benson, *Ancient Greek Coins*, 45; Larson,
Greek Nymphs, 219

Methe

A NYMPH of Greek mythology, Methe ("drunkenness") was one of the MAENADS, the collective
name of the daughter born of the CANONICAL
MUSE, Mnemosyne, the personification of memory, and the god Zeus (Jupiter), after nine days
of continuous intercourse. Methe was such a
wonderful dancer she was defied because of her
ability.

Sources: Avant, *Mythological Reference*, 287; Monaghan, *Encyclopedia of Goddesses and Heroines*, 418–
19

Methone

A NYMPH of the town of Methone in Pieria in
northern Greece, Methone was the NAIAD wife
of King Pireros, according to Greek mythology.
She gave birth to Oeager who became a Thracian
hero and king. Methone was also one of the many
lovers to the god of the sea, Poseidon (Neptune).
In some sources Methone was named as one of
the ALKYONIDES.

Sources: Falkner, *Mythology of the Night Sky*, 195;
Hesiod, *Hesiod, the Homeric Hymns, and Homerica*,
571

Metioche

Variations: Metiokhe

In Greek mythology, Metioche was a NYMPH
of Boiotia in central Greece; she and her sister,
MENIPPE were collectively known as the KO-
RONIDES.

Sources: Fontenrose, *Orion*, 16–17; Monaghan, *Encyclopedia of Goddesses and Heroines*, 415

Metis

Born one of the 3,000 daughters of the Titians,
Oceanus and Tethys, Metis ("craft," "skill," or
"wisdom") was one of the named OCEANIDS in
Greek mythology; she was the first wife of the
god, Zeus (Jupiter) and the mother of the goddess
of war and wisdom, Athena (Minerva).

Sources: Boswell, *What Men or Gods Are These*,
58; Day, *God's Conflict with the Dragon and the Sea*,
64; Hesiod, *Works of Hesiod, Callimachus, and Theognis*, 20; Westmoreland, *Ancient Greek Beliefs*, 24

Metope

Metope was a NYMPH of the river Stymphalis
from the mythology of classical Greece and
Rome. One of the NAIADS, as the wife of Asopos,
a river god of Boiotia in central Greece, she was

the NYMPH of the Arcadian River, Ladon; together they had two daughters, Aegina and KORKYRA.

Sources: Illes, *Encyclopedia of Spirits*, 126; Larson, *Greek Nymphs*, 39, 139

Micol

Believed to be the Queen of the TROOPING FAIRIES by seventeenth century European magicians, diminutive Micol was invoked by medieval sorcerers during magical ceremonies (see FAIRY QUEEN). After chanting "O Micol, Micol regina Pigmeorum veni" a soft wind would rise up giving way to whirlwind and develop into a hurricane; during the storm Micol was said to then appear.

Sources: Briggs, Encyclopedia of Fairies, 295; Lilly, *William Lilly's History of his Life and Times from the Year 1602 to 1681*, 229–30; Rose, *Spirits, Fairies, Leprechauns, and Goblins*, 220, 351

Midar

Variations: Midhr, Midir, Midir the Proud

In the folklore of Ireland, Midar is a King of the TUATHA DÉ DANANN; his home was once called Brí Léith but it is now known as Slieve Glory, located in County Longfeford.

According to Lady Wild's *Ancient Legends of Ireland*, Midar chose Etain, the wife of King EOCHAID, to be his second wife, however, his first wife, Fuarnnach, became jealous and changed her into a midge, a type of very small fly. After a long search Midar found her with King EOCHAID and won her in a game of chess. Midhar changed them both into swans joined together with a golden chain; as they flew home they encountered King EOCHAID and his armies. After many battles, Etain returned to her husband.

Sources: Evan-Wentz, *Fairy Faith in Celtic Countries*, 374; Matson, *Celtic Mythology A to Z*, 83–4; Monaghan, *Encyclopedia of Celtic Mythology and Folklore*, 330; Rose, *Spirits, Fairies, Leprechauns, and Goblins*, 220, 351

Midea

In Greek mythology Midea was a water–NYMPH and one of the named DANAIDS, the collective name for the daughters of Danaus; her name appears in a list of the DANAIDS generated by Gaius Julius Hyginus (ca. 64 B.C.–A.D. 17), a Latin author. Midea was wedded to Antimachus and killed him on their wedding night.

Sources: Bell, *Women of Classical Mythology*, 149, 307; Parada, Genealogical Guide to Greek Mythology, 22, 59

Milân Shâh Peri

In Persian fairy lore, Milân Shâh Peri and his brother DÂL PERI, tried to save their sister the beautiful PERI MERJÂN ("fairy pearl"), from the fierce DEEV, DEMRUSH, but failed.

Sources: Hunt, *Leigh Hunt's London Journal*, Volumes 1–2, 235; Keightly, *World Guide to Gnomes, Fairies, Elves, and Other Little People*, 18

Milk-White Milch Cow

A FAIRY ANIMAL of Welsh lore Milk-White Milch Cow (Y Fuwh Laethwen Lefrith) had the ability to give just enough milk every day to everyone who wanted it, no matter how many households milked her. It was said to drink her milk would cure nearly any illness, make a foolish man wise, and a miserable person happy. Milk-White Milch Cow was owned by no one and wandered the land as she pleased leaving calves in her wake. One of her calfs was a long-horned ox called Ychen Bannog; it killed a monstrous KELPIE. According to legend the residents of the Vale of Towy tried to capture her with the intent of slaughtering her to eat but the elfin cow literally disappeared from their grasp and was never seen again.

Sources: Monaghan, *Encyclopedia of Celtic Mythology and Folklore*, 141; Sikes, *British Goblins*, 41

Mimis

Tiny NATURE SPIRITS living in rock crevices in the mythology of the Arnhem Land in northern Australia; mimis are described as being fragile, lightweight, and long limbed a gust of wind could blow them away, breaking their petite bodies. The mimis only leave their home to seek out roots and yams to eat but there are many tales of them also eating humans they happen across. Typically these good natured fairies are accredited with having taught the aboriginals how to paint and hunt.

Sources: Finley, *Aboriginal Art of Australia*, 20; Sykes, *Who's Who in Non-Classical Mythology*, 130

Minthe

Variations: Mentha, Menthe, Mintho

Minthe ("mint") was once a mountain NYMPH of Triphylia associated with the river Cocytus however, just as she was about to be seduced by Hades (Pluto), the king of the Underworld, his wife, Queen Persephone (Proserpina) transformed the NYMPH into the pungently sweet-smelling mint plant which some call *hedyosmus*.

Sources: Day, *God's Conflict with the Dragon and*

the Sea, 410; Hard, *Routledge Handbook of Greek Mythology*, 129; Larson, *Greek Nymphs*, 159

Miodvitnir

Variations: Mjodvitnir, Mjöðvitnir, Mjothvitnir

Miodvitnir was one of the many DWARFS named in the *Voluspa*, the first and best known poem of the *Poetic Edda*, a collection of Old Norse poems dating back to about A.D. 985.

Sources: Grimes, *Norse Myths*, 288; Wägner, *Asgard and the Gods*, 311

Mist

In Nordic and Teutonic mythology Mist ("cloud grey") was one of the named VALKYRIES, a NYMPH of battle. Always depicted as beautiful women who are sometimes immortal, they are the attendants of the god, Odin.

Sources: Grimm *Teutonic Mythology*, Volume 1, 422; Sigfusson, *Elder Eddas of Saemund Sigfusson Younger Eddas of Snorre Sturleson*, 57, 313

Mither o' the Sea

Variations: Sea Mither

Possibly one of the oldest surviving aspects of Orcadian folklore, Mither o' the Sea ("mother of the sea") is the personification of the benign force of the summer sea.

Teran, the spirit of winter, is the very hostile and powerful enemy of Mither o' the Sea; his BANSHEE-like cries could be heard in the winter gails and his angry roar as the waves crashed against the mountain coastline. In the spring Mither o' the Sea and Teran would battle against one another for weeks causing the deadly seasonal storms known as the Vore Tullye ("spring struggle"). After an exhausting summer of work Teran would return to battle Mither o' the Sea again, this time their battle is referred to as the Gore Vellye ("autumn tumult") and drained Mither o' the Sea would be forced to retreat.

Sources: Marwick, *Folklore of Orkney and Shetland*, 185; Sjoholm, *Pirate Queen*, 45

Mjödvitnir

Variations: Modvitnir

Mjödvitnir ("mead wolf") was one of the many DWARFS named in the *Voluspa*, the first and best known poem of the *Poetic Edda*, a collection of Old Norse poems dating back to about A.D. 985.

Sources: Crossley-Holland, Norse Myths, 183; Daly, *Norse Mythology A to Z*, 22; Sykes, *Who's Who in Non-Classical Mythology*, 53; Universität Münster, *Frühmittelalterliche Studien*, 106

Mneme

One of the original three MUSES in Greek mythology according to Pausanias, a second century Greek geographer and traveler, Mneme ("memory") was a MUSE associated with Mount Helicon.

Sources: McLean, *Triple Goddes*, 54; Peterson, *Mythology in Our Midst*, 121

Mnestra

In Greek mythology Mnestra was a water–NYMPH and one of the named DANAIDS, the collective name for the daughters of Danaus. In a list compiled by Apollodorus, a Greek scholar and grammarian, she was one of the daughters of an unnamed Ethiopian woman and was wedded to Aegius, one of the sons of an unnamed Phoenician woman.

Sources: Grimal, *Dictionary of Classical Mythology*, 127; Lemprière, *Classical Dictionary*, 236

Moddey Dhoo

Variations: Moddey Dohe, Mauthe Doog

The nocturnal BARGUEST of Peel Castle on the Isle of Man, the Moddey Dhoo ("black dog") was a singular entity; it was described as looking like a large black spaniel standing as big as a calf with curly black hair and glowing red eyes. Although it was seen in every room of the castle at one time or another, Moddey Dhoo frequented the guard chambers most often; as soon as the candles were lit there, this FAIRY ANIMAL would appear and lay down before the fireplace. Those guards who claimed to have seen it said they feared it would harm them should they use profanity in its presence; the guards also walked the castle in pairs whenever Moddey Dhoo was apparent as it created a presence of dread.

Sources: Cumming, *Guide to the Isle of Man*, 119–20; Eberhart, *Mysterious Creatures*, 344; Evan-Wentz, *Fairy Faith in Celtic Countries*, 129; Glover, *Glover's Illustrated Guide and Visitors' Companion*, 86–7

Modsognir

Variations: Modsogner

In old German lore Modsognir ("frenzy-roarer," "frenzy seeker"), one of the first of the DUERGAR, was one of three powerful DWARF leaders; he along with DURIN and DVALIN, forged many fantastic and magical weapons. Any weapon demanded from them would ultimately kill its owner. According to the Voluspa, the first and best known poem of the *Poetic Edda*, Modsognir was born of the blood and bones of YMIR.

Sources: Keightly, *World Guide to Gnomes, Fairies, Elves, and Other Little People*, 67; Rose, *Spirits, Fairies, Leprechauns, and Goblins*, 93; Sturluson, *Younger Edda*, 70

Moerae

Variations: FATE, Moirae, Parcae

In ancient Greek mythology the moerae appeared as a trio, one a young girl, one a middle-aged woman, and the last an old woman representing the three stages of human life; less commonly they appeared as three middle-aged women. The names of these three sisters were ATROPOS who decides how a life will end, Clotho ("the spinner") who gives life, and Lachesis ("drawer of lots") who determines a person's fortunes. The moerae were neither evil nor good but rather they determined the fate of children; at their most helpful they would assist with inspiration and divination. The ancient Roman equivalent to ATROPOS, Clotho, and Lachesis were Decuma, Morta, and Nona.

Sources: Bennett, *The Gods and Religions of Ancient and Modern Times*, Volume 1, 269; McCoy, *Witch's Guide to Faery Folk*, 139, 274–5; Rose, *Spirits, Fairies, Leprechauns, and Goblins, an Encyclopedia*, 254

Moin

Variations: Moinn

Moin was one of the many DWARFS named in the *Voluspa*, the first and best known poem of the *Poetic Edda*, a collection of Old Norse poems dating back to about A.D. 985.

Sources: Daly, *Norse Mythology A to Z*, 22; Sykes, *Who's Who in Non-Classical Mythology*, 53; Wilkinson, *Book of Edda called Völuspá*, 12

Mokotiti

Variations: Waihoetoto

One of the ATUA from the mythology of the Maori people of New Zealand, Mokotiti, was described as looking lizard-like and was believed to cause lung disease, such as pulmonary consumption.

Sources: Hamilton, *Transactions of the Royal Society of New Zealand*, Volume 37, 14, 17; Illes, *Encyclopedia of Spirits*, 44

Mokumokuren

The mokumokuren of Japanese mythology are fairy spirits living in *torn shoji*, the paper sliding walls. If the *torn shoji* has holes in it the eyes of the mokumokuren can be seen peeking through; if the eyes are stared at long enough the person

may go blind. The only way to banish these fairies is to patch the holes.

Sources: Frater, *Listverse.Com's Ultimate Book of Bizarre Lists*, 533

Molione

According to Greek mythology Molione was a NYMPH of the god Poseidon (Neptune), or Actor, sources conflict; she was said to be the mother of the Moliondis twins, Cleatus and Eurytus, who were hatched from a silver egg.

Sources: Bell, *Bell's New Pantheon*, 10; Room, *Who's Who in Classical Mythology*, 207

Molpe

Variations: Molpa, Molpea, Molpee, Molpey, Molpi, Molpie, Molpy

In classical Greek mythology, Molpe ("music" or "song") was one of the named SIRENS, a type of malicious NYMPH born the offspring of the ancient sea god, Phorcys. Half bird and half woman, she and her sisters would perch on the rocky Sicilian coastline and lure in sailor with their melodious song; once caught, their prey were eaten alive. Although they hunted the coastline, Molpe and her kind lived inland in a meadow.

Sources: Austern, *Music of the Sirens*, 40; Roman, *Encyclopedia of Greek and Roman Mythology*, 443; Smith, *Dictionary of Greek and Roman Biography and Mythology*, 817

Monachetto

In Italian folklore the monachetto are GNOME-like NATURE SPIRITS associated with caves, crevices, tunnels, and valleys; they are similar to the sub-species of NYMPHS known as OREADS.

Sources: Arrowsmith *Field Guide to the Little People*, 240; Grimassi, *Hereditary Witchcraft*, 83

Monaciello

In Naples Italy, Monaciello ("little monk") is a singular, nocturnal fairy being, similar to INCUBO. Describd as looking like a short and thick-bodied little man dressed like a monk in a broad-rimed hat it would appear in the middle of the night and beckon a person to follow it. If Monaciello was obliged the little fairy would lead the person to a concealed treasure. In some lore he is said to wear red clothing and stagger about perpetually drunk.

Sources: Euvino, *Complete Idiot's Guide to Italian History and Culture*, 274; Keightly, *World Guide to Gnomes, Fairies, Elves, and Other Little People*, 449; McCoy, *Witch's Guide to Faery Folk*, 275–6

Mondull

Mondull ("mill handle") was a DWARF appearing in the Norwegian saga *Göngu-Hrólfs* ("Walking Wolf"); as a character he was interesting only because he completely lacked individuality, his use of magical abilities was in truth an extension of the hero's, Hrólfs, will. On one occasion in the story Mondull prevented a fiendish necromancer, Grimr, from resurrecting the slain from the day's battlefield by arriving first and casting preventative spells.

Sources: De Walsh, *Grillparzer as a Poet of Nature*, 9; Herbert, *Catalogue of Romances in the Department of Manuscripts in the British Museum*, Volume 2, 54

Montana

A FATE of neutral alignment, Montana sought to avenge the fate of her lover who had been slain by Alidoro in the Italian poem *Amadigi* written by the poet Bernado Tasso in 1560. Montana enchanted a warrior within the confines of a temple she erected with her magic to commemorate the memory of her fallen beloved.

Sources: Keightly, *World Guide to Gnomes, Fairies, Elves, and Other Little People, 454*; Proto, *Sul Rinaldo di Torquato Tasso*, 175

Monuste

In Greek mythology Monuste was a NYMPH and one of the named DANAIDS, the collective name for the daughters of Danaus; her name appears in a list of the DANAIDS generated by Gaius Julius Hyginus (ca. 64 B.C.–A.D. 17), a Latin author. Monuste was wedded to Eurysthenes and killed him on their wedding night.

Sources: Bell, *Women of Classical Mythology*, 312, 446; Hyginus, *Myths of Hyginus*, 133

Morea

In Greek mythology Morea was one of the eight HAMADRYADS who was born of HAMADRYAS; she was the HAMADRYAD of the mulberry (oleaster) tree.

Sources: Buxton, *Forms of Astonishment*, 211; Larson, *Greek Nymphs: Myth, Cult, Lore*, 283

Morgan

Variations: Maries Morgan, Morganes, Morgen, Sea Morgan

In Breton, the MERMAID is called a morgan ("sea-women") or morverc'h ("sea-daughters"); fond of combing out their long hair these fair beings are known to lure in sailors with their beautiful singing voice, let their ship dash on the rocks, snatch up the sailors, and take them down to the bottom of the sea or a deep ponds where their palace of crystal and gold resides.

Sources: Archibald, *Sixpence for the Wind*, 38–9; Keightly, *World Guide to Gnomes, Fairies, Elves, and Other Little People*, 433

Morgan Le Fey

Variations: Dame d' Avalon, FATA MORGANA, Margot-La-Fee, Mergain, Mergiana, Morgain la Fee, Morgaine, Morgan lá Fée, Morgan la Fay, Morgan the Fairy, Morgan the Goddess, Morgana, Morgane la fée, Morgane, Morganetta, Morgen, Morgue le Faye

Morgan le Fey is a complicated figure in history and mythology. She has had many names and fulfilled many roles in religion and folklore including Badb, the Irish goddess of war; Dahut (or Ahes) a Breton goddess; a daughter of the Celtic god, Avallach; Modron, a Welsh goddess; Morrigan, the Celtic goddess of death and war; Morrigan, an Irish goddess; a species of the MERMAID; as well as the daughter of King Gorlois (or Hoel) of Cornwall and his wife, Queen Igraine; lady-in-waiting for Queen Guinevere; and the wife of King Urien and mother of the hero Owain (or Yvain).

Some Arthurian scholars make the claim she is the LADY OF THE LAKE but as many will say the two FAIRY QUEENS were enemies and rivals as one gave the King his sword, Excalibur, while the other sought to steal it. In British Arthurian lore and according to Sir Thomas Malory's *Le Morte Darthur* (1469), Morgan le Fay ("Morgan the Fairy") was the consistently evil and malicious half-sister to King Arthur. Determined to kill her half-brother and see to the defamation of his court, it was most unexpected when she appeared with three other FAIRY QUEENS, Queen of the Nimue (Niniane), Queen of the Northgales, and the Queen of the Wasteland, to ferry Arthur to the Isle of Apples to tend to his wounds after the battle of Camlan.

As this character Morgan la Fey also appears in *Ogier le Danois* ("*Ogier the Dane*"); *Orlando Furioso* ("*Mad Orlando*") the Italian epic poem by Ludovico Ariosto published in 1516; and *Orlando Innamorato* ("*Orlando in Love*") the Renaissance epic peom by Matteo Maria Boiardo.

Outside of Arthurian lore FATA MORGANA is a fay of the sea comparable to the Morgans of Brenton. In Italy, it is said when the MERMAIDS cause mirages to appear over the straights of

Messina these illusions are referred to as FATA MORGANAS.

No matter when or where Morgan le Fey appeared she was always portrayed as a cunning, intelligent, and powerful woman. Gifted with supernatural skills in herbal medicine, and occult magical knowledge, she was also a proficient shape-shifter. She has been described as a deeply beautiful woman as well as an old crone with a deformed face, a vicious HAG, and uncountable animal forms, particularly a crow, a heifer crowned with a silver crescent rather than horns, and a she-wolf.

Morgan le Fey had many strongholds throughout the course of the history, among them were the Castle of the Maidens in Edinburg, filled with beautiful but malicious fairy-servants; the fortress Mongibel (also known as Mongibello and Mount Etna) in England; the Island of AVALON (Isle of Apples) where she lived with her husband, Guingamar; and an underwater paradise.

Sources: Briggs, *Encyclopedia of Fairies*, 303–4; Gardner, *Arthurian Legend in Italian Literature*, 12; Keightly, *World Guide to Gnomes, Fairies, Elves, and Other Little People*, 34; Rose, *Spirits, Fairies, Leprechauns, and Goblins*, 224, 351; Wallace, *Folk-lore of Ireland*, 90

Morgana Fata

In Italy, MORGANA FATA ("fairy Morgana") is the personification of the goddess, Fortune.

Source: Keightly, *World Guide to Gnomes, Fairies, Elves, and Other Little People*, 451

Morgens

Variations: Mari-Morgans, Mary Morgens, Morganezed, Morgans, Sea Morgens

Brenton and Welsh water fairies, morgens, will sit MERMAID-like upon the rocks combing out their long hair. Then, like SIRENS, they will use their beautiful singing voice to lure fishermen and sailors alike towards them, wrecking their ships. Anyone who survives the initial wreck will be snatched up by the morgens and taken to the ocean's depths where they are drowned.

These fairies are also blamed for any heavy flooding that destroyed crops or villages.

Sources: Briggs, *Encyclopedia of Fairies*, 304; Rhys, *Celtic folklore: Welsh and Manx*, Volume 1, 299; Tongue, *Forgotten Folk-Tales of the English Counties*, N.p.

Moria

Moria ("oleaster") was a NYMPH of the river Hermos in Lydia, Anatolia from the mythology of classical Greece and Rome; she was one of the NAIADS. MORIA was born of from the incestuous relationship between the NATURE SPIRIT Oxylus and his sister, HAMADRYAS.

Sources: Larson, *Greek Nymphs*, 283; Parada, *Genealogical Guide to Greek Mythology*, 128

Moss People

Variations: Greenies, Wild, Wood, Timber

The moss people of southern Germany were described as DWARF-life beings standing about as tall as a three-year old child and lived in a communal environment. Overall, these fairies appeared to be aged, grey-skinned, hairy, and clad in moss. The females of the species wore cocked hats and green clothes faced with red; they would approach wood cutters to ask for or trade for food by cooking, giving advice, or washing clothes. The female moss people were of a nicer disposition than the males who lived deep in the woods. Sometimes the moss people were described as being very small and having wings attached to their back; when this was the case, these fairies were then oftentimes mistaken for being butterflies.

These fairies were relentlessly hunted by their flying, invisible natural enemy, the Wild Huntsman (see WILD HUNT).

Sources: Keightly, *World Guide to Gnomes, Fairies, Elves, and Other Little People*, 230–31; McCoy, *Witch's Guide to Faery Folk*, 276–7; Telesco, *Kitchen Witch Companion*, 21

Moth

Moth is a FLOWER FAIRY and an attendant of TITANIA, the FAIRY QUEEN. Along with fellow fairies COBWEB, MUSTARDSEED, and PEASE BLOSSOM, she attended a human peasant named Bottom whose head was changed into an ass' by OBERON, the FAIRY KING.

Sources: Lamb, *Works of Charles and Mary Lamb*, 18; Rose, *Spirits, Fairies, Leprechauns, and Goblins*, 255, 351; Shakespeare, *Shakespeare's a Midsummer Night's Dream*, 26

Motsognir

Motsognir ("battle roarer" or "the mighest") was one of the many DWARFS named in the *Voluspa*, the first and best known poem of the *Poetic Edda*, a collection of Old Norse poems dating back to about A.D. 985. Motsognir became the master of all DWARFS.

Sources: Daly, *Norse Mythology A to Z*, 22; Wilkinson, *Book of Edda called Völuspá*, 12, 26

The Mouse Fairy

In the fairy-tale *The Good Little Mouse* by Madame d'Aulnoy, the kind and unnamed good fairy of the story is never mentioned by name but typically took the form of a beautiful little mouse. In the service of the sulky and savage king of the Land of Tears, the fairy was supposed to guard over a captive and her infant princess but rather the mouse fairy befriended the captive queen and assisted her in her escape. The fairy CANCALINE was the sworn enemy of the mouse fairy.

Source: Lang, *Red Fairy Book*, 146–57

Mrs. Bedonebyasyoudid

Described as an elderly and strict schoolmarm, Mrs. Bedoneasyoudid, along with fellow fairy MRS. DOASYOUWOULDBEDONEBY, instructed the WATER BABIES in the nineteenth-century story *The Water Babies* (1863), by Charles Kingsley.

Sources: Manguel, *Dictionary of Imaginary Places*, 588; Rose, *Spirits, Fairies, Leprechauns, and Goblins*, 36; Zipes, *Victorian Fairy Tales*, xix

Mrs. Doasyouwouldbedoneby

Described as the loveliest fairy in the world, Mrs. Doasyouwouldbedoneby, along with fellow fairy MRS. BEDONEBYASYOUDID, instruct the WATER BABIES in the nineteenth-century story *The Water Babies* (1863), by Charles Kingsley. She was described as being cuddly, fat, and soft, Mrs. Doasyouwouldbedoneby understood babies thoroughly as she was the mother of several hundred babies herself.

Sources: Manguel, *Dictionary of Imaginary Places*, 588; Rose, *Spirits, Fairies, Leprechauns, and Goblins*, 36, 351; Zipes, *Victorian Fairy Tales*, xix

Mu

The mu are NATURE SPIRITS or NATS from Burmese folklore; they are sky NATS controling the people's overall prosperity and their wealth. The core mu NATS are a collection of seven, eight, or nine brothers and although there is little argument over what their names are, there is a great deal of uncertainty over the order of their birth. Names commonly appearing on the list of the brothers' names include Hkringwan, JAN, Madai, Mu-Iam, Musheng, and SINLAP. It has been established the chief of mu NATS is La N'Roi Madai; he is also the youngest of the brothers.

Sources: Leach, *Essential Edmund Leach*, Volumes 1–2, 21–2; Porteous, *Forest in Folklore and Mythology*, 125; Scott, *The Burman: His Life and Notions*, Volume 1, 286

Muireartach

Variations: HAG of the Seas, Muileartach

In Celtic lore the Muireartach ("eastern sea") was a bald (or white haired, sources conflict), blue-skinned, one-eyed HAG with jagged teeth. Traditionally she is said to be malevolent, but her motivations in the folklore's story has never been made clear.

Wife of the ocean-smith, Muireartach was the embodiment of the storm-raging sea; ultimately slain by the hero, Fionn MacCumhail. She was such a violent and formidable opponent the only way to kill her was to drown her in calm waters or bury her in the earth up to her shoulders.

Sources: MacKenzie, *Scottish Folk-Lore and Folk Life*, 156; Monaghan, *Women in Myth and Legend*, 208; Mountain, *Celtic Encyclopedia*, Volume 4, 878–9

Mum-Poker

Variations: Mumpoker

A GOBLIN, Mum-Poker was a NURSERY-BOGY from the folklore of England. His two brothers were HODGE-POKER and TOM-POKER. The word "mum" alludes to his silent and stealthy approach. Parents would use the threat of this fairy to quiet children who are screaming.

Sources: American Philological Association, *Transactions of the American Philological Association*, Volume 26, 118; Halliwell, *Dictionary of Archaic and Provincial Words*, 453; Long, *Dictionary of the Isle of Wight Dialect*, 42; Narváez, *Good People*, 469

Mumiai

The mumiai of Indian lore are well known for their persecution of the peasantry; they particularly single out those who are of the lowest castes, demonstrated bad habit, and have stolen from their neighbors. Taking hold of their possessions the mumiai break their pottery and trample down their gardens until the victim finally relents and moves away.

Sources: Allardice, *Myths, Gods and Fantasy*, 153; Avant, *Mythological Reference*, 479

Murdhuachas

Variations: Sea Cows, Walrus People

A race of Irish sea fairies, the murdhuachas are sometimes mistakenly labeled as a merperson, like the MERMAID or MERMAN, because they have the lower body of a fish. However these fay have the upper body and head of an animal. Murdhuachas are of a divided nature, as they are as likely to help a sailor find his home port on a foggy night as they are to lure them into rock jetties with their haunting SIREN-like songs.

Sources: Kynes, *Sea Magic*, 136; McCoy, *Witch's Guide to Faery Folk*, 278–9; Newcomb, *Faerie Treasury*, 16, 54

Murgatroyd

An individual, specific LEPRECHAUN from Irish folklore, Murgatroyd, standing only two feet tall, claimed he was a descendant of the TUATHA DE DANANN. Always dressing in green and tan, Murgatroyd cast no shadow and loved to ride in taxis. Acting as a guardian spirit to a particular family, Murgatroyd would appear whenever they were in distress.

Source: Bord, *Fairies*, 117–18

Murigen

Variations: Morgan

Originally a lake goddess associated with flooding in Welsh mythology, Murigen ("born of the sea") is possibly a not only a FAIRY QUEEN but also a specific individual from the species of fairy known as MORGENS.

Sources: Seamon, *Dwelling, Place, and Environment*, 144; Sykes, *Who's Who in Non-Classical Mythology*, 133

Muryan

Variations: Meryan, Meryon, Myryan

In Cornish fairy belief the muryan ("ant") are the returned souls of ancient, non-Christians who were too good to be condemned to Hell but unable to enter into Heaven. Over time, muryans were believed to decrease in size until they were the size of ants; then, then the fairy disappeared. The mythology did not offer any idea as to what then happened to the soul.

Because it was believed ants were the decomposing souls of fairies it was considered very unlucky to destroy an ant hill.

Sources: Hunt, *Popular Romances of the West of England*, Volume 1, 131; Stepanich, *Faery Wicca*, Book One, 272; Wright, *English Dialect Dictionary*, 209

Musail

Variations: The Forest Tsar

FAIRY KING Musail was once a god in the Slavic pantheon but after the introduction of Christianity he was reduced to a NATURE SPIRIT and guardian of forest animals. Musail has dominion over the SATYER-like, LESHY. Peasants would write a letter to Musail asking him to restore a particular individual to health and if this was not done then it would leave the family of the sick man not recourse but to travel to Moscow and ask the Tsar to send regiments of men to cut down the rowan trees of the forest. This letter was then left in a rowan tree for Musail to discover and read.

Sources: Illes, *Encyclopedia of Spirits*, 628; Oinas, *Agents and Audiences*, 481

Muse

Variations: Aganippides

In Greek and Roman mythology a muse was a beautiful NYMPH known for its dancing and singing; it recited poetry as the gods ate their meals. Over time the role of the muse changed and they evolved to beings akin to lesser gods inspiring human artist. There is no unified mythology explaining the parentage of the muses; a wide array of gods and goddesses have been accredited with it.

Throughout Greek mythology the muses have been associated with many events; they gave the Sphinx her riddle, taught ECHO how to play music, and taught healing and prophecy. However, they were malicious and vindictive when contradicted.

According to Pausanias, a second century Greek geographer and traveler, there were originally three muses, AOIDE ("song" or "voice"), MELETE ("occasion" or "practice"), and MNEME ("memory"). Collectively, they formed the ideals of the poetic arts. Later, a fourth muse was introduced, ARCHE. In Hellenistic times, the muses were assigned divisions of poetry to which they were said to oversee and inspire.

Sources: Littleton, *Gods, Goddesses, and Mythology*, Volume 11, 921–26; Peterson, *Mythology in Our Midst*, 121–23; Parker, *Mythology: Myths, Legends and Fantasies*, 44

Mustardseed

Mustardseed is a FLOWER FAIRY and an attendant of TITANIA, the FAIRY QUEEN. Along with fellow fairies COBWEB, MOTH, and PEASE BLOSSOM, attends a human peasant named Bottom whose head was changed into an ass' by OBERON, the FAIRY KING.

Sources: Lamb, *Works of Charles and Mary Lamb*, 18; Rose, *Spirits, Fairies, Leprechauns, and Goblins*, 255, 351; Shakespeare, *Shakespeare's a Midsummer Night's Dream*, 26

Mykene

A NYMPH of the town of Mykenai in Argos located in southern Greece; the NAIAD from Greek mythology Mykene was born the daughter of Inakhos and the wife of King Arestor.

Sources: Larson, *Greek Nymphs*, 149; Pausânias, *Guide to Greece: Central Greece*, 167

Myrmidone

In Greek mythology Myrmidone was a water–NYMPH and one of the named DANAIDS, the collective name for the daughters of Danaus; her name appeared in a list of the DANAIDS generated by Gaius Julius Hyginus (ca. 64 B.C.–A.D. 17), a Latin author. Myrmidone was wedded to Mineus and killed him on their wedding night.

Sources: Bell, *Women of Classical Mythology*, 149, 315, Hyginus, *Myths of Hyginus*, 132; Parada, *Genealogical guide to Greek mythology*, 59, 123

Myrtoessa

Myrtoessa was a CRINAEAE, a sub-species of the NAIAD, a NYMPH of a fountain in Arcadia, and one of the OCEANID from Greek mythology; she was associated with the care and feeding of the infant god, Zeus (Jupiter). In art, she and the NYMPH ARCHIROE were depicted holding a water pot from which water is flowing from.

Sources: Larson, *Greek Nymphs*, 153; Pausanias, *Pausanias's Description of Greece*, Volume 1, 414, 434

Mystis

One of the BAKKHAI in Greek mythology, Mystis was a NYMPH of the island of Euboia; she was one of the nurses to the infant god, Dionysus (Bacchus).

Sources: Dowden, *Companion to Greek Mythology*, 102; Smith, *Dictionary of Greek and Roman Biography and Mythology*, 1047

Näcken

Variations: Fosse-Grim, Grim, Naecken, NECK, Nix, Nøkk, Nøkken, Strom Karl, STRÖM-KARL ("Strong Man of the Stream"), Strömkarlennäck

The näcken ("nude") was a male, solitary, water fairy in Scandinavia lore. Similar to the SIREN, a näcken would play, naked upon a rock, its violin, luring children and women into lakes and streams where they would drown. Pregnant women and unbaptized children were said to particularly susceptible it its music. Many fiddlers have claimed after they made a sacrifice this fay it shared its knowledge on how to play the Hardanger fiddle beautifully; common offerings were a black animal, *brännvin* (Scandinavian vodka), snus (wet snuff), and three drops of blood.

As the fossegrim, this fairy would appear as an especially attractive young man playing a fiddle wearing little or no clothes, but it could also appear as an animal or some floating bit of treasure on or just below the surface of the water to lure its prey in. Most often a fossegrim would appear as a horse. There are some folktales of a fossegrim living with a woman who professed her love for it, but by the end of the story it almost always becomes depressed and returns back to its watery home.

Sources: Blind, *Contemporary Review*, Volume 40, 560; Keightley, *Fairy Mythology*, 162; Moorey, *Fairy Bible*, 122–3; Morgan, *Baron Bruno*, 96–8, 100–01, 108–09; Vanberg, *Of Norwegian Ways*, 139

Naga

In Buddhist, Hindu, and Jainism mythology the naga are a complicated and diverse being. As the deified guardians and NATURE SPIRITS of the elixir of immortality, pearls, and raindrops they wield great power as they confer fertility and wealth upon mankind but only if properly worshiped. Residing in the aquatic underworld of the earth called Patala the naga are described as serpentine beings with cobra hoods and human heads. The naga were said to have been born the sons of Kadru, the daughter of Daksha, and it is believed one day this race will destroy the world in fire. A female nagas is called a nagini and their King is named ANANTA-SHESHA.

As WATER SPIRITS the naga are said to reside at the bottom of lakes, rivers, and the sea in gem encrusted palaces filled with never-ending dance and song.

Sources: Avant, *Mythological Reference*, 345; Chopra, *Academic Dictionary of Mythology*, 198; Leeming, *Oxford Companion to World Mythology*, 277

Naglfar

Naglfar was one of the many DWARFS named in the *Voluspa*, the first and best known poem of the *Poetic Edda*, a collection of Old Norse poems dating back to about A.D. 985.

Sources: Daly, *Norse Mythology A to Z*, 22; Sykes, *Who's Who in Non-Classical Mythology*, 53

Nai

Nai was the golden-haired fairy of Irish folklore from the land of "ever young."

Source: Wallace, *Folk-lore of Ireland*, 90

Naiad

Variations: The Heleionomai, Naiade, Naide, NAIS

The Naiad ("to flow" or "running water") of Greek mythology were one of twelve species of NYMPHS, they were associated to freshwater lakes, rivers, and springs whereas the NEREIS were specifically associated to the Mediterranean Sea and the OCEANIDS of saltwater sources in general.

It was believed by the ancient Greeks all the water of the world was connected by one underground system, therefore Naiad were not restricted to remaining locked to their water source, they could travel through the subterranean waterways from one water source to another. However, if their body of water ever dried up or was somehow destroyed, the associated water fairy would die. Naiads were said to have the ability to foretell mortals their destiny and generally predict the future. These NATURE SPIRITS were typically said to have been born the daughter of the god Poseidon (Neptune), Zeus (Jupiter), the goddess Ge, or one of the many OCEANIDS or river gods, but individual origin stories are not uncommon. Because naiads are not mortal women they have the privilege of being sexually aggressive and active without shame.

Although generally benign, naiads could prove to be very dangerous as they were well known to act on their jealous tendencies. Punishments from a naiad ranged from being drowned to having been struck blind.

Accord to the Greek oral poet, Hesiod, in one of his fragmented poems a naiad declares "a crow lives for nine human generations, a stag lives four times as long as a crow, a raven three times as long as a stag, a phoenix nine times as long as a raven, and a NYMPH 10 times as long as a phoenix." Assuming a human generation is 20 years, a NYMPH can reasonable expect to live 194,000 years. A DRYAD lives only as long as its tree and a naiad similarly coexist with her spring.

Many times in Greek mythology when the name of a character was introduced it was given as, for instance, "daughter of Asopos," to which ancient Greeks would have known Asopos was a lesser known river god, therefore his daughter was a NAIAD. Very often naiads' names had the suffex–nais (naiad") or–rhoe, but not always. Some of the historical known and named naiads are ABA, ABARBAREA, ABARBAREE, Aegina, AEGLE, Aia, ALCINOE, ALEXIRHOE, ANCHIRHOE, ANIPPE, ANNAED, ANTHEDON, ARETHUSA, ARGYRA, BATEIA, BISTONIS, BYZIA, CALIADNE, CALLIRRHOE, CASTALIA, CHARYBDIS, CHLIDANOPE, CLEOCHAREIA, CORYCIA, CREUSA, DAPHNE, DIO-

GENEIA, DIOPATRE, DROSERA, ECHENAIS, HARPINA, ISMENIS, KALYBE, KLEODORA (CLEODORA), LANGIA, LARA, LETHE, LILAEA, LIRIOPE (LEIRIOPE), MELAINA, MELITE, MEMPHIS, METOPE, MINTHE, MORIA, NANA, NEAERA, NICAEA, NOMIA, ORSEIS, PEGASIS, PERIBOEA, PITANE, POLYXO, PRAXITHEA, SALMACIS, SPARTA, STRYMO, STYX, TELPHOUSA, THRONIA, TIASA, and ZEUXIPPE.

Sources: Day, *God's Conflict with the Dragon and the Sea*, 391–95; Hansen, *Classical Mythology*, 41, 242; Keightly, *World Guide to Gnomes, Fairies, Elves, and Other Little People*, 444; Larson, *Greek Nymphs*, 2–4; Littleton, *Gods, Goddesses, and Mythology, Volume 11*, 999

Nain

Variations: Nainn

Nain ("corpse") was one of the many DWARFS named in the *Voluspa*, the first and best known poem of the *Poetic Edda*, a collection of Old Norse poems dating back to about A.D. 985.

Sources: Daly, *Norse Mythology A to Z*, 22; Sykes, *Who's Who in Non-Classical Mythology*, 53; Wägner, *Asgard and the Gods*, 311

Nain Rouge

Variations: Demon of the Strait, Le Petit Homme Rouge ("the little RED MAN")

A LUTIN that originated in the folklore of Normandy, France nain rouge ("red DWARF") is similar to HOUSE-SPIRITS in England, Germany, and Scandinavia except he is especially kind to fishermen, giving them invaluable aid when need and dulling out punishment to those who are not respectful of him. Described as looking like a small, red faced child-like creature with blazing red eyes, and rotting teeth; it also wore black or red fur boots.

In Detroit, Michigan the Nain Rouge has a reputation for only appearing on the eve of disaster. It is said when the founder of Detroit, the French explorer Antoine Laumet de Lamothe Cadillac struck it, he soon thereafter lost his fortune. It was seen shortly before the Battle of Bloody Run in 1763, and again in 1805 when the city was nearly destroyed by fire.

When nain rouge shape-changes into the form of a horse it is then called LE CHEVAL BAYARD.

Sources: Hamlin, *Legends of Le Détroit*, 22–29; Keightly, *World Guide to Gnomes, Fairies, Elves, and Other Little People*, 478

Nais

Variations: ABARBAREA

Nais ("water"), one of the HOMERIC NYMPHS

of Greek mythology was known to have "blessed the bed" of many of the heroes and warriors who fought at the battle of Troy. As one of the OCEANIDS, she was the mother of Chiron or Glaucus ("grey green") the prophetic sea-god by Magnes, a son of Zeus (Jupiter); she was also the mother of twins who fought and were slain at Troy, Aeseopus and Pedasus.

In one story, a cowhearder named Daphnis fell in love with Nais and began to waste away because she did not return his affection. Moved with compassion she promised to be his if he swore to remain forever faithful to her. Not long after his vow was given to the river NYMPH, a mortal woman named Xenia fell in love with Daphnis; she was able to get him drunk and trick him into making love to her. For his infidelity Nais struck him blind. He wandered the countryside singing of his misfortune until he accidentally fell into a river; because he had broken his vow to Nais, the NYMPH of the river let him drown.

Living on an island in the Red Sea, Nais would use her magic to turn her lovers into fishes after she was no longer interested in them. Eventually she was changed into a fish by the god, Apollo.

Sources: Grant, *Who's Who in Classical Mythology*, 103, 144; Keightly, *World Guide to Gnomes, Fairies, Elves, and Other Little People*, 445; Lemprière, *Classical Dictionary*, 34

Näkki

Variations: Näkk, NECK, Vesihiisi, Vetehinen ("Water dweller")

In Finnish mythology the näkki is a water fairy living in murky pools, wells and under docks, piers and under bridges that cross rivers. Descriptions of the fairy vary; it has been described as being very beautiful in the front but extremely hairy and ugly in the back but also as an ugly fisherman that can shape-shift at will into a beautiful woman who has three breasts, a beautiful woman who is extremely voluptuous, a horse, a hound, or a silvery fish.

Used by parents as a NURSERY BOGIE, the näkki has a reputation for grabbing children and pulling them into the water, drowning them.

Sources: Bray, *World of Myths*, 45; Keightly, *World Guide to Gnomes, Fairies, Elves, and Other Little People*, 489

Nali

Nali was one of the many DWARFS named in the *Voluspa*, the first and best known poem of the

Poetic Edda, a collection of Old Norse poems dating back to about A.D. 985.

Sources: Daly, *Norse Mythology A to Z*, 22; Sykes, *Who's Who in Non-Classical Mythology*, 53; ; Wägner, *Asgard and the Gods*, 311; Wilkinson, *Book of Edda called Völuspá*, 12

Nana

Nana was a river-NYMPH of the River Saggarios in Phrygia, Anatolia from the mythology of classical Greece and Rome; she was born the daughter of the river god, Sangarios. According to the story, the hermaphroditic godling child of Zeus (Jupiter), Agdistis, was castrated by the gods and from his discarded sexual organs an almond or pomegranate tree sprang forth. The NAIAD Nana ate the beautiful fruit (or hide it on her lap, sources conflict) and became pregnant with a son she named Attis, a vegetation god.

Sources: Kerényi, *Gods of the Greeks*, 89; Leeming, *Mythology*, 26; Roman, *Encyclopedia of Greek and Roman Mythology*, 94

Nanny Button-Cap

In Yorkshire, England Nanny Button-Cap is a fairy known to watch over young children, ensuring they are safe and warm in their bed when it is time to go to sleep.

Sources: Monaghan, *Encyclopedia of Celtic Mythology and Folklore*, 348; Rose, *Spirits, Fairies, Leprechauns, and Goblins*, 231, 351; Wright, *Rustic Speech and Folk-Lore*, 207

Napaeae

The Napaeae ("a wooded dell") of Greek mythology are a beautiful but shy sub-species of the NAPAEA; they are the NYMPHS of glens in mountain valleys. Associated with the goddess Artemis (Diana), they often accompany her.

Sources: Avant, *Mythological Reference*, 291; Bell, *Bell's New Pantheon*, 95, 112; Daly, *Greek and Roman Mythology A to Z*, 102

Napf-Hans

Variations: Jack-of-the-bowl, Jean de la Bolieta, Napfhans

Napf-hans is a HOBGOBLIN form German lore. It was customary to leave a bowl of fresh, sweet cream for him each evening on the roof of the cow house. Whenever a dangerous weather event rose up the napf-hans would assist the farmers in bringing in the cow herds safely.

Sources: Croker, *Fairy Legends and Traditions of the South of Ireland*, 111; Keightly, *World Guide to*

Gnomes, Fairies, Elves, and Other Little People, 265; Rose, *Spirits, Fairies, Gnomes, and Goblins*, 235

Nár

Variations: Nar, Narr ("fool")

Nár was one of the many DWARFS named in the *Voluspa*, the first and best known poem of the *Poetic Edda*, a collection of Old Norse poems dating back to about A.D. 985.

Sources: Daly, *Norse Mythology A to Z*, 22; Sykes, *Who's Who in Non-Classical Mythology*, 53; ; Wägner, *Asgard and the Gods*, 311; Wilkinson, *Book of Edda called Völuspá*, 12

Nat

In the Burmese folk belief and religion nats is the generic name for the indigenous NATURE SPIRITS of the air, cultivated fields, earth, forest, hills, households, rain, rivers sky, streams, wind, and the like. They can also be persuaded to act as tutelary spirits to boats, house, personal property, treasure, tribe, and village.

Generally nats are considered to be malicious unles they are constantly appeased or placated. Buddhist monks and Nat-priests alike see to their worship by performing the required periodic ceremonies; a *natsin* ("nat house" or "spirit shrine") is located in every pagoda and in each village.

There are different types of nats envoked for different needs; one group consisting of four species is similar to the HAMADRYADS of classical Greek mythology, AKAKASOH, BOOMASOH, HMIN, and SHEKKASOH. Another group of four has dominion over the air: JAN, MBŌN, MU, and SHITTA. Other types of nats include the SABA-LEIPPYA, SINLAP, THIEN, TRIKURAT, and the UPAKA.

Sources: Porteous, *Forest in Folklore and Mythology*, 125; Scott, *The Burman: His Life and Notions*, Volume 1, 286

Nature Spirit

Variations: Elemental, KAMI, Nature Deities

Nature spirits are common in many of the world's folklore, mythologies, religions, and spiritual beliefs; they have appeared in Aborigine, African, ancient Greek and Roman, Hawaiian, Japanese, Native American, Norse, Polynesian, and Shinto to name but a scant few. These beings are perhaps best described as being the energy of the animals and plants of nature. Nature spirits are also decribed as being ther spirits or returned souls of deceased ancestors. In most cases nature spirits have the ability to shape-shift, taking on an unlimited array of animal forms; these fairies can be female, male, or genderless. As beings of nature, they are neither good nor evil but are labeled as such by human perceptions. When these fairies are described as wearing clothing they are said to dress in green.

Sources: Barstow, *Elementally Speaking*, 16–17; Bord, *Fairies*, 111–12; Keightly, *World Guide to Gnomes, Fairies, Elves, and Other Little People*, 34; McCoy, *Witch's Guide to Faery Folk*, 32–34

Nausithoe

A sea–NYMPH, Nausithoe, was the NEREIDS of swift ships in classical Greek mythology; she was born the daughter of Nerues and DORIS.

Sources: Apollodorus of Athens, *Apollodorus' Library and Hyginus' Fabulae*, 2; Bell, *Bell's New Pantheon*, 97; Trzaskoma, *Anthology of Classical Myth*, 18

Navky

Variations: Latawci, Majky, Mavje, Mavky, Nakki, Navi, Navjaci, Navje, Nejky

A type of NATURE SPIRIT, the navky ("dead") is the collective name for the returned spirits of children who died without having been baptized or were born to mothers who met with a violent death. Navky are very similar to the RUSALKY ("WATER SPIRIT").

The latawci of Poland will wander the earth for seven years begging for someone to baptize it; if no one does it will transform into a navje.

As the Mavky, these fairies are created when a child was drowned by its mother; it appears as a beautiful young girl with curly hair or as small baby. Angry at those who permitted their death they can be banished by shouting a baptism prayer at them. After a few years if not laid to rest, it will dissolve into a water NYMPH.

In Bulgaria the navky, created when an unbaptized child dies, are described as invisible bird-like beings with a cry sounding like an infant; they single out troubled mothers to attack but can be banished if a baptismal prayer is said over it. In Slovenia these beings appear as large black birds crying out to be baptized; doing so gains their blessing by mocking them will rise their wrath.

Sources: Allardice, *Myths, Gods and Fantasy*, 157; Gray, *Mythology of All Races*, Volume 3, 253–5; Monaghan, *New Book of Goddesses and Heroines*, 227

Neaera

Variations: Neaira

In Greek mythology Neaera was a NYMPH and the mother of a daughter by the god Zeus (Jupiter) named Aegel. In Homer's epic poem *The Odyssey*, Neaira was a NYMPH from the mythical island of Thrinakie; by the sun god, Helios (Sol), she had two daughters, Lamperia (LAMPETIE) and Phaëthousa (PHAETHUSA); collectively the sisters were known as the Neaireides.

Sources: Bell, *Women of Classical Mythology*, 319; Dixon-Kennedy, *Encyclopedia of Greco-Roman Mythology*, 149; Lemprière, *Lempriere's Classical Dictionary for Schools and Academies*, 17

Neasa

A sea–NYMPH from Greek mythology, Neasa, was the friendly, generous NEREIDS; she was born the daughter of Nerues and DORIS.

Source: Betham, *Transactions of the Royal Irish Academy*, Volume 17, 88

Neck

Variations: Bäckahästen ("brook horse"), Fossegrim, KELPIE, NÄCKEN, NÄKKI, Nickur, Nikar, Ninner, 'Nix, NIXIE, Nixe, Nökke, Nyx, Rügen Nickle, Strömkarlen, Water-Spirit

The neck of Scandinavian lore is similar to the AUGHISKY of Ireland, the HNIKUR of the Faroe Islands, the KELPIE of Scotland, and the NÄKKI of Finland; a shape-shifting WATER SPIRIT, the neck take on an appearance found to be very sexually attractive to humans. Sitting upon a rock near a water source a neck will play a musical instrument and using its hypnotic singing voice, lure in close its prey and then drown them. Sometimes the neck is described as a horse, an old man with long beard, having the upper body of a man and the lower body of a horse, or a golden locked young man wearing a red cap.

Like the NÄCKEN, the neck will teach his art of harp playing if he is given a black lamb and the solemn promise of Christian redemption and resurrection.

Particular to Iceland the neck is said to appear as fine apple-grey horse running along the seashore. Except for the fact that its hooves are facing backward, it can pass as a mortal horse. Anyone who mounts this FAIRY ANIMAL will be carried off into the sea and likely drowned. If a neck can be bridled with a bit of tack known as a *binda neckon* ("to bind the neck") while in its equine form, this fairy being will make for an excellent plow horse. This special halter likely contains elements of steel in it.

Sources: Keightly, *World Guide to Gnomes, Fairies, Elves, and Other Little People*, 1447–49; McCoy, *Witch's Guide to Faery Folk*, 279; Thorpe, *Northern Mythology*, Volume 2, 78–9

Neda

Variations: Nede

Neda was a NYMPH charged with the care and feeding of the infant god, Zeus (Jupiter), along with HAGNO and THEISOA in ancient Greek mythology. In art, Neda was depicted holding the infant god in her arms. It was said she was the first river to appear in a waterless land in Messene; this was unique because usually in Greek lore rivers have gods, not NYMPHS, associated with them.

Sources: Larson, *Greek Nymphs*, 153; Pausanias, *Pausanias's Description of Greece*, Volume 1, 414, 434

Nelly Longarms

Variations: Nelly Long-Arms

In the folklore of England, Nelly Longarms was a NYMPH or water-fairy who lived in ponds and rivers with green scum floating on the surface. When children came to close to her domain, she reached out, grabbed, and held them under the water until they drowned. She had been known to take up temporary residence in trees and could be heard moaning in the night. Similar to JENNY GREENTEETH and PEG POWLER, she was used by parents as a NURSERY BOGIE. The male equivalent of Nelly Longarms is called NICKY NYE.

Sources: Briggs, *Encyclopedia of Fairies*, 339; Rose, *Giants, Monsters, and Dragons*, 264; Simpson, *Dictionary of English Folklore*, N.p.; Wright, *Rustic Speech and Folk-Lore*, 198–9

Nelo

In Greek mythology Nelo was a water–NYMPH and one of the named DANAIDS, the collective name for the daughters of Danaus. In a list compiled by Apollodorus, a Greek scholar and grammarian, she was one of the daughters of an unnamed Ethiopian woman and was wedded to Menemachus, one of the sons of an unnamed Phoenician woman.

Sources: Apollodorus, *Gods and Heroes of the Greeks*, 69; Grimal, *Dictionary of Classical Mythology*, 127; Lemprière, *Classical Dictionary*, 236

Nemea

A NYMPH from the town of Nemea in Argos located in southern Greece, Nemea ("she is Nemeia") was born the daughter the daughter of the god Zeus (Jupiter) and the moon goddess, Selene.

Sources: Avant, *Mythological Reference*, 292; Hard, *Routledge Handbook of Greek Mythology*, 256

Nemertes

A sea–NYMPH, Nemertes ("the giver") was the NEREID of unerring (good council), she is said to be the wisest of the sisters as stated by the Greek oral poet, Hesiod, she had "the mind of her immortal father." She was one of the named NEREID who accompanied THETIS in mourning the loss of her son, Achilles.

Sources: Betham, *Transactions of the Royal Irish Academy*, Volume 17, 89; Apollodorus, *Apollodorus' Library and Hyginus' Fabulae*, 95; Collignon, *Manual of Mythology*, 18; Gould, *Historic Magazine and Notes And Queries*, Volume 14, 212; Hesiod, *Works of Hesiod, Callimachus, and Theognis*, 15

Nemesis

Born one of the 3,000 daughters of the Titians, Oceanus and Tethys, Nemesis ("an agent") was one of the named OCEANIDS from Greek mythology. Not to be confused with the goddess of the night and vengeance who has the same name, there also was, according to Strabo the Greek geographer, historian, and philosopher, an ash-tree NYMPH bearing the title ADRASTEIA ("inescapable"). She was one of the nurses who took care of the infant god, Zeus (Jupiter).

Sources: Daly, *Greek and Roman Mythology A to Z*, 89; Littleton, *Gods, Goddesses, and Mythology*, Volume 11, 959–61

Nemglan

Nemglan was the Irish FAIRY KING of birds. Appearing on only one myth, Nemglan appeared to the heroine Mess Buachalla in the form of a bird and seduced her. Their son, Conaire went on to become a king of Tara; he was forbidden to ever harm a bird because of his origins. Before Conaire is crowned king, his father, Nemglan appears to him and explains to his son the secrets of success.

Sources: Monaghan, *Encyclopedia of Celtic Mythology and Folklore*, 354; Wallace, *Folk-lore of Ireland*, 90

Neomeris

A sea–NYMPH, Neomeris, was one of the named NEREIDS in classical Greek mythology; she was born the daughter of Nerues and DORIS.

Sources: Apollodorus, *Apollodorus' Library and Hyginus' Fabulae*, 2; Bell, *Women of Classical Mythology*, 321; Trzaskoma, *Anthology of Classical Myth*, 18

Nephelai

According to the ancient Greek oral poet, Hesiod, the nephelai were the NYMPHS of rainclouds.

Sources: Rigoglioso, *Cult of Divine Birth in Ancient Greece*, 87

Nephele

Variations: Nephelê

Born one of the 3,000 daughters of the Titians, Oceanus and Tethys, Nephele ("cloud") was one of the named OCEANIDS; one of the younger OCEANIDS, she was also one of the NEREIDS. According to the ancient Greek oral poet, Hesiod, Nephele was one of the OCEANID NYMPHS which formed the retinue of the goddess, Artemis (Diana).

In another version of the myth Nephele began life as a cloud-like mass created by the god Zeus (Jupiter) to trick Ixion who was attempting to seduce his wife, the goddess Hera (Juno). The cloud resembled the goddess and through her union with Ixion became the parents to Centauros, the progenitors of the centaur race. Nephele went on to marry Athamas and have three more children, Helle, Leucon, and Phrixus.

Sources: Daly, *Greek and Roman Mythology A to Z*, 89; Day, *God's Conflict with the Dragon and the Sea*, 47; Dixon-Kennedy, *Encyclopedia of Greco-Roman Mythology*, 217

Nera

Variations: Le Fate Nera

Nera is one of the two FATES appearing in Matteo Maria Boiardo's epic poem *Orlando Innamorato* ("*Orlando in Love*," 1495) from the Italian Renaissance period. In the poem, Nera and fellow Fate BIANCA are the protectors of Aquilante, son of Ricciardetto, and Guidone, likely the son of Boveto d'Antona, the poem is vague as to his parentage.

Sources: Brewer, *Character Sketches of Romance, Fiction and the Drama*, 5; Keightly, *World Guide to Gnomes, Fairies, Elves, and Other Little People*, 452

Nereids

Variations: Neriads, Nereides, Nêreïdes, Nêrêïdes, NEREIS, Nerine

Nereids are one of the twelve different species of NYMPH in classical Greek mythology; they are the NYMPHS of the Mediterranean Sea in general and the Aegean Sea in particular. Born the daughters of Nereus and DORIS, an OCEANID, the Nereids ("wet ones") are blue- and golden-haired sea NYMPHS, often found in the company of Poseidon (Neptune), the god of the sea. Always friendly and well known to help sailors who are caught in dangerous storms, the nereids are described as being both beautiful and youthful. Typically they are depicted naked, holding fish in their hands, and surrounded by dolphins, hippokampoi, and various sea animals. On occasion they have been portrayed as being half maiden and half fish, like a MERMAID.

Living in the underwater palace of their father, these sea–NYMPHS each have a golden throne of their own within the palace. They pass their time riding dolphins, spinning, and weaving. THETIS, the wife of Peleus and mother of Achilles, is portrayed as their leader.

Typically, the nereids are said to be fifty in number, although some sources claim there are as many as a hundred. Homer names thirty-three of the nereids in his works. In modern Greek folklore the word *nereid* is used when referring to all fairies and NYMPHS and not strictly the sea–NYMPHS.

The hermetic and neo-Platonic doctrine from which all medieval medicine and science was founded describes four Elemental classes, Air, Earth, Fire, and Water; accordingly the Nereids (see UNDINES) belong to the Water class, GNOMES to Earth, SALAMANDERS to Fire, and SLYPHS to Air.

Sources: Briggs, *Encyclopedia of Fairies*, 192–3; Daly, *Greek and Roman Mythology A to Z*, 90; Dixon-Kennedy, *Encyclopedia of Greco-Roman Mythology*, 217; Evan-Wentz, *Fairy Faith in Celtic Countries*, 290' Littleton, *Gods, Goddesses, and Mythology, Volume 11*, 999

Nereis

One of the HOMERIC NYMPHS from ancient Greek mythology, Nereis was known to have "blessed the bed" of many of the heroes and warriors who fought at the battle of Troy. Born the daughter of the sea–NYMPH, Nereus, Nereis was said to have been one of the constant companions to Neptune, the god of the sea. She, like all but THETIS of the NEREIDS has no individual character traits.

Sources: *Columbian Cyclopedia*, Volume 20, 20; Keightly, *World Guide to Gnomes, Fairies, Elves, and Other Little People*, 445; Larson, *Greek Nymphs*, 61

Nesaea

A sea–NYMPH from Greek mythology, Nesaea was one of the named NEREID who accompanied THETIS in mourning the loss of her son, Achilles.

Sources: Apollodorus, *Apollodorus' Library and Hyginus' Fabulae*, 95; Hesiod, *Works of Hesiod, Callimachus, and Theognis*, 15; Perry, *Women of Homer*, 146

Nesaie

Variations: Nesaia

Nesaie was the NEREIS of islands in classical Greek mythology; she was born the daughter of Nerues and DORIS. Nesaie was one of the named NEREID who accompanied THETIS in mourning the loss of her son, Achilles.

Sources: Apollodorus, *Apollodorus' Library and Hyginus' Fabulae*, 2; Collignon, *Manual of Mythology*, 18; Trzaskoma, *Anthology of Classical Myth*, 18

Nesnas Mhiccallain

Variations: DIREACH, Direach Ghlinn Eitidh ("DWARF of Glen Etive")

The desert creature of glen Eiti, Nesnas Mhiccallain was a FACHAN, GIANT, and a woodcutter. When the would-be king of Ireland, Murachadh Mac Brian, lost his red eared hounds while out on a hunt, he was challenged to a race by the fairy. In spite of his greater size, Nesnas Mhiccallain lost the race.

Sources: Campbell, *Popular Tales of the West Highlands*, 297–8; Cowan, *Ley Lines and Earth Energies*, 236; Rose, *Giants, Monsters, and Dragons*, 99

Neso

A sea–NYMPH from Greek mythology, Neso ("nimble") was the NEREID of the islands, according to Hesiod.

Sources: Bell, *Bell's New Pantheon or Historical Dictionary of the Gods*, 112; Betham, *Transactions of the Royal Irish Academy*, Volume 17, 88

Nete

Variations: MELETE

One of the MUSES from Greek mythology, Nete ("lowest," literally "our highest") was the MUSE of the last and most acute cord of the lyre, a popular Greek musical instrument (see also HYPATE and MESE). Nete was associated with Delphi, Greece.

Sources: McLean, *Triple Goddess*, 54; Monro, *Modes of Ancient Greek Music*, 31; Peterson, *Mythology in Our Midst*, 121

Niägruisar

In the Feroe Islands the niägruisar are a species of BROWNIE or NISSES; they are described as small beings wearing a red cap. Bringing luck to any place they take up residence

Sources: Brewer, *Dictionary of Phrase and Fable*, 631; Campbell, *Superstitions of the Highlands and Islands of Scotland*, 191; Keightly, *World Guide to Gnomes, Fairies, Elves, and Other Little People*, 163

Niamh

Variations: Neeve, Niam, Niamh of the Golden Hair, Niau, Niave

In the folklore of Ireland, Niamh ("bright" or "radiant") is one of the fairies of the TUATHA DÉ DANANN; she was said to have been so beautiful no mortal man could resist her. A FAIRY QUEEN, Niamh was married to Osiam; together they live in the land of Tir Nan Og ("land of the young"). Niamh on an island called Tir Tairngiri ("land of promise").

Sources: Joyce, *Ancient Celtic Romances*, 390; Monaghan, *Encyclopedia of Celtic Mythology and Folklore*, 358; Rose, *Spirits, Fairies, Leprechauns, and Goblins*, 235, 351

Nibelung

Variations: Nibelungen

Nibelung was one of the many DWARFS named in the *Voluspa*, the first and best known poem of the *Poetic Edda*, a collection of Old Norse poems dating back to about A.D. 985; he was named as being a king of the DWARFS. Nibelung lived in a crystal palace in a subterranean domain; his treasure hoard was guarded by the dragon, FAFNIR.

Sources: Daly, *Norse Mythology A to Z*, 22; Keightly, *World Guide to Gnomes, Fairies, Elves, and Other Little People*, 206; McCoy, *Witch's Guide to Faery Folk*, 281–2; Sykes, *Who's Who in Non-Classical Mythology*, 53

Nicaea

Variations: Nixoia

Nicaea was a NYMPH from the mythology of classical Greece and Rome; she was worshiped in Bithynia, Anatolia. One of the NAIADS, she was the daughter of the goddess Cyble and the river god, Sangarius. A sworn virgin hunter dedicated to the goddess Artemis (Diana), Nicaea, similar to NYMPH KALYBE, continually rejected the love of a shepherd named Hymnus. When he would not desist, she shot him through the heart with an arrow, angering the god, Eros (Cupid) who inspired the god, Dionysus (Bacchus) to fall in love with her. Because she rejected his love as well, the god temporarily turned the waters of her fountains into wine and while she was in a stupor, raped her. Failing a suicide attempt, she gave birth to the mainad, Telete.

Sources: Bell, *Women of Classical Mythology*, 323, 412; Rigoglioso, *Cult of Divine Birth in Ancient Greece*, 97, 99; Smith, *Dictionary of Greek and Roman Biography and Mythology*, 1173

Nicky Nye

In the folklore of England, Nicky Nye was a male NYMPH or water-fairy who lived in ponds and rivers with green scum floating on the surface. When children came too close to his domain, he reached out, grabbed, and held them under the water until they drowned. Similar to JENNY GREENTEETH and PEG POWLER, he was used by parents as a NURSERY BOGIE. The female equivalent of Nicky Nye was called NELLY LONGARMS.

Sources: Briggs, *Dictionary of British Folk-Tales in the English Language*, 422–35; Simpson, *Dictionary of English Folklore*, N.p.; Tongue, *Forgotten Folk Tales of the English Counties*, 113–14

Nicnevin

Variations: The Bone Mother, GYRE-CARLIN, Nicnevan

In the Scottish Lowlands it was believed Nicnevin was a FAIRY QUEEN; originally a goddess with the ability to transform water into dry land, she would fly through the air invisibly by night leading the FAIRY RADE.

Sources: Briggs, *Encyclopedia of Fairies*, 319; Illes, *Encyclopedia of Spirits*, 760; Jamieson, *Etymological Dictionary of the Scottish Language*, n.p.

Nidi

Nidi ("fading moon" or "kinsman") was one of the many DWARFS named in the *Voluspa*, the first and best known poem of the *Poetic Edda*, a collection of Old Norse poems dating back to about A.D. 985.

Sources: Crossley-Holland, *Norse Myths*, 183; Daly, *Norse Mythology A to Z*, 22; Wägner, *Asgard and the Gods*, 311; Wilkinson, *Book of Edda called Völuspá*, 12

Nikaia

A NYMPH of the town of Nikaia in Bithynia, Nikaia was, according to Greek mythology, raped by the god of wine, Dionysus (Bacchus), and by him bore a daughter named Telete.

Sources: Avant, *Mythological Reference*, 324; Rose, *Handbook of Greek Mythology*, 156

Nilus

Born one of the 3,000 daughters of the Titians, Oceanus and Tethys, Nilus was one of the named OCEANIDS from Greek mythology.

Sources: Boswell, *What Men or Gods Are These*, 58; Day, *God's Conflict with the Dragon and the Sea*, 64; Hesiod, *Works of Hesiod, Callimachus, and Theognis*, 20

Ningyo

First recorded in A.D. 619 during the twenty-seventh year of the reign of Empress Suiko, the ningyo ("human fish") are FAIRY ANIMALS from Japanese lore; its name is typically translated as MERMAID, but it is in fact not human or MERMAID-like in appearance.

Originally they were described as having a crest of thick fur atop its head; humanoid, webbed fingers; a monkey-like mouth; small fish-like teeth; and golden scales. Like the SIREN, these beings have a hauntingly beautiful voice, similar to a flute or skylark; their song does not consist of words but is nevertheless still hypnotic.

In their underwater domain, the ningyo lived in a highly intricate society; they were believed to be highly skilled in the art of healing and magic. If a fisherman caught one, it was considered to bring about misfortune and storms so these fairies were usually thrown back. If a ningyo was willing to offer up a bit of itself, anyone who consumed any amount of its flesh would grant immortality. The blood of the ningyo was said to have the ability to heal any wound. However to take these elements from the fairy without its permission was to be the victim of dire consequences.

In the modern telling the mythology the ningyo is now described as looking like a traditional MERMAID, having long black hair rather than the golden or green of Celtic lore. Elusive and avoiding human contact, it is believed the sighting of a ningyo brings good luck. It is also believe when they cry their tears are precious pears of considerable value.

Sources: Loar, *Goddesses for Every Day*, 72; Rosen, *Mythical Creatures Bible*, 132; Yamaguchi, *We Japanese*, 318

Nípingr

Variations: Niping

Nípingr ("pinch") was one of the many DWARFS named in the *Voluspa*, the first and best known poem of the *Poetic Edda*, a collection of Old Norse poems dating back to about A.D. 985.

Sources: Daly, *Norse Mythology A to Z*, 22; Sykes, *Who's Who in Non-Classical Mythology*, 53; Wägner, *Asgard and the Gods*, 311

Nippel

A tutelary, individual NATURE SPIRIT from Czech and German folklore the nipple kills poachers in the same method the criminal used to kill his ill-gotten game. When being helpful to good or poor people by gifting them food or gold or by alerting them when danger is approaching Nippel looks like a nobleman, otherwise, he appears as a DWARF. It is said he lives on Niklasberg Hill, located between Bela and Radbuzou and Tremesna in the Moravian-Silesian Region of the Czech Republic. There was a similar NATURE SPIRIT from Bavarian lore called Tyllenberger.

Source: Maberry, *Crytopedia*, 111

Nisaea

Variations: Nisæa

A sea–NYMPH, Nisaea was one of the named NEREID in classical Greek mythology; she was born the daughter of Nerues and DORIS.

Sources: Bell, *Bell's New Pantheon or Historical Dictionary of the Gods*, 112; Gould, *Historic Magazine and Notes and Queries*, Volume 14, 212

Nisse (plural: nissess)

Variations: Nicls, Niclsen, Nisse God-Deng, TOMTE

A fairy from Scandinavian folklore, a nisse is similar to the BROWNIE of Scotland or the NIÄGRUISAR of the Feroe Islands, helping farmers in both the barn and in the home. Bringing luck wherever they go, nissess are most active at night, particularly when the family is asleep.

Described as small, standing between a few inches to a few feet tall, having a single cyclopean eye, and wearing red caps, the nissess are social, living communally with their own kind. However, folklore says claims these fairies are also shape-shifters who are additionally skilled illusionists and able to become invisible at will.

Sources: Ashliman, *Fairy Lore*, 46, 203; Bringsværd, *Phantoms and Fairies*, 95–6; Keightly, *World Guide to Gnomes, Fairies, Elves, and Other Little People*, 163

Nixen

Variations: Nis, Nix, Urchins

In Germany and Switzerland the nixen are water fairies, living in lakes and rivers, they have been known to lure sailors and swimmers alike to their death on the rocky shoreline. Although seen in both human genders the females, alluring and lovely, are more commonly sighted, sometimes at the market purchasing meat. The male nixen are also physically attractive but are described as having green teeth. Both sexes are said to wear green hats.

There are a few stories of nixen intentionally choosing to be helpful to a human either by preventing a prowing or giving a warning of an approaching storm; however these instances are notably rare. Typically, these water fairies are said to dance along the surface of the water when a person is about to drown and will steal a child, leaving a CHANGELING in its place. The male nixen will abduct a mortal woman and keep her as its wife; later, when it is necessary, it will hire a mortal midwife to assist in the delivery of their child.

Nixen are particularly susceptible to metals, more so than other fay. When used against them, they are rendered powerless. Long term exposure to metal will kill them.

Sources: Keightly, *World Guide to Gnomes, Fairies, Elves, and Other Little People*, 258–59; McCoy, *Witch's Guide to Faery Folk*, 30; Thorpe, *Northern Mythology*, Volume 1, 246–7

Nixie

The nixie of German and Norse lore are water fairies of dubious motivations; in some stories they are malicious, luring people into the water and drowning them, while in others they are considered to be benign and friendly. The males, sometimes referred to as a nix, are shape-shifters able to assume many forms, including fish, humans, and snakes. The female of the species are described as looking like the traditional MERMAID. When these fay assume a human guise they can always be discerned for what they are as their clothes will always be wet.

Nixies, like many water fairies, live in palatial underwater castles resplendent with their riches. Mortals who have been fortunate enough to visit and were allowed to return claim the only fault with the aquatic kingdom is the food which is served at their lavish banquets are served without salt seasoning.

Sources: Illes, *Encyclopedia of Spirits*, 762; Snowe, *Rhine, Legends, Traditions, History, From Cologne to Mainz*, Volume 2, 90–2; Spence, *Hero Tales and Legends of the Rhine*, 52–4

Nokke

Variations: NECK, Nikke

In Danish fairy lore the nokke, a species of water fairy, can live in either fresh or salt water. Most often the folklore claims the nokke are always male, and will reveal themselves to about their waist from the water; however, below the surface the rest of their body is horse-like. On warm days they will sit upon the rock and beautifully play their harps wearing nothing but their

trademark red caps. Attractive and with very agreeable personalities there are many stories of a nokke falling in love with a mortal woman. As with many water-fairies, the nokke are easily repelled by metal, especially steel.

Sources: Conway, *Magickal Mystical Creatures*, 50; Keightly, *World Guide to Gnomes, Fairies, Elves, and Other Little People*, 148; McCoy, *Witch's Guide to Faery Folk*, 284–5

Nomia

Nomia was a NYMPH of Arcadia from the mythology of ancient Greece and Rome. One of the NAIADS and an OREAD, she fell in love with a handsome Sicilian goat-herder and hunter named Daphnis, son of the god, Hermes (Mercury) (see ECHENAIS); before she would fully give her herself to him she either solicited a promise he would resist the temptations of all other women or foretold if he should ever fall into the arms of another he would become blind (or be turned to stone, sources conflict). The daughter of the king fell in love with Daphnis and seduced him by giving him too much wine to drink; in his drunken stupor, he forgot his vow to Nomia and consequently became blind.

Sources: Fontenrose, *Orion*, 189–92; Larson, *Greek Nymphs*, 155–6; Lemprière, *Classical Dictionary*, 14

Nonakris

Variations: Nonacris, SYRINX

Nonakris was a NAIAD in classical Greek mythology; she was the NYMPH of the town of Nonakril in Arcadia lovated in southern Greece. Nonakris was the wife of king Lykaon.

Sources: Grant, *Who's Who in Classical Mythology*, 395, 485; Pausânias, *Guide to Greece: Southern Greece*, 414

Nonnus' Nymphs

Nonnus of Panopolis, a Greek epic poet of late antiquity, probably having lived at the end of the 4th or early 5th century described three separate species of NYMPHS. The first, hydriades (water-nymphs), were described in his principal work, *Dionysiaca*, an epic poem of 20,426 lines; in book twenty-four he describes the hydriades as mingling with the HAMADRYADS of the trees.

The second species of NYMPHS he paired together, the Neiades and Hadryades; of them in book four-teen he wrote "One all-comprehending summons was sounded for Trees and for Rivers, one call for Neiades and Hadryades, the troops of the forest."

The third and final species of Nonnus' NYMPHS appear in book fourteen of *Dionysiaca*, the wild OREIADES. The poet describes them as being very long lived, much desired by men, and wearing long robes. Of this species were the Alseides (see ALSEID), who lived in wooded glades; the EPI-MELIDES, who lived high up in the pastoral hills mingling with the shepherds; and the MELIAI who lived in the ash-tree covered mountains.

Sources: Clark, *Classical Manual,* 587; Custer, *Treasury of New Testament Synonyms*, 76; Larson, *Greek Nymphs*, 168; Rigoglioso, *Cult of Divine Birth in Ancient Greece*, 87

Nootaikok

A NATURE SPIRIT from Inuit mythology, Noo-taikok lives in the icebergs; when invoked, he will lead hunters to seals.

Sources: Andrews, *Dictionary of Nature Myths*, 15; Drew, *Wiccan Bible*, 367

Nordi

Variations: Nodri, NORDRI

Nordi ("little scrap" or "north") was one of the many DWARFS named in the *Voluspa*, the first and best known poem of the *Poetic Edda*, a collection of Old Norse poems dating back to about A.D. 985. One of the four DWARFS of the four main compass points, Nordi, along with AUSTRI ("east"), and SUDRI ("south") and WESTRI ("west") each held up one corner of the earth which is de-scribed as a flat, plate-like piece of land.

Sources: Crossley-Holland, Norse Myths, 183; Wägner, *Asgard and the Gods*, 311

Nordri

Nordri ("northerly") was one of the many DWARFS named in the *Voluspa*, the first and best known poem of the *Poetic Edda*, a collection of Old Norse poems dating back to about A.D. 985.

Sources: Daly, *Norse Mythology A to Z*, 22; Sykes, *Who's Who in Non-Classical Mythology*, 53; Wil-kinson, *Book of Edda called Völuspá*, 12

Nóri

Variations: Nori

Nóri was one of the many DWARFS named in the *Voluspa*, the first and best known poem of the *Poetic Edda*, a collection of Old Norse poems dating back to about A.D. 985; he is described as being one of the great Dwarven lords.

Sources: Crossley-Holland, Norse Myths, 183; Daly, *Norse Mythology A to Z*, 22; Sykes, *Who's Who in Non-Classical Mythology*, 53; Wägner, *Asgard and the Gods*, 311

Nornir

Variations: Norns

The nornir are a type of DJINN or FATE of Scan-dinavian lore that unequally direct and shape the destiny of mankind. Described as three old women named SKULLD (Skuldr), UDR, and VER-DANDI, they spin the threads of destiny shaping human lives; they live under the shade of the tree, Yggdrasil. SKULLD is the youngest of the three and personifies the future. VERDANDI, the middle nornir, personifies the future; Urdr the eldest per-sonifies the past. The nornir reside in a sanctuary called Gimle or Vingolf; their hall was by Urdar-brunnr Well under the branches of Yggdrasyll.

There also lesser nornir and racially descend from the ALFS, Æser (the gods), and the DWARFS; these fairies were said to assist in the birth of fu-ture eminent individuals, bestow gifts upon them, and foretell their future. The nornir are the one who apply a good life and future to a person; those individuals who seem to fall into one mis-fortune after another are the victims of a malig-nant alignment of nornir.

Sources: Du Chaillu, *Viking Age*, 385, 387, 389; Keightly, *World Guide to Gnomes, Fairies, Elves, and Other Little People*, 64–5; Norroena Society, *Satr Edda*, 4, 34

Norori

Norori was one of the many DWARFS named in the *Voluspa*, the first and best known poem of the *Poetic Edda*, a collection of Old Norse poems dating back to about A.D. 985.

Sources: Daly, *Norse Mythology A to Z*, 22; Sykes, *Who's Who in Non-Classical Mythology*, 53

Nuada Airgetlam

Variations: Nuada Argatlam, Nuada of the Sil-ver Arm, Nuada of the Silver Hand, Nuadha Airgeatlámh, Nuadhu, Nuadu

The first king of the TUATHA DÉ DANANN, Nuada Airgetlam ("Nuada of the silver arm") a great leader and powerful warrior had his right arm or hand cut off in the battle in the war against the FIRBOLGS, Magh-Tuiredh. As tradition de-manded a king must not have any physical de-formity, Nuada lost his throne for seven years to the half-Fomorian, Bres Mac Elathan. The great healer, Dian Cecht, forged a silver replacement and Miach cause skin to grow over it. Nuada was now considered to be restored and able to reclaim his throne; he then ruled for twenty years. Nuada was the personification of divine justice, justice, sovereignty, and war.

Sources: Monaghan, *Encyclopedia of Celtic Mythology and Folklore*, 361; O'Conor, *Battles and Enchantments, Retold from Early Gaelic Literature*, 7

Nuala

Queen of the Munster fairies, Nuala, according to some Irish legends, was a FAIRY QUEEN and the wife of the King of the TUATHA DÉ DANANN, FINVARRA.

Sources: Briggs, *Encyclopedia of Fairies*, 311; McCoy, *Witch's Guide to Faery Folk*, 21; Rose, *Spirits, Fairies, Leprechauns, and Goblins*, 240, 351

el Nuberu

Variations: Nuberos

El nuberu was a NATURE SPIRIT in Austrian and Spanish lore; sometime he was considered to be an individual entity while other tales say it was a species of deformed DWARF-like beings living in the clouds. Both mythologies were very similar to one another.

As an individual entity, el Nuberu was called a "lord of tempests"; this bright eyed, big eared, and dark skinned fairy was described as wearing furs, a cloak, and a large hat. If a farmer was respectful to him, el Nuberu would see to it the proper amount of rain fell so crops will be plentiful. However, if he felt he had been treated poorly this vindictive fairy would send destructive hail and rain storms. If el Nuberu actually hated an individual he would send a plague of frogs to the offender's farm. He, like many fairies from the region, such as BASA-ANDRE, BASA-JUAN and the LAMINAK, could be driven off by the ringing of bells.

Sources: Maberry, *Cryptopedia*, 112; Mountain, *Celtic Encyclopedia*, Volume 5, 1108

Nuckelavee

Variations: Knoggelvi, Mukkelevi, Nuckalavee, Nuchlavis

In Scotland, on the Orkney Islands, there was a vampiric fay known as Nuckelavee. Described as looking like a skinless centaur, it had a piglike nose that snorts steam, an overly wide mouth, and one large bloodshot eye in the middle of its forehead, which was about three feet wide. Its body was covered in thick yellow veins pumping its black blood; its overly long arms almost reached the ground as it walked.

Nuckelavee was the bane to all animals, humans, and plants; it even caused its own particular disease, *mortasheen*. Should it breathe upon a person, they would begin to wither up and die.

Nuckelavee caused droughts, epidemics, and had been known to drive herds of animals off cliffs and into the sea, where it was said to live. In fact, any area of unexplained ruin or destruction was said to be its handiwork.

Nuckelavee was repelled by the smell of burning seaweed; oftentimes it was gathered and burnt as a precaution. Like all fay, it was repelled by iron, but Nuckelavee was also deterred by fresh water and falling rain, and it couldnot cross running water. During the summer months, it was locked away by MITHER O' THE SEA, the Orcadian concept of Mother Nature.

Sources: Douglas, *Scottish Fairy Tales, Folklore, and Legends*, 160; McCoy, *Witch's Guide to Faery Folk*, 285; Monaghan, *Encyclopedia of Celtic Mythology and Folklore*, 362

Nuggie

Variations: Neugle, Noggle, Nogle, Nuggie, NUGGLE, Nygel

A water FAIRY ANIMAL from the lore of Scalloway, Scotland, it was believed to live in the Njugals Water. Described as looking like a horse with a wheel-like tail arching up and over its back, the nuggie, like the EACH UISGE would appear as a bridled and saddled horse. When a rider would climb up on its back, the nuggie would dash off into the water and attempt to drown its victim. Fond of mills and water wheels, the nuggie would take great pleasure in making the wheel stop spinning by backing up into it.

In the folklore, of Cornwall, England, there was a type of fairy also called a nuggie said to live in tin-mines; they were very similar to KNOCKERS.

Sources: Briggs, *Encyclopedia of Fairies*, 255; Rose, *Spirits, Fairies, Leprechauns, and Goblins*, 235; Wright, *English Dialect Dictionary*, 309

Nuggle

Variations: Noggle, Nygel, Nyuggle

A FAIRY ANIMAL from the Shetland Islands, the nuggle is similar to the other water horses, such as the KELPIE; it will use its shape-shifting abilities to take the form of a magnificent grey Shetland pony and entice a weary traveler to ride it whereupon it. As soon as it is mounted, the nuggle will bolt running, delivering a wild ride to its passenger; the ordeal only begins to end when the fairy crashes into a lake or river, attempting to drown its prey.

Never seen far from water the nuggle will also torment mill owners; this most frequently happens as they attempt to grind corn. Using it back the FAIRY ANIMAL will back up against the water wheel and prevent it from spinning, no matter how much water is rushing over the top of it. The only way to make the creature more is drop a fire brand as close to it as possible, as they are terrified of fire.

Sources: Briggs, Encyclopedia of Fairies, 277; Littell, *Living Age*, Volume 150, 811–12; Monaghan, *Encyclopedia of Celtic Mythology and Folklore*, 362–63

Nukir Mai Tore

Similar to the fey of western lore the Nukir Mai Tore ("people of the otherworld") of Polynesian mythology were not as injurious as the ATUA from New Zealand; rather they were reclusive, shy, and lived in the trees of the forest. On occasion, one of the Nukir Mai Tore would marry a human. It was not acceptable to say their real name aloud; anyone who attempted to do so would discover their tongue had become paralyzed and rendered them speechless.

Source: Illes, *Encyclopedia of Spirits*, 44

Number Nip

Variations: The Great King, RUBEZAHL ("turnip counter"), Spirit of the GIANT Mountains

Number Nip seems to be the British equivalent of a German FAIRY KING called RUBEZAHL. A GNOME or ELF king of Das Riesengebirge ("GIANT Mountain"), the highest mountain in the Czech Republic and overlooking the Black Forest, Number Nip was the most powerful of the FAIRY KINGS in German and Scandinavian folklore.

In British lore he rules over all the DWARFS and fire spirits in his underground kingdom. His subjects spend their days forging and mining copper, diamonds, gold, iron, silver, and an array of precious gems while he rules from his throne surrounded by the wisest of his subjects as laws and pertinent decisions are made regarding his rulership. On occasion he will visit his lands above and amuse himself by playing pranks on humans, punishing those who do evil and rewarding those who do well. A consummate shape-shifter there is no telling what appearance or form he will assume while entertaining himself.

Sources: Brinton, *Science*, Volume 4, 135–36; Brewer, *Dictionary of Phrase and Fable*, 901; Grahame, *Stories about Number Nip*, 1–5

Nunnehi

Variations: The Gentle People, the Immortals, Nunne'hi, the People Who Live Anywhere

The Elves of the Cherokee people of Pilot Knob, North Carolina, the nummehi ("people who live anywhere"), described as looking like the Indians themselves, these fairies live in subterranean towns. In some telling of their folklore the nunnehi are said to be very small while in others they are as tall as a man; they are otherwise gourd- headed and hairless.

According to the legend the nummehi foresaw a great disaster coming that would destroy the Cherokee people so the fairies approached the tribe and begged them to follow them to a safe place to live. The tribe agreed and after a week's long trek they arrived in an earthly paradise. For a long time they peacefully co-existed but one day the nummehi came to them again and warned them of a terrible time approaching; the nummehi wanted the Cherokee to follow them into their subterranean home and live there with them, but the tribe did not want to leave their beautiful home. The nummehi warned once the stone was rolled across the opening to their underground lands it would not open again for many, many years, if at all. Determined to stay, the nummehi retreated below the surface and sealed the way behind them; not long later the Cherokee were forced to walk the Trail of Tears and were relocated to Oklahoma.

Sources: Avant, *Mythological Reference*, 475; Duncan, *Living Stories of the Cherokee*, 71–3; Taylor, *Native American Myths and Legends*, 16–17

Nuno

Variations: Lamang-Lupa, Nuno sa Punso ("grandparent of the anthill"), Taong-Lupa ("man of the earth")

In Philippine mythology the nuno ("grandfather") was a DWARF-like being living in anthills and termite mounds and was described as looking like a small old man with long beard standing only a few feet tall. If ever an anthill was stepped upon offerings of rice and viand was made while forgiveness was asked.

Sources: Demetrio, *Encyclopedia of Philippine Folk Beliefs and Customs*, Volume 2, 403; Licauco, *Dwarfs and Other Nature Spirits*, 172

Nursery Bogie

Variations: Frightening Figures

A nursery bogie is any FAIRY ANIMAL or being used by parents to frighten their children into good behavior; they appear in many cultures. Generally, these beings not only have a frightening physical appearance but also extremely harsh, if not deadly means, by which they deal with mortals. Nursery bogies are not only used to urge children into proper social behavior but also to protect crops and keep children away from dangerous environments and situations.

Some examples of a nursery bogie are APO-TAMKIN, AWD GOGGIE, BERCHTA, BILLY WINKER, BLACK ANNIS, BLOODY-BONES, BODACH, BOGEY-MAN, BUCCA DHU, BUGBEAR, BUGUL-NOZ, CHURN MILK PEG, CLAP-CANS, CUCO, GRINDYLOW, JENNY GREENTEETH, LAZY LAWRENCE, MELSH DICK, NÄKKI, NUT-NANS, RAWHEAD REX, TAN-KERABOGUS, TOM DOCKIN, and TOM-POKER.

Sources: Briggs, *Encyclopedia of Fairies*, 313; Rose, *Spirits, Fairies, Leprechauns, and Goblins*, 241; Wright, *Rustic Speech and Folk-Lore*, 198

Nut-Nans

Nut-Nans is an invisible NURSERY-BOGEY from the folklore of England that makes scary sounds.

Sources: Buckton, *Notes and Queries*, 156; Wright, *English Dialect Dictionary*, 313

Ny

Ny was one of the many DWARFS named in the *Voluspa*, the first and best known poem of the *Poetic Edda*, a collection of Old Norse poems dating back to about A.D. 985. Ny was the son of Modsogner-Mimmer in the sense it was he who created and gave the DWARF life.

Sources: Daly, *Norse Mythology A to Z*, 22; Rydberg, *Teutonic Mythology*, Volume 2, 640

Nyamatsane

In the fairy-tale *The Little Hare* the nyamatsane are a species of Fairy whose liver is considered to be a rare delicacy. These fairies live in large family units near marshy areas; they have the ability to smell a human if one is nearby. Nyamatsane eat pebbles and amuse themselves by leaping over ditches. With the ability to track by scent and being very fast runners, the nyamatsane will tear apart a man if they capture one; fortunately, they will not enter into a human settlement because they are hated by dogs who are their natural enemy.

Source: Lang, *Pink Fairy Book*, 321–33

Nycheia

Variations: Nykheia

Nycheia was a NYMPH of a fountain on the island of Propontis in Greek mythology; she was described as having "spring time in her eyes." Along with the NYMPHS EUNICA and MALIS, as they were preparing to dance saw a young boy name Hylas who traveled with the Argonauts; instantly enamored with him, they took him by the hand and pulled him into the fountain.

Sources: *Encyclopaedia Britannica*, Volume 16, Issue 1, 313; Lang, *Tales of Troy and Greece*, 196; Larson, *Greek Nymph*, 67, 155–6; Pache, *Moment's Ornament*, 161

Nýi

Variations: Nyi

Nýi ("new") was one of the many DWARFS named in the *Voluspa*, the first and best known poem of the *Poetic Edda*, a collection of Old Norse poems dating back to about A.D. 985.

Sources: Crossley-Holland, Norse Myths, 183; Daly, *Norse Mythology A to Z*, 22; Sykes, *Who's Who in Non-Classical Mythology*, 53; Wägner, *Asgard and the Gods*, 311

Nymph

In ancient Greek lore, the nymphs were lesser deities or NATURE SPIRITS, whose dominion or realm was over a cave, glade, landform, ocean, river, stream, tree, well, or the like. Depicted nude and having a reputation for being promiscuous, these beings frequently were the companion or lovers to the gods. Small and beautiful these seductive fairies could also choose to marry and live out a life with a mortal man. They were honored with prayers and sacrifices made to them at cairns and shrines.

There are twelve different species of nymph: the ATLANTID were any and all the offspring of the primordial Titan, Atlas; DRAYAD were the nymphs of the forests and trees, the oak in particular; HAMADRYAD were the nymphs of trees in general; the HYAD were the daughters of Atlas and AETHRA; LIMNIAD were the nymphs of lakes, marshes, and swamps, they were dangerous to travelers; LIMONIAD were the nymphs of the flowers and meadows; NAIAD were nymphs of the freshwater lakes, rivers, and springs; the NAPAEA were the nymphs of valleys that have grazing herds; the NEREID were the sea-nymphs of the Mediterranean Sea in general and the Aegean sea in particular; OCEANID were the nymphs of the oceans as well as fountains and streams; the OREAD were the nymphs of mountains and grottoes; and the PLEIADES were any one of the seven daughters born of Atlas and Pleione.

Originally the word *nymph* signified a newly married woman, taken from the Greek word "bride" and "veiled."

Some of the named nymphs are: ABA, BEN-
THESIKYME, CHALCIS, DROSERA, and ERATO.

Sources: Keightly, *World Guide to Gnomes, Fairies,
Elves, and Other Little People*, 444; Littleton, *Gods,
Goddesses, and Mythology, Volume 11*, 999; McCoy, *A
Witch's Guide to Faery Folk*, 286; Rose, *Spirits, Fairies,
Leprechauns, and Goblins, an Encyclopedia*, 242

Nýr

Variations: Nyr

Nýr ("new") was one of the many DWARFS
named in the *Voluspa*, the first and best known
poem of the *Poetic Edda*, a collection of Old
Norse poems dating back to about A.D. 985.

Sources: Crossley-Holland, *Norse Myths*, 183; Daly,
Norse Mythology A to Z, 22; Wägner, *Asgard and the
Gods*, 311

Nyrad

Variations: Nýrádr

Nyrad ("cunning") was one of the many
DWARFS named in the *Voluspa*, the first and best
known poem of the *Poetic Edda*, a collection of
Old Norse poems dating back to about A.D. 985.

Sources: Crossley-Holland, *Norse Myths*, 183; Daly,
Norse Mythology A to Z, 22; Sykes, *Who's Who in Non-
Classical Mythology*, 53; Wilkinson, *Book of Edda
called Völuspá*, 12

Nysa

Variations: Thysa

A NYMPH from the mythical Mount Nysa,
Nysa was a nurse to the infant god, Dionysus
(Bacchus), in classical Greek mythology. Collec-
tively these NYMPHS were known as the BAC-
CHANTS; their names were BACCHE, BROMIE,
ERATO, MACRIS, and NYSA.

Sources: Daly, *Greek and Roman Mythology A to Z*,
22; Hyginus, *Myths of Hyginus*, 140

Nyyrikki

In Finnish folk beliefs Nyyrikki was a singular
entity, a male NATURE SPIRITS who lived in the
forests. Born the son of the god of the forest,
Tapio, and the mistress of the woods, Miellikki,
Nyyrikki was described as being well built,
noble, and very handsome; he wore a blue vest
and red cap. In bogs, Nyyrikki was said to lay
stones in such a way as to allow travelers to cross
safely and looked after the safety of hunters.

Although Nyyrikki had many sisters he only
had one who was named in the mythology with
an actual name as opposed to being called by her
most notable attribute, a female NATURE SPIRIT,
named TUULIKKI.

Sources: Latham, *Russian and Turk*, 269–271; Rose,
Spirits, Fairies, Leprechauns, and Goblins, 319

Oaf

Variations: Aufe, Aulf, Aulfe, Kielkropf, Oph

In English folklore an oaf was a deformed or
simple child believed to be a CHANGELING left by
the fairies in exchange for the human child they
stole.

Sources: Hunter, *American Encyclopedic Dictionary*, Volume 7, 2879; Merriam-Webster, *Merriam-Webster New Book of Word Histories*, 325; Rose, *Spirits,
Fairies, Leprechauns, and Goblins, an Encyclopedia*,
243

Oak King

Variations: Erl King, ROBIN GOOD FELLOW

According to contemporary folklore the Oak
King rules over the waxing year, from Yule Time
to Midsummer and represents the expansion of
growth as the days grow longer; the second half
of the year is ruled over by the HOLLY KING. As
a FAIRY KING the Oak King is depicted wearing
a breech cloth and a crown of acorns and oak
leaves.

Sources: McCoy, *Witch's Guide to Faery Folk*, 139,
286–7; Monaghan, *Encyclopedia of Celtic Mythology
and Folklore*, 248, 364; Rose, *Spirits, Fairies, Leprechauns, and Goblins, an Encyclopedia*, 103

Oakmen

Variations: Oak Men

Oakmen are male DWARFS in German fairy
lore who are the guardians of the sacred oak
groves. Although they are not friendly to mankind there are no stories of an oakman ever
having harmed a human. In British lore oakmen
are more akin to the HAMADRYADS of Greek lore,
a type of NATURE SPIRIT liveing within oak trees,
protecting the forest and wildlife while harassing
humans.

Sources: Briggs, *Folklore of the Cotswalds*, 121;
McCoy, *Witch's Guide to Faery Folk*, 288; Monaghan,
Encyclopedia of Celtic Mythology and Folklore, 365;
Rose, *Spirits, Fairies, Leprechauns, and Goblins, an
Encyclopedia*, 243

Oannes

Variations: Dagon

Originally worshiped as fish-headed god-like
being from another world by the ancient Chal-
deans the singular entity known as Oannes was
believed to have built the ancient Sumerian civilization as well as having taught art, the compilation of laws, how to build cities and found tem-

ples, and general sciences to mankind. By day Oannes lived among men but by night he entered into the Erythraean Sea (the Persian Gulf) and swam freely through the ocean in his MERMAID-like appearance. Identified with floods, Oannes is identified as a sun god and the giver of civilization and knowledge.

Sources: Jewitt, *Reliquary*, Volume 19, 195; Patrick, *Chambers's Encyclopædia*, Volume 7, 19

Obda

Variations: Koza Ia, Koza Oza, Koza Peri, Surali

A NATURE SPIRIT from the folklore of the Mari people of the former Soviet Republic it is described as being a hairy, naked, squat, human with long, pendulous breasts it keeps thrown over its shoulders. The obda typically faces backward, the direction its feet face; should it ever be seen mounted upon a horse, it will be seated there backwards as well. If ever an obda captures a person they should clog up the holes in the creatures armpits, as doing so will cause it to lose its power. If ever an obda is harmed, each drop of blood it loses and hits the earth will create a new obda; otherwise a new obda is created each time an unbaptized child dies.

Sources: Rose, *Spirits, Fairies, Leprechauns, and Goblins, an Encyclopedia*, 243; Sebeok, *Studies in Cheremis*, 86–87

Oberon

Variations: Albrich, Auberich, Auberon, Auberon, ELBERICH, Oberon le Fayé, Oseron, Oberycome

Originating in Celtic lore from the ninth century Oberon was the fairy who owned a magical cup. For the virtuous, this vessel could provide not only food but fine wine. In this oldest story of the ELF, he was said to be the child of Julius Caesar and MORGAN LE FEY.

Later in the early thirteenth century Oberon the FAIRY KING DWARF appears in a French heroic song entitled titled *Les Prouesses et faitz du noble Huon de Bordeaux*. In the song the fairy assists a noble hero named Huon in clearing his name by completing a series of seemingly impossible tasks.

Popularized in British folklore and made immortal in William Shakespeare's play *A Midsummer Night's Dream*, Oberon is presented as the FAIRY KING and the ruler of FAIRYLAND; he was said to be the husband to the FAIRY QUEEN, TITANIA. Shakespeare described the king as looking

like a DWARF but having a beautiful face and a kingly bearing. Like many fairies Oberon enjoys playing pranks on humans.

Although Oberon is more of a literary figure than a mythological one he has managed to make his way into many folkloric telling involving the fay, such as being the father of ROBIN GOOD FELLOW.

Sources: Keightly, *World Guide to Gnomes, Fairies, Elves, and Other Little People*, 40, 208; Monaghan, *Encyclopedia of Celtic Mythology and Folklore*, 365; Rose, *Spirits, Fairies, Leprechauns, and Goblins*, 244, 351

Oceanid (plural: oceanids or oceanides)

Variations: Nymphae Artemisiae ("NYMPHS of Artemis"), Nymphae Oceanides ("Oceanid Nymphs"), Nymphai Artemisiai, Nymphai Okeaninai, Ocean Nymphs, Oceanide, Okeanides, Okeanids, Okeaninai

The Oceanid of Greek and later Roman mythology are one of twelve species of NYMPHS; they are the NYMPHS of the oceans as well as fountains and streams. Generally considered to be alluring, gentle, and sweet by nature the oceanids, unlike the DRYADS, wander the ancient world, visiting glades, plains, and woodlands; there are numerous stories of how their beauty attract the attention of the gods, SATYERS, and various sylvan creatures. According to the ancient Greek oral poet, Hesiod, the OCEANID were the NYMPHS which formed the retinue of the goddess, Artemis (Diana); they were likely NEPHELAI (cloud NYMPHS).

The Titans, Oceanus and Tethys, were the parents to some 6,000 children, 3,000 of which were their daughters who were known collectively as the Oceanids; each one was the patroness of a particular cloud, flower lake, pasture, pond, river, sea, or spring; they are described as being beautiful even compared to the Greek goddesses. Although most sources will say the Oceanids were strictly females, others include their brothers among them; traditionally the sons of Oceanus and Tethys are considered to be river gods, collectively known as the Potamoi ("rivers"). The Ocenids are closely related to the NEREIDS, the NYMPHS of the Mediterranean Sea.

There are many ancient sources naming the individual Oceanids, some of them include: CALLIANASSA, EIDYIA, HESIONE, IAKHE, KHRYSEIS, and LYRIS.

Sources: Daly, *Greek and Roman Mythology A to Z*,

92; Hesiod, *Works of Hesiod, Callimachus, and Theognis*, 20; Roman, *Encyclopedia of Greek and Roman Mythology*, 341

Ocypete

Variations: Ocypeta, Okypete ("rapid")

In Greek mythology Ocypete was a water–NYMPH and one of the named DANAIDS, the collective name for the daughters of Danaus. In a list compiled by Apollodorus, a Greek scholar and grammarian, she was one of the daughters of Pieria and was wedded to Lampus, one of the sons of Gorgo.

Sources: Grimal, *Dictionary of Classical Mythology*, 127; Lemprière, *Classical Dictionary*, 236; Rose, *Spirits, Fairies, Leprechauns, and Goblins, an Encyclopedia*, 245

Ocyroe

Born one of the 3,000 daughters of the Titians, Oceanus and Tethys, Ocyroe was one of the named OCEANIDS from Greek mythology.

Sources: Bell, *Bell's New Pantheon or Historical Dictionary of the Gods,* 112; Boswell, *What Men or Gods Are These*, 58; Hesiod, *Works of Hesiod, Callimachus, and Theognis*, 20

Ocyrrhoe

Born one of the 3,000 daughters of the Titians, Oceanus and Tethys, Ocyrrhoe was one of the named OCEANIDS from Greek mythology; with the sun god, Helios (Sol), she was the mother of Phasis. According to Ovid, Ocyrrhoe was born the daughter of the centaur Chiron by the NYMPH Chariolo.

Sources: Bell, *Women of Classical Mythology*, 329; Westmoreland, *Ancient Greek Beliefs*, 24

Odmience

In Polish lore an odmience ("changed one") was a species of malicious CHANGELING. When a type of vampiric NYMPH-like demon known as the boginki ("little princess") attacked a newborn child, it left the odmience in its place so it could consume to infant.

Sources: Deck-Partyka, *Poland, a Unique Country and Its People*, 278; Maberry, *Crytopedia*, 232

O'Donoghue

The FAIRY KING of the Lough Lean fairies in Ireland, O'Donoghue rules over his fairy subjects with justice, kindness, and wisdon. It is said in Irish folklore each May Day this renowned warrior known for his pacific virtue rides forth from his underwater home mounted upon his war horse, disappearing into the lakeside mist of Loch Kjllarney.

Sources: Croker, *Fairy Legends and Traditions of the South of Ireland*, Volumes 1–3, 132; Yeats, *Fairy and Folk Tales of the Irish Peasantry*, 201

Oeme

In Greek mythology Oeme was a water–NYMPH and one of the named DANAIDS, the collective name for the daughters of Danaus; her name appears in a list of the DANAIDS generated by Gaius Julius Hyginus (ca. 64 B.C.–A.D. 17), a Latin author. Oeme was wedded to Polydector and killed him on their wedding night. In a list compiled by Apollodorus, a Greek scholar and grammarian, she was one of the daughters of Crino and was wedded to the son of Hephaestine, Arbelus.

Sources: Grimal, *Dictionary of Classical Mythology*, 127; Parada, *Genealogical Guide to Greek Mythology*, 59, 130

Oenis

Oenis was a NYMPH and alleged to have been one of the possible mothers of the god, Pan (Faunus) fathered by the god, Jupiter.

Sources: Bell, *Bell's New Pantheon*, 154, 116; King, *Historical Account of the Heathen Gods and Heroes*, 149

Oennerbanske

Variations: Oennereeske, Unnerorske ("underground folks")

In the Friesland islands, DWARFS are called oennerbanske; according to folklore they steal young girls they have fallen in love with, keeping them for a period of time before setting them free. Oennerbanske also steal human infants leaving a CHANGELING in its place; borrow money, plates and pots, and assist in the construction of churches and homes. There are also numerous accounts of the oennerbanske assisting the farmers in the field by bringing them fresh water to drink and pancakes to eat.

Sources: Keightly, *World Guide to Gnomes, Fairies, Elves, and Other Little People*, 231

Oenoe

Oenoe was a NAIAD who, in Greek mythology, married Sicinus, the son of Thoas, the king of Lemnos.

Sources: Bell, *Bell's New Pantheon*, 116; Parada, *Genealogical Guide to Greek Mythology*, 119, 130

Oenone

Variation: Oenone, Oinone

Oenone was an OREAD NYMPH of Troad in north-western Mysia, Anatolia from classical Greek mythology; she was the daughters of the river god, Cebren (Kebren) and lived in the town of Kebrene located near Mount Ida. Gifted with the gift of prophecy and a skilled physician Oenone was the first wife of Paris who abandoned her for the love of Helen of Troy. According to the story when she was confronted with the body of her former husband she was so distraught with grief she committed suicide but there are numerous version as to how the act was committed included burying herself with his body, flinging herself from the top of a high tower, leaping into his funeral pyre, strangling herself to death, and waning away with sorrow.

Sources: Bell, *Bell's New Pantheon*, 116; Lang, *Tales of Troy and Greece*, 16–7, 78–9; Larson, *Greek Nymphs: Myth, Cult, Lore*, 11, 82; Roman, *Encyclopedia of Greek and Roman Mythology*, 386

Ogre

Variations: ORCULLI, Norrgens

All throughout fairy lore exists the ogre, a cannibalistic humanoid fairy-being with an extremely malicious temperament. Described as being larger and more broad than a man but not quite the size and strength of a GIANT, the ogre is variously defined as being hairy, carrying a club and having an overly large head. The female of the species is called an ogress.

It has been suggested the word ogre originated in the pre–Christian legends of the Scandinavian Vikings. The Norse term, *yggr* ("Lord of death") was a title of the god Odin who whom human sacrifices were made. As the stories of Odin spread to the British Isles and were retold over the years the god eventually evolved into a GIANT living in the clouds and consumed human flesh and the word *yggr* transformed into the word *ogre*. Some sources claim *ogre* was a French word originally created by author Charles Perrault (1628–1703) for his book, *Histoires ou Contes du temps Passé* (1697) while other sources say it was first used by his contemporary, Marie-Catherine Jumelle de Berneville, Comtesse d' Aulnoy (1650–1705).

The fairy mythology of Yorkshire, England has more GIANT and ogre lore than any other location in the world. In Scandinavian folklore the words ogre and TROLL is oftentimes used interchangeably.

Some famous ogres from folklore, literature and mythology are Allewyn, BABAU, Babou, Balardeu, Croque-Mitaine (CROQUEMITAINE), Dents Rouge, Fine Oreille, Galaffre, GRAND COLIN, HUORCO, L'Homme Rouge, Orch, Orlo, PACOLET, PÈRE FOUETTARD, Père Lustucru, Pier Jan Claes, Raminagrobis, SAALAH, and TARTARO.

Sources: Hamilton, *Ogres and Giants*, 16–18; McCoy, *Witch's Guide to Faery Folk*, 29, 230–31; Perrault, *Histoires ou Contes du temps Passé*, 60–2, 112–18

Ogue Fairy

In Irish lore the invisible ogue fairy's kisses became the sound of singing birds whose song could inspire love. This fairy can be found around wells and romantic locations, anyplace where lovers are likely to meet.

Source: Wallace, *Folk-lore of Ireland*, 90

Ohdows

Variations: Ohdowas

The Ohdows ("underground people") are one of three types of mountain dwelling NYMPH or *JOGAH* ("DWARF people") from the folklore of the Iroquois people of North America; the GAHONGA and the GANDAYAH are the other two. Ohdows are small in size but well formed, these NATURE SPIRITS control the Underworld, a dim and sunless place populated with monstrous spirit animals all of which are very desirous of escaping into the sunlit world above. The ohdow, small, strong and sturdy, prevent this disaster from happening. They also use their magic to subdue the spirits that cause earthquakes.

Sources: Chopra, *Academic Dictionary of Mythology*, 216; Gray, *Mythology of All Races*, Volume 10, 28; Rose, *Spirits, Fairies, Leprechauns, and Goblins, an Encyclopedia*, 245

Oinia

In classical Greek mythology Oinia was one of the NAIADS daughters of the river god ASOPUS in Sikyonia and Boiotia, central and southern Greece.

Sources: Classical Association, *Classical Review*, Volume 12, 125; Quiggin, *Essays and Studies Presented to William Ridgeway*, 224

Óinn

Variations: Oin

Óinn ("shy") was one of the many DWARFS named in the *Voluspa*, the first and best known poem of the *Poetic Edda*, a collection of Old Norse poems dating back to about A.D. 985.

Sources: Crossley-Holland, *Norse Myths*, 183; Daly, *Norse Mythology A to Z*, 22; Sykes, *Who's Who in Non-Classical Mythology*, 53

Oinoe

Variations: Oeroe

Oinoe ("vine" or "wine") was an Arcadian NYMPH and one of the OCEANID from classical Greek mythology who nursed the god, Zeus (Jupiter), while he was an infant with goat's milk. She and Aither, first-born elemental god (or Hermes (Mercury), sources conflict), are sometimes said to be the mother of the god, Pan (Faunus). Oinoe was the personification of wine, as she had the ability to produce it at will. She was the wife of King Thoas.

Sources: Chambers, *Chambers's Encyclopaedia*, 582: Garland, *Introducing New Gods*, 61; Larson, *Greek Nymphs*, 309

Oinoie

In Greek mythology, Oinoie was a NYMPH of North Aegean; by Thoas, the mythical ruler of Lemnos, she bore a child named Sikinos.

Sources: Larson, *Greek Nymphs: Myth, Cult, Lore*, 54; Pache, *Moment's Ornament*, 162

Oiolyka

Variations: Oeolyca

A NYMPH in classical Greek mythology, Oiolyka was born a daughter of Briareos (Briareus) the hundred-handed GIANT.

Source: Campbell, *Greek Lyric*, 106–07

Oite

In Greek mythology, Oite was a NYMPH of Thessaly; Mount Oite in central Greece, the place where Herakles (Hercules) cremated himself, is named for her.

Sources: Larson, *Greek Nymphs*, 168; Rose, *Handbook of Greek Mythology*, 10

Okyrhoe

Born one of the 3,000 daughters of the Titians, Oceanus and Tethys, Okyrhoe ("swift flowering") was one of the named OCEANIDS in ancient Greek mythology; she was described as having a "flowering face" and was blessed to be "infinitely beautiful." She was one of the playmates of Persephone (Proserpina) and present when the goddess was kidnapped.

Another NYMPH with the name of Okyrhoe was said to have been born the daughter of the centaur Cheiron and had the gift of prophecy. Ac-cording to the mythology, after predicting the fate of Asklepios and her father, she was at Zeus's command, transformed into a horse.

Sources: Avant, *Mythological Reference*, 298; Crudden, *Homeric Hymns*, 19; Fowler, *Archaic Greek Poetry*, 14; Larson, *Greek Nymphs*, 8, 201

Ol' Doofus

Variations: Devil Hound

Ol' doofus was a FAIRY ANIMAL from the fairy lore of New Hampshire, Unites States of America; it was very similar to the BARGUEST, the BLACK SHUCK, and the GALLY-TROT.

Source: Buckland, *Weiser Field Guide to Ghosts*, 25

Old Man Winter

Variations: Father Frost, Father Winter, Frost King, JACK FROST

Old Man Winter, the personification of winter was a SEASONAL FAIRY in various Asian, European, and Scandinavian mythologies. In Lapp folklore, for instance, it was said when the snow comes off the mountain it was Old Man Winter driving his reindeer close to the earth while in Russia he was said to bring death to those who travel in winter.

Sources: McCoy, *Witch's Guide to Faery Folk*, 172; Walsh, *Were They Wise Men or Kings*, 14

Old Roger

Old Roger of British folklore is the red-faced guardian of apple-trees; it was a Celtic custom to plant a fruit-bearing tree over the grave of the recently deceased, particularly an apple tree, as the apple was the fruit of life and granted passage into the land of the gods.

Sources: Rose, *Spirits, Fairies, Leprechauns, and Goblins, an Encyclopedia*, 245; Spence, *Minor Traditions of British Mythology*, 107

Old Woman of the Mountain

Variations: Old Woman

In Welsh lore the Old Woman of the Mountain was a GWYLLION who lived on Lanhyddel Mountain in Monmouthshire. Described as looking like an old, poor woman wearing ash-colored clothes and a four-corned hat her apron; she carried a milking pail and her apron was tossed over her shoulder. This fairy was typically seen at night or on exceptionally overcast or misty day; following her was a guaranteed way to become lost. Old Woman of the Mountain was said to exclaim "Wow up!" when seen, a Welsh expression of distress; her call was said to be loud enough to be heard a parish away. In South Wales Old Woman of the Mountain was said to haunt mines and coal pits.

Sources: Illes, *Encyclopedia of Spirits*, 458; Sikes, *British Goblins*, 51; Spence, *Minor Traditions of British Mythology*, 98

Ole Luk Øj

Variations: Lukøje ("eye-closer"), Ole Luk Oie, Ole Luk Öie, Ole Lukøje

In Danish lore and as popularized by Hans Christian Anderson, Ole Luk Øj was a type of nocturnal fairy known as a SANDMAN; each night he gently lulled children to sleep and depending on their behavior distributed appropriate dreams to them. In the Anderson version of this tale Ole Luk Øj reveals not only was he the Greek god of dreams, Morpheus but his brother, also called Ole Luk Øj was the god of death.

Sources: Andersen, *Hans Christian Andersen's Stories for the Household*, 191–97; Rose, *Spirits, Fairies, Leprechauns, and Goblins*, 351

Olsen

In Danish folklore Olsen is an invisible household spirit who is the cause for any slight annoyance or inconvenience which happens in the home, such as cake missing, door being found ajar, items missing or misplaced, or toys found broken.

Sources: Rose, *Spirits, Fairies, Leprechauns, and Goblins, an Encyclopedia*, 247

Olwen

A fairy woman from Arthurian mythology, the SÍDHE, Olwen ("golden wheel" or "leaving white footprints") was likely originally a goddess of the sun; she was described having streaming yellow hair and as wearing many golden rings and red gold necklace. Having the power to spring forth white flowers with every step she took, Olwen's father, Yspaddaden Penkawr ("GIANT hawthorn tree") opposed her marriage to the hero, Kulhwch. According to the tale, *Kulhwcn and Olwen* thirteen obstacles were placed before the suitor and with the help of his beloved, was able to overcome them all and finally win consent to marry.

Sources: Evan-Wentz, *Fairy Faith in Celtic Countries*, 318; Monaghan, *Encyclopedia of Celtic Mythology and Folklore*, 369

Ombwiri

Similar to the Hamadryads from the mythology of ancient Greece, the ombwiri are a species of tree spirits in the beliefs of West Africa. Small offerings are left at trees the ombwiri are known to occupy; they are especially fond of the apa tree, the ashorin tree, and silk-cotton tree.

Sources: Hastings, *Encyclopædia of Religion and Ethics*, Volume 8, 286; Rose, *Spirits, Fairies, Leprechauns, and Goblins, an Encyclopedia*, 248

Onagh

Variations: Oonagh

In Irish folklore, Onagh was the supreme FAIRY QUEEN of the SÍDHE; she was the wife of the FAIRY KING, FINVARRA. Described as being absolutely beautiful with long golden hair sweeping the ground and wearing gowns made of glittering silver gossamer, her husband was unfaithful to her and had numerous trysts with mortal women.

Onagh had the allegiance of her provincial Queens, AINE, AOIBHINN, and CILODNA.

Sources: Briggs, *Encyclopedia of Fairies*, 317; Rose, *Spirits, Fairies, Leprechauns, and Goblins*, 248, 351; Squire, *Celtic Myth and Legend*, 162

Ónarr

Variations: Ánaar, Anar, Ánarr, ANNAR, Annarr, Annaver, Fjorgyn, Onar, Ónar, Onarr, Ónarr

Ónarr was one of the many DWARFS named in the *Voluspa*, the first and best known poem of the *Poetic Edda*, a collection of Old Norse poems dating back to about A.D. 985. As the second husband of Nott, they had a daughter named Jordr.

Sources: Grimes, *Norse Myths*, 254; Sturluson, *Prose Edda*, 25; Wägner, *Asgard and the Gods*, 311

Opis

Variations: Oupis

A sea–NYMPH, Opis was one of the named NEREID in classical Greek mythology; she was born of Nereus and DORIS.

Sources: Apollodorus, *Apollodorus' Library and Hyginus' Fabulae*, 95; Bell, *Bell's New Pantheon or Historical Dictionary of the Gods*, 112; Lemprière, *Classical Dictionary*, 468

The One with the White Hand

In Somerset, England there was a malignant NATURE SPIRIT who lived on the moors within the birch trees by the name of the One with the White Hand. Described as looking like a gaunt and pale young maiden, she darts from tree to tree and waylays any young man she happens upon. If she touches his head he will go insane but if she touches his chest he will die instantly.

Sources: Briggs, *Fairies in Tradition and Literature*,

49; Rose, *Spirits, Fairies, Leprechauns, and Goblins, an Encyclopedia*, 248

Orang Bunian

Variations: Borrowers of the Forest, Orang Bunyian, Voice People

The orang bunian ("chattering" or literally "men making a noise") are fairy-like race of invisible elves in Malay folklore. These fairies are said to live in caves containing stalactites capable of producing musical tones. The orang bunian, just like the fairy folk of Europe, are well known borrowers; whenever an item has gone missing it is said the orang bunian have taken it. The orang bunian are not very intelligent and are easily tricked. Typically these NATURE SPIRITS are only heard, their voices sounding exactly like a person calling out in distress from some distance away. Anyone who falls for this ply and tries to track down the sources of the voiceb by calling out to it as they try to find the person will be transformed into an orang bunian themselves, fading away until only their voice remains.

Sources: Forth, *Images of the Wildman in Southeast Asia*, 300; Moore, *West Malaysia and Singapore*, 160; Rose, *Spirits, Fairies, Leprechauns, and Goblins, an Encyclopedia*, 249

Orc

Variations: Orch, Ork, Orke

According to Pliny the Elder an orc was a huge sea-creature "armed with teeth." In the Galeic language the word orc means "a small sort of whale," like the orcas living in pods all around the Orkney Islands. Michael Drayton (1563–1631) described the orcs as being man eating sea-monsters. In John Milton's *Paradise Lost* (1667) he writes of "seals, orcs, and sea-mews (gulls)" living in the ocean. The idea of the orc as a large barbaric, brutish, uncivilized, humanoid first appeared in J.R.R. Tolkien's novel *Lord of the Rings* (1954).

Sources: Dasent, *Orkneyingers Saga*, 10; Manser, *Facts on File Dictionary of Allusions*, 349; Milton, *Paradise Lost*, 641

Orculli

A species of GIANT said to live in the clouds coming to earth only to gather food, the clumsy and malicious orculli are cannibals. Rarely seen they are described as being bearded males; their touch can cause cattle to die. Adept thieves these GIANTS are said to smell like rotting corpses.

Sources: Euvino, *Complete Idiot's Guide to Italian History and Culture*, 274; Livo, *Storytelling Folklore Sourcebook*, 38; McCoy, *Witch's Guide to Faery Folk*, 288–89

Orea

In ancient Greek mythology Orea was a HAMADRYAD of the ash tree; she was born from the incestuous relationship between Oxylus and his sister.

Sources: Athenaeus of Naucratis, *Deipnosophists*, Volume 1, 131

Oread

Variations: Orends, Orestiad

The Oread ("mountain") of classical Greek mythology were one of the twelve species of NYMPHS, they were the NYMPHS of grottoes, mountains, ravines, and valleys. Living lives virtually identical to human females, the oreads were associated with the goddess Artemis (Diana) because when she hunted she preferred mountains and rocky precipices.

An oread was usually known by the name of the mountain or hill on which she lived, for example, the Claea were the oreads of Mount Calathion, the Daphnis were the oreads of Mount Parnassos, the Idae were the oreads of Mount Ida, the NOMIA were the Oreads of Mount Nomia in Arcadia, the OTHREIS were the oreads of Mount Othrys, Malis, and the Peliades were the oreads of Mount Pelia.

Some of the commonly known oreads are ALCYONE, BRITOMARTIS, Celaeno, CYNOSURA, ECHO, ELECTRA, Kola, KYLLENE, Kouratni, MAIA, MEROPE, NOMIA, OENONE, PITYS, PLEIADES, STEROPE (ASTEROPE), and TAYGETE.

Sources: Antoninus Liberalis, *Metamorphoses of Antoninus Liberalis*, 60; Keightly, *World Guide to Gnomes, Fairies, Elves, and Other Little People*, 444; Littleton, *Gods, Goddesses, and Mythology, Volume 11*, 999; Pausanias, *Pausanias' Description of Greece*, Volume 2, 279

Oreande la Fée

A benevolent fairy from European lore, Oreande la Fée appears in legends and romances from the fifteenth century in Europe.

Source: Rose, *Spirits, Fairies, Leprechauns, and Goblins*, 351

Oreiades

Variations: OREAD

Oreiades was a NYMPH of the ancient Greek city Ossa. Oreiades was also the name for the species of NYMPH that were the guardians of caves, fir trees, and mountains.

Sources: Avant, *Mythological Reference*, 298; Hard, *Routledge Handbook of Greek Mythology*, 210; Larson, *Greek Nymphs*, 238; Rigoglioso, *Cult of Divine Birth in Ancient Greece*, 87

Oreithuia

Oreithuia was one of the named NEREID who accompanied THETIS in mourning the loss of her son, Achilles. According to ancient Greek legend, Oreithuia was carried off by the North-East wind and thereafter lived with him as his wife.

Sources: Homer, *Iliad of Homer*, Volume 2, 155; Pausânias, *Guide to Greece*, 55; Perry, *Women of Homer*, 146

Óri

Variations: Ori ("delirious (with love)")

Óri ("raving") was one of the many DWARFS named in the *Voluspa*, the first and best known poem of the *Poetic Edda*, a collection of Old Norse poems dating back to about A.D. 985.

Sources: Daly, *Norse Mythology A to Z*, 22; Puryear, *Nature of Ásatrú*, 229

Oriana

Oriana was one of the FATES appearing in Matteo Maria Boiardo's epic poem *Orlando Innamorato* ("*Orlando in Love*," 1495) from the Italian Renaissance period. In the poem, Oriana and fellow FATE, URGANDA, were the protectors of Amadigi. She was the most accomplished and beautiful of the fairy-ladies in court and when wedded to Amadigi lived a happy and love-filed life with him.

Sources: Boiardo, *Orlando Innamorato Di Bojardo*, 393–95; Keightly, *World Guide to Gnomes, Fairies, Elves, and Other Little People*, 453

Oriande la Fée

Variations: Oriande

Living atop Mount Etna (Mongibel) Oriande la Fée was the fairy caretaker to the hero, Maugis.

Sources: Brewer, *Reader's Handbook of Famous Names in Fiction*, 686; Keightly, *World Guide to Gnomes, Fairies, Elves, and Other Little People, 32*

Orithya

Variations: Orythia

A sea–NYMPH, Orithya ("sandy") is the NEREID of the beach. She was one of the named NEREID who accompanied THETIS in mourning the loss of her son, Achilles.

Sources: Apollodorus, *Apollodorus' Library and Hyginus' Fabulae*, 95; Gould, *Historic Magazine and Notes and Queries*, Vol 14, 212; Homer, *Iliads of Homer*, 137

Orithyia

Variations: Oreithyia

A sea–NYMPH, Orithyia was the NEREIS of raging seas; named in Homer's *The Illiad* she was described as a "divine maid." Orithyia was one of the NEREID who accompanied THETIS in mourning the loss of her son, Achilles. According to traditional Greek mythology Orithyia was kidnapped and raped by Boreas, the north wind, along the banks of the Illissus River; their coupling bore two winged children Calais and Zetes who grew to become great warriors.

Sources: Avant, *Mythological Reference*, 298; Bulfinch, *Bulfinch's Mythology*, 162–63; Homer, *Iliad of Homer*, 161

Orphne

Variations: Gorgyra

In classical Greek mythology, Orphne was a NYMPH of the Underworld River, Akheron (ACHERON); she was the mother of the demon, Askalaphos (Ascalaphus). As the female personification of Chaos she was also known as Nyx and Skotia.

Sources: Boccaccio, *Genealogy of the Pagan Gods*, Volume 1, 357; Fontenrose, *Python*, 229, 288

Orsa

In Dukagjin, Albania the Orsa was a FAIRY-GODMOTHER-like being appearing in three diferent colors. White orsas bring good luck and prosperity and do good deeds, yellow orsas commit acts of evil and bring bad luck; black orsas bring death.

Source: Elsie, *Dictionary of Albanian Religion, Mythology, and Folk Culture*, 59

Orseis

Orseis was a NYMPH from the mythology of classical Greece and Rome. One of the NAIADS, she was the wife of King Hellen of the Hellenes; he was the son of Deucallim and PYRRHA. Together Orseis and Hellen had three children, Aeolus, Dorus, and Xuthus.

Sources: Bell, *Women of Classical Mythology*, 355, 389; Larson, *Greek Nymphs*, 166; Parada, *Genealogical Guide to Greek Mythology*, 134

Orthone

Orthone was a French HOUSE-SPIRIT who was said to attend the Lord of Corasse in Gascony, France. Orthone was similar to the German house fairy, HINZELMAN; he served the knight for one season. Orthone claimed he was physically incapable of harming anyone, the worst he could do would be to rouse a person from a sound sleep. He has the ability to travel to other countries, such as England and Hungary and return a few hours later with all of the latest news and gossip. He appeared to the Lord as two pieces of straw twisting about in the wind, as well as a thin sow.

Sources: Keightly, *World Guide to Gnomes, Fairies, Elves, and Other Little People*, 468; Scott, *Minstrelsy of the Scottish Border*, 405–06

Ortygia

A NYMPH of the sacred Ortygian grove in Lykia, Turkey, Ortygia was a NAIAD and a nurse to the infant god, Apollo in Greek mythology.

Sources: Clark, *Classical Manual*, 301; Larson, *Greek Nymphs*, 213–14

Oschaert

A type of malicious BLACK DOG from Belgian folklore, specifically in and around the town of Hamme, Oschaert would wander along the road seeking to attack and otherwise terrorize travelers; it was especially fond of singling out individuals with an uneasy conscience. Unlike a BARGUEST, Oschaert has no set form and has been sighted in the shape of dog, donkey, horse, and rabbit. Like the KLUDDE of Belgium it would play pranks of lost travelers, but the oschaert being far more vicious would jump on people's backs, pin them to the ground and increasing its body mass, crush them beneath its weight. The only means by which to escape an attacking oschaert would be to stand in a crossroads or present it with a picture of the Virgin Mary.

Sources: Henderson, *Notes on the Folk-Lore of the Northern Counties of England and the Borders*, 273; Rose, *Giants, Monsters, and Dragons*, 282

Othreis

A NYMPH of Mount Othrys in Malis in northern Greece, Orthreis was the lover to both the god Apollo and the god Zeus (Jupiter) in Greek mythology. By the god, Apollo, Othreis bore a son named Phagros; by the mortal king Hellen she bore three sons, Aiolos, Doros, and Xouthos; and by the god Zeus (Jupiter) she bore a son named Meliteus (Melitus).

Sources: Lemprière, *Classical Dictionary* (1839), 365; Rigoglioso, *Cult of Divine Birth in Ancient Greece*, 111

Ótr

Variations: Odr

Ótr ("otter") was a son of the magician DWARF king, HREIDMAR and the brother of FAFNIR and REGIN in Norse mythology. A loner who ate with his eyes closed because he coud not stand to see his food disappear, Ótr was an expert shapeshifter who typically took the form of an otter, Ótr. One day he was tragically killed when the god Loki threw a stone at believing he was aiming nothing more than a common otter. When HREIDMAR saw the god carrying his son's body like a hunting trophy over his shoulder, he demanded to be compensated for his son's death, insisting on enough treasure to cover an otter's pelt and fill its insides. HREIDMAR was given by the god Loki a treasure hoard of gems and gold as compensation for slaying his son. This tragic story is told in the legendary thirteenth century saga, *Volsunga Saga* ("*Saga of the Völsungs*").

Sources: Daly, *Norse Mythology*, 78–9; Gentry, *Nibelungen Tradition*, 109

Ouphe

Variations: OAF, Ouph

Ouphe was a common name for elves, fairies, and NYMPHS in European folklore. Not as agile or quick-witted as the TROOPING FEY, the ouphe were left as CHANGELINGS whenever a human baby was stolen. Their variant name, *oaf*, came into use to mean a person of low intelligence. This species of fairy was written about by Joseph Rodman Drake in the poem, *The Culprit Fay* (1819).

Sources: Poe, *Complete Works of Edgar Allan Poe*, Volume 7, 285–86; Roget, *Roget's Thesaurus of English Words and Phrases*, 341; Rose, *Spirits, Fairies, Leprechauns, and Goblins*, 250, 351

Ourania

Born one of the 3,000 daughters of the Titians, Oceanus and Tethys, Ourania was one of the named OCEANIDS in ancient Greek mythology; she was one of the playmates of Persephone (Proserpina) and present when the goddess was kidnapped.

Sources: Crudden, *Homeric Hymns*, 19; Fowler, *Archaic Greek Poetry*, 14; Trzaskoma, *Anthology of Classical Myth*, 509

Ovinnik

In Slavic folklore an ovinnik is a fairy spirit living in the thrashing barn; it takes on the appearance of a large and disheveled looking black cat with burning eyes. Offerings of *blini*, a type of pancake, is left for it; if the ovinnik is ever angered or shown disrespect it burns down the barn with the farmer's children inside of it. On the first of November a rooster is beheaded and its blood sprinkled in each corner of the barn to appease the fairy. It is customary to enter the barn on New Year's Eve and allow the fairy to touch you; if the ovinnik's touch was soft or warm the person could expect good fortune for the upcoming year, however, if the touch was harsh or cold than misfortune and unhappiness were so come.

Sources: Ivanits, *Russian Folk Belief*, 58–62; Mack, *Field Guide to Demons*, 195; Rose, *Spirits, Fairies, Leprechauns, and Goblins, an Encyclopedia*, 250

Oxun

In the Batuque mythology Oxun was a type of MERMAID derived from the spirits of the Yourba people of Nigeria; she is worshiped as a NATURE SPIRIT or goddess of beauty, flirtation, and love. Oxun is depicted in art as holding a fan and wearing jewels.

Sources: Monaghan, *Encyclopedia of Goddesses and Heroines*, 42; Rose, *Spirits, Fairies, Leprechauns, and Goblins, an Encyclopedia*, 251

Pachatusan

Variations: Pachatosa, Payatusan

Pachatusan is an APU who lives on a mountain peak in the Andes Mountains. Pachatusan is also the name of the tallest and most gold rich mountain in the area; mined intensely by the Spanish locals still recognize this place as the home of the Apus.

Sources: Illes, *Encyclopedia of Spirits*, 198; Parry, *Money and the Morality of Exchange*, 212

Pacolet

A famous DWARF or familiar spirit from medieval lore, Pacolet created a wooden horse bridled with *bast* which had the ability to run through the air. Pacolet was described as being a "venerable gentleman" who was born the heir to one of the wealthiest families in Great Britain but was accidently drowned at the age of one month.

Sources: Grimm, *Teutonic Mythology*, Volume 4, 1423, 1626; Lindahl, *Medieval Folklore*, 161; White, *Notes and queries*, Volume 115, 225

Padfoot

Variations: Padfooit

A monstrously large BLACK DOG from the folklore of Leeds, England, Padfoot was a sheep-sized bogey. Like the KLUDDE and OSCHAERT of Belgium, Padfoot was normally invisible but it

could shape-shift; most often it would take the form of a bear; a gigantic black or white dog walking on two or three legs; a demonic-looking sheep with burning eyes, a calf; or an enormous black donkey. Its eyes were said to be as large as tea-plates. No matter the form this FAIRY ANIMAL assumes it would always be accompanied by the sound of dragging chains. To see Padfoot was a death omen; sometime to see it would cause a person to die of fright. Any attempt to fend off the fairy would guarantee the creature will maul its victim.

Sources: Cole, *Glossary of Words Used In South-West Lincolnshire*, 96; Henderson, *Notes on the Folk-Lore of the Northern Counties of England and the Borders*, 274; Rose, *Giants, Monsters, and Dragons*, 285

Paian

A paian is the fairy gathering of all the DWARFS of Scandinavia. Although no human has ever been witness to one of these events it is said they meet in secret to discuss business, play and worship. The most famous ruling ever made at a paian was against the DWARF, Ammaze; because he chose to live as a human he was censured and then excommunicated from his people.

Sources: McCoy, *Witch's Guide to Faery Folk*, 139, 289–90; Scott, *Fantastic People*, 80

Painajainen

Variations: Alp

In the folklore throughout Western Europe the painajainen ("presser") are a species of fairy who can live to be 4,000 years old; they are described as looking like small white horses and are seen racing through the Alps. The painajainen enjoy teasing children and although sometimes they are harmed by the prank no child has ever been killed by one. Although these fay do not steal children they do bring them terrible nightmares; an effective means to repel them from this form of harassment is to place a broom or a bit or iron under the child's pillow.

Sources: Keightly, *World Guide to Gnomes, Fairies, Elves, and Other Little People*, 488; McCoy, *Witch's Guide to Faery Folk*, 290

Palatyne

Born one of a set to triplets to the fountain NYMPH, PRESSYNE and King Elynas of Albany, Palatyne was condemned to guard her father's treasure hoard atop a mountain top in Arragon, according to medieval French folklore; her only companions were a bear and a serpent with one large eye. Because of the crime she and sisters perpetrated against their father only a knight from her father's lineage could break the enchantment her mother, PRESSYNE, place on her, keeping her bound to the treasure. Many knights tried and failed; one of Tristan's lineage from King Arthur's court made the quest, defeating every obstacle and killing both the bear and hundreds of snakes, however, because the knight was not a descendant of Elynas, was consumed by the one eyed snake. Another knight by the name of Geoffrey-with-the-great tooth, Elynas' own grandson made the quest but took too long in both making preparation and journeying to the mountain. By the time the would-be hero arrived, he was too old to make the ascent to the top of the mountain.

Sources: D'Arras, *Melusine*, 7–17; Foubister, *Goddess in the Grass*, 88

Pallas

Born one of the 3,000 daughters of the Titians, Oceanus and Tethys, Pallas ("maiden"), the waker of battle, was one of the named OCEANIDS in ancient Greek mythology; she she was one of the playmates of Persephone (Proserpina) and present when the goddess was kidnapped. Pallas was the NYMPH of the salt-lake Tritonis in Libya, North Africa.

Sources: Crudden, *Homeric Hymns*, 19; Fowler, *Archaic Greek Poetry*, 14

Pallene

In Greek mythology, Pallene was a NYMPH of Chalkidike, the peninsula of Pallene in the Thrakian Khersonesos located in northern Greece.

Source: Larson, *Greek Nymphs*, 170

Pamarindo

A male DWARF in Italian fairy lore Pamarindo was a lazy, mean, obese, and small individual who was disliked by the other fay; he was described as wearing a fur hat and red clothes stained with animal fat. Pamarindo was a scavenger because he was either forbidden or unable to kill animals for himself. He was known to run animals off cliffs or cause them to impale themselves on low branches. In some of the folklore from northern Italy Pamarindo was not an individual fay but rather a species.

Sources: Livo, *Storytelling Folklore Sourcebook*, 38; McCoy, *Witch's Guide to Faery Folk*, 290–1

Panope

Variations: Panopeia, Panopae

A sea–NYMPH of Halikarnassos, Panope ("of the beautiful husband") was the NEREID of the sea panorama in classical Greek mythology; she was born the daughter of Nerues and DORIS. She was one of the named NEREID who accompanied THETIS in mourning the loss of her son, Achilles.

Sources: Apollodorus, *Apollodorus' Library and Hyginus' Fabulae*, 95; Bell, *Bell's New Pantheon or Historical Dictionary of the Gods*, 112; Collignon, *Manual of Mythology*, 18; Gould, *Historic Magazine and Notes And Queries*, Vol 14, 212; Hesiod, *Works of Hesiod, Callimachus, and Theognis*, 15; Perry, *Women of Homer*, 146

Papa Bois

Variations: Daddy Bouchon ("hairy man"), Jab Molasi, Maître Bois ("master of the woods")

In Trinidad folklore Papa Bois ("papa farce" or "oods") is the custodian of the trees and guardian of the animals. He has many different forms he appears in, such as a deer, a man in ragged clothes or as an extremely hairy old man who is very muscular and strong but has cloven hooves for feet and leaves growing out of his beard. In the original mythology, Papa Bois traveled the woods at night with his walking stick and his nocturnal companion, a witch, because they could not tolerate the light of day.

Sources: Besson, *Folklore and Legends of Trinidad and Tobago*, 1–3; Siefker, *Santa Claus, Last of the Wild Men*, 26–7

Para

The para are a species of KOBOLD in Finland that steals milk from the neighbor's cows. After he drinks all he can, the fairy takes it back to his family's churn, disgorges the milk into it, and then churns it into butter.

Sources: Conway, *Magickal Mystical Creatures*, 215; Keightly, *World Guide to Gnomes, Fairies, Elves, and Other Little People*, 488

Paralda

Variations: The King of the Element of Air

In ancient Greek lore Paralda was the leader of the SYLPHS, a type of beautiful and small fairy.

Sources: Briggs, *Encyclopedia of Fairies*, 192–3; Hall, *Secret Teachings of All Ages*, 317

Pareia

Pareia was a NYMPH of Crete, the main town of the island of Paros; she was loved by King Minos of Crete and by which she had four children, Chryses, Eurymedon, Nephalion, and Philolaus.

Sources: Bell, *Women of Classical Mythology*, 341; Larson, *Greek Nymphs: Myth, Cult, Lore*, 181; Smith, *Dictionary of Greek and Roman Biography and Mythology*, 122

Paribanou

In the fairy-tale *The story of Prince Ahmed and the Fairy Paribanou* from the collected story of the *Arabian Nights*, the fairy Paribanou lives deep in a cave with her retinue of ladies. Described as having a majestic air, exceedingly beautiful, and always lavishly dressed, she is one of the daughters of the most powerful and distinguished GENIE. Her brother is the fairy, SCHAIBAR.

Source: Lang, *Blue Fairy Book*, 342–53

Paridamie

In the Comte de Caylus fairy-tale entitled *Rosanella*, Paridamie was one of two viable candidates worthy of earning the position of FAIRY QUEEN; SURCANTINE was the other. As each of the two candidates was equally matched for the position a contest was held to determine the winner and win the title of queen.

SURCANTINE promised she would raise a human prince whom nothing could make constant while Paridamie set out to create a mortal princess so charming none who saw her could help but fall instantly and deeply in love with her. Paridamie ultimately won the contest as she was clever enough to use her fairy magic to divide the character of Princess Rosanella into twelve parts so each one would charm the fickle Prince Mirliflor. Once the twelve parts were united the prince was cured of his inconstancy.

Sources: Lang, *Green Fairy Book*, 48–55; Quiller-Couch, *Twelve Dancing Princesses and Other Fairy Tales*, 97–98, 110

Parthenope

In classical Greek mythology, Parthenope ("maiden-face") was one of the named SIRENS, a type of malicious NYMPH born the offspring of the ancient sea god, Phorcys. Half bird and half woman, she and her sisters would perch on the rocky Sicilian coastline and lure in sailor with their melodious song; once caught their prey were eaten alive. Although they hunted the coastline these creatures lived inland in a meadow.

Sources: Smith, *Dictionary of Greek and Roman Biography and Mythology*, 817; Smith, *Smaller Classical Mythology*, 34

Pasiphae

Born one of the 3,000 daughters of the Titians, Oceanus and Tethys, the NYMPH Pasiphae ("all shining") was one of the named OCEANIDS from Greek mythology.

Source: Apollodorus of Athens, *Apollodorus' Library and Hyginus' Fabulae*, 95

Pasithea

A sea–NYMPH from Greek mythology, Pasithea ("all-divine") was one of the named NEREID; she was the gentle NYMPH who deviously sports in the waves.

Sources: Betham, *Transactions of the Royal Irish Academy*, Volume 17, 88; Hesiod, *Works of Hesiod, Callimachus, and Theognis*, 15

Pasithoe

Born one of the 3,000 daughters of the Titians, Oceanus and Tethys, Pasithoe was one of the eldest of the named OCEANIDS from Greek mythology.

Sources: Bell, *Bell's New Pantheon or Historical Dictionary of the Gods*, 112; Boswell, *What Men or Gods Are These*, 58; Hesiod, *Works of Hesiod, Callimachus, and Theognis*, 20; Westmoreland, *Ancient Greek Beliefs*, 24

Patch

Patch was one of the fairies mentioned being in the company of ROBIN GOOD FELLOW in a seventeenth century pamphlet. He and his fellow fairies, GRIM, GULL, and PINCH are all said to have shape-shifting abilities.

Sources: Briggs, *Encyclopedia of Fairies*, 327; Wilson, *Life in Shakespeare's England*, 42

Patupaiarehe

Variations: Ngati Hotu, Paiarehe, Pakehakeha, Parehe, Patu-Paiarehe, Patupairehe, Patuparehe, Patu Paiarehe, Pukehakeha, TUREHU, Urukehu ("red heads")

According to Maori mythology, the patupaiarehe are the pale-skinned fairy spirits dwelling in the forests and mountain tops of New Zealand. Only three things are able to ward off the patupaiarehe, ashes, fire, and the red ochre used to mark taboo objects. Patupaiarehe themselves are considered taboo as they only eat raw meat; these fay are particularly fond of uncooked fish.

Described as being pale-skinned, tall, and having a head or red hair, the cautious patupaiarehe are most active at night or during days with a heavy fog. Considered to be generally peaceful the patupaiarehe have been known to take a human and keep it as its mate; children produced from such a union are always albino. In Maori society this union is never viewed as a case of kidnap or rape, as the patupaiarehe have very poor memories and forgets they already have a mate when they set out to find a new one.

Sources: Baker, *Origins of the Words Pakeha and Maori*, 223–31; Hyland, *Paki Waitara*, 67–8; Maberry, *They Bite*, 361–63

Peallaidh

Variations: Pealldaidh

The peallaidh ("shaggy one") is one of the FUATH, a collective name for the malicious and monstrous water fay in Scottish folklore. As an individual being, Peallaidh is believed to be the chief of the URISK, a type of SOLITARY FAIRY water KELPIE living in isolated pools in the Scottish Highlands.

Sources: Gordon, *Highways and Byways in the Central Highlands*, 105; Rose, *Spirits, Fairies, Leprechauns, and Goblins*, 121, 255; Thompson, *Supernatural Highlands*, 154

Pease Blossom

Pease Blossom is a FLOWER FAIRY and an attendant of TITANIA, the FAIRY QUEEN. Along with fellow fairies COBWEB, MOTH, and MUSTARDSEED, attends a human peasant named Bottom whose head was changed into an ass' by OBERON, the FAIRY KING.

Sources: Lamb, *Works of Charles and Mary Lamb*, 18; Rose, *Spirits, Fairies, Leprechauns, and Goblins*, 255, 351; Shakespeare, *Shakespeare's a Midsummer Night's Dream*, 26

Pech

Variations: Pecht, Pehts

In Scottish Lowland mythology the pech was a short GNOME-like fairy being who, although small of stature was extremely strong. Described as having long arms, wide feet, and wild red hair, the pech were believed to have been the builders of the ancient the stone megaliths of ancient Scotland.Pechs were strictly nocturnal fairies, as they could not stand the light of day.

Sources: Spence, *Fairy Tradition in Britain*, 17, 32; Stevenson, *Scottish Antiquary, or, Northern Notes and Queries*, Volume 14, 135; Stepanich, *Faery Wicca*, Book One, 272

Pechamnderlin

A subspecies of the WICHTLN from the folklore of southern Germany the Pechamnderlin are said to glue the eyes of sleepy children closed.

Source: Arrowsmith, *Field Guide to the Little People*, 51–3

Pedile

According to Greek mythology Pedile was a HYAD and a NYMPH of the mythical Mount Nysa; she was a BAKKHAI, and one of the nurses to the infant god, Dionysus (Bacchus).

Sources: Parada, *Genealogical Guide to Greek Mythology*, 92; Smith, *Dictionary of Greek and Roman Biography and Mythology: Earinus-Nyx*, 533

Peerifool

Variations: Perifoal

From the folklore of the Orkney Islands north of Scotland comes Peerifool, one of the LITTLE PEOPLE. Similar to the stories of GIRLE GUAIRLE, HABETROT, RUMPELSTILTSKIN and TIT TOT, in this Scottish tale the youngest princess of a king is captured by an OGRE, imprisoned in his dungeon, and forced to spin thread. Unfortunately the princess never learned this skill and sobbed so much the nearby Little People came to investigate, one of which was the flaxen-haired Peerifool. This fairy told the princess he would do all her spinning for her on the condition that she guesses his name before a certain date or "all would be lost" for her. With no other choice the princess agrees, the fairy spins the thread and the OGRE releases her but the time is approaching for when she must correctly guess the name. Nearly at her wits end and just as the final hour is upon her she meets an old beggar woman who tells the princess a story of how she came upon a fairy lodge and overheard a flaxen-haired Little Person declaring to himself the princess will never guess his odd name of Peerifool. The beggar woman is rewarded and the Princess is able to save herself from the fairy's intended curse.

Sources: Henderson, *Scottish Fairy Belief*, 31; Rose, *Spirits, Fairies, Leprechauns, and Goblins*, 256, 351; Seal, *Encyclopedia of Folk Heroes*, 103

Peg O'Nell

Variations: Peggy O'Nell

Peg O'Nell was a malicious water fairy haunting a well at Waddow near the Ribble River in Clitheroe, Lancashire, England. It is believed every seven years she drowns someone. According to local lore Peg O'Nell was originally a servant girl at Waddow Hall in Waddington; one day she had a bitter fight with the lord and lady of the house. Peg stormed off to fetch a bucket of water for the house and while she was gone the master of the Hall wished she would fall in the well and break her neck rather than return as angry as she was. The wish came to pass and Peg O'Nell returned as an angry NYMPH set to punish those who wished her dead and everyone in the parish. Chickens disappeared, calves were born deformed, cows fell sick, and young adults fell sick. In order to appease the water fairy every seven years a good, sound, living sacrifice had to be made to her well.

Sources: Henderson, *Notes on the Folk-Lore of the Northern Counties of England*, 265; Monaghan, *Encyclopedia of Celtic Mythology and Folklore*, 377; Parkinson, *Yorkshire Legends and Traditions*, 106–07

Peg Powler

One of the many NURSERY BOGIES of British folklore, Peg Powler is believed to live in the warm water wells supported by the River Tees. Said to be bottomless and referred to as "Hell's Kettles" these wells are where the green haired Peg Powler, just like JENNY GREENTEETH of Lancashire, hunts for her prey, children, who venture too close to the edge of her watery domain; she was especially active on Sundays. It is possible this fairy being was once worshiped as a river goddess who was offered human sacrifices.

The foam that gathers on the stream's surface is called Peg Powler's suds, implying she is doing her laundry; the scum that accumulates on the surface is known as Peg Powler's Cream, the runoff of her sloppily milking her cow.

Sources: Briggs, *Encyclopedia of Fairies*, 323; Monaghan, *Encyclopedia of Celtic Mythology and Folklore*, 377; Spence, *Minor Traditions of British Mythology*, 13, 23

Pegaea

Variation: Pegaia, Pegaia
A NAIAD from classical Greek mythology Pegaea ("she of the springs") was one of the four NYMPHS of the healing springs of the river Kytheros in Elis, located in southern Greece. Collectively they were known as the IODINES and they names were CALLIPHAEA, IASIS, PEGAEA, and SYNALLAXIS and it was believed to bathe in one of their springs was a cure-all for an array of illnesses and pains.

Sources: Larson, *Greek Nymphs*, 158; Pausanias, *Commentary on Book I: Attica*, 319

Pegaeae

Variations: The Pegaiai
The pegaeae were a sub-species of the NAIADS, they are the NYMPHS of fresh water springs and fountains in classical Greek mythology.

Sources: Avant, *Mythological Reference*, 295; Conner, *Everything Classical Mythology Book*, 17, 276; Maberry, *Cryptopedia*, 112

Pegasis

A NYMPH of a spring of the river Grenikos in the Troad, Anatolia, Pegasis was loved by the Trojan prince, Emathion and described by the ancient Roman poet, Ovid, as being "fair-tressed."

Sources: Ovid, *Ovid*, 142; Parada, *Genealogical Guide to Greek Mythology*, 32

Peirene

Peirene was a NYMPH of the spring Peirene in the town of Korinthos located in southern Greece; the NAIAD was a daughter of the Spartan, Oilbalos. Peirene loved by the god of the sea, Poseidon (Neptune). When her son, Kenchrias, died, Peirene wept so heavily she transformed into a fountain.

Sources: Irving, *Metamorphosis in Greek Myths*, 301; Larson, *Greek Nymphs*, 307

Peisinoe

In classical Greek mythology, Peisinoe ("persuading the mind") was one of the named SIRENS, a type of malicious NYMPH born the offspring of the ancient sea god, Phorcys. Half bird and half woman, she and her sisters would perch on the rocky Sicilian coastline and lure in sailor with their melodious song; once caught, their prey were eaten alive. Although they hunted the coastline, Peisinoe and her kind lived inland in a meadow.

Sources: Austern, *Music of the Sirens*, 40; Hard, *Library of Greek Mythology*, 167; Monaghan, *Encyclopedia of Goddesses and Heroines*, 434

Peitho

Variations: Suada
Born one of the 3,000 daughters of the Titians, Oceanus and Tethys, Peitho ("winning eloquence") was one of the named OCEANIDS although some sources say she was the minor goddess of the persuasive tricks of love born the daughter of the goddess of love, Aphrodite (Venus) and the god, Hermes (Mercury), who by nature was tricky.

Sources: Hesiod, *Theogony*, 113; Monaghan, *Encyclopedia of Goddesses and Heroines*, 428; Westmoreland, *Ancient Greek Beliefs*, 24

Peloris

Variations: Pelorias
Peloris was a NYMPH of Sicily in Greek mythology.

Sources: Bell, *Bell's New Pantheon*, 112; Larson, *Greek Nymphs*, 219

Pelznickel

Variations: Pelze Nocol, Weinachts Man ("white night man") Schimmel Reiter ("rider of the white horse")

In northern Germany, Pelznickel ("furry Nick") is the name of the Christmas spirit; his name was one of the epithets of the god, Odin indicating Pelznickel was likely demoted from god to fairy even before the introduction of Christianity. Prior to the Lutheran reformation, Pelznickel was a jovial NATURE SPIRIT of Winter who was described as wearing furs. Flying through the night sky Pelznickel would visit homes and deliver toys to children. After the reformation Pelznickel was described as wearing religious robes and would deliver toys on Saint Nicholas' Feast Day.

In the Volga German colonies Pelznickel was utilized as a NURSERY BOGIE; he was described as wearing an illfitting sheep-skin coat and a shaggy hat and having a stringy beard and moustache and bushy eyebrows. Here, Pelznickel handed switches out to parents and would whip children who were unruly, somehow magically knowing the history of their behavior. He would appear each New Year Eve.

Sources: Koch, *Volga Germans*, 193; Rose, *Spirits, Fairies, Leprechauns, and Goblins, an Encyclopedia*, 257

Penates

In the mythology of the ancient Romans penates ("the inner ones") were originally the gods of the storeroom but grew to become the gods of the entire household. Worshiped at the hearth a portion of each meal was given to them these house hold fairies are similar to the BROWNIES of Scotland, as the Penates will do good deeds and household chores for the family at night. Unaffected by the sunlight these fairies chose to live nocturnally.

Sources: Keightly, *World Guide to Gnomes, Fairies, Elves, and Other Little People*, 448–9; McCoy, *Witch's Guide to Faery Folk*, 147, 291–92; Rose, *Spirits, Fairies, Leprechauns, and Goblins, an Encyclopedia*, 257

Penelopeia

A NYMPH of Mount Kyllene in Arcadia located in southern Greece, Penelopeia a DRYAD, was born the daughter of Dryops. Penelopeia was the mother of the god Pan (Faunus) by the god, Hermes (Mercury). The THYMBRIS was also said to be Pan's mother.

Sources: Grant, *Who's Who in Classical Mythology*, 185; Rose, *Handbook of Greek Mythology*, 168

Peneus

Born one of the 3,000 daughters of the Titians, Oceanus and Tethys, Peneus was one of the named OCEANIDS from Greek mythology.

Sources: Boswell, *What Men or Gods Are These*, 58; Day, *God's Conflict with the Dragon and the Sea*, 64; Hesiod, *Works of Hesiod, Callimachus, and Theognis*, 20

Pénghoú

Variations: Count P'eng, P'eng-hou

A type of HAMADRYAD from Chinese lore the pénghoú were associated with the camphor tree. Described as having the body of a black dog with no tail and the face of a man these NATURE SPIRITS were said to taste quite good when properly steamed. In Japan this same being is call a *hōkō*.

Sources: Gan, *In Search of the Supernatural*, 215; White, *Myths of the Dog-Man*, 282, 285

Le Père Fouettard

Variations: Father Birch Rod, Father Whipper, Père Fouchette

A famous BOGEYMAN from Dutch, French, and German lore, the mean-spirited and ugly Père Fouettard was a well-known figure in Christmas mythology. Dressed in black or dark grey and sometimes described as having horns and a pointed tail this NURSERY BOGIE would accompany Père Noël ("Father Christmas") on his rounds on St. Nicolas' Day and whip with his birch rod all the naughty children.

Sources: Del Re, *Christmas Almanack*, 117; Mould, *Routledge Dictionary of Cultural References in Modern French*, 28; World Book, Inc., *Christmas in France*, 16

Peri

Variations: Parikas, Pairikas

In ancient Persian lore the peri ("to surround") were pre–Zoroastrian forest and river goddesses who late came to seen as fairy beings, the descendants of the fallen angels and seen as related to the DJINN; as such they had been denied entry into paradise until they have performed their penance. In the original mythology the peri were considered to be evil beings but evolved into benevolent beings. Said to live in the mountains of

Kâf they are described as being exquisitely beautiful beings whose bodies were made of fire these winged fairies existed off of a diet of the scents of perfume. Peri do not have nor do they serve a FAIRY QUEEN; when overcome by their enemies the peri seek the assistance of a mortal hero.

The mortal enemies of the peri were the DEVS; the animosity between the two originated in the peri's lack of confidence in the rebellion against Heaven. When DEVS captured the peri were locked up in iron cages and hug high up in the branches of trees.

Sources: Geddie, *Chambers's Encyclopaedia*, Volume 7, 399; Keightly, *World Guide to Gnomes, Fairies, Elves, and Other Little People*, 15–17, 21–23; McClintock, *Cyclopaedia of Biblical*, Volume 7, 949; Sykes, *Who's Who in Non-Classical Mythology*, 154

Peri Merjân

Variations: Mergiana

In Persian fairy lore, the beautiful Peri Merjân ("fairy pearl") is captured by the fierce and ugly DEV, DEMRUSH and chained to the center of a mountain. Her brothers DÂL PERI and MILÂN SHÂH PERI tried to save her but failed; ultimately she was rescued by the hero, Tahmuras.

Sources: Hunt, *Leigh Hunt's London Journal*, Volumes 1–2, 235; Keightly, *World Guide to Gnomes, Fairies, Elves, and Other Little People*, 18

Periboea

Variations: MEROPE

Periboea was a NYMPH from the mythology of classical Greece and Rome. One of the NAIADS, she is the mother of Aura by Lelantos and the wife of the mortal hero, Icarius. There are also four mortal queens of ancient Greece named Periboea as well as a lesser goddess of love.

Sources: Bernhardt, *Gods and Goddesses in the Garden*, 59; Parada, *Genealogical Guide to Greek Mythology*, 128

Periboia

Variations: Periboée

Periboia was a NAIAD married to the river god, Axios. By the hero Icarius she had five sons named Aletes, Damasippos, Imeusimos, Perileos, and Thoas, as well as a daughter named Penelope.

Sources: Apollodorus of Athens, *Apollodorus' Library and Hyginus' Fabulae*, 60; Hard, *Library of Greek Mythology*, n.p.; Larson, *Greek Nymphs*, 308

Periklymene

In Greek mythology, Periklymene was a NAIAD of Halikarnassos; she was born the daughter of Minyas and was married to Pheres to whom she bore him two sons, Admetos and Lykourgos.

Sources: Hard, *Routledge Handbook of Greek Mythology*, 425; Larson, *Greek Nymphs*, 207

Perit

In Albanian folklore the perit were female NATURE SPIRITS living in the mountains. Described as being extremely beautiful these benign fairies dress entirely in white. Although considered to be kindly, the perit would harshly punish anyone who was wasteful with bread.

Sources: Avant, *Mythological Reference*, 460; Lurker, *Routledge Dictionary of Gods and Goddesses*, 150; ose, *Spirits, Fairies, Leprechauns, and Goblins, an Encyclopedia*, 259

Pero

According to Acousilaos, the ancient Greek logographer and mythographer, the NYMPH Pero was a NAIAD from the area of Sikyonia in southern Greece. Pero bore a lame son, the river god Asopos, to Poseidon (Neptune), god of the sea.

Sources: Apollodorus of Athens, *Library of Greek Mythology*, 126; Fontenrose, *Python*, 232

Perse

Variations: Persa, Perseis

Born one of the 3,000 daughters of the Titians, Oceanus and Tethys, Perse, wife of Helios (Sol), was one of the named OCEANIDS in Greek mythology; him bore Aeëtes, CIRCE, and Pasiphaë.

Sources: Bell, *Bell's New Pantheon or Historical Dictionary of the Gods*, 112; Boswell, *What Men or Gods Are These*, 58; Day, *God's Conflict with the Dragon and the Sea*, 64; Hesiod, *Works of Hesiod, Callimachus, and Theognis*, 20

Peseias

In Slavic lore the peseias was a household spirit and the guardian of domestic animals.

Sources: Dixon-Kennedy, *Encyclopedia of Russian and Slavic Myth and Legend*, 218; Rose, *Spirits, Fairies, Leprechauns, and Goblins, an Encyclopedia*, 259

Petraea

Variations: Petrae

Born one of the 3,000 daughters of the Titians, Oceanus and Tethys, Petraea ("the comely") was one of the named OCEANIDS from Greek mythology.

Sources: Boswell, *What Men or Gods Are These*, 58; Hesiod, *Works of Hesiod, Callimachus, and Theognis*, 20; Westmoreland, *Ancient Greek Beliefs*, 24

Le Petit Colin

Variations: P'tit Colin

A famous household fairy from France, le Petit Colin and his constant companion, LE GRAND COLIN, lived in or on the hearth. Normally invisible this fairy would show its appreciation from time-to-time by assisting in household chores, similar to the BROWNIE, le Petit Colin and his companion enjoy playing ball on the fields of les Paysans; one of the large standing stones there is said to be the bat of LE GRAND COLIN planted firmly into the ground during a moment's annoyance with Petit Colin for losing the ball as they played.

Sources: Bois, *Jersey Folklore and Superstitions* Volume Two, 113, 396; MacCulloch, *Guernsey Folk Lore*, 214–15

Pexy

Variations: Colepexy

In Dorset, England pixies are pexy and are said to live in coppices and woods. Used as a NURSERY BOGIE, children are told to behave properly or the pexy will punish them.

Sources: Briggs, *Encyclopedia of Fairies*, 78; Keightly, *World Guide to Gnomes, Fairies, Elves, and Other Little People*, 305

Phaeno

Variations: Phaeo, Phaio

Born one of the 3,000 daughters of the Titians, Oceanus and Tethys, Phaeno was one of the named OCEANIDS in ancient Greek mythology; she was one of the playmates of Persephone (Proserpina) and present when the goddess was kidnapped.

Sources: Allen, *Homeric Hymns*, 51; Morford, *Classical Mythology*, 613

Phaethousa

In Greek mythology Phaethousa was a NYMPH and sometimes named as one of the HELIADES, the daughters of the sun god Helios (Sol) and the OCEANID, CLYMENE.

Sources: Cox, *Mythology of the Aryan Nations*, Volume 2, 280; Hansen, *Handbook of Classical Mythology*, 220

Phaethusa

Variations: Phaëtusa

In Greek mythology Phaethusa ("radiance"), was a NYMPH of the sun and one of the named DANAIDS; she was said to be one of the possible candidates to be the mother of Myrtilus by the god, Myrtilus. Other sources say she and her sister, LAMPETIE, were born the daughters of the Titan, Hyperion (Heilos) and tended after his sacred herds on the mythical island of Thrinakie. Each sister was described by Homer, the greatest ancient Greek epic poet, in *The Odyssey* as having "redundant locks" of hair.

Sources: Homer, *The Odyssey*, Volume 1, 307; Keightley, *Mythology of Ancient Greece and Italy*, 56

Phaino

Born one of the 3,000 daughters of the Titians, Oceanus and Tethys, Phaino ("to appear" or "show") was one of the named OCEANIDS from Greek mythology. Phaino was one of the playmates of Persephone (Proserpina) and present when the goddess was kidnapped.

Sources: Crudden, *Homeric Hymns*, 102; Fowler, *Archaic Greek Poetry*, 14, 338

Phaisyle

A NYMPH in Greek mythology, Phaisyle was one of the nurses of the infant god, Dionysus (Bacchus).

Sources: Dalby, *Bacchus*, 46; Rigoglioso, *Cult of Divine Birth in Ancient Greece*, 144

Phartis

In Greek mythology Phartis was a water–NYMPH and one of the named DANAIDS, the collective name for the daughters of Danaus. In a list compiled by Apollodorus, a Greek scholar and grammarian, she was one of the daughters of an unnamed Ethiopian woman and was wedded to Eurydamas, one of the sons of an unnamed Phoenician woman; she slew her husband on their wedding night.

Sources: Apollodorus of Athens, *Apollodorus' Library and Hyginus' Fabulae*, 22; Bell, *Women of Classical Mythology*, 362; Grimal, *Dictionary of Classical Mythology*, 127

Phasyleia

A NYMPH in classical reek mythology, Phasyleia was one of the MAENADS, the collective name of the daughter born of the CANONICAL MUSE, Mnemosyne, the personification of memory, and the god Zeus (Jupiter), after nine days of continuous intercourse. Phasyleia along with her sister CHAROPEIA would oftentimes lead her sisters and religious followers in dance.

Sources: Monaghan, *Encyclopedia of Goddesses and Heroines*, 418

Pherousa

A sea–NYMPH, Pherousa ("converter" or "the first") was the NEREID of carrying fish and sailors in ancient Greek mythology; she was born the daughter of Nerues and DORIS. She was one of the named NEREID who accompanied THETIS in mourning the loss of her son, Achilles.

Sources: Apollodorus, *Apollodorus' Library and Hyginus' Fabulae*, 2; Collignon, *Manual of Mythology*, 18; Gould, *Historic Magazine and Notes and Queries*, Volume 14, 212; Trzaskoma, *Anthology of Classical Myth*, 18

Pherusa

A sea–NYMPH from Greek mythology, Pherusa was one of the named NEREID who accompanied THETIS in mourning the loss of her son, Achilles.

Sources: Apollodorus, *Apollodorus' Library and Hyginus' Fabulae*, 95; Bell, *Bell's New Pantheon or Historical Dictionary of the Gods,* 112; Hesiod, *Works of Hesiod, Callimachus, and Theognis*, 15; Perry, *Women of Homer*, 146

Phi Nang Mai

Similar to the DRYADS and WOOD NYMPHS from Greek lore, the phi nang mai ("phi female tree") live in the sacred trees which surround Buddhist temples in Thailand. These female fairy spirits were generally considered to be benign and were believed to refill the bowls of tired pilgrims.

Sources: Evan-Wentz, *Fairy Faith in Celtic Countries*, 229; Spence, *British Fairy Origins*, 108

Phi-Suk

Originally worshiped like gods before the introduction of Buddhism to Thailand the phi-suk are now regarded as NATURE SPIRITS who assist humans by teaching them the lessons they will need to know in order to leave the cycle of reincarnation. In some of the more remote regions, the phi-suk are regaining their former god-head status. Described as wearing traditional native dress these fairies are considered to be neither good nor bad but neutrally aligned entities.

Source: McCoy, *Witch's Guide to Faery Folk*, 292

Phiale

Variations: Phialê
According to the ancient Greek oral poet, Hesiod, Phiale ("water bowl") was one of the OCEANID, the NYMPHS which formed the retinue of the goddess, Artemis (Diana).

Sources: Ovid, *Four Books of the Metamorphoses*, 173, 311; Parada, *Genealogical Guide to Greek Mythology*, 128, 145

Phigalia

Phigalia was a DRYAD and a NYMPH in Greek mythology; the ancient Greek town of Phigalia in Arcadia, southern Greece was named after her.

Sources: Larson, *Greek Nymphs*, 309; Monaghan, *Encyclopedia of Goddesses and Heroines*, 426; Pausanias, *Pausanias' Description of Greece*, Volume 2, 310

Phila

In Greek mythology Phila was a water–NYMPH and one of the named DANAIDS, the collective name for the daughters of Danaus; her name appears in a list of the DANAIDS generated by Gaius Julius Hyginus (ca. 64 B.C.–A.D. 17), a Latin author. Phila was wedded to Philinus and killed him on their wedding night.

Sources: Bell, *Women of Classical Mythology*, 149; Hyginus, *Myths of Hyginus*, 132

Philia

A Naxian NYMPH, Philia, along with KLEIDE and KORONIS, was according to ancient Greek mythology, entrusted by the god Zeus (Jupiter) to care for the infant god, Dionysus (Bacchus).

Sources: Dalby, *Bacchus*, 105; Larson, *Greek Nymphs: Myth, Cult, Lore*, 81

Philodike

Variations: Philodice
In Greek mythology, Philodike was a NAIAD born the daughter of the river god, Inuchus; she was the wife of King Leucippus (Leukippos) of Messenia.

Sources: Barthell, *Gods and Goddesses of Ancient Greece*, 45; Bell, *Bell's New Pantheon, 175*

Philomela

In Greek mythology Philomela was a water–NYMPH from Greek mythology and one of the named DANAIDS, the collective name for the daughters of Danaus; her name appears in a list of the DANAIDS generated by Gaius Julius Hyginus (ca. 64 B.C.–A.D. 17), a Latin author. Philomela was wedded to Panthius and killed him on their wedding night.

Sources: Bell, *Women of Classical Mythology*, 149, 365; Grimal, *Dictionary of Classical Mythology*, 127; Hyginus, *Myths of Hyginus*, 132

Philyra

Born one of the 3,000 daughters of the Titians, Oceanus and Tethys, Philyra was one of the named OCEANIDS in ancient Greek mythology. Philyra was also named as being the HAMADRYAD of the lime tree.

Sources: Boswell, *What Men or Gods Are These*, 58; Buxton, *Forms of Astonishment*, 211; Hesiod, *Works of Hesiod, Callimachus, and Theognis*, 20; Conti, *Natale Conti's Mythologiae: Books VI–X*, 701

Philyre

An OCEANIAD of Mount Pelion in Thessalia in northern Greece Philyre was a NYMPH beloved by the god Cronos (Saturn); when their affair was discovered by his wife, the god transformed his lover into a horse. Philyre gave birth to the Centaur, Chiron (Kheiron).

Sources: Lemprière, *Classical Dictionary* (1839), 52; Smith, *New Classical Dictionary of Greek and Roman Biography, Mythology and Geography*, Volume 2, 655

Phoebe

Variations: Phoibe

Phoebe ("bright") was a NYMPH in the mythology of classical Greece and Rome. According to the Greek oral poet, Hesiod, when her brother, Phaethon, died, she and her sisters were transformed into amber-weeping poplar tree. The seven sisters were collectively known as The Daughters of Helios (Sol); their names are AEGLE, AETHERIE, DIOXIPPE, Helie (see THE HELIADES), LAMPETIE, MEROPE, and PHOEBE.

Sources: Hyginus, *Myths of Hyginus*, 26, 125; Roman, *Encyclopedia of Greek and Roman Mythology*, 200; Trzaskoma, *Anthology of Classical Myth*, 264

Phoeno

Born one of the 3,000 daughters of the Titians, Oceanus and Tethys, Phoeno was a NYMPH and one of the named OCEANIDS in ancient Greek mythology; she was one of the companions of Persephone (Proserpina) and present when the goddess was kidnapped.

Sources: Conti, *Natale Conti's Mythologiae: Books VI–X*, 701; Homer, *Odyssey of Homer*, 432

Phooka

Variations: Bookhas, Bwcas, Dgèrnésiais, GLASHTYN, GRUAGACH, KORNBOCKES, Phouka, Pooka, Pouka, Pouke, Pouque, Púca, Púka, Pwca

In Irish fairy lore the malicious phooka is the bane of the countryside. It is said when it rains while the sun is shining the phooka will be out that night.

A shape-shifting trickster takes great delight in tormenting travelers, this fairy being will assume the form of a wild colt dragging chains, enticing a weary traveler to mount up upon its back. As soon as it has a rider the phooka takes it victim on a wild ride, kicking and bucking hard enough to break human bones; ultimately it dumps its prey off in a ditch. In the guise of an eagle it will snatch up a man and fly him toward the moon. As a black goat with an impressive set of horns the phooka will jump upon a person back and claw at him with its hooves until the victim is dead or has managed to bless himself three times. It is also known to take on the form of a demonic horse, black, huge, and well muscles breathing blue flames from its nostrils and smelling like sulfur.

When blackberries begin to go to seed and rot on the vine children are told not to eat them because the phooka "dirtied" them. When the berries are killed by a frost it is said the phooka spit upon them. After the first of November it is tradition not to eat blackberries as the phooka has defecated or urinated over the remaining crop.

According to legend only one man, the High King of Ireland, Brian Boru, was ever able to successfully ride upon a phooka. By use of a magical bridle containing three hairs from the creature's own tail he managed to stay mounted on it until the FAIRY ANIMAL was too exhausted to move and surrendered to the King. Boru solicited two promises from the phooka—first, it would no longer torment Christians or ruin their land; second, it would never again attack an Irishman unless he was drunk or intended to harm another.

Sources: Froud, *Faeries*, 93; Keightly, *World Guide to Gnomes, Fairies, Elves, and Other Little People*, 371; McCoy, *Witch's Guide to Faery Folk*, 293–4; Monaghan, *Encyclopedia of Celtic Mythology and Folklore*, 384–85; Wallace, *Folk-lore of Ireland*, 91

Phra Phum

In Thailand Phra Phum ("lord of the place") is a house hold spirit and guardian of the home. To ensure her good will small houses or *sams* are placed near the entrance of the home where daily offerings are made.

Sources: Rose, *Spirits, Fairies, Leprechauns, and Goblins, an Encyclopedia*, 260; Smith, *Historical Dictionary of Thailand*, 65–66

Phrixa

Phrixa was a NYMPH of Arcadia and one of the named OCEANID from Greek mythology; she was associated with the care and feeding of the infant god, Zeus (Jupiter).

Sources: Larson, *Greek Nymphs*, 153; Pausanias, *Pausanias's Description of Greece*, Volume 1, 434

Phyllodoce

A sea–NYMPH, Phyllodoce was one of the named NEREID in classical Greek mythology; she was born of Nereus and DORIS and described by Virgil as having bright, waving locks of hair and a slender pale neck.

Sources: Apollodorus, *Apollodorus' Library and Hyginus' Fabulae*, 95; Lemprière, *Classical Dictionary*, 468; Virgil, *Fourth Georgic of Virgil*, 49

Phylodameia

In Greek mythology Phylodameia, was a NYMPH, daughter of Danaos, and one of the named DANAIDS; she was said to be the mother of Pharis by the god, Hermes (Mercury).

Sources: Bell, *Women of Classical Mythology*, 151; Pausânias, *Guide to Greece: Southern Greece*, 172

Phynnodderee

Variations: BUGGANES, FENODEREE

In Manx fairy lore the phynnodderee ("hairy one") were a species of SOLITARY FAIRY similar to the BROWNIE and KOBOLD. Described as being very kind and obliging to the family of the farm it occupies, the phynnodderee assisted in daily chores, particularly in driving sheep and gathering hay if a storm is rolling in.

According to the folklore the Phynnodderee was once a singular individual who was courting a beautiful human maiden and missed participating in *Re-hollys vodar yn oury*, the fairy's Harvest Moon celebration. Because he chose the mortal over his own kind Phynnodderee was exiled from FAIRYLAND and condemned to wander the Isle until Doomsday. As the years passed he took on a grotesque form, his body becoming shriveled, his skin leathery, and covered with log, shaggy hair. In the Glashtin region, Fenodyree was said to look like a GOBLIN, half cow and half horse in appearance.

Sources: Keightly, *World Guide to Gnomes, Fairies, Elves, and Other Little People*, 402; Evan-Wentz, *Fairy Faith in Celtic Countries*, 129; McCoy, 294–5, *Witch's Guide to Faery Folk*

Physadeia

In Greek mythology Physadeia, was a NYMPH of a spring in Argos and as a daughter of Danaus, one of the named DANAIDS; a freshwater sources is named after her.

Sources: Bell, *Women of Classical Mythology*, 369; Callimachus, *Callimachus*, 157; Keightley, *Mythology of Ancient Greece and Italy*, 366; Larson, *Greek Nymphs*, 53

Phyto

One of the NYMPHS of the mythical Mount Nysa, Phyto ("rot") was one of the BAKKHAI and a nurse to the infant god, Dionysus (Bacchus).

Sources: Clark, *Classical Manual*, 246; Hansen, *Handbook of Classical Mythology*, 75

Pickleharin

Variations: Pickle Harin

Likely originating in Teutonic mythology Pickleharin is a singular, sea-going fairy. Covered with hair and wearing garments of leaves like the Scottish BROWNIE, he lived aboard ships.

Sources: Brewer, *Dictionary of Phrase and Fable*, 684; Edwards, *Hobgoblin and Sweet Puck*, 149; Keightly, *World Guide to Gnomes, Fairies, Elves, and Other Little People*, 316

Picktree Brag

A shape-shifting BARGUEST or GOBLIN haunting the roads of North England, Picktree Brag would, the like the PHOOKA of Ireland, appear as a horse enticing travelers to mount up upon its back. When it had its victim it would bolt off taking them on a wild chace across the countryside and ultimately dumping its rider off in a pond. Picktree Brag is also known to appear as a calf with a white handkerchief around its neck, a donkey, a naked man without a head, and as four men holding up a white sheet.

Sources: Henderson, *Notes on the Folk-Lore of the Northern Counties of England*, 270; Keightly, *World Guide to Gnomes, Fairies, Elves, and Other Little People*, 310; Wright, *English Dialect Dictionary, A–C*, 371

Pigwidgeon

Variations: PILLYWIGGINS

In England the pigwidgeons are a species of diminutive fairies looking after the wellbeing of wildflowers. When sighted, they are often mounted upon the back of a bee.

Source: Rose, *Spirits, Fairies, Leprechauns, and Goblins*, 261

Pijchu

Pijchu is an APU who lives on a mountain peak in the Andes Mountains.

Source: Illes, *Encyclopedia of Spirits*, 198

Pikol

Pikol is an APU who lives on a mountain peak in the Andes Mountains.

Source: Illes, *Encyclopedia of Spirits*, 198

Pillan

Powerful male NATURE SPIRITS in the Mapuche mythology, the pillan resides high up in the Andean mountains; they control catastrophic natural disasters such as droughts, earthquakes, thunder, tidal waves, and volcanic eruptions. Considered to be a sort of ancestral spirit, shamans would consult the pillan to determine the source of an illness.

Associated with fire, initiation rites, shamanism, and volcanoes the pallan were associated with the Devil by Christian missionaries.

Sources: Briones, *Contemporary Perspectives on the Native Peoples of Pampa*, 156; Faron, *Hawks of the Sun*, 51, 143, 156

Pillywiggins

Variations: Flower Faeries, Spring Faeries

Diminutive winged, SEASONAL FAIRIES associated with spring, the playful pillywiggins live in the wildflowers growing at the base of oak trees. These TROOPING FAIRIES have no particular interest in humans but have been seen acting out events of human life, such as parties and weddings. Unlike other fay, they do not play pranks of any kind. Pillywiggins are led by their beautiful and seductive FAIRY QUEEN, ARIEL; while her people ride upon the backs of bees she rides upon a bat.

Sources: McCoy, *Witch's Guide to Faery Folk*, 139, 295; Rose, *Spirits, Fairies, Leprechauns, and Goblins*, 261

Pinari

In the mythology from the people of the Solomon Islands the pinari are the fairies of the Islanders. These NATURE SPIRITS are described as having human-like bodies with hairy bodies and long legs.

Source: Rose, *Spirits, Fairies, Leprechauns, and Goblins, an Encyclopedia*, 261

Pinch

Pinch was one of the fairies mentioned being in the company of ROBIN GOOD FELLOW in a seventeenth century pamphlet. He and his fellow fairies, GRIM, GULL, and PATCH are all said to have shape-shifting abilities. According to Shakespeare, Pinch goes about at night checking on household doors; if he finds any of them left unlocked he would pinch the servant who neglected their duty "until their bodies were as many colors as a mackerel's back." When the beating was finished he would then leave the servant in the open doorway to be discovered in the morning. Pinch also bruises the arms and legs of house maids who are sleeping when they should be working or intentionally leave bones or egg shells on the floor behind doors. He likewise punishes anyone who does not keep their shoes clean and goes to bed wearing their stockings.

Sources: Briggs, *Encyclopedia of Fairies*, 327; Wilson, *Life in Shakespeare's England*, 42–43

Pincoy

The pincoy of the Chilote mythology of Chiloé, Chile was a water fairy described as being half fish and half man; it was often seen in the presence of its sister and wife, PINCOYA. If this fairy was seen on the beach and facing the water the weather would be good. Many sailors who lost their ship at sea and were fortunate enough to wash up on shore credit the pincoy with the deed. The pincoy had the natural ability to attract fish and shellfish in abundance.

Sources: Fergusson, *Chile*, 61; Porterfield, *Chile*, 47

Pincoya

The pincoya of the chilote mythology of Chiloé, Chile was a water fairy described as being the most beautiful woman ever seen from the waist up, having long blond hair and blue eyes, from the waist down she had the body of a fish. Cheerful and sensual by nature this SIREN of the sea personifies the fertility of marine species; she is married to her brother, PINCOY. If she is seen on shore dancing while facing the sea there will be an abundance of fish; however if she is dancing and facing the mountains fishing will be poor.

Sources: Fergusson, *Chile*, 61; Porterfield, *Chile*, 47

Pinket

Variations: Ignis Fatuus, Pinkett, Piuket

In the parish of Badsey, England the Ignis Fatuus (see ELF-FIRE and ESPRIT FOLLET) was known as the pinket, a Dutch word which means "to wink." One of the attendants of FAIRY QUEEN, MAB was named Pinket.

Sources: Allies, *On the Ignis Fatuus*, 18; Briggs, *Encyclopedia of Fairies*, 327; Wright, *English Dialect Dictionary M–Q*, 514

Piranu

In the fresh-water rivers of Argentina, South American fairy lore says the piranu is a malicious water fairy known for overturning boats. Described as looking like a large black fish with the head of a horse, the large eyed piranu is particularly aggressive.

Sources: Eberhart, *Mysterious Creatures*, 437; Rose, *Giants, Monsters, and Dragons*, 293

Pirene

In Greek mythology Pirene was a water–NYMPH and one of the named DANAIDS, the collective name for the daughters of Danaus; her name appears in a list of the DANAIDS generated by Gaius Julius Hyginus (ca. 64 B.C.–A.D. 17), a Latin author. Pirene was wedded to Dolichus and killed him on their wedding night. In a list compiled by Apollodorus, a Greek scholar and grammarian, she was one of the daughters of an unnamed Ethiopian woman and was wedded to Agaptolemus, the son of an unnamed Phoenician woman.

Sources: Classical Association, *Classical Review*, Volume 12, 125; Grimal, *Dictionary of Classical Mythology*, 127; Lemprière, *Classical Dictionary*, 236

Pisinoe

Variations: Peisinoë, Pisinōe, Peisithoe, Peisinoë

In classical Greek mythology, Pisinoe was one of the named SIRENS, a type of malicious NYMPH born the offspring of the ancient sea god, Phorcys. Half bird and half woman, she and her sisters would perch on the rocky Sicilian coastline and lure in sailor with their melodious song; once caught, their prey were eaten alive. Although they hunted the coastline they lived inland in a meadow.

Sources: Rose, *Giants, Monsters, and Dragons*, 293; Smith, *Dictionary of Greek and Roman Biography and Mythology*, 817

Pitane

Pitane ("lady of the pine") was a NYMPH of Sparta from the mythology of classical Greece and Rome. One of the NAIADS, she was raped by the god Poseidon (Neptune) and bore a daughter named EUADNE.

Sources: Bell, *Women of Classical Mythology*, 371;

Grant, *Who's Who in Classical Mythology*, 75; Larson, *Greek Nymphs*, 197

Pitho

Born one of the 3,000 daughters of the Titians, Oceanus and Tethys, Pitho was one of the named OCEANIDS from Greek mythology.

Sources: Bell, *Bell's New Pantheon or Historical Dictionary of the Gods*, 112; Boswell, *What Men or Gods Are These*, 58; Hesiod, *Works of Hesiod, Callimachus, and Theognis*, 20

Pitys

Pitys ("pine") was one of the OREADS and a NYMPH of Arcadia from ancient Greek mythology. She was beloved by the god Pan (Faunus) but refused his advances, ultimately transforming into a pine tree. Anoter version of the story says she and Pan (Faunus) were lovers but the god of the wind, Boreas, desired her. When Pitys rejected him, the angered god blew her off a cliff. Gain moved by the NYMPH's devotion to Pan saved her by transforming her into a pine tree; whenever the wind would touch its bark the tree would weep sap.

Sources: Hard, *Routledge Handbook of Greek Mythology*, 216; Larson, *Greek Nymphs*, 96, 155; Monaghan, *Encyclopedia of Goddesses and Heroines*, 426

Pitzln

A subspecies of the WICHTLN from the folklore of southern Germany the pitzln are well known as extreme pranksters and mischief-makers.

Source: Arrowsmith, *Field Guide to the Little People*, 51–3

Pixie

Variations: Colepexy, Dusters, Grigs, HEATHER PIXIES, PECH, Pechs, Pechts, PEXY, Picker, Pickers, Pigseys, Pigsies, Pisgy, Piskies, Piskies-Pisgies, Pisky, Pisky-pow, Pixies, Pixy, Púcaí, Pucksy, Urchins

A species of friendly, playful, and small fairy from British and Welsh folklore; there are various traditions regarding their appearance, origin, and physical size, but all accounts agree pixies wear green clothing and delight in misleading travelers. Pixies are a specific type of fairy, like the BROWNIE, ELF, and GOBLIN.

One of the favorite pastimes of the pixies is to lead travelers astray; to be pixie-led is to fall for their WILL O' THE WISP like trick and be led astray. To prevent this trick from happening it is advised to turn an article of clothing, such as one's coat, inside out. Pixies enjoy dancing to the musical sounds of crickets, grasshoppers, and frogs; their nocturnal dancing creates FAIRY RINGS. From the safety of the FAIRY RING on moonlit nights their FAIRY KING will emerge and give his subjects their nightly charges. The only reference to a female pixie was made of JOAN THE WAD, their FAIRY QUEEN.

In Devonshire and Cornwall, England the pixie are said to be beautifully handsome, small, and winged mischievous fairies with long legs and springy feet, allowing them to hop. Always dressed in green, dancing is their favorite hobby. It is locally believed pixies are the returned souls of infants who had the misfortune of dying before they were baptized.

In Dorset, England pixies were believed to live in coppices and woods while in Cornwall England and in Scotland pixies were described as being small, winged beings whose heads were slightly larger than the rest of their body. They were also described as having arched eyebrows and pointed ears and noses.

Sources: Board, *Fairies*, 2, 101; Froud, *Faeries*, 87–89; Keightly, *World Guide to Gnomes, Fairies, Elves, and Other Little People*, 298–99; McCoy, *Witch's Guide to Faery Folk*, 147, 243–4, 296–7, 305

Plaksy

Variations: Kriksy ("scream")

In Russian folklore Plaksy ("sniveler") was a HAG who tormented children at night. Offerings of bread and salt are made to her. A part of the offering is rubbed on the child and rest if left for her under the stove.

Sources: Hastings, *Encyclopedia of Religion and Ethics,* Part 8, 625; Khanam, *Demonology*, 256

Plant Annwn

The plant annwn ("the family of the Otherworld") was the Welsh name used to describe the fairies; the name likely came from the underwater entrance to their kingdom located underground. Females were called GWRAGEDD ANNWN, their speckled cattle called GWARTHEG Y LLYN, and their white hounds were known as the Cwn Annwn (see ANNWN, HOUNDS OF; CWN ANNWFN; GABRIEL HOUNDS; and GWYN AP NUDD). The FAIRY KING of the plant annwn was said to be Arawn or GWYN AP NUDD, sources conflict.

Sources: Croker, *Fairy Legends and Traditions of the South of Ireland*, Volumes 1–3,182; Monaghan, *Encyclopedia of Celtic Mythology and Folklore*, 381–82; Sikes, *British Goblins*, 30, 37

Plant Rhys Dwfen

The Plant Rhys Dwfen ("the family of Rhys of the Deep") was a specific family of Welsh fairies; they lived on a hidden land where the plant of invisibility grew. Generally, the Plant Rhys Dwfen were friendly and would spend a great deal of money every time they went to market. Described as being particularly handsome and only slightly smaller than the average person the Plant Rhys Dwfen appreciated fair dealings and would invite honest farmers and merchants back to their land with them.

Sources: Briggs, *Encyclopedia of Fairies*, 331; Moorey, *Fairy Bible*, 392; Monaghan, *Encyclopedia of Celtic Mythology and Folklore*, 382

Pleiades

Variations: Pleiad, Seven Sisters

The pleiades ("flock of doves" or "sailing ones") are one of the twelve species of NYMPHS; they were any one of the seven daughters born of the primordial Titian, Atlas and of the OCEANID, Pleione ("sailing queen"). The pleiades, with their half sisters, the Hyades, were the attendants of the goddess, Artemis (Diana). The pleiades were romantically persued by Orion for seven years and were only able to escape his advances when the god Zeus (Jupiter) answered their prayers for help and transformed them all into doves.

The names of the seven pleiades are ALCYONE ("Queen who wards off evil [storms]"); ASTEROPE (also known as STEROPE) ("lightening," "sun-face," and "twinkling"); and CELAENO (also known as Celaino) ("swarthy"); DRYOPE (also known as MEROPE) ("bee-eater," "eloquent," and "mortal"); ELECTRA ("Amber," "bright" or "shining"); MAIA ("mother" or "Nurse");and TAYGETE (also known as Taygeta) ("long-necked").

Sources: Larson, *Greek Nymphs*, 7; Littleton, *Gods, Goddesses, and Mythology*, Volume 11, 999; Rigoglioso, *Cult of Divine Birth in Ancient Greece*, 163; Rose, *Spirits, Fairies, Leprechauns, and Goblins, an Encyclopedia*, 263

Pleione

Born one of the 3,000 daughters of the Titians, Oceanus and Tethys, Pleione was one of the named OCEANIDS from Greek mythology. She was also the NEREIDS of rain-bringing clouds, the wife of the Titian Atlas, and the mother of the PLEIADES.

Sources: Boswell, *What Men or Gods Are These*, 58; Day, *God's Conflict with the Dragon and the Sea*,

64; Hesiod, *Works of Hesiod, Callimachus, and Theognis*, 20; Westmoreland, *Ancient Greek Beliefs*, 24

Plentin Newid

Variations: Plentyn-newid

In Welsh folklore the plentin newid ("changed child") was a CHANGELING left behind by the TYLWYTH TEG when they took a human child. At first, the plentin newid looks exactly like the infant it replaced but quickly begins to change form, becoming ill-tempered, shriveled, and ugly. Biting and screaming the fairy become a terror to its "mother" using its supernatural cunning to cause not end of trouble. To test if a child is a plentin newid it was placed on a shovel and held over a fire or bathed in a bath of foxglove. If the child died, it was a CHANGELING.

Sources: Briggs, *Encyclopedia of Fairies*, 332; Sikes, *British Goblins*, 57; Spence, *Fairy Tradition in Britain*, 232

Plexaure

Variations: Plexaura

Born one of the 3,000 daughters of the Titians, Oceanus and Tethys, Plexaure ("like a dashing brook") was one of the named OCEANIDS in ancient Greek mythology. Plexaure was also the name of one of the NEREIDS; she was born the daughter of Nerues and DORIS.

Sources: Bell, *Bell's New Pantheon or Historical Dictionary of the Gods*, 112; Boswell, *What Men or Gods Are These*, 58; Hesiod, *Works of Hesiod, Callimachus, and Theognis*, 20; Trzaskoma, *Anthology of Classical Myth*, 18; Westmoreland, *Ancient Greek Beliefs*, 24

Ploto

A sea–NYMPH from Greek mythology, Ploto ("she is the joy of sailing"), was the NEREID of sailing in classical Greek mythology; she was born the daughter of Nerues and DORIS. Ploto was described by Hesiod, the Greek oral poet, as having "bright-dilated eyes."

Sources: Anthon, *Classical Dictionary*, 330; Hesiod, *Works of Hesiod, Callimachus, and Theognis*, 299

Plouto

Variations: PLUTO

Born one of the 3,000 daughters of the Titians, Oceanus and Tethys, Plouto was one of the named OCEANIDS in ancient Greek mythology; she was married to Tmolus, the stepfather of Tantalus. Plouto was one of the playmates of Persephone (Proserpina) and present when the goddess was kidnapped. Plouto was a NYMPH of Mount Sipylos in Lydia, Anatolia.

Sources: Crudden, *Homeric Hymns*, 19; Fowler, *Archaic Greek Poetry*, 14

Pluto

Born one of the 3,000 daughters of the Titians, Oceanus and Tethys, Pluto was one of the named OCEANIDS from Greek mythology.

Sources: Boswell, *What Men or Gods Are These*, 58; Hesiod, *Works of Hesiod, Callimachus, and Theognis*, 20; Westmoreland, *Ancient Greek Beliefs*, 24

Pluvush

In Transylvania, there is an EARTHMAN by the name of Pluvush. According to the folklore, he steals infants in the night.

Source: Mennes, *Gnome and Garden*, 40

Poake

Variations: Ignis Fatuus, Poke, PUCK, Puck-Ball Fungus, Pug-Fiest

In the fairy lore of Worcestershire, England the poake, similar to the WILL O' THE WISP, was said to be a mischievous spirit that led travelers into bogs, ditches, and pools and then laughed manically about it.

Sources: Allies, *On the Ignis Fatuus*, 7–8, 12; Keightly, *World Guide to Gnomes, Fairies, Elves, and Other Little People*, 317; Rose, *Spirits, Fairies, Leprechauns, and Goblins*, 263

Podarce

In Greek mythology Podarce was a water–NYMPH and one of the named DANAIDS, the collective name for the daughters of Danaus. In a list compiled by Apollodorus, a Greek scholar and grammarian, she was one of the daughters of Pieria and was wedded to Oeneus, one of the sons of Gorgo.

Sources: Grimal, *Dictionary of Classical Mythology*, 127; Lemprière, *Classical Dictionary*, 236

Pokey-Hokey

Pokey-Hokey is frightening GOBLIN from East Anglian British folklore. Similar to a poltergeist, the pokey-hokey would make knocking sounds from within the walls.

Sources: Briggs, *Encyclopedia of Fairies*, 333; Rose, *Spirits, Fairies, Leprechauns, and Goblins, an Encyclopedia*, 263; Wright, *Rustic Speech and Folk-Lore*, n.p.

Polevik

Variations: Polevoi, Polevoy, Polewik

The polevik of Polish fairy lore are described as looking bipedal goats, they are NATURE SPIRITS and protectors of fields. Sometimes their appearance would vary from region to region; it has been said to have a body "as black as earth," two different colored eyes, and even long green grass rather than hair.

Generally regarded as benign the polevik will assist in reaping and bringing in the harvest; however, they expect to be paid an excessive amount at the harvest's end. To prevent this from happening it is said a contract must be drawn up in advance stating exactly what will be paid for their assistance and the payment will be left in the field for them at night. Typically the polevik will decide it is not worth the trouble and move along. Nevertheless, farmers to this day will leave some extra grain in the fields as a libation to them. Poleviks fear and will flee from sickles.

Sources: Aldington, *Larousse Encyclopedia of Mythology*, 290; Gray, *Mythology of All Races*, Volume 3, 269; McCoy, *Witch's Guide to Faery Folk*, 298

Poludnica

Variations: Lady Midday, Poludniowka, Poludnitsa, Polunditsa ("noon-wife"), Pscipolnitsa, Psezpolnica, Rzanica

In Slovenia there is a malicious NATURE SPIRIT that looks like a beautiful, tall woman wearing white or dressed as if in mourning. In either guise, a *poludnica* ("noon") is said to be carrying a scythe or shears. During harvest time, right around noon, a poludnica attacks laborers who are working and not taking their proper rest, causing them to be afflicted with heat stroke or madness if they are lucky. If not, the poludnica will lure them off with her beauty and when she has them in a secluded place, attack viciously, draining them of their blood. It has also been said it will break the arms and legs of anyone it happens to come across. If a poludnica comes up to a field worker, it will start to ask him difficult questions. As soon as he cannot answer one, it will chop off his head. It was said if a poludnica was seen, immediately drop to the ground and lie perfectly still until it meanders off. The male version of the poludnica is called *polevoy*.

Typically a bundle of grain is decorated when harvest starts to keep poludnica at bay, and when harvest time is over, the effigy is burned.

In addition to attacking laborers, it is said to also steal children it finds wandering unattended as the adults worked. Most likely the poludnica is a NURSERY BOGEY used by parents to keep their children from wandering off and damaging the crops. It is also an excellent story for a worker who wants to take a break.

Sources: Gray, *Mythology of All Races*, Volume 3, 267–68; Oinas, *Essays on Russian Folklore and Mythology*, 103–05; Perkowski, *Vampires of the Slavs*, by Jan L. Perkowski

Poluvirica

A NATURE SPIRIT in Slavic lore the poluvirica ("half-believer") is described as appearing naked and holding a child in her arms; she is said to have a long face and long hanging breasts; her hair is kept in three braids hanging down her back. Reported to be a malicious being the poluvirica would claim to be Orthodox yet chant the Devil's creed.

Source: Oinas, *Essays on Russian Folklore and Mythology*, 128

Polybe

In Greek mythology Polybe was a water–NYMPH and one of the named DANAIDS, the collective name for the daughters of Danaus; her name appears in a list of the DANAIDS generated by Gaius Julius Hyginus (ca. 64 B.C.–A.D. 17), a Latin author. Polybe was wedded to Itonomus and killed him on their wedding night.

Sources: Apollodorus of Athens, *Apollodorus' Library and Hyginus' Fabulae*, 170; Hyginus, *Myths of Hyginus*, 133; Parada, *Genealogical Guide to Greek Mythology*, 59

Polydora

Born one of the 3,000 daughters of the Titians, Oceanus and Tethys, Polydora ("the shapely") was one of the named OCEANIDS of ancient Greek mythology. A NYMPH and one of the named DANAIDS; Polydora was said to be the mother of Dryops (Oeta) by the river god, Spercheus.

Sources: Bell, *Bell's New Pantheon or Historical Dictionary of the Gods*, 112; Boswell, *What Men or Gods Are These*, 58; Hesiod, *Works of Hesiod, Callimachus, and Theognis*, 20; Westmoreland, *Ancient Greek Beliefs*, 24

Polyhymnia

One of the nine CANONICAL MUSES Polyhymnia ("many hymns") was the MUSE of oratory and sacred songs in the mythology of ancient Greece; she is depicted in art as having a pensive expression, sometimes she even has one of her fingers placed over her lips. Her intent was to lift the soul of man to heavenly heights. When referred to as the inventor of myths she is portrayed as wearing a veil across her face.

Sources: Hunt, *Masonic Symbolism*, 470; Littleton, *Gods, Goddesses, and Mythology*, Volume 11, 921; Peterson, *Mythology in Our Midst*, 121

Polyhymno

One of the NYMPHS from Greek mythology of the mythical Mount Nysa, Polyhymno was one of the BAKKHAI and a nurse to the infant god, Dionysus (Bacchus).

Sources: Cook, *Zeus*, 1022; Smith, *Smaller Classical Mythology*, 144

Polynome

A sea–NYMPH from the folklore of ancient Greece, Polynome was the NEREID of the seacaverns; she was born the daughter of Nerues and DORIS.

Sources: Apollodorus, *Apollodorus' Library and Hyginus' Fabulae*, 2; Betham, *Transactions of the Royal Irish Academy*, Volume 17, 89; Hesiod, *Works of Hesiod, Callimachus, and Theognis*, 15; Trzaskoma, *Anthology of Classical Myth*, 18

Polyphe

Variations: Koryphe

Born one of the 3,000 daughters of the Titians, Oceanus and Tethys, Polyphe was one of the named OCEANIDS. In very rare instances she was referred to as the mother of the goddess, Athena (Minerva) by the god of the sea, Poseidon (Neptune).

Sources: Cook, *Journal of Hellenic Studies*, Volume 14, 143, 145; Day, *God's Conflict with the Dragon and the Sea*, 251

Polyxena

In Greek mythology Polyxena ("many strangers") was a water–NYMPH in Greek mythology and one of the named DANAIDS, the collective name for the daughters of Danaus; her name appears in a list of the DANAIDS generated by Gaius Julius Hyginus (ca. 64 B.C.–A.D. 17), a Latin author. Polyxena was wedded to her uncle, Aegyptus, and killed him on their wedding night.

Sources: Bell, *Women of Classical Mythology*, 378; Hyginus, *Myths of Hyginus*, 133

Polyxo

Polyxo was a NYMPH from the mythology of classical Greece and Rome. One of the NAIADS, her twelve daughters were wed to the twelve sons of her sister, the NAIAD NYMPH, CALIADNE and her husband the Egyptian king, Aigyptos.

Sources: Apollodorus of Athens, *Apollodorus' Library and Hyginus' Fabulae*, 95; Larson, *Greek Nymphs*, 307; Lemprière, *Classical Dictionary*, 245; Parada, *Genealogical Guide to Greek Mythology*, 128

Ponaturi

In Maori mythology the ponaturi ("knee-joint") are a species of malevolent water-fairy living in deep ocean water. These fay are described as having a light, greenish colored skin with a phosphorescent radiance; their hair is red and their fingers are long and tipped with claw-like talons. By day they live in their undersea kingdom Manawa-Tane, but by night they come onto land. The ponaturi are fearful of fire and will die is subjected to direct sunlight.

Sources: Craig, *Dictionary of Polynesian Mythology*, 213; Tregear, *Maori-Polynesian Comparative Dictionary*, 350

Ponphyoi

The ponphyoi is a species of NAT from the mythology of Kachin people of Burma.

Source: Rose, *Spirits, Fairies, Leprechauns, and Goblins, an Encyclopedia*, 264

Pontomedusa

A sea–NYMPH from Greek mythology, Pontomedusa, was one of the named NEREIDS; she was born the daughter of Nerues and DORIS.

Sources: Apollodorus, *Apollodorus' Library and Hyginus' Fabulae*, 2; Bell, *Women of Classical Mythology*, 379; Trzaskoma, *Anthology of Classical Myth*, 18

Pontoporeia

A sea–NYMPH, Pontoporeia was the NEREID of sea-crossings in ancient Greek mythology; she was a NYMPH of springs and wells.

Sources: Betham, *Transactions of the Royal Irish Academy*, Volume 17, 89; Hesiod, *Works of Hesiod, Callimachus, and Theognis*, 15

Pontoporia

A sea–NYMPH, Pontoporia ("sea-passage"), was one of the named NEREIDS in ancient Greek mythology; she was born the daughter of Nerues and DORIS.

Sources: Parada, *Genealogical Guide to Greek Mythology*, 125, 154; Sluiter, *Free Speech in Classical Antiquity*, 33

Porpoise Girl

Similar to the South American ENCANTADO and the SELKIES of the Orkney and Shetland Islands, porpoise girl of Micronesian folklore is a well know water fairy. According to the legend, porpoise girl had the ability to come up onto land, remove her tail and pass as human; the tail was always well hidden, as without it she would not be able to return to her home beneath the waves. One night as she was watching people enjoy themselves at a dace a fisherman discovered the tail and took it home with him. Unable to return to the sea, the porpoise girl married the fisherman and became the mother to his children. Many years later the fairy accidently discovered the hidden tail; she took it, solicited a promise from her children to never eat porpoise meat, and then after slipping on her tail, dove into the ocean never to be seen again.

Sources: Cavendish, *Man, Myth and Magic*, Volume 4, 2233; Lessa, *Tales From Ulithi Atoll*, 38–39, 120; Rose, *Spirits, Fairies, Leprechauns, and Goblins, an Encyclopedia*, 265

Portune

Variations: Neptune, Wish Maker

These inch-tall fairies of medieval British folklore were described as looking like old men with wrinkled faces; portunes loved to play harmless pranks on humans and were otherwise very wily. The portunes were among the very first of the fay to be recorded in English manuscripts. Similar to the LEPRECHAUN of Ireland the portunes were guardians of treasure hoards and would grant its captor a wish if it is ever caught. Friendly and helpful these BROWNIE-like fairies worked on human farms; however at night they were not above grabbing the bridle of a horse and leading it, rider and all, into a pond. These fay were known to eat frogs they roasted over human fires.

Sources: Briggs, *Fairies in Tradition and Literature*, 3, 8; McCoy, *Witch's Guide to Faery Folk*, 299; Monaghan, *Encyclopedia of Celtic Mythology and Folklore*, 385

Potameides

The potameides of ancient Greek mythology were a sub-species of the NAIADS, they were the NYMPHS of fresh water rivers.

Sources: Avant, *Mythological Reference*, 295; Day, *God's Conflict with the Dragon and the Sea*, 394; Maberry, *Cryptopedia*, 112

Poulunoe

A sea–NYMPH, Poulunoe, was one of the named NEREIDS in ancient Greek mythology; she was born the daughter of Nerues and DORIS.

Sources: Day, *God's Conflict with the Dragon and the Sea*, 390; Parada, *Genealogical Guide to Greek Mythology*, 125

Poulynoe

A sea–NYMPH, Poulynoe ("richness of mind" or "thoughtful"), was one of the named NEREIDS in ancient Greek mythology; she was born the daughter of Nerues and DORIS.

Sources: Sluiter, *Free Speech in Classical Antiquity*, 33; Westmoreland, *Ancient Greek Beliefs*, 26

Pozemne Vile

Variations: Pcûvushi, Pûvushi

In Slavic gypsy lore the pozemne vile are a type of NATURE SPIRIT that are amiable, companionable, and noble fairy beings who give good counsel to mankind; they, like the GNOMES they resemble, live underground.

Sources: Grimassi, *Encyclopedia of Wicca and Witchcraft*, 383; Leland, *Gypsy Sorcery and Fortune Telling*, 69; Spence, *Encyclopædia of Occultism*, 371

Praxidike

Variations: Praxidika

In Greek mythology, Praxidike was a NYMPH of a Lykia; he was born the daughter of either Ogygos or the Sibros River.

Source: Larson, *Greek Nymphs*, 209, 323

Praxithea

Praxithea was a river NYMPH of the city of Athens in Attika, southern Greece according to the mythology of classical Greece and Rome. One of the NAIADS, she married King Erichthonius and bore him a son named Pandion.

Sources: Apollodorus of Athens, *Gods and Heroes of the Greeks*, 205; Parada, *Genealogical Guide to Greek Mythology*, 134, 156

Pressyne

According to medieval French folklore Pressyne was a beautiful fountain fairy who had captured the eye of Elynas, the King of Albany. After the wedding the NYMPH became pregnant and made her husband promise he would not look upon her while she was in labor. The king agreed but when the time came he discovered his wife was delivering triplets. In an excited state he forgot his promise and watched their birth. Unhappily, Pressyne had to leave the kingdom with her three daughters, MELUSINE, MELIOR, and PALATYNE, to the Island of AVALON. For seven years Elynas mourned the loss of his wife and children; his son, Nathas, by his first wife, became the king.

When the daughters were fifteen years old they discovered the reason they were living on the Island of AVALON was because their father had broken his promise and sought revenge against him. The sisters captured their father and locked him and his treasure hoard up in a mountain. When Pressyne discovered what her daughters had done she punished them for their great disrespect. Melusine was condemned to have the lower half of her body change into a snake every Saturday. If she was able to marry a man who agrees to never see her on Saturday, she would remain a woman but he broke his promise she would be transformed until Judgment Day. MELIOR was burdened with keeping a sparrow hawk in a castle in Armenia until she was rescued. PALATYNE was imprisoned with the treasure hoard atop a mountain in Arragon.

Sources: D'Arras, *Melusine*, 7–17; Foubister, *Goddess in the Grass*, 88

Prigirstitis

Similar to the BROWNIE of Scottish lore, the prigirstitis is a household fairy in Slavic-European homes. Described as looking like a little grey-haired old man the prigirstitis was said to have very acute hearing, sensitive to even the slightest whisper and because of this loathed any excessive noise, especially screaming. Those who offended this fairy could expect some form of retribution to fall upon them.

Sources: Dixon-Kennedy, *Encyclopedia of Russian and Slavic Myth and Legend*, 227; Rose, *Spirits, Fairies, Leprechauns, and Goblins, an Encyclopedia*, 266

Priparchis

A NATURE SPIRIT in Polish folklore Priparchis was a guardian of domestic animals; he ensured they were healthy and remained unharmed. Working in collaboration with another NATURE SPIRIT, KREMARA, Priparchis paid particular attention to sows in farrow and the weaning of piglets.

Sources: Dixon-Kennedy, *Encyclopedia of Russian and Slavic Myth and Legend*, 228; Rose, *Spirits, Fairies, Leprechauns, and Goblins, an Encyclopedia*, 266–67

Prone

A sea–NYMPH, Prone ("forethought"), was one of the named NEREIDS in ancient Greek mythology; she was born the daughter of Nerues and DORIS.

Source: Sluiter, *Free Speech in Classical Antiquity*, 33

Pronoe

Variations: PRONE ("forethought")

A sea–NYMPH, Pronoe ("bewailing" or "complaining") was the named NEREID of sailing forethought in ancient Greek mythology; she was born the daughter of Nerues and DORIS.

Sources: Betham, *Transactions of the Royal Irish Academy*, Volume 17, 89; Hesiod, *Works of Hesiod, Callimachus, and Theognis*, 15; Sluiter, *Free Speech in Classical Antiquity*, 33

Pronoia

Born one of the 3,000 daughters of the Titians, Oceanus and Tethys, Pronoia ("consort") was one of the named NEREID and OCEANIDS in ancient Greek mythology. By the Titian Prometheus, she was the mother of Deucalion, the single individual the god Zeus (Jupiter) determined had too many good qualities to die in the cataclysmic world flood he was sending to destroy the wickedness of the earth. As the consort to the demiurge, Ialdabaoth, she was the mother to the god of love, Eros.

Sources: Bonnefoy, *Roman and European Mythologies*, 192; Westmoreland, *Ancient Greek Beliefs*, 238, 799

Prosymna

Prosymna was a NYMPH of the river Asterion in Argos, southern Greece; she was born the daughter of the river god, Asterion. Prosymna, along with AKRAIA and EUBOIA, was a nurse to the infant goddess, Hera (Juno).

Sources: Larson, *Greek Nymphs*, 150; Lemprière, *Classical Dictionary*, 642

Proto

A sea–NYMPH, Proto ("the receiver") was the NEREID of the first or maiden voyage in classical Greek mythology; she was born the daughter of Nerues and DORIS. Proto was one of the named NEREID who accompanied THETIS in mourning the loss of her son, Achilles.

Sources: Apollodorus, *Apollodorus' Library and Hyginus' Fabulae*, 95; Bell, *Bell's New Pantheon or Historical Dictionary of the Gods*, 112; Collignon, *Manual of Mythology*, 18; Gould, *Historic Magazine and Notes and Queries*, Volume 14, 212; Hesiod, *Works of Hesiod, Callimachus, and Theognis*, 15, 48; Perry, *Women of Homer*, 146

Protomedeia

A sea–NYMPH, Protomedeia ("first counsel" or "first queen") was one of the named NEREID in ancient Greek mythology; she was born the daughter of Nerues and DORIS.

Sources: Hesiod, *Works of Hesiod, Callimachus, and Theognis*, 15; Sluiter, *Free Speech in Classical Antiquity*, 33

Protomelia

Variations: Protomedusa

A sea–NYMPH from Greek mythology, Protomelia, was the NEREIDS who sports in the phosphoric spark of the waves; she was born the daughter of Nerues and DORIS.

Sources: Bell, *Bell's New Pantheon or Historical Dictionary*, 199; Betham, *Transactions of the Royal Irish Academy*, Volume 17, 88

Prousa

In Greek mythology, Prousa was a NYMPH in ancient Greek mythology.

Source: Larson, *Greek Nymphs*, 196

Prymno

Born one of the 3,000 daughters of the Titians, Oceanus and Tethys, Prymno ("like a cascade which falls down over a great height") was one of the named OCEANIDS from Greek mythology.

Sources: Bell, *Bell's New Pantheon or Historical Dictionary of the Gods,* 112; Boswell, *What Men or Gods Are These*, 58; Hesiod, *Works of Hesiod, Callimachus, and Theognis*, 20; Westmoreland, *Ancient Greek Beliefs*, 24

Psamathe

A sea–NYMPH of summer breezes, Psamathe was the NEREID of sand in classical Greek mythology; she was born the daughter of Nerues and DORIS, was the wife of the sea-god Proteus, and was loved by King Aiakos of Aigina. According to the Greek oral poet, Hesiod, she was "graceful in person."

Sources: Apollodorus, *Apollodorus' Library and Hyginus' Fabulae*, 2; Hesiod, *Works of Hesiod, Callimachus, and Theognis*, 15; Trzaskoma, *Anthology of Classical Myth*, 18

Psekas

Variations: Psecas ("drops of dew")

Born one of the 3,000 daughters of the Titians, Oceanus and Tethys, Psekas ("rain-shower") was one of the named OCEANID in ancient Greek mythology. According to the ancient Greek oral poet, Psekas was one of the OCEANID NYMPHS which formed the retinue of the goddess, Artemis (Diana); they were likely NEPHELAI (cloud NYMPHS).

Sources: Ovid, *Metamorphoses of Publius Ovidius Naso*, 213; Parada, *Genealogical Guide to Greek Mythology*, 128

Ptelea

In ancient Greek mythology Ptelea was one of the eight HAMADRYAD who was born of the incestuous relationship between the NATURE SPIRIT Oxylus and his sister, HAMADRYAS. Ptelea was the HAMADRYAD of the elm tree.

Sources: Athenaeus of Naucratis, *Deipnosophists*, Volume 1, 131; Buxton, *Forms of Astonishment*, 211; Larson, *Greek Nymphs*, 283

Pteleades

Pteleades was a NYMPH of elm trees in ancient Greek mythology.

Source: Larson, *Greek Nymphs*, 11

Pterides

In ancient Greek mythology, Pterides was a NYMPH of ferns.

Sources: Larson, *Greek Nymphs*, 11; Monaghan, *Encyclopedia of Goddesses and Heroines*, 425

Ptoides

Ptoides was a NYMPH of Ptoion in ancient Greek mythology.

Source: Larson, *Greek Nymphs*, 364

Puck

Variations: Butz, HOBGOBLIN, Poake-Ledden, Pocker, Pouke, Pucke, PUK, Putz, ROBIN GOOD FELLOW, Robin Hood

Originally the word puck was used to refer to all of fairy-kind; eventually it refered to a specific NATURE SPIRIT called Puck, an impish trickster in pre–Christianized Europe. Perhaps the most familiar use of the name is for the character in William Shakespeare's play *A Midsummer Night's Dream*. In the play, the merry and mischievous Puck of medieval English folklore boasted of pranks, shape-changing abilities, and milk spoiling. With his willow-tree flute, he accompanied the fay on their moonlight dancing.

In Elizabethan folklore, Puck was an ill-behaved BROWNIE-like fairy, similar to the PHOOKA of Ireland; it was also used to refer to the WILL O' THE WISP.

Sources: Keightly, *World Guide to Gnomes, Fairies, Elves, and Other Little People*, 314, 316–17; Rose, *Spirits, Fairies, Leprechauns, and Goblins*, 267, 351; Sikes, *British Goblins*, 25

Puck the French

In the fairy-tale *A French Puck* by Paul Sebillot there is a mischievous SPRITE called Puck who was particularly fond of playing tricks on people during the midnight hour; he was especially fond of pranking cowboys and shepherds. Puck had the ability to shape-shift into a child, goat, man, ploughshare, stick, and a woman; he also had the ability to shape-shift into a needle however he could not manage to make the hole. Puck would not play his tricks in the same place and was always on the move from village to village.

Source: Lang, *Lilac Fairy Book*, 91–94

Puddlefoot

A singular being, Puddlefoot was a BROWNIE believed to live in a small barn on the road between Dunkeld and Pitlochry, Scotland; he gained his name for his habit of splashing in puddles and in the Altmor Burn, a stream running near Clochfoldich Farm. It was always obvious to those who worked the farm whenever Puddlefoot tidied up an area or came and made a mess because his wet footprints were always left behind.

Sources: Briggs, *Encyclopedia of Fairies*, 337; Henderson, *Scottish Fairy Belief*, 16; Rose, *Spirits, Fairies, Leprechauns, and Goblins, an Encyclopedia*, 267

Puk

Variations: Nise-Bok, Niske, Niske-Puk, Nis-Kuk, Niss-Puk, Pulter-Class (Nick Knocker)

In Friesland, the puk is very similar to the KOBOLD of German fairy lore; it is described as wearing a long green or gry jacket, a pointed red cap, and slippers on its feet. When the puk is treated well it will do basic household chores and tend to the cattle; occasionally it will amuse itself by pulling the clothes off of sleeping servants and tickling their noses. A bowl of gruel must be left for it each evening and if there is no butter in it, the puk will grow angry.

Sources: Guiney, *Brownies and Bogles*, 82; Keightly, *World Guide to Gnomes, Fairies, Elves, and Other Little People*, 233, 315

Pukin

Pukin is an APU who lives on a mountain peak in the Andes Mountains.

Source: Illes, *Encyclopedia of Spirits*, 198

Pūkis

Variations: Pujke, Pukis, Pukys, Puuk

Possibly of German origin, in Lithuanian mythology, the Pūkis is a household fairy, similar to the Latvian AITVARAS; it is described as being GOBLIN-like or as having the appearance of a dragon. Said to be a trickster and a treasure hoarding fairy it was said to have the ability to shape-shift into a cat or rooster while standing on the ground or a dragon with a fiery tail while in the air.

Sources: Lurker, *Routledge Dictionary of Gods and Goddesses*, 156; Rose, *Spirits, Fairies, Leprechauns, and Goblins, an Encyclopedia*, 268

Pukwudgies

In the folklore of the Wampanoag Nation, a Native American tribe of Massachusetts and Southern New England, Unites States of America, the elusive, small, and TROLL-like pukwudgies have the ability to appear and disappear at will; shape-shift in animals; possess magical arrows that can create fire at will; and have control over Tei-Pai-Wankas, the spirits of the people they have killed. Standing no more than three feet tall, the face of the pukwudgies have facial features similar to those of the Wampanoag people, however their ears, fingers, and noses are greatly enlarged and their skin is grey and smooth.

These malicious NATURE SPIRITS were known to lure people to cliffs and then push them off. They would also use balls of light to lure victims into the woods where they are then killed or kidnapped.

Sources: Fritz, *Good Giants and the Bad Pukwudgies, 40;* Mood, *American Regional Folklore*, 79–81; South, *Mythical and Fabulous Creatures*, 74–5

Pulch

A singular individual and NATURE SPIRIT from German lore, Pulch was believed to be the guardian of the trees making up the Kammerfrost, old ban-forest near Trier. Anyone who walked through it with *gesteppten leimeln* ("nailed shoes"), harmed one of the trees, or took their wood without his permission could expect to suffer some sort of retribution.

Sources: Grimm, *Teutonic Mythology*, Volume 4, 1360; Porteous, *Lore of the Forest*, 90; Rose, *Spirits, Fairies, Leprechauns, and Goblins, an Encyclopedia*, 269

Pwca'r Trwyn

Variations: Pwca of Trwyn, Yr Arglwydd Hywel ("Lord Howell")

Pwca'r Trwyn was the name of a fairy said to haunt a farmhouse in Mynyddyslwyn, Wales.

Traditionally the name of this fairy was Yr Arglwydd Hywel and it is likely he was a vanquished lord who went into hiding from the British forces at Pantygassg Trwyn Farm.

Sources: Sikes, *British Goblins*, 126–27; Thomas, *Welsh Fairy Book*, 172

Pwcca

Variations: BUCCA, Bucca-Boo, BWBACH, Bwci, Bwciod, COBLYN, Pooca, Pwca

Similar to the BROWNIE of Scottish lore, the pwcca will do household chores each night while the family sleeps so long as they remember to leave out a bowl of cream or milk for it. To forget the treat it with respect or ask the pwcca its name would cause this fairy to leave in a fit of disgust. It is sometimes described as having a birdlike head and a tadpole-like body.

Sources: Keightly, *World Guide to Gnomes, Fairies, Elves, and Other Little People,* 418; Monaghan, *Encyclopedia of Celtic Mythology and Folklore*, 64

Pylarge

In Greek mythology Pylarge was a water–NYMPH and one of the named DANAIDS, the collective name for the daughters of Danaus. In a list compiled by Apollodorus, a Greek scholar and grammarian, she was one of the daughters of Pieria and was wedded to Idmon, one of the sons of Gorgo.

Sources: Apollodorus of Athens, *Apollodorus' Library and Hyginus' Fabulae*, 22; Grimal, *Dictionary of Classical Mythology*, 127; Parada, *Genealogical Guide to Greek Mythology*, 59, 96

Pyrante

In Greek mythology Pyrante was a water–NYMPH and one of the named DANAIDS, the collective name for the daughters of Danaus; her name appears in a list of the DANAIDS generated by Gaius Julius Hyginus (ca. 64 B.C.–A.D. 17), a Latin author. Pyrante was wedded to Athamas and killed him on their wedding night.

Sources: Bell, *Women of Classical Mythology*, 149; Hyginus, *Myths of Hyginus*, 132; Parada, *Genealogical Guide to Greek Mythology*, 59

Pyrantis

In Greek mythology Pyrantis was a water–NYMPH and one of the named DANAIDS, the collective name for the daughters of Danaus; her name appears in a list of the DANAIDS generated by Gaius Julius Hyginus (ca. 64 B.C.–A.D. 17), a Latin author. Pyrantis was wedded to Plexippus and killed him on their wedding night.

Sources: Bell, *Women of Classical Mythology*, 150, 388; Hyginus, *Myths of Hyginus*, 133; Parada, *Genealogical Guide to Greek Mythology*, 59, 159

Pyreness

In Cornwall, England the pyreness is a type of earth fairy and is believed to live inside the stone megaliths in the area. Although there is no description of these being their energy is said to be felt radiating from the stones.

Source: McCoy, *Witch's Guide to Faery Folk*, 299–300

Pyrrha

Pyrrha was a NYMPH of Lesbos; she was the wife of Deucalion, the son of the Titian, Prometheus and the NYMPH, PRONOIA. After they and their son, Hellen, survived the Great Flood sent by the god, Zeus (Jupiter) to cleanse the earth of evil, Pyrrha and Deucalion had two additional children, Amphictyon and Protogenia ("first born").

Sources: Larson, *Greek Nymphs*, 197; Monaghan, *Encyclopedia of Goddesses and Heroines*, 431; Westmoreland, *Ancient Greek Beliefs*, 801

Pyrrhakidai

Pyrrhakidai was a NYMPH of Delos in the mythology of ancient Greece.

Source: Larson, *Greek Nymphs*, 183

Querciola

Variations: Querciuola

The querciola ("walnut tree") of Italian lore are a species of DRYAD, HAMADRYAD, NATURE SPIRIT, or SYLVAN generally living in trees. It is believed when lovers are separated sitting beneath an oak tree and singing to the querciola will ease tension between them.

Sources: Euvino, *Complete Idiot's Guide to Italian History and Culture*, 274; Leland, *Etruscan Magic and Occult Remedies*, 103–06

Qutrub

Originating in pre–Islamic demonology, qutrub are the male demonic ghouls or DJINN born from eggs as the children of IBLIS and a wife created especially for him by God out of the fire of Samūn. The females are called ghūl. Qutrub wander graveyards consuming human corpses.

Sources: Hughes, *Dictionary of Islam*, 137; Knappert, *Encyclopaedia of Middle Eastern Mythology and Religion*, 234; Rose, *Spirits, Fairies, Leprechauns, and Goblins*, 126; Turner, *Dictionary of Ancient Deities*, 251

Radande

Variations: Ra

In Swedish folklore it was believed if a particular tree was growing faster than the others in its proximity this was because the tree was occupied by a type of NATURE SPIRIT known as a radande ("to be able"). Similar to the DRYAD and HAMADRYAD of Greek mythology, the invisible radande lived in the tree and tended to its health and prosperity; it was especially fond of lime trees. The radande would punish anyone who cause any harm to a tree under its protection but the fairy could go not travel beyond the shadow of the tree. In Westmanland there was once a pine tree growing out from a boulder said to be under the protection of a MERMAID who acted as its radande.

Sources: Hastings, *Encyclopedia of Religion and Ethics,* Part 1, 23; Rose, *Spirits, Fairies, Leprechauns, and Goblins, an Encyclopedia,* 273; Thorpe, *Northern Mythology,* Volume 2, 71

Rade

Variations: FAIRY RADE

A *rade* is the spectacular procession the TROOPING FAIRIES; these events can be grandly celebratory or extremely solem. During the rade the fairies decorates their horses and don their finest clothes. Sometimes the fay would take cattle, goods, or people during this time.

SEELIE fairies fly through the air on their beautiful white horses for their rades while the UNSEELIE fairies present a howling terror the likes of which if witnessed by a mortal my frighten them to death. A FAIRY PATH is said to be created when TROOPING FAIRIES parade along the ground.

Sources: Briggs, *Vanishing People,* 162; McCoy, *Witch's Guide to Faery Folk,* 13, 23, 43; Newcomb, *Faerie Treasury,* 70

Radgrid

In Nordic and Teutonic mythology Radgrid was one of the named VALKYRIES, a NYMPH of battle. Always depicted as beautiful women who are sometimes immortal, they are the attendants of the god, Odin.

Sources: Grimm *Teutonic Mythology,* Volume 1, 421; Sigfusson, *Elder Eddas of Saemund Sigfusson Younger Eddas of Snorre Sturleson,* 57, 316

Radspakr

Radspakr ("counsel wise") was one of the many DWARFS named in the *Voluspa,* the first and best known poem of the *Poetic Edda,* a collection of Old Norse poems dating back to about A.D. 985.

Source: Acker, *Poetic Edda,* 218

Rádsvidr

Variations: Radsvid, Radsvinn

Rádsvidr ("swift in counsel") was one of the many DWARFS named in the *Voluspa,* the first and best known poem of the *Poetic Edda,* a collection of Old Norse poems dating back to about A.D. 985.

Sources: Daly, *Norse Mythology A to Z,* 22; Sturluson, *Prose Edda,* 30

Radsvithr

Radsvithr was one of the many DWARFS named in the *Voluspa,* the first and best known poem of the *Poetic Edda,* a collection of Old Norse poems dating back to about A.D. 985.

Sources: Daly, *Norse Mythology A to Z,* 22; Sykes, *Who's Who in Non-Classical Mythology,* 53

Ragotte

In the fairy-tale *The Wonderful Sheep* by Madame d'Aulnoy there was an ugly but powerful fairy by the name of Ragotte who owned a beautiful slave he kept in chains of gold. Ragotte was in love with a king who did not return her affection; no amount of her promises of power and wealth or threat of death could convince the king to marry her, as he was already in love with her slave. The fairy became so enraged she killed the slave-girl with a hard look; with a touch of her wand she transformed the king into a sheep, a spell which would last for five years. The king became the leader of Ragotte's flock of talking sheep, all princes who in some way or another displeased her. From time to time the spell on one of the sheep would end and the prince was able to make his way back to his home and return to his life.

Sources: Aulnoy, *Fairy Tales of Madame d'Aulnoy,* 181–86; Lang, *Blue Fairy Book,* 222–23

Raidne

In classical Greek mythology, Raidne ("improvement") was one of the named SIRENS, a type of malicious NYMPH born the offspring of the ancient sea god, Phorcys. Half bird and half woman, she and her sisters would perch on the rocky Sicilian coastline and lure in sailors with their melodious song; once caught, their prey were eaten alive. Although they hunted the coastline they lived inland in a meadow.

Sources: Roman, *Encyclopedia of Greek and Roman Mythology*, 443; Smith, *Dictionary of Greek and Roman Biography and Mythology*, 817

Raja Jinn Peri

In Malay mythology, Raja Jinn Peri ("king DJINN fairy") is the King of the DJINN (see FAIRY KING).

Source: Chopra, *Academic Dictionary of Mythology*, 243

Rambha

In Hindu mythology Rambha is one of the twelve apsaras but only four of them stand out in Sanskirt literature, MENAKA, RAMBHA, TILOTTAMA and URVASI. Rambha, along with MENAKA, and URVASI are the three celebrated dancers of INDRA's court; whenever his throne is threatened by an aspiring rishis, INDRA send one of these three apsaras down to earth to distract them during their meditations. Rambha appeals specifically to those who have attained the first degree of concentration.

Sources: Kallury, *Symbolism in the Poetry of Sri Aurobindo*, 84–5; Rajan, *Complete Works of Kālidāsa*, 168, 373

Randgrid

In Nordic and Teutonic mythology Randgrid was one of the named VALKYRIES, a NYMPH of battle. Always depicted as beautiful women who are sometimes immortal, they are the attendants of the god, Odin.

Sources: Grimm *Teutonic Mythology*, Volume 1, 421; Sigfusson, *Elder Eddas of Saemund Sigfusson Younger Eddas of Snorre Sturleson*, 57, 316

Raosvior

Raosvior was one of the many DWARFS named in the *Voluspa*, the first and best known poem of the *Poetic Edda*, a collection of Old Norse poems dating back to about A.D. 985.

Source: Acker, *Poetic Edda*, 218

The Raspberry King

In the fairy-tale *The Raspberry King* from Zacharias Topelius, the Raspberry King was a benevolent fairy who lived in the raspberry bushes. Described as looking like a small but kindly old man, this fairy wore a white coat and a red hat; when he walked, he did so with a limp as he left foot was deformed. Reigning over all the raspberry bushes for more than a thousand years he must spend one week every one-hundred

years as a worm by decree of the Great Spirit who rules over the sea, sky, and woods. The Raspberry always shows his gratitude to anyone who helps him while he is in his insect form.

Source: Lang, *Lilac Fairy Book*, 233–34

Ratainitsa

A singular being, this female domestic fairy from Russian mythology, Ratainitsa, was the guardian of horses and the stables they slept in.

Sources: Dixon-Kennedy, *Encyclopedia of Russian and Slavic Myth and Legend*, 232; Graves, *Larousse Encyclopedia of Mythology*, 290; Rose, *Spirits, Fairies, Leprechauns, and Goblins, an Encyclopedia*, 274

Rath

Variations: Burghs, Fairy Knowe, Fairy Hill, FAIRY MOUND, Fairy Mount, Sithean ("house of the fairies"), Taigh Shidhe

In Ireland a rath is the traditional home of a fairy; it is described as looking like a mound of earth or one of the countries many prehistoric earthen mounds. The inside is called the BRUGH. Although Irish fay are typically only a few inches tall, inside the mounds, the space was vast; sometimes they are seen departing the rath mounted upon their tiny horses.

Sources: *Bord*, Fairies, 3; Keightly, *World Guide to Gnomes, Fairies, Elves, and Other Little People*, 363; McCoy, *Witch's Guide to Faery Folk*, 42

Raviyoyla

A Serbian NATURE SPIRIT and a VILA, Raviyoyla had the ability to appear as a mortal woman. According to the folklore, Raviyoyla possessed the gift of clairvoyance and had supreme knowledge of the healing properties of every single plant; although she accidently killed Prince Marko's *pobratim* ("brother-in-God"), Voyvode Miloshshe, she was able by use of herbology, to restore him to life once again.

Sources: Petrovitch, *Serbia*, 220; Rose, *Spirits, Fairies, Leprechauns, and Goblins, an Encyclopedia*, 274–75

Rawhead

Variations: Tommy Rawhead

From the folklore of England and the Unites States of America, Rawhead and his companion, BLOODY-BONES, were often used as NURSERY BOGIES by parents to trick children into good behavior or for avoiding a certain activity or area, which ever was appropriate. Rawhead was said to dwell in bogs and ponds as well as in little used cabinets and under stairs. Exceedingly ugly and with a continuous flow of blood drooling from his mouth, Rawhead sits atop a pile of bones waiting for his next prey.

Sources: Brewer, *Reader's Handbook of Famous Names in Fiction,* 129, Monaghan, *Encyclopedia of Celtic Mythology and Folklore*, 450; Wright, *Rustic Speech and Folk-Lore*, 198

Red Cap

Variations: Bloodycap, DUNTER, Fir Larrig, Powries, Red-comb, Redcap

The red cap is perhaps one of the most evil and malicious of all the fairies of Scotland. Prowling the ruins in the Scottish Lowlands and along the English boarder this hatful SOLITARY FAIRY is described as looking like an emaciated man with leathery skin and with little or no hair atop its head. Its eyes are fire red, its hands are tipped in razor-sharp claws, its mouth is full of sharp teeth, and it has a long pointed nose. This fairy is also very strong and can out wrestle any man. Once engage in combat there is little chance of survival for the victim unless they are quick witted enough to shout out a few verses from the bible in order to drive it away. The red cap is capable of moving remarkably quickly despite the fact it wears boots made of iron, a rather interesting point as typically iron is the bane of the fay.

The red hat it wears and for which it is named for has been dyed with human blood. After each kill the red cap will clean up the murder site, mopping up the blood with its hat. In some folklore the red cap is also said to be a cannibal, consuming fairy and human flesh alike.

Once the red cap has laid claim to an abandoned castle or cairn it will guard the location with extreme violence, using its sharp scythe to fell anyone it perceived as invading its territory. It will also shove someone off a rampart as well as pushing boulders off a cliff down on unsuspecting prey it see the opportunity.

The red cap is constantly making strange sounds and they are described as resembling those of the beating of flax. It is believed when this noise is especially loud it is a sign of misfortune or death.

Robin RED CAP was perhaps the most infamous of its kind; it was believed to have been the familiar to Lord William de Soulis of Hermitage Castle. Robin RED CAP cruelly abused women, murdered men, and practiced black magic.

Sources: Briggs, *Encyclopedia of Fairies*, 339; Froud, *Faeries*, 154; McCoy, *Witch's Guide to Faery*

Folk, 213, 300–01; Monaghan, *Encyclopedia of Celtic Mythology and Folklore*, 392

Red Cloak Woman

On the Isle of Man at Keeill Moirrey ("Mary's church") there was often sighted a little old woman wearing a red cloak. Believed to be a fairy, the apt named Red Cloak Woman was seen coming over the mountain ringing a bell just about an hour before church services were about to start.

Source: Evan-Wentz, *Fairy Faith in Celtic Countries*, 118

Red Fairies

There was a well-documented tradition of a race of fairies called the red fairies ("y gwylliaid cochion") who lived in Coed y Dugoed Mawr ("wood of the great dark wood") in Merionethshire, Wales during the middle of the sixteenth century. These fairies were described as having red hair and long strong arms, lived in den located underground. They were well known to steal cattle and sheep during the night however placing a scythe in the family's chimney would ward them off.

Sources: Curran, *Celtic Lore and Legend*, 73, 76, 92; Sikes, *British Goblins*, 125–26

Red-Haired Man

The red-haired man of Irish lore has an affinity for humans, although its reasons are never made clear. This fairy will lead spell-drugged young men out of FAIRY FORTS and warn young maidens to refuse fairy wine. In stories, the Red-Haired Man acts as *deus ex machina*, assisting the hero in solving or escaping an unsolvable situation.

Sources: Wilde, *Ancient Legends, Mystic Charms, and Superstitions of Ireland*, 32; White, *History of Irish Fairies*, 101

Red Man

Variations: Far Darrig, Fear Dearg, FIR DARRIG

Akin to the LEPRECHAUN, the short and stocky, yellow-faced red man ("far darrig") of Irish folklore is named for his choice of attire. From his red top hat to the toe-tips of his red wool stockings this fairy take tremendous delight in causing mischief and playing gruesome practical jokes, as mortal terror amuses it. Usually the red man plans his tricks so well in advance its prey is caught before they realize they are in of fairy protection. However, if in doubt, say aloud "Na dean maggadh fum" ("do not mock me") as this will prevent the red man from victimizing you with pranks.

With the ability to move about invisibly the red man, a master of mimicry and ventriloquism will terrorize men by making scary and strange sounds. Its favorite trick of this sort is to make the sound of a dead man laughing emit from a grave. It can also make the sound of angels singing, bird calls, and waves crashing against the rocks.

The red man enjoys its creature comforts, such as a cozy couch, a pipe full of good tobacco, a warm hearth, and a glass of poteen. If these few items are routinely left for the red man to find in the house it will become as docile and helpful as the BROWNIE, even assisting in household chores.

Sources: Croker, *Fairy Legends and Traditions of the South of Ireland*, 360; Evan-Wentz, *Fairy Faith in Celtic Countries*, 32, 48; Monaghan, *Encyclopedia of Celtic Mythology and Folklore*, 180; White, *History of Irish Fairies*, 89

Redsvid

Redsvid was one of the many DWARFS named in the *Voluspa*, the first and best known poem of the *Poetic Edda*, a collection of Old Norse poems dating back to about A.D. 985.

Sources: Crossley-Holland, *Norse Myths*, 183; Sturluson, *Younger Edda*, 298

Regin

Variations: Reginn

Regin ("mighty") was a son of the magician DWARF king, HREIDMAR and the brother of FAFNIR and ÓTR in Norse mythology. A fierce and wise DWARF, albeit small, he was highly skilled in magic. After his brother FAFNIR kills his father, Regin spends many years seeking out his murderous sibling. He journeys to the court of King Hjalpreck and convinces the cultural hero, Sigurd, to slay kill his brother who has since transformed into a dragon. He told the young hero of place on the dragon's belly where a single scale was missing, its only weakness. Once the dragon was defeated Sigurd discovers he has not only had been used by Regin as a weapon of revenge but the DWARF intended to kill him. Before Regin gets a chance to kill Sigurd, the hero slays him, consumes the dragon's heart thereby gaining its power, and lays claim to the dragon's hoard. This tragic story is told in the legendary thirteenth century saga, *Volsunga Saga* ("*Saga of the Völsungs*").

Sources: Daly, *Norse Mythology*, 84; Dekirk, *Dragonlore*, 72–3; Sykes, *Who's Who in Non-Classical Mythology*, 53

Rekkr

Variations: Rek, Rekk

Rekkr ("warrior") was one of the many DWARFS named in the *Voluspa*, the first and best known poem of the *Poetic Edda*, a collection of Old Norse poems dating back to about A.D. 985.

Sources: Crossley-Holland, *Norse Myths*, 183; Sturluson, *Younger Edda*, 71

Rhanis

According to the ancient Greek oral poet, Hesiod, Rhanis ("rain drop") was one of the name OCEANID NYMPHS from Greek mythology formed part of the retinue of the goddess, Artemis (Diana).

Sources: Bell, *Bell's New Pantheon*, 211; Lemprière, *Classical Dictionary*, 669; Parada, *Genealogical Guide to Greek Mythology*, 128

Rhapso

In Greek mythology, Rhapso ("stitcher") was a NYMPH of healing in Athans.

Sources: Larson, *Greek Nymphs*, 132; Matthews, *Greek Personal Names*, 60

Rhea

Rhea was a NYMPH from the mythology of ancient Greece; she was charged with the care and feeding of the infant god, Zeus (Jupiter). Rhea was associated with a cave on Mount Methydrion, the place where the deception of Kronos and the subsutiting of stones occurred.

Sources: Larson, *Greek Nymphs*, 153; Pausanias, *Pausanias's Description of Greece*, Volume 1, 434

Rhene

Rhene was a NYMPH of the island of Samothrake in the Greek Aegean Sea in the mythology of ancient Greece. Rhene was the mother of Samon, the first settler of Samothrace, by the god, Hermes (Mercury).

Sources: Larson, *Greek Nymphs*, 178, 315; Parada, *Genealogical Guide to Greek Mythology*, 87, 128

Rhetia

Variations: Rhoiteia

A NYMPH of Greek mythology from the island of Samothrake (Samothrace) in the Greek Aegean Sea, Rhetia was the mother of nine children by the god, Apollo; collectively their children were known as the Corybantes (Korybantes). Rhetia was born one of three daughters to the sea god, Proteus and Torone.

Sources: Bell, *Bell's New Pantheon*, 198; Larson, *Greek Nymphs*, 315

Rhode

Variations: Rhodea, Rhodope

Born one of the 3,000 daughters of the Titians, Oceanus and Tethys, Rhode was one of the named OCEANIDS in the mythology of ancient Greece. She was also a NYMPH and one of the named DANAIDS, the collective name for the daughters of Danaus. In a list compiled by Apollodorus, a Greek scholar and grammarian, Rhode was one of the daughters of HAMADRYAD, AT-LANTEIA or (PHOEBE, sources vary) and was wedded to Hippolytus, one of the sons of an unnamed Arabic woman.

Sources: Boswell, *What Men or Gods Are These*, 58; Day, *God's Conflict with the Dragon and the Sea*, 64; Grimal, *Dictionary of Classical Mythology*, 127; Hesiod, *Works of Hesiod, Callimachus, and Theognis*, 20; Westmoreland, *Ancient Greek Beliefs*, 24

Rhodeia

Born one of the 3,000 daughters of the Titians, Oceanus and Tethys, Rhodeia ("flowering among rose-trees") was one of the named OCEANIDS in ancient Greek mythology; she was one of the playmates of Persephone (Proserpina) and present when the goddess was kidnapped.

Sources: Fowler, *Archaic Greek Poetry*, 14; Murray, *Manual of Mythology*, 154

Rhodia

In ancient Greek mythology Rhodia was a water–NYMPH and one of the named DANAIDS, the collective name for the daughters of Danaus. In a list compiled by Apollodorus, a Greek scholar and grammarian, she was one of the daughters of HAMADRYAD, ATLANTEIA or (PHOEBE, sources vary) and was wedded to Chalcodon, one of the sons of an unnamed Arabic woman.

Sources: Grimal, *Dictionary of Classical Mythology*, 127; Lemprière, *Classical Dictionary*, 236

Rhodina

Born one of the 3,000 daughters of the Titians, Oceanus and Tethys, Rhodina was one of the named OCEANIDS.

Sources: Boswell, *What Men or Gods Are These*, 58; Hesiod, *Theogony*, 114; Hesiod, *Works of Hesiod, Callimachus, and Theognis*, 20

Rhodos

A NYMPH in classical Greek mythology of the island Rhodes in the Greek Aegean Sea, Rhodos was born of the god of the sea, Poseidon (Neptune) and the goddess of love, Aphrodite (Venus); her brother was the NYMPH, HEROPHILOS. In very ancient Greek mythology, her parents were said to be Poseidon and Alia, one of the TEL-CHINES.

Sources: Budin, *Origin of Aphrodite* 18; Dalby, *Story of Venus*, 43, 131

Ri

Similar to a MERMAID or SIREN, Ri was a female sea-spirit in the folklore of the Maori people of New Zealand.

Sources: Meurger, *Lake Monster Traditions*, 21–22; Rose, *Spirits, Fairies, Leprechauns, and Goblins, an Encyclopedia*, 275

The Riesengebirges

Inhabiting the Riesengebirge Mountains ("GIANT Mountains") these DWARFS of German mythology were ruled by their monarch, NUMBER NIP. Well known for their malignant nature and strictly nocturnal the Riesengebirges harassed anyone who traveled through their territory. The only means to defeat these malicious DWARFS was to outlast their assault and wait for the first rays of sunlight to strike their bodies and turn them into stone.

Sources: Brewer, *Dictionary of Phrase and Fable*, 901; Rose, *Spirits, Fairies, Leprechauns, and Goblins*, 276

The Roane

Variations: Roan, Seal Maidens, SELKIE

In Ireland the roane ("seal") are seal fairies of the Scottish Highlands; in some lore it is says a roane is a MERMAN who has the ability to take the form of a seal. The roane are the gentlest of the fairy creatures, so benign they do not even seek revenge upon those mortals who kill seals and their fellow roane. On occasion one of the roane will wed a human and produce offspring; these children will have webbed fingers and toes. If the webbing is cut to allow for greater range of movement, bumpy horn-like knobs will appear on their feet and hands.

Sources: Briggs, *Encyclopedia of Fairies*, 340; Narváez, *Good People*, 245; Stewart, *Popular Superstitions and Festive Amusements of the Highlanders of Scotland*, 65

Roaring Bull of Bagbury

A fairy ghost from the folklore of England, the Roaring Bull of Bagbury was once an evil Squire who ran Bagbury Manor, a farm between Hyssington and Snead churches. According to one version of the legend, one of the household staff wished the squire to be transformed into a bull, but in another the squire was so evil in life when he died he returned as a gigantic, raging bull. No matter how the bull came into being the story goes on to say it was terror of the countryside. It took many men several days to round up the beast and corral it into the church at Hyssington. There, twelve clergy surrounded the FAIRY ANIMAL and "read him down," causing him to shrink in size. Eventually the fairy was small enough to be trapped in a snuff box and buried. The location of the snuff box varies in tellings, but possible locations are the Red Sea and the underside of the Bagbury Bridge.

Sources: Allardice, *Myths, Gods and Fantasy*, 184; Briggs, *Encyclopedia of Fairies*, 341; Jones *Collections Historical and Archaeological*, Volume 34, 201

Robin Good Fellow

Variations: Green Man, HOBGOBLIN, HOLLY KING, Jack Robinson, OAK KING, Owen, Pan (Faunus), Phouka, Pooka, Pouke, Puca, PUCK, Pwca, ROBIN GOOD FELLOW, Robin Hood

In British folklore, ROBIN GOOD FELLOW was a type domestic fairy, very similar to the BROWNIE. Born the son of a fairy father and a mortal mother, Robin loved to play pranks on anyone he came across in the woods. He was also adept at mimicking animal and bird calls.

The first time ROBIN GOOD FELLOW appeared in print was in a letter written by Thomas Norton to Sir Christopher Hatton, dated December 30, 1580 and inserted in Sir H. Nicolas's *Life of Hatton*.

In the work, *Mad Pranks and Merry Jests of Robin Goodfellow* (1629) Robin was born the child of a proper young woman and a FAIRY KING. Always a mischievous child, at the age of six years he ran away from home. Eventually he came into the service of a tailor and soon thereafter they eloped. In the second part of the story Robin had a vision of his father, OBERON, while he slept and upon waking discovered a scroll explaining to him anything he wished for would be granted. The note, evidently left by his father, went on to explain how to shape-shift into the form of an ape dog, hog, and horse. The letter closed with a warning, Robin was only to harm knaves and queens and, love those who were honest, and help honest people when they are in need. In this second part of the story, Robin's behavior is more in line with that of a BROWNIE or a Nis, as he plays many pranks. In the end, OBERON takes his son to FAIRYLAND.

Robin Good Fellow was also known as PUCK in William Shakespeare's play *A Midsummer Night's Dream*; there, he was described as looking like a Greek SATYR. Having a lusty and playful nature, he played pranks on humans and danced while he played on his pan pipes.

Sources: Brewer, *Dictionary of Phrase and Fable*, 1062; Collier, *Bibliographical and Critical Account of the Rarest Books in the English Language*, 330; Keightly, *World Guide to Gnomes, Fairies, Elves, and Other Little People*, 281, 287, 289, 314; McCoy, *Witch's Guide to Faery Folk*, 301–02

Robin Round-Cap

Variations: HOBTHRUST

In British fairy lore Robin Round-Cap is a singular individual domestic fairy. Similar to a BROWNIE or HOBGOBLIN, the good natured Robin Round-Cap of East Yorkshire, England, would assist servant maids by doing their chores for them in the early hours of the morning. However, it is said when he was in a bad mood, he would undo his earlier work.

Sources: Briggs, *Encyclopedia of Fairies*, 344; Hope, *Legendary Lore of the Holy Wells of England*, 198; Rose, *Spirits, Fairies, Leprechauns, and Goblins*, 277

Rota

In Nordic and Teutonic mythology Rota was one of the named VALKYRIES, a NYMPH of battle. Always depicted as beautiful women who are sometimes immortal, they are the attendants of the god, Odin.

Source: Grimm *Teutonic Mythology*, Volume 1, 421

Ruamano

A TANIWHA or fairy from the mythology of the Maori people, Ruamano lives in the ocean off of the east coast of the North Sea; he is known to assist drowning people, helping them to return to shore. He was born the offspring of the god, Tutara-kauika.

Sources: Best, *Māori Religion and Mythology*, 510; Reed, *Reed Book of Māori Mythology*, 284

Ruatane

A species of PATUPAIAREHE fairy from the myths of the Native New Zealanders Ruatane was a singular, individual fay who had once stolen a human woman named Tarapikau. When Tarapikau, her lover discovered she was missing he prayed to his god for advice and was told to find the fellow fairies of Rutane and ask them to dance. Tarapikau did as he was told and upon finding Ruatane and his people was able to persuade them to perform the Haka dance, a ceremony lasting all throughout the night, ending with the arrival of the dawn. When the fairies fell from exhaustion, Tarapikau made his escape with Tarapikau. Rutane discovered how he had been tricked and raised a fairy arm to kill Tarapikau; however, Tarapikau had already raised a much larger army of his own. Upon seeing how greatly outnumber he and his army was, Ruatane conceded the battle and left.

Sources: Cowan, *Journal of the Polynesian Society*, Volume 30, 145; Reed, *Reed Book of Māori Mythology*, 203–04

Rubezahl

Variations: He-Manner, Herr Johannes, Hey-Hey Men, Hoioimann, Huamann, NUMBER NIP, Riibezahl, Ropenkerl, Rubheyzahl, Rübezahl, Schlocherl

In Eastern Europe, particularly in the German mountains, Rubezahl ("turnip counter") is a singular entity, a male DWARF, dressed in heavy black cloaks and carries a thin, spiky walking stick. Hostile to climbers, tourists, and travelers this fairy has the ability to command to the rain and wind. Rubezahl lives in the mountain range which separates Poland and Czechoslovakia; it is known as Riesengebirge ("GIANT Moutains"). In some of the folktales Rubezahl is not a singular individual but rather a species of DWARFS.

In the fairy-tale *Rübezahl* the lord mountain GNOME, Rübezahl, ruled over the vast underworld. He had a vast treasure hoard and love pretty things. Rübezahl would occasionally travel to the surface world and enjoy all of the beautiful and wonderful sights he beheld. Rübezahl had the ability to shape change into a human and a raven and could also shrink his size small enough to pass through a keyhole. He had the magical ability to alter the natural terrain into beautifully landscaped settings. Sadly, Rübezahl fell in love with a princess whose heart already belonged to Prince Ratibor. When Rübezahl discovered he would never be able to win her love he stomped the earth three times and retreated into his underground world taking all of his treasures with him.

Sources: Brewer, *Dictionary of Phrase and Fable*, 901; Lang, *Brown Fairy Book*, 283–299; Mccoy, *Witch's Guide to Faery Folk*, 302–03

Rumpelstiltskin

Variations: Cruickshanks, Päronskaft, Repelsteeltje, Ricdin Ricdon, Robiquet, Rosania, Rumpelstilzchen, Sheepshanks, Spindleshanks, Titiliture, TOM-TIT-TOT, WHOOPITY STOORIE, Winterkolbe

A blackmailer and oppressor, Rumpelstiltskin ("little rattle stilt") was one of the many German tales collected by the Brothers Grimm and published in their 1812 book, *Children's and Household Tales*. Although there are many version of the story, the basis of it says a miler tried to impress the king by saying his daughter could spin straw into gold. The king summoned the woman to his castle and locking her in a tower room demanded for the next three days she spin straw into gold for him or she would be executed. The daughter who did not even have the skill to spin began to cry by was soon visited by a little fairy. It promised her in exchange for completing her task for her she would deliver her first born child to him. Feeling she had no other choice, the daughter agreed. The king was so please with the work she had done fell in love and married the miller's daughter. A year later, shortly the birth of her first child the fairy reappeared to the now queen demanding his fee. The queen managed to stall for more time by asked for three days, and if at the end of the allotted time she could not guess the fairy's name she would turn over her child. The fairy agreed and disappeared. Luckily for the queen one of her retinue overheard the little fairy singing a victory song which contained its name. When the fairy appeared, the queen as correctly able to guess the fairy name, causing it to run away and never return.

Sources: Grimm, *Grimm's Fairy Tales*, 92–8; Lang, *Blue Fairy Book*, 96–99; McCoy, *Witch's Guide to Faery Folk*, 64; Watts, *Encyclopedia of American Folklore*, 342

Rusalka (plural: rusalki)

A rusalka is a species of Succubus-like water NYMPH from Slavic lore. Its name loosely translates to mean "MERMAID." Rusalki are seen as the demons of the dualistic quality of nature, created when a woman dies an unnatural death, such as in a drowning, dying unbaptized, dying a virgin, or having committed suicide. They are described as looking like pale, lithe, startlingly beautiful women with loose and wild-looking green hair or as ugly large-breasted creatures. Most commonly seen in the summer and winter, rusalki prey upon men, using their charms to lure men into the water where they will tickle them to death. Controlling the cycles of the moon, these demonic creatures are also said to direct the clouds across the sky, as well as control the weather and the amount of rainfall. The rusalki are the symbol of life and death and are said to live in the forest near the edge of a river or lake during spring and summer months; they live in the water in the winter months. Each individual rusalka is a unique personage with her own tale.

Sources: Andrews, *Dictionary of Nature Myths*, 165; Mack, *Field Guide to Demons, Fairies, Fallen Angels, and Other Subversive Spirits*, 19–21; Phillips, *Forests of the Vampire*, 67; Riasanovsky, *California Slavic Studies*, Vol.11, 65–6; *Slavic and East European Folklore Association Journal*, Vol. 3, Issue 2, 59, 62

Saalah

Variations: SEALAH

In Arabic lore, the saalah were believed to be the offspring between DJINN and Humans and although partially mortal these fairy-beings are considered to be a sub-species of the DJINN. Living in forests and loving to dance the saalah have been said to capture people and force them to be their dancing partners. Hated by wolves saalah were also said to be fearful of them, so much so even the image of a wolf would repel them. When attacked by a wolf the saalah would cry out for assistance, but it was custom to ignore these cries and leave the hybrid to its fate.

Sources: Fraser, *Turkey, Ancient and Modern*, 25; Illes, *Encyclopedia of Spirit*, 872; Lane, *Arabian Society in the Middle Ages*, 43

Sa-Bdag

Variations: Sa bDag

NATURE SPIRITS in the Bon religion of Tibet the sa-bdag ("earth movers") live within the earth, lakes, and springs. Each region has its own sa-bdag acting as its protective guardian and its image, which also widely varies, is portrayed on the local temple.

Sources: Rennie, *Bhutan*, 131; Rose, *Spirits, Fairies, Leprechauns, and Goblins*, 281

Saba-Leippya

Similar to the HAMADRYADS of classical Greek mythology, the saba-leippya ("paddy-butterfly") are tree spirits or NATS from Burmese folklore; they are specifically the guardian of the rice crops

and appear as a butterfly. After the harvest has been taken in and the crop sold off, a small amount of rice from each field is kept in a container so before replanting next season the token rice can be returned to the area from where it came.

Sources: Porteous, *Forest in Folklore and Mythology*, 125; Rose, *Spirits, Fairies, Leprechauns, and Goblins*, 281; Scott, *The Burman: His Life and Notions*, Volume 1, 286

Sabdh

In the folklore of Ireland, Sabdh was a woman of the SÍDHE; she was also the fairy mother of Oisin, the legendary greatest poet of Irish history.

Sources: Leach, *Funk and Wagnalls Standard Dictionary of Folklore, Mythology, and Legend*, n.p.; Rose, *Spirits, Fairies, Leprechauns, and Goblins*, 281, 351

Saci

Variations: Saci-Perere

In in Afro-Brazilian folklore the saci was a one-legged primordial DWARF; described as wearing a red hood and smoking a pipe made of a sea-shell, he also had holes in his hands in some stories. The saci have magical powers and travel by means of whirlwinds. Less of a prankster and more of a minor annoyance, saci cause eggs to not hatch, release animals from their pens, and spill salt. Saci do not have the ability to cross running water and are compelled to untie knots.

Sources: Maberry, *They Bite!*, 320–21; Peek, *African Folklore*, 179

Sagaritis

In Greek mythology Sagaritis was a NYMPH and a NAIAD of the river Saggarios in Phrygia, Anatolia but she was also a HAMADRYAD. Sagaritis had an affair with the god of vegetation, Attis, the lover of the goddess, Cybele (Kybele) breaking the vow of fidelity he swore to her. When the goddess discovered the deception she cut down Sagaritis' tree, killing the HAMADRYAD; Attis, overcome with grief, castrated himself.

Sources: Hard, *Routledge Handbook of Greek Mythology*, 218; Roman, *Encyclopedia of Greek and Roman Mythology*, 94

Saivo-Neita

Saivo-Neita ("sea maiden") was a MERMAID from the folklore of the Lapp people of Finland and Norway.

Source: Rose, *Spirits, Fairies, Leprechauns, and Goblins*, 281

Salamander

The hermetic and neo-Platonic doctrine from which all medieval medicine and science were founded describes four Elemental classes, Air, Earth, Fire, and Water; accordingly the Salamanders belong to the Fire class, GNOMES to Earth, NEREIDS (see UNDINE) to water, and SLYPHS to Air. Salamanders look exactly like the amphibians they are named after and were believed to be powerful beings; they were well aware of their own value to magicians and are considered to be supreme in the elemental hierarchies.

Sources: Briggs, *Encyclopedia of Fairies*, 192–3; McCoy, *Witch's Guide to Faery Folk*, 304; Rose, *Spirits, Fairies, Leprechauns, and Goblins*, 282; Stepanich, *Faery Wicca*, Book One, 31

Salamis

In classical Greek mythology Salamis was one of the NAIADS daughters of the river god ASOPUS in Sikyonia and Boiotia, central and southern Greece.

Sources: Classical Association, *Classical Review*, Volume 12, 125; Quiggin, *Essays and Studies Presented to William Ridgeway*, 224

Salbanelli

Born of the union between the SALVANELLI and a *strega* ("witch") the salbanelli are quarter-fairy being from the folklore of northern Italy; they are considered to be fairy hybrids.

Sources: Arrowsmith, *Field Guide to the Little People*, 105; Grimassi, *Hereditary Witchcraft: Secrets of the Old Religion*, 83

Saleerandees

Bipedal lizards in Welsh fairy lore the saleerandees are benign but their sudden appearance can be startling. These fay are naturally always cold and do not have the ability to create fire for themselves; when they are seen it is always near a fireplace.

Source: McCoy, *Witch's Guide to Faery Folk*, 305

Salgfraulein

A type of WOOD NYMPH form the Tyrol region of Austria, salgfraulein, similar to the HAMADRYAD of Greek mythology, was a fairy of the larch tree. Typically the salgfraulein would take on the appearance of a young maiden dressed in all white; they could be said to be heard singing throughout the woods.

Sources: Porteous, *Forest Folklore*, 93; Rose, *Spirits, Fairies, Leprechauns, and Goblins*, 282

Salkanaty

Salkanaty is an APU who lives on a mountain peak in the Andes Mountains.

Source: Illes, *Encyclopedia of Spirits*, 198

Salmacis

Variations: Salmachis, Salmakis

Salmacis was a NYMPH from the mythology of classical Greece and Rome. One of the NAIADS, she was written of in Ovid's *Metamorphoses* as a sexually aggressive individual. In the story, the son of the god Hermes (Mercury) and Aphrodite (Venus), Hermaphroditus, happened by her while traveling and upon seeing him, Salmacis fell deeply and instantly in love with him. She offered herself to him but he refused; wandering off he had the misfortune to come upon her pool and wanting to refresh himself entered into it. Salmacis dove into the pool after him and entwining her body around his prayed to the gods they would never be separated. The gods granted their prayers, melding them together, creating the first hermaphrodite. What remained of Hermaphroditus prayed to the gods asking them to transform any man who bathed in his fountain into *semivir*, an individual who has lost his masculinity and have become infertile; his impassioned prayer was answered.

Sources: Anderson, *Ovid's Metamorphoses*, Books 1–5, 442; Larson, *Greek Nymphs*, 142; Littleton, *Gods, Goddesses, and Mythology*, Volume 11, 1000; Parker, *Mythology: Myths, Legends and Fantasies*, 61

Salvanelli

Variations: Sanguanello

Born of the union between the AGUANE and the SILVANI, the Salvanelli were half-fay being from the folklore of northern Italy. The name of these hybrids referes to the glint of light which gleams off the surface of a mirror or the sparkling surface of water. It was not unusual for a salvanelli to take a *strega* ("witch") as its mate, as Italian fay and witches were said to share a common bloodline. Children produced from this coupling are known as *SALBANELLI*.

Sources: Arrowsmith, *Field Guide to the Little People*, 107; Grimassi, *Hereditary Witchcraft: Secrets of the Old Religion*, 83; Rose, *Spirits, Fairies, Leprechauns, and Goblins*, 282

Samhanach

A BOGIE or GOBLIN from Scottish lore the samhanach ("a savage") is most active on the feast of Samhain (October 31), from which its name is derived. These malignant fairies are believed to steal children and cause general mischief.

Sources: Hastings, *Encyclopedia of Religion and Ethics,* Part 9, 104; MacRitchie, *Fians, Fairies, and Picts,* 36; Rose, *Spirits, Fairies, Leprechauns, and Goblins,* 283

Samia

In Greek mythology Samia was a NAIAD and a NYMPH of the main town on the island of Samos in the Greek Aegean Sea; she was the wife of Ankaios (Ancaeus), the island's first king; their son was named Samos. Samia was born the daughter of the giver god, Maiandros (Meander).

Sources: Larson, *Greek Nymphs,* 127; Smith, *Dictionary of Greek and Roman Biography and Mythology,* 167

Sand Yan Y Tad

Similar to the ELLYDAN of Welsh fairy lore, the sand yan y tad ("Saint John and Father") of Brenton lore leads travelers astray at night exactly as the WILL O' THE WISP does. The sand yan y tad is sometimes described as ELVES holding candels and dancing around, causing the firelight to become beguiling.

Sources: Guiney, *Brownies and Bogles,* 116; Keightly, *World Guide to Gnomes, Fairies, Elves, and Other Little People,* 441; Rose, *Spirits, Fairies, Leprechauns, and Goblins,* 283

Sandman

Variations: Mister Sandman, Mr. Sandman

Originally, in Scandinavian folklore, the sandman was a NURSERY BOGIE used to frighten children into going to bed willingly; those who did not were likely candidates to be victimized by this fairy. First he would rub sane in their eyes until their eyes popped out of their heads, then he would collect their eyeballs and take them home to feed to his own children who lived on the crescent moon. Over time, the sandman was a household fairy with a clown-like appearance that threw sand into the eyes of children who would not go to bed and go to sleep; the sand had magical properties making them sleepy.

Sources: Dalley, Nightmare Encyclopedia, 274–75; Rose, *Spirits, Fairies, Leprechauns, and Goblins,* 283; Walsh, *Heroes and Heroines of Fiction,* 273

Sangye Khado

Sangye Khado is the Queen of the KHADO (the female DJINN). She is a Succubus-like DJINN who can fly through the air and is especially kind to

humans. This demonic-fairy does not have a humanlike mind but rather acts on animal instinct. Sangye Khado is essentially the Buddha Dakini from Hindu lore and LILITH of Hebrew lore.

Sources: Blavatsky, *Secret Doctrine,* 298; Schlagintweit, *Buddhism in Tibet,* 248; Turner, *Dictionary of Ancient Deities,* 268, 414

Santa Claus

Variations: Father Christmas, HOLLY KING, Julienisse, King of the Waning Year, Klaubauf, Knecht Ruprecht, Knecht, Krampus, Kris Kringle, Kriss Kringle, Meister Strohbart, Père Fouettard, Pierre Le Noir, Rampus, ROBIN GOOD FELLOW, Sumerklas Ruppels, Sankt Herr Nikolaus, Sante Klaas ("Saint Nicholas"), Sinter Klass Hans Trapp, Sinter Klass, Saint Nicholas, Zwarte Piet

Santa Claus is a singular, benevolent, happy, and smiling fairy being who has always been portrayed as being portly, symbolic of the abundance he delivers onto others. Dressed in either green or red winter clothing he sports a sprig of holly in his hat.

The mythology of Santa Claus as a guardian of children who gives them presents once a year may have originated in Durope, Turkey; he is said to live in a grand palace high up in the sky or in the further reaches of the north. Deer are sacred to him and elves are in his service. Santa visits houses during the "fairy hour," which is midnight and uses a fairy whip to dive his team as he flies through the night sky crying out the call of ROBIN GOOD FELLOW "Ho, ho, ho!"

Different regions of the world have their own name for this fairy; in Christian mythology, Santa Claus is the personification of the spirit of Christmas and did not wholly come into use until the 18th century in America; this is largely due to the Clement Clark Moore 1823 poem *The Night Before Christmas.* The illustrator Thomas Nast gave Santa Claus his current appearance, as the figure was widely used in Christmas ads in Harper's Magazine from 1860 to 1880. Nast portrayed Santa Claus as a bearded, fur-clad, obese, older man.

Sources: McCoy, *Witch's Guide to Faery Folk,* 305–06; Rouse, *History, Legends and Folklore of Christmas,* 187–90; Seal, *Encyclopedia of Folk Heroes,* 226; Watts, *Encyclopedia of American Folklore,* 348–9

Sânziana (plural: sânziene)

Variations: Dragaice, Sanziene

The Romanian name for benign and gentle

fairies, the sânziene ("saint fairies") are believed to live in the Baneasa and the Bucium forests. On June 24, an annual festival is held each year to honor these fairies; the unwed girls in the village dress in white and spend the day speaking to no one and remaining unseen, picking *Galium verum*. Wreaths are made from the plants they picked and at nightfall the girls dance around a huge bonfire where the remains of last year's harvest are thrown into it. During this time it is believed the girls are possessed by the sânziene.

Sources: *Journal of Religion*, Volume 59, 219; Whitmore, *Trials of the Moon*, 40–41

Sao

A sea–NYMPH, Sao ("flitting light") was the NEREID of safe passage in classical Greek mythology; she was born the daughter of Nerues and DORIS.

Sources: Apollodorus, *Apollodorus' Library and Hyginus' Fabulae*, 2; Hesiod, *Works of Hesiod, Callimachus, and Theognis*, 14; Trzaskoma, *Anthology of Classical Myth*, 18

Saqsaywaman

Saqsaywaman ("satiated eagle") is an APU who lives on a mountain peak in the Andes Mountains.

Sources: Cohen, *Chasing the Sun*, n.p.; Illes, *Encyclopedia of Spirits*, 198

Saradine

In the fairy-tale *Prince Featherhead and the Princess Celandine* by Le Prinze Muguet the Fairy Saradine was an acquaintance of the FAIRY OF THE BEECH-WOODS.

Source: Lang, *Green Fairy Book*, 99

Sasabonsam

Variations: Kasampere

In the folklore of the Ashanti and Tschwi people of West Africa the sasabonsam are a collection of NATURE SPIRITS who live in the forests in and around the silk-cotton tree. Like the HAMADRYADS of ancient Greek mythology the sasabonsam will protect the tree it lives in, but will do so with extreme violence; the soil around the base of a tree which is occupied by one of these fairies has turned red, because this is where the sasabonsam wipes itself clean of its victim's blood. Appearing as a small and think humanoid, these fairies have red skin, large blood-shot eyes, and long straight hair. When walking through the forests travelers need to be weary when walking beneath the cotton-silk trees, as the sasabonsam sits in its branches dangling down its feet. When a person passes beneath the highly territorial fairy will grab them up with its legs and drain the person of all their blood.

In some versions of this myth Sasabonsam is an individual and singular being; his wife's name is SHAMANTIN.

Sources: Budd, *Weiser Field Guide to Cryptozoology*, 23; Rose, *Spirits, Fairies, Leprechauns, and Goblins*, 285; Shuker, *Beasts That Hide from Man*, 103–04

Satnioeis

In Greek mythology, Satnioeis was a NAIAD and a NYMPH of the river Satnioeis in the Troad, Anatolia; she was the lover of the Dardanian prince, Enops, to whom she bore a son named Satnios.

Sources: Larson, *Greek Nymphs*, 22; Kirk, *The Iliad: A Commentary:* Volume 2, 158

Satyer

Variations: Satry

In Greek mythology, satyers are a type of fairy being or NATURE SPIRIT; living in the mountains and woods they were described as having the upper half of a man and the lower half of a goat, curly hair, flat noses, full beards, pointed ears, a long thick tail, and short goat horns atop their head, In art the satyers was often depicted wearing a wreath of ivy on its head and carrying a *thyrsus* (the rod of Dionysus (Bacchus) tipped with a pine cone) in their hand.

There are many origin stories for the creation of satyers but according to the Greek oral poet, Hesiod, the satyers were born of the five OREAD granddaughters of Phoroneus; satyers were described by the poet as being "worthless and unsuitable for work." The satyer's fondness for uninhibited carousing made them perfect companions for the gods Dionysus (Bacchus) and Pan (Faunus). As Dionysiac creatures they are natural born lovers of boys, women, and wine; they play bagpipes, cymbals, castanets, and pipes and love to dance with NYMPHS, their fellow, ageless, immortals. Older satyers were referred to as *sileni* and younger ones were called *satyrisci*.

Sources: Conner, *Everything Classical Mythology Book*, 191–92; Hansen, *Classical Mythology: A Guide to the Mythical World of the Greeks and Romans*, 279–80; Littleton, *Gods, Goddesses, and Mythology*, Volume 11, 1256

Satyra

Satyra was a NYMPH of Tarsa according to ancient Greek mythology; she was named after named after Satyrion, a locality near Tarentum. By the god of the sea, Poseidon (Neptune), Satyra was believed to be the mother of Taras, the historical founder of the city bearing his name.

Sources: Sourvinou-Inwood, *Hylas, the Nymphs, Dionysos and Others*, 113; Larson, *Greek Nymphs*, 221; Malkin, *Myth and Territory in the Spartan Mediterranean*, 133

Scaea

Variations: Scea

In ancient Greek mythology Scaea was a water–NYMPH and one of the named DANAIDS, the collective name for the daughters of Danaus. In a list compiled by Apollodorus, a Greek scholar and grammarian, she was one of the daughters of Europe and was wedded to Daiphron, one of the sons of Argyphia.

Sources: Grimal, *Dictionary of Classical Mythology*, 127; Lemprière, *Classical Dictionary*, 236

Scamander

Born one of the 3,000 daughters of the Titians, Oceanus and Tethys, Scamander was one of the named OCEANIDS from ancient Greek mythology.

Sources: Boswell, *What Men or Gods Are These*, 58; Day, *God's Conflict with the Dragon and the Sea*, 64; Hesiod, *Works of Hesiod, Callimachus, and Theognis*, 20

Scantlie Mab

In British folklore Scantlie Mab was one of the assistant to HABETROT, the spinning fairy. Described as having a deformed lip and a long hooked nose Scantlie Mab is admired for her devotion to her FAIRY QUEEN mistress.

Sources: Briggs, *Encyclopedia of Fairies*, 347; Henderson, *Notes on the Folk-Lore of the Northern Counties of England and the Borders*, 259; Monaghan, *Encyclopedia of Celtic Mythology and Folklore*, 410

Sceolan

Variations: Sceolang

In British folklore Sceolan was one of the hounds of Finn Mac Cumhaill. This FAIRY ANIMAL was bound to its master by a secret blood-tie, for it was born while its mother, Uirne, Finn's aunt, had been bewitched and transformed into a hound. Had Uirne been in human form when she gave birth her twin sons, Bran and Secolan would have been born human. Both hounds were excellent hunters, fighters, and sentinels.

Sources: Briggs, *Encyclopedia of Fairies*, 347; Monaghan, *Encyclopedia of Celtic Mythology and Folklore*, 410

Schaibar

In the fairy-tale *The story of Prince Ahmed and the Fairy Paribanou* from the collected story of the *Arabian Nights*, the Fairy Schaibar is the brother of the fairy PARIBANOU. Although the siblings have the same father Schaibar had a violent nature and was quick to chastise with harsh cruelties for even the slightest offence. In spite of his renown cruelty he was also known to oblige anyone in whatever they desired. Described as standing a foot and a half tall and having a beard over thirty-feel long he carries a bar of iron on his shoulders which weight more than five-hundred pound; he uses this bar as his quarterstaff.

Source: Lang, *Blue Fairy Book*, 369

Schellenrock

Jacob Grimm states in his work, *Deutsche Mythologie* the Schellenrock ("bell-coat") so named from the coat it wears, a vestment covered in little bells, is the same fairy as the SHELLYCOAT of Scotland.

Sources: Grimm, *Deutsche Mythologie*, 148; Thorpe, *Northern Mythology*, Volume 2, 22

Scothniamh

Born the daughter of Bodhb Derg, the son of Daghda, Scothniamh ("flower luster") was one of the TUATHA DE DANANN.

Sources: Evan-Wentz, *Fairy Faith in Celtic Countries*, 286; Löffler, *Voyage to the Otherworld Island in Early Irish Literature*, Volume 1, 108

Scrat

Variations: Schrat, Schretel, Schretlein, Sehretel

In German fairy lore, scrat was a type of domestic fairy or NATURE SPIRIT. It has been speculated by no less than Jacob Grimm, the Old English slang for the Devil, Old Scratch, originated from this Old and Middle High German language word.

Sources: Jones, *Notes and Queries*, 14; Keightly, *World Guide to Gnomes, Fairies, Elves, and Other Little People*, 229; Ruoff, *Standard Dictionary of Facts*, 811

Scylla

Variations: Skylla

In ancient Greek mythology Scylla was a water–NYMPH and one of the named DANAIDS, the collective name for the daughters of Danaus; her name appears in a list of the DANAIDS generated by Gaius Julius Hyginus (ca. 64 B.C.–A.D. 17), a Latin author. Scylla unlike other NYMPHS had no interest in love, lust, or men; sadly she had gained the attention of a sea-deity named Glaucus ("grey green") who was aware of her mindset. Glaucus sought the evil and powerful witch CIRCE for a magical means by which to win Scylla's heart, but CIRCE who loved Glaucus became enraged. The witch poured poison into the whirlpool where the NYMPH bathed; the magical poison transformed the beautiful and fun-long NYMPH into a hideous monster with twelve feet and six heads; each of her mouth held three rows of teeth. Unable to move well, she rooted to the spot and destroyed everything within her reach.

Sources: Andrews, *Dictionary of Nature Myths*, 171; Conner, *Everything Classical Mythology Book*, 201–02; Littleton, *Gods, Goddesses, and Mythology*, Volume 11, 1274

Sea-Trow

Variations: Seal, Sellkie, SELKIE

In the Shetland Islands the grotesque sea-trows are believed to live on the bottom of the sea in their own region; they are said to remove the fish from the fishermen's hooks and nets to eat for themselves. Whenever they want to come on land they must don the skin of some animal that is able of breathing while in the water, such as a haa fish or seal, although they are known to assume the form of a MERMAN or MERMAID. Each sea-TROW only has one skin and should it ever become lost its owner would not be able to return. Generally the sea-trow are considered to be dangerous and are avoided whenever possible but there are a scant few tales of one being helpful or taking a human as a mate and marrying them.

Sources: Keightly, *World Guide to Gnomes, Fairies, Elves, and Other Little People*, 167; Kynes, *Sea Magic*, 137; Narváez, *Good People*, 120–21

Sea Witch

Many cultures have the mythology of the sea witch, being who are widely described as supernatural beings who have sway over the fate of men at sea. According to British folklore Sir Francis Drake sold his soul to the Devil to have the ability to be a skilled admiral and seaman; in one story the Devil sent an army of sea witches to Drake's assistance, sinking the Spanish Armada in 1588. In the Hans Christian Anderson tale *The Little Mermaid* the physically repulsive

sea witch lives in a house of bones and is a powerful and cruel if not honest enchantress; her bargain with the MERMAID has been compares to Faust's pact with the Devil.

Sources: Andersen, *Annotated Hans Christian Andersen*, 142–44; Littleton, *Gods, Goddesses, and Mythology*, Volume 11, 1273

Sealah

Variations: DJINN, Saaláh, Sealáh

A sealah is a demonic species of creature in Arabic lore. It is a type of DJINN born the offspring of a human and a DJINN that ate human flesh. Absolutely hideous in its appearance, the sealah prey upon men, hunting and capturing them, forcing them to dance, torturing them, and using them to practice their hunting techniques.

Sealah live in the forests and ancient Arabic geographers have marked an island off the coast of China named "the island of the sealah," believing it is populated by these demons.

Hated by wolves, when attacked by one the sealah will cry out "*Come to my help, for the wolf devoureth me!*" or "*Who will liberate me? I have a hundred deenars, and he shall receive them!*" But be forewarned, and do not answer its call for help. The wolf will destroy the demon and consume its body.

Sources: Campbell, *Popular Tales of the West Highlands*, 297; *Chambers's Encyclopaedia: A Dictionary of Universal Knowledge*, 749; Poole, *The Thousand and One Nights*, 32–3

Seasonal Fairies

Seasonal fairies are present in many cultures but are especially popular in African and Russian fairy lore. These fairies are generally said to be able to shape-shift in various forms and assist in the changing of the seasons, a task well suited to their playful nature. Examples of well-known seasonal fairies are JACK FROST, JIMANINOS, MITHER O' THE SEA, OLD MAN WINTER, PILLYWIGGINS, and SANTA CLAUS to name a few.

Sources: Bord, *Fairies*, 1; Briggs, Fairies in Tradition and Literature, 126; McCoy, *Witch's Guide to Faery Folk*, 33, 172

Sebille

Variations: Sebille l'Enchanteresse

Sebille ("fairy") was associated as a queen of the underworld and a FAIRY QUEEN of the Sidh. Another fairy with this name, Sebille la DAME DU LAC was said to live within a castle in Perceforest surrounded by a river and a layer of fog so dence the water could not be seen. She was said to have incredible healing powers and used them both on Alexander the Great and Floridas; each man spent two weeks under her care but within the castle only one day passed.

Sources: Jacobs, *Folklore*, Volume 14, 441; Keightley, *Fairy Mythology Illustrative of the Romance and Superstition of Vairous Countries*, 33; Newcomb, *Faerie Treasury*, 66

Seelie Court

Variations: Blessed Ones, Kindlt Fairy Host, Seely Court, the Sluagh

In Scottish fairy lore the Seelie Court ("blessed court") are the aristocratic and benign TROOPING FAIRIES; they are believed to be made up of the last of the TUATHA DE DANANN and the most heroic and beautiful faeries of Scotland. They act as arbiters and judges in fairy disputes. Fond of riding upon their fairy horses in long processions known as RADES during twilight. Sometimes the fairies are described as having a vaporous physical form when sighted but other lore claims they have never been seen but only heard.

Although the Seelie fairies once interacted with humans they are now indifferent to mortals and their affairs, although the fairies of the Seelie Court are quick to avenge an insult or injury delivered on them.

The counterpart to the Seelie Court is the malicious and malignant UNSEELIE COURT.

Sources: McCoy, *Witch's Guide to Faery Folk*, 23, 307–08; Monaghan, *Encyclopedia of Celtic Mythology and Folklore*, 413–14; Rose, *Spirits, Fairies, Leprechauns, and Goblins*, 286

Seemänlein

In Germany's Black Forest the seemänlein ("water-man") was a type of BROWNIE that would work along people the whole day long and by evening return to his home in the lake. Food was set aside for him would be accepted and eaten and he would insist everyone be appointed a fair amount of work daily work least he become angry and toss things about. Seemänlein are described as wearing very old and worn clothing. Like all BROWNIES, if ever he were to be given clothes, he would leave his current location forever.

Source: Keightly, *World Guide to Gnomes, Fairies, Elves, and Other Little People*, 261

Segesta

Variations: Segeste

Segesta was river NYMPH from ancient Greek mythology. Originally from Try, she was one of the many who fled the city for fear of being offered up in sacrifice to the sea-monster. Upon arriving in Sicily, she was raped by the river god, Krimissos (Crimesus) in the form of a dog, Segesta conceived a child and named him Egestos (alternatively spelled Aigetes and Akestes).

Sources: Head, *Historia Numorum*, 164; Sources: Larson, *Greek Nymphs*, 221; Winckelmann, *Essays on the Philosophy and History of Art*, Volume 1, 259

Selkie

Variations: ROANE, Seal Fairy, Seal-Faeries, Seal People, Selchies, Selkie Folk, SILKIES, Water KELPIES

Living in the seas around the Orkney and Shetlands Islands the shape-shifting selkies ("seal") often takes the form of grey seals or great seals as they travel through the ocean. There is the regional beliefe the selkies are fallen angels who were not so evil they partook in the war against heaven but were condemned to earth to live as they do for some far less trivial sin.

When a selkie comes upon land it removes its seal-skin covering and appears in all ways to be a human; however sometimes the folklore will say, like the MERROW, the selkie have wide palms or webbing between their fingers and toes. It will hide the skin or guard it carefully, as it cannot return back to the ocean without it. Unlike the ROAN of the Scottish Highlands the male selkies not only have the ability to raise storms and capsize boats but are also very willing to avenge the indiscriminate slaughter of seals.

Occasionally a selkie will make contact with a human and on rare occasions will take one as a mate, but those relationships never last. If the selkie is female she will eventually return to the sea; if the selkie is male it will after seven years offer its mate a fee for rearing the child, wanting to return to the ocean with it.

Unlike the MERMAID, the selkie always appear in groups, and do not reside in a magical underwater kingdom decked out beautifully; rather the selkie are considered to be a completely different species of fairy who prefer to live in their own company on an outlying skerry.

Sources: Briggs, *Dictionary of British Folk-Tales in the English Language*, Volumes 1–2, 226–28; Froud, *Faeries*, 119; McCoy, *Witch's Guide to Faery Folk*, 307–08; Stevenson, *Scottish Antiquary, or, Northern Notes and Queries*, Volume 7–8, 172–73

Selnozoura

In the fairy-tale *A Fairy's Blunder* the fairy Selnozoura, who had fallen into poor health, was ordered by her doctors to tour the world for some fresh air. Selnozoura happened upon Fountain Island, the land under the protection of the fairy DINDONETTE, in her airship which flew a "thousand nine hundred and fifty times" faster than the fastest ship. While visiting the island, her adopted son, Cornichon, and ward Toupette, drank from the ill-enchanted fountain.

Sources: Lang, *Grey Fairy Book*, 355–65; Romanowski, *Homage to Paul Bénichou*, 284

Senq'a

Senq'a is an APU who lives on a mountain peak in the Andes Mountains.

Source: Illes, *Encyclopedia of Spirits*, 198

Servan

Although no one has ever seen the servan of Swiss fairy lore it is well known to have a very mischievous nature. Like the TROW of the Shetland Islands, the servan, hide things at night in odd places but also, like the GROGAN of the Scottish Highlands, it will assist farmers in threshing corn and other chores.

Sources: Andrews, *Ulster Folklore*, 50; McCoy, *Witch's Guide to Faery Folk*, 309–10

Seven Inches

In the fairy-tale *The Three Crows* the fairy Seven Inches, so named as this was exactly how tall he stood, used an enchanted boat to kidnap the king's daughters and took them to his home in Tir-na-n-Oge (the underworld).

Source: Lang, *Lilac Fairy Book*, 95–109

The Seven Whistlers

Similar to GABRIEL HOUNDS and WISH HOUNDS only in appearance the Seven Whistlers are less like a FAIRY ANIMAL and more akin to the BANSHEE, as they are harbingers of death. These spiritual fairies fly through the night sky making a frightful baying sound; by morning seven people will have been found to have passed away. Sometimes they are described as looking like a flock of seven birds.

Sources: Briggs, *Encyclopedia of Spirits*, 359–60; Henderson, *Notes on the Folk-Lore of the Northern Counties*, 129; Rose, *Spirits, Fairies, Leprechauns, and Goblins*, 289

Shag-Foal

Variations: Tatter-Foal, Tatterfoal, Tatter Foal

In Lincolnshire England there is a shape-shifting BRAG known as a shag-foal; it travels the roads in the guise of a shaggy donkey or horse with fiery eyes. Frightening in appearance, this FAIRY ANIMAL will chase a person but there are no tales of it actually catching or hurting anyone. PICKTREE BRAG is a well-known shag-foal.

Sources: Briggs, *Encyclopedia of Fairies*, 360; Rose, *Spirits, Fairies, Gnomes, and Goblins*, 289; Westwood, *Lore of the Land*, 560–61

Shaitans

Variations: MAZIKEEN Shaytans, Shedeem, SHEDIM, Sheitan, Sheytan

Created by the fire of Allah, the shaitans, a type of DJINN, appear in their natural form as wisps of smoke, very ugly, and with the feet of a rooster, although they do have the ability to take on a solid form, according to Arabic lore, shape-shifting to look like an animal, a regular person, or a seductive woman. Ruled over by IBLIS, King of the Shaitans, their behavior varies from mildly mischievous to purely evil. The purpose of the shaitans is to tempt mankind into sin; however, some of these beings have been converted to Islam and are faithful servants of Allah.

Living off a diet of dirt and excrement, the shaitans send tempting and unclean thoughts to those who miss morning prayers. These demons have the ability to create mental illusions, sending visions of pleasure to entice mankind to sin. If a person does not wash their hands after supper and goes to bed without having done so, the shaitans will lick their hands to bloody stumps. They can also possess a corpse or a person. Shaitans have an aversion to water. The word in Arabic means "the heat from the sun."

Sources: Davidson, *Dictionary of Angels*, 270; Hughes, *Dictionary of Islam*, 134; Mack, *Field Guide to Demons, Fairies, Fallen Angels, and Other Subversive Spirits*, 151

Shakespearian Fairies

The fairies written about by the Elizabethan English playwright and poet, William Shakespeare, are superior to man, as they often speak of human frailty and weakness; they are not mortal and seem to imply they will live on into eternity. By night these fairies sing, dance and make merry beneath the moon and stars. Shakespeare's fairies are not the fay of the popular rustic belief; his fairies were as small as a bee and has tiny wings upon their back, they were friendly, helpful and happy whereas the fairies of the countryside were the size of mortals, abducted children, left CHANGELINGS behind, spread illness, and stole cattle. Shakespearian Fairies were amusing, beautiful, fascinating, harmless, poetic, and struck a chord with the populace, as after his interpretation and introduction of OBERON and TATIANA, the traditionally malicious fairy began to disappear from literature.

Shakespeare was aware of the folklore of the fay but preferred to invent his own mythology for his plays and poems where they were concerned. With no control over humans and no particular powers or special abilities, his fairies do little more than entertain. His fairies mix freely with men, and even their nature is more in line with those of the DRYADS and NYMPHS of ancient Greece.

The fairies of the Elizabethan age were mischievous and bothersome; NYMPHS were a newly discovered subject matter and two species of fairy were invented during this era, the HOBGOBLIN and Shakespeare's small flower fairies with gossamer wings which appeared in his play, *Midsummer Night's Dream*. It is during this period we are first given insight into the social aspects of fairy life.

Sources: Cumberland, *Shakespeare and the Supernatural*, 33, 47–9; Keightly, *World Guide to Gnomes, Fairies, Elves, and Other Little People*, 327–28, 331; Stepanich, *Faery Wicca*, Book One, 21–22, 27

Shamantin

Variations: Srahman

In the folklore of the Ashanti and Tschwi people of West Africa Shamantin ("tall ghost") is the wife of the NATURE SPIRIT known as SASABONSAM. Like her husband, Shamantin lives in the forest and sitting in the cotton-silk tree waits for travelers to pass beneath her so she may grab them up with her legs; unlike her husband she only detains for a few months people she captures. While in her custody, Shamantin forcibly teaches her prisoners the lore of the forest. Described as being immensely tall and completely white

Sources: Eberhart, *Mysterious Creatures*, 473; Porteous, *Forest Folklore*, 137; Rose, *Spirits, Fairies, Leprechauns, and Goblins*, 289–90

Sheean-ny-Feaynid

On the Isle of Man, on Dalby Mountain, it is believed if you put your ear to the ground you can hear the Sheean-ny-Feaynid ("sound of the infinite"), the voices of the fairies who live underground.

Sources: Evans-Wentz, *Fairy-Faith in Celtic Countries*, 130; McCoy, *Witch's Guide to Faery Folk*, 22

Shefro

Variations: Siofra ("CHANGELING" or "phantom")

Male, Irish TROOPING FAIRIES, fond of dancing, feasting, horseback riding, hunting game, and RADES, are described as wearing green coats and red caps. The shefro live communally in castles beneath their FAIRY FORT. Like most fairies who live underfround the shefro are shape-shifters.

Sources: Croker, *Fairy Legends and Traditions of the South of Ireland*, 107; Rose, *Spirits, Fairies, Leprechauns, and Goblins*, 290

Shekkasoh

Similar to the HAMADRYADS of classical Greek mythology, the Shekkasoh are tree spirits or NATS from Burmese folklore. They live in the trunk of the tree.

Sources: Porteous, *Forest in Folklore and Mythology*, 125; Rose, *Spirits, Fairies, Leprechauns, and Goblins*, 290; Scott, *Burman: His Life and Notions*, Volume I, 286

Shellycoat

Variations: Shellicoat, Shelly Coat

The shellycoat is one of the FUATH, a collective name for the malicious and monstrous water fay and BOGIE in Scottish folklore. Found in freshwater stream and wearing a coat of shells that rattles when it moves, the shellycoat takes great pleasure in leading travelers astray. There are many tales of this fairy and his little trick but it never does any harm nor does it lead the person into a dangerous area, simply just out of their way.

Sources: Briggs, *Encyclopedia of Fairies*, 362; McCoy, *Witch's Guide to Faery Folk*, 310; Rose, *Spirits, Fairies, Leprechauns, and Goblins*, 290

Sheoques

Variations: Sidheog ("a little fairy")

In the folklore of Ireland the sheoques are the fairies who live in the thorn bushes they hold sacred. Generally these fay are benign, their worse crime perhaps is their dancing and singing are so beautiful and relaxing mortals forget their cares and stop to listen—except for their habit of stealing human infants and replacing them with CHANGELINGS. It is very rare to hear a tale where one of the sheoques has injured a human, but in Down County two people were said to have been killed by them because, after having been warned, they pulled up some thorn bushes which belonged to the fay.

Sources: Wallace, *Folk-lore of Ireland*, 92; Welsh, *Catholic World*, Volume 79, 754

Shinseen

In Chinese lore the diminutive shinseen live in a state of blissful ease, exempt from the cares of human life, however they hold an influence over mortal affairs. These NATURE SPIRITS are believed to live in the mountains and woods. They have appeared as both old men with long beards and young maidens.

Sources: Keightley, *Fairy Mythology Illustrative of the Romance and Superstition of Vairous Countries*, 511; Penwyche, *World of Fairies*, 108; Porteous, *Forest Folklore*, 127

Shitta

According to Burmese folklore, the shitta ("the moon") are one of the four different species of the NATS of the Air; generally they are considered to be beneficial towards mankind. Once a year they are worshiped by the village chief; sacrifices are not required.

Sources: Hastings, *Encyclopedia of Religion and Ethics*, Part 5, 22; Hastings, *Encyclopedia of Religion and Ethics*, Part 5, 22; Porteous, *Forest in Folklore and Mythology*, 125; Scott, *The Burman: His Life and Notions*, Volume 1, 286

Shock

A BOGIE and BARGUEST from northern England lore, Shock has been described as a GOBLIN-like, monstrous, dog sporting a mouth full of teeth and large claws on its paws. Regionally, it is said he has only one eye. Completely nocturnal, it was believed anyone who clearly saw Shock would die soon thereafter but if they only caught a glimpse of him would die a few months later.

BARGUESTS seem to become a staple fixture in an area or community and several have been named, such as the Barghest of Burnley, the BLACK DOG of Winchester, BLACK SHUCK, the Demon of Tidworth, the Dogs of Hell, Gwyllgi the Dog of Darkness, Hounds of Annwn (see ANNWN, HOUNDS OF), Mauthe Doog, MODDEY DHOO, the PADFOOT of Wakefield, PICKTREE BRAG, SKRIKER, STRIKER, and TRASH.

Sources: Chisholm, *Encyclopædia Britannica: A Dictionary of Arts* Volume 3, 399; Spence, *Minor Traditions of British Mythology*, 97; Westwood, *Lore of the Land*, 561

Shony

Variations: SHELLYCOAT, Shoney, Shoney of the Lews, Sjofn

Shony, a sea- or NATURE SPIRIT of death in ancient Scottish lore, was originally a sea demon described as a large man with thick, shaggy hair covering his head and a ridge of fins running down his back. This ancient sea-spirit was especially well known on the Isle of Lewis. Yearly human sacrifices were once made to Shony by slitting the throat of a crewman and throwing him overboard. Ship builders would bind a man to the logs used to roll a new boat into the water in the hopes it would please the spirit. Shony later evolved into a god of the sea who appeared on land, wearing strands of shells that clattered, announcing his presence. Offerings of ale were made to Shony at Hallowtide in hopes it would let seaweed wash up on the shore. Evolving yet again, this time into a trickster spirit, it would pretend to be a drowning man and when about to be rescued would laugh and swim away.

Preying on fishermen and sailors, Shony keeps the souls it captures in its castle of jagged coral which lies on the ocean floor in the North Sea. Sometimes the location is said to be off the coast of Scotland.

When a man falls overboard it was the ancient custom to not attempt a rescue of the man because Shony must receive his annual quota of souls. If an attempt was made it was said Shony would take the rescuer and leave the would-be victim alive in his place.

Shony is similar to, and possibly the predecessor of, Davey Jones and "the old John" in that he keeps those who drown at sea eternally in his realm.

Sources: Evans-Wentz, *Fairy-Faith in Celtic Countries*, 93, 101; Henderson, *Norse Influence on Celtic Scotland*, 101; Hyatt, *Book of Demons*, 83; MacKenzie, *Scottish Folk-Lore and Folk Life*, 252–3; Spence, *Magic Arts in Celtic Britain*, 91

Shoopiltee

Variations: CABYLL-USHTEY

In the Shetland and Ornkey Islands, shoopiltee are playful little water horses; they are said to be friendly to humans they encounter along the shoreline as well as sailors. It has been over one-hundred years since a shoopiltee has been sited, but at one time they were said to be numerous in the North Sea.

Sources: Briggs, *Encyclopedia of Fairies*, 363; Keightly, *World Guide to Gnomes, Fairies, Elves, and Other Little People*, 171; McCoy, *Witch's Guide to Faery Folk*, 311

Short Hoggers

Variations: Whittinghame

In the Whittinghame region of Scotland there was believed to be a fairy named Short Hoggers who would run back and forth through the community wailing and otherwise causing disturbances. According to the lore, this fairy came into being because a local child died without having been baptized. For many years the residents were afraid of it but one night a drunkard on his way home came across the fairy and addressed it as "Short Hoggers." As is often the case in fairy lore, naming the fairy was enough to banish it forever, such as in RUMPELSTILTSKIN.

Sources: Briggs, *Fairies in Tradition and Literature*, 137; McPherson, *Primitive Beliefs in the Northeast of Scotland*, 117; Rose, *Spirits, Fairies, Leprechauns, and Goblins*, 292

Shriker

Variations: Shuck, SKRIKER, Striker

A monstrous BLACK DOG with glowing yellow eyes from the regional folklore of Lancashire, England, Shriker is a death omen and, like the BANSHEE, his distinctive bay can be hear from miles away. Taking the form of a cow, dog, or horse, it follows people down the road and when they notice it, attacks.

Sources: Eberhart, *Mysterious Creatures: A Guide to Cryptozoology*, Volume 1, 555; Mitchell, *Slow Norfolk and Suffolk*, 159; Monaghan, *Encyclopedia of Celtic Mythology and Folklore*, 47

Shug Monkey

Shug Monkey is a FAIRY ANIMAL from the fairy lore of Holland. Described as looking like it is half ape and half black massif, it is very similar to the BARGUEST, the BLACK SHUCK, and the GALLY-TROT.

Sources: Buckland, *Weiser Field Guide to Ghosts*, 113; Westwood, *Lore of the Land*, 70

Shvod

In Armenian folklore the household spirit known as the shvod is active only in the beginning of March; a shape-shifter, this BROWNIE-like fairy takes on the appearance of a cat in order to enter into a home. As a household spirit a well-treated shvod would reward the occupants with little gifts of gold, however, if it was mistreated it would cause no end of strife before it would finally leave. It is sometimes used as a NURSERY BOGIE to keep misbehaving children in line. Its agricultural counterpart was known as the *shvaz*.

Sources: Ananikian, *Armenian Mythology*, 81; Franklin, *Working with Fairies*, 133; Rose, *Spirits, Fairies, Leprechauns, and Goblins*, 292

Siabra

Variations: Sheevra, Siabrae

Mentioned in the medieval Irish Manuscript *The Book of Leinster* (1160), in the poem of *Eochais*, the TUATHA DE DANANN were said to be the hosts of the siabra ("fairies") a species of contemptible, dangerous, powerful, and malicious fairy. So feared and hated, to call an unruly child a "little sheevra" was an expression of the greatest disappointment. These fay were often called upon by the ancient druids to do harm to their enemies; once such tale claims the siabra choked King Cormac mac Art to death with the bone of a salmon while he ate dinner one evening because he was considering converting to Christianity.

Sources: Evans-Wentz, *Fairy-Faith in Celtic Countries*, 285; Mahon, *Ireland's Fairy Lore*, 111; Spence, *Fairy Tradition in Britain*, 89

Siar

Siar was one of the many DWARFS named in the *Voluspa*, the first and best known poem of the *Poetic Edda*, a collection of Old Norse poems dating back to about A.D. 985.

Source: Sturluson, *Prose Edda*, 30

Sib

Sib was one of the fairies mentioned in the literature of ROBIN GOOD FELLOW. She had three brothers, GRIM, PATCH, and PINCH and four sisters, GULL, LICKE, LULL, and TIB. Sib acted as a spokeswoman for her siblings and explains their nightly actions, such as of leaving behind money to those people who leave out clean water and towels for them to bathe in.

Sources: Briggs, *Encyclopedia of Fairies*, 364; Davis, *Life in Elizabethian Days*, 217; Wilson, *Life in Shakespeare's England*, 42, 44

Sicksa

In Slavic lore the sicksa was a NATURE SPIRIT who had the ability to shape-shift at will. This fairy was known for playing pranks on people who made a living working in the woods as well as on travelers.

Sources: Dixon-Kennedy, *Encyclopedia of Russian and Slavic Myth and Legend*, 257; Graves, *Larousse Encyclopedia of Mythology*, 291; Rose, *Spirits, Fairies, Leprechauns, and Goblins*, 292

Sídhe

Variations: Aes Sídhe, Aos Sí, Si, Sidhe, Sith

Sídhe ("people of the (fairy) hills" or "something which controls the elements") is the word used in Ireland and the highlands of Scotland to name the very tall, shining race of fairy people who are believed to belong to both the earthly and heavenly realms. The word *sidhe* and TUATHA DE DANANN are used interchangeably. Their name is derived from the ancient barrows or FAIRY FORTS where they are believed to reside.

The sídhe are said to be extremely beautiful and although youthful in appearance give the impression of being aristocratic, mature, and powerful, not just in body but in ability and mind as well. Sídhe were generally skillful artisans but were considered experts and excelled in baking, crafts, dancing, hunting, metalwork, music, RADES, spinning, and weaving. As many of their tale will show they held beauty, fertility, generosity, love, loyalty, order, and truth in very high regard; they would repay in kind any generosity or hospitality afforded to them. They would offer their assistance to their favorite humans and would on occasion take one as a lover or spouse. There are some families who still lay claim to the fact their bloodline caries sídhe blood, such as with the MacLeodse of Scotland.

Many animals, both domestic and wild, are associated with sidhe and there are numerous stories of their great love of horses. Although as general rule fairy horses were beautiful they were also too dangerous and wild for a mortal to ride, fairy cattle were generally benign and helpful to mankind.

Sources: Evan-Wentz, *Fairy Faith in Celtic Countries*, 59; MacLeod, *Celtic Myth and Religion*, 149–50; McCoy, *Witch's Guide to Faery Folk*, 20; Rose, *Spirits, Fairies, Leprechauns, and Goblins*, 4

Sigrun

In Nordic and Teutonic mythology Sigrun was one of the named VALKYRIES, a NYMPH of battle. Always depicted as beautiful women who are sometimes immortal, they are the attendants of the god, Odin. Sigrun, the wound-giving VALKYRIE, was from the land of Sefafell and was unsuccessfully courted by Hodbrodd, the son of Granmar. In the *Poem of Helgi Hundingsbani*, Sigrun is a VALKYRIE bride, and her marriage to the hero ultimately brings about his death.

Sources: Grimm *Teutonic Mythology*, Volume 1, 423, 435; Sigfusson, *Elder Eddas of Saemund Sigfusson Younger Eddas of Snorre Sturleson*, 282, 317

Sila

Variations: Si'lah

Sila are said to be the weakest of all the types of the DJINN. They have the ability to appear in any form.

Sources: Britannica, *Students' Britannica India*, Vol. 1–5, 142; Carta, *Djinn Summoning*, 26; Hughes, *Dictionary of Islam*, 135; Knowles, *Nineteenth Century*, Volume 31, 449; Rose, *Spirits, Fairies, Leprechauns, and Goblins*, 363

Silent Moving Folk

Variations: People of Peace, Still Folk

In Scotland the silent moving folk are the fairies living in the knolls and mountains of the Highlands.

Sources: Avant, *Mythological Reference*, 478; Evans-Wentz, *Fairy-Faith in Celtic Countries*, 22; McCoy, *Witch's Guide to Faery Folk*, 24

Silenus

Variations: Sileni

In classical Greek mythology Silenus was the oldest and the wisest of the SATYERS. An attendant of the god Dionysus (Bacchus), Silnenus was often depicted as a comical, drunken, obese, old man riding upon a mule. If a person was able to capture Silenus and tie him up, he would reveal his captor's destiny, as Silenus possessed the ability to see both the future and the past. In some myths Silenus was said to be born the son of the god Pan while others said he was born the son of the god Hermes and the goddess Gaia. Silenus was the father of three sons, two SATYERS named Astraeus and Maron, and a centaur named Pholus. In later myths the older SATYERS were all named Silenus and had the lower body of a horse; the younger ones had goat legs.

Sources: Graves, *Larousse Encyclopedia of Mythology*, 161; Littleton, *Gods, Goddesses, and Mythology*, Volume 11, 1305–06; Rose, *Spirits, Fairies, Leprechauns, and Goblins*, 293

Sili Ffrit

Variations: Sili-go-Dwt, Trwtyn-Tratyn

In Welsh lore there was a fragmented tale of a fairy woman or woman of the SÍDHE who made a habit of borrowing from a local widow woman. Although there was no deviation to the tale except for the name being sung in the song, the story is the same for all three fay, Sili Ffrit, Sili-go-Dwt and Trwtyn-Tratyn.

Sili Ffrit was a fairy who routinely would visit a woman and borrow her padell and gradell; upon returning these items would reward the woman with some loaves bread. One day the fairy asked the use of her spinning wheel so she may spin some flax. The woman was inclined to extend the favor and asked the fairy its name, but the fairy would not give it; however, the woman listened to the fairy who sang as she spun and in her song, revealed her name *"little did she know that Sili Ffrit is my name."*

Sources: Briggs, *Encyclopedia of Fairies*, 364; Rhys, *Celtic folklore: Welsh and Manx*, Volume 1, 64, 229; Rose, *Spirits, Fairies, Leprechauns, and Goblins*, 293

Siliniets

In Polish folklore the siliniets were a species of NATURE SPIRIT who resided in the forest.

Sources: Dixon-Kennedy, *Encyclopedia of Russian and Slavic Myth and Legend*, 194; Graves, *Larousse Encyclopedia of Mythology*, 291; Rose, *Spirits, Fairies, Leprechauns, and Goblins*, 293

Silkie

Variations: ROAN, SELKIE, Silky

In Scottish folklore Selkie is a type of domestic fairy similar to a BROWNIE; she would sneak into homes and to whatever chores had been left undone. However, if a house was left in perfect order, she would mess it up a little bit. Taking her name from the silk, white gown she wore, Silkie is associated with the harvest. The word silkie is also connected to the seal people known as the ROAN.

Sources: Briggs, *Encyclopedia of Fairies*, 364–65; Monaghan, *Encyclopedia of Celtic Mythology and Folklore*, 420; Rose, *Spirits, Fairies, Leprechauns, and Goblins*, 293–94

Siltim

A DEEV from Persian lore, Siltim lives in the forests, groves, and solitary places. Taking a human form she is known to do injury to man.

Sources: Porteous, *Forest Folklore*, 121; Rose, *Spirits, Fairies, Leprechauns, and Goblins*, 294

Silvanella

A fairy in Italian lore Silvanella found the body of Narcissus and immediately fell in love with him. Knowing they could never be together, she raised a marble tomb over him and then unable to stop crying, dissolved away into the fountain. As she disappeared she cast a spell on the fountain causing its water to reflect the face of a young girl so beautiful and captivating than any man who saw it would not be able to leave the fountain.

Sources: Boiardo, *Orlando Innamorato Di Bojardo*, 385, 391–92; Keightly, *World Guide to Gnomes, Fairies, Elves, and Other Little People*, 452

Silvanes

Italian weather fairies or NATURE SPIRITS, silvanes ("wood women") have backward-facing toes; these nearly invisible fay mate with the SILVANI and produce little babies called FOLLETTI.

Source: Arrowsmith, *Field Guide to the Little People*, 105

Silvani

The NATURE SPIRITS of the mountains of northern Italy known as the AGUANE were said to be able to successfully mate with the silvani ("wooded") thereby producing offspring known as *SALVANELLI.* Described as looking like winged wood-NYMPHS, they had a ghost-like appearance and dressed in animal furs and red clothing.

Sources: Euvino, *Complete Idiot's Guide to Italian History and Culture*, 274; Grimassi, *Hereditary Witchcraft: Secrets of the Old Religion*, 83; McCoy, *Witch's Guide to Faery Folk*, 311–12

Simona

Simona is an APU who lives on a mountain peak in the Andes Mountains.

Source: Illes, *Encyclopedia of Spirits*, 198

Sindri

Variations: Sindre

Sindri ("sparky") was one of the many DWARFS named in the *Voluspa*, the first and best known poem of the *Poetic Edda*, a collection of Old Norse poems dating back to about A.D. 985. Sindri was the brother to AWL and BROC. Sindri was also the name of the golden hall the DWARFS were said to reside within.

Sources: Dronke, *Poetic Edda*, 141; Wilkinson, *Book of Edda called Völuspá*, 12

Sinlap

According to Burmese folklore, the sinlap, the givers of wisdom, were a species of the NATS; generally they were considered to be beneficial towards mankind. Once a year they are worshiped by the village chief; sacrifices are not required.

Sources: Hastings, *Encyclopedia of Religion and Ethics*, Part 5, 22; Porteous, *Forest in Folklore and Mythology*, 125; Scott, *Burman*, Volume 1, 286

Sinoe

In Greek mythology Sinoe was an OREAD and a NYMPH of Mount Sinoe in Arcadia located in southern Greece; she was one of the nurses to the infant god, Pan (Faunus). She was transformed in a reed to avoid being raped by the god when he reached adulthood; to commemorate the beautiful NYMPH who raised him he invented and named the seven-reed flute after her, the SYRINX.

Sources: Kent, *Mythological Dictionary*, 89–90; Pausânias, *Guide to Greece: Southern Greece*, 448

Sinope

In classical Greek mythology Sinope was one of the NAIAD daughters of the river god ASOPUS in Sikyonia and Boiotia, central and southern Greece.

Sources: Classical Association, *Classical Review*, Volume 12, 125; Quiggin, *Essays and Studies Presented to William Ridgeway*, 224

Sir Calidore

A fairy knight named in Spencer's *Fairy Queen*, Sir Calidore was renowned for being courteous and honest. He quested to defeat the Blatant Beast; his lady is called Pastorella.

Sources: Keightly, *World Guide to Gnomes, Fairies, Elves, and Other Little People*, 59; Spenser, *Faery Queen and Her Knights*, 294

Siren

Variations: Seirenes

In classical Greek mythology the sirens ("bewitching ones") were a type of malicious NYMPH born the offspring of the ancient sea god, Phorcys (Phorkys) or from the drops of blood that hit the earth from the broken horn of Acheloos, ancient sources conflict. Half bird and half woman, she and her sisters would perch on the rocky Sicilian coastline and lure in sailor with their melodious song; once caught, their prey were eaten alive. Although they hunted the coastline they lived inland in a meadow.

Homer, the greatest ancient Greek epic poet an author of *The Iliad* and *Odyssey* named only two sirens, but on vases they were usually depicted as three. Occasionally, the sirens were depicted as being bearded. As time progressed their number increased to five and grew as authors continued to add to their flock. Some of the named sirens are AGLAOPHEME, LEUCOSIA, LIGIA, MOLPE, PARTHENOPE, PISINOE, RAIDNE, TELES, and THELXIEPIA.

Over time, ancient writers evolved the sirens into MERMAID-like beings who would sit on the rocky shoreline using their beautiful singing voice to lure sailors into the jetty where their ships would wreck. In these late myths the only way to kill a siren was to resist their song; if this was accomplished, the being would kill itself.

Some ancient writers say the sirens lived on the island Anthemoessa but other authors say they lived on three small rocky islands called Sirenum scopuli.

Sources: Daly, *Greek and Roman Mythology A to Z*, 118; Fox, *Greek and Roman*, 262–63; Littleton, *Gods, Goddesses, and Mythology*, Volume 11, 1269; Smith, *Dictionary of Greek and Roman Biography and Mythology*, 817

Sithnides

In Greek mythology the sithnides were a group of NYMPHS associated with a fountain in Megara. The sithnides were so greatly venerated their fountain was surrounded with a magnificent enclosure of columns. By the god Jupiter, one of the sithnides became the mother of Megarus, the ancestral hero of the Megarians.

Sources: Bell, *Bell's New Pantheon*, 27; McClintock, *Cyclopaedia of Biblical, theological, and Ecclesiastical Literature*, Volume 9, 787

Sjarr

Sjarr ("sparky") was one of the many DWARFS named in the *Voluspa*, the first and best known poem of the *Poetic Edda*, a collection of Old Norse poems dating back to about A.D. 985.

Sources: Daly, *Norse Mythology A to Z*, 22; Sykes, *Who's Who in Non-Classical Mythology*, 53

Skáfidr

Variations: Skafidr ("crooked Finn")

Skáfidr was one of the many DWARFS named in the *Voluspa*, the first and best known poem of the *Poetic Edda*, a collection of Old Norse poems dating back to about A.D. 985.

Sources: Daly, *Norse Mythology A to Z*, 22; Wilkinson, *Book of Edda called Völuspá*, 12

Skafinn

Skafinn one of the many DWARFS named in the *Voluspa*, the first and best known poem of the *Poetic Edda*, a collection of Old Norse poems dating back to about A.D. 985.

Source: Sturluson, *Edda*, 17

Skandar

Skandar was one of the many DWARFS named in the *Voluspa*, the first and best known poem of the *Poetic Edda*, a collection of Old Norse poems dating back to about A.D. 985.

Sources: Daly, *Norse Mythology A to Z*, 22; Sykes, *Who's Who in Non-Classical Mythology*, 53

Skavaerr

Skavaerr ("crooked") was one of the many DWARFS named in the *Voluspa*, the first and best known poem of the *Poetic Edda*, a collection of Old Norse poems dating back to about A.D. 985.

Source: Sykes, *Who's Who in Non-Classical Mythology*, 57–8

Skavidr

Skavidr ("slanting board") was one of the many DWARFS named in the *Voluspa*, the first and best known poem of the *Poetic Edda*, a collection of Old Norse poems dating back to about A.D. 985.

Source: Crossley-Holland, *Norse Myths*, 183

Skeggold

Variations: Skeggiold

In Nordic and Teutonic mythology Skeggold was one of the named VALKYRIES, a NYMPH of battle. Always depicted as beautiful women who are sometimes immortal, they are the attendants of the god, Odin

Sources: Grimm *Teutonic Mythology*, Volume 1, 421; Sigfusson, *Elder Eddas of Saemund Sigfusson Younger Eddas of Snorre Sturleson*, 282, 317

Skilly Widden

Variations: Skillywidden

Skilly Widden was an individual fairy child who was said to have been adopted by a farmer of Terridge in Cornwall, England and raised as his son; he called the foot-tall child Bobby Griglans. One day the fairy's mother came looking for her child, and no sooner has she found him then the two of them disappeared.

Sources: Ashliman, *Fairy Lore*, 78; Briggs, *Encyclopedia of Fairies*, 370; Rose, *Spirits, Fairies, Leprechauns, and Goblins*, 295, 351

Skirfir

Skirfir was one of the many DWARFS named in the *Voluspa*, the first and best known poem of the *Poetic Edda*, a collection of Old Norse poems dating back to about A.D. 985.

Source: Crossley-Holland, Norse Myths, 183

Skirvir

Variations: SKIRFIR, Skirpir

Skirvir ("craftsman") was one of the many

DWARFS named in the *Voluspa*, the first and best known poem of the *Poetic Edda*, a collection of Old Norse poems dating back to about A.D. 985.

Sources: Daly, *Norse Mythology A to Z*, 22; Sturluson, *Edda*, 17; Sykes, *Who's Who in Non-Classical Mythology*, 53; Wilkinson, *Book of Edda called Völuspá*, 12

Skogsfru

Variations: Skogsnufa, Skogsnufvar

A type of WOOD NYMPH form Danish and Swedish lore, the skogsfru ("lady (ruler) of the forest" or "WOOD-WIFE") are dangerous and predatory fairies seeking out foolish young men; their typical victims are lumberjacks and hunters. Although they have the ability to shape-shift into an owl, a skogsfru will appear in a camp as a small but beautiful woman; it will make merry drinking and singing songs around the campfire until she is able to lure one man away. If the man goes off with it, he will never been seen again; the best way to avoid an encounter with this fay is to prtend not to see it when it wanders into camp.

Sources: Keightly, *World Guide to Gnomes, Fairies, Elves, and Other Little People*, 153; MacCulloch, *Celtic and Scandinavian Religions*, 133; Rose, *Spirits, Fairies, Leprechauns, and Goblins*, 295

Skogsra (plural: skogsran)

Variations: Skogs Fru, Skogsrå

Swedish folklore the skogsrå are a race beautiful WOOD NYMPHS with a SIREN-like voice; they are described as having a back as hollow as an old tree and a fox tail. Any man who falls for her charms and engages in sexual intercourse with it will lose his immortal soul. Theses SOLITARY FAIRIES skogsra hold power over the forest; particularly interactive with humans, they often take men as lovers and frequently give very good, albeit unwitting advice in the form of herbal recipes. There are no male skogsra. The skogsran takes great delight in causing poor hunting, causing travelers to become lost in the woods, sending unacceptable erotic dreams to men, stealing cattle and sheep, and tricking or marrying Christians. Most of the tales of the skogsran are between it and a mortal hero; the exchange ends victorious for the man, as he avoids an unpleasant consequence of some sort.

In once story a skogsra had taken a husband as a lover and placed a spell on him so no force on earth could compel him not to visit her nightly. The wife went into the woods one evening and found the skogsra who had entrapped her husband and ask the fairy how she would keep a wandering bull from leaving the barn; the skogsra advised feeding it a mixture of garlic, tar and grass from the north side of the chimney. The wife followed the skogsra's advice and no sooner had her husband consumed the elixir than the desire to visit the fairy vanished. In another story a hunter had become tire of being the skogsra lover and wanted to end it but was unable to resist her spell. The hunter told the fairy he could shoot and kill any creature in the woods but one and wanted to know how to kill it; the skogsra said by missing bulbs, grass from the north side of the chimney, and roots with gunpowder there would be no creature he could not shoot and kill. The hunter followed her advice and was able to rid himself of the fairy once and for all.

Sources: Lindow, *Swedish Legends and Folktales*, 36–7, 111–12; McCoy, *Witch's Guide to Faery Folk*, 312; Thorpe, *Scandinavian Popular Traditions and Superstitions*, 74

Skogul

In Nordic and Teutonic mythology Skogul ("carrier-through") was one of the named VAL-KYRIES, a NYMPH of battle. Always depicted as beautiful women who are sometimes immortal, they are the attendants of the god, Odin.

Sources: Grimm *Teutonic Mythology*, Volume 1, 421; Sigfusson, *Elder Eddas of Saemund Sigfusson Younger Eddas of Snorre Sturleson*, 8, 318

Skovtrolde

Variations: Wood Troll

In the mythology of Denmark, Norway, and Sweden the skovtrolde ("wood TROLLS") are a type of forest NYMPH, malicious and constantly trying to injury mankind. Typically they are found in the densest areas of the woods.

Sources: Dunham, *History of Denmark, Sweden, and Norway*, Volume 2, 64; Keightly, *World Guide to Gnomes, Fairies, Elves, and Other Little*, 63

Skrat

Variations: SCRAT, Scrato, Skraethins

In Teutonic, German lore there is a FAIRY AN-IMAL called a skrat similar to the British BOGART and the Irish CLURICAUNES; it is described as looking like a chicken caught out in the rain; its wingtips and tail drags along the ground. Reported to live in beech trees or caves the skrat has the ability to shape-shift into a cat, dog, goose, or a hair-covered man. Any family the skrat lives with soon became rich, however in

Saxon lore the skrat were reputed to attack women.

Sources: Knight, *Sexual Symbolism*, 163; Forlong, *Faiths of Man*, 317

Skriker

Originating from the fairy lore of Yorkshire England, Skriker is a FAIRY ANIMAL appearing as a BLACK DOG or BARGUEST; it also has the ability to become invisible. This fairy received its name for the horrific scream it makes while invisible. It has been said Skriker is a death omen appearing to someone who will soon have a death in their family; it also splashes in ponds creating a disturbance, and stalk behind travelers as walk down lonely roads at night. Those who have attacked this fairy have never been able to deliver any sort of damage to it, as there has never been a successful solid blow hitting it; it is likely weapons are passing right through the creature.

Sources: Briggs, *Fairies in Tradition and Literature*, 279; Eberhart, *Mysterious Creatures*, 555; Turner, *Yorkshire Notes and Queries*, Volumes 1–2, 203

Skrimsl

A FAIRY ANIMAL from the folklore of Iceland, the skrimsl is said to live in lakes and along the coastline. Malevolent and malicious fairies, they are especially unfriendly towards humans, sinking fishing vessels that sail along the Thorska-fjord. The skrimsl are described as looking like an overturned ship between 180 and 240 feet (54 to 73 meters), bobbing along the surface of the water; they have a hump on their back and a blow-hole that sprays up jets like water, similar to a whale.

Sources: Baring-Gould, *Iceland*, 345–46, 348; Rose, *Spirits, Fairies, Leprechauns, and Goblins*, 296

Skritek

A household fairy from the folklore of Germany, the skritek ("HOBGOBLIN") is described as looking like a small boy. Living behind the oven or in the stable this BROWNIE-like fay would not only assist in doing household chores, such as herding animals sweeping, and weaving, but also share in the family's joys and sorrows. To this day little wooden images of him, standing with his arms folded across his chest and wearing a crown upon his head, are found in many traditional homes.

Sources: Gray, *Mythology of All Races*, Volume 3, 244–45; MacCulloch, *Celtic Mythology*, 224; Perkowski, *Vampires of the Slavs*, 34

Skulld

Variations: Skuld, Skuldr

Similar to the FATES of ancient Greece, there were three principle NORNIRS in the mythology of the ancient Norse; Skulld ("future") was the youngest of the three sisters; she represented the future. In addition to being one of the NORNIR, Skulld was also one of the VALKYRIE. In art she was depicted as being veiled and holding an un-opened book in her hand, looking away from her sister, UDR; she had some golden threads in her hand she was giving to her other sister, VER-DANDI, to weave into the fabric of time.

Sources: Arrowsmith, *Field Guide to the Little People*, 208; Grimes, *Norse Myths*, 23; Keightly, *World Guide to Gnomes, Fairies, Elves, and Other Little People*, 64

Skye

In ancient Greek mythology Skye was one of the HAMADRYAD who was born of from the incestuous relationship between Oxylus and his sister, HAMADRYAS. Skye was the HAMADRYAD of the fig tree.

Source: Larson, *Greek Nymphs*, 283

The Slaugh

The slaugh ("the host') was what the UNSEELIE COURT was called in Scotland; the fairies of the slaugh were believed to be fallen angels who roam the sky at night looking for lost souls. Slaugh were said to be responsible for causing death and sickness in domestic animals.

Sources: Avant, *Mythological Reference*, 480; Rose, *Spirits, Fairies, Leprechauns, and Goblins*, 296

Sleigh Beggey

Variations: Beggys, Ny Mooinjer Veggey ("little kindred"), Sleigh Veggy

On the Isle of Man the sleigh beggey ("little people") were a species of shy, stocky Manx domestic TROOPING FAIRIES which usually lived in underground burghs; it was believed they were the island's original inhabitants. Living lives just as humans did, the sleigh beggeys enjoyed going on hunts and to war. These diminutive fairies were fond of playing music and would use it to lure and abduct humans. Sleigh Beggeys did not like artificial light, ashes, or the taste of salt; they were seldom ever found in modern homes. These fairies never wore clothing; as they walked the foot prints they left behind resembled those of a crow's.

Sources: Briggs, *Encyclopedia of Fairies*, 373; Livo, *Storytelling Folklore Sourcebook*, 41; McCoy, *Witch's Guide to Faery Folk*, 313

Sluag

Variations: Host of the Unforgiven Dead, SLAUGH

Fairies of the Scottish Highlands, the sluag ("host") were considered by some scholars to be fallen angels rather than fairies or ancestral spirits, but no matter what they are, these being were generally considered to be the returned souls of mortal sinners. Flying through the sky from west to east like a flock of birds these fairy spirits seek out the souls of those who have recently died. It was custom a baby never be left near a west-facing window for fear the sluag would take it, even if the baby had been baptized.

Sources: Campbell, *Superstitions of the Highlands and Islands of Scotland*, 8; Curran, *Dark Fairies*, n.p.; Evan-Wentz, *Fairy Faith in Celtic Countries*, 108; Moorey, *Fairy Bible*, 392

Smiera-Gatto

A domestic fairy from the folklore of the Lapp people of northern Scandinavia the smiera-gatto ("butter cat") was a popular familiar spirit; it was well known to steal butter and bring it back to its master. Described as looking like a cat this fairy was oftentimes a blessing to the household to the family it adopted and assisted in prospering; however any wealth or prosperity it bestowed was taken from the neighbors and nearby farms.

Sources: Hastings, *Encyclopædia of Religion and Ethics*, Volume 7, 798; Rose, *Spirits, Fairies, Leprechauns, and Goblins*, 296

Smilax

In Greek mythology, Smilax was a NYMPH who was loved by a mortal named Crocus (Krokos); in some versions of the tale they were each other's constant companion while in others Smilax could not decide if she should accept the affection of a mortal or not. No matter the reason the gods were irritated by their behavior transforming Crocus into the flower which to this day bears his name while Smilax was transformed into a yew tree.

Sources: Folkard, *Plant Lore, Legends, and Lyrics*, 299; Rose, *Spirits, Fairies, Leprechauns, and Goblins*, 245296

Snow Fairies

Variations: Father Frost, Frost Fairies, Frost King, JACK FROST, OLD MAN WINTER, SNOW QUEEN, Winter Faeries

SEASONAL FAIRIES, the snow fairies appear in various apparent ages, forms, and genders, depending on the region. Collectively, their goal is to assist in bringing the winter season into being.

Source: McCoy, *Witch's Guide to Faery Folk*, 313–14

Snow Queen

In the folklore from Denmark the Snow Queen is the queen of fairies; she is described as being a dazzlingly beautiful as ice crystals. The Snow Queen lives in the Ice Realm and travels down from the arctic in blizzards. She incites men to follow her but to love her means instant death.

Sources: Moorey, *Fairy Bible*, 374–77; Rose, *Spirits, Fairies, Leprechauns, and Goblins*, 296–7, 351

Sojo-Bo

Sojo-bo is the leader of the TENGU, a type of BOGEYMAN from Japanese folklore.

Sources: Gray, *Mythology of All Races,* Volume 8, 309; McCoy, *Witch's Guide to Faery Folk*, 319

Solblindi

Solblindi ("sun-blind") was one of the many DWARFS named in the *Voluspa*, the first and best known poem of the *Poetic Edda*, a collection of Old Norse poems dating back to about A.D. 985. It was his three sons who constructed the lattice, Thrymgioll.

Sources: Bellows, *Poetic Edda*, 241; Crossley-Holland, *Norse Myths*, 123

Solitary Fairy

In British and Irish fairy lore, there are essentially two group of fay, the solitary fairies and the TROOPING FAIRIES. Although there are a few BROWNIES and NATURE SPIRITS who are counted among the solitary fay, they are, generally speaking, ominous, outcasts, malicious renegade fairies who wear brown, grey, or red clothing. Many solitary fay are individual, one-of-a-kind beings associated with a certain place. These fairies are quick to anger and have a heightened sense of entitlement; they are known to bestow bad luck on people, consume human flesh, steal babies and leave CHANGELINGS in their place, and take people for slaves. Solitary fairies do not participate in fairy dances but would rather prefer to interact with human on a one-on-one basis. When these fairies give a mortal a gift, it is not always a trick, but the receiver would be advised to proceed with caution.

Examples of solitary fairies are the BANSHEE, BOGIES, BRAG, BROWN MAN OF THE MUIRS, DUERGAR, FENODEREE, FIR DARRIG, HEDLEY KOW, LEPRECHAUN, NUCKELAVEE, PHOOKA, and SHELLEYCOAT to name a few.

Sources: Briggs, *Encyclopedia of Fairies*, 375–76; McCoy, *Witch's Guide to Faery Folk*, 13; White, *History of Irish Fairies*, 82–4; Narváez, *Good People*, 244–45; Rosen, *Mythical Creatures Bible*, 259

El Sombrerón

Variations: Tzipitio, the GOBLIN; Tzizimite

El Sombrerón ("big hat") is a BOGEYMAN figure in Guatemala South America; he is described as being a short, strong man dressed in black with boots, a large hat, and thick belt. He makes a great deal of noise as he walks so he usually rides upon his deer with the golden horns. El Sombrerón is a NATURE SPIRIT, a protector of the forest and the animals who live within it. According to Mexican lore el Sombrerón is a BOGEYMAN, a GIANT headless man who flies through the sky on a white horse; they believe he copulates with mares and then braids their tails.

Sources: Havens, *People's Guide to Mexico*, 306; Kunst, *Journal of American Folklore*, Volume 28, 354–55

Sons of Ivaldi

In ancient Norse mythology there were said to be four son of the DWARF, Ivaldi; collectively they were known as the Ijosalfar. The sons of Ivaldi were the individuals who created many of the magical items of the gods, including the golden wig of Sif; the ship, Skidbladnir; and the spear of Odin. The names of the four sons were BARI ("feisty"), FINNR, IRI, and LIDSKJALFR ("limb shaker").

Sources: Crossley-Holland, Norse Myths, 183; Grimes, *Norse Myths*, 9, 285; Rydberg, *Teutonic Mythology*, 356

Sose

In Greek mythology, Sose was a prophetic OREAD and NYMPH of the mountainous region of Arcadia in southern Greece. By the god Hermes (Mercury), Sose was the mother of two sons, Agreus and Nomios.

Sources: Day, *God's Conflict with the Dragon and the Sea*, 452; Parada, *Genealogical Guide to Greek Mythology*, 11, 87

Le Souin-Souin

A kindly NURSERY BOGIE invoked in French folklore of la Breesse region, this sleepy-time fairy guides children into a deep slumber filled with wonderful dreams. A popular nursery rhyme goes *Le poupon voudrait bien donir,/ Le souin-souin ne veut pas venir./ Souin-souin, vene, vene, vene /Souin-souin, vene, vene, done!* ("Little baby wants to sleep,/ The souin-souin doesn't want to come,/ Souin-souin, come, come, come,/ Souin-souin, come, come, please!").

Similar to BILLY WINKER of English and the SANDMAN Scandinavian folklore le Souin-souin has a female counterpart; she is known as la DORMETTE.

Sources: Martinengo-Cesaresco, *Essays in the Study of Folk-Songs*, 318; Rose, *Spirits, Fairies, Leprechauns, and Goblins*, 297

Spae-Wife

Variations: ELF Damsel

In Icelandic folklore the spae-wives ("prophecy-wives") were described as looking like a diminutive peasant woman who was believed to live in ancient burial places, barrows, and mounds considered being sacred to the SÍDHE. Similar to the WOOD-WIFE of German and Swiss lore, these fairies were experts in herbal magic and healing; there are tales of mortally wounded heroes who would smear their blood on a FAIRY FORT and make offering of meat; in return the resident spae-wife would heal his wounds. Spae-wives were blessed with the gift of prophecy and could easily divine the future by means of reading natural omens, runes, and tea leaves.

Sources: Rose, *Spirits, Fairies, Leprechauns, and Goblins*, 297; Rosen, *Mythical Creatures Bible*, 269

Sparta

Sparta was a NYMPH from the mythology of classical Greece and Rome. One of the NAIADS, she was born the daughter of the river god, Eurotas and his wife Cletas. Sparta was the mother of EURYDICE.

Sources: Bell, *Women of Classical Mythology*, 310; Pausânias, *Pausanias's Description of Greece*, 311

Sparte

In Greek mythology, Sparte was a NYMPH of the town if Sparta in Lakedaimonia located in southern Greece; she was born the daughter of the river god, Eurotas. Sparte was the wife of King Lakedaimon, the son of the OREADS, TAYGETE. Sparte has six sisters, ALCYONE, CELAENO, ELECTRA, MAIA, MEROPE, and STEROPE.

Sources: Larson, *Greek Nymphs*, 152; Westmoreland, *Ancient Greek Beliefs*, 117

Speio

A sea–NYMPH, Speio was the NEREIS of the sea cave in classical Greek mythology; she was born the daughter of Nerues and DORIS. Speio was one of the named NEREID who accompanied THETIS in mourning the loss of her son, Achilles.

Sources: Apollodorus, *Apollodorus' Library and Hyginus' Fabulae*, 2; Collignon, *Manual of Mythology*, 18; Gould, *Historic Magazine and Notes and Queries*, Vol 14, 212; Perry, *Women of Homer*, 146; Trzaskoma, *Anthology of Classical Myth*, 18

Spencer's Fay

English poet and premier craftsmen of Modern English verse Edmund Spencer is perhaps best known for his epic poem entitled *The Faerie Queene* (1590), a fantastical allegory about the morality of life and what conditions are necessary to live a life of virtue.

Throughout *The Faerie Queene* Spence used the word Elfins, Elfs, Fairies, Farys, Fays, and Fées, freely and interchangeably when speaking of fairies. It was through this work all distraction between the different species of fay was lost and fairies became the established name of popular elves.

Source: Keightly, *World Guide to Gnomes, Fairies, Elves, and Other Little People*, 57, 59

Spio

A sea–NYMPH from Greek mythology, Spio ("reproachful") was one of the named NEREID.

Sources: Apollodorus, *Apollodorus' Library and Hyginus' Fabulae*, 95; Betham, *Transactions of the Royal Irish Academy*, Volume 17, 88; Hesiod, *Works of Hesiod, Callimachus, and Theognis*, 15

Spoorn

Variations: Spurn

A type of HOBGOBLIN from folklore of Dorset England, the spoorn was said to be a malevolent type of NURSERY BOGIE; parents would tell their children if they did not behave the spoorn would come and get them.

Source: Rose, *Spirits, Fairies, Leprechauns, and Goblins*, 299

Spor

The tutelary NATURE SPIRIT that embodying fertility, the spor watches over cattle in the stable and the growth of corn.

Sources: Bonnefoy, *American, African, and Old European Mythologies*, 244; Grimal, *Larousse World Mythology*, 414

Spriggans

Members of the UNSEELIE COURT in Scottish fairy lore, spriggans are bearded, short, ugly GOBLIN-like fairies with large feet and spindly limbs; they are utilized by the UNSEELIE COURT as bodyguards. Wearing clothes covered with ornamental bits of stone allowing them to be mistaken for a rock pile, these vicious fairies are often seen at old ruins where they are the guardian of a lost treasure. Spriggans are generally dangerous and destructive fay; they have the ability to blight crops, create whirlwinds to destroy crops, grow large in size and pretend to be the ghost of a GIANT, create bad weather, kidnap human children, and are skilled thieves.

Hanging a horseshoe over a window will keep a spriggan from entering a household. If a toad should enter into the home, it may invite one of these malicious fay in. Should a spriggan gain entry into the home throw a garment that has been turned inside-out at it; if struck, the spriggan will vanish.

Sources: Ashliman, *Fairy Lore*, 208; Avant, *Mythological Reference*, 478; Froud, *Faeries*, 15; McCoy, *Witch's Guide to Faery Folk*, 26, 315; Moorey, *Fairy Bible*, 389

Sprite

Variations: Spret, Spright, Spryte

The word sprite is used as a general term to refer to an ELF, fairy, or PIXIE with an unpredictable nature; it is also used to reference NEREIDS and SYLPHS.

Sources: Avant, *Mythological Reference*, 478; Rose, *Spirits, Fairies, Leprechauns, and Goblins*, 299

Spunkies

Variations: Spunky

In English and Scottish folklore spunkies are always spoken of in the plural tense and are said to appear as a malignant GOBLIN. Like the WILL O' THE WISP, the spunkies will act as a light off in the distance and lure travelers off a path, causing them to become lost as they travel at night; whenever they can these injurious and malicious fairies will lead a person off a cliff or into a morass. Off the Scottish coast they are also sometimes blamed for causing shipwrecks, as they will mimic the light of a lighthouse, luring ships into the rocks.

Sources: Arrowsmith, *Field Guide to the Little People*, 19; Briggs, *Encyclopedia of Fairies*, 381; McCoy, *Witch's Guide to Faery Folk*, 315–16; Rose, *Spirits, Fairies, Leprechauns, and Goblins*, 299

Squant

In the folklore of the Mampanoag people of Massachusetts, United States of America comes the lore of Squant, the sea woman or MERMAID living along the coast of Cape Cod. Described as a square-eyed GIANT with a head of seaweed hair and webbed fingers. Like the SIREN of ancient Greece she has a beautiful singing voice but Squant uses her song to push violent storms back out to sea. When angered, these storms return and crash along the shore.

Source: Belanger, *Weird Massachusetts*, 64

Stalo

Variations: Yityatya

In Andrew Lang's *The Orange Fairy Book*, Stalo ("ogre ") was an OGRE appearing in a Sámi fairy tale collected by J. C. Poestion. In the folklore of Lapland he is described as being one-eyed and wearing clothing of iron Stalo was a fierce man-eater.

Sources: Grimm, *Teutonic Mythology*, Volume 2, 554–55; Lang, *Orange Fairy Book*, 333–337

Staphyle

A NYMPH from classical Greek mythology, Staphyle ("a bunch of grapes") was a lover of the god, Dionysus (Bacchus); he transformed her into a grapevine.

Sources: Porteous, *Forest Folklore*, 112; Rose, *Spirits, Fairies, Leprechauns, and Goblins*, 300

Sterope

Variations: ASTEROPE

One of the OREADS from classical Greek mythology, Sterope ("lightening") was one of the twelve PLEIADES, the companions to the goddess Artemis (Diana); she was married to Oenomaus, one of the sons of the god of war, Ares (Mars) and together had a daughter named Hippodameia.

Sources: Larson, *Greek Nymphs*, 308; Littleton, *Gods, Goddesses, and Mythology*, Volume 11, 1130; Rigoglioso, *Cult of Divine Birth in Ancient Greece*, 135

Sthenele

In ancient Greek mythology Sthenele ("strong light") was a water–NYMPH and one of the named DANAIDS, the collective name for the daughters of Danaus. In a list compiled by Apollodorus, a Greek scholar and grammarian, she was one of the daughters of MEMPHIS and was wedded to Sthenelos, one of the sons of Tyria; since these children were namesakes of one another, they were matched up without drawing lots.

Sources: Apollodorus of Athens, *Apollodorus' Library and Hyginus' Fabulae*, 22; Grimal, *Dictionary of Classical Mythology*, 127

S'thich

A s'thich ("fairy") is a mischievous fairy spirit in Scottish Highland lore; it is especially bothersome to women who are suffering with labor pains and is known to take newborn infants.

Source: Eberhart, *Mysterious Creatures*, 169

Stilbe

In Greek mythology Stilbe ("brilliance") was a NAIAD and a NYMPH of the main town of the Lapithai located in northern Greece; she was born the daughter of the river god, Peneios. Stilbe was a lover of the god, Apollo and bore him a son named Lapithes. In later mythologies the Greek historian Diodorus claimed she and Apollo were the parents of Kentauros, the progenitor of the centaur race.

Sources: Hard, *Routledge Handbook of Greek Mythology*, 555; Larson, *Greek Nymphs*, 165, 311

Stilbo

Born one of the 3,000 daughters of the Titians, Oceanus and Tethys, the NYMPH Stilbo was one of the named OCEANIDS from Greek mythology.

Source: Apollodorus of Athens, *Apollodorus' Library and Hyginus' Fabulae*, 95

Storm Hag

On the bottom of Lake Erie near Presque Isle Peninsula, Unites States of America lives a water fairy by the name of Storm HAG. Described as being hideously ugly she has pale green skin, poisonous talon tipped fingertips, shark-like teeth, and yellow cat-like eyes. Custom says before she attacks, the storm HAG will sing a song few have lived to tell. Traditionally her goes *"Come into the water, love, Dance beneath the waves, Where dwell the bones of sailor lads Inside my saffron caves."* Once the song has ended she calls up a violent storm and riding the waves reaches up onto the ship and snatches up the crew, one by one with her long and strong arms.

Sources: Schlosser, *Spooky Pennsylvania*, 164–66; Swope, *Eerie Erie*, 35–6

Strabo, Types of Nymph

According to Strabo, an ancient geographer, there are four different types of NYMPHS, all of which are the attendants of the god, Dionysus (Bacchus); they are the Lenai (wine-press dancers), Mimallones (musical), Naiades (freshwater) and the Thyiai (orgiastic).

Sources: Conti, *Natale Conti's Mythologiae*, Volume 1, 401; Sourvinou-Inwood, *Hylas, the Nymphs*, 107

Strätteli

In Swiss folklore Strätteli ("a nightmare") and her malignant cohort, STRUDELI, were WOOD NYMPHS living in the forest near Lake Lucerne. Taking particular delight in destroying the fertility of fruit trees, they would then move in and occupy the lifeless tree. These two fairies were said to have destroyed entire orchards. Local tradition had it on January 6, the Feast of the Twelfth Night boys would walk the woods and orchards banging gongs, ringing bells, and sounding horns in the hopes of frightening these two malicious HAMADRYADS away.

Sources: Frazer, *Golden Bough*, 571; Porteous, *Forest Folklore*, 119; Rose, *Spirits, Fairies, Leprechauns, and Goblins*, 301

Strömkarl

Variations: FOSSEGRIN, Fosse-Grim (Waterfall-Grim), GRIM, Stromkarl

In Germany, the strömkarl ("river-spirit) is a musical fairy who will, if a black lamb or a white kid is sacrificed to it, will teach a person how to play beautiful music; this is similar to the NECK of Scandinavian lore. If the sacrificial animal is fattened, the strömkarl will seize the hand of its student and wing it back and fort vigorously until blood runs from their fingertips. After this, the student is then able to play music so masterfully the trees will dance and waterfalls will stop to listen.

Sources: Cora Linn, *Encyclopedia of Superstitions, Folklore, and the Occult Sciences of the World*, Volume 3, 1417; Croker, *Fairy Legends and Traditions of the South of Ireland*, Volumes 1–3, 91; Keightly, *World Guide to Gnomes, Fairies, Elves, and Other Little People*, 152

Strudeli

In Swiss folklore Strudeli ("a witch") and her malignant cohort, STRÄTTELI, were WOOD NYMPHS living in the forest near Lake Lucerne. Taking particular delight in destroying the fertility of fruit trees, they would then move in and occupy the lifeless tree. These two fairies were said to have destroyed entire orchards. Local tradition had it on January 6, the Feast of the Twelfth Night boys would walk the woods and orchards banging gongs, ringing bells, and sounding horns in the hopes of frightening these two malicious HAMADRYADS away.

Sources: Frazer, *Golden Bough*, 571; Porteous, *Forest Folklore*, 119; Rose, *Spirits, Fairies, Leprechauns, and Goblins*, 301

Strymo

Variations: Rhoio, ZEUXIPPE

Strymo was a NYMPH from of the town of Troy in the Troad, Anatolia in the mythology of classical Greece and Rome. One of the NAIADS, she was the born the daughter of SCAMANDER, a river god in Troy. As one of the many wives of the Trojan King Laomedon, Strymo was the mother of Priam and Tithonus.

Sources: Apollodorus of Athens, *Apollodorus: The Library*, Volume 2, 43; Larson, *Greek Nymphs*, 364; Littleton, *Gods, Goddesses, and Mythology*, Volume 6, 805

Sturluson

Sturluson was one of the many DWARFS named in the *Voluspa*, the first and best known poem of the *Poetic Edda*, a collection of Old Norse poems dating back to about A.D. 985.

Sources: Crossley-Holland, Norse Myths, 183; Sturluson, *Prose Edda*, 223

Stygne

In ancient Greek mythology Stygne was a water–NYMPH and one of the named DANAIDS, the collective name for the daughters of Danaus. In a list compiled by Apollodorus, a Greek scholar and grammarian, she was one of the daughters of the NAIAD, POLYXO and was wedded to Polyctor, one of the sons of the NAIAD, CALIADNE.

Sources: Apollodorus, *Gods and Heroes of the Greeks*, 69; Grimal, *Dictionary of Classical Mythology*, 127; Lemprière, *Classical Dictionary*, 236

Styx

Born one of the 3,000 daughters of the Titians, Oceanus and Tethys, Styx was one of the named OCEANIDS as well as a NYMPH from the mythology of classical Greece and Rome.

Sources: Bell, *Bell's New Pantheon or Historical Dictionary of the Gods*, 112; Boswell, *What Men or Gods Are These*, 58; Day, *God's Conflict with the Dragon and the Sea*, 64; Hesiod, *Works of Hesiod, Callimachus, and Theognis*, 20; Westmoreland, *Ancient Greek Beliefs*, 24

Suartalfar

Suartalfar was the DWARF who made the golden replacement hair for the goddess Sif, when the god Loki shaved her head.

Sources: Dunham, *History of Denmark, Sweden, and Norway*, Volume 2, 70; Keightly, *World Guide to Gnomes, Fairies, Elves, and Other Little People*, 68

Sudri

Sudri ("south") was one of the many DWARFS named in the *Voluspa*, the first and best known poem of the *Poetic Edda*, a collection of Old Norse poems dating back to about A.D. 985. One of the four DWARFS of the four main compass points, Sudri, along with AUSTRI ("east"), and NORDI ("north") and WESTRI ("west") each held up one corner of the earth which is described as a flat, plate-like piece of land.

Sources: Crossley-Holland, *Norse Myths*, 183; Daly, *Norse Mythology A to Z*, 22; Sykes, *Who's Who in Non-Classical Mythology*, 53

Suke

In ancient Greek mythology Suke was a HAMADRYAD of the fig tree; she was born from the incestuous relationship between Oxylus and his sister.

Sources: Athenaeus of Naucratis, *Deipnosophists*, Volume 1, 131; Buxton, *Forms of Astonishment*, 211

Sumascazzo

Variations: GRANDINILLI

In Sardinia, Italy, it is believed wind twirls are cause by a NATURE SPIRIT called sumascazzo; sighting one is an omen of an upcoming misfortune. In southern Italy these little fairies are said to wear red clothing and live in the hollow of oak trees.

Sources: Arrowsmith, *Field guide to Little People*, 22; Bois, *Jersey Folklore*, 436; McCoy, *Witch's Guide to Faery Folk*, 223

Surcantine

In the Comte de Caylus fairy-tale entitled *Rosanella*, Surcantine was one of two viable candidates worthy of earning the position of FAIRY QUEEN; PARIDAMIE was the other. As each of the two candidates was equally matched for the position a contest was held to determine the winner and win the title of queen.

Surcantine promised she would raise a human prince, Mirliflor, whom nothing could make constant while PARIDAMIE set out to create a mortal princess, Rosanella, so charming none who saw her could help but fall instantly and deeply in love with her.

Sources: Lang, *Green Fairy Book*, 48–55; Quiller-Couch, *Twelve Dancing Princesses and Other Fairy Tales*, 97, 103, 105

Svartálfar

Variations: ALFAR, Dökkálfar ("DARK ELVES")

In Norse mythology, the Svartálfar ("black spirits") are fairies who live in the underground world of Svartálfaheim; their name likely is derived from their habit of avoid the light as opposed to their nature. Described as looking like ugly and misshaped humans with skin darker than a starless night, the svartálfar are often used interchangeably in stories with the DWARFS and DARK ELVES. Greedy and troublesome the Svartálfar, like the DWARFS, were created from the maggots of the GIANT'S YMIR's rotting flesh and are reputed as being magnificent smiths, creating magical armor and weapons. The Svartalfar are associated with fertility, giving them a substantial following among the ancient Norse people.

Sources: Illes, *Encyclopedia of Spirits*, 17; Keightly, *World Guide to Gnomes, Fairies, Elves, and Other Little People*, 68; Littleton, *Gods, Goddesses, and Mythology*, Volume ll, 58; Rose, *Spirits, Fairies, Leprechauns, and Goblins*, 10

Svíarr

Variations: Sviar, Sviarr

Svíarr was one of the many DWARFS named in the *Voluspa*, the first and best known poem of the *Poetic Edda*, a collection of Old Norse poems dating back to about A.D. 985.

Source: Sturluson, *Prose Edda*, 25

Svior

Variations: Svidr

Svior ("wise") was one of the many DWARFS named in the *Voluspa*, the first and best known poem of the *Poetic Edda*, a collection of Old Norse poems dating back to about A.D. 985.

Sources: Acker, *Poetic Edda*, 218; Wägner, *Asgard and the Gods*, 311; Wilkinson, *Book of Edda called Völuspá*, 12

Sviurr

Variations: Sviarr

Sviurr ("waner") was one of the many DWARFS named in the *Voluspa*, the first and best known poem of the *Poetic Edda*, a collection of Old Norse poems dating back to about A.D. 985.

Sources: Bellows, *Poetic Edda,* 7; Crossley-Holland, *Norse Myths*, 183

The Swan Fairy

In the Arabic fairy-tale *The Blue Parrot* the swan fairy was a FAIRY QUEEN who ruled a kingdom near the lands of the young king, Lino. The swan fairy had only one child, a daughter named Princess Hermosa. The swan fairy owned a magical mirror that allowed her to see whatever she wished as it truly was and not as it appeared. Although the images it showed were accurate it did not allow the viewer to hear anything being said. Although she was a skilled magician the swan fairy was not as well versed in the magical arts as her enemy, the magician Ismenor. Fortunately, she was more clever, prudent, and vengeful than her foe. The swan fairy traveled great distances by a magical flying chariot disguised to look like a beautiful white cloud.

Source: Lang, *Olive Fairy Book*, 9–26

Swan Maidens

Variations: Fairy Brides

The idea of a swan maiden is a very old one and exists in several cultures, such as Celtic, Oriental, Slavic, and Teutonic traditions. The topic of swan maidens was very popular in Victorian England. As the name implies, these beings have the ability to shape-shift between bird and human form in one of two ways: either of their own free will by means of a magical garment or as a secret magical condition, such as a lover promising to never break a specific promise or taboo.

Usually swan maidens appear in groups of three; they are beautiful beyond measure and can be found near a water source spinning or weaving. They love to dance and swim. In Celtic lore they also always wear a magical golden chain that allows them to leave Midgard.

Swan maidens, unlike other fairy brides, are sexually aggressive, oftentimes approaching the man of her intent and seducing him. Among stories of swan maidens, once the marriage takes place, even if it is against her will, and children have been born and her domestic duties established, a happy ending to the tale is impossible. The supernatural world the fairy left behind will reclaim her; she will either return of her own free will, her spouse breaks his promise or taboo, or a tragic event will take her life.

Sources: Grimm, *Teutonic Mythology*, Volume 4, 429; Hastings, *Encyclopedia of Religion and Ethics*, Part 23, 125–26; Welch, *Goddess of the North*, 71–2

Swawa

In Nordic and Teutonic mythology Swawa was one of the named VALKYRIES, a NYMPH of battle. Always depicted as beautiful women who are sometimes immortal, they are the attendants of the god, Odin. Swawa took the hero, Helgi, as her lover and accompanied him into battles.

Sources: *Library of Universal Knowledge*, Volume 15, 136; Rose, *Spirits, Fairies, Leprechauns, and Goblins, an Encyclopedia*, 293

Swor Skogsfru

Variations: Sky Skogsfru

In Sweden the swor skogsfru ("wood wives") are utterly beautiful and seductive fairy women; when viewed from behind these being are revealed to be made of tree bark and are hollow as a log. The male equivalent of this fair is known as the skogsman ("forest man").

Sources: Datlow, *Green Man*, 9–10; Hastings, *Encyclopedia of Religion and Ethics*, Part 12, 485

Syen

Variations: Syenovik

A type of household spirit from the Slavic folklore of the people living in southeastern Europe, the syen are a type of DJINN who enter into the home under the guise of a domestic animal. Once within, the syen become the tutelary guardian of the family. It is also believed each forest, lake, and mountain also has a tutelary syen.

Sources: Avant, *Mythological Reference*, 461; Rose, *Spirits, Fairies, Leprechauns, and Goblins*, 304; Petrovitch, *Hero Tales and Legends of the Serbians*, 18–19

Syke

In ancient Greek mythology Syke was one of the HAMADRYAD who was born of the incestuous relationship between Oxylus and his sister, HAMADRYAS; she was the NYMPH of the fig tree.

Sources: Kloppenborg, *Tenants in the Vineyard*, 227; Larson, *Greek Nymphs*, 283

Syllis

Syllis was a NYMPH of a Sikyon in ancient Greek mythology; by the god Apollo, she was the mother of Zeuxippus.

Sources: Larson, *Greek Nymphs*, 364; Pausanias, *Pausanias's Description of Greece*, Volume 6, 151

Sylph

Variations: Aurae, Windsingers

The hermetic and neo-Platonic doctrine from which all medieval medicine and science was founded describes four Elemental classes, Air, Earth, Fire, and Water; accordingly the Sylphs belong to the Air class, GNOMES to Earth, NEREIDS (see UNDINE) to water, and SALAMANDERS to Fire.

In ancient Greek lore a sylph ("butterfly") was said to be a beautiful, long-lived, small fairy with the ability to shape-shift into human guise. These fairies lived atop mountains and were inclined to grant wishes involving the air. Female sylphs were called sylphids; the leader of the sylphs is named PARALDA.

Sources: Briggs, *Encyclopedia of Fairies*, 192–3; Evan-Wentz, *Fairy Faith in Celtic Countries*, 241; Hall, *Secret Teachings of All Ages*, 317; Rose, *Spirits, Fairies, Leprechauns, and Goblins*, 304; Stepanich, *Faery Wicca*, Book One, 31

Symaithis

In Greek mythology Symaithis was a NAIAD and NYMPH of the river Symaithos in Sicily. Symaithis was a lover of the god, Pan (Faunus) to whome she bore a son named Acis who became the lover of the sea–NYMPH and NEREID, GALATEA.

Source: Parker, *Mythology*, 118

Synallaxis

Variations: Synallasis

A NAIAD from classical Greek mythology Synallaxis ("intercourse") was one of the four NYMPHS of the healing springs of the river Kytheros in Elis, located in southern Greece. Synallaxis was likely the personification of the change toward recovery. Collectively they were known as the IODINES and they names were CALLIPHAEA, IASIS, PEGAEA, and SYNALLAXIS and it was believed to bathe in one of their springs was a cure-all for an array of illnesses and pains.

Sources: Larson, *Greek Nymphs*, 158; Pausanias, *Commentary on Book I: Attica*, 319; Selbie, *Encyclopædia of Religion and Ethics*, 548

Syrinx

In ancient Greek mythology the NYMPH Syrinx had caught the attention of the god Pan (Faunus) who relentlessly perused her. Syrinx had always rejected the advances of the NATURE SPIRITS and SATYERS preferring to live as a virgin huntress; she did not want to be raped by Pan and begged the gods to save her. Taking pity on the NYMPH they transformed her into a patch of reeds. Pan cut some of the reeds and fashioned them into a set of musical pipes. In other telling, Syrinx was saved by being consumed by the earth and from the place where she disappeared a patch of reeds grew. Pan, engaged, tore the reeds apart but realizing his loss, released a sigh of sorrow, his breath passing through the broken reeds and creating the first set of pan pipes.

Sources: Bell, *Bell's New Pantheon or Historical*

Dictionary of the Gods, 112; Hard, *Routledge Handbook of Greek Mythology*, 216; Larson, *Greek Nymphs*, 155

Szepasszony

Variations: FAIR LADY, White Maiden of the Storm, Winter Witch

Szepasszony is a taboo word in Hungarian folklore as it is the name of an injurious and malicious NATURE SPIRIT who dances in hailshowers and storms and seduces young men. Described as being stunningly beautiful with long, silvery-white hair, and wearing a white dress this fairy-woman appears at noon when she is most powerful.

It is considered to be unlucky to enter into a circle of short grass surrounded by taller grass, as it is believd this area was created when the Szepasszony was dancing. After a rain storm, where water drips down from an eave and collects into a puddle is an invitation for the Szepasszony to cause trouble, as she uses puddles as a tool for casting her magical spells.

Sources: Klaniczay, *Witchcraft Mythologies and Persecutions*, 230; Moorey, *Fairy Bible*, 382; Pócs, *Between the Living and the Dead*, 50

Tallemaja

Variations: Talle-maja

In Scandinavian folklore, the tallemaja ("lady of the woods" or "pine tree Mary") was a female HULDRA; it lived deep in the birch forests.

Source: Lindow, *Swedish Legends and Folktales*, 111

Talonhaltija

A guardian spirit of the home in in the folk beliefs of the Estonian people the talonhaltija typically attach themselves to a household rather than an individual. This FAIRY is said to be the spirit of either the first person who lit a fire in the house or was the first person to have died within the home. The sighting of this fairy is said to precede a death or a horrible misfortune is about to occur. The talonhaltija is said to not be fond of loud noises.

Sources: Hastings, *Encyclopedia of Religion and Ethics*, Part 11, 23; Rose, *Spirits, Fairies, Leprechauns, and Goblins*, 305

Tanagra

In classical Greek mythology Tanagra was one of the NAIAD daughters of the river god ASOPUS in Sikyonia and Boiotia, central and southern Greece.

Sources: Classical Association, *Classical Review*, Volume 12, 125; Quiggin, *Essays and Studies Presented to William Ridgeway*, 224

Tangie

A water FAIRY from Scottish lore, the tangie ("seaweedy"), a FAIRY ANIMAL similar to the NUGGLE, was covered in seaweed; it would appear as either a horse or a man in both fresh and salt-water in and around the Orkney Islands.

Sources: Eberhart, *Mysterious Creatures*, 580; Keightly, *World Guide to Gnomes, Fairies, Elves, and Other Little People*, 173; Monaghan, *Encyclopedia of Celtic Mythology and Folklore*, 440

Tangotango

Tangotango ("pitch-black night") was a beautiful FAIRY maiden with an illustrious lineage in the Maori mythology Having heard of a handsome young god named Tawhaki, she sought him out and laid with him each evening until she became pregnant. Tangotango gave birth to a daughter named Arahuta.

Sources: Buse, *Cook Islands Maori Dictionary*, 416; Grey, *Maori Lore*, 86–7

Taniwha

In Māori mythology, the taniwha are a species of tutelary FAIRY ANIMAL living in dark caves, deep pools, or in the sea; they are particularly fond of living in places where the current is dangerous; each tribal group is believed to have its own taniwha. In some traditions the taniwha are seen less are guardians and more as dangerous, predatory snake-like sea monsters kidnapping women to keep as wives.

Sources: Dekirk, *Dragonlore*, 105; Rosen, *Mythical Creatures Bible*, 67

Tankerabogus

Variations: Tanterabobus

A NURSERY BOGIE from the folklore of Devon and Somerset, England, Tankerabogus was invoked by parents to frighten children into good behavior; if the children did not listen, then they ran the risk Tankerabogus would kidnap them, taking them back to his pit-home.

Sources: Briggs, *Encyclopedia of Fairies*, 389; Rose, *Spirits, Fairies, Leprechauns, and Goblins*, 61; Wright, *Rustic Speech and Folk-Lore*, 198

Taotaomonas

The Chamorro people of Guam believe in a type of NATURE SPIRIT called taotaomonas ("old people"); these FAIRY spirits are believed to be the returned sous of their ancestors who are, similar to the HAMADRYAD, guardians of the banyan trees. When walking through their territory, it is necessary to ask for their permission.

Sources: Carlson, *Folklore and Folktales around the World*, Issues 15–19, 155; Curran, *Dark Fairies*, 110–11

Tapairu

In the folk belief of the Mangaia people of the Pacific, the tapairu ("peerless ones") are the four FAIRY daughters of the female demon, Miru. The sisters are described as having long silken hair; at sunset they can enter into our realm and dance at festivals to honor their brother, Tautiti. The tapairu will only appear at dances where a carpet of fresh banana leave have been laid out for them, as their feet are especially delicate.

Sources: Porteous, *Forest in Folklore and Mythology*, 141; Rose, *Spirits, Fairies, Leprechauns, and Goblins*, 304–305

Tarakika

One of the ATUA from the mythology of the Maori people of New Zealand, Tarakika caused swellings in people's ankles and toes.

Source: Illes, *Encyclopedia of Spirits*, 44

Tarans

Variations: SPUNKIES

In the north-east of Scotland babies who have died without first having been baptized are said to return as a type of FAIRY spirit known as a tarans. These little fairies are most often seen flying through the forests crying out in their soft voices of their sad fate.

Sources: Briggs, *Encyclopedia of Fairies*, 389; McPherson, *Primitive Beliefs in the Northeast of Scotland*, 114

Tarbh Uisge

Variations: Tairbh Uisge

Living in Lochan an Tarbh-Uisge, near the Tarmachans Mountains in Scotland, the tarbh uisge ("water bull") is a FAIRY ANIMAL; unlike the EACH UISGE and the KELPIE, it is not prone to assaulting those who happen upon it. Described as being all black, having no ears, and with a soft and velvety appearance, the nocturnal tarbh uisge makes a sound similar to the call of a rooster. Calves born with short ears are said to be the offspring of a tarbh-uisge; these animals were often killed in order to prevent the bad luck they could bring.

Sources: Eberhart, *Mysterious Creatures*, 580; Rose, *Giants, Monsters, and Dragons*, 353

Tarroo-Ushtey

Variations: Tarbh Eithre

Exclusive to the Isle of Man, the tarroo-ushtey is a water bull that although is far less dangerous than the EACH UISGE is still risky to encounter. Living in pools and swamps it is described as looking like an ordinary bull but with and glittering eyes and rounder ears, this FAIRY ANIMAL will mingle with mundane cattle and occasionally produce offspring with very short ears. The tarroo-ushtey is unable to be captured or domesticated, and although there are no stories of one ever having hurt a human there are numerous stories of it having done a great deal of damage ripping up fencing.

Sources: Conway, *Magickal Mermaids and Water Creatures*, 72; Moore, *Folk-Lore of the Isle of Man*, 59–60; Rhys, *Celtic folklore: Welsh and Manx*, Volume 1, 284

Tartaro

Tartaro was an OGRE or Cyclopes of Basque lore. Described as a huge man or GIANT having one eye in the middle of its forehead the tartaro first appeared in Basque mythology during the thirteenth century. In folktale the dim-witted but incredibly strong tartaro is use to replace a GIANT, OGRE or even the NATURE SPIRIT known as BASA-JUAN. In many of the tartaro stories it is the owner of a magical, talking ring which ultimately, because of the low intelligence of the tartaro, is the cause of its death.

Sources: Daniels, *Encyclopædia of Superstitions, Folklore, and the Occult Sciences of the World*, 1378; Rose, *Giants, Monsters, and Dragons*, 355; Webster, *Basque Legends*, 1–6

Tatiana

Variations: Titania ("FAIRY QUEEN" or "great one")

In Shakespearean fairy lore Tatiana was a FAIRY QUEEN, wife to the FAIRY KING, OBERON; together they lead a community of diminutive fairies who were fond of cleanliness and dancing and were prone to child abductions. Tatiana had a persona place of repose, a river bank where musk-roses, oxlip, thyme, and violets grew under a canopied woodbine. Tatiana was dignified whereas MAB was made to be frivolous.

In Shakespeare's *A Midsummer Night's Dream* Tatiana was very proud but the personification of ethical commitment, as she was raising the child of her favorite human companion who passed away in childbirth. Additionally in spite of the fact she had committed at least one act of adultery, she had declared she will no long share her bed with her husband, OBERON, as he had been unfaithful to her one at least two known occasions. Throughout the play Tatiana defends the right of woman to choose for herself, for sexual independence, and to have sovereignty over their body and soul.

Sources: Briggs, *Encyclopedia of Fairies*, 401; Kehler, *Midsummer Night's Dream*, 317; Keightly, *World Guide to Gnomes, Fairies, Elves, and Other Little People*, 325–7

Taygete

One of the OREADS, Taygete was a NYMPH from classical Greek mythology; she was born one of the daughters of the Titian, Atlas and the ocean NYMPH, PLEIONE. She and her sisters, ALCYONE, ASTEROPE, CELAENO, DRYOPE (Aero or MEROPE), ELECTRA, and MAIA, are sometimes referred to as the ATLANTIDES or the Seven Sisters (see PLEIADES).

Sources: Ardinger, *Pagan Every Day*, 190; Illes, *Encyclopedia of Spirits*, 158; Smith, *Dictionary of Greek and Roman Biography and Mythology*, 389

Te-Ihi

In the folklore of the Maori of New Zealand the chief of the *TANIWHA* ("fairy") known as te-ihi ("the dread") was once a mortal man who was out canoeing on Lake Rotoma and Taupo. He dove into the water and came out as a large reptilian man. Since that day the te-ihi, as he has come to be called, has cause trouble on the lake, creating huge waves.

Sources: Reed, *Maori Fables and Legendary Tales*, 18; Taylor, *Te Ika a Maui*, 50

Telchines

In the mythology of ancient Greece, the telchines ("sea children") were the first inhabitants of the Isle of Rhodes. In the oldest myths the telchines were said to have been nine dog-headed enchantresses who had flippers for hands. They were believed to have founded Iaiysos, Kamros, and Lindos; created the first statues of the god, and the sickle Cronus used to castrate Uranus. The telchines were the nurses to the god of the sea, Poseidon, and created his trident for him; the god fell in love with the telechines sister, Alia, and by her had six sons and a daughter, the NYMPH, RHODOS.

In later versions of the myth, the telchines no longer had dog heads and flippers and were born the sons of Pontos and Thalassa; as artisans and magicians they were also the ministers of the god, Zeus. Alia, one of the sisters of the telchines became the lover of Poseidon and the parents of the NYMPH, RHODOS. When the male telchines would not let the goddess of love, Aphrodite, land upon their island she cast an incestuous love spell upon them which caused the brothers to rape their mother, Alia. In their shame the brothers hid in the bowels of the earth and became demons. Poseidon, in a rage, flooded the island but the goddess Artemis alerted the remaining telchines allowing them to escape.

There are some scholars who believe the telchines were a race of ancient people, DWARF-like in appearance, which were conquered by Greek invaders, similar to how the FORMORIANS were invaded and defeated by the TUATHA DE DANANN.

Sources: Facaros, *Greek Islands*, 405; Graves, *The Greek Myths*, 54; Rose, *Spirits, Fairies, Leprechauns, and Goblins*, 307

Teledike

Teledike was a NYMPH of Argos in classical Greek mythology; she was the wife of King Phoroneus and had two children by him, Apis and Niobe.

Sources: Hard, *Routledge Handbook of Greek Mythology*, 228; Larson, *Greek Nymphs*, 149

Teles

In classical Greek mythology, Teles ("perfect") was one of the named SIRENS, a type of malicious NYMPH born the offspring of the ancient sea god, Phorcys. Half bird and half woman, she and her sisters perched on the rocky Sicilian coastline and lured in sailor with their melodious song; once caught, their prey were eaten alive. Although they hunted the coastline they lived inland in a meadow.

Sources: Roman, *Encyclopedia of Greek and Roman Mythology*, 443; Smith, *Dictionary of Greek and Roman Biography and Mythology*, 817

Telesto

Variations: Telestho

Born one of the 3,000 daughters of the Titians, Oceanus and Tethys, Telesto ("NYMPH of the cool springs," "saffron-clad" or "success") was one of the named OCEANIDS. Hesiod describes her as "wearing a yellow peplos."

Sources: Boswell, *What Men or Gods Are These*, 58; Day, *God's Conflict with the Dragon and the Sea*, 64; Hesiod, *Theogony*, 115; Hesiod, *Works of Hesiod, Callimachus, and Theognis*, 20; Westmoreland, *Ancient Greek Beliefs*, 24

Telonnesos

Telonnesos was a NYMPH of Telos in classical Greek mythology.

Sources: Larson, *Greek Nymphs*, 364; Müller, *Ancient Art and Its Remains*, 540; Murray, *Manual of Mythology*, 207

Telphousa

Telphousa was a NYMPH from the mythology of classical Greece and Rome. One of the NAIADS, her fountain was guarded by a fierce dragon. According to the *Homeric Hymn to Apollo*, the god was on a quest to find a place to establish his oracle; when he came upon Telphousa's fountain he decided the spot was nearly perfect but the NYMPH did not want to share her location with a god who would so outshine her. Telphousa recommended another location to Apollo claiming the noise of the hoof beats from the horses and mules that watered at her fountain would soon annoy the god. Apollo did move on and find a better location but soon realized he had been tricked into doing so. Returning to the fountain he killed Telephousa's guardian dragon with one of his arrows and to punish her hid her stream under a cliff.

Sources: Hard, *Routledge Handbook of Greek Mythology*, 144; Richardson, *Three Homeric Hymns*, 120

Tereine

In Greek mythology Tereine was a NAIAD and a NYMPH of the river Strymon located north of Greece; she was a lover of the god Ares (Mars).

Source: Larson, *Greek Nymphs*, 314

Terpsichore

One of the nine CANONICAL MUSES Terpsichore ("delight in dancing") was the MUSE of dance; she was depicted in art as dancing with her dress, girted up, carrying a lyre, and having cymbals on her fingertips. Terpsichore was also the name of one of the MAENADS, the collective name of the daughter born of the CANONICAL MUSE, Mnemosyne, the personification of memory, and the god Zeus (Jupiter), after nine days of continuous intercourse; as such she was said to be the MUSE of epic poetry.

Sources: Hunt, *Masonic Symbolism*, 470; Littleton,

Gods, Goddesses, and Mythology, Volume 11, 921; Monaghan, *Encyclopedia of Goddesses and Heroines*, 434; Peterson, *Mythology in Our Midst*, 121

Terrytop

Terrytop is a devil from the Cornish folktale of *Duffy and the Devil*. In the story a young maiden named Duffy is physically beaten by her stepmother for romping about town with boys rather than tending to her knitting. A handsome squire, having seen the beating take place, is instantly smitten by her good looks and takes Duffy back to his home. There, the old woman who runs his household sets Duffy to spinning and knitting. Angry at having to work, she curses at the spinning wheel, which summons up a devil. The devil then offers to do her work and fulfill any wish she has if at the end of three years she becomes his, but only if by that time she cannot correctly guess his name. Duffy agrees to the bargain.

The squire soon marries Duffy and they have a wonderful life, but as the time draws near to the end of the three-year contract she made with the devil, Duffy grows more and more despondent. The day before her time is up the squire tells his wife of a sight he saw in the woods with the hopes it will cheer her up. He tells here he saw a devil dancing in a circle around a coven of witches singing a song that went "*Duffy, my lady, you'll never know—what? That my name is Terrytop, Terrytop, top!*" The next day when the devil appears he taunts Duffy and gives her three guesses at his name. She plays with him, pretending to be nervous and tossing out two names she knows will not work, but on her last try uses the correct name. Enraged, the devil leaves in a flash of fire, taking his knitting and spinning wheel with him.

Sources: Briggs, *Encyclopedia of Fairies*, 390; Cooper, *Fairy Tales*, 70; Folklore Society, *Folk-Lore Journal*, Vol. 7, 143–4; Hunt, *Popular Romances of the West of England*, 239–47; Rose, *Spirits, Fairies, Leprechauns, and Goblins*, 307

Tethra

A Fomorian king associated with the sea, Tethra was called the FAIRY KING of the Underworld. He was one of the two known kings to rule Magh Mell and seems to have died in the second battle of Moytura, as his sword was found and cleaned by Ogma the Champion.

Sources: Evan-Wentz, *Fairy Faith in Celtic Countries*, 335; Jacobs, *Folklore*, Volume 18, 132–34; Monaghan, *Encyclopedia of Celtic Mythology and Folklore*, 445

Teursapouliet

Appearing in the likeness of a various domestic animals, the teursapouliet of Morlaix, France is a TEURST that in all ways is similar to the BARGUEST of Yorkshire England.

Sources: Keightly, *World Guide to Gnomes, Fairies, Elves, and Other Little People*, 442

Teurst

In Morlaix, France there is specie of FAIRY ANIMAL known as a teurst; these fearsome creatures appear as a large black version of various domestic animals.

Sources: Croker, *Fairy Legends and Traditions of the South of Ireland*, Volumes 1–3, 149; Spence, *Legends and Romances of Brittany*, 71

Teus

Variations: Bugelnoz

In Vannes, France there is a TEURST by the name of Teus who is described as a colossal being clothed in white. Appearing between midnight and 2 A.M., he takes it upon himself to protect people who are about to fall victim to the Devil. Spreading his mantle over the person and hiding them from the Devil's sight, they are rendered safe as the Devil cannot stand to look upon a good being.

Sources: Croker, *Fairy Legends and Traditions of the South of Ireland*, Volumes 1–3, 149; Keightly, *World Guide to Gnomes, Fairies, Elves, and Other Little People*, 442, Spence, *Legends and Romances of Brittany*, 71

Thaleia

Thaleia ("bloom") was one of the named NEREID who accompanied THETIS in mourning the loss of her son, Achilles. Thaleia fell in love with a handsome Sicilian goat-herder and hunter named Daphnis, son of the god, Hermes (Mercury) (see ECHENAIS); before she would fully give her herself to him she either solicited a promise he would resist the temptations of all other women or foretold if he should he fall into the arms of another he would become blind (or be turned to stone, sources conflict). The daughter of the king fell in love with Daphnis and seduced him by giving him too much wine to drink; in his drunken stupor, he forgot his vow to Thaleia and consequently became blind.

Sources: Collignon, *Manual of Mythology*, 18; Fontenrose, *Orion*, 189–92; Perry, *Women of Homer*, 146

Thalia

A sea–NYMPH, Thalia was the NEREID of the clam in classical Greek mythology; she was born of Nereus and DORIS. As one of the nine CANONICAL MUSES in classical Greek mythology, Thalia was the MUSE of bucolic poetry and comedy; she was depicted in art as carrying a comic mask. Thalia was also the name of one of the CHARITIES.

Sources: Apollodorus, *Apollodorus' Library and Hyginus' Fabulae*, 95; Betham, *Transactions of the Royal Irish Academy*, Volume 17, 88; Littleton, *Gods, Goddesses, and Mythology*, Volume 11, 921; Peterson, *Mythology in Our Midst*, 121

Theano

In Greek mythology Theano was a water–NYMPH and one of the named DANAIDS, the collective name for the daughters of Danaus. In a list compiled by Apollodorus, a Greek scholar and grammarian, she was one of the daughters of the NAIAD, Polyxo and was wedded to Phantes, one of the sons of the NAIAD, CALIADNE.

Sources: Apollodorus, *Gods and Heroes of the Greeks*, 69; Grimal, *Dictionary of Classical Mythology*, 127; Lemprière, *Classical Dictionary*, 236

Thebe

In classical Greek mythology Thebe was one of the NAIADS daughters of the river god ASOPUS in Sikyonia and Boiotia, central and southern Greece.

Sources: Classical Association, *Classical Review*, Volume 12, 125; Quiggin, *Essays and Studies Presented to William Ridgeway*, 224

Theisoa

Theisoa was a NYMPH of the springs of the town of Theisoa in Arcadia, southern Greece in classical Greek mythology; she was connected with the care and feeding of the infant god, Zeus (Jupiter), along with HAGNO and NEDA. She was associated with a spring in a town named for her.

Sources: Larson, *Greek Nymphs*, 153; Pausanias, *Pausanias's Description of Greece*, Volume 1, 414, 434

Thelpousa

In Greek mythology, Thelpousa was a NAIAD and a NYMPH of the town of Thelpousa in Arcadia located in southern Greece; she was one of the daughters of the river god, Ladon.

Sources: Larson, Greek Nymphs, 156; Pausânias, *Guide to Greece: Southern Greece*, 432

Thekk

Variations: Thekkr ("clever"), Thror

Thekk was one of the many DWARFS named in the *Voluspa*, the first and best known poem of the *Poetic Edda*, a collection of Old Norse poems dating back to about A.D. 985. Thekk may be one of the many aliases and forms used by the god, Odin.

Sources: Crossley-Holland, Norse Myths, 183; Daly, *Norse Mythology A to Z*, 22; Wilkinson, *Book of Edda called Völuspá*, 12; Sykes, *Who's Who in Non-Classical Mythology*, 53

Thelxiepia

Variations: Thelxiepeia ("beguiling with her words"), Thelxinoe ("beguiling of speech"), Thelxiope ("persuasive face")

In classical Greek mythology, Thelxiepia was one of the named SIRENS, a type of malicious NYMPH born the offspring of the ancient sea god, Phorcys. Half bird and half woman, she and her sisters would perch on the rocky Sicilian coastline and lure in sailor with their melodious song; once caught, their prey were eaten alive. Although they hunted the coastline they lived inland in a meadow.

Sources: Austern, *Music of the Sirens*, 40; Smith, *Dictionary of Greek and Roman Biography and Mythology*, 817

Themistagora

Variations: Thémistaoora

In ancient Greek mythology Themistagora was a water–NYMPH and one of the named DANAIDS, the collective name for the daughters of Danaus; her name appears in a list of the DANAIDS generated by Gaius Julius Hyginus (ca. 64 B.C.–A.D. 17), a Latin author. Themistagora was wedded to Podasimus and killed him on their wedding night.

Source: Hyginus, *Myths of Hyginus*, 133

Themiste

A sea–NYMPH from ancient Greek mythology, Themiste was the NYMPH of the flowing tide.

Sources: Betham, *Transactions of the Royal Irish Academy*, Volume 17, 89; Hard, *Library of Greek Mythology*, 123

Themisto

Variations: Karmentis

A sea–NYMPH from ancient Greek mythology, Themisto ("justice") is the NEREID of the law of the sea; one of the named NEREIDS in ancient Greek mythology, she was born the daughter of Nerues and DORIS.

Sources: Hesiod, *Works of Hesiod, Callimachus, and Theognis*, 15; Sluiter, *Free Speech in Classical Antiquity*, 33

Thero

In Greek mythology Thero was a NAIAD and a NYMPH of the town of Therapne, in Lakedaimonia located in southern Greece. Thero was a nurse to the infant god Ares (Mars).

Sources: Bell, *Bell's New Pantheon*, 112; Pausânias, *Guide to Greece: Southern Greece*, 69

Thespia

Variations: Thespeia

Thespia was a NYMPH of the town of Thespiae in Boiotia located in central Greece; she was the daughter of the river god, ASOPUS. The NAIAD Thespia was loved by the god, Apollo according to ancient Greek mythology.

Sources: Bell, *Bell's New Pantheon*, 112; Pausanias, *Pausanias's Description of Greece: Indices, Maps*, 159

Thespian

In classical Greek mythology Thespian was one of the NAIADS daughters of the river god ASOPUS in Sikyonia and Boiotia, central and southern Greece.

Sources: Classical Association, *Classical Review, Volume 12*, 125; Quiggin, *Essays and Studies Presented to William Ridgeway*, 224

Thetis

A sea–NYMPH from classical Greek mythology, Thetis was the NEREID of the spawning of fish and deep water; she was born the daughter of Nerues and DORIS. Considered the leader of his sisters, she was the mother of the famed Greek hero, Achilles. Thetis is the only one of all the NEREIDS who had her own individual character traits; she was described as being exceptionally beautiful and was at one time courted by both Zeus (Jupiter) and Poseidon (Neptune) before marrying the mortal king, Thessaly.

Sources: Bell, *Bell's New Pantheon or Historical Dictionary of the Gods*, 112; *Columbian Cyclopedia*, Volume 20, 20; Hesiod, *Works of Hesiod, Callimachus, and Theognis*, 15

Thiasse

A GIANT in Norse mythology, Thiasse, who had the ability to shape-shift into an eagle, was the father of the beautiful FRIDUR. Thiasse was slain by the hero, Suaforlami with the magical sword, Tirfing.

There is also a story where a GIANT named Thiasse who lived in the mountains at Thrymheim who had a daughter named Skada. Thiasse was killed by the god Thor while he flew in the form of an eagle. When Skada discovered how her father had died, she set out to avenge his death but was appeased and married Njord.

Sources: Pigott, *Manual of Scandinavian Mythology*, 192–93; Tegnér, *Fritiof's Saga*, xxxv

Thien

A NAT from the folk belief of Burma, the thien were NATURE SPIRITS of rain and were believed to live near the stars. During times of drought people would hold tug-of-war contests because during rainfalls the thien would stage mock battles between themselves, the flashes of lightening said to be the clashing of their weapons.

Source: Rose, *Spirits, Fairies, Leprechauns, and Goblins*, 307

Thisbe

A NYMPH of the village of Thisbe in Bioiotia located in central Greece, Thisbe was a NAIAD in classical Greek mythology.

Source: Larson, *Greek Nymphs*, 143

Thisoa

Thisoa was a NYMPH from classical Greek mythology; she was, along with HANGO and NEDA, associated with the care and feeding of the infant god, Zeus (Jupiter).

Sources: Pausanias, *Pausanias's Description of Greece*, Volume 1, 434; Smith, *New Classical Dictionary of Greek and Roman Biography, Mythology and Geography*, Volume 2, 953

Thiua

THIUA was one of the names given as being one of the NYMPHS of the cave at Corycian. She was said to be one of the "triple muses of divination at Delphi" along with CORYCIA, DAPHNUS, KLEODORA and MELAINA. She was one of the NAIADS AND one of a trio of NYMPHS known collectively as the Thriae or the Thriai.

Source: Monaghan, *Goddesses in World Culture*, 147

Thoe

Born one of the 3,000 daughters of the Titians, Oceanus and Tethys, Thoe ("the runner") was one of the named OCEANIDS in Greek mythology. She

was the NEREID of running waves and a speedy voyage as well as one of the named NEREID who accompanied Thetis in mourning the loss of her son, Achilles.

Sources: Apollodorus, *Apollodorus' Library and Hyginus' Fabulae*, 95; Bell, *Bell's New Pantheon or Historical Dictionary of the Gods*, 112; Boswell, *What Men or Gods Are These*, 58

Thoosa

A NYMPH from classical Greek mythology, Thoosa was born the daughter of Phorcys, a gigantic sea creature. During an affair with the god of the sea, Poseidon (Neptune), she gave birth to Polypemon the Cyclops. Thooa, described as having a MERMAID-like appearance, was known for her swiftness; she was the NYMPH of dangerous currents.

Sources: Apollodorus of Athens, *Apollodorus' Library and Hyginus' Fabulae*, 89; Conner, *Everything Classical Mythology Book*, 87

Thorinn

Variations: Thorin

Thorinn was one of the many DWARFS named in the *Voluspa*, the first and best known poem of the *Poetic Edda*, a collection of Old Norse poems dating back to about A.D. 985.

Sources: Crossley-Holland, Norse Myths, 183; Daly, *Norse Mythology A to Z*, 22; Sykes, *Who's Who in Non-Classical Mythology*, 53; Wilkinson, *Book of Edda called Völuspá*, 12

Thouria

Thouria was a NYMPH in classical Greek mythology of a spring in Italy.

Source: Larson, *Greek Nymphs*, 223

Thrainn

Variations: Thrain

Thrainn ("craver") was one of the many DWARFS named in the *Voluspa*, the first and best known poem of the *Poetic Edda*, a collection of Old Norse poems dating back to about A.D. 985.

Sources: Crossley-Holland, Norse Myths, 183; Daly, *Norse Mythology A to Z*, 22; Wilkinson, *Book of Edda called Völuspá*, 12

Thrar

Thrar ("contumax" or "insolent") was one of the many DWARFS named in the *Voluspa*, the first and best known poem of the *Poetic Edda*, a collection of Old Norse poems dating back to about A.D. 985.

Sources: Grimm, *Teutonic Mythology*, Volume 2, 453; Wägner, *Asgard and the Gods*, 311

Thrasir

Thrasir ("against") was one of the many DWARFS named in the *Voluspa*, the first and best known poem of the *Poetic Edda*, a collection of Old Norse poems dating back to about A.D. 985.

Source: Sturluson, *Prose Edda*, 248

Thrassa

A NYMPH of the Triballoi tribe of Thrake in north of Greece Thrassa was born the daughter of the god Ares (Mars); she bore him a daughter named Polyphonte. Thrassa was the wife of King Hipponous.

Sources: Lemprière, *Classical Dictionary* (1839), 36; Parada, *Genealogical Guide to Greek Mythology*, 25, 179

Thridi

Thridi ("the third") was one of the many DWARFS named in the *Voluspa*, the first and best known poem of the *Poetic Edda*, a collection of Old Norse poems dating back to about A.D. 985. Thridi was a king.

Sources: Clarke, *Ten Great Religions*, 370; Keightly, *World Guide to Gnomes, Fairies, Elves, and Other Little People*, 61

Thronia

Variations: Babylon ("of the throne"), Babylon Thronia

Thronia was a NYMPH from the mythology of classical Greece and Rome. One of the NAIADS, she was born the daughter of the god of Babylon, Bel; Thronia was said to be the mother of the hero, Arabos, who was killed by the mares of Diomedes.

Sources: Larson, *Greek Nymphs*, 174; Tarn, *Greeks in Bactria and India*, 253

Thronie

A NYMPH of the town of Abdera in Bistonia, Thrake located in north of Greece, she was born a daughter of Belos, the son of the goddess, Io. Thronie was a NAIAD loved by the god, Poseidon (Neptune) but by Hermes (Mercury) gave birth to the eponyms, Arabos.

Sources: Dowden, *Companion to Greek Mythology*, 462; Gantz, *Early Greek Myth*, 208

Thrór

Variations: Thror

Thrór ("burgeoning") was one of the many DWARFS named in the *Voluspa*, the first and best known poem of the *Poetic Edda*, a collection of Old Norse poems dating back to about A.D. 985. Thrór may be one of the many aliases and forms used by the god, Odin.

Sources: Crossley-Holland, Norse Myths, 183; Daly, *Norse Mythology A to Z*, 22; Sykes, *Who's Who in Non-Classical Mythology*, 53; Wilkinson, *Book of Edda called Völuspá*, 12

Thrud

In Nordic and Teutonic mythology Thrud ("power") was one of the named VALKYRIES, a NYMPH of battle. Always depicted as beautiful women who are sometimes immortal, they are the attendants of the god, Odin.

Source: Sigfusson, *Elder Eddas of Saemund Sigfusson Younger Eddas of Snorre Sturleson*, 57, 320

Thrummy-Cap

Variations: Thrummy, Trom, Tromie, Troomie

In the folklore of the northern counties of England, particularly Northumberland, Thrummy-Cap was a fairy described as a "queer look little man" wearing a cap made of "thrums," the short ends of wool that is clipped off a loom at the end of weaving. Thrummy-Cap lived in the cellars of old houses.

Sources: Briggs, *Fairies in Tradition and Literature*, 280; Halliwell, *Dictionary of Archaic and Provincial Words* Volume 2, 871; Narváez, *Good People*, 138

Thrumpin

Along the British and Scottish boarder there was the belief in a species of fairy known as the thrumpin; they acted like a guardian spirit or a FATE, who had the power to take away or end a person's life. One thrumpin was assigned to each person upon birth. Sometimes it was said the thrumpin acted like a guardian angel, actually taking action to protect its charge.

Sources: Briggs, *Encyclopedia of Fairies*, 395; Henderson, *Notes on the Folk-Lore of the Northern Counties of England and the Borders*, 262; Rose, *Spirits, Fairies, Leprechauns, and Goblins, an Encyclopedia*, 308

Thussers

Variations: Huldre Folk, Vardogls

Living in the earthen mounds on the fjords of Norway are communities of diminutive fairies known as thussers. These elusive fay love to dance and are expert fiddle players; they are not malicious and will quickly disappear when humans approach.

Sources: Bois, *Jersey Folklore and Superstitions*, 210; McCoy, *Witch's Guide to Faery Folk*, 319

Thyia

Variations: Thyad

A NYMPH in classical reek mythology, Thyia was one of the MAENADS, the collective name of the daughter born of the CANONICAL MUSE, Mnemosyne, the personification of memory, and the god Zeus (Jupiter), after nine days of continuous intercourse. Thyia was a NAIAD of a shrine in Phokis located in central Greece and was a lover of the god, Apollo, and bore him a son named Delphus.

Sources: Monaghan, *Encyclopedia of Goddesses and Heroines*, 418; Zacharia, *Converging Truths*, 115

Thyiades

Variations: Thyades

In ancient Greek mythology the Thyiades were the orgiastic NYMPHS of Dionysus (Bacchus), according to Alkman, an ancient Greek lyrical poet from Sparta who worked in the 7th century B.C. Thyiades were the NYMPHS of *thyrsus*, staves of fennel covered with vines and leaves and topped with a pinecone. They took their name from the NYMPH THYIA, daughter of the river god, Kephisos.

Sources: Brooks, *Myths, Games and Conflict*, 53; Rigoglioso, *Cult of Divine Birth in Ancient Greece*, 87

Thymbris

A prophetic NYMPH of Arcadia, Thymbris was the mother of the god Pan (Faunus) by the god, Zeus (Jupiter), according to some ancient Greek myths; the NYMPH PENELOPEIA was also said to be Pan's mother.

Sources: Anthon, *Classical Dictionary*, 967; Keightley, *Mythology of Ancient Greece and Italy*, 123, 229

Tiasa

Tiasa was a NYMPH from the mythology of classical Greece and Rome. One of the NAIADS, she was born the daughter of Eurotas, a river god of Lakedaimonia in southern Greece; she inhabited a river in Laconia which ran alongside the road between Amyklai and Sparta.

Sources: Larson, *Greek Nymphs*, 152; Lemprière, *Classical Dictionary*, 52

Tib

Tib was one of the fairies mentioned in the literature of ROBIN GOOD FELLOW. She had three brothers, GRIM, PATCH, and PINCH and four sisters, GULL, LICKE, LULL, and SIB. A lieutenant to her sister, SIB, Tib was second in command among her group of siblings.

Sources: Briggs, *Encyclopedia of Fairies*, 395; Davis, *Life in Elizabethian Days*, 217; Wilson, *Life in Shakespeare's England*, 42, 44

Tiberinus

Born one of the 3,000 daughters of the Titians, Oceanus and Tethys, Tiberinus was one of the named OCEANIDS from Greek mythology.

Sources: Boswell, *What Men or Gods Are These*, 58; Day, *God's Conflict with the Dragon and the Sea*, 64; Hesiod, *Works of Hesiod, Callimachus, and Theognis*, 20

Tiddy Ones

Variations: Tiddy Men, Tiddy Mun, Tiddy People, Strangers, YARTHKINS

In the folklore of Lincolnshire, England the tiddy ones were a drifting mass of NATURE SPIRITS or YARTHKINS; although they were thought of as a collective, one of them stood apart from the others, Tiddy Mun. This particular fairy was called upon in times of flood to cause the water to recede. Generally, the tidy ones were considered benign but if they were emotionally or physically hurt they would cause a pestilence to befall cattle and children.

Sources: Avant, *Mythological Reference*, 479; Briggs, *Fairies in Tradition and Literature*, 280, 395, 398; Rose, *Spirits, Fairies, Leprechauns, and Goblins*, 308

Tighe

Variations: BEAN TIGHE

Similar to the BROWNIE of Scottish lore, tighe fairies attach themselves to a home and each night will finish any chores not completed during the day. These fairies get along well with all domestic animals but will not take up occupancy in any home with a cat or is continuously excessively loud. Any offering other than food will be taken as an insult by the tighe.

Sources: Evans-Wentz, *Fairy-Faith in Celtic Countries*, 81; McCoy, *Witch's Guide to Faery Folk*, 320–21

Tilottama

In Hindu mythology Tilottama was a type of celestial NYMPH known as an apsaras. In all there are twelve apsaras but only four of them stand out in Sanskirt literature, MENAKA, RAMBHA, Tilottama and URVASI. Tilottama was the apsaras who appeared before Lord Brahma while he was performing his austerities; eventually she was able to humiliate him.

Sources: Rajan, *Complete Works of Kālidāsa*, 168, 373; Ryan, *Encyclopedia of Hinduism*, 42

Tilphossa

Variations: Telphusa, Thelpusa

Tilphossa was a NYMPH of a spring in classical Greek mythology; she was the mother of Draken the Theban dragon by the god, Ares (Mars).

Sources: Fontenrose, *Python*, 367, 613; Larson, *Greek Nymphs*, 143

Tingoi

Variations: Njaloi

A water base NATURE SPIRIT from the folklore of the Mende people of Sierra Leone, the tingoi were a type of GENIE described as looking like a beautiful young woman with soft, white skin or as a MERMAID. Sometime the tingoi was described as being a singual being; as such, Tingoi epitomized the ideal yet unattainable perfection of physical feminine beauty and oversaw female initiation ceremonies.

Sources: Mittman, *Ashgate Research Companion to Monsters and the Monstrous*, 81–82; Rose, *Spirits, Fairies, Leprechauns, and Goblins*, 309

Tiphaine

Bertrand du Guesclin (c. 1320–1380), a Breton knight and French military commander during the Hundred Years' War was popularly believed to have married a fairy woman by the name of Tiphaine. Considered to be educated, learned, and wise, she was also an accomplished astrologer and well known for her accurate prophecies.

Sources: Keightley, *Fairy Mythology*, Volume 2, 479; Vernier, *Flower of Chivalry*, 32, 54

Tisiphone

One of the three FURIES from classical Greek mythology, Tisiphone ("rage") was the sister who specialized in avenging act of evil. As a guardian of the gates of Tartaros, Tisiphone wears a bloody robe and whips the wicked dead who had been locked up in a steel cage. She like her sisters, were described as looking like an old HAG with bat wings, bloodshot eyes, and snakes in her hair; sometime they were confused as being a gorgon. The ancient Greek tragedian, Aeschylus (525 B.C.–456 B.C.), claimed the sisters were the daughters of Night while the tragedian Sophocles (497 B.C.–406 B.C.) said they were the daughter of Skotos, the personification of darkness, and the earth.

Sources: Chopra, *Academic Dictionary of Mythology*, 112, 284; Drury, *Dictionary of the Esoteric*, 93; Hard, *Routledge Handbook of Greek Mythology*, 39, 124

Tithorea

Tithorea was a NYMPH of of the town of Tithorea in Phokis, central Greece in classical Greek mythology.

Sources: Larson, *Greek Nymphs,* 147; Roman, *Encyclopedia of Greek and Roman Mythology*, 71

Titihal

One of the ATUA from the mythology of the Maori people of New Zealand, Titihal caused general pain in the feet.

Source: Illes, *Encyclopedia of Spirits*, 44

The Toads and Diamonds Fairy

In the fairy-tale *Toads and Diamonds* by Charles Perrault the fairy who had disguised herself as an old woman in order to test the manners of beautiful girls blessed one so each time she spoke either a diamond or a flower would fall from her lips. This same fairy also cursed beautiful girls who acted as if ill-breed so each time they spoke a snake or a toad would fall from her lips.

Sources: Lang, *Blue Fairy Book*, 274–76; Olcott, *Book of Elves and Fairies*, 121–22

Tod-Lowery

Variations: Tod Lowery, Tom Lowery, Tomloudy

In the folklore of Lincolnshire, England todlowery ("fox-fox") was a species of GOBLIN; they were frightening in appearance and used as a NURSERY BOGIE. In the lowlands of Scotland, this is used as the nickname of a fox.

Sources: Briggs, *Encyclopedia of Fairies*, 401; Folklore Society (Great Britain), *County Folk-Lore*, Volume 37, 58; Rose, *Spirits, Fairies, Leprechauns, and Goblins*, 311

Toice Bhrean

Variations: LIBAN

In Irish folklore Toice Bhrean ("lazy wench" or "untidy") was originally the guardian of a sacred well but due to her neglect, she left its lid off one day causing the well to overflow, thereby creating Lough Gur. In these stories she was also known as LIBAN, the daughter of EOCHAID (also known as Eochaidh Finn). According to legend, Toice Bhrean was punished for forgetfulness; she must spend eternity beneath a magical tree growing at the bottom of the lake. Once every seven years when the water evaporates just enough she is able to see sunlight for a few moments.

It is still held in modern times to be an entrance

way to Tir-Na-Nog ("land of eternal youth"), a fairy Otherworld (see FAIRYLAND).

Sources: Evan-Wentz, *Fairy Faith in Celtic Countries*, 78; Monaghan, *Encyclopedia of Celtic Mythology and Folklore*, 450

Tolcarne Troll

Variations: Odin the Wanderer, the Wandering One

Dating back to the times of the Phoenicians, the tolcarne troll was described as looking like a little, old pleasant-faced man who was dressed in a tight fitting leather jerkin and wore a hood on his head. This fairy being lived invisibly in the rocks and wherever he chose he could make himself seen to mortals. It was also believed this TROLL could be summoned by holding three shriveled leaves, one ash, one oak, and one thorn, and reciting a secret incantation. The magical spell was passed from one believer to another, from a man to a woman.

Sources: Evan-Wentz, *Fairy Faith in Celtic Countries*, 176; Hastings, *Encyclopædia of Religion and Ethics*, Volume 12, 452

Tolv

A Danish FAIRY KING, Tolv ("twelve") will not allow a mortal prince to cross over the bridge of Kjelskör in Skjelskör, Zealand. It is isad each New Year's Eve he takes from a random smith's forge nine new horse shoes and accompanying nails. When sighted, Tolv is seen on sunny days rolling in the grass.

Source: Keightly, *World Guide to Gnomes, Fairies, Elves, and Other Little People*, 92

Tom Cockle

Tom cockle was an individual BROWNIE or domestic fairy from Irish lore who attached himself to a family rather than a location. According to the legend, when the family fell into poverty and had to move they bid a tearful farewell to their beloved fairy. When they arrived at their new home they discovered the fire was lit in the fireplace and food was set on the table, as Tom Cockle moved with them.

Sources: Briggs, *Encyclopedia of Fairies*, 402; Moorey, *Fairy Bible*, 388; Rose, *Spirits, Fairies, Leprechauns, and Goblins*, 311, 351

Tom Dockin

Variations: Tom Donkin, Tommy Dockin

Tom Dockin in a NURSERY BOGY from the folklore of Yorkshire, England; he has iron teeth in which he use to bit naughty children.

Sources: Briggs, *Encyclopedia of Fairies*, 402; Rose, *Spirits, Fairies, Leprechauns, and Goblins*, 311; Wright, *Rustic Speech and Folk-Lore*, 198

Tom-Poker

Variations: Tom Po, Tom Poker, TOMTE-Pocke

GOBLIN Tom-Poker was a NURSERY-BOGY from the folklore of East Anglia, England; he lived in *poker-holes*, dark closets, holes under stairs, and unoccupied lofts. His two brothers were HODGE-POKER and MUM-POKER.

Sources: American Philological Association, *Transactions of the American Philological Association*, Volume 26, 141–42; Briggs, *Encyclopedia of Fairies*, 402; Wright, *Rustic Speech and Folk-Lore*, 198

Tom Thumb

Variations: Le Petit Poucet

First appearing in print in 1621 by pamphleteer Richard Johnson, the tale of the diminutive boy was already considered proverbial. The story tells us once a farmer and his wife beseeched Merlin to give them a son, even if it was only as big as the tip of his thumb. When they returned home the wife discovered she was with child and within moments gave birth to a tiny boy who grew to his full size of a few inches. Tom never grew any larger than his father's thumb but because of his size drew the attention of the fay. A FAIRY QUEEN became his godmother and supplied him with clothing. She also blessed him so not only could he hang pots and pans on sunbeams but also he had no need to breath, drink or eat.

The incomplete story ends with Tom returning to King Arthur's court but in various versions he went on to have a wide array of adventures. In the *Mad Pranks and Merry Jests of Robin Goodfellow* (1841) Tom was the bagpipe player of FAIRYLAND.

The female counterpart to Tom Thumb is called Thumbelina. A Danish version of Tom exists, his name is Tommelise.

Sources: Briggs, *Encyclopedia of Fairies*, 402–04; Keightly, *World Guide to Gnomes, Fairies, Elves, and Other Little People* 289; Rose, *Spirits, Fairies, Leprechauns, and Goblins*, 311

Tom-Tit-Tot

In English folklore, Tom-Tit-Tot was similar to the German story of RUMPELSTILTSKIN. A beautiful maiden was sworn as wife to the king on the promise of her mother that she could spin five skeins of flax per day for a month. Set with the task and unable to complete it she is approached by a fairy; it is described as being a "black little thing with a long tail." The fairy says it will do her spinning on the condition if at the end of the month she cannot correctly guess its name she will go away with it. The would-be bride agrees and just when all seems lost, she happens to overhear the fairy singing a boastful song to itself "Niminy niminy not, My name's Tom-Tit-Tot." When the month ends and the chore is complete the fairy returns demanding the answer or the woman. The bride correctly guesses the name the fairy then angrily vanished forever.

Sources: Haase, *Greenwood Encyclopedia of Folktales and Fairy Tales*, 464; McCoy, *Witch's Guide to Faery Folk*, 64; Yearsley, *Folklore of Fairytale*, 153–57

Tomte (plural: tomtar)

Like the BROWNIE of Scotland and the KOBOLD of Germany, tomte is a NIS of Sweden a domestic house fairy is very helpful when it is treated with respect. Proud and sensitive by nature if ever he is made fun or if it observed social proprieties being ignored, a misfortune would befall, such as, the cows could dry up, the harvest may fail, or the milk could turn sour. Typically to prevent calamity a bowl or porridge or rice is left outdoors for it. Each Christmas day the tomte is paid its wages; along with the food a piece of grey cloth, a pinch of tobacco, and a shovelful of clay is left for it as well. The tomte was not shy about boxing a person's ears if it found their behavior to be unacceptable by either its or the community's standards; otherwise this fairy was completely benign and content to do household chores and look after the farm's animals.

Sources: Ashliman, *Fairy Lore: A Handbook*, 46, 209; Keightly, *World Guide to Gnomes, Fairies, Elves, and Other Little People*, 139; Lindow, *Swedish Legends and Folktales*, 142–43

Tomtegubbe

Variations: Tomte Gubbe, Tomtgubbe ("old man of the house"), Tontty, Tonttu

A house hole Nis in Swedish lore the tomtegubbe is described as being as small as a child but looking like an old man; dressed in homemade grey clothing and clumsy looking shoes, he keeps a red nightcap atop his head. A benign fairy, the tomtegubbe may be kept in good spirits by being left little treats of cake, drink, and tobacco placed either on the barn or kitchen floor. An extremely hard worker the tomtegubbe gift the house hold he lives with good fortune but in exchange, he expect the home to be particularly clean and neat.

Sources: Grimm, *Teutonic Mythology*, Volume 4, 1414; Keightly, *World Guide to Gnomes, Fairies, Elves, and Other Little People*, 139, 488; Newton, *Spiritual Magazine*, Volume VI, 218–19

Tonx

The Vogul people of western Serbia believed in benign water based NATURE SPIRIT called Tonx. This fairy would bestow good hunting and fishing on those who venerated him; he also could be persuaded to cure those who were ill.

Sources: Dixon-Kennedy, *Encyclopedia of Russian and Slavic Myth and Legend*, 281; Rose, *Spirits, Fairies, Leprechauns, and Goblins*, 313

Tootega

A water NATURE SPIRIT from the folklore of the Inuit people of northern Canada, Tootega appears as a small, old woman walking along the surface of the water. It was believed she lived in a small stone house on an unspecified island.

Sources: Avant, *Mythological Reference*, 49; Rose, *Spirits, Fairies, Leprechauns, and Goblins*, 313

Tooth Fairy

Variations: Tooth Faery, Toothy Fairy

The tooth fairy is a fey that exists in the folklore of European cultures and contemporary North America; originally she ensured when a child's milk-tooth fell out a new one grew back in its place. During the course of the fairy's evolution it became important to place the tooth under the child's pillow so she would leave money or a small gift it its place. Descriptions of the tooth fairy vary widely, from a small gossamer winged being to an adult-sized princess; it can be male or female, lean or chubby, young or old; no matter its appearance, children are willing to accept it without drawing suspicion.

Sources: Narváez, *Good People*, 406, 439; Rose, *Spirits, Fairies, Leprechauns, and Goblins*, 313, 351

Torrhebia

Torrhebia was a lake NYMPH of Lydia in ancient Greek mythology. By the god Zeus (Jupiter) she was the mother of the hero, Karios (Carius).

Sources: Cramer, *Geographical and Historical Description of Asia Minor*, 474; Larson, *Greek Nymphs*, 200

Tot Grid

Variations: Tot, Tut, Tut gut

A HOBGOBLIN from Lincolnshire, England, Tot Grid was typically regarded as a harmless household spirit.

Sources: Briggs, *Vanishing People*, 200; Rose, *Spirits, Fairies, Leprechauns, and Goblins*, 315

Tragasia

Tragasia was a NYMPH of Lykia in classical Greek mythology. Miletus, one of the godling sons of Apollo, and Tragasia are sometimes said to be the mother of BYBLIS who fell in love with her twin brother, Caunus; sometimes their mother is said to be the NYMPH, KYANEE.

Sources: Larson, *Greek Nymphs*, 210; Smith, *Dictionary of Greek and Roman Biography and Mythology*, 520

El Trasgu

Variations: Trasgos

In the folklore of northern Spain, el trasgu was believed to live in old houses; they were especially fond of those with large rooms, although it was not the house they were attached to but rather the family who lived there. These fairies would even follow the family should they move. Described as looking like a DWARF dressed in red or has having horns, a tail, and walking with a limp, trasgu loved doing domestic house hold chores however similar to the BROWNIE, if they were not compensated with food and a warm place to sleep they would become very angry, breaking dishes, moving objects, and waking people as they slept.

Sources: Rose, *Spirits, Fairies, Leprechauns, and Goblins*, 315; Vicente, *El Gran Libro de la Mitología Asturiana*, 111–114

Trash

Variations: Guy Trash, SKRIKER

In Lancashire, England Trash was a regionally specific spectral hound; its name, Trash, was said to have originated from the sound the BARGUEST'S paws make as it would splashe through mud and puddles.

Sources: Briggs, *Encyclopedia of Fairies*, 412; Choron, *Planet Dog*, 28; Haughton, *Famous Ghost Stories*, 104

Trauco

Variations: Huelli, Pompo'n del monte

In the fairy lore of Chile, the virile Trauco, is a GOBLIN or TROLL so ugly woman cannot resist his sexual advance. Described as standing less than three foot tall and having a body covered with thick hair it wears a conical hat upon its head and walks with a staff. Active during both the day and night the fruit-eating trauco uses its powerful hypnotism when assaulting women.

Sources: Eberhart, *Mysterious Creatures*, 555; Roth, *American Elves*, 59

Trikurat

Variations: Kyam

In the Burmese folk belief and religion Trikurat is a type of NATURE SPIRIT known as a NAT. Trikurat assists hunters by luring game towards them. If the hunter was lucky enough to have Trikurat's assistance he will venerate the NAT by sprinkling the blood of the game and walking upon the ashes of home's hearth.

Sources: Hastings, *Encyclopaedia of Religion and Ethics*, Volume 3, 22; Porteous, *Forest in Folklore and Mythology*, 125; Scott, *The Burman: His Life and Notions*, Volume 1, 286

Trite

In classical Greek mythology Trite was a water–NYMPH and one of the named DANAIDS, the collective name for the daughters of Danaus; her name appears in a list of the DANAIDS generated by Gaius Julius Hyginus (ca. 64 B.C.–A.D. 17), a Latin author. Trite was wedded to Enceladus and killed him on their wedding night.

Sources: Apollodorus, *Apollodorus' Library and Hyginus' Fabulae*, 170; Hyginus, *Myths of Hyginus*, 132

Triteia

A sea–NYMPH of the town of Triteia in Akhaia located in southern Greece, Triteia was an Oceaniad born of the North African river god, Triton. Triteia was a lover to the god, Apollo and by him gave birth to a son named Melanippus, the founder of the city named for his mother, Tritaia.

Sources: Larson, *Greek Heroine Cults*, 80; Rigoglioso, *Cult of Divine Birth in Ancient Greece*, 80–81

Tritonis

The NYMPH of a salt-water lake in Libya, Tritonis was said to have been the mother of Caphaurus (or Cephalion) and Nasamon by a son of the god Apollo, Amphithemis, according to classical Greek mythology. In older traditions, Tritonis was also said to have been the mother of Athena (Minerva) by the god, Poseidon (Neptune).

Sources: Apollodorus of Athens, *Apollodorus' Library and Hyginus' Fabulae*, 103; Grant, *Who's Who in Classical Mythology*, 43; Smith, *New Classical Dictionary of Greek and Roman Biography, Mythology and Geography*, Volume 2, 908

Tritons

According to classical Greek and Roman mythology, the Tritons were born the sons of the god of the sea, Poseidon (Neptune) and AMPHITRITE; they are depicted as Mermen and carry conch shell horns and tridents (see MERMAN). The tritons were the escorts of the NEREIDS and acted as the attendants of Poseidon and GALATEA. The individual known as Triton was considered to be a god of the sea; his appearance was always preceded by the sounding of a conch shell horn.

Sources: Hard, *Routledge Handbook of Greek Mythology*, 105–06; Rose, *Spirits, Fairies, Leprechauns, and Goblins*, 315

Troll

Variations: BERG PEOPLE, Foddenskkmaend, Guild Neighbors, GUILD-FOLK, Hill Men, Hill-People, Holder-Folk, Hollow-Men, Jutul, Orcs, Rise, Trolds, Trows, Tusse, Underground-People

In Scandinavian myth, trolls are one of the four types of fairies and are generally described as being the enemies of mankind; they also appear as such in the folklore of Finland, Germany Russia, and Siberia. Larger and stronger than humans these cannibalistic fairy beings came to be the size of humans over time. Usually trolls have a hunchback and a long, bent nose, and dress in grey coats and wear red hats. By use of a magical hat, trolls can walk about invisibly; they also have the ability to bestow bodily strength on anyone, foresee the future, shape-shift into any form, and an array of feats beyond the power of man as needed in folklore. Only in ballads do the trolls have a king ruling over them, they do not in lore or mythology.

On the Fero Islands trolls are called foddenskkmaend, holder-folk, hollow-men, and underground-people. There it is believed trolls carry humans into their underground lairs and detain them there.

Troll who dwell on the land are called GUILD-FOLK; they live beneath the green hills. The walls of their homes are said to be lined with gold and silver. Those troll who live in the woods are called *SKOVTROLDE*; these trolls constantly seek to injure and torment mankind. Hill trolls ("BJERG-TROLDE") are the trolls living in the hills, sometimes alone or with their family.

It is said because of a racial memory from the time when the god of thunder, Thor, used to throw his hammer at them, trolls disdain loud noises. Trolls are believed to be virtually indestructible due to their hard skin and size; however, if they are exposed to sunlight they will retreat into the shadows or they will turn into stone.

Sources: Keightly, *World Guide to Gnomes, Fairies, Elves, and Other Little People*, 63, 95–6, 162, 164; McCoy, *Witch's Guide to Faery Folk*, 322–23; Rose, *Spirits, Fairies, Leprechauns, and Goblins*, 316

Tronc

Variations: Tronc le Nain

A deformed but witty DWARF and principal character in *Ysaie le Triste* (c. 1400), Tronc was born the son of Julius Creaser and MORGAN LA FEY. By the end of the story, it is revealed Tronc was in fact the FAIRY KING, OBERON who had been transformed by a curse.

Sources: Dunlop, *History of Prose Fiction*, Volume 1, 218–19; Keightly, *World Guide to Gnomes, Fairies, Elves, and Other Little People*, 42

Trooping Fairies

Variations: Aristocratic Fairies, Heroic Fairies, Trooping Faery

Throughout the British Isles there are two basic classifications of fairies, SOLITARY FAIRIES and Trooping Fairies. Large and small, benign and malignant, the trooping fay tends to wear green jacket and live in social communities overseen by a monarch, although popular consensus seems to rule. FAIRY RADES are popular with trooping fairies, as it allows them dress both themselves and their beloved horses in the finest of clothing and accessories; as they travel they create a FAIRY TRAIL, a long path of dark grass; sometimes these paths are miles long. Trooping fairies are far more approachable than SOLITARY FAIRIES, although it is not always safe to do so; on occasion one of the trooping fay will take a mortal human as its spouse.

Sources: Briggs, *Encyclopedia of Fairies*, 412; McCoy, *Witch's Guide to Faery Folk*, 13–14, 23, 43, 68; Newcomb, *Faerie Treasury*, 70; Rosen, *Mythical Creatures Bible*, 259–61

Trow

Variations: Bannafeet (bannock feet), Creepers, Grey Neighbors, Night Stealers, Trowe, Truncherface (trencher face)

On the Shetland Islands the trow are small GOBLINS dressed in grey. In many ways they are similar to the TROLL such as living inside earth mounds which are alleged to be filled with gold, precious metals, and silver; they serve only the finest drink and food upon their tables. Trows have a fondness for music and are not above kidnapping a musician and bringing him back to its home to play for one of its feasts. While only a few days may pass within the mound, years could pass in the real world. Trow are also known to kidnap human babies and leave a CHANGELING in its place. Descriptions of trows vary greatly in the specifics but generally they are described as being short and ugly.

Sources: Briggs, *Encyclopedia of Fairies*, 414; Avant, *Mythological Reference*, 196–97; Emick, *Everything Celtic Wisdom Book*, 144–45; Frazer, *Golden Bough*, 169

Tuatha de Danann

Variations: De Danaan, Feadh-Ree, Fir, Dea ("men of the goddess"), People of god whose mother was Dana, Sidhe, Spirit Race

The Tuatha de Danann ("people of the goddess Dana") were the magical and mythological race who lived in Ireland and defeated both the FIRBOLGS and FOMORIANS for control of the country. According to the *Book of Invasions*, which details the mythological history of the country, they arrived in Ireland on May 1 upon on the mountains of Conmaicne Rein in Connachta having come from four northern cities Falias, Finias, Gorias, and Murias. Dark clouds came with them and were said to hang in the air for three days. They were the fifth group of people to have settled the island.

For three thousand years the Tuatha de Danann ruled Ireland until the Milesians fought them for control. Neither side was able to gain the advantage so an accord was struck—the Milesians would rule the surface world and the Tuatha de Danann would have dominion over the rest. This bargin included the fairy mounds, the invisible islands, and the Underworld. Becoming a race of fairy people these timeless immortal still interact with the surface would, but only when the veil between the two realms is thin. When occasion permits, theses TROOPING FAIRIES will parade, dressed in their finest, upon their magnificent horses. Described as being aristocratic, fair-skinned, perfectly physically fit, red-headed, and tall, the Tuatha de Danann were skilled in poetry, magic and science.

The Tuatha de Danann were named after the goddess they are descended from, Danu. Many of the Tuatha de Danann were worshiped as gods in ancient Ireland. Each member of the race established his or her own FAIRY FORT, some of which are well known to this day, such as Knockshegowna.

Sources: Board, *Fairies*, 117; Evan-Wentz, *Fairy*

Faith in Celtic Countries, 27; Koch, *Celtic Heroic Age*, 245; McCoy, *Witch's Guide to Faery Folk*, 324–26; MacKillop, Myths and Legends of the Celts, 136; Marstrander, *Dictionary of the Irish Language*, 612; Monaghan, *Encyclopedia of Celtic Mythology and Folklore*, 475; Stepanich, *Faery Wicca*, Book One, 23

Tündér

Variations: DAME HIRIP, Dame Jenö, Dame Rampson, Dame Vénétur, Fairy Helen, Mika

In Hungarian lore the tündér ("fairy") are a type of beautiful and being NATURE SPIRIT; exclusively female these fairies are immensely wealthy and live atop mountains in luxurious castles surrounded by exquisite gardens. They spend their nights dancing beneath the moon. In lore the tündér look after the destitute and orphans, gifting them with priceless pearls they use as adornment in their hair. Additionally, the breast milk, saliva, and tears contain magical properties that are used in spell casting. The tündér themselves are skilled magic users and have many magical herbs and jewels.

In Hungarian folklore there are many popular tündér, such as Dame Rampson, Dame Venetur, Tündér Ilona ("fairy Helen"), Tündér Maros.

Sources: Illes, *Encyclopedia of Spirits*, 974; Rose, *Spirits, Fairies, Leprechauns, and Goblins*, 318

Turehu

Variations: Heketoro, Korakorako, Nuku-mai-tore, Patu-pai-arehe, PATUPAIAREHE, Tahurangi

In Polynesian mythology the turehu were a race of fair haired and skinned fairies living in an underworld region known as Raro-henga. These fairies only ate uncooked food, were fond of dancing, and would on occasion take a human as a spouse. The turehu, when the landed on the island of New Zealand conquered the residence, the Tutu-mai-ao, interbreeding and driving their species to extinction.

Sources: Andersen, *Myths and Legends of the Polynesians*, 126, 288; Craig, *Handbook of Polynesian Mythology*, 105

Tutara-Kauika

A TANIWHA from the lore of the native people of New Zealand, the Tutara-Kauika was a FAIRY ANIMAL, a sperm whale said to accompany the hero Takitimu in his voyage to the island Aotearoa. Tutara-Kauika was the chief of all the whales in the ocean and commands a large army of them.

Sources: Cowan, *Tales of the Maori*, 33–4; Orbell, *Concise Encyclopedia of Māori Myth and Legend*, 195

Tutumaiao

NATURE SPIRITS from the lore of the native people of New Zealand, the tutumaiao are said to look like people from a distance and are often seen dancing on the beach; however these fairies are made of air and disappear as one draws closer. It is believed they live in the ocean. According to legend, one evening a man called Kahukura saw a group of tutumaiao on the beach pulling in their fishing nets and decided to assist them. As soon as the tutumaiao realized a mortal was among them, they vanished but left their nets behind. Kahukura took the net with him and became the first human to discover the art of net-fishing.

Sources: Craig, *Handbook of Polynesian Mythology*, 104–05; Orbell, *Concise Encyclopedia of Māori Myth and Legend*, 197

Tuulikki

In Finnish folk beliefs Tuulikki was a singular entity, a female NATURE SPIRITS who lived in the forests. Born the daughter of the god of the forest, Tapio, good-natured Tuulikki who was invoked for good luck when hunting, had a brother, a male NATURE SPIRIT, named NYYRIKKI.

Sources: Latham, *Russian and Turk*, 271; Rose, *Spirits, Fairies, Leprechauns, and Goblins*, 319

Tyche

Variations: Tykhe

Born one of the 3,000 daughters of the Titians, Oceanus and Tethys, Tyche ("luck") was one of the named OCEANIDS and the goddess of good luck in ancient Greek mythology; she was one of the playmates of Persephone (Proserpina) and present when the goddess was kidnapped.

Sources: Bell, *Bell's New Pantheon or Historical Dictionary of the Gods*, 112; Boswell, *What Men or Gods Are These*, 58; Day, *God's Conflict with the Dragon and the Sea*, 64; Hesiod, *Works of Hesiod, Callimachus, and Theognis*, 20; Westmoreland, *Ancient Greek Beliefs*, 24

Tylwyth Teg

Variations: BENDITH Y MAMAU, DAOINE SIDHE, Dynnon Bach Teg, FAIR FAMILY, Plant Rhys Ddwfn, Tylwyth Têg, Tylwyth Teg y Mwn ("fair folks of the mine"), Twlwwyth Tegs, y Tylwyth Teg yn y Coed ("the FAIR FAMILY in the woods")

After the Milesians and the TUATHA DÉ DANANN divided up Ireland the Tylwyth Tegs were said to live off of the Welsh coast on FAIRY ISLANDS which were connected to the mainland by tunnels. While visiting the mainland the Tegs had FAIRY FORTS they stayed in. As was the case with many fairy dwellings, time moves differently inside their homes. The Twlwwyth Teg, like all Wesh fairies, preferred to play the harp but on especially grand occasions they would play the bag pipes or the bugle. Their music has been described with much vagueness but generally as a sweet, intangible harmony.

Described as beautiful, fair-haired and ethereal, the Teg were generally considered to be benign but occasionally inclined towards playing a prank. When the Teg were inclined they liked to reward a housewife who kept a neat house with a silver coin. Like many of the fay, they were fearful of iron.

As a species, the Twlwwyth Tegs were capable of interbreeding with both humans and other species of fairy; these off-springs are called Bendith y Mauman ("mother's blessing") and were considered to be the native elves of Wales. At one time the Teg was accused of kidnapping fair-haired mortal babies and replacing them with CHANGELINGS, but over time the belief died out.

Goats, which possess more knowledge than they appear to possess, were believed to be favorites of the Teg. Each Friday night the fairies would comb out the animals' beards so they would have a presentable appearance on Sunday.

Sources: McCoy, *Witch's Guide to Faery Folk*, 326–27; MacKillop, *Dictionary of Celtic Mythology*, 368; Wentz, *Fairy-Faith in Celtic Countries*, 138–9, 141–2; Sikes, *British Goblins*, 55

Udr

Variations: Udur, Urd, Urdhr, Urdr, Urdur, Urth, Wurd, Wyrd

Similar to the FATES of ancient Greece, there were three principles NORNIR in the mythology of the ancient Norse. Udr ("past" or literally "that which has taken place") was one of the three NORNIR, a type of FATE in Scandinavian lore; she was the eldest of the three sisters and personifies the past; her sisters were SKULLD ("future") and VERDANDI ("present").

Sources: Arrowsmith, *Field Guide to the Little People*, 208; Ripley, *American Encyclopaedia: A Popular Dictionary of General Knowledge*, Volume 7, 400; Sturluson, *Prose Edda*, 28, 30

Uilebheist

Variations: Draygan

Appearing as multi-headed sea-monsters these water fairies' guards known as uilebheist ("monsters") protect coastal inlets and the rocky coastline of the Orkney and Shetland Islands.

Sources: Eberhart, *Mysterious Creatures*, 426; McCoy, *Witch's Guide to Faery Folk*, 147, 327–28; Spence, *Minor Traditions of British Mythology*, 136

Ukulan-Tojon

In the folk belief of the Yakut people of Siberia, Ukulan-Tojon ("water-master") was a powerful NATURE SPIRIT; no body of water would ever be crossed without first asking his permission and making a libation or suitable offering such as bread, fish, gin, or salt. Shamans would offer up an annual sacrifice to Ukulan-Tojon of a black bull to ensure good fishing.

Sources: Cotterell, *Macmillan Illustrated Encyclopedia of Myths and Legends*, 172; Gray, *Mythology of All Races,* Volume 4, 469; Rose, *Spirits, Fairies, Leprechauns, and Goblins*, 321

Umskiptingar

In Norway the umskiptingar are the offspring of the fairies who live underground but have been taken to the surface and left in the place of a stolen unbaptized human child, much as in the CHANGELING tradition. The fairy parents singled out unbaptized children so their own offspring may have the benefit of receiving that particular sacrament and eternal salvation. Typically these fairy children were dull-witted and physically weak.

Sources: Fergusson, *Rampling Sketches in the Far North*, 199–200; Keightly, *World Guide to Gnomes, Fairies, Elves, and Other Little People*, 160–1, Thorpe, *Northern Mythology*, Volume 2, xxv

Undine

Variations: Un'Dine

The Renaissance alchemist, astrologer, botanist, general occultist, and physician, Paracelsus believed nature, both the visible and invisible, was inhabited by a host of being aligned with the elements. On the invisible side he determined there were four distinct groups, the GNOMES of the earth, the SALAMANDERS of fire, the SYLPHS of the air and the Undines of the water.

The undines were water fairies or NATURE SPIRITS who had the ability to control the element of water to a certain degree. Always depicted in art as being beautiful and nearly always in a female form the undines of ancient lore were said to resemble humans in appearance and size; the ones who inhabited smaller water sources were proportionally smaller but all were capable of assuming a human guise and intermingling with

mankind. In Greek lore undines resembled the goddess portrayed in statuaries; rising up from the water and draped in mist they could not retain from for very long out of the water. There are ancient Roman tales of an undine taking a mortal as a spouse but in all cases the call of the sea is too much for her to resist and she eventually returns to the water and the god of the sea, Neptune.

Generally it was believed these NYMPH-like fairies lived in coral cave under the oceans or in the reeds along the banks of rivers. In Celtic lore undines lived under lily pads and in houses made of moss located underneath waterfalls. It is believed when the TUATHA DE DANNA retreated underground the undines also fell back to their homes where they remain to this day.

The ruler of the undines is named Necksa; she is honored, loved, and served untiringly by them. Emotional, friendly beings they occasionally ride upon the backs of dolphins and other sea creatures.

Examples of species of undines would be CRINAEAE, DANAIDS, ELEIONOMAE, GWRAGEDD ANNWN, KALLRADEN, KATAW, LIMNADES, MERMAIDS, MERROW, MIENGU, MORGENS, NÄCKEN, NÄKKI, NECK, NIXEN, NOKKE, NYMPHS, OCEANID, PINCOY, PONATURI, POTAMEIDES, RUSALKA, SHELLYCOAT, SIRNES, STRÖMKARL, and SWAN MAIDEN.

Examples of individual beings falling under the classification of undine would be JENNY GREENTEETH, LORELEI, MAMMA D'LO, MARY PLAYER, MELUSINA, NADDAHA, NELLY LONGARMS, NICKY NYE, PEG POWLER, PEISINOE, PICKLEHARIN, SCYLLA, STORM HAG, and SZEPASSZONY.

Sources: Hall, *Secret Teachings of All Ages*, 313–14; Evan-Wentz, *Fairy Faith in Celtic Countries*, 241; McCoy, *Witch's Guide to Faery Folk*, 328–29; Silver, *Strange and Secret Peoples*, 38

Uni

Uni ("calm") in Norse mythology was named as being one of the Ijosalfar, the SONS OF IVALDI. These DWARFS were the ones who created many of the magical items of the gods, including the golden wig of Sif; the ship, Skidbladnir; and the spear of Odin.

Sources: Crossley-Holland, *Norse Myths* 124; Grimes, *Norse Myths*, 9, 285; Hollander, *Poetic Edda*, 150

Unknown

In Greek mythology an unknown a water–NYMPH appears in a list of the DANAIDS generated by Gaius Julius Hyginus (ca. 64 B.C.–A.D. 17), a Latin author. This unknown DANAIDS was wedded to Armoasbus and killed him on their wedding night.

Source: Hyginus, *Myths of Hyginus*, 132

Unseelie Court

Variations: The Hoard, the Host, SLAUGH

In Scottish fairy lore the Unseelie Court ("unblessed court") are the injurious and malicious fairies consisting most of Solitary Fairies, especially those associated with ancestral spirits and the dead. In Cornish lore the vicious and bloodthirsty, illusion-wielding SPRIGGANS were used as their body-guards. According to legend, the members of the Unseelie court are those fairies who fell out of favor or were cast out of the SEELIE COURT.

As the SEELIE COURT has their beautiful FAIRY RADES along the ground leaving a FAIRY PATH as they travel the Unseelie Court has their Horde, their own procession which flies through the night sky with cried of unnerving howls. Any mortal unfortunate enough to cross their path is snatched up and taken along for the ride. Victims are beaten and forced to take part in their bizarre nocturnal activities; as they have mean of reproduction the people they prefer to take are those who will never be missed, as they are transformed into one of these fay.

Examples of the member of the Unseelie court would be BAOBHAN SITH, BENDITH Y MAMAU, BROWN MAN OF THE MUIRS, DARK ELVES, DARK MAN, DULLAHAN, DWARF, NUCKELAVEE, RED CAP, SHELLYCOAT, the SLAUGH, and SPRIGGANS.

Sources: Briggs, *Encyclopedia of Fairies*, 419–20; Ashliman, *Fairy Lore*, 55, 208; Froud, *Faeries*, 97–98; McCoy, *Witch's Guide to Faery Folk*, 23, 26, 329–30; Monaghan, 413–14, 462; Rosen, *Mythical Creatures Bible*, 258–59, Stepanich, *Faery Wicca*, Book One, 274

Upaka

The upaka are NATURE SPIRITS or NATS from Burmese folklore, specifically of the air; they fly about through the clouds and sky on the hunt for men they can swoop down and snatch up.

Sources: Porteous, *Forest in Folklore and Mythology*, 125; Scott, *The Burman: His Life and Notions*, Volume 1, 286

Upis

Variations: Oupis

In classical Greek mythology Upis was one of the three NYMPH attendants of the goddess Arte-mis (Diana) who came from the mythical land to the north, Hyperborea (see HEKAERGE and LOXO).

Sources: Hard, *Routledge Handbook of Greek Mythology*, 190; Keightley, *Mythology of Ancient Greece and Italy*, 119

Urania

Born one of the 3,000 daughters of the Titians, Oceanus and Tethys, Urania ("divine in form") was one of the named OCEANIDS and should not to be confused with the MUSE, Urania.

One of the nine CANONICAL MUSES was also named Urania and was the MUSE of astronomy; she was depicted in art as carrying a celestial globe and a pointed staff.

Sources: Bell, *Bell's New Pantheon or Historical Dictionary of the Gods*, 112; Boswell, *What Men or Gods Are These*, 58; Hesiod, *Works of Hesiod, Callimachus, and Theognis*, 20; Hunt, *Masonic Symbolism*, 470; Littleton, *Gods, Goddesses, and Mythology*, Volume 11, 921; Peterson, *Mythology in Our Midst*, 121; Westmoreland, *Ancient Greek Beliefs*, 24

Urganda

Variations: Urganda la Desconecida

Urganda is one of the FATES appearing in Matteo Maria Boiardo's epic poem *Orlando Innamorato* ("*Orlando in Love*," 1495) from the Italian Renaissance period. In the poem, Urganda and fellow FATE, ORIANA, are the protectors of Amadigi.

Sources: Boiardo, *Orlando Innamorato Di Bojardo*, 396; Keightly, *World Guide to Gnomes, Fairies, Elves, and Other Little People*, 453

Uri

Uri ("smith") in Norse mythology is named as being one of the Ijosalfar, the SONS OF IVALDI. These DWARFS were the ones who created many of the magical items of the gods, including the golden wig of Sif; the ship, Skidbladnir; and the spear of Odin.

Sources: Grimes, *Norse Myths*, 9, 285; Rydberg, *Teutonic Mythology*, 356

Urisk

Variations: Ùruisg ("water man")

The urisk is one of the FUATH, a collective name for the malicious and monstrous water fay in Scottish folklore. A SOLITARY FAIRY from Scottish lore the urisk is described as looking half-goat and half-human with flowing yellow hair and wearing a broad, blue bonnet. Associated with waterfalls and said to live in remote pools and rivers the friendly urisk is desperately lonely because of its hideously ugly appearance. His physical appearance will frighten away, if not frighten to death, any mortal who sees it.

Sources: Bord, *Fairies*, 2; Briggs, *Encyclopedia of Fairies*, 420; McCoy, *Witch's Guide to Faery Folk*, 330; Rose, *Spirits, Fairies, Leprechauns, and Goblins*, 323

Ursitory

Variations: Oursitori ("white women"), Ourmes

In the folk beliefs of the Romany Gypsies of Poland and Russia the ursitory are male fairies of fate who appear in groups of three to three-day old infants in order to determine its future; once the child's fate has been revealed, it cannot be altered. One of the ursitory is benign, one is malevolent, and the third is of a neutral disposition. Only the mother of the child is able to see these fairies. The female equivalent of the ursitory is known as the urme.

Sources: Bonnefoy, *Roman and European Mythologies*, 230; Rose, *Spirits, Fairies, Leprechauns, and Goblins*, 323

Urvasi

Variations: Urvashi

In Hindu mythology Urvasi was the most beautiful of all of the apsaras. In all there are twelve apsaras but only four of them stand out in Sanskirt literature, MENAKA, RAMBHA, TILOTTAMA and URVASI. All the Apsarases are well versed in the art of dancing and music.

Sources: Hudson, *Body of God*, 406; Rajan, *Complete Works of Kālidāsa*, 168, 373; Rose, *Spirits, Fairies, Leprechauns, and Goblins*, 232

Vadleany

According to Hungarian folklore the Vadleany ("wild girl") is a NATURE SPIRIT similar to a forest NYMPH or DRYAD. Described as having hair so long it touches the ground, long fingernails and completely naked, it seduced shepherds and steals their strength. When a vadleany is present, the trees of the forest make a rustling sound.

Sources: Franklin, *Working with Fairies*, 47, 236; Hoppál, *Studies on Mythology and Uralic Shamanism*, 66

Vættir

Variations: De Underjordiske ("the subterranean ones"), Huldrefolk ("concealed people"), Maahinen, Vättar, Wights

In the Norse religion Vættir ("beings") are NATURE SPIRITS; they are divided up into different groups, the Æsir, Álfar (elves), Dvergar (DWARFS), the gods, Jötnar (GIANTS), and the Vanir. The vættir consists of those among the dead, especially individuals in the Underworld, Hel.

Peasants were cautious about hurting or offending the vættir, as doing so would result in accidents occurring, disease spreading, or livestock deaths. The vættir have the power of invisibility and carry about them a feeling of otherworldliness, they were described as being strikingly beautiful, clad in grey clothing, and living underground. In addition to having their own breed of cattle that gave tremendous amounts of milk these fairies could shape-shift in animals making them difficult to observe; frogs were said to be their preferred form. After the introduction of Christianity the human sized vættir begin to shrink in size. Through Christian Europe tales of the Scandinavian vættir kidnapping unbaptized babies and leaving CHANGELINGS in their place begin to spread. In some cases it was said the vættir themselves would remain behind in the infant's place.

Sources: Croker, *Fairy Legends and Traditions of the South of Ireland*, Volumes 1–3, 68–69; Grimm, *Teutonic Mythology*, Volume 4, 1407; Norroena Society, *Satr Edda*, 56–59

Vairies

In the fairy lore of Somerset, England vairies are described as looking like diminutive people who, because of their natural-born vanity, wear high-heeled shoes. It is locally believed if a pie is made and not marked with a cross upon the crust the vairies will tread across it, leaving their shoe prints behind.

Sources: Arrowsmith, *Field Guide to the Little People*, 77; Briggs, *Anatomy of Puck*, 231; Keightly, *World Guide to Gnomes, Fairies, Elves, and Other Little People*, 299

Váli

Váli ("foreign") was one of the many DWARFS named in the *Voluspa*, the first and best known poem of the *Poetic Edda*, a collection of Old Norse poems dating back to about A.D. 985. Váli is not to be confused with the son of Loki who was named in the poem *Gylfaginning*; in the poem Váli was used as a means of punishing his father for the death of the god, Baldr. Váli was transformed into a wolf and made to kill his brother Nair.

Sources: Crossley-Holland, Norse Myths, 183; Lindow, *Norse Mythology*, 309

Valkyrie

Variations: Battle Maidens, Shield Maiden, Vakkijnor, Walkries, Wish Maiden, Wish Wife

In Nordic and Teutonic mythology the Valkyries ("choosers of the slain") were the NYMPHS of battle. These being were always beautiful women and sometimes immortal. The attendants of the god Odin would don suits of armor and ride through the sky on powerful horses or as SWAN MAIDENS to wherever battle was taking place. Then, hovering overhead the Valkyries would guide heroes throughout the combat; those who were selected to die or did so bravely would be given the kiss of death and then their soul would be taken up to Valhalla by the Valkyries where they would be regaled as the newest member of the Einherjar, feasting with Odin and preparing to do battle at Ragnarok ("doom of the gods"). Although they dressed for battle while on earth, wearing helmets, corsets, armor, and carried spears, the Valkyries were not warriors. At Walhalla they wore white robes and attended to the Einherjar, typically keeping the tables full of food and their skull chalices filled with mead.

The concept of the Valkyries have changed over time; at first they were thought of as little more than carrion goddesses who would appear after a battle, collect the intestines of the dead and feed them to their pet wolves. When the Valkyrie appeared in the *Prose Edda* (circa 1220) it was as fierce spirits but later, in the *Volsungo Saga* (late 13th century) they were give a more important role. At this point in time it was also believed a mortal princess could become a Valkyrie upon her death. During the Middle Ages (500 c to 1500 c) it was believed the Northern Lights were the Valkyrie flying across the sky; they were now also acting as the bodyguard and messengers of Odin.

The number of Valkyries varies anywhere from between three and 27, depending on the source; some of the better known ones are BRUNHILDE (Brynhilde), GEIROLUL ("spear-alimentrix"), Goil, GOLL ("herald"), GONDUL ("she wolf"), Held ("hero"), Herfijtur, HILDE ("war"), HILDUR ("warrior"), HLOKK, HRIST ("storm"), Judur, MIST ("cloud grey"), RADGRID, RANDGRID, Reiginlief, ROTA, SIGRUN, SKEGGOLD, SKOGUL ("carrier-through"), Skuld (see SKULLD), SWAWA, THRUD ("power"), Thrudur ("maiden" or "virgin"), and WOLKENTHRUT ("cloud power").

Sources: Daly, *Norse Mythology A to Z*, 115; Littleton, *Gods, Goddesses, and Mythology*, Volume 11, 1400–1402; Rose, *Spirits, Fairies, Leprechauns, and Goblins*, 325

Vanadevatas

In the Vedic mythology of India, the vanadevatas were considered to be benign NATURE SPIRITS not so different from the HAMADRYADS of ancient Greek mythology; these fairies were intent on going good and were typically friendly to those who looked after the tree they spirits lived in but were especially vengeful to anyone who felled one of their trees. Easily frightened the vanadevatas will flee an area where a god or monster appears.

Sources: Begde, *Living Sculpture*, 2; Hopkins, *Epic Mythology*, 57; Rose, *Spirits, Fairies, Leprechauns, and Goblins*, 325

Var

Variations: Varr

Var ("careful") in Norse mythology was named as being one of the Ijosalfar, the SONS OF IVALDI. These DWARFS were the ones who created many of the magical items of the gods, including the golden wig of Sif; the ship, Skidbladnir; and the spear of Odin. According to the Edda, he "existed before Valhalla was walled" and should not be confused with the Norse goddess Var who heard men's oaths and punished them if they were ever broken.

Sources: Grimes, *Norse Myths*, 9, 285; Puryear, *Nature of Ásatrú*, 246

Vasily

DWARFS of Russian lore the vasily were believed to live in barns with the horses they loved and looked-after; at best they were indifferent to mankind. Although there are no stories of these fairies ever killing anyone, they do have a reputation of being mean toward anyone who harms or mistreats their favorite horses. It was believed hearing sleigh bells when no sleighs were around was a sign the vasily were tending to your horses. Although vasily females exist most stories and folklore contain male vasily.

Sources: Llewellyn, *Llewellyn's Magical Almanac*, 166; McCoy, *Witch's Guide to Faery Folk*, 147, 331

Vedenhaltia

The vedenhaltia ("water ruler") was a water based NATURE SPIRIT from the the mythology of Estonia.

Sources: Gray, *Mythology of All Races*, Volume 4, 215; Monaghan, *Encyclopedia of Goddesses and Hero-*

ines, 358; Rose, *Spirits, Fairies, Leprechauns, and Goblins*, 326

Veggr

Veggr ("wedge") was one of the many DWARFS named in the *Voluspa*, the first and best known poem of the *Poetic Edda*, a collection of Old Norse poems dating back to about A.D. 985.

Sources: Faulkes, *Edda*, 176; Universität Münster, *Frühmittelalterliche Studien*, 106

Veigr

Veigr ("brew") was one of the many DWARFS named in the *Voluspa*, the first and best known poem of the *Poetic Edda*, a collection of Old Norse poems dating back to about A.D. 985.

Sources: Wägner, *Asgard and the Gods*, 311; Wilkinson, *Book of Edda called Völuspá*, 12

Veigur

Veigur was one of the many DWARFS named in the *Voluspa*, the first and best known poem of the *Poetic Edda*, a collection of Old Norse poems dating back to about A.D. 985.

Sources: Daly, *Norse Mythology A to Z*, 22; Sykes, *Who's Who in Non-Classical Mythology*, 53

Vejasmate

A female NATURE SPIRIT from the folk belief of the Latvian people Vejasmate ("mother of the wind") is the guardian fairy of the wind. Her male counterpart from Lithuanian folk belief is known as Vejopatis ("master of the wind").

Sources: Greimas, *Of Gods and Men*, 74, 127; Rose, *Spirits, Fairies, Leprechauns, and Goblins*, 326

Venusleute

Diminutive NATURE SPIRITS in German lore the venusleute ("people of Venus") are beautiful and said to possess a truly generous spirit. Small enough to sit in a person's palm these fairies are known to give food to lost children; they bathe, cook, and wash their clothes in bowl-like indentions found in the rocks near Zulova in the Czech Republic.

Source: Maberry, *Cryptopedia*, 116

Verdandi

Variations: Verthandi

Similar to the FATES of ancient Greece, there were three principles NORNIR in the mythology of the ancient Norse. Verdandi ("present" or "that which is growing") was one of the three NORNS, a type of FATE in Scandinavian lore; she was associated with adulthood.

Sources: Keightly, *World Guide to Gnomes, Fairies, Elves, and Other Little People*, 64; Littleton, *Gods, Goddesses, and Mythology*, Volume 11, 992; Sturluson, *Prose Edda*, 113; Welch, *Goddess of the North*, 173

Vestri

Vestri ("west") was one of the many DWARFS named in the *Voluspa*, the first and best known poem of the *Poetic Edda*, a collection of Old Norse poems dating back to about A.D. 985.

Sources: Crossley-Holland, *Norse Myths*, 183; Daly, *Norse Mythology A to Z*, 22; Wilkinson, *Book of Edda called Völuspá*, 12

Vidyesvaras

The vidyesvaras are Hindu NATURE SPIRITS and masters of knowledge. Presiding over Pasupati, the Lord of the Animals, these fairies are described as looking like SATYERS. If one of the eight vidyesvara are properly persuaded it may be inclined to teach its ancient techniques of wisdom. In all there are eight vidyesvaras; their names are Anantesa (or Ananta, sources vary) ("endless"), Ekanetra ("one-eyed"), Ekaruda, Sikhandin ("with a tuft of hair"), Sivottama ("highest siva"), Srikantha (or SrTkantha, sources vary) ("beautiful throat"), Suksma ("very small"), and Trimurti.

Sources: Bühler, *Grundriss der indo-arischen Philologie und Altertumskunde*, 125; Chandra, *Encyclopaedia of Hindu Gods and Goddesses*, 16, 89, 303, 320, 322, 327

Viggr

Variations: Vig, Vigg

Viggr ("horse") was one of the many DWARFS named in the *Voluspa*, the first and best known poem of the *Poetic Edda*, a collection of Old Norse poems dating back to about A.D. 985.

Sources: Crossley-Holland, Norse Myths, 183; Daly, *Norse Mythology A to Z*, 22

Vila

Variations: Veela, Vilia, Vilya, Vilishkis, Vily, Willi

From the lore of Serbia, the vilas were the beautiful and young mountain NYMPHS clad in white; their voice was said to resemble the call of the woodpecker and was a warning of some mountain catastrophe, such as an avalanche. Vilas were known to carry off children whose mothers had, in a fit of anger, condemned them to the Devil or Hell. The vilas were said to injure those who interrupt their revelries as they dance beneath the branches of the ash or cherry trees, shooting them with deadly accuracy with their bow and arrows. Vilas would heal deer that have been wounded, foretell heroes of their imminent death, and spoke the languages of the animals. These fairies were said to bridle seven year old harts with snakes so they could ride them as mounts.

It is possible the vilas may have at one time not been a species of NYMPH but rather a singular goddess.

In Western Europe the vilia is a type of NYMPH or NATURE SPIRIT; nearly always female they are described as being captivatingly beautiful. These fairies will attract the attention and love of men but will eventually end the relationship; according to some tales it was said if a vilia ever found true love it would die a slow and terrible death. In Dalmatia, a man who is lucky enough have the blessings of a vila is called *vilenik*.

As the vily, they are similar to Greek NYMPHS, and found in the mountains of the European Alps and Poland are beautiful, female NATURE SPIRITS who prefer not to become involved in human affairs. Although there are a few stories of the vily rescuing a person from an alpine disaster by guiding the team of rescue dogs it is not because the vily are inclined to help the human but rather because they love dogs over all other animals. The vily are believed to protect and watch over the Saint Bernard Monastery houses and trains the much acclaimed rescue dogs.

Sources: Keightly, *World Guide to Gnomes, Fairies, Elves, and Other Little People*, 491–2; McCoy, *Witch's Guide to Faery Folk*, 331–32; Porteous, *Forest in Folklore and Mythology*, 109

Vili

Vili ("drudge") was one of the many DWARFS named in the *Voluspa*, the first and best known poem of the *Poetic Edda*, a collection of Old Norse poems dating back to about A.D. 985.

Sources: Wägner, *Asgard and the Gods*, 311; Wilkinson, *Book of Edda called Völuspá*, 12

Vindalf

Variation: Vindálfr

Vindalf ("wind ELF") was one of the many DWARFS named in the *Voluspa*, the first and best known poem of the *Poetic Edda*, a collection of Old Norse poems dating back to about A.D. 985.

Sources: Crossley-Holland, Norse Myths, 183; Daly, *Norse Mythology A to Z*, 22; Sykes, *Who's Who in Non-Classical Mythology*, 53; Wägner, *Asgard and the Gods*, 311

Virfir

Virfir was one of the many DWARFS named in the *Voluspa*, the first and best known poem of the *Poetic Edda*, a collection of Old Norse poems dating back to about A.D. 985. Virfir was allied to the sons of FINNR.

Sources: Crossley-Holland, Norse Myths, 183; Rydberg, *Teutonic Mythology*, 119; Sturluson, *Prose Edda*, 265

Virginial

Variations: Virginal

FAIRY QUEEN, Virginial, first appears in the ancient German work compiled in the fifteenth century by Kaspar von der Rhon, *Book of Heroes*. Her palace is called Jeraspunt. Although she is guarded over and protected by the unconquerable DWARF, BIBUNG, Virginal is captured by the magician Ortgis. BIBUNG solicited the assistance of the cultural hero, Hildebrand and his comrade in arms, Dietrich, to rescue the queen who was being held in a castle. Each month on the new mood Virginal was forced to deliver up to the magician one of her personal attendants, known as the Snow Maidens; first they were to be fattened up and then consumed. Ortgis was ultimately slain by Hildebrand.

Sources: Guerber, *Legends of the Middle Ages*, 113–14.; Rose, *Spirits, Fairies, Leprechauns, and Goblins*, 40; Wägner, *Epics and Romances of the Middle Ages*, 114

Virpir

Virpir one of the many DWARFS named in the *Voluspa*, the first and best known poem of the *Poetic Edda*, a collection of Old Norse poems dating back to about A.D. 985.

Source: Sturluson, *Edda*, 179

Virra Birro

Variations: Willy Willy

In the Dreamtime myths of the Native Australians the virra birro is a NATURE SPIRIT; he appears as a whirlwind.

Sources: Božić, *Aboriginal Myths*, 83; Rose, *Spirits, Fairies, Leprechauns, and Goblins*, 327

Virvir

Virvir ("dyer") was one of the many DWARFS named in the *Voluspa*, the first and best known poem of the *Poetic Edda*, a collection of Old Norse poems dating back to about A.D. 985.

Sources: Daly, *Norse Mythology A to Z*, 22; Sykes, *Who's Who in Non-Classical Mythology*, 53; Wilkinson, *Book of Edda called Völuspá*, 12

Vithur

Vithur was one of the many DWARFS named in the *Voluspa*, the first and best known poem of the *Poetic Edda*, a collection of Old Norse poems dating back to about A.D. 985.

Sources: Daly, *Norse Mythology A to Z*, 22; Sykes, *Who's Who in Non-Classical Mythology*, 53

Vitore

A benign and helpful household fairy from Albanian lore the vitore is described as looking like a golden snake with horns although in Permet it is said to look like a bird; in southern Cameria it is more likened to a FATE, present three days after the birth of child to determine the course it will take in life. Living inside the walls of a home whenever this FAIRY ANIMAL hisses aloud an important family event is about to occur.

Source: Elsie, *Dictionary of Albanian Religion*, 260

Vitr

Variations: Vit

Vitr ("wise") was one of the many DWARFS named in the *Voluspa*, the first and best known poem of the *Poetic Edda*, a collection of Old Norse poems dating back to about A.D. 985.

Sources: Acker, *Poetic Edda*, 218; Crossley-Holland, Norse Myths, 183; Wilkinson, *Book of Edda called Völuspá*, 12

Vivian

Variations: Nimue, Vivienne

One of the SÍDHE from Arthurian mythology, the beautiful Vivian at one time placed her lover, the wizard Merlin, under an enchantment rendering him unable to exert his control over spirits, including fairies. The reasons for her turning on Merlin vary, sometimes it is said she was angry he would not share his magical knowledge with her, because of his affairs, or she wish to save him from the hardship of growing old. Whatever her actual reason was, Vivian encased her lover in a tree, which according to legend, and he remains to this day. The location of this tree is said to be in the legendary forest of Broceliande in Brittany. Some Arthurian scholars believe Vivian to be the LADY OF THE LAKE.

Sources: Evan-Wentz, *Fairy Faith in Celtic Countries*, 329; Monaghan, *Encyclopedia of Celtic Mythology and Folklore*, 465

Vodianikha

In Russian folklore Vodianikha is a water-fairy and the wife of VODYANOI. Appearing as a naked woman with enormous breasts and long, tangled hair this fairy is most often seen sitting on the riverbank trying to comb out its hair. It is likely she is the returned soul of a drowned maiden or a RUSALKA.

Sources: Ivanits, *Russian Folk Belief*, 77; Rose, *Spirits, Fairies, Leprechauns, and Goblins*, 328

Vodianoi

Variations: Vodianoi Chert ("water devil")

Particularly malevolent, vale water fairy of Slavic lore the vodianoi exists only to drown swimmers, especially those who are boastful or proud by nature. Although it's it has the ability to shape-shift into a fish, descriptions of its true-form vary; sometimes it is said to look like a bloated, hairy, naked old man covered in slimy fish scales while other times it is said to look like a simple bearded peasant wearing a red shirt. Sometimes the vodianoi appeared looking like a hunchback with cow's feet and tailor a MERMAN.

Living in deep pool with mills, a vodianoi came into being whenever an unbaptized child died, someone committed sucide or a person passed away without having received the Catholic sacrament Anointing of the Sick, more popularly known as Last Rites.

The female of this species of fairy is known as a VODIANIKHA; they are described as looking like women with large breasts. The vodianoi never come out of the water more, emerging only as high as their waist; their spouses however will sit upon the rocks and comb out their hair in MERMAID-like fashion.

Sources: Dixon-Kennedy, *Encyclopedia of Russian and Slavic Myth and Legend*, 145; Ivanits, *Russian Folk Belief*, 70–71; Rose, *Spirits, Fairies, Leprechauns, and Goblins*, 329

Vodianoy

Small, green-haired, nocturnal fairies the vodianoy of Russian lore look bloated and wet, as if they had recently drowned. These dangerous and malicious fay spread illnesses associated with polluted water, such as cholera.

Sources: McCoy, *Witch's Guide to Faery Folk*, 147, 332–3; Meurger, *Lake Monster Traditions*, 153

Vodni Panny

Variations: Bile Pani ("white women")

In Celtic mythology the vodni panny ("water NYMPHS") are pale, tall water–NYMPHS dressed in transparent green robes. Living in crystal palaces under the water their gravel pathways are made up of bits of gold and silver. Sitting in trees these fairies sing SIREN-like, luring in young men. In the evenings, the vodni panny will go to local villages and partake in festival dances.

Sources: Eberhart, *Mysterious Creatures*, 573; Mac-Culloch, *Celtic Mythology*, Volume 3, 271–72

Vodyanoi

Variations: Lord Wodjanoj; Vodyanoy, plural vodyanoyovia; Vodník, plural vodníci; Wodjanoj

One of the many malicious water fairies in Slavic folklore the vodyanoi lives on the bottom of lakes, mill ponds, rivers, or the sea and snatch people up, pulling them into the water, and drowning them. Descriptions of these creatures vary widely, including a floating log, a large fish, a monster with fiery eyes, a seal with a human face, an enormous frog, and an old man with green beards and hair.

The vodyanoi live an entire life cycle in a single lunar phase, young at the new moon and growing older with each phase. When the lunar cycle begins anew the vodyanoi is rejuvenated and young again.

Sources: Bartlett, *Mythology Bible*, 139; Conway, *Magickal Mystical Creatures*, 181

Volturnus

Born one of the 3,000 daughters of the Titians, Oceanus and Tethys, Volturnus was one of the named OCEANIDS in Greek mythology.

Sources: Boswell, *What Men or Gods Are These*, 58; Day, *God's Conflict with the Dragon and the Sea*, 64; Hesiod, *Works of Hesiod, Callimachus, and Theognis*, 20

Vough

The vough ("hatred") is one of the FUATH, a collective name for the malicious and monstrous water fay in Scottish folklore. This female KELPIE-like fay is one of the most fearful and terrifying apparitions in the Highlands. Described being dressed in green and having a noseless face and webbed feet they preferred to live a nocturnal life but would come out during the day if occasion called for it. The vough are said to enjoy the intellectual and sexual companionship of humans and some Scottish families, such as the Munroes even claim to have vough blood in their family line.

Sources: Briggs, *Encyclopedia of Fairies*, 43; Monaghan, *Encyclopedia of Celtic Mythology and Folklore*, 466; Rose, *Spirits, Fairies, Leprechauns, and Goblins*, 329

Vrikshakas

In the Hindu mythology of India the vrikshakas are a benign species of tree spirit similar to the HAMADRYADS of ancient Greek mythology. Like the DRYADS the vrikshakas can be attached to either a singular specific tree or an entire forest. These NATURE SPIRITS are described as looking like voluptuous women and in art are representative of fertility.

Sources: Begde, *Living Sculpture*, 160; Rose, *Spirits, Fairies, Leprechauns, and Goblins*, 329

Vu-Kutis

A benevolent fresh-WATER SPIRIT from the folk lore of the Ostyak and Votyak people of the Vyatka region of Russia, the vu-kutis ("aquatic aggressor") was invoked to fight the demons of disease that afflict people.

Sources: Aldington, *Larousse Encyclopedia of Mythology*, 307; Rose, *Spirits, Fairies, Leprechauns, and Goblins*, 330

Vu-Nuna

A benevolent fresh-WATER SPIRIT from the folk lore of the Ostyak and Votyak people of the Vyatka region of Russia, the vu-nuna ("aquatic uncle") was invoked to fight the water based demon of disease known as Yanki-murt.

Sources: Aldington, *Larousse Encyclopedia of Mythology*, 307; Rose, *Spirits, Fairies, Leprechauns, and Goblins*, 330

Wag-at-the-Wa'

Variations: Droll, Droll-Teller, Wag-by-the-Way

A household BROWNIE in Scottish folklore, wag-at-the-wa' was something of a family monitor and especially fond of children seeking to keep the home happy; however, it was a torment to the kitchen-maid. Typically this fairy would sit on the hook within the hearth that held a cooking pot. When this hook was empty the wag-at-the-Wwa' would sit there and swing back and forth, secured in place by its prehensile little tail. In modern times a cross or witch's mark would be etched onto the hook to prevent the fairy from sitting upon it.

This species of fairy disapproved of any liquor being consumed in the home unless it was a home-made brew. Described as looking like a grizzled old man with crooked legs the wag-at-the-wa' would wear blue pants, a grey mantle, a red jacket, and a *pirnicap* covering the side of its head, as these fairies were particularly susceptible to toothaches.

Sources: Briggs, *Fairies in Tradition and Literature*, 43; Guiney, *Brownies and Bogles*, 74; Henderson, *Notes on the Folk-Lore of the Northern Counties of England and the Borders*, 256–57

Waldgeister

A type of NATURE SPIRIT in the folk lore of Germany and Scandinavia the waldgeister, similar to the HAMADRYADS from Greek lore, lived within the trees of the more ancient forests. While some of the waldgeister were benign other was malicious but they all held the knowledge of the healing herbs of the forest. FRAU HOLLE who was said to live in the elder trees, was one of the waldgeister.

Sources: Porteous, *Forest in Folklore and Mythology*, 90; Rose, *Spirits, Fairies, Leprechauns, and Goblins*, 331

Walgino

In Polish folklore the walgino was a NATURE SPIRIT who watched over cattle.

Sources: Dixon-Kennedy, *Encyclopedia of Russian and Slavic Myth and Legend*, 218; Rose, *Spirits, Fairies, Leprechauns, and Goblins*, 331

Wanakauri

Wanakauri is an APU who lives on a mountain peak in the Andes Mountains.

Source: Illes, *Encyclopedia of Spirits*, 198

Wassermann

A WATER SPIRIT from the folklore of Germany, the wassermann ("waterman") was similar to the NIXEN.

Sources: Aldington, *Larousse Encyclopedia of Mythology*, 279; Rose, *Spirits, Fairies, Leprechauns, and Goblins*, 332

Water Leaper

Variations: LLAMHIGYN Y DWR

Living in the sea off the Welsh coast the water leapers are a species of vicious water fairy preying off fishermen by luring their ships into rocks where they will wreck and drown or by tricking them into falling overboard and into the water. These FAIRY ANIMALS have been described as being winged toad-like creatures with long, barbed tails. When these fay cannot successfully hunt fishermen they have been known to eat sheep.

Sources: Eberhart, *Mysterious Creatures*, 299; McCoy, *Witch's Guide to Faery Folk*, 33–34; Rose, *Giants, Monsters, and Dragons*, 225

Water Spirit

Appearing in many different folklores and mythologies water spirit are typically considered to be dangerous and numerous. When not protecting the boundaries of their watery kingdoms these fairies are seeking out humans to kidnap and keep as mates. It is not unheard of for a water spirit to assist a fisherman in increasing his catch or lead a sailor to safety however they are far more likely to cut the seamen's net, wreck his boat, and be the cause of the sailor's drowning. Examples of water spirits are the benevolent AS-IGA of Siberia; the AUGHISKY of Ireland; the benevolent BEREGINI of Russia; the FUATH of Scotland; the HNIKUR of the Faroe Islands; the KELPIE of Scotland; the NAGAS of Buddhist, Hindu, and Jainism mythology; the NAVKY of Slavic lore; and the NECK of Scandinavia.

Individual interties classified as water spirits are BAR of Scandinavia and EAGER of British folklore

Sources: Briggs, *Fairies and Traditions in Literature*, 52; Chopra, *Academic Dictionary of Mythology*, 198; Dixon-Kennedy, *Encyclopedia of Russian and Slavic Myth and Legend*, 18; McCoy, *Witch's Guide to Faery Folk*, 172; Spence, *Minor Traditions of British Mythology*, 14

Water Women

Variations: Dones d'aigo

These malicious water fairies of Spanish lore often disguise themselves as local fauna or seaweed. Although their special name is feminine there have been androgynous and male versions of these fay reported. In the older tales the water women were diurnal and lived equally on land as in the water; they had broad and mysterious powers and were capable of speaking with the birds, trees, water, and the wind. After the introduction of Christianity the water women were literally driven underground where they lived in wonderful palaces in lakes and waterfalls. Like the NYMPHS of ancient Greece, each water woman was the guardian of a spring.

Sources: Haase, *Greenwood Encyclopedia of Folktales and Fairy Tales*, 1001–02; McCoy, *Witch's Guide to Faery Folk*, 172

Water-Wraith

The water-wraith of Scotland is described as looking like a ragged, scowling, tall, thin, and withered woman dressed in green; most often she is sighted by inebriated people as they make their way home. Whenever possible she will attempt to mislead them into the water where they will drown.

Sources: Emoto, *Healing Power of Water*, 213; McPherson, *Primitive Beliefs in the Northeast of Scotland*, 63; Wilson, *Wilson's Tales of the Borders and of Scotland*, 68

Wayland Smith

Variations: Weiland Smith, Weland Smith

In British folklore Wayland Smith was an invisible DWARF, ELF, or GIANT who was a renowned armorer and swordsmith. On the ancient Ridgeway of Berkshire stands a megalithic dolmen called, to this day, Wayland's Smithy. It was believed if a horse was left there overnight with a coin fastened to its saddle by morning it would be newly shod.

Wayland Smith was mentioned by King Alfred the Great (A.D. 899) as being a "famous and wise goldsmith"; Wayland was also named in the *Saga of Beowulf*. Sir Walter Scott introduced the legend of this fairy in his 1821 novel, *Kenilworth* and Rudyard Kipling also told the tale in his 1906 novel *Puck of Pook's Hill*.

Sources: Kipling, *Puck of Pook's Hill*,, 11, 21–23; Rose, *Spirits, Fairies, Leprechauns, and Goblins*, 332; Scott, *Kenilworth*, 106–107, 126

Die Weisse Frau

Variations: Ahnfrau ("ancestress")

A German fairy spirit believed to haunt royal castles, to see the weisse Frau ("white lady") was said to be a death omen, similar to the BANSHEE of Irish lore. Virtually every noble German family claimed to have one such spirit in their castle. Although the imperial family Hohenzollern had a weisse Frau they believed to be the spirit of Kunigunda von Orlamonde; typically these fay were named BERTHA and has some sort of deformity on its foot, be it club-footed, flat-footed, large-footed, or swan-footed. Associated with the goddess Freia, the weisse Frau had a deep interest in the welfare of her descendants.

Sources: Lynch, *Famous Ghosts and Haunted Places*, 116; Walsh, *Heroes and Heroines of Fiction, Classical Mediæval, Legendary*, 354

Well Spirit

Variations: Guardian Spirit

Similar to the Nymphs of ancient Greece, well spirits are the guardians of their individual, hot springs, sacred wells, and wishing well all throughout Europe. Occasionally mistaken as a deity or the ghost of a human, well spirits are be-lieved to be sympathetic to human needs but accepting their assistance is said to be burdened with a huge price. Expert shape-shifters these fairies will often take the form of a human, whose bodies they envy; when they manifest in this form they are always dangerously beautiful. It was not uncommon for offerings to be made to the fairy before the well was utilized.

Sources: Bonwick, *Irish Drunids and Old Irish Religions*, 234; Evans-Wentz, *Fairy-Faith in Celtic Countries*, 341; McCoy, *Witch's Guide to Faery Folk*, 173, 334–45

Westri

Variations: Westre

Westri ("west") was one of the many DWARFS named in the *Voluspa*, the first and best known poem of the *Poetic Edda*, a collection of Old Norse poems dating back to about A.D. 985. One of the four DWARFS of the four main compass points, Westri, along with AUSTRI (east), NORDI (north), and Sudri (south) each held up one corner of the earth which is described as a flat, plate-like piece of land.

Sources: Crossley-Holland, *Norse Myths*, 183; Wägner, *Asgard and the Gods*, 311

White Dwarfs

Living on the Isle of Rügen in Germany the white DWARFS were believed to be the most beautiful and delicate of the DWARF having the most gentle and innocent of dispositions. Their principal residence is in an area called the nine hills, small mounds believed to be *hünengräber*, or the graves of GIANTS; the white DWARFS occupy only two of these hills.

Throughout the winter months the white DWARF stay within their hills and work diligently constructing the finest creations of gold and silver. In the spring these DWARFS would move above ground and live there until the end of summer enjoying both the sun and starlight albeit in an assumed form during the day typically, a colored little bird or snow-white dove. White DWARFS are said to enjoy both dancing and music.

Sources: Keightly, *World Guide to Gnomes, Fairies, Elves, and Other Little People*, 174–76

The White Ladies

The white ladies are both a type of ghost and a fairy being, as there is a nearly indiscernible separation between fairies and the deceased. Named for their appearance, dressed in long, flowing, silky gowns, they are similar to the BAN-SHEE, as they appear near the time of a family member's death.

In British lore the white ladies were believed to be fairies and sometimes associated with fertility; in Northumberland they were believed to be attached to a place rather than a family.

German lore they were associated with elves. Irish lore white ladies were said to be the direct descendants of the TUATHA DE DANANN. In Normandy HABUNDIA is said to be the Queen of the white ladies.

Sources: Avant, *Mythological Reference*, 480; Briggs, *Fairies in Tradition and Literature*, 33; Gerwig, *Crowell's Handbook for Readers and Writers*, 711; Siefker, *Santa Claus, Last of the Wild Men*, 183

White Merle

In ancient Basque lore the white merle is a FAIRY ANIMAL, a bird whose singing could restore sight to the blind.

Sources: Brewer, *Wordsworth Dictionary of Phrase and Fable*, 1137; Daniels, *Encyclopedia of Superstitions, Folklore, and the Occult Sciences of the World*, 1417

Whoopity Stoorie

Variations: Fittletot, Whippity Stourie, Whuppity Stoorie

A fairy of the Scottish Lowlands Whoopity Stoorie is described as looking like a deformed elderly woman dressed entirely in green. Similar to TOM-TIT-TOT in that her name must be correctly guessed within three days or some previously avoided tragedy will return; this is more often achieved by luck rather than skill. Versions of Whoopity Stoorie involve her restoring a sow to life and spinning fine thread into shirts.

Sources: Henderson, *Scottish Fairy Belief: A History*, 16; Rose, *Spirits, Fairies, Leprechauns, and Goblins*, 333–34

Wichtlan (plural: wichtlein)

Variations: HAUS-SCHMIEDLEIN ("little house-smiths")

In southern Germany the wichtlein ("little wights") were a species of mining fairy similar to GOBLINS. The wichtlein were overall harmless as the stone they threw at miners never hurt anyone unless the fairy was deeply insulted; they would announce the death of a miner by tapping loudly three times, and when a disaster was about to occur they could be heard imitating the sounds of miners working. Described as standing less than three feet tall and looking like old men with

long beards they dressed like miners carrying hammers, lanterns, and mallets and wore leather aprons and white hoods. In areas where there was abundant ore the wichtlein appeared to be working very hard but it was all show, as no progress was ever accomplished.

In Istria a place was set aside in the mine for the wichtlein where food was left for them in a pot. On various days throughout the year a little red coat suitable for a child was left as a gift for them.

Sources: Froud, *Faeries*, 81; Keightly, *World Guide to Gnomes, Fairies, Elves, and Other Little People*, 229–30; Rose, *Spirits, Fairies, Leprechauns, and Goblins*, 334; Sikes, *British Goblins*, 29, 32

Wichtln

In southern Germany and Austria, the wichtln are tireless in their pursuit of fun which when perpetrated upon unsuspecting animals and people range between mischievous and malicious. Described as looking like diminutive elves the wichtln have very bulbous bodies, overly long arms and legs, and wear brown fur coats. Similar to the BROWNIE of Scotland the wichtln will adopt a home and assist the family in completing household tasks however most families who have one of these fairies living with them claim the benefits do not outweigh their poltergeist pinching, pranks, and tripping in addition to letting the livestock loose and spilling over any unattended filled container. To placate these fay gifts and displays of affection will usually keep them placated.

Subspecies of the wichtln are the FÜTTERMAR-INCHEN who specialize in feeding farm animals; the PECHAMNDERLIN who glue the eyes of children shut with pitch, and the extreme pranksters known as the PITZLN.

Sources: Arrowsmith, *Field Guide to the Little People*, 51–3; Bois, *Jersey Folklore and Superstitions*, 235; McCoy, *Witch's Guide to Faery Folk*, 335–56

Wild Hunt

Variations: Åsgårdsreia ("ride of Asgard"), Chasse de Cain (cain's hunt), Chasse deHerode (Hunt of Herodias), Chasse Sauvage, Compaña, Divoký Hon ("wild hunt"), Dziki Gon, Dziki Łów, Estantiga ("the old army"), FAIRY RADE, Herlaþing ("herla's assembly"), Herod's Hunt, Hostia, Hunt of Arthur O'Bower, Mesnée d'Hellequin ("household of hellequin"), Oskoreia, Wilde Jagd ("wild chase"), Wildes Heer ("wild army"), Woden's Hunt, Wutan's Army

The idea of the Wild Hunt, a pack of spectral hounds racing through the air lead by a fairy hunt-master, has been adopted by many different mythologies; it originates in ancient lore but was demonized after the introduction of Christianity. During the Middle Ages the Wild Hunt was associated with witches and the leader of the hunt was a demonic spirit or Satan himself. Many of the witches who were charged during the Inquisition were accused of taking part in this activity.

In German lore the hunt is led by Frau BERCHTA with her ghostly dogs, chasing unlucky mortals to their death.

In Scotland the SLUAG of the SEELIE COURT will use the opportunity of a FAIRY RADE or Wild Hunt to fly through the sky and kidnap travelers who are on the road at midnight. They always fly towards the West in order to catch the souls of dying men before the souls dissipate.

In Wales the leader of the hunt is GWYN AP NUDD who heads up the TYLWYTH TEG fairies.

There have been many hunters have been said to lead the Wild Hunt such as Abonde, the Angel of Death, Black Vaughan, Callow of Feckenham, Denmark's King Waldemar, the Devil, Diana, Edric the Wild (or Wild Edric), Finn mac Cumhail and his hounds, Fraw Selga, the Ghost Riders in the Sky, GRIM, Harlequin (also known as Erlequin and Herlequin), Gulfora, Harry-ca-Nab, the Headless Horseman, Herne the Hunter and his GABRIEL HOUNDS, Hulde, King Arthur, King Stakh, King Vold, Lady Abonde, Odin, Old Mother Darky (a rare female manifestation), Sir Francis Drake driving a hearse, Sir Peter Corbet, the UNSEELIE COURT, Wild Darrell, and Wotan.

Sources: Eason, *Fabulous Creatures, Mythical Monsters, and Animal Power Symbols*, 105–08; Grimm, *Teutonic Mythology*, Volume 4, 1588–89; Guerber, *Hammer of Thor*, 17–19; Howey, *Horse in Magic and Myth*, 51–60; Thorpe, *Northern Mythology,* Volume 3, 61, 218–19

Wild Women

Variations: DZUNUKWA, ELLE-MAIDS, Tsonoqua, Wilde Frauen

The wild women of German mythology were believed to be a species of NATURE SPIRITS who live on the Wunderberg (also known as Unaerberg), a great moor near Salzburg; there they would appear to children who tended cattle and give them bread to eat. Wild women, standing only about three feet tall, were also sighted in places where people were reaping early in the mornings. These fairies were said to live in hills where within were stately palaces made of silver and gold were surrounded by beautiful gardens and springs. Like the ELLE-MAIDS of Scandinavian lore, the wild women were described as being very beautiful and having fine, flowing hair. These fairies were only ever sighted alone or in groups and on occasion would brazenly abduct a child. When confronted by a parent the fairy would sometimes leave the child behind, but weep bitterly as it left empty-handed.

Sources: Conway, *Magickal Mystical Creatures*, 208; Keightly, *World Guide to Gnomes, Fairies, Elves, and Other Little People*, 234–35; McCoy, *Witch's Guide to Faery Folk*, 139, 336–7; Spence, *Encyclopedia of Occultism and Parapsychology*, 986

Wildbean

Variations: Little Wildbean

A BOGGART of who was said to have once haunted the home of a Quaker, Wildbean of Irish lore would, if the cook did not leave him a proper meal, take his vengeance out on the family by clogging the tap to the beer kegs.

Sources: Keightly, *World Guide to Gnomes, Fairies, Elves, and Other Little People*, 369

Will o' the Wisp

Variations: Bob-a-Longs, CANDELAS, Canwyllgorff, Corpse Candles, Dick o' Tuesday, Eclaireux, Ellylldan, Faery Lights, Fairy Lights, Fox Fire, Friar's Lantern, Friar-with-the Rush, Hinky-Puck, HOB-and-his-Lantern, Hobany's-Lantern, Hobbedy's Lantern; Hobby Lantern, Hobredy's Lanthorn, Huckpoten, Ignis Fatuus, Ignus Fatuus ("fools fire"), Irrbloss, Jack O'Lantern, Jack-O-Lantern, Jacky Lantern, Jenny Burnt-Tail, Jenny with the Lantern, JOAN THE WAD, Jock-'o-the-Lantern, Kit with the Candlestick, Lantern Man, Peg-a-Lantern, PINKET, PUCK, Pwca, Ruskaly, Spunkie, Spunky, Saint Elmo's Fire, Teine Sith, Walking Fire, Will o the Wikes, Will the Smith, Will-O'-the-Wykes, Will-with-the-Wisp, Willy Wisp

Described as looking like floating balls of blue flame in the British folklore the will o' the wisp is sometimes said to be the souls of deceased children. Living in the marshes these nocturnal fairies will mislead travelers appearing as a lantern light in the distance. Those who follow the light will at least become lost but many times the will o' the wisp will lead the person into mortal danger.

In German lore the will o' the wisp, believed

to be the souls of children who died before having been baptized, will assist a lost traveler on occasion, but there are only a few tales of this occurring. To ward off this fairy it is said to walk with one foot in a wagon rut or to throw some graveyard dirt at it.

Sources: Ashliman, *Fairy Lore*, 126–27; Bord, *Fairies*, 5; McCoy, *Witch's Guide to Faery Folk*, 53; Keightly, *World Guide to Gnomes, Fairies, Elves, and Other Little People* 318; Rose, *Spirits, Fairies, Leprechauns, and Goblins*, 86

Wiraqochan

Wiraqochan is an APU who lives on a mountain peak in the Andes Mountains.

Source: Illes, *Encyclopedia of Spirits*, 198

Wirry-Cowe

Variations: Worriecowe, Worrikow, Worry-Cow, Wurricowe, Wurrycow

In Scotland a wirry-cowe is a BUGBEAR, ghost, ghoul, GOBLIN, or any other unpleasant being; sometimes it was used as euphuism for the Devil or to refer to a scarecrow.

Sources: Mackay, *Dictionary of Lowland Scotch*, 283; Wright, *English Dialect Dictionary*, T-Z, 545

Wish Hounds

Variations: Wisked Hounds, Yell-Hounds, Yeth-Hounds

In Cornwall and Dartmoor, England, the headless wish hounds are said to be seen walking along the oldest roads and across the moors during the midnight hours; it is believed if mortal dogs hear the baying call of these FAIRY ANIMALS, they will die. Similar to the folklore of CHENEY'S HOUNDS, the wish hounds have a headless pack master who follows them; described as being dressed all in black, this spectral huntsman is believed to lead the WILD HUNT in the Devonshire region.

Sources: Briggs, *Encyclopedia of Fairies*, 440; Hardwick, *Traditions, Superstitions, and Folklore*, 153, 192; Hunt, *Popular Romances of the West of England*, 29, 145

Witte Wieven

Variations: Witte Juffers, Witte Vrouwen, Witte, Wijven, Wittewijven

In the folklore of Belgium, France, Friesland, Germany, and Holland the witte wieven ("wise women") are a species of fairy living near mounds near lakes or in swamps; they are described as looking like women dressed in white and are said

to have the ability to make prophecies as they are the fairy spirits of priestess and wise women.

It is believed in Friesland the witte wieven are prone not only to take children but also pregnant women, shepherds, watchmen and those who travel by night. On the other hand the witte juffers are inclined to assist lost travelers and women in labor.

Sources: Saille, *Walking the Faery Pathway*, 91; Thorpe, *Northern Mythology*, Volume 3, 269–70

Wolkenthrut

In Nordic and Teutonic mythology Wolkenthrut ("cloud power") was one of the named VALKYRIES, a NYMPH of battle. Always depicted as beautiful women who are sometimes immortal, they are the attendants of the god, Odin.

Sources: Lurker, *Routledge Dictionary of Gods and Goddesses*, 195; Sykes, *Who's Who in Non-Classical Mythology*, 212

Woman Ruler

Woman ruler was a fairy from Irish folklore; along with the FAIRY ANIMAL, BLACK SHANGLAN, they lived invisibly inside their FAIRY FORT. These two fairies come out only when it involves the freeing of Ireland in order to aid and comfort the people during a national uprising.

Source: Wallace, *Folk-lore of Ireland*, 81

Wood Nymph

Variations: DRAYAD

The attendants and companions of the goddess of the hunt and the moon, Artemis (Diana), wood nymphs featured prominently in many of the myths of ancient Greece. Nymphs were lesser deities or NATURE SPIRITS who had dominion over a specific dominion or realm; wood nymphs or DRAYAD had dominion over the forests and stands of trees.

Sources: Keightly, *World Guide to Gnomes, Fairies, Elves, and Other Little People*, 444; Littleton, *Gods, Goddesses, and Mythology, Volume 11*, 999; McCoy, *A Witch's Guide to Faery Folk*, 286; Roman, *Encyclopedia of Greek and Roman Mythology*, 86

Wood-Wife

Variations: Skoggra, SWOR SKOGSFRU ("WOOD-WIFE"), Wish Wife, Wood Maid, Wood Women

The wood-wife of German and Swiss lore were said to live in dense groves in old forest; these fairy beings are described as being petite and beautifully dressed. These fairies were believed to be connected to the trees of the forest in a way similar to the DRYAD of ancient Greece; there was a belief that if the bark of a tree was twisted off, a wood-wife will die. In the oldest mythology, the wood wives made up the court of the ancient gods who dwelled in the forests.

Oftentimes these fay would approach people in the woods asking for assistance in baking bread or mending a broken wheelbarrow. Anyone one who assisted them was richly rewarded as wood chips in the area would turn into gold coins and remain thus so long as their origin was not revealed.

Wood Wives were the prey of the relentless Wild Huntsman; the only way these diminutive fairies could save themselves would be to find a tree a woodcutter had cut a cross into and dive into the center of the cross.

Sources: Keightly, *World Guide to Gnomes, Fairies, Elves, and Other Little People*, 491; Porteous, *Forest Folklore*, 91–93; Siefker, *Santa Claus, Last of the Wild Men*, 183

Woodwose

Variations: Ooser, Wild Men of the Woods, Wodwose, Wooser, Wuduwasa

A race of fairy beings from pre–Christian Gaul, the woodwose were the guardians of the forests. Completely covered in long hair the woodwose was often depicted in art as carrying a club. In the Middle Ages these beings were symbolic of prohibited desires and were described in British and Scottish lore as wearing animal skins; in art were drawn carrying a young boy tied to their club as if to eat it although they were believed to be shy and never causing harm to anyone; sometimes they also had a tail.

Sources: Conway, *Magickal Mystical Creatures*, 90–91; Knoppers, *Monstrous Bodies*, 26, 28; Simpson, *Dictionary of English Folklore*, n.p.; Monaghan, *Encyclopedia of Celtic Mythology and Folklore*, 474

Wulver

A race of fairy beings from Scottish lore the wulvers were said to be half human and half wolf. Living alone in the woods and generally keeping away from humans these fairies would on occasion leave wild game on the doorsteps of those in need.

In the Shetland Islands the wulver was described as having the body of a man covered in short brown hair and having the head of a wolf. Wulvers lives in caves they dug out of the side steep hills; they enjoy fishing in deep water.

Sources: Briggs, *Encyclopedia of Fairies*, 445;

Monaghan, *Encyclopedia of Celtic Mythology and Folklore*, 475; Shuker, *Beasts That Hide from Man*, 227

Wünschelwib

In German romance lore the wünschelwib ("wish-woman") was a fairy lover; all her human partner needed to do for her to appear was wish for it and in an instant, she would materialize.

Sources: Keightly, *World Guide to Gnomes, Fairies, Elves, and Other Little People*, 425

Xana

Variations: Xmas

In the Asturian mythology of northern Spain, the xana were a species of water–NYMPH or NATURE SPIRIT of amazing beauty; they were said to have lived in forested regions with pure water, fountains, rivers, and waterfalls. These fairies were described as slender beings with curly, long, blond or light brown hair; they comb their hair with gold and silver combs made from moon- and sun-beams. Sometimes the xana is said to be a singular entity who represents the balance of nature and is a moral trickster. If you pass her test she will reward you with a gift from her vast treasure hoar but if you fail she will publically shame you.

The children of the xana are called *xaninos*; because the mothers cannot produce breast milk they will take their children and swap them out with a human child. When the xaninos is no longer dependent on milk and is weaned the xana will return and take her child back but will not necessarily return the human baby. Many stories say the xana drown the human infant as they do not have the means to properly care for it.

Sources: Bahrami, *Spiritual Traveler Spain*, 139–40; Curran, *Dark Fairies*, 135; Mountain, *Celtic Encyclopedia*, Volume 5, 1109–1110

Xanthe

Born one of the 3,000 daughters of the Titians, Oceanus and Tethys, Xanthe ("blond haired") was one of the named OCEANIDS from ancient Greek mythology.

Sources: Boswell, *What Men or Gods Are These*, 58; Hesiod, *Works of Hesiod, Callimachus, and Theognis*, 20; Conti, *Natale Conti's Mythologiae: Books VI–X*, 701; Westmoreland, *Ancient Greek Beliefs*, 24

Xantho

A sea–NYMPH, Xantho ("golden-haired") was one of the named NEREID from ancient Greek mythology; she was born of Nereus and DORIS and described by Virgil as having bright, waving locks of hair and a slender pale neck.

Sources: Apollodorus, *Apollodorus' Library and Hyginus' Fabulae*, 95; Lemprière, *Classical Dictionary*, 46; Virgil, *The Fourth Georgic of Virgil*, 49

Xindhi

In Albanian folklore the xindhi are a type of ELF or elflike creature; the males of the species are called xindhi and the females are xindha. Typically these fairies are cruel to humans but on occasion they can be friendly or helpful; the presence of these fairies is made known by the creaking of a door or floorboard, or by the flickering of a flame.

Source: Maberry, *Cryptopedia*, 119

Yallery Brown

Described as being no larger than a year-old child, having long, soft, golden hair, and a face that is brown and withered, Yallery Brown of British folklore was a malicious CHANGELING. Discovered by Tom Tiver under the Stranger Stone, a place where children were left to die of exposure, Yallery offered his would-be savior a gift but instead places a curse upon him.

Sources: Monaghan, *Encyclopedia of Celtic Mythology and Folklore*, 476; Narváez, *Good People*, 232–33; Rose, *Spirits, Fairies, Leprechauns, and Goblins*, 341, 351

Yama-Uba

Variations: Yamamba, Yamanba

In Japanese beliefs Yama-Uba ("mountain grandmother") was said to be the female NATURE SPIRIT of the mountains. As old as time itself this singular being would work constantly to maintain the cycle of human life; occasionally she appeared to travelers as a beautiful young woman.

Sources: Monaghan, *Goddesses in World Culture*, 164; Rose, *Spirits, Fairies, Leprechauns, and Goblins*, 341

Yann-An-Od

In Brittany, Yann-an-Od ("John of the coast") was described as looking like a kindly, old shepherd with a long white beard, wearing a long robe and carrying a staff. Once a FAIRY KING, he now acts as a protector of sheep. When approached by humans, this shy fairy fades away.

Associated with the coast of Brittany, Yann-an-Od was a skilled shape-shifter, appearing as a DWARF, GIANT or a seaman wearing an oil-cloth hat. Walking along the shore, this fairy would let loose with a long oiercing cry to frighten away fishermen who are still working late at night.

Sources: Avant, *Mythological Reference*, 480; Evan-Wentz, *Fairy Faith in Celtic Countries*, 193; McCoy, *Witch's Guide to Faery Folk*, 147

Yann-an-Ord

In Breton folklore figure Yann-an-Ord ("John of the dunes") was a fairy being very similar to the SIREN. Walking along the shoreline and calling out like a sea-bird, Yann-an-Ord was described as looking like a man in a raincoat or a DWARF. His call was said to be a clear and ringing as a church bell. There are an equal numbers of tales of this fairy using his voice to warn sailors of fog banks hiding dangerous rock jetties as there are of him luring ships against those same rocks to sink their ships.

Sources: Curran, *Mysterious Celtic Mythology in American Folklore*, 235; Monaghan, *Encyclopedia of Celtic Mythology and Folklore*, 476

Yarthkins

In the folklore of Lincolnshire, England, yarthkins were believed to be a drifting mass of NATURE SPIRITS but were also said to be small and very ugly; although they were thought of as a collective being, some stood apart from others, such as TIDDY ONES and the GREENCOATIES. Once the fens of Lincolnshire were drained, the yarthkins disappeared.

Sources: Avant, *Mythological Reference*, 479; Briggs, *Encyclopedia of Fairies*, 447

Yech

Variations: Yach

In Indian folklore the yech is a humorous, power FAIRY ANIMAL described as looking like a dark civet cat with a small white hat on its head. If someone manages to gain possession of the creature's hat, the yech will then become the devoted servant; wearing the hat will make a person invisible. Making catlike noises, and having the ability to shape-shift into any form, the feet of the yech are so small they are mistaken for being invisible.

Sources: Crooke, *Popular Religion and Folk-Lore of Northern India*, Volume 2, 80; Spence, *Encyclopedia of Occultism and Parapsychology*, 1005

Yehasuri

Two-foot tall GNOME-like humanoids from the Catawba and Lumbee Indian folklore of South Carolina, America, the yehasuri ("little people") are believed to live in tree stumps or underground and play little tricks, such as braiding horses tails.

Sources: Boughman, *Herbal Remedies of the Lumbee Indians*, 49; Lyon, *Encyclopedia of Native American Healing*, 326

The Yellow Dwarf

In the fairy-tale *The Yellow Dwarf* by Madame d'Aulnoy, the Yellow Dwarf was described as having an ugly yellow face, bald head, long ears, and wore a yellow coat and wooden shoes; he lived in an orange tree. This Dwarf tricked a queen into agreeing to marry her favorite and most beautiful daughter, Bellissima, The Yellow Dwarf is malicious and has a spiteful laugh; he rides upon a Spanish cat.

Sources: Aulnoy, *Fairy Tales of Madame d'Aulnoy*, 239–41; Lang, *Blue Fairy Book*, 30–50

Yingi

Yingi was one of the many DWARFS named in the *Voluspa*, the first and best known poem of the *Poetic Edda*, a collection of Old Norse poems dating back to about A.D. 985.

Sources: Daly, *Norse Mythology A to Z*, 22; Sykes, *Who's Who in Non-Classical Mythology*, 53

Ymir

In Norse mythology, the primordial GIANT Ymir was created when the hot air from Muspell came into contact with the ice of Niflheim. Ymir was progenitor of the frost GIANTS, from his sleeping body a son sprung froth from one of his legs and a daughter crawled out from his armpit. Next, Audumla the divine cow was born from the melting ice of his body; Ymir fed Ymir from her udders while she sustained herself by licking hoar frost and salt from the ice.

The god Odin was not happy with the growing number of GIANTS Ymir was creating. When the god slew Ymir the rush of blood drowned all but two GIANTS. The corpse of Ymir was used to create the earth and heavens; his blood became the lakes, rivers, and seas; bones were used to make the mountains; teeth became boulders, rocks, and stones, his hair became the trees, and his brains were the clouds. The eyebrow was used to create Midgard, the world of man. The maggots which crawled on Ymir's decomposing flesh transformed and became the DWARFS who lived under the hills and mountains.

Sources: Fontenrose, *Python*, 522–24; Lindow, *Norse Mythology*, 322–25; Littleton, *Gods, Goddesses, and Mythology*, Volume 11, 1428

Yngvi

Yngvi ("lordly") was one of the many DWARFS named in the *Voluspa*, the first and best known poem of the *Poetic Edda*, a collection of Old Norse poems dating back to about A.D. 985.

Sources: Daly, *Norse Mythology A to Z*, 22; Wilkinson, *Book of Edda called Völuspá*, 12

Yōsei

Yōsei ("bewitching spirit") are the fairies of Japan; humans can only see them as birds; typically they take on the guise of cranes or swans.

Sources: Nakao, *Random House Japanese-English English-Japanese Dictionary*,265; Roberts, *Japanese Mythology A to Z*, 127

Yr Wyll

In the folk lore of Wales the yr wyll were described as being invisible but their presence could be physically felt. Like the PIXIE of England, the yr wyll enjoyed taking horses and ride them all night long only to return them to the barn covered in lather and with tangled manes.

Sources: Jones, *Welsh folklore and Folk-Custom*, 33; Rose, *Spirits, Fairies, Leprechauns, and Goblins*, 343

Yumbo

Variations: BACHNA RACHNA ("the good people")

On Goree Island, south of the Cape Verde Peninsula in Senegal, West Africa the white skinned, silver haired race of fairies known as the yumboes. Living underground in the hills located about three miles from the coast, each evening they dress in their pangs revealing only their eyes and sneak into the nearby villages. There the yumboes steal cuscus and cornmeal by putting it into their calabashes and arranging themselves into a row by which to pass their loot downward. Fond of fish yumboes will borrow canoes and take fire in order to cook their catch. Beating on their jaloff drums these little fairies, standing only about two foot tall will drink palm wine until they become intoxicated; they greatly enjoy dancing and feasting. Akin to the BANSHEE of Ireland the yumboes will attach themselves to a particular family; when one of them dies the fairies are hear wailing and lamenting.

Sources: Brewer, *Wordsworth Dictionary of Phrase and Fable*, 973; Keightly, *World Guide to Gnomes, Fairies, Elves, and Other Little People*, 496; Maberry, *Cryptopedia*, 119

Yunw Tsunsdi

The Cherokee and Iroquois Indians of North Carolina, United States, tell of a small race of ELF-like people they call the yunw tsunsdi. As these little fairies move through the wilderness they leave behind small footprints; if anyone follows them the yunw tsunsdi will pelt them with stones or cast a spell on them.

Source: Board, *Fairies*, 82

Zemyna

Variations: Mati Syra Zemyna ("moist mother earth"), Žemyna

A NATURE SPIRIT from the folk lore of Lithuania, Zemyna ("mistress of the earth") is primarily concerned with the abundance of crops and fertility; her male counterpart was known as Zemepatis. Zemyna played an important part in daily life and was shown great respect; when an oath was sworn dirt was rubbed in the hands, when a couple married they would each bit into a clump of earth, and if a person were to spit upon the ground, they were then expect to apologize to her.

Sources: Monaghan, *Encyclopedia of Goddesses and Heroines*, 522; Rose, *Spirits, Fairies, Leprechauns, and Goblins*, 345

Zephir

A NATURE SPIRIT intimate with MORGAN LE FEY, Zephir was "repairing to her from her youth up"

Source: Keightly, *World Guide to Gnomes, Fairies, Elves, and Other Little People*, 34

Zeuxippe

Zeuxippe was a NYMPH from the mythology of classical Greece and Rome; daughter of the river god, Eridanus. One of the NAIADS, she was married to the sixth mythical king of Athens, Pandion; together they had twin sons, Butes and Erechtheus, as well as two daughters, PHILOMELA and Prokne.

Sources: Apollodorus of Athens, *Apollodorus' Library and Hyginus' Fabulae*, 101; Grant, *Who's Who in Classical Mythology*, 55, 68; Grote, *History of Greece*, Volume 1, 196

Zeuxo

Born one of the 3,000 daughters of the Titians, Oceanus and Tethys, Zeuxo was one of the named OCEANIDS from Greek mythology.

Sources: Bell, *Bell's New Pantheon or Historical Dictionary of the Gods*, 112; Boswell, *What Men or Gods Are These*, 58; Hesiod, *Theogony*, 116; Hesiod, *Works of Hesiod, Callimachus, and Theognis*, 20; Westmoreland, *Ancient Greek Beliefs*, 24

Zips

Shy and thin fairies from the folklore of Central America and Mexico the nocturnal zips are a race of male fairies who look after herds of deer. Described as wearing a cap or helmet and carrying a spear the zips are reclusive and will avoid human contact.

Source: McCoy, *Witch's Guide to Faery Folk*, 340

Bibliography

Acker, Paul, and Carolyne Larrington. *The Poetic Edda: Essays on Old Norse Mythology.* London: Psychology Press, 2002.

Adams, H. G. *A Cyclopaedia of Female Biography; Consisting of Sketches of all Women, who have been Distinguished by Great Talents, Strength of Character, Piety, Benevolence, or Moral Virtue of any kind; Forming a Complete Record of Womanly Excellence or Ability: Edited by H. G. Adams.* London: Groombridge, 1857.

Addy, Sidney Oldall. *Folk Tales and Superstitions.* Totowa, NJ: Rowman & Littlefield, 1973.

Adelson, Betty M. *The Lives of Dwarfs: Their Journey from Public Curiosity Toward Social Liberation.* New Brunswick: Rutgers University Press, 2005.

Adkins, Lesley, and Roy A. Adkins. *Handbook to Life in Ancient Rome.* Oxford: Oxford University Press, 1998.

_____, and _____. *Handbook to Life in Ancient Rome.* New York: Infobase, 2004.

Aguilar, Filomeno V. *Clash of Spirits: The History of Power and Sugar Planter Hegemony on a Visayan Island.* Honolulu: University of Hawaii Press, 1998.

Akehurst, F. R. P., and Stephanie Cain Van D'Elden. *The Stranger in Medieval Society.* Minneapolis: University of Minnesota Press, 1997.

Aldhouse-Green, Miranda Jane. *Celtic Myths.* Austin: University of Texas Press, 1995.

_____. *The Gods of Roman Britain.* London: Osprey, 1983.

Aldington, Richard, and Delano Ames, trans. *The Larousse Encyclopedia of Mythology.* New York: Barnes & Noble, Incorporated, 1994.

Aldrich, Thomas Bailey. *The Young Folks' Library: A Book of Famous Fairy Tales.* Boston: Hall and Locke, 1901.

Alexander, Hartley Burr. *North American [mythology].* Boston: Marshall Jones, 1916.

Alexander, Marc. *British Folklore.* New York: Crescent Books, 1982.

Allardice, Pamela. *Myths, Gods and Fantasy.* Santa Barbara: ABC-CLIO, 1991.

Allen, Henry G., ed. *The Encyclopedia Britannica: A Dictionary of Arts, Sciences and General Literature,* Volume 14. New York: Henry G. Allen, 1890.

Allen, Thomas William, and Edward Ernest Sikes. *The Homeric Hymns.* London: Macmillan, 1904.

Allies, Jabez. *On the Ignis Fatuus: Or, Will-O'-The-Wisp, and the Fairies.* London: Simpkin, Marshall, and Company, 1846.

Altmann, Anna E. *The Seven Swabians, and Other German Folktales.* Westport, CT: Libraries Unlimited, 2005.

Ambrosetti, Juan Bautista. *Supersticiones y Leyendas.* Buenos Aires: Ediciones Siglo Veinte, 1976.

American Philological Association. *Transactions of the American Philological Association,* Volume 26. Boston: Ginn and Company, 1895.

Ames, Winthrop. *What Shall We Name the Baby?* New York: Simon & Schuster, 1990.

Ananikian, Mardiros Harootioon. *Armenian Mythology: Stories of Armenian Gods and Goddesses, Heroes and Heroines, Hells and Heavens, Folklore and Fairy Tales.* Los Angeles: Indo-European, 2010.

Andersen, Hans Christian. *Hans Christian Andersen's Stories for the Household.* New York: McLoughlin Brothers, 1893.

_____. *Tales and Fairy Stories.* London: G. Routledge and Company, 1852.

Andersen, Hans Christian, and Maria Tatar. *The Annotated Hans Christian Andersen.* London: W.W. Norton, 2008.

Andersen, Johannes Carl. *Myths and Legends of the Polynesians.* Mineola, NY: Courier Dover, 1928.

Anderso, Rasmus Björn. *Norse Mythology.* Chicago: S.C. Griggs and Company, 1884.

Anderson, Graham. *King Arthur in Antiquity.* London: Psychology Press, 2004.

Anderson, Linda, Janis Lull, and Thomas Clayton. *"A Certain Text." Close Readings and Textual Studies on Shakespeare and Others in Honor of Thomas Clayton.* Newark: University of Delaware Press, 2002.

Andrews, Elizabeth. *Ulster Folklore.* New York: E. P. Dutton, 1919.

Andrews, Tamra. *Dictionary of Nature Myths: Legends of the Earth, Sea, and Sky.* New York: Oxford University Press, 2000.

Andrews, Ted. *Enchantment of the Faerie Realm: Communicate with Nature Spirits and Elementals.* St. Paul: Llewellyn Worldwide, 1993.

Anthon, Charles. *A Classical Dictionary: Containing the Principle [sic] Proper Names Mentioned in Ancient Authors.* Whitefish, MT: Kessinger, 2005.

Antoninus Liberalis, and Francis Celoria. *The Metamorphoses of Antoninus Liberalis: A Translation with Commentary.* London: Psychology Press, 1992.

Apollodorus of Athens, and Sir James George Frazer, trans. *Apollodorus: The Library,* Volume 2. London: William Heinemann, 1921.

Apollodorus of Athens, and Robin Hard, trans. *The Library of Greek Mythology.* Oxford: Oxford University Press, 1999.

Apollodorus of Athens, and Michael Simpson. *Gods and*

Heroes of the Greeks: The Library of Apollodorus. Amherst: University of Massachusetts Press, 1976.

Apollodorus of Athens, R. Scott Smith, Stephen Trzaskoma, and C. Julius Hyginus. *Apollodorus' Library and Hyginus' Fabulae: Two Handbooks of Greek Mythology.* Indianapolis: Hackett, 2007.

Archibald, Elizabeth, and David F. Johnson. *Arthurian Literature XXVII.* Cambridge: Boydell and Brewer, 2010.

Archibald, Malcolm. *Sixpence for the Wind: A Knot of Nautical Folklore.* Tonawanda, NY: Dundurn Press, 1998.

Ardinger, Barbara. *Pagan Every Day: Finding the Extraordinary in Our Ordinary Lives.* San Francisco: Weiser, 2007.

Argyle, William John. *The Fon of Dahomey: A History and Ethnography of the Old Kingdom.* Oxford: Clarendon Press, 1966.

Arndt, Ernst Moritz. *Fairy Tales from the Isle of Rügen.* London: David Nutt, 1896.

Arnold, Albert James. *Monsters, Tricksters, and Sacred Cows: Animal Tales and American Identities.* Charlettesville: University of Virginia Press, 1996.

Arnott, W. *Birds in the Ancient World from A to Z.* New York: Psychology Press, 2007.

Arrowsmith, Nancy. *Field Guide to the Little People: A Curious Journey into the Hidden Realm of Elves, Faeries, Hobgoblins and Other Not-So-Mythical Creatures.* St. Paul: Llewellyn Worldwide, 2009.

Asante, Molefi K., and Ama Mazama. *Encyclopedia of African Religion,* Volume 1. Thousand Oaks, CA: SAGE, 2008.

Ashliman, D. L. *Fairy Lore: A Handbook.* Westport, CT: Greenwood, 2005.

Ashton, John. *Romances of Chivalry Told and Illustrated in Facsimile.* London: T. Fisher Unwin, 1890

Asiatic Journal and Monthly Miscellany, Volume 6. London: Parbury, Allen and Company, 1831.

Athenaeus of Naucratis, Charles Duke Yonge, trans. *The Deipnosophists; or, Banquet of the Learned,* Volume 1. London: H.G. Bohn, 1854.

Aulnoy, Marie-Catherine, Madame d. *The Fairy Tales of Madame d'Aulnoy, Newly Done into English.* London: Lawrence and Bullen, 1892.

Austen, Ralph A., and Jonathan Derrick. *Middlemen of the Cameroons Rivers: The Duala and Their Hinterland, c.1600-c.1960.* Cambridge: Cambridge University Press, 1999.

Austern, Linda Phyllis, and Inna Naroditskaya. *Music of the Sirens.* Bloomington: Indiana University Press, 2006.

Avant, G. Rodney. *A Mythological Reference.* Bloomington: AuthorHouse, 2005.

Bahrami, Beebe. *The Spiritual Traveler Spain: A Guide to Sacred Sites and Pilgrim Routes.* Mahwah, NJ: Paulist Press, 2009.

Baker, Margaret. *Discovering the Folklore of Plants.* Oxford: Shire, 1996.

Baker, Sidney John. *Origins of the Words Pakeha and Maori.* New Plymouth, New Zealand: T. Avery, 1945.

Ballentine, Floyd G. *The Nymphs as Water-deities Among the Greeks and Roman.* Philadelphia: Journal Office, 1906.

Barbanson, Adrienne. *Fables in Ivory: Japanese Netsuke and their Legends.* Tokyo: C. E. Tuttle Company, 1961.

Barber, Dulan. *Monsters Who's Who.* New York: Crescent, 1974.

Barchiesi, Alessandro, Jörg Rüpke, Susan A. Stephens, and the Stanford University Dept. of Classics. *Rituals in Ink: A Conference on Religion and Literary Production in Ancient Rome Held at Stanford University in February 2002.* Munich: Franz Steiner Verlag, 2004.

Baring-Gould, Sabine. *Curious Myths of the Middle Ages,* Volume 2. London: Rivingtons, 1868.

Baring-Gould, Sabine, and Alfred Newton. *Iceland: Its Scenes and Sagas.* London: Smith, Elder and Company, 1863.

Barnstone, Willis, and William E. McCulloh. *Ancient Greek Lyrics.* Bloomington: Indiana University Press, 2010.

Barstow, Cheri, and Trafford. *Elementally Speaking: The Nature Spirits' Guide to Their World.* Bloomington: Trafford, 2006.

Barthell, Edward E. *Gods and Goddesses of Ancient Greece.* Miami: University of Miami Press, 1971.

Bartlett, Sarah. *The Mythology Bible: The Definitive Guide to Legendary Tales.* New York: Sterling, 2009.

Bayley, Harold. *Archaic England: An Essay in Deciphering Prehistory from Megalithic Monuments, Earthworks, Customs, Coins, Placenames, and Faeric Superstitions.* Philadelphia: Chapman and Hall Limited, 1920.

Beachem, Walton. *Critical Survey of Poetry: Authors A–Z 1–1728.* Englewood Cliffs, NJ: Salem Press, 1984.

Beauchamp, William Martin, and the Onondaga Historical Association. *Iroquois Folk Lore: Gathered From the Six Nations of New York.* New York: AMS Press, 1976.

Bechtel, John Hendricks. *A Dictionary of Mythology.* Philadelphia: The Penn Publishing Company, 1905.

Beck, Horace. *Folklore and the Sea.* Edison, NY: Castle, 1999.

Beeler, Kent D. *(More) Parents, Family and the New College Student Experience.* Indianapolis: University of Indianapolis Press, 2002.

Begde, Prabhakar V. *Living Sculpture: Classical Indian Culture as Depicted in Sculpture and Literature.* New Delhi: Sagar, 1996.

Begley, Brandon. *The Faith of Legacy.* Morrisville: Lulu.com, 2007.

Belanger, Jeff, Mark Moran, and Mark Sceurman. *Weird Massachusetts: Your Travel Guide to Massachusetts's Local Legends and Best Kept Secrets.* New York: Sterling, 2008.

Belanger, Michelle. *The Dictionary of Demons: Names of the Damned.* St. Paul: Llewellyn Worldwide, 2010.

Beliefnet. *The Big Book of Angels: Angelic Encounters, Expert Answers, Listening to and Working with Your Guardian Angel.* Emmaus, PA: Rodale, 2002.

Bell, John. *Bell's New Pantheon; Or Historical Dictionary of the Gods, Demi-Gods, Heroes and Fabulous Personages of Antiquity.* London: J. Bell, 1790.

Bell, Robert E. *Place-Names in Classical Mythology: Greece.* Santa Barbara: ABC-CLIO, 1989.

_____. *Women of Classical Mythology: A Biographical Dictionary.* Oxford: Oxford University Press, 1993.

Bellows, Henry Adams. *The Poetic Edda: The Mythological Poems.* Mineola, NY: Courier Dover, 2004.

Benjamin, Samuel Greene Wheeler. *The Story of Persia.* New York: G. P. Putnam's Sons, 1887.

_____. *Troy: Its Legend, History and Literature, with a Sketch of the Topography of the Troad in the Light of Recent Investigation.* New York: Charles Scribner's Sons, 1888.

Bennett, DeRobingne Mortimer. *The Gods and Religions of Ancient and Modern Times*, Volume 1. New York: Bennett, 1880.

Benson, Frank Sherman. *Ancient Greek Coins: pt. XI–XIV. Sicily*. Boston: T. R. Marvin, 1904.

Benson, Margaret, Janet A. Gourlay, and Percy Edward Newberry. *The Temple of Mut in Asher: An Account of the Excavation of the Temple and of the Religious Representations and Objects Found Therein, as Illustrating the History of Egypt and the Main Religious Ideas of the Egyptians*. London: Murray, 1899.

Berens, E M. *The Myths and Legends of Ancient Greece and Rome: Being a Popular Account of Greek and Roman Mythology*. London: Blackie and Son, 1880.

Berg, Wendy. *Red Tree, White Tree: Faeries and Humans in Partnership*. Gloucestershire: Skylight Press, 2010.

Bernal, Martin. *Black Athena: The Linguistic Evidence*. New Brunswick: Rutgers University Press, 2006.

Bernhardt, Peter. *Gods and Goddesses in the Garden: Greco-Roman Mythology and the Scientific Names of Plants*. New Brunswick: Rutgers University Press, 2008.

Besson, Gérard A. *Folklore and Legends of Trinidad and Tobago*. Port of Spain: Paria, 1989.

Best, Elsdon. *Māori Religion and Mythology: Being an Account of the Cosmogony, Anthropogeny, Religious Beliefs and Rites, Magic and Folk Lore of the Māori Folk of New Zealand, Part 2*. Wellington: Te Papa Press, 2005.

Best, Elsdon, and the New Zealand Institute. "Maori Forest Lore: Being Some Account of the Native Forest Lore and Woodcraft, and also of Many Myth, Rites, Customs, and superstitions connected with the Flora and Fauna of the Tuhoe or Ure-wera District, Part One." *Transactions and Proceedings of the New Zealand Institute*, Volume 40, New Zealand Institute, ed., 185–254. Wellington: John Hughes, Printer, 1908.

Betham, Sir William. "On the Affinity og the Hiberno-Celtic and Phenician Languages." *The Transactions of the Royal Irish Academy*, Volume 17, 73–89. Dublin: P. Dixion Hardy, 1837.

Bilby, Julian W. *Among Unknown Eskimo: An Account of Twelve Years Intimate Relations with the Primitive Eskimo of Ice-Bound Baffin Land: With a Description of their Ways of Living, Hunting Customs and Beliefs*. Philadelphia: J.B. Lippincott, 1923.

Bingham, Ann, and Jeremy Roberts. *South and Meso-American Mythology A to Z*. New York: Infobase, 2010.

Birch, Samuel. *History of Ancient Pottery*, Volume 1. London: John Murray, 1858.

Blacket, William Stephens. *Researches into the Lost Histories of America: or, The Zodiac Shown to Be an Old Terrestrial Map in Which the Atlantic Isle Is Delineated; So That Light Can Be Thrown upon the Obscure Histories of the Earthworks and Ruined Cities of America*. London: Trubner and Company, 1883.

Blackman, W. Haden. *Field Guide to North American Monsters: Everything You Need to Know About Encountering Over 100 Terrifying Creatures in the Wild*. New York: Three Rivers Press, 1998.

Blankner, Frederika, and Giovanni Bach. *The History of the Scandinavian Literatures: A Survey of the Literatures of Norway, Sweden, Denmark, Iceland, and Finland, from their Origins to the Present Day, Including Scandinavian-American Authors, and Selected Bibliographies*. Westport, CT: Greenwood Press, 1975.

Blavatsky, Helena Petrovna. *Anthropogenesis*. Point Loma, CA: Aryan Theosophical Press, 1917.

_____. *Isis Unveiled: Science, Volume 1 of Isis Unveiled: A Master-key to the Mysteries of Ancient and Modern Science and Theology*. New York: J.W. Bouton, 1877.

_____. *The Secret Doctrine: Anthropogenesis*. Point Loma, CA: Aryan Theosophical Press, 1888.

Blind, Karl. "Scottish, Shetlandic, and Germanic Water Tales, Part Three." *The Contemporary Review*, Volume 40, Karl Blind, ed., 534–564. London: A. Strahan and Company, Limited, 1881.

Boccaccio, Giovanni, and Jon Solomon. *Genealogy of the Pagan Gods*, Volume 1. Cambridge: Harvard University Press, 2011.

Boiardo, Matteo Maria, Lodovico Ariosto, and Sir Anthony Panizzi. *Orlando Innamorato Di Bojardo: Orlando Furioso Di Ariosto*, Volume 1. London: William Pickering, 1830.

Bois, G. J. C. *Jersey Folklore and Superstitions: A Comparative Study with the Traditions of the Gulf of St. Malo (The Channel Islands, Normandy and Brittany)*. Central Milton Keynes: AuthorHouse, 2010.

_____. *Jersey Folklore and Superstitions*, Volume Two. Central Milton Keynes: AuthorHouse, 2010.

Bolin, Inge. *Growing Up in a Culture of Respect: Child Rearing in Highland Peru*. Austin: University of Texas Press, 2006.

Bond-Freeman, Tara, and Southern Methodist University. *The Maya Preclassic Ceramic Sequence at the Site of Ek Balam, Yucatan, Mexico*. Ann Arbor: ProQuest, 2007.

Bonnefoy, Yves. *American, African, and Old European Mythologies*. Chicago: University of Chicago Press, 1993.

_____. *Greek and Egyptian Mythologies*. Chicago: University of Chicago Press, 1992.

_____. *Roman and European Mythologies*. Chicago: University of Chicago Press, 1992.

Bonnerjea, Biren. *The Allborough New Age Guide: Biren Bonnerjea's a Dictionary of Superstition and Mythology*. London: Allborough Publishing, 1991.

Bonwick, James. *Irish Drunids and Old Irish Religions*. London: Griffith, Farran, and Company, 1894.

_____. *Our Nationalities*. London: David Bouge, 1880.

Booss, Claire, and William Butler Yeats. *A Treasury of Irish Myth, Legend, and Folklore*. New York: Gramercy, 1986.

Bord, Janet. *Fairies: Real Encounters with Little People*. New York: Carroll & Graf, 1997.

Borrero, Mauricio. *Russia*. New York: Infobase, 2004.

Boswell, Fred, and Jeanetta Boswell. *What Men or Gods Are These? A Genealogical Approach to Classical Mythology*. Lanham, MD: Scarecrow, 1980.

Bottrell, William. *Stories and Folk-Lore of West Cornwall*. Penzance: Fernando Alanso Rodda, 1880.

Boughman, Arvis Locklear, and Loretta O. Oxendine. *Herbal Remedies of the Lumbee Indians*. Jefferson, NC: McFarland, 2004.

Bové, Frank James. *The Story of Ergot: For Physicians, Pharmacists, Nurses, Biochemists, Biologists and Others Interested in the Life Sciences*. Unionville, CT: S. Karger, 1970.

Bowersock, Glen Warren. *Hellenism in Late Antiquity*. Ann Arbor: University of Michigan Press, 1990.

Bowlby, Rachel. *Freudian Mythologies: Greek Tragedy and Modern Identities*. New York: Oxford University Press, 2007.

Božić, Sreten, and Alan Marshall. *Aboriginal Myths*. Melbourne: Gold Star, 1972.

Brand, John, and Sir Henry Ellis. *Observations on the Popular Antiquities of Great Britain: Chiefly Illustrating the Origin of our Vulgar and Provincial Customs, Ceremonies, and Superstitions*, Volume 3. London: George Bell, 1901.

_____, _____, and _____, eds. *Brand's Popular Antiquities of Great Britain: Faiths and Folklore; A Dictionary of National Beliefs, Superstitions and Popular Customs, Past and Current, with Their Classical and Foreign Analogues, Described and Illustrated*. London: Reeves and Turner, 1905.

Brand, John, Sir Henry Ellis, William Carew Hazlitt, editors. *Brand's Popular Antiquities of Great Britain: Faiths and Folklore; a Dictionary of National Beliefs, Superstitions and Popular Customs, Past and Current, with their Classical and Foreign Analogues, Described and Illustrated*. London: Reeves and Turner, 1905.

Brann, Eva. *Homeric Moments: Clues to Delight in Reading the Odyssey and the Iliad*. Philadelphia: Paul Dry, 2002.

Bray, Frank Chapin. *The World of Myths: A Dictionary of Mythology*. New York: Thomas Y. Crowell Company, 1935.

Brayley, Edward Wedlake. *The Graphic and Historical Illustrator, edited by Edward Wedlake Brayley*. London: J. Chidley, 1834.

Brewer, Ebenezer Cobham. *Dictionary of Phrase and Fable: Giving the Derivation, Source, or Origin of Common Phrases, Allusions, and Words That Have a Tale to Tell*. London: Cassell and Company, 1900.

_____. *The Reader's Handbook of Famous Names in Fiction, Allusions, References, Proverbs, Plots, Stories, and Poems*. London: Chatto and Windus, 1902.

_____. *The Wordsworth Dictionary of Phrase and Fable*. Hertfordshire: Wordsworth Editions, 2001.

Brewer, Ebenezer Cobham, and Marion Harland. *Character Sketches of Romance, Fiction and the Drama*. New York: E. Hess, 1892.

Briggs, Katharine Mary. *Abbey Lubbers, Banshees, and Boggarts: An Illustrated Encyclopedia of Fairies*. New York: Pantheon, 1979.

_____. *The Anatomy of Puck: An Examination of Fairy Beliefs among Shakespeare's Contemporaries and Successors*. London: Routledge and Paul, 1959.

_____. *A Dictionary of British Folk-Tales in the English Language: Folk Narratives*, Volumes 1–2. New York: Taylor & Francis, 1991.

_____. *An Encyclopedia of Fairies: Hobgoblins, Brownies, Bogies, and Other Supernatural Creatures, Volume 1976*. New York: Pantheon, 1976.

_____. *The Fairies in Tradition and Literature*. London: Psychology Press, 2002.

_____. *Folklore of the Cotswalds*. London: B. T. Batsford, 1974.

_____. *The Vanishing People: Fairy Lore and Legends*. New York: Pantheon, 1978.

Bringsværd, Tor Åge. *Phantoms and Fairies: From Norwegian Folklore*. Oslo: Tanum, 1970.

Brinton, D. G. "The Story of 'Number Nip.'" *Science*, Volume 4, the staff of the American Association for the Advancement of Science, eds. 135–36. Boston: Moses King, 1896.

Briones, Claudia, and José Luis Lanata. *Contemporary Perspectives on the Native Peoples of Pampa, Patagonia, and Tierra Del Fuego: Living on the Edge*. Westport, CT: Greenwood, 2002.

Britannica, Dale Hoiberg, and Indu Ramchandani. *Students' Britannica India*, Volumes 1–5. Mumbai: Popular Prakashan, 2000.

Broedel, Hans Peter. *The Malleus Maleficarum and the Construction of Witchcraft: Theology and Popular Belief*. Manchester: Manchester University Press, 2003.

Brooks, Allan. *Myths, Games and Conflict*. Raleigh: Lulu.com, 2008.

Brown, Arthur, and Peter Godfrey Foote, eds. *Early English and Norse Studies: Presented to Hugh Smith in Honour of his Sixtieth Birthday*. London: Methuen, 1963.

Brown, Robert. *Eridanus: River and Constellation : A Study of the Archaic Southern Asterisms*. London: Longmans, Green, 1883.

_____. *The Great Dionysiak Myth*, Volume 2. London: Longmans, 1878.

Bruce, C. *The Arthurian Name Dictionary*. New York: Taylor & Francis, 1998.

Bruce, Christopher W. *The Arthurian Name Dictionary*. New York: Taylor & Francis, 1999.

Bruun, Ole, Arne Kalland, and the Nordic Institute of Asian Studies. *Asian Perceptions of Nature: A Critical Approach*. London: Psychology Press, 1995.

Buckland, Raymond. *The Weiser Field Guide to Ghosts: Apparitions, Spirits, Spectral Lights and Other Hauntings of History and Legend*. San Francisco: Weiser, 2009.

Buckton, T. J. *Notes and Queries*. London: Spottelwood and Company, 1870.

Budd, Deena West. *The Weiser Field Guide to Cryptozoology: Werewolves, Dragons, Skyfish, Lizard Men, and Other Fascinating Creatures Real and Mysterious*. San Francisco: Weiser, 2010.

Budin, Stephanie Lynn. *The Origin of Aphrodite*. Bethesda, MD: CDL Press, 2003.

Bühler, Georg, Franz Kielhorn, Heinrich Lüders, and Jacob Wackernagel, eds. *Grundriss der indo-arischen Philologie und Altertumskunde (Encyclopedia of Indo-Aryan research)*. Strassburg: K. J. Trübner, 1897.

Bulfinch, Thomas. *Bulfinch's Mythology*. Whitefish, MT: Kessinger, 2004.

_____. *The Golden Age of Myth and Legend*. Hertfordshire: Wordsworth Editions, 1915.

_____. *The Illustrated Age of Fable*. New York: Stewart, Tabori and Chang, 1998.

Bunce, John Thackray. *Fairy Tales, Their Origin and Meaning: With Some Account of Dwellers in Fairyland*. London: Macmillan, 1878.

Bunkśe, Edmunds Valdemārs. *Geography and the Art of Life*. Baltimore: Johns Hopkins University Press, 2004

Bunsen, Christian Karl Josias. *God in History: Or, the Progress of Man's Faith in the Moral Order of the World*. London: Longmans, Green, 1868.

Burke, Sir Bernard J. "Fairy Land." *Saint James's Magazine, and Heraldic and Historical Register*, Volume 1, 413–27. London: E. Churton, 1850.

Burns, William E. *Witch Hunts in Europe and America: An Encyclopedia*. Westport, CT: Greenwood, 2003.

Buse, Jasper, and Raututi Taringa. *Cook Islands Maori Dictionary*. Canberra: Ministry of Education of Cook Island, 1995.

Buxton, R. G. A. *Forms of Astonishment: Greek Myths of Metamorphosis*. Oxford: Oxford University Press, 2009.

Bynum, Edward Bruce. *The African Unconscious.* New York: Cosimo, 2001.

Caldwell, Richard S. *The Origin of the Gods: A Psychoanalytic Study of Greek Theogonic Myth.* Oxford: Oxford University Press, 1993.

Callaway, Henry Canon. *Nursery Tales, Traditions, and Histories of the Zulus: In Their Own Words.* London: Trubner and Company, 1868.

_____. *The Religious System of the Amazulu: Izinyanga and Zokubula.* London: Trubner and Company, 1870.

Callimachus. *Hymn 5: Teiresias and Athena on the Nature of Poetry.* Columbus: Ohio State University, 1987.

Callimachus, and Stanley Lombardo. *Callimachus: Hymns, Epigrams, Select Fragments.* Baltimore: Johns Hopkins University Press, 1988.

Cameron, Alan. *Greek Mythography in the Roman World.* Oxford: Oxford University Press, 2004.

Campbell, David A. *Greek Lyric: Anacreon, Anacreontea Choral Lyric from Olympus to Alcman.* Cambridge: Harvard University Press, 1979.

Campbell, J. G. *Superstitions of the Highlands and Islands of Scotland: Collected Entirely from Oral Sources.* Glasgow: James MacLehose and Sons, 1900.

Campbell, John Francis. *Popular tales of the West Highlands: Orally Collected,* Volume 2. Paisley: Alexander Gardner, 1890.

_____. *Popular Tales of the West Highlands,* Volume 3. Edinburgh: Edmonston and Douglas, 1862.

_____. *Popular Tales of the West Highlands: Orally Collected,* Volume 4. Paisley: Alexander Gardner, 1893.

_____, ed. *Popular Tales of the West Highlands: Orally Collected.* London: Alexander Gardner, 1893.

Campbell, John Francis, and George Henderson. *The Celtic Dragon Myth.* Lampeter: Llanerch, 1911.

Campbell, John Francis, and the Scottish Anthropological and Folklore Society. *More West Highland Tales,* Volume 2. Harlow: Oliver and Boyd, 1994.

Campbell, John Gregorson. *Superstitions of the Highlands and Islands of Scotland: Collected Entirely from Oral Sources.* Glasgow: James Maclehose and Sons, 1900.

_____, trans. *Witchcraft and Second Sight in the Highlands and Islands of Scotland: Tales and Traditions Collected Entirely from Oral Sources.* London: J. MacLehose and Sons, 1902.

Campbell, Marie. *Strange World of the Brontës.* Wilmslow, Cheshire: Sigma Leisure, 2001.

Canney, Maurice Arthur. *An Encyclopaedia of Religions.* London: George Routledge and Sons, 1921.

Carlson, Ruth Kearney, ed. *Folklore and Folktales Around the World,* Issues 15–19, 1972.

Carlyle, Thomas. *Essays on the Greater German Poets and Writers.* London: Walter Scott, 1893.

Carta, Dalida. *Djinn Summoning.* Raleigh: Lulu.com, 2008.

Cartwright, Julia. "Undine." *The English Illustrated Magazine,* Volume 4, 298–308. London: Macmillan, 1887.

Cau, Jean, Jacques Laurent Bost, D. Chambry, Nagel Publishers, and Paul Wagret. *Brazil.* Geneva: Nagel, 1979.

Cavallo, Jo Ann. *Boiardo's Orlando Innamorato: An Ethics of Desire.* Madison, NJ: Fairleigh Dickinson University Press, 1993.

Cavanagh, Sheila T. *Wanton Eyes and Chaste Desires: Female Sexuality in the Faerie Queene.* Bloomington: Indiana University Press, 1994.

Cavendish, Richard. *Man, Myth and Magic: An Illustrated Encyclopedia of the Supernatural,* Volume 3. London: Purnell, 1971.

_____. *Man, Myth and Magic: An Illustrated Encyclopedia of the Supernatural,* Volume 4. London: Purnell, 1971.

Chamberlain, Alexander Francis. *The Child and Childhood in Folk Thought (The Child in Primative Culture).* New York: Macmillan, 1895.

Chambers, Robert, ed. *The Book of Days: A Miscellany of Popular Antiquities in Connection with the Calendar, Including Anecdote, Biography and History, Curiosities of Literature, And Oddities of Human Life and Character,* Volume 2. London: W. and R. Chambers, 1888.

Chambers, William, ed. *Chambers's Encyclopaedia: A Dictionary of Universal Knowledge for the People,* Volume 10. Philadelphia: J. B. Lippincott and Company, 1869.

_____, ed. *Chambers's Encyclopaedia: A Dictionary of Universal Knowledge for the People,* Volume 3. London: W. and R. Chambers, 1878.

Chambers, William, and Robert Chambers. *Chambers's Journal,* Volumes 19–20. Edinburg: William and Robert Chambers, 1853.

Chambers 21st Century Dictionary. New Delhi: Allied, 2001.

Chambers's Encyclopaedia: A Dictionary of Universal Knowledge, Volume 3. London: William and Robert Chambers, 1901.

Chandra, Suresh. *Encyclopaedia of Hindu Gods and Goddesses.* New Delhi: Sarup and Sons, 1998.

Chaniótis, Ángelos. *From Minoan Farmers to Roman Traders: Sidelights on the Economy of Ancient Crete.* Stuttgart: Franz Steiner Verlag, 1999.

Chapuis, Oscar. *A History of Vietnam: From Hong Bang to Tu Duc.* Westport, CT: Greenwood, 1995.

Charlesworth, James H. *The Good and Evil Serpent: How a Universal Symbol Became Christianized.* New Haven: Yale University Press, 2010.

Chaucer Geoffrey, and Marijane Osborn. *Romancing the Goddess: Three Middle English Romances about Women.* Urbana: University of Illinois Press, 1998.

Chisholm, Hugh, ed. *The Encyclopedia Americana: A Library of Universal Knowledge,* Volume 10. New York: Encyclopedia Americana Corporation, 1918.

_____, ed. *The Encyclopædia Britannica: A Dictionary of Arts, Sciences, Literature and General Information,* Volume 3. Cambridge: University Press, 1910.

_____, ed. *The Encyclopædia Britannica: A Dictionary of Arts, Sciences, Literature and General Information,* Volume 14. New York: The Encyclopedia Britannica Co., 1910.

_____, ed. *The Encyclopædia Britannica: A Dictionary of Arts, Sciences, Literature and General Information,* Volume 16. New York: The Encyclopedia Britannica Company, 1910.

_____, ed. *The Encyclopædia Britannica: A Dictionary of Arts, Sciences, Literature and General Information,* Volume 19. New York: Cambridge University Press, 1911.

Chopra, Ramesh. *Academic Dictionary of Mythology.* New Delhi: Gyan, 2005.

Choron, Sandra, and Harry Choron. *Planet Dog: A Doglopedia.* New York: Houghton Mifflin Harcourt, 2005.

Cirlot, J. C. *A Dictionary of Symbols.* New York: Philosophical Library, 1971.

Clark, Jerome. *Unexplained! Strange Sightings, Incredible Occurrences and Puzzling Physical Phenomena.* Detroit: Visible Ink Press, 1999.

Clark, Joseph H. *A Classical Manual: Being a Mytholog-*

ical, Historical, and Geographical Commentary on Pope's Homer and Dryden's Aeneid of Virgil. London: John Murray, 1833.

Clarke, James Freeman. *Ten Great Religions: An Essay in Comparative Theology,* Volume 1. Boston: James R. Osgood and Company, 1871.

Classical Association (Great Britain). *The Classical Review,* Volume 12. London: David Nutt, 1898.

Clébert, Jean-Paul. *The Gypsies.* New York: Penguin, 1963.

Clifford, Sir Hugh Charles, and Sir Frank Athelstane Swettenham. *A Dictionary of the Malay Language: Malay-English, Parts 1–4.* Taiping: Government Printing Office, 1894.

Clouston, William Alexander. *Popular Tales and Fictions: Their Migrations and Transformations,* Volume 1. Edinburgh: W. Blackwood and Sons, 1887.

Cobham, E. *Character Sketches of Romance, Fiction and the Drama,* Volume 1. Whitefish, MT: Kessinger, 2004.

_____. *Character Sketches of Romance, Fiction and the Drama,* Volume 4. Whitefish, MT: Kessinger, 2004.

Cohen, Jeffrey Jerome. *Cultural Diversity in the British Middle Ages: Archipelago, Island, England.* London: Macmillan, 2008.

Cohen, Richard. *Chasing the Sun: The Epic Story of the Star That Gives Us Life.* New York: Random House Digital, 2010.

Cohen, Simona. *Animals as Disguised Symbols in Renaissance Art.* Leiden: BRILL, 2008.

Colburn, Henry, and Richard Bently, eds. "A Few Ghosts for Christmas." *The New Monthly Magazine.* Volume 25, 77–80. London: Henry Colburn and Richard Bently, 1829.

Cole, Fay-Cooper. *Traditions of the Tinguian: A Study in Philippine Folklore.* Chicago: Field Museum of Natural History, 1915.

Cole, Robert Eden George. *A Glossary of Words Used In South-West Lincolnshire (Wapentake of Graffoe).* London: Trübner and Company, 1886.

Coleman, Loren, and Jerome Clark. *Cryptozoology A to Z: The Encyclopedia of Loch Monsters, Sasquatch, Chupacabras, and Other Authentic Mysteries of Nature.* New York: Simon & Schuster, 1999.

Collier, John Payne. *A Bibliographical and Critical Account of the Rarest Books in the English Language, Alphabetically Arranged.* New York: David G. Francis, 1866.

Collier, John Payne, and the Percy Society. *The Mad Pranks and Merry Jests of Robin Goodfellow.* London: Percy Society, 1628.

Collignon, Maxime. *Manual of Mythology: In Relation to Greek Art.* London: H. Grevel and Company, 1890.

Columbian Cyclopedia, Volume 20. Buffalo: Garretson, Cox and Company, 1897.

Conner, Nancy. *The Everything Classical Mythology Book: From the Heights of Mount Olympus to the Depths of the Underworld—All You Need to Know About the Classical Myths.* Avon, NA: Everything Books, 2010.

Conti, Natale. *Natale Conti's Mythologiae,* Volume 1. Tempe: ACMRS, 2006

Conti, Natale, John Mulryan, and Steven Brown. *Natale Conti's Mythologiae: Books VI–X.* Tempe: ACMRS, 2006.

Converse, Harriet Maxwell. *Myths and Legends of the New York State Iroquois.* Albany: University of the State of New York, 1908.

Conway, Deanna J. *Magickal Mermaids and Water Creatures: Invoke the Magick of the Waters.* Franklin Lakes, NJ: New Page, 2005.

_____. *Magickal Mystical Creatures: Invite Their Powers Into Your Life.* St. Paul: Llewellyn Worldwide, 2001.

_____. *Maiden, Mother, Crone: The Myth and Reality of the Triple Goddess.* St. Paul: Llewellyn Worldwide, 1994.

_____. *The Mysterious, Magickal Cat.* St. Paul: Llewellyn, 1998.

_____. *Norse Magic.* St. Paul: Llewellyn Worldwide, 1990.

Cook, A. B. "Animal Worship in the Mycenaen Age." *The Journal of Hellenic Studies,* Volume 14, Society for the Promotion of Hellenic Studies (London), eds., 81–169. London: Macmillan, 1894.

Cook, Arthur Bernard. *Zeus: A Study in Ancient Religion,* Volume 1. Cambridge: Cambridge University Press, 1914.

Cambridge. *Zeus: A Study in Ancient Religion,* Volume 2. Cambridge: Cambridge University Press, 1914.

Cambridge. *Zeus: A Study in Ancient Religion,* Volume 3. Cambridge: Cambridge University Press, 1914.

Cooper, Jean C., and Ebenezer Cobham Brewer. *Brewer's Book of Myth and Legend.* Oxford: Helicon, 1993.

Cork Historical and Archaeological Society. *Journal of the Cork Historical and Archaeological Society.* Cork: Cork Historical and Archaeological Society, 1908.

Corsaro, William A. *The Sociology of Childhood.* Thousand Oaks, CA: Pine Forge Press, 2005.

Cotterell, Arthur. *The Macmillan Illustrated Encyclopedia of Myths and Legends.* London: Macmillan, 1989.

Courtney, Margaret Ann. *Cornish Feasts and Folk-Lore.* Penzance: Beare and Son, 1890.

Cowan, David. *Ley Lines and Earth Energies: An Extraordinary Journey into the Earth's Natural Energy System.* Kempton, IL: Adventures Unlimited Press, 2003.

Cowan, James, and the New Zealand Department of Tourist and Publicity. *New Zealand: Or Ao-teä-roa (The Long Bright World): Its Wealth and Resources, Scenery, Travel-Routes, Spas, and Sport.* Wellington: John Mackay, 1908.

Cowan, James. "The Patu-Paiarehe." *Journal of the Polynesian Society,* Volume 30, 142–151. New Plymouth: Polynesian Society, 1921.

Cox, George William. *The Mythology of the Aryan Nations.* London: Keagan Paul, Trench and Company, 1882.

_____. *The Mythology of the Aryan Nations,* Volume 2. London: Longmans, Green, 1870.

_____. *Tales of the Maori.* Auckland: Reed, 1982.

Crabb, George. *The Mythology of All Nations Adapted to the Biblical, Classical and General Reader.* Whitefish, MT: Kessinger, 2006.

Craig, R. D. *Dictionary of Polynesian Mythology.* Westport, CT: Greenwood Press, 1989.

Craig, Robert D. *Handbook of Polynesian Mythology.* Santa Barbara: ABC-CLIO, 2004.

Craigie, Sir William Alexander, translator. *Scandinavian Folk-Lore: Illustrations of the Traditional Beliefs of the Northern Peoplest.* London: Alexander Gardner, 1896.

Cramer, John Anthony. *A Geographical and Historical Description of Asia Minor.* Oxford: Oxford University Press, 1832.

Cramer, Marc. *The Devil Within.* London: W. H. Allen, 1979.

Croker, Thomas Crofton. *Fairy Legends and Traditions*

of the South of Ireland, Volumes 1–3. London: John Murray, 1828.

Crooke, William. *The Popular Religion and Folk-Lore of Northern India*, Volume 2. Westminster: Archibald Constable and Company, 1896.

_____, ed. *North Indian Notes and Queries*, Volumes 1–2. Allahabad: Pioneer Press, 1891.

Crooke, William, and Reginald Edward Enthoven. *Religion and Folklore of Northern India*. Oxford: Oxford University Press, H. Milford, 1926.

Crossley-Holland, Kevin. *The Norse Myths*. New York: Random House Digital, 1981.

Crudden, Michael. *The Homeric Hymns*. Oxford: Oxford University Press, 2002.

Cumberland, Clark. *Shakespeare and the Supernatural*. New York: Haskell House, 1931.

Cumming, Joseph George. *A Guide to the Isle of Man*. London: Edward Stanford and Sons, 1861.

Cunliffe, Henry. *A Glossary of Rochdale-With-Rossendale Words and Phrases*. London: John Heywood, 1886.

Cunningham, Scott. *Cunningham's Encyclopedia of Magical Herbs*. St. Paul: Llewellyn Worldwide, 2000.

Curran, Bob. *Celtic Lore and Legend: Meet the Gods, Heroes, Kings, Fairies, Monsters, and Ghosts of Yore*. Franklin Lakes, NJ: New Page, 2005.

_____. *Mysterious Celtic Mythology in American Folklore*. Gretna, LA: Pelican, 2010.

Curran, Bob, and Andrew Whitson. *A Field Guide to Irish Fairies*. San Francisco: Chronicle, 1998.

Curran, Bob, and eBook Architects, LLC. *Dark Fairies*. New York: Open Road Media, 2012.

Currie, Stephen. *Goblins*. San Diego: Capstone Press, 2011.

Curtin, Jeremiah. *Hero-Tales of Ireland*. Boston: Little, Brown, 1894.

Custer, Stewart. *A Treasury of New Testament Synonyms*. Greenville, SC: Bob Jones University Press, 1975.

da Cherda, Macc. "Mythology of Finnland." *The Eclectic Magazine of Foreign Literature, Science, and Art*, Volume 42, W. H. Bidwell, ed., 354–66. New York: Leavitt, Trow, and Company, 1857.

Dalby, Andrew. *Bacchus: A Biography*. Los Angeles: Getty, 2004.

_____. *The Story of Venus*. London: British Museum, 2005.

Daly, Kathleen N., and Marian Rengel. *Greek and Roman Mythology A to Z*. New York: Infobase, 2009.

_____, and _____. *Norse Mythology A to Z*. New York: Infobase, 2009.

D'Amato-Neff. Adam L. *Book of Clouds: A Handbook for Practitioners of the Pagan*. Lincoln: iUniverse, 2002.

Daniel, Antoine B., and Alex Gilly. *Incas: The Light of Machu Picchu*. New York: Simon & Schuster, 2003.

Daniels, Cora Linn, and C. M. Stevans, eds. *Encyclopedia of Superstitions, Folklore, and the Occult Sciences of the World*. Doral, FA: The Minerva Group, 2003.

_____, and _____, editors. *Encyclopaedia of Superstitions, Folklore, and the Occult Sciences of the World: A Comprehensive Library of Human Belief and Practice in the Mysteries of Life*, Volume 2. Chicago: J. H. Yewdale and Sons, 1903.

_____, and _____. *Encyclopedia of Superstitions, Folklore, and the Occult Sciences of the World*, Volume 3. Doral: The Minerva Group, Inc., 2003.

D'Arras, Jean. *Melusine*. London: Kegan Paul, Trench, Tribner and Company, 1895.

Dasent, George Webbe. *The Orkneyingers Saga: And Other Historical Documents Relating to the Settlements and Descents of the Northmen on the British Isles*. Charleston, SC: Forgotten Books, 2008.

Datlow, Ellen, and Terri Windling. *The Green Man: Tales from the Mythic Forest*. New York: Viking, 2001.

Davidson, Gustav. *A Dictionary of Angels: Including the Fallen Angels*. New York: Free Press, 1971.

Davidson, Hilda Ellis. *Roles of the Northern Goddess*. London: Psychology Press, 1998.

Davis, Frederick Hadland. *Myths and Legends of Japan*. New York: Cosimo, 2007.

Davis, William S. *Life in Elizabethan Days*. New York: Biblo and Tannen, 1988.

Day, John. *God's Conflict with the Dragon and the Sea: Echoes of a Canaanite Myth in the Old Testament*. Cambridge: CUP Archive, 1985.

de Almeida, Livia, Ana Portella, and Margaret Read MacDonald. *Brazilian Folktales*. Westport, CT: Libraries Unlimited, 2006.

de Claremont, Lewis. *The Ancient's Book of Magic: Containing Secret Records of the Procedure and Practice of the Ancient Masters and Adepts 1940*. Whitefish, MT: Kessinger, 2004.

de Jubainville, Henry Arbois. *The Irish Mythological Cycle and Celtic Mythology*. Paris: Hodges, Figgis, 1903.

de Vere, Nicholas. *The Dragon Legacy: The Secret History of an Ancient Bloodline*. San Diego: Book Tree, 2004.

De Walsh, Faust Charles. *Grillparzer as a Poet of Nature*. New York: Columbia University Press, 1910.

Deck-Partyka, Alicja. *Poland, a Unique Country and Its People*. Bloomington: AuthorHouse, 2006.

Dégh, Linda, and Harry Gammerdinger. *Folklore on Two Continents: Essays in Honor of Linda Dégh*. Bloomington: Trickster Press, 1980.

Degidon, N. F. "As the Sun Went Down." *New Catholic World*, Volume 85, Paulest Fathers, ed., 98–102. New York: Office of the Catholic World, 1907.

Dekirk, Ash. *Dragonlore: From the Archives of the Grey School of Wizardry*. Franklin Lakes, NJ: New Page Books, 2006.

Del Re, Gerard, and Patricia Del Re. *The Christmas Almanack*. New York: Random House Reference, 2004.

Demetrio, Francisco R. *Encyclopedia of Philippine Folk Beliefs and Customs*, Volume 2. Cincinnati: Xavier University Press, 1991.

_____. *Myths and Symbols, Philippines*. Manila: National Book Store, 1981.

Denham, Michael Aislabie. *The Denham Tracts: A Collection Of Folklore: Reprinted From the Original Tracts and Pamphlets Printed by Mr. Denham Between 1846 and 1859*, Volume 2. London: David Nutt, 1895.

Devereux, George. *Dreams in Greek Tragedy: An Ethno-Psycho-Analytical Study*. Berkeley: University of California Press, 1976.

Dewdney, Christopher. *Acquainted with the Night: Excursions Through the World After Dark*. New York: Bloomsbury USA, 2005.

Dexter, Miriam Robbins. *Whence the Goddesses: A Source Book*. New York: Pergamon Press, 1990.

Di Lauro, Frances. *Through a Glass Darkly: Collected Research*. Sydney: Sydney University Press, 2006.

Dibbley, Dale Corey. *From Achilles' Heel to Zeus's Shield*. New York: Fawcett Columbine, 1993.

Dixon-Kennedy, Mike. *Encyclopedia of Greco-Roman Mythology*. Santa Barbara: ABC-CLIO, 1998.

_____. *Encyclopedia of Russian and Slavic Myth and Legend*. Santa Barbara: ABC-CLIO, 1998.

Dömötör, Tekla. *Hungarian Folk Beliefs*, Volume 1981. Bloomington: Indiana University Press, 1982.

Dorson, Richard Mercer. *Peasant Customs and Savage Myths: Selections from the British Folklorists*, Volume 1. Chicago: University of Chicago Press, 1969.

Doty, W. G. *Mythosphere*. Issue 4. New York: Taylor & Francis United States, 2000.

Douglas, Sir George. *Scottish Fairy Tales*. Whitefish, MT: Kessinger, 2006.

_____. *Scottish Fairy Tales, Folklore, and Legends*. London: Gibbings, 1902.

Dow, Joseph A. *Ancient Coins Through the Bible*. Mustang, OK: Tate, 2011.

Dowden, Ken. *Death and the Maiden: Girls' Initiation Rites in Greek Mythology*. London: Routledge, 1989.

Dowden, Ken, and Niall Livingstone. *A Companion to Greek Mythology*. West Sussex: John Wiley and Sons, 2011.

Dowe, William. "A Talk About the Fairies." *Sharpe's London Magazine: A Journal of Entertainment and Instruction*, Anna Maria Hall, ed., 10–16. London: Virtue, Hall and Virtue, 1849.

Drew, A. J. *A Wiccan Bible: Exploring the Mysteries of the Craft from Birth to Summerland*. Franklin Lakes, NJ: New Page Books, 2003.

Dronke, Ursula. *The Poetic Edda: Mythological Poems*. Oxford: Clarendon Press, 1997.

Drury, Nevill. *The Dictionary of the Esoteric: 3000 Entries on the Mystical and Occult Traditions*. Delhi: Motilal Banarsidass, 2004.

Du Chaillu, Paul Belloni. *The Viking Age: The Early History, Manners, and Customs of the Ancestors of the English-Speaking Nations. Illustrated from the Antiquities Discovered in Mounds, Cairns, and Bogs as Well as from the Ancient Sagas and Eddas*. Volume 1. Boston: Adamant Media, 1889.

Dumont, Jean-Paul. *Visayan Vignettes: Ethnographic Traces of a Philippine Island*. Chicago: University of Chicago Press, 1992.

Duncan, Barbara R., and Davey Arch. *Living Stories of the Cherokee*. Chapel Hill: University of North Carolina Press, 1998.

Duncan, Thomas Shearer. *The Influence of Art on Description in the Poetry of P. Papinius Statius*. Balitmore: J.H. Furst, 1914.

Dunham, Samuel Astley. *History of Denmark, Sweden, and Norway*, Volume 2. London: Longman, Orme, Brown, Green and Longmans and John Taylor, 1839.

Dunlop, John Colin, and Henry Wilson. *History of Prose Fiction*, Volume 1. London: George Bell and Sons, 1906.

Dunwich, Gerina. *Witch's Halloween: A Complete Guide to the Magick, Incantations, Recipes, Spells, and Lore*. Avon, MA, Adams Media, 2007.

Dutt, William Alfred. *Highways and Byways in East Anglia*. London: Macmillian, 1901.

Dyer, T. F. Thiselton. *Folklore of Shakespeare*. Whitefish, MT: Kessinger, 2004.

Eason, Cassandra. *A Complete Guide to Faeries and Magical Beings: Explore the Mystical Realm of the Little People*. Boston: Weiser, 2002.

_____. *Fabulous Creatures, Mythical Monsters, and Animal Power Symbols: A Handbook*. Westport, CT: Greenwood, 2008.

_____. *The Mammoth Book of Ancient Wisdom*. London: Robinson, 1997.

_____. *Scrying the Secrets of the Future: How to Use Crystal Balls, Water, Fire, Wax, Mirrors, Shadows, and Spirit Guides to Reveal Your Destiny*. Franklin Lakes, NJ: New Page Books, 2007.

Eberhart, George M. *Mysterious Creatures: A Guide to Cryptozoology*, Volume 1. Santa Barbara: ABC-CLIO, 2002.

Eco, Umberto. *The Infinity of Lists: An Illustrated Essay*. New York: Rizzoli, 2009.

Edel, May Mandelbaum. *The Chiga of Uganda*. New Brunswick: Transaction, 1996.

Edinburgh Geological Society. *Transactions of the Edinburgh Geological Society*, Volume 4. Edinburgh: Turnbull and Spears, 1883.

Edwards, Elizabeth, and Kaushik Bhaumik. *Visual Sense: A Cultural Reader*. New York: Berg, 2008.

Edwards, Gillian Mary. *Hobgoblin and Sweet Puck: Fairy Names and Natures*. London: Bles, 1974.

Elliott, A. Marshal, Johns Hopkins University, and JSTOR, eds. *Modern Language Notes*, Volume 16. Baltimore: Johns Hopkins Press, 1901.

Ellis, Peter Berresford. *Celtic Myths and Legends*. New York: Carroll & Graf, 1999.

_____. *The Chronicles of the Celts: New Tellings of their Myths and Legends*. London: Robinson, 1999.

Elsie, Robert. *A Dictionary of Albanian Religion, Mythology, and Folk Culture*. New York: New York University Press, 2000.

_____. *A Dictionary of Albanian Religion, Mythology, and Folk Culture*. New York: New York University Press, 2001.

Elworthy, Frederick Thomas. *The Evil Eye: An Account of this Ancient and Widespread Superstition*. Mineola, NY: Courier Dover, 2004.

Emick, Jennifer. *The Everything Celtic Wisdom Book: Find Inspiration Through Ancient Traditions, Rituals, and Spirituality*. Avon, MA: Everything Books, 2009.

Emoto, Masaru. *The Healing Power of Water*. Carlsbad, CA: Hay House, 2008.

Encyclopaedia Britannica, or Dictionary of Arts, Sciences, and General Literature, Volume 16, Issue 1.Edinburgh: Adam and Charles Black, 1842.

Endsjø, Dag Øistein. *Greek Resurrection Beliefs and the Success of Christianity*. New York: Macmillan, 2009.

Euvino, Gabrielle, and Michael San Filippo. *The Complete Idiot's Guide to Italian History and Culture*. New York: Penguin, 2001.

Evans, Cheryl, and Anna Millard. *Greek and Norse Legends*. Tulsa: EDC, 2003.

Evans, Sir John. *The Ancient Stone Implements, Weapons and Ornaments of Great Britain*. London: Longmans, Green, 1897.

Evans, Thomas Christopher. *History of Llangynwyd Parish*. Llanelly: Llanelly and County Guardian Office, 1887.

Evans-Wentz, W. Y. *The Fairy-Faith in Celtic Countries*. Mineola, NY: Courier Dover, 2003.

_____. *The Fairy Faith in Celtic Countries: The Classic Study of Leprechauns, Pixies, and Other Fairy Spirits*. New York: Citadel Press, 1994.

Facaros, Dana, and Michael Pauls. *Greek Islands*, 9th ed. London: New Holland, 2007.

Falkner, David E. *The Mythology of the Night Sky: An Amateur Astronomer's Guide to the Ancient Greek and Roman Legends*. New York: Springer, 2011.

Falkner, Thomas. *A Description of Patagonia and the Adjoining parts of South America*. New York: AMS Press, 1976.

Faron, L. C. *Hawks of the Sun: Mapuche Morality and Its Ritual Attributes.* Pittsburgh: University of Pittsburgh Press, 1964.

Farrell, Joseph. *Vergil's Georgics and the Traditions of Ancient Epic: The Art of Allusion in Literary History.* Oxford: Oxford University Press, 1991.

Faulkes, Anthony, ed. *Edda: Prologue and Gylfaginning.* Oxford: Clarendon Press, 1982.

Fenster, Thelma. *Arthurian Women: A Casebook.* New York: Psychology Press, 1996.

Fergusson, Erna. *Chile.* New York: A. A. Knopf, 1943.

Fergusson, Robert Menzies. *Rampling Sketches in the Far North, and Orcadian Musings.* London: Alexander Gardner, 1884.

Figal, Gerald A. *Civilization and Monsters: Spirits of Modernity in Meiji Japan.* Durham: Duke University Press, 1999.

Finley, Carol. *Aboriginal Art of Australia: Exploring Cultural Traditions.* Minneapolis: Lerner, 1999.

Fish, Lydia M. *The Folklore of the Coal Miners of the Northeast of England.* Norwood, PA: Norwood Editions, 1975.

Fisher, Teresa. *National Geographic Traveler Switzerland.* Washington, D.C.: National Geographic Books, 2012.

Folk-Lore and Legends: Scandinavian. Whitefish, MT: Kessinger, 2006.

Folk-Lore and Legends: Scotland. Teddington, Middlesex: Echo Library, 2006.

Folkard, Jr., Richard. *Plant Lore, Legends, and Lyrics: Embracing the Myths, Traditions, Superstitions, and Folk-Lore of the Plant Kingdom.* London: Sampson Low, Marston, Searle, and Rivington, 1884.

Folklore Society (Great Britain). *County Folk-Lore*, Volume 37. Lincolnshire: Folk-Lore Society, 1908.

_____. *The Folk-Lore Journal*, Volume 6. London: Published for the Folk-lore Society, by Elliot Stock, 1888.

Fontenrose, Joseph Eddy. *Orion: The Myth of the Hunter and the Huntress.* Berkley: University of California Press, 1981.

_____. *Python: A Study of Delphic Myth and Its Origins.* Berkley: University of California Press, 1959.

Fontenrose, Joseph. *Didyma: Apollo's Oracle, Cult, and Companions.* Berkley: University of California Press, 1988.

Ford, Michael. *Luciferian Witchcraft.* Raleigh: Lulu.com, 2005.

Forde, Cyril Daryll, Wendy James, and the International African Institute. *African Worlds: Studies in the Cosmological Ideas and Social Values of African Peoples, Classics in African Anthropology.* Hamburg: LIT Verlag Berlin-Hamburg-Münster, 1999.

Forlong, James George Roche. *Faiths of Man: A Cyclopædia of Religions.* London: Benard Quaritch, 1906.

Forth, Gregory L. *Images of the Wildman in Southeast Asia: An Anthropological Perspective.* New York: Taylor & Francis, 2008.

Foubister, Linda. *Goddess in the Grass: Serpentine Mythology and the Great Goddess.* Victoria, British Columbia: Ecce Nova Editions, 2003.

Fowke, Edith. *Canadian Folklore.* Oxford: Oxford University Press, 1988.

Fowler, Barbara Hughes. *Archaic Greek Poetry: An Anthology.* Madison: University of Wisconsin Press, 1992.

Fox, William Sherwood. *Greek and Roman [mythology].* Boston: Marshall Jones Company, 1916.

Foxhall, Lin. *When Men Were Men: Masculinity, Power and Identity in Classical Antiquity.* London: Psychology Press, 1999.

Francillon, Robert Edward. *Gods and Heroes, or, The Kingdom of Jupiter.* Boston: Ginn and Company, 1894.

Franklin, Anna. *Working with Fairies: Magick, Spells, Potions and Recipes to Attract and See Them.* Franklin Lakes, NJ: New Page Books, 2005.

Fraser, Robert William. *Turkey, Ancient and Modern: A History of the Ottoman Empire from the Period of its Establishment to the Present Time.* Edingurgh: A. and C. Black, 1854.

Frater, Jamie. *Listverse.Com's Ultimate Book of Bizarre Lists: Fascinating Facts and Shocking Trivia on Movies, Music, Crime, Celebrities, History, and More.* Brooklyn: Ulysses Press, 2010.

Frazer, Sir James George. *Folk-Lore in the Old Testament.* London: Macmillan, 1919.

_____. *The Golden Bough: A Study in Magic and Religion.* Charleston, SC: Forgotten Books, 1922.

Freeman, Edward Augustus. *The History of Sicily from the Earliest Times.* Oxford: Clarendon Press, 1891.

Freyre, Gilberto. *The Masters and the Slaves.* Berkeley: University of California Press, 1986.

Friend, Hilderic. *Flowers and Flower-Lore.* London: W. Swan Sonnenschein, 1884.

Fritz, Jean. *The Good Giants and the Bad Pukwudgies.* New York: G.P. Putnam's Sons, 1982.

Froud, Brian, and Alan Lee. *Faeries.* New York: Harry N. Abrams, 1978.

Fujii, Daryl. *The Neuropsychology of Asian-Americans.* New York: Psychology Press, 2010.

Gale, Albert, and Fay-Cooper Cole. *The Tinguian: Social, Religious, and Economic Life of a Philippine Tribe.* Chicago: Chicago Natural History Museum, 1922.

Gall, Timothy L., and Susan B. Gall. *The Lincoln Library of Greek and Roman Mythology.* Cleveland: Lincoln Library Press, 2006.

Gan, Bao, Kenneth J. DeWoskin, and J. I. Crump, Jr., trans. *In Search of the Supernatural: The Written Record.* Palo Alto: Stanford University Press, 1996.

Gantz, Timothy. *Early Greek Myth: A Guide to Literary and Artistic Sources.* Baltimore: Johns Hopkins University Press, 1993.

Gardner, Edmund Garratt. *Arthurian Legend in Italian Literature.* Whitefish, MT: Kessinger, 2003.

Gardner, James. *Faiths of the World*, Part 2. Whitefish, MT: Kessinger, 2003.

Gardner, Percy. "Countries and Cities in Ancient Art." *The Journal of Hellenic Studies, Volume 9*, Society for the Promotion of Hellenic Studies (London), eds., 47–82. London: Macmillan, 1888.

Garland, Robert. *Introducing New Gods: The Politics of Athenian Religion.* Ithaca: Cornell University Press, 1992.

Garza, Xavier. *Creepy Creatures and Other Cucuys.* Houston: Arte Público Press, 2004.

Geddie, William. *Chambers's Encyclopaedia: Dictionary of Universal Knowledge for the People*, Volume 7. Edinburgh: W. and R. Chambers, 1874.

Geertz, Clifford. *The Religion of Java.* Chicago: University of Chicago Press, 1976.

Gentry, Francis G. *The Nibelungen Tradition: An Encyclopedia.* London: Psychology Press, 2002.

Gerber, Douglas E. *Greek Iambic Poetry: From the Seventh to the Fifth Centuries BC.* New Haven: Harvard University Press, 1999.

Gerwig, Henrietta. *Crowell's Handbook for Readers and Writers: A Dictionary of Famous Characters and Plots in Legend, Fiction, Drama, Opera and Poetry, Together with Dates and Principal Works of Important Authors, Literary and Journalistic Terms, and Familiar Allusions*. New York: Thomas Y. Crowell, 1925.

Gibb, Sir Hamilton Alexander Rosskeen, Johannes Hendrik Kramers, and Koninklijke Nederlandse Akademie van Wetenschappen. *Shorter Encyclopaedia of Islam*. Leiden: E. J. Brill, 1961.

Gigante, Marcello. *Philodemus in Italy: The Books from Herculaneum*. Ann Arbor: University of Michigan Press, 2002.

Gilchrist, Cherry. *Russian Magic: Living Folk Traditions of an Enchanted Landscape*. Wheaton, IL: Quest, 2009.

Gilman, Daniel Coit, Harry Thurston Peck, and Frank Moore Colby, eds. *The New International Encyclopædia*, Volume 5. New York: Dodd, Mead, 1907.

Gimbutas, Marija, and Miriam Robbins Dexter. *The Living Goddesses*. Berkeley: University of California Press, 2001.

Ginswick, Jules. *Labour and the Poor in England and Wales 1849–1851: Northumberland and Durham, Staffordshire, the Midlands*. London: Frank Cass, 1983.

Glover, Matthew. *Glover's Illustrated Guide and Visitors' Companion Through the Isle of Man: With Sea and Trout Fishing*. London: Matthew Glover, 1873.

Godfrey, Linda S., and Rosemary Ellen Guiley. *Mythical Creatures*. New York: Infobase, 2009.

Gomme, George Laurence. *A Dictionary of British Folklore*. London: David Nutt, 1898.

Gordon, Seton Paul. *Highways and Byways in the Central Highlands*. London: Macmillan, 1949.

Gordon, Seton Paul, and William John Watson. *Highways and Byways in the West Highlands*. London: Macmillan, 1935.

Gorrell, Robert M. *What's in a Word? Etymological Gossip About Some Interesting English Words*. Reno: University of Nevada Press, 2001.

Gould, S. C., ed. *Historic Magazine and Notes and Queries: A Monthly of History, Folk-Lore, Mathematics, Literature, Art, Arcane Societies, Etc*, Volume 14, Number 9. Manchester: S. C. and L. M. Gould, 1896.

Grahame, Walter. *Stories about Number Nip: The Spirit of the Giant Mountains*. London: Chatto and Windus, 1881.

Grant, Michael, and John Hazel. *Gods and Mortals in Classical Mythology*. Springfield, MA: G. and C. Merriam Company, 1973.

_____, and _____. *Who's Who in Classical Mythology*. London: Psychology Press, 2002.

Graves, Robert. *The Greek Myths: Classics Deluxe Edition*. New York: Penguin, 2012.

_____. *The Larousse Encyclopedia of Mythology*. New York: Barnes & Noble, 1994.

Gray, Louis Herbert. *The Mythology of All Races*, Volume 2. Boston: Marshall Jones Company, 1964.

_____. *The Mythology of All Races*, Volume 3. Boston: Marshall Jones Company, 1964.

Gray, Louis Herbert, George Foot Moore, and John Arnott MacCulloch. *The Mythology of All Races*, Volume 3. Boston: Marshall Jones Company, 1918.

_____, _____, and _____. *The Mythology of All Races*, Volume 4. Boston: Marshall Jones Company, 1918.

_____, _____, and _____. *The Mythology of All Races*, Volume 10. Boston: Marshall Jones Company, 1916.

_____, _____, and _____. *The Mythology of All Races*, Volume 12. Boston: Marshall Jones Company, 1918.

_____, _____, and _____. *The Mythology of All races*, Volume 17. Boston: Marshall Jones Company, 1925.

_____, _____, and _____. *The Mythology of All Races*, Chinese, by J. C. Ferguson. Japanese, by M. Anesaki, Volume 8. New York: Cooper Square, 1964.

Green, Jonathon. *Cassell's Dictionary of Slang*. London: Sterling, 2005.

Green, Miranda. *Animals in Celtic Life and Myth*. New York: Routledge, 1998.

Greene, Liz, and Juliet Sharman-Burke. *The Mythic Journey: The Meaning of Myth as a Guide for Life*. London: Eddison-Sadd, 2000.

Greer, John Michael. *The New Encyclopedia of the Occult*. St. Paul: Llewellyn Worldwide, 2003.

Gregory, Lady. *Gods and Fighting Men: The Story of the Tuatha de Danaan and of the Fianna of Ireland*. Charleston, SC: Forgotten Books, 1976.

Gregory, Lady, Finn MacCumhaill, and William Butler Yeats. *Gods and Fighting Men: The Story of Tuatha de Danann and of the Fianna of Ireland*. London: John Murray, 1905.

Greimas, Algirdas Julien. *Of Gods and Men: Studies in Lithuanian Mythology*. Bloomington: Indiana University Press, 1992.

Grey, Sir George. *Maori Lore: The Traditions of the Maori People, with the more Important of their Legends*. Wellington: J. Mackay, 1904.

Grimal, Pierre. *The Dictionary of Classical Mythology*. Malden, MA: Wiley-Blackwell, 1996.

_____. *Larousse World Mythology*. New York: Hamlyn, 1973.

Grimassi, Raven. *Encyclopedia of Wicca and Witchcraft*. St. Paul: Llewellyn Worldwide, 2000.

_____. *Hereditary Witchcraft: Secrets of the Old Religion*. St. Paul: Llewellyn Worldwide, 1999.

Grimes, Heilan Yvette. *The Norse Myths*. Boston: Heilan Yvette Grimes, 2010.

Grimm, Jacob. *Deutsche Mythologie*. Gottingen: In der Dieterichschen Buchhandlung, 1835.

_____. *Grimm's Goblins, Grimm's Household Stories, Translated by E. Taylor*. London: R. Meek and Company, 1876.

_____. *Teutonic Mythology*, Volume 1. London: George Bell, 1882.

_____. *Teutonic Mythology*, Volume 2. London: George Bell, 1882.

_____. *Teutonic Mythology*, Volume 3. London: George Bell, 1888.

_____. *Teutonic Mythology*, Volume 4. London: George Bell, 1888.

Grimm, Jacob, and Wilhelm Grimm. *The German Legends of the Brothers Grimm*, Volume 1. Philadelphia: Institute for the Study of Human Issues, 1981.

_____, and _____. *Grimm's Fairy Tales*. New York: Merrill, 1903.

Grote, George. *A History of Greece from the Earliest Period to the Close of the Generation Contemporary with Alexander the Great*, Volume 1. New York: Harper & Brothers, 1858.

_____. *History of Greece*, Volume 2. London: John Murray, 1859.

Gudgeon, Lt. Col. "Maori Superstitions." *The Journal of the Polynesian Society*, Volume 14. The Polynesian Society, New Zealand, eds., 167–199. Wellington: The Polynesian Society, 1906.

Guelden, Marlane. *Thailand into the Spirit World.* Singapore: Times Editions, 1995.

Guerber, Hélène Adeline. *Hammer of Thor—Norse Mythology and Legends—Special Edition.* El Paso: El Paso Norte Press, 2010.

_____. *Legends of the Middle Ages: Narrated with Special Reference to Literature and Art.* New York: American Book Company, 1896.

Guiley, Rosemary. *The Encyclopedia of Angels.* New York: Infobase, 2004.

_____. *The Encyclopedia of Magic and Alchemy.* New York: Infobase, 2006.

_____. *An Encyclopedia of Vampires, Werewolves and other Monsters.* New York: Checkmark, 2004.

_____. *The Encyclopedia of Witches, Witchcraft and Wicca.* New York: Infobase, 2008.

Guiley, Rosemary Ellen, and John Zaffis. *The Encyclopedia of Demons and Demonology.* New York: Infobase, 2009.

Guiney, Louise Imogen. *Brownies and Bogles.* Boston: D. Lothrop, 1888.

Guirand, Félix. *New Larousse Encyclopedia of Mythology.* New York: Hamlyn, 1968.

Guthrie, William Keith Chambers. *The Greeks and Their Gods.* Boston: Beacon Press, 1955.

Gwynn, Stephen Lucius. *The Fair Hills of Ireland.* London: Maunsel, 1914.

Haase, Donald. *The Greenwood Encyclopedia of Folktales and Fairy Tales.* Westport, CT: Greenwood, 2008.

Haining, Peter. *Ghosts: The Illustrated History.* London: Macmillan, 1975.

Hall, Alaric. *Elves in Anglo-Saxon England: Matters of Belief, Health, Gender and Identity.* Woodbridge, Suffolk: Boydell Press, 2007.

Hall, Granville Stanley. *The Pedagogical Seminary*, Volume 10. Worcester, MA: Clark University Press, 1903.

Hall, Manly P. *The Secret Teachings of All Ages: An Encyclopedic Outline of Masonic, Hermetic, Qabbalistic, and Rosicrucian Symbolical Philosophy.* Charleston, SC: Forgotten Books, 1928.

Hall, S. C. *The Book of South Wales, the Wye, and the Coast.* London: Arthur Hall, Virtue, 1861.

Halliday, William Reginald. *Greek Divination: A Study of its Methods and Principles.* London: Macmillan, 1913.

Halliwell, John Orchard. *A Dictionary of Archaic and Provincial Words: Obsolete Phrases, Proverbs and Ancient Customs from the Fourteenth Century J-Z*, Volume 2. Whitefish, MT: Kessinger, 2006.

Hamilton, A., ed., and the New Zealand Institute (Wellington), Royal Society of New Zealand. *Transactions of the Royal Society of New Zealand*, Volume 37. Wellington: John Mackay, 1905.

Hamilton, Duncan. *Am Bratach Sith of Dunvegan.* Bloomington: AuthorHouse, 2008.

Hamilton, John. *Ogres and Giants.* Edina, MN: ABDO, 2004.

Hamlin, Marie Caroline Watson, and James Valentine Campbell. *Legends of Le Détroit.* Detroit: Thorndike Nourse, 1883.

Hankins, John Erskine. *Source and Meaning in Spenser's Allegory: A Study of The Faerie Queene.* Oxford: Clarendon Press, 1971.

Hansen, William F. *Handbook of Classical Mythology.* Santa Barbara: ABC-CLIO, 2004.

Hansen, William, and William F. Hansen. *Classical Mythology: A Guide to the Mythical World of the Greeks and Romans.* Oxford: Oxford University Press, 2005.

Hard, Robin. *The Library of Greek Mythology.* Oxford: Oxford University Press, 2008.

_____. *The Routledge Handbook of Greek Mythology: Based on H.J. Rose's "Handbook of Greek Mythology."* London: Psychology Press, 2004.

Hardiman, John Percy. *Gazetteer of Upper Burma and the Shan States*, Part 1, Volume 2. Rangoon: The Superintendent, Government Printing, Burma, 1900.

Hardwick, Charles. *Traditions, Superstitions, and Folklore: Chiefly Lancashire and the North of England: Their Affinity to Others in Widely-distributed Localities; Their Eastern Origin and Mythical Significance.* London: Simpkin, Marshall, 1872.

Harland, John. *A Glossary of Words Used in Swaledale, Yorkshire*, Volume 4, Issue 1. London: Trübner and Company, 1876.

Harpur, Patrick. *The Philosophers' Secret Fire: A History of the Imagination.* Victoria, Australia: Blue Angel Gallery, 2007.

Harrison, Constance Burton. *Bric-A-Brac Stories.* New York: Charles Scribner's Sons, 1885.

Harrison, Jane Ellen. *Mythology.* Whitefish, MT: Kessinger, 2006.

Hartland, Edwin Sidney. *English Fairy and Folk Tales.* Whitefish, MT: Kessinger, 2006.

_____. *Mythology and Folktales: Their Relation and Interpretation*, Volume 7. New York: AMS Press, 1900.

_____, ed. *English Fairy and Other Folk Tales.* Charleston, SC: Forgotten Books.

_____, ed. *Gloucestershire.* London: David Nutt, 1895.

Harvey, Paul B., and Celia E. Schultz. *Religion in Republican Italy.* Cambridge: Cambridge University Press, 2006.

Hastings, James, ed. *Encyclopedia of Religion and Ethics*, Part 1. Whitefish, MT: Kessinger, 2003.

_____, ed. *Encyclopedia of Religion and Ethics*, Part 5. Whitefish, MT: Kessinger, 2003.

_____, ed. *Encyclopedia of Religion and Ethics*, Part 6. Whitefish, MT: Kessinger, 2003.

_____, ed. *Encyclopedia of Religion and Ethics*, Part 7. Whitefish, MT: Kessinger, 2003.

_____, ed. *Encyclopedia of Religion and Ethics*, Part 8. Whitefish, MT: Kessinger, 2003.

_____, ed. *Encyclopedia of Religion and Ethics*, Part 9. Whitefish, MT: Kessinger, 2003.

_____, ed. *Encyclopedia of Religion and Ethics*, Part 10. Whitefish, MT: Kessinger, 2003.

_____, ed. *Encyclopedia of Religion and Ethics*, Part 11. Whitefish, MT: Kessinger, 2003.

_____, ed. *Encyclopedia of Religion and Ethics*, Part 12. Whitefish, MT: Kessinger, 2003.

_____, ed. *Encyclopedia of Religion and Ethics*, Part 23. Whitefish, MT: Kessinger, 2003.

_____, ed. *Encyclopedia of Religion and Ethics*, Part 24. Whitefish, MT: Kessinger, 2003.

_____, ed. *Encyclopedia of Religion and ethics*, Volumes 3–4. New York: Scribner, 1951.

Hastings, James, John Alexander Selbie, and Louis Herbert Gray, eds. *Encyclopaedia of Religion and Ethics*, Volume 3. New York: Scribner, 1951.

_____, _____, and _____, eds. *Encyclopædia of Religion and Ethics*, Volume 7. Edinburgh: T. and T. Clark, 1917.

_____, _____, and _____, eds. *Encyclopædia of Religion and Ethics*, Volume 8. Edinburgh: T. and T. Clark, 1917.

_____, _____, and _____, eds. *Encyclopædia of Religion and Ethics*, Volume 9. Edinburgh: T. and T. Clark, 1917.

_____, _____, and _____, eds. *Encyclopædia of Religion and Ethics*, Volume 12. Edinburgh: T. and T. Clark, 1917.

Hathaway, Nancy. *The Friendly Guide to Mythology: A Mortal's Companion to the Fantastical Realm of Gods, Goddesses, Monsters, and Heroes.* New York: Penguin, 2003.

Haugen, Einar Ingvald. *Language and Its Ecology: Essays in Memory of Einar Haugen.* Chicago: de Gruyter, 1997.

Haughton, Brian. *Famous Ghost Stories: Legends and Lore.* New York: Rosen, 2011.

_____. *Hidden History: Lost Civilizations, Secret Knowledge, and Ancient Mysteries.* Franklin Lakes, NJ: New Page Books, 2007.

Haughton, Rosemary. *Tales from Eternity: The World of Fairytales and the Spiritual Search.* New York: Seabury Press, 1973.

Hausman, Gerald, and Loretta Hausman. *The Mythology of Horses: Horse Legend and Lore throughout the Ages.* New York: Random House Digital, 2003.

Havens, Lorena, and Steve Rogers. *The People's Guide to Mexico.* Emeryville, CA: Avalon Travel, 2006.

Hay, M. Cameron. *Remembering to Live: Illness at the Intersection of Anxiety and Knowledge in Rural Indonesia.* Ann Arbor: University of Michigan Press, 2004.

Hazlitt, William Carew, and John Brand. *Faiths and Folklore: A Dictionary of National Beliefs, Superstitions and Popular Customs, Past and Current, with Their Classical and Foreign Analogues, Described and Illustrated,* Volume 2. London: Reeves and Turner, 1905.

Head, Barclay Vincent. *Historia Numorum: A Manual of Greek Numismatics.* Oxford: Spink, 1963.

Hearn, Lafcadio, Grace James, and Basil Hall Chamberlain. *Japanese Fairy Tales.* New York: Boni and Liveright, 1918.

Heath, Jennifer. *The Echoing Green: The Garden in Myth and Memory.* New York: Plume, 2000.

Heckman, Andrea M. *Woven Stories: Andean Textiles And Rituals.* Albuquerque: University of New Mexico Press, 2003.

Helms, Mary W. *Creations of the Rainbow Serpent: Polychrome Ceramic Designs from Ancient Panama.* Albuquerque: University of New Mexico Press, 1995.

Hemming, John. *Red Gold: The Conquest of the Brazilian Indians.* New Haven: Harvard University Press, 1978.

Henderson, George. *The Norse Influence on Celtic Scotland.* Glasgow: J. Maclehose, 1910.

Henderson, George. *The Norse Influence on Celtic Scotland.* Glasgow: Sine Nomine, 1901.

Henderson, Lizanne, and Edward J. Cowan. *Scottish Fairy Belief: A History.* Tonawanda, NY: Dundurn Press, 2001.

Henderson, William. *Folk-Lore of the Northern Countries.* London: Folk-Lore Society, 1897.

_____. *Notes on the Folk-Lore of the Northern Counties of England and the Borders.* London: Folk-lore Society by W. Satchell, Peyton, 1879.

Hendry, Joy. *Interpreting Japanese Society: Anthropological Approaches.* London: Psychology Press, 1998.

Henig, Martin. *Religion in Roman Britain.* London: Psychology Press, 1995.

Henry, Rodney L. *Filipino Spirit World: A Challenge to the Church.* Denver: iAcademic Books, 2001.

Herbert, John Alexander, Harry Leigh Douglas Ward, and the British Museum Department of Manuscripts. *Catalogue of Romances in the Department of Manuscripts in the British Museum,* Volume 2. London: Longmans and Company, 1893.

Heron-Allen, Edward. *Violin-Making, as It Was and Is: Being A Historical, Theoretical, and Practical Treatise on the Science and Art of Violin-Making, for the Use of Violin Makers and Players, Amateur and Professional. Preceded by an Essay on the Violin and its Position as a Musical Instrument.* Boston: E. Howe, 1914.

Herrera-Sobek, Maria. *Celebrating Latino Folklore.* Santa Barbara: ABC-CLIO, 2012.

_____. *Chicano Folklore: A Handbook.* Westport, CT: Greenwood, 2006.

Herrmann, Paul. *Deutsche Mythologie in gemeinverständlicher Darstellung.* Leipzig: W. Engelmann, 1898.

Herskovits, Melville Jean. *The Myth of the Negro Past.* Boston: Beacon Press, 1990.

Hesiod. *Hesiod, the Poems and Fragments, Done into English Prose.* Oxford: Clarendon Press, 1908.

Hesiod, Callimachus, Theognis, James Davies, Sir Charles Abraham Elton, Henry William Tytler, and John Hookham Frere. *The Works of Hesiod, Callimachus, and Theognis.* London: H.G. Bohn, 1856.

Hesiod, James Davies, Sir Charles Abraham Elton, Henry William Tytler, Callimachus, and Theognis. *The Works of Hesiod, Callimachus, and Theognis.* London: George Bell and Sons, 1879.

Hesiod, and Hugh Gerard Evelyn-White, trans. *Hesiod, the Homeric Hymns, and Homerica.* New Haven: Harvard University Press, 1914.

Hesiod, and Hugh Gerard Evelyn-White, trans. *The Theogony, Works and Days, and The Shield of Heracles.* Stilwell: Digireads.com, 2008.

Hesiod, and R. M. Frazer, ed. *The Poems of Hesiod.* Norman: University of Oklahoma Press, 1983.

Hesiod, Homer, and Hugh Gerard Evelyn-White, trans. *The Homeric Hymns and Homerica.* New York: William Heinemann, 1920.

Hesiod, Catherine Schlegel, and Henry Weinfield. *Theogony; and, Works and Days.* Ann Arbor: University of Michigan Press, 2006.

Hewitt, John Napoleon Brinton. *Seneca Fiction, Legends, and Myths.* Washington, D.C.: United States Government Printing Office, 1918.

Hill, G. F. "Adonis, Baal, and Astarte." *The Church Quarterly Review,* Volume 66, Arthur C. Headlam, ed., 118–142. London: Spottiswoode and Company, 1908.

Hiltebeitel, Alf. *Criminal Gods and Demon Devotees: Essays on the Guardians of Popular Hinduism.* Albany: SUNY Press, 1989.

History of Civilization: A Complete History of Mankind from Pre-Historic Times: Greek Civilization. New York: Taylor & Francis, 1997.

Hitchins, Fortescue, and Samuel Drew. *The History of Cornwall: From the Earliest Records and Traditions, to the Present Time,* Volume 1. Helston, England: W. Penaluna, 1824.

Ho, Oliver. *Mysteries Unwrapped: Mutants and Monsters.* New York: Sterling, 2008.

Hodson, Geoffrey. *The Fairy Kingdom.* Palo Alta: Book Tree, 2003.

Holden, Robert, and Nicholas Holden. *Bunyips: Australia's Folklore of Fear.* Canberra: National Library Australia, 2001.

Hole, Christina. *English Folklore.* London: B.T. Batsford, 1945.

Hollander, Lee M. *The Poetic Edda,* Volume 1. Austin: University of Texas Press, 1986.

Homer, and Apostolos N. Athanassakis. *The Homeric*

Hymns. Baltimore: Johns Hopkins University Press, 1976.

Homer, and George Chapman. *Chapman's Homer: The Iliad*. Princeton: Princeton University Press, 1998.

Homer, and James Morrice. *The Iliad of Homer*, Volume 2. London: Richard Taylor and Company, 1809.

Homer, Thomas Starling Norgate. *The Iliad; or, Achilles' Wrath: At the Siege of Ilion*. London: Williams and Norgate, 1864.

Homer, Alexander Pope, and Gilbert Wakefield. *The Iliad*, Volume 1. London: Longman, 1796.

Homer, Robert Porter Keep, ed. *The Iliad of Homer, Books 1–6*. Boston: Allyn and Bacon, 1883.

Homer, and William Cullen Bryant, trans. *The Odyssey*, Volume 1. Boston: James R. Osgod, 1871.

Homer, and Theodore Alois Buckley, trans. *The Odyssey of Homer: With the Hymns, Epigrams, and Battle of the Frogs and Mice*. London: George Bell and Sons, 1891.

Homer, and George Chapman, trans. *The Iliads of Homer: Prince of Poets*. London: John Russell Smith, 1888.

Homer, and James MacPherson trans. *The Iliad of Homer, in two Volumes*. London: J. R. Osgood and company, 1773.

Hooke, Della. *Trees in Anglo-Saxon England: Literature, Lore and Landscape*. Woodbridge, Suffolk: Boydell and Brewer, 2010.

Hope, Robert Charles. *The Legendary Lore of the Holy Wells of England: Including Rivers, Lakes, Fountains and Springs*. London: Elliot Stock, 1893.

Hopkins, Edward Washburn. *Epic Mythology*. New York: Biblo and Tannen, 1968.

Hopkins, Lisa. *Shakespeare on the Edge: Border-Crossing in the Tragedies and the Henriad*. Burlington, VT: Ashgate, 2005.

Hoppál, Mihály. *Studies on Mythology and Uralic Shamanism*. Budapest: Akadémiai Kiadó, 2000.

Houtsma, Martijn Theodoor. *E.J. Brill's First Encyclopaedia of Islam, 1913–1936*, Volume 3. Leiden: E.J. Brill, 1993.

Howe, George, and Gustave Adolphus Harrer. *A Handbook of Classical Mythology*. Redwood Shores, CA: Oracle, 1996.

Howels, William. "Cambrian Superstitions and Fugitive Subjects." *Cambrian Quarterly Magazine and Celtic Repertory*, Volume 3, 63–76. London: H. Hughes, 1831.

Howey, M. Oldfield. *The Cults of the Dog*. London: Daniel, 1972.

_____. *The Horse in Magic and Myth*. Mineola, NY: Courier Dover, 2002.

Hudson, D. Dennis. *The Body of God: An Emperor's Palace for Krishna in Eighth-Century Kanchipuram*. Oxford: Oxford University Press, 2008.

Huffington, Arianna Stassinopoulos. *The Gods of Greece*. New York: Atlantic Monthly Press, 1993.

Hughes, David. *The British Chronicles*, Volume 1. Westminster, MD: Heritage, 2007.

Hughes, Thomas Patrick. *A Dictionary of Islam: Being a Cyclopaedia of the Doctrines, Rites, Ceremonies, and Customs, Together With the Technical and Theological Terms, of the Muhammadan Religion*. London: W. H. Allen and Company, 1885.

Hultkrantz, Åke. *The Supernatural Owners of Nature: Nordic Symposion on the Religious Conceptions of Ruling Spirits (Genii Loci, Genii Speciei) and Allied Concepts*. Stockholm: Almqvist ach Wiksell, 1961.

Hunt, Charles Clyde. *Masonic Symbolism*. Whitefish, MT: Kessinger, 1997.

Hunt, Leigh. *Leigh Hunt's London Journal*, Volumes 1–2. London: Charles Knight, 1834.

Hunt, Robert. *Popular Romances of the West of England; or, the Drolls, Traditions, and Superstitions of Old Cornwall*. London: Chatto and Windus, 1881.

_____, ed. *Popular Romances of the West of England, Or, The Drolls, Traditions and Superstitions of Old Cornwall, Volume 1*. London: John Camden Hotten, 1865.

Hunter, Robert, John Alfred Williams, and Sidney John Hervon Herrtage. *American Encyclopedic Dictionary*, Volume 7. Chicago: R.S. Peale and J.A. Hill, 1897.

Hunter-Duvar, John. *The Stone, Bronze and Iron Ages: A Popular Treatise on Early Archaeology*. London: Swan Sonnenschein and Company, 1892.

Hupfeld, Henry. *Encyclopedia of Wit and Wisdom: A Collection of Over Nine Thousand Anecdotes, And Illustrations of Life, Character, Humor and Pathos*. Philadelphia: David McKay, 1897.

Hurd, Ryan. *Sleep Paralysis: A Guide to Hypnagogic Visions and Visitors of the Night*. Los Altos: Hyena Press, 2011.

Hyatt, Victoria, and Joseph W. Charles. *The Book of Demons*. New York: Simon & Schuster, 1974.

Hyde, Douglas. *Beside The Fire: A Collection of Irish Gaelic Folk Storie*. Charleston, SC: Forgotten Books, 1973.

_____. *Giolla an Fhiugha (Lad of the Ferrule)*. London: Irish Text Society, 1899.

Hyginus, and Mary Amelia Grant, ed. *The Myths of Hyginus*. Lawrence: University of Kansas Publications, 1960.

Hyland, Queenie Rikihana. *Paki Waitara: Myths and Legends of the Māori*. Auckland: Reed, 1997.

Illes, Judika. *Encyclopedia of Spirits: The Ultimate Guide to the Magic of Fairies, Genies, Demons, Ghosts, Gods and Goddesses*. New York: HarperCollins, 2009.

Indick, William. *Movies and the Mind: Theories of the Great Psychoanalysts Applied to Film*. Jefferson, NC: McFarland, 2004.

Ingemann, Frances. *Studies in Cheremis: The Supernatural*. New York: Johnson Reprint Corporation, 1964.

Ingpen, Robert R., and Molly Perham. *Ghouls and Monsters*. Philadelphia: Chelsea House, 1996.

Irving, Paul M. C. Forbes. *Metamorphosis in Greek Myths*. Oxford: Clarendon Press, 1990.

Ivanits, Linda J. *Russian Folk Belief*. New York: M.E. Sharpe, 1989.

Jacobs, Joseph. *English Fairy Tales Collected by Joseph Jacobs*. London: David Nutt, 1892.

_____, ed. *Celtic Fairy Tales*. London: David Nutt, 1892.

Jacobs, Joseph, Donald Haase, and John Dickson Batten. *English Fairy Tales: And, More English Fairy Tales*. Santa Barbara: ABC-CLIO, 2002.

Jacobs, Joseph, Alfred Trübner Nutt, Arthur Robinson Wright, and William Crooke, eds. *Folklore*, Volume 4. London: David Nutt, 1893.

_____, _____, _____, and _____, eds. *Folklore*, Volume 14. London: David Nutt, 1903.

_____, _____, _____, and _____, eds. *Folklore*, Volume 18. London: David Nutt, 1907.

Jamieson, John. *An Etymological Dictionary of the Scottish Language: Illustrating the Words in their Different Significations by Examples from Ancient and Modern Writers*, Volume 1. Edinburgh: Edinburgh University Press for W. Creech, 1808.

_____. *Scottish Dictionary and Supplement: In Four Volumes. A–Kut*, Volume 1. Edinburgh: Tail, 1841.

_____. *Scottish Dictionary and Supplement: In Four Volumes. Suppl. Aai–Jux*, Volume 3. Edinburgh: Tail, 1841.

Jastrow, Morris. *The Civilization of Babylonia and Assyria: Its Remains, Language, History, Religion, Commerce, Law, Art, and Literature*. Philadelphia: J.B. Lippincott, 1915.

Jayne, Walter Addison. *Healing Gods of Ancient Civilizations*. Whitefish, MT: Kessinger, 2003.

Jeaffreson, Joseph Russell. *The Faröe Islands*. London: S. Low, Marston, 1898.

Jenkinson, Henry Irwin. *Jenkinson's Practical Guide to the Isle of Man*. London: Edward Stanford and Sons, 1878.

Jestice, Phyllis G. *Encyclopedia of Irish Spirituality*. Santa Barbara: ABC-CLIO, 2000.

Jewitt, Llewellyn. "The Mermaid and the Symbolism of the Fish in Art, Literature, and Legendary Lore." *The Reliquary*, Volume 19, April 1879, Llewellyn Jewitt, ed., 193–200. London: John Russell Smith, 1879.

Johns, Andreas. *Baba Yaga: The Ambiguous Mother and Witch of the Russian Folktale*. New York: Peter Lang, 2004.

Johnson, Kenneth. *Slavic Sorcery: Shamanic Journey of Initiation*. St. Paul: Llewellyn, 1998.

Jolly, Karen Louise, Catharina Raudvere, and Edward Peters. *Witchcraft and Magic in Europe: The Middle Ages*. London: Athlone Press, 2002.

Joly, Henri L. *Legend in Japanese Art: A Description of Historical Episodes, Legendary Characters, Folk-Lore, Myths, Religious Symbolism, Illustrated in the Arts of old Japan*. New York: John Lane Company, 1908.

Jones, David E. *Evil in Our Midst: A Chilling Glimpse of Our Most Feared and Frightening Demons*. Garden City Park, NY: Square One, 2001.

Jones, Lindsay. *Encyclopedia of Religion*, Volume 1. New York: Macmillan Reference USA, 2005.

_____. *Encyclopedia of Religion*, Volume 6. Now York: Macmillan Reference USA, 2005.

Jones, Marie D. *Modern Science and the Paranormal*. New York: Rosen, 2009.

Jones, Noragh. *Power of Raven, Wisdom of Serpent*. Hudson, NY: Lindisfarne Press, 1995.

Jones, Richard. "The Roaring Bull of Bagbury." *Collections Historical and Archaeological Relating to Montgomeryshire and its Borders*, Volume 34. Oswestry: Woodall, Minshall, Thomas and Company, 1907.

Jones, Thomas Gwynn. *Welsh Folklore and Folk-Custom*. Folcroft, PA: Folcroft Library Editions, 1977.

Jones, W. Henry, and the Oxford Journals. *Notes and Queries*. London: Oxford University Press, 1884.

Journal of Religion, Volume 59. Chicago: University of Chicago Press, 1979.

Jōya, Moku. *Japanese Customs and Manners*. Tokyo: Sakurai Shoten, 1949.

Joyce, P.W. *Ancient Celtic Romances*. London: Parkgate Books, 1997.

_____. *The Origin and History of Irish Names of Places*. Dublin: McGlashan and Gill, 1869.

Kallury, Syamala. *Symbolism in the Poetry of Sri Aurobindo*. New Delhi: Abhinav, 1989.

Karr, Phyllis Ann. *The Arthurian Companion*. Oakland: Green Knight, 2001.

Keegan, John. *Legends and Poems: Now First Collected*. Dublin: Sealy, Bryers and Walker, 1907.

Kehler, Dorothea. *A Midsummer Night's Dream: Critical Essays*. London: Psychology Press, 2001

Keightley, Thomas. *The Fairy Mythology*, Volume 2. London: W. H. Ainsworth, 1828.

_____. *The Fairy Mythology: Illustrative of the Romance and Superstition of Various Countries*. London: H. G. Bohn, 1850.

_____. *The Mythology of Ancient Greece and Italy*. London: Whittaker and Company, 1838.

Keltie, Sir John Scott. *A History of the Scottish Highlands, Highland Clans and Highland Regiments with an Account of the Gaelic Language, Literature, and Music by the Rev. Thomas Maclauchlan*. London: A. Fullarton and Company, 1875.

Kennedy, Patrick. *Legendary Fictions of the Irish Celts*. Charleston, SC: Forgotten Books.

Kent, William Charles M. *A Mythological Dictionary*. London: Charlton Tucker, 1870.

Kenyon, Sherrilyn, and the Writer's Digest Books. *The Writer's Digest Character Naming Sourcebook*. Cincinnati: Writer's Digest Books, 2005.

Kerényi, Karl. *Eleusis: Archetypal Image of Mother and Daughter*. Princeton: Princeton University Press, 1991.

_____. *The Gods of the Greeks*. New York: Grove Press, 1960.

Khanam, R. *Demonology: Socio-religious Belief of Witchcraft*. New Delhi: Global Vision, 2003

Killikelly, Sarah Hutchins. *Curious Questions in History, Literature, Art, and Social Life: Designed as a Manual of General Information*, Volume 2. Pittsburg: Joseph Eichbaum and Company, 1895.

Killip, Margaret. *The Folklore of the Isle of Man*. Totowa: Rowman & Littlefield, 1976.

King, Richard John. "The Folk-Lore of Devonshire." *Fraser's Magazine*, Volume 88, James Anthony Froude, ed., 773–791. London: Longmans, Green, and Company, 1873.

King, William. *An Historical Account of the Heathen Gods and Heroes: Necessary for the Understanding of the Ancient Poets: Being an Improvement of Whatever Has Been Hitherto Written, by the Greek, Latin, French, and English Authors, Upon That Subject*. London: Henry Lintot, 1750.

Kingsley, Charles. *The Heroes*. New York: Taylor & Francis, 1895.

Kipling, Rudyard, and Charles Wolcott Balestier. *Puck of Pook's Hill, 1905–1906. Rewards and Fairies*. Garden City: Doubleday, Page, 1910.

Kirk, G. S. *The Iliad: A Commentary*: Volume 1. Cambridge: Cambridge University Press, 1985.

_____. *The Iliad: A Commentary*: Volume 2, Books 5–8. Cambridge: Cambridge University Press, 1990.

Kirk, Robert. *The Secret Commonwealth of Elves, Fauns, and Fairies*. Stirling, Scotland: Mackay, 1933.

Kisacky, Julia. *Magic in Boiardo and Ariosto*. New York: Peter Lang, 2000.

Klaniczay, Gábor, Éva Pócs, and Eszter Csonka-Takács. *Witchcraft Mythologies and Persecutions*. Budapest: Central European University Press, 2008.

Kloppenborg, John S. *The Tenants in the Vineyard: Ideology, Economics, and Agrarian Conflict in Jewish Palestine*. Tübingen, Germany: Mohr Siebeck, 2006.

Kmietowicz, Frank A. *Slavic Mythical Beliefs*. Windsor, Ontario: F. Kmietowicz, 1982.

Knapp, Bettina Liebowitz. *Women, Myth, and the Feminine Principle*. Albany: SUNY Press, 1998.

Knappert, Jan. *The Aquarian Guide to African Mythology*.

Wellingborough, Northamptonshire: Aquarian Press, Ltd, 1990.

_____. *Bantu Myths and Other Tales*, Volume 7. Leiden: Brill Archive, 1977.

_____. *The Encyclopaedia of Middle Eastern Mythology and Religion.* Rockport, MA: Element, 1993.

Knight, Richard Payne, and Thomas Wright. *Sexual Symbolism: A History of Phallic Worship.* Mineola, NY: Courier Dover, 2006.

Knight, Sirona. *Celtic Traditions: Druids, Faeries, and Wiccan Rituals.* New York: Citadel Press, 2000.

_____. *Little Giant Encyclopedia: Runes.* New York: Sterling, 2008.

Knoppers, Laura Lunger, and Joan B. Landes. *Monstrous Bodies/Political Monstrosities in Early Modern Europe.* Ithaca: Cornell University Press, 2004.

Knowles, James. *The Nineteenth Century,* Volume 31. London: Henry S. King and Company, 1892.

Koch, Fred C., and Jacob Eichhorn. *The Volga Germans: In Russia and the Americas, from 1763 to the Present.* University Park: Pennsylvania State University Press, 1978.

Koch, John Thomas. *Celtic Culture: A Historical Encyclopedia.* Santa Barbara: ABC-CLIO, 2006.

Koch, John T., and John Carey. *The Celtic Heroic Age: Literary Sources for Ancient Celtic Europe and Early Ireland and Wales.* Andover, MA: Celtic Studies, 2003.

Koch, Kurt E. *Occult ABC: Exposing Occult Practices and Ideologies.* Grand Rapids: Kregel, 1978.

Kohl, Johann Georg. *Travels in Scotland.* London: Darling, 1849.

Kölbing, Eugen, Johannes Hoops, Arthur Kölbing, and Albert Wagner, eds. *Englische Studien,* Volume 5. Heilbronn: Verlag von Gebr. Henninger, 1882.

Kravchenko, Maria. *The World of the Russian Fairy Tale.* New York: Peter Lang, 1987.

Kunst, J. "Some Animal Fables of the Chuh Indians." *Journal of American Folklore,* Volume 28, American Folklore Society, ed., 553–57. New York: G. E. Stechert, 1915.

Kynes, Sandra. *Sea Magic: Connecting with the Ocean's Energy.* St. Paul: Llewellyn Worldwide, 2008.

Laing, Jeanie M. *Notes on Superstition and Folk Lore.* Edinburgh: John Menzies and Company, 1885.

Lamb, Charles, and Mary Lamb. *The Works of Charles and Mary Lamb: Books for Children.* North Andover, MA: Methuen and Company, 1903.

Lambe, Robert. *An Exact and Circumstantial History of the Battle of Floddon. In verse: Written about the Time of Queen Elizabeth. In which are Related many Particular Facts not to be found in the English History.* London: R. Taylor and E. and C. Dilly, 1774.

Lambright, Anne. *Creating the Hybrid Intellectual: Subject, Space, and the Feminine in the Narrative of José María Arguedas.* Cranbury, NJ: Associated University Press, 2007.

Landy, David, and the University of Puerto Rico (Río Piedras Campus) Social Science Research Center. *Tropical Childhood: Cultural Transmission and Learning in a Rural Puerto Rican Village.* New York: Harper & Row, 1959.

Lane, Edward William. *Arabian Society in the Middle Ages: Studies from The Thousand and One Nights.* London: Chatto and Windus, 1883.

Lang, Andrew. *The Blue Fairy Book.* London: Longmans, Green, and Company, 1906.

Lang, Andrew. *Tales of Troy and Greece.* Rockville: Wildside Press LLC, 2008.

_____. *The Brown Fairy Book.* Mineola, NY: Dover, 1965.

_____. *The Green Fairy Book.* Mineola, NY: Dover, 1965.

_____. *The Grey Fairy Book.* Mineola, NY: Dover, 1967.

_____. *The Lilac Fairy Book.* Mineola, NY: Dover, 1968.

_____. *The Olive Fairy Book.* Mineola, NY: Dover, 1968.

_____. *The Orange Fairy Book.* London: Longmans, Green, and Company, 1906.

_____. *The Pink Fairy Book.* Mineola, NY: Dover, 1967.

_____. *The Red Fairy Book.* Mineola, NY: Dover, 1966.

_____. *The Red Romance Book.* London: Longmans, Green, and Company, 1905.

_____. *Tales of Troy and Greece.* Rockville, MD: Wildside Press, 2008.

_____. *The Yellow Fairy Book.* Mineola, NY: Dover, 1966.

Langond, Stephen, H. "Lilith." *Semitic Mythology of All Races,* Volume V. June, 1932. New York: Cooper Square Pub, 1932.

Lanier, Henry Wysham. *A Book of Giants: Tales of Very Tall Men of Myth, Legends, History, and Science.* New York: E. P. Dutton, 1922.

Larkin, Rochelle. *Snow White and Other Stories.* Edina, MN: ABDO, 2005.

Larned, Augusta. *Old Tales Retold from Grecian Mythology in Talks Around the Fire.* Whitefish, MT: Kessinger, 1998.

Larrington, Carolyne. *King Arthur's Enchantresses: Morgan and Her Sisters in Arthurian Tradition.* London: I.B. Tauris, 2006.

Larson, Emily. *The Best Baby Names Treasury: Your Ultimate Naming Resource.* Naperville, IL: Sourcebooks, 2011.

Larson, Jennifer Lynn. *Greek Heroine Cults in their Social and Literary Contexts,* Volume 2. Madison: University of Wisconsin–Madison, 1992.

_____. *Greek Nymphs: Myth, Cult, Lore.* Oxford: Oxford University Press, 2001.

Latham, Minor White. *The Elizabethan Fairies: The Fairies of Folklore and the Fairies of Shakespeare.* Ely, Cambridgeshire: Octagon, 1972.

Latham, Robert Gordon. *Russian and Turk: From a Geographical, Ethnological, and Historical Point of View.* London: Wiliam H. Allen and Company, 1878.

Lawson, John Cuthbert. *Modern Greek Folklore and Ancient Greek Religion: A Study in Survivals.* Cambridge: Cambridge University Press, 2012.

Layzer, Varese. *Signs of Weakness: Juxtaposing Irish Tales and the Bible.* Sheffield, Somerset: Sheffield Academic Press, 2001.

Leach, Edmund, Stephen Hugh-Jones, and James Laidlaw. *The Essential Edmund Leach,* Volumes 1–2. New Haven: Yale University Press, 2001.

Leach, María. *Funk and Wagnalls Standard Dictionary of Folklore, Mythology, and Legend.* New York: Funk and Wagnalls, 1972.

Leach, María, and Jerome Fried. *Dictionary of Folklore: Mythology and Legend.* New York: Funk and Wagnalls, 1950.

Leake, William Martin. *Numismata Hellenica: A Catalogue of Greek Coins Collected by William Martin Leake.* London: J. Murray, 1856.

Lee, Sir Sidney. *The Boke of Duke Huon of Burdeaux.* London: Trübner and Company, 1882.

Leeming, David Adams. *Mythology: The Voyage of the Hero.* New York: Oxford University Press, 1998.

_____. *The Oxford Companion to World Mythology.* Oxford: Oxford University Press, 2005.

Legey, Françoise. *The Folklore of Morocco.* London: G. Allen and Unwin, 1935.

Leland, Charles Godfrey. *Etruscan Magic and Occult Remedies.* Whitefish, MT: Kessinger, 2003.

_____. *Gypsy Sorcery and Fortune Telling: Illustrated by Incantations, Specimens of Medical Magic, Anecdotes, and Tales.* New York: Charles Scribner's Sons, 1891.

Lemprière, John. *A Classical Dictionary, Containing a Copious Account of All the Proper Names Mentioned in Ancient Authors.* London: T. Cadell, 1839.

_____. *A Classical Dictionary: Containing a Copious Account of All the Proper Names Mentioned in Ancient Authors with the Value of Coins, Weights, and Measures used among the Greeks and Romans and a Chronological Table.* New York: Evert Duyckinck, George Long, W.H. Gilley, Collins, and Company, 1825.

Lempriere. *A Classical Dictionary Containing a Copious Account of all Mentioned Proper Names Mentioned in Ancient Authors and Cronologicae Table The Sixteerth Edition, Corrected.* London: T. Cadell, 1831.

Lemprière, John. *Lempriere's Classical Dictionary for Schools and Academies: Containing Every Name and All That is Either Important or Useful in the Original Work.* Boston: Richardson, Lord and Holbrook, 1832.

Lemprière, John. *Classical Dictionary, Containing a Full Account of all the Proper Names Mentioned in Ancient Authors, with Tables of Coins, Weights, and Measures in use Among the Greeks and Romans: To Which is Prefixed, a Chronological Table.* New York: G. P. Putnam's Sons, 1875.

Lenormant, François. *Chaldean Magic: Its Origin and Development.* Boston: Weiser Books, 1999.

Lerner, Martin, and Steven Kossak. *The Lotus Transcendent: Indian and Southeast Asian Art from the Samuel Eilenberg Collection.* New York: Metropolitan Museum of Art, 1991.

Lessa, William Armand. *Tales From Ulithi Atoll: A Comparative Study in Oceanic Folklore.* Berkeley: University of California Press, 1961.

Lethbridge, Thomas Charles. *Gogmagog: The Buried Gods.* New York: Taylor & Francis, 1957.

Levin, Eve. *Sex and Society in the World of the Orthodox Slavs, 900–1700.* Ithaca: Cornell University Press, 1989.

Lewis, Maureen Warner. *Guinea's Other Suns: The African Dynamic in Trinidad Culture.* Dover, MA: The Majority Press, 1991.

Library of Universal Knowledge: Being a Reprint Entire of the Last (1879) Edinburgh and London Edition of Chambers's Encyclopaedia; A Dictionary of Universal Knowledge for the People. With very Large Additions upon Topics of Special Interest to American Readers, Volume 15. New York: American Book Exchange, 1879.

Licauco, Jaime T. *Dwarves and Other Nature Spirits: Their Importance to Man.* Quezon City: Rex Bookstore, 2005.

_____. *Dwarves and Other Nature Spirits, 2005 Edition.* Quezon City: Rex Bookstore, 2005.

Lilly, William. *William Lilly's History of his Life and Times from the Year 1602 to 1681.* London: C. Baldwyn, 1822.

Lima, Robert. *Stages of Evil: Occultism in Western Theater and Drama.* Lexington: University Press of Kentucky, 2005.

Lincoln, Bruce. *Death, War, and Sacrifice: Studies in Ideology and Practice.* Chicago: University of Chicago Press, 1991.

Lindahl, Carl, John McNamara, and John Lindow. *Medieval Folklore: A Guide to Myths, Legends, Tales, Beliefs, and Customs.* Oxford: Oxford University Press, 2000.

Lindow, John. *Handbook of Norse Mythology.* Santa Barbara: ABC-CLIO, 2001.

_____. *Norse Mythology: A Guide to the Gods, Heroes, Rituals, and Beliefs.* Oxford: Oxford University Press, 2001.

_____. *Swedish Legends and Folktales.* Berkeley: University of California Press, 1978.

Littell, Eliakim, Robert S. Littell, and the Making of America Project. "Scottish, Shetlandic, and Germanic Water Tales." *The Living Age,* Volume 150. 809–17. Boston: The Living Age Company, 1881.

Little, Don. *Spirits, Angels, Demons, and Gods: Experiences on the Road to the Heavens and to the Hells.* Pittsburgh: Dorrance, 2010.

Littleton, C. Scott, and Linda A. Malcor. *From Scythia to Camelot: A Radical Reassessment of the Legends of King Arthur, the Knights of the Round Table, and the Holy Grail.* New York: Taylor & Francis, 2000.

Littleton, C. Scott, and the Marshall Cavendish Corporation. *Gods, Goddesses, and Mythology,* Volume 4. Tarrytown, NY: Marshall Cavendish, 2005.

_____, and _____. *Gods, Goddesses, and Mythology,* Volume 6. Tarrytown, NY: Marshall Cavendish, 2005.

_____, and _____. *Gods, Goddesses, and Mythology,* Volume 11. Tarrytown, NY: Marshall Cavendish, 2005.

Livia, Anna, and Kira Hall. *Queerly Phrased: Language, Gender, and Sexuality.* New York: Oxford University Press, 1997.

Livo, Norma J., and Sandra A. Rietz. *Storytelling Folklore Sourcebook.* Englewood Cliffs, NJ: Libraries Unlimited, 1991.

Llamzon, Teodoro A. *Handbook of Philippine Language Groups.* Quezon City: Ateneo de Manila University Press, 1978.

Llewellyn's Magical Almanac. St. Paul: Llewellyn, 2002.

Loar, Julie. *Goddesses for Every Day: Exploring the Wisdom and Power of the Divine Feminine Around the World.* Novato, CA: New World Library, 2010.

Löffler, Christa Maria. *The Voyage to the Otherworld Island in Early Irish Literature,* Volume 1. Salzburg: Institut für Anglistik und Amerikanistik, Universität Salzburg, 1983.

Logan, Patrick. *The Holy Wells of Ireland.* Dublin: Smythe, 1980.

Long, William Henry. *A Dictionary of the Isle of Wight Dialect, and of Provincialisms Used in the Island: With Illustrative Anecdotes and Tales; to Which is Appended the Christmas Boy's Play, an Isle of Wight "Hooam Harvest," and Songs Sung by the Peasantry; Forming a Treasury of Insular Manners and Customs of Fifty Years Ago.* London: Reeves and Turner, 1886.

Lorenz, Brenna E. *The Pacific Islander's Book of Names: A Dictionary of Modern and Ancient First Names Used by People From Guam and other Pacific Islands.* Mangilao, Guam: Three Furies Press, 1996.

Luce, T. James. *Ancient Writers: Greece and Rome.* New York: Scribner, 1982.

Lurker, Manfred. *The Routledge Dictionary of Gods and Goddesses, Devils and Demons.* London: Psychology Press, 2004.

Lyly, John. *Endymion*. Manchester: Manchester University Press, 1997.

Lynch, Gordon J., Diane Canwell, and Jonathan Sutherland. *Famous Ghosts and Haunted Places*. New York: Rosen, 2011.

Lynch, Patricia Ann, and Jeremy Roberts. *African Mythology A to Z*. New York: Infobase, 2010.

_____, and _____. *Native American Mythology A to Z*. New York: Infobase, 2010.

Lyon, William S. *Encyclopedia of Native American Healing*. London: W. W. Norton and Company, 1996.

Lysaght, Patricia, Séamas Ó Catháin, and Dáithí Ó hÓgáin. *Islanders and Water-Dwellers: Proceedings of the Celtic-Nordic-Baltic Folklore Symposium held at University College Dublin, 16–19 June, 1996*. Dublin: DBA Publications, 1999.

Maberry, Jonathan. *Vampire Universe: The Dark World of Supernatural Beings That Haunt Us, Hunt Us, and Hunger for Us*. New York: Kensington, 2006.

Maberry, Jonathan, and David F. Kramer. *The Cryptopedia: A Dictionary of the Weird, Strange, and Downright Bizarre*. New York: Citadel Press, 2007.

_____, and _____. *They Bite: Endless Cravings of Supernatural Predators*. New York: Citadel Press, 2009.

MacCulloch, J. A. *The Celtic and Scandinavian Religions*. New York: Cosimo, 2005.

MacCulloch, John Arnott. *Eddic*. New York: Cooper Square, 1964.

MacCulloch, John Arnott, Jan Máchal, and Louis Herbert Gray. *Celtic [Mythology]*. New York: Cooper Square, 1964.

_____, _____, and _____. *Celtic Mythology*. Boston: Marshall Jones Company, 1918.

_____, _____, and _____. *Celtic Mythology*, Volume 3. Boston: Marshall Jones Company, 1918.

MacCulloch, Sir Edgar. *Guernsey Folk Lore: A Collection of Popular Superstitions, Legendary Tales, Peculiar Customs, Proverbs, Weather Sayings, etc., of the People of that Island*. London: Eliot Stock, 1903.

MacDonald, Margaret Read. *Earth Care: World Folktales to Talk About*. Little Rock: August House, 2005.

MacDonnell, Arthur A. *Vedic Mythology*. Whitefish, MT: Kessinger, 2006.

Macdowall, Maria Wilhelmina, and Johann Wilhelm E. Wägner. *Asgard and the Gods, Tales and Traditions of Our Northern Ancestors, Adapted from the Work of W. Wägner by M.W. Macdowall and Edited By W.S.W. Anson*. London: W. Swan Sonnenschein, 1884.

Mack, Carol K., and Dinah Mack. *A Field Guide to Demons, Fairies, Fallen Angels, and Other Subversive Spirits*. New York: Arcade, 1998.

_____, and _____. *A Field Guide to Demons, Vampires, Fallen Angels and Other Subversive Spirits*. New York: Skyhorse, 2011.

Mackay, Charles, and Allan Ramsay. *A Dictionary of Lowland Scotch: With an Introductory Chapter on the Poetry, Humour, and Literary History of the Scottish Language and an Appendix of Scottish Proverbs*. London: Whittaker and Company, 1888.

MacKenzie, Donald Alexander. *Migration of Symbols*. Whitefish, MT: Kessinger, 2003.

_____. *Scottish Folk-Lore and Folk Life: Studies in Race, Culture and Tradition*. Glasgow: Blackie and Sons, 1935.

_____. *Scottish Wonder Tales from Myth and Legend*. Mineola, NY: Courier Dover, 1997.

_____. *Wonder Tales from Scottish Myth and Legend*. Glasgow: Blackie and Sons, 1924.

MacKillop, James. *Dictionary of Celtic Mythology*. Oxford: Oxford University Press, 2004.

_____. *Myths and Legends of the Celts*. New York: Penguin, 2006.

Maclaren, Archibald. *The Fairy Family: A Series of Ballads and Metrical Tales Illustrating the Fairy Mythology of Europe*. London: Longman, Brown, Green, Longmans, and Roberts, 1857.

Macleod, Norman. *A Dictionary of the Gaelic Language, in two Parts: I. Gaelic and English.—II. English and Gaeli*. Edinburgh: W. R. M'Phun, 1853.

MacLeod, Sharon Paice. *Celtic Myth and Religion: A Study of Traditional Belief, with Newly Translated Prayers, Poems and Songs*. Jefferson, NC: McFarland, 2011.

MacManus, Diarmuid A. *The Middle Kingdom: The Faerie World of Ireland*. Dublin: Smythe, 1973.

MacManus, Seumas. *The Story of the Irish Race: A Popular History of Ireland*. New York: The Irish Publishing Company, 1922.

MacRitchie, David. *Fians, Fairies, and Picts*. London: Kegan Paul, Trench, Trübner and Company, Limited, 1893.

Mageo, Jeannette Marie, and Alan Howard. *Spirits in Culture, History, and Mind*. New York: Psychology Press, 1996.

Magnanini, Suzanne. *Fairy-Tale Science: Monstrous Generation in the Tales of Straparola and Basile*. Toronto: University of Toronto Press, 2008.

Mahon, Michael Patrick. *Ireland's Fairy Lore*. Boston: Thomas J. Flynn and Company, 1919.

Malinowski, Sharon. *The Gale Encyclopedia of Native American Tribes: Northeast, Southeast, Caribbean*. Detroit: Gale, 1998.

Malkin, Irad. *Myth and Territory in the Spartan Mediterranean*. Cambridge: Cambridge University Press, 2003.

Manguel, Alberto, and Gianni Guadalupi. *The Dictionary of Imaginary Places*. New York: Houghton Mifflin Harcourt, 2000.

Manser, Martin H. *The Facts On File Dictionary of Allusions*. New York: Infobase, 2008.

Mark, Colin B. D. *The Gaelic-English Dictionary*. London: Psychology Press, 2003.

Markale, Jean. *Women of the Celts*. Rochester, NY: Inner Traditions, Bear and Company, 1986.

Marstrander, Carl Johan Sverdrup, ed. *Dictionary of the Irish Language, Compact Edition*. Dublin: Royal Irish Academy, 1990.

Martinengo-Cesaresco, Countess Evelyn Lilian Hazeldine Carrington. *Essays in the Study of Folk-Songs*. London: J. M. Dent, 1886.

Marwick, Ernest W. *The Folklore of Orkney and Shetland*. Totowa, NY: Rowman & Littlefield, 1975.

Matson, Gienna, and Jeremy Roberts. *Celtic Mythology A to Z*. New York: Infobase, 2010.

Matthews, Elaine, Simon Hornblower, and Peter Marshall Fraser, eds. *Greek Personal Names: Their Value as Evidence*. Oxford: Oxford University Press, 2000.

Matthews, John, and Caitlin Matthews. *The Element Encyclopedia of Magical Creatures: The Ultimate A–Z of Fantastic Beings from Myth and Magic*. New York: Barnes and Noble, 2005.

_____, and _____. *The Encyclopaedia of Celtic Myth and*

Legend: A Definitive Sourcebook of Magic, Vision, and Lore. London: Globe Pequot, 2004.

Mauss, Marcel. *A General Theory of Magic.* London: Psychology Press, 2001.

Mbiti, John S. *Introduction to African Religion.* Westlands, Nairobi: East African, 1992.

McCann, Michelle Roehm, Marianne Monson-Burton, and David Hohn. *Finding Fairies: Secrets for Attracting Little People from Around the World.* Tulsa: Council Oak Books, 2005.

McCarthy, Carolyn, and Jean-Bernard Carillet. *Chile and Easter Island.* Oakland: Lonely Planet, 2009.

McClintock, John, and James Strong. *Cyclopaedia of Biblical, Theological, and Ecclesiastical Literature*, Volume 7. New York: Harper and Brothers, 1894.

_____, and _____. *Cyclopaedia of Biblical, Theological, and Ecclesiastical Literature*, Volume 9. New York: Harper and Brothers, 1880.

McConnell, Winder. *A Companion to the Nibelungenlied.* Columbia, SC: Camden House, 1998.

McCoy, Edain. *Celtic Myth and Magick: Harness the Power of the Gods and Goddesses.* St. Paul: Llewellyn Worldwide, 1995.

_____. *A Witch's Guide to Faery Folk: Reclaiming Our Working Relationship with Invisible Helpers.* St. Paul: Llewellyn, 1995.

McEwan, Gordon F. *The Incas: New Perspectives.* New York: W.W. Norton, 2008.

McHugh, James Noel. *Hantu Hantu: An Account of Ghost Belief in Modern Malaya.* Singapore: Donald Moore for Eastern Universities Press, 1959.

McInerney, Jeremy. *The Folds of Parnassos: Land and Ethnicity in Ancient Phokis.* Austin: University of Texas Press, 1999.

McKinnell, John. *Meeting the Other in Norse Myth and Legend.* Rochester: D.S. Brewer, 2005.

McLean, Adam. *The Triple Goddess: An Exploration of the Archetypal Feminine.* Boston: Red Wheel/Weiser, 1989.

McNamara, Kenneth J., and Ken McNamara. *The Star-Crossed Stone: The Secret Life, Myths, and History of a Fascinating Fossil.* Chicago: University of Chicago Press, 2010.

McNeese, Tim. *Myths of Native America.* New York: Running Press, 2003.

McPherson, J. M. *Primitive Beliefs in the Northeast of Scotland.* Whitefish, MT: Kessinger, 2003.

Meisch, Lynn. *A Traveler's Guide to El Dorado and the Inca Empire.* New York: Penguin, 1977.

Mennes, Marcus. *Gnome and Garden: A Gnovelty Kit.* Philadelphia: Quirk, 2004.

Meredith, George. *The Works of George Meredith*, Volume 23. New York: Charles Scribner's Sons, 1910.

Merriam-Webster, Inc. *The Merriam-Webster New Book of Word Histories.* Springfield, MA: Merriam-Webster, 1991.

_____. *Merriam-Webster's Encyclopedia of Literature.* Springfield, MA: Merriam-Webster, 1995.

_____. *Merriam-Webster's Encyclopedia of World Religions.* Springfield, MA: Merriam-Webster, 1999.

Meurger, Michel, and Claude Gagnon. *Lake Monster Traditions: A Cross-Cultural Analysis.* London: Fortean Tomes, 1988.

Meyer, Kuno. *Contributions to Irish Lexicography.* London: Max Niemeyer, 1906.

Milton, John, and Alastair Fowler. *Paradise Lost.* London: Longman, 1998.

Mitchell, Laurence. *Go Slow Norfolk and Suffolk.* Chalfont St. Peter: Bradt Travel Guides, 2010.

Mittman, Asa Simon, and Peter J. Dendle. *The Ashgate Research Companion to Monsters and the Monstrous.* Surrey, England: Ashgate, 2012.

Monaghan, Patricia. *The Encyclopedia of Celtic Mythology and Folklore.* New York: Infobase, 2004.

_____. *Encyclopedia of Goddesses and Heroines.* Santa Barbara: ABC-CLIO, 2009.

_____. *Goddesses in World Culture.* Santa Barbara: ABC-CLIO, 2010.

_____. *New Book of Goddesses and Heroines.* St. Paul: Llewellyn, 1997.

_____. *The Red-Haired Girl from the Bog: The Landscape of Celtic Myth and Spirit.* Novato, NY: New World Library, 2004.

_____. *Women in Myth and Legend.* London: Junction, 1981.

Monro, David Binning. *The Modes of Ancient Greek Music.* London: Henry Frowde, 1894.

Montemayor, Carlos, and Donald H. Frischmann, *Words of the True Peoples: Anthology of Contemporary Mexican Indigenous-Language Writers.* Austin: University of Texas Press, 2005.

Montgomery, Sy. *Journey of the Pink Dolphins: An Amazon Quest.* White River Junction, VT: Chelsea Green, 2009.

Mood, Terry Ann. *American Regional Folklore: A Sourcebook and Research Guide.* Santa Barbara: ABC-CLIO, 2004.

Moore, Arthur William. *The Folk-Lore of the Isle of Man: Being an Account of its Myths, Legends, Superstitions, Customs, and Proverbs, Collected from many Sources; with a General Introduction; and with Explanatory Notes to Each Chapter.* London: David Nutt, 1891.

_____, ed. *Manx Note Book*, Volume 1. Douglas, 1885.

Moore, Wendy. *West Malaysia and Singapore.* Tokyo: Tuttle, 1998.

Moorey, Teresa. *The Fairy Bible: The Definitive Guide to the World of Fairies.* New York: Sterling, 2008.

Morel, Héctor V., and José Dalí Moral. *Diccionario Mitológico Americano.* Buenos Aires: Editorial Kier, 1987.

Morford, Mark P. O., and Robert J. Lenardon. *Classical Mythology.* Oxford: Oxford University Press, 1999.

Morgan, Louisa. *Baron Bruno; or, The Unbelieving Philosopher, and other Fairy Stories.* London: Macmillan, 1875.

Morgan, Octavius, and Thomas Wakeman. *Notes on Wentwood, Castle Troggy, and Llanvair Castle.* Newport, South Wales: Monmouthshire and Caerleon Antiquarian Association, by H. Mullock, 1863.

Morley, Henry, and William Hall Griffin. *English Writers: An Attempt Towards a History of English Literature*, Volume 11. London: Cassell and Company, 1892.

Morphy, Howard. *Ancestral Connections: Art and an Aboriginal System of Knowledge.* Chicago: University of Chicago Press, 1991.

Morton, Lisa. *The Halloween Encyclopedia.* Jefferson, NC: McFarland, 2003.

Morvan, F. *Legends of the Sea.* Geneva: Minerva, 1980.

Motley, James. *Tales of the Cymry: With Notes Illustrative and Explanatory.* London: Longmans, 1848.

Mould, Michael. *The Routledge Dictionary of Cultural References in Modern French.* New York: Taylor & Francis, 2011.

Mountain, Harry. *The Celtic Encyclopedia*, Volume 2. Aveiro, Portugal: Universal-Publishers, 1998.

_____. *The Celtic Encyclopedia*, Volume 3. Aveiro, Portugal: Universal-Publishers, 1998.

_____. *The Celtic Encyclopedia*, Volume 4. Aveiro, Portugal: Universal-Publishers, 1998.

_____. *The Celtic Encyclopedia*, Volume 5. Aveiro, Portugal: Universal-Publishers, 1998.

Mowat, Farley. *People of the Deer.* New York: Carroll & Graf, 2004.

Müller, Karl Otfried. *Ancient Art and its Remains: Or, a Manual of the Archaeology of Art.* London: Bernard Quaritch, 1852.

Muirithe, Diarmaid Ó, and Alan Tuffery. *Words We Use.* Dublin: Gill and Macmillan, 2006.

Munn, Mark Henderson. *The Mother of the Gods, Athens, and the Tyranny of Asia: A Study of Sovereignty in Ancient Religion.* Berkley: University of California Press, 2006.

Murray, Alexander Stuart. *Manual of Mythology: For the use of Schools, Art Students, and General Readers Founded on the Works of Petiscus, Preller, and Welcker.* London: Asher, 1873.

_____. *Manual of Mythology: Greek and Roman, Norse, and Old German, Hindoo and Egyptian Mythology: Reprinted from the Second Revised London Edition.* New York: Charles Scribner's Sons, 1891.

Museo Nacional de Historia (Peru) and the Instituto Nacional de Cultura (Peru). *Historia y Cultura*, Volume 16. Cuzco: Instituto Nacional de Cultura., 1983.

Myers, K. Sara. *Ovid's Causes: Cosmogony and Aetiology in the Metamorphoses.* Ann Arbor: University of Michigan Press, 1994.

Nagy, Gregory. *Greek Mythology and Poetics.* Ithaca: Cornell University Press, 1992.

_____. *Homer the Preclassic.* Berkeley: University of California Press, 2012.

Nakao, Seigo. *Random House Japanese-English English-Japanese Dictionary.* New York: Random House Digital, 1997.

Nardo, Don. *The Gods and Goddesses of Greek Mythology.* San Diego: Capstone Press, 2011.

Nares, Robert. *A Glossary of Words, Phrases, Names: And Allusions in the Works of English Authors, Particularly of Shakespeare and His Contemporaries.* London: G. Routledge, 1905.

Narváez, Peter. *The Good People: New Fairylore Essays.* Lexington: University Press of Kentucky, 1997.

Native American Legendary Creatures: Aztec Legendary Creatures, Inuit Legendary Creatures, Maya Legendary Creatures. Memphis: General Books LLC, 2010.

Neal, Derek G. *The Masculine Self in Late Medieval England.* Chicago: University of Chicago Press, 2008.

New International Encyclopedia, Volume 15. New York: Dodd, Mead, 1916.

Newcomb, Jacky, and Alicen Geddes-Ward. *A Faerie Treasury.* London: Hay House, 2008.

Newell, William Well, and the American Folklore Society. "The Ignis Fatuus." *Journal of American Folklore*, Volumes 17–18, American Folklore Society, 39–60. New York: American Folklore Society, 1904.

Newton, A. E. "A Rational View of the Evidence of a Life After Death." *The Spiritual Magazine*, Volume VI, A. E. Newton, ed., 210–221. London: F. Pitman, 1871.

Nicholson, John. *Folk Lore of East Yorkshire.* London:

Simpkin, Marshall, Hamilton, Kent, and Company, 1890.

The Norroena Society. *The Satr Edda: Sacred Lore of the North.* Bloomington: iUniverse, 2009.

Nzita, Richard, and Mbaga-Niwampa. *Peoples and Cultures of Uganda.* Kampala, Uganda: Fountain, 1995.

Ó Hógáin, Dáithí. *Myth, Legend and Romance: An Encyclopaedia of the Irish Folk Tradition.* New York: Prentice Hall Press, 1991.

_____. *The Sacred Isle: Belief and Religion in Pre-Christian Ireland.* Rochester: Boydell and Brewer, 1999.

O'Connor, Frank, ed. *A Book of Ireland.* London: Collins, 1959.

O'Conor, Norreys Jephson. *Battles and Enchantments, Retold from Early Gaelic Literature.* Boston: Houghton Mifflin, 1922.

O'Hanlon, John. *Irish Folk Lore: Traditions and Superstitions of the Country, With Humorous Tales.* Glasgow: Cameron and Ferguson, 1870.

_____. *Legend Lays of Ireland.* Dublin: John Mullany, 1870.

O'Reilly, Edward. *An Irish-English Dictionary.* Dublin: James Duffy, 1864.

O'Sheridan, Mary Grant. *Gaelic Folk Tales: A Supplementary Reader.* Chicago: W.F. Roberts, 1911.

Oden, Thomas C. *Early Libyan Christianity: Uncovering a North African Tradition.* Downer Grove, IL: InterVarsity Press, 2011.

Oesterley, W. O. E. *Immortality and the Unseen World: A Study in Old Testament Religion 1921.* Whitefish, MT: Kessinger, 2004.

Ogden, Daniel. *A Companion to Greek Religion.* Chichester, West Sussex: Wiley-Blackwell, 2010.

Oinas, Felix J. *Essays on Russian Folklore and Mythology.* Columbus, OH: Slavica, 1985.

_____. "Historical Reality and Russian Supernatural Beings." *Agents and Audiences,* Agrhananda Bharati, ed., 475–485. Chicago: Walter de Gruyter, 1976.

Olcott, Frances Jenkins. *The Book of Elves and Fairies.* Mineola, NY: Courier Dover, 2002.

_____. *Baltic Wizards.* Charleston: Forgotten Books.

Olupọna, Jacob Obafẹmi Kẹhinde. *Beyond Primitivism: Indigenous Religious Traditions and Modernity.* London: Psychology Press, 2004.

Orbell, Margaret Rose. *A Concise Encyclopedia of Māori Myth and Legend.* Christchurch, New Zealand: Canterbury University Press, 1998.

Osborn, Marijane. *Nine Medieval Romances of Magic: Re-Rhymed in Modern English.* Toronto: Broadview Press, 2010.

Ouseley, William. *The Oriental Collections: Consisting of Original Essays and Dissertations, Translations and Miscellaneous Papers; Illustrating the History and Antiquities, the Arts, Sciences, and Literature, of Asia.* London: Cooper and Graham, 1797.

Ovid. *Four Books of the Metamorphoses of Publius Ovidius Naso, Expurgated, and Freed from Everything Objectionable. With a Dictionary Giving the Meaning of All Words with Critical Exactness.* New York: Arthur Hinds and Company, 1890.

Ovid, Nathan Covington Brooks, ed. *The Metamorphoses of Publius Ovidius Naso.* New York: A. S. Barnes and Burr, 1860.

Ovid, Peter E. Knox, ed. *Ovid: Heroides: Select Epistles.* New York: Cambridge University Press, 1996.

Ovid, and William S. Anderson. *Ovid's Metamorphoses,*

Books 1–5. Norman: University of Oklahoma Press, 1998.

Ovid, and Frank Justus Miller, trans. *Ovid: Metamorphoses*, Volume 2. London: William Heinemann, 1916.

Ovid, John Dryden, Alexander Pope, William Congreve, Joseph Addison, trans. *Mythological Fables.* New York: W.E. Dean, 1837.

Ovid, and George Gilbert Ramsay. *Ovid: Selections for the Use of Schools, with Introductions and Notes and an Appendix on the Roman Calendar.* Oxford: Clarendon Press, 1868.

Pache, Corinne Ondine. *A Moment's Ornament: The Poetics of Nympholepsy in Ancient Greece.* Oxford: Oxford University Press, 2010.

Page, Michael F., and Robert R. Ingpen. *Encyclopedia of Things That Never Were: Creatures, Places, and People.* New York: Viking Press, 1987.

Palmer, Robin. *Dragons, Unicorns, and Other Magical Beasts: A Dictionary of Fabulous Creatures with Old Tales and Verses about Them.* New York: H. Z. Walck, 1966.

Parada, Carlos. *Genealogical Guide to Greek Mythology.* Jonsered, Sweden: P. Aströms Forlag,, 1993.

Parker, H. *Village Folktales of Ceylon*, Part 2. Whitefish, MT: Kessinger, 2003.

Parker, Janet, Alice Mills, and Julie Stanton. *Mythology: Myths, Legends and Fantasies.* Cape Town: Struik, 2007.

Parker, Robert. *On Greek Religion.* Ithaca: Cornell University Press, 2011.

_____. *Polytheism and Society at Athens.* Oxford: Oxford University Press, 2007.

Parkinson, Thomas. *Yorkshire Legends and Traditions as Told by Her Ancient Chroniclers, Her Poets and Journalists*, Volume 2. London: E. Stock, 1889.

Parratt, John. *Papuan Belief and Ritual.* New York: Vantage, 1976.

Parrinder, Edward Geoffrey. *Religion in Africa.* New York: Praeger, 1969.

Parry, Jonathan P., and Maurice Bloch. *Money and the Morality of Exchange.* Cambridge: Cambridge University Press, 1989.

Parry-Jones, Daniel. *Welsh Legends and Fairy Lore.* London: Batsford, 1953.

Parsons, Elsie Clews. *Pueblo Indian Religion*, Volume 2. Lincoln: University of Nebraska Press, 1996.

_____. *Pueblo Indian Religion*, Volume 2. Chicago: University of Chicago Press, 1939.

Paton, Lucy Allen. *Studies in the Fairy Mythology of Arthurian Romance.* Boston: Ginn and Company, 1903.

Patrick, David. ed. *Chambers's Encyclopædia*, Volume 4. New York: Collier, 1888.

_____, ed. *Chambers's Encyclopædia*, Volume 7. New York: Collier, 1888.

Pausânias, and Sir James George Frazer, trans. *Commentary on Book I: Attica. Appendix: The Pre-Persian Temple on the Acropolis.* London: Macmillan, 1898.

_____, and _____, trans. *Pausanias's Description of Greece*, Volume 1. New York: Macmillan and Company, Limited, 1898.

_____, and _____. *Pausanias's Description of Greece*, Volume 3. New York: Macmillan and Company, Limited, 1898.

_____, and _____. *Pausanias's Description of Greece*, Volume 6. New York: Macmillan and Company, Limited, 1898.

_____, and _____. *Pausanias's Description of Greece:*

Commentary on books II–V: Corinth, Laconia, Messenia, Elis. London: Macmillan and Company, Limited, 1913.

_____, and _____, *Pausanias's Description of Greece: Indices, Maps.* Whitefish, MT: Kessinger, 2006.

Pausânias, and Peter Levi. *Guide to Greece: Central Greece.* New York: Penguin, 1971.

_____, and _____, trans. *Guide to Greece: Southern Greece.* Middlesex: Penguin, 1971.

Pausânias, and Arthur Richard Shilleto, trans. *Pausanias' Description of Greece*, Volume 2. London: George Bell, 1900.

Pavlock, Barbara. *The Image of the Poet in Ovid's Metamorphoses.* Madison: University of Wisconsin Press, 2009.

Peach, Howard. *Curious Tales of old East Yorkshire.* Wimslow, Cheshire: Sigma Leisure, 2001.

Peacock, Edward. "Ghostly Hounds at Horton." *The Folklore Journal*, Volume 18. The Folklore Society. London: Folklore Society, 1886.

Peacock, Mable. "The Folklore of Lincolnshire." *Folklore*, Volume 12, Joseph Jacobs, Alfred Trübner Nutt, Arthur Robinson Wright, and William Crooke, eds., 161–256. London: David Nutt, 1901.

Peck, Harry Thurston. *Harper's Dictionary of Classical Literature and Antiquities*, Volume 1. New York: Harper, 1897.

Peek, Philip M. *African Divination Systems: Ways of Knowing.* Bloomington: Indiana University Press, 1991.

Peek, Philip M., and Kwesi Yankah. *African Folklore: An Encyclopedia.* New York: Taylor & Francis, 2004.

Penglase, Charles. *Greek Myths and Mesopotamia: Parallels and Influence in the Homeric Hymns and Hesiod.* London: Psychology Press, 1997.

Pentikäinen, Juha. *Shamanism and Northern Ecology.* New York: Walter de Gruyter, 1996.

Penwyche, Gossamer. *The World of Fairies.* New York: Sterling, 2001.

Perkowski, Jan Louis. *Vampire Lore: From the Writings of Jan Louis Perkowsk.* Columbus, OH: Slavica, 2006.

_____. *Vampires of the Slavs.* Columbus, OH: Slavica, 1976.

Perrault, Charles. *Histoires ou contes du temps passé avec des moralités.* Montpezat-en-Provence: AURORÆ LIBRI, Éditeur, 1982.

Perry, Bliss. *A Study of Poetry.* Whitefish, MT: Kessinger, 2004.

Peterson, Amy T., and David J. Dunworth. *Mythology in Our Midst: A Guide to Cultural References.* Westport, CT: Greenwood, 2004.

Petiscus, August Heinrich. *The Gods of Olympos: or, Mythology of the Greeks and Romans.* London: T. Fisher Unwin, 1892.

Petrovitch, Woislav M. *Hero Tales and Legends of the Serbians.* New York: Cosimo, 2007.

_____. *Serbia: Her People History and Aspirations.* New York: Cosimo, 2007.

Pfeiffer, Ida, and Frédéric Guillaume Bergmann. *Visit to Iceland and the Scandinavian North.* London: Ingram, Cooke, 1853.

Phillips, Charles, and Michael Kerrigan. *Forests of the Vampire.* Amsterdam: Time-Life Books BV, 1999.

Philpott, Don, and Hunter Publishing. *Trinidad and Tobago.* Madison: Hunter Publishing, 2002.

Phylactopoulos, George. *History of the Hellenic World: The Archaic Period.* Athens: Ekdotikē Athēnōn, 1975.

Pigott, Grenville. *A Manual of Scandinavian Mythology*. London: William Pickering, 1839.

Pindar, and Roy Arthur Swanson. *Pindar's Odes*. New York: Ardent Media, 1974.

Pinkerton, John. *A General Collection of the Best and Most Interesting Voyages and Travels in all Parts of the World: Many of Which are Now First Translated into English: Digested on a New Plan; Illustrated with Plates, Volume 14*. London: Longman, 1813.

Plain, David D. *Ways of Our Grandfathers: Our Traditions and Culture*. Bloomington: Trafford, 2007.

Platthy, Jenő. *The Mythical Poets of Greece*. Washington, D.C.: Federation of International Poetry Associations, 1985.

Playfair, Alan. *The Garos*. Guwahati, Assam: Spectrum, 1998.

Pliny the Elder, John Bostock, and Henry Thomas Riley. *The Natural History of Pliny*, Volume 2. London: Henry G. Bohn, 1855.

Pócs, Éva. *Between the Living and the Dead: A Perspective on Witches and Seers in the Early Modern Age*. Budapest: Central European University Press, 1999.

Poe, Edgar Allan. *The Complete Works of Edgar Allan Poe*, Volume 7. New York: Williams-Barker Company, 1908.

Polynesian Society. *The Journal of the Polynesian Society*, Volume 6. Wellington, New Zealand: Polynesian Society, 1897.

Poole, Edward Stanley. *The Thousand and One Nights: Commonly Called In England, the Arabian Nights' Entertainments: A New Translation From the Arabic, with Copious Notes, Volume 1*. London: Routledge, Warne, and Routledge, 1865.

Pope, Alexander. *The Iliad of Homer*. Whitefish, MT: Kessinger, 2004.

Pope, Paul Russel. *German Composition: With Notes and Vocabularies*. New York: Henry Holt and Company, 1908.

Porteous, Alexander. *Forest Folklore: Mythology and Romance*. Whitefish, MT: Kessinger, 2006.

_____. *The Forest in Folklore and Mythology*. Mineola, NY: Courier Dover, 2001.

_____. *The Lore of the Forest*. New York: Cosimo, 2005.

Porter, Darwin, and Danforth Prince. *Frommer's England 2011: With Wales*. Hoboken, NJ: John Wiley and Sons, 2010.

Porterfield, Jason, and Corona Brezina. *Chile: A Primary Source Cultural Guide*. New York: Rosen, 2003.

Pratt, Terry Kenneth, and T. K. Pratt. *Dictionary of Prince Edward Island English*. Toronto: University of Toronto Press, 1996.

Pritchett, Robert Taylor. *"Gamle Norg" Rambles and Scrambles in Norway*. London: Virtue and Company, 1879.

Proto, Errico. *Sul Rinaldo di Torquato Tasso; Note Letterarie e Critiche*. Naples: Cav. A. Tocco, 1895.

Proudfit, S. V. "The Hobyas: A Scottish Nursery Tale." *The Journal of American Folk-Lore*, Volume 4, Parts 1–2, the American Folklore Society, ed., 173–4. Boston: Houghton Mifflin, 1891.

Pu, Muzhou. *Rethinking Ghosts in World Religions*. Leiden: BRILL, 2009.

Puryear, Mark. *The Nature of Ásatrú: An Overview of the Ideals and Philosophy of the Indigenous Religion of Northern Europe*. New York: iUniverse, 2006.

Quiggin, Edmund Crosby, ed. *Essays and Studies Pre-sented to William Ridgeway on His Sixtieth Birthday, 6 August, 1913*. Cambridge: Cambridge University Press, 1914.

Quiller-Couch, Sir Arthur Thomas, and Kay Nielsen. *The Twelve Dancing Princesses and Other Fairy Tales*. Mineola, NY: Courier Dover, 2012.

Quint, David. *Epic and Empire: Politics and Generic from Virgil to Milton*. Princeton: Princeton University Press, 1993.

Radford, Edwin, and Mona A. Radford. *Encyclopedia of Superstitions 1949*. Whitefish, MT: Kessinger, 2004.

Radford, Ken. *Tales of South Wales*. London: Skilton and Shaw, 1979.

Rajan, Chandra, and Sahitya Akademi. *The Complete Works of Kālidāsa: Poems*. New Delhi: Sahitya Akademi, 1997.

Ramos, Maximo D. *The Creatures of Midnight: Faded Deities of Luzon, the Visayas and Mindanao*. Quezon City: Island, 1967.

_____. *Creatures of Philippine Lower Mythology*. Quezon City: Phoenix, 1990.

Randall, Alice Elizabeth Sawtelle. *The Sources of Spenser's Classical Mythology*. New York: Silver, Burdett and Company, 1896.

Randles, Jenny. *Super Natural Isle of Man*. London: Robert Hale, 2003.

Ransome, Hilda M. *The Sacred Bee in Ancient Times and Folklore*. Mineola, NY: Courier Dover, 2004.

Read, James. *The Rough Guide to Bolivia*. New York: Penguin, 2008.

Reclus, Élie. *Les Primitifs: Études D'ethnologie Compare*. Paris: Schleicher frères et cie, 1903.

Reed, Alexander Wyclif. *Maori Fables and Legendary Tales*. Auckland, New Zealand: Reed, 1964.

_____. *Reed Book of Māori Mythology*. Auckland, New Zealand: Reed, 2004.

Reidling, Kisma. *Faery Initiations*. Bloomington: AuthorHouse, 2005.

Reinhard, Johan. *The Ice Maiden: Inca Mummies, Mountain Gods, and Sacred Sites in the Andes*. Washington D.C.: National Geographic, 2006.

Renner, George Thomas. *Primitive Religion in the Tropical Forests: A Study in Social Geography*. New York: Columbia University Press, 1927.

Rennie, Frank, and Robin Mason. *Bhutan: Ways of Knowing*. Charlotte, NC: Information Age, 2008.

Rhyne, George N., George V. Rhyne, and Edward J. Lazzerini. *The Supplement to the Modern Encyclopedia of Russian, Soviet and Eurasian History*, Volume 3. Gulf Breeze, FL: Academic International Press, 1995.

Rhys, John. *Celtic Folklore Welsh and Manx*, Volume 1. Whitefish, MT: Kessinger, 2006.

_____. *Celtic Folklore: Welsh and Manx*, Volume 1. Charleston: Forgotten Books, 1983.

_____. *Celtic Folklore: Welsh and Manx*, Volume 2. Whitefish, MT: Kessinger, 2006.

Riasanovsky, Nicholas Valentine, Thomas Eekman, and Gleb Struve. *California Slavic Studies*, Volume 11. Berkeley: University of California Press, 1980.

Richardson, John. *A Dissertation on the Languages, Literature, and Manners of Eastern Nations*. Oxford: Claredon Press, 1777.

Richardson, John, and Charles Wilkins. *A Dictionary, Persian, Arabic and English*, Volume 1. London: William Bulmer and Company, 1806.

Richardson, Nicholas. *Three Homeric Hymns: To Apollo,*

Hermes, and Aphrodite: Hymns 3, 4, and 5. Cambridge: Cambridge University Press, 2010.

Rigoglioso, Marguerite. *The Cult of Divine Birth in Ancient Greece.* New York: Macmillan, 2009.

Ripley, George, and Charles Anderson Dana, eds. *The American Cyclopaedia: A Popular Dictionary of General Knowledge,* Volume 7. New York: D. Appleton, 1883.

_____, and _____. *The New American Encyclopaedia: A Popular Dictionary of General Knowledge,* Volume 7. New York: D. Appleton, 1872.

Robbins, Eliza. *Elements of Mythology, or, Classical Fables of the Greeks and Romans: To Which are Added some Notices of Syrian, Hindu, and Scandinavian Superstitions: Together with Those of the American Nations: The Whole Comparing Polytheism with True Religion: For the Use of Schools.* Philadelphia: Hogan and Thompson, 1849.

Roberts, Jeremy. *Japanese Mythology A to Z.* New York: Infobase, 2009.

Robinson, Agnes Mary Frances, and the National American Woman Suffrage Association Collection (Library of Congress). *Margaret of Angoulême, Queen of Navarre.* Boston: Roberts Brothers, 1890.

Rogers, Robert William. *The Religion of Babylonia and Assyria, Especially in its Relations to Israel: Five Lectures Delivered at Harvard University.* New York: Eaton and Mains, 1908.

Roget, Peter Mark. *Roget's Thesaurus of English Words and Phrases.* New York: T.Y. Crowell Company, 1911.

Rolfe, Robert Thatcher, and F. W. Rolfe. *The Romance of the Fungus World: An Account of Fungus Life in Its Numerous Guises, Both Real and Legendary.* Mineola, NY: Courier Dover, 1974.

Rolleston, T. W. *Celtic Myths and Legends.* Mineola, NY: Courier Dover, 1990.

Roman, Luke, and Mónica Román. *Encyclopedia of Greek and Roman Mythology.* New York: Infobase, 2010.

Romanowski, Sylvie. *Homage to Paul Bénichou.* Birmingham, AL: Summa, 1994.

Room, Adrian. *Who's Who in Classical Mythology.* New York: Random House Value, 2003.

Roscher, Wilhelm Heinrich, and James Hillman. *Pan and the Nightmare.* Zurich: Spring, 1972.

Roscoe, Thomas. *The German Novelists: Tales Selected from Ancient and Modern Authors.* London: Henry Colburn, 1826.

Rose, Carol. *Giants, Monsters, and Dragons: An Encyclopedia of Folklore, Legend, and Myth (in English).* New York: W.W. Norton, 2001.

_____. *Spirits, Fairies, Leprechauns, and Goblins, an Encyclopedia.* New York: W.W. Norton, 1996.

Rose, Herbert Jennings. *A Handbook of Greek Mythology.* London: Psychology Press, 1990.

Rosen, Brenda. *The Mythical Creatures Bible: The Definitive Guide to Legendary Beings.* New York: Sterling, 2009.

Roth, John E. *American Elves: An Encyclopedia of Little People from the Lore of 380 Ethnic Groups of the Western Hemisphere.* Jefferson, NC: McFarland, 1997.

Rouse, Judy M. *History, Legends and Folklore of Christmas.* Lincoln: iUniverse, 2001.

Rowthorn, Chris, Andrew Bender, Matthew D. Firestone, and Timothy N. Hornyak. *Japan.* Oakland: Lonely Planet, 2010.

Roza, Greg. *Incan Mythology and Other Myths of the Andes.* New York: Rosen, 2007.

Ruoff, Henry Woldmar, ed. *The Standard Dictionary of Facts: History, Language, Literature, Biography, Geography, Travel, Art, Government, Politics, Industry, Invention, Commerce, Science, Education, Natural History, Statistics and Miscellany.* Buffalo: Frontier Press, 1919.

Russell, John Rutherfurd. *The History and Heroes of the Art of Medicine.* London: John Murray, 1861.

Russell, Matthew. *The Irish Monthly,* Volume 20. Dublin: M. H. Gill and Sons, 1892.

Ryan, James D., and Constance Jones. *Encyclopedia of Hinduism.* New York: Infobase, 2010.

Ryan, William Francis. *The Bathhouse at Midnight: An Historical Survey of Magic and Divination in Russia.* University Park: Pennsylvania State University Press, 1999.

Rydberg, Viktor, Rasmus Björn Anderson, and James William Buel. *Teutonic Mythology: Gods and Goddesses of the Northland,* Volume 2. London: Norrœna Society, 1907.

_____, _____, and _____. *Teutonic Mythology: Gods and Goddesses of the Northland,* Volume 3. London: Norrœna Society, 1907.

Rye, Walter, and Robert Forby. *A Glossary of Words used in East Anglia,* Volume 31, Issue 3. London: Henry Frowde, Oxford University Press, 1895.

Sacks, David, Oswyn Murray, and Lisa R. Brody. *Encyclopedia of the Ancient Greek World.* New York: Infobase, 2009.

Saille, Harmonia. *Walking the Faery Pathway.* Ropley, Hamptonshire: O-Books, 2009.

Sakihara, Mitsugu, Stewart Curry, and Leon Angelo Serafim. *Okinawan-English Wordbook: A Short Lexicon of the Okinawan Language With English Definitions And Japanese Cognates.* Honolulu: University of Hawaii Press, 2006.

Salisbury, Joyce E. *Women in the Ancient World.* Santa Barbara: ABC-CLIO, 2001.

Salmonson, Jessica Amanda. *The Encyclopedia of Amazons: Women Warriors from Antiquity to the Modern Era.* New York: Paragon House, 1991.

Sammons, Benjamin. *The Art and Rhetoric of the Homeric Catalogue.* Oxford: Oxford University Press, 2010.

Samuelson, Pamela, and Albry Montalbano. *Baby Names for the New Generation: A Comprehensive, Mulitcultural Guide to Finding the Perfect Name for Your Baby.* New York: HarperCollins, 2006.

Savill, Sheila, Geoffrey Parrinder, Chris Cook, and Lilian Mary Barker. *Pears Encyclopaedia of Myths and Legends: Oceania and Australia, the Americas,* Book 4. London: Pelham, 1978.

Saxby, Jessie Margaret Edmondston. *Shetland Traditional Lore.* Norwood, PA: Norwood Editions, 1974.

Scales, Helen. *Poseidon's Steed: The Story of Seahorses, From Myth to Reality.* New York: Penguin, 2009.

Schimmel, Annemarie. *Islamic Names.* Edinburgh: Edinburgh University Press, 1989.

Schlagintweit, Emil. *Buddhism in Tibet: Illustrated by Literary Documents and Objects of Religious Worship, with an Account of the Buddhist Systems Preceding it in India.* Leipzig: F.A. Brockhaus, 1863.

Schlosser, S. E., and Paul G. Hoffman. *Spooky Pennsylvania: Tales of Hauntings, Strange Happenings, and Other Local Lore.* Guilford, CT: Globe Pequot, 2006.

Schmidt, Joël, and Seth Benardete. *Larousse Greek and Roman Mythology*. New York: McGraw-Hill, 1980.

Schofield, William Henry. *English Literature*. 1906.

_____. *Mythical Bards and the Life of William Wallace*. Cambridge: Harvard University Press, 1920.

Schreiber, Charlotte. *The Mabinogion: From the Llyfr. Cocho Hergest, and Other Ancient Welsh Manuscripts. Part 3, Containing Geraint the Son of Erbin*, Volume 2. London: Longman, Brown, Green, and Longmans, 1849.

Schreiber, Lady Charlotte, Jo Nathan, and Sir Owen Morgan Edwards. *The Mabinogion: From the Llyfr Coch o Hergest, and Other Ancient Welsh Manuscripts*, Volume 2. London: Longman, Brown, Green and Longmans, 1849.

Scott, Allan, and Michael Scott Rohan. *Fantastic People*. New York: Galahad Books, 1980.

Scott, Delilah, and Emma Troy. *The Upside-Down Christmas Tree: And Other Bizarre Yuletide Tales*. Guildford, CT: Globe Pequot, 2009.

Scott, James George. *The Burman: His Life and Notions*, Volume 1. London: Macmillan, 1882.

Scott, Sir Walter. *Kenilworth*. London: Marcus Ward and Company, 1877.

Scott, Walter Bart. *Minstrelsy of the Scottish Border: Ballads, Collected By Sir W. Scott*. London: Alex Mury and Sons, 1869.

Scott, Walter. *Minstrelsy of the Scottish Border: Consisting of Historical and Romantic Ballads, Collected in the Southern Counties of Scotland: With a Few of Modern Date, Founded Upon Local Traditions; in Three Volumes*, Volume 1. Edinburgh: Longman, 1812.

Seal, Graham. *Encyclopedia of Folk Heroes*. Santa Barbara: ABC-CLIO, 2001.

Seamon, David, and Robert Mugerauer. *Dwelling, Place, and Environment: Towards a Phenomenology of Person and World*. Dordrecht, the Netherlands: M. Nijhoff, 1985.

Sebeok, Thomas Albert, and Frances Ingemann. *Studies in Cheremis: The Supernatural*. New York: Johnson Reprint Corporation, 1956.

Selbie, John A. *Encyclopædia of Religion and Ethics*. Elibron.com, 1999.

Seligman, Charles G. *The Melanesians of British New Guinea*. Cambridge: Cambridge University Press Archive, 1975.

Seltman, Charles Théodore. *Masterpieces of Greek Coinage: Essay and Commentary*. Oxford: B. Cassirer, 1949.

Senior, Michael. *The Illustrated Who's Who in Mythology*. London: Orbis, 1985.

Sered, Susan Starr. *Women of the Sacred Groves: Divine Priestesses of Okinawa*. Oxford: Oxford University Press, 1999.

Sergent, Bernard. *Homosexuality in Greek Myth*. Boston: Beacon Press, 1986.

Serviss, Garrett Putman. *Astronomy with the Naked Eye: A New Geography of the Heavens, with Descriptions and Charts of Constellations, Stars, and Planets*. New York: Harper and Brothers, 1908.

Seth, Kailash Nath, and B. K. Chaturvedi. *Gods and Goddesses of India*. New Delhi: Diamond Pocket Books, 2000.

Shah, Sirdar Ikbal Ali. *Occultism: Its Theory and Practice*. Whitefish, MT: Kessinger, 2003.

Shakespeare, William. *The Tempest*. London: Macmillan, 1864.

Shakespeare, William, Sir Israel Gollancz, Walter Bagehot, Sir Leslie Stephen, Richard Grant White, and Thomas Spencer Baynes. *The Complete Works of William Shakespeare: With Historical and Analytical Prefaces, Comments, Critical and Explanatory Notes, Glossaries, a Life of Shakespeare and a History of the Early English Drama*, Volume 1. London: University Society, 1901.

Shakespeare, William, Henry Chichester Hart, ed. *The Merry Wives of Windsor*. London: Methuen and Company, 1904.

_____, and _____, ed. *Othello*. London: Methuen and Company, 1904.

Shakespeare, William, John Hort, and Leela Hort. *Shakespeare's a Midsummer Night's Dream: A Shortened and Simplified Version in Modern English*. Nottingham: The Kabet Press, 1992.

Sharp, Sir Cuthbert. *The Bishoprick Garland: Or, A collection of Legends, Songs, Ballads, etc Belonging to the County of Durham*. London: Nichols, and Baldwin and Cradock, 1834.

Shaw, Carol P. *Scottish Myths and Customs*. New York: HarperCollins, 1997.

Shearar, Cheryl. *Understanding Northwest Coast Art: A Guide to Crests, Beings, and Symbols*. Vancouver: Douglas and McIntyre, 2000.

Sheard, K. M. *Llewellyn's Complete Book of Names: For Pagans, Wiccans, Druids, Heathens, Mages, Shamans and Independent Thinkers of All Sorts Who Are Curious about Names from Everyday Places and Times*. St. Paul: Llewellyn Worldwide, 2011.

Shendge, Malati J. *The Civilized Demons: The Harappans in Rgveda*. New Delhi: Abhinav, 2003.

Sherman, Josepha, and David Boston. *Trickster Tales: Forty Folk Stories from Around the World*. Little Rock: August House, 1996.

Shuker, Karl. *The Beasts That Hide from Man: Seeking the World's Last Undiscovered Animals*. New York: Cosimo, 2003.

Siefker, Phyllis. *Santa Claus, Last of the Wild Men: The Origins and Evolution of Saint Nicholas, Spanning 50,000 Years*. Jefferson, NC: McFarland, 2006.

Siefring, Judith. *The Oxford Dictionary of Idioms*. Oxford: Oxford University Press, 2005.

Sievers, Ann H. ed. *Master Drawings from the Smith College Museum of Art*. New York: Hudson Hills, 2000.

Sigfusson, Saemund, and Snorre Sturleson. *The Elder Eddas of Saemund Sigfusson Younger Eddas of Snorre Sturleson*. Middlesex: Echo Library, 2007.

Sikes, Wert. *British Goblins: Welsh Folklore, Fairy Mythology, Legends and Traditions*. Doylestown, PA: Wildside Press, 2002.

Silver, Carole G. *Strange and Secret Peoples: Fairies and Victorian Consciousness*. Oxford: Oxford University Press, 1999.

Simpson, Evelyn Blantyre. *Folk Lore in Lowland Scotland*. London: J.M. Dent and Company, 1908.

Simpson, Jacqueline, and Stephen Roud. *A Dictionary of English Folklore*. Oxford: Oxford University Press, 2000.

Singer, Isaac Basheris. *Stories for Children*. New York: Harper and Row, 1966.

Singer, Isidore, and Cyrus Adler. *The Jewish Encyclopedia: A Descriptive Record of the History, Religion, Literature, and Customs of the Jewish People from the Earliest Times to the Present Day, Volume 1*. New York: Funk and Wagnalls, 1912.

Sjoholm, Barbara. *The Pirate Queen: In Search of Grace O'Malley and Other Legendary Women of the Sea.* Emeryville, CA: Seal Press, 2004.

Skamble, Skimble (pseud.). *Fairy Tales.* Durham: Andrews, 1869.

Skeat, Walter William, and Charles Otto Blagden. *Malay Magic: Being an Introduction to the Folklore and Popular Religion of the Malay Peninsula.* London: Macmillan, 1900.

Sluiter, Ineke, and Ralph Mark Rosen. *Free Speech in Classical Antiquity.* Leiden: BRILL, 2004.

Smart, T. H. *Norroena, the History and Romance of Northern Europe: A Library of Supreme Classics Printed in Complete Form*, Volume 2. London: Norroena Society, 1906.

Smedley, Edward, William Cooke Taylor, Henry Thompson, and Elihu Rich. *The Occult Sciences: Sketches of the Traditions and Superstitions of Past Times, and the Marvels of the Present Day.* London: R. Griffin and Company, 1855.

Smith, Harold Eugene, Gayla S. Nieminen, and May Kyi Win. *Historical Dictionary of Thailand.* Lanham, MD: Scarecrow Press, 2005.

Smith, Herbert Huntington. *Brazil, the Amazons and the Coast.* London: Sampson Low, Marston, Searle and Rivington, 1879.

Smith, James Reuel. *Springs and Wells in Greek and Roman Literature: Their Legends and Locations.* New York: G. P. Putnam's Sons, 1922.

Smith, Nigel J. H. *The Enchanted Amazon Rain Forest: Stories from a Vanishing World.* Gainesville: University Press of Florida, 1996.

Smith, Peter Alderson. *W.B. Yeats and the Tribes of Danu: Three Views of Ireland's Fairies.* Dublin: Smythe, 1987.

Smith, Sir William. *A Classical Dictionary of Biography, Mythology, and Geography Based on the Larger Dictionaries.* London: John Murray, 1891.

_____. *A Dictionary of Greek and Roman Biography and Mythology.* London: John Murray, 1880.

_____. *A Dictionary of Greek and Roman Geography: Abacaenum-Hytanis.* London: John Murray, 1878.

_____. *New Classical Dictionary of Biography, Mythology, and Geography.* London: John Murray, 1850.

Smith, William, and Charles Anthon. *A New Classical Dictionary of Greek and Roman Biography, Mythology and Geography*, Volume 1. Whitefish, MT: Kessinger, 2006.

Smith, William. *Dictionary of Greek and Roman Biography and Mythology.* New York: Taylor and Walton, 1844.

_____. *Dictionary of Greek and Roman Biography and Mythology*, Volume 1. London: John Murray, 1890.

_____. *A Dictionary of Greek and Roman Biography and Mythology: Earinus-Nyx.* London: John Murray, 1880.

_____. *A Smaller Classical Dictionary.* London: J. M. Dent and Sons, 1910.

_____. *A Smaller Classical Dictionary of Biography, Mythology, and Geography: Abridged from the Larger Dictionary.* New York: Harper and Brothers, 1883.

_____. *A Smaller Classical Mythology: With Translations from the Ancient Poets, and Questions Upon the Work.* London: John Murray, 1882.

Snow, Edward Rowe. *Incredible Mysteries and Legends of the Sea.* New York: Dodd, Mead, 1967.

Snowe, Joseph. *The Rhine, Legends, Traditions, History, From Cologne to Mainz*, Volume 2. London: F. C. Westley, 1839.

Society for the Diffusion of Useful Knowledge. *The Penny Cyclopædia of the Society for the Diffusion of Useful Knowledge,* Volume 17. London: Charles Knight and Company, 1840.

Sourvinou-Inwood, Christiane. *Hylas, the Nymphs, Dionysos and Others: Myth, Ritual, Ethnicity : Martin P. Nilsson Lecture on Greek Religion, Delivered 1997 at the Swedish Institute at Athens.* Stockholm: Paul Aaström, 2005.

South, Malcolm. *Mythical and Fabulous Creatures: A Source Book and Research Guide.* Westport, CT: Greenwood Press, 1987.

Sparling, Henry Halliday, Eiríkr Magnússon, and William Morris. *Völsunga Saga: The Story of the Volsungs and Niblungs.* London: The Walter Scott Publishing Company, 1888.

Spence, Lewis. *British Fairy Origins.* Wellingborough, Northamptonshire: Aquarian Press, 1981.

Spence, Lewis. *A Dictionary of Medieval Romance and Romance Writers.* London: George Routledge and Sons, 1913.

Spence, Lewis. *A Dictionary of Non-Classical Mythology.* New York: Cosimo, 2005.

Spence, Lewis. *An Encyclopædia of Occultism: A Compendium of Information on the Occult Sciences, Occult Personalities, Psychic Science, Magic, Demonology, Spiritism and Mysticism.* New York: Dodd, Mead, 1920.

Spence, Lewis. *Encyclopedia of Occultism and Parapsychology.* Whitefish, MT: Kessinger, 2003.

Spence, Lewis. *The Fairy Tradition in Britain.* London: Rider, 1948.

Spence, Lewis. *Hero Tales and Legends of the Rhine.* Charleston, SC: Forgotten Books.

Spence, Lewis. *History and Origins of Druidism.* Whitefish, MT: Kessinger, 2003.

Spence, Lewis. *Legends and Romances of Brittany.* Charleston, SC: Forgotten Books.

Spence, Lewis. *The Magic Arts in Celtic Britain.* Mineola, NY: Courier Dover, 1998.

Spence, Lewis. *The Minor Traditions of British Mythology.* London: Ayer, 1948.

Spence, Lewis. *Myths and Legends of the North American Indians.* Whitefish, MT: Kessinger, 1997.

Spenser, Edmund. *The Faery Queen and Her Knights: Stories.* New York: Macmillan, 1914.

Spencer, Edmund, and M. C. Jussawala. *Faerie Queen, Book 1 (A.O.L.T.).* New Delhi: Orient Blackswan, 1981.

Spiro, Melford E. *Burmese Supernaturalism.* Philadelphia: Transaction, 1978.

Springborg, Patricia. *Western Republicanism and the Oriental Prince.* Austin: University of Texas Press, 1992.

Squire, Charles. *Celtic Myth and Legend. The Gaelic Gods: Chapter XV. The Decline and Fall of the Gods.* London: Gresham, 191?.

_____. *Celtic Myth and Legend: Poetry and Romance.* Lexington, KY: Forgotten Books.

_____. *The Mythology of the British Islands: An Introduction to Celtic Myth, Legend, Poetry, and Romance.* London: Blackie and Son, 1905.

Stafford, Emma, and Judith Herrin. *Personification in the Greek World: From Antiquity to Byzantium.* Aldershot, England: Ashgate, 2005.

Stanford, John Frederick. *The Stanford Dictionary of Anglicised Words and Phrases.* London: C. J. Clay and Son, 1892.

Stanley, David. *South Pacific Handbook*. Fort Leaven-worth, KS: David Stanley, 2000.

Steele, Paul Richard, and Catherine J. Allen. *Handbook of Inca Mythology*. Santa Barbara: ABC-CLIO, 2004.

Steiger, Brad. *Real Monsters, Gruesome Critters, and Beasts from the Darkside*. Canton, OH: Visible Ink Press, 2010.

Stepanich, Kisma K. *Faery Wicca*, Book One. St. Paul: Llewellyn Worldwide, 1997.

Steward, Julian Haynes, ed. *Handbook of South American Indians*, Volume 2. Washington D.C.: U.S. Government Printing. Office, 1946.

_____. *The Scottish Antiquary, or, Northern Notes and Queries*, Volume 7–8. Edinburgh: Lorimer and Gillies, 1900.

_____. *The Scottish Antiquary, or, Northern Notes and Queries*, Volume 14. Edinburgh: Lorimer and Gillies, 1900.

Stewart, William Grant. *The Popular Superstitions and Festive Amusements of the Highlanders of Scotland*. Edinburgh: Archibald Constable and Company, 1823.

Stookey, Lorena Laura. *Thematic Guide to World Mythology*. Westport, CT: Greenwood, 2004.

Sturluson, Snorri. *The Prose Edda: Or, Younger Edda*. Charleston, SC: Forgotten Books, 1916.

_____. *The Younger Edda, also Called Snorre's Edda of the Prose Edda: An English Version of the Foreword; the Fooling of Gylfe, the Afterword; Brage's Talk, the Afterword to Brage's Talk, and the Important Passages in the Poetical Diction (Skaldskaparmal)*. Chicago: S.C. Griggs, 1879.

Sturtevant, William C., and the Smithsonian Institution. *Handbook of North American Indians*, Volume 17. Washington, D.C.: Smithsonian Institution, 1978.

Súilleabháin, Seán Ó. *A Handbook of Irish Folklore*. Detroit: Singing Tree Press, 1970.

Sullivan, Michael. *An Introduction to Chinese Art*. Berkley: University of California Press, 1961.

Summers, Montague. *Geography of Witchcraft*. Whitefish, MT: Kessinger, 2003.

Susej, Tsirk. *The Demonic Bible*. Raleigh, NC: Lulu, 2006.

Sutton, Max Keith. *The Drama of Storytelling in T.E. Brown's Manx Yarns*. Newark: University of Delaware Press, 1991.

Swatos, William H., and Loftur Reimar Gissurarson. *Icelandic Spiritualism: Mediumship and Modernity in Iceland*. New Brunswick, NJ: Transaction, 1997.

Swire, Otta F., and Ronald Black. *Skye: The Island and Its Legends*. Edinburgh: Birlinn, 2006.

Swope, Robin S. *Eerie Erie: Tales of the Unexplained from Northwest Pennsylvania*. New York: The History Press, 2011.

Sykes, Egerton, and Alan Kendall. *Who's Who in Non-Classical Mythology*. London: Psychology Press, 2001.

Ṭabarī. *The Sāsānids, the Byzantines, the Lakhmids, and Yemen*. Albany: SUNY Press, 1999.

Talve, Ilmar. *Finnish Folk Culture*. Helsinki: Finnish Literature Society, 1997.

Tan, Michael T., and Michael L. Tan. *Revisiting Usog, Pasma, Kulam*. Quezon City: University of the Philippines Press, 2008.

Tarn, W. W. *The Greeks in Bactria and India*. Cambridge: Cambridge University Press Archive, 1938.

Taylor, Colin F. *Native American Myths and Legends*. New York: Smithmark, 1994.

Taylor, Richard. *Te Ika a Maui: Or, New Zealand and Its Inhabitants: Illustrating the Origin, Manners, Customs, Mythology, Religion, Rites, Songs, Proverbs, Fables, and Language of the Natives: Together with the Geology, Natural History, Productions, and Climate of the Country: Its State as Regards Christianity: Sketches of the Principal Chiefs, and Their Present Position*. Wellington, New Zealand: A.H. and Alexander Wyclif Read, 1855.

Tegnér, Esaias, Frans Michael Franzén, Bror Emil Hildebrand, and Matilda Maria Valeria Beatrix d'Orozco Gyllenhaal. *Fritiof's Saga: A Legend of the North*. Stockholm: A. Bonnier, 1839.

Telesco, Patricia. *The Kitchen Witch Companion: Simple and Sublime culinary Magic*. New York: Citadel Press, 2005.

Tennant, William. *Thane of Fife: A Poem*. Philadelphia: Hickman and Hazzard, 1822.

Terry, Patricia Ann. *Poems of the Elder Edda*. University Park: University of Pennsylvania Press, 1990.

Thomas, Leslie. *My World of Islands*. London: Methuen, 1993.

Thomas, William Jenkyn. *The Welsh Fairy Book*. Charleston, SC: Forgotten Books, 1979.

Thomassen, Einar. *Canon and Canonicity: The Formation and Use of Scripture*. Copenhagen: Museum Tusculanum Press, 2010.

Thompson, Francis. *The Supernatural Highlands*. London: R. Hale, 1976.

Thompson, Mary Pickering. *Landmarks in Ancient Dover, New Hampshire*. Durham, NC: Concord Republican Press Association, 1892.

Thompson, Robert Farris, and the Museum for African Art. *Face of the Gods: Art and Altars of Africa and the African Americas*. New York: Museum for African Art, 1993.

Thoms, William John. *Lays and Legends of Various Nations: Illustrative of their Traditions, Popular Literature, Manners, Customs, and Superstitions*, Volumes 2–4. London: George Cowie, 1834.

Thorburn, John E. *Facts on File Companion to Classical Drama*. New York: Infobase, 2005.

Thornton, David E. *Kings, Chronologies, and Genealogies: Studies in the Political History of Early Medieval Ireland and Wales*. Oxford: Occasional Publications UPR, 2003.

Thorpe, Benjamin. *Northern Mythology, Comprising the Principal Popular Traditions and Superstitions of Scandinavia, North Germany and the Netherlands: Compiled from Original and Other Sources. In Three Volumes. Scandinavian Popular Traditions and Superstitions*, Volume 1. London: Edward Lumley, 1851.

_____. *Northern Mythology, Comprising the Principal Popular Traditions and Superstitions of Scandinavia, North Germany and the Netherlands: Compiled from Original and Other Sources. In Three Volumes. Scandinavian Popular Traditions and Superstitions*, Volume 2. London: Edward Lumley, 1851.

_____. *Northern Mythology, Comprising the Principal Popular Traditions and Superstitions of Scandinavia, North Germany and the Netherlands: Compiled from Original and Other Sources. In Three Volumes. Scandinavian Popular Traditions and Superstitions*, Volume 3. London: Edward Lumley, 1851.

_____. *Scandinavian Popular Traditions and Supersititions: Volume 2 of Northern Mythology: Comprising the Principal Popular Traditions and Superstitions of*

Scandinavia, North Germany, and the Netherlands, Benjamin Thorpe. London: Edward Lumley, 1851.

_____. *Scandinavian Popular Traditions and Superstitions,* Volume 2. London: Edward Lumley, 1851.

Thury, Eva M., and Margaret Klopfle Devinney. *Introduction to Mythology: Contemporary Approaches to Classical and World Myths.* Oxford: Oxford University Press, 2009.

Tibbits, Charles John. *Folk-Lore and Legends: England and Scotland.* Whitefish, MT: Kessinger, 2006.

_____. *Folk-Lore and Legends, Scandinavian.* Philadelphia: J. B. Lippincott, 1891.

Tolstoy, Nikolai. *The Oldest British Prose Literature: The Compilation of the Four Branches of the Mabinogi.* Lewiston, NY: Edwin Mellen Press, 2009.

Tomita, Kumasaku, and Gordon Ambrose De Lisle Lee. *Japanese Treasure Tales.* London: Yamanaka and Company, 1906.

Tongue, Ruth L. *Forgotten Folk-Tales of the English Counties.* London: Routledge and Kegan Paul, 1970.

Toor, Frances. *Three Worlds of Peru.* New York: Crown, 1949.

Torr, Cecil. *Rhodes in Ancient Times.* Oxford: Oxford University Press, 1885.

Townsend, Chris. *Scotland.* Milnthorpe, Cumbria: Cicerone, 2011.

Tregarthen, Enys. *North Cornwall Fairies and Legends.* London: Wells Gardner, Darton and Company, 1906.

Tregear, Edward. *The Maori-Polynesian Comparative Dictionary.* Wellington, New Zealand: Lyon and Blair, 1891.

Trevelyan, Marie. *Folk-Lore and Folk-Stories of Wales.* Whitefish, MT: Kessinger, 1973.

Trinkauske, Eglute, and the Syracuse University Graduate School. *Seeing the Swarming Dead: Of Mushrooms, Trees, and Bees.* Ann Arbor: ProQuest, 2008.

Tripp, Edward. *The Meridian Handbook of Classical Mythology.* New York: Plume, 2007.

Trzaskoma, Stephen. *Anthology of Classical Myth: Primary Sources in Translation.* Indianapolis: Hackett, 2004.

Turner, Joseph Horsfall. *Yorkshire Notes and Queries,* Volumes 1–2. Bingley, West Yorkshire: T. Harrison, 1888.

Turner, Patricia, and Charles Russell Coulter. *Dictionary of Ancient Deities.* New York: Oxford University Press, 2001.

Tyson, Edward. *A Philological Essay Concerning the Pygmies of the Ancients.* London: David Nutt, 1894.

Universität Münster Institut für Frühmittelalterforschung. *Frühmittelalterliche Studien: Jahrbuch des Instituts für Frühmittelalterforschung der Universität Münster,* Volume 7. Munster: W. de Gruyter, 1973.

Vallee, Jacques. "Taken by the Wind." *Other Worlds, Other Universes,* Brad Steiger and John White, eds., 83–110. Mokelumne Hill, CA: Health Research Books, 1986.

van Doorn-Harder, Pieternella, and Lourens Minnema. *Coping with Evil in Religion and Culture: Case Studies.* New York: Rodopi, 2007.

Vanberg, Bent. *Of Norwegian Ways.* Minneapolis: Dillon Press, 1970.

Varner, Gary R. *Creatures in the Mist: Little People, Wild Men and Spirit Beings Around the World: A Study in Comparative Mythology.* New York: Algora, 2007.

_____. *The Mythic Forest, the Green Man and the Spirit of Nature: The Re-Emergence of the Spirit of Nature* from Ancient Times into Modern Society. New York: Algora, 2006.

Venable, Shannon L. *Gold: A Cultural Encyclopedia.* Santa Barbara: ABC-CLIO, 2011.

Venedey, Jacob. *Excursions in Normandy: Illustrative of the Character, Manners, Customs, and Traditions of the People of the State of Society in General; and of the History, Arts, Sciences, Commerce, Manufactures, Antiquities, Scenery, etc., of that Interesting province of France.* London: Henry Colburn, 1841.

Vernaleken, Theodor. *In the Land of Marvels: Folk-Tales from Austria and Bohemia.* London: W. Swan Sonnenschein and Company, 1884.

Vernier, Richard. *The Flower of Chivalry: Bertrand Du Guesclin and the Hundred Years War.* Woodbridge, Suffolk: Boydell Press, 2007.

Vicente, Xuan Xosé Sánchez, and Xesús Cañedo Valle. *El Gran Libro de la Mitología Asturiana.* Oviedo: Trabe, 2003.

Virgil, and R. M. Millington, trans. *The Fourth Georgic of Virgil, Containing an Account of the Treatment of Bees, the Story of Aristæus and his Bees, the Episode of Orpheus and Eurydice; and an Article on the Gladiators.* London: Longmans, Green, Reader, and Dyer, 1870.

Vives, Juan Luis, and Denise Albanese. *The Instruction of a Christen Woman.* Urbana: University of Illinois Press, 2002.

Waardenburg, Jean Jacques. *Islam: Historical, Social, and Political Perspectives.* New York: Walter de Gruyter, 2002.

Wägner, W. *Asgard and the Gods: Tales and Traditions of our Northern Ancestors: Told for Boys and Girls.* London: W. Swan Sonnenschein and Allen, 1880.

_____. *Epics and Romances of the Middle Ages.* London: W. Swan Sonnenschein, 1883.

_____. *Great Norse, Celtic and Teutonic Legends.* Mineola, NY: Courier Dover, 2004.

Wägner, Wilhelm, and M. W. Macdowall. *Asgard and the Gods.* New York: E. P. Dutton, 1917.

Waldman, Carl. *Encyclopedia of Native American Tribes.* New York: Infobase, 2006.

Wallace, Kathryn. *Folk-lore of Ireland: Legends, Myths and Fairy Tales.* Chicago: J.S. Hyland, 1910.

Walsh, Joseph J. *Were They Wise Men or Kings?: The Book of Christmas Questions.* Louisville: Westminster John Knox Press, 2001.

Walsh, William Shepard. *Heroes and Heroines of Fiction: Famous Characters and Famous Names in Novels, Romances, Poems and Dramas, Classified, Analyzed and Criticised, with Supplementary Citations from the Best Authorities.* Philadelphia: J. B. Lippincott, 1914.

_____. *Heroes and Heroines of Fiction, Classical Mediæval, Legendary: Famous Characters and Famous Names in Novels, Romances, Poems and Dramas, Classified, Analyzed and Criticised, With Supplementary Citations from the Best Authorities.* Philadelphia: J.B. Lippincott, 1915.

Warner, Elizabeth. *Russian Myths.* Austin: University of Texas Press, 2002.

Watson, James Carmichael, and Angus Matheson. *Carmina Gadelica: Hymns and Incantations with Illustrative Notes on Words, Rites, and Customs, Dying and Obsolete,* Volume 2. Edinburgh: T. and A. Constable, 1900.

Watson, William John. *Place-Names of Ross and Cromarty.* Edinburgh: The Northern Counties Printing and Publishing Company, 1904.

Watts, Donald. *Dictionary of Plant Lore.* Burlington, MA: Academic Press, 2007.

Watts, Linda S. *Encyclopedia of American Folklore.* New York: Infobase, 2007.

Webster, Richard. *Flower and Tree Magic: Discover the Natural Enchantment Around You.* St. Paul: Llewellyn Worldwide, 2008.

Webster, Wentworth, and Julien Vinson. *Basque Legends.* London: Griffith and Farran, 1877.

Weinreich, Max. *Lantukh: A Jewish Hobgoblin.* YIVO Annual of Jewish Social Sciences 2–3. New York, 1947–48.

Welch, Lynda C. *Goddess of the North: A Comprehensive Exploration of the Norse Godesses, from Antiquity to the Modern Age.* York Beach, ME: Weiser, 2001.

Wells, Evelyn. *A Treasury of Names.* New York: Essential, 1946.

Wells, John Edwin, and the Modern Language Association of America Middle English Group. *A Manual of the Writings in Middle English, 1050–1500,* Volume 1. New Haven: Connecticut Academy of Arts and Sciences, 1967.

Welsh, Charles. "Irish Fairy and Folk Tales." *Catholic World,* Volume 79, Paulist Fathers and Making of America Project, eds., 753–60. New York: Office of the Catholic World, 1904.

Wentz, Walter Yeeling Evans. *The Fairy-Faith in Celtic Countries.* New York: Henry Frowde, 1911.

Werner, E. T. C. *Myths and Legends of China.* Rockville, MD: Wildside Press, 2005.

Westervelt, William Drake, trans. *Legends of Gods and Ghosts: Hawaiian Mythology.* Boston: George H. Ellis, 1915.

Westmoreland, Perry L. *Ancient Greek Beliefs.* San Ysidro, CA: Lee and Vance, 2007.

Westwood, Jennifer. *Albion: A Guide to Legendary Britain.* London: Granada, 1985.

Westwood, Jennifer, and Jacqueline Simpson. *The Lore of the Land: A Guide to England's Legends, from Spring-Heeled Jack to the Witches of Warboys.* New York: Penguin, 2005.

White, Carolyn. *A History of Irish Fairies.* New York: Carroll & Graf, 2005.

White, David Gordon. *Myths of the Dog-Man.* Chicago: University of Chicago Press, 1991.

White, John. *The Ancient History of the Maori: His Mythology and Traditions,* Volume 1. Wellington, New Zealand: G. Didsbury, 1887.

White, William. *Notes and queries,* Volume 96. London: Oxford University Press, 1897.

_____. *Notes and queries,* Volume 115. London: Oxford University Press, 1907.

Whitmore, Ben. *Trials of the Moon: Reopening the Case for Historical Witchcraft.* Auckland: Briar Books, 2010.

Whittier, John Greenleaf, and Elizabeth Whittier. *The Writings: Narrative and Legendary Poems,* Volume 1. Boston: Houghton, Mifflin, 1894.

Wikimedia Foundation. *Slavic Mythology.* Würzburg: eM Publications.

Wilborn, Bruce K. *Witches' Craft: A Multidenominational Wicca Bible.* New York: Skyhorse, 2011.

Wilby, Emma. *Cunning Folk and Familiar Spirits: Shamanistic Visionary Traditions in Early Modern British Witchcraft and Magic.* Portland, OR: Sussex Academic Press, 2005.

Wilde, Lady Jane Francesca Elgee. *Ancient Legends, Mystic Charms, and Superstitions of Ireland: With Sketches of the Irish Past. To which is Appended a Chaper on "The Ancient Race of Ireland."* Boston: Ticknor and Company, 1888.

Wilde, Lady Jane Francesca Elgee, and William Robert Wilde. *Ancient Legends, Mystic Charms, and Superstitions of Ireland: With Sketches of the Irish Past. To which is appended a chapter on "The ancient race of Ireland."* Boston: Ticknor and Company, 1888.

Wilkinson, James John Garth. *The Book of Edda called Völuspá: A Study in its Scriptural and Spiritual Correspondences.* London: J. Speirs, 1897.

Williams, John Ellis Caerwyn, and Patrick K. Ford. *The Irish Literary Tradition.* Cardiff: University of Wales Press, 1992.

Wilson, Colin, and Damon Wilson. *The Mammoth Encyclopedia of the Unsolved.* New York: Carroll & Graf, 2000.

Wilson, John Dover. *Life in Shakespeare's England: A Book of Elizabethan Prose.* Cambridge: Cambridge University Press, 1913.

Wilson, L. M., and Alexander Leighton. *Wilson's Tales of the Borders and of Scotland.* London: Walter Scott, 1888.

Winckelmann, Johann Joachim. *Essays on the Philosophy and History of Art,* Volume 1. New York: Continuum, 2006.

Woodfield, Stephanie. *Celtic Lore and Spellcraft of the Dark Goddess: Invoking the Morrigan.* St. Paul: Llewellyn Worldwide, 2011.

Wood-Martin, William Gregory. *Traces of the Elder Faiths of Ireland: A Folklore Sketch; A Handbook of Irish Pre-Christian Traditions,* Volume 1. New York: Longmans, Green, and Company, 1902.

_____. *Traces of the Elder Faiths of Ireland: A Folklore Sketch; a Handbook of Irish Pre-Christian Traditions,* Volume 2. London: Longmans, Green, and Company, 1902.

World Book, Inc. *Christmas in France.* Chicago: World Book, 1996.

World Book, Inc. *The World Book Encyclopedia,* Volume 7. Chicago: World Book, 2000.

Wright, Dudley. *Eleusinian Mysteries and Rites.* Whitefish, MT: Kessinger, 2003.

Wright, Elizabeth Mary. *Rustic Speech and Folk-Lore.* London: Humphrey Milford, 1913.

Wright, G. Frederic, Frederick Bennett Wright, and the Records of the Past Exploration Society. *Records of the Past,* Volume 10. Washington, D.C.: Records of the Past Exploration Society, 1911.

Wright, Joseph. *The English Dialect Dictionary, Being the Complete Vocabulary of All Dialect Words Still in Use, Or Known to Have Been in Use During the Last Two Hundred Years: A–C.* London: Henry Frowde, 1900.

_____. *The English Dialect Dictionary, Being the Complete Vocabulary of All Dialect Words Still in Use, Or Known to Have Been in Use During the Last Two Hundred Years: D–G.* London: Henry Frowde, 1900.

_____. *The English Dialect Dictionary, Being the Complete Vocabulary of All Dialect Words Still in Use, Or Known to Have Been in Use During the Last Two Hundred Years: M–Q.* London: Henry Frowde, 1900.

_____. *The English Dialect Dictionary, Being the Complete Vocabulary of All Dialect Words Still in Use, Or Known to Have Been in Use During the Last Two Hundred Years: T–Z.* London: Henry Frowde, 1900.

Wright, Thomas. *Dictionary of Obsolete and Provincial English: Containing Words from the English Writers Previous to the Nineteenth Century Which Are No Longer in Use, or Are Not Used in the Same Sense. And Words Which Are Now Used Only in the Provincial Dialects.* London: Henry G. Bohn, 1857.

_____. *Dictionary of Obsolete and Provincial English, Containing Words from the English Writers Previous to the Nineteenth Century Which Are No Longer in Use, or Are Not Used in the Same Sense. And Words Which Are Now Used Only in the Provincial Dialects.* London: George Bell and Sons, 1904.

Wylie, William P. *The Pattern of Love.* London: Longmans, Green, 1958.

Yamaguchi, Kenkichi, Frederic De Garis, Atsuharu Sakai, and Fujiya Hoteru. *We Japanese: Being Descriptions of many of the Customs, Manners, Ceremonies, Festivals, Arts and Crafts of the Japanese, besides Numerous other Subjects.* Miyanshita: Fujiya Hotel, 1964.

Yardley, Edward. *The Supernatural in Romantic Fiction.* London: Longmans, Green, and Company, 1880.

Yar-Shater, Ehsan. *Encyclopædia Iranica.* London: Routledge and Kegan Paul, 1989.

Yearsley, MacLeod. *The Folklore of Fairytale.* Whitefish, MT: Kessinger, 2005.

Yeats, William Butler. *Fairy and Folk Tales of the Irish Peasantry.* London: Walter Scott, 1888.

_____. *Visions and Beliefs in the West of Ireland*, Volume 1. New York: G. P. Putman's Sons, 1920.

Yeats, William Butler, and Lady Augusta Gregory. *Gods and Fighting Men: The Story of the Tuatha De Danaan and of the Fianna of Ireland.* London: John Murray, 1905.

Yolen, Jane, Shulamith Levey Oppenheim, and Paul Hoffman. *The Fish Prince and Other Stories: Mermen Folk Tales.* New York: Interlink Books, 2001.

Yonge, Charlotte Mary. *History of Christian names*, Volume 2. London: Macmillian, 1878.

Zacharia, Katerina. *Converging Truths: Euripides' Ion and the Athenian Quest for Self-Definition.* Leiden: BRILL, 2003.

Zipes, Jack David. *Victorian Fairy Tales: The Revolt of the Fairies and Elves.* New York: Psychology Press, 1989.

Žižek, Slavoj. *The Plague of Fantasies.* London: Verso, 1997.

Index

A-senee-ki-wakw 9
Aafreeda 14
Aba 9, 242, 255
Abapansi 26
Abarbarea 9, 242
Abarbaree 9, 196, 242
Abatwa 9
Abbey Lubbers 9, 71
Abcán 10
Abcán mac Bicelmois 10
Abdera, Greece 324
Abdullah al-Kazwini 10
Abeille, Princess 200–01
Abenaki 9, 23, 108
Aberdeen, Scotland 123
Aberdover 218
Aberystruth 171
Abhartach 10
Abhartach's Grave 10
Abonde 10, 95, 96, 171,
  344
Abruzzo, Italy 227
Abuelo 92
Abundantina 10
Abunde 10
Abundia 10, 11, 95, 171
Acacia 107, 116
Acacila 11
Acalica 11
Acamantis 11, 98
Acaste 11
Accadia 152
Acesidas 94
Achachilas 11
Acheloides 11
Acheloos 19, 106, 198,
  306
Achelous 11, 77
Acheron 11, 262
Achilles 15, 20, 27, 33,
  74, 104, 110, 111, 117,
  162, 172, 187, 196, 203,
  207, 208, 217, 230, 246,
  247, 262, 265, 272,
  282, 311, 231, 322, 323
Achtan 118
Acis 155, 316
Acmon 94
Acorn 45, 80, 81, 84, 173
Acorn Lady 84

Acousilaos 270
Acraia 19
Actaea 11, 97
Actaeon 91
Actaia 12
Actea 12
Ad-Hene 12
Adam 22, 174, 227
Adam and Eve 174
Adhunall 12
Adiante 12, 97
Adite 12, 97
Admeta 12
Admete 12
Admeto 12
Admetos 270
Adone of Marini 143
Adonis 27, 55, 143
Adraste 12, 24, 186, 188
Adrastea 12, 188
Adrasteia 12, 246
Aeacus 13
Aebhel 14
Aebill 14, 16
Aectes, King 189
Áed 10, 17
Aed Abrat 13
Áed Abrat 13, 139, 215
Aed Srónmár 10
Aedh 94
Aeëtes 270
Aeetes, King 119
Aegean Sea 12, 19, 24,
  27, 102, 188, 195, 197,
  202, 203, 204, 228,
  246, 254, 289, 290, 295
Aegeirus 13
Aegel 13, 245
Ægina 13, 37, 234, 242
Aegina 13, 37, 234, 242
Ægir 118
Aegis 19, 133
Aegius 98, 235
Ægle 13
Aegle 13, 34, 81, 106, 112,
  129, 176, 178, 210, 232,
  242, 271
Aegyptus 97, 99, 106,
  280
Ælf 22

Aelfdane 13
Aelfraed 14
Aelfric 20
Aelfwen 25
Aelfwenn 25
Aelfwenne 25
Aelfwin 25
Aelfwine 25
Aelfwinn 25
Aelfwyne 25
Aelfwynn 25
Aelfwynne 25
Aello 122
Aengus 13, 29
Aengus Mac Óg 29
Aengus MacOg 13
Aeolus 262
Aero 37, 38, 79, 112, 122,
  224, 319
Aes Sídhe 32, 304
Aesacus 21
Æsar 113
Aeschylus 21, 228, 326
Aeseopus 243
Æsepus 9
Aesepus 9
Æser 23, 251
Æsir 25, 335
Aethelwine 25
Aethelwyne 25
Aetherie 13, 106, 176, 210,
  232, 273
Aethra 13, 128, 186, 254
Aeval 14, 16, 85, 141
Afanc 198
Affric 14
Affrica 14
Afreda 14
Afredah 14
Afreeda 14
Afreedah 14
Afreet 107, 158, 189, 194
Afric 14
Africa 2, 14, 35, 38, 41,
  43, 56, 117, 123, 208,
  260, 265, 296, 301, 348
African Fairy Lore 2, 14,
  26
Afrida 14
Afridah 14

Afrit 17, 189
Afrite 189
Afryda 14
Afrydah 14
Agamenmon 191
Aganippe 14, 151
Aganippides 240
Agaptolemus 98, 276
Agate 223
Agaue 15
Agave 15, 40, 97, 132, 186
Agdistis 243
Agenor 85, 97, 98, 133
Aglaia 81
Aglaope 15
Aglaopheme 15, 306
Aglaophonos 15
Aglaurides 15, 23
Aglauros 15, 23
Agloolik 15
Agnes Barre 166
Agraulos 15
Agreus 310
Aguane 15, 16, 294, 305
Agun Kuguza 16
Ahermanabad 16, 35
Ahermanabâd 16, 35
Ahes 237
Ahi At-Trab 16
Ahnfrau 342
Ai 16
Aia 16, 242
Aia, Greece 16
Aiaia 16, 84
Aiaia, island 16, 84
Aiakos, King 126, 283
Aibell 14, 16, 17
Aíbell 17, 141
Aibell, Queen 16–17
Aibell's well 17
Aibheaeg 17
Aibheag, Queen 141
Aibheall 141
Aibhinn 14, 16
Aicha Kandida 17
Aideen 118
Aigeiros 17, 173
Aigel 17
Aigetes 299
Aigina 13, 65

Aigina, island 126, 283
Aigypans 24
Aigyptos 74, 280
Aiken Drum 17
Ailbill 17
Ailill 17–18, 139
Ailill of Leinster 17
Aillen Mac Midhna 18
Aillen Mac Midna 18
Aillen MacModha 18
Aine 18, 41, 51, 86, 105, 141, 148, 158, 260
Ainé 18, 41
Aine Cliach 18
Aine Marina 18
Aine Marine 18
Aine of Knockaine 18
Aine of the Sight 18
Aine of the Whip 18
Aine's Hill 18
Ainsel 18, 82
Aiolid 37
Aiolos 228, 263
Aira 35
Airmed 18
Airmid 18
Aisakos 21, 78
Aithadh 123
Aithech Tuatha 149
Aither 259
Aithousa 19
Aitvaras 19, 45, 284
Aiuka 193
Aiwel 19
Aiwel Longar 19
Aix 19
Ajnan 107
Akaia 19, 130
Akakanaza 200
Akakasoh 19, 244
Akan people 56
Akaste 19
Akeste 19
Akestes 127, 299
Akhaia, Greece 34, 63, 329
Akheloides 19
Akheloios 19
Akheron, river 262
Akraia 20, 282
Aktaie 20
Aktaion 156
Akvan 55
Al-A'war 20
Alan 20
Alb 22
Albania 48, 74, 145, 262
Albany 229, 264, 281
Albastor 20
Alberich 20, 21, 22, 122
Albrich 20, 121, 256
Alces 98, 161
Alcheringa 21
Alcina 21, 219
Alcina Island 219
Alcinda 21
Alcinoe 21, 242

Alcmenor 98, 180
Alcyineus 23
Alcyone 19, 21, 37, 38, 79, 112, 122, 224, 261, 277, 311, 319
Alder tree 85
Alder, King 125
Ale 71, 72, 121, 164, 302
Alecto 21, 153
Alekto 21
Aletes 270
Alexander the Great 209, 299
Alexirhoe 21, 78, 242
Alf 22
Alf (2) 22
Alf-gust 23
Alf-heim 22
Alfa 22, 172
Alfa-blot 22
Alfa-folk 22
Alfar 22, 108, 335
Alfavakir 123
Alfavakir 123
Alferich 20
Alfheim 22, 124, 216
Alfheimr 124
Alfhime 22, 217
Alfquarnar 123
Álfr 22
Alfred the Great, King 342
Alfreikr 22
Alfrigg 22, 55, 65, 115, 158
Alfrik 23
Alfs 23, 108, 216, 251
Álfur 162
Algonquin Indians 125, 226
Algue 69
Algul 158
Alia 290, 319
Alidoro 237
Alien Big Cats 59
Alkinoe 23
Alkippe 23, 151
Alkman 210, 325
Alkyone 21
Alkyoneus 23
Alkyonides 23, 233
All Hallows Eve 73, 221
All Saints' Day 93
Allah 107, 188, 300
Allewyn 258
Allvar 25
Allvaro 25
Allvarso 25
Almo 211
Almond tree 243
Alom-bag-winno-sis 23
Alom-begwi-no-sis 23
Alp 264
Alp-Luachra 23
Alpheios 34
Alpheios River 34
Alpheus 24, 26, 28

Alpris 20
Alriche 122
Alsatian 54
Alsea 24, 183
Alseid 24, 251
Alseides 24, 251
Alston 24
Althaea 12, 24, 186, 188
Althaia 24
Althiof 24
Althiolf 24
Althjof 24
Althjófr 24
Altmor Burn 284
Aluche 24
Alundyne 211
A'lus 24
Alux 24–25
Aluxob 24–25
Alva 25
Alvar 25
Alvara 25
Alvare 25
Alvaria 25
Alvarie 25
Alvarr 25
Alvarso 25
Alven 25
Alvie 25
Alvin 25
Alvina 25
Alvis 25
Alvis-Mal-Edda 25
Alviss 25
Alvíss 25
Alwis 25
Alyxothoe 21
Am Fear Liath Mor 145
Amadáin 25
Amadáin Mhóir 25
Amadán 25, 57
Amadán Mór 25
Amadán na Briona 25
Amadán na Bruidne 25
Amadigi 237, 262, 334
Amalthea 26
Amalthéa 26
Amaltheia 19, 24, 26
Amáltheia 26
Amathea 26
Amathëa 26
Amatheia 26
Amathia 26
Amatongo 26
Amazon Basin 44
Amazon River 188
Amazonian, Brazil 32
Amber 13, 65, 176, 210, 232, 273, 277
Amber City 26
Amber-weeping popular tree 13, 210, 232, 273
Amberabad 26
Amberabâd 26
Ambrosia 27, 108, 186, 215
Ameer Ali, Prince 140

Amesha Spentas 104
A' Mharcachd-Shith 141
Ammaze 264
Amnisiades 27
Amnisides 27
Amnisos, river 27
Amoret 27, 53
Ampelos 27, 173
Ampelus 27
Amphicomone 27, 98
Amphictyon 285
Amphidamas 83
Amphimedusa 99
Amphinome 27
Amphion 106
Amphirho 27
Amphiro 27
Amphissos 112
Amphithemis 329
Amphithoe 27
Amphithoë 27
Amphitrite 23, 27–28, 93, 94, 102, 207, 330
Amphytrite 27
Amykos 229
Amymone 28, 97, 99, 132
Amyntor 96, 98
An 28
An Nighechain 51
Ana 28, 136, 199, 200, 217, 219
Ánaar 29, 260
Analida 211
Anank 12
Ananta 28, 337
Ananta Sesha 28
Ananta-Shesha 28, 241
Anantesa 337
Anapos 207
Anar 29, 260
Anarr 29
Ánarr 29, 260
Anatolia, Greece 19, 37, 162, 178, 188, 207, 238, 243, 248, 258, 268, 278, 293, 296, 317
Anatolian peninsula 36, 198
Anaxibia 29, 97
Anaxithea 29, 99
Ancaeus 295
Ancestral god 1, 231
Ancestral spirit 5, 14, 21, 26, 38, 47, 100, 106, 126, 157, 231, 275, 309, 334
Anchirhoe 29, 72, 127, 224, 230, 242
Anchiroe 29
Ancho 183
Ancient Legends of Ireland 234
Ande 107
Anderson, Hans Christian 260
Andes Mountains 11, 33, 39, 40, 225, 226, 264,

275, 284, 294, 296, 300, 341, 345
Andorra 135
Andreus 90
Androgynous 214, 341
Andromachus 98, 177
Andvaranaut 29
Andvari 20, 29
Andvari's Gift 29
Angel of Death 344
Anglesey 29
Anglitora 73
Angry Ones 153
Angus 29
Angus Mac Og 94
Angus Oc 29
Angus of the Birds 29
Angus Og 29, 30, 61
Anhanga 30
Anigriades 30
Anigrides 30
Anigros 30
Anippe 30, 242
Anjanas, las 30
Ankaios 295
Anklets 140
Ankore people 126
Ankou 30
Anna Perenna 30
Annaed 31, 242
Annamuttu 204
Annar 29, 31, 260
Annarr 29
Annaver 29, 260
Annwn, Hounds of 35, 48, 59, 92, 93, 137, 154, 171, 184, 277, 302
Anointing of the Sick 339
Anser segetum 154
Anthedon 31, 242
Antheia 81
Antheli 97
Anthelia 31
Anthemoessa, island 306
Anthills 253
Anthousai 31
Anthoussai 31
Anthracia 31
Anthrakia 31
Anthropohagi 31
Anthropophagi 31, 198
Antimachus 98, 234
Antiochus 98, 192
Antiope 31
Antipaphus 91, 98
Antonoe 31
Antrim 167
Anu 158
Anvil 154, 174
Aobiheall 14
Aoede 32
Aoibheal 14
Aoibheall 16, 31
Aoibhell 14, 16, 17
Aoibhil 14, 16

Aoibhinn 18, 32, 86, 148, 260
Aoide 32, 240
Aonghus 13, 29
Aos Sí 32, 304
Aotearoa, island 331
Apa tree 260
Apayao people 54
Apayao River 54
Apci'lnic 32
Ape-men 21, 219
Aphaia 65
Aphrodite 55, 81, 106, 178, 188, 204, 268, 290, 294, 319
Apis 319
Apoiaueue 32
Apollo 19, 63, 77, 81, 87, 89, 100, 112, 127, 128, 129, 198, 205, 207, 208, 215, 228, 243, 263, 289, 313, 320, 322, 325, 329
Apollodorus of Athens 4, 28
Apopa 32
Apotamkin 32
Appiades 33
Appian 33
Appias 33
Apple-grey horse 181, 199, 245
Apple Island 40
Apple trees 13, 33, 34, 127, 129, 178, 228, 259
Appletree Man 33
Apsaras 156, 231, 287, 325, 335
Apseudes 33
Apsyrtus 189
Apu 33, 40, 225, 226, 264, 275, 284, 294, 296, 300, 305, 341, 345
Apu Putukusi 225
Apuku 33, 45
Apus 11, 264
Aquatic devil 225
Aquilante 56, 246
Arabian Nights 10, 194, 266, 297
Arabos 324
Arada 191
Aradia 191
Arahuta 317
Arallu 33
Arapteš 33
Arawn 184, 277
Arbelus 98, 257
Arcadia 33–34
Arcadia, Greece 2, 23, 31, 37, 50, 83, 98, 128, 176, 179, 207, 229, 241, 250, 261, 269, 272, 274, 276, 306, 310, 321, 325
Arcadians 83
Arcas 2, 75, 83, 231
Archangel 108, 154
Archangel's Day 93

Archbishop Baldwin 137
Arche 34, 240
Archelaus 29, 97
Archiroe 34, 241
Arcturus 2, 75
Ares 23, 99, 132, 165, 174, 312, 320, 322, 324, 326
Arestor, King 241
Arethusa 13, 24, 129, 178, 242
Aretusa 34
Argante 34, 141
Arge 176
Argentina 206, 276
Argia 34
Argiope 34
Argius 98, 133
Argolis, Greece 129
Argonauts 131, 225, 254
Argos, Greece 20, 34, 72, 127, 129, 186, 190, 192, 211, 224, 228, 240, 245, 274, 282, 319
Argos, King 129
Argus 190
Argyllshire, island 76
Argyphia, Queen 15, 28, 40, 97, 98, 165, 187, 297
Argyra 34
Argyra, Greece 34
Ariā 35
Ariadne 13
Ariel 35, 275
Ariosto, Ludovico 237
Aristaios 208
Aristocratic Fairies 330
Aristonoos 79, 98
Arkan Sonney 35, 137
Arkas 83, 128
Arke 122
L'Armée Furieuse 35
Armenia 282
Armoasbus 98, 334
Armorica 205
Arne 228
Arnhem, Australia 46, 234
Arragon, France 264, 284
Arrow 53, 123, 196, 248
Arrowheads 137
Arsalte 35, 98
Arshenk 35, 102, 103
Art 52, 103, 165, 303
Artemis 24, 27, 34, 65, 91, 95, 156, 176, 187, 220, 224, 228, 229, 243, 246, 248, 256, 261, 272, 277, 283, 289, 312, 319, 345
Arthelwine 25
Arthur, King 34, 58, 73, 144, 177, 237, 344
Arthurian lore 34, 44, 58, 96, 125, 208, 211, 228, 237

Arthurian mythology 121, 208, 211, 260, 339
Arunta, tribes 21
Arvon 177
Aryas 101
Arzshenk 35, 102
As-Iga 35
Asamanukpai 35, 36
Ascalaphus 262
Asdeev 36, 102
Åsgårdsreia 343
Ash Boys 36
Ash tree 136, 229, 246, 251, 261
Ash-tree 246, 251
Ashanti people 296, 301
Ashes 36, 200, 221, 266, 309, 329
Ashes Man 36
Ashinaga and Tenaga 36
Ashorin tree 260
Ashray 36
Asia 36
Asie 36
Askalaphos 262
Asklepios 259
Askra, Boiotia 37
Askre 37
Aso Sidhe 99
Asopides 37, 79, 85, 89
Asopis 37
Asopos 198, 204, 233, 242, 270
Asopos, river 37, 79, 85, 89, 198, 204, 233, 242, 270
Asopus 13, 31, 37, 79, 85, 89, 174, 258, 294, 306, 317, 321, 322
Asrai 36
Assaracus, Prince 178
Assarakos, Prince 178
Assyria 209
Astakides 37
Asteria 36, 97
Asteriai 37
Asterides 83, 98
Asterion 19
Asterion, river 20, 282
Asterius 85, 98
Asterodeia 37
Asterodia 37
Asterope 37, 38, 79, 112, 122, 178, 224, 261, 312, 319
Astraeus 304
Astris 37, 79
Astynome 83
Astyoche 37
Astyokhe 37
Asyn 178
Ataman 38
Atargatis 38, 232
Athach 38, 106, 221
Athamas 99, 246, 285
Athelstan, King 88

Athena 15, 81, 99, 199, 204, 233, 280, 329
Athenaeus 63, 173
Athens, Greece 4, 15, 28, 120, 126, 196, 281, 349
Athletes 98, 132
Atlanteia 36, 38, 85, 97, 98, 161, 164, 180, 191, 290
Atlantic 151
Atlantid 2, 38, 231, 254
Atlantides 21, 37, 38, 79, 112, 122, 224, 233, 319
Atlantis 75
Atlas 13, 21, 36, 37, 38, 79, 87, 110, 112, 128, 129, 178, 186, 224, 233, 254, 277, 319
Atropos 38, 144, 236
Attercroppe 38
Attica 105, 128, 130, 173
Attika, Greece 95, 196, 216, 281
Attis 217, 243, 293
Attorcroppe 38
Atua 35, 38, 204, 224, 236, 253, 318, 326
Au Co 38–39
Auberich 121, 256
Auberon 121, 256
Audumla 348
Aufe 255
Aughisky 39, 117, 118, 161, 198, 199, 245, 341
Auki 39
El Auki 39
Aulanerk 39
Aulf 255
Aulfe 255
Auloniad 39
Aumanil 39
Aura 270
Aurae 316
Aurai 39
Aurora Borealis 148
Aurvang 39
Aurvangr 39
Ausangate 40
Australia 21, 46, 234
Austri 40, 251, 314, 342
Austria 58, 128, 135, 294, 343
Austrian Alps 15
Autodice 40, 98
Automate 40, 97, 132
Autone 186
Autonoe 15, 40, 97
Autumn Tumult 235
Autychos 208
Avalanche 337
Avallach 237
Avalon 34, 40, 139, 141, 238, 281, 282
Aveline 40
Avon, river 199
Awd Goggie 40, 254
Awd Goggin 164

Awki 41
Awl 41, 305
Axios 270
Aymara people 11, 121
Aynia 41, 141
Aynia's Chair 41
'Azâzeel 41, 174
Azimo 26
Aziza 41
Azizan 41
Azrail 41

Bà-Dúc-Chúa 43, 113
Baba 42
Баба Яга 42
Бába-Яга́ 42
Baba Yaga 42, 194
Baba Yaga Kostianaya Noga 42
Baba Yaga's Hut 42
Babau 43, 258
Babban Ny Mheillea 43
Babou 258
Babylon 324
Babylon Thronia 324
Bacchantes 44
Bacche 43, 65, 128, 223, 255
Bacchus 15, 31, 40, 43, 44, 80, 89, 95, 106, 128, 155, 186, 201, 202, 204, 214, 223, 224, 241, 248, 255, 267, 271, 272, 27, 280, 296, 304, 312, 313, 325
Bachna Rachna 43, 348
Bäckahästen 43, 98, 245
Bacon family of Seafeild 215
Badb 237
Bademagu 44, 228, 231
Badgers 165
Badsey, England 275
Baennik 47
Baetata 44
Bafur 44
Báfurr 44
Bagbury Bridge 291
Bagbury Manor 291
Baghlet el Qebour 44
Bagpipe 327
Bahaman 44
Bahasa kapor 59
Bahlindjo 44
Bainik 47
Bainikha 47
Bainushko 47
bakat 104
Bakemono 44
Bakgest 59
Bakhna Rakhna 43
Bakkhai 44, 223, 241, 267, 274, 280
Bakkhe 43
Bakru 44–45
Bakš Ia 45
Bakš Kuba 45

Bakš Kuguza 45
Bakš Oza 45
Baku 45, 137
Bakwas 70
Balandjo 44
Balanos 45, 173
Balanus 45
Balar 46
Balardeu 258
Baldarich 45
Balder 217
Balderich 45
Baldr 335
Balendjo 44
balete 107, 116, 126
Balior 46
Balkin 45–46, 226
Ballad 125, 225
Ballafletcher 215
Balls of blue flame 344
Balls of light 104, 284
Ballybog 46
Balmung 20
Balor 46, 79, 129
Balor mac Doit 46
Balor of the Evil Eye 46
Balrog 46
Balroth 46
Balte 46
Baltic Sea 45, 201
Balur 46
Bamapama 46
Ban-na-Naomha 46
Ban Naomha 46
Ban Nighechain 46
Ban-Shoan 51
Banana tree 208, 318
Baneasa forest 296
Bannafeet 330
Bannaia 47
Bannik 47
Banshee 1, 14, 16, 20, 31, 47, 48, 51, 62, 76, 86, 93, 101, 110, 114, 121, 148, 155, 161, 166, 214, 224, 230, 235, 300, 320, 342, 343, 348
Baobhan Sith 48, 334
Baptized 56, 166, 189, 244, 277, 303, 309, 318, 345
Bar 48, 341
Barbarian Nymph 9
Barbegazi 48
Bardha 48
Bargeist 48
Bargest 48
Bargheist 48
Barghest 48, 59, 302
Barghest of Burnley 48, 302
Bargtjest 48
Barguest 48, 59, 60, 155, 172, 235, 259, 263, 274, 302, 303, 308, 321
Barguist 48
Bari 48, 310

Bariaua 49
Barley 77, 177
Barley cake 140
Barley meal 140
Barn 7, 48, 62, 115, 249, 263, 264, 284, 308, 328, 348
Barrie, Sir James Matthew 6
Barrow Mound 138
Barstukai 198
Barux 24
Basa-Andre 49, 210, 252
Basa-Juan 49, 183, 210
Basaandre 49
Basadone 49
Basajuan 49
Basile, Giambattista 185
Basilisk 49
Basmus 173
Basque 49, 210, 318, 343
Bassai 50
Bat 21, 35, 152, 165, 170, 202, 228, 271, 275, 326
Bateia 50, 242
Bath-Slough 155
Bathhouse 20, 47
Bathing Fairies 50
Bathurst, lake 71
Battle Maidens 336
Battle of Bloody Run 242
Battle of Camlan 237
Battle of Clontarf 16, 31
battle of Moytura 320
Battle of Troy 183, 243, 247
Bauchan 50, 62, 88, 89
Bauchans 62
Bauken 62
Baumbur 50
Baumesel 50
Bavor 50
Bavorr 50
Bawken 62
Bayard 50
Bayard, King 226
Bažaloshtsh 51
Bazimo 26
Be Bind 52
Be Find 52
Beach 32, 68, 120, 262, 275, 323
Beafhola 52
Bean a'Tighe 51
Bean Chaointe 47
Bean Fionn 51
Bean Goose 154
Bean-nigh 46
Bean Nighe 47, 51, 146
Bean-Nighe 47
Bean-nighidh 46
Bean Si 47, 51
Bean Sidhe 51
Bean Sídhe 51
Bean Tighe 51, 325
Bean-Tighe 51
Beansidhe 47, 51, 76

Bear 2, 42, 69, 75, 106, 167, 264, 265
Beara 74
Beara Peninsula 137
Beast of Odail Pass 56
Beautiful woman 17, 20, 48, 49, 78, 86, 118, 119, 140, 152, 159, 189, 215, 225, 238, 243, 275, 307
Bebo 192
Bebrykes 228
Becfhola 52, 141, 150
Becfola 52
Becuma 52, 103
Becuma Cneisgel 52
Beden 56
Bediadari 52, 135
Bedonebyasyoudid, Mrs. 239
Beer 25, 57, 68, 69, 80, 81, 205, 207
Beer kegs 344
Bees 66, 177, 229, 274, 275, 300
Befana 52
Befind 52
Béfind 52, 141
Befionn 52
Beggys 309
Behir 53, 153
Beithir 53
Bel 30, 324
Bela, Czech Republic 249
Belelah 221
Belgium, Germany 200, 202, 263, 264, 345
Belial 221
Belize 113
Bell 66, 2887
Bellissima 348
Belly Blin 58
Belos 324
Belphoebe 27, 53
Beltane 171
Ben Baynac 53, 84
Ben MacDhui 146
Ben Socia 53
Ben Varrey 53, 232
Ben-Varrey 53, 232
Bendith Y Mamau 53–54, 66, 134, 137, 334
Benshi 47
Bensocia 53
Benthesikyme 54, 255
Berberoka 54
Berchta 54, 254, 344
Beregini 55, 341
Bereginya 55
Berehynias 55
Berg-Mänlein 115
Berg People 55, 330
Bergfolk 55
Berggeist 55
Bergmanli 128
Bergsmiedlein 128
Berkhyas 55, 102

Berkta 54
Berling 23, 55, 65, 115, 158
Berlingr 55
Bero 55
Beroe 55
Bertha 54, 56, 342
Bertha of Rosenberg 56
Beside the Fire 24
Bethen 56
Betikhân 56
Bezdukai 198
Bia 56
Bianca 56, 246
Biasd Bheulach 56
Bib 169
Bibung 56, 338
Biča Ia 56, 57
Biča Kuba 57
Biča Kuguza 57
Biča Oza 56, 57
Bidadari 52
Biddy Early 25, 57
Bielobog 69
Biersal 57
Bifurr 57
Big Ears 57, 74
Bild 57
Bile Pani 339
Billie Blin 58
Billingr 58
Billy Blin 58
Billy Blind 58
Billy Blynde 58
Billy Winker 58, 311
Biloko 58
Bilwis 58
Bilwis Reaping's 58
Bimesschneider 58
Binda neckon 245
Bioiotia, Greece 323
Birch tree 42, 159, 260, 317
Bird 15, 20, 50, 64, 156, 160, 187, 192, 211, 215, 216, 227, 236, 246, 266, 268, 276, 286, 289, 291, 315, 319, 322, 339, 342, 343, 347
Birds of Rhiannon 58
Birth of the Gods 178
Bisan 59
Bishop of Skalholt 116, 135
The Bishoprick Garland 65
Bistonia, Greece 324
Bistonis 59, 242
Bithynia, Anatolia 37, 228, 248
Bitias 187
Bivaurr 57
Bivor 59
Bivorr 57
Bjerg-trolde 59, 330
Bjerg-Trolds 55
Bjergfolk 179

Bjergtrolde 59
Black Agnes 59
Black Alfs 108
Black Angus 59
Black Annis 59, 73, 158
Black Annis' Bower 59
Black Bogey 198
Black bucca 68, 69
Black cattle 154, 218
Black Dog 48, 59–61, 76, 112, 202, 263, 264, 269, 302, 303, 308
Black Dog of Winchester 48, 302
Black Dwarf 60, 203
Black Elf 60
Black Forest, Germany 125, 253, 299
Black God 69
Black lamb 245, 313
Black magic 288
Black poplar tree 17, 173
Black Sea 37
Black Shanglan 60, 345
Black Shuck 48, 59, 60, 155, 259, 302, 303
Black Shug 59
Black thorn tree 221
Black Vaughan 344
Black Werewolf 198
Blackberries 273
Blackmailer 292
Blainn 61
Blanid 61
Blarney stone 1, 86
Blatant Beast 306
Blathnad 61
Blathnait 61
Blathnat 61
Blathnet 61
Blednoch, Scotland 17
Blessed Folk 134
Blessed Ones 134, 299
Blind Barlow 58
Blini 263
Blizzards 310
Blobins 163
Blobs 62, 111
Bloodstone 148
Bloody-Bones 61, 254, 287
Bloodycap 288
Blud 61
Blue bird 227
The Blue Bird 227
Blue-Bonnet 61
Blue Britches 61
Blue Burches 61
Blue-Cap 61
Blue Hag 73
Blue Men 62, 232
Blue Men of the Minch 62
The Blue Parrot 315
Bo-guest 48
Boand 62
Boann 13, 62

Boanna 62
Boar 55, 65, 92, 121, 165
Boat 10, 52, 121, 146, 201, 217, 300, 302, 341
Bob-a-Longs 344
Bobby Griglans 307
Bocan 38, 50, 62, 106
Bòcan 50
Boccan 62
Bocian 62
Bockle 66
Bodach 62, 66, 254
Bodach a Chipein 62
Bodach Glas 62
Bodachan Sabhaill 62
Bodaich 62
Bodhb Derg 297
Bodmin Moor 66
Boe Bulbagger 70
Boetia, Greece 14
Bofur 44
Bog 201
Bog-a-boo 46
Bogan 50, 62
Bogans 62
Bogart 62–63, 308
Bogey 69, 264
Bogey-beast 63
Bogeyman 69, 91, 92, 185, 213, 226, 254, 269, 310
Bogeymen 63
Boggan 46
Boggane 70
Boggans 62
Boggart 62, 63, 66, 67, 69, 72, 86, 87, 203, 344
Boggle 62
Boggle-Boo 69
Bogie 40, 58, 59, 63, 294, 301, 302
Bogies 163
Bóginki 55
Boginki 55, 257
Bogle 46, 62, 63, 93, 129
Bogle Boo 69
Bogles 163
Bogy 63
Boh-Thing 203
Bohemia 174
Boialoshtsh 51
Boiardo, Matteo Maria 129
Boind 62
Boiotia, Greece 14, 31, 37, 79, 85, 89, 101, 106, 192, 202, 208, 228, 233, 258, 294, 306, 317, 321, 322
Boiotos 228
Boks 70
Bokwus 63
Bolar 46
Bolbe 63, 217
Bolbe, lake 63
Bolina 63
Bolina, Akhaia 63

Bolivia 11, 206
Bolotnyi 64
Bombor 64
Bömburr 64
Bon Garcon 64
Bon Garçon 64, 221
Bone Mother 248
Boneless 175
Bonfire 296
Bonga 64
Bonga Maidens 64
Boobach 71, 72
Boobrie 64, 137
Boogey Man 62
Boogeyman 63
Boogies 62
Book of Heroes 56, 116, 338
Book of Invasions 5, 331
The Book of Leinster 303
Book of Revelation 188
Book of Settlements 210
Book of the Yezidi 188
Bookha 66
Bookhas 273
Booman 64
Boomasoh 64, 244
Boreas 39, 199, 262, 276
Bornnholm 124
Borrowers of the Forest 261
Boruta 64
Bostonis 64
Boto 126
Bottom 88, 238, 240, 267
Boukolai 127
Boukolion 9, 196
Bouvindea 62
Boveto d'Antona 56, 246
Bow and arrows 338
Bowden, Roxburghshire 90
Bowers 139
Bowis 70
Boyne, Ireland 62
Brabant, Belgium 202
Brag 64, 65, 88, 300, 310
Bragi 169
Brags 163
Brahma 156, 325
Bran 12, 93, 297
Brandy 105, 116, 232
Brännvin 241
Bras-de-Fer 91
Brazil 30, 32, 74, 92, 121, 206
Bread 68, 69, 71, 72, 109, 114, 115, 138, 139, 165, 175, 189, 220, 270, 277, 305, 333, 344, 346
Breadcrumbs 152
Brechta 54, 56
Bredbedal, Sir 58
Breena 65
Brenin Llwyd 65
Brenton 116, 146, 222, 237, 238, 295

Bres Mac Elathan 251
Breton 53, 70, 89, 237, 326, 347
Brí Léith 234
Brian Boru 16, 273
Briareos 207, 259
Briareus 207, 259
Bridge of Kjelskör 327
Bridges 96, 126, 184, 231, 243, 327
Bridle 78, 199, 273, 281, 338
Brigid 128
Brique-à-Brac 91
Brisgein 138
Brisinga Men 65
Brísingamen 23, 55, 65, 115, 158
Brísingamen Dwarfs 23, 55, 65, 115, 158
Britomartis 29, 65, 72, 127, 224, 230, 261
Britomatis 65
Brittany, France 14, 30, 53, 70, 76, 89, 91, 124, 139, 141, 144, 145, 146, 205, 224, 321, 339, 347
Broc 41, 65, 121, 305
Broceliande, France 68, 339
Brock 65
Brocket deer 92
Brokk 65
Brokkr 65, 192
Brollachan 18
Bromia 186
Bromie 43, 65, 128, 223, 255
Bromius 97, 128
Broom 42, 264
Broome, Dora 53
Broonie 66
Brosingamene 65
Brother Mike 66
Brothers Grimm 292
Brounie 66
Brouny 66
Brown Dwarfs 66
Brown Man of the Moors 66
Brown Man of the Moors and Mountains 66
Brown Man of the Muirs 66, 310, 334
Brown Men 66
Browney 66
Brownie 17, 54, 58, 61, 62, 63, 64, 66, 67, 70, 71, 72, 73, 77, 92, 93, 109, 110, 112, 113, 115, 125, 128, 146, 154, 157, 158, 163, 165, 166, 168, 169, 175, 180, 182, 183, 193, 195, 200, 201, 203, 219, 220, 221, 224, 228,

247, 249, 271, 274, 276, 281, 282, 283, 284, 285, 289, 291, 299, 303, 305, 325, 327, 328, 329, 340, 343
Brownie-Clod 67, 228
Brownie of Blednoch 17
The Brownie of Blednoch 17
Brownie of the Lake 67
Brownie Stone 67
Browny 66
Bru 67
Brucie 67
Brugh 67–68, 258
Bruigh na Bóinne, Ireland 30
Bruighean 67
Bruighin Sithein 67
Bruised One 188
Brujos 39
Brùnaidh an Easain 67
Brunhilde 68, 336
Bruni 68
Brunissen 68, 141
Bruthain 136
Bryce 68, 97
Brynhilde 68, 336
Buachailleen 68
Bub 169
Bucca 68, 69, 72, 87, 285
Bucca Boo 68, 69, 285
Bucca-Boo 68, 285
Bucca Dhu 69
Bucca-Du 68
Bucca Guidder 69
Bucca Gwidden 69
Bucca-Widn 69
Buccas 203
Bucium forest 296
Buckawn 50
Bucolion 9, 196
Budagh 66
Buddha 41, 113, 295
Buddha Dakini 295
Buddhist monks 244
Buecubu 69
Buefo Colorado 129
Buffardello 72
Bug 63, 68, 69
Bug-A-Boo 62, 63, 68, 69
Bug Boy 69
Bugaboo 69
Bugan 62
Bugarik 69
Bugbear 62, 63, 69, 71, 254, 345
Bugbeare 69
Bugell 63
Bugelnoz 321
Buggane 69–70, 274
The Buggane of Saint Trinion 70
Buggar 70
Buggare 70
Bugger 63

Buggy Bow 69
Bugil 63
Bugle 137, 332
Bugul Noz 70, 254
Bugul-Noz 70, 254
Bukura e detit 70
Bukura e dheut 70
E Bukura e Dheut 70, 117
E Bukura e Dynjas 70
Bukwas 70
Bulgaria 198, 244
Bull 35, 70, 92, 106, 132, 142, 154, 190, 291, 308, 333
Bull-Beggar 70
Bullbeggar 70–71
Bullebeggar 70
Bullerkate 203
Bullerkater 203
Bullermann 203
Bullihann 203
Bumburr 71
Buneep 71
Bungaya 200
Bunyip 71
Burghs 136, 138, 287, 309
Buri 71
Burial mound 61
Burial shroud 51, 115
Burinn 71
Burma 120, 205, 280, 323
Burman people 120
Burton, Sir Richard F. 194
Buschfrauen 71
Buschgrossmutter 71
Buschweiber 71
Busiris 30, 40, 97
Butes 349
Butter 45, 62, 86, 99, 125, 136, 138, 154, 265, 284, 309
Butterfly 145, 153, 293, 316
Buttery Sprites 9, 71
Butz 283
Butzemann 203
Butzenbercht 54
Bwaganod 71
Bwbach 68, 71, 72, 285
Bwbachod 66, 72
Bwca 66, 68, 72, 203, 273
Bwcca 72
Bwci 68, 72, 285
Bwciod 68, 285
Bwgan 72
Bwganod 72
Bwyd ellyllon 72, 138
Byblis 72, 151, 207, 329
Byzantine 72
Byze 29, 72, 127, 224, 230
Byzia 72, 242

Caapora 74, 92
Cabeiro 195

Cabyll-Ushtey 72, 302
Caccavecchia 72
Cachaça 74
Cachina 195
Cacy Taperere 73
Cadair Idris 93
Cadillac, Antoine Laumet de Lamothe 242
Cadmus 192
Caelia 73
Caer 73, 170
Caer Gwydion 170
Caer Ibormeith 73
Caerphilly 166
Caesar Augustus 98
Caillagh ny Groamagh 73
Cailleac Bhuer 73, 74, 158
Cailleach Beara 74
Cailleach Beare 74
Cailleach Bearra 74
Cailleach Bera 74
Cailleach Bhearra 74
Cailleach Bheirre 74
Cailleach Bherri 74
Cailliagh ny Gueshag 73
Caimito 116
Cain 46, 343
Cain's Hunt 343
Cainte 104
Caipira 92
Caipora 74, 92
Cairngorm Mountains 146
Cait Sith 57, 74
Caitlín 79
Calabria, Italy 227
Calaca 92
Calais 262
Calf 60, 64, 65, 74, 76, 235, 264, 274
Caliadna 74
Caliadne 74, 85, 97, 122, 128, 132, 162, 242, 280, 314, 321
Calidore, Sir 306
Calliagh Birra 74
Callianassa 74, 256
Callianira 74
Callicantzaroi 74
Callicanzaris 80
Callidice 75, 97
Calliope 75, 76
Calliphaea 75, 188, 190, 268, 316
Callirrhoe 75, 242
Callirrhoë 75
Callisto 2, 75, 83, 128, 231
Callow of Feckenham 344
Cally Berry 73
Calybe 196
Calypso 75, 197
Camenae 76, 151
Cameria 339
Camphor language 59
Camphor tree 59, 269

Canada 32, 255, 328
Cancaline 76, 239
Candelas 76, 344
Candle 89, 101
Cannered-Noz 76
Cannibal 56, 117, 288
Cannibalistic fairy 330
Cano 90
Canoe 49
Canonical Muses 14, 75, 76, 86, 128, 230, 279, 334
Canta 104
Canthus 98, 132
Canwyllgorff 344
Caoineag 47, 76, 93, 153
Caointeach 76
Cap of oblivion 125
Cape Cod 312
Cape Verde Peninsula, Senegal 348
Capelthwaite 59, 76
Caphaurus 329
Capheira 77
Carabibounet 91
Carabosse 77
Carian 213
Carius 328
Carlin 77
Carline 77
Carmarthenshire, Wales 54
Carme 65
Carnac 91
Carpathian mountains 28
Carrig Cliodna 1, 85
Carrigcleena 86
Carrion goddesses 149, 336
Carvilia 144
Carya 77
Caryatid 77
Carystus 81
Cashel 138
Cassus 98, 176
Castalia 77, 242
Castanets 296
Castle 1, 16, 20, 21, 28, 30, 35, 41, 46, 56, 70, 78, 91, 117, 121, 134, 137, 141, 166, 177, 180, 200, 217, 219, 224, 227, 228, 229, 230, 235, 238, 282, 288, 292, 298, 299, 302, 338, 342
Castle Lusinia 230
Castle of the Maidens 238
Cat 7, 14, 17, 19, 21, 57, 59, 74, 78, 82, 109, 164, 202, 219, 263, 303, 308, 313, 325, 347, 348
Cat-men 21, 219
Cat Sidhe 74
Cat Sith 74
Catalogues of Women 178
Catarrhal illness 217

Catawba Indian 347
Catenes, island of 45
Caterpillar 164
Catholic sacrament 339
Cattle 25, 39, 64, 72, 78, 91, 105, 107, 115, 116, 118, 125, 135, 137, 150, 154, 160, 166, 168, 169, 170, 174, 175, 185, 195, 218, 222, 261, 277, 284, 286, 288, 301, 304, 307, 311, 318, 325, 335, 341, 344
Catyatids 77
Cauld Lad 77, 184
Cauld Lad of Hylton 77
Caunos 72
Caunus 207, 329
Cave 25, 49, 59, 84, 89, 100, 103, 143, 165, 166, 179, 184, 202, 224, 228, 254, 266, 289, 311, 323, 333
Cavutayi 204
Ccoa 78
Cearb 78
Ceasg 78
Ceathach 84
Cebren 21, 78, 258
Cecht 18, 104, 251
Cecrops 15
Ceffyl-Dwr 78–79
Ceithlenn 79
Celaeno 37, 79, 97, 112, 122, 224, 261, 277, 311, 319
Celaino 277
Celestial goat 26
Celestial nymph 82, 325
Cellar 87, 198, 200, 213
Cellar Demon 71
Celmis 94
Celoeno 38, 79
Celusa 198
Centaur 81, 126, 246, 252, 257, 259, 273, 304, 313
Centfind 85
Central Australia 21
Cephalion 329
Cephissus 79, 101, 105, 216
Cephissus River 105
Cephisus 213, 216
Cerberus 70
Cerceis 79
Cercestis 79
Cercetes 97, 110
Cercropids 15
Ceres 196, 229
Cesme 82
Cethleann 79
Cethlenn 46
Cethlion 79, 141
Céthlionn 79
Ceto 37, 79, 199
Cetus 199
Chaetus 36, 97

Chaetus 36, 97
Chair of Aynia 41
Chair of lunatics 41
Chalcis 37, 79, 225
Chalcodon 98, 290
Chalcomede 80, 223
Chalice 144
Chalkidike 265
Chamber-maid 224
Chamorro people 317
Chamucho 92
Changeling 54, 55, 80–81, 88, 89, 90, 121, 135, 146, 147, 169, 205, 250, 255, 257, 278, 301, 331, 333, 347
Changeling child 80, 88
Chao Phum Phi 81
Charicio 81
Charicol 126
Chariklo 81
Chariolo 81, 257
Chariot 77, 120, 139, 140, 150, 315
Charioteer 233
Charissa 73
Charities 81, 132, 321
Charlemagne 50
Charming, King 227
Charms 125, 145, 156, 288, 293, 307
Charon 101
Charopeia 81, 223, 271
Charybdis 81, 242
Chasse de Cain 343
Chasse deHerode 343
Chasse Sauvage 343
Cheese 114, 136, 140, 154, 174, 183
Cheiron 228, 259
Chelone 82
Cheney old squire 82
Cheney's Downs 82
Cheney's Hounds 82, 245
Cherokee Indian 253, 349
Cherry tree 337
Chesiad 82
Chesma 82
Chesme 82, 151
Chess 52, 99, 148, 234
Le Cheval Bayard 82, 220, 221, 242
Ch'i His 82
Chi Spirits 82
Chicken 42, 74, 109, 200, 268, 308
Chief Alter Washer 84
Chih Nü 82
Children of pride 135
Children's and Household Tales 292
Chile 149, 275, 329
Chili 69
Chimmeken 203
Chimney 18, 62, 80, 210, 228, 288, 308

Chin-Chin Kobakama 66, 83
China 36, 80, 83, 184, 298
Chiron 81, 126, 243, 257, 273
Chlidanope 83, 242
Chloris 150
Choa Phum Phi 66
Choin Dubh 59
Cholera 339
Chrétien de Troyes 211
Christianity 6, 14, 17, 18, 22, 49, 53, 54, 55, 56, 63, 69, 85, 102, 106, 111, 129, 134, 148, 179, 183, 184, 189, 205, 206, 211, 223, 240, 269, 303, 335, 341, 344
Christmas 10, 52, 54, 74, 93, 192, 269, 295, 328
Chronicon Anglicanum 166
Chrysa 75, 83
Chrysaor 75
Chryse 83, 87, 99, 191, 199, 266
Chryseis 83, 87, 199
Chryses 83, 99, 191, 266
Chrysippus 98, 99, 103
Chrysis 83
Chrysogonee 27, 53
Chrysopeleia 83
Chrysopelia 2, 83
Chrysothemis 83, 98
Chthonius 68, 281
Chu Pa-Chiai 84, 135
Chu Pa-chieh 84
Chucklebud 169
Chumcho 92
Church 6, 49, 70, 76, 116, 124, 134, 201, 218, 257, 288, 291
Church bell 49, 134, 205, 210, 347
Church Grim 201
Church Lamb 201
Churchyard 112, 201, 220
Churchyard Dog 155
Churn Milk Peg 84, 230, 254
Churnmilk Peg 84
Cian 129
Cicada 59
Cigar 74
Cin 107
Cinderella 6, 138, 163, 164
Cinler 107
Cinnamonium camphora 59
Circe 70, 75, 84, 270, 298
Circeis 84
Cisseus 31, 97
Citheach 84
City of Jewels 107

City of Principal Evil 16
Ciuthach 84
Civet cat 347
Clach-an-duine-mbairbh 67
Claea 261
Clairvoyance 287
Clap-Cans 84, 254
Clapcans 84
Clare County 14
Clashnichd Aulniac 53, 84
Claus 10, 203
Clay pipe 156
Cleary, Bridget 80
Cleatus 236
Cleeia 186, 202
Cleena 85, 86
Cleeona 86
Cleio 85
Cleis 186
Cleo 85, 98
Cleochareia 85, 242
Cleocharia 202
Cleodora 85, 202, 242
Cleodore 85, 97
Cleone 37, 85
Cleopatra 85, 97, 98
Cletas 311
Clethrad 85
Clidna 1, 14, 17, 85–86, 141
Clídna 85
Clídna of the Fair Hair 85
Cliff 72, 113, 167, 169, 202, 276, 288, 312, 320
Climbers 292
Clio 76, 86
Cliodhna 86
Cliodna 17, 18, 51, 86, 141
Clíodna 85
Clíona 85
Clite 86, 97
Clitemneste 86
Clitunno 86
Clitus 86, 97
Cloak of Darkness 16
Cloan ny moyrn 135
Clochfoldich Farm 284
Clommel, Ireland 80
Clontarf 16, 31
Clooracaun 86
Clotho 144, 236
Cloud Grey 235, 336
Cloud Power 336, 345
Clouds 25, 32, 136, 20, 252, 258, 261, 277, 293, 331, 334, 348
Club 94, 133, 159, 193, 206, 230, 258, 342, 346
Cluracaun 86
Cluricaun 86–87
Cluricaune 86
Cluricauns 86
Clyde River 121

Clymene 38, 87, 110, 176, 271
Clytia 87
Clytic 87
Clytie 87
Clytus 40, 98
Cnoc Aine 18
Cnoc Finnine 148
Cnoc Greine 165
Cnoc Ma Fairies 203
Cnoc Meadha 99, 148
Cnoc Meadhe 203
Cnossia 203
Co-Walker 87
Coal 61, 214, 260
Coastline 15, 60, 93, 215, 216, 235, 236, 266, 268, 276, 286, 306, 308, 319, 322, 333
Cobald 203
Coblyn 68, 72, 87, 203, 285
Coblynau 87–88
Cobweb 88, 238, 240, 237
Cobylnaus 203
Cobylynau 87
Coca 92
Coco 92
Coco Man 92
Cocytus, river 234
Codex Regius 95
Coed y Dugoed Mawr 288
Coggeshall Abby 166, 224
Cohuleen druith 232, 233
Coin 152, 201, 332, 342
Coinchend, Queen 103
Cointeach 47, 51
Cóiste Bodhar 101
Colann Gun Cheann 88
Colbentz 220
Colbrand 88
Colbrond 88
Colbronde 88
Colbronde Guy of War-wick 88
Cóle, King 139
Coleman Gray 88
Colepexy 271, 276
Coll ap Collfrewy 176
Cologne, Germany 175
Colt 88, 273
Colt-Pixy 88
Coluinn Gan Ceann 88
Coluinn gun Chean 88–89
Comb 49, 149, 175, 288, 332, 339, 346
Compaña 343
Companion 87
Comte de Caylus 140, 150, 157, 164, 226, 266, 314
Conaire 246
Conall 148

Conc 132
Concealed ones 107
Conch shell 232, 330
Conchobar 129
Condená 149
Conelock, King of Noweay 88
Conmaicne Rein 331
Conn, King 52
Conn of the Hundred Battles 103
Connacht 17, 73, 139, 141
Connachta, Ireland 331
Connaugh, Ireland 227
Connaught Fairies 32, 148
Connla 139
Consort of Jack o' Lantern 194
Constellation 2, 26, 176, 186, 208
Cooper, Durrant 212
Copenhagen, Denmark 186
Copper 253
Copper Woods 139
Copy 87
Coral 141, 167, 232, 302, 333
Corbet, Sir Peter 344
Corcyra 37, 89, 204
Corinth 162
Cork, Scotland 74
Cork County, Ireland 46, 86
Cormac Mac Art, King 165, 303
Corn 43, 62, 67, 77, 103, 104, 120, 125, 131, 202, 204, 220, 252, 300, 311
Corn mills 131
Corn mother 204
Cornel 90
Cornel-cherry 205
Cornichon 300
Cornik 205
Cornwall, England 30, 33, 66, 82, 125, 134, 135, 176, 183, 194, 203, 208, 224, 237, 252, 277, 285, 307, 345
Cornwall, Scotland 147, 277
Coronia 186
Coronis 89, 108, 186, 223
Corpse Candles 344
Corrigan 89, 205
Corrigans 81, 146
Corriket 89
Corybantes 95, 290
Corycae 89
Corycia 89, 100, 202, 228, 242, 323
Cotton tree 117, 260, 296
Count P'eng 269
Country of Delight 107
County Longfeford 234

Couril 89, 205
Cow 69, 89, 90, 91, 108, 109, 123, 154, 161, 169, 170, 193, 197, 218, 234, 243, 268, 274, 303, 345, 348
Cowboys 284
Cowlug E'en 90
Cowlug Sprites 90
Cowslip 167
Craganeevul 14
Crageevil 16
Craig Aulniac, Scotland 53, 84
Craneia 90
Craneus 90
Cranto 90
Crazyman 46
Cream 67, 72, 168, 175, 193, 243, 268, 285
Cream cheese 140
Cred 90, 141
Créd 90
Creiddylad 171
Creide ingen Guaire 90
Crenaeis 90
Crenaeus 192
Crendé 90
Creneis 90
Crenis 90
Crescent moon 295
Cressida 83
Crete 12, 19, 24, 27, 46, 65, 94, 132, 176, 188, 203, 208, 229, 265
Creusa 90, 242
Cricket 167
Crimbils 54, 80, 90
Crimesus 299
Crimthann 52
Crinaeae 14, 33, 90, 151, 241, 333
Crinisus 91
Crion 205
Crions 91
Critomedia 91, 98
Crocale 91
Crocodile 157
Crocus 309
Crodh Mara 91, 137, 170
Crodh Sidhe 91
Cron Annwn 154
Crones 165
Cronios 179
Cronos 273
Cronus 94, 176, 192, 319
Croque-Mitaine 91, 258
Croquemitaine 91, 258
Cross 20, 124, 340, 346
Crossroad 60, 93, 170, 189, 211, 226, 263
Crow 73, 77, 178, 202, 223, 238, 242
Crown 128, 140, 255, 308
Cruickshanks 292
Crunniuc, Queen 141
Cryfaglach 90

Cu Chulain 61
Cu Chulainn 148
Cu Chulsinn 215
Cu Roi 61
Cu Sith 92, 137
Cu Sith 137
Cuachag 92
Cuarahu-Yara 92
Cuca 92
Cuchulainn 143
Cúchulainn 39
Cuchullain tales 223
Cuco 92, 163, 254
Cucui 92
Cucuy 92
Cuddlepie 169
Cuilenn 92
Cuiseagan an fhraoich 138
Culann 92
Cullen 92
Culprit Fay 263
Cultural hero 9, 12, 19, 36, 56, 61, 102, 122, 133, 143, 185, 289, 338
Cumberland, England 112
Cunnere Noe 170
Cupid 27, 53, 248
Curetes 95, 176
Curinqueans 24
Current of Destruction 62
Currie, family 76
Curupira 92, 206
Curupiras 24
Curupiri 206
Curupura 92
Cururipur 93
CuSith 59
Cusith 92
Cutty Soams 93
Cuzo peak, Andes Mountains 225
Cwn Annw 59
Cwn Annwfn 93
Cwn Annwn 93, 154, 171, 184, 277
Cwn Cyrff 93
Cwn Mamau 93
Cwn Wyber 93
Cwrw da 72
Cy-oer-aeth 94
Cyane 207
Cyanea 207
Cyanee 207
Cybele 95, 293
Cyble 248
Cycais 93
Cyclone 95
Cyclops 155, 323
Cydippe 93
Cyhiraeth 47
Cyhyraeth 93
Cyllene 207
Cyllenus 94
Cymadoce 93
Cymatolege 28, 93, 94
Cymbals 220, 296, 320

Cymodoce 94
Cymodocè 94
Cymothoe 28, 93, 94
Cynosura 94, 176, 208, 261
Cyoeraeth 94
Cyoerraeth 47, 51
Cyrenaica 49
Cyrene 83, 206
Cyrfaglach 90
Cyrhiraeth 51
Cyriac's Mead 80
Cyriacc's well 80
Cytos 179
Czech Republic 249, 253, 337
Czechoslovakia 173, 292
Czernobog 69

Dactyl 94
Dactylic rhythm 94
Daddy Bouchon 265
Dadga 79
Daeira 95
Daemones 95
Daeva 101
Dagda 13, 30, 73, 94, 153
Dagda the Good God 94
Dagfinn 94
Dagfinnr 94
Daghda 297
Dagon 255
Dagr 102
Dagwano'ĕñ'iĕn 95
Dagwanoenyent 95
Dagworthy Castle 224
Dahomey people 41
Dahut 237
Daimones 95
Dain 95, 101, 114, 115
Dáinn 95
Daiphron 12, 97, 98
Daira 95
Daksha 241
Dâl Peri 95, 103, 234, 270
Dalby Mountain, Isle of Man 301
Dalcassians 16, 51
Dallwyr, Cornwall 176
Dallwyr Dallben 176
Dalmatia 223, 338
Dama Dagenda 95
Damasippos 270
Dame Ab 10, 171
Dame Abonde 10, 95, 171
Dame Abunde 10
Dame Abundia 95
Dame Croquemitaine 91
La Dame d' Aprigny 10, 96
Dame d' Avalon 237
Dame du Lac 96, 298
Dame Hab 171
Dame Habonde 10, 95
Dame Habundia 95, 171, 172, 343

Dame Hirip 96, 331
Dame Jenö 331
Dame Mab 171
Dame Rampson 331
Dame Tryamoug 96
Dame Tryamour 96
Dame Venetur 331
Dame Vénétur 331
Dames blanches 10, 96
Dames Blanches 96
Damone 96, 98
Dana O'Shee 97
Danaid 85, 97, 98, 99, 132, 191
Danaides 97
Danaïdes 97
Danaids 11, 12, 15, 27, 28, 29, 31, 33, 34, 35, 36, 40, 68, 75, 79, 83, 86, 91, 96, 97, 99, 100, 103, 106, 110, 122, 127, 130, 131, 132, 133, 161, 162, 164, 175, 176, 177, 180, 181, 186, 187, 191, 192, 210, 234, 235, 237, 241, 245, 257, 271, 272, 274, 276, 278, 279, 280, 285, 290, 297, 298, 312, 314, 321, 322, 329, 333, 334
Danais 98, 99
Danaïs 98, 99
Danaus 11, 12, 15, 27, 28, 29, 31, 33, 35, 36, 38, 40, 68, 75, 79, 83, 85, 86, 91, 96, 97, 99, 100, 103, 106, 110, 122, 127, 130, 131, 132, 133, 161, 162, 164, 175, 179, 177, 180, 181, 186, 187, 191, 192, 234, 235, 237, 241, 257, 271, 272, 274, 276, 278, 279, 280, 285, 290, 297, 298, 312, 314, 321, 322, 329
Dancing 35, 89, 91, 95, 97, 101, 107, 118, 118, 124, 125, 131, 134, 135, 136, 137, 142, 146, 178, 205, 211, 213, 216, 218, 220, 240, 266, 275, 277, 283, 293, 295, 301, 304, 314, 317, 318, 320, 331, 332, 335, 342, 348
Dando's and his Dogs 82
Dandy-Dogs 82
Dane Hills 59, 158
Dani 109
Danu 62, 90, 141, 331
Daoi-Sith 99, 100
Daoine Beaga 99
Daoine Maithe 99
Daoine Matha 99
Daoine O'Sidhe 97
Daoine Shi' 99
Daoine Sidh 32

Daoine Sidhe 97, 99, 110, 134, 135, 332
Daoine Sith 32
Daoine uaisle 158
Daphne 100, 112, 242
Daphnis 118, 175, 243, 250, 261, 321
Daphnus 89, 100, 202, 228, 323
Daplidice 98, 100
Dark Elf 60
Dark Elves 20, 22, 60, 99, 100, 108, 123, 315, 334
Dark Grey Man 62
Dark Man 100, 334
Dark ones 107
Darling, Prince 142
Darrant 100
Dartmoor, England 82, 345
Dasyus 101
Datan 101
Dathkin 101
Daughter of Grianan 73
Daughters of Danaus 11, 12, 15, 27, 28, 29, 31, 33, 35, 36, 40, 68, 75, 79, 83, 85, 86, 91, 96, 97, 99, 100, 103, 106, 110, 122, 127, 130, 131, 132, 161, 162, 164, 175, 176, 180, 181, 186, 187, 191, 192, 234, 235, 237, 241, 245, 257, 271, 272, 276, 278, 279, 280, 285, 290, 297, 298, 312, 314, 321, 322, 329
Daughters of Helios (Sol) 13, 106, 210, 232, 273
Daughters of the Sea 37
Daulis 101
D'Aulnoy, Madame 76, 77, 239, 258
Davalin 95, 101, 114, 115
Davey Jones 302
Dawn 44, 89, 139, 153, 179, 292
Day of the Dead festival 194
De Danaan 331
Death 10, 15, 16, 17, 20, 23, 25, 26, 30, 41, 46, 47, 48, 53, 59, 61, 62, 67, 69, 70, 72, 75, 76, 78, 80, 82, 86, 92, 93, 94, 97, 100, 101, 106, 108, 109, 113, 114, 115, 209, 212, 125, 126, 127, 134, 141, 142, 153, 154, 155, 156, 159, 161, 165, 166, 167, 170, 172, 174, 179, 182, 184, 192, 200, 201, 202, 203, 209, 212, 214, 215, 218, 223, 227, 237, 244, 249, 258, 259, 260, 262, 263,

264, 288, 292, 300, 302, 303, 304, 308, 309, 310, 317, 318, 323, 335, 336, 338, 342, 343, 344
Death Candle 101
Death Coach 101, 114
Death omen 17, 20, 23, 47, 48, 59, 61, 70, 93, 94, 101, 172, 179, 182, 200, 264, 303, 308, 342
Death shrouds 76
De Berneville, Marie-Catherine Jumelle 258
Deceased children 194, 344
Decuma 236
Dedek 109
Dedushka Dobrokhot 109
Deer 30, 92, 108, 133, 138, 199, 212, 265, 295, 310, 338, 349
Deev 35, 95, 101, 102, 103, 184, 234, 305
Deev Akvan 102
Deev-Binder 184
Deev Sefeed 35, 102
Deeve 101, 102
Deeve Akvan 102
Deeve Sefeed 102
Deianeira 207
Deified guardians 241
Deimakhos 162
Deino 165, 199
Deion 37
Deiopea 102
The Deipnosophistae 173
Deive 102
Delas 94
Delbchaem 102
Deliades 102
Delicia, Princess 76
Dellingr 102
Delos, island 102, 105, 285
Delphi, Greece 77, 89, 100, 186, 198, 202, 228, 233, 247, 323
Delphian temples 77, 89
Delphin 102
Delphinus 102
Delphus 325
Delucaem 52, 102–03
Delvcaem 102
Demarchus 98, 130
Demeter 196
Demetrius 83
Demoditas 98, 103
Demogorgon 103
Demon 9, 20, 22, 28, 43, 48, 71, 104, 107, 121, 136, 173, 189, 199, 217, 219, 226, 242, 257, 262, 298, 302, 318, 340
Demon of debauchery 20
Demon of the Strait 242

Demon of Tidworth 48, 302
Demonic-fairy 295
Demonic spirit 344
Demophile 98, 103
Demrush 95, 102, 103, 234, 270
Denmark 13, 88, 111, 124, 125, 175, 187, 308, 310
Denmark's King Waldemar 344
Dents Rouge 258
Deohako 103
Deopea 103
Derbyshire, England 100
Derketo 232
Dero 103
Derrick 104
Derwent River 100
De Soulis, Lord William 288
Destines 144
Detroit, Michigan 242
Deucalion 282, 285
Deucallim 262
Deukalion 262
Deutsche Mythologie 297
Dev 16, 35, 36, 55, 101, 102, 104, 270
Dev Akvan 102
Deva 101
Devas 104, 156
Deve 101
Devi 101
Devil 55, 82, 88, 93, 174, 214, 225, 275, 297, 298, 320, 321, 337, 344, 345
Devil Dog 59
Devil Hound 259
Devon, England 33, 154, 317
Devonshire, England 104, 227, 345
Devs 104, 270
Dewas 104
Dewcup charms 156
Dexamene 104
Dgèrnésiais 273
Dhundh 114
Di Manes 225
Diamond 49, 60, 326
Dian Cecht 18, 104, 251
Dian Cécht Diancécht 104
Diana 24, 27, 34, 53, 65, 91, 95, 119, 156, 176, 186, 191, 220, 224, 228, 229, 243, 246, 248, 256, 261, 272, 277, 283, 289, 312, 334, 344, 345
Diancecht 104
Dianceht 129
Diaphana, Princess 160
Diarmaid and Grainne 84
Diarmuid of the Love Spot 165
Dick o' Tuesday 344
Dickenpoten 61

Dictaea 12, 188
Dictionaire Infernale 214
Dictynna 65
Dietrich 212, 338
Dieva 102
Dievini 104
Dike 104, 120, 131, 183
Diktynna 105
Diktynnaion 65
Diminutive fairy 105, 113, 227
Dindonette 105, 300
Dinh Tien Hoang 39
Dinka people 19
Dinnshenchas 105
Dinny-Mara 105, 232
Diocorystes 98, 180
Diogeneia 105, 213, 242
Dione 106, 108, 186
Dionysiaca 250, 251
Dionysus 15, 31, 40, 43, 44, 55, 65, 80, 89, 95, 128, 155, 186, 201, 202, 204, 214, 223, 224, 241, 248, 255, 267, 271, 272, 274, 280, 296, 304, 312, 313, 325
Diopatre 242
Dioxippe 13, 97, 106, 176, 210, 273
Dip 106
Dirae 130, 153
Direach 38, 106, 247
Direach Ghlinn Eitidh 106, 247
Dirke 106
Dirne Weibl 106
Disathing 106
Discordia 214
Disease 28, 33, 114, 124, 136, 218, 236, 252, 335, 340
Disir 106
Disir salen 106
Dithreach 106
Diuturna 106–07, 151, 195
Div 101, 102, 104, 107
Div Akvan 102
Dive 101
Divoký Hon 343
Divous 107
Divozenky 107, 200
Divs 104
Diwata 107
Djadek 109
Djendoes 162
Djin 107
Djinn 17, 20, 33, 35, 41, 43, 44, 95, 104, 107, 108, 157, 158, 173, 174, 188, 189, 193, 209, 226, 227, 251, 269, 285, 287, 293, 295, 298, 300, 304, 316
Djinnee 107
Djinni 107
Djinny 107

Djude 162
Do-gakw-ho-wad 108
Doamna Zinelor 191
Dobbie 66, 67
Dobbs 108
Dobby 108
Dobie 108
Döcalfar 108
Döckalfar 22, 108
Dodlin 154
Dodone 108
Dodonides 27, 108
Dodore 108–09
Dofri 152
Dog 35, 48, 59, 60, 61,
    69, 70, 74, 76, 82, 92,
    108, 112, 142, 144, 155,
    172, 202, 219, 235, 263,
    264, 269, 291, 299, 302,
    303, 308, 319, 329
Dog-men 21, 219
Dogs of Hell 48, 154,
    302
Dogwood tree 173
Doinney Marrey 105
Dökkálfar 100, 315
Dola 109
Dolgthrasir 109
Dolgthvari 109
Dólgthvari 109
Dolichus 99, 276
Dolphins 126, 247, 333
Dolya 109
Domaći 109
Domania 109, 200
Domavichka 109
Domavikha 109
Domawiczka 109, 110
Domestic animals 270,
    282, 309, 321, 325
Domestic fairy 56, 57,
    66, 184, 195, 211, 287,
    291, 297, 305, 309, 327
Domestic Fay 134, 158,
    184
Domestic spirit 184, 209
Domikha 109
Domina Abundia 10
Domonvoi 66
Domovik 109, 200
Domovikha 109, 200
Domoviyr 109
Domovoi 109–10, 136, 162
Domovoi Djedoe 109, 162
Domovoj 109, 184
Domovoj House Fairy
    184
Domovoy 109
Domovye 109
Domowije 109
Domowoj 109
Dona Janaina 193
Dona Maria 193
Donagh 110
Donegal, Ireland 17, 141,
    145
Dones d'aigo 341

Donkey 108, 188, 217,
    263, 264, 274, 300
Donn Fírinne, King 110,
    139
Donnerstag 139
Doodweg 141
Dooiney-oie 184
Dooinney-Oie 110
Dooinney Marrey 105,
    232
Doom Dog 60
Doom of the Gods 336
Doomsday 274
Doonie 110, 114
Dorani 190
Dorch 115
Dori 110
Dóri 110
Dorion 97, 110
Doris 11, 12, 15, 26, 27,
    28, 33, 55, 77, 79, 85,
    87, 90, 93, 94, 102, 103,
    106, 110, 111, 112, 117,
    120, 127, 129, 130, 131,
    132, 147, 155, 162, 172,
    180, 181, 187, 190, 191,
    199, 202, 207, 211, 212,
    215, 216, 217, 222, 224,
    229, 230, 244, 245,
    246, 247, 249, 260,
    265, 272, 274, 278,
    280, 281, 282, 283, 29,
    311, 321, 322, 346
La Dormette 111, 311
La Dormette de Poitou
    111, 311
Doros 263
Dorset, England 271, 277,
    311
Dorus 262
Dosemary Pool 208
Doto 111
Doubleman 87
Dove 108, 142, 208, 281,
    294, 319, 342
Down County 301
Drac 111
Dracae 111
Drachen 111
Drachma 173
Dragaice 295
Dragon 19, 36, 38, 77, 79,
    92, 111, 116, 120, 133,
    139, 142, 152, 164, 178,
    206, 248, 284, 289,
    320, 325, 326
Dragon Prince of the Sea
    38
Dragontina 111, 143
Drake 111, 112
Drake, Joseph Rodman
    263
Drake, Sir Francis 298,
    344
Draken 326
Drauga 104
Draupnir 65, 112

Draygan 332
Drayton, Michael 223,
    261
Dream 26, 45, 73, 88, 140
Dreamtime myth 338
Drerge 115
Drimachos 162
Droll 340
Droll-Teller 340
Dronningstolen 124
Drosera 112, 242, 255
Drought 323
Drow 100
Druggen Hill Boggle 112
Druidic bards 221
Drumashie, Scotland 67
Drupner 121
Dryad 2, 13, 64, 77, 83,
    112, 119, 128, 129, 142,
    159, 173, 178, 200, 242,
    256, 261, 272, 285, 286,
    294, 296, 301, 314, 335,
    340, 346
Dryades 183
Dryas 98, 132, 162, 173,
    175, 237
Drymo 112
Dryope 37, 38, 79, 112,
    122, 224, 277, 319
Dryops 99, 269, 279
Dryp 223
Dschin 107
Duala people 194
Dualin 112–13, 117
Duallach 113
Dublin, Ireland 31
Dúc-Bà 41, 113
Dúc-Thành Bà 41, 113
Dudeen 156
Dudje 162
Duende 24, 113, 162
Dueño de casa 113
El Dueno del Sol 92
Duergar 100, 113, 115, 235
Duergarrs 113
Du Guesclin, Bertrand
    326
Duf 114
Duffy 320
Duffy and the Devil 320
Dufr 114
Dúfr 114
Dugani 114
Duh 107
Dukagjin, Albania 262
Du Lac 96
Dulachan 114
Dullaghan 114
Dullahan 100, 101, 114,
    334
Duln Glichd 114
Dumbarton 121
Dumfries Magazine 17
Dun Cow 161
Dun Cow of Kirkham 161
Dun Cow of Mac
    Brandy's Thicket 161

Dunany, Ireland 41
Dund 114
Duneyr 95, 101, 114, 115
Dunkeld, Scotland 284
Dunnie 110, 114
Dunter 114, 288
Duny Mara 105
Dunya Mara 232
Durahan 100, 114
Durathror 95, 101, 114, 115
Durham, England 154
Durham County 108
Duri 114
Durin 115, 235
Durinn 114, 115
Durope, Turkey 295
Durrachan 100
Durugh 104
Dush 115, 163
Dusii 115
Dusk 30, 70, 72, 153, 218
Dusters 276
Dustman 58
Duwende 116
Dvalin 23, 55, 65, 115,
    158, 235
Dvalin Brisings 115
Dvalinn 115
Dverg 115, 116
Dvergar 335
Dvergr 113
Dvergur 162
Dvoroi 115
Dvorovoi 115
Dwalin 115
Dwarf 10, 14, 20, 22, 25,
    29, 32, 33, 35, 44, 55,
    56, 57, 58, 60, 64, 65,
    66, 67, 68, 71, 73, 80,
    89, 95, 102, 104, 112,
    113, 115, 116, 117, 121,
    122, 128, 129, 130, 133,
    134, 135, 140, 146, 154,
    156, 167, 174, 177, 184,
    192, 195, 206, 212, 217,
    221, 235, 237, 238, 242,
    247, 249, 252, 253,
    254, 256, 258, 263,
    264, 265, 289, 292,
    293, 310, 314, 329, 334,
    338, 342, 347, 348
Dwarf of Glen Etive 247
Dweeorg 115
Dwende 116
Dwerger 115
Dwergugh 115
Dworh 115
Dyinyinga 157
Dyn cynnil 72
Dynamene 117
Dynamenè 117
Dynnon Bach Teg 332
Y Dynon Bach Têg 137
Dyombie 117
Dyren 112, 117
Dyrin 113, 115
Dyved 177

Dziki Gon 343
Dziki Łów 343
Džin 107
Dziwitza 117
Dziwozony 71, 107
Dzsinn 107
Dzunukwa 117, 344

Ea 33, 323
Eač Uisge 117
Each Uisce 39, 72, 91, 117, 118, 161
Each Uisge 117, 198, 199, 252, 318
Eager 118, 341
Eagle 140, 147, 156, 177, 273, 322, 323
Eaia 90
Earl Fitzgerald 18, 158
Earl Gerald Fitzgerald of the Desmond Geraldines 86
Earl of Desmond 18, 151, 158
Earth 22, 122, 162, 178, 217, 239, 247, 294, 316
Earth-Men 118
Earth People 118, 128
Earth-spirits 14, 130
Earthmen 118
East Anglia, England 60, 187, 278, 327
East Yorkshire, England 40, 291
Eastern Russia 16
Ebchester, England 175
The Ecclesiastical History of Iceland 116, 135
Echenais 118, 175, 222, 242, 250, 321
Echidna 75, 199
Echo 87, 118, 127, 146, 192, 240, 261
Echu 127
Ecnomius 11, 98
Eczema 219
Edain 17, 118, 153
Édáin 118
Eddy winds 119
Edinburg 238
Edric the Wild 344
Eevell 14
Eevil 14
Eevinn 14
Eeyeekalduk 119
Efreet 189
Egeria 119
Egestus 127
Egg 38, 78, 86, 78, 112, 167, 188, 236, 275, 285
Eggmoinn 119
Egypt 20, 30, 74, 97, 132, 172, 190, 192, 193, 215, 280
Eido 119
Eidothea 119
Eidyia 119, 189, 252

Eight Fairies of the Kingdom of Matakin 119
Eikinskjaldi 120
Eilian of Garth Dorwen 120
Eingsaung 120
Einherjar 336
Eione 120
Eirene 104, 120, 131, 183
Eisenberta 54
Eisges 198
Eithne 120, 129
Eitri 65, 121
Ekako 121
Ekanetra 337
Ekaruda 337
Ekeko 121
Ekho 118
Ekimmu 121
Ekke Nekkepem 121
Ekkekko 121
El-Harith 41, 174, 188
El-Hârith 41, 174, 188
Elaby Gathan 121
Elain 121
Elaine 121
Elane 121
Elatus 83
Elayne 121
Elayne of Astolat 121
Elb 122
Elbe, river 25
Elben 22
Elberich 20, 121, 122, 256
Elbgast 122
Elder Graces 81
Elder tree 60, 125, 186, 341
Elder-mother 186
Elder-wife 186
Elderberry 138
Eldrich 122
Eldriche 122
Eldritch 122
Elea 186
Electra 37, 38, 79, 97, 98, 112, 122, 224, 261, 277, 311, 319
Eleionomae 122, 333
Elektra 122
Elemental 122, 162, 244, 247, 294, 316
Elemental god 259
Elephantis 98, 165, 187
Elerkonge 125
Eleusis, Attika 95, 196
Eleuther 19
Elf 13, 14, 17, 21, 22, 23, 25, 54, 60, 80, 95, 122, 123, 124, 125, 134, 136, 137, 142, 145, 156, 174, 192, 217, 253, 256, 275, 311, 312, 338, 342, 347, 349
Elf Arrows 123, 137
Elf-blast 23
Elf-Bolt 123

Elf Circle 142
Elf Damsel 311
Elf-Dart 123
Elf-Fire 123, 125, 275
Elf King of Denmark 125
Elf-King's Tune 123
Elf-like 192, 217, 349
Elf-Mills 123
Elf-Quarnor 123
Elf-Shot 124
Elfame 123
Elfdans 136
Elfin 18, 74, 122, 123, 218, 234
Elfin Arrow 123
Elfin Cats 74
Elfin cow 218, 234
Elfinmills 123
Elfins 134, 311
Elfland 124, 142
Elflike creature 347
Elfs 134, 311
Elfvor 22
Elgin 221
Elis, Greece 30, 75, 99, 174, 188, 190, 268, 316
Elixir 111, 129, 241, 308
Elixir of blissful oblivion 111
Elixir of immortality 241
Elle Folk 125, 128
Elle-Folk 125
Elle-King 124
Elle-maid 124, 125
Elle Maids 124, 344
Elle-people 125
Ellefolk 123, 125
Ellen 22, 125
Ellerkonge 125, 128
Ellydan 125, 222, 295
Ellyll 122, 137
Ellylldan 124, 344
Ellyllon 72, 122, 123, 125, 138
Elm tree 173, 283
Elokos 58
Elrage 122
Elraige 122
Elrisch 122
Elrish 122
Eltrich 122
Elv 22
Elve-Woman 124
Elven 22
Elver-Konge 128
Elverkonge 125, 128
Elves 14, 21, 22, 25, 60, 72, 73, 99, 100, 108, 116, 122, 123, 124, 125, 128, 134, 135, 136, 179, 184, 216, 217, 253, 261, 265, 295, 311, 315, 332, 334, 335, 343
Elves of Light 123, 125
Elynas 229, 264, 265, 281
Elysium Fields 215
Emandwa 126

Emandwa Zabakazi 126
Emathion, Prince 268
Emer 143
Empedo 126
Emperor of the Fairies 223
Empress Suiko 249
Enais 188
Encantada 107
Encantada 107
Encantado 107
Encantado 126, 280
Encante 126
Encanto 107
Enceladus 28, 97, 99
Enchantress 54, 84, 111, 143, 144, 227, 298
Endeis 126
Endrop 198
Endymion 37
Engel 130
Engelein 130
Engkantada 126
Engkanto 126
England 7, 9, 10, 18, 23, 29, 33, 38, 40, 43, 46, 48, 50, 51, 52, 53, 56, 58, 59, 61, 64, 66, 67, 71, 76, 77, 82, 84, 88, 89, 99, 100, 104, 105, 108, 112, 113, 114, 115, 116, 118, 121, 122, 183, 135, 136, 139, 146, 154, 163, 164, 166, 167, 169, 171, 172, 175, 181, 182, 183, 187, 189, 193, 194, 203, 208, 212, 224, 230, 238, 239, 242, 243, 245, 248, 252, 254, 258, 260, 263, 264, 267, 271, 274, 275, 277, 278, 284, 285, 287, 291, 300, 302, 303, 307, 308, 311, 315, 317, 321, 324, 325, 326, 327, 328, 329, 335, 345, 347, 348
English Channel 111
English Chronicle 166
Engus Mac Og 29
Enig Saung 120
Enipeus 126
Enkanto 107
Enki 33
Ennesiades 127
Enops, Prince 296
Entella 127
The Entertainment at Althorp 223
Enyo 165, 199
Eoachaid Ollathif 94
Eochaid 118, 127, 149, 215, 234, 326
Eochaid, King 118, 127, 215, 234, 326
Eochaid Mac Eirc 127
Eochaide 127

Eochaidh Finn 326
Eochaidhe 127
Eochaidu 127
Eochais 303
Eoched 127
Eocho 127
Eochu 127
Eochy 127
Eogabal 146
Eoghainn 147
Epaphos 216, 231
Epens 104
Ephesos 229
Ephesus 127
Ephialtes 35, 98
Ephira 127
Ephyra 127
Ephyre 127
Epidemic 93
Epimedes 94
Epimeliad 127
Epimeliades 127
Epimelides 127
Epimetheus 36, 87, 127
Epiphania 52
Epiphany 33, 52, 54
Eq'eq'o 121
Eranno 127
Erasinides 127
Erasinos, river 72, 127
Erasinus 29
Erata 127
Erato 43, 65, 76, 83, 97, 98, 127, 128, 186, 223, 255
Erchia 128
Erd-Mänlein 115, 162
Erdbibberli 128
Erdleute 128
Erdluitle 128
Erdmanlein 162
Erdmannlein 128
Erdweibchen 128
Erechtheus 349
Ergiske 9
Ergiskos 9
Eri 128
Eri of the Golden Hair 128
Erichthonius, King 281
Eridanus 349
Erikhthonios 38
Erinyes 130, 153
Eriphia 128, 186
Eris 214
Erl King 122, 125, 255
Erlequin 344
Erlking 125
The Erlking's Daughter 125
ErlKonig 125, 128
Erlkonig 125
Erlkönig 128
Eros 248, 282
Errinys 153
Erytheia 13, 34, 129
Erytheir 129, 178

Erytheis 129
Erythraean Sea 256
Erythras 99
Esa 119
Esclandos, Sir 211
Espiet 129
Esprit Follet 129, 163, 275
Essex, England 60
Estantiga 343
Esterel 129
Esterelle 129
Esterello 129
Estonia 336
Etain 17, 118, 148, 215, 234
Étain 118
Etain Echraide 118
Etaine 118
Eternal salvation 333
Ethal 73
Etheline 46
Ethne 120, 129
Ethniu 129
Etruscan 72, 285
Euadne 129, 276
Euagora 131
Euagore 129
Euagoreis 129
Euarne 129
Euboia 19, 20, 130, 282
Euboia, island 241
Eubule 98, 130
Euchenor 98, 191
Eucrante 130
Eucrate 130
Eudaemon 98, 127
Eudaimonia 81
Eudora 130, 186
Eudore 108, 130
Eugel 130
Euis 130
Eukrante 130
Eulimene 130
Eulimine 130
Eumendies 130
Eumenides 153, 154
Eumolpe 131
Eunica 131, 151, 224, 254
Eunice 131
Eunika 131
Eunike 131
Eunoe 131
Eunomia 104, 120, 131, 183
Eunoste 131
Eupheme 98, 131
Euphemos 196
Euphrosyne 81
Eupome 131
Eupompe 131
Eur-Cunnere Noe 47, 51
Euripides 106
Europa 36, 132
Europe 132
European Alps 338
European Wildcats 74

Europome 98, 132
Eurotas 85, 202, 311, 325
Eurotas, river 325
Euryale 199
Eurydamas 98, 271
Eurydice 39, 98, 132, 311
Eurylochus 40, 97
Eurymedon 266
Eurynome 81, 132
Eurysthenes 98, 237
Eurythoe 99, 132
Eurytus 236
Euterpe 76, 132
Evagora 132
Evagore 132
Evarne 133
Eve of the Epiphany 33
Evidea 98, 133, 176
Evil bucca 69
Evippe 98, 133
Excalibur 208, 237
Excommunicated 227, 264
Fachan 106, 133, 153, 247
Fachen 133
Fachin 133
Fada 133, 134, 136, 144, 145
Fades 144
Fadet 144
Fadhas 144
Fae 145
Fae Eire 134
Faerie 134
Faërie 134
The Faerie Queene 311
Faërieland 142
Faery 134
Faery Folk 134
Faery Godmother 138
Faery Lights 344
Faeryland 142
Faes 134
Fafner 133
Fafnir 133, 184, 248, 263, 289
Fáfnir 133
Fai 134
Faierie 134
Faiery 134
Faine 134
Fair Family 133, 134, 332
Fair family in the woods 332
Fair Folk 133, 134, 137
Fair folks of the mine 332
Fair Head 167
Fair Lady 133–34, 148, 317
Fairies of fate 335
Fairy Animal 38, 43, 50, 56, 71, 74, 91, 92, 105, 137, 145, 160, 161, 176, 218, 221, 226, 234, 245,

252, 297, 300, 317, 318, 331
Fairy Arrows 123
Fairy Artifacts 137
Fairy avenue 141
Fairy being 7, 80, 107, 114, 163, 175, 186, 191, 192, 193, 200, 223, 226, 236, 245, 258, 267, 268, 273, 294, 295, 296, 327, 342, 347
Fairy-being 107, 114, 175, 192, 223, 258
Fairy brides 170, 315
Fairy Bush 138
Fairy Butter 125, 138
Fairy circle 142
Fairy creature 71, 76, 106, 137
Fairy cup 137, 215
Fairy Cup of Ballafletcher 215
Fairy Cup of Edenhal 215
Fairy Family 134, 137
Fairy Flag of Dunvegan Castle 137
Fairy Food 72, 138
Fairy Fort 14, 18, 60, 120, 138, 141, 148, 301, 311, 331, 345
Fairy gathering 264
Fairy ghost 51, 291
Fairy Godmother 40, 53, 76, 138–39, 140, 150, 157, 160, 163, 164, 227
Fairy Helen 331
Fairy hill 1, 85, 99, 110, 287
Fairy-hill 99
Fairy hour 295
Fairy house 138
Fairy hunt-master 344
Fairy Island 40, 139
Fairy King 6, 13, 17, 22, 44, 52, 88, 92, 94, 96, 110, 118, 139, 141, 147, 148, 150, 153, 170, 190, 192, 201, 203, 215, 220, 228, 238, 240, 246, 253, 255, 256, 257, 260, 267, 277, 287, 291, 318, 320, 327, 330, 347
Fairy kingdom 140, 142
Fairy knight 76, 306
Fairy knowe 287
Fairy-Land 142
Fairy light 101
Fairy loaf 139
Fairy lover 131, 346
Fairy money 139
Fairy mound 138, 139, 287
Fairy mount 287
Fairy of the Beech-Woods 139, 296
Fairy of the Dawn 139
Fairy of the Desert 140

Fairy of the Fields 140
Fairy of the Forest 140
Fairy of the Meadows 140
Fairy of the Well 140
Fairy oil 114
Fairy pass 141
Fairy passage 141
Fairy path 141, 286, 334
Fairy people 99, 134, 182, 220, 304, 331
Fairy Pig of Man 35
Fairy piper 113
Fairy place 67
Fairy Queen 1, 6, 10, 11, 13, 14, 16, 17, 18, 28, 30, 32, 34, 35, 41, 51, 52, 53, 56, 70, 71, 85, 86, 88, 90, 95, 110, 117, 125, 136, 141, 143, 146, 148, 153, 165, 168, 170, 171, 189, 191, 192, 194, 199, 208, 215, 217, 218, 219, 223, 227, 234, 238, 240, 248, 252, 256, 260, 266, 267, 270, 275, 277, 297, 298, 314, 315, 318, 327, 338
Fairy Queen 306
Fairy rade 138, 141, 142, 146, 158, 248, 286, 343, 344
Fairy riding 141
Fairy ring 32, 142, 146, 160, 277
Fairy servant 191, 225
Fairy shoe 137
Fairy spirit 16, 30, 33, 36, 46, 51, 71, 76, 89, 94, 101, 103, 114, 115, 126, 145, 158, 169, 179
Fairy Tales from the Isle of Man 53
Fairy trail 30, 138, 142, 330
Fairy triad 112, 142
Fairy Truth 142
Fairy whip 295
Fairy wine 288
Fairy woman 51, 185, 211, 260, 304, 317, 326
Fairye 134
Fairyland 21, 26, 52, 86, 100, 123, 124, 138, 141, 142–43, 144, 146, 149, 169, 190, 203, 256, 247, 291, 327
A Fairy's Blunder 105, 299
Fal 143
Falerina 111, 143
Falias 5, 331
Fallen angels 62, 99, 116, 135, 149, 188, 269, 299, 309
Falr 143
Falsirena 143

Family of Rhys of the Deep 277
Fand 13, 141, 143, 215
Fantine 143
Far Darric 143
Far Darrig 145, 288
Far Dorocha 100, 114
Far Gorta 145
Far Liath 167
Farfadet 144, 163
Farie 134
Farin Faeries 149
Farisees 149
Farm 67, 76, 92, 146, 149, 154, 161, 168, 195, 221, 227, 252, 274, 284, 285, 291, 343
Farm faeries 149
Faroe Islands 181, 245, 341
Farvann 144
Fary 122, 134
Farys 134, 311
Fas 134, 145
Fasti 150
Fata 134, 135, 144, 145, 190
Fata Bianca 56
Fata della Fonte 144
Fata della Fonti 144
Fata Morgana 144, 237, 238
Fata Morga'na 144
Fata Silvanella 144
Fatal Sisters 144
Le Fate Bianca 56, 246
Le Fate Nera 246
Fates 38, 56, 111, 143, 144–45, 199, 209, 246, 262, 309, 332, 334, 337
Father Birch Rod 269
Father Christmas 10, 269, 295
Father Frost 192, 259, 309
Father of the Sheitans 188
Father Rhine 220
Father Time 30
Father Whipper 269
Father Winter 259
Fati 145
Fatit 145
Faun 49, 56, 145
Fauna 145
Faunus 39, 95, 128, 145, 192, 257, 259, 269, 276, 291, 296, 306, 316, 325
Fauths 5, 153
Faye 134
Fayerie 134, 145
Fayery 134
Faylinn 142, 192
Fayry 134
Fays 134, 210, 218, 220, 311
Fdnn 148

Feadh-Ree 331
Feakle 57
Fear Darrig 145
Fear Dearc 145
Fear Dearc of Donegal 145
Fear Dearg 145, 288
Fear-Dearg 145
Fear Durgs 149
Fear gorta 145
Fear gorta stone 145
Fear Liath Mór 145
Fear Liath More 145–46
Fearghal 148
Feast of the Epiphany 52
Feast of the Twelfth Night 313
Feather of Finist the Falcon 42
Fee 122, 134, 135, 138, 145, 146, 173
Feen 134
Feeorin 146
Feerieland 142
Fees 89, 134, 136, 311
Fées 89, 134, 136
Fees des Houles 146
Feinen Feiri 134
Felisinda 143
Fennel 18, 148
Fennel 325
Fenoderee 134, 146, 182, 274, 182
Fenodoree 66
Fenodrerr 134
Fenodyree 146, 274
Fer Fi 68, 146
Fer-Las Mhór 145
Ferier 134
Ferisher 134
Ferla Mór 145
Ferlie More 145
Ferns 174, 283
Ferrie 134
Ferrish 146–47
Ferrishin 146
Ferrishyn 134, 146, 147
Ferryman 101
Ferusa 147
Fery 134
Fetes 145, 146
Feux follets 147
Feyrie 134
Feyrye 134
Fi-follet 147
Fiachra 139, 147
Fiaghra 147
Fialarr 147
Fianna 18
Fib 223
Fid 147
Fidchell 118
Fiddle 137, 179, 241, 324
Fideal 147, 153
Fidelia 73
Fidr 147

Fields of les Paysans 165, 271
Fig tree 309, 314, 316
Fili 147
Fíli 147
Fin Bheara 148
Fin finn 147
Fin folk 147
Fin wizards 147
Finbheara 148
Fincastle 67
Findabair 148
Findchóem 141, 148
Fine Oreille 258
Finias 5, 331
Fininne 148
Finland 46, 116, 173, 201, 245, 265, 293, 330
Finn 148
Finn Bheara 148
Finn MacCool 165
Finn Mac Cumhaill 12, 18, 297
Finn-Men 147
Finnachaidh, Ireland 18
Finncaev 148
Finncháem 148
Finnen 18, 148
Finnine 148
Finnine's Hill 148
Finnoderee 146
Finnr 148, 310, 338
Finvara 148, 203
Finvarr 148
Finvarra 32, 86, 99, 110, 139, 148, 252, 260
Fion 147
Fionn MacCumhail 239
Fionn macCumhil 171
Fionnbharr 148
Fionnchaomh 148
Fions 146
Fiordelisa, Princess 227
Fir Bholg 149
Fir Bolg 149, 331
Fir chlis 148
Fir darrig 148, 149, 213, 288, 210
Fir Dhearga 145, 149
Fir ghorma 62
Fir gorm 62
Fir gorta 145
Fir larrig 288
Fir Liath 167
Fir tree 47, 64, 261
Firbolgs 127, 149, 151, 251
Firbourage 149
Fire 7, 17, 18, 23, 25, 28, 35, 36, 46, 57, 65, 67, 68, 71, 74, 77, 80, 81, 82, 101, 107, 109, 111, 115, 116, 122, 123, 127, 136, 137, 139, 145, 162, 165, 167, 169, 183, 188, 189, 195, 217, 219, 221, 229, 241, 242, 247, 253, 266, 270, 275, 278,

280, 284, 285, 288, 294, 300, 316, 317, 320, 327, 333, 344, 348
Fire Boys 36
Fire brand 253
Fire god 219
Firedrake 111
Fireesin 149, 163
First Branch of the Mabinogi 184
Firth of Cromarty, Scotland 158
Fish 25, 36, 41, 54, 69, 105, 130, 149, 156, 162, 167, 173, 189, 193, 197, 198, 200, 212, 217, 226, 230, 231, 232, 239, 243, 247, 250, 255, 266, 272, 275, 276, 298, 322, 339, 340, 348
Fish-god 232
Fishermen 10, 15, 19, 53, 54, 63, 65, 68, 69, 78, 107, 141, 175, 183, 189, 193, 200, 201, 220, 222, 238, 242, 243, 249, 289, 302, 341, 347
Fishing nets 38, 69, 332
Fith 149
Fittletot 343
Fiura 143
Fjalar 149, 155
Fjalarr 149
Fjolsvidr 150
Fjolsvinnr 150
Fjolsvior 150
Fjords 324
Fjorgyn 29, 260
Flanders, Belgium 202
Flann ua Fedach 52, 139, 150
Flateyjarbok 23, 55
Flax 115, 152, 160, 171, 192, 288, 305, 327
Fletcher family 215
Flint boys 36
Flood 2, 151, 282, 285, 325
Flora 150
Floridas 299
Flower Fairies 150, 169, 301
Flower Fairy 88, 150, 238, 240, 267
Flowers 30, 31, 64, 136, 138, 140, 143, 150, 152, 156, 167, 187, 188, 216, 217, 254, 260
Flute 95, 132, 249, 283, 306
Flying Heads 95
Foawr 150
Foddenskkmaend 162, 330
Fog 167, 183, 266, 298, 347
Foliage 173, 214

Folk 134
Follet 150, 162, 163
Folletti 49, 150–51, 305
Fomhoraiah 151
Fomor 145
Fomori 100
Fontus 195
Food 5, 11, 23, 36, 54, 59, 64, 66, 70, 71, 72, 84, 92, 101, 107, 109, 124, 138, 140, 145, 150, 157, 166, 169, 177, 200, 203, 224, 238, 249, 250, 256, 261, 263, 299, 325, 327, 328, 329, 330, 331, 336, 337, 343
Fool of the Irish Sídhe 25
Fools fire 344
Fords 46, 51, 96
Forest 2, 10, 19, 25, 30, 33, 41, 42, 49, 50, 63, 67, 68, 74, 92, 106, 107, 113, 117, 124, 125, 128, 136, 140, 152, 157, 163, 166, 170, 173, 181, 185, 193, 214, 225, 240, 244, 250, 253, 255, 261, 269, 284, 293, 294, 299, 301, 305, 307, 308, 310, 313, 316, 332, 335, 339, 340, 341, 345
Forest lore 214
Forest man 214, 316
Forest sprite 67
Forest Tsar 240
Forfarshire, Scotland 202
Forgetful People 105, 134
Formor 151
Formori 151
Formorian 46, 79, 128, 129, 143, 149, 150, 151, 319
Fornbogi 151
Forth 138
Fortress Mongibel 238, 262
Fortune 144, 238
Fosse-Grim 151, 241, 313
Fossegrim 241, 245
Fossegrin 151, 313
Fountain 14, 23, 72, 82, 105, 106, 107, 119, 131, 139, 140, 151, 156, 176, 195, 211, 225, 229, 241, 254, 264, 268, 281, 294, 300, 305, 306, 320
Fountain Fairies 151
Fountain Island 105, 300
Fourche 205
Fox 74, 106, 169, 184, 191, 307, 344
Fox Fire 344
Fox-fox 326
Foxglove 80, 81, 278
Fraegr 151
Frænir 133
Frag 151

Frairiesv 134
France 10, 48, 53, 76, 80, 82, 89, 91, 111, 113, 115, 124, 129, 133, 136, 142, 146, 150, 165, 183, 201, 217, 242, 262, 271, 231, 245
Frankincense tree 215
Frar 152
Frarr 152
Frau Berchta 54, 344
Frau Berta 54
Frau Hilde 53
Frau Holle 152, 341
Frau Wachholder 152
Frau Welt 152
Fraw Selga 344
Fray Holle 152
Freia 342
A French Puck 284
Fresh water 63, 122, 150, 178, 198, 217, 230, 252, 257, 268, 276, 281, 340
Fresh-water spirit 340
Freshwater lake 242, 254
Freya's necklace 20
Freyja 65
Freyr 22, 23, 55, 115, 158
Friar-with-the Rush 344
Friar's Lantern 129, 344
Frid 152
Frideag 152
Fridean 152
Fridich 152
Fridur 152, 322
Friesland 116, 257, 284, 345
Frigg 53
Frightening Figures 253
Frog 92, 116, 202, 340
Frost Fairies 309
Frost King 259, 309
Frosti 153, 192
Fruit trees 228, 259, 313
Fu-Lung Mountains 84
Fuaieach 153
Fuaimnech 153
Fuamnach 118, 153
Fuarnnach 234
Fuath 53, 92, 147, 153, 160, 198, 224, 267, 301, 334, 340, 341
Fuathan 153
Full moon 95, 106, 158, 182
Fullangr 53
Fundin 153
Fundinn 153
Funeral boat 217
Fungus 125, 138, 142, 278
Furies 21, 130, 153, 154, 228, 326
Furl of Fairy Wind 119
Furry Nick 269
Füttermarinchen 154, 343
Y Fuwch Frech 154

Fuwch Gyfeiliorn 154, 170
Y Fuwch Gyfeiliorn 154
Y Fuwh Laethwen Lefrith 234
Fyfe, Scotland 171
Fynnoderee 146

Gabble Retchets 154
Gabriel 154
Gabriel Hounds 93, 154, 171, 277, 344
Gabriel Ratchets 154
Gabriel Ratchet's Hounds 154
Gaea 228
Gahonga 154, 156, 195, 258
Gaia 13, 34, 81, 129, 130, 178, 304
Gaibnenn 164
Gairloch, Scotland 147, 159
Gaius Julius Hyginus 11, 27, 28, 34, 35, 40, 79, 83, 85, 91, 96, 98, 99, 100, 103, 122, 127, 130, 131, 132, 133, 162, 175, 176, 177, 180, 181, 186, 187, 192, 234, 237, 241, 257, 272, 276, 279, 280, 285, 298, 322, 329, 334
Galaffre 258
Galahad, Sir 121, 208
Galar 150, 154
Galarr 154
Galas 155
Galatea 155, 315, 330
Galateia 155
Galates 155
Galaxaura 155
Galaxaure 155
Galene 155
Galium verum 296
Gallena 155
Galley-Beggar 155
Galleytrot 60, 155
Galloway, Scotland 17
Gally-Trot 155, 259, 303
Galway 99, 148
Gamanraide 149
Gan Ceanach 155–56, 164
Gan Ceann 88, 100, 114
Gancanagh 155, 164
Ganconagh 164
Ganconer 155
Gandalf 156
Gandalfr 156
Gandálfr 156
Gandaruwo 157
Gandayah 154, 156, 258
Gandhabba 156
Gandharbas 156
Gandharvas 156
Gangana 156

Ganges 217
Gans 156
Ganymede 75
Gardarike 113, 317
Garden Gnome 162
Garden of Eden 227
Gargaphia 151, 156
Gargaphie 156
Gargettus 190
Garos of Assam 69
Gartenzwerg 162
Gascony, France 262
Gates of Tartaros 326
Gateside, Roxburghshire 90
Gaul 155, 158, 205, 346
Ge 242
Gean-Canach 155, 164
Gean-Cannah 155
Geancanach 155, 157
Geer 158
Geese 154
Geirolul 157, 336
Geisterweg 141
Gemology 145
Gems 20, 116, 133, 141, 253, 263
Genderuwa 157
Genderuwo 157
Gendruwo 157
Genesta 157
Genie 107, 157, 194, 266, 326
Génie 107
Genii 95, 107, 157, 158, 211
Genii cucullati 157–58
Genii loci 211
Gênio 107
Genius cucullatus 157
Gentle Annie 158
Gentle Annis 59, 158
Gentle People 253
Gentraighe 146
Gentry 99, 105, 134, 158
Geoffrey of Monmouth 40
Geoffrey-with-the-great tooth 230
Geoffrey with the Tooth 230
Gerald of Wales 137
Gerald, the Earl of Desmond 18, 51, 158
Gereonsu 117
Geri 158
Germany 50, 51, 56, 57, 58, 80, 91, 116, 125, 128, 136, 141, 142, 152, 154, 158, 164, 165, 166, 175, 179, 180, 182, 200, 204, 206, 221, 238, 242, 249, 267, 269, 276, 308, 313, 328, 330, 341, 342, 343, 345
Geroid 18, 146, 158
Geroid Iarla 18, 158

Geroid Iarla, Earl Fitzgerald 18
Gerr 23, 55, 65, 115, 158
Gervase of Tilbury 165
Geryon 75
Gesteppten leimeln 284
Ghaddar 107
Ghana, West Africa 35, 56
Ghilan 107, 158–59, 194
Ghillan 158
Ghillie Dhu 159
Ghillie Yu 159
Ghlaistig Uaine 160
Ghost 1, 36, 51, 56, 63, 72, 77, 89, 108, 124, 130, 141, 145, 170, 208, 225, 291, 301, 305, 312, 342, 344, 345
Ghost-like 1, 170, 305
Ghost Riders in the Sky 344
Ghostly dog 344
Ghoul 158, 345
Ghul 107, 158, 285
Ghūl 285
Gia 153
Gianes 159
Giant 20, 22, 23, 36, 38, 41, 45, 51, 59, 69, 75, 84, 88, 102, 108, 113, 125, 150, 152, 159–60, 185, 193, 194, 206, 207, 209, 219, 247, 253, 258, 259, 260, 261, 290, 292, 310, 312, 318, 322, 323, 342, 347, 348
Giant's graves 66
Gibbs, Cecelia May 169
Gibraltar 135
Giflet 68
Gille Dubh 159
Gillee Doo 159
Gillee Yoo 159
Gillette, Queen 140
Gimle 251
Gin 333
Ginar 160
Ginn 107
Ginnar 160
Ginnarr 160
Ginneyya 20
Girle Guairle 160, 267
Girouette 160
Girp 160
Giver of Abundance 95
Gladfly 190
Glaestig 160
Glaistig 153, 160–61, 171
Glaistyn 161
Glamorganshire, Wales 54, 93
Glandore Harbor 86
Glas Gaivlen 161
Glas Ghailbhleann 161, 170
Glasgavlen 161

Glashan 161
Glashtin 274
Glashtin, Man 160, 161
Glashtinhe 72
Glashtyn 161
Glastig 160
Glastonbury Tor 40, 141
Glastyn 161
Glauce 98, 161
Glaucè 161
Glaucia 162
Glaucippe 98, 161–62
Glauconome 162
Glaucus 243, 298
Glaueippe 161
Glauke 151, 162
Glaukia 162
Glaukonome 162
Glen Cuaich, Inverness 92
Glen Liadail 152
Glen of Eiti, Ballachulish 247
Glen Rushen, Isle of Man 146
Glenmore, Scotland 222
Glenullin, Londonderry 10
Gloi 162
Gloinn 162
Glóinn 162
Glooskap 125
Glove 142
Gluskab 9
Gnom 162
Gnome 20, 48, 118, 145, 162–63, 173, 231, 253, 267, 278, 292, 347
Gnomiko 162
Gnomo 162
Gnomos 162
Goat 16, 19, 26, 33, 49, 145, 151, 160, 171, 183, 210, 214, 222, 224, 227, 250, 273, 284, 296, 304, 321
Gob 163
Gobbies 163
Gobble-ratches 154
Gobelin 163
Gobelins 62
Goblin 44, 50, 53, 57, 62, 63, 64, 66, 68, 70, 72, 84, 87, 125, 139, 144, 149, 152, 161, 162, 163, 182, 221, 226, 239, 274, 276, 278, 284, 294, 302, 310, 312, 326, 327, 329, 345
Goblin pony 163
Gobnenn 164
Goborchinu 198
Gobs 62
God 14, 22, 69, 107, 109, 116, 121, 172, 174, 188, 205, 285
God of Babylon 324

God of Darkness 69
God of death 260
God of dreams 260
God of light 69
God of love 73, 153, 165, 282
God of the forest 255, 332
God of the sea 9, 19, 21, 23, 28, 37, 52, 54, 55, 68, 79, 85, 110, 118, 129, 130, 143, 172, 178, 197, 204, 207, 228, 232, 233, 246, 247, 268, 270, 280, 290, 297, 302, 319, 323, 330, 333
God of vegetation 293
God of war 23, 171, 174, 312
Goda 163
Godda 163
Goddess 10, 13, 14, 15, 16, 17, 18, 19, 20, 23, 24, 26, 27, 28, 29, 34, 41, 52, 53, 54, 55, 56, 63, 65, 70, 72, 75, 81, 84, 85, 91, 102, 104, 105, 106, 109, 115, 117, 118, 119, 120, 122, 125, 127, 128, 129, 130, 131, 139, 143, 145, 148, 152, 156, 157, 158, 165, 172, 174, 176, 177, 178, 183, 186, 178, 183, 186, 187, 188, 191, 196, 197, 199, 200, 204, 210, 211, 214, 215, 220, 223, 224, 228, 230, 233, 237, 238, 240, 242, 243, 245, 246, 248, 256, 259, 260, 261, 263, 264, 265, 268, 270, 271, 272, 273, 277, 278, 280, 282, 283, 289, 290, 293, 304, 312, 314, 319, 324, 331, 332, 334, 336, 337, 338, 342, 345
Goddess of beauty, flirtation, and love 264
Goddess of death and war 237
Goddess of discord and strife 214
Goddess of love 178, 270, 290, 319
Goddess of the hunt and the moon 345
Goddess of the night and vengeance 246
Goddess of the sun 260
Goddess of war 233, 237
Goddess of war and wisdom 233
Godling 13, 23, 34, 112, 117, 127, 129, 162, 207, 210, 243, 329

Gods of the entire house-
    hold 269
Gods of the storeroom
    269
Gofannon 164
Goibhniu 164
Goibne 164
Goibniu 164
Goil 336
Gold 17, 18, 20, 21, 29,
    44, 65, 66, 83, 101, 111,
    113, 116, 121, 129, 133,
    134, 139, 140, 142, 143,
    159, 164, 168, 184, 201,
    213, 237, 249, 253, 260,
    263, 264, 286, 292,
    303, 330, 340, 342,
    344, 346
Gold Woods 139
Goldemar, King 200
Golden apple tree 13, 34,
    129, 178
Golden apples 13, 34,
    129, 178
Golden hair 30, 53, 65,
    70, 71, 128, 168, 175,
    220, 230, 248, 260, 347
Goldmar, King 20, 122,
    200
Goldsmith 213, 342
Goll 164, 336
Gommes 162, 203
Goncoter 164
Gondul 163, 164, 336
Göngu-Hrólfs 237
Good bucca 69
Good Folk 66, 134
Good fortune 29, 56, 109,
    117, 145, 145, 156, 157,
    264, 328
Good Friday 93
The Good Little Mouse
    76, 239
Good Lubber 164
Good Neighbors 32, 105,
    134
Good People 43, 52, 99,
    134, 348
Goona 169
Goose 108, 177, 210, 308
Gooseberry Wife 64
Gore Vellye 235
Goree Island, Senegal 43,
    348
Gorge 98, 164
Gorgo 11, 12, 97, 98, 106,
    257, 278, 285
Gorgon 21, 103, 228, 326
Gorgone 232
Gorgons 79, 153, 165, 199
Gorgonzola 164
Gorgophone 98, 164
Gorgyra 262
Gorias 5, 331
Goric 205
Gorics 91
Gorlois, King 237

Gorre 44
Gorta man 145
Görzoni 165
Gottfried von Herder,
    Johann 125
Gotwergi 128
Gouvelin 163
Gower, Wales 137
Graces 81
Graeae 79, 165
Gragedd annwn 170
Graia 165
Graiae 165
Graiai 165, 199
Grain 165
Grain of the Bright
    Cheeks 165
Grainne 84, 165
Le Grand Colin 165, 258,
    271
Grandfather Well-Wisher
    109
Grandinilli 150, 165, 314
Grandmother Bony-
    shanks 42
Grandmother in the Forest
    42
Grandmother of the
    Bushes 71
Grandparent of the anthill
    253
Granfather Lausks 212
Grania 165
Granicus 21
Granmar 21
Grant 165
Grants of Strathspey 228
Grapevine 312
Grass 9, 42, 58, 124, 136,
    141, 142, 147, 161, 214,
    216, 265, 279, 282, 308,
    317, 327, 330
Grasshopper 193, 227
Gratiae 81
Grave 10, 17, 64, 68, 87,
    101, 159, 201, 215, 259,
    289
Graves of giants 342
Graveyards 107, 155, 285
Gray, James 53
Great Britain 80, 264
Great Dagda 94
Great Flood 151, 285
Great Lakes 226
Great Spirit 287
Greeba Mountain, Isle of
    Mann 70
Greece 2, 7, 9, 11, 12, 13,
    14, 19, 20, 21, 23, 27,
    29, 30, 31, 34, 37, 46,
    50, 59, 63, 74, 75, 79,
    80, 81, 83, 85, 89, 90,
    95, 99, 100, 101, 105,
    106, 112, 118, 127, 129,
    133, 134, 156, 165, 172,
    173, 174, 175, 177, 186,
    188, 190, 192, 196, 198,

199, 202, 204, 206, 208,
    209, 210, 211, 214, 216,
    220, 222, 224, 228,
    229, 231, 232, 233, 238,
    240, 243, 245, 247,
    248, 250, 258, 259,
    260, 262, 263, 265,
    268, 269, 270, 272,
    273, 276, 279, 280, 281,
    282, 285, 289, 290,
    294, 301, 306, 309, 310,
    311, 312, 313, 314, 316,
    317, 319, 320, 321, 322,
    323, 324, 325, 326,
    329, 337, 341, 342, 345,
    346, 349
Greek Aegean 12, 19, 24,
    102, 188, 195, 196, 197,
    202, 203, 204, 228,
    289, 290, 295
Green 17, 30, 35, 47, 50,
    51, 58, 60, 67, 76, 77,
    86, 92, 99, 101, 103, 113,
    116, 134, 135, 136, 137,
    140, 144, 146, 147, 150,
    153, 154, 159, 160, 161,
    162, 166, 167, 168, 170,
    175, 185, 187, 188, 194,
    195, 197, 201, 208, 213,
    224, 227, 231, 232, 233,
    238, 240, 295, 296,
    298, 301, 313, 330, 339,
    340, 341, 343
Green beards 340
Green Children 166, 267
Green Children of Wolf
    Pit 166
Green Children of Wool-
    pit 166
Green Friend 134
Green glaistig 160
Green goons 134
Green hair 92, 194, 201,
    208, 233, 293
Green hat 311, 249
Green Knight 58
Green Lady of Caerphilly
    166
Green Maiden 160, 224
Green Man 291
Green men 134
Green teeth 92, 232, 233,
    249
Greencoaties 134, 233,
    249
Greenies 134, 166, 193,
    238
Greentoothed Woman 51
Gregory, Lady Isabella
    Augusta 25
Greine 165
Gremlin 80, 166–67
Grenikos, river 21, 268
Grer 158, 167
Grerr 167
Gresholm 139
Grey Man 167

Grey Man's Breath 167
Grey neighbours 134
Grey rock 16
Grian 165
Grian of the Bright
    Cheeks 165
Griffin 140
Grig 167
Grigging apples 167
Grigs 276
Grim 163, 167, 168, 169,
    216, 221, 241, 266, 275,
    303, 313, 325, 344
Grim Reaper 30
Grimm, Jacob 80, 204,
    292, 297
Grimm, Wilhelm 80, 292
Grimr 237
Grindylow 167, 254
Groac'h 167
Groagach 168
Grogach 168
Grogan 168, 300
Grogoch 168
Grottes des fees 146
Grottoe 254, 261
Ground manikins 162
Ground-mannikins 115
Gruagach 160, 168, 182,
    273
Gruagach Sheombair 160
Gruel 284
Grumedan 229
Guam 317
Guaraní people 32, 44,
    74, 206
Guardian angel 95, 121,
    173, 324
Guardian fairy 337
Guardian of forest ani-
    mals 240
Guardian spirit 148, 184,
    205, 207, 240, 317, 324,
    342
Guardians of the forests
    346
Guatemala 24, 310
Guayazis 24
Gudrun 68
Guecubu 69
Gugner 65
Guidone 56, 246
Guild-folk 168, 330
Guild neighbors 168, 330
Guillen 210
Guillyn veggey 134
Guinevere, Queen 44, 96,
    228, 231, 237
Guingamar 238
Gulfora 344
Gull 167, 168, 216, 221,
    266, 275, 303, 325
Gullinbursti 65, 121
Gumnut Babies 169
Gumnut Town 169
Gungnir 115
Gunlod 169

Gunn 169
Gunna 169
Gunnold 169
Guriuz 128, 169
Gurt Dog 59
Gustr 169
Guy of Warwick 88
Guy Trash 329
Guytrash 169
Guytrash Padfoot 169
Gwartheg y llyn 91, 161, 170, 218, 277
Gwarwyn-a-throt 72
Gwenhidw, Queen 170
Gwenhidwy 170
Gwenhudwy 170
Gwenhwyvar 231
Gwent 177
Gwrach Y Rhibyn 47, 51, 94, 170
Gwrachyribin 170
Gwragedd Annwn 170, 218, 277, 333
Gwrarch Er Hreebin 170
Gwydion ab Don 170
Gwyllgi the Dog of Darkness 48, 302
Y Gwylliaid Cochion 288
Gwyllion 170, 171, 259
Gwyn ap Nudd 93, 141, 171, 277, 344
Gwyneb y Nyth 171
Gwynn ap Nudd, King 139, 171
Gwythyr ap Greidal 171
Gy-Carlin 171
Gy-Carling 171
Gyergyo-Szens-Miklos 96
Gyl burnt-tayl 171
Gylfaginning 335
Gymro, Gerallt 137
Gyre-Carlin 171, 248
Gyre-Carling 171
Gytrash 59, 154, 169

Habetrot 59, 154, 169, 171, 219, 267, 297
Habetrot the Spinstress 171
Habitrot 171
Habonde 10, 95, 171
Habtrot 171
Habundia 95, 171, 172, 343
Hada 133, 134
Hadada 133, 134
Hadas 134
Hades 28, 39, 204, 207, 210, 211, 214, 215, 234
Hadryades 250
Hag 7, 21, 42, 52, 54, 59, 73, 74, 89, 109, 158, 164, 168, 170, 172, 194, 218, 228, 238, 239, 277, 313, 326, 333
Hag of the Seas 239

Hag of Warning 170
Hagno 172, 245, 321
Hail storms 150
Hairy Jack 172
Hairy Meg 227
Haka dance 292
Haks Oza 45
Half bird 15, 20, 215, 216, 236, 266, 268, 276, 286, 306, 319, 32
Half-fay being 294
Half-kin 174
Half-kyn 174
Halia 172, 179
Haliai 172
Halie 172
Haliè 172
Halikarnassos 265, 270
Halimede 172
Halirrhotios 23
Halloween 77
Hallowtide 305
Halmus 83
Haltija 107, 173
Halykos 173
Hamadryad 13, 17, 27, 36, 38, 45, 85, 90, 112, 127, 152, 161, 164, 173, 180, 183, 191, 198, 205, 214, 228, 237, 254, 269, 273, 283, 285, 286, 290, 293, 309, 316, 318
Hamadryádes 173
Hamadryadnik 173
Hamadryas 27, 45, 127, 173, 180, 198, 205, 258, 283, 309, 316
Hamme 263
Hammer 65, 116, 121, 330
Hammer of the Witches 209
Hammerlinge 162
Hamou Ukaiou 17, 173
Hampshire, England 88, 212, 289
Hamu Ukaiou 17, 173
Hanarr 173
Handkerchief 87, 159, 274
Hannar 173
Hannarr 173
Hans 173
Har 174
Harbingers of death 300
Hardenstein Castle, Germany 200
Härdmandle 115, 128, 174
Härdmändlen 128, 174
Härdmandlene 128
Haris 188
Hârith, El 41, 174, 188
Harlequin 125, 344
Harp 16, 17, 18, 94, 125, 137, 151, 200, 245, 332
Harper's Magazine 295
Harpies 79, 122
Harpina 174, 242

Hárr 174
Hárr Hall 174
Harry-ca-Nab 334
Harts 338
Harvard University 137
Harvest Moon 146
Harvesters 149
Hatdedases 95
Hatekin 182
Hathors 174
Hatton, Sir Christopher 291
Haugspori 174
Haumia 174
Haumia-tiketike 174
Haur 174
Haus-schmiedlein 174, 343
Hausmanner 174
Havelock, King of Denmark 88
Havfrue 175
Havman 175
Havmand 175, 232
Hawaii 231
Hawlaa 161
Hazelnut tree 173
He-Manner 292
Headingley Hill, Yorkshire 48
Headless 30, 31, 48, 61, 65, 88, 100, 101, 114, 167, 189, 310, 344, 345
Headless coach 101
Headless horseman 114, 344
Heaprides 79
Hearse 344
Heart of Ice 157, 164, 226
Hearth 51, 77, 112, 157, 165, 269, 271, 289, 329, 340
Heath hounds 154
Heather 138, 175, 276
Heather pixies 175, 276
Heaven 99, 123, 135, 174, 240, 270
Heavens 26, 153, 299
Hebrides Islands, Scotland 74, 219
Hecabe 98, 175
Hecate 172
Hecla 221
Hector 144
Hedina 118, 175
Hedley Kow 175, 310
Hedley, England 175
Hedyosmus 234
Hegetoria 175
Heiaus 136
Heidenmanndli 128
Heidenweibchen 128
Heifer 144, 190, 238
Heilos 210, 271
Heinsel-mannchen 203
Heinzelmanchen 175–76

Heinzelmännchen 66
Heinzelmännchenbrunnen 176
Heinzelmannchens 203
Heinzemannchens 162
Heione 120
Hekaerge 176, 220, 334
Hekate 210
Hekaterides 176
Hekateros 176
Heketoro 331
Hel 125, 172, 335
Hel-kaplein 115
Hel keplein 212
Held 336
The Heldenbuch 116
Heleionomai 241
Helen of Troy 258
Helgi 315
Heliades 13, 87, 106, 176, 232, 271, 273
Helice 98, 176
Heliconian 176
Helicta 98, 176
Helie 13, 106, 176, 210, 232, 273
Helike 94, 176, 208
Helios 13, 17, 37, 79, 81, 87, 106, 175, 176, 210, 232, 245, 257, 270, 271, 273
Heliotrope 87, 148
Hell 48, 59, 99, 123, 135, 154, 188, 240, 302, 337
Hell beast 155
Hell hounds 154, 184
Helle 246
Hellekin 125
Hellen, King 262, 263, 285
Hell's Kettles 168
Helmet 133, 349
Helweg 141
Hemp 192
Hen Wen 176–77
Hen-Wen 176
Hengetär 107
Henkie knows 177
Henkies 177
Henks 177
Henry II 166
Henwen 176
Hephaestine 12, 79, 97, 180, 187, 257
Hephaistos 195
Hepti 177
Heptifili 177
Hera 2, 13, 19, 20, 34, 75, 82, 102, 118, 129, 130, 178, 190, 192, 211, 228, 246, 282
Herakles 13, 23, 34, 63, 83, 129, 162, 178, 259
Herbal medicine 238
Herbaline 177
Herbalism 136
Herbology 107, 287

Herbs 18, 104, 114, 142, 157, 159, 331, 341
Hercules 13, 23, 34, 63, 83, 129, 162, 178, 259
Herfijtur 336
Heri 177
Herkyna 177
Herkyna, river 177
Herlaþing 343
Herla's Assembly 343
Herla's Hounds 184
Herla's Rade 184
Herleekin 125
Herleking 125
Herlequin 125, 344
Hermaphrodite 188, 294
Hermaphroditus 294
Hermes 81, 95, 99, 118, 175, 197, 207, 211, 222, 224, 250, 259, 268, 274, 289, 294, 304, 310, 321, 324
Hermitage Castle 288
Hermos, river 238
Hermosa, Princess 315
Hermus 85, 97, 98
Herne the Hunter and his Gabriel Hounds 344
Hero 9, 10, 12, 19, 20, 36, 42, 43, 46, 50, 54, 56, 61, 68, 70, 75, 83, 84, 102, 103, 112, 117, 122, 130, 133, 143, 148, 152, 156, 177, 185, 192, 195, 196, 202, 205, 206, 212, 215, 233, 237, 239, 256, 260, 262, 265, 270, 288, 289, 304, 306, 307, 315, 322, 323, 324, 328, 331, 338
Hero 98, 159
Herod's hunt 343
Herodiada 191
Herodias 191
Heroic Fairies 178, 330
Herophilos 178, 290
Herr Johannes 292
Herse 12, 15, 97, 98, 180
Hesiod 4, 13, 15, 28, 81, 84, 106, 131, 133, 144, 155, 162, 172, 176, 178, 180, 181, 186, 199, 210, 211, 212, 230, 231, 232, 242, 246, 247, 256, 272, 273, 278, 283, 289, 296, 319
Hesiod, type of nymph 178
Hesione 178, 256
Hespera 178
Hespere 178
Hespereia 178
Hesperethoosa 178
Hesperia 13, 34, 129, 178
Hesperian dragon 79
Hesperides 13, 34, 81, 129, 178

Hesperidian nymphs 178
Hesperusa 178
Hestyaea 178
Hesychia 104, 131
Hexenringe 142
Hey-Hey Men 292
Hieromneme 178
High elves 216
High king 16, 94, 218, 273
High King of Ireland 273
Hilde 53, 179, 336
Hildebrand 56, 338
Hildesheim, Germany 182
Hildur 179, 336
Hill crowd 134
Hill folk 105, 134
Hill manikins 162
Hill-mannikins 115
Hill men 55, 330
Hill-men 55
Hill of Fennel 148
Hill of the Plain 203
Hill People 179, 330
Hill-people 179, 330
Hill trolls 115, 330
Hille Bingels 179, 180
Hillmen 182
Hillocks 99, 185
Hilton Hall, England 77
Himalia 179
Himba people 14
Himera 179
Hina 197
Hindustan 190
Hine-Korako 179
Hine-pukohu-rangi 179
Hine-Pukohurangi 179, 180
Hine-Ruru 179
Hine-Wai 180
Hinekorako 179
Hinerary of Giraldus Cambrensis 137
Hinky-puck 344
Hinzelmann 179, 180
Hipparete 98, 180
Hippo 180
Hippocoon 50
Hippocorystes 98, 187
Hippodamia 98, 99, 132, 180
Hippodice 98, 180
Hippokampoi 247
Hippolytus 98, 290
Hippomedusa 98, 180
Hipponay 180
Hipponoe 180
Hipponous, King 324
Hippothe 181
Hippothoe 98, 181
Hippothous 98, 164
His nibs 86
Histoires ou Contes du temps Passé 258
Historia rerum Anglicarum 166

History of English Affairs 166
History of Places 62
Hjalpreck, King 289
Hkringwan 239
Hlaevang 181
Hlaevangr 181
Hledjólfr 181
Hliodolf 181
Hljodjolfr 181
Hlokk 181
Hmin 181, 244
Hnikur 181, 198, 199, 245, 341
Hnitbjorg Mountain 169
Hoard 28, 29, 53, 91, 111, 122, 133, 184, 199, 213, 248, 263, 264, 282, 289, 292
Hoard 334
Hob 10, 66, 162, 181, 182
Hob-and-his-Lantern 344
Hob-goblin 181
Hob-thrush 163
Hob Thrust 181, 182
Hob of T'hurst 181
Hob-thrust 182
Hobany 10, 95
Hobany's-Lantern 344
Hobbedy's Lantern 344
Hobbers 62
Hobby Lantern 344
Hobgoblin 50, 58, 61, 62, 63, 64, 66, 69, 71, 72, 84, 115, 122, 134, 167, 181–82, 184, 211, 220, 243, 283, 291, 301, 308, 311, 328
Hobgoblinet 181
Hobgobs 163
Hobmen 182
Hobredy's lanthorn 344
Hobthrust 181, 182, 291
Hobtrust 181
Hobyahs 182
Hodbrodd 304
Hödeken 182
Hodge-Poker 182, 239
Hoel, King 237
Hog 74, 197, 291
Högfolk 179
Hoggstari 182
Hogmen 182
Hoioimann 292
Holder-Folk 330
Holland 195, 200, 213, 303, 345
Hollantide 182
Holle 152
Hollenmadchen 182
Hollow-men 330
Holly 73, 92, 138, 183, 295
Holly King 183, 255, 291, 295
Holly trees 183

Holy Thursday 151
Homer 4, 16, 19, 26, 27, 75, 81, 83, 87, 144, 151, 178, 183, 191, 206, 210, 247, 271, 306
Homeric Hymn to Apollo 320
Homeric Nymphs 183, 242, 247
Homme de Bouc 49, 183
L'Homme Rouge 258
Honest folks 134
Honey 138, 229
Honey Tongued 17
Honeycomb 67, 229
Honeysuckle 139
Honolulu 231
Hooded crow 223
Hook of Prosnitz 45
Hooper of Sennen Cove 83
Hop 223
Hopi Indians 195
Hor 183
Horae 104, 120, 131, 183
Horn of Plenty 11
Hornbori 183
Horny Siegfred 130
Horr 183
Hörr 183
Horse 9, 16, 39, 40, 43, 45, 50, 61, 64, 69, 71, 72, 78, 79, 82, 100, 108, 109, 110, 114, 117, 118, 121, 127, 133, 137, 138, 146, 156, 158, 161, 165, 167, 169, 181, 191, 193, 197, 198, 199, 200, 202, 214, 220, 221, 227, 241, 242, 243, 245, 250, 252, 256, 257, 259, 263, 264, 269, 273, 274, 276, 281, 291, 300, 303, 304, 310, 317, 327, 337, 342
Horseshoe 213, 312
Horton, England 169
Hosentefel 80
Host 309
Host of the unforgiven dead 309
Hostia 343
Houndkonz 102, 184
Hounds of Annwn 35, 48, 59, 92, 93, 137, 184, 302
Hounds of the Hills 184
Hour of the Ox 83
House brownie 66
House-fairy 52, 108, 154
House of the Gorics 91
House-spirit 19, 66, 110, 111, 113, 121, 129, 184, 262
Household brownie 340
Household chores 51, 110, 125, 165, 175, 181, 195,

220, 269, 271, 284, 285, 289, 308, 328
Household fairy 58, 72, 73, 104, 114, 165, 193, 200, 271, 282, 284, 295, 308, 339
Household of hellequin 343
Household spirit 109, 122, 204, 260, 270, 303, 316, 328
Household task 213
Housekeeper's little seat 51
Houses of the alux 25
Housewife 53, 84, 133, 332
Howa-a 184
Howaa 110, 184
Howlaa 110, 184
Howlers 161
Howlies 161
Hreidmar 133, 184, 263, 289
Hrist 184, 336
Hrólfs 237
Hu hsien 184
Huacas 184
Huamann 292
Huckpoten 344
Hüdemuhlen Luneburg, Germany 180
Huecuvu 69
Huelli 239
Huerco 185
Huergo 185
Hugh MacLeod 144
Hugstari 185
Hulda-folk 185
Huldafolk 185
Hulde 344
Huldra 185, 317
Huldrafolk 122, 123, 185
Huldraslaat 185
Huldre 185, 324
Huldre folk 324
Huldre-men 185
Huldrefolk 185, 335
Huldreslaut 123
Huldubyggd 185
Huldufólk 185
Huli people 95
Hulla 185
Hummam 209
Humuhumu 185
Hunchback 330, 339
Hundred Years' War 326
Hünengräber 342
Hung Sheung Tree 36
Hungary 42, 135, 263
Hunt of Herodias 343
Hunting hounds 59, 117, 137
Huon de Bordeaux 225, 226
Huorco 185, 258
Hurnen Sifrift 130

Hustomte 162
Hütchen 182
Hutchens 203
Hy Brasil 139
Hyad 12, 24, 128, 185, 188, 254, 267
Hyades 13, 185, 277
Hyale 91, 98, 186
Hyalê 186
Hyamos 198
Hybrid animal 74, 107
Hybrids 74, 294
Hydaspes 37
Hyde 186
Hydra 15
Hydriades 250
Hyele 186
Hylas 131, 225, 254, 297, 313
Hylde-moer 186
Hyldemoer 152, 186
Hyldeqvinde 186
Hyldermoder 186
Hylleis 186
Hylton, Baron 77, 78
Hymnos 9, 196
Hymnus 248
Hypate 186, 233, 247
Hyperantus 98, 122
Hyperbius 79, 97, 98, 131
Hyperborea 176, 220, 334
Hypereia 186
Hyperion 210, 271
Hyperippe 98, 186
Hypermnestra 28, 98, 99, 187
Hypseus 83, 90
Hyria, Greece 202
Hyrieus, King 202
Hyssington 291
Hyster 187
Hyter sprite 187

Iache 187
Iæneria 187
Iaera 187
Iaira 187
Iaiysos 319
Iakhe 187, 256
Ialdabaoth 282
Iamos 129
Ianassa 187
Ianeria 187
Ianesse 187
Ianira 187
Ianthe 188
Iapetos 36
Iapetus 87
Iara 188
Iasis 75, 188, 190, 268, 316
Iberia 135
Iberian peninsula 226
Iblees 174
Iblis 20, 96, 158, 188, 193, 194, 226, 285, 300
Ibormeith 30, 73

Icarios 50
Icarius 270
Ice Realm 310
Icebergs 251
Iceland 46, 116, 123, 135, 181, 185, 199, 221, 245, 308
Ida 12, 188
Idae 261
Idaean Mother 188
Idaia 188
Idaia 188
Idas 94, 98, 180
Ide 188
Idmon 98, 285
Idothea 12, 186, 188
Idya 188
Idyia 119, 189
Iele 189
Ieles 189
Ielle 189, 191
Ifreet 189
Ifrit 107, 158, 189, 194
Ifrita 189
Ignis fatuus 123, 129, 275, 276, 278, 344
Ignis-fatuus 123
Ignus fatuus 344
Igosha 189
Igraine, Queen 237
Ihalmiut 32
Ijosalfar 48, 148, 216, 310, 333, 334, 336
Iliad 16, 26, 27, 75, 81, 83, 87, 144, 151, 183, 206, 306
Illes 189
Illissus River 262
Illyria 70, 117
Imbrus 98
Imeusimos 270
Immortality 63, 81, 107, 161, 188, 197, 241, 249
Immortals 253, 296
Ina Pic Winna 189
Inachus 190
Inakhos 34, 190, 228, 241
Incantations 104
Incantatori 190
Incantatrice 144, 190
Incense 109, 209, 215
Inchiquin Lake 14
Inconstancy 40, 190
Incubo 190, 236
Incubus 107, 226
India 50, 56, 64, 69, 101, 103, 114, 120, 121, 156, 204, 217, 336, 340
Indra 101, 190, 287
Infant 46, 76, 77, 120, 129, 139, 186, 189, 209, 239, 244, 257, 259, 278, 346
Infant god 12, 15, 19, 20, 21, 23, 24, 26, 27, 29, 31, 34, 40, 43, 65, 94, 128, 130, 161, 172, 176, 186, 188, 192, 201, 202,

204, 207, 208, 223, 241, 245, 246, 255, 263, 267, 271, 272, 274, 280, 282, 289, 306, 321, 322, 323
Ing 190
Inge of Rantum 121
Ingi 190
Ingkanto 107
Initiation rites 275
Ino 15, 40, 186
Inopos, river 102
Inquisition 344
Insect 35, 64, 118, 190, 287
Insuls Avallonis 40
Inti huatana 184
Inuchus 272
Inuit 15, 32, 39, 119, 191, 251, 328
Inverness, Scotland 67
Inverness-Shire 92, 137
Invisible 13, 14, 16, 21, 24, 26, 32, 35, 42, 43, 46, 60, 66, 67, 76, 82, 84, 88, 91, 97, 102, 105, 107, 109, 110, 111, 116, 122, 126, 134, 135, 141, 143, 150, 157, 158, 160, 168, 170, 172, 180, 200, 212, 215, 223, 224, 225, 227, 238, 244, 249, 254, 258, 260, 261, 264, 271, 286, 305, 308, 331, 333, 342, 347, 348
Invisible islands 5
Io 190, 231, 324
Ion 190
Ione 190
Ionia 72
Ioniades 190
Ionides 190
Iormungrundar i iodyr 100
Iöunn 159
Iphianassa 191
Iphiklos 203
Iphimedusa 98, 191
Ircenrraat 191
Ircenrraq 191
Ireland 1, 5, 10, 17, 18, 30, 31, 39, 41, 46, 51, 52, 60, 62, 65, 68, 73, 74, 80, 85, 86, 99, 103, 105, 110, 118, 127, 135, 137, 138, 139, 141, 142, 146, 147, 148, 149, 151, 153, 155, 157, 158, 161, 165, 168, 169, 170, 192, 19, 208, 218, 227, 234, 245, 247, 248, 257, 273, 274, 281, 283, 287, 290, 293, 301, 304, 331, 341, 345, 348
Iri 191, 310
Iris 122
Irish mythology 12, 13,

17, 32, 41, 52, 79, 92, 94, 100, 102, 104, 105, 118, 128, 143, 148, 213, 215
Irish potato famine 114
Irish Sea 29, 143, 239
Irodeasa 189, 191
Irodiada 191
Iron 48, 55, 68, 82, 94, 101, 113, 170, 173, 182, 212, 213, 252, 253, 264, 270, 288, 297, 312, 327, 332
Iron Age 138
Iron Nosed Witch 42
Iron Nosed Woman 42
Ironworking 49
Iroquois people 103, 154, 156, 195, 258, 349
Irrbloss 344
Irrlicht 61
Iseult 90
Isione 99, 191
Iskrzycki 184, 191
Island of Avalon 34, 40, 141, 238, 281
Islands of the Blessed 150
Isle of Apples 40, 238
Isle of Lewis 302
Isle of Man, England 12, 35, 43, 53, 69, 70, 73, 105, 135, 146, 149, 150, 161, 182, 184, 212, 213, 215, 235, 288, 301, 309, 318
Isle of Rhodes 319
Isle of Rügen, Germany 45, 60, 66, 342
Isle of Skye 56, 88
Isle of the Blest 139
Isle of Tyree, Ireland 169
Isle of Wails 16
Isle of Wight 164
Isles des Saints 205
Ismene 191
Ismenian spring 228
Ismenis 192, 242
Ismenor 315
Ismenus 192
Isonoe 99, 192
Issa 192
Istria 343
Istrus 98, 180
Italian Renaissance 56, 129, 144, 246, 262, 334
Italy 16, 49, 52, 74, 107, 128, 159, 165, 186, 197, 227, 236, 237, 238, 265, 294, 305, 314, 323
Itea 98, 192
Ithome 192
Itonomus 99, 279
Itonus 228
Iubdan, King 139, 192
Ivald 192
Ivalde 148

Ivaldi 48, 148, 191, 192, 216, 310, 333, 334, 336
Ívaldi 192
Ivallda 65, 192
Iwain, Sir 211
Ixion 246
Ixtabay 24
Iynx 192
Izanagi 197
Izanami 197

Jab Molasi 265
Jack Frost 192, 259, 298, 309
Jack-In-Irons 193
Jack-Muh-Lantern 193
Jack-o'-Lantern 92
Jack o' Lanthorn 123
Jack o' the Bowl 193
Jack-of-the-bowl 243
Jack Robinson 291
Jacky Lantern 125, 344
Jade Emperor 41, 113
Jafnhar 193
Jaga Baba 42
Jaloff drum 348
Jaloff people 348
Jan 38, 193, 239, 244
Jan bin Jan 193
Jan-Ibn-Jan 193
Jan the Sun 193
Janaina 193
Jann 107, 158, 193–94
Jann al-Jann 193
Janus 195
Japan 83, 197, 200, 269, 348
Jari 194
Jasius 94
Jasmine 139
Jean de la Bolieta 243
Jem 177
Jengu 194
Jenny Burnt-Tail 344
Jenny Greenteeth 7, 51, 100, 194, 245, 248, 254, 268, 333
Jenny Greentooth 51
Jenny with the Lantern 344
Jeraspunt 338
Jerusalem 221
Jewels 164, 264, 331
Jezi-Baba 42
Jezibaba 42, 194
Jil 223
Jimaninas 194
Jimaninos 194, 298
Jimmy Squarefoot 194
Jin 107, 223
Jineeyeh 107
Jinn 101, 102, 104, 107
Jinnee 107
Jinnestan 193
Jinnestân 35
Jinni 107
Jinnie 107

Jinnistan 26, 107
Jinniy 107
Jinniyah 107
Joac-O-Lantern 193
Joan of the torch 194
Joan the Wad 194, 227, 344
Jock-'o-the-Lantern 344
Jocosa 140
Jogah 154, 156, 195, 258
Johannaeus, Finnus 116, 135
John of the Coast 347
John of the Dunes 347
Johnson, Richard 327
Joint eater 23
Jokul 192
Jonson, Ben 223
Jordr 260
Jötnar 335
Joyous Isle 121
Judgment Day 123, 188, 282
Judur 336
Julienisse 295
Julius Caesar 256
Juniper 109
Juniper tree 152
Juno 2, 13, 19, 20, 34, 75, 82, 102, 118, 129, 130, 178, 190, 192, 211, 228, 246, 282
Jupiter 12, 13, 15, 19, 21, 23, 24, 26, 27, 29, 31, 34, 37, 40, 65, 75, 76, 80, 81, 82, 85, 89, 94, 99, 104, 106, 107, 108, 120, 131, 132, 140, 161, 172, 176, 179, 180, 183, 188, 190, 191, 192, 195, 201, 202, 204, 208, 211, 223, 224, 229, 231, 233, 241, 242, 243, 245, 246, 257, 259, 263, 271, 272, 274, 277, 282, 285, 289, 306, 320, 321, 322, 323, 325, 328
Jutul 330
Juturna 106, 151, 195, 211

Ka-jinn 107
Ka-ka 204
Kabauter 162
Kabeirides 165
Kabeiro 195
Kabeiroi 195
Kabira 195
Kabouter 162, 195, 203
Kaboutermannekin 195
Kaboutermannikin 195, 203
Kachin people 195, 204, 280
Kachina 195, 204
Kacina 195
Kadmilos 195
Kadru 241

Kâf 101, 270
Kafizin 196
Kahiki-ula 197
Kahtal alux 25
Kahukura 332
Kakamora 108, 196
Kakangora 108
Kalfater 201
Kaliadne 74
Kaliya 196
Kallianassa 196
Kallianeira 196
Kalligeneia 196
Kalliphaeia 75
Kallirhoe 196
Kalliste, island 196, 216
Kallisto 75
Kallithyia 190
Kallraden 196, 333
Kalybe 9, 196, 242, 248
Kalypso 75, 197
Kamapua'a 197
Kamarina 197
Kamarina, Sicily 197
Kami 197, 244
Kamillos 195
Kamros 319
Kankantree tree 117
Kannerez-noz 47
Kapheira 172, 197
Kapok tree 92
Kappa 197
Karakoncolos 198
Karakondjol 198
Karakondjul 198
Karia, Anatolia 207
Karios 328
Karmentis 322
Karuppayi 204
Karya 173, 198
Karyatis 77
Karzeł 198
Karzelek 198
Kasampere 296
Kaspar von der Rhon 56, 338
Kassotis 198
Kastalia 198
Kastalios 198
Kataw 198, 333
Katchina 195
Kattavarayan 204
Katu 108
Kaukai 198
Kaukas 198
Kaukasos Mountains, Greece 16, 37
Kaukis 162
Kaunos 72
Kavanaghs 47
Kawako 197
Kax 24
Kebren 258
Kebrene, Greece 258
Keeill Moirrey, Isle of Man 288
Keeill Vrisht 70

Keening 47
Keening woman 51
Kekropides 15
Kelaino 198
Kellas Cats 74
Kelly, family 76
Kelouse 198
Kelpie 39, 43, 62, 64, 78,
    118, 135, 153, 181, 198–
    99, 234, 245, 252, 267,
    299, 318, 340, 341
Kenchrias 268
Kenilworth 342
Kentauros 313
Keos, Greece 228
Kepec 162
Kephalos 203
Kephisos 213, 216
Kepler, Johannes 199
Kepler's Fairy 199
Kerana 206
Kerese Indians 195
Kerkeis 199
Keshalyi 199, 217, 219
Kethlenda of the Crooked
    Teeth 79
Keto 165, 199
Kewach 84
Khalkis 130
Khariklo 199
Kharites 17
Kheiron 273
Khione 199
Khloris 150
Khryseis 199–200, 256
Khrysopeleia 83
Ki no mono 200
Kidnap 62, 68, 110, 134,
    141, 158, 182, 267, 300,
    312, 317, 331, 341, 344
Kidnapping 42, 108, 126,
    207, 317, 330, 332,
    335
Kielkropf 255
Kiji-mun 200
Kijimun 200
Kijimuna 200
Kijimunaa 200
Kijini 107
Kikimera 200
Kikimora 109, 200
Kikonia, Greece 9
Kili 200
Kili 200
Killaloe 14, 16
Killmoulis 45, 66, 182,
    200
Kiltubrid, Ireland 145
Kindlt Fairy Host 299
Kindly Ones 153
King Arthur 58, 73, 144,
    177, 228, 237, 344
King David 221
King Diarmaite 52
King Djinn Fairy 287
King Egobagal 18
King Goldemar 200

King Goldmar 20, 122,
    200
King Gunnar 68
King Melisseus 26
King Oebalus 50
King of Albany 229, 281
King of Athens 15, 341
King of Demons 28
King of the Dead 30
King of the Djinn 287
King of the Dwarfs 20,
    248
King of the Element of
    Air 265
King of the Elves 125,
    128
King of the Gold Mine
    140
King of the Sea 48
King of the Shaitans 193,
    300
King of the Underworld
    57, 234, 320
King of the Waning Year
    295
King-trows 206
Kingsley, Charles 239
Kintyre, Scotland 168
Kios, Greece 131, 224,
    228
Kipling, Rudyard 342
Kirk, Reverend Rovert 87
Kirke 84
Kirkegrim 201
Kirkonwaki 201
Kisseis 43, 65, 128, 201
Kissel 192
Kisthene 165
Kit o' the Canstick 123
Kit with the Candlestick
    344
Klabauter 162
Klabautermann 201
Klaboutermannikins 201
Klaia 202
Klaubauf 295
Kleeia 186, 202
Kleide 202, 204, 272
Kleine volk 115, 134
Kleinmanneken 162
Kleocharia 202
Kleodora 85, 89, 100,
    202, 228, 323, 242
Kleokhareia 202
Kleone 85
Klepsydra 126
Kleure 202
Klintekonger 124
Klippe 134, 202
Kloka 60
Kloka män 136
Klonia 202
Klonie 202
Kludde 202, 263, 264
Kluterman 201
Klymene 203
Klytie 87

Knecht 295
Knecht Ruprecht 295
Knenye 117
Knife 80, 81, 171, 173, 185
Knight 27, 58, 65, 68, 73,
    96, 100, 111, 121, 177,
    208, 211, 218, 224, 225,
    232, 233, 262, 265,
    306, 308, 326
Knock Aine 18
Knock Fennel 148
Knock Ma 203
Knock Ma Fairies 203
Knockaine 18
Knockers 88, 163, 203,
    252
Knockfierna mountain,
    Ireland 110
Knockma 99, 148
Knockshegouna 110
Knockshegowna 331
Knocky-Boh 203
Knoggelvi 252
Knolls 41, 177, 304
Knossia 203
Knossos, Greece 203
Kobauld 203
Koblernigh 87, 203
Kobold 32, 66, 135, 163,
    175, 180, 195, 200, 203–
    04, 265, 274, 284, 328
Kobolde 203
Kodin-haltia 204
Kokko 204
Koko 204
Kolbalds 203
Kollhos, Greece 16
Kollimalaikanniyarka
    204
Kongsbjerg, Zealand 124
Kontsodaimonas 80
Korakorako 331
Koran 20, 158, 167, 188
Korandon 167
Korea 83
Kores 205
Korid-gwen 139
Koril 91, 205
Korinthos, Greece 127,
    268
Korkyra 204
Kornbocke 204, 273
Kornmutter 204
Kornmutter-korn 204
Korokiorwek 38, 204
Koronides 204, 231, 233
Koronis 43, 65, 108, 128,
    202, 204, 272
Korred 205
Korrig 205
Korrigan 67, 89, 116, 124,
    205
Korrs 205
Korybantes 95, 290
Korykia 205
Koryphe 280
Koumyoumin 205

Kouril 91
Koza ia 256
Koza oza 256
Koza Peri 256
Kramer, Heinrich 209
Krampus 295
Kraneia 173, 205
Kransnoludi 220
Kranto 90
Krasnoludek 162
Krasnoludki 220
Kremara 205, 207, 282
Krênai 183
Kreousa 206
Kretheis 206
Kriksy 277
Krimissos 299
Kris Kringle 295
Krokalê 91
Kronos 289
Kruzimugeli 206
Kulhwch 260
Kulhwcn and Olwen 260
Kunal-trow 206
Kunene 14
Kunhild 212
Kupara 206
Kuperan 206
Kuppiron 206
Kuprian 206
Kura 206
Kurana 206
Kurene 206
Kuru-Pira 206
Kurupira 206
Kurwaichin 205, 207
Kvasir 150, 155, 169
Kwakiutl people 63, 70
Kwan Yin 84
Kyam 329
Kyane 207
Kyanee 207, 329
Kyankse, Burma 205
Kybele 188, 293
Kykais 207
Kyllene 207, 261, 269
Kymatolege 93, 207
Kymo 207
Kymodoke 207
Kymopoleia 207
Kymothoe 208
Kynosoura 94, 208
Kyrene 206, 208
Kyrtones 208
Kytheros, river 75, 188,
    190, 268, 316

Labasta 20
Labrador, Canada 32
Lac Long Quan 38
Lachesis 144, 236
Laconia 99, 129, 325
Ladon 178, 321
Ladon, river 234
Lady Abonde 344
Lady Banana Ghost 208
Lady Bertha 56

Lady Fortune 144
Lady Janaina 193
Lady Midday 279
Lady of Death 47
Lady of Gollerus 208
Lady of Shalott 121
Lady of the Fountain 211
Lady of the Lake 96, 125, 208, 237, 339
Lady of the woods 317
Lady Perchta 56
Lady Rekya Daughter of the Red One 209
Lady's Own 147
Lagoon 225
Laimos 209
Lake 14, 37, 39, 63, 67, 73, 92, 96, 125, 148, 154, 158, 167, 169, 170, 194, 201, 208, 209, 218, 237, 240, 252, 256, 265, 293, 299, 313, 316, 319, 326, 328, 329, 339
Lake Astakos 37
Lake Erie 313
Lake goddess 240
Lake Lucerne 313
Lake Rotoma 319
Lake Volvi 63
Lakedaimon, King 311
Lakedaimonia, Greece 202, 228, 311, 325
Lakes of Len 213
Lakonia 202
Lalla Malika 209
Lalla Mira 209
Lalla Mira al-Mtiriyya 209
Lalla Mira Bent Hartya 209
Lalla Mirra 209
Lalla Mkouna Bent Mkoun 209
Lalla Raqya 209
Lalla Rekya Bint el Khamar 209
Lalla Reqya 209
Lalla Rkia 209
Lamang-lupa 253
Lamas 209
Lamb 64, 88, 201, 245, 313
Lambana 107
Lamia of the Sea 209
Lamia of the Shore 209
Lamiae 209
Lamiarum sagittas 213
Laminak 210, 252
Lamin'ak 210
Lamnia 85
Lampades 210
Lamperia 245
Lampetia 210
Lampetie 13, 106, 176, 210, 232, 245, 271, 273
Lampus 98, 257
Lancaster, England 84

Lancelot 96, 121, 208
Land of Eternal Youth 327
Land of Perpetual Youth 134
Land of Promise 248
Land of Saint Martin 166
Land of Tears 239
Land of the Ever-Young 97
Land of the Young 142, 148
Land of Women 208
Landnámabók 210
Landvaettir 210
Landvaettir 210
Landvættir 210
Laneria 210
Langia 210, 242
Lanhyddel Mountain, Monmouthshire 171, 259
Lantern 92, 116, 123, 125, 129, 193, 194, 200, 344
Lantern man 344
Lanthe 210
Lantukh 211
Laodice 191
Laomedeia 211
Laomedia 211
Laomedon, King 196, 314
Lapithai, Greece 313
Lapiths 83
Lapland 46, 446, 185, 312
Lapp 259, 293, 309
Lara 211, 242
Larch tree 294
Lares 211, 213, 225
Lares compitales 211
Lares domestici 211
Lares familiars 211
Lares patria 211
Lares permarini 211
Lares praestitis 211
Lares private 211
Lares rurales 211
Lares viales 211
Larissa 211
Larunda 211
Larvae 213
Lases 211
Last Rites 339
Latawci 244
Latin 7, 11, 27, 28, 34, 35, 40, 79, 83, 85, 91, 96, 98, 99, 100, 103, 113, 118, 122, 127, 130, 131, 132, 133, 162, 175, 176, 177, 180, 181, 186, 187, 192, 224, 234, 237, 241, 257, 272, 276, 279, 280, 285, 280, 285, 298, 322, 329, 334
Latinus 75
Latium, Italy 107, 195
Latvian people 104, 211, 212, 284, 337

Laudine 211
Lauma 211–12
Laume 211
Laumiukas 212
Launfal, Sir 96
Laurel tree 100, 112
Laurin 212
Lauskis 212
Lausks 212
Lauza de la Fado 129
Laxey, Isle of Mann 70
The Lay of Saint Gregory the Theologian of the Idols 55
Layamon 34
Lazio, Italy 227
Lazy Larrence 212
Lazy Laurence 212
Lazy Lawrence 212, 254
Lazy Lawrence, Sir 212
Lazy Lawrence of Lubberland 212
Leagore 212
Leanan-sidhe 212
Leanhaum-shee 212
Leanhaun-shee 212
Leanhaun-sidhe 212
Lebadeia, Greece 177
Lechies 214
Leeds, England 48, 264
Legia 215
Leiagore 212
Leicester, England 59
Leimakid 213
Leimenides 217
Leimonides 183, 213
Leinster 17, 139
Leinster, Ireland 165
Leiriope 213, 242
Lelantos 270
Lelegian 213
Lelex, King 85, 202
Lemanja 193
Lemnos, island 83, 195, 259
Lemuralia 213
Lemures 213, 225, 226
Len 213
Len of Killarney 213
Len of the Many Hammers 213
Lenai 313
Lepracaun 213
Leprechaun 86, 195, 213, 240, 281, 288, 310
Lerna 28
Lešak 214
Lesbos 127, 192, 285
Leshes 214
Leshii 214
Leshiye 214
Leshouikha 214
Leshy 214, 240
Lesidhe 214
Lesiy 214
Lesní mužík 214
Lesnik 214

Lesný mužík 214
Lesny mužik/ded 214
Lesovij 214
Lesovik 214
Lesovikha 214
Lesovy 214
Lesun 214
Lešy 214
Leszi 214
Leszy 214
Lethe 214, 242
Leuce 214
Leucippe 214
Leucippus, King 272
Leucon 246
Leucosia 215, 306
Leucothoe 215
Leuka 214
Leukas 214
Leuke 215
Leukippe 215
Leukippos, King 272
Leukothea 172
Leurre 80
Lhiannah-Shee 215
Lhiannan Shee 48, 212, 215
Lhiannan-Shee 215
Li Ban 215
Li Ponz de L' Espee 231
Li Ponz Evages 231
Liagora 215
Liagore 215
Lianhan shee 215
Liban 13, 215, 326
Libya 196, 215, 231
Libya, North Africa 38, 208, 265, 329
Lick 216
Licke 216
Lidscialfr 216
Lidskjalfr 216, 310
Liega 216
Lieutenant of the Great Architect 103
Life of Hatton 219
The Life of Robin Good-fellow 216, 221
Ligea 216
Ligeia 215, 216
Light elves 22, 25, 123, 216, 217
Ligia 216, 306
Li'l Fellas 135
Lilaea 216, 242
Lilaia 216
Lily pads 333
Lily plant 213
Lilyi 217
Lime tree 273, 286
Limerick County 18, 210
Limnades 63, 217, 333
Limnaee 217
Limnatides 217
Limniace 217
Limniad 122, 217, 254
Limnoria 217

Limoniad 24, 213, 217, 254
Linchetto 72, 217
Lincolnshire, England 166, 169, 172, 187, 264, 300, 325, 326, 328, 347
Lindos 319
Lino, King 315
Lion 33, 45, 142, 208, 211
Lios 138
Liosalfar 22, 125, 217
Liosálfar 217
Liquor 340
Liriope 213, 242
Lit 217
Lithuania 349
Litr 217
Little boys 68, 134
Little fair people 137
Little fellas 134
Little folk 99, 105, 134
Little folks 134
The Little Hare 254
Little kindred 309
Little King Loc 200, 201
Little man 66
Little men of Morlaix 217
The Little Mermaid 6, 298
Little people 32, 35, 115, 134, 135, 218, 220, 267, 309, 347
Little People of the Passamaquoddy Indians 218
Little red man 242
Little sheevra 303
Little Washer by the Ford 47
Little Washer of Sorrow 51
Little Wights 116, 343
Little Wildbean 344
Litur 218
Livestock 33, 54, 56, 109, 115, 141, 172, 335, 343
Living picture 87
Lixus 85, 97
Lizard 26, 107, 164, 236, 294
Llamhigyn y dwr 218, 341
Llanllughan-Adfa-Cefn Coch 72
Lliannan-She 215
Llyn barfog 154, 218
Loathly Lady 218
Lob 181, 219, 220, 221
Lob Lie-by-the-fire 219, 220
Lobaircin 213
Loby 219
Loc, King 200–01
Loch a Druing, Scotland 159
Loch Bunachton, Scotland 67
Loch Ewe, Scotland 60

Loch Gur, Scotland 68
Loch Kjllarney, Scotland 257
Loch Maree Hotel 147
Loch na Fideil, Scotland 147
Loch nam Breacan Dubha, Scotland 221
Loch of the Black Trout, Scotland 221
Locha Lein, Scotland 213
Lochan an Tarbh-Uisge, Scotland 318
Locolico 199, 217
Locolico 28
Lofar 219
Lofarr 219
Lofnheid 133, 184
Logheryman 213
Logistilla 21, 219
Loireag 219
Loki 29, 65, 184, 219, 263, 314, 355
Lokria 219
Lokros 224
Lolmischo 219
Lolotte 208
Long Island, Scotland 62
Loni 220
Looby 219
Lord Brahma 325
Lord Howell 284
Lord Kirwan 148
Lord of Annwn 184
Lord of Corasse 262
Lord of Love 30
Lord of tempests 252
Lord of the Animals 337
Lord of the Nine Towns 205
Lord of the Northern Mountains 45, 221
Lord of the Rings 261
Lord Wodjanoj 340
Lordly ones 134
Lorelei 20, 194, 220, 226, 333
Lorelei with Green Tresses 194
Lorraine, France 10, 95
Lorryack 219
Lotis 220
Lotos-tree 220
Lough Bel Dracon, Ireland 30
Lough Erne, Ireland 52, 150
Lough Gur, Ireland 18, 146, 148, 158, 326
Lough Lean, Ireland 257
Love potion 192
Loxo 176, 220, 334
Luath Luchar 12
Lubbard 182, 219, 220
Lubbard fiend 182, 220
Lubber 9, 219
Lubberkin 213, 219, 220

Lubin 220, 221
Lubrican 213
Luchorpain 213
Luchuiro 213
Lucius Caecilius Firmianus Lactantius 103
Luck 35, 41, 45, 78, 95, 109, 121, 141, 200, 201, 210, 213, 214, 247, 249, 262, 310, 318, 332, 343
Lucky charm 213
Lucky Piggies 35
Lucky Piggy 35
Ludki 220–21
Lug 94, 219
Lugh 46
Lugovik 221
Lugovnik 221
Luideag 36, 108, 221
Lukøje 260
Lull 169, 216, 221, 303, 325
Lumbee Indian 347
Lunantishee 221
Lunantishess 221
Lunantisidhe 221
Lunar cycle 340
Luneburg, Germany 165, 179, 180
Luporipan 213
Lurdane 220
Luridan 46, 221
Luring 180
Lusatia, Germany 116, 135, 220
Lutin 64, 82, 144, 163, 221–22, 242
Lutinos 221
Lutky 220
Luxuria 152
Ly Erg 222
Lycaon 229
Lyce 118
Lycoreus 89
Lycorias 222
Lycorua 89
Lycorus 89
Lycus 15, 97
Lydia, Anatolia 238, 278
Lyka 118, 222
Lykaon, King 207, 250
Lykia 163
Lykia, Turkey 263, 329
Lykoros 205
Lykos 198, 202
Lykourgos 270
Lyktgubhe 222
Lymax, river 132
Lyncaeus 98, 187
Lynceus 97, 99
Lyngheid 133, 184
Lyr 48
Lyre 128, 186, 233, 247, 320
Lyris 222, 256
Lysianassa 222

Lysithea 222
Lytgubhe 222

Maahinen 162, 355
Maahiset 222–23
Maanalaiset 222
Mab 125, 171, 172, 223, 275, 318
Mab's Maids of Honor 223
Mabinogi of Branwen, Daughter of Llyr 58
MacCarthy, family 1, 51, 86
Macdonalds of Morar 88
MacEndroe, Ean 60
Macha 223
Machu Pichu 225
Mac Ian, family 161
Macieh 223
Mackay, family 76
Mackenzie, Donald A. 4, 78
Macleod, "Big" John 89
Macleod, Hugh 144
Macleods of Raasay 89
MacLeodse 304
Macmillan, family 76
MacQuarries family 161
Macris 43, 65, 128, 223, 255
Mad Orlando 237
Mad Pranks and Merry Jests of Robin Goodfellow 291, 327
Madai 239
Mae d'Agua 188
Maeander 207
Maebhe 223
Maelwas 231
Maen Du, Wales 177
Maenad 44, 80, 81, 89, 155, 223, 233, 271, 320, 325
Maenades 44
Maera 29, 72, 127, 223, 224, 230
Mæra 223
Maeve 141, 223, 247
Mag Tuired 79
Maga 144, 190
Maggie Moloch 227
Maggots 22, 113, 152, 315, 348
Magh Mell 320
Magh-Tuiredh 251
Magic 10, 21, 38, 70, 77, 96, 99, 115, 120, 121, 126, 140, 142, 143, 144, 159, 177, 204, 208, 212, 219, 227, 237, 243, 249, 258, 266, 288, 289, 311
Magic mirror 121
Magic potion 143
Magical arts 96, 151, 315
Magical cup 256
Magical items 20, 48, 113,

148, 191, 216, 310, 333, 334, 336
Magician 56, 96, 129, 133, 148, 184, 163, 289, 315, 338
Magnes 243
Mahuhu 185
Maia 37, 38, 79, 112, 122, 224, 261, 277, 311
Maiandros 295
Maid 72
Maiden 30, 43, 54, 73, 96, 104, 109, 120, 131, 138, 156, 190, 220, 224, 247, 260, 265, 266, 274, 282, 293, 294, 217, 320, 327, 336, 339
Maidservant 120
Maighdean-Mara 232
Maighdean mhara 78
Maighdean na tuinne 78
Maighdean sheombair 160
Maighdean uaine 160, 224
Mainades 224
Maira 224
Maître Bois 265
Majky 244
Makawe 38, 224
Makris 223
Mal-de-mer 224
Malaita people 108
Malay people 52, 59, 261, 287
Malekin 224
Malewas 228
Maliarda 190
Malicious spirit 121
Malis 131, 224, 254, 261
Malis, Greece 220, 263
Maliseet-Passamaquoddy people 32
Malkin 224
Mallebron 225
Mallet 116
Malleus Maleficarum 209
Mallow 86
Malory, Sir Thomas 237
Mama Dglo 225
Mama Dlo 225
Mama Glow 225
Mama Putukusi 225
Mama Simona 225
Mama Veronica 225
Mamagwasewug 225
Maman de l' eau 225
Mamita Putukusi 225
Mampanoag people 312
Man of the earth 253
Mana 211
Manannan mac Lir 25, 139, 143
Manawa-Tane 280
Manchester, England 48
Mandricardo 144
Mane 225

Manesto 226
Mango trees 116
Manidoo 226
Manito 226
Manitou 226
Manittoes 226
Manitu 226
Mannikin 122
Mannittos 226
Mano 162
Manó 162
Mansfield, Germany 164
Manuel Pinta 226
Manukau 174
Manx 12, 48, 53, 70, 72, 73, 90, 110, 120, 135, 136, 143, 154, 170, 194, 218, 238, 274, 305, 309, 318
Maori people 38, 179, 180, 185, 201, 224, 236, 266, 267, 280, 288, 290, 291, 317, 318, 319, 326
Mara 223, 226, 232
Marcachd Shith 141
Marcachd-Shith 141
Marcan, King 90
March 30, 303
Marc'h 90
Märchen, Rümänische 139
Mareed 107
Mares of Diomedes 324
Margot-La-Fee 237
Mari-Morgans 238
Mari people 16, 20, 33, 45, 56, 57, 238, 256
Marid 107, 158, 194, 226
Maride 109
Maries morgan 237
Markis 130
Marko, Prince 287
Maron 304
Marool 226
Mars 23, 99, 132, 165, 174, 312, 320, 322, 324, 326
Marsh grass 147
Marshes 122, 141, 149, 217, 254, 344
Marsontine 226
Mary Magdalene 44
Mary Morgan 232
Mary Morgens 238
Mary Player 226, 333
Mary's Church, Isle of Man 288
Massachusetts 284, 312
Masseriol 226
Master Dobbs 108
Master of the wind 337
Master of the woods 265
Mathison, family 76
Mati Syra Zemyna 349
Matuyus 24
Maug Moulach 228

Maug Moulack 227
Maug Vuluchd 227
Maugis 50, 129, 262
Maugis Renadu 50
Mauthe dhoog 50
Mauthe doog 235, 302
Mavje 244
Mavky 244
Mawkin 224
May Day 221, 257
May Eve 73
Maybush 138
Mayence 220
Mazapegolo 72
Mazikeen 227, 300
Mazilla 227
Mazzamarelle 227
Mbōn 227, 244
Mcfarlane, family 76
Mead 80, 150, 155, 169, 227, 229, 235, 336
Mead of Poetry 150, 155, 169
Meadhbh 227
Meadow 15, 140, 165, 170, 215, 216, 221, 236, 266, 268, 276, 286, 306, 319, 322
Meander 295
Meave 227
Medb 227
Medba 129
Medbh 17, 227
Medea 119, 189
Medhbh 227
Mediterranean Sea 34, 149, 242, 246, 254, 256, 297
Medma 297
Medusa 199
Meerweibers 226
Meg Mullach 227–28
Megaera 153, 228
Megaira 228
Megalithic dolmen 342
Megarians 306
Megarus 306
Meister Strohbart 295
Mekumwasuck 218
Melaina 89, 100, 202, 228, 242, 323
Melalo 217, 219
Melampus 228
Melanesia 49
Melanippe 228
Melanippus 329
Melch Dick 230
Meleagant 44, 139, 228
Meleagraunce 228
Meles 206, 228
Melete 228, 240, 247
Melia 34, 127, 190, 228
Meliade 228
Meliades 127
Meliads 228
Meliae 228, 229
Meliai 178, 228, 229, 251

Melian 229
Melias 127
Meliboea 229
Meliboia 207, 229
Melides 127
Melinette 229
Melior 229, 281, 282
Melissa 229
Melissai 229
Melita 229, 230
Melite 29, 72, 127, 224, 230, 242
Melité 230
Meliteus 263
Melitus 263
Mellyagraunce 228
Melobosis 230
Melolosis 230
Melpomene 76, 230
Melsh Dick 84, 230, 254
Melusina 230, 333
Melusine 230, 281, 282
Melwas 44, 228, 231
Memedis 157
Memphis 86, 97, 98, 216, 231, 242, 312
Men Made of Bark 231
Men of Peace 99, 134
Men of the goddess 331
Mena 2, 231
Menaka 231, 287, 325, 335
Menalces 12, 97
Mende people 156, 326
Menehuna 212, 231
Menehunes 231
Menelaos, King 203
Menelaus, King 119
Menemachus 98, 245
Menestho 231
Mengloth's hall 48
Menihuni 231
Menippe 204, 231, 233
Menninkäinen 162
Menoetius 13, 87
Menoitios 36
Mentha 234
Menthe 234
Mentis 231
Menyn tylna teg 138
Mera 226
Mercury 81, 95, 99, 118, 175, 197, 207, 211, 222, 224, 250, 259, 268, 274, 289, 294, 310, 321, 324
Merfolk 232, 233
Mergain 237
Mergiana 237
Merionethshire, Wales 288
Merlin 96, 144, 162, 327, 339
Mermaid 6, 20, 49, 53, 55, 78, 119, 132, 136, 173, 175, 193, 194, 198, 209, 230, 232, 233,

238, 239, 247, 249, 256, 264, 286, 290, 292, 293, 298, 299, 306, 312, 218, 323, 326, 333, 339
Mermen 10, 39, 105, 136, 175, 232, 239, 290, 330, 339
Merope 13, 37, 38, 79, 106, 112, 122, 176, 210, 224, 232, 261, 270, 273, 277, 311, 319
Merrow 105, 208, 233, 333
Merry dancers 148
The Merry Wives of Windsor 31
Meryan 240
Meryon 240
Mese 186, 233, 247
Mesma 227
Mesnée d'Hellequin 343
Mess Buachalla 246
Messana 233
Messenia, Greece 272
Mestizos people 121
Metalces 85, 98
Metallurgy 104
Metamorphoses 118, 294
Methe 233
Methone 233
Methone, Pieria 233
Metioche 204, 233
Metiokhe 233
Metis 233
Metope 13, 204, 233, 242
Metsän väki 173
Meuse, river 50
Miach 18, 104, 251
Miare-couette 91
Micaraouda 91
Mice 164, 219
Micol 234
Midanus 28, 98
Midar 234
Middle Ages 43, 58, 145, 336, 344, 346
Middle world ones 134
Midea 98, 234
Midgard 115, 3115, 348
Midhir, King 139
Midhr 234
Midir 17, 118, 139, 153, 234
Midir the Proud 153, 234
Midnight 14, 44, 47, 114, 117, 125, 141, 164, 284, 295, 321, 344, 345
Midnight Court 14
Midsummer 121, 183, 255, 256
A Midsummer Night's Dream 167, 168, 318
Midwife 114, 120, 168, 223, 250
Miellikki 255
Miengu 194, 333

Mika 331
Milân Shâh Peri 95, 103, 234, 270
Milesians 94, 99, 331, 332
Miletos, Anatolia 207
Miletus 207, 329
Milk 26, 54, 67, 72, 84, 86, 94, 99, 111, 120, 121, 125, 135, 136, 137, 138, 140, 144, 152, 154, 155, 160, 161, 168, 170, 183, 185, 203, 217, 219, 230, 234, 254, 259, 265, 283, 285, 331, 335, 346
Milk-White Milch Cow 234
Milkmaids 164
Mill 45, 67, 200, 252, 340
Mill Devil 45
Mill Master 45
Mill Old Woman 45
Mill ponds 340
Miloshshe, Voyvode 287
Mimallones 313
Mimis 234
Mine 61, 100, 116, 140, 163, 203, 332, 343
Minerva 15, 192, 199, 204, 233, 280, 329
Mineus 99, 241
Mining fairy 343
Min-magayi 120
Minos, King 65, 265
Mint 234
Minthe 234, 242
Mintho 234
Minyas 75, 270
Miodvitnir 235
Miolner 121
Miren 145
Mirliflor, Prince 266, 314
Miru 318
Misfortune 35, 109, 124, 165, 192, 200, 221, 243, 249, 251, 264, 277, 288, 294, 314, 317, 328
Mist 84, 156, 175, 179, 183, 201, 235, 257, 333, 336
Mister Sandman 295
Mr. Sandman 295
Mither o' the Sea 235, 252, 298
Mittwoch 139
Mjodvitnir 235
Mjödvitnir 235
Mjolner 65
Mjöðvitnir 235
Mjothvitnir 235
Mneme 235, 240
Mnemosyne 76, 80, 81, 89, 223, 233, 271, 325
Mnestra 98, 235
Mockingbirds 214

Moddey Dhoo 48, 60, 235, 302
Moddey Dhoo of Norfolk 60
Moddey Dohe 235
Modron 237
Modsogner 113, 235, 254
Modsogner-Mimmer 254
Modsognir 115, 235
Modvitnir 235
Möen 124
Moerae 38, 236
Moin 236
Moinn 236
Moipa 144
Moirae 236
Moirai 144
Moist Mother Earth 349
Mokotiti 38, 236
Mokumokuren 236
Moliondis twins 236
Molione 236
Molpa 236
Molpe 236, 306
Molpea 236
Molpee 236
Molpey 236
Molpi 236
Molpie 236
Molpy 236
Monachetto 236
Monaciello 236
Monarch of the Mists 65
Monciello 86
Mondull 237
Money 81, 106, 116, 1339, 156, 214, 218, 223, 257, 264, 277, 303, 328
Mongan 17
Mongibello 238
Monmouthshire, Wales 171, 259
Monster of trees 200
Montagnais 32
Montana 237
Monuste 98, 237
Mooinjer-veggey 134, 135
Moon 25, 33, 43, 56, 95, 106, 124, 137, 146, 158, 182, 232, 245, 248, 273, 274, 293, 295, 296, 300, 302, 331, 340, 345
Moon goddess 245
Moor 66, 344
Moor men 344
Moore, Clement Clark 295
Moosfraulein 71
Mop 223
Moqo 41
Morar House, Isle of Skye 88
Moravian-Silesian Region, Czech Republic 249
Mordillard 91
Morea 173, 237

Morecambe Bay 108
Morgain 34
Morgain la Fee 237
Morgaine 237
Morgan 103, 232, 237, 240
Morgan, King 103
Morgan lá Fée 237
Morgan Le Fay 237
Morgan Le Fey 34, 40, 96, 237,-38, 256, 330, 349
Morgan the Fairy 237
Morgan the Goddess 237
Morgana 21, 144, 219, 237, 238
Morgana Fata 238
Morgane 237
Morgane la feé 237
Morganes 237
Morganetta 144, 237
Morganezed 238
Morgans 238
Morgans of Brenton 237
Morgause 208
Morgen 237
Morgens 232, 238, 240, 333
Morgue le Faye 237
Moria 173, 238, 242
Morlaix, France 91, 217, 321
Morocco 17
Morpheus 260
Morphing Shuck 59
Morrigan 237
Mórrígan 223
Morrough 232
Mors 152
Morta 236
Mortasheen 252
Le Morte Darthur 237
Moruach 232, 233
Moruadh 232, 233
Morverc'h 237
Moscow 240
Moss 116, 149, 159, 212, 238, 333
Moss people 115, 238
Moss-damsels 71
Moth 88, 238, 240, 267
Mother Holle 152
Mother Nature 152
Mother of the Water 225
Mother Spirit 152
Mother's blessing 54, 66, 134, 137, 332
Motsognir 238
Mound 14, 18, 51, 61, 120, 138, 148, 189, 287, 331
Mount Calathion 261
Mount Dikte 105
Mount Djandjavaz 41
Mount Drios 202, 204
Mount Etna 238, 262
Mount Hekla 64

Mount Helicon 14, 32, 228, 235
Mount Helikon 14, 32, 228, 235
Mount Ida, Crete 12, 19, 21, 24, 94, 176, 178, 188, 258, 261
Mount Ithome 192
Mount Kalathion, Greece 202
Mount Keretes 82
Mount Kithairon, Boiotia 106
Mount Kyllene 207, 261, 269
Mount Lykaion 2, 75
Mount Lykaios 23, 31
Mount Nomia 118, 242, 261
Mount Nysa 43, 65, 128, 186, 201, 202, 223, 255, 267, 274, 280
Mount Oite 259
Mount Olympus 76, 104, 120, 131, 183
Mount Othrys 220, 261, 263
Mount Parnassos 34, 77, 198, 202, 261
Mount Parnassus 85, 223
Mount Pelia 261
Mount Pelion 126, 199, 273
Mount Sipylos 278
Mountain 2, 4, 11, 16, 17, 28, 32, 33, 37, 38, 39, 40, 43, 45, 46, 48, 49, 55, 56, 65, 70, 74, 82, 83, 84, 87, 90, 92, 93, 95, 101, 102, 103, 104, 107, 108, 110, 117, 118, 122, 124, 134, 136, 139, 145, 146, 149, 153, 154, 156, 157, 158, 159, 169, 170, 171, 178, 179, 180, 183, 184, 185, 187, 188, 199, 204, 206, 207, 212, 220, 221, 224, 225, 226, 229, 234, 235, 243, 251, 253, 254, 258, 259, 260, 261, 264, 265, 266, 269, 270, 275, 282, 284, 288, 290, 292, 294, 296, 300, 302, 304, 305, 310, 3216, 318, 323, 331, 337, 338, 341, 345, 346, 347, 348
Mountain ash tree 229
Mountain grandmother 347
Mousai 76
Mousai Titanides 34
Mouse 109, 137, 140, 141, 219, 239
Mouse Fairy 76, 239
Mrs. Doasy-ouwouldbedoneby 239

Mrs. Bedonebyasyoudid 239
Mu 239, 244
Mu-Iam 239
Muckle black tyke 59
Muckle men 147
Mudbog 46
Muguet, Prinze 139, 296
Muileartach 239
Muintir bheaga 134
Muir-gheilt 232
Muireartach 239
Mukkelevi 252
Mulberry tree 173, 237
Mule 44, 169, 304
Mule of the Graves 44
Mumiai 239
Mum-Poker 182, 239, 327
Mumpoker 239
Mumu 108
Mumulou 108
Munster, Ireland 14, 16, 18, 31, 32, 51, 85, 86, 141, 145, 148, 181, 235, 252
Murachadh Mac Brian 247
Murbhheo 10
Murbhheo 10
Murdhuachas 239
Murgatroyd 240
Murgin people 46
Murias 5, 331
Murigen 240
Murky pool 243
Murray River 71
Muryan 240
Musail 240
Muse 14, 32, 34, 75, 76, 80, 81, 86, 89, 100, 128, 132, 153, 186, 202, 223, 228, 230, 233, 235, 240, 247, 271, 279, 320, 321, 323, 325, 334
Musheng 239
Mushroom 72, 138, 142
Music 17, 35, 54, 60, 76, 80, 83, 90, 94, 113, 123, 124, 134, 135, 137, 146, 151, 178, 185, 189, 205, 236, 240, 241, 304, 309, 313, 330, 332, 335, 342
Musk-roses 318
Muslim-Tureg lore 16
Muspell 348
Mustardseed 88, 238, 240
Muta 211
Mykenai, Greece 240
Mykene 240–41
Myles 85
Mynyddyslwyn, Wales 284
Myrmidone 241
Myrtilus 99, 271
Myrtoessa 34, 241
Myryan 240
Mysia 258

Mystis 241
Mythological race 331

Na Marcachd-Shìth 141
Näcken 43, 241, 245, 333
Naddaha, al 20, 333
Naecken 241
Naga 28, 196, 241
Nagini 241
Naglfar 241
Nagumwasuck 218
Nai 241
Naiad 7, 13, 14, 31, 33, 34, 37, 40, 68, 72, 75, 76, 79, 85, 90, 97, 98, 122, 128, 129, 131, 132, 151, 162, 174, 178, 183, 186, 188, 190, 198, 202, 203, 204, 206, 207, 208, 211, 216, 220, 224, 233, 240, 241–42, 243, 250, 254, 257, 263, 268, 270, 272, 280, 293, 295, 296, 306, 313, 314, 316, 317, 320, 321, 322, 323, 324, 325
Naiade 241
Naiades 18, 183, 313
Naide 241
Nain 242
Nain rouge 222, 242
Nainn 242
Nains 91, 146, 162
Nair 335
Nais 207, 241, 242, 243
Näkk 243
Nakki 243, 244
Näkki 245, 254, 333
Nali 243
Nallatankaj 204
Nallatankal 204
Nalli 204
Nana 242, 243
Nanna 33
Nanny Button-Cap 243
Nanu 162
Naori people 174
Napaeae 16, 243
Napææ 39
Napf-hans 243
Napfhans 243
Naples, Italy 236
Nar 107
Nár 277
Nara 107
Narcissus 105, 118, 213, 305
Narcissus, Prince 229
Narnywo 169
Narr 244
Nasamon 329
Nast, Thomas 295
Nat 120, 205, 244, 280, 323, 329
Nat house 244
Nat-priests 244
Nathas 281

Native Americans 63, 80, 136
Natives 134
Natsin 244
Natural disasters 275
Naturalis Historia 49
Nature Deities 244
Nature spirit 5, 15, 19, 25, 32, 33, 39, 41, 45, 49, 56, 58, 63, 64, 66, 69, 70, 74, 78, 89, 92, 93, 94, 95, 96, 101, 102, 104, 106, 108, 110, 113, 116, 117, 118, 119, 120, 131, 134, 143, 145, 147, 153, 156, 159, 173, 179, 180, 183, 184, 185, 194, 197, 204, 205, 206, 207, 208, 211, 212, 214, 223, 225, 226, 238, 240, 244, 249, 251, 252, 255, 256, 260, 264, 269, 279, 281, 282, 283, 284, 285, 286, 287, 296, 297, 301, 302, 303, 305, 310, 311, 314, 317, 318, 326, 337, 338, 341, 346, 347, 349
Nausinous 75
Nausithoe 244
Nausithous 75
Navi 244
Navjaci 244
Navje 244
Navky 244, 341
Naxos, island 202, 204
Neaera 242, 244
Neaira 244, 245
Neaireides 245
Neasa 245
Nechtan 62
Neck 181, 198, 199, 241, 243, 245, 250, 333, 341
Necksa 333
Necklaces 73, 140
Necromancer 129, 237
Nectar 167, 215
Neda 132, 172, 192, 245, 321, 323
Nede 245
Nedolya 109
Needle 54, 54, 284
Neeve 248
Neiades 250
Neighbors 134
Neighbours 134
Neilgherry Hills 56
Neilos 132
Neilus 75
Neith 174
Nejky 244
Nelly Long-Arms 245
Nelly Longarms 245, 248
Nelo 98, 245
Nelson Island 191
Nemea 245
Nemea, Argos 245

Nemean games 210
Nemedians 149, 151
Nemertes 146
Nemesis 12, 188, 246
Nemglan 246
Nemi 119
Neomeris 246
Nephalion 266
Nephelai 246, 256, 283
Nephele 91, 246
Nephelê 246
Neptune 9, 19, 21, 23, 28,
  30, 37, 54, 55, 75, 85,
  99, 102, 129, 130, 172,
  178, 197, 198, 202, 204,
  207, 220, 228, 232,
  233, 236, 242, 246,
  247, 268, 270, 276,
  280, 281, 290, 297, 322,
  323, 324, 329, 330, 333
Nera 56, 246
Nereides 246
Nêrèïdes 246
Nêrêïdes 246
Nereids 11, 12, 77, 79, 87,
  90, 94, 103, 106, 122,
  129, 130, 131, 147, 162,
  187, 190, 191, 195, 224,
  229, 244, 245, 246,
  247, 256, 277, 248,
  280, 281, 282, 283, 294,
  322, 330
Nereis 26, 27, 83, 93, 94,
  130, 131, 161, 187, 197,
  199, 207, 208, 211, 212,
  217, 230, 232, 242, 246,
  247, 262, 311
Nereus 11, 15, 26, 27, 33,
  55, 85, 90, 93, 102, 103,
  112, 127, 130, 132, 187,
  199, 202, 215, 216, 222,
  224, 246, 247, 260,
  274, 321, 346
Neriads 246
Nerine 246
Nerues 11, 12, 28, 77, 79,
  87, 90, 93, 94, 103, 106,
  110, 111, 117, 120, 127,
  129, 130, 131, 147, 155,
  162, 172, 180, 181, 187,
  190, 191, 207, 212, 217,
  222, 229, 230, 244,
  245, 246, 247, 249,
  265, 272, 278, 280, 281,
  282, 283, 296, 311, 322
Nesaea 247
Nesaie 247
Nesnas Mhiccallain 133,
  247
Neso 247
Nete 186, 228, 233, 247
Nether Stowey, England
  155
Netherlands 25, 116
Netun 221
Neugle 252
Neuhausen, Germany 80

Never-failing purse 96
New England 23, 284
New Hampshire 259
New South Wales 71
New Year 93
New Year's Day 10
New Year's Eve 7, 264,
  327
New Zealand 35, 38, 174,
  179, 204, 224, 236, 253,
  266, 290, 318, 319, 326,
  331, 332
Newborn child 257
Ngati hotu 266
Niagruisar 66, 203, 247
Niägruisar 66, 247
Niam 248
Niamh 141, 248
Niamh of the Golden Hair
  248
Niau 248
Niauius 98
Niave 248
Nibelung 248
Nibelungen 248
Nibelungen Saga 22
Nibelungenlied 122, 206
Nicaea 242, 248
Nicholson, William 17
Nick Knocker 284
Nicker 199
Nickur 181, 199, 245
Nicky Nye 245, 248, 333
Nicls 249
Niclsen 249
Nicnevan 248
Nicnevin 248
Nicolas, Sir H. 291
Nidavellir 113
Nidi 248
Niflheim 348
Nigeria 44, 136, 264
Nigheag 46, 51
Nigheag bheag a bhroin
  46
Nigheag Na H-Ath 46, 51
Night 228
Night 9, 10, 11, 14, 17, 18,
  21, 22, 23, 25, 27, 28,
  33, 34, 35, 40, 43, 44,
  45, 47, 48, 53, 56, 58,
  59, 60, 61, 62, 66, 68,
  70, 72, 73, 76, 77, 79,
  83, 84, 85, 87, 88, 89,
  90, 91, 93, 96, 97, 99,
  100, 102, 103, 105, 109,
  110, 115, 116, 118, 119,
  120, 121, 122, 124, 125,
  126, 127, 130, 131, 132,
  133, 134, 137, 140, 144,
  146, 150, 151, 153, 154,
  157, 158, 160, 161, 162,
  163, 165, 167, 168, 171,
  173, 175, 176, 177, 179,
  180, 181, 182, 184, 186,
  187, 191, 192, 193, 198,
  200, 201, 202, 205, 212,

217, 218, 221, 222, 231,
  234, 236, 237, 240, 241,
  245, 246, 248, 249,
  256, 257, 259, 265,
  266, 271, 272, 273, 275,
  276, 277, 278, 279,
  280, 281, 285, 288, 292,
  295, 300, 303, 308,
  309, 312, 313, 315, 317,
  322, 325, 329, 330, 331,
  332, 334, 335, 347, 348
The Night Before Christ-
  mas 295
Night Born Sisters 153
Night Man 184, 189
Night Shepherd 70
Night Stealers 330
Night walkers 134, 137
Nightingale 77, 120
Nightman 110
Nightmare 22, 45, 56, 66,
  73, 115, 143, 213, 217,
  226, 264, 295, 313
Nikaia, Bithynia 248
Nikar 181, 245
Nikke 250
Niklasberg Hill, Czech
  Republic 249
Nile River 20, 30, 74,
  190, 231
Nilus 248
Nimble men 148
Nimue 208, 237, 339
Ningyo 249
Niniane 96, 237
Ninner 181, 99, 245
Niobe 319
Niping 249
Nipingr 249
Nippel 249
Nirgallu 209
Nis 66, 86, 163, 1882,
  203, 230, 249, 291, 328
Nis-kuk 284
Nisaea 249
Nisæa 249
Nise-bok 284
Niske 284
Niske-puk 284
Nisse 162, 249
Nisse god-deng 249
Nissen 162
Nissess 249
Niss-puk 284
Nit 223
Nittersing 169
Niu Lang 82
Nivetta 144
Nix 199, 241, 245, 249,
  250
'nix 245
Nix dracae 111
Nixe 245
Nixen 43, 135, 196, 249,
  250, 333, 341
Nixie 245, 250
Nixies 250

Nixoia 248
Njaloi 326
Njord 323
Njugals Water 252
Nkundo people 58
Nocturnal fairies 36, 56,
  67, 73, 87, 92, 106, 107,
  124, 159, 171, 173, 175,
  179, 182, 189, 193, 198,
  224, 235, 236, 260,
  265, 267, 277, 290,
  302, 318, 334, 339, 340,
  344, 349
Nodri 251
Noggle 252
Nogle 252
Nok 181
Nøkk 241
Nokke 254, 250, 333
Nökke 245
Nøkken 241
Nomia 118, 242, 250, 261
Nomios 310
Nona 236
Nonacris 250
Nonakril, Greece 250
Nonakris 250
Nonchalante et Papillon
  208
Nonnus' Nymphs 250
Nonnus of Panopolis 250
Noon 117, 211, 279, 317
Nootaikok 251
Nordi 40, 251, 314, 342
Nordri 251
Norfolk, England 60, 189
Nori 251
Nóri 251
Normandy, France 64,
  82, 96, 136, 146, 171,
  220, 221, 222, 242, 343
Nornir 23, 251, 309, 332,
  337
Norns 251, 232, 337
Norori 251
Norrgens 258
Norse goddess 53, 223,
  336
North Carolina 253, 349
North Devon, England
  154
North Munster, England
  16, 18, 51, 86
North Sea 291, 302
North Somerset, England
  189
Northern Europe 14, 22
Northern Lights 248, 336
Northern Mountains 45,
  221
Northumberland, England
  18, 108, 324, 343
Northumbria, England 114
Norton, Thomas 291
Norway 22, 91, 124, 151,
  221, 293, 308, 324, 333
Nott 102, 260

Nottingham, England 118
November 30, 39, 118, 182, 194, 221, 264, 273
November Eve 30
Novgorod manuscript 55
La N'Roi Madai 239
Nuada Airgetlam 251
Nuada Argatlam 251
Nuada of the Silver Arm 251
Nuada of the Silver Hand 251
Nuadha Airgeatlámh 251
Nuadhu 251
Nuadu 251
Nuala 148, 252
Nuberos 252
El Nuberu 252
Nuchlavis 252
Nuckalavee 252
Nuckelavee 252, 310, 334
Nudd 171
Nuggie 252
Nuggies 199
Nuggle 252, 317
Nukir Mai Tore 38, 253
Numa 119
Number-nip, King 163, 253, 290, 292
Numicus, river 30
Nunne'hi 253
Nunnehi 253
Nuno 253
Nuno sa Punso 253
Nur 201
Nursery bogie 7, 32, 43, 54, 58, 59, 61, 62, 63, 69, 70, 84, 92, 167, 194, 212, 230, 243, 245, 248, 253, 254, 269, 295, 303, 310, 311, 317, 326
Nut 77, 84, 173
Nut-Nans 254
Ny 254
Ny mooinjer veggey 309
Nyamatsane 254
Nycheia 131, 225, 254
Nygel 252
Nyi 254
Nýi 254
Nyiwa 104
Nykheia 254
Nykteus 202
Nykur 43
Nymph 2, 7, 9, 11, 12, 12, 14, 15, 16, 36, 37, 38, 40, 43, 44, 46, 50, 53, 54, 55, 59, 63, 65, 68, 71, 72, 74, 75, 76, 77, 78, 79, 80, 81, 82, 83, 85, 86, 87, 89, 90, 91, 93, 94, 95, 96, 97, 99, 100, 101, 102, 103, 104, 105, 106, 110, 111, 112, 117, 118, 119, 120, 122, 126, 127, 128, 129, 130, 131, 133, 139, 147, 150,

154, 155, 156, 157, 161, 162, 164, 137, 172, 173, 174, 175, 176, 177, 178, 179, 180, 181, 184, 185, 186, 187, 188, 189, 190, 191, 192, 194, 195, 196, 197, 198, 199, 200, 201, 202, 203, 204, 205, 206, 207, 208, 209, 210, 211, 212, 213, 214, 215, 216, 217, 219, 220, 221, 222, 223, 224, 227, 228, 229, 230, 231, 233, 234, 235, 236, 237, 238, 240, 241, 242, 243, 244, 245, 246, 247, 248, 249, 250, 254, 255, 257, 258, 259, 260, 261, 262, 263, 264, 265, 266, 267, 268, 269, 270, 271, 272, 273, 274, 276, 278, 279, 280, 281, 282, 283, 285, 286, 287, 289, 290, 291, 292, 293, 294, 295, 296, 297, 298, 299, 304, 306, 307, 308, 309, 310, 311, 312, 313, 314, 315, 316, 319, 320, 321, 322, 323, 324, 325, 326, 328, 329, 333, 334, 335, 338, 345, 346, 349
Nymph-like 71, 139, 257, 333
Nymph of battle 157, 164, 179, 181, 184, 235, 286, 287, 291, 304, 307, 308, 315, 324, 345
Nymphae artemisiae 256
Nymphae oceanides 256
Nymphai artemisiai 256
Nymphai Okeaninai 256
Nymphidia 223
Nymphs of Artemis 256
Nyr 255
Nýr 255
Nyrad 255
Nýrádr 255
Nyrdra 100
Nysa 43, 128, 186, 223, 255
Nyuggle 252
Nyx 144, 210, 245, 262
Nyyrikki 255, 332

Oaf 255, 263
Oak King 119, 125, 183, 255, 291
Oak men 255
Oak tree 2, 45, 83, 108, 119, 285
Oakmen 255
Oannes 232, 255–56
Oatmeal 138
Obda 156
Oberon 88, 121, 122, 139,

223, 225, 238, 240, 256, 267, 291, 301, 318, 319, 330
Oberon le Fayé 256
Obol 173
Oborotni 55
O'Brian clan 14
O'Briens 16
Obrimus 98, 181
Obscure elves 100
Occult magical knowledge 238
Ocean 21, 28, 41, 45, 69, 79, 82, 86, 101, 140, 163, 199, 232, 239, 254, 256, 261, 280, 281, 291, 299, 302, 331, 332
Ocean nymphs 21, 37, 79, 112, 224, 256, 319
Oceanid 11, 12, 31, 34, 36, 79, 81, 86, 91, 110, 155, 172, 176, 178, 186, 190, 192, 195, 197, 199, 206, 241, 246, 254, 256, 259, 271, 272, 274, 283, 289, 333
Oceanid nymphs 36, 91, 186, 246, 256, 283, 289
Oceanide 256
Oceanides 256
Oceanids 2, 11, 13, 19, 24, 26, 27, 28, 29, 34, 36, 37, 63, 74, 75, 78, 79, 83, 84, 85, 86, 87, 90, 91, 95, 106, 108, 119, 122, 126, 130, 132, 155, 178, 180, 187, 188, 189, 190, 197, 200, 210, 214, 215, 217, 222, 226, 229, 230, 231, 232, 233, 242, 243, 246, 248, 256, 257, 259, 263, 265, 266, 268, 269, 270, 271, 273, 276, 277, 278, 279, 280, 282, 283, 290, 297, 313, 314, 319, 323, 325, 332, 334, 340, 346, 349
Ocean-smith 239
Oceanus 11, 12, 13, 19, 24, 26, 27, 28, 29, 34, 36, 37, 63, 74, 75, 77, 78, 79, 83, 83, 84, 85, 86, 87, 90, 91, 95, 106, 108, 110, 119, 122, 126, 130, 132, 155, 178, 180, 187, 188, 189, 196, 197, 200, 210, 214, 215, 222, 226, 229, 230, 231, 232, 233, 246, 248, 256, 257, 259, 263, 265, 266, 268, 269, 270, 271, 273, 276, 277, 278, 279, 280, 282, 283, 290, 297, 313–14, 319, 323, 325, 332, 334, 340, 346, 349

Ochimus, King 176
O'Connors 47
Ocypeta 257
Ocypete 98, 122, 257
Ocyroe 81, 257
Ocyrrhoe 257
Odail Pass 56
Odin 49, 60, 68, 113, 117, 148, 157, 164, 169, 179, 181, 184, 191, 216, 235, 258, 259, 286, 287, 291, 304, 308, 310, 315, 322, 324, 327, 333, 334, 336, 344, 345, 348
Odin the Wanderer 327
Odmience 55, 257
O'Donoghue 257
Odr 263
Odysseus 75, 84, 197
The Odyssey 26, 75, 84, 144, 151, 183, 197, 206, 210, 245, 271, 273, 306
Oeager, King 75, 233
Oeme 98, 99, 257
Oeneus 99, 278
Oengus, Young Son 29
Oenis 257
Oennerbanske 115, 257
Oennereeske 115, 116, 257
Oenoe 257
Oenomaus 99, 312
Oenone 258, 261
Oeolyca 259
Oeroe, Plataia 156, 259
Oeta 99, 279
Ogier le Danois 237
Ogier the Dane 237
Ögir the Dane 48
Ogma the Champion 320
Ogme 94
O'Gradys 47
Ogre 43, 69, 160, 185, 258, 267, 312, 318
Ogre-like 69
Ogres 159, 258
Ogress 258
Ogue Fairy 258
Ogun River 44
Ogygia, island 75, 197
Ogygos 281
O'Hartigan, Dunlang 31
Ohdowas 258
Ohdows 154, 156, 258
Oil 114, 209, 347
Oilbalos 268
Oilill 17
Oin 258
Oinia 37, 258
Óinn 258
Oinoe 259
Oinoie 259
Oinomaos 174
Oinone 258
Oiolyka 259
Oirig 14
Oisin 293
Oite 259

Oiteag Sluaigh 119
Okeanides 256
Okeanids 256
Okeaninai 256
Okeanos, river 150
Okinawa, Japan 200
Oklahoma, United States
of America 253
Okypete 257
Okyrhoe 259
Ol' doofus 259
Old Army 343
Old Bloody Bones 61
Old Luk Oie 58
Old man 16, 20, 35, 47,
57, 61, 62, 66, 92, 110,
125, 157, 183, 192, 195,
212, 245, 253, 259, 265,
282, 287, 298, 304,
309, 328, 340
Old man of the house 66,
328
Old Man of the Sea 195
Old Man Winter 192, 212,
259, 298, 309
Old Man with a Peg 62
Old Mother Darky 344
Old people 134, 135, 317
Old Roger 259
Old Scratch 297
Old Shock 60
Old Shuck 60
Old woman 40, 42, 45,
46, 57, 73, 77, 19, 110,
140, 171, 214, 218, 236,
259, 260, 288, 320,
326, 328
Old woman Jadwiga 42
Old Woman of the Moun-
tain 117, 259–60
Old woman Yaga 42
Ole Luk Oie 260
Ole Luk Öie 260
Ole Luk Øj 260
Ole Lukøje 260
Oleaster 173, 237, 238
Olenus 29, 99
Olive trees 136
L'Olseau Bleu 227
Olsen 260
Olwen 260
Olympia 154
Olympus 76, 104, 120,
131, 183
Olynthus 63
Ombwiri 260
Omen 17, 20, 23, 47, 48,
59, 61, 68, 70, 78, 93,
94, 101, 115, 134, 163,
165, 172, 175, 179, 182,
184, 200, 264, 303, 308,
314, 342
Onagh 32, 86, 110, 148,
260
Onar 29, 260
Ónar 29, 260
Onarr 29, 260

Ónarr 29, 260
Onatha 103
Onaugh 110
*One Thousand and One
Arabian Nights* 194
One with the White Hand
260
O'Neills 47
Onesippus 83
Ontayi 204
Oona 110
Oonagh 260
Oonagy 110
Ooser 346
Oph 255
Opis 260
Oracle 103, 108, 109, 320
Orang Bunian 261
Orang Bunyian 135, 261
The Orange Fairy Book
312
Orc 261, 330
Orch 261
Orchomenus 99, 192
Orco 185
Orculli 258, 261
Orea 138, 261
Oread 94, 176, 192, 232,
250, 254, 258, 261, 296,
306, 310
Oreande la Fée 261
Oreiades 178, 183, 251,
261
Oreithuia 262
Oreithyia 199, 262
Orends 261
Orestiad 261
Ori 262
Óri 262
Oriana 262, 334
Oriande 262
Oriande la Fée 262
Orion 204, 277
Orithya 262
Orithyia 262
Orixas 193
Ork 261
Orke 261
Orkney Islands 67, 100,
136, 221, 252, 261, 267,
317
Orlando 111, 143
Orlando Furioso 237
Orlando in Love 56, 129,
144, 237, 246, 262, 334
Orlando Innamorato 56,
129, 144, 237, 246, 262,
334
Orlo 258
Orontes 229
Orpheus 39, 75
Orphne 262
Orsa 262
Orseis 242, 262
Ortgis 56, 338
Orthone 184, 162
Ortygia 24, 34, 263

Ortygia, Sicily 34
Orythia 262
Oschaert 263, 264
Oseron 256
Osiam 248
Ossa, Greece 261
Ostyak people 340
Othello 31
Otherworld 10, 164, 171,
208, 216, 253, 277, 327
Othreis 161, 263
Ótr 133, 184, 263, 289
Otrynteus 186
Otter 263
Ottermaaner 25
Ouph 122, 263
Ouphe 263
Oupis 260, 334
Our Housekeeper 51
Ourania 263
Ourmes 335
Oursitori 335
Over Stowey, England
155
Ovid 158, 257, 268
Ovinnik 7, 263
Owain 237
Owen 291
Owl 140, 167, 179, 214,
307
Oxlip 318
Oxun 264
Oxylos 173
Oxylus 13, 27, 45, 77, 90,
127, 180, 238, 261, 283,
309, 314, 316
Ozeganned 89, 205
Ozeganned 89, 205
Ozomene 122

Paca 92
Pachatosa 264
Pachatusan 264
Pacific Northwest 70, 117
Pacolet 258, 264
Paconius 94
Padasus 9
Padfooit 264
Padfoot 48, 59, 62, 169,
264, 302
Padfoot of Wakefield 48,
302
Paian 264
Paiarehe 266
Paidia 81
Painajainen 264
Pairikas 269
Pakehakeha 266
Palace 16, 17, 21, 35, 111,
139, 140, 150, 153, 167,
182, 201, 203, 209, 212,
228, 230, 237, 247,
248, 295, 338
Palatyne 264, 282
Pallas 165, 265
Pallas Green Hill 165
Pallene 265

Palm wine 348
Pamarindo 265
Pamphilus 98, 103
Pan 39, 95, 128, 145, 192,
257, 259, 269, 276, 291,
296, 306, 316, 325
Pan pipes 291, 316
Pancake 263
Pandaisia 81
Pandarus 187
Pandion 75, 97, 281, 349
Pandora 229
Pandrosos 15
Pannonia 158
Pannykhis 81
Panopae 265
Panope 264
Panopeia 265
Panther 223, 224
Panthius 99, 272
Pantygassg Trwyn Farm
285
Pap Mountain 43
Papa 174
Papa Bois 265
Papa Farce 265
Papotchantel 91
Paps of Danu, Ireland 90,
141
Papua New Guinea 95
Para 203, 265
Paracelsus 162, 333
Paradise 84, 96
Paradise Lost 103, 261
Paraguay 206
Paralda 265, 316
Paralysis 141, 158
Parcae 144, 236
Parehe 266
Pareia 265
Paribanou, Fairy 266,
297
Paridamie 266, 314
Parikas 269
Paris 258
Parish of Saint Teath,
England 82
Parnasso 205
Parnassos 34, 77, 198,
202, 261
Parnassus 85
Parnassus 233
Päronskaft 292
Paros, island 265
Parrot 143
Parthalons 149
Parthenope 229, 266, 305
Parthenopex of Blois 229
Parvati 204, 231
Pasiphae 266, 270
Pasiphaë 266, 270
Pasithea 266
Pasithoe 266
Passamaquoddy Indians
32, 218
Pastorella 306
Pasupati 337

Patala 241
Patch 167, 168, 169, 216, 221, 266, 275, 303, 325
Patu-pai-arehe 331
Patu paiarehe 266
Patu-paiarehe 266
Patuljak 162
Patupaiarehe 266–67, 291, 331
Patupaiarehe fairy 291
Patupairehe 266
Patuparehe 266
Pau 201
Pausanias 32, 81, 228, 240, 235
Payatusan 264
Pcûvushi 281
Peallaidh 67, 153, 267
Peallaidh an Spùit 67
Peallaidh of the Spout 67
Pealldaidh 267
Pease Blossom 88, 238, 240, 267
Peat faeries 46
Pebel vean 134
Pecari 74
Peccaries 92
Pech 267, 276
Pechamnderlin 267, 343
Pechs 267, 276
Pecht 267, 276
Pedair Cainc y Mabinogi 184
Pedasus 9, 243
Pedile 186, 276
Peel Castle 235
Peerifool 160, 267
Peg Leg Jack 133
Peg O'Nell 267–68
Peg Powler 51, 194, 245, 248, 268, 333
Peg Powler's Cream 268
Pegaea 75, 188, 190, 268, 316
Pegaeae 268
Pegai potamon 183
Pegaia 268
Pegaiai 268
Peg-a-lantern 123, 344
Pegasis 242, 268
Pegasus 14
Peggy O'Nell 167
Pehts 267
Peirene 268
Peisinoe 268, 333
Peisinoë 267
Peisithoe 276
Peitho 192, 268
Pelasgos 207, 229, 231
Pele 197
Peleus 247
Peliades 261
Peloponessos, Greece 30
Peloponnese, Greece 229
Peloponnesos, Greece 23, 186
Pelops 98, 99

Pelops, King 98
Pelorias 268
Peloris 268
Pelze Nocol 269
Pelznickel 269
Pemphredo 165, 199
Penates 81, 269
Peneios 100, 186, 206, 231, 313
Penelope 270
Penelopeia 269, 325
Peneus 90, 269
P'eng-hou 269
Pénghoú 269
Peninsula of Drigge 45
The Pentamerone 185
Pentheus 15
People of god whose mother was Dana 331
People of Peace 32, 99, 105, 134, 304
People of the goddess Dana 331
People of the hills 134
People of the otherworld 253
People of Venus 337
People who live anywhere 253
People's puff of wind 119
Perceforest 298
Percht Perchta 54
Perchta 54, 56
Père Fouchette 269
Père Fouettard 258, 269, 295
Père Lustucru 258
Père Noël 269
Peri 269, 270
Peri Merjân 95, 103, 234, 270
Periboea 242, 270
Periboée 270
Periboia 270
Perifoal 267
Periklymene 270
Perileos 270
Periphas 11, 97
Peristhenes 97, 122
Perit 270
Perius 98, 186
Perkunas 19
Permet 339
Pero 270
Perrault, Charles 163, 258, 326
Perry Dancers 148
Persa 270
Perse 270
Perseis 270
Persephone 12, 19, 122, 177, 187, 188, 196, 197, 200, 204, 214, 215, 230, 234, 259, 263, 265, 271, 273, 278, 290, 332
Perseus 210
Persia 103

Persian Gulf 256
Personification of beans, corn, and squash 103
Personification of beauty, charm, and grace 81
Personification of Chaos 262
Personification of darkness 21, 228, 326
Personification of divine justice, justice, sovereignty, and war 251
Personification of ethical commitment 318
Personification of memory 80, 81, 233, 271, 320, 325
Personification of mother earth 90
Personification of the benign force of the summer sea 235
Personification of the change toward recovery 316
Personification of the cold 212
Personification of the cyclone 95
Personification of the entangling marsh grass and reeds 147
Personification of the goddess, Fortune 238
Personification of the island 196
Personification of the mist 179
Personification of the mountains 179
Personification of the sovereignty of Ireland 218
Personification of the spirit of Christmas 295
Personification of the tenacity of life 183
Personification of the terror of the sea 165
Personification of the Trent River Tidal Bore 118
Personification of the whirlpools 81
Personification of twilight 102
Personification of wine 259
Personification of winter 73, 259
Peru 33, 39, 41, 78, 121, 225
Peseias 270
Petaldo 156
Peter Pan 6
Le Petit Colin 271
Le Petit Homme Rouge 242

Le Petit Poucet 327
Petrae 270
Petraea 270
Pexy 271, 276
Phaeno 108, 186, 271
Phaeo 186, 271
Phaeote 186
Phaesyla 186
Phaethon 13, 276, 210, 232, 273
Phaethonides 176
Phaethousa 176, 271
Phaëthousa 245
Phaethusa 99, 210, 245, 271
Phaëtusa 271
Phagros 263
Phaiak 204
Phaino 271
Phaio 108, 271
Phairie 134
Phaisyle 108, 3271
Phantes 98, 321
Pharaildis 53
Pharie 134
Pharis 99, 274
Pharisee loaf 139
Phartis 98, 271
Phasis 16, 257
Phasyleia 81, 223, 271
Phaunos 145
Phelegyas 83
Phemonoe 198
Phenodyree 134
Phereceydes of Syros 26
Pheres 270
Pherie 134
Pherousa 272
Pherusa 272
Phi Nang Mai 272
Phi-suk 272
Phiale 272
Phialê 272
Phigalia 272
Phigalia, Greece 272
Phila 99, 272
Philammon 34
Phileto 186
Philia 186, 202, 204, 272
Philinus 99, 272
Philippines 20, 54, 107, 113, 126, 198
Philodemus 120
Philodice 272
Philodike 272
Philomela 99, 272, 349
Philtrum 107, 126
Philyra 273
Philyre 273
Phit Nang Tani 208
Phoebe 13, 36, 85, 97, 98, 106, 161, 164, 176, 180, 191, 210, 232, 273, 290
Phoenix 178, 242
Phoeno 273
Phoeus 31
Phoibe 273

Phokis, Greece 34, 216, 325, 326
Phokos 37
Phooka 654, 163, 182, 204, 273, 274, 283, 310
Phorcids 199
Phorcys 15, 79, 215, 216, 236, 266, 268, 286, 306, 319, 322, 323
Phorkys 165, 199, 305
Phoroneos 190
Phouka 273, 291
Phra Phum 273
Phrasimos 105
Phrixa 274
Phrixus 246
Phrygia 94, 187, 217, 243, 293
Phyllodoce 274
Phylodameia 99, 274
Phynnodderee 146, 168, 213, 274
Physadeia 99, 274
Phyto 274
Piazza Euclide, Rome 30
Picker 276
Pickers 276
Pickle Harin 274
Picklehain 274, 333
Picktree Brag 48, 65, 274, 300, 302
Pie 335
Pier Jan Claes 258
Pieria 11, 12, 76, 97, 98, 106, 233, 257, 278, 285
Pierides 76
Pierre Le Noir 295
Pig (gnome) 201
Pig 35, 61, 74, 84, 176, 194, 197
Pig fairy 84
Piglet 84, 177
Pigseys 276
Pigsies 276
Pigwidgeon 274
Pijchu 275
Pi'kis 70
Pikol 275
Pillan 275
Pillywiggins 35, 274, 275, 298
Pilosi 115
Pilot Knob, North Carolina 253
Pilwiz 58
Pin 223
Pinari 275
Pinch 167, 168, 169, 216, 221, 223, 266, 275, 303, 325
Pincoy 275, 333
Pincoya 275
Pindar 26
Pine tree 276, 286
Pine tree Mary 185, 317
Pinecone 325
Pinket 275, 344

Pinkett 275
Pip 223
Pipe 71, 73, 84, 156, 164, 201, 230, 289, 293
Piranu 276
Pirene 37, 98, 99, 276
Pireros, King 233
Pirnicap 340
Pisa, Elis 99, 174
Piscean 232
Pisgy 276
Pisinoe 276, 306
Pisinõe 276, 306
Piskies 194, 276
Piskies-pisgies 276
Pisky 276
Pisky-pow 276
Pitane 129, 242, 276
Pitho 276
Pitlochry, Scotland 248
Pitys 261, 276
Pitzln 276, 343
Piuket 275
Pixie 66, 142, 195, 276–77, 312, 348
Pixie circle 142
Pixies 56, 81, 88, 134, 175, 182, 271, 276, 277
Pixy 88, 276
Pixy-puffs 138
Place of the Fairies 138
Placida, Princess 208
Plaksy 277
Plant annwn 277
Plant rhys ddwfn 332
Plant Rhys Dwfen 277
Plataia 156
Pleiad 277
Pleiades 13, 21, 37, 38, 79, 112, 122, 129, 178, 224, 232, 254, 261, 277, 312, 319
Pleione 13, 21, 37, 38, 79, 112, 122, 129, 178, 224, 232, 254, 261, 277, 312, 319
Plentin newid 278
Plentyn-newid 278
Plexaris 186
Plexaura 278
Plexaure 278
Plexippus 27, 98, 99, 285
Pliny the Elder 49, 261
Ploto 278
Ploughshare 284
Plouto 278
Pluto 28, 39, 204, 207, 210, 211, 214, 215, 234
Pluvush 204, 278
Poake 278
Poake-ledden 283
Pobratim 287
Pocker 283
Podarce 98, 278
Podasimus 99, 322
Poem of Helgi Hundings-bani 304

Poestion, J. C. 312
Poetic Edda 16, 22, 24, 28, 29, 31, 39, 40, 41, 44, 48, 49, 50, 57, 58, 59, 61, 64, 68, 71, 95, 101, 109, 110, 112, 114, 115, 119, 120, 143, 147, 148, 149, 150, 151, 152, 153, 155, 156, 160, 162, 167, 169, 173, 174, 177, 181, 182, 183, 185, 190, 191, 192, 193, 194, 200, 217, 218, 220, 235, 236, 238, 241, 242, 243, 244, 248, 249, 251, 254, 255, 258, 260, 262, 286, 287, 289, 303, 305, 306, 307, 310, 314, 315, 322, 323, 324, 333, 335, 337, 338, 339, 342, 348
Poitou, France 111
Poke 278
Poker boys 36
Pokey-hokey 278
Pokwas 70
Poland 244, 292, 335, 338
Polevik 278–79
Polevoi 278
Polevoy 278, 279
Polewik 278
Poliahu 197
Polo 150
Polperro, Cornwall 194
Poltergeist 62, 203, 226, 278, 343
Poltergeist-like spirit 226
Poludnica 279
Poludniowka 279
Polunditsa 279
Polušan 162
Polutan 162
Poluvirica 279
Polybe 99, 279
Polycaon 85
Polyctor 98, 314
Polydector 99, 257
Polydora 99, 279
Polyhymnia 279
Polyhymno 186, 280
Polynesian 38, 136, 137, 213, 231, 244, 253, 331
Polynome 280
Polypemon 323
Polyphe 155, 280
Polyphemus 155
Polyphonte 324
Polyxena 99, 280
Polyxo 31, 40, 68, 74, 85, 97, 98, 108, 122, 128, 132, 162, 186, 242, 280, 314, 321
Pomegranate tree 243
Pomerania 45
Pomonia 221
Pompo'n del monte 329

Ponaturi 280, 333
Ponca 32
Ponphyoi 280
Pontomedusa 280
Pontoporeia 280
Pontoporia 280
Pontos 319
Pony 110, 163, 252
Pooca 285
Pooka 59, 125, 273, 291
Pool 23, 148, 153, 208, 225, 294, 339
Poole, Joshua 223, 298
Popanz 203
Poplar forest 225
Poplar tree 13, 210, 214, 215, 232, 273
Porpoise Girl 280–81
Porridge 45, 77, 109, 328
Portugal 113, 135, 136
Portune 281
Poseidon 9, 19, 21, 23, 28, 30, 37, 54, 55, 75, 85, 99, 102, 129, 130, 172, 178, 197, 198, 202, 204, 207, 220, 228, 232, 233, 236, 242, 246, 247, 268, 270, 276, 280, 281, 290, 297, 322, 323, 324, 329, 330, 333
Pot of gold 213
Potameides 281, 333
Potamoi 183, 256
Potamon 98, 162
Poteen 289
Pouka 273
Pouke 273, 283, 291
Poulpikan 205
Poulunoe 281
Poulynoe 281
Pouque 273
Powries 114, 288
Pozemne vile 281
Prank 77, 114, 163, 264, 332
Prankster 293
Praxidika 281
Praxidike 281
Praxithea 242, 281
Precht 54
Precious gems 20, 116, 141, 253
Precious metal 330
Pregnant women 9, 119, 241, 345
Premien 107
Presque Isle Peninsula 313
Pressyne 229, 264, 265, 281–82
Prester John 73
Priam 21, 314
Priapus 220
Prigirstitis 282
Prince Featherhead and the Princess Celandine 139, 296

Prince Narcissus and the Princess Potentilla 229
Princess of the Sea 193
Priparchis 205, 282
Proetus 228
Prokne 349
Prometheus 36, 87, 178, 190, 282
Promontory-Kings 124
Prone 282
Pronoe 282
Pronoia 178, 282, 285
Prophecy 46, 190, 221, 240, 258, 259, 311
Propontis, island 151, 254
Prose Edda 22, 336
Proserpina 12, 19, 122, 177, 187, 188, 196, 197, 200, 204, 207, 214, 215, 230, 234, 259, 263, 265, 271, 273, 278, 290, 332
Prosymna 19, 20, 130, 282
Protective spirit 95, 109
Protector of sheep 347
Proteus 98, 99, 119, 165, 195, 283, 290
Protheon 98, 180
Proto 282
Protogenia 285
Protomedeia 282
Protomedusa 283
Protomelia 283
Les Prouesses et faitz du noble Huon de Bordeaux 256
Prousa 283
Provence, France 68, 129
Prowlies 134
Prymno 283
Psamathe 283
Pscipolnitsa 279
Psecas 283
Psekas 283
Psezpolnica 279
Psgie 66
Ptelea 173, 283
Pteleades 283
Pterides 283
P'tit Colin 271
Ptoides 283
Puca 134, 173, 276, 291
Púca 173, 291
Púcaí 134, 276
Puck 32, 72, 182, 278, 283, 284, 291, 344
Puck-ball fungus 278
Puck of Pook's Hill 342
Puck the French 284
Pucke 283
Pucksy 276
Puddlefoot 284
Pueblo Indians 195
Pug-fiest 278
Pugno 98, 100
Pujke 284

Puk 203, 284
Púka 273
Pukehakeha 266
Pukin 284
Pukis 284
Pūkis 284
Pukmis 70
Puks 70
Pukwubis 70
Pukwudgies 284
Pukys 284
Pulch 284
Pulmonary consumption 236
Pulter-class 284
Putz 283
Puuk 284
Puvayi 204
Pûvushi 281
Pwaronga 108
Pwca 68, 125, 273, 284, 285, 291, 344
Pwca of Trwyn 284
Pwca'r Trwyn 284
Pwcca 285
Pylarge 98, 285
Pyrante 99, 285
Pyrantis 99, 285
Pyrenean Mountains 49
Pyrenee 205
Pyreness 285
Pyrrha 262, 285
Pyrrhakidai 285
Python 186

Qrennah 206
Quaker 344
Quartz 35, 65
Quebec 147
Quechua people 33, 39, 41
Quechua tribes 78
Queen of the Elves of Light 125
Queen of the Fish 193
Queen of the Khado 295
Queen of the Nimue 237
Queen of the Niniane 237
Queen of the Northgales 237
Queen of the Piskies 194
Queen of the Sea-Nymphs 209
Queen of the Wasteland 237
Queen of the White Ladies 172, 343
Queen who wards off evil [storms] 277
Queen's Chair 124
Querciola 285
Querciuola 285
Quick 223
Qutrub 107, 285

Ra 286
Rabbit 263

Radande 286
Radbuzou, Czech Republic 249
Rade 138, 141, 142, 146, 158, 248, 286, 343, 344
Radgrid 286, 336
Radspakr 286
Radsvid 286
Rádsvidr 286
Radsvinn 286
Radsvithr 286
Ragged Blossom 169
Ragnarok 336
Ragotte 286
Raidne 286, 306
Rainclouds 188, 246
Raja Jinn Peri 287
Ralph Coggeshall 166
Ralph of Coggeshall 224
Rambha 231, 287, 325
Raminagrobis 258
Rampus 295
Randgrid 287, 336
Rangi 174
Raosvior 287
Rape 7, 13, 28, 80, 129, 197, 220, 267, 319
Raro-henga 331
Raspberry bushes 287
Raspberry King 287
The Raspberry King 287
Rat boys 149
Ratainitsa 287
Ratepenate 91
Rath 138, 237
Ratibor, Prince 292
Raven 178, 242, 292
Ravine 96
Raviyoyla 287
Rawhead 61, 194, 254, 287–88
Reaping 67, 146, 279, 344
Red cap 114, 288, 334
Red cap, clothing 9, 73, 245, 247, 255, 284, 288
Red Cloak Woman 288
Red-comb 288
Red dwarf 242
Red Earl 158
Red fairies 288
Red-haired man 288
Red hat 287, 288
Red Man 145, 149, 242, 288, 289
Red Rose Fairy Knight 73
Red Sea 72, 243, 291
Redcap 288
Redsvid 289
Reflex-man 87
Regin 133, 184, 263, 289
Regina Falls 179
Reginn 289
Regulus 49
Re-hollys vodar yn oury 274

Reidmar 184
Reiginlief 336
Reincarnation 272
Reindeer 259
Rek 289
Rekk 289
Rekkr 289
Rent-paying people 149
Repelsteeltje 292
Republic of Senegal, Africa 43
Republic of Trinidad and Tobago 225
Resemblance 87
Restless people 134
Revenant 10
Rhanis 289
Rhapso 289
Rhea 289
Rhene 289
Rhetia 289, 290
Rhine River 220
Rhiwgyverthwch, Wales 117
Rhode 98, 177, 290
Rhodea 290
Rhodeia 290
Rhodia 98, 290
Rhodina 290
Rhodope 290
Rhodos 175, 178, 290, 319
Rhoio 314
Rhoiteia 289
Ri 46
Ri Balor 290
Ribble River 267
Ricciardetto 56, 246
Ricdin Ricdon 292
Rice 104, 253, 293, 328
Ride of Asgard 343
Rider of the white horse 269
Ridgeway of Berkshire 342
Das Riesengebirge 253, 290, 292
Riibezahl 292
Ring fort 138
Ring of Gullion 92
Ringworm 222
River god 14, 16, 19, 21, 24, 29, 31, 34, 37, 99, 100, 132, 174, 188, 190, 192, 198, 204, 206, 211, 213, 216, 217, 228, 229, 231, 233, 242, 243, 248, 258, 270, 272, 279, 282, 294, 299, 306, 311, 313, 314, 317, 321, 322, 325, 329, 349
River goddesses 269
River Tees 268
Roane 29, 299, 305
Roaring Bull of Bagbury 291
Rob goblin 181
Rob-goblin 181

Robin goblin 163
Robin Good Fellow 108, 167, 138, 181, 184, 221, 255, 256, 266, 275, 283, 291, 295, 303, 325
Robin Hood 283, 291
Robin Red Cap 288
Robin Round-Cap 291
Robiquet 292
Rock of Aeval 14
Roggenmutter 204
Romany Gypsy 219
Rome, Italy 7, 9, 12, 13, 14, 21, 29, 30, 31, 0, 74, 81, 83, 85, 90, 100, 105, 112, 118, 119, 175, 192, 195, 210, 213, 214, 216, 222, 226, 228, 231, 233, 238, 243, 248, 250, 262, 270, 273, 276, 280, 281, 294, 311, 314, 320, 324, 325, 349
Romeo and Juliet 168, 223
Roostem 36, 102
Rooster 59, 179, 264, 284, 300, 318
Rope-traces 93
Ropenkerl 292
Rosanella 266, 314
Rosanella, Princess 266, 314
Rosania 292
Rose-tree 140
Rota 291, 336
Rothly, England 18
Round Table 68
Rowan tree 240
Ruad 10, 94
Ruad Rofessa 94
Ruamano 291
Ruatane 291
Rubezahl 253, 292
Rübezahl 163, 253, 292
Rübezahl 292
Rubheyzahl 292
Rue Saint Quentin, France 96
Rug 201
Rügen Nickle 245
Ruhr River, Germany 200
Rumpelgeist 203
Rumpelstiltskin 121, 160, 206, 67, 292, 303, 327
Rumpelstilzchen 292
Running water 39, 47, 118, 242, 252, 293
Rusalii 189
Rusalka 35, 292–93, 333, 339
Rusalki 292, 293
Rusheen 138
Ruskaly 344
Russia 16, 20, 33, 45, 46, 56, 57, 110, 113, 115, 117, 192, 221, 259, 330, 335, 340, 341

Rustam 36
Rye mother 204
Rzanica 279

Sa bdag 293
Sa Maraine qui estoit Fée 138
Saalah 258, 293, 298
Saaláh 298
Saba-leippya 244, 293
Sabdh 293
Saci 293
Saci-Perere 293
Sacrament 333, 339
Saga of Beowulf 342
Saga of the *Völsungs* 133, 184, 263, 289
Sagaritis 293
Saggarios, river 243, 293
Sahara desert 16
Sailor 15, 201, 215, 216, 22, 236, 266, 268, 276, 268, 276, 306, 313, 319, 322, 341
Saining 111
Saint Agnes' Day 93
Saint Befana 52
Saint Bernard Monastery 338
Saint-Cast, Brittany 146
Saint David's Day 93
Saint Elmo's Fire 344
Saint John and Father 295
Saint John's Day 93, 95, 125
Saint John's wort 125
Saint Martin's Day 93
Saint Michael 93
Saint Nicholas 269, 295
Saint Nicholas' Feast Day 269
St. Nicolas' Day 269
Saint Trinian's Church 70
Saint Valentine's Day 82
Saivo-neita 293
Salamander 294
Salamis 294
Salbanelli 294
Saleerandees 294
Salgfraulein 294
Salkanaty 294
Salmachis 294
Salmacis 242, 294
Salmakis 294
Salmon 59, 63, 78, 303
Salt 107, 109, 118, 153, 172, 217, 250, 277, 293, 309, 333, 348
Salt marshes 217
Salt water 64, 118, 153, 250, 317, 329
Salt-lake 265
Salvanelli 16, 150, 294, 305
Salzburg, Germany 344
Samhain 18, 77, 221, 294

Samhanach 294
Samhghubh'a 232
Samia 295
Samildannach 129
Samos, island 295
Samothrace, island 289
Samothrake, island 195, 289
Sams 273
Samūn 285
Sand yan y tad 222, 295
Sandman 111, 260, 295, 311
Sangarios 243
Sangarius 248
Sanguanello 294
Sangye Khado 295
Sankaikyo 36
Sankt Herr Nikolaus 295
Santa Claus 10, 295, 298
Sante Klaas 295
Sante Klaas 295
Sânziana 295
Sanziene 295, 296
Sânziene 295, 296
Sao 296
Saqsaywaman 296
Saradine 296
Sarafan 214
Sardinia, Italy 159, 165, 314
Saronic Gulf 13
Sasabonsam 296, 301
Sasquatch 117
Sasy Perere 73
Satan 344
Satnioeis 296
Satnioeis, river 296
Satnios 296
Satry 296
Saturday 282
Saturn 273
Satyer 28, 45, 49, 214, 240, 291, 296
Satyra 297
Satyrion 297
Satyrisci 296
Scaea 98, 132, 297
Scalloway, Scotland 252
Scamander 188, 297, 314
Scandinavia 118, 136, 201, 241, 242, 264, 309, 341
Scantlie Mab 297
Scare bug 70
Scarecrow 69, 345
Scea 297
Sceolan 12, 297
Sceolang 297
Schaibar 266, 297
Schellenrock 297
Schimmel Reiter 269
Schlocherl 292
Schrat 297
Schretel 297
Schretlein 297
Scorpion 107
Scothniamh 297
Scotland 5, 45, 53, 58,

59, 62, 66, 67, 68, 70, 74, 77, 80, 84, 106, 111, 114, 115, 123, 133, 136, 139, 141, 144, 147, 149, 152, 157, 158, 168, 170, 171, 199, 202, 219, 220, 221, 226, 245, 249, 252, 267, 269, 277, 284, 288, 297, 299, 302, 303, 304, 309, 318, 326, 328, 341, 343, 344, 345
Scott, Sir Walter 342
Scottish Folk-Lore and Folk Life 78
Scottish Highland Folk Museum 137
Scottish Highlands 39, 56, 57, 64, 67, 73, 74, 91, 92, 99, 137, 148, 168, 170, 267, 290, 299, 300, 309
Scottish Lowland 267
Scottish moors 175
Scrat 297, 308
Scrato 308
Scudamour 27
Scylla 28, 82, 99, 297–98, 333
Scythe 136, 279, 288
Scythes 94
Sea cows 239
Sea creature 53, 261, 323, 333
Sea-daughters 237
Sea demon 302
Sea-foam 79, 226
Sea gardeners 147
Sea god 15, 119, 215, 216, 232, 236, 243, 266, 268, 276, 283, 286, 290, 306, 319, 323
Sea maidens 232
Sea Mither 235
Sea-monster 199, 261, 299, 332
Sea morgan 237
Sea morgens 237
Sea-nymph 11, 12, 14, 15, 26, 27, 31, 33, 34, 40, 54, 55, 83, 85, 90, 93, 94, 102, 103, 132, 133, 147, 155, 161, 162, 165, 172, 180, 181, 187, 190, 191, 199, 202, 207, 209, 211, 212, 215, 216, 222, 223, 229, 230, 231, 244, 245, 246, 247, 249, 254, 260, 262, 265, 266, 272, 274, 278, 280, 281, 282, 283, 296, 311, 316, 321, 322, 329, 346
Sea panorama 265
Sea-shell 293
Sea-trow 298
Sea-urchins 139
Sea witch 298

Seal 15, 62, 71, 184, 218, 251, 253, 261, 290, 298, 299, 305, 340
Seal-faeries 299
Seal fairy 299
Seal maidens 290
Seal people 299, 305
Seal women's coat 232
Sealah 293, 298
Sealáh 298
Seals 62, 71, 218, 251, 261, 290, 299
Sear Dugh 12
Seasonal fairies 14, 35, 123, 136, 194, 275, 298, 310
Seaweed 91, 252, 302, 317, 341
Sea-weed hair 312
Sebille 298
Sebille l'Enchanteresse 298
Sebille la Dame du Lac 298
Sebu, Morocco 17
Seelie court 123, 134, 141, 299, 334, 344
Seely court 299
Seemänlein 299
Sefafell 304
Segesta 299
Segeste 299
Sehretel 297
Seilenos 228
Seine River 111
Seirenes 306
Se'irim 107
Selchies 299
Selemnos 34
Selene 245
Selkie 290, 298, 299, 305
Selkie folk 299
Sellkie 298
Selnozoura 299–300
Semele 86
Semivir 294
Semnai Theai 130
Seneca people 95, 103
Sennen Cove, England 183
Senq'a 300
Serbia 42, 220, 328, 337
Serpent 19, 28, 53, 69, 111, 112, 197, 206, 207, 230, 264
Servan 300
Setan 157
Setek 109
Seven Inches 300
Seven Maidens 204
Seven Maidens from the Kolli Mountains 204
Seven Sisters 13, 31, 37, 79, 106, 112, 122, 210, 224, 232, 273, 277, 319
Seven Whistlers 300
Seventh son 219

Seyfrid 206
Shagfoal 169
Shag-foal 300
Shaitans 193, 300
Shakespeare, William 4, 223, 256, 300, 301
Shakespearian Fairies 300–01
Shaman 95, 156
Shamantin 296, 301
Shape-shift 20, 30, 47, 64, 66, 78, 105, 116, 126, 133, 134, 135, 157, 163, 166, 180, 185, 187, 188, 189, 199, 205, 210, 212, 220, 243, 244, 264, 284, 291, 298, 303, 307, 308, 315, 316, 322, 330, 335, 339, 347
Sharp, Sir Cuthbert 65
Shaw, family 76
Shaytan 188
She who intoxicates 227
She who is mead 227
She Wolf 164, 336
Shears 38, 279
Shedeem 227, 300
Shedland Island 123
Shee 134
Sheean-ny-feaynid 301
Sheeè 134
Sheeidh 134
Sheep 44, 49, 64, 67, 68, 76, 87, 116, 127, 128, 142, 146, 159, 205, 207, 212, 218, 219, 264, 269, 274, 286, 288, 307, 341, 347
Sheepshanks 292
Sheevra 303
Shefro 301
Shehireem 227
Sheitan 107, 188, 300
Shekkasoh 244, 301
Shellfish 70, 275
Shellicoat 301
Shelly coat 301
Shellycoat 64, 66, 153, 297, 301, 302, 334
Sheoques 301
Shepherd 34, 118, 248, 347
Shepherdesses 164
Shetland Islands 64, 100, 136, 177, 206, 252, 280, 298, 300, 330, 333, 346
Sheytan 300
Sheytân 174
Shia 134
Shians 99, 135
Shiant Islands 62
Shicáre 134
Shield 17, 60, 120, 193, 206, 336
Shield maiden 336
Shifra 134
Shining ones 134

Shinseen 302
Ship 19, 49, 52, 62, 64, 65, 82, 105, 115, 129, 148, 167, 191, 201, 216, 226, 232, 237, 275, 300, 302, 308, 310, 313, 333, 334, 336
Shishimora 109, 200
Shitta 244, 302
Shock 48, 60, 302
Shoney 199, 302
Shoney of the Lews 302
Shony 302
Shoopiltee 118, 199, 302
Short Hoggers 303
Shriker 303
Shropshire, England 163
Shuck 59, 303
Shucky dog 60
Shug monkey 303
Shukir 60
Shvaz 303
Shvod 303
Si 304
Siabra 303
Siabrae 303
Siar 303
Sib 169, 216, 303, 325
Siberia 35, 330, 333, 341
Sibhreach 80
Sibros River 281
Sicilian coastline 15, 215, 216, 236, 266, 268, 276, 286, 306, 319
Sicily 34, 82, 127, 150, 155, 179, 197, 206, 227, 233, 268, 299, 316
Sicinus 257
Sickle 319
Sicksa 303
Sídhe 13, 18, 25, 32, 41, 47, 52, 57, 61, 74, 86, 99, 134, 143, 147, 148, 158, 211, 215, 227, 260, 293, 304, 311, 339
Sidhe 13, 51, 99, 331
Sídhe blood 304
Sidheog 301
Siegfried 122, 206
Sierra Leone 157, 326
Sif 49, 115, 148, 191, 216, 310, 314, 333, 334, 336
Sifrift 130
Sighe Finncaev 148
Sigrun 304, 336
Sigurd 68, 133, 289
Sikhandin 337
Sikinos 259
Sikyonia, Greece 37, 79, 85, 89, 198, 258, 270, 294, 306, 317, 321, 322
Sila 107, 304
Si'lah 304
Sileni 95, 296, 304
Silent moving folk 134, 304
Silenus 304

Sili Ffrit 304, 305
Sili-go-Dwt 304
Siliniets 305
Silk-cotton tree 260, 296
Silkie 305
Silky 305
Silphium 206
Siltim 305
Silvanella 144, 305
Silvanes 305
Silvani 16, 294, 305
Silver 17, 18, 30, 34, 35, 42, 43, 45, 65, 66, 87, 104, 110, 121, 138, 139, 152, 164, 168, 236, 238, 251, 253, 260, 330, 332, 333, 340, 342, 344, 346, 348
Silver Queen 34
Silver-smiths 66
Silver weed 138
Silver Woods 139
Simona 305
Simple Jacks 159
Sin 33
Sindre 305
Sindri 41, 192, 305
Sinlap 239, 244, 305
Sinoe 306
Sinope 37, 306
Sinter Klass 295
Siofra 301
Siren 20, 69, 82, 121, 188, 198, 220, 226, 232, 240, 241, 249, 275, 290, 306, 307, 312, 340, 347
Sirena 232
Sirenum scopuli, island 306
Sisth 134
Sith 136, 304
Sithean 136, 287
Sithnides 306
Siva 204
Sivottama 337
Sjarr 306
Sjofn 199, 302
Skada 323
Skáfidr 306
Skafinn 306
Skalsd 198
Skamander 162
Skamandros 162, 188
Skandar 306
Skavaerr 307
Skavidr 307
Skeggiold 307
Skeggold 307, 336
Skeleton 30, 92, 155
Skelton, Robert 78
Skidbladnir 49, 115, 148, 191, 216, 310, 333, 334, 336
Skilly Widden 307
Skillywidden 307
Skip 223
Skirfir 307

Skirpir 307
Skirvir 307
Skjelskör, Zealand 327
Skoggra 345
Skogs fru 307
Skogsfru 185, 307, 316,
    345
Skogsman 316
Skogsnerte 185
Skogsnufa 307
Skogsnufvar 307
Skogsrå 185, 307
Skogsra 307–08
Skogsran 307
Skogul 308, 336
Skotia 262
Skotos 21, 228, 326
Skovtrolde 55, 308, 330
Skraethins 308
Skrat 308
škriatok 162
Skriker 48, 59, 302, 303,
    308, 329
Skrimsl 308
Skritek 162, 308
Skřítek 308
Skrzat 162
Skuld 309, 336
Skuldr 251, 309
Skulld 251, 309, 332, 336
Sky Skogsfru 316
Sky yelpers 154
Skyddsande 107
Skye, Scotland 56, 76,
    88, 91, 173, 221, 224,
    309
Skylark 249
Skylla 297
Slagfiu 148
Slaugh 309, 334
Slaughtaverty, Ireland 10
Sleagh maith 134
Sleeth ma 134
Sleigh beggey 309
Sleigh bells 336
Sleigh veggy 309
Sleighs 336
Sleight beggey 134
Sleih beggey 146
Slieve-an-irain 145
Slieve Glory 234
Slieve Gullion 92, 139
Slovenia 16, 244, 279
Sluag 141, 309, 344
Sluagh 299
Small people 134
Small people of Cornwall
    134
Smallfolk 134
Småtomte 163
Smerwick, Ireland 208
Smiera-gatto 309
Smilax 309
Smyrna, Lydia 206
Snake 15, 26, 38, 49, 110,
    142, 157, 225, 265, 282,
    317, 326, 339

Snead 291
Snow fairies 309–10
Snow Maidens 56, 338
Snow Queen 309, 310
Snugglepot 169
Snus 241
Sojo-Bo 310
Sol 13, 17, 37, 79, 81, 87,
    106, 175, 176, 210, 232,
    245, 257, 270, 271, 273
Solblindi 310
Solemnos 34
Solitary fairy 66, 73, 113,
    159, 168, 169, 175, 213,
    267, 274, 288, 310, 334
Solomon, King 21, 108,
    193, 221
Solomon Islands 196
El Sombrerón 310
Somerset, England 33, 61,
    88, 139, 155, 167, 189,
    212, 228, 260, 317, 335
Song 15, 19, 30, 32, 54,
    58, 75, 76, 77, 89, 90,
    121, 147, 152, 160, 179,
    185, 206, 215, 216, 219,
    220, 223, 226, 236,
    240, 241, 249, 256, 258,
    266, 268, 276, 286,
    292, 304, 305, 306, 312,
    313, 319, 320, 322, 328
The Song of the Nibelungs
    122, 206
Sons of Iblis 20
Sons of Ivaldi 48, 148,
    191, 216, 310, 333, 334,
    336
Sons of Ivallda 65
Sophocles 21, 228, 326
Sorceress 49, 52, 70, 103,
    118, 119, 208
Sorla Thattr 23, 55
Sose 310
Souci 40, 190
Le Souin-Souin 310–11
Soul 2, 55, 45, 63, 78,
    101, 104, 105, 113, 120,
    133, 158, 172, 201, 203,
    232, 240, 279, 298,
    307, 319, 336
South Africa 117
South America 126, 136,
    310
South Carolina 347
South Cork 86
South Munster 51, 86
Sovereignty 52
Soviet Republic 256
Sow of Dallweir Dallpenn
    176
Spae-wife 311
Spain 49, 113, 135, 136,
    183, 329, 346
Spandule 166
Spanish Armada 298
Spanish cat 348
Sparta 311

Sparta, ancient 50, 203,
    210, 242, 276, 311, 325
Spartacos 179
Sparte 311
Spear 18, 19, 49, 65, 79,
    115, 148, 157, 191, 216,
    310, 336, 349
Spear Masters 19
Spear of Odin 49, 148,
    191, 216, 310, 333, 334,
    336
Spear-alimentrix 157, 336
Species of fairy 20, 52,
    60, 62, 96, 102, 105,
    108, 114, 115, 124, 126,
    133, 138, 145, 163, 168,
    186, 191, 193, 198, 205,
    211, 219, 220, 224, 240,
    254, 263, 264, 299, 301,
    324, 332, 339, 340, 345
Spectral hounds 154, 344
Speio 311
Spencer, Edmund 311
Spencer's Fay 311
Speranza 73
Spercheus 99, 279
Sperm whale 331
Sphinx 240
Spindle 120
Spindleshanks 292
Spinning 54, 82, 109, 110,
    123, 144, 159, 160, 171,
    172, 200, 212, 219, 247,
    252, 253, 267, 297,
    304, 305, 315, 320, 328,
    343
Spinning Damsel 82
Spinning wheel 54, 82,
    109, 159, 171, 212, 305,
    320
Spinnstubenfrau 54
Spio 311
Spirit of the air 41, 47,
    221
Spirit of the Forest 113,
    214
Spirit of the Giant Moun-
    tains 253
Spirit of winter 54, 235,
    269
Spirit paths 141
Spirit race 331
Spirit shrine 244
Spirits of children 244
Spiritual fairies 300
Spoorn 311
Spor 311
Spreader 108
Sprenger, Jacob 209
Spret 312
Spriggans 203, 312, 334
Spright 312
Spring 9, 16, 18, 24, 28,
    30, 71, 73, 77, 105, 106,
    120, 125, 126, 131, 143,
    150, 156, 171, 172, 173,
    182, 184, 186, 196, 198,

206, 207, 208, 210, 211,
    219, 224, 227, 228, 235,
    242, 254, 256, 260,
    268, 274, 275, 293, 321,
    323, 326, 341, 342
Spring faeries 275
Spring-nixen 196
Spring struggle 235
Springs of Arethusa 34
Sprite 17, 49, 67, 72, 85,
    86, 87, 144, 187, 284,
    312
Spryte 312
Spunkie 125, 344
Spunkies 312, 318
Spunky 3112, 344
Spurn 311
Squant 312
Srahman 301
Srikantha 337
SrTkantha 337
St. Nicolas' Day 269
Staff 30, 54, 73, 164, 183,
    329, 334, 347
Staffordshire, England
    154
Stag 178, 242
Stakh, King 344
Stalo 312
Staphyle 312
Steel 60, 81, 107, 153, 159,
    245, 250, 326
Stele volk 115
Stenni 199
Sterope 261, 277, 311,
    312
Stevns, Zealand 124
Sthenele 98, 312
Sthenelus 98
S'thich 313
Stilbe 90, 313
Stilbo 313
Still folk 134
Still-folk 99
Still people 134
Stillevolk 128
Stochdail a' Chùirt 67
Stomach-Slasher 54
Stone Age 141
Stone fort 138
Stone megaliths 267, 285
Stone of the dead man 67
Stone Woman 73
Stopan 109
Store Hedding, Holland
    124
Storm Hag 313, 333
Storm kelpies 62
Storms 83, 107, 110, 126,
    128, 140, 150, 151, 161,
    171, 183, 189, 226, 235,
    246, 249, 252, 277,
    299, 312, 317
The Story of Prince
    Ahmed and the Fairy
    Paribanou 266, 297
Stove 109, 200, 277

Strabo, type of nymph 313
Strabo the Greek 246
Straits of Messina 144
Stranger Stone 347
Strangers 134, 166, 325
Strätteli 313
Straw 54, 62, 119, 175, 198, 263, 292
Stray Cow 154
Stream 23, 24, 27, 34, 37, 62, 75, 111, 153, 155, 186, 224, 241, 254, 284, 301, 320
Stream of Love 111
Strega 294
La Strega (the Witch) 54
Streghe 190
Striker 48, 302, 303
Stroke lad 25
Strom Karl 241
Strömkarl 151, 313, 333
Strömkarlen 245
Strömkarlennäck 241
Strong Limbed 101
Strong Man of the Stream 241
Strong ones 153
Strudeli 313
Strymo 242, 314
Sturluson 314
Sturluson, Snorri 24
Stygne 98, 314
Stymphalis, river 233
Styx 242, 314
Suada 268
Suaforlami 112, 117, 152, 323
Suantraighe 146
Suartalfar 314
Subterranean ones 222, 335
Succubus 20, 292, 295
Succubus-like djinn 295
Suculae 186
Sudan 19
Sudri 40, 251, 314, 342
Suffolk, England 60, 66, 224, 303
Suicide 72, 73, 89, 248, 258, 292
Suicide Shuck 59
Suidheachan 51
Suire 232
Suke 314
Suksma 337
Suleyman 107
Sulfur 77, 273
Sulphur springs 188
Sumascazzo 150, 165, 314
Sumerklas Ruppels 295
Sumerset, England 40
Summer 53, 60, 62, 125, 141, 175, 221, 228, 235, 252, 283, 293, 342
Summer feast of Lugh-nasa 221

Summer Land 228
Summerland 30
Sun god 17, 37, 81, 176, 232, 245, 256, 257, 271
Sunday 23, 41, 123, 136, 268, 332
Sunset 89, 165, 318
Surali 256
Surcantine 266, 314
Surinam 33, 44, 117
Surrey, England 71, 155
Sussex Vocabulary 212
Sutherland, island 45
Svartalfaheim 60
Svartálfaheim 315
Svartalfar 22, 108
Svartálfar 315
Svartálfheim 100
Sviar 315
Sviarr 315
Sviarr 315
Svidr 315
Svior 315
Sviurr 315
Swampland 71
Swamps 54, 64, 71, 193, 197, 217, 225, 254, 318, 345
Swan 30, 73, 130, 147, 167, 197, 232, 234, 315, 342, 348
Swan Fairy 315
Swan Maidens 315, 336
Swan Maiden's cloak 232
Swart elves 60
Swartalfar 108
Swartelves 100
Swarthy-elves 100
Swawa 315, 336
Swiss 35, 54, 55, 101, 143, 300, 311, 313, 345
Switzerland 48, 116, 128, 135, 174, 193, 249
Swooning shadow 155
Swor skogsfru 316, 345
Sword 10, 20, 29, 47, 60, 61, 80, 96, 112, 113, 115, 117, 119, 143, 152, 163, 206, 208, 212, 230, 231, 237, 320, 323, 342
Sword bridge 231
Swordsmith 342
Syen 316
Syenovik 316
Syke 173, 316
Syllis 316
Sylph 122, 265, 312, 316, 333
Sylvain 140
Symaithis 316
Symaithos, river 316
Synallasis 316
Synallaxis 75, 188, 190, 268, 316
Syracuse 207
Syria 229
Syrinx 250, 306, 319

Szellem 107
Szepasszony 317, 333

Taboo 46, 102, 109, 137, 170, 266, 315, 317
Tad 201
Taghairm 57
Tahmuras 102, 103, 270
Tahurangi 331
Taigh shidhe 138, 287
Tairbh uisge 318
Takitimu 331
Talaing people 120
Talle-maja 317
Tallemaja 185, 317
Talonhaltija 317
Tamnuras, King 184
Tanagra 37, 131, 317
Tane-Kino 179
Tangie 317
Tangotango 317
Taniwha 174, 291, 317, 319, 331
Taniwha whale 174
Tankerabogus 317
Tantalus 278
Tanterabobus 317
Taong-Lupa 253
Taotaomonas 317
Tapairu 318
Tapio 255, 332
Tara 18, 52, 141, 150, 227, 246
Tarakika 38, 318
Tarans 318
Tarapikau 292
Taras, Greece 297
Tarbh eithre 318
Tarbh uisge 318
Tarentum 297
Tarmachans Mountains 318
Tarnkapppe 115
Tarroo-ushtey 318
Tarsa 297
Tartaro 258, 318
Tartaros 326
Tasso, Bernado 144, 237
Tata Duende 113
Tatermann 203
Tatiana 301, 318–19
Tatter foal 300
Tatter-foal 300
Tatterfoal 300
Tau 206
Taupo 319
Tautiti 318
Tawhaki 317
Taygeta 277
Taygete 37, 38, 79, 112, 122, 224, 261, 277, 319
Tchian du bouolay 59
Te-ihi 319
Te Makawe 224
Te Maunga 179
Tei-Pai-Wankas 284
Teine sith 344

Teir-nos ysprydion 163
Teiresias 199
Telchines 319
Tele volk 115
Teledike 319
Telegonus 84
Teles 306, 319
Telestho 319
Telesto 319
Telete 248
Telonnesos 320
Telos, city of 93, 127, 191, 207, 320
Telphousa 242, 320
Telphusa 326
The Tempest 35, 167
Teran 235
Tereine 320
Tereus 59
Termessus 14
Termite mounds 253
Terpsichore 76, 223, 320
Terrestrial devil 214
Terridge, Cornwall 307
Terrytop 320
Tethra 320
Tethys 11, 12, 13, 19, 24, 26, 27, 28, 29, 34, 36, 37, 63, 74, 75, 77, 78, 79, 83, 84, 85, 86, 87, 90, 91, 95, 106, 108, 110, 119, 122, 126, 130, 132, 155, 177, 180, 187, 188, 189, 190, 196, 197, 200, 210, 214, 215, 222, 226, 229, 230, 21, 232, 233, 246, 248, 256, 257, 259, 263, 265, 266, 268, 269, 270, 271, 273, 276, 277, 278, 279, 280, 282, 283, 290, 297, 313, 314, 319, 323, 325, 332, 334, 340, 346, 349
Teursapouliet 321
Teurst 321
Teus 321
Teutonic mythology 20, 22, 54, 68, 100, 102, 106, 122, 157, 164, 179, 181, 184, 217, 235, 254, 264, 274, 284, 286, 287, 291, 304, 307, 308, 315, 324, 336, 345
Teuz 205
Tewa Indians 195
Thailand 208, 272, 273
Thalassa 319
Thaleia 118, 321
Thalia 81, 321
Thames, river 199
Thamyris 34
Thaumas 122
Theano 98, 321
Theban dragon 326
Thebe 37, 321

Thebes, Greece 15, 204, 228
Thefford Forest 166
Their mother's blessing 134, 137
Theisoa, Greece 172, 245, 321
Thekk 322
Thekkr 322
Thelpousa 321
Thelpousa, Greece 321
Thelpusa 326
Thelxiepeia 322
Thelxiepia 306, 322
Thelxinoe 322
Thelxiope 322
Them That's in It 134
Them Who Be 134
Them Who Prowl 134
Themis 104, 120, 131, 183
Themistagora 99, 322
Thémistaoora 322
Themiste 322
Themisto 75, 322
Themselves 134
Theogony 178
Theonoe 119
Thera, Greece 186
Therapne 85
Therapne, Greece 322
Thero 322
Theseus 13
Thespeia 322
Thespia 322
Thespiae River 14
Thespiae, Greece 322
Thespian 37, 322
Thessalia, Greece 126, 199, 206, 208, 273
Thessaly, King 322
Thessaly, Greece 229, 259
Thetis 15, 20, 27, 33, 74, 104, 110, 111, 117, 162, 172, 187, 196, 203, 207, 208, 217, 230, 246, 247, 262, 265, 272, 282, 311, 321, 322, 333
Thiasse 152, 322, 323
Thien 244, 323
Thisbe 323
Thisoa 323
Thiua 89, 100, 202, 228, 323
Thoas, King 257, 259, 270
Thoe 323
Гном 162
Thoosa 323
Thor 25, 55, 60, 100, 121, 217, 323, 330
Thorin 323
Thorinn 323
Thorn bushes 301
Thorn tree 10, 221
Thorska-fjord 308
Thouria 323

Thousand and One Tales of the Arabian Nights 10
Thrace, Greece 59, 75, 149, 151, 289
Thrain 323
Thrainn 323
Thrake, Greece 199, 324
Thrar 323
Thrashing barn 263
Thrasir 324
Thrassa 324
Threads of destiny 251
The Three Crows 300
Three-headed dog 70
Three Mothers 41, 113
Threshing 62, 220, 300
Thriai 89, 100, 202, 228, 323
Thridi 324
Thrinakie, island 210, 245, 271
Throne 21, 52, 140, 201, 219, 247, 251, 253, 287, 324
Thronia 242, 324
Thronie 324
Thror 322
Thrór 322, 324
Thrud 25, 324, 336
Thrudur 336
Thrummy 324
Thrummy-Cap 324
Thrumpin 324
Thrymgioll 310
Thueyd 85
Thumbelina 327
Thunder 19, 139, 275, 330
Thunderstorm 49, 62, 77
Thuringia, Germany 56
Thurse 181
Thussers 324
Thyad 184, 325
Thyades 185, 325
Thyia 223, 325
Thyiades 44, 325
Thyiai 313
Thymbris 269, 325
Thyme 318
Thyone 186
Thyrsus 296, 325
Thysa 255
Ti Goriquet 91
Tiasa 242, 325
Tib 169, 219, 221, 223, 3003, 325
Tiberinus 325
Tick 223
Tidal Bore 118
Tidal waves 275
Tiddy Men 325
Tiddy Mun 166, 325
Tiddy ones 325, 347
Tiddy people 166, 325
Tiger 45, 140, 157
Tighe 66, 325

Tilottama 231, 287, 325, 335
Tilphossa 326
Timbaru 156
Timber 115, 238
Tingoi 326
Tinguian people 20
Tinker Bell 6
Tinne 117
Tiphaine 326
Tipperary County 110
Tir na Mban 208
Tir-na-n-Oge 300
Tír na nÓg 142, 327
Tir-Na-Nog 327
Tir Nan Og 97, 142, 248
Tir-nan-Og 97
Tir Tairngiri 248
Tirfing 152, 323
Tisiphone 153, 326
Tit 223
Titania 88, 14, 238, 240, 256, 267, 318
Tithe 80
Tithonus 314
Tithorea 326
Titian 21, 34, 36, 37, 38, 79, 87, 104, 120, 131, 183, 224, 233, 277, 282, 285, 319
Titian Muses 34
Titias 94
Titihal 38, 326
Titiliture 292
Патуљак 162
Полушан 162
Toads and Diamonds 326
Toads and Diamonds Fairy 326
Toadstool 125, 138, 142
Tobacco 74, 109, 116, 201, 289, 328
Tober Kil-na-Greina 46
Tobereevil 17
Tobereevul 14
Tod lowery 326
Tod-lowery 326
Toice Bhrean 326
Toku 108
Tolcarne troll 327
Tolkien, J. R. R. 261
Tolv 327
Tom a' Lincoln 73
Tom Cockle 327
Tom Dockin 252, 327
Tom Donkin 327
Tom lowery 326
Tom Po 327
Tom Poker 182, 239, 254, 327
Tom-Poker 182, 239, 254, 327
Tom Thumb 327
Tom-Tit-Tot 292, 327–28, 343
Tom Tiver 347

Tomhans 99, 135
Tommelise 327
Tommy Dockin 327
Tommy Rawhead 194, 287
Tommyknockers 203
Tomor 70, 117
Tomtar 328
Tomte 162, 249, 328
Tomte Gubbe 328
Tomte-Pocke 327
Tomtegubbe 3238
Tomtgubbe 66, 328
Tomtra 66
Tontti 162
Tonttu 328
Tontty 148, 328
Tonx 328
Tootega 328
Tooth faery 328
Tooth fairy 328
Toothy fairy 328
Topelius, Zacharias 287
Tor Mor 46
Toradh 138
Torn shoji 236
Torone 290
Torrey Island 151
Torrhebia 328
Tortoises 93
Tory Island 46
Tot 328
Tot Grid 328
Toupette 300
Tourists 1, 292
Tragasia 207, 329
Tragic mask 230
Trail of Tears 253
Transylvania 217, 278
Trasgo 113
Trasgos 329
El trasgu 329
Trash 48, 59, 169, 302, 329
Trauco 149, 329
Traveler 6, 32, 65, 70, 71, 96, 159, 193, 228, 235, 240, 252, 273, 345
Travelers 11, 24, 78, 106, 108, 110, 113, 125, 141, 147, 169, 170, 202, 211, 214, 217, 222, 254, 263, 273, 274, 276, 278, 292, 295, 296, 301, 303, 307, 308, 312, 344, 345, 347
Treasure 29, 35, 36, 53, 91, 95, 103, 111, 122, 160, 184, 190, 205, 213, 217, 236, 241, 244, 248, 263, 264, 265, 281, 282, 284, 292, 312, 346
Tree spirit 340
Tremella 138
Tremesna, Czech Republic 249
Trencher face 330

Trent River 118
Tresmalaouen 89
Tresmalouen 91
Tretyakov 42
Trickster 46, 175, 224, 273, 283, 284, 302, 346
Trident 319
Trier 284
Trifing 112, 117
Trikurat 244, 329
Trimurti 337
Trinidad 225, 265
Trip 223
Triphylia 234
Triple goddess 223
Triple muses of divination at Delphi 89, 100, 202, 228, 323
Tristan 90
Trite 99, 329
Triteia 329
Triteia, Greece 329
Triton 196, 216, 329, 330
Tritonis 329
Tritonis, lake 265
Tritons 232, 330
Troad, Anatolia 37, 313, 162, 178, 188, 196, 258, 268, 296, 314
Trojan War 83
Trold 115, 116
Troll 55, 59, 100, 115, 116, 121, 149, 163, 168, 169, 177, 179, 189, 210, 258, 284, 308, 327, 329, 330
Troll's butter 138
Trom 324
Tromie 324
Tronc 330
Tronc le Nain 330
Troomie 324
Trooping Faery 330
Trooping fairies 74, 97, 122, 134, 135, 142, 146, 175, 234, 275, 286, 299, 301, 309, 310, 330, 331
Trophonios 177
Tros 75
Trow 100, 123, 163, 177, 206, 300, 330–31
Trowe 330
Troy 21, 37, 183, 196, 243, 247, 314
Truncherface 330
Trwtyn-Tratyn 304
Try 299
Tschwi people 296, 301
Tsonokwa 117
Tsonoqua 117, 344
Tuarenga 179
Tuatha de Danann 5, 10, 13, 18, 30, 32, 52, 62, 68, 85, 86, 90, 94, 97, 104, 120, 129, 134, 139, 149, 151, 153, 164, 213, 223, 227, 234, 240,

248, 251, 252, 297, 299, 303, 319, 331, 343
Tubetube people 49
Tucky Piggy 35
Tuinpan 18
Tulla 57
Tullochgorm Castle 228
Tullochgorm 67, 228
Tünder 96, 331
Tündér 331
Tündér Ilona 311
Tündér Maros 311
Tupi Guarani people 32, 44, 74
Turehu 266, 331
Turkey 37, 198, 263, 295
Turnip Counter 292
Turnus 195
Turritella 227
Turtle 82
Tuscany 217
Tusse 330
Tut 328
Tut gut 328
Tutara-kauika 291, 331
Tutelary Apu 225
Tutu-Langi 108
Tutumaiao 332
Tuulikki 108, 255, 332
Twelfth Night 52, 313
Twilight 59, 70, 102, 124, 140, 166, 220, 299
Twin-brother 87
Y Tylwyth Teg 134, 137
Y Tylwyth Teg yn y Coed 332
Twlwwyth Tegs 332
Y Tylwyth Tegyny Coed 332
Tyche 186, 332
Tychios 130
Tykhe 332
Tyllenberger 249
Tylwyth Teg 53, 120, 133, 134, 137, 170, 278, 332, 344
Tylwyth Têg 332
Tylwyth Teg y Mwn 332
Tyndareus 50
Tyria 86, 97, 98, 312
Tyrol, Austria 294
Tyroleso mountains 212
Tyrone, Ireland 41
Tzipitio 310
Tzizimite 310

Udr 251, 309, 332
Udur 332
Uerco 185
Uganda 126
Uilebheist 332
Uirne 297
Uisges 153, 199
Ukantalaki 204
Ukulan-Tojon 333
Uldra 185

Ulster 118, 139, 141, 148, 168, 192
Ulster, Ireland 168
Umskiptingar 333
Umvelinqangi 26
Umzimu 26
Una 110
Unaerberg 344
Unbaptized child 81, 201, 241, 244, 256, 333, 339
Under-Wave, King 201
Underground folks 257
Underground-people 330
De Underjordiske 335
Underworld 57, 70, 93, 110, 153, 178, 184, 210, 214, 234, 258, 262, 298, 300, 320, 331, 335
Undine 122, 201, 247, 294, 316, 333
Un'Dine 333
Uni 191, 333
United Kingdom 6, 213
United States of America 32, 61, 213, 287, 313
Unknown 2, 22, 52, 138, 157, 166, 169, 223, 333, 334
Unnerorske 115, 257
Unseelie Court 53, 100, 114, 116, 123, 134, 136, 299, 309, 312, 334, 344
Unterirdische 128
Unterjordiske 128
Upaka 244, 334
Upis 176, 220, 334
Upper Brittany 145, 146
Urania 76, 334
Uranus 34, 153, 228, 319
Urchin 139, 249, 276
Urd 332
Urdarbrunnr Well 251
Urdhr 186
Urdr 251, 332
Urdur 332
Ureia 174
Urganda 262, 334
Urganda la Desconecida 334
Uri 334
Urien, King 237
Urisk 66, 84, 153, 267, 334
Ursa Major 2, 75, 176, 179
Ursa Minor 208
Ursitory 335
Urth 332
Úruisg 334
Urukehu 266
Urvashi 335
Urvasi 231, 287, 325, 335
Uterpe 132

Vadleany 335
Vættir 162, 335
Vættir 162, 335

Vairies 335
Väki 173
Vakkijnor 336
Vale of the Wear, England 77
Vale of Towy 234
Valhalla 191, 336
Váli 335
Valkyrie 25, 68, 163, 164, 179, 181, 184, 235, 286, 287, 291, 304, 307, 309, 315, 324, 336, 345
Valleys 164, 174, 236, 243, 254, 261
Vallhalla 102
Valli 204
Vampiric fairy 82, 170
Vampiric fairy-spirit 101
Vanadevatas 336
Vancouver Island 70
Vanir 25, 335
Vannes, France 321
Var 336
Vardogls 324
Varoldal, Hungary 96
Varr 336
Vasily 336
Vasitris 24
Vättar 335
Vaudois valley, Switzerland 143
La Vecchia (the Old) 52
Veden väki 173
Vedenhaltia 336
Veela 337
Vega 82
Vegetation god 217, 243
Veggr 337
Veigr 337
Veigur 337
Vejasmate 337
Vejopatis 337
Velia 186
Vends of Lüneburg, Germany 165
Venus 27, 33, 53, 55, 106, 140, 178, 204, 268, 290, 294, 337
Venus Genetrix 33
Venusleute 337
Verdandi 251, 332, 337
Verry volk 137
Verthandi 337
Vesihiisi 243
Vestal Virgins 195
Vestri 337
Vetehinen 243
Viand 253
Vicuñas 39
Vidyesvaras 337
Vietnam 38, 39, 41, 113
Vig 337
Vigg 337
Viggr 337
Vila 287, 337, 338
Vilenik 338
Vili 338

Vilia 337, 338
Vilishkis 337
Vily 337, 338
Vilya 337
Vindalf 338
Vindálfr 338
Vineri 140
Vines 27, 170, 173, 325
Vingolf 251
Violets 318
Violin 151, 241
Vipérine 91
Vira 188
Virfir 148, 338
Virgil 112, 216, 274, 347
Virgin 2, 63, 65, 97, 100,
    128, 187, 195, 205, 248,
    263, 292, 316, 336
Virgin Mary 205, 263
Virginal 56, 338
Virpir 338
Virra Birro 338
Virvir 338
Visayan islands, Philip-
    pines 198
Vishnu 28
Vit 339
Vita 152
Vithur 339
Vitis 27, 173
Vitore 339
Vitr 339
Vivian 208
Vivien, Prince 208
Vivienne 96, 339
Vodianikha 339
Vodianoi 339
Vodianoi Chert 339
Vodianoy 339
Vodka 241
Vodni Panny 339, 340
Vodníci 340
Vodník 340
Vodyaniye 214
Vodyanoi 339, 340
Vodyanoy 340
Vodyanoyovia 340
Vogul people 328
Voice people 261
Volcanic eruptions 275
Vold, King 344
Volga German 269
Vollmar, King 200
Volmar, King 200
Volsunga Saga 133, 184,
    263, 289
Volsungo Saga 336
Voltaire 103
Volturnus 340
Voluspa 16, 22, 24, 28,
    29, 31, 39, 40, 41, 44,
    48, 50, 57, 58, 59, 61,
    64, 68, 71, 95, 102, 109,
    110, 112, 114, 115, 119,
    120, 143, 147, 148, 149,
    150, 151, 152, 153, 155,
    156, 160, 162, 167, 169,

173, 174, 177, 181, 182,
    183, 185, 190, 191, 192,
    193, 194, 200, 217, 218,
    220, 235, 236, 238, 241,
    242, 243, 244, 248,
    249, 251, 254, 255, 258,
    260, 262, 286, 287,
    289, 303, 305, 306,
    307, 310, 314, 315, 322,
    323, 324, 335, 337,
    338, 339, 342, 348
Von der Rhon, Kaspar 56,
    338
Von Hardenberg, Nevel-
    ing 200
Von Orlamonde, Kuni-
    gunda 342
Vore Tullye 235
Votive offerings 119
Votyak people 340
Vough 153, 340
Vrikshakas 340
Vrouelden 53
Vu-Kutis 340
Vu-Nuna 340
Vyatka, Russia 340

Wadd 221
Waddington 267
Waddow, England 267
Waddow Hall 267
Waff 87
Wag-at-the-Wa' 340
Wag-by-the-Way 340
Wagawaga people 49
Waihoetoto 236
Wainscoting 203
Wairoa River 179
Waitarohia 108
Wakay Willca 225
Waldgeister 341
Wales 30, 46, 54, 65, 71,
    78, 79, 81, 93, 118, 123,
    125, 137, 139, 141, 147,
    161, 170, 221, 222, 260,
    284, 288, 332, 344,
    348
Walgino 341
Walhalla 336
Walking Fire 344
Walking Wolf 237
Walkries 336
Walnut tree 198, 285
Walrus People 239
Wampanoag Nation 284
Wanakauri 341
Wandering Dame Abonde
    10, 171
Wandering One 327
Wap 223
War god 234
Warhorse 60
Warwickshire, England
    171
Washer at the Banks 47,
    51
Washer at the Ford 47, 51

Washer of the Shrouds
    47, 51
Wassermann 341
Watchmen 345
The Water Babies 239
Water Bridge 231
Water devil 339
Water dweller 243
Water fairies 62, 111, 135,
    201, 238, 249, 250, 332,
    333, 340, 341
Water fairy 54, 69, 92,
    194, 198, 219, 233, 241,
    242, 243, 250, 252,
    267, 268, 275, 276,
    280, 313, 317, 339, 241
Water-fairy 100, 167, 179,
    181, 194, 196, 245, 248,
    280, 339
Water horse 39, 72, 78,
    79, 117, 161, 252, 302
Water kelpies 299
Water leaper 218, 341
Water Lover 36
Water maiden 220
Water-nymph 11, 12, 27,
    29, 31, 33, 35, 36, 40,
    68, 75, 79, 83, 85, 86,
    91, 97, 99, 100, 103, 106,
    110, 122, 130, 131, 132,
    133, 161, 164, 175, 176,
    177, 180, 186, 187, 191,
    192, 234, 235, 241, 245,
    257, 271, 272, 276, 278,
    279, 280, 285, 290,
    297, 312, 314, 321, 322,
    329, 333, 339, 346
Water of Life 117
Water spirit 35, 44, 48,
    55, 118, 153, 194, 199,
    241, 244, 245, 340, 341
Water-Spirit 44, 194, 199,
    245
Water-sprite 85
Water women 341
Water-Wraith 341
Waterfall 67, 69, 76, 149,
    151, 168, 313, 333, 334
Waterfall-Grim 151, 313
Wayland Smith 342
Wayland's Smithy 342
Weather fay 11
Weaving 82, 160, 219,
    247, 304, 308, 324
Weaving Sister 82
Webbed fingers 170, 197,
    249, 290, 312
Wee folk 134
Wee Folk 134
Wee ones 134
Wee Willie Winkie 58
Weiland Smith 342
Weinachts Man 269
Weiss Frau 51
Die Weisse Frau 342
Weland Smith 342
Well 14, 17, 33, 46, 62,

64, 72, 78, 80, 107, 109,
    111, 140, 148, 167, 184,
    195, 211, 243, 254, 258,
    267, 268, 280, 326, 342
Well of Aeval 14
Well of Fire 17
Well of the Font of the
    Sun 46
Well of Wisdom 62
Well spirit 342
Welsh coast 332, 341
Welwa 139
West Africa 35, 45, 260,
    296, 301, 348
West Cornwall, England
    183
West Malaysia 52, 59
West Riding, Yorkshire
    230
West Yorkshire, England
    48, 84
Western Europe 10, 264,
    338
Westmanland 286
Westre 342
Westri 40, 251, 314, 342
Wéwé 157
Whales 39, 331
Wheat bread 72
Whippity Stourie 343
Whirlpools 81
Whirlwinds 119, 165, 227,
    293, 312
White bucca 69
White Corn country 67
White dwarfs 342
White elves 136, 216
White god 69
White hat 347
White ladies 10, 96, 172,
    342, 343
White Ladies 172, 342,
    343
White Lady of Lough Gur
    148
White Lady of Sorrow 47
White Maiden of the
    Storm 317
White Merle 343
White Night Man 269
White poplar tree 214
Whitethorn 138
Whittinghame, Scotland
    303
Whoopity Stoorie 292,
    343
Whuppity Stoorie 343
Wichlein Paras 203
Wichtel 162
Wichtelmannchen 116
Wichtelweib 116
Wichtlan 343
Wichtlein 116, 343
Wichtln 154, 267, 276,
    343
Wig of Sif 49, 148, 191,
    216, 310, 333, 334, 336

Wight 116, 122, 134, 164, 335, 343
Wijven 345
Wild, Lady 234
Wild Army 343
Wild Chase 343
Wild Darrell 344
Wild Eric 163
Wild Hunt 35, 82, 93, 128, 141, 152, 154, 171, 238, 343, 344, 345
Wild Huntsman 238, 346
Wild Men of the Woods 346
Wild Women 344
Wildbean 344
Wilde Frauen 344
Wilde Jagd 343
Wildes Heer 343
Wildflowers 274, 275
Will o the Wikes 344
Will O' the Wisp 61, 101, 123, 125, 129, 147, 171, 222, 276, 278, 283, 295, 312, 344
Will-O'-the-Wykes 344
Will the Smith 61, 344
Will-with-the-Wisp 344
Willi 337
William of Newburgh 166
Willoughton, England 172
Willow tree 176, 283
Willy Willy 338
Willy Wisp 344
Win 223
Winchester, England 48, 88, 302
Wind Knots 150
Wind-fairy 227
Windsingers 316
Wine 11, 25, 44, 87, 124, 138, 150, 153, 175, 202, 214, 222, 223, 248, 250, 256, 259, 288, 296, 321, 348
Winter 18, 48, 54, 62, 73, 74, 110, 125, 149, 169, 172, 183, 185, 189, 192, 198, 212, 221, 235, 259, 269, 293, 295, 298, 309, 310, 317, 342
Winter faeries 309
Winter feast of Samhain 221
Winter Witch 317
Winterkolbe 292
Wiraqochan 345
Wirry-Cowe 345
Wise Woman Early 57
Wise women 345
Wish hounds 82, 154, 300, 345
Wish maiden 336
Wish maker 281
Wish wife 336, 345
Wish-woman 346

Wisk 154, 345
Wisked hound 345
Witch 42, 44, 52, 54, 57, 73, 74, 95, 103, 138, 141, 142, 161, 163, 170, 171, 172, 182, 194, 209, 219, 227, 265, 294, 298, 313, 317, 320, 340, 344
Witch Rhibyn 170
Witch ring 142
Witch's butter 138
Witte 345
Witte Juffers 345
Witte Vrouwen 345
Witte Wieven 345
Wittewijven 345
Wizard 9, 147, 227, 339
Woden's Hunt 343
Wodjanoj 340
Wodwose 346
Wolf 39, 107, 142, 164, 166, 177, 181, 191, 214, 235, 237, 238, 293, 298, 335, 336, 346
Wolfgang von Goethe, Johann 125
Wolkenthrut 336, 345
Wolterken 203
Woman of Peace 47
Woman Ruler 60, 345
The Wonderful Sheep 286
Wondrous Elfin Man 18
Wood maid 345
Wood nymph 100, 272, 294, 305, 307, 313, 345
Wood-nymph 100, 305
Wood of the Great Dark Wood 288
Wood spirit 49
Wood troll 55, 308
Wood wife 106, 307, 311, 345, 346
Wood-Wife 106, 307, 311, 345, 346
Wood-Woman 124
Wood women 173, 305, 345
Woodbridge 155
Woodcutter 116, 247, 346
Woodpecker 337
Woodwose 346
Wool 62, 115, 212, 288, 324
Woolpit, England 166
Wooser 346
Worcestershire, England 10, 278
World Mill 115
World Tree 95, 101, 113, 114, 115
Worlebury Hill, England 189
Worm 111, 148, 152, 287
Worriecowe 345
Worrikow 345

Worry-Cow 345
Wort 67, 125
Wotan 344
Wreath 96, 172, 183, 296
Wreghorn, Yorkshire 48
Wrthin 221
Wuduwasa 346
Wulver 346
Wunderberg 344
Wünschelwib 346
Wurd 332
Wurm 111
Wurricowe 345
Wurrycow 345
Wutan's Army 343
Wyrd 332
Wyrm 111

Xana 346
Xaninos 346
Xanthe 346
Xantho 346
Xanthus 34, 98
Xenia 243
Xenodamus 203
Xenon 118
Xhind 107
Xindha 347
Xindhi 347
Xmas 346
Xouthos 263
Xuthus 262

Yach 347
Yakut people 333
Yallery Brown 166, 347
Yama-Uba 347
Yamamba 347
Yamuna, river 196
Yanki-murt 340
Yann-An-Od 347
Yann-an-Ord 347
Yara 188
Yarthkins 166, 325, 347
Ychen Bannog 234
Yech 347
Yefimenko 42
Yehasuri 347
Yell Hound 154, 345
Yellow Dwarf 140, 348
The Yellow Dwarf 140, 348
Yesk 154
Yeth Hounds 345
Yeth-Hounds 345
Yew tree 309
Yggdrasil 95, 101, 113, 114, 115, 251
Yingi 348
Yityatya 312
Ymir 22, 108, 113, 235, 315, 348
Yn Foldyr Gastey 146
Yngvi 348
Yogurt 136
Yorba 117

Yorkshire River 194
Yorkshire, England 7, 40, 48, 76, 84, 135, 154, 167, 169, 175, 193, 194, 230, 243, 258, 291, 308, 321, 327
Yōsei 348
Youkai 45
Young man 41, 64, 72, 82, 103, 124, 142, 147, 156, 173, 215, 241, 245, 260
Younger Graces 81
Yourba people 264
Yr Arglwydd Hywel 284, 285
Yr Wyll 348
Ysaie le Triste 330
Yspaddaden Penkawr 260
Yucatán Peninsula 24
Yugoslavia 173
Yule Time 75, 255
Yumbo 14, 43, 66, 348
Yumboes 14, 43, 66, 348
Yunw Tsunsdi 349
Yup'ik, Alaska 191
Yvain 211, 237
Yvain, the Knight with the Lion 211, 237
Ywain, Sir 211

Zaire 58
Zemepatis 349
Zemyna 349
Žemyna 349
Zephir 349
Zephyrus 150
Zetes 262
Zethos 106
Zeus 2, 12, 13, 19, 21, 23, 24, 26, 27, 29, 31, 34, 37, 65, 75, 76, 80, 81, 82, 85, 89, 94, 99, 104, 106, 108, 120, 131, 132, 161, 172, 176, 179, 180, 183, 188, 190, 191, 192, 201, 202, 204, 208, 211, 223, 224, 229, 231, 233, 241, 242, 243, 244, 245, 246, 259, 263, 271, 272, 274, 277, 282, 285, 289, 319, 320, 321, 322, 323, 325, 328
Zeuxippe 242, 314, 349
Zeuxippus 316
Zeuxo 349
Zips 349
Zuibotshniks 214
Zulova, Czech Republic 337
Zuni Indians 36, 195, 204
Zwarte Piet 295
Zwerge 116
Zylba 117
Zzwerg 116

www.ingramcontent.com/pod-product-compliance
Lightning Source LLC
Chambersburg PA
CBHW040248290326
41929CB00058B/3480